NEW PERSPECTIVES

Microsoft® Office 365™ & Office 2016

INTERMEDIATE

Ann Shaffer
Patrick Carey
Katherine T. Pinard

Mark Shellman
Gaston College

June Jamrich Parsons
Dan Oja

Carol A. DesJardins
St. Clair County Community College

CENGAGE Learning®

Australia • Brazil • Mexico • Singapore • United Kingdom • United States

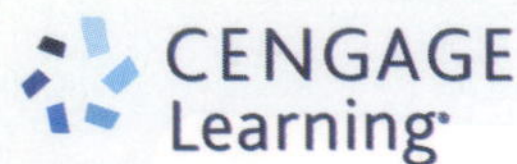

New Perspectives Microsoft® Office 365™ & Office 2016, Intermediate

SVP, GM Science, Technology & Math: Balraj S. Kalsi

Senior Product Director: Kathleen McMahon

Senior Product Team Manager: Lauren Murphy

Product Team Manager: Andrea Topping

Associate Product Manager: Melissa Stehler

Senior Director, Development: Julia Caballero

Product Development Manager: Leigh Hefferon

Senior Content Developers: Kathy Finnegan, Marjorie Hunt

Developmental Editors: Kim T. M. Crowley, Robin M. Romer, Mary Pat Shaffer, Sasha Vodnik

Manuscript Quality Assurance: Chris Scriver, John Freitas, Nicole Spoto, Serge Palladino

Product Assistant: Erica Chapman

Marketing Director: Michele McTighe

Marketing Manager: Stephanie Albracht

Production Director: Patty Stephan

Senior Content Project Managers: Jennifer Goguen McGrail, Stacey Lamodi

Manufacturing Planner: Fola Orekoya

Art Director: Diana Graham

Text Designer: Althea Chen

Cover Template Designer: Wing-Ip Ngan, Ink Design, Inc.

Cover image(s): danielo/Shutterstock.com

Composition: GEX Publishing Services

For product information and technology assistance, contact us at **Cengage Learning Customer & Sales Support, 1-800-354-9706**

For permission to use material from this text or product, submit all requests online at **www.cengage.com/permissions**.
Further permissions questions can be e-mailed to
permissionrequest@cengage.com

Mac users: If you're working through this product using a Mac, some of the steps may vary. Additional information for Mac users is included with the Data Files for this product.

Disclaimer: The material in this text was written using Microsoft Office 365 ProPlus and Microsoft Office 2016 running on Microsoft Windows 10 Professional and was Quality Assurance tested before the publication date. As Microsoft continually updates the Microsoft Office suite and the Windows 10 operating system, your software experience may vary slightly from what is presented in the printed text.

Library of Congress Control Number: 2016931360
Soft-cover Edition ISBN: 978-1-305-87919-5
Loose-leaf Edition ISBN: 978-1-337-25155-6

Cengage Learning
20 Channel Center Street
Boston, MA 02210
USA

Cengage Learning is a leading provider of customized learning solutions with employees residing in nearly 40 different countries and sales in more than 125 countries around the world. Find your local representative at **www.cengage.com.**

Cengage Learning products are represented in Canada by Nelson Education, Ltd.

To learn more about Cengage Learning, visit **www.cengage.com**

Purchase any of our products at your local college store or at our preferred online store **www.cengagebrain.com**

Printed in the United States of America
Print Number: 02 Print Year: 2016

TABLE OF CONTENTS

EXCEL MODULES

ACCESS MODULES

POWERPOINT MODULES

Productivity Apps for School and Work

OneNote
Sway
Office Mix
Edge

Corinne Hoisington

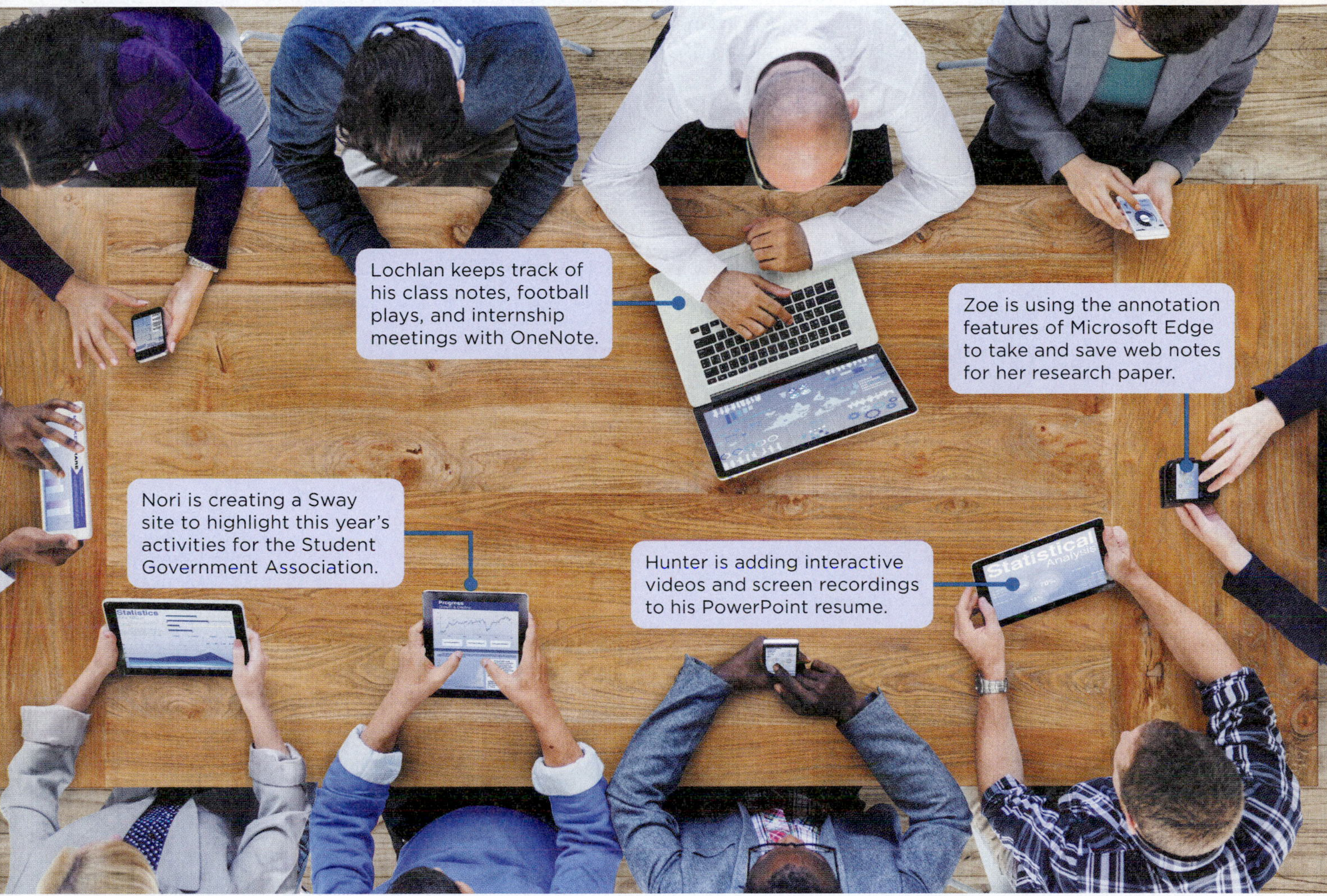

Lochlan keeps track of his class notes, football plays, and internship meetings with OneNote.
Zoe is using the annotation features of Microsoft Edge to take and save web notes for her research paper.
Nori is creating a Sway site to highlight this year's activities for the Student Government Association.
Hunter is adding interactive videos and screen recordings to his PowerPoint resume.
Statistical Analysis
Statistics
Progress

Being computer literate no longer means mastery of only Word, Excel, PowerPoint, Outlook, and Access. To become technology power users, Hunter, Nori, Zoe, and Lochlan are exploring Microsoft OneNote, Sway, Mix, and Edge in Office 2016 and Windows 10.

In this Module

Learn to use productivity apps!
Links to companion **Sways**, featuring **videos** with hands-on instructions, are located on www.cengagebrain.com.

Introduction to OneNote 2016

Bottom Line
- OneNote is a note-taking app for your academic and professional life.
- Use OneNote to get organized by gathering your ideas, sketches, webpages, photos, videos, and notes in one place.

notebook | section tab | To Do tag | screen clipping | note | template | Microsoft OneNote Mobile app | sync | drawing canvas | inked handwriting | Ink to Text

As you glance around any classroom, you invariably see paper notebooks and notepads on each desk. Because deciphering and sharing handwritten notes can be a challenge, Microsoft OneNote 2016 replaces physical notebooks, binders, and paper notes with a searchable, digital notebook. OneNote captures your ideas and schoolwork on any device so you can stay organized, share notes, and work with others on projects. Whether you are a student taking class notes as shown in **Figure 1** or an employee taking notes in company meetings, OneNote is the one place to keep notes for all of your projects.

Figure 1: OneNote 2016 notebook

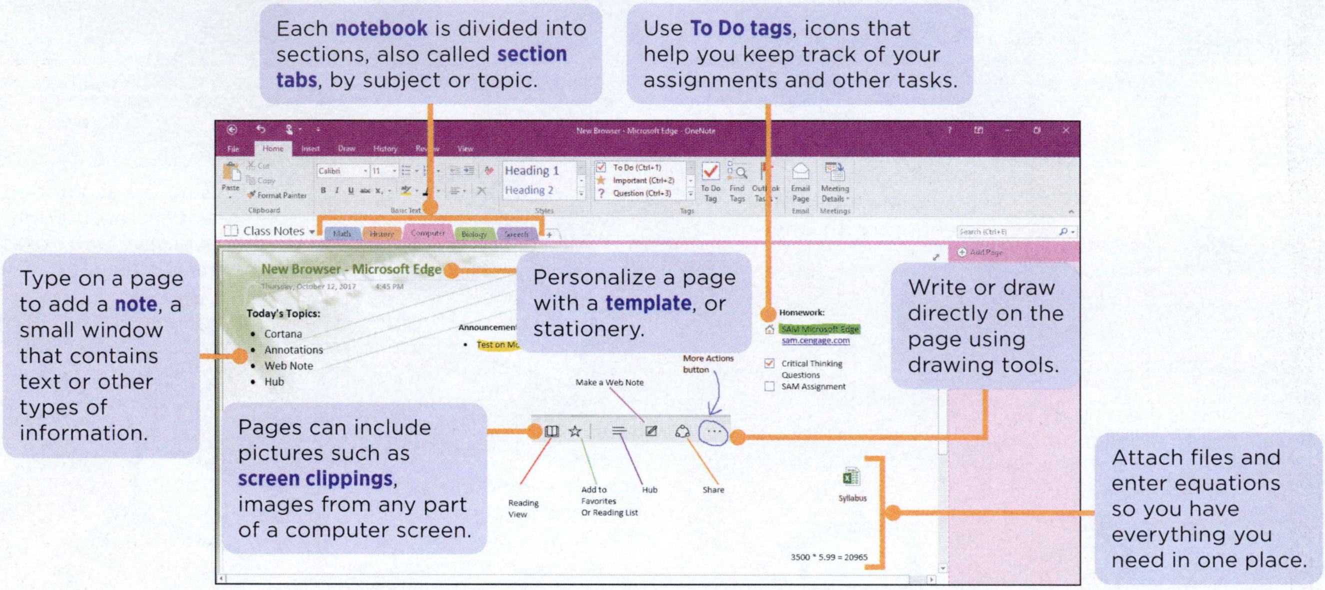

Each **notebook** is divided into sections, also called **section tabs**, by subject or topic.

Use **To Do tags**, icons that help you keep track of your assignments and other tasks.

Type on a page to add a **note**, a small window that contains text or other types of information.

Personalize a page with a **template**, or stationery.

Write or draw directly on the page using drawing tools.

Pages can include pictures such as **screen clippings**, images from any part of a computer screen.

Attach files and enter equations so you have everything you need in one place.

Creating a OneNote Notebook

OneNote is divided into sections similar to those in a spiral-bound notebook. Each OneNote notebook contains sections, pages, and other notebooks. You can use OneNote for school, business, and personal projects. Store information for each type of project in different notebooks to keep your tasks separate, or use any other organization that suits you. OneNote is flexible enough to adapt to the way you want to work.

When you create a notebook, it contains a blank page with a plain white background by default, though you can use templates, or stationery, to apply designs in categories such as Academic, Business, Decorative, and Planners. Start typing or use the buttons on the Insert tab to insert notes, which are small resizable windows that can contain text, equations, tables, on-screen writing, images, audio and video recordings, to-do lists, file attachments, and file printouts. Add as many notes as you need to each page.

Learn to use OneNote!
Links to companion **Sways**, featuring **videos** with hands-on instructions, are located on www.cengagebrain.com.

Syncing a Notebook to the Cloud

OneNote saves your notes every time you make a change in a notebook. To make sure you can access your notebooks with a laptop, tablet, or smartphone wherever you are, OneNote uses cloud-based storage, such as OneDrive or SharePoint. **Microsoft OneNote Mobile app**, a lightweight version of OneNote 2016 shown in **Figure 2**, is available for free in the Windows Store, Google Play for Android devices, and the AppStore for iOS devices.

If you have a Microsoft account, OneNote saves your notes on OneDrive automatically for all your mobile devices and computers, which is called **syncing**. For example, you can use OneNote to take notes on your laptop during class, and then open OneNote on your phone to study later. To use a notebook stored on your computer with your OneNote Mobile app, move the notebook to OneDrive. You can quickly share notebook content with other people using OneDrive.

Figure 2: Microsoft OneNote Mobile app

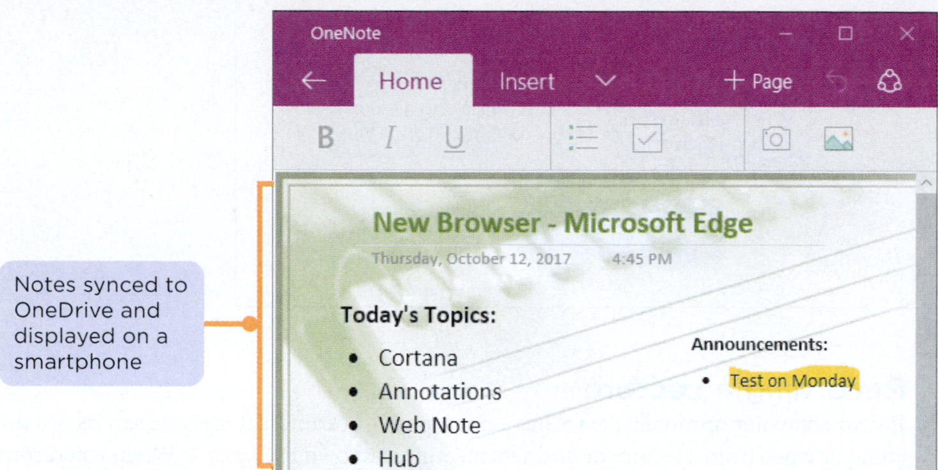

Taking Notes

Use OneNote pages to organize your notes by class and topic or lecture. Beyond simple typed notes, OneNote stores drawings, converts handwriting to searchable text and mathematical sketches to equations, and records audio and video.

OneNote includes drawing tools that let you sketch freehand drawings such as biological cell diagrams and financial supply-and-demand charts. As shown in **Figure 3**, the Draw tab on the ribbon provides these drawing tools along with shapes so you can insert diagrams and other illustrations to represent your ideas. When you draw on a page, OneNote creates a **drawing canvas**, which is a container for shapes and lines.

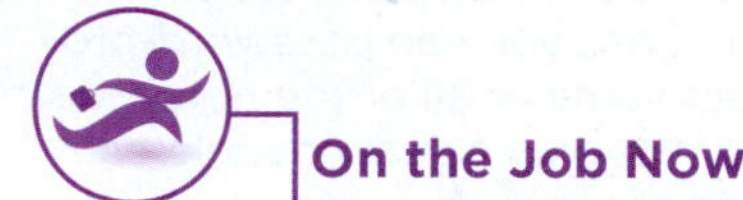

On the Job Now

OneNote is ideal for taking notes during meetings, whether you are recording minutes, documenting a discussion, sketching product diagrams, or listing follow-up items. Use a meeting template to add pages with content appropriate for meetings.

Figure 3: Tools on the Draw tab

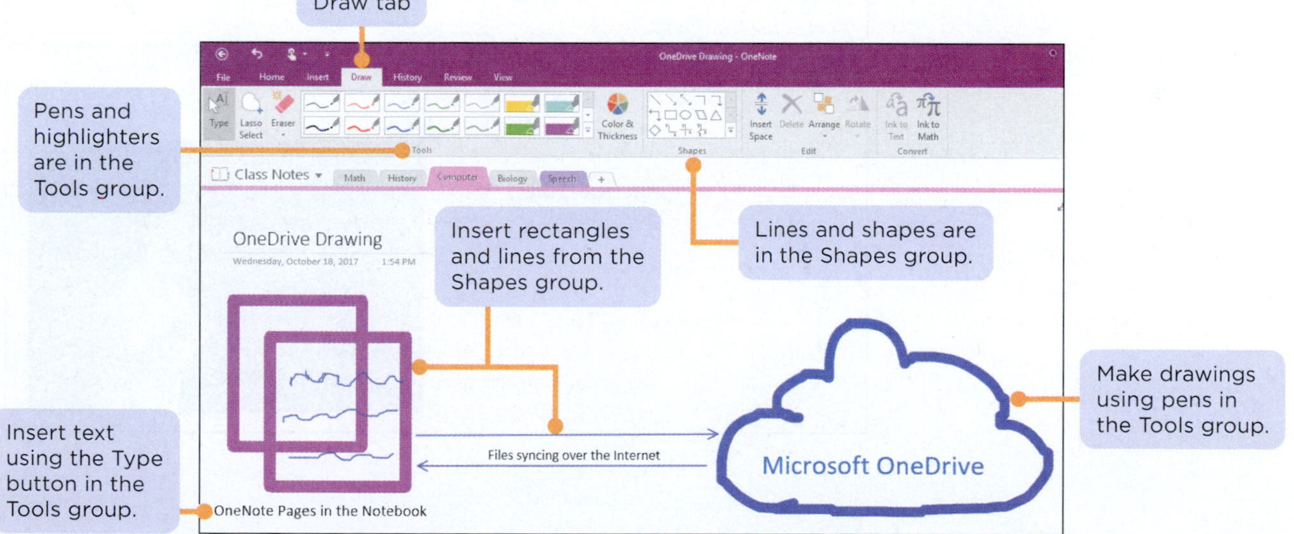

Converting Handwriting to Text

When you use a pen tool to write on a notebook page, the text you enter is called **inked handwriting**. OneNote can convert inked handwriting to typed text when you use the **Ink to Text** button in the Convert group on the Draw tab, as shown in **Figure 4**. After OneNote converts the handwriting to text, you can use the Search box to find terms in the converted text or any other note in your notebooks.

Figure 4: Converting handwriting to text

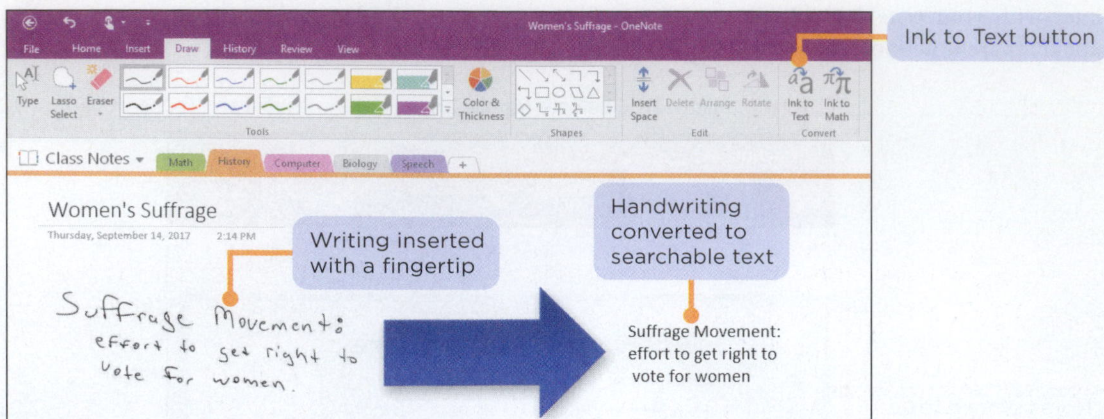

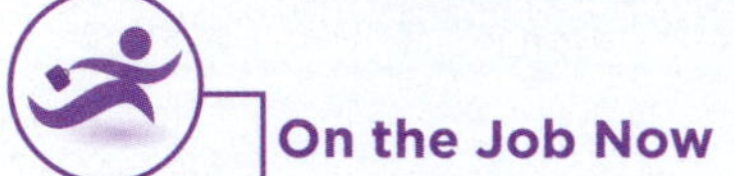

On the Job Now

Use OneNote as a place to brainstorm ongoing work projects. If a notebook contains sensitive material, you can password-protect some or all of the notebook so that only certain people can open it.

Recording a Lecture

If your computer or mobile device has a microphone or camera, OneNote can record the audio or video from a lecture or business meeting as shown in **Figure 5**. When you record a lecture (with your instructor's permission), you can follow along, take regular notes at your own pace, and review the video recording later. You can control the start, pause, and stop motions of the recording when you play back the recording of your notes.

Figure 5: Video inserted in a notebook

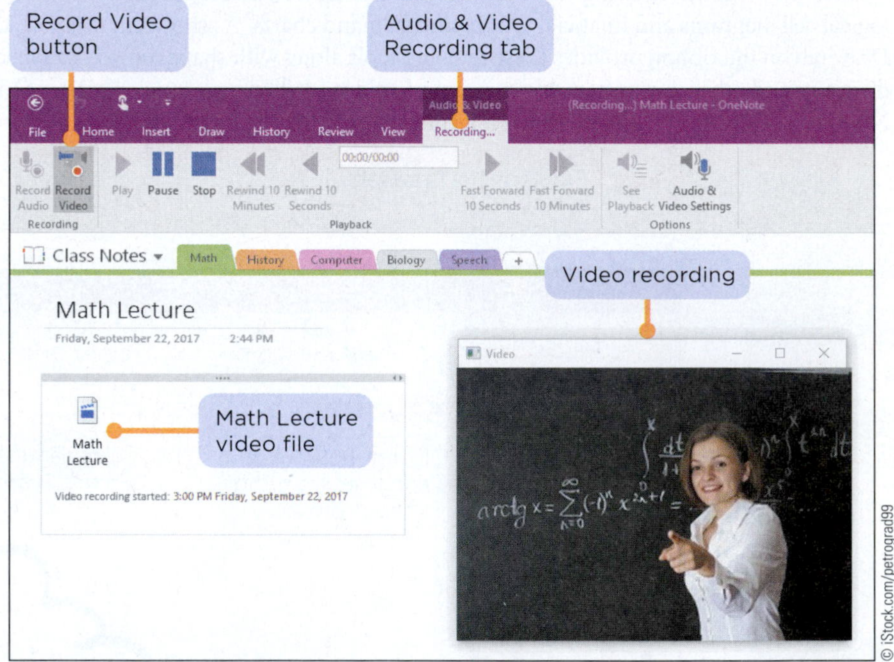

Try This Now

Learn to use OneNote!
Links to companion **Sways**, featuring **videos** with hands-on instructions, are located on www.cengagebrain.com.

1: Taking Notes for a Week

As a student, you can get organized by using OneNote to take detailed notes in your classes. Perform the following tasks:

a. Create a new OneNote notebook on your Microsoft OneDrive account (the default location for new notebooks). Name the notebook with your first name followed by "Notes," as in **Caleb Notes**.
b. Create four section tabs, each with a different class name.
c. Take detailed notes in those classes for one week. Be sure to include notes, drawings, and other types of content.
d. Sync your notes with your OneDrive. Submit your assignment in the format specified by your instructor.

2: Using OneNote to Organize a Research Paper

You have a research paper due on the topic of three habits of successful students. Use OneNote to organize your research. Perform the following tasks:

a. Create a new OneNote notebook on your Microsoft OneDrive account. Name the notebook **Success Research**.
b. Create three section tabs with the following names:
   - **Take Detailed Notes**
   - **Be Respectful in Class**
   - **Come to Class Prepared**
c. On the web, research the topics and find three sources for each section. Copy a sentence from each source and paste the sentence into the appropriate section. When you paste the sentence, OneNote inserts it in a note with a link to the source.
d. Sync your notes with your OneDrive. Submit your assignment in the format specified by your instructor.

3: Planning Your Career

Note: This activity requires a webcam or built-in video camera on any type of device.

Consider an occupation that interests you. Using OneNote, examine the responsibilities, education requirements, potential salary, and employment outlook of a specific career. Perform the following tasks:

a. Create a new OneNote notebook on your Microsoft OneDrive account. Name the notebook with your first name followed by a career title, such as **Kara - App Developer**.
b. Create four section tabs with the names **Responsibilities, Education Requirements, Median Salary**, and **Employment Outlook**.
c. Research the responsibilities of your career path. Using OneNote, record a short video (approximately 30 seconds) of yourself explaining the responsibilities of your career path. Place the video in the Responsibilities section.
d. On the web, research the educational requirements for your career path and find two appropriate sources. Copy a paragraph from each source and paste them into the appropriate section. When you paste a paragraph, OneNote inserts it in a note with a link to the source.
e. Research the median salary for a single year for this career. Create a mathematical equation in the Median Salary section that multiplies the amount of the median salary times 20 years to calculate how much you will possibly earn.
f. For the Employment Outlook section, research the outlook for your career path. Take at least four notes about what you find when researching the topic.
g. Sync your notes with your OneDrive. Submit your assignment in the format specified by your instructor.

Introduction to Sway

Sway site | responsive design | Storyline | card | Creative Commons license | animation emphasis effects | Docs.com

Bottom Line

- Drag photos, videos, and files from your computer and content from Facebook and Twitter directly to your Sway presentation.
- Run Sway in a web browser or as an app on your smartphone, and save presentations as webpages.

Expressing your ideas in a presentation typically means creating PowerPoint slides or a Word document. Microsoft Sway gives you another way to engage an audience. Sway is a free Microsoft tool available at Sway.com or as an app in Office 365. Using Sway, you can combine text, images, videos, and social media in a website called a **Sway site** that you can share and display on any device. To get started, you create a digital story on a web-based canvas without borders, slides, cells, or page breaks. A Sway site organizes the text, images, and video into a **responsive design**, which means your content adapts perfectly to any screen size as shown in **Figure 6**. You store a Sway site in the cloud on OneDrive using a free Microsoft account.

Figure 6: Sway site with responsive design

You can display a Sway presentation in a web browser.
Sway uses responsive design to make sure pages fit perfectly on any device.
The Market for Commercial Drones
Medical Defibrillator
• Ambulance drone can help heart attack victims in under 2 minutes with
The Market for Commercial Drones
Medical Defibrillator

Creating a Sway Presentation

Learn to use Sway!
Links to companion **Sways**, featuring **videos** with hands-on instructions, are located on www.cengagebrain.com.

You can use Sway to build a digital flyer, a club newsletter, a vacation blog, an informational site, a digital art portfolio, or a new product rollout. After you select your topic and sign into Sway with your Microsoft account, a **Storyline** opens, providing tools and a work area for composing your digital story. See **Figure 7**. Each story can include text, images, and videos. You create a Sway by adding text and media content into a Storyline section, or **card**. To add pictures, videos, or documents, select a card in the left pane and then select the Insert Content button. The first card in a Sway presentation contains a title and background image.

Figure 7: Creating a Sway site

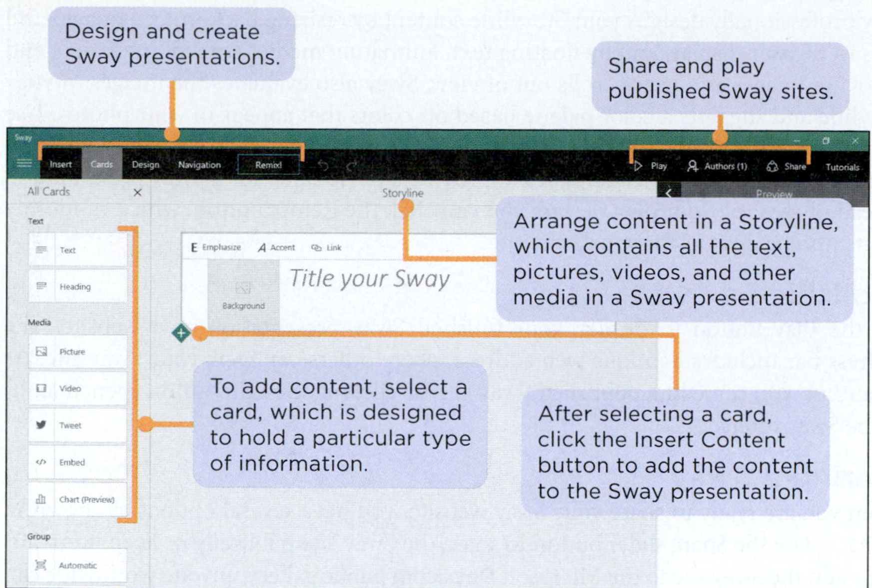

Adding Content to Build a Story

As you work, Sway searches the Internet to help you find relevant images, videos, tweets, and other content from online sources such as Bing, YouTube, Twitter, and Facebook. You can drag content from the search results right into the Storyline. In addition, you can upload your own images and videos directly in the presentation. For example, if you are creating a Sway presentation about the market for commercial drones, Sway suggests content to incorporate into the presentation by displaying it in the left pane as search results. The search results include drone images tagged with a **Creative Commons license** at online sources as shown in **Figure 8**. A Creative Commons license is a public copyright license that allows the free distribution of an otherwise copyrighted work. In addition, you can specify the source of the media. For example, you can add your own Facebook or OneNote pictures and videos in Sway without leaving the app.

On the Job Now

If you have a Microsoft Word document containing an outline of your business content, drag the outline into Sway to create a card for each topic.

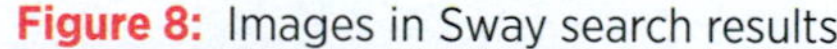

Figure 8: Images in Sway search results

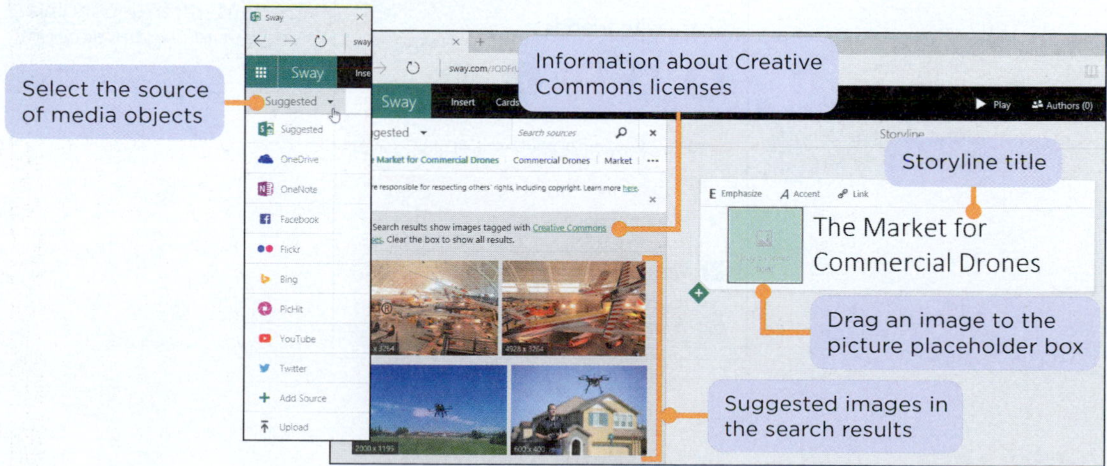

If your project team wants to collaborate on a Sway presentation, click the Authors button on the navigation bar to invite others to edit the presentation.

Designing a Sway

Sway professionally designs your Storyline content by resizing background images and fonts to fit your display, and by floating text, animating media, embedding video, and removing images as a page scrolls out of view. Sway also evaluates the images in your Storyline and suggests a color palette based on colors that appear in your photos. Use the Design button to display tools including color palettes, font choices, **animation emphasis effects**, and style templates to provide a personality for a Sway presentation. Instead of creating your own design, you can click the Remix button, which randomly selects unique designs for your Sway site.

Publishing a Sway

Use the Play button to display your finished Sway presentation as a website. The Address bar includes a unique web address where others can view your Sway site. As the author, you can edit a published Sway site by clicking the Edit button (pencil icon) on the Sway toolbar.

Sharing a Sway

When you are ready to share your Sway website, you have several options as shown in **Figure 9**. Use the Share slider button to share the Sway site publically or keep it private. If you add the Sway site to the Microsoft **Docs.com** public gallery, anyone worldwide can use Bing, Google, or other search engines to find, view, and share your Sway site. You can also share your Sway site using Facebook, Twitter, Google+, Yammer, and other social media sites. Link your presentation to any webpage or email the link to your audience. Sway can also generate a code for embedding the link within another webpage.

Figure 9: Sharing a Sway site

Share button
Play
Authors (1)
Share
Share
Just me
Drag the slider button to Just me to keep the Sway site private
Share with the world
Post the Sway site on Docs.com
Docs.com - Your public gallery
Share with friends
Options differ depending on your Microsoft account
Send friends a link to the Sway site
https://sway.com/JQDFrUaxmg4lEbbk
More options
Viewers can duplicate this Sway
Stop sharing

Try This Now

> **Learn to use Sway!**
> Links to companion **Sways**, featuring **videos** with hands-on instructions, are located on www.cengagebrain.com.

1: Creating a Sway Resume

Sway is a digital storytelling app. Create a Sway resume to share the skills, job experiences, and achievements you have that match the requirements of a future job interest. Perform the following tasks:

a. Create a new presentation in Sway to use as a digital resume. Title the Sway Storyline with your full name and then select a background image.
b. Create three separate sections titled **Academic Background, Work Experience**, and **Skills**, and insert text, a picture, and a paragraph or bulleted points in each section. Be sure to include your own picture.
c. Add a fourth section that includes a video about your school that you find online.
d. Customize the design of your presentation.
e. Submit your assignment link in the format specified by your instructor.

2: Creating an Online Sway Newsletter

Newsletters are designed to capture the attention of their target audience. Using Sway, create a newsletter for a club, organization, or your favorite music group. Perform the following tasks:

a. Create a new presentation in Sway to use as a digital newsletter for a club, organization, or your favorite music group. Provide a title for the Sway Storyline and select an appropriate background image.
b. Select three separate sections with appropriate titles, such as Upcoming Events. In each section, insert text, a picture, and a paragraph or bulleted points.
c. Add a fourth section that includes a video about your selected topic.
d. Customize the design of your presentation.
e. Submit your assignment link in the format specified by your instructor.

3: Creating and Sharing a Technology Presentation

To place a Sway presentation in the hands of your entire audience, you can share a link to the Sway presentation. Create a Sway presentation on a new technology and share it with your class. Perform the following tasks:

a. Create a new presentation in Sway about a cutting-edge technology topic. Provide a title for the Sway Storyline and select a background image.
b. Create four separate sections about your topic, and include text, a picture, and a paragraph in each section.
c. Add a fifth section that includes a video about your topic.
d. Customize the design of your presentation.
e. Share the link to your Sway with your classmates and submit your assignment link in the format specified by your instructor.

Introduction to Office Mix

add-in | clip | slide recording | Slide Notes | screen recording | free-response quiz

Bottom Line

- Office Mix is a free PowerPoint add-in from Microsoft that adds features to PowerPoint.
- The Mix tab on the PowerPoint ribbon provides tools for creating screen recordings, videos, interactive quizzes, and live webpages.

To enliven business meetings and lectures, Microsoft adds a new dimension to presentations with a powerful toolset called Office Mix, a free add-in for PowerPoint. (An **add-in** is software that works with an installed app to extend its features.) Using Office Mix, you can record yourself on video, capture still and moving images on your desktop, and insert interactive elements such as quizzes and live webpages directly into PowerPoint slides. When you post the finished presentation to OneDrive, Office Mix provides a link you can share with friends and colleagues. Anyone with an Internet connection and a web browser can watch a published Office Mix presentation, such as the one in **Figure 10**, on a computer or mobile device.

Figure 10: Office Mix presentation

Adding Office Mix to PowerPoint

Learn to use Office Mix!
Links to companion **Sways**, featuring **videos** with hands-on instructions, are located on www.cengagebrain.com.

To get started, you create an Office Mix account at the website mix.office.com using an email address or a Facebook or Google account. Next, you download and install the Office Mix add-in (see **Figure 11**). Office Mix appears as a new tab named Mix on the PowerPoint ribbon in versions of Office 2013 and Office 2016 running on personal computers (PCs).

Figure 11: Getting started with Office Mix

Capturing Video Clips

A **clip** is a short segment of audio, such as music, or video. After finishing the content on a PowerPoint slide, you can use Office Mix to add a video clip to animate or illustrate the content. Office Mix creates video clips in two ways: by recording live action on a webcam and by capturing screen images and movements. If your computer has a webcam, you can record yourself and annotate the slide to create a **slide recording** as shown in **Figure 12**.

On the Job Now

Companies are using Office Mix to train employees about new products, to explain benefit packages to new workers, and to educate interns about office procedures.

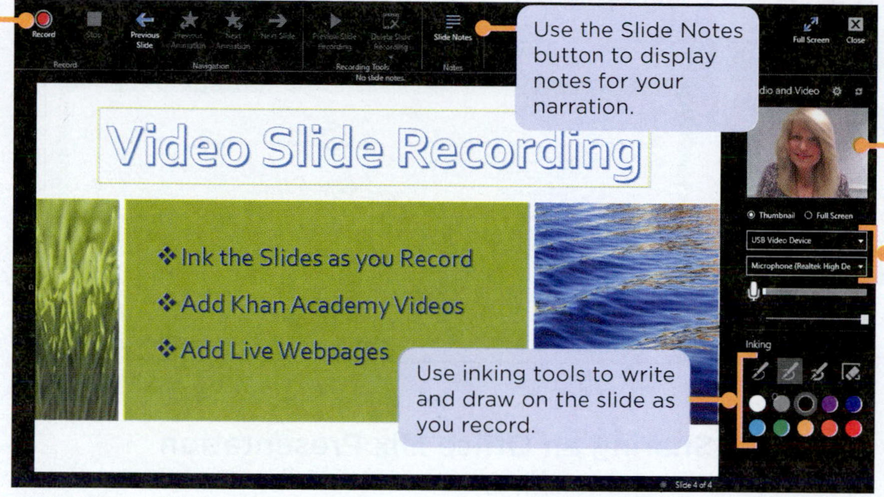
Record your voice; also record video if your computer has a camera.
Use the Slide Notes button to display notes for your narration.
For best results, look directly at your webcam while recording video.
Video Slide Recording
Ink the Slides as you Record
Add Khan Academy Videos
Add Live Webpages
Choose a video and audio device to record images and sound.
Use inking tools to write and draw on the slide as you record.

Figure 12: Making a slide recording

When you are making a slide recording, you can record your spoken narration at the same time. The **Slide Notes** feature works like a teleprompter to help you focus on your presentation content instead of memorizing your narration. Use the Inking tools to make annotations or add highlighting using different pen types and colors. After finishing a recording, edit the video in PowerPoint to trim the length or set playback options.

The second way to create a video is to capture on-screen images and actions with or without a voiceover. This method is ideal if you want to show how to use your favorite website or demonstrate an app such as OneNote. To share your screen with an audience, select the part of the screen you want to show in the video. Office Mix captures everything that happens in that area to create a **screen recording**, as shown in **Figure 13**. Office Mix inserts the screen recording as a video in the slide.

On the Job Now

To make your video recordings accessible to people with hearing impairments, use the Office Mix closed-captioning tools. You can also use closed captions to supplement audio that is difficult to understand and to provide an aid for those learning to read.

Record the action on the screen within the red dashed outline.
Record audio while capturing your on-screen actions.
Select Area button
Watched Mixes
Uploaded Mixes

Figure 13: Making a screen recording

Inserting Quizzes, Live Webpages, and Apps

To enhance and assess audience understanding, make your slides interactive by adding quizzes, live webpages, and apps. Quizzes give immediate feedback to the user as shown in **Figure 14**. Office Mix supports several quiz formats, including a **free-response quiz** similar to a short answer quiz, and true/false, multiple-choice, and multiple-response formats.

Figure 14: Creating an interactive quiz

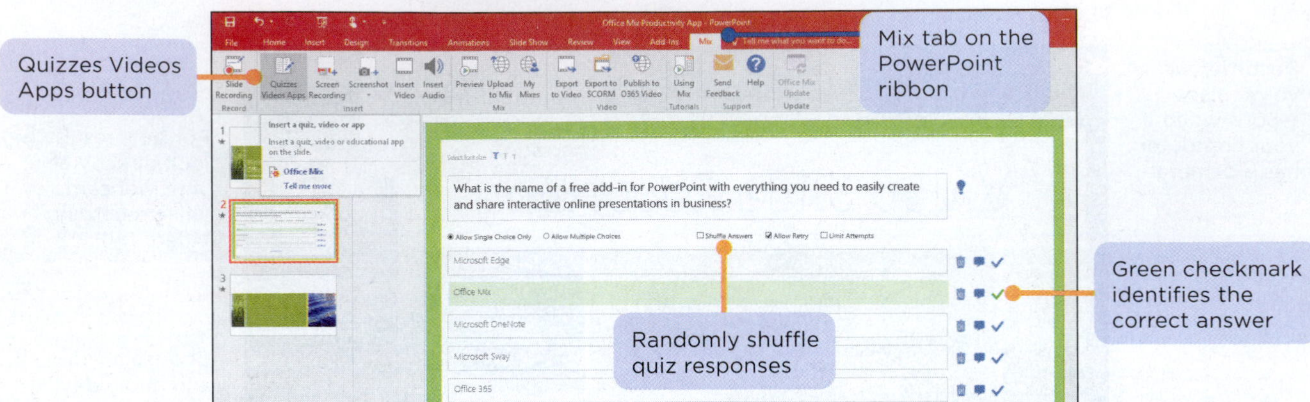

Sharing an Office Mix Presentation

When you complete your work with Office Mix, upload the presentation to your personal Office Mix dashboard as shown in **Figure 15**. Users of PCs, Macs, iOS devices, and Android devices can access and play Office Mix presentations. The Office Mix dashboard displays built-in analytics that include the quiz results and how much time viewers spent on each slide. You can play completed Office Mix presentations online or download them as movies.

Figure 15: Sharing an Office Mix presentation

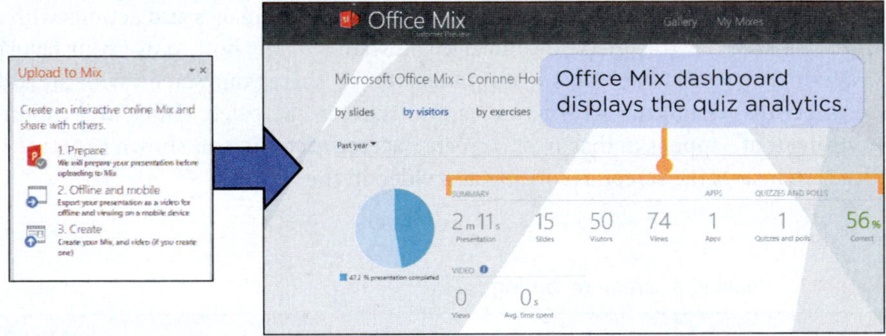

Try This Now

Learn to use Office Mix!

Links to companion **Sways**, featuring **videos** with hands-on instructions, are located on www.cengagebrain.com.

1: Creating an Office Mix Tutorial for OneNote

Note: This activity requires a microphone on your computer.

Office Mix makes it easy to record screens and their contents. Create PowerPoint slides with an Office Mix screen recording to show OneNote 2016 features. Perform the following tasks:

a. Create a PowerPoint presentation with the Ion Boardroom template. Create an opening slide with the title **My Favorite OneNote Features** and enter your name in the subtitle.
b. Create three additional slides, each titled with a new feature of OneNote. Open OneNote and use the Mix tab in PowerPoint to capture three separate screen recordings that teach your favorite features.
c. Add a fifth slide that quizzes the user with a multiple-choice question about OneNote and includes four responses. Be sure to insert a checkmark indicating the correct response.
d. Upload the completed presentation to your Office Mix dashboard and share the link with your instructor.
e. Submit your assignment link in the format specified by your instructor.

2: Teaching Augmented Reality with Office Mix

Note: This activity requires a webcam or built-in video camera on your computer.

A local elementary school has asked you to teach augmented reality to its students using Office Mix. Perform the following tasks:

a. Research augmented reality using your favorite online search tools.
b. Create a PowerPoint presentation with the Frame template. Create an opening slide with the title **Augmented Reality** and enter your name in the subtitle.
c. Create a slide with four bullets summarizing your research of augmented reality. Create a 20-second slide recording of yourself providing a quick overview of augmented reality.
d. Create another slide with a 30-second screen recording of a video about augmented reality from a site such as YouTube or another video-sharing site.
e. Add a final slide that quizzes the user with a true/false question about augmented reality. Be sure to insert a checkmark indicating the correct response.
f. Upload the completed presentation to your Office Mix dashboard and share the link with your instructor.
g. Submit your assignment link in the format specified by your instructor.

3: Marketing a Travel Destination with Office Mix

Note: This activity requires a webcam or built-in video camera on your computer.

To convince your audience to travel to a particular city, create a slide presentation marketing any city in the world using a slide recording, screen recording, and a quiz. Perform the following tasks:

a. Create a PowerPoint presentation with any template. Create an opening slide with the title of the city you are marketing as a travel destination and your name in the subtitle.
b. Create a slide with four bullets about the featured city. Create a 30-second slide recording of yourself explaining why this city is the perfect vacation destination.
c. Create another slide with a 20-second screen recording of a travel video about the city from a site such as YouTube or another video-sharing site.
d. Add a final slide that quizzes the user with a multiple-choice question about the featured city with five responses. Be sure to include a checkmark indicating the correct response.
e. Upload the completed presentation to your Office Mix dashboard and share your link with your instructor.
f. Submit your assignment link in the format specified by your instructor.

Introduction to Microsoft Edge

Reading view | Hub | Cortana | Web Note | Inking | sandbox

Bottom Line

- Microsoft Edge is the name of the new web browser built into Windows 10.
- Microsoft Edge allows you to search the web faster, take web notes, read webpages without distractions, and get instant assistance from Cortana.

Microsoft Edge is the default web browser developed for the Windows 10 operating system as a replacement for Internet Explorer. Unlike its predecessor, Edge lets you write on webpages, read webpages without advertisements and other distractions, and search for information using a virtual personal assistant. The Edge interface is clean and basic, as shown in **Figure 16**, meaning you can pay more attention to the webpage content.

Figure 16: Microsoft Edge tools

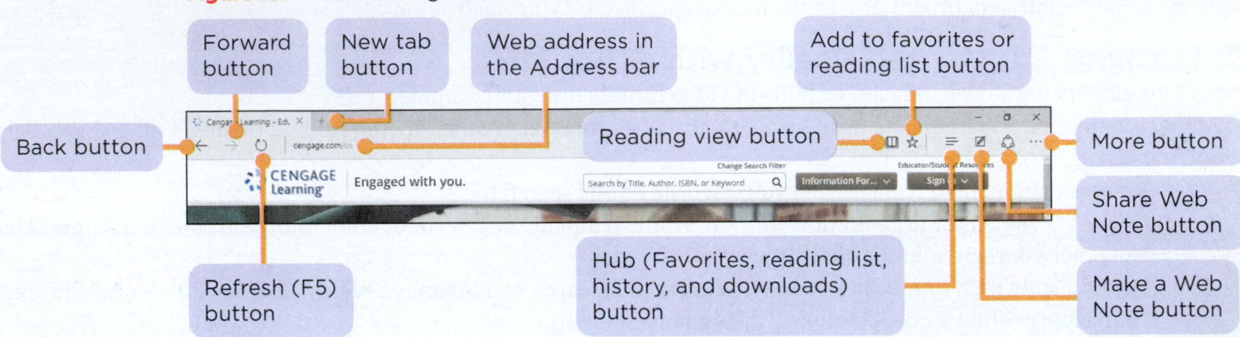

Learn to use Edge!

Links to companion **Sways**, featuring **videos** with hands-on instructions, are located on www.cengagebrain.com.

Browsing the Web with Microsoft Edge

One of the fastest browsers available, Edge allows you to type search text directly in the Address bar. As you view the resulting webpage, you can switch to **Reading view**, which is available for most news and research sites, to eliminate distracting advertisements. For example, if you are catching up on technology news online, the webpage might be difficult to read due to a busy layout cluttered with ads. Switch to Reading view to refresh the page and remove the original page formatting, ads, and menu sidebars to read the article distraction-free.

Consider the **Hub** in Microsoft Edge as providing one-stop access to all the things you collect on the web, such as your favorite websites, reading list, surfing history, and downloaded files.

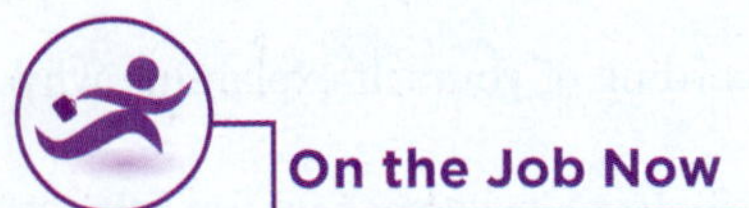

On the Job Now

Businesses started adopting Internet Explorer more than 20 years ago simply to view webpages. Today, Microsoft Edge has a different purpose: to promote interaction with the web and share its contents with colleagues.

Locating Information with Cortana

Cortana, the Windows 10 virtual assistant, plays an important role in Microsoft Edge. After you turn on Cortana, it appears as an animated circle in the Address bar when you might need assistance, as shown in the restaurant website in **Figure 17**. When you click the Cortana icon, a pane slides in from the right of the browser window to display detailed information about the restaurant, including maps and reviews. Cortana can also assist you in defining words, finding the weather, suggesting coupons for shopping, updating stock market information, and calculating math.

Figure 17: Cortana providing restaurant information

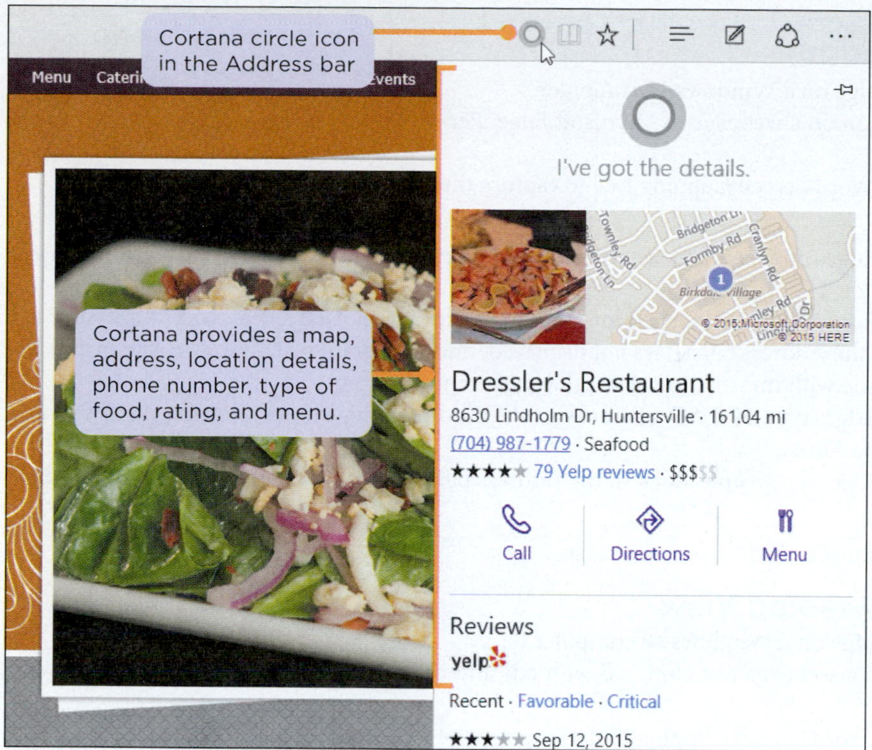

Annotating Webpages

One of the most impressive Microsoft Edge features are the **Web Note** tools, which you use to write on a webpage or to highlight text. When you click the Make a Web Note button, an **Inking** toolbar appears, as shown in **Figure 18**, that provides writing and drawing tools. These tools include an eraser, a pen, and a highlighter with different colors. You can also insert a typed note and copy a screen image (called a screen clipping). You can draw with a pointing device, fingertip, or stylus using different pen colors. Whether you add notes to a recipe, annotate sources for a research paper, or select a product while shopping online, the Web Note tools can enhance your productivity. After you complete your notes, click the Save button to save the annotations to OneNote, your Favorites list, or your Reading list. You can share the inked page with others using the Share Web Note button.

To enhance security, Microsoft Edge runs in a partial sandbox, an arrangement that prevents attackers from gaining control of your computer. Browsing within the **sandbox** protects computer resources and information from hackers.

Figure 18: Web Note tools in Microsoft Edge

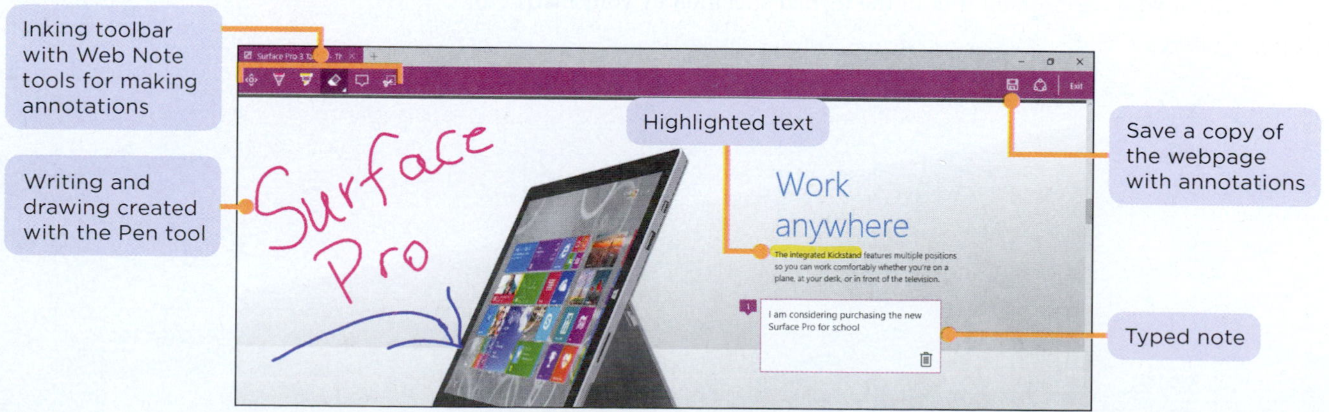

Try This Now

> **Learn to use Edge!**
> Links to companion **Sways**, featuring **videos** with hands-on instructions, are located on www.cengagebrain.com.

1: Using Cortana in Microsoft Edge

Note: This activity requires using Microsoft Edge on a Windows 10 computer.

Cortana can assist you in finding information on a webpage in Microsoft Edge. Perform the following tasks:

a. Create a Word document using the Word Screen Clipping tool to capture the following screenshots.
   - Screenshot A—Using Microsoft Edge, open a webpage with a technology news article. Right-click a term in the article and ask Cortana to define it.
   - Screenshot B—Using Microsoft Edge, open the website of a fancy restaurant in a city near you. Make sure the Cortana circle icon is displayed in the Address bar. (If it's not displayed, find a different restaurant website.) Click the Cortana circle icon to display a pane with information about the restaurant.
   - Screenshot C—Using Microsoft Edge, type **10 USD to Euros** in the Address bar without pressing the Enter key. Cortana converts the U.S. dollars to Euros.
   - Screenshot D—Using Microsoft Edge, type **Apple stock** in the Address bar without pressing the Enter key. Cortana displays the current stock quote.

b. Submit your assignment in the format specified by your instructor.

2: Viewing Online News with Reading View

Note: This activity requires using Microsoft Edge on a Windows 10 computer.

Reading view in Microsoft Edge can make a webpage less cluttered with ads and other distractions. Perform the following tasks:

a. Create a Word document using the Word Screen Clipping tool to capture the following screenshots.
   - Screenshot A—Using Microsoft Edge, open the website **mashable.com**. Open a technology article. Click the Reading view button to display an ad-free page that uses only basic text formatting.
   - Screenshot B—Using Microsoft Edge, open the website **bbc.com**. Open any news article. Click the Reading view button to display an ad-free page that uses only basic text formatting.
   - Screenshot C—Make three types of annotations (Pen, Highlighter, and Add a typed note) on the BBC article page displayed in Reading view.

b. Submit your assignment in the format specified by your instructor.

3: Inking with Microsoft Edge

Note: This activity requires using Microsoft Edge on a Windows 10 computer.

Microsoft Edge provides many annotation options to record your ideas. Perform the following tasks:

a. Open the website **wolframalpha.com** in the Microsoft Edge browser. Wolfram Alpha is a well-respected academic search engine. Type **US$100 1965 dollars in 2015** in the Wolfram Alpha search text box and press the Enter key.

b. Click the Make a Web Note button to display the Web Note tools. Using the Pen tool, draw a circle around the result on the webpage. Save the page to OneNote.

c. In the Wolfram Alpha search text box, type the name of the city closest to where you live and press the Enter key. Using the Highlighter tool, highlight at least three interesting results. Add a note and then type a sentence about what you learned about this city. Save the page to OneNote. Share your OneNote notebook with your instructor.

d. Submit your assignment link in the format specified by your instructor.

MODULE 5

Working with Templates, Themes, and Styles

Creating a Summary Report

WORD

OBJECTIVES

Session 5.1
- Create a new document from a template
- Move through a document using Go To
- Use the thesaurus to find synonyms
- Customize a document theme
- Save a custom theme
- Select a style set
- Customize a style
- Change character spacing

Session 5.2
- Create a new style
- Inspect styles
- Reveal and compare text formatting details
- Review line and page break settings
- Generate and update a table of contents
- Create and use a template
- Create a Quick Part

Case | *Dakota Tech Incubator*

The Sioux Falls Center for Business and Technology, in Sioux Falls, South Dakota, is spearheading construction of the Dakota Tech Incubator. The facility will house new, technically oriented companies (known as startups) that require the specialized kind of support needed in the fast-moving technology world. Benjamin Witinski, a project manager at the Sioux Falls Center for Business and Technology, is responsible for creating a report designed to help generate interest in the Dakota Tech Incubator. Benjamin has asked you to help him prepare the report. He's also interested in learning more about Word templates, so he'd like you to do some research by opening a few templates and examining the styles they offer. Next, he wants you to modify the formatting currently applied to his report document, including modifying the theme and one of the styles, creating a new style, and adding a table of contents. Then he wants you to create a template that can be used for all reports produced by his organization, as well as a reusable text box containing the current mailing address and phone number for the Sioux Falls Center for Business and Technology, which his coworkers can insert into any Word document via the Quick Parts gallery.

STARTING DATA FILES

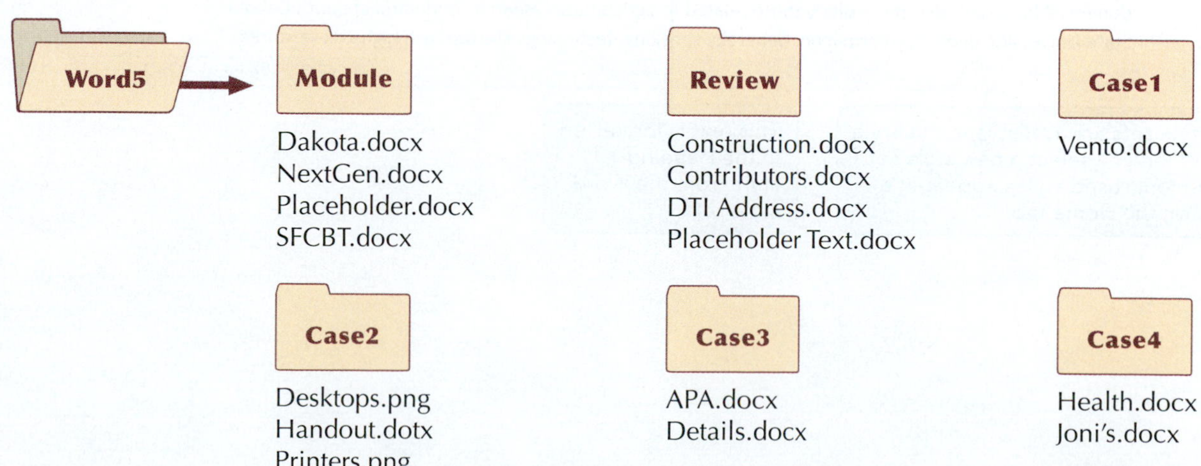

Session 5.1 Visual Overview:

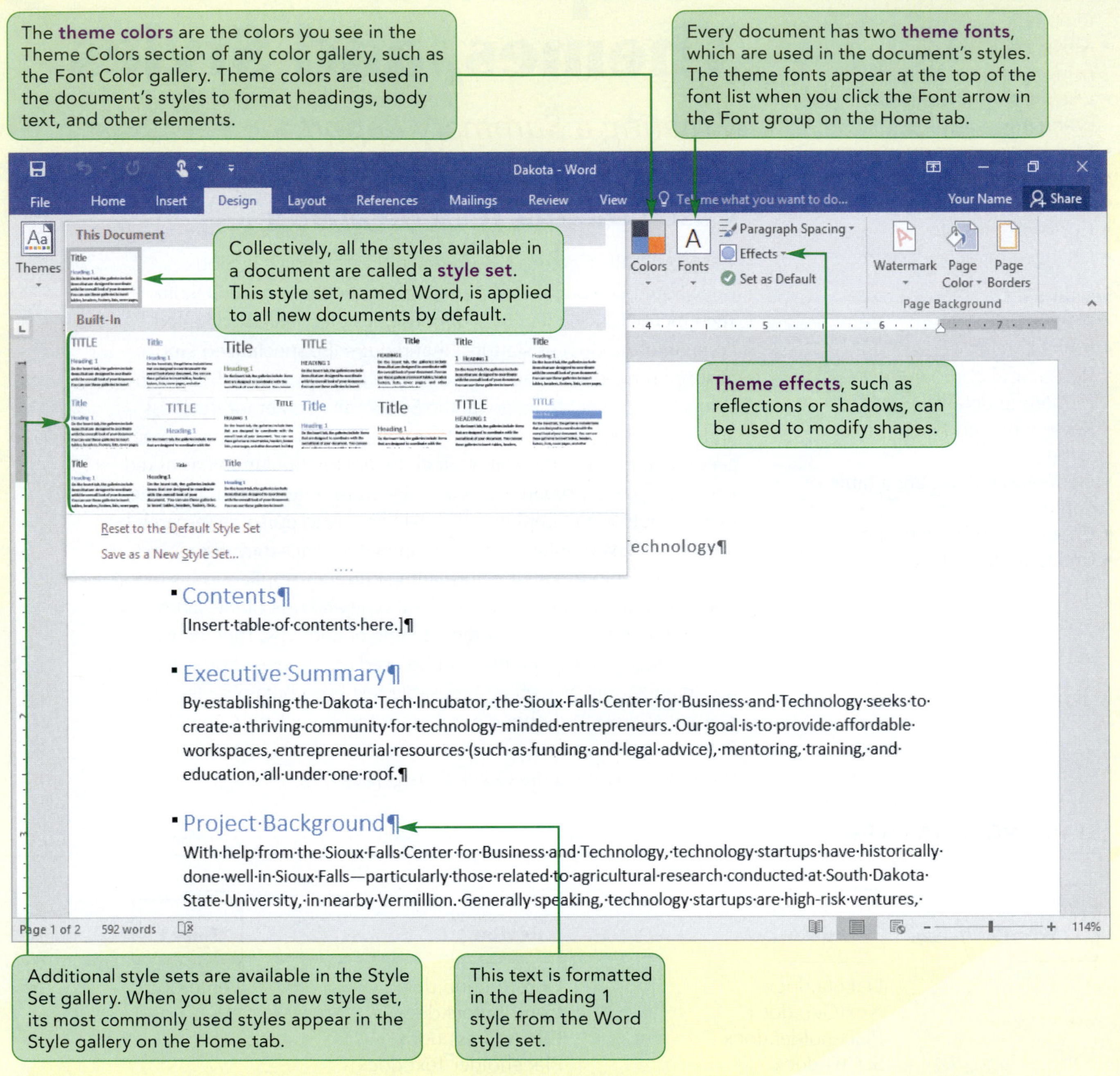
The theme colors are the colors you see in the Theme Colors section of any color gallery, such as the Font Color gallery. Theme colors are used in the document's styles to format headings, body text, and other elements.
Every document has two theme fonts, which are used in the document's styles. The theme fonts appear at the top of the font list when you click the Font arrow in the Font group on the Home tab.
Dakota - Word
File
Home
Insert
Design
Layout
References
Mailings
Review
View
Tell me what you want to do...
Your Name
Share
Themes
This Document
Built-In
Collectively, all the styles available in a document are called a style set. This style set, named Word, is applied to all new documents by default.
Colors
Fonts
Paragraph Spacing
Effects
Set as Default
Watermark
Page Color
Page Borders
Page Background
Theme effects, such as reflections or shadows, can be used to modify shapes.
Reset to the Default Style Set
Save as a New Style Set...
Technology¶
Contents¶
[Insert·table·of·contents·here.]¶
Executive·Summary¶
By·establishing·the·Dakota·Tech·Incubator,·the·Sioux·Falls·Center·for·Business·and·Technology·seeks·to·create·a·thriving·community·for·technology-minded·entrepreneurs.·Our·goal·is·to·provide·affordable·workspaces,·entrepreneurial·resources·(such·as·funding·and·legal·advice),·mentoring,·training,·and·education,·all·under·one·roof.¶
Project·Background¶
With·help·from·the·Sioux·Falls·Center·for·Business·and·Technology,·technology·startups·have·historically·done·well·in·Sioux·Falls—particularly·those·related·to·agricultural·research·conducted·at·South·Dakota·State·University,·in·nearby·Vermillion.·Generally·speaking,·technology·startups·are·high-risk·ventures,·
Page 1 of 2
592 words
114%
Additional style sets are available in the Style Set gallery. When you select a new style set, its most commonly used styles appear in the Style gallery on the Home tab.
This text is formatted in the Heading 1 style from the Word style set.

Custom Themes and Style Sets

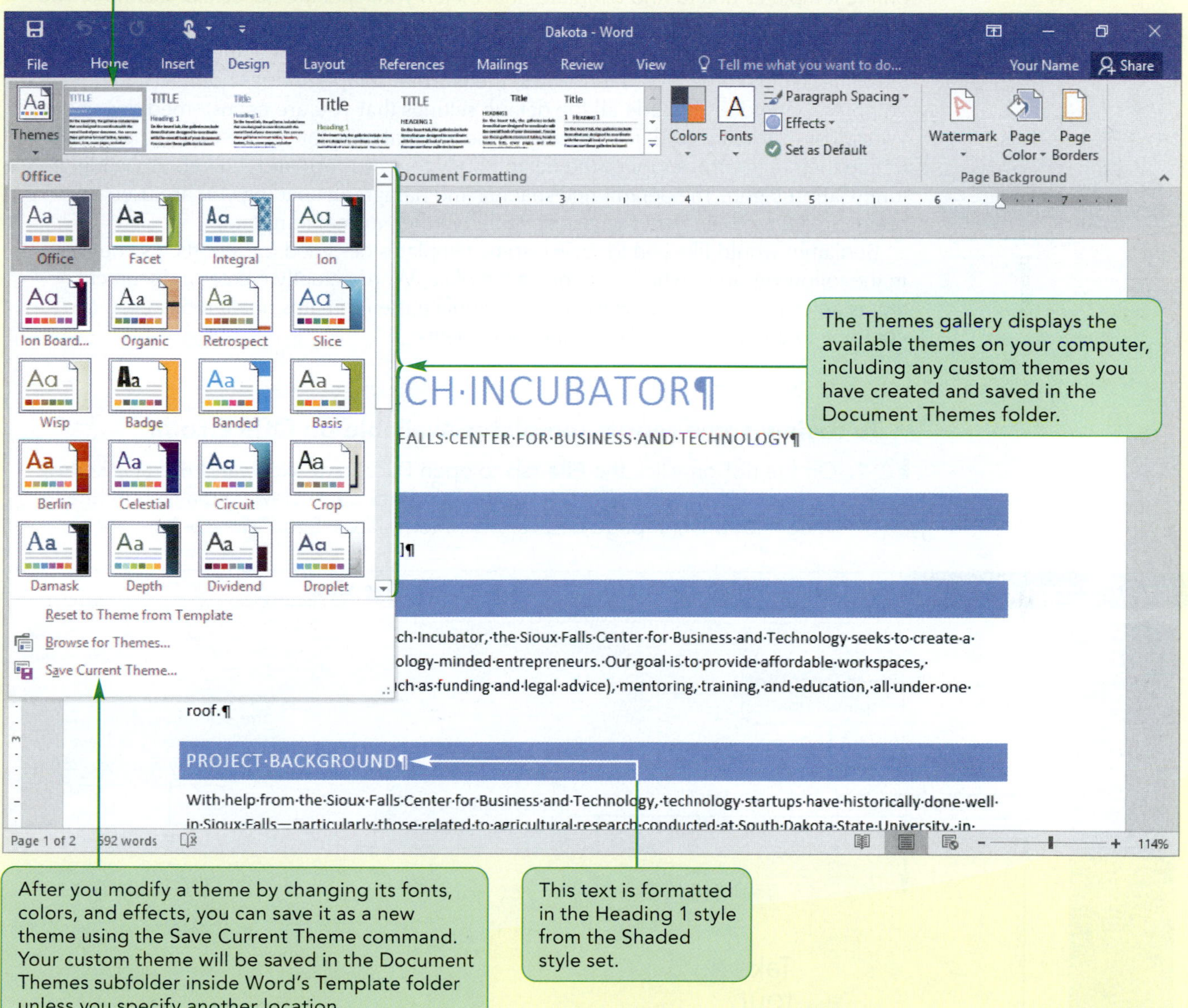
This style set, named Shaded, is applied to the Dakota document, shown below. In the Shaded style set, the Heading 1 style formats text with blue paragraph shading and a white font color.
The Themes gallery displays the available themes on your computer, including any custom themes you have created and saved in the Document Themes folder.
After you modify a theme by changing its fonts, colors, and effects, you can save it as a new theme using the Save Current Theme command. Your custom theme will be saved in the Document Themes subfolder inside Word's Template folder unless you specify another location.
This text is formatted in the Heading 1 style from the Shaded style set.
Dakota - Word
File
Home
Insert
Design
Layout
References
Mailings
Review
View
Tell me what you want to do...
Your Name
Share
Themes
Colors
Fonts
Paragraph Spacing
Effects
Set as Default
Watermark
Page Color
Page Borders
Page Background
Document Formatting
Office
Office
Facet
Integral
Ion
Ion Board...
Organic
Retrospect
Slice
Wisp
Badge
Banded
Basis
Berlin
Celestial
Circuit
Crop
Damask
Depth
Dividend
Droplet
Reset to Theme from Template
Browse for Themes...
Save Current Theme...
CH·INCUBATOR¶
FALLS·CENTER·FOR·BUSINESS·AND·TECHNOLOGY¶
ch·Incubator,·the·Sioux·Falls·Center·for·Business·and·Technology·seeks·to·create·a·
ology-minded·entrepreneurs.·Our·goal·is·to·provide·affordable·workspaces,·
ch·as·funding·and·legal·advice),·mentoring,·training,·and·education,·all·under·one·
roof.¶
PROJECT·BACKGROUND¶
With·help·from·the·Sioux·Falls·Center·for·Business·and·Technology,·technology·startups·have·historically·done·well·
Page 1 of 2
592 words
114%

Creating a New Document from a Template

A template is a file that you use as a starting point for a series of similar documents so that you don't have to re-create formatting and text for each new document. A template can contain customized styles, text, graphics, or any other element that you want to repeat from one document to another. In this module, you'll customize the styles and themes in a Word document and then save the document as a template to use for future documents. Before you do that, however, you will investigate some of the ready-made templates available at Office.com.

When you first start Word, the Recent screen in Backstage view displays a variety of templates available from Office.com. You can also enter keywords in the Search for online templates box to find templates that match your specific needs. For example, you could search for a calendar template, a birthday card template, or a report template.

TIP

Templates have the file extension .dotx to differentiate them from regular Word documents, which have the extension .docx.

Every new, blank document that you open in Word is a copy of the Normal template. Unlike other Word templates, the **Normal template** does not have any text or graphics, but it does include all the default settings that you are accustomed to using in Word. For example, the default theme in the Normal template is the Office theme. The Office theme, in turn, supplies the default body font (Calibri) and the default heading font (Calibri Light). The default line spacing and paragraph spacing you are used to seeing in a new document are also specified in the Normal template.

Benjamin would like you to review some templates designed for reports. As you'll see in the following steps, when you open a template, Word actually creates a document that is an exact copy of the template. The template itself remains unaltered, so you can continue to use it as the basis for other documents.

To review some report templates available on Office.com:

1. On the ribbon, click the **File** tab to open Backstage view, and then click **New** in the navigation bar. The New screen in Backstage view displays thumbnail images of the first page of a variety of templates. See Figure 5-1.

Figure 5-1 Featured templates on the New screen in Backstage view

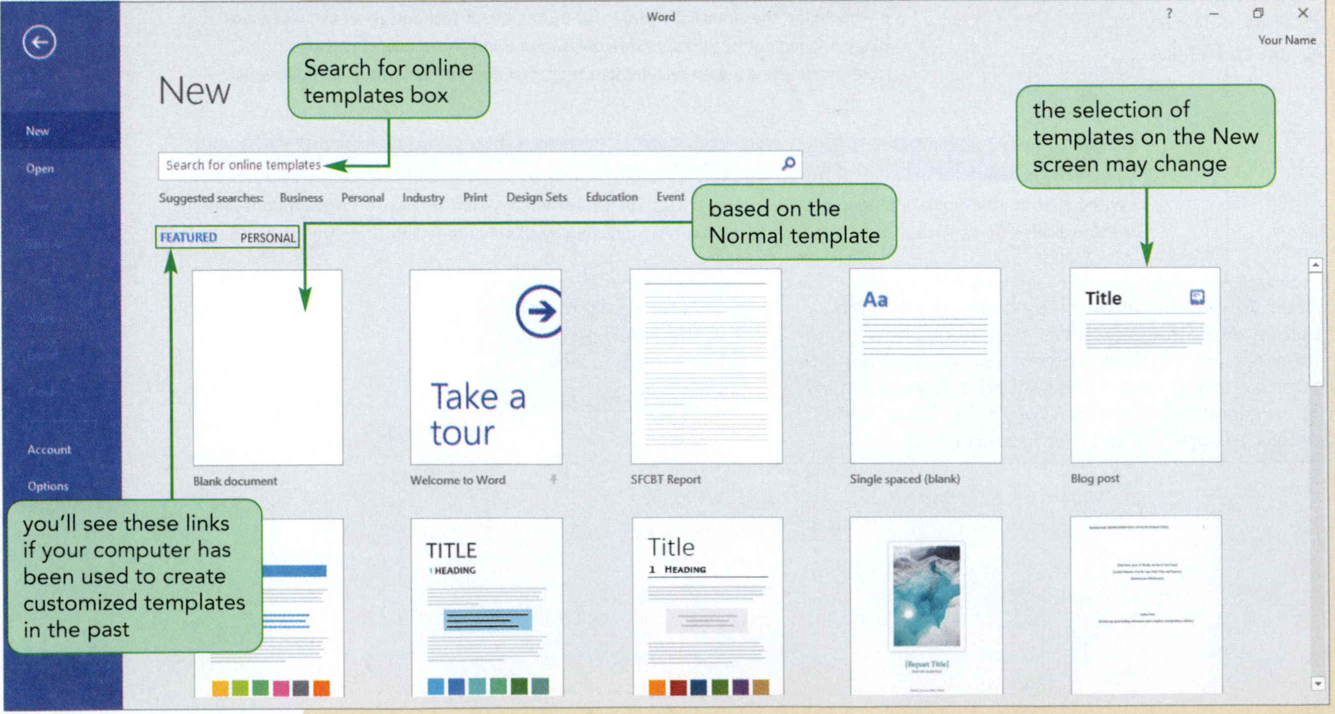

Trouble? If you just started Word, you'll see the list of templates on the Recent screen. You'll be able to complete the next step using the Search for online templates box on the Recent screen.

Below the Search for online templates box are template options available from Office.com. You've already used the Blank document template to open a new, blank document that is based on the Normal template. The list of templates changes as new templates become available, so your screen probably won't match Figure 5-1 exactly.

If your computer has been used to create customized templates, two additional links are displayed below the Search for online templates box—FEATURED and PERSONAL. You can ignore those links for now. In this case, you want to open a document based on a template designed specifically for reports.

2. Click the **Search for online templates** box, type **report** and then press the **Enter** key. The New screen displays thumbnail images for a variety of report templates. If you scroll down to the bottom, you'll see options for searching for templates to use in other Office applications. The Category pane on the right displays a list of report categories. You could click any category to display only the templates in that category.
3. Click the first template in the top row. A window opens with a preview of the template. Note that the template indicates it is provided by Microsoft Corporation. Figure 5-2 shows the Student report with cover photo template. The template that opens on your computer might be different.

Figure 5-2 **Previewing a template**

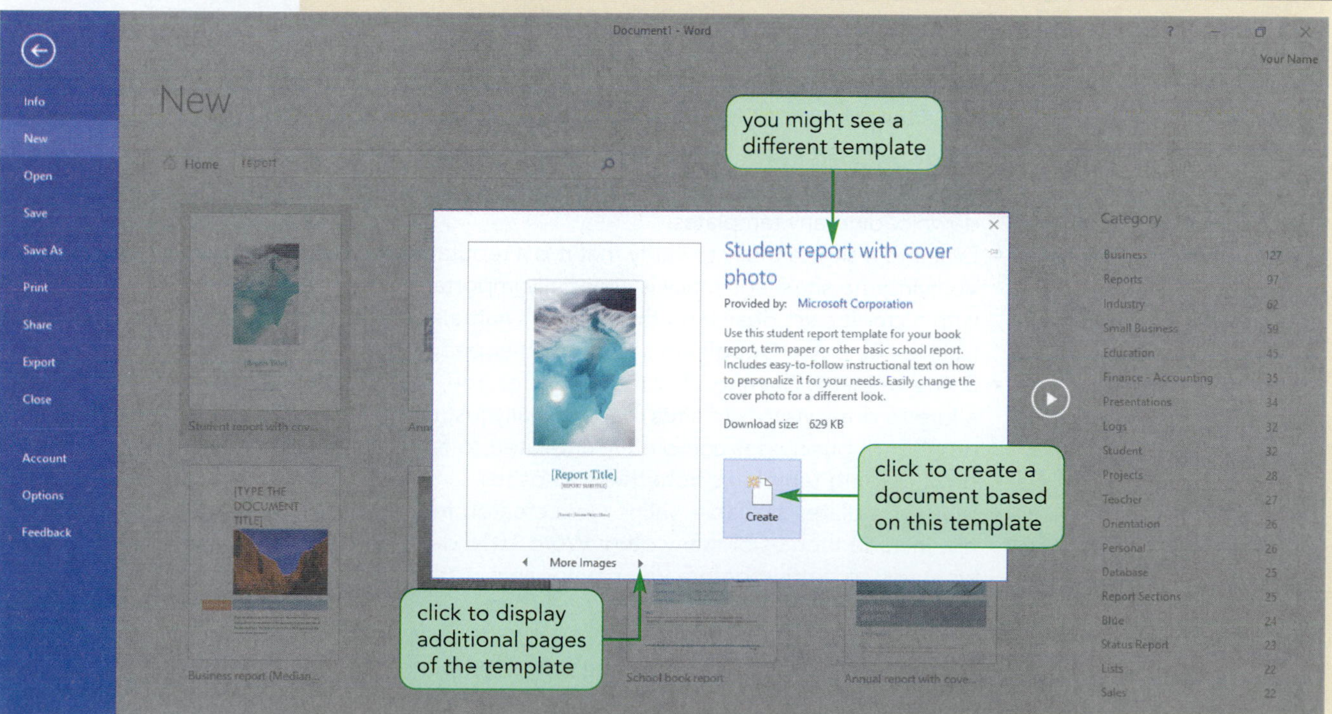

You could click the Close button to close the preview window and browse other report templates, but Benjamin asks you to continue investigating the current template.

4. Click the **Create** button. A new document based on the Student report with cover photo template opens. It begins with a cover page and contains a number of content controls designed specifically for the template, similar to the content controls you've seen in other documents. It also contains some placeholder text, a footer, and graphics.

   At this point, you could save the document with a new name and then begin revising it to create an actual report. But since your goal now is to review various templates, you'll close the document.

5. Close the document without saving any changes.
6. On the ribbon, click the **File** tab, and then click **New** in the navigation bar.
7. Search online for newsletter templates, open a document based on one of the templates, and then review the document, making note of the various elements it includes.
8. Close the newsletter document without saving it.
9. Return to the New screen, and search for templates for flyers. Open a new document based on one of the templates, review the document, and then close it without saving it.

PROSKILLS

Decision Making: Using Templates from Other Sources

The Office.com website offers a wide variety of templates that are free to Microsoft Office users. Countless other websites offer templates for free, for individual sale, as part of a subscription service, or a combination of all three. However, you need to be wary when searching for templates online. Keep in mind the following when deciding which sites to use:

- Files downloaded from the Internet can infect your computer with viruses and spyware, so make sure your computer has up-to-date antivirus and anti-malware software before downloading any templates.
- Evaluate a site carefully to verify that it is a reputable source of virus-free templates. Verifying the site's legitimacy is especially important if you intend to pay for a template with a credit card. Search for the website's name and URL using different search engines (such as Bing and Google) to see what other people say about it.
- Some websites claim to offer templates for free, when in fact the offer is primarily a lure to draw visitors to sites that are really just online billboards, with ads for any number of businesses completely unrelated to templates or Word documents. Avoid downloading templates from these websites.
- Many templates available online were created for earlier versions of Word that did not include themes or many other Word 2016 design features. Make sure you know what you're getting before you pay for an out-of-date template.

Now that you are finished reviewing report templates, you will open the document containing the report about the Dakota Tech Incubator.

To open Benjamin's report document:

1. Open the document **Dakota** from the Word5 > Module folder, and then save it as **Dakota Report** in the location specified by your instructor.
2. Display nonprinting characters and the rulers, switch to Print Layout view if necessary, and then change the Zoom level to **120%**, if necessary. See Figure 5-3.

Figure 5-3 Dakota Report document

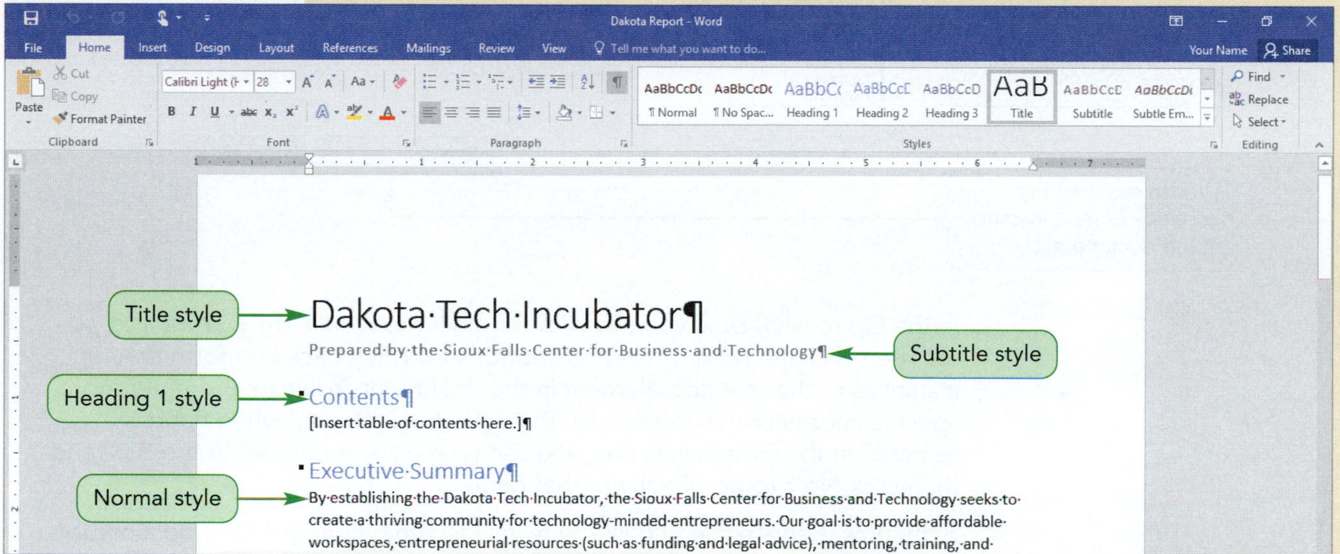

The report is formatted using the default settings of the Normal template, which means its current theme is the Office theme. Text in the report is formatted using the Title, Subtitle, Heading 1, Heading 2, and Normal styles. The document includes a footer containing "Dakota Tech Incubator" and a page number field.

Before you begin revising the document, you should review its contents. To get a quick overview of a document, it's helpful to use the Go To feature.

Using Go To

The Go To tab in the Find and Replace dialog box allows you to move quickly among elements in a document. For example, you can use it to move from heading to heading, from graphic to graphic, or from table to table. In a long document, this is an efficient way to review your work. Although the Dakota Report document is not very long, you can still review its contents using Go To.

To use the Go To feature to review the Dakota Report document:

1. If necessary, press the **Ctrl+Home** keys to move the insertion point to the beginning of the document.
2. On the ribbon, make sure the Home tab is displayed.

3. In the Editing group, click the **Find button arrow** to display the Find menu, and then click **Go To**. The Find and Replace dialog box opens, with the Go To tab displayed. See Figure 5-4.

Figure 5-4 Go To tab in the Find and Replace dialog box

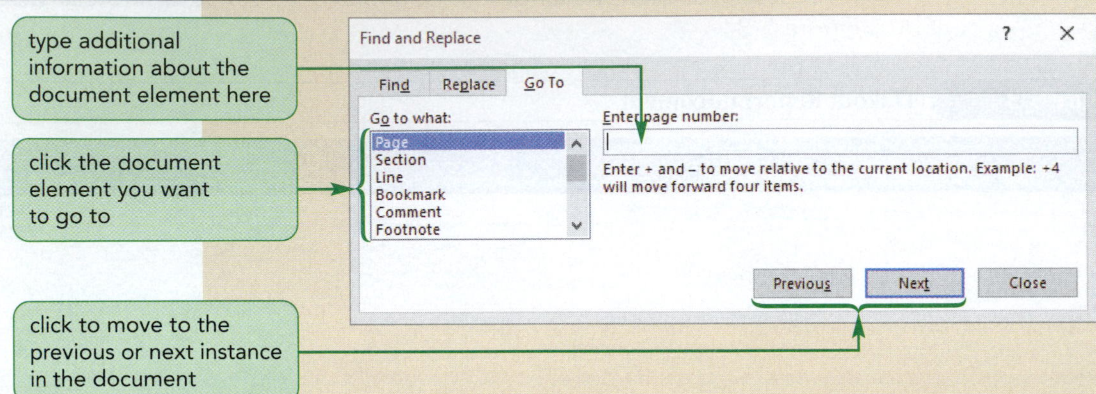

In the Go to what box, you can click the document element you want to go to. Then click the Next or Previous buttons to move back and forth among instances of the selected element in the document. You can also enter more specific information in the box on the right. For instance, when Page is selected in the Go to what box, you can type a page number in the box, and then click Next to go directly to that page.

Right now, Benjamin would like to review all the headings in the document—that is, all the paragraphs formatted with a heading style.

4. Scroll down to the bottom of the Go to what box, click **Heading**, and then click the **Next** button. The document scrolls down to position the first document heading, "Contents," at the top of the document window.
5. Click the **Next** button again. The document scrolls down to display the "Executive Summary" heading at the top of the document window.
6. Click the **Next** button five more times to display the last heading in the document, "Accelerate Investments," at the top of the document window.
7. Click the **Previous** button to display the "Coleman 3D Printing" heading at the top of the document window, and then close the Find and Replace dialog box.

INSIGHT

Choosing Between Go To and the Navigation Pane

Both the Go To tab in the Find and Replace dialog box and the Navigation pane allow you to move through a document heading by heading. Although you used Go To in the preceding steps, the Navigation pane is usually the better choice for working with headings; it displays a complete list of the headings, which helps you keep an eye on the document's overall organization. However, the Go To tab is more useful when you want to move through a document one graphic at a time, or one table at a time. In a document that contains a lot of graphics or tables, it's a good idea to use the Go To feature to make sure you've formatted all the graphics or tables similarly.

Next, before you begin formatting the document, Benjamin asks you to help him find a synonym for a word in the text.

Using the Thesaurus to Find Synonyms

In any kind of writing, choosing the right words to convey your meaning is important. If you need help, you can use Word's thesaurus to look up a list of synonyms, or possible replacements, for a specific word. You can right-click a word to display a shortcut menu with a short list of synonyms or open the Thesaurus task pane for a more complete list.

Benjamin is not happy with the word "innovators" in the paragraph about Coleman 3D Printing because he thinks it is overused in writing about technical entrepreneurs. He asks you to find a synonym.

To look up a synonym in the thesaurus:

1. In the last line one page 1, right-click the word **innovators**. A shortcut menu opens.
2. Point to **Synonyms**. A menu with a list of synonyms for "innovators" is displayed, as shown in Figure 5-5.

Figure 5-5 Shortcut menu with list of synonyms

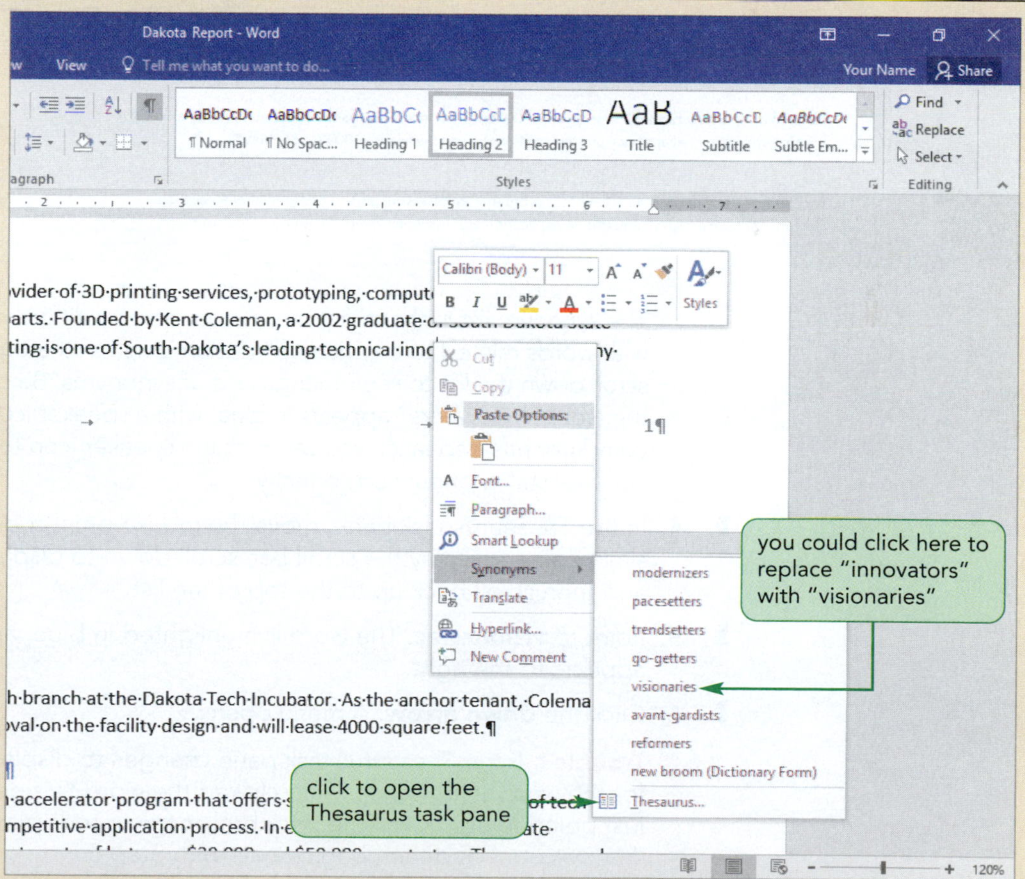

Benjamin thinks one word in the list, "visionaries," is a good replacement for "innovators." You could click "visionaries" to insert it in the document in place of "innovators," but Benjamin asks you to check the Thesaurus task pane to see if it suggests a better option.

3. At the bottom of the shortcut menu, click **Thesaurus**. The Thesaurus task pane opens on the right side of the document window, with the word "innovators" at the top and a more extensive list of synonyms below. The word "innovators" is also selected in the document, ready to be replaced. See Figure 5-6.

Figure 5-6 **Thesaurus task pane**

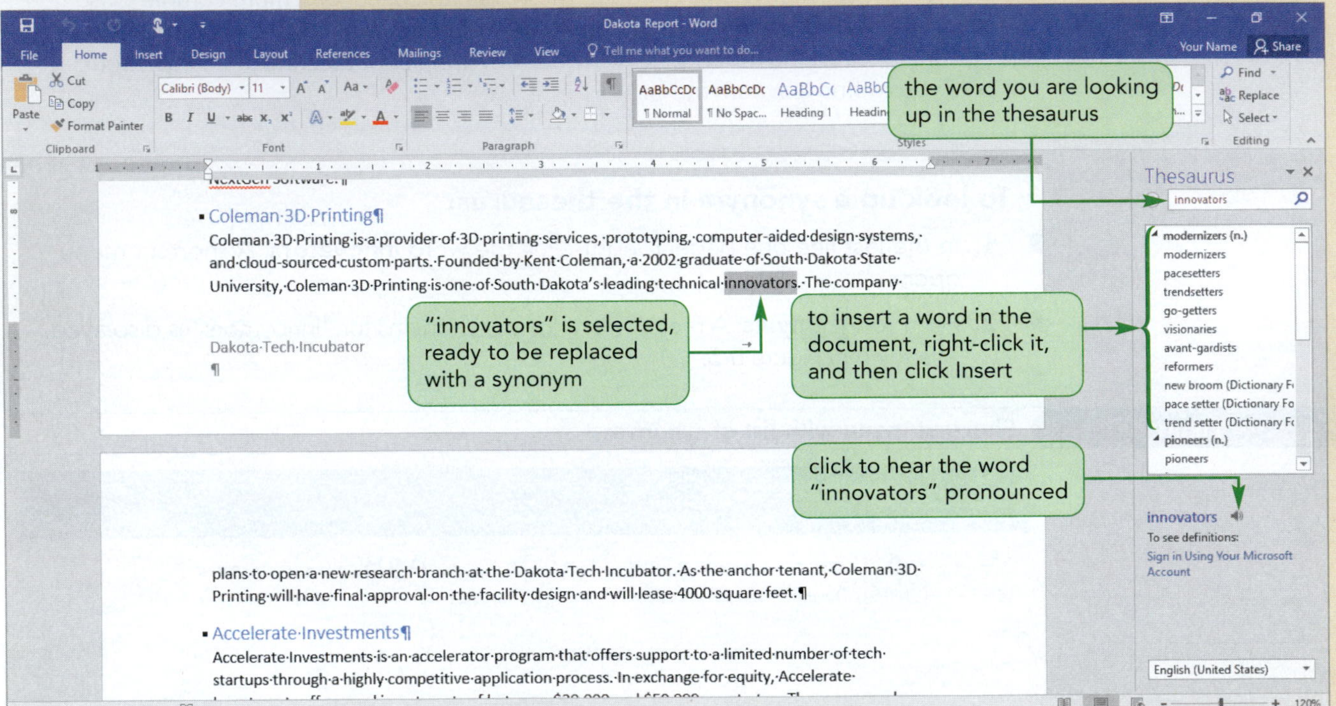

The synonym list in the task pane is organized by different shades of meaning, with words related to the idea of "modernizers" at the top of the list. You can scroll down the list to see other groups of synonyms. Below the list of synonyms, the word "innovators" appears in blue, with a speaker icon next to it. If your computer has a speaker, you can click the speaker icon to hear the word "innovators" pronounced correctly.

4. In the Thesaurus task pane, move the mouse pointer over the list of synonyms to display the scroll bar, scroll down to display other synonyms, and then scroll back up to the top of the list.
5. Point to **visionaries**. The word is highlighted in blue, and a down arrow appears to the right.
6. Click the **down arrow**. A menu opens.

   Trouble? If the Thesaurus task pane changes to display a set of synonyms for the word "visionaries," you clicked the word "visionaries" instead of just pointing at it. Click the Back button to redisplay the synonyms for "innovators," and then begin again with Step 5.

7. Click **Insert** to replace "innovators" with "visionaries" in the document, and then close the Thesaurus task pane.
8. Save the document.

INSIGHT

Looking Up Information in the Insight Pane

Word's Smart Lookup feature makes it easy to search the web for information about a topic in your document. To get started, select a word or phrase in your document, click the Review tab, and then click the Smart Lookup button in the Insights group. This opens the Insights task pane, with links to various sources related to your selected topic. Depending on the topic, the task pane might also display thumbnails of relevant images. Click any link or picture to display its complete web page in your browser. When you're finished, return to Word, and close the Insights task pane.

Now that the document text is finished, you can get to work on the formatting. You'll start by customizing the document theme.

Customizing the Document Theme

A document theme consists of three main components—theme colors, theme fonts, and theme effects. A specific set of colors, fonts, and effects is associated with each theme, but you can mix and match them to create a customized theme for your document. The theme fonts are the fonts used in a document's styles. You see them at the top of the font list when you click the Font arrow in the Font group on the Home tab. The theme colors are displayed in the Theme Colors section of any color gallery. The colors used to format headings, body text, and other elements are all drawn from the document's theme colors. Theme effects alter the appearance of shapes. Because they are generally very subtle, theme effects are not a theme element you will typically be concerned with.

When you change the theme colors, fonts, or effects for a document, the changes affect only that document. However, you can also save the changes you make to create a new, custom theme, which you can then use for future documents.

The Dakota Report document, which was based on the Normal template, is formatted with the Office theme—which applies a blue font color to the headings by default and formats the headings in the Calibri Light font. Benjamin wants to select different theme colors and theme fonts. He doesn't plan to include any graphics, so there's no need to customize the theme effects. You'll start with the theme colors.

Changing the Theme Colors

The theme colors, which are designed to coordinate well with each other, are used in the various document styles, including the text styles available on the Home tab. They are also used in shape styles, WordArt styles, and picture styles. So when you want to change the colors in a document, it's always better to change the theme colors rather than selecting individual elements and applying a new color to each element from a color gallery. That way you can be sure colors will be applied consistently throughout the document—for example, the headings will all be shades of the same color.

Reports created by the Sioux Falls Center for Business and Technology are typically emailed to many recipients, some of whom might choose to print the reports. To keep printing costs as low as possible for all potential readers of his report, Benjamin wants to format his document in black and white. He asks you to apply a set of theme colors consisting of black and shades of gray.

To change the theme colors in the document:

1. Press the **Ctrl+Home** keys to display the beginning of the document.
2. On the ribbon, click the **Design** tab.

3. In the Document Formatting group, move the mouse pointer over the **Colors** button. A ScreenTip is displayed, indicating that the current theme colors are the Office theme colors.
4. Click the **Colors** button. A gallery of theme colors opens, with the Office theme colors selected at the top of the gallery. See Figure 5-7.

Figure 5-7 Theme Colors gallery

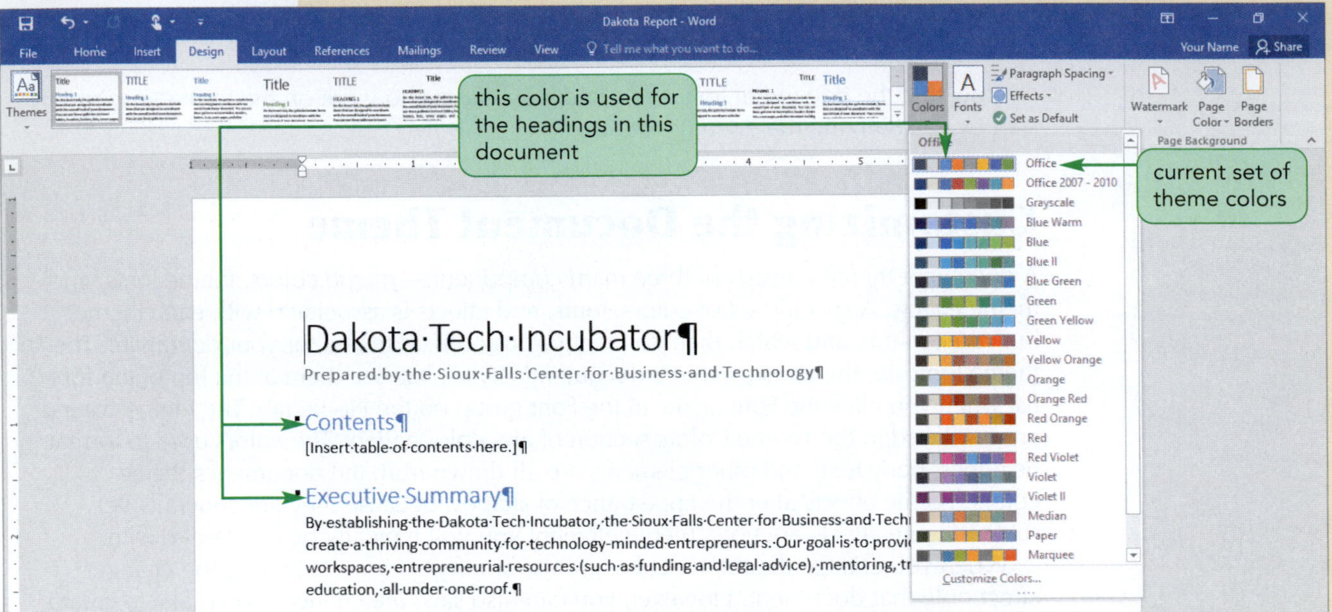

Each set of colors contains eight colors, with each assigned to specific elements. For example, the third color from the left is the color used for headings. The remaining colors are used for other types of elements, such as hyperlinks, page borders, shading, and so on.

Trouble? If you see additional theme colors at the top of the gallery under the "Custom" heading, then custom theme colors have been created and stored on your computer.

5. Move the mouse pointer over the options in the gallery to observe the Live Preview of the colors in the document.
6. Near the top of the gallery, click the **Grayscale** color set, which is the third from the top. The document headings are now formatted in gray.
7. Save the document.

The new colors you selected affect only the Dakota Report document. Your changes do not affect the Office theme that was installed with Word. Next, Benjamin asks you to customize the document theme further by changing the theme fonts.

Changing the Theme Fonts

As with theme colors, you can change the theme fonts in a document to suit your needs. Each theme uses two coordinating fonts—one for the headings and one for the body text. In some themes, the same font is used for the headings and the body text. When changing the theme fonts, you can select from all the font combinations available in any of the themes installed with Word.

To select a different set of theme fonts for the document:

1. In the Document Formatting group, move the mouse pointer over the **Fonts** button. A ScreenTip is displayed, indicating that the current fonts are Calibri Light for headings and Calibri for body text.
2. Click the **Fonts** button. The Theme Fonts gallery opens, displaying the heading and body font combinations for each theme.
3. Scroll down to review the fonts. Benjamin prefers the Franklin Gothic set of theme fonts, which includes Franklin Gothic Medium for headings and Franklin Gothic Book for the body text.
4. In the Theme Fonts gallery, point to **Franklin Gothic** to display a Live Preview in the document. See Figure 5-8.

Figure 5-8 Theme Fonts gallery

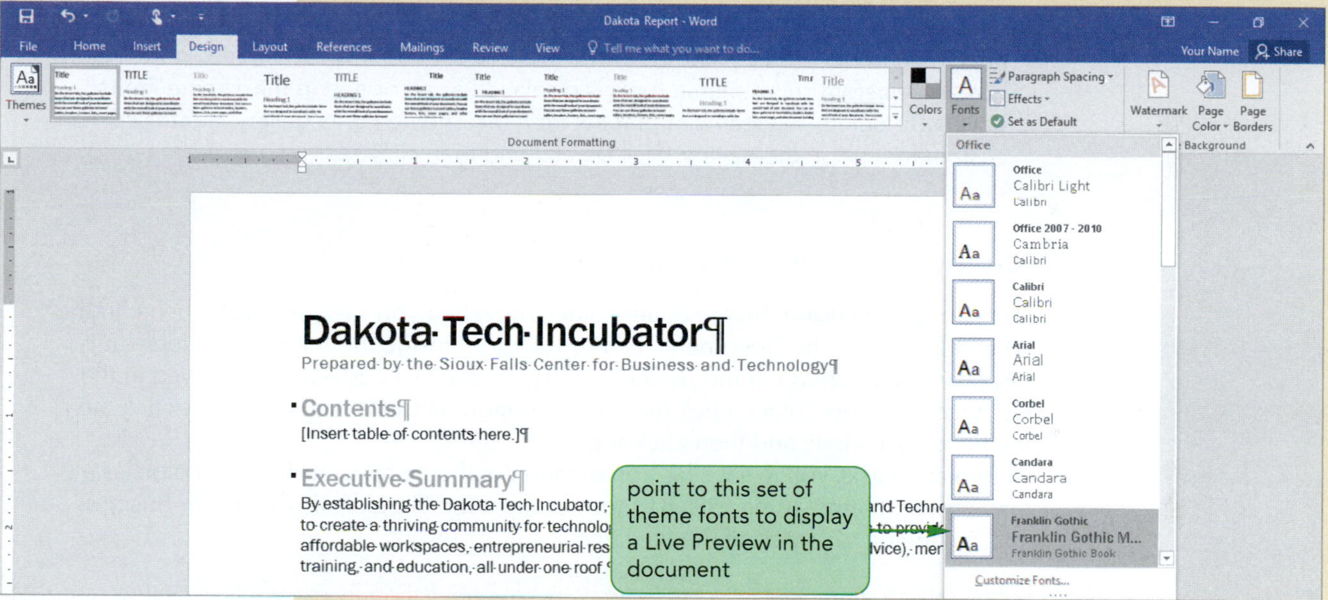

5. Click **Franklin Gothic**. The Theme Fonts gallery closes, and the new fonts are applied to the document.
6. Save the document.

The changes you have made to the theme fonts for the Dakota Report document do not affect the original Office theme that was installed with Word and that is available to all documents. To make your new combination of theme fonts and theme colors available to other documents, you can save it as a new, custom theme.

INSIGHT

Creating Custom Combinations of Theme Colors and Fonts

The theme color and font combinations installed with Word were created by Microsoft designers who are experts in creating harmonious-looking documents. It's usually best to stick with these preset combinations rather than trying to create your own set. However, in some situations you might need to create a customized combination of theme colors or fonts. When you do so, that set is saved as part of Word so that you can use it in other documents.

To create a custom set of theme colors, you click the Colors button in the Document Formatting group on the Design tab and then click Customize Colors to open the Create New Theme Colors dialog box, in which you can select colors for different theme elements and enter a descriptive name for the new set of theme colors. The custom set of theme colors will be displayed as an option in the Theme Colors gallery. To delete a custom set of colors from the Theme Colors gallery, right-click the custom color set in the gallery, click Delete, and then click Yes.

To create a custom set of heading and body fonts, you click the Fonts button in the Document Formatting group on the Design tab, click Customize Fonts, select the heading and body fonts, and then enter a name for the new set of fonts in the Name box. The custom set of theme fonts is displayed as an option in the Theme Fonts gallery. To delete a custom set of fonts from the Theme Fonts gallery, right-click the custom font set in the gallery, click Delete, and then click Yes.

Saving a Custom Theme

You can save a custom theme to any folder, but when you save a custom theme to the default location—the Document Themes subfolder inside the Templates folder—it is displayed as an option in the Themes gallery. To delete a custom theme saved in the Document Themes folder, click the Themes button on the Design tab, right-click the theme, click Delete, and then click Yes.

Benjamin asks you to save his combination of theme fonts and theme colors as a new custom theme, using "SFCBT," the acronym for "Sioux Falls Center for Business and Technology," as part of the filename.

To save the new custom theme:

1. In the Document Formatting group, click the **Themes** button, and then click **Save Current Theme**. The Save Current Theme dialog box opens. See Figure 5-9.

Figure 5-9 Save Current Theme dialog box

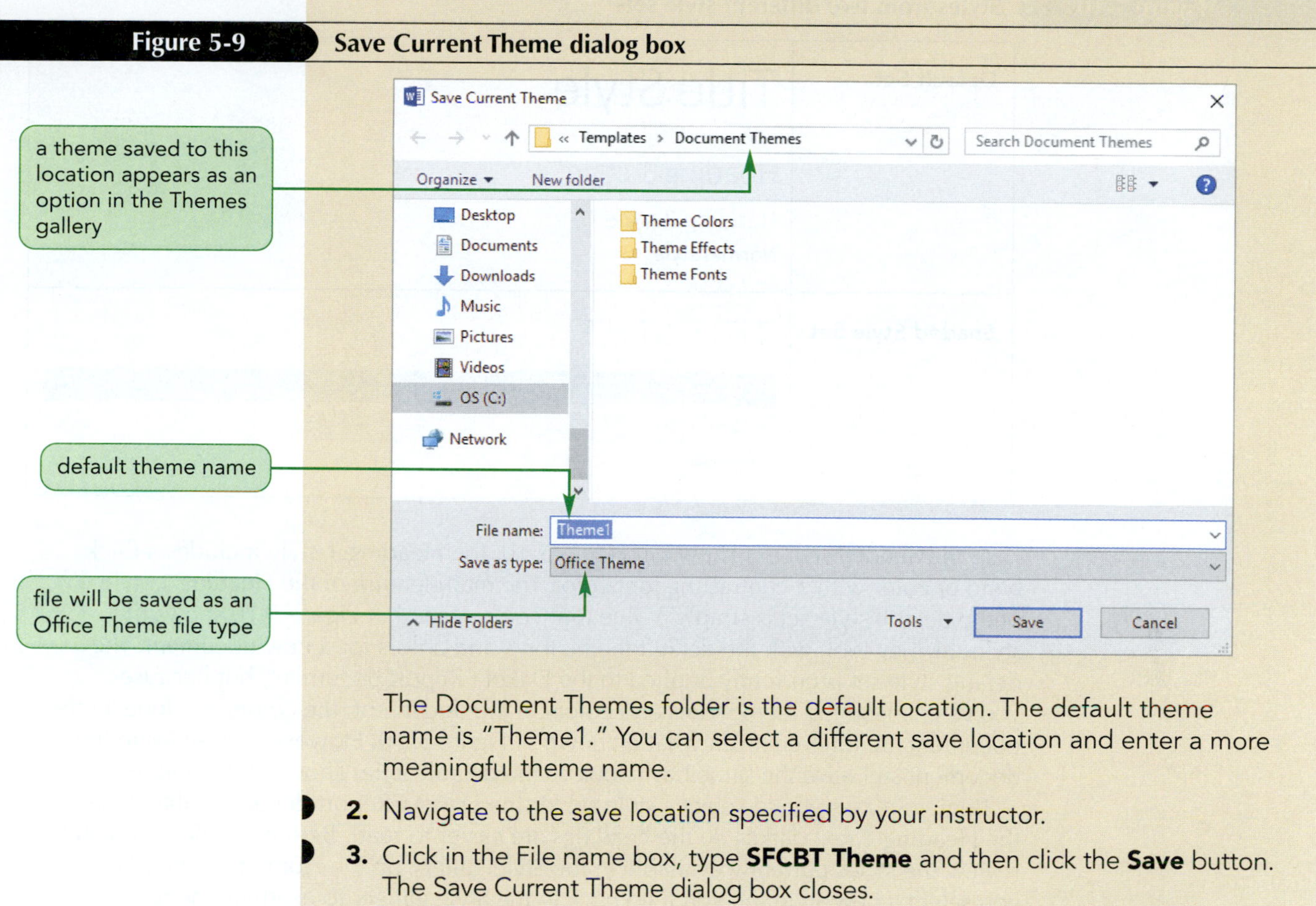

The Document Themes folder is the default location. The default theme name is "Theme1." You can select a different save location and enter a more meaningful theme name.

2. Navigate to the save location specified by your instructor.
3. Click in the File name box, type **SFCBT Theme** and then click the **Save** button. The Save Current Theme dialog box closes.

Benjamin plans to use the new theme to help standardize the look of all documents created in his department. When he is ready to apply it to a document, he can click the Themes button in the Document Formatting group on the Design tab, click Browse for Themes, navigate to the folder containing the custom theme, and then select the theme. If he wants to be able to access his theme from the Themes gallery instead, he will need to save it to the Document Themes folder first.

Benjamin likes the document's new look, but he wants to make some additional changes. First, he wants to select a different style set.

Selecting a Style Set

Recall that a style is a set of formatting options that you can apply to a specific text element in a document, such as a document's title, heading, or body text. So far, you have used only the default set of styles available in the Style gallery on the Home tab. You can access 16 additional style sets, or groups of styles, in the Style Set gallery, which is located in the Document Formatting group on the Design tab.

Each style set has a Normal style, a Heading 1 style, a Heading 2 style, and so on, but the formatting settings associated with each style vary from one style set to another. See Figure 5-10.

Figure 5-10 Styles from two different style sets

Default Set	Title Style Heading 1 style Heading 2 style Normal style
Shaded Style Set	TITLE STYLE HEADING 1 STYLE HEADING 2 STYLE Normal style

In the Shaded style set shown in Figure 5-10, the Heading 1 style includes a thick band of color with a contrasting font color. The main feature of the Heading 1 style of the default style set is simply a blue font color. Note that Figure 5-10 shows the styles as they look with the default theme fonts and colors for a new document. The default style set is currently applied to the Dakota Report document; but because you've changed the theme fonts and colors in the document, the colors and fonts in the document are different from what is shown in Figure 5-10. However, the styles in the document still have the same basic look as the default styles shown in the figure.

Benjamin asks you to select a style set for the Dakota Report document that makes the Heading 1 text darker, so the headings are easier to read. Before you do that, you'll review the styles currently available in the Style gallery on the Home tab. Then, after you select a new style set, you'll go back to the Style gallery to examine the new styles.

To review the styles in the Style gallery and select a new style set for the document:

1. On the ribbon, click the **Home** tab.
2. In the Styles group, click the **More** button, and then review the set of styles currently available in the Style gallery. Note that the icon for the Heading 1 style indicates that it applies a light gray font color.
3. On the ribbon, click the **Design** tab.
4. In the Document Formatting group, click the **More** button to open the Style Set gallery. Move the mouse pointer across the icons in the gallery to display their ScreenTips and to observe the Live Previews in the document.
5. Point to the **Lines (Stylish)** style set, which is on the far-right side of the top row. In the Lines (Stylish) style set, the Heading 1 style applies a black font color, with a light gray line that spans the width of the document. See Figure 5-11.

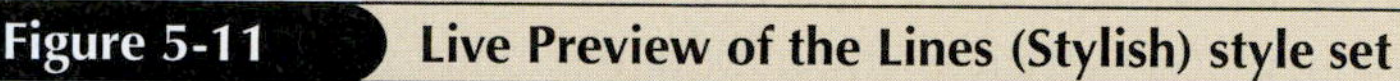

Figure 5-11 Live Preview of the Lines (Stylish) style set

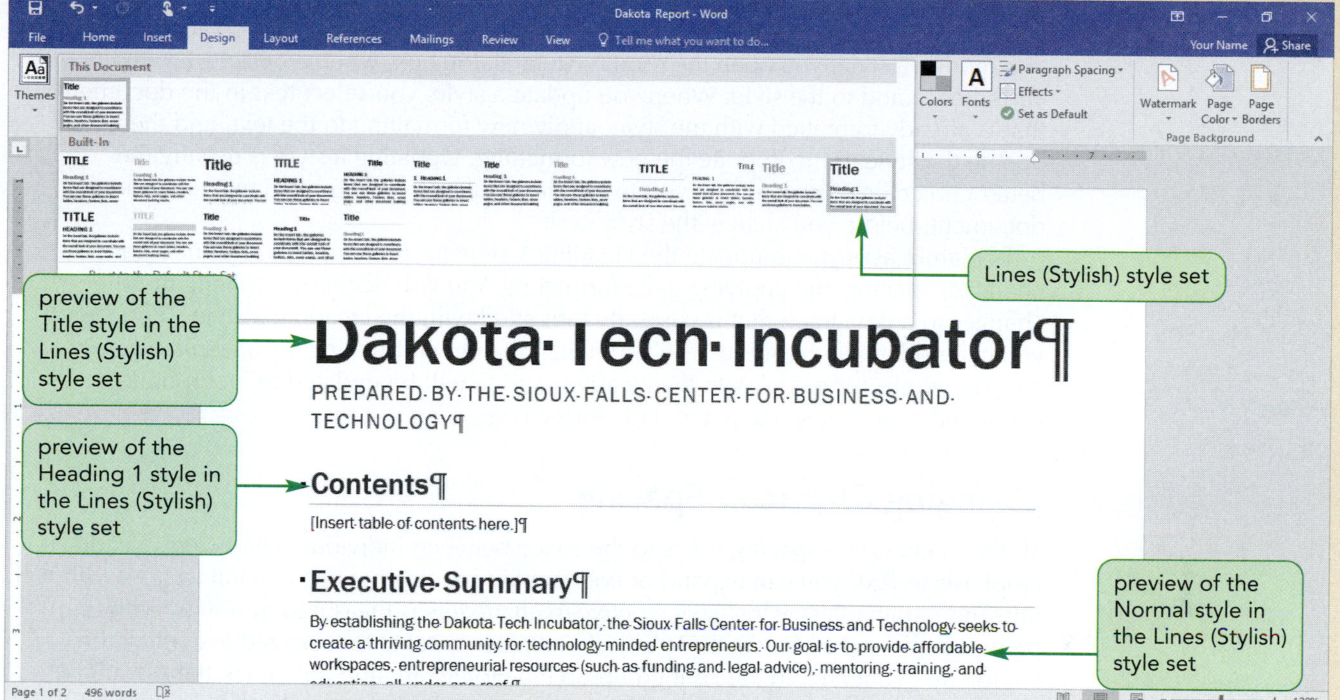

Notice that the theme fonts you specified earlier—Franklin Gothic Medium for headings and Franklin Gothic Book for body text—are still applied, as are the Grayscale theme colors.

6. Click the **Lines (Stylish)** style set. The styles in the document change to reflect the styles in the Lines (Stylish) style set. You can verify this by looking at the Style gallery on the Home tab.
7. On the ribbon, click the **Home** tab.
8. In the Styles group, click the **More** button to review the styles available in the Style gallery. The icon for the Heading 1 style indicates that it now applies a black font color. The style also applies a light gray underline, although that is not visible in the Style gallery icon.
9. Click anywhere in the document to close the Style gallery, and then save the document.

INSIGHT

The Set as Default Button: A Note of Caution

The Set as Default button in the Document Formatting group on the Design tab saves the document's current formatting settings as the default for any new blank documents you create in Word. In other words, it saves the current formatting settings to the Normal template. You might find this a tempting option, but, as you will learn in Session 5.2, when working with styles, modifying the Normal template is almost never a good idea. Instead, a better option is to save a document with the formatting you like as a new template, which you can then use as the basis for future documents. Exercise similar caution with the Set as Default button in the Font dialog box, which allows you to change the default font for the Normal template.

Customizing Styles

The ability to select a new style set gives you a lot of flexibility when formatting a document. However, sometimes you will want to customize an individual style to better suit your needs. To do so, you can modify the style or you can update it. When you modify a style, you open the Modify Style dialog box, where you select formatting attributes to add to the style. When you update a style, you select text in the document that is already formatted with the style, apply new formatting to the text, and then update the style to incorporate the new formatting. Updating a style is usually the better choice because it allows you to see the results of your formatting choices in the document, before you change the style itself.

Benjamin asks you to update the Heading 1 style for the report by expanding the character spacing and applying italic formatting. You will begin by applying these changes to a paragraph that is currently formatted with the Heading 1 style. Then you can update the Heading 1 style to match the new formatting. As a result, all the paragraphs formatted with the Heading 1 style will be updated to incorporate expanded character spacing and italic formatting.

Changing Character Spacing

The term **character spacing** refers to the space between individual characters. To add emphasis to text, you can expand or contract the spacing between characters. As with line and paragraph spacing, space between characters is measured in points, with one point equal to 1/72 of an inch. To adjust character spacing for selected text, click the Dialog Box Launcher in the Font group on the Home tab, and then click the Advanced tab in the Font dialog box. Of the numerous settings available on this tab, you'll find two especially useful.

First, the Spacing box allows you to choose Normal spacing (which is the default character spacing for the Normal style), Expanded spacing (with the characters farther apart than with the Normal setting), and Condensed spacing (with the characters closer together than with the Normal setting). With both Expanded and Condensed spacing, you can specify the number of points between characters.

Second, the Kerning for fonts check box allows you to adjust the spacing between characters to make them look like they are spaced evenly. Kerning is helpful when you are working with large font sizes, which can sometimes cause evenly spaced characters to appear unevenly spaced. Selecting the Kerning for fonts check box ensures that the spacing is adjusted automatically.

To add expanded character spacing and italic formatting to a paragraph formatted with the Heading 1 style:

1. In the document, scroll down if necessary, and select the **Executive Summary** heading, which is formatted with the Heading 1 style.
2. Make sure the Home tab is selected on the ribbon.
3. In the Font group, click the **Dialog Box Launcher**. The Font dialog box opens.
4. Click the **Advanced** tab. The Character Spacing settings at the top of this tab reflect the style settings for the currently selected text. The Spacing box is set to Normal. The more advanced options, located in the OpenType Features section, allow you to fine-tune the appearance of characters.
5. Click the **Spacing** arrow, and then click **Expanded**. See Figure 5-12.

Figure 5-12 Changing character spacing in the Font dialog box

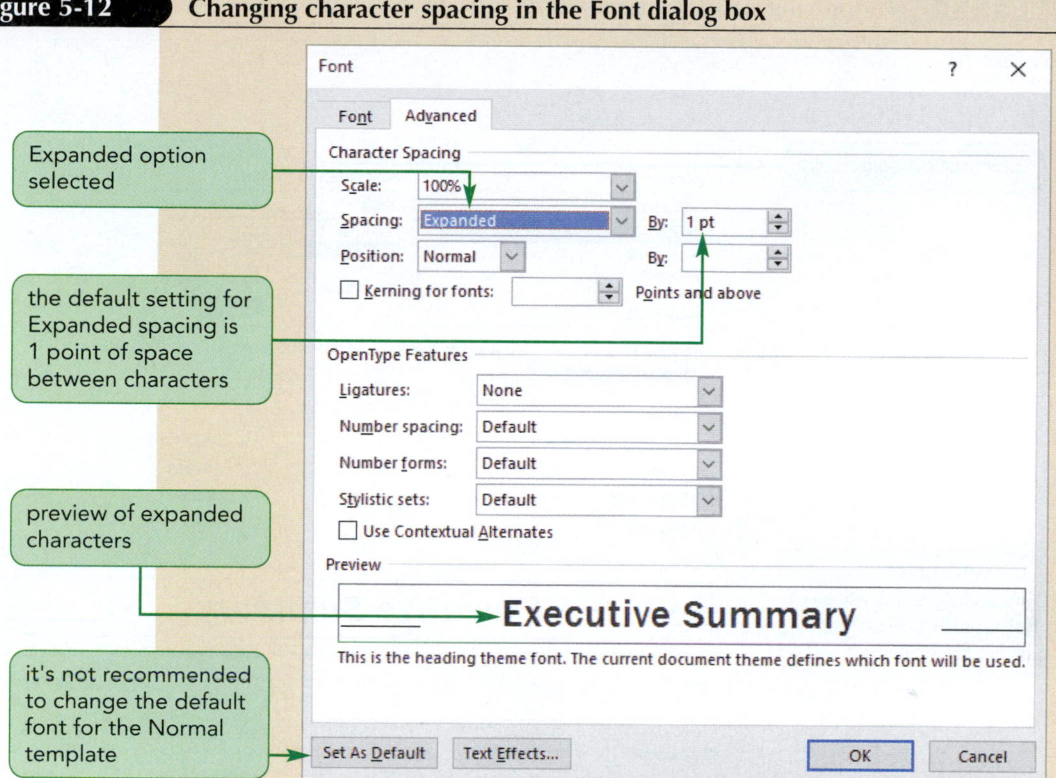

The By box next to the Spacing box indicates that each character is separated from the other by 1 point of space. You could increase the point setting; but in the current document, 1 point is fine. The Preview section shows a sample of the expanded character spacing.

Next, you need to apply italic formatting, which you could do from the Font group on the Home tab. But since you have the Font dialog box open, you'll do it from the Font tab in the Font dialog box instead.

6. In the Font dialog box, click the **Font** tab.

   Here you can apply most of the settings available in the Font group on the Home tab and a few that are not available in the Font group—such as colored underlines and **small caps** (smaller versions of uppercase letters). You can also hide text from view by selecting the Hidden check box.

TIP

Text formatted as hidden is visible only when nonprinting characters are displayed.

7. In the Font style box, click **Italic**. The Preview section of the Font tab shows a preview of the italic formatting applied to the "Executive Summary" heading. See Figure 5-13.

Figure 5-13 Applying italic formatting to text using the Font dialog box

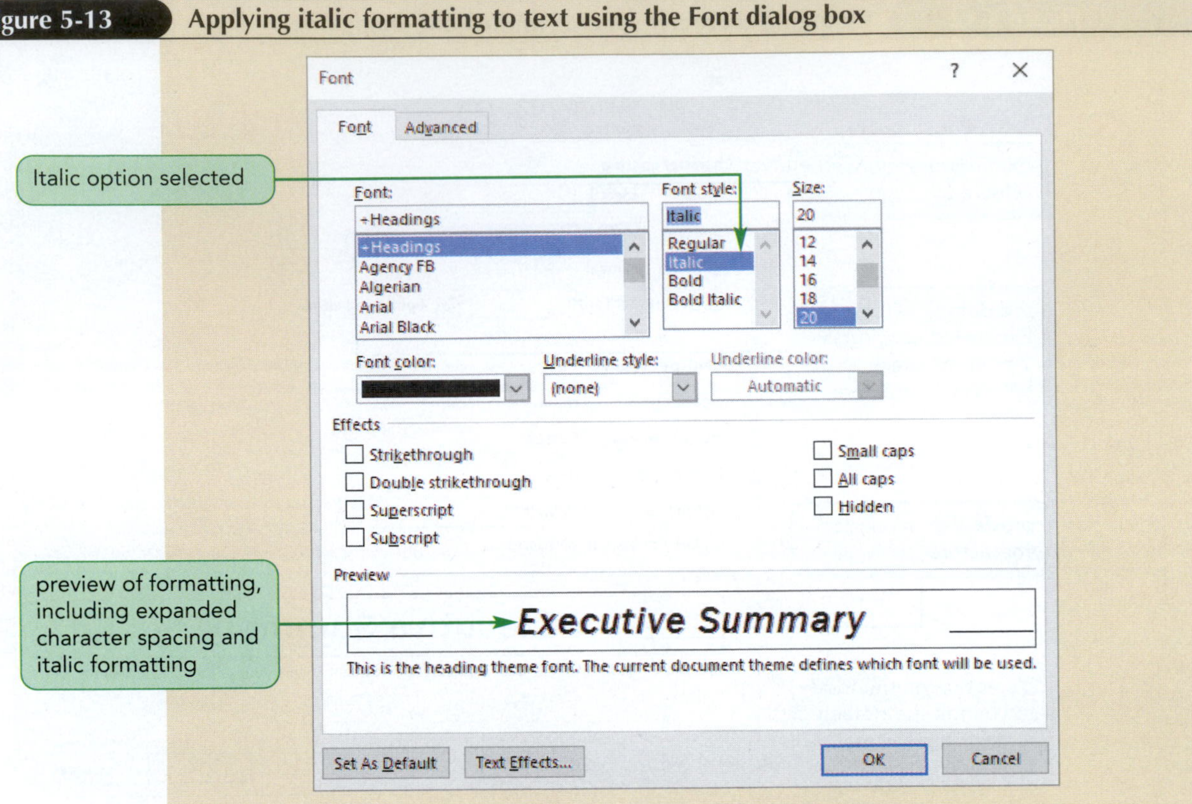

The other font attributes associated with the Heading 1 style are also visible on the Font tab.

8. Click the **OK** button to close the Font dialog box. The selected heading is now italicized, with the individual characters spread slightly farther apart.
9. Click anywhere in the "Executive Summary" heading to deselect the text, and then save the document.

Now that the selected heading is formatted the way you want, you can update the Heading 1 style to match it. When working with styles, it's helpful to open the Styles pane to see more information about the styles in the current style set, so you'll do that next.

Displaying the Styles Pane

The Styles pane shows you more styles than are displayed in the Style gallery. You can click a style in the Styles pane to apply it to selected text, just as you would click a style in the Style gallery.

The Styles pane provides detailed information about each style. In particular, it differentiates between character styles, paragraph styles, and linked styles. A **character style** contains formatting options that affect the appearance of individual characters, such as font style, font color, font size, bold, italic, and underline. When you click a character style, it formats the word that contains the insertion point or, if text is selected in the document, any selected characters.

A **paragraph style** contains all the character formatting options as well as formatting options that affect the paragraph's appearance—including line spacing, text alignment, tab stops, and borders. When you click a paragraph style, it formats the entire paragraph that contains the insertion point, or, if text is selected in the document, it formats all selected paragraphs (even paragraphs in which just one character is selected).

A **linked style** contains both character and paragraph formatting options. If you click in a paragraph or select a paragraph and then apply a linked style, both the paragraph styles and character styles are applied to the entire paragraph. If you apply a linked style to a selected word or group of words rather than to an entire paragraph, only the character styles for that linked style are applied to the selected text; the paragraph styles are not applied to the paragraph itself. All of the heading styles in Word are linked styles.

To open the Styles pane to review information about the styles in the current style set:

1. Make sure the Home tab is selected on the ribbon.
2. In the Styles group, click the **Dialog Box Launcher**. The Styles pane opens on the right side of the document window. See Figure 5-14.

Figure 5-14 Styles pane

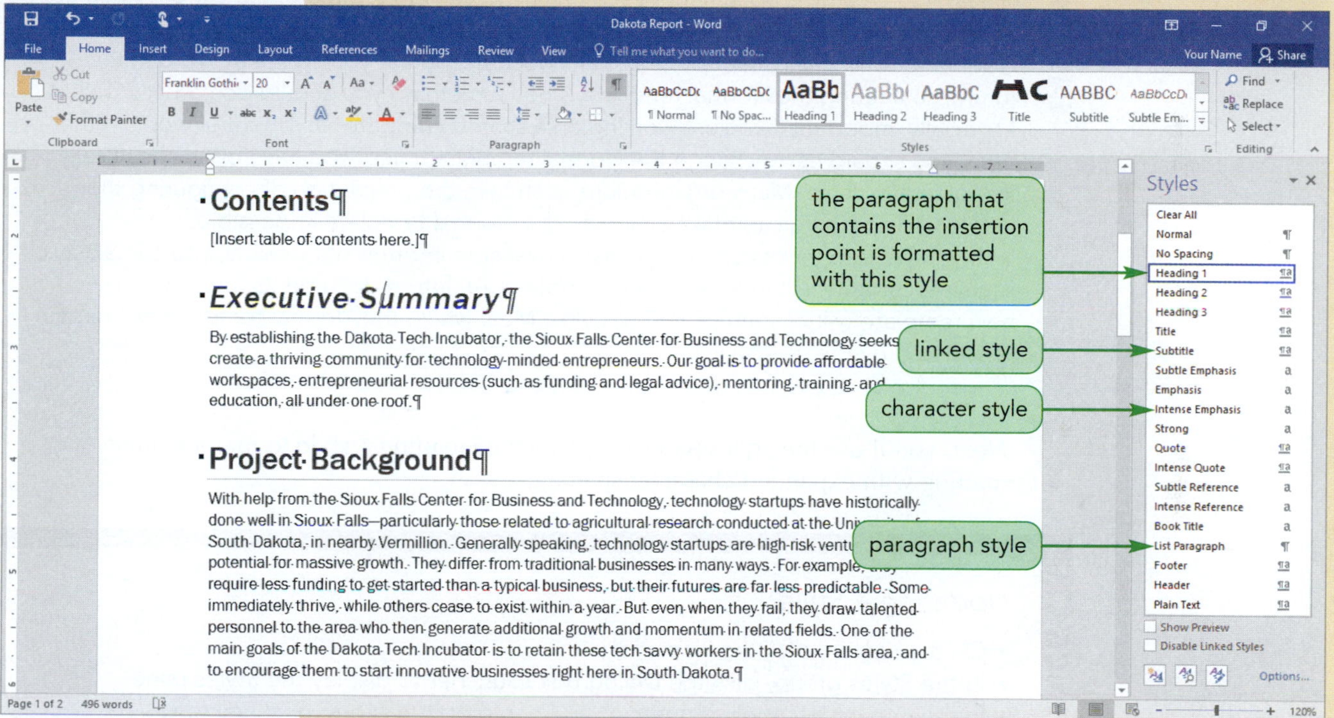

TIP

If the Styles pane is floating over the top of the document window, you can double-click the pane's title bar to dock it on the right side of the document window.

The outline around the Heading 1 style indicates that the insertion point is currently located in a paragraph formatted with that style. A paragraph symbol to the right of a style name indicates a paragraph style, a lowercase letter "a" indicates a character style, and a combination of both indicates a linked style. You can display even more information about a style by moving the mouse pointer over the style name in the Styles pane.

3. In the Styles pane, move the mouse pointer over **Heading 1**. An arrow is displayed to the right of the Heading 1 style name, and a ScreenTip with detailed information about the Heading 1 style opens below the style name.

The information in the ScreenTip relates only to the formatting applied by default with the Heading 1 style; it makes no mention of italic formatting or expanded character spacing. Although you applied these formatting changes to the "Executive Summary" heading, they are not yet part of the Heading 1 style.

You'll incorporate the new formatting into the Heading 1 style in the next section, when you update the style.

Updating a Style

Word is set up to save all customized styles to the current document by default. In fact, when you update a style, you don't even have a choice about where to save it—the updated style is automatically saved to the current document, rather than to the current template. If for some reason you needed to save a customized style to the current template instead, you would need to modify the style using the Modify Style dialog box, where you could then select the New documents based on this template button to save the modified style to the current template.

INSIGHT

Preserving the Normal Template

Unless you created a document based on an Office.com template, the current template for any document is probably the Normal template. Any changes you make to the Normal template will affect all new, blank documents that you create in Word in the future, so altering the Normal template is not something you should do casually. This is especially important if you are working on a shared computer at school or work. In that case, you should never change the Normal template unless you have been specifically instructed to do so. Many organizations even take the precaution of configuring their networked computers to make changing the Normal template impossible.

If you want to make customized styles available in other documents, you can always save the current document as a new template. All future documents based on your new template will contain your new styles. Meanwhile, the Normal template will remain unaffected by the new styles.

Next, you'll use the Styles pane to update the Heading 1 style to include italic formatting with expanded character spacing.

REFERENCE

Updating a Style

- On the ribbon, click the Home tab.
- In the Styles group, click the Dialog Box Launcher to display the Styles pane.
- In the document, apply formatting to a paragraph or group of characters.
- Click in the formatted paragraph (if you are updating a paragraph or linked style) or in the formatted group of characters (if you are updating a character style).
- In the Styles pane, right-click the style you want to update to display a shortcut menu.
- Click Update Style to Match Selection (where Style is the name of the style you want to update).

The insertion point must be located in the "Executive Summary" heading to ensure that you update the Heading 1 style with the correct formatting.

To update the Heading 1 style:

1. In the document, make sure the insertion point is located in the paragraph containing the "Executive Summary" heading, which is formatted with the Heading 1 style.
2. In the Styles pane, right-click **Heading 1**. A menu opens with options related to working with the Heading 1 style. See Figure 5-15.

Figure 5-15 Heading 1 style menu

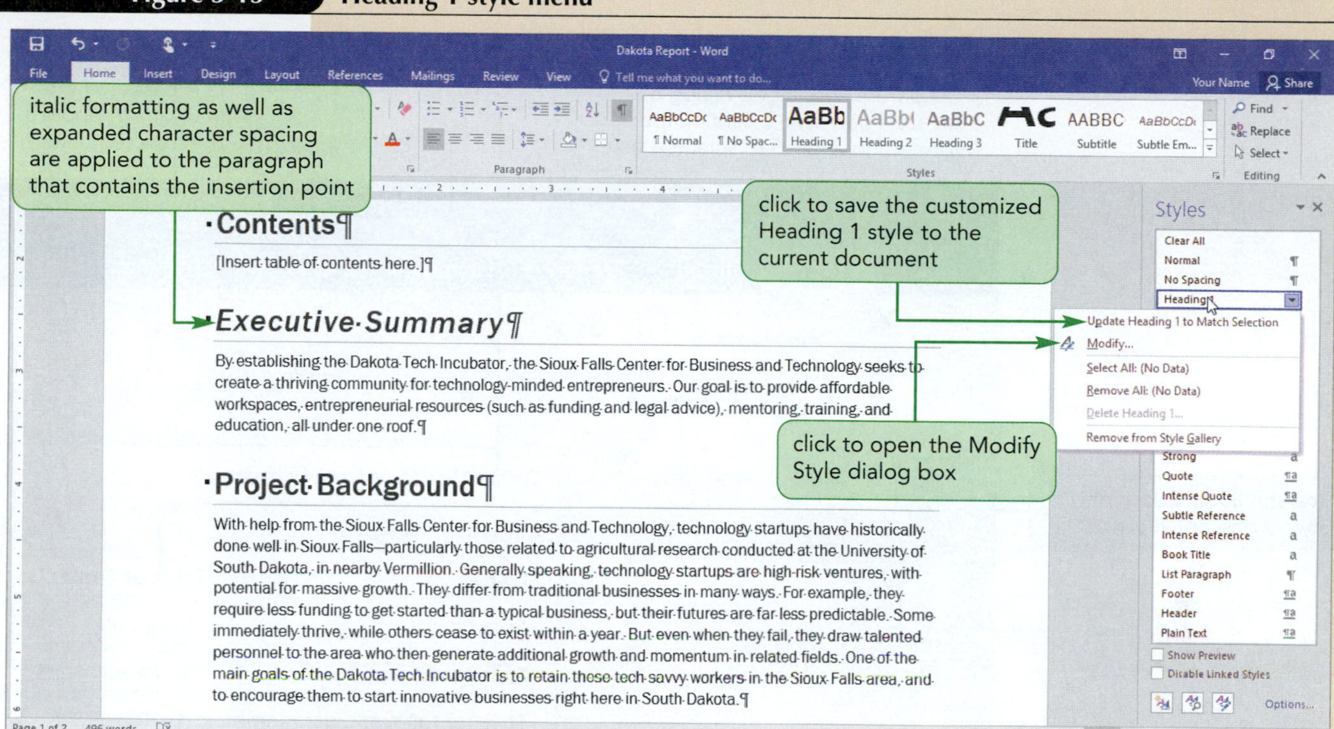

3. Click **Update Heading 1 to Match Selection**. The Heading 1 style is updated to reflect the changes you made to the "Executive Summary" heading. As a result, all the headings in the document formatted in the Heading 1 style now have italic formatting with expanded character spacing.
4. Save the document. The updated Heading 1 style is saved along with the document. No other documents are affected by this change to the Heading 1 style.

You can also use the Styles pane to create a new style for a document. You will do that in the next session.

REVIEW

Session 5.1 Quick Check

1. What is a template?
2. Suppose you want to move through a document one graphic at a time. Should you use the Navigation pane or the Go To tab in the Find and Replace dialog box?
3. Explain how to change a document's theme colors.
4. Explain how to select a new style set.
5. Suppose you create a new, blank document by clicking Blank document on the New screen in Backstage view. What is the name of the document's template?
6. What is the difference between a character style and a paragraph style?

Session 5.2 Visual Overview:

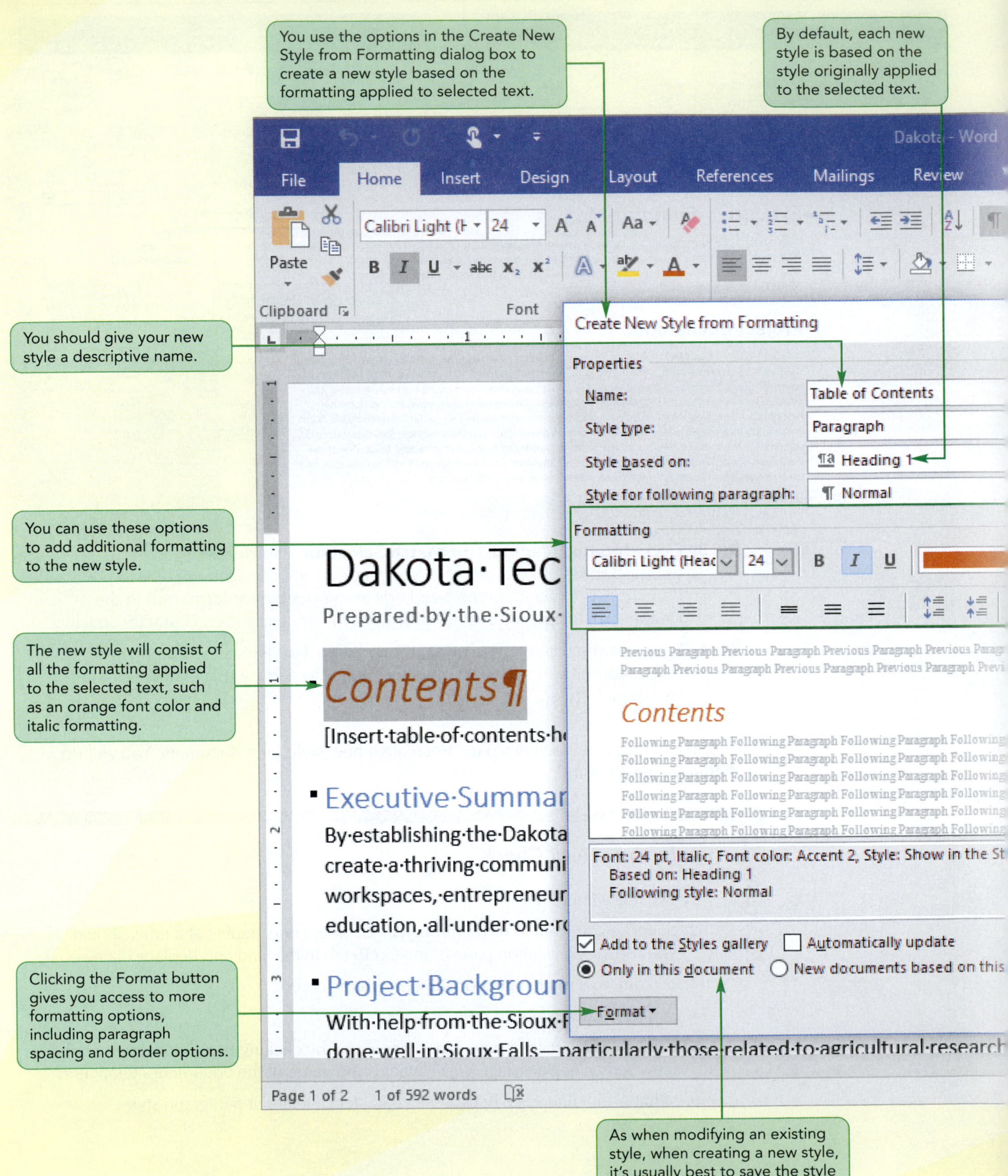
You use the options in the Create New Style from Formatting dialog box to create a new style based on the formatting applied to selected text.
By default, each new style is based on the style originally applied to the selected text.
You should give your new style a descriptive name.
You can use these options to add additional formatting to the new style.
The new style will consist of all the formatting applied to the selected text, such as an orange font color and italic formatting.
Clicking the Format button gives you access to more formatting options, including paragraph spacing and border options.
As when modifying an existing style, when creating a new style, it's usually best to save the style only to the current document.
Dakota - Word
File
Home
Insert
Design
Layout
References
Mailings
Review
Paste
Clipboard
Font
Create New Style from Formatting
Properties
Name:
Table of Contents
Style type:
Paragraph
Style based on:
Heading 1
Style for following paragraph:
Normal
Formatting
Calibri Light (Head
24
Dakota·Tec
Prepared·by·the·Sioux·
Contents¶
[Insert·table·of·contents·h
Executive·Summar
By·establishing·the·Dakota
create·a·thriving·communi
workspaces,·entrepreneur
education,·all·under·one·r
Project·Backgroun
With·help·from·the·Sioux·F
done·well·in·Sioux·Falls—particularly·those·related·to·agricultural·research
Contents
Font: 24 pt, Italic, Font color: Accent 2, Style: Show in the St
Based on: Heading 1
Following style: Normal
Add to the Styles gallery
Automatically update
Only in this document
New documents based on this
Format
Page 1 of 2
1 of 592 words

Creating a New Style

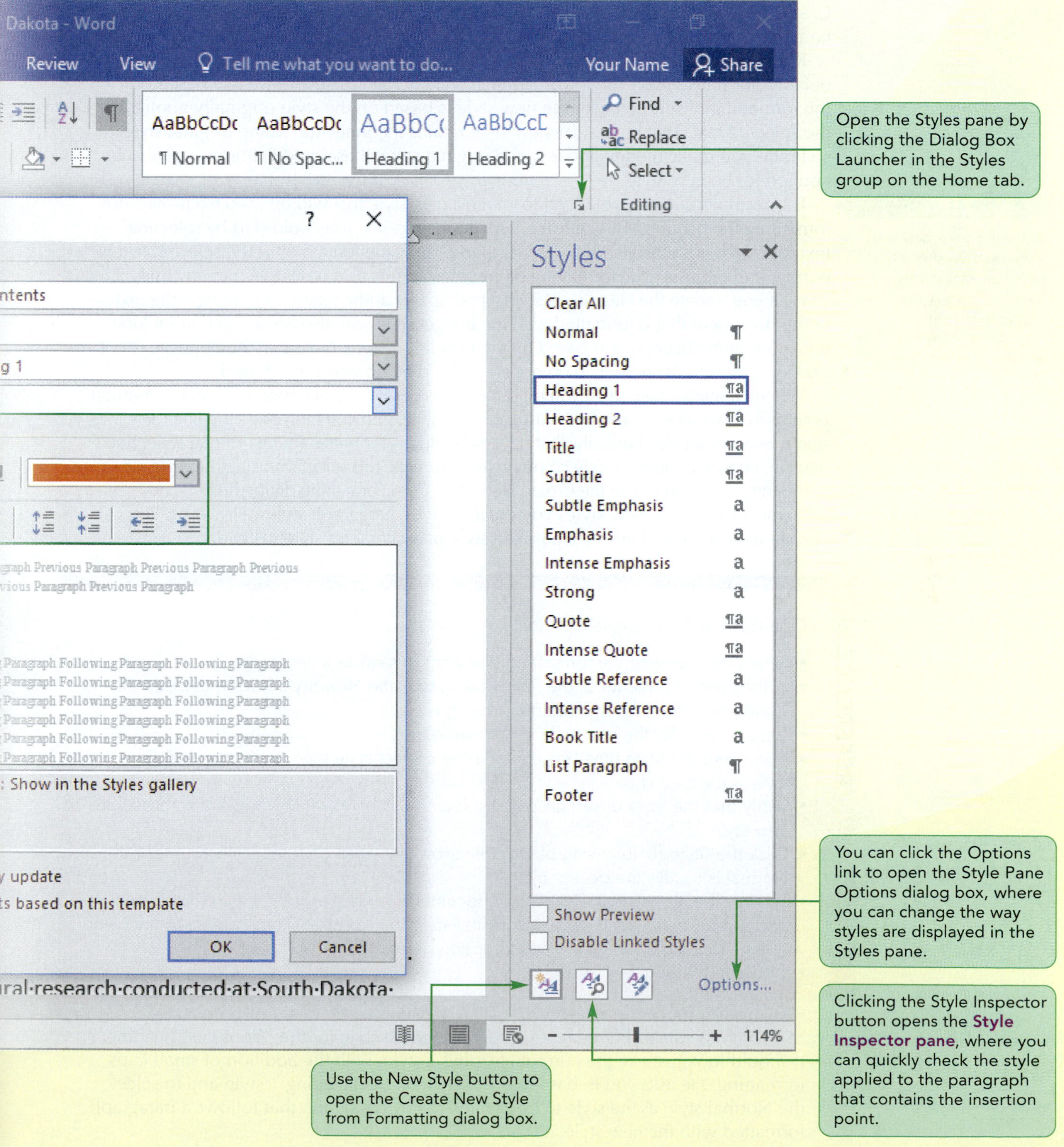

Creating a New Style

Creating a new style is similar to updating a style, except that instead of updating an existing style to match the formatting of selected text, you save the text's formatting as a new style. By default a new style is saved to the current document. You can choose to save a new style to the current template, but, as explained earlier, that is rarely advisable.

To begin creating a new style, select text with formatting you want to save, and then click the New Style button in the lower-left corner of the Styles pane. This opens the Create New Style from Formatting dialog box, where you can assign the new style a name and adjust other settings.

Remember that all text in your document has a style applied to it, whether it is the default Normal style or a style you applied. When you create a new style based on the formatting of selected text, the new style is based on the style originally applied to the selected text. That means the new style retains a connection to the original style, so that if you make modifications to the original style, these modifications will also be applied to the new style.

TIP

To break the link between a style and the style it is based on, click the Style based on arrow in the Create New Style from Formatting dialog box, and then click (no style).

For example, suppose you need to create a new style that will be used exclusively for formatting the heading "Budget" in all upcoming reports. You could start by selecting text formatted with the Heading 1 style, then change the font color of the selected text to purple, and then save the formatting of the selected text as a new style named "Budget." Later, if you update the Heading 1 style—perhaps by adding italic formatting—the text in the document that is formatted with the Budget style will also be updated to include italic formatting because it is based on the Heading 1 style. Note that the opposite is not true—changes to the new style do not affect the style on which it is based.

When creating a new style, you must also consider what will happen when the insertion point is in a paragraph formatted with your new style, and you then press the Enter key to start a new paragraph. Typically, that new paragraph is formatted in the Normal style, but you can choose a different style if you prefer. You make this selection using the Style for following paragraph box in the Create New Style from Formatting dialog box.

In most cases, any new styles you create will be paragraph styles. However, you can choose to make your new style a linked style or a character style instead.

REFERENCE

Creating a New Style

- Select the text with the formatting you want to save as a new style.
- In the lower-left corner of the Styles pane, click the New Style button to open the Create New Style from Formatting dialog box.
- Type a name for the new style in the Name box.
- Make sure the Style type box contains the correct style type. In most cases, Paragraph style is the best choice.
- Verify that the Style based on box displays the style on which you want to base your new style.
- Click the Style for following paragraph arrow, and then click the style you want to use. Normal is usually the best choice.
- To save the new style to the current document, verify that the Only in this document option button is selected; or to save the style to the current template, click the New documents based on this template option button.
- Click the OK button.

Benjamin wants you to create a new paragraph style for the "Contents" heading. It should look just like the current Heading 1 style, with the addition of small caps formatting. He asks you to base the new style on the Heading 1 style and to select the Normal style as the style to be applied to any paragraph that follows a paragraph formatted with the new style.

To format the "Contents" heading in small caps:

1. If you took a break after the last session, make sure the Dakota Report document is open in Print Layout view with the nonprinting characters and the ruler displayed. Confirm that the document Zoom level is set at 120% and that the Styles pane is docked on the right side of the document window.
2. Make sure the Home tab is selected on the ribbon.
3. In the document, select the **Contents** heading.
4. In the Font group, click the **Dialog Box Launcher**, and then, in the Font dialog box, click the **Font** tab, if necessary.
5. In the Effects section, click the **Small caps** check box to select it. See Figure 5-16.

Figure 5-16 Formatting the "Contents" heading

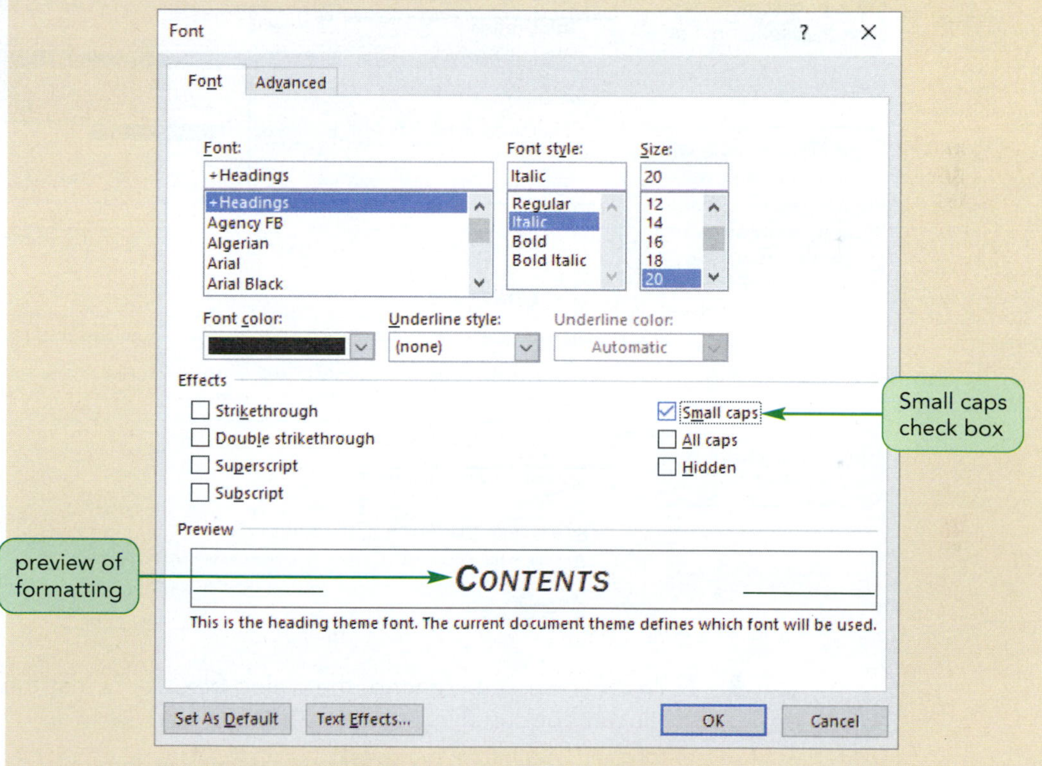

6. Click the **OK** button. The Font dialog box closes, and the "Contents" heading is formatted in small caps.

Now that the text is formatted the way you want, you can save its formatting as a new style.

To save the formatting of the "Contents" heading as a new style:

1. Verify that the "Contents" heading is still selected.
2. In the lower-left corner of the Styles pane, click the **New Style** button. The Create New Style from Formatting dialog box opens. A default name for the new style, "Style1," is selected in the Name box. The name "Style1" is also displayed in the Style for following paragraph box.

3. Type **Contents** to replace the default style name with the new one. The Style type box contains Paragraph by default, which is the type of style you want to create. The Style based on box indicates that the new Contents style is based on the Heading 1 style, which is also what you want. Notice that the Style for following paragraph box is now blank. You need to select the Normal style.
4. Click the **Style for following paragraph** arrow, and then click **Normal**. See Figure 5-17.

Figure 5-17 Creating a new style

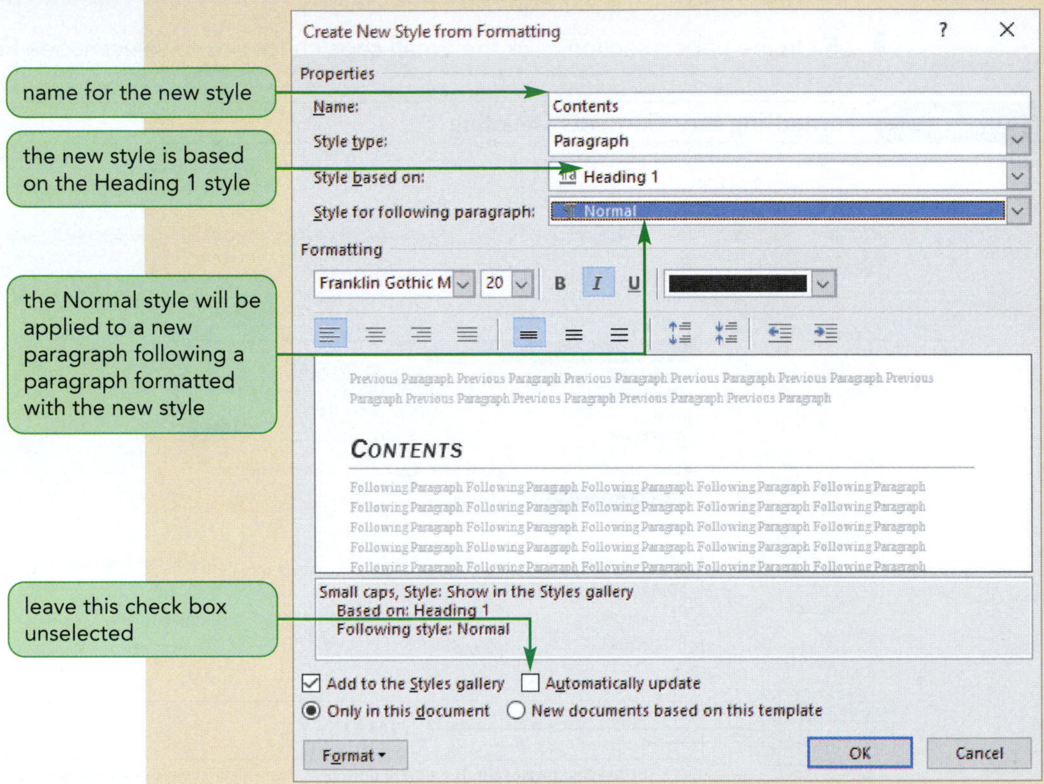

5. In the lower-left corner of the dialog box, verify that the Only in this document button is selected.

   Note that, by default, the Automatically update check box is not selected. As a general rule, you should not select this check box because it can produce unpredictable results in future documents based on the same template.

   If you plan to use a new style frequently, it's helpful to assign a keyboard shortcut to it. Then you can apply the style to selected text simply by pressing the keyboard shortcut.

TIP

To assign a keyboard shortcut to an existing style, right-click the style in the Styles pane, click Modify, click the Format button, and then click Shortcut key.

6. In the lower-left corner of the Create New Style from Formatting dialog box, click the **Format** button, and then click **Shortcut key** to open the Customize Keyboard dialog box. If you wanted to assign a keyboard shortcut to the Contents style, you would click in the Press new shortcut key box, press a combination of keys not assigned to any other function, and then click the Assign button. For now, you can close the Customize Keyboard dialog box without making any changes.
7. Click the **Close** button. You return to the Create New Style from Formatting dialog box.

8. Click the **OK** button. The Create New Style from Formatting dialog box closes. The new Contents style is added to the Style gallery and to the Styles pane. See Figure 5-18.

Figure 5-18 Contents style added to Style gallery and Styles pane

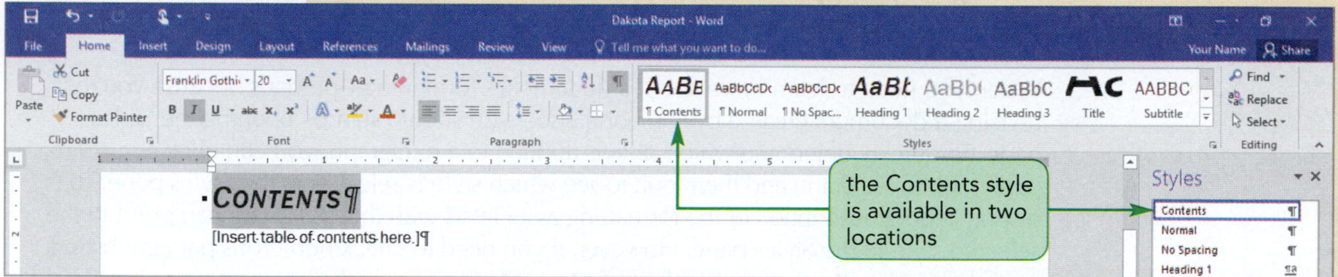
the Contents style is available in two locations

After you update a style or create a new one, you can create a custom style set that contains the new or updated style.

9. On the ribbon, click the **Design** tab.
10. In the Document Formatting group, click the **More** button, and then click **Save as a New Style Set**. The Save as a New Style Set dialog box opens, with the QuickStyles folder selected as the save location by default. Only style sets saved to the QuickStyles folder will appear in the Style Set gallery.

    In this case, you don't actually want to create a new style set, so you can close the Save as a New Style Set dialog box.

11. Click the **Cancel** button, and then save the document.

INSIGHT

Managing Your Styles

If you create a lot of styles, the Style gallery can quickly become overcrowded. To remove a style from the Style gallery without deleting the style itself, right-click the style in the Style gallery, and then click Remove from Style Gallery.

To delete a style entirely, open the Styles pane, and then right-click the style. What happens next depends on the type of style you are trying to delete. If the style was based on the Normal style, you can click Delete *Style* (where *Style* is the name of the style you want to delete), and then click Yes. If the style was based on any other style, you can click Revert to *Style* (where *Style* is the style that the style you want to delete was based on), and then click Yes.

If you create a new style and then paste text formatted with your style in a different document, your new style will be displayed in that document's Style gallery and Styles pane. This means that a document containing text imported from multiple documents can end up with a lot of different styles. In that case, you'll probably reformat the document to use only a few styles of your choosing. But what do you do about the remaining, unused styles? You could delete them, but that can be time-consuming. It's sometimes easier to hide the styles that are not currently in use in the document. At the bottom of the Styles pane, click the Options link to open the Style Pane Options dialog box, click the Select styles to show arrow, and then click In current document.

The styles used in the Dakota Report document are relatively simple. However, in a long document with many styles, it's easy to lose track of the style applied to each paragraph and the formatting associated with each style. In that case, it's important to know how to display additional information about the document's formatting.

Displaying Information About Styles and Formatting

When you need to learn more about a document's formatting—perhaps because you're revising a document created by someone else—you should start by opening the Styles pane. To quickly determine which style is applied to a paragraph, you can click a paragraph (or select it) and then look to see which style is selected in the Styles pane. To display a brief description of the formatting associated with that style, you can point to the selected style in the Styles pane. However, if you need to check numerous paragraphs in a long document, it's easier to use the Style Inspector pane, which remains open while you scroll through the document and displays only the style for the paragraph that currently contains the insertion point. To see a complete list of all the formatting applied to a paragraph, you can use the **Reveal Formatting pane**. Within the Reveal Formatting pane, you can also choose to compare the formatting applied to two different paragraphs.

Inspecting Styles

You can use the Style Inspector to examine the styles attached to each of the paragraphs in a document. When you are using the Style Inspector, it's also helpful to display the Home tab on the ribbon so the Style gallery is visible.

To use the Style Inspector pane to examine the styles in the document:

1. On the ribbon, click the **Home** tab.
2. On page 1, click anywhere in the **[Insert table of contents here.]** paragraph. The Normal style is selected in both the Style gallery and the Styles pane, indicating that the paragraph is formatted with the Normal style.
3. At the bottom of the Styles pane, click the **Style Inspector** button. The Style Inspector pane opens and is positioned next to the Styles pane. See Figure 5-19.

Figure 5-19 Style Inspector pane

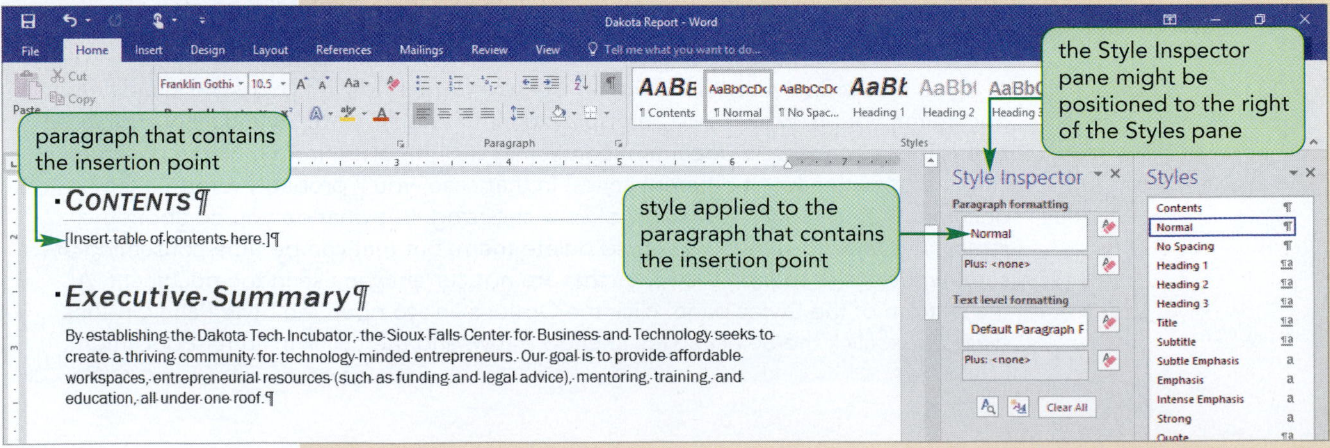

Trouble? If the Style Inspector pane on your computer is floating over the top of the document window, drag it to position it the left of the Styles pane, and then double-click the pane's title bar to dock the Style Inspector pane next to the Styles pane.

In the Style Inspector pane, the top box under "Paragraph formatting" displays the name of the style applied to the paragraph that currently contains the insertion point.

4. Press the **Ctrl+↓** keys. The insertion point moves down to the next paragraph, which contains the "Executive Summary" heading. The Style Inspector pane tells you that this paragraph is formatted with the Heading 1 style.
5. Press the **Ctrl+↓** keys as necessary to move the insertion point down through the paragraphs of the document, observing the style names displayed in the Style Inspector pane as well as the styles selected in the Styles pane. Note that the bulleted paragraphs below the "Dakota Tech Incubator Board of Directors" heading are formatted with the List Paragraph style. This style is applied automatically when you format paragraphs using the Bullets button in the Paragraph group on the Home tab.
6. Scroll up, and select the paragraph **[Insert table of contents here.]**.

INSIGHT

Finding Styles

Suppose you want to find all the paragraphs in a document formatted with a specific style. One option is to right-click the style in the Styles pane, and then click Select All *Number* Instances, where *Number* is the number of paragraphs in the document formatted with the style.

Another way to find paragraphs formatted with a particular style is by using the Find tab in the Find and Replace dialog box. If necessary, click the More button to display the Format button in the lower-left corner of the Find tab. Click the Format button, click Style, select the style you want in the Find Style dialog box, and then click the OK button. If you want to find specific text formatted with the style you selected, you can type the text in the Find what box on the Find tab, and then click Find Next to find the first instance. If, instead, you want to find any paragraph formatted with the style, leave the Find what box blank.

You can also use the Find and Replace dialog box to find paragraphs formatted with one style and then apply a different style to those paragraphs. On the Replace tab, click in the Find what box and use the Format button to select the style you want to find. Then, click in the Replace with box and use the Format button to select the style you want to use as a replacement. Click Find Next to find the first instance of the style, and then click Replace to apply the replacement style. As you've probably guessed, you can also type text in the Find what and Replace with boxes to find text formatted with a specific style and replace it with text formatted in a different style.

Next, Benjamin wants you to use the Reveal Formatting panes to learn more about the formatting applied by the Normal and Heading 2 styles.

Examining and Comparing Formatting in the Reveal Formatting Pane

You access the Reveal Formatting pane by clicking a button in the Style Inspector pane. Because the Reveal Formatting pane describes only formatting details without mentioning styles, it's helpful to keep the Style Inspector pane open while you use the Reveal Formatting pane.

To examine formatting details using the Reveal Formatting pane:

1. At the bottom of the Style Inspector pane, click the **Reveal Formatting** button. The Reveal Formatting pane opens, displaying detailed information about the formatting applied to the selected paragraph. It is positioned to the right of the Styles pane in Figure 5-20, but on your computer it might be to the left of the Styles pane or to the left of the Style Inspector.

Figure 5-20 Displaying formatting details in the Reveal Formatting pane

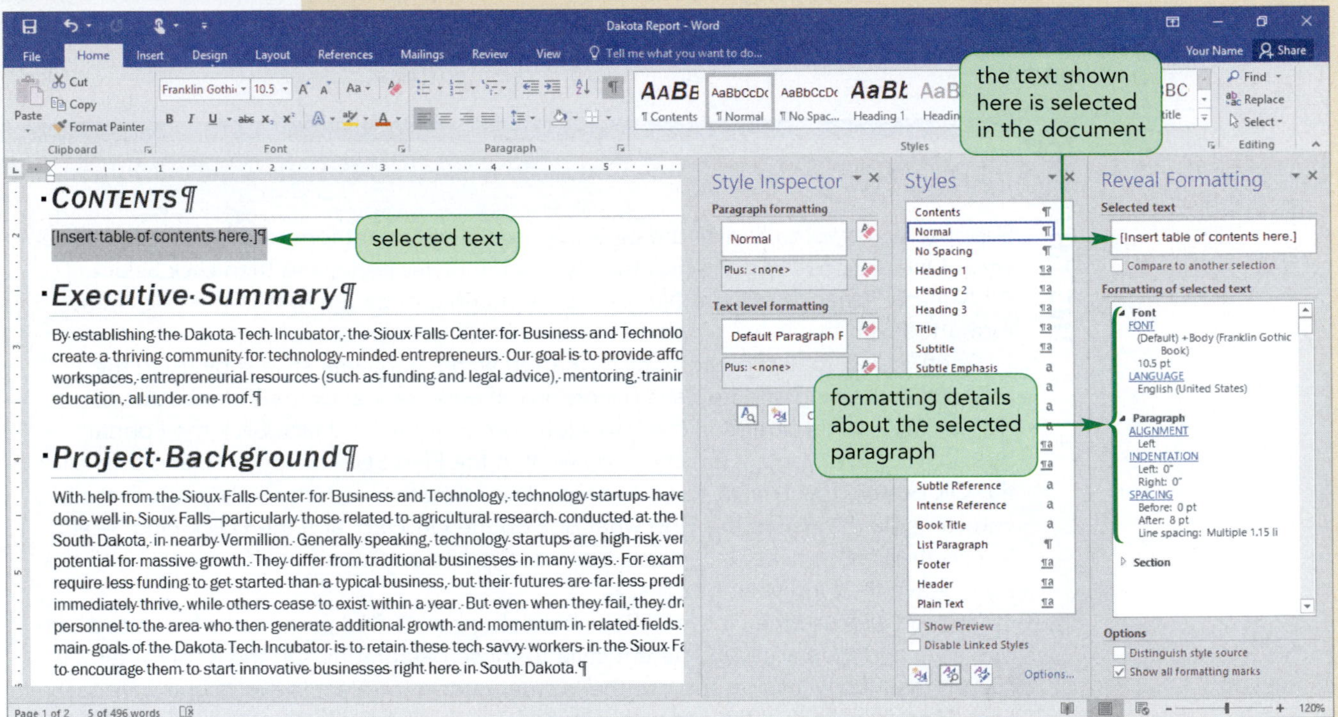

Trouble? If the Reveal Formatting pane on your computer is floating over the top of the document window, double-click the pane's title bar to dock the Reveal Formatting pane next to the other two task panes.

The Formatting of selected text box displays information about the formatting applied to the paragraph that contains the insertion point. Note that this information includes no mention of the style used to apply this formatting, but you can still see the style's name, Normal, displayed in the Style Inspector pane.

Now that you have the Reveal Formatting pane open, you can use it to compare one paragraph's formatting to another's. Benjamin asks you to compare text formatted with the Normal style to text formatted with the Heading 2 style.

To compare the formatting of one paragraph to another:

1. In the Reveal Formatting pane, click the **Compare to another selection** check box to select it. The options in the Reveal Formatting pane change to allow you to compare the formatting of one paragraph to that of another. Under Selected text, both text boxes display the selected text, "[Insert table of contents here.]" This tells you that, currently, the formatting applied to the selected text is being compared to itself.

   Now you'll compare this paragraph to one formatted with the Heading 2 style.

2. In the document, scroll down to page 2 and select the heading text **Coleman 3D Printing**, which is formatted with the Heading 2 style. The text "Coleman 3D Printing" is displayed in the Reveal Formatting pane, in the text box below "[Insert table of contents here.]" The Formatting differences section displays information about the formatting applied to the two different paragraphs. See Figure 5-21.

Figure 5-21 Comparing one paragraph's formatting with another's

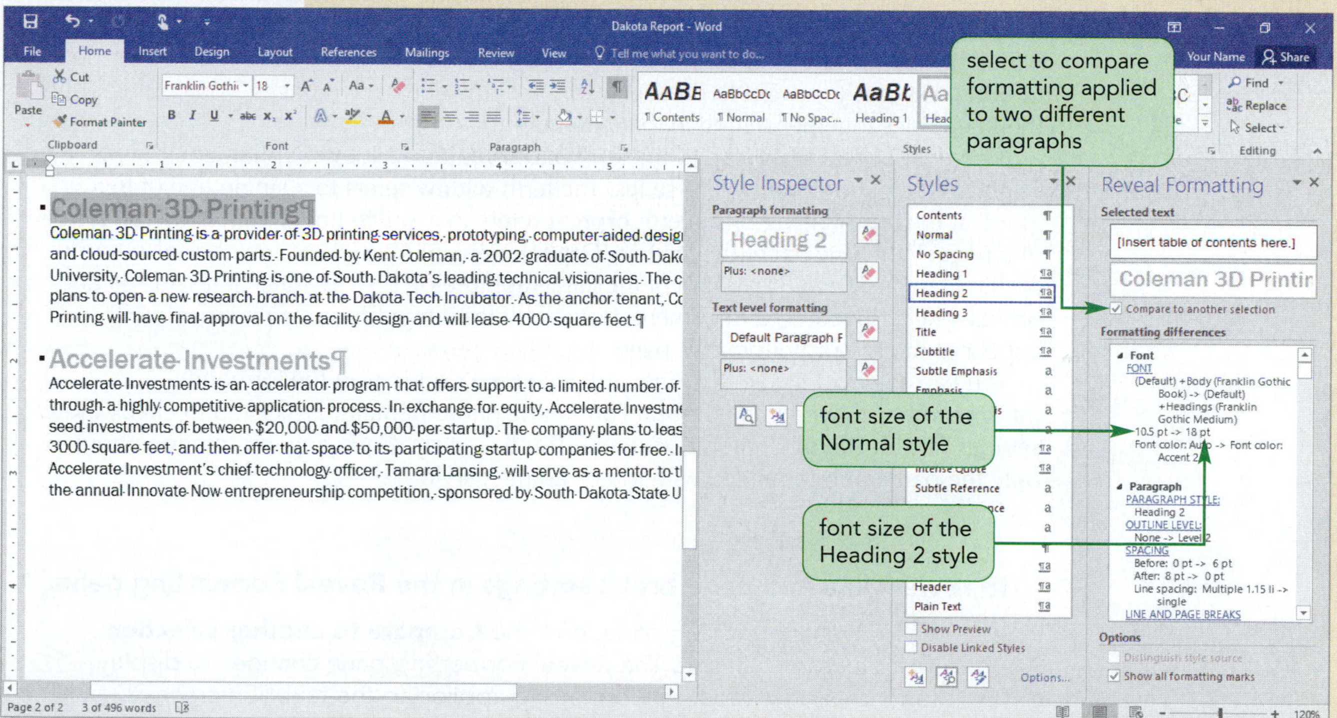

TIP

Text formatted in a white font is not visible in the text boxes at the top of the Reveal Formatting pane. To use the Reveal Formatting pane with white text, temporarily format it in black.

The information in the Reveal Formatting pane is very detailed. But, generally, if you see two settings separated by a hyphen and a greater than symbol, the item on the right relates to the text in the bottom box. For example, in the Font section, you see "10.5 pt -> 18 pt." This tells you that the text in the top text box, "[Insert table of contents here.]," is formatted in a 10.5-point font, whereas the text in the bottom text box, "Coleman 3D Printing," is formatted in an 18-point font.

The Paragraph section of the Reveal Formatting pane provides some information about two important default settings included with all of Word's heading styles—line and page break settings.

Reviewing Line and Page Break Settings

By default, all of Word's heading styles are set up to ensure that a heading is never separated from the paragraph that follows it. For example, suppose you have a one-page document that includes a heading with a single paragraph of body text after it. Then suppose you add text before the heading that causes the heading and its paragraph of body text to flow down the page so that, ultimately, the entire paragraph of body text moves to page 2. Even if there is room for the heading at the bottom of page 1, it will move to page 2, along with its paragraph of body text. The setting that controls this is the **Keep with next** check box on the Line and Page Breaks tab in the Paragraph dialog box. By default, the Keep with next check box is selected for all headings.

A related setting on the same tab is the **Keep lines together** check box, which is also selected by default for all headings. This setting ensures that if a paragraph consists of more than one line of text, the lines of the paragraph will never be separated by a page break. This means that if one line of a paragraph moves from page 1 to page 2, all lines of the paragraph will move to page 2.

A nonprinting character in the shape of a small black square is displayed next to any paragraph for which either the Keep lines together setting or the Keep with next setting is selected. Because both settings are selected by default for all the heading styles (Heading 1 through Heading 9), you always see this nonprinting character next to text formatted with a heading style. By default, the Keep lines together setting and the Keep with next setting are deselected for all other styles. However, if you have a paragraph of body text that you want to prevent from breaking across two pages, you could apply the Keep lines together setting to that paragraph.

One helpful setting related to line and page breaks—Widow/Orphan control—is selected by default for all Word styles. The term **widow** refers to a single line of text alone at the top of a page. The term **orphan** refers to a single line of text at the bottom of a page. When selected, the **Widow/Orphan control** check box, which is also found on the Line and Page Breaks tab of the Paragraph dialog box, ensures that widows and orphans never occur in a document. Instead, at least two lines of a paragraph will appear at the top or bottom of a page.

You can see evidence of the line and page break settings in the formatting information displayed in the Reveal Formatting pane. Benjamin asks you to check these settings for the Dakota Report document. You'll start by displaying information about only the paragraph formatted with the Heading 2 style.

To review line and page break settings in the Reveal Formatting pane:

1. In the Reveal Formatting pane, click the **Compare to another selection** check box to deselect it. The Reveal Formatting pane changes to display information only about the formatting applied to the text "Coleman 3D Printing," which is currently selected in the document.

   The Style Inspector pane tells you that "Coleman 3D Printing" is formatted with the Heading 2 style, so all the information in the Reveal Formatting pane describes the Heading 2 style.

2. In the Formatting of selected text box, scroll down to display the entire Paragraph section.
3. Review the information below the blue heading "LINE AND PAGE BREAKS." The text "Keep with next" and "Keep lines together" tells you that these two settings are active for the selected text. The blue headings in the Reveal Formatting pane are actually links that open a dialog box with the relevant formatting settings.

4. In the Formatting of selected text box, click **LINE AND PAGE BREAKS**. The Paragraph dialog box opens, with the Line and Page Breaks tab displayed. See Figure 5-22.

Figure 5-22 **Line and Page Breaks tab in the Paragraph dialog box**

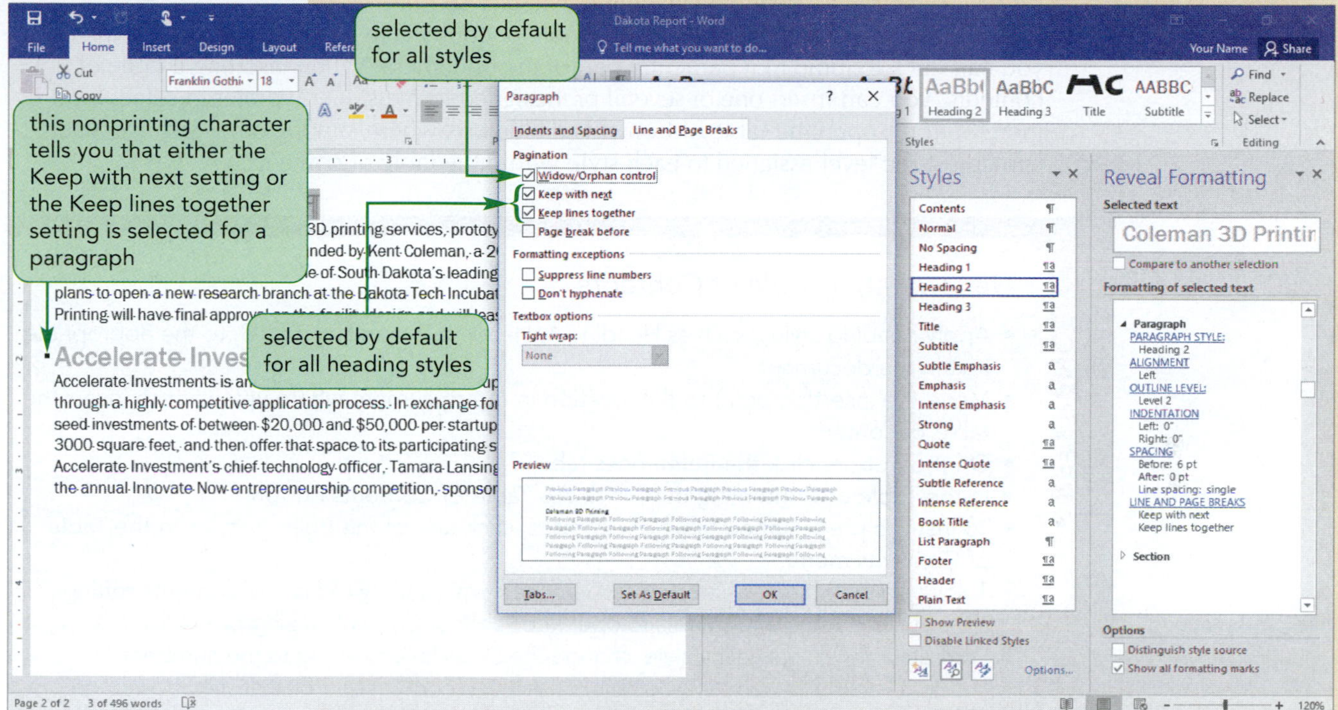

The settings on the tab are the settings for the selected paragraph, which is formatted with the Heading 2 style. The Widow/Orphan control, Keep with next, and Keep lines together check boxes are all selected, as you would expect for a heading style.

You are finished reviewing formatting information, so you can close the Paragraph dialog box and the Reveal Formatting pane.

5. In the Paragraph dialog box, click the **Cancel** button; and then, in the Reveal Formatting pane, click the **Close** button ✕.
6. In the Style Inspector pane, click the **Close** button ✕; and then, in the Styles pane, click the **Close** button ✕.
7. Click anywhere in the document to deselect the "Colman 3D Printing" heading.

You are almost finished working on the Dakota Report document. Your next task is to add a table of contents.

Generating a Table of Contents

TIP

To delete a table of contents, click the Table of Contents button, and then click Remove Table of Contents.

You can use the Table of Contents button in the Table of Contents group on the References tab to generate a table of contents that includes any text to which you have applied heading styles. A **table of contents** is essentially an outline of the document. By default, in a table of contents, Heading 1 text is aligned on the left, Heading 2 text is indented slightly to the right below the Heading 1 text, Heading 3 text is indented slightly to the right below the Heading 2 text, and so on.

The page numbers and headings in a table of contents in Word are hyperlinks that you can click to jump to a particular part of the document. When inserting a table of contents, you can insert one of several predesigned formats. If you prefer to select from more options, open the Table of Contents dialog box where, among other settings, you can adjust the level assigned to each style within the table of contents.

REFERENCE

Generating a Table of Contents

- Apply heading styles, such as Heading 1, Heading 2, and Heading 3, to the appropriate text in the document.
- Move the insertion point to the location in the document where you want to insert the table of contents.
- On the ribbon, click the References tab.
- In the Table of Contents group, click the Table of Contents button.
- To insert a predesigned table of contents, click one of the Built-In styles in the Table of Contents menu.
- To open a dialog box where you can choose from a variety of table of contents settings, click Custom Table of Contents to open the Table of Contents dialog box. Click the Formats arrow and select a style, change the Show levels setting to the number of heading levels you want to include in the table of contents, verify that the Show page numbers check box is selected, and then click the OK button.

The current draft of Benjamin's report is fairly short, but the final document will be much longer. He asks you to create a table of contents for the report now, just after the "Contents" heading. Then, as Benjamin adds sections to the report, he can update the table of contents.

To insert a table of contents into the document:

1. Scroll up to display the "Contents" heading on page 1.
2. Below the heading, delete the placeholder text **[Insert table of contents here.]**. Do not delete the paragraph mark after the placeholder text. Your insertion point should now be located in the blank paragraph between the "Contents" heading and the "Executive Summary" heading.
3. On the ribbon, click the **References** tab.
4. In the Table of Contents group, click the **Table of Contents** button. The Table of Contents menu opens, displaying a gallery of table of contents formats. See Figure 5-23.

Figure 5-23 Table of Contents menu

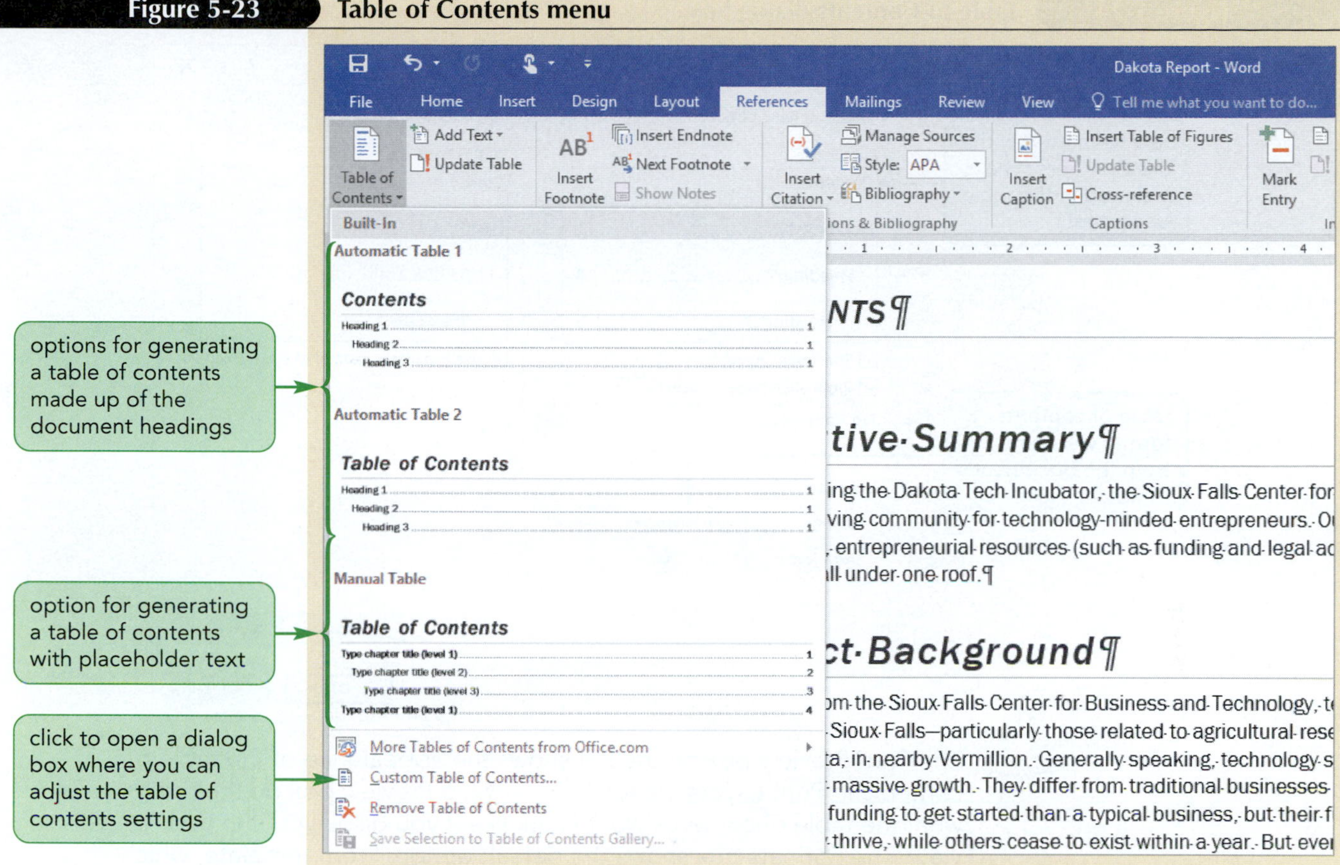

The Automatic Table 1 and Automatic Table 2 options each insert a table of contents made up of the first three levels of document headings in a predefined format. Each of the Automatic options also includes a heading for the table of contents. Because Benjamin's document already contains the heading "Contents," you do not want to use either of these options.

The Manual option is useful only in specialized situations, when you need to type the table of contents yourself—for example, when creating a book manuscript for an academic publisher that requires a specialized format.

You'll use the Custom Table of Contents command to open the Table of Contents dialog box.

5. Below the Table of Contents gallery, click **Custom Table of Contents**. The Table of Contents dialog box opens, with the Table of Contents tab displayed. See Figure 5-24.

Figure 5-24 Table of Contents dialog box

text formatted with the Contents style is included in the table of contents

table of contents format will come from the document's template

Table of Contents

Index | Table of Contents | Table of Figures | Table of Authorities

Print Preview

Contents....................1
Heading 1....................1
Heading 2....................3
Heading 3....................5

Show page numbers
Right align page numbers
Tab leader: ....

Web Preview

Contents
Heading 1
Heading 2
Heading 3

Use hyperlinks instead of page numbers

General
Formats: From template
Show levels: 3

Options... Modify...
OK Cancel

The Print Preview box on the left shows the appearance of the table of contents in Print Layout view, while the Web Preview box on the right shows what the table of contents would look like if you displayed it in Web Layout view. The Formats box shows the default option, From template, which applies the table of contents styles provided by the document's template.

In the Print Preview section, notice that the Contents heading style, which you created in Session 5.1, appears in the table of contents at the same level as the Heading 1 style.

6. In the lower-right corner of the Table of Contents dialog box, click the **Options** button. The Table of Contents Options dialog box opens. The Styles check box is selected, indicating that Word will compile the table of contents based on the styles applied to the document headings.

7. In the TOC level list, review the priority level assigned to the document's styles, using the vertical scroll bar, if necessary. See Figure 5-25.

Figure 5-25 Checking the styles used in the table of contents

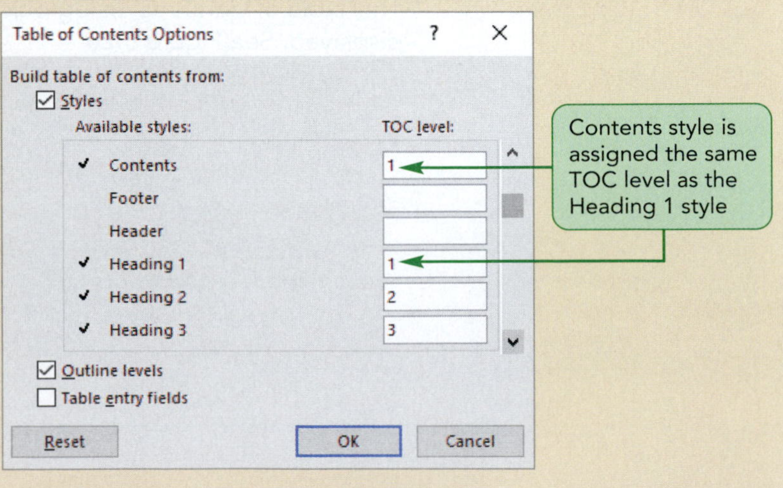

If the box next to a style name is blank, then text formatted with that style does not appear in the table of contents. The numbers next to the Contents, Heading 1, Heading 2, and Heading 3 styles tell you that any text formatted with these styles appears in the table of contents. Heading 1 is assigned to level 1, and Heading 2 is assigned to level 2.

Like Heading 1, the Contents style is assigned to level 1; however, you don't want to include the "Contents" heading in the table of contents itself. To remove any text formatted with the Contents style from the table of contents, you need to delete the Contents style level number.

8. Delete the **1** from the TOC level box for the Contents style, and then click the **OK** button. "Contents" is no longer displayed in the sample table of contents in the Print Preview and Web Preview sections of the Table of Contents dialog box.
9. Click the **OK** button to accept the remaining default settings in the Table of Contents dialog box. Word searches for text formatted with the Heading 1, Heading 2, and Heading 3 styles, and then places those headings and their corresponding page numbers in a table of contents. The table of contents is inserted at the insertion point, below the "Contents" heading. See Figure 5-26.

Figure 5-26 **Table of contents inserted into document**

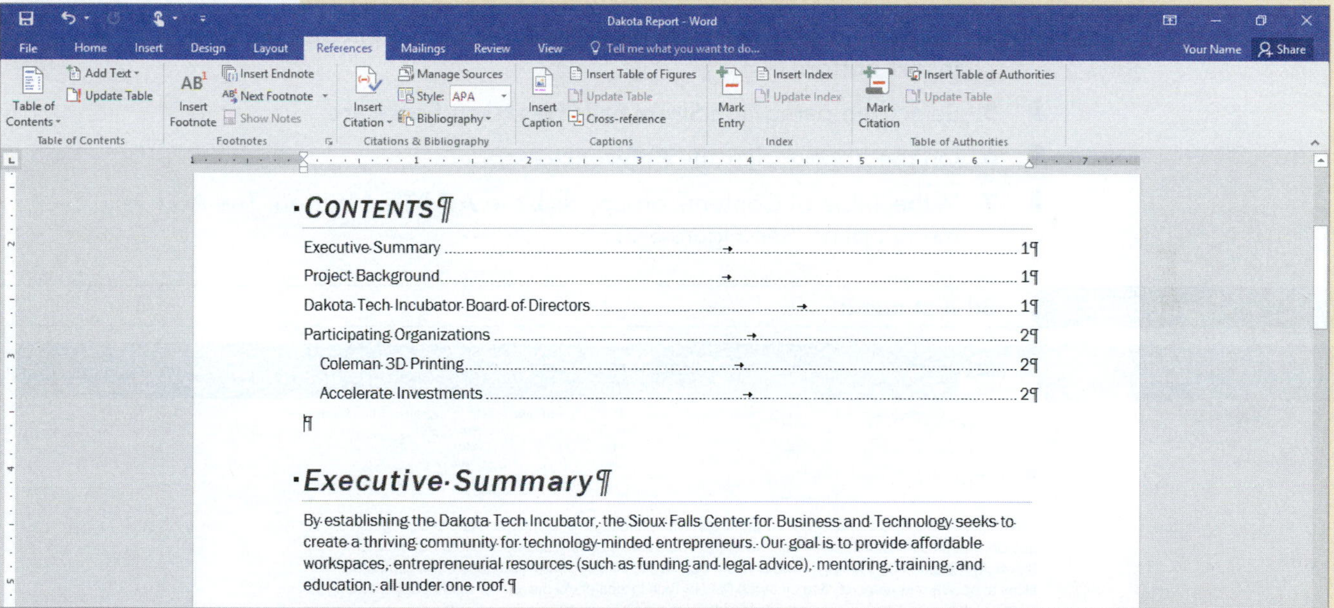

The text in the table of contents is formatted with the TOC styles for the current template. Depending on how your computer is set up, the table of contents might appear on a light gray background.

You can check the hyperlink formatting to make sure the headings really do function as links.

10. Press and hold the **Ctrl** key while you click **Coleman 3D Printing** in the table of contents. The insertion point moves to the beginning of the "Coleman 3D Printing" heading near the bottom of page 2.
11. Save the document.

Updating a Table of Contents

If you add or delete a heading in the document or add body text that causes one or more headings to move to a new page, you can quickly update the table of contents by clicking the Update Table button in the Table of Contents group on the References tab. To add text that is not formatted as a heading to the table of contents, you can select the text, format it as a heading, and then update the table of contents. However, if you already have the References tab displayed, it's more efficient to select the text in the document, use the Add Text button in the Table of Contents group to add a Heading style to the selected text, and then update the table of contents.

Benjamin has information on a third participating organization saved as a separate Word file, which he asks you to insert at the end of the Dakota Report document. You will do this next and then add the new heading to the table of contents.

To add a section to the Dakota Report document and update the table of contents:

1. Press the **Ctrl+End** keys to move the insertion point to the end of the document, and then press the **Enter** key.
2. On the ribbon, click the **Insert** tab.
3. In the Text group, click the **Object button arrow**, and then click **Text from File**.
4. Navigate to the **Word5 > Module** folder, click **NextGen**, and then click the **Insert** button.
5. Select the paragraph **Sioux Falls NextGen Software**.
6. On the ribbon, click the **References** tab.
7. In the Table of Contents group, click the **Add Text** button. The Add Text menu opens. See Figure 5-27.

Figure 5-27 Add Text menu

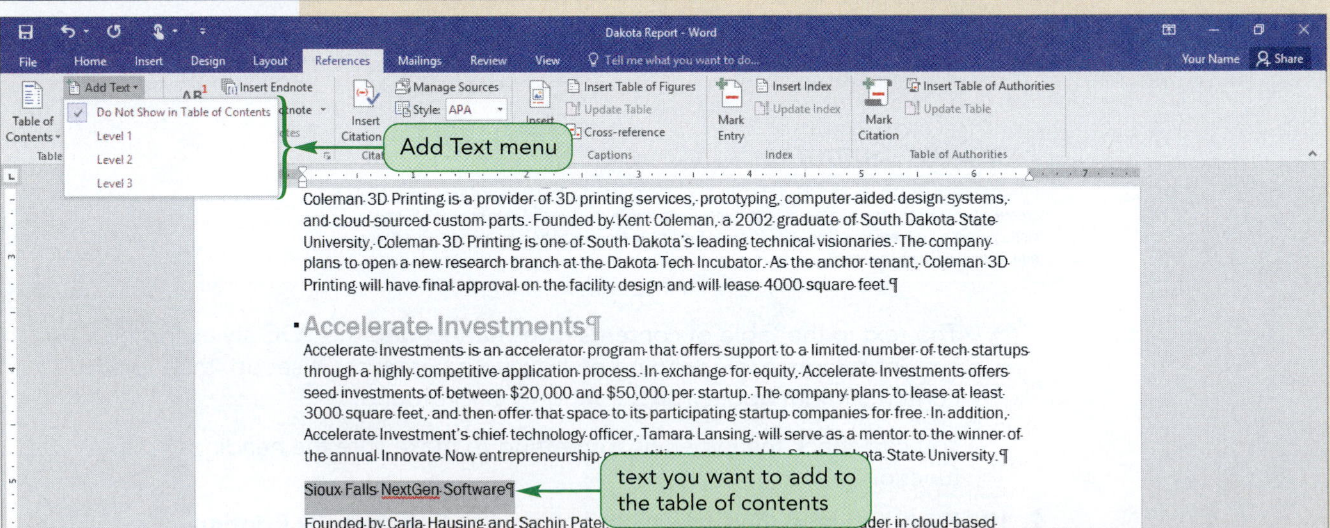

8. Click **Level 2**. The text is formatted with the Heading 2 style to match the headings for the sections about the other participating organizations. Now that the text is formatted with a heading style, you can update the table of contents.

9. Scroll up so you can see the table of contents, and then, in the Table of Contents group, click the **Update Table** button. The Update Table of Contents dialog box opens.

   You can use the Update page numbers only option button if you don't want to update the headings in the table of contents. This option is useful if you add additional content that causes existing headings to move from one page to another. In this case, you want to update the entire table of contents.

10. Click the **Update entire table** option button to select it, and then click the **OK** button. The table of contents is updated to include the "Sioux Falls NextGen Software" heading. See Figure 5-28.

Figure 5-28 Updated table of contents

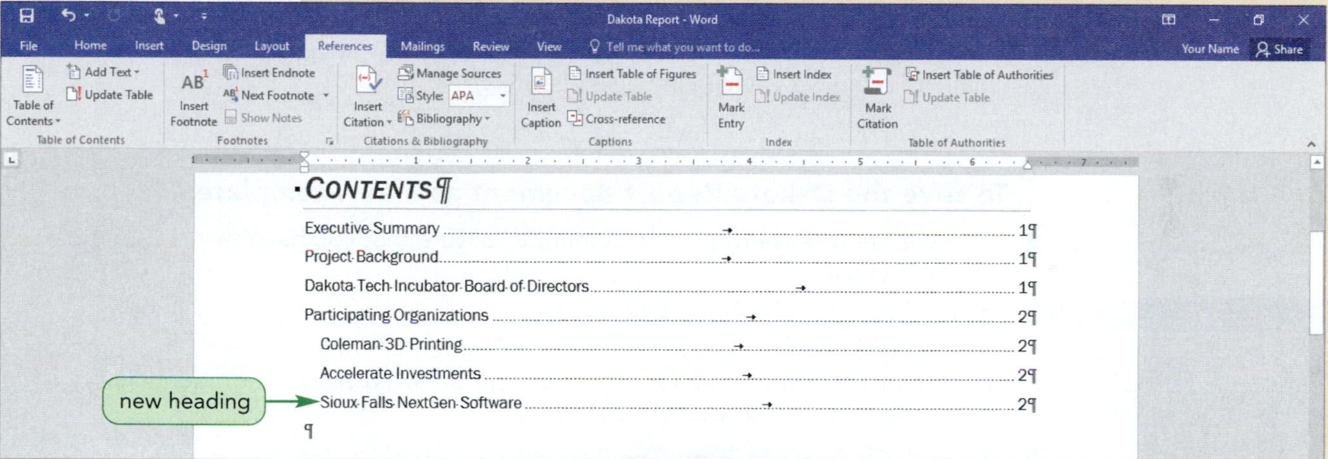

11. In the document, scroll down below the "Dakota Tech Incubator Board of Directors" heading on page 1, and replace "Lana Rivers" with your first and last names.

12. Press the **Ctrl+End** keys to move the insertion point to the last paragraph in the document, which is blank, and then press the **Delete** key to delete the blank paragraph.

13. Save the document.

Now that you are finished working on the Dakota Report document, Benjamin asks you to use the document to create a template that can be used for all reports issued by the Sioux Falls Center for Business and Technology.

Saving a Document as a Template

If you frequently need to create a particular type of document, it's a good idea to create your own template for that type of document. Organizations often use templates to ensure that all employees use the same basic format for essential documents. When creating a template, you can save it to any folder on your computer. After you save it, you can open the template to revise it just as you would open any other document. You can also use the Save As option in Backstage view to create a new document based on the template, in which case Word Document will be selected as the file type in the Save As dialog box. If you want to be able to open a new document based on the template from the New screen, you need to save your template to the Custom Office Templates folder that is installed with Word.

REFERENCE

Saving a Document as a Template

- On the ribbon, click the File tab, and then click Export in the navigation bar.
- Click Change File Type, click Template, and then click the Save As button to open the Save As dialog box with Word Template selected in the Save as type box.
- Navigate to the folder in which you want to save the template. To save the template to the Custom Office Templates folder that is installed with Word, click the Documents folder in the navigation pane of the Save As dialog box, and then click Custom Office Templates.
- In the File name box, type a name for the template.
- Click the Save button.

You will save the new Sioux Falls Center for Business and Technology template in the location specified by your instructor; however, you'll also save it to the Custom Office Templates folder so you can practice opening a new document based on your template from the New screen in Backstage view.

To save the Dakota Report document as a new template:

1. Save the **Dakota Report** document to ensure that you have saved your most recent work.
2. On the ribbon, click the **File** tab, and then click **Export** in the navigation bar. On the Export screen, you could click Create PDF/XPS to save the document as a PDF. However, the Change File Type option gives you additional file type possibilities, which you will review next.
3. Click **Change File Type**. The Export screen displays options for various file types you can use when saving a file. For example, you could save a Word document as a Plain Text file that contains only text, without any formatting or graphics. See Figure 5-29.

TIP

You can also click the File tab, click Save As, and then select Template as the file type.

Figure 5-29 Export screen with Change File Type options in Backstage view

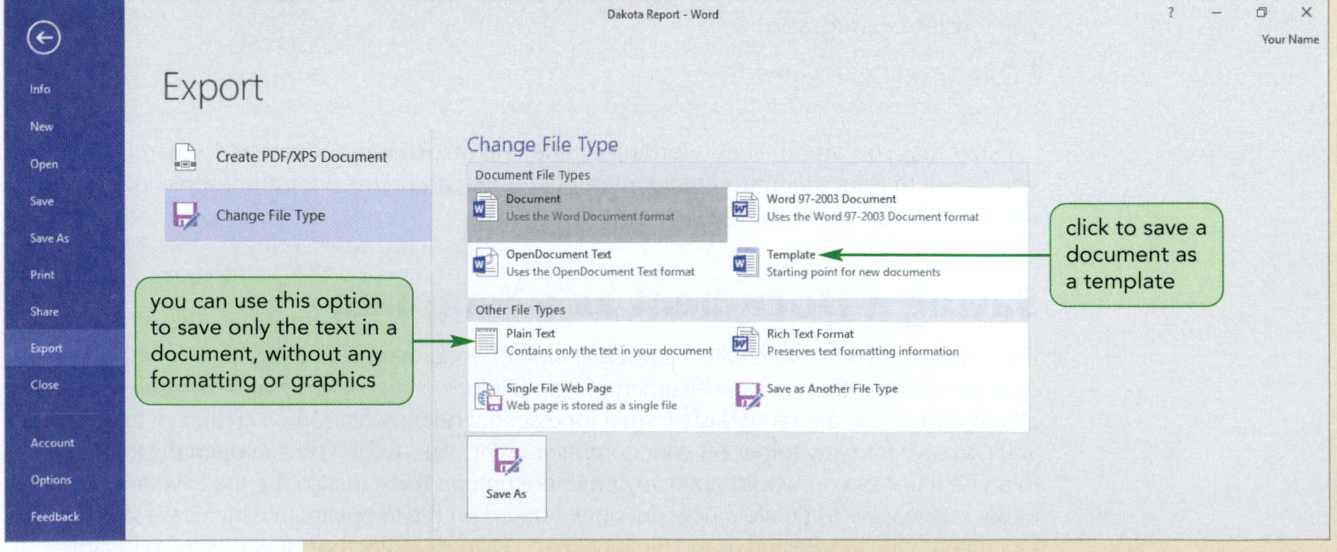

4. Under Change File Type, click **Template**, and then click the **Save As** button. The Save As dialog box opens with Word Template selected in the Save as type box.
5. If necessary, navigate to the location specified by your instructor. Next, you'll replace the selected, default filename with a new one that includes the acronym for the Sioux Falls Center for Business and Technology.
6. In the File name box, type **SFCBT Report**. See Figure 5-30.

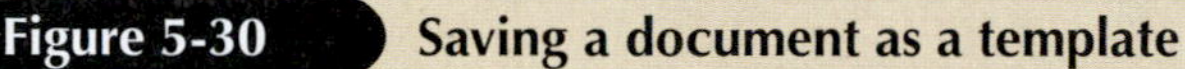

Figure 5-30 Saving a document as a template

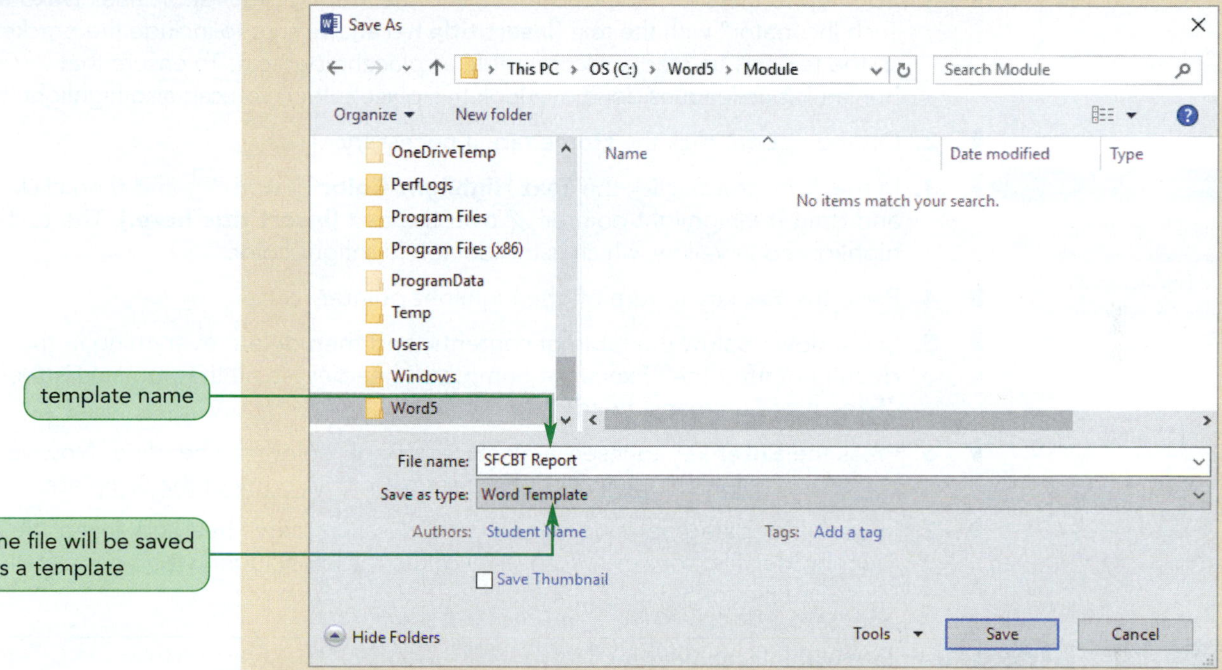

7. Click the **Save** button. The Save As dialog box closes, and the document, which is now a template with the .dotx file extension, remains open.

PROSKILLS

Written Communication: Standardizing the Look of Your Documents

Large companies often ask their employees to use a predesigned template for all corporate documents. If you work for an organization that does not require you to use a specific template, consider using one anyway in order to create a standard look for all of your documents. A consistent appearance is especially important if you are responsible for written communication for an entire department because it ensures that colleagues and clients will immediately recognize documents from your department.

Be sure to use a professional-looking template. If you decide to create your own, use document styles that make text easy to read, with colors that are considered appropriate in your workplace. Don't try to dazzle your readers with design elements. In nearly all professional settings, a simple, elegant look is ideal.

To make the new SFCBT Report template really useful to Benjamin's colleagues, you need to delete the specific information related to the Dakota Tech Incubator and replace it with placeholder text explaining the type of information required in each section. In the following steps, you will delete the body of the report and replace it with some placeholder text. Benjamin wants to use the current subtitle, "Prepared by the Sioux Falls Center for Business and Technology," as the subtitle in all reports, so there's no need to change it. However, the title will vary from one report to the next, so you need to replace it with a suitable placeholder. You'll retain the table of contents. When Benjamin's colleagues use the template to create future reports, they can update the table of contents to include any headings they add to their new documents.

To replace the information about the Dakota Tech Incubator with placeholder text:

1. Scroll up to the top of the document, and then replace the report title "Dakota Tech Incubator" with the text **[Insert title here.]**. Be sure to include the brackets so the text will be readily recognizable as placeholder text. To ensure that Benjamin's colleagues don't overlook this placeholder, you can also highlight it.
2. On the ribbon, click the **Home** tab, if necessary.
3. In the Font group, click the **Text Highlight Color** button, and then click and drag the highlight pointer over the text **[Insert title here.]**. The text is highlighted in yellow, which is the default highlight color.
4. Press the **Esc** key to turn off the highlight pointer.
5. Scroll down below the table of contents, and then delete everything in the document after the "Executive Summary" heading so all that remains is the "Executive Summary" heading.
6. Press the **Enter** key to insert a blank paragraph below the heading. Now you can insert a file containing placeholder text for the body of the template.
7. In the blank paragraph under the "Executive Summary" heading, insert the **Placeholder** file from the Word5 > Module folder included with your Data Files. See Figure 5-31.

TIP

To remove highlighting from selected text, click the Text Highlight Color button arrow, and then click No Color.

Figure 5-31 Template with placeholder text

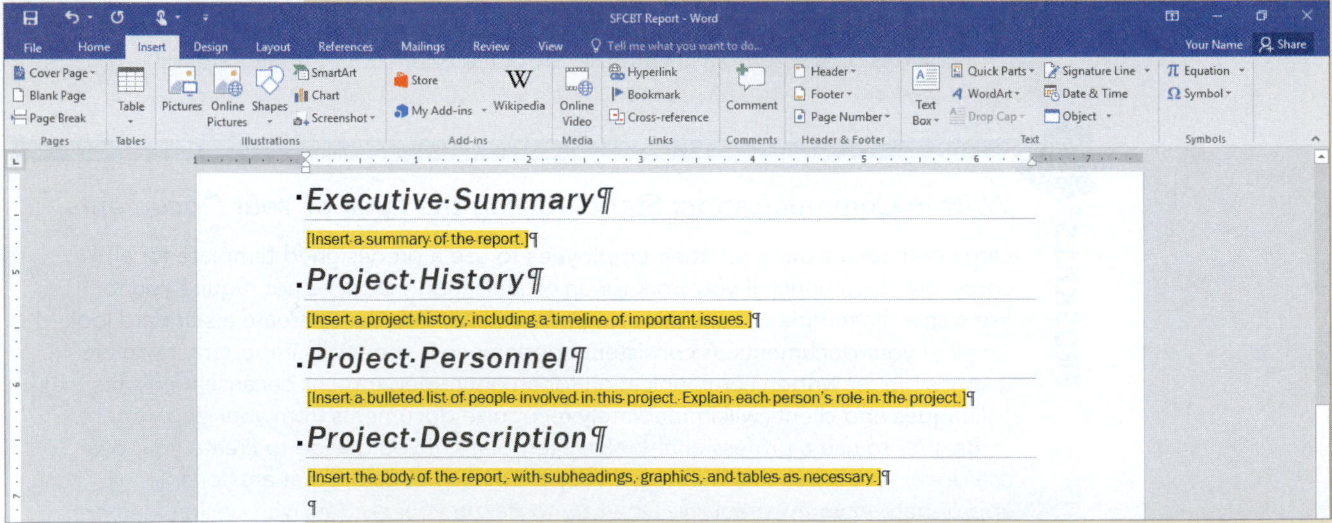

Scroll up to review the document, and notice that the inserted placeholder text is highlighted and the headings are all correctly formatted with the Heading 1 style. When Benjamin created the Placeholder document, he formatted the text in the default Heading 1 style provided by the Office theme. But when you inserted the file into the template, Word automatically applied your updated Heading 1 style. Now you can update the table of contents.

8. On the ribbon, click the **References** tab.
9. In the Table of Contents group, click the **Update Table** button. The table of contents is updated to include the new headings.
10. On the Quick Access Toolbar, click the **Save** button to save your changes to the template just as you would save a document.

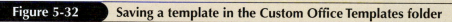

At this point, you have a copy of the template stored in the location specified by your instructor. If you closed the template, clicked the File tab, and then opened the template again from the same folder, you would be opening the template itself and not a new document based on the template. If you want to be able to open a new document based on the template from the New screen, you have to save the template to the Custom Office Templates folder. You'll do that next. You can also open a new document based on a template by double-clicking the template file from within File Explorer. You'll have a chance to try that in the Case Problems at the end of this module.

To save the template to the Custom Office Templates folder:

1. On the ribbon, click the **File** tab, and then click **Save As** in the navigation bar.
2. Click **Computer** if necessary, and then click the **Browse** button to open the Save As dialog box.
3. In the navigation pane of the Save As dialog box, click the **Documents** folder, and then, in the folder list on the right, double-click **Custom Office Templates**. See Figure 5-32.

Figure 5-32 Saving a template in the Custom Office Templates folder

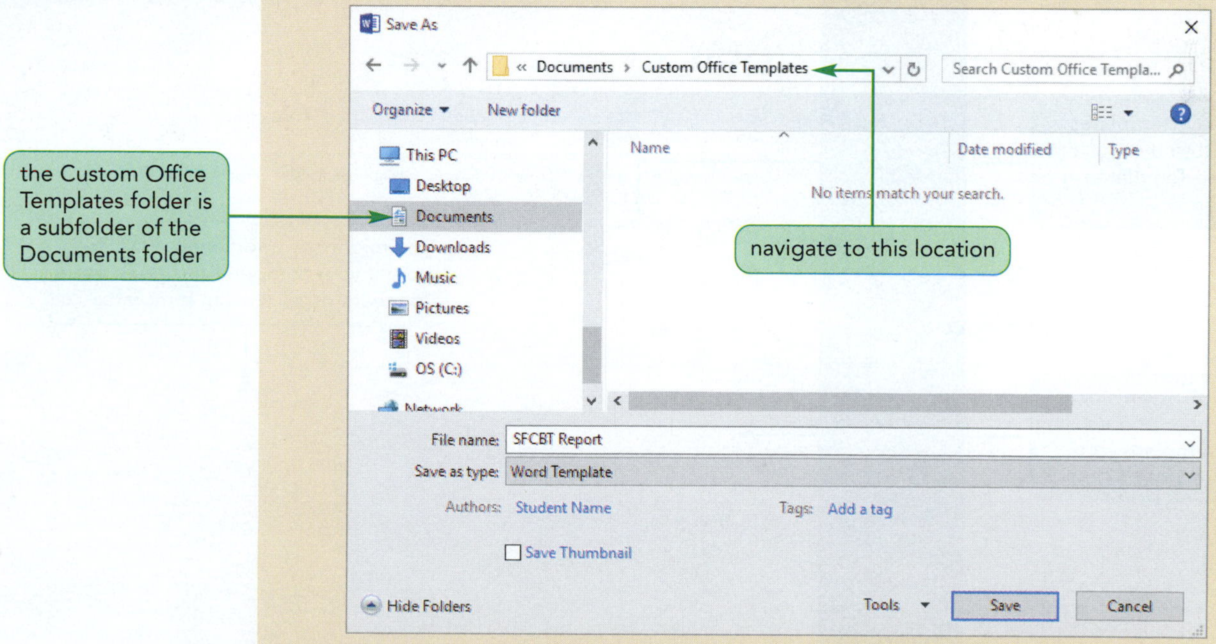

4. Click the **Save** button to save the template to the Custom Office Templates folder and close the Save As dialog box.
5. On the ribbon, click the **File** tab, and then click **Close** in the navigation bar to close the template, just as you would close a document.

The template you just created will simplify the process of creating new reports in Benjamin's department.

Opening a New Document Based on Your Template

Documents created using a template contain all the text and formatting included in the template. Changes you make to this new document will not affect the template file, which remains unchanged in the Custom Office Templates folder.

Benjamin would like you to use the SFCBT Report template to begin a report on SFCBT's annual coding academy.

To open a new document based on the SFCBT Report template:

1. On the ribbon, click the **File** tab, and then click **New** in the navigation bar.

   Because you have created and saved a template, the New screen in Backstage view now includes two links—FEATURED and PERSONAL. The FEATURED link is selected by default, indicating that the templates currently featured by Office.com are displayed. To open the template you just saved to the Custom Office Templates folder, you need to display the personal templates instead.

2. Click **PERSONAL**. The SFCBT Report template is displayed as an option on the New screen. See Figure 5-33.

Figure 5-33 Opening a document based on the SFCBT Report template

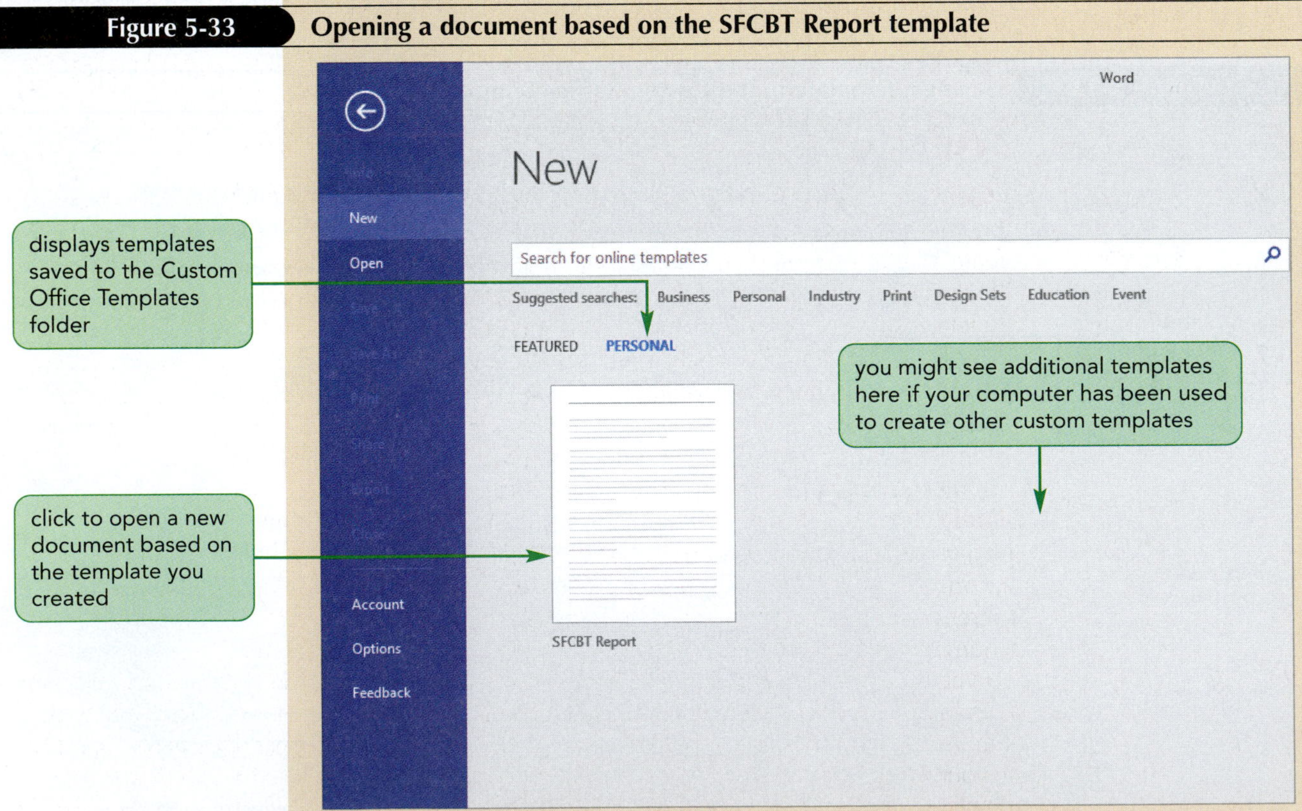

3. Click **SFCBT Report**. A new document opens, containing the text and formatting from the SFCBT Report template.

4. Delete the placeholder **[Insert title here.]**, and type **Annual Coding Academy** in its place.

   Benjamin and his colleagues will add new material to this report later. For now, you can close it.

5. Save the document as **Coding Academy** in the location specified by your instructor, and then close the document.

   Next, to ensure that you can repeat the steps in this module if you choose to, you will delete the SFCBT Report template from the Custom Office Templates folder. You can delete it from within the Open dialog box.

6. On the ribbon, click the **File** tab, and then click **Open** in the navigation bar.
7. Click the **Browse** button.
8. In the navigation pane of the Open dialog box, click the **Documents** folder, and then double-click **Custom Office Templates**. The SFCBT Report template is displayed in the file list.
9. Right-click **SFCBT Report** to display a shortcut menu, and then click **Delete**. The template file is removed from the file list.

   Trouble? If you see a message box asking you to confirm that you want to move the file to the Recycle Bin, click Yes.

10. Click the **Cancel** button to close the Open dialog box, and then close Backstage view.

Creating a template makes it easy to create a series of similar documents. But what if you want to insert specific text such as an address or email address or a graphic such as a logo in many different documents? In that case, you can save the item as a Quick Part.

Creating a New Quick Part

A **Quick Part** is reusable content that you create and that you can then insert into any document later with a single click in the Quick Parts gallery. For example, you might create a letterhead with your company's address and logo. To save the letterhead as a Quick Part, you select it and then save it to the Quick Parts gallery. Later, you can insert the letterhead into a document by clicking it in the Quick Parts gallery.

By default, a new Quick Part appears as an option in the Quick Parts gallery. However, you can assign a Quick Part to any gallery you want. For example, you could assign a text box Quick Part to the Text Box gallery so that every time you click the Text Box button on the Insert tab, you see your text box as one of the options in the Text Box gallery.

Quick Parts are just one type of a larger category of reusable content known as **building blocks**. All of the ready-made items that you can insert into a document via a gallery are considered building blocks. For example, preformatted headers, preformatted text boxes, and cover pages are all examples of building blocks. Some reference sources use the terms "building block" and "Quick Part" as if they were synonyms, but in fact a Quick Part is a building block that you create.

When you save a Quick Part, you always save it to a template; you can't save a Quick Part to an individual document. Which template you save it to depends on what you want to do with the Quick Part. If you want the template to be available to all new documents created on your computer, you should save it to the Building Blocks template. The **Building Blocks template** is a special template that contains all the building blocks installed with Word on your computer, as well as any Quick Parts you save to it. If you want to restrict the Quick Part to only documents based on the current template, or if you want to be able to share the Quick Part with someone else, you should save it to the current template. To share the Quick Part, you simply distribute the template to anyone who wants to use the Quick Part.

REFERENCE

Creating and Using Quick Parts

- Select the text, text box, header, footer, table, graphic, or other item you want to save as a Quick Part.
- On the ribbon, click the Insert tab.
- In the Text group, click the Quick Parts button, and then click Save Selection to Quick Parts Gallery.
- In the Create New Building Block dialog box, replace the text in the Name box with a descriptive name for the Quick Part.
- Click the Gallery arrow, and then choose the gallery to which you want to save the Quick Part.
- To make the Quick Part available to all documents on your computer, select Building Blocks in the Save in box. To restrict the Quick Part to the current template, select the name of the template on which the current document is based.
- Click the OK button.

Benjamin has created a text box containing the address and phone number for the Sioux Falls Center for Business and Technology. He asks you to show him how to save the text box as a Quick Part. He wants the Quick Part to be available to all new documents created on his computer, so you'll need to save it to the Building Blocks template.

To save a text box as a Quick Part:

1. Open the document **SFCBT** from the Word5 > Module folder, and then save it as **SFCBT Address** in the location specified by your instructor.
2. Display nonprinting characters and the rulers, switch to Print Layout view, and then change the Zoom level to **120%**, if necessary.
3. Click the **text box** to select it, taking care to select the entire text box and not the text inside it. When the text box is selected, you'll see the anchor symbol in the left margin.
4. On the ribbon, click the **Insert** tab.
5. In the Text group, click the **Quick Parts** button. If any Quick Parts have been created on your computer, they will be displayed in the gallery at the top of the menu. Otherwise, you will see only the menu shown in Figure 5-34.

Figure 5-34 Quick Parts menu, with no Quick Parts visible

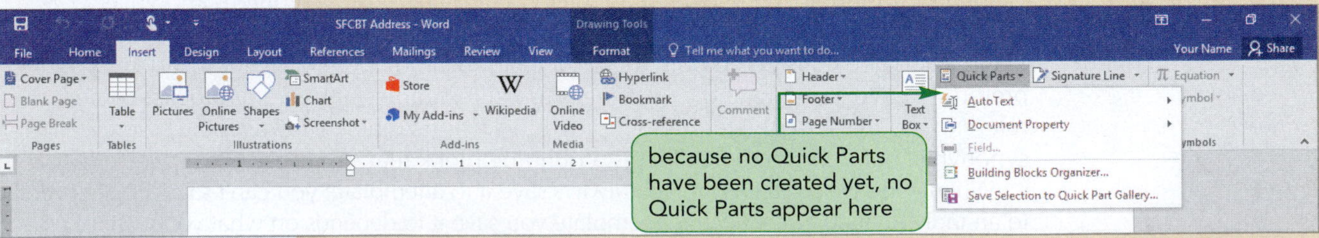

6. At the bottom of the menu, click **Save Selection to Quick Part Gallery**. The Create New Building Block dialog box opens. The name of this dialog box is appropriate because a Quick Part is a type of building block. See Figure 5-35.

Figure 5-35 Create New Building Block dialog box

the first two words in the text box are used as the name of the new building block by default

Create New Building Block

Name: Sioux Falls

Gallery: Quick Parts

Category: General

Description:

Save in: Building Blocks

Options: Insert content only

OK Cancel

the new building block will be saved in the Quick Parts gallery by default

the new building block will be saved to the Building Blocks template by default

By default, the first two words in the text box, "Sioux Falls," are used as the default name for the new building block. You could type a new name, but Benjamin is happy with the default. Also, the default setting in the Gallery box tells you that the new building block will be saved in the Quick Parts gallery. You could change this by selecting a different gallery name. The Save in box indicates that the Quick Part will be saved to the Building Blocks template, which means it will be available to all documents on your computer.

Benjamin asks you to accept the default settings.

7. Click the **OK** button to accept your changes and close the Create New Building Block dialog box.

You've finished creating the new Quick Part. Now you can try inserting it in the current document.

To insert the new Quick Part into the current document:

1. Press the **Ctrl+End** keys to move the insertion point to the end of the document.
2. In the Text group, click the **Quick Parts** button. This time, the Quick Parts gallery is displayed at the top of the menu. See Figure 5-36.

Figure 5-36 New Quick Part in the Quick Parts gallery

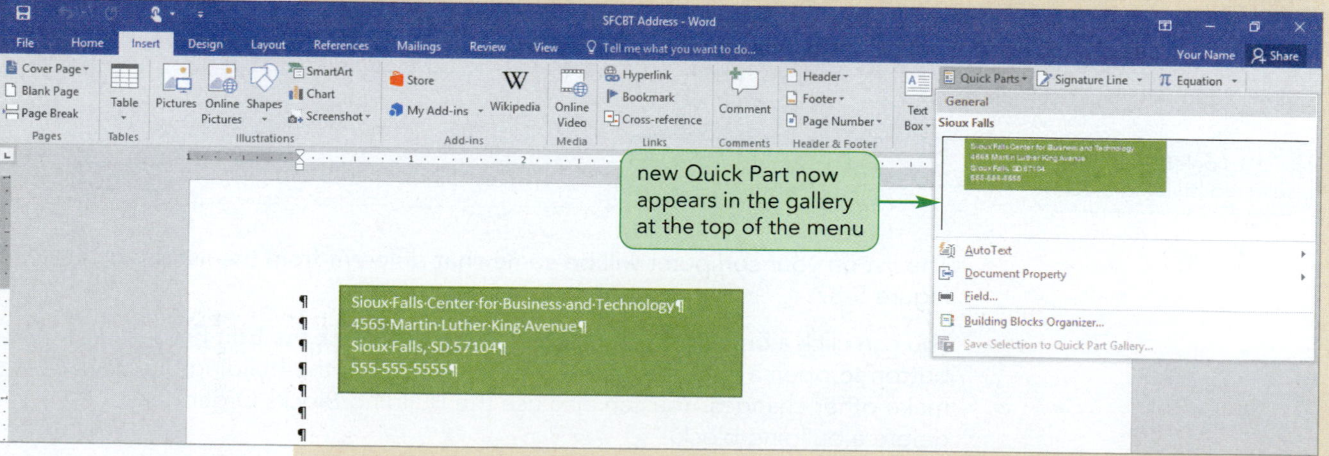

3. Click the **Sioux Falls** Quick Part. A copy of the green text box is inserted at the end of the document, at the insertion point.
4. In the newly inserted text box, replace the phone number with your first and last names, and then save the document.

The new Quick Part is stored in the Quick Parts gallery, ready to be inserted into any document. However, after reviewing the Quick Part, Benjamin has decided he wants to reformat the address text box and save it as a new Quick Part later. So you'll delete the Quick Part you just created.

To delete a Quick Part:

1. In the Text group, click the **Quick Parts** button, and then click **Building Blocks Organizer** to open the Building Blocks Organizer dialog box. Here you see a list of all the building blocks available in your copy of Word, including Quick Parts. See Figure 5-37.

Figure 5-37 Building Blocks Organizer dialog box

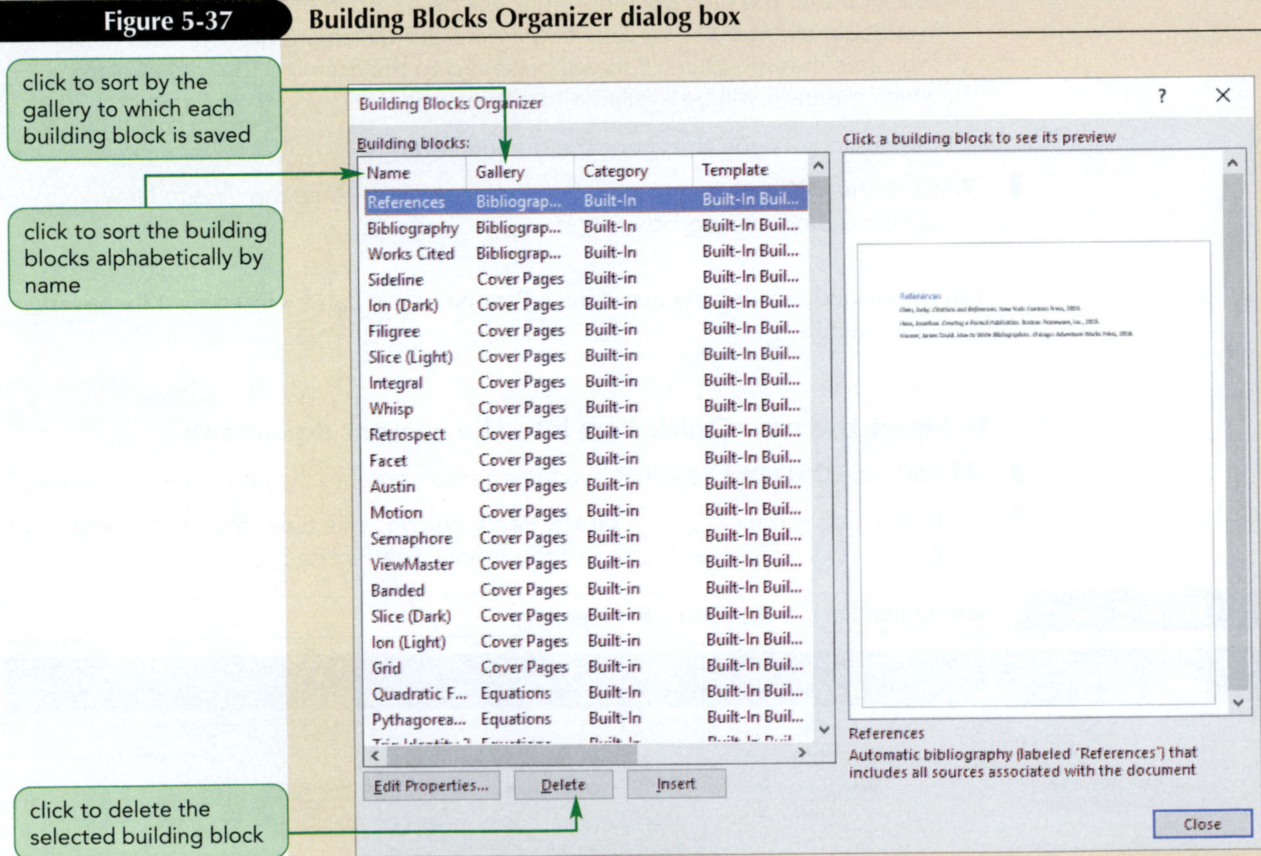

The list on your computer will be somewhat different from the list shown in Figure 5-37.

You can click a building block in the list and then click the Edit Properties button to open a dialog box where you can rename the building block and make other changes. You can also use the Building Blocks Organizer to delete a building block.

2. Click the **Name** column header to sort the building blocks alphabetically by name, scroll down and click **Sioux Falls**, click the **Delete** button, and then click the **Yes** button in the warning dialog box. The Department Quick Part is deleted from the list in the Building Blocks Organizer.
3. Click the **Close** button.
4. In the Text group, click the **Quick Parts** button, and verify that the Sioux Falls Quick Part is no longer displayed in the Quick Parts gallery.

   Finally, to completely delete the Quick Part from the Building Blocks template, you need to save the current document. In the process of saving the document, Word will save your changes to the Building Blocks template, which controls all the building blocks available in your copy of Word. If you don't save the document now, you'll see a warning dialog box later, when you attempt to close the document. It's easy to get confused by the wording of this warning dialog box, and you might end up restoring your Quick Part rather than deleting it. To avoid seeing this warning dialog box entirely, remember to save the current document after you delete a Quick Part.
5. Save the **SFCBT Address** document, and then close it.

Benjamin is happy to know how to save Quick Parts to the Building Blocks template. He'll create a new Quick Part later and save it to a custom template so that he can make it available to everyone at the Sioux Falls Center for Business and Technology.

REVIEW

Session 5.2 Quick Check

1. By default, is a new style saved to the current document or to the current template?
2. Explain how to create a new style.
3. What pane displays information about the style applied to the paragraph that currently contains the insertion point?
4. Which setting on the Line and Page Breaks tab of the Paragraph dialog box ensures that if a paragraph consists of more than one line of text, the lines of the paragraph will never be separated by a page break?
5. What must you do to your document before you can create a table of contents for it?
6. Where should you save a custom template if you want to be able to access it from the New screen in Backstage view?
7. What is a Quick Part?

PRACTICE

Review Assignments

Data Files needed for the Review Assignments: Construction.docx, Contributors.docx, DTI Address.docx, Placeholder Text.docx

Benjamin's SFCBT Report template is now used for all reports created by employees of the Sioux Falls Center for Business and Technology. Inspired by Benjamin's success with the template, a project manager for the Dakota Tech Incubator Planning Commission, Layla Farhad, wants you to help with a report on construction plans for the new facility. After you format the report, she'd like you to save the document as a new template and then create a Quick Part. Complete the following steps:

1. Create a new document based on the Report (Essential design) template from Office.com. (If you can't find that template, choose another.) Replace the first placeholder in the document with your name, and then save the document as **Document from Office.com Template** in the location specified by your instructor. If you see a dialog box explaining that the document is being upgraded to the newest file format, click the OK button.
2. Close the document.
3. Open the document **Construction** from the Word5 > Review folder included with your Data Files, and then save it as **Construction Report** in the location specified by your instructor.
4. Use the Go To feature to review all the headings in the document.
5. In the fourth line of the "Project Background" section, use the Thesaurus task pane to replace "ancillary" with a synonym. Use the fourth synonym in the list of words related to "auxiliary."
6. Change the theme colors to Grayscale, and then change the theme's fonts to the Georgia fonts.
7. Save the new colors and fonts as a theme named **DTI Theme** in the location specified by your instructor.
8. Change the style set to Minimalist.
9. Change the formatting of the "Project Background" heading by adding italic formatting and by changing the character spacing so that it is expanded by 1 point between characters.
10. Update the Heading 1 style to match the newly formatted "Project Background" heading.
11. Revise the "Likely Challenges" heading by changing the font size to 16 points, and then update the Heading 2 style to match the newly formatted "Likely Challenges" heading.
12. Create a new paragraph style for the "Contents" heading that is based on the Heading 1 style but that also includes Gray-50%, Accent 3 paragraph shading, and the White, Background 1 font color. Name the new style **Contents**, select Normal as the style for the following paragraph, and then save the new style to the current document.
13. Open the Style Inspector pane, and check the style applied to each paragraph in the document. Then use the Reveal Formatting pane to compare the formatting applied to the "Contents" heading with the formatting applied to the "Project Background" heading.
14. Delete the placeholder text below the "Contents" heading, and then insert a custom table of contents that does not include the Contents style. Except for excluding the Contents style, use the default settings in the Table of Contents dialog box.
15. Insert a blank paragraph at the end of the document, and then insert the **Contributors** file from the Word5 > Review folder. Add the text **Contributing Staff Members** to the table of contents as a Level 1 heading, and then delete the blank paragraph at the end of the document.
16. At the end of the report, replace "Student Name" with your first and last names.
17. Save your changes to the Construction Report document.
18. Save the Construction Report document as a Word Template named **DTI Report** in the location specified by your instructor.
19. On page 1, replace the title "CONSTRUCTING THE DAKOTA TECH INCUBATOR" with the placeholder text **[INSERT TITLE HERE.]**, and then highlight the placeholder in the default yellow color.
20. Delete everything in the report after the blank paragraph after the table of contents.

21. In the blank paragraph below the table of contents, insert the **Placeholder Text** file from the Word5 > Review folder.
22. In the Business Community Personnel section, replace "Student Name" with your first and last names, and then update the table of contents.
23. Save the template, save it again to the Custom Office Templates folder, and then close it.
24. Open a new document based on the DTI Report template, enter **PROJECTIONS FOR GROWTH** as the document title, save the new document as **Projections** in the location specified by your instructor, and then close it.
25. Delete the DTI Report template from the Custom Office Templates folder.
26. Open the document **DTI Address** from the Word5 > Review folder, and then save it as a Word Template named **DTI Address Box** in the location specified by your instructor.
27. Save the green text box as a Quick Part named **Address**. Save it to the DTI Address Box template, not to the Building Blocks template.
28. Save the template and close it.

APPLY

Case Problem 1

Data File needed for this Case Problem: Vento.docx

Vento Energy Experts Haley Porter is a consultant for Vento Energy Experts, a firm that helps clients lower their energy bills by replacing outdated heating and cooling systems with more efficient options. For each client, Haley needs to prepare an "Energy Efficiency Report for Existing and Proposed Systems." These reports can be quite long, so it's necessary to include a table of contents on the first page. Your job is to create a template that Haley and her fellow consultants can use when compiling their reports. Complete the following steps:

1. Open the document **Vento** from the Word5 > Case1 folder included with your Data Files, and then save it as **Vento Report** in the location specified by your instructor.
2. Use Go To to review all the tables in the document.
3. Change the document's theme to the Facet theme, and then change the theme colors to Blue Green. Change the style set to Basic (Stylish).
4. Highlight in yellow the three instances of placeholder text below the company name and above the "Contents" heading.
5. Format the "Contents" heading by changing the character spacing to Expanded, with the default amount of space between the expanded characters. Increase the font size to 22 points, add italic formatting, and then change the font color to one shade darker, using the Blue, Accent 6, Darker 50% font color. Update the Heading 1 style for the current document to match the newly formatted heading.
6. Create a new paragraph style for the company name at the top of the document that is based on the Heading 1 style but that also includes Blue, Accent 6, Darker 50% paragraph shading; White, Background 1 font color; 36-point font size; and center alignment. Reduce the points of paragraph spacing before the paragraph to 0, and increase the points after the paragraph to 36. Name the new style **Company**. Select the Normal style as the style for the following paragraph, and save the style to the current document.
7. Remove the Company style from the Style gallery.
8. Below the "Contents" heading, replace the placeholder text with a custom table of contents that does not include the Company style.

9. In the document, delete the paragraph containing the "Contents" heading, and then update the table of contents to remove "Contents" from it.
10. Click in the paragraph before the table of contents, and increase the spacing after it to 24 points.
11. Add the "General Recommendations" heading, in the second to last paragraph of the document, to the table of contents at the same level as the "Project Summary" heading.
12. In the document's last paragraph, replace "improving" with a synonym. In the Thesaurus task pane, use the second synonym in the list of words related to "bettering."
13. Save your changes to the Vento Report document, and then save the Vento Report document as a template named **Vento Template** in the location specified by your instructor.
14. On page 4, save the complete "Analysis, Proposed System X" section (including the heading, the placeholder text, the table, and the blank paragraph below the table) as a Quick Part named **Additional Analysis**. Save the Quick Part to the Vento Template template.
15. Delete the complete "Analysis, Proposed System X" section from the body of the template, including the heading, the placeholder text, the table, and the blank paragraph after the table.
16. Update the table of contents to remove the "Analysis, Proposed System X" heading.
17. Save the template to its current location, and then save the template again to the Custom Office Templates folder. Close the template.
18. Open a document based on your new template, and then save the new document as **Bachman Report** in the location specified by your instructor.
19. Replace the first placeholder with the current date, replace the second placeholder with **Robert Bachman**, and then replace the third placeholder with your first and last names.
20. To the left of the "G" in the "General Recommendations" heading, insert the Additional Analysis Quick Part.
21. Replace the "X" in the new heading with the number "2" so that the heading reads "Analysis, Proposed System 2."
22. Update the table of contents to include the new heading.
23. Save and close the document, and then delete the Vento Template template from the Custom Office Templates folder.

CREATE

Case Problem 2

Data Files needed for this Case Problem: Desktops.png, Handout.dotx, Printers.png

Turnaround Solutions Isaiah Chandler is the founder of Turnaround Solutions, a volunteer organization that accepts outdated electronics from local businesses, refurbishes them, and then donates them to schools and social service agencies. Isaiah's organization hosts recycling fairs several times a year, with each fair focusing on a different type of electronic device, such as printers or desktop computers. He has created a template that he hopes will simplify the task of creating handouts announcing these recycling fairs, but it's not quite finished. He asks you to finish the template by adding two graphics as Quick Parts: one graphic for desktop recycling fairs, and one for printer recycling fairs. Then he would like you to use the new template to create a handout for an upcoming printer recycling fair. Your completed handout should look like the one shown in Figure 5-38.

Figure 5-38 Flyer for Turnaround Solutions

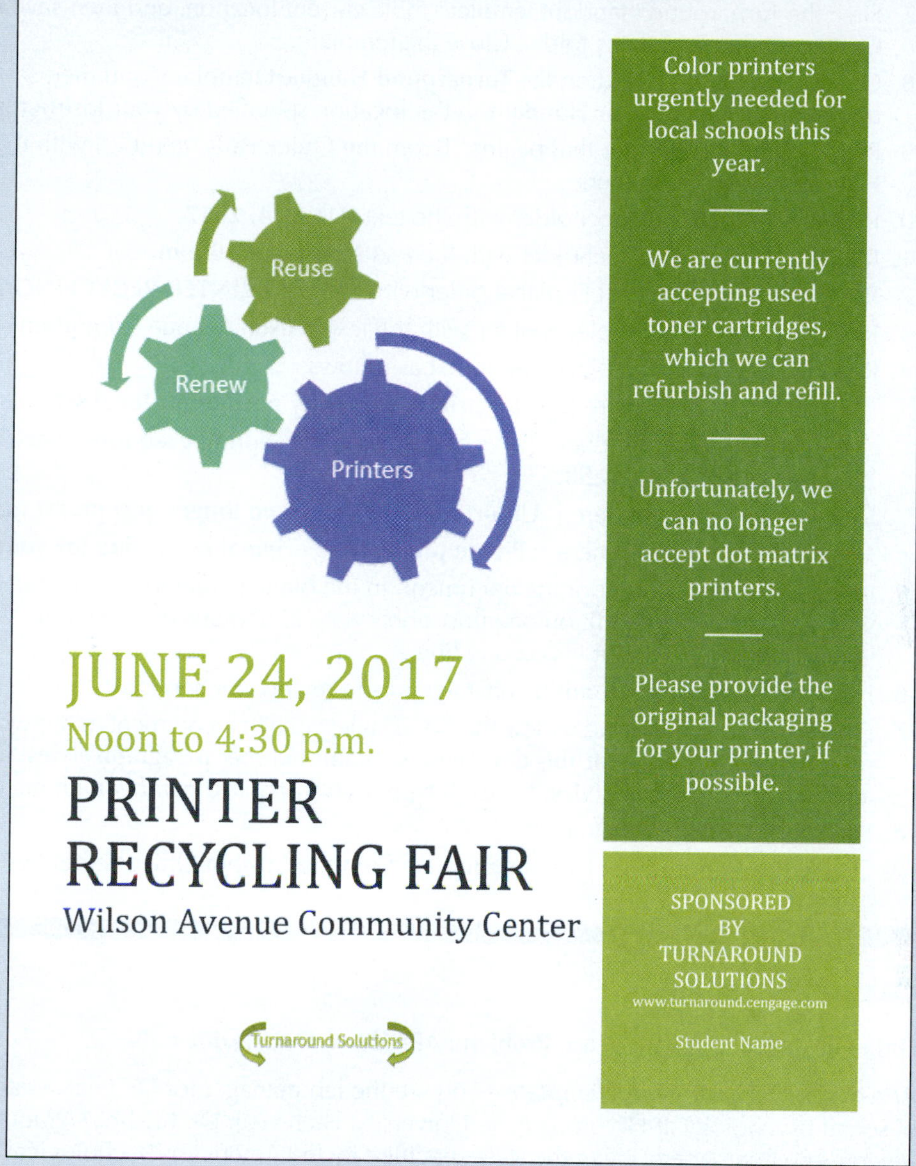

Complete the following steps:

1. Open the template **Handout** from the Word5 > Case2 folder included with your Data Files, then save it as a template named **Turnaround Handout** in the location specified by your instructor. Notice that the parts of the template are laid out using a table structure. If necessary, display the table gridlines so you can see the template's structure.
2. Replace the [Insert Graphic 1 here.] placeholder with the picture in the file **Desktops.png** located in the Word5 > Case2 folder, and then change the picture's height to 4".
3. Save the picture as a Quick Part named **Handout Graphic, Desktops** to the Turnaround Handout template.
4. Delete the picture and, in its place, insert the file **Printers.png** from the Word5 > Case2 folder. Change the picture's height to 4".
5. Save the picture as a Quick Part named **Handout Graphic, Printers** to the Turnaround Handout template.

6. Delete the picture, and insert the placeholder text **[From the Quick Parts menu, insert the graphic for the type of device that will be collected at the recycling fair.]**.
7. Save the Turnaround Handout template in its current location, and then save it again to the Custom Office Templates folder. Close the template.
8. Open a document based on the **Turnaround Handout** template, and then save the new document as **Printer Fair Handout** in the location specified by your instructor.
9. Replace the placeholder that begins "[From the Quick Parts menu…" with the Quick Part named Handout Graphic, Printers.
10. Replace the [DATE] placeholder with the text **JUNE 24, 2017**.
11. Replace the [Time] placeholder with the text **Noon to 4:30 p.m.**
12. Replace the [EVENT TITLE] placeholder with the text **PRINTER RECYCLING FAIR**.
13. Replace the [Location] placeholder with the text **Wilson Avenue Community Center.**
14. Replace the remaining placeholder text as follows:
    - [Insert first point here.]: **Color printers urgently needed for local schools this year.**
    - [Insert second point here.]: **We are currently accepting used toner cartridges, which we can refurbish and refill.**
    - [Insert third point here.]: **Unfortunately, we can no longer accept dot matrix printers.**
    - [Insert fourth point here.]: **Please provide the original packaging for your printer, if possible.**
15. In the lower-right corner of the document, in the blank paragraph below the web address, insert your name. If it doesn't fit on one line, abbreviate it, perhaps by using only your first initial and your last name, so that it fits on one line.
16. Hide gridlines and nonprinting characters, and review the handout.
17. Open the Styles pane and review the list of styles. Attach a comment to the word "JUNE" that reads: **The Styles pane for this document contains *number* paragraph styles, number linked styles, and number character styles.** For each type of style, replace *number* with the correct number.
18. Save and close the document.
19. Delete the Turnaround Handout template from the Custom Office Templates folder.

RESEARCH

Case Problem 3

Data Files needed for this Case Problem: APA.docx, Details.docx

APA-Style Research Paper Template You are the lab manager for Dr. Leah Krishna, a professor of social psychology at Holbrook State University. Each year, Dr. Krishna's graduate students write several research papers, using the style specified by the American Psychological Association (APA). To make it easier for her students to focus on writing about their research, rather than the formatting details of the APA style, Dr. Krishna wants to provide them with a Word template for an APA-style research paper. She asks you to create the template for her. You'll start by doing some research on specifications for the APA style, and, in the process, you will create a custom theme that Dr. Krishna can use for other lab documents. Complete the following steps:

1. Open the document **Details** from the Word5 > Case3 folder included with your Data Files, and then save it as **APA Details** in the location specified by your instructor.
2. In the second paragraph, insert your name where indicated.
3. Change the document's theme to the Office theme, and then change the theme colors to Red. Change the style set to Centered.
4. Save the customized theme as **KrishnaLab.thmx** in the location specified by your instructor.
5. Using a source on the web or an up-to-date print publication, research the characteristics of an APA-style research paper.
6. In the APA Details document, fill in the table with the necessary information about APA-style research papers.

7. Save the APA Details document, and then use it for reference as you complete the remaining steps in this Case Problem.
8. Open the document **APA** from the Word5 > Case3 folder, and then save it as a Word template named **APA Paper** in the location specified by your instructor.
9. Review the template, which contains all the necessary headings and placeholder text, along with paragraphs that Dr. Krishna generated by typing =lorem() and pressing the Enter key. You can use this text as body text to separate placeholder headings in the template.
10. Change the margins as necessary to match the APA style, and add page breaks where necessary.
11. Format the entire document using the appropriate font, font size, line spacing, and character spacing.
12. Edit the comment to insert the appropriate examples after each colon, and then add your name where indicated. In the comment, format the citation examples and your name with yellow highlighting.
13. Add an APA-style document header. Use the placeholder text **"[INSERT TITLE.]"** where appropriate. Remember to create a different header for the title page, as specified by the APA style.
14. Format the text on the first two pages appropriately.
15. In the main body of the paper, format the title placeholder, the headings placeholders, and the sample body text appropriately.
16. Format the "References" title appropriately.
17. Save the APA Paper template, and then close it.

CHALLENGE

Case Problem 4

Data File needed for this Case Problem: Health.docx, Joni's.docx

Health Time Software You are the assistant to Joni Duboff, a technical writer at Health Time Software, a medical software company in Paterson, New Jersey. Joni often uses Word styles in the reports and other publications she creates for the company, and she wants to learn more about managing styles. In particular, she wants to learn how to copy styles from one document to another. She's asked you to help her explore the Style Pane Options, Manage Styles, and Organizer dialog boxes. She would also like your help creating a Quick Part for a memo header. Complete the following steps:

1. Open the document **Health** from the Word5 > Case4 folder included with your Data Files, and then save it as **Health Time Memo** in the location specified by your instructor. This document contains the text you will eventually save as a Quick Part. It contains all the default styles available in any new Word document, as well as one style, named "Memorandum," which Joni created earlier. In the following steps, you will copy styles from another document to this document. For now, you can close it.
2. Close the Health Time Memo document.
3. Open the document **Joni's** from the Word5 > Case4 folder, and then save it as **Joni's Styles** in the location specified by your instructor. This document contains styles created by Joni, which you will copy to the Health Time Memo document. It also includes sample paragraphs formatted with Joni's styles, and one paragraph that you will format with a style later in this Case Problem.
4. **Explore** Open the Style Pane Options dialog box, and then change the settings so the Styles pane displays only the styles in the current document, in alphabetical order. Before closing this dialog box, verify that these settings will be applied only to the current document rather than to new documents based on this template.
5. **Explore** Open a new, blank document, and then use the Screenshot button in the Illustrations group on the Insert tab to create a screenshot of the Joni's Styles document.
6. Copy the screenshot to the Clipboard, and then paste it in the blank paragraph at the end of the Joni's Styles document, just as you would paste text that you had previously copied to the Clipboard. Close the document in which you created the screenshot without saving it.

Explore 7. At the bottom of the Styles pane, click the Manage Styles button, and then click the Import/Export button to open the Organizer dialog box. Close the Normal template, and open the Health Time Memo document instead. (*Hint*: On the right, under the In Normal.dotm box, click the Close File button, and then click the Open File button. In the Open dialog box, you'll need to display all files.)

Explore 8. Copy the following styles from the Joni's Styles document to the Health Time Memo document: Company Name, Department, Documentation Heading, and Product Description. Then copy the Memorandum style from the Health Time Memo document to the Joni's Styles document.

9. Close the Organizer dialog box, and then save your changes to the Health Time Memo document.
10. In the Joni's Styles document, apply the Memorandum style to the text "Sample of Memorandum style," in the document's third to last paragraph.
11. Save the Joni's Styles document, and then close it.
12. Open the **Health Time Memo** document, and then review the list of styles in the Styles pane to locate the styles you just copied to this document from the Joni's Styles document.
13. Apply the Company Name style to "Health Time Software" in the second paragraph.
14. Save the Health Time Memo document, and then save it again as a template named **Health Time Memo Template** in the location specified by your instructor.
15. Select all of the text in the document, and then save it as a Quick Part named **Gray Memo**. Save the Quick Part to the current template, not to the Building Blocks template.
16. Change the Paragraph shading for the first paragraph to gold, using the Gold, Accent 4, Darker 25% color, and then save the document text as a new Quick Part named **Gold Memo**. Again, save the Quick Part to the current template.
17. Delete all the text from the document, save the Health Time Memo Template file, and then close it.

Explore 18. Open a File Explorer window, and then navigate to the location where you saved the Health Time Memo Template file. Open a new document based on the template by double-clicking the template's filename in File Explorer.

19. Save the new document as **Sample Health Time Memo** in the location specified by your instructor, insert the Gold Memo Quick Part in the document, and then save and close the document.

MODULE 6

Using Mail Merge

Creating a Form Letter, Mailing Labels, and a Telephone Directory

WORD

OBJECTIVES

Session 6.1
- Insert a Date field
- Select a main document
- Create a data source
- Insert mail merge fields into a main document
- Edit a main document
- Preview a merged document
- Complete a mail merge

Session 6.2
- Reopen a main document
- Edit a data source
- Sort and filter records
- Create mailing labels
- Create a phone directory
- Convert a table to text

Case | *Tupelo Family Farm*

Chris Tupelo owns and manages Tupelo Family Farm, a peach orchard and packing facility in Fort Valley, Georgia. The company has just opened its newly expanded farm market store. To generate business, Chris plans to send a form letter to regular customers announcing the new market store and offering a dozen free peaches to customers who bring their copies of the letter to the store.

The form letter will also contain specific details for individual customers, such as name, address, and favorite variety of peach. Chris has already written the text of the form letter. She plans to use the mail merge process to add the personal information for each customer to the form letter. She asks you to revise the form letter by inserting a Date field in the document that will display the current date. Then she wants you to use the Mail Merge feature in Word to create customized letters for her customers. After you create the merged letters, Chris would like you to create mailing labels for the envelopes and a directory of employee phone numbers. Finally, you'll convert some text to a table so that it can be used in a mail merge.

STARTING DATA FILES

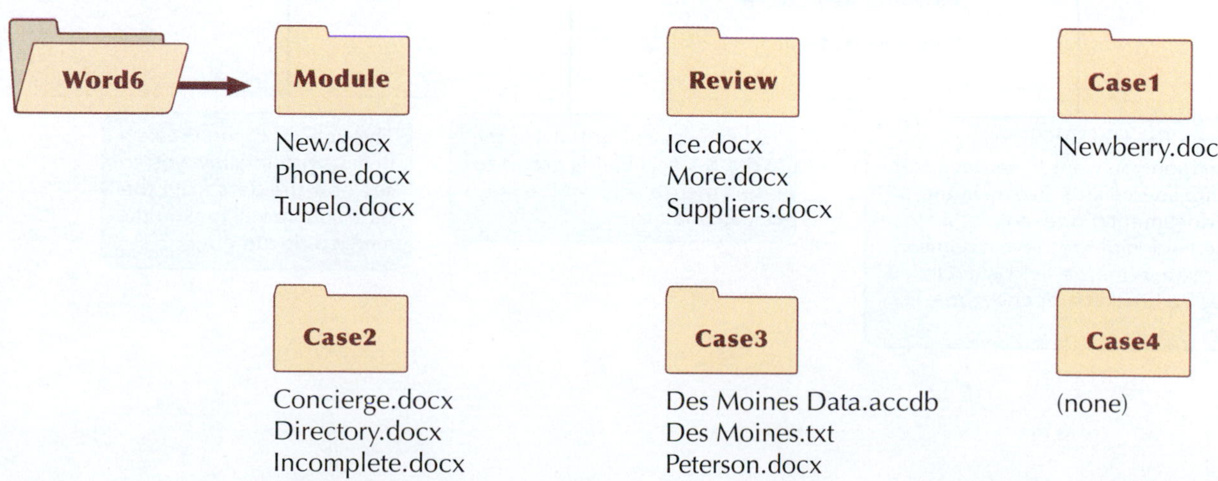

Module: New.docx, Phone.docx, Tupelo.docx

Review: Ice.docx, More.docx, Suppliers.docx

Case1: Newberry.docx

Case2: Concierge.docx, Directory.docx, Incomplete.docx, Residents.xlsx

Case3: Des Moines Data.accdb, Des Moines.txt, Peterson.docx

Case4: (none)

Session 6.1 Visual Overview:

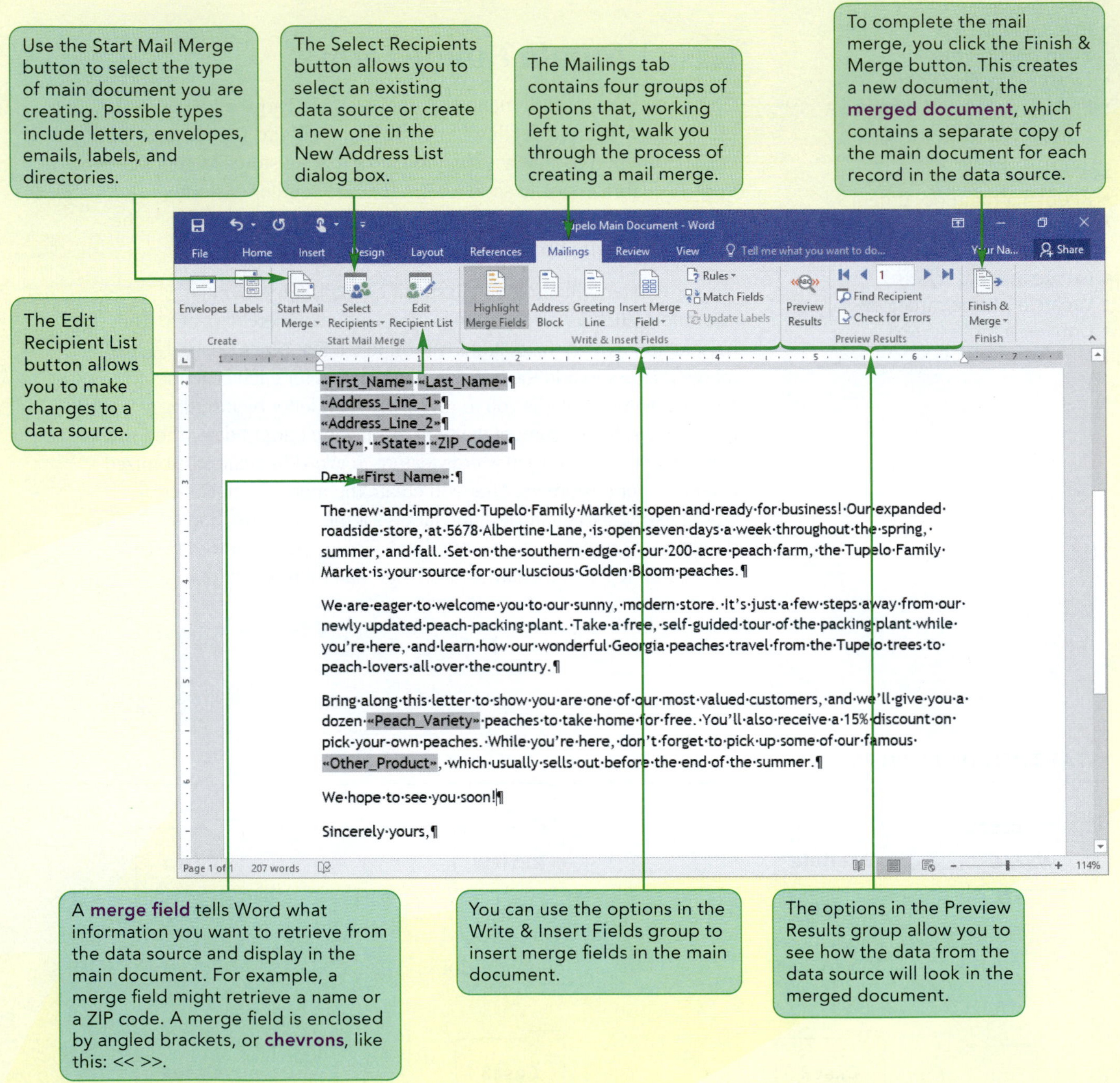

Mail Merge

A **data source** is a file that contains information, such as names and addresses, that is organized into fields and records; the merge fields cause the information in the data source to be displayed in the main document. You can use a Word table, an Excel spreadsheet, or other types of files as data sources, or you can create a new data source using the New Address List dialog box.

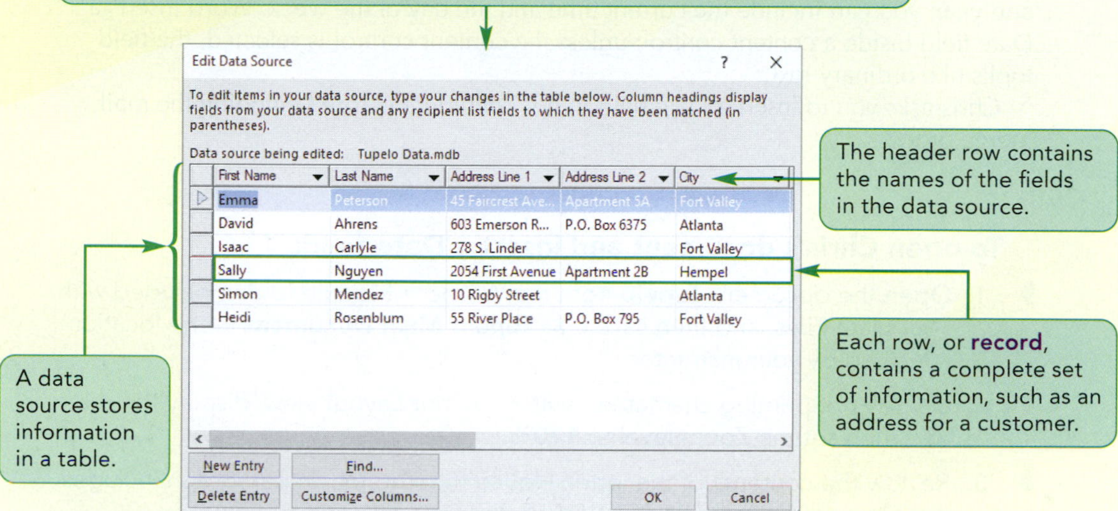

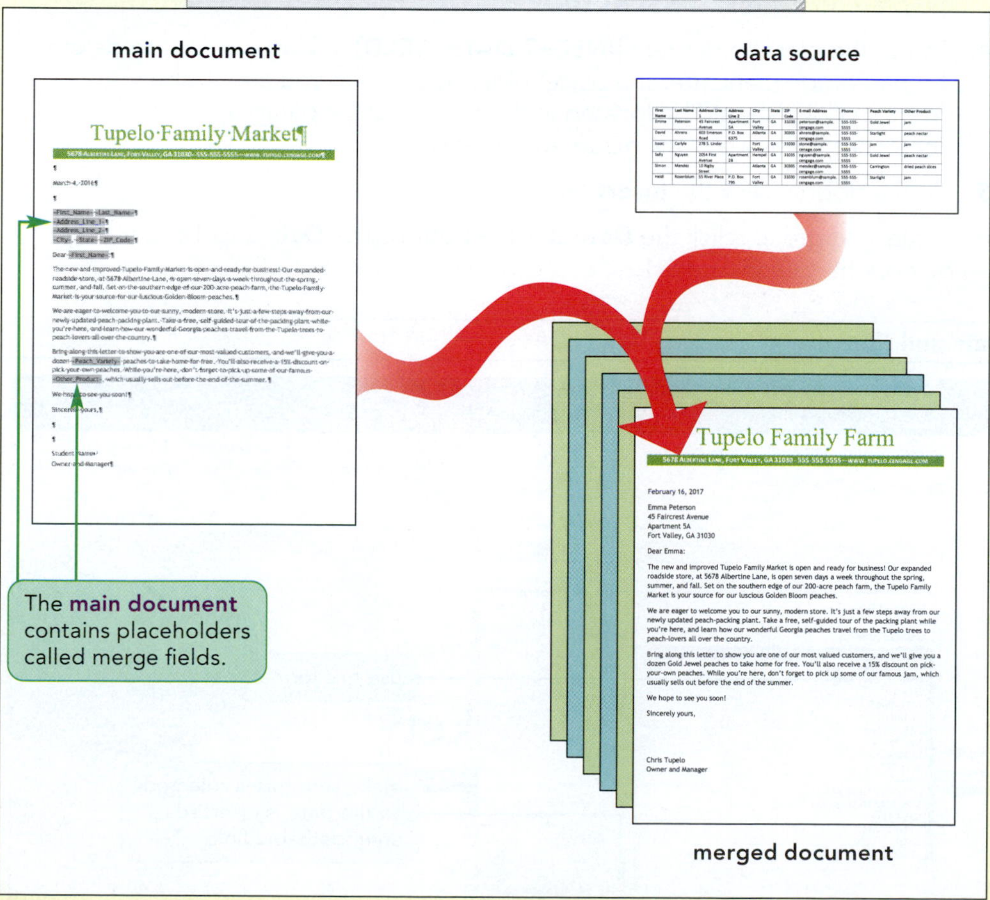

Inserting a Date Field

A **Date field** is an instruction that tells Word to display the current date in a document. Although a Date field is not a merge field, it's common to use Date fields in mail merge documents to ensure that the main document always includes the current date. Every time you open a document containing a Date field, it updates to display the current date. To insert a Date field, you use the Date and Time dialog box to select from a variety of date formats. In addition to displaying the date with the current day, month, and year, you can include the current time and the day of the week. Word inserts a Date field inside a content control; unless the content control is selected, the field looks like ordinary text.

Chris asks you to insert a Date field in her document before beginning the mail merge process.

To open Chris's document and insert a Date field:

1. Open the document **Tupelo** from the Word6 > Module folder included with your Data Files, and then save it as **Tupelo Main Document** in the location specified by your instructor.
2. Display nonprinting characters, switch to Print Layout view, display the rulers, and then set the Zoom level to **120%**.
3. Review the contents of the letter. Notice that the fourth paragraph includes the placeholder text "[INSERT DATE FIELD]."
4. Delete the placeholder text **[INSERT DATE FIELD]**, taking care not to delete the paragraph mark after the placeholder text. When you are finished, the insertion point should be located in the second blank paragraph of the document, with two blank paragraphs below it.
5. On the ribbon, click the **Insert** tab.
6. In the Text group, click the **Date & Time** button. The Date and Time dialog box opens. See Figure 6-1.

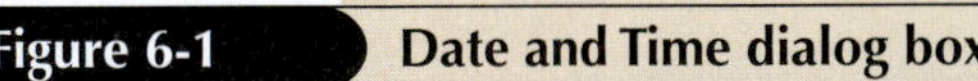
Figure 6-1 Date and Time dialog box

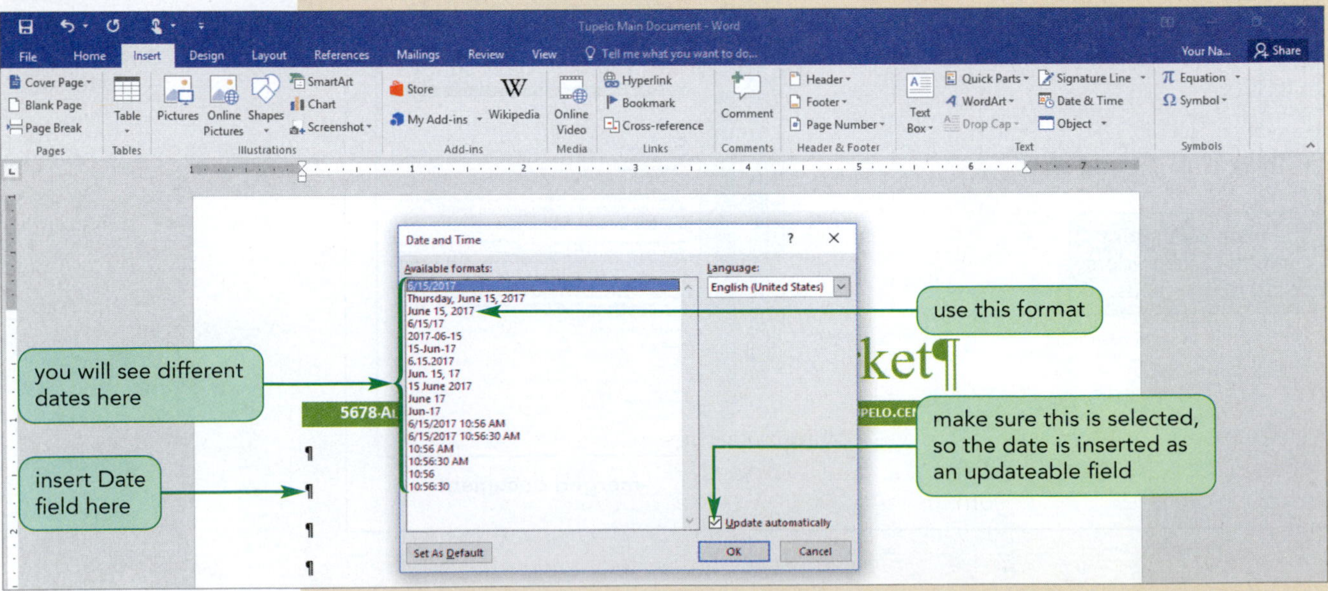

The Available formats list provides options for inserting the current date and time. In this case, you want to insert the date as a content control in a format that includes the complete name of the month, the date, and the year (for example, March 11, 2017).

7. In the Available formats list, click the third format from the top, which is the month, date, and year format.

8. Make sure the **Update automatically** check box is selected so the date is inserted as a content control that updates every time you open the document.

9. Click the **OK** button. The current date is inserted in the document. At this point, it looks like ordinary text. To see the content control, you have to click the date.

10. Click the date to display the content control. If you closed the document and then opened it a day later, the content control would automatically display the new date. See Figure 6-2.

TIP

If you use a date format that includes the time, you can update the time while the document is open by clicking the Update tab at the top of the content control.

Figure 6-2 Date field inside content control

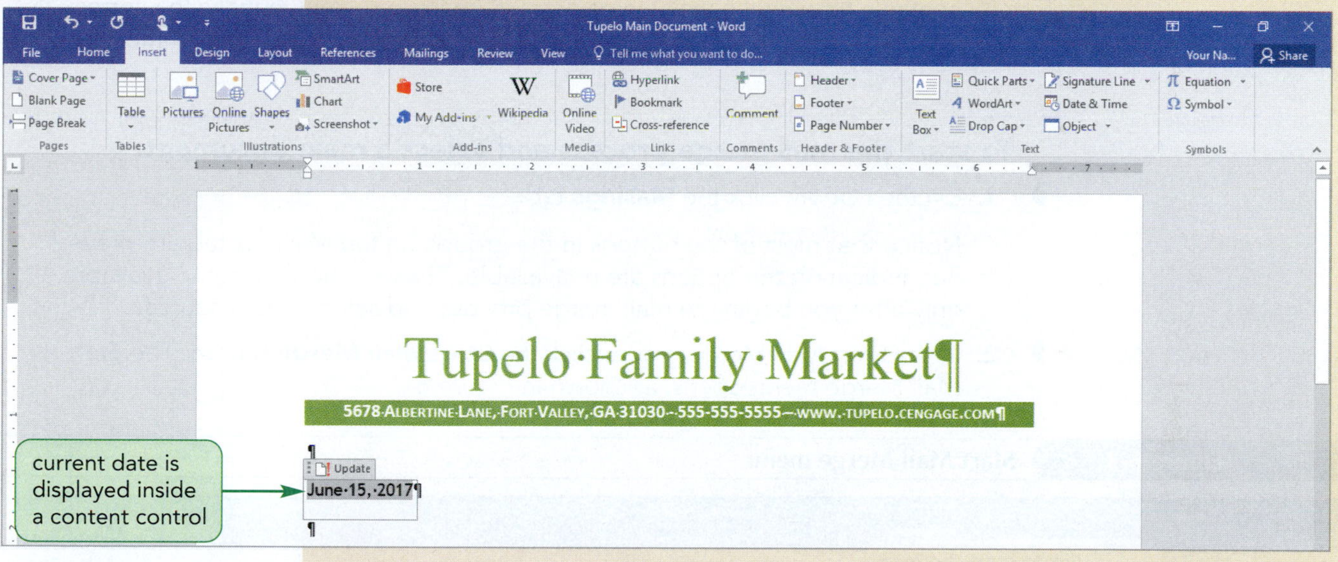

11. Scroll down to display the letter's closing, change "Chris Tupelo" to your first and last names, and then scroll back up to the beginning of the letter.

12. Save the document.

Now that the document contains the current date, you can begin the mail merge process.

Performing a Mail Merge

When you perform a mail merge, you insert individualized information from a data source into a main document. A main document can be a letter or any other kind of document containing merge fields that tell Word where to insert names, addresses, and other variable information from the data source. When you **merge** the main document with information from the data source, you produce a new document called a merged document. The Session 6.1 Visual Overview summarizes mail merge concepts.

Chris's main document is the letter shown in the Session 6.1 Visual Overview. In this session, you will insert the merge fields shown in this letter. You'll also create Chris's data source, which will include the name and address of each customer. The data source will also include information about each customer's favorite items at the store.

You can perform a mail merge by using the Mail Merge task pane, which walks you through the steps of performing a mail merge. You access the Mail Merge task pane by clicking the Start Mail Merge button in the Start Mail Merge group on the Mailings tab and then clicking the Step-by-Step Mail Merge Wizard command on the menu. You can also use the options on the Mailings tab, which streamlines the process and offers more tools. In this module, you'll work with the Mailings tab to complete the mail merge for Chris. The Mailings tab organizes the steps in the mail merge process so that you can move from left to right across the ribbon using the buttons to complete the merge.

Starting the Mail Merge and Selecting a Main Document

The first step in the mail merge process is selecting the type of main document. Your choice of main document type affects the commands that are available to you later as you continue through the mail merge process, so it's important to make the correct selection at the beginning. In this case, you will use a letter as the main document.

To start the mail merge process and select a main document:

1. On the ribbon, click the **Mailings** tab.

   Notice that most of the buttons in the groups on the Mailings tab are grayed out, indicating the options are unavailable. These options become available only after you begin the mail merge process and select a data source.

2. In the Start Mail Merge group, click the **Start Mail Merge** button. The Start Mail Merge menu opens, as shown in Figure 6-3.

Figure 6-3 Start Mail Merge menu

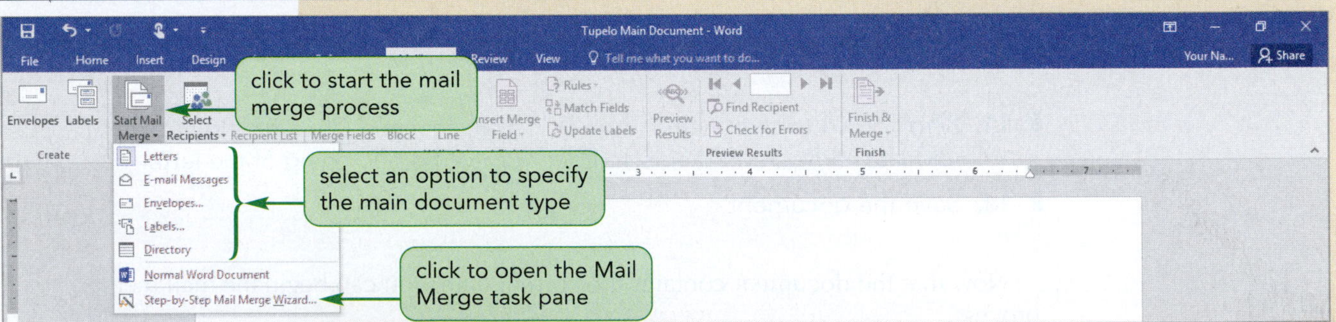

   The first five options on the menu allow you to specify the type of main document you will create. Most of the options involve print items, such as labels and letters, but you can also select an email message as the type of main document. In this case, you'll create a letter.

3. Click **Letters**. The Start Mail Merge menu closes.

   Next, you need to select the list of recipients for Chris's letter; that is, you need to select the data source.

4. In the Start Mail Merge group, click the **Select Recipients** button. The Select Recipients menu allows you to create a new recipient list, use an existing list, or select from Outlook Contacts (the address book in Outlook).

   Because Chris hasn't had a chance to create a data source yet, she asks you to create one.

5. Click **Type a New List**. The New Address List dialog box opens, as shown in Figure 6-4.

Figure 6-4 New Address List dialog box

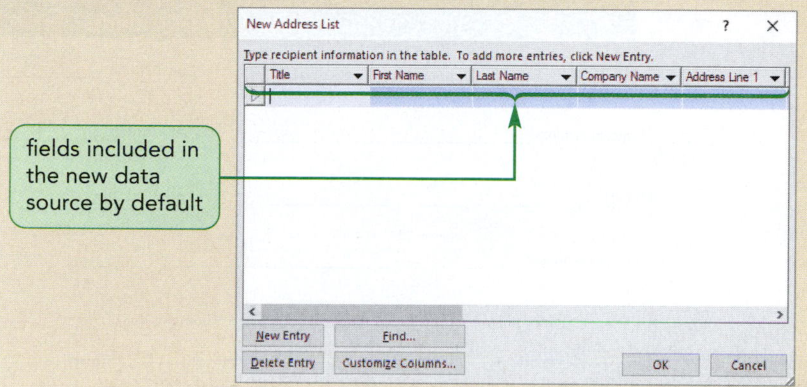

The default fields for a data source are displayed in this dialog box. Before you begin creating the data source, you need to identify the fields and records Chris wants you to include.

Creating a Data Source

As described in the Session 6.1 Visual Overview, a data source is a file that contains information organized into fields and records. Typically, the data source for a mail merge contains a list of names and addresses, but it can also contain email addresses, telephone numbers, and other data. Various kinds of files can be used as the data source, including an Excel workbook or an Access database. You can also use a file from another kind of database, such as one created by a company to store its sales information. For a simple mail merge project, such as a telephone directory, you can use a table stored in a Word document.

When performing a mail merge, you'll usually select an existing data source file—created in another application—that already contains the necessary information. However, in this module, you'll create a new data source in Word and then enter the data into it so you can familiarize yourself with the basic structure of a data source. After creating the new data source, you'll save the file in its default format as an Access database file, with an .mdb file extension. Microsoft Outlook also uses MDB files to store contact information—in which case they are referred to as Microsoft Office Address Lists files.

When you create a new data source, Word provides a number of default fields, such as First Name, Last Name, and Company. You can customize the data source by adding new fields and removing the default fields that you don't plan to use. When creating a data source, keep in mind that each field name must be unique; you can't have two fields with the same name.

The Microsoft Office Address Lists file you will create in this session will contain information about Chris's customers, including each customer's name, address, preferred variety of peach, and another favorite product. Chris collected all the necessary information by asking customers to sign up for the farm's mailing list. Figure 6-5 shows one of the forms she used to collect the information.

Figure 6-5 **Customer comment card**

Tupelo Family Market

Sign up for our mailing list to receive special offers and information about our latest products.

First Name ______________ Last Name ______________

Street Address ______________ Apartment ______________

City ______________ Zip Code ______________

Email Address ______________

Home delivery customers, please include a phone number (home or cell) ______________

Which variety of peach do you like best? ______________

Which of our other peach products do you like best? ______________

The information on each form will make up one record in the data source. Each blank on the form translates into one field in the data source as shown in Figure 6-6.

Figure 6-6 **Fields to include in the data source**

Field Names	Description
First Name	Customer's first name
Last Name	Customer's last name
Address Line 1	Customer's street address
Address Line 2	Additional address information, such as an apartment number
City	City
State	State
ZIP Code	ZIP code
E-mail Address	Customer's email address
Phone	Customer's home or cell phone number
Peach Variety	Customer's favorite peach variety
Other Product	Customer's favorite other peach product

Even though you won't need the customers' email addresses or phone numbers to complete the mail merge, you can still include them in the data source. That way, Chris can reuse the data source in future mail merges to send emails to her customers or when creating a directory of phone numbers for home delivery customers.

REFERENCE

Creating a Data Source for a Mail Merge

- On the ribbon, click the Mailings tab.
- In the Start Mail Merge group, click the Select Recipients button, and then click Type a New List to open the New Address List dialog box.
- To select the fields for your data source, click the Customize Columns button to open the Customize Address List dialog box.
- To delete an unnecessary field, select it, click the Delete button, and then click the Yes button.
- To add a new field, click the Add button, type the name of the field in the Add Field dialog box, and then click the OK button.
- To rearrange the order of the field names, click a field name, and then click the Move Up button or the Move Down button.
- To rename a field, click a field name, click the Rename button to open the Rename Field dialog box, type a new field name, and then click the OK button to close the Rename Field dialog box.
- Click the OK button to close the Customize Address List dialog box.
- In the New Address List dialog box, enter information for the first record, click the New Entry button, and then enter the information for the next record. Continue until you are finished entering all the information for the data source, and then click the OK button to open the Save Address List dialog box.
- Type a name for the data source in the File name box. By default, Word will save the file to the My Data Sources folder unless you specify another save location. Click the Save button. The file is saved with the .mdb file extension.

You're ready to create the data source for the form letter using information Chris has given you for three of her customers. However, before you begin entering information, you need to customize the list of fields to include only the fields Chris requires.

To customize the list of fields before creating the data source:

1. In the New Address List dialog box, click the **Customize Columns** button. The Customize Address List dialog box opens. Here you can delete the fields you don't need, add new ones, and arrange the fields in the order you want. You'll start by deleting some fields.
2. In the Field Names box, verify that **Title** is selected, and then click the **Delete** button. A message is displayed, asking you to confirm the deletion.
3. Click the **Yes** button. The Title field is deleted from the list of field names.
4. Continue using the Delete button to delete the following fields: **Company Name**, **Country or Region**, and **Work Phone**.

   Next, you need to add some new fields. When you add a new field, it is inserted below the selected field, so you'll start by selecting the last field in the list.
5. In the Field Names box, click **E-mail Address**, and then click the **Add** button. The Add Field dialog box opens, asking you to type a name for your field. See Figure 6-7.

Figure 6-7 **Add Field dialog box**

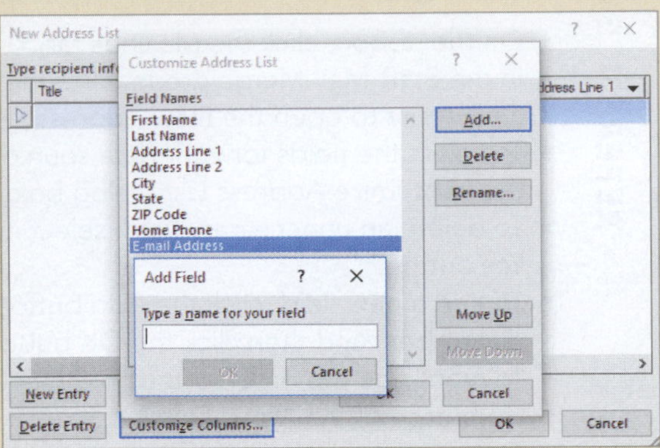

6. Type **Peach Variety** and then click the **OK** button. The field "Peach Variety" is added to the Field Names list.
7. Use the Add button to add the **Other Product** field below the Peach Variety field.

   Next, you need to move the E-mail Address field up above the Home Phone field, so that the fields are in the same order as they appear on the form shown in Figure 6-5.

8. Click **E-mail Address**, and then click the **Move Up** button. The E-mail Address field moves up, so it is now displayed just before the Home Phone field.

   Finally, because Chris's form asks customers to fill in a home or cell phone number, you need to change "Home Phone" to simply "Phone."

9. Click **Home Phone**, and then click the **Rename** button to open the Rename Field dialog box.
10. In the To box, replace "Home Phone" with **Phone** and then click the **OK** button to close the Rename Field dialog box and return to the Customize Address List dialog box. See Figure 6-8.

Figure 6-8 **Customized list of field names**

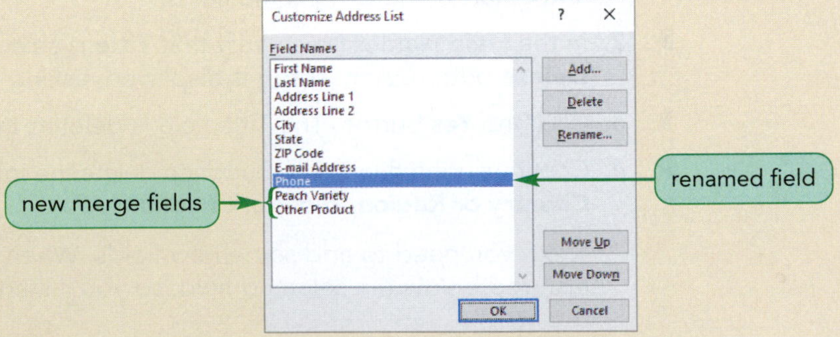

11. Click the **OK** button in the Customize Address List dialog box to close it and return to the New Address List dialog box. This dialog box reflects the changes you just made. For instance, it no longer includes the Title field. The fields are listed in the same order as they appeared in the Customize Address List dialog box.
12. Use the horizontal scroll bar near the bottom of the New Address List dialog box to scroll to the right to display the Peach Variety and Other Product fields. See Figure 6-9.

Figure 6-9 **Changes made to New Address List dialog box**

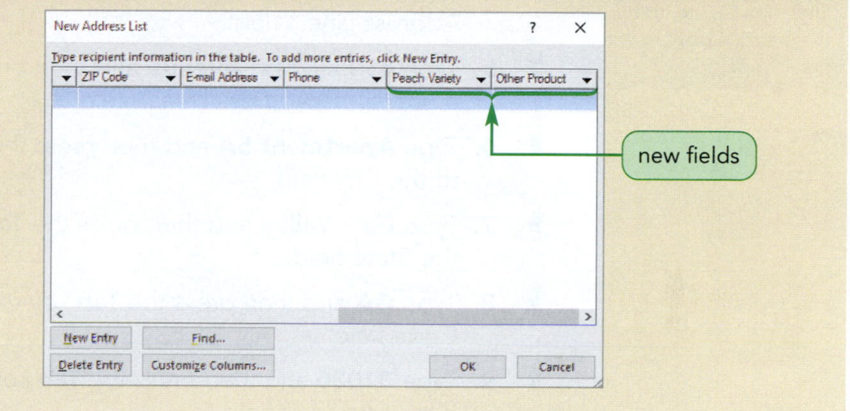

INSIGHT

Organizing Field Names

Although the order of field names in the data source doesn't affect their placement in the main document, it's helpful to arrange field names logically in the data source so you can enter information quickly and efficiently. For example, you'll probably want the First Name field next to the Last Name field. To make it easier to transfer information from a paper form to a data source, it's a good idea to arrange the fields in the same order as on the form, just like you did in the preceding steps. Also, note that if you include spaces in your field names, Word will replace the spaces with underscores when you insert the fields into the main document. For example, Word transforms the field name "First Name" into "First_Name."

Now that you have specified the fields you want to use, you are ready to enter the customer information into the data source.

Entering Data into a Data Source

Chris has given you three completed customer information forms and has asked you to enter the information from the forms into the data source. You'll use the New Address List dialog box to enter the information. As you press the Tab key to move right from one field to the next, the dialog box will scroll to display fields that are not currently visible.

To enter data into a record using the New Address List dialog box:

1. In the New Address List dialog box, scroll to the left to display the First Name field.
2. Click in the **First Name** field, if necessary, and then type **Emma** to enter the first name of the first customer.

   Do not press the spacebar after you finish typing an entry in the New Address List dialog box.
3. Press the **Tab** key to move the insertion point to the Last Name field.
4. Type **Peterson** and then press the **Tab** key to move the insertion point to the Address Line 1 field.
5. Type **45 Faircrest Avenue** and then press the **Tab** key to move the insertion point to the Address Line 2 field.
6. Type **Apartment 5A** and then press the **Tab** key to move the insertion point to the City field.
7. Type **Fort Valley** and then press the **Tab** key to move the insertion point to the State field.
8. Type **GA** and then press the **Tab** key to move the insertion point to the ZIP Code field.
9. Type **31030** and then press the **Tab** key to move the insertion point to the E-mail Address field.
10. Type **peterson@sample.cengage.com** and then press the **Tab** key to move the insertion point to the Phone field.
11. Type **555-555-5555** and then press the **Tab** key to move the insertion point to the Peach Variety field.
12. Type **Gold Jewel** and then press the **Tab** key. The insertion point is now in the Other Product field, which is the last field in the data source.
13. Type **jam** and then stop. Do not press the Tab key.
14. Use the horizontal scroll bar to scroll to the left, and then review the data in the record. See Figure 6-10.

TIP

You can press the Shift+Tab keys to move the insertion point to the previous field.

Figure 6-10 Completed record

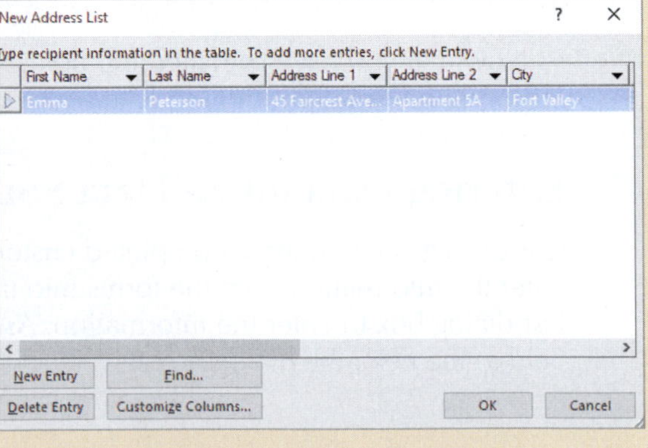

You have finished entering the information for the first record of the data source. Now you're ready to enter information for the next two records. You can create a new record by clicking the New Entry button, or by pressing the Tab key after you have finished entering information into the last field for a record. Note that within a record, you can leave some fields blank. For example, only two of Chris's three customers included information for the Address Line 2 field.

To add additional records to the data source:

1. In the New Address List dialog box, click the **New Entry** button. A new, blank record is created.
2. Enter the information shown in Figure 6-11 for the next two records. To start the Isaac Carlyle record, press the **Tab** key after entering the Other Product field for the David Ahrens record.

Figure 6-11 Information for records 2 and 3

First Name	Last Name	Address Line 1	Address Line 2	City	State	ZIP Code	E-mail Address	Phone	Peach Variety	Other Product
David	Ahrens	603 Emerson Road	P.O. Box 6375	Atlanta	GA	30305	ahrens@sample.cengage.com	555-555-5555	Starlight	peach nectar
Isaac	Carlyle	278 S. Linder		Fort Valley	GA	31030	carlyle@sample.cengage.com	555-555-5555	Starlight	jam

Note that the Address Line 2 field should be blank in the Isaac Carlyle record.

Trouble? If you start a fourth record by mistake, click the Delete Entry button to remove the blank fourth record.

You have entered the records for three customers. Chris's data source eventually will contain hundreds of records for Tupelo Family Farm customers. The current data source, however, contains the records Chris wants to work with now. Next, you need to save the data source.

Saving a Data Source

TIP

In File Explorer, the file type for a Microsoft Office Address Lists file is "Microsoft Access Database."

After you finish entering data for your new data source, you can close the New Address List dialog box. When you do so, the Save Address List dialog box opens, where you can save the data source using the default file type, Microsoft Office Address Lists.

To save the data source:

1. In the New Address List dialog box, click the **OK** button. The New Address List dialog box closes, and the Save Address List dialog box opens, as shown in Figure 6-12.

Figure 6-12 **Saving the data source**

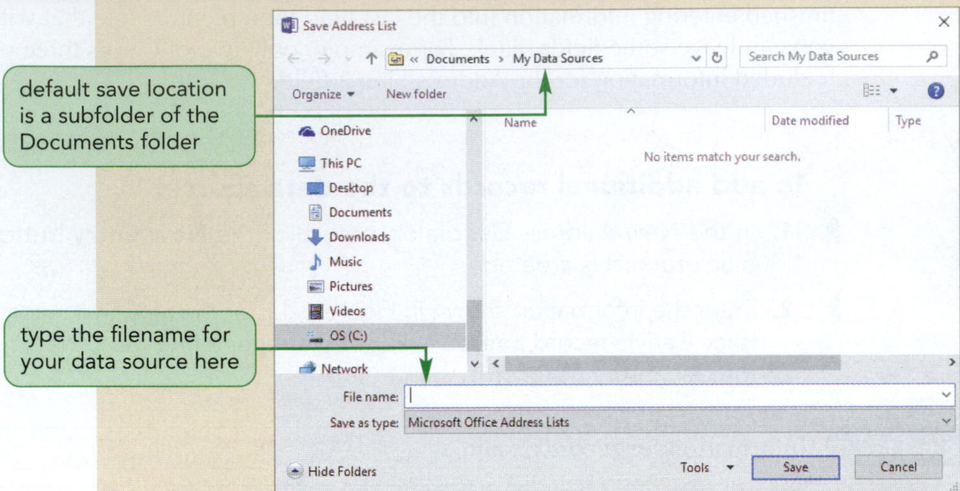

The Save as type box indicates that the data source will be saved as a Microsoft Office Address Lists file. The File name box is empty; you need to name the file before saving it.

2. Click the **File name** box, if necessary, and then type **Tupelo Data**.

   Unless you specify another save location, Word will save the file to the My Data Sources folder, which is a subfolder of the Documents folder.

   In this case, you'll save the data source in the same location in which you saved the main document.

3. Navigate to the location in which you saved the main document, and then click the **Save** button. The Save Address List dialog box closes, and you return to the main document.

The next step in the mail merge process is to add the necessary merge fields to the main document. For Chris's letter, you need to add merge fields for the inside address, for the salutation, and for each customer's favorite variety of peach and other product.

PROSKILLS

Decision Making: Planning Your Data Source

When creating a data source, think beyond the current mail merge task to possible future uses for your data source. For example, Chris's data source includes both an E-mail Address field and a Phone field—not because she wants to use that information in the current mail merge project, but because she can foresee needing these pieces of information at a later date to communicate with her customers. Having all relevant customer information in one data source will make it easier to retrieve and use the information effectively.

In some cases, you'll also want to include information that might seem obvious. For example, Chris's data source includes a State field even though all of her current customers live in or around Fort Valley, Georgia. However, she included a State field because she knows that her pool of addresses could expand sometime in the future to include residents of other states.

Finally, think about the structure of your data source before you create it. Try to break information down into as many fields as seems reasonable. For example, it's always better to include a First Name field and a Last Name field, rather than simply a Name field, because including two separate fields makes it possible to alphabetize the information in the data source by last name. If you entered first and last names in a single Name field, you could alphabetize only by first name.

If you're working with a very small data source, breaking information down into as many fields as possible is less important. However, it's very common to start with a small data source and then, as time goes on, find that you need to continually add information to the data source, until you have a large file. If you failed to plan the data source adequately at the beginning, the expanded data source could become difficult to manage.

Another important issue is what type of file you use to store your data source. In this session, you created a data source from within Word and saved it as a Microsoft Office Address Lists file. However, in most situations, you should save your data source in a spreadsheet or database file so that you can utilize the data manipulation options a spreadsheet program or database program provides.

Inserting Merge Fields

When inserting merge fields into the main document, you must include proper spacing around the fields so that the information in the merged document will be formatted correctly. To insert a merge field, you move the insertion point to the location where you want to insert the merge field, and then click the Insert Merge Field button arrow in the Write & Insert Fields group.

For Chris's letter, you will build an inside address by inserting individual merge fields for the address elements. The letter is a standard business letter, so you'll place merge fields for the customer's name and address below the date.

To insert a merge field in the main document:

1. Click in the second blank paragraph below the date.
2. In the Write & Insert Fields group, click the **Insert Merge Field button arrow**. A menu opens with the names of all the merge fields in the data source. Note that the spaces in the merge field names have been replaced with underscores. See Figure 6-13.

Figure 6-13 Insert Merge Field menu

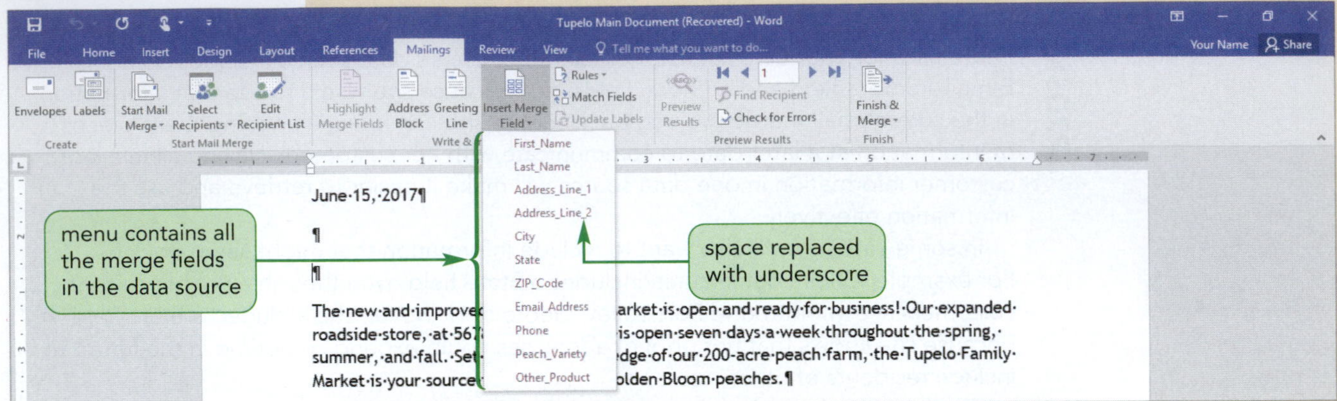

Trouble? If the Insert Merge Field dialog box opens, you clicked the Insert Merge Field button instead of the Insert Merge Field button arrow. Close the dialog box and repeat Step 2.

3. Click **First_Name**. The Insert Merge Field menu closes, and the merge field is inserted into the document.

The merge field consists of the field name surrounded by double angled brackets << >>, also called chevrons.

Trouble? If you make a mistake and insert the wrong merge field, click to the left of the merge field, press the Delete key to select the field, and then press the Delete key again to delete it.

4. In the Write & Insert Fields group, click the **Highlight Merge Fields** button. The First_Name merge field is displayed on a gray background, making it easier to see in the document. See Figure 6-14.

TIP

You can only insert merge fields into a main document using the tools on the Mailings tab or in the Mail Merge task pane. You cannot type merge fields into the main document—even if you type the angled brackets.

Figure 6-14 First_Name merge field highlighted in main document

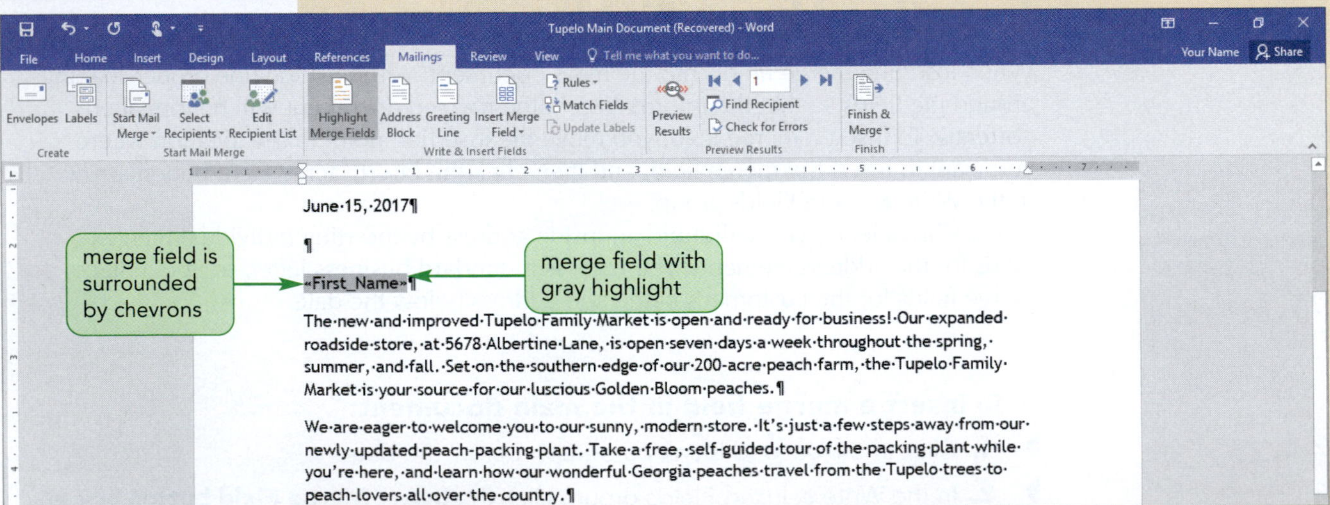

Later, when you merge the main document with the data source, Word will replace the First_Name merge field with information from the First Name field in the data source.

Now, you're ready to insert the merge fields for the rest of the inside address. You'll add the necessary spacing and punctuation between the merge fields as well. You might be accustomed to pressing the Shift+Enter keys to start a new line in an inside address without inserting paragraph spacing. However, because your data source includes a record in which one of the fields (the Address Line 2 field) is blank, you need to press the Enter key to start each new line. As you will see later in this Module, this ensures that Word hides the Address Line 2 field in the final merged document whenever that field is blank. To maintain the proper spacing in the main document, you'll adjust the paragraph spacing after you insert all the fields.

To insert the remaining merge fields for the inside address:

1. Press the **spacebar** to insert a space after the First_Name merge field, click the **Insert Merge Field button arrow**, and then click **Last_Name**.
2. Press the **Enter** key to start a new paragraph, click the **Insert Merge Field button arrow**, and then click **Address_Line_1**. Word inserts the Address_Line_1 merge field into the form letter.
3. Press the **Enter** key, click the **Insert Merge Field button arrow**, and then click **Address_Line_2**. Word inserts the Address_Line_2 merge field into the form letter.
4. Press the **Enter** key, insert the **City** merge field, type **,** (a comma), press the **spacebar** to insert a space after the comma, and then insert the **State** merge field.
5. Press the **spacebar**, and then insert the **ZIP_Code** merge field. The inside address now contains all the necessary merge fields. See Figure 6-15.

Figure 6-15 Main document with merge fields for inside address

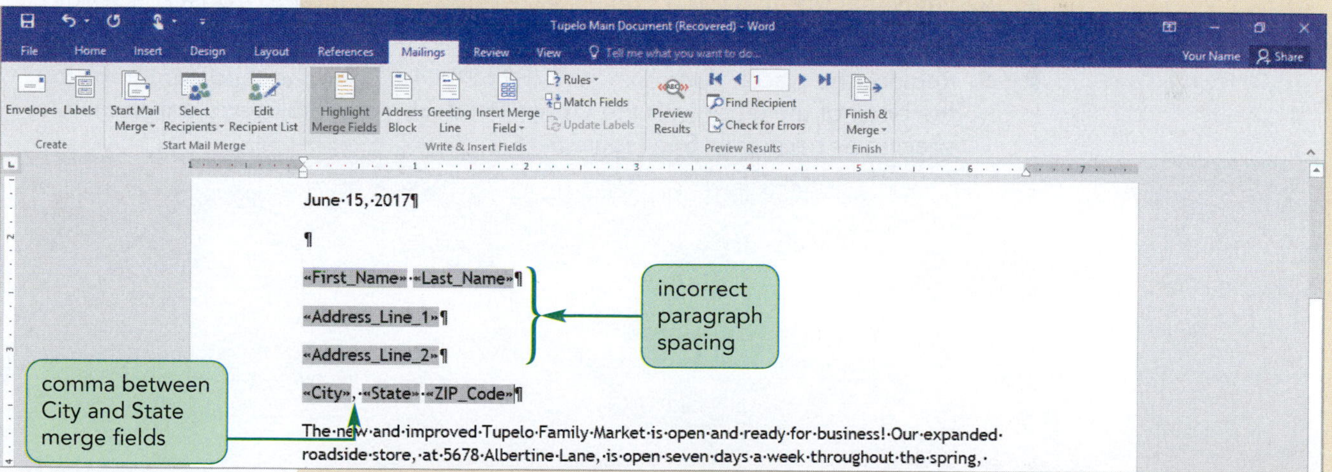

Next, you will adjust the paragraph spacing for the inside address.

6. Select the first three paragraphs of the inside address.
7. On the ribbon, click the **Home** tab.
8. In the Paragraph group, click the **Line and Paragraph Spacing** button, and then click **Remove Space After Paragraph**. The paragraph spacing is removed, so that the paragraphs of the inside address are now correctly spaced.

You can now add the salutation of the letter, which will contain each customer's first name.

To insert the merge field for the salutation:

1. Insert a new paragraph after the ZIP_Code field, type **Dear** and then press the **spacebar**.
2. On the ribbon, click the **Mailings** tab.
3. In the Write & Insert Fields group, click the **Insert Merge Field button arrow**, click **First_Name** to insert this field into the document, and then type **:** (a colon).
4. Save the document.

You'll further personalize Chris's letter by including merge fields that will allow you to reference each customer's favorite variety of peach and favorite other product.

To add merge fields for each customer's favorite items:

1. If necessary, scroll down to display the complete third paragraph in the body of the letter, which begins "Bring along this letter...."
2. In the third paragraph in the body of the letter, select the placeholder text **[PEACH VARIETY]**, including the brackets. You'll replace this phrase with a merge field. Don't be concerned if you also select the space following the closing bracket.
3. Insert the **Peach_Variety** merge field. Word replaces the selected text with the Peach_Variety merge field.
4. Verify that the field has a single space before it and after it. Add a space on either side if necessary.
5. Replace the placeholder text "[OTHER PRODUCT]" in the third paragraph in the body of the letter with the **Other_Product** merge field, and adjust the spacing as necessary. See Figure 6-16.

Figure 6-16 Main document after inserting merge fields

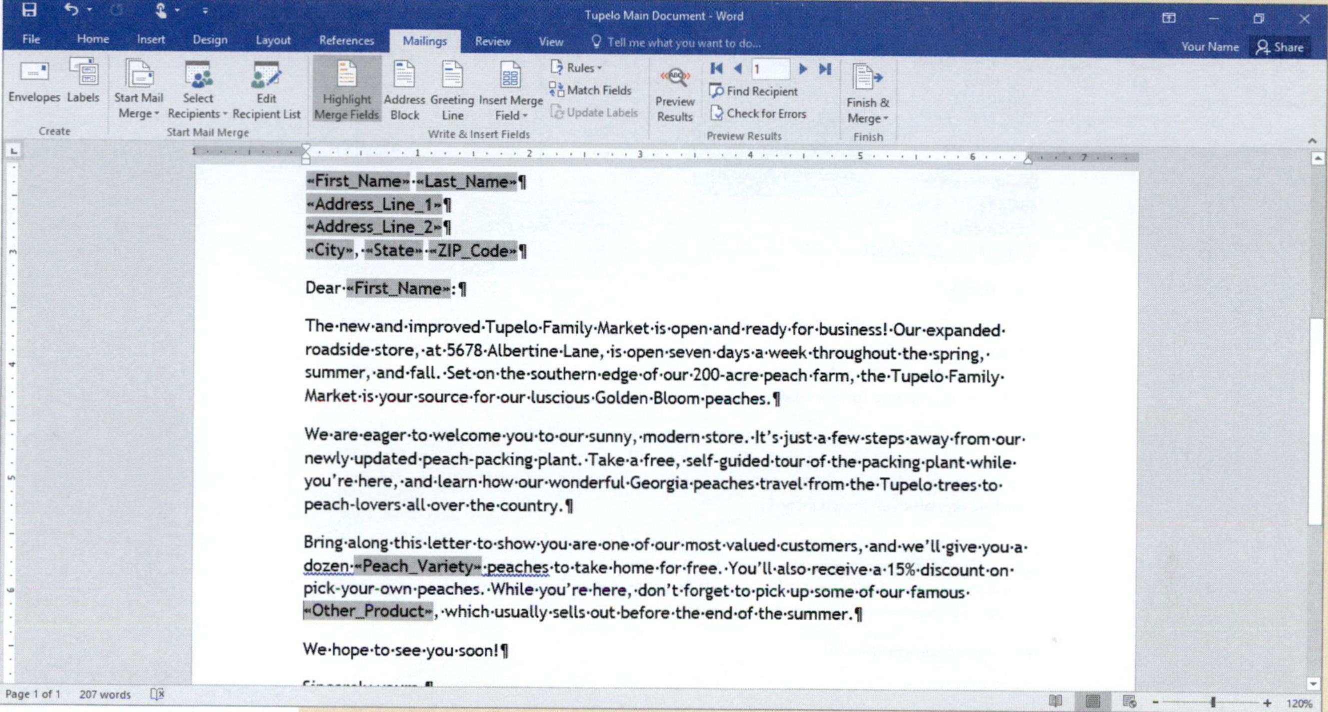

Trouble? The text before and after the inserted merge fields might be marked with a wavy blue underline because Word mistakenly identifies the text as a grammatical error. You can ignore the wavy underlines.

6. Save the document.

The main document now contains all the necessary merge fields.

Previewing the Merged Document

Your next step is to preview the merged document to see how the letter will look after Word inserts the information for each customer. When you preview the merged document, you can check one last time for any missing spaces between the merge fields and the surrounding text. You can also look for any other formatting problems, and, if necessary, make final changes to the data source.

To preview the merged document:

1. In the Preview Results group, click the **Preview Results** button, and then scroll up to display the inside address. The data for the first record (Emma Peterson) replaces the merge fields in the form letter. On the ribbon, the Go to Record box in the Preview Results group shows which record is currently displayed in the document. See Figure 6-17.

Figure 6-17 Letter with merged data for first record

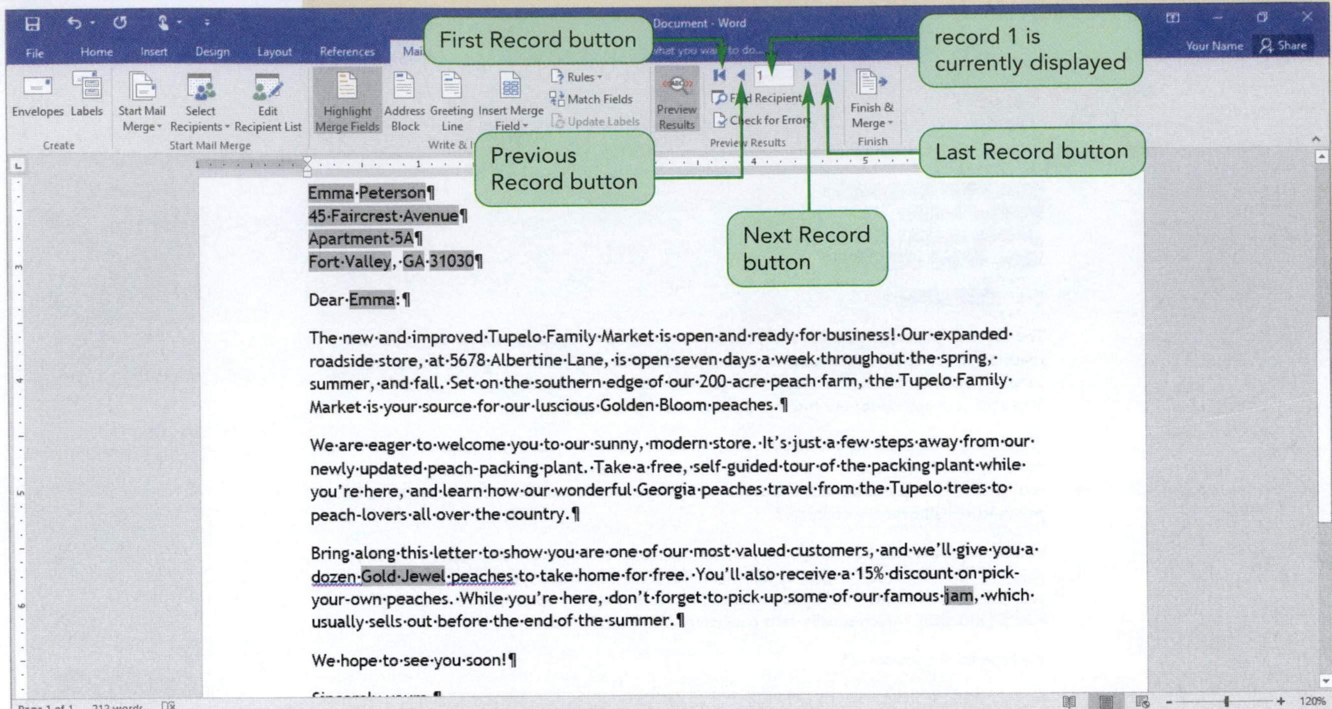

Note that the inside address, which includes information from the Address Line 2 field, contains a total of four lines.

2. Carefully check the Emma Peterson letter to make sure the text and formatting are correct, and make any necessary corrections. In particular, make sure that the spacing before and after the merged data is correct; it is easy to accidentally omit spaces or add extra spaces around merge fields.

3. In the Preview Results group, click the **Next Record** button. The data for David Ahrens is displayed in the letter. As with the preceding record, the inside address for this record includes four lines of information.

4. Click the **Next Record** button again to display the data for Isaac Carlyle in the letter. In this case, the inside address includes only three lines of information. See Figure 6-18.

Figure 6-18 Address for third record

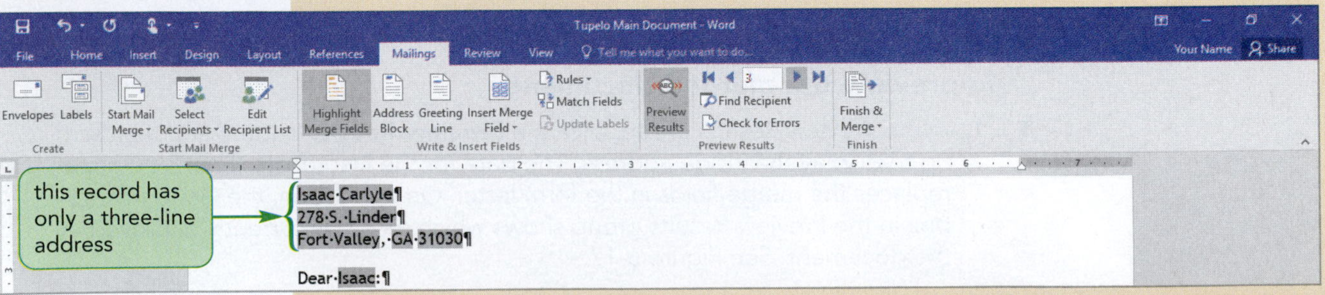

5. In the Preview Results group, click the **First Record** button to redisplay the first record in the letter (with data for Emma Peterson).

The main document of the mail merge is complete. Now that you have previewed the merged documents, you can finish the merge.

Merging the Main Document and the Data Source

When you finish a merge, you can choose to merge directly to the printer. In other words, you can choose to have Word print the merged document immediately without saving it as a separate file. Alternatively, you can merge to a new document, which you can save using a new filename. If your data source includes an E-mail Address field, you can also create a mail merge in email format, generating one email for every email address in the data source.

Chris wants to save an electronic copy of the merged document for her records, so you'll merge the data source and main document into a new document.

To complete the mail merge:

1. In the Finish group, click the **Finish & Merge** button. The Finish & Merge menu displays the three merge options. See Figure 6-19.

Figure 6-19 Finishing the merge

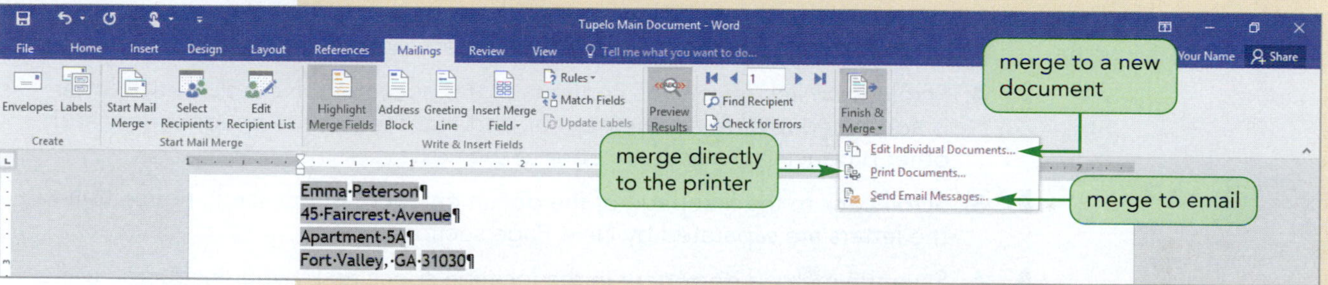

2. In the Finish & Merge menu, click **Edit Individual Documents**. The Merge to New Document dialog box opens. Here, you need to specify which records to include in the merge. You want to include all three records from the data source.
3. Verify that the **All** option button is selected, and then click the **OK** button. Word creates a new document named Letters1, which contains three pages—one for each record in the data source. See Figure 6-20.

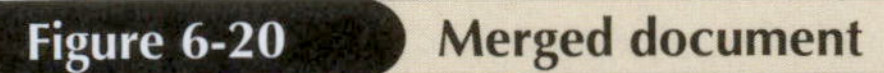

Figure 6-20 Merged document

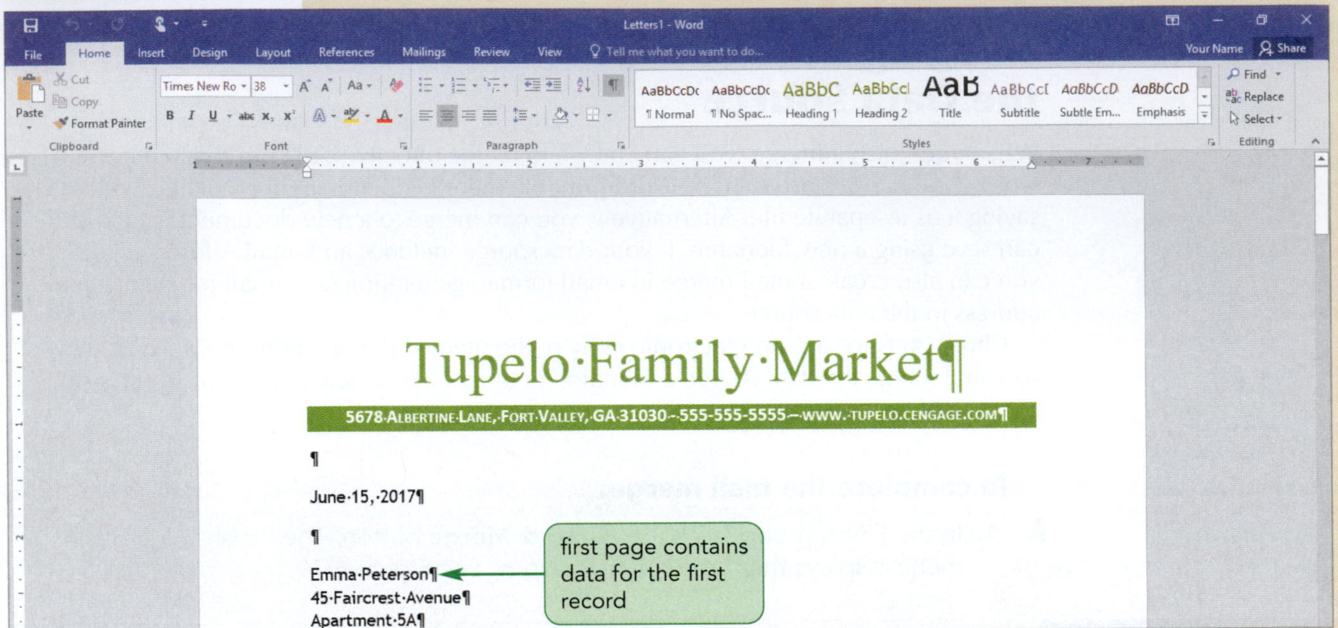

In this new document, the merge fields have been replaced by the specific names, addresses, and so on from the data source.

4. Scroll down and review the contents of the document. Note that each letter is addressed to a different customer, and that the favorite peach variety and other product vary from one letter to the next.
5. Scroll back to the first page of the document, and as you scroll, notice that the letters are separated by Next Page section breaks.
6. Save the merged document in the location specified by your instructor, using the filename **Tupelo Merged Letters 1**.
7. Close the **Tupelo Merged Letters 1** document. The document named "Tupelo Main Document" is now the active document.

   After completing a merge, you need to save the main document. That ensures that any changes you might have made to the data source during the course of the mail merge are saved along with the main document.
8. Save and close the **Tupelo Main Document** file.

Note that if you need to take a break while working on a mail merge, you can save the main document and close it. The data source and field information are saved along with the document. When you're ready to work on the merge again, you can open the main document and update the connection to the data source. You'll see how this works at the beginning of the next session, when you will learn how to use additional mail merge features.

REVIEW

Session 6.1 Quick Check

1. Explain how to insert a Date field that updates automatically every time the document is opened.
2. Define the following:
   a. merge field
   b. record
   c. main document
   d. data source
3. List at least three types of files that you can use as data sources in a mail merge.
4. What is the first step in performing a mail merge?
5. Explain how to use the options on the Mailings tab to insert a merge field into a main document.
6. What are the last two steps in the mail merge process?

Session 6.2 Visual Overview:

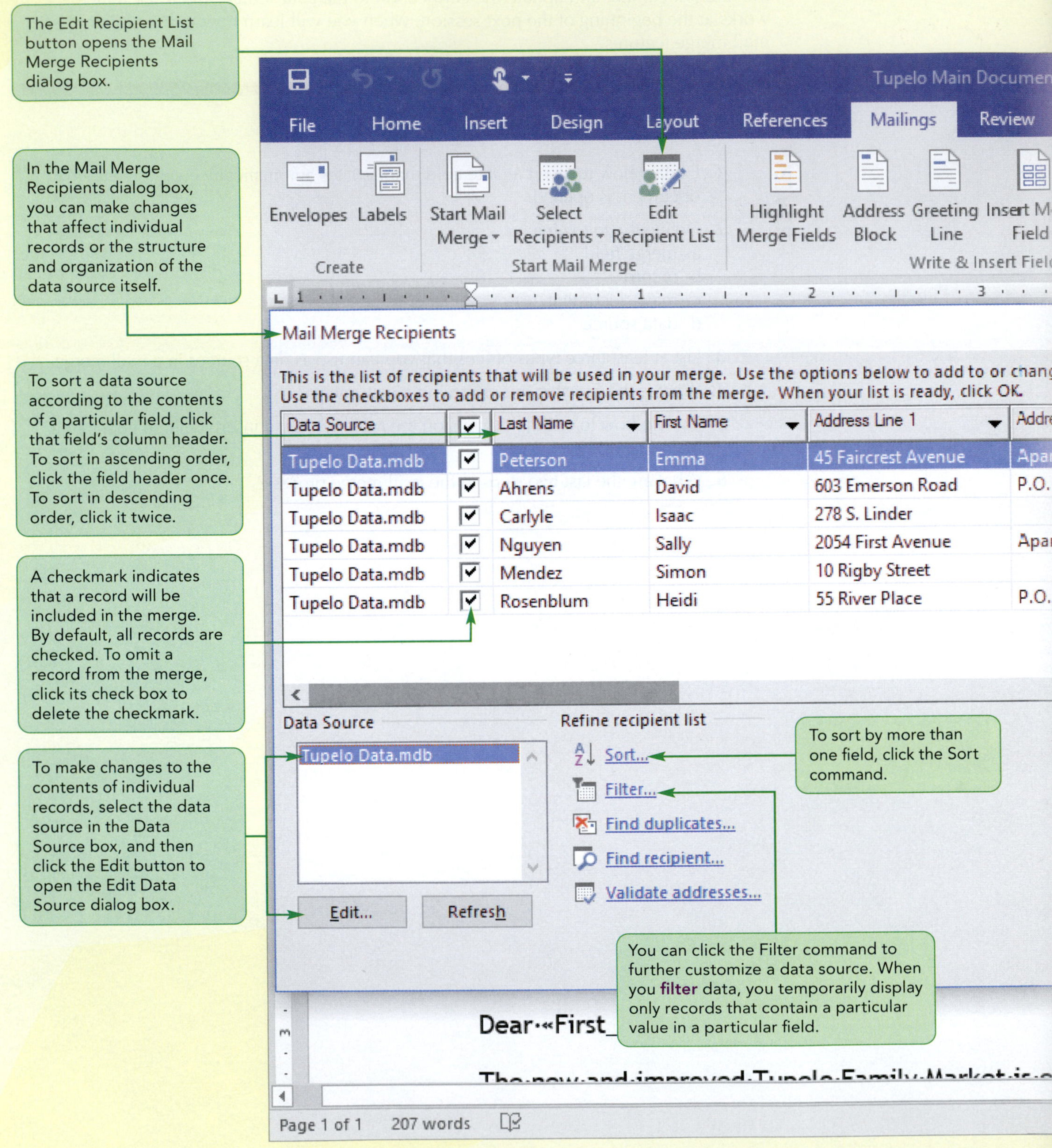

The Edit Recipient List button opens the Mail Merge Recipients dialog box.
In the Mail Merge Recipients dialog box, you can make changes that affect individual records or the structure and organization of the data source itself.
To sort a data source according to the contents of a particular field, click that field's column header. To sort in ascending order, click the field header once. To sort in descending order, click it twice.
A checkmark indicates that a record will be included in the merge. By default, all records are checked. To omit a record from the merge, click its check box to delete the checkmark.
To make changes to the contents of individual records, select the data source in the Data Source box, and then click the Edit button to open the Edit Data Source dialog box.
To sort by more than one field, click the Sort command.
You can click the Filter command to further customize a data source. When you filter data, you temporarily display only records that contain a particular value in a particular field.
Tupelo Main Documen
File
Home
Insert
Design
Layout
References
Mailings
Review
Envelopes
Labels
Start Mail Merge
Select Recipients
Edit Recipient List
Highlight Merge Fields
Address Block
Greeting Line
Insert M Field
Create
Start Mail Merge
Write & Insert Field
Mail Merge Recipients
This is the list of recipients that will be used in your merge. Use the options below to add to or chang
Use the checkboxes to add or remove recipients from the merge. When your list is ready, click OK.
Data Source
Last Name
First Name
Address Line 1
Tupelo Data.mdb
Peterson
Emma
45 Faircrest Avenue
Ahrens
David
603 Emerson Road
P.O.
Carlyle
Isaac
278 S. Linder
Nguyen
Sally
2054 First Avenue
Mendez
Simon
10 Rigby Street
Rosenblum
Heidi
55 River Place
Data Source
Refine recipient list
Sort...
Filter...
Find duplicates...
Find recipient...
Validate addresses...
Edit...
Refresh
Dear·«First_
Page 1 of 1
207 words

Editing a Data Source

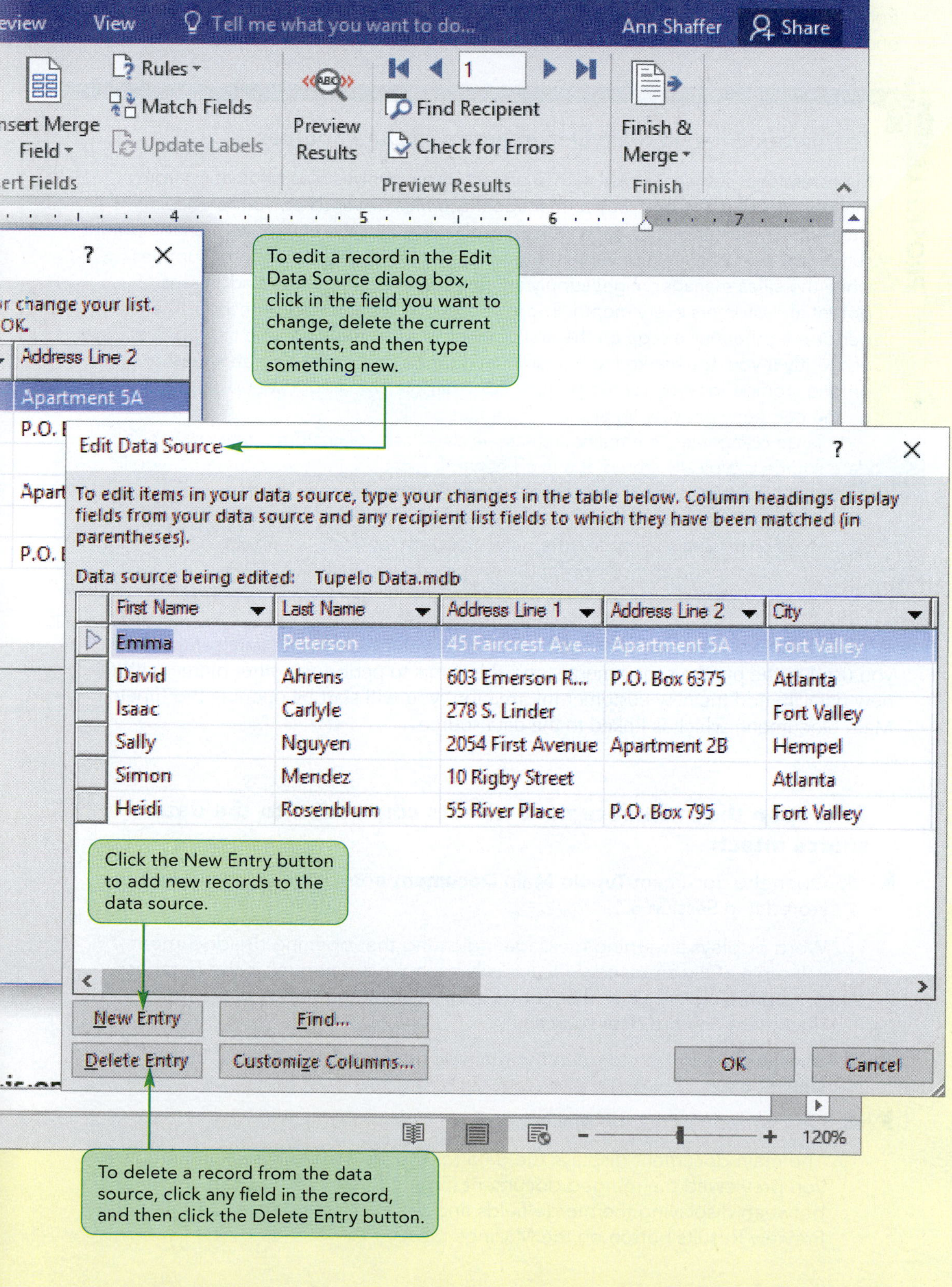
ocument.docx - Word
Review View Tell me what you want to do... Ann Shaffer Share
Rules
Match Fields
Update Labels
Insert Merge Field
sert Fields
Preview Results
Find Recipient
Check for Errors
Preview Results
Finish & Merge
Finish
To edit a record in the Edit Data Source dialog box, click in the field you want to change, delete the current contents, and then type something new.
Edit Data Source
To edit items in your data source, type your changes in the table below. Column headings display fields from your data source and any recipient list fields to which they have been matched (in parentheses).
Data source being edited: Tupelo Data.mdb
First Name Last Name Address Line 1 Address Line 2 City
Emma Peterson 45 Faircrest Ave... Apartment 5A Fort Valley
David Ahrens 603 Emerson R... P.O. Box 6375 Atlanta
Isaac Carlyle 278 S. Linder Fort Valley
Sally Nguyen 2054 First Avenue Apartment 2B Hempel
Simon Mendez 10 Rigby Street Atlanta
Heidi Rosenblum 55 River Place P.O. Box 795 Fort Valley
Click the New Entry button to add new records to the data source.
New Entry
Find...
Delete Entry
Customize Columns...
OK
Cancel
120%
To delete a record from the data source, click any field in the record, and then click the Delete Entry button.

Reopening a Main Document

Performing a mail merge creates a connection between the main document file and the data source file. This connection persists even after you close the main document and exit Word. The connection is maintained as long as you keep both files in their original locations. The two files don't have to be in the same folder; each file just has to remain in the folder it was in when you first performed the mail merge.

When you reopen a main document, you see a warning dialog box explaining that data from a database (that is, the data source) will be placed in the document you are about to open. You can click Yes to open the document with its connection to the data source intact.

PROSKILLS

Teamwork: Sharing Main Documents and Data Sources

In professional settings, a mail merge project often involves files originating from multiple people. The best way to manage these files depends on your particular situation. For instance, at a small office supply company, the marketing manager might supply the text of a main document introducing monthly sales on printer supplies, while the sales manager might supply an updated list of names and addresses of potential customers every month. Suppose that you are the person responsible for performing the mail merge on the first of every month. You'll be able to work more efficiently if you, the marketing manager, and the sales manager agree ahead of time on one storage location for the project. For example, you might set up a special folder on the company network for storing these files.

In large companies that maintain massive databases of customer information, a data source is typically stored at a fixed network location. In those situations, you'll probably need to work with the technical staff who manage the databases to gain access to the data sources you need for your mail merge projects. Maintaining the security of such data sources is extremely important, and you usually can't access them without a password and the appropriate encryption software.

Chris has new customer information she wants you to add to the data source that you used in the previous mail merge, and she wants to perform another merge with the new data. To add the new customer information, you will start by opening the Tupelo Main Document, which is linked to the data source.

To reopen the main document with its connection to the data source intact:

1. Open the document **Tupelo Main Document** from the location in which you stored it in Session 6.1.

   Word displays a warning message indicating that opening the document will run a SQL command. SQL (usually pronounced *sequel*) is the database programming language that controls the connection between the main document and the data source.

2. Click the **Yes** button to open the main document with its link to the data source intact.
3. On the ribbon, click the **Mailings** tab.

   The main document displays the data for the last record you examined when you previewed the merged document (Emma Peterson). You can alternate between displaying the merge fields and the customer data by toggling the Preview Results button on the Mailings tab.

Trouble? If you see the merge fields instead of the data for one of the customers, skip to Step 5.

4. In the Preview Results group, click the **Preview Results** button to deselect it. The merge fields are displayed in the main document. At the beginning of the letter, the Date field, which is not a merge field, continues to display the current date.
5. If necessary, highlight the merge fields by clicking the **Highlight Merge Fields** button in the Write & Insert Fields group.

INSIGHT

Maintaining, Breaking, and Reestablishing the Connection to a Data Source

As you have seen, when you reopen a main document, Word displays a warning dialog box, where you can click Yes to open the document with its connection to the data source intact. But what if you want to break the connection between the main document and the data source? One option is to click No in the warning dialog box. In that case, the main document opens with no connection to the data source. If the main document is currently open and already connected to the data source, you can break the connection by clicking Normal Word Document on the Start Mail Merge menu. You can reestablish the connection at any time by starting the mail merge over again and using the Select Recipients button to select the data source.

Keep in mind that you could also break the connection between a main document and its data source if you move one or both of the files to a different folder. Exactly what happens in this case depends on how your computer is set up and where you move the files. In the case of a broken connection, when you open the main document, you'll see a series of message boxes informing you that the connection to the data source has been broken. Eventually, you will see a Microsoft Word dialog box with a button labeled Find Data Source, which you can click, and then use the Select Data Source dialog box to locate and select your data source.

If you are creating mail merges for personal use, it's a good idea to either store the data source in the default My Data Sources folder and keep it there, or store the data source and the main document in the same folder (a folder other than the My Data Sources folder). The latter option is best if you think you might need to move the files to a different computer. That way, if you do need to move them, you can move the entire folder.

Editing a Data Source

After you complete a mail merge, you might need to make some changes to the data source and redo the merge. You can edit a data source in two ways—from within the program used to create the data source, or via the Mail Merge Recipients dialog box in Word. If you are familiar with the program used to create the data source, the simplest approach is to edit the file from within that program. For example, if you were using an Excel worksheet as your data source, you could open the file in Excel, edit it (perhaps by adding new records), save it, and then reselect the file as your data source. To edit the Microsoft Office Address Lists file that you created as a data source for this project, you can use the Mail Merge Recipients dialog box.

REFERENCE

Editing a Microsoft Office Address Lists Data Source in Word

- Open the main document for the data source you want to edit.
- On the ribbon, click the Mailings tab.
- In the Start Mail Merge group, click the Edit Recipient List button.
- In the Data Source box in the Mail Merge Recipients dialog box, select the data source you want to edit, and then click the Edit button.
- To add a record, click the New Entry button, and then enter the data for the new record.
- To delete a record, click any field in the record, and then click the Delete Entry button.
- To add or remove fields from the data source, click the Customize Columns button, click Yes in the warning dialog box, make any changes, and then click the OK button. Remember that if you remove a field, you will delete any data entered into that field for all records in the data source.
- Click the OK button in the Edit Data Source dialog box, click the Yes button in the Microsoft Office Word dialog box, and then click the OK button in the Mail Merge Recipients dialog box.

Chris would like you to add information for three new customers to the data source.

To edit the data source by adding records:

1. In the Start Mail Merge group, click the **Edit Recipient List** button. The Mail Merge Recipients dialog box opens, displaying the contents of the data source that is currently connected to the main document—the Tupelo Data file.

   This dialog box is designed to let you edit any data source, not just the one currently connected to the main document. To edit the Tupelo Data file, you first need to select it in the Data Source box in the lower-left corner. If you had multiple data sources stored in the same folder as the Tupelo Data file, you would see them all in this list box.

2. In the Data Source box, click **Tupelo Data.mdb**. The filename is selected.

   Note that the file has the extension .mdb, which is the file extension for an Access database file—the default format for a data source created in Word. See Figure 6-21.

Figure 6-21 Tupelo Data.mdb file selected in the Data Source box of the Mail Merge Recipients dialog box

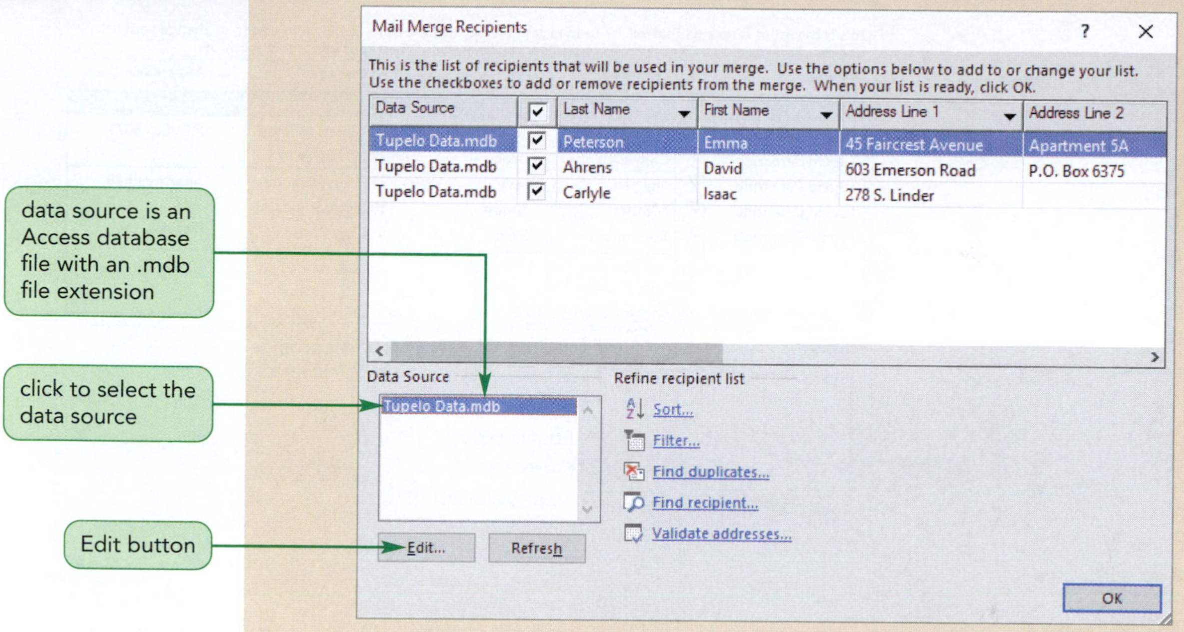

3. Click the **Edit** button. The Edit Data Source dialog box opens.
4. Click the **New Entry** button, and then enter the information for the three new records shown in Figure 6-22.

Figure 6-22 New Customer data

First Name	Last Name	Address Line 1	Address Line 2	City	State	ZIP Code	E-Mail Address	Phone	Peach Variety	Other Product
Sally	Nguyen	2054 First Avenue	Apartment 2B	Hempel	GA	31035	nguyen@sample.cengage.com	555-555-5555	Gold Jewel	peach nectar
Simon	Mendez	10 Rigby Street		Atlanta	GA	30305	mendez@sample.cengage.com	555-555-5555	Carrington	dried peach slices
Heidi	Rosenblum	55 River Place	P.O. Box 795	Fort Valley	GA	31030	rosenblum@sample.cengage.com	555-555-5555	Starlight	jam

When you are finished, you will have a total of six records in the data source. Notice that the record for Simon Mendez contains no data in the Address Line 2 field.

5. Click the **OK** button, and then click the **Yes** button in the message box that asks if you want to update the Tupelo Data.mdb file. You return to the Mail Merge Recipients dialog box, as shown in Figure 6-23.

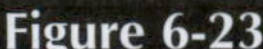

Figure 6-23 New records added to data source

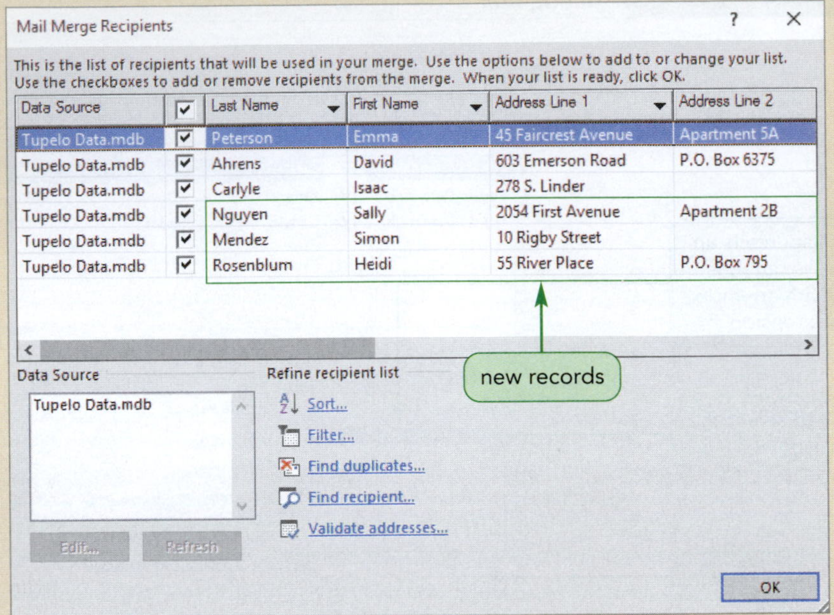

Trouble? If your records look different from those in Figure 6-23, select the data source, click the Edit button, edit the data source, and then click the OK button.

You'll leave the Mail Merge Recipients dialog box open so you can use it to make other changes to the data source.

Sorting Records

You can sort, or rearrange, information in a data source table just as you can sort information in any other table. To quickly sort information in ascending order (*A* to *Z*, lowest to highest, or earliest to latest) or in descending order (*Z* to *A*, highest to lowest, or latest to earliest), click a field's heading in the Mail Merge Recipients dialog box. The first time you click the heading, the records are sorted in ascending order. If you click it a second time, the records are sorted in descending order.

To perform a more complicated sort, you can click the Sort command in the Mail Merge Recipients dialog box to open the Filter and Sort dialog box, where you can choose to sort by more than one field. For example, you could sort records in ascending order by last name, and then in ascending order by first name. In that case, the records would be organized alphabetically by last name, and then, in cases where multiple records contained the same last name, those records would be sorted by first name.

REFERENCE

Sorting a Data Source by Multiple Fields

- On the ribbon, click the Mailings tab.
- In the Start Mail Merge group, click the Edit Recipient List button to open the Mail Merge Recipients dialog box.
- Click Sort to open the Sort Records tab in the Filter and Sort dialog box.
- Click the Sort by arrow, select the first field you want to sort by, and then select either the Ascending option button or the Descending option button.
- Click the Then by arrow, select the second field you want to sort by, and then select either the Ascending option button or the Descending option button.
- If necessary, click the Then by arrow, select the third field you want to sort by, and then select either the Ascending option button or the Descending option button.
- Click the OK button to close the Filter and Sort dialog box.
- Click the OK button to close the Mail Merge Recipients dialog box.

As Chris looks through the letters to her customers in the merged document, she notices one problem—the letters are not grouped by ZIP codes. Currently, the letters are in the order in which customers were added to the data source file. Chris plans to use business mail (also known as bulk mail) to send her letters, and the U.S. Postal Service offers lower rates for mailings that are separated into groups according to ZIP code. She asks you to sort the data file by ZIP code and then by last name, and then merge the main document with the sorted data source.

To sort the data source by ZIP code:

1. In the Mail Merge Recipients dialog box, click **Sort**. The Filter and Sort dialog box opens, with the Sort Records tab displayed.
2. Click the **Sort by** arrow to display a menu, scroll down in the menu, and then click **ZIP Code**. The Ascending button is selected by default, which is what you want.
3. In the Then by box, directly below the Sort by box, click the **Then by** arrow, and then click **Last Name**. See Figure 6-24.

Figure 6-24 Sorting by ZIP code and by last name

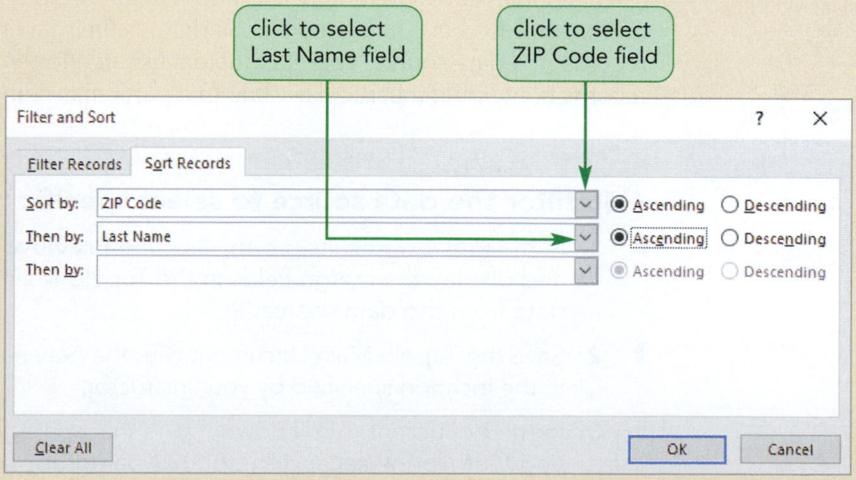

4. Click the **OK** button. Word sorts the records from lowest ZIP code number to highest; and then, within each ZIP code, it sorts the records by last name.

   In the Mail Merge Recipients dialog box, the record for David Ahrens, with ZIP code 30305, is now at the top of the data source list. The record for Simon Mendez, which also has a ZIP code of 30305, comes second. The remaining records are sorted similarly, with the record for Sally Nguyen the last in the list. When you merge the data source with the form letter, the letters will appear in the merged document in this order.

5. Click the **OK** button. The Mail Merge Recipients dialog box closes.
6. On the Mailings tab, in the Preview Results group, click the **Preview Results** button. The data for David Ahrens is displayed in the main document.
7. In the Finish group, click the **Finish & Merge** button, and then click **Edit Individual Documents**.
8. In the Merge to New Document dialog box, verify that the **All** option button is selected, and then click the **OK** button. Word generates the new merged document with six letters—one letter per page as before, but this time the first letter is addressed to David Ahrens.
9. Scroll down and verify that the letters in the newly merged document are arranged in ascending order by ZIP code and then in ascending order by last name.
10. Save the new merged document in the location specified by your instructor, using the filename **Tupelo Merged Letters 2**, and then close it. You return to the Tupelo Main Document.
11. Save the **Tupelo Main Document** file, and keep it open for the next set of steps.

Next, Chris would like you to create a set of letters to send to customers who listed "Starlight" as their favorite peach variety.

Filtering Records

TIP

To omit an individual record from a merge, you can deselect the corresponding check box in the Mail Merge Recipients dialog box rather than using a filter.

Chris wants to inform customers that Starlight peaches are now available fresh or frozen. She asks you to modify the form letter and then merge it with the records of customers who have indicated that Starlight is their favorite variety. To select specific records in a data source, you filter the data source to temporarily display only the records containing a particular value in a particular field.

To filter the data source to select specific records for the merge:

1. In the Preview Results group, click the **Preview Results** button to deselect it and display the merge fields in the Tupelo Main Document file instead of the data from the data source.
2. Save the Tupelo Main Document with the new name **Starlight Main Document** in the location specified by your instructor.
3. In the document, scroll down to the third paragraph in the body of the letter, and then, in the second line of that paragraph, click to the right of the word "peaches."

4. Insert a space, type **(now available fresh or frozen)** and then verify that the sentence reads "...and we'll give you a dozen <<Peach_Variety>> peaches (now available fresh or frozen) to take home for free."

5. In the Start Mail Merge group, click the **Edit Recipient List** button to open the Mail Merge Recipients dialog box, and then scroll to the right so you can see the Peach Variety field.

6. In the header row, click the **Peach Variety** arrow. A menu opens, listing all the entries in the Peach Variety field, as well as a few other options. See Figure 6-25.

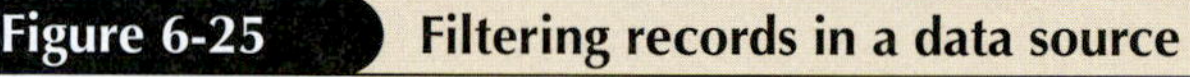

Figure 6-25 Filtering records in a data source

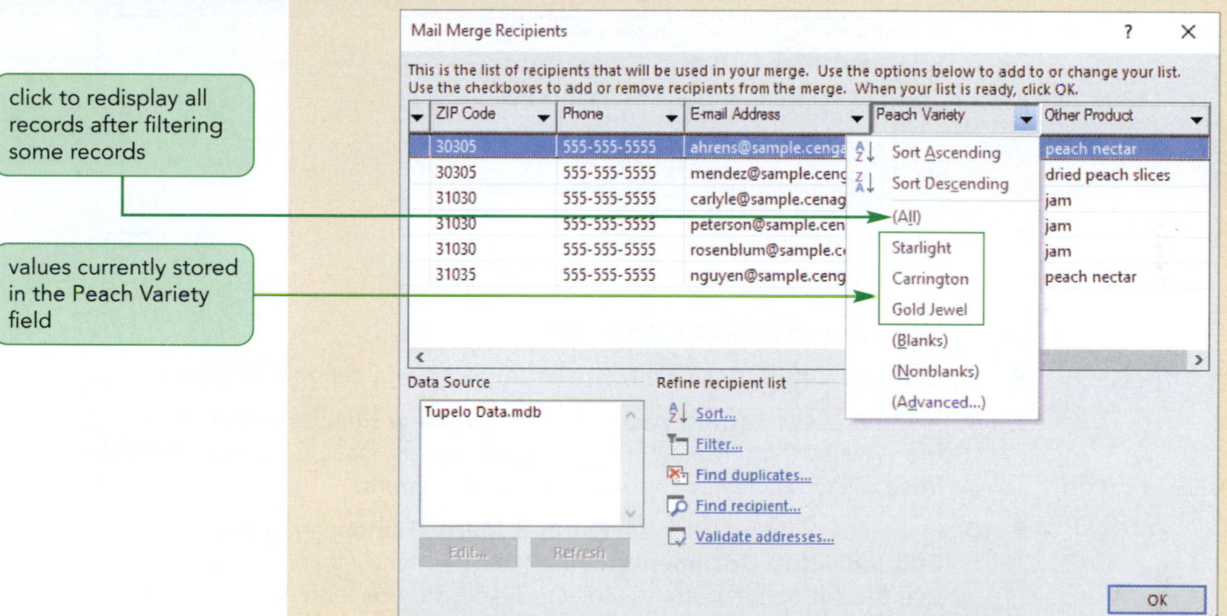

Trouble? If the records sort by Peach Variety, with the record for Carrington peaches at the top, you clicked the Peach Variety column header instead of the arrow. That's not a problem; you don't need to undo the sort. Repeat Step 6, taking care to click the arrow.

You can use the "(All)" option to redisplay all records after previously filtering a data source. The "(Advanced)" option takes you to the Filter Records tab in the Filter and Sort dialog box, where you can perform complex filter operations that involve comparing the contents of one or more fields to a particular value to determine whether a record should be displayed. In this case, however, you can use an option in this menu.

7. Click **Starlight**. Word temporarily hides all the records in the data source except those that contain "Starlight" in the Peach Variety field. See Figure 6-26.

Figure 6-26 Filtered data source

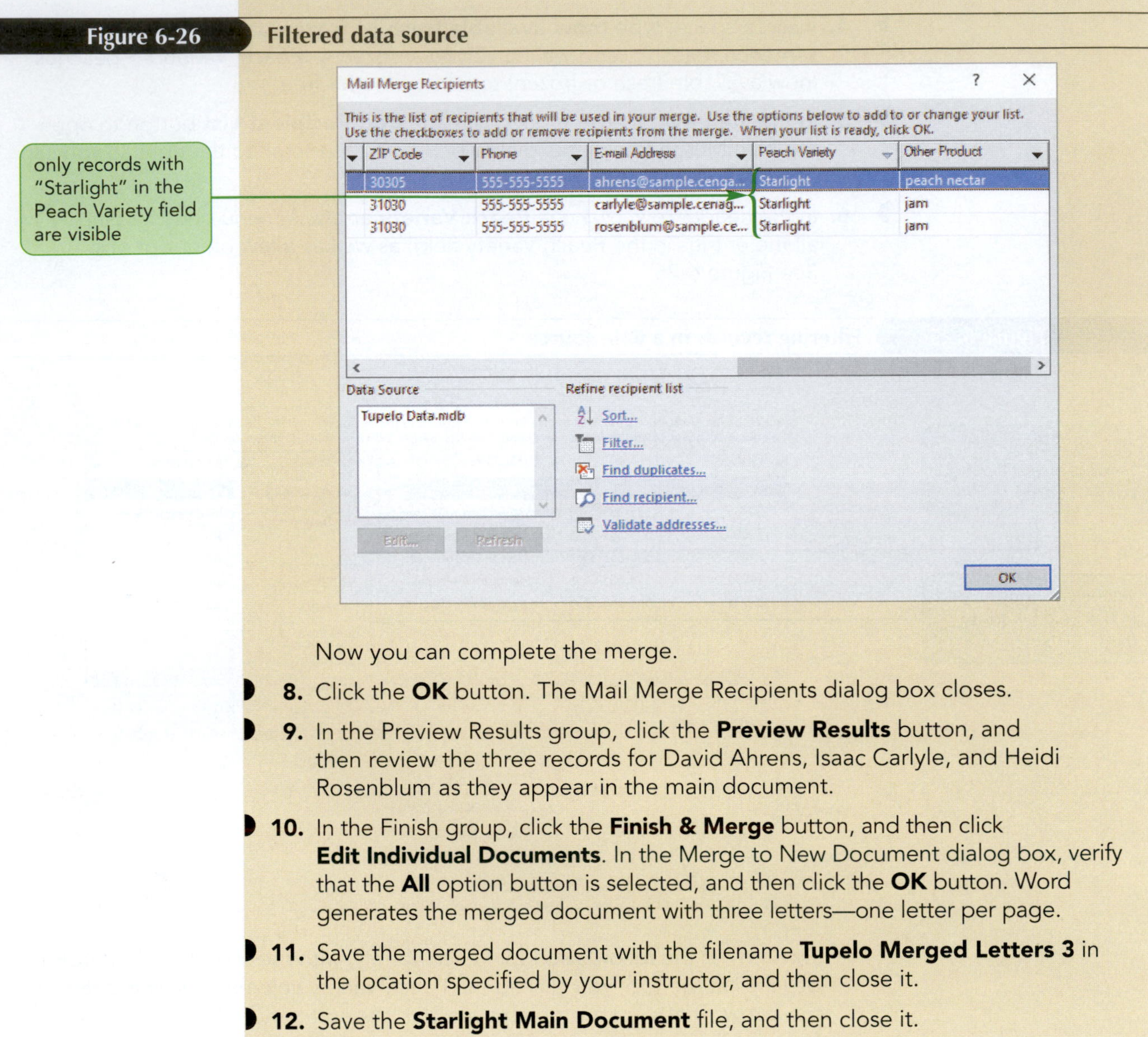

Now you can complete the merge.

8. Click the **OK** button. The Mail Merge Recipients dialog box closes.
9. In the Preview Results group, click the **Preview Results** button, and then review the three records for David Ahrens, Isaac Carlyle, and Heidi Rosenblum as they appear in the main document.
10. In the Finish group, click the **Finish & Merge** button, and then click **Edit Individual Documents**. In the Merge to New Document dialog box, verify that the **All** option button is selected, and then click the **OK** button. Word generates the merged document with three letters—one letter per page.
11. Save the merged document with the filename **Tupelo Merged Letters 3** in the location specified by your instructor, and then close it.
12. Save the **Starlight Main Document** file, and then close it.

Next, you'll create and print mailing labels for the form letters.

Creating Mailing Labels

Chris could print the names and addresses for the letters directly on envelopes, or she could perform a mail merge to create mailing labels. The latter method is easier because she can print 14 labels at once rather than printing one envelope at a time.

Chris has purchased Avery® Laser Printer labels, which are available in most office-supply stores. Word supports most of the Avery label formats, allowing you to choose the layout that works best for you. Chris purchased labels in 8 1/2 × 11-inch sheets that are designed to feed through a printer. Each label measures 4 × 1.33 inches. Each sheet contains seven rows of labels, with two labels in each row, for a total of 14 labels. See Figure 6-27.

TIP

It is a good idea to print one page of a label document on regular paper so you can check your work before printing on the more expensive sheets of adhesive labels.

Figure 6-27 Layout of a sheet of Avery® labels

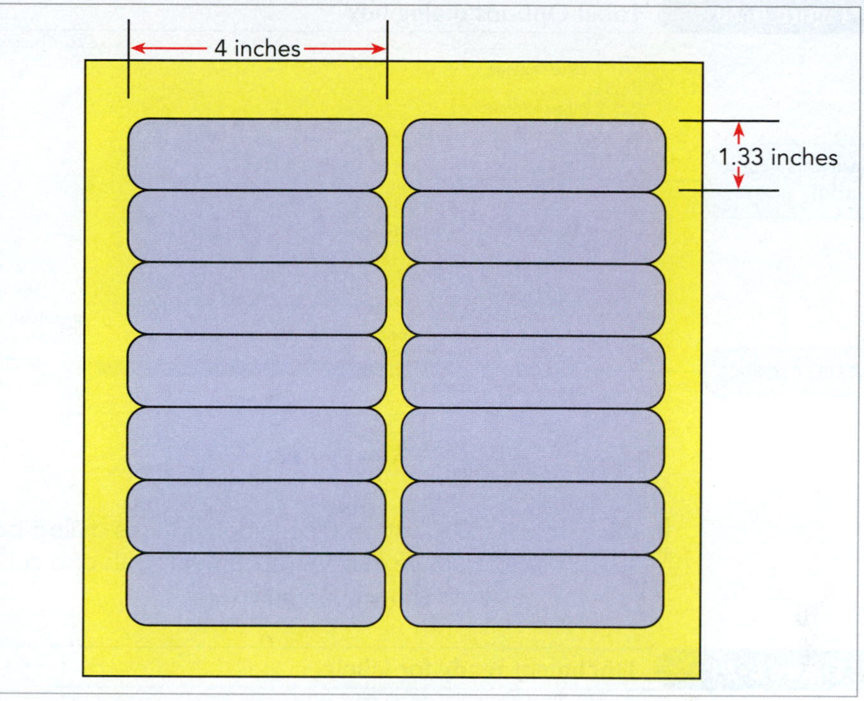

Performing a mail merge to create mailing labels is similar to performing a mail merge to create a form letter. You begin by selecting Labels as the type of main document and then you specify the brand and product number for the labels you are using. You will also need to specify a data source file. In this case, you'll use the Microsoft Office Address Lists data source file, Tupelo Data.mdb, which you created and used in the form letter mail merges.

To specify the main document for creating mailing labels:

1. Open a new, blank document, and then save the document as **Tupelo Labels Main Document** in the location specified by your instructor.
2. Make sure nonprinting characters are displayed, and zoom out so you can see the whole page.
3. On the ribbon, click the **Mailings** tab.
4. In the Start Mail Merge group, click the **Start Mail Merge** button.

   At this point, if you wanted to merge to envelopes instead of labels, you could click Envelopes to open the Envelope Options dialog box, where you could select the envelope size you wanted to use. In this case, however, you want to merge to labels.
5. Click **Labels**. The Label Options dialog box opens.
6. Click the **Label vendors** arrow to display a list of vendors, scroll down, and then click **Avery US Letter**.
7. Scroll down the Product number box, and then click **5162 Easy Peel Address Labels**. See Figure 6-28.

Figure 6-28 **Label Options dialog box**

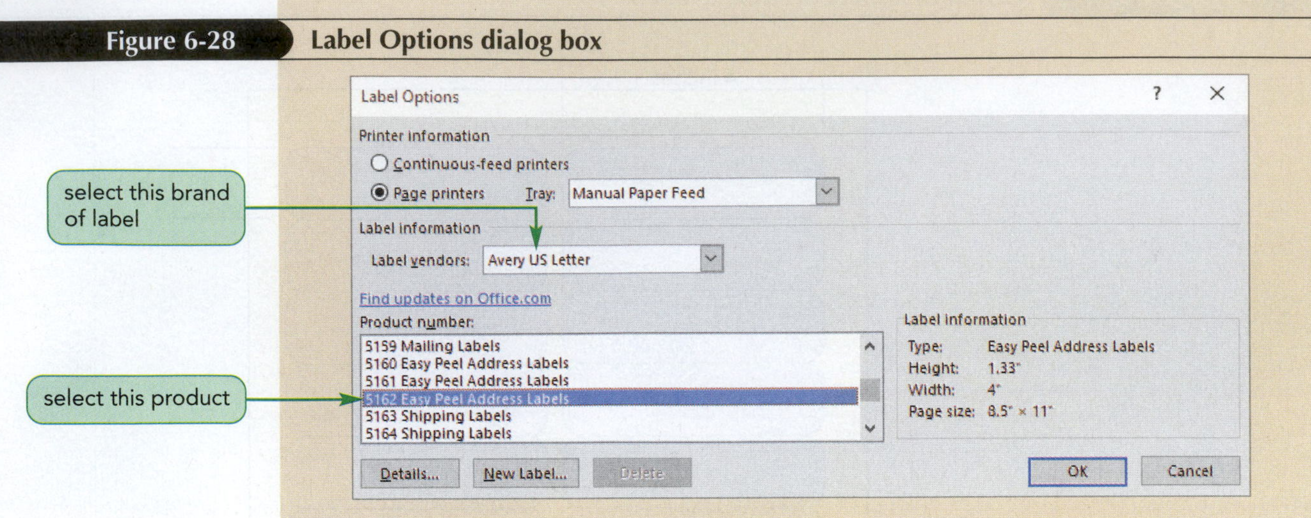

8. Click the **OK** button. The Label Options dialog box closes, and Word inserts a table structure into the document, with one cell for each of the 14 labels on the page, as shown in Figure 6-29.

Figure 6-29 **Document ready for labels**

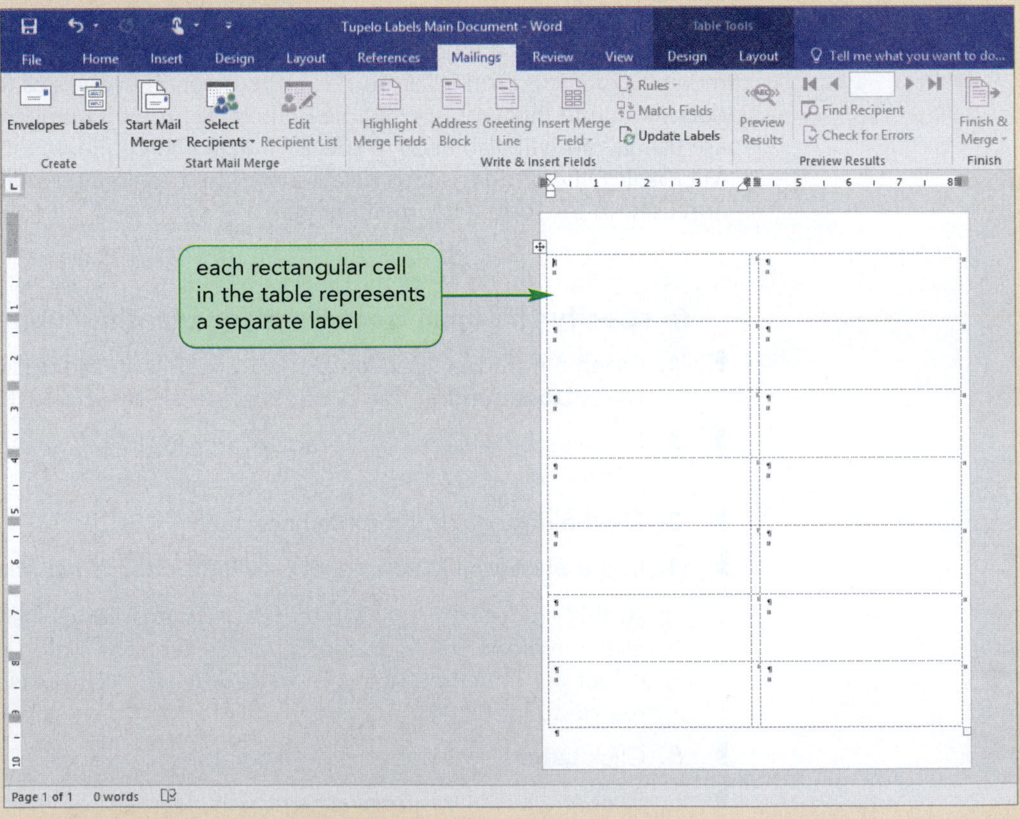

As with all table gridlines, these gridlines are visible only on the screen; they will not be visible on the printed labels.

Trouble? If you don't see the table gridlines, click the Table Tools Layout tab, and then, in the Table group, click the View Gridlines button to select it.

You have finished setting up the document. Next, you need to select the data source you created earlier. Note that the changes you made to the data source as a whole earlier in this session (sorting the records and selecting only some records) have no effect on the data source in this new mail merge. However, the changes you made to individual records (such as editing individual records or adding new records) are retained.

To continue the mail merge for the labels:

1. In the Start Mail Merge group, click the **Select Recipients** button, and then click **Use an Existing List**. The Select Data Source dialog box opens.
2. Navigate to the location where you stored the Tupelo Data file, select the **Tupelo Data** file, and then click the **Open** button. The Select Data Source dialog box closes, and you return to the main document.
3. Change the Zoom level to **120%** so you can read the document.

   In each label except the first one, the code <<Next Record>> is displayed. This code tells Word to retrieve the next record from the data source for each label.
4. Verify that the insertion point is located in the upper-left label, and make sure the Mailings tab is still selected on the ribbon.
5. In the Write & Insert Fields group, click the **Address Block** button. The Insert Address Block dialog box opens. The left pane displays possible formats for the name in the address block. The default format, "Joshua Randall Jr.," simply inserts the first and last names, which is what Chris wants. The Preview pane on the right currently shows the first address in the data source, which is the address for Emma Peterson.
6. In the Preview section of the Insert Address Field dialog box, click the **Next** button ▷. The record for David Ahrens is displayed in the Preview pane, as shown in Figure 6-30.

TIP

You can use the AddressBlock merge field only if you include a State field in your data source.

Figure 6-30 Previewing addresses in the Insert Address Block dialog box

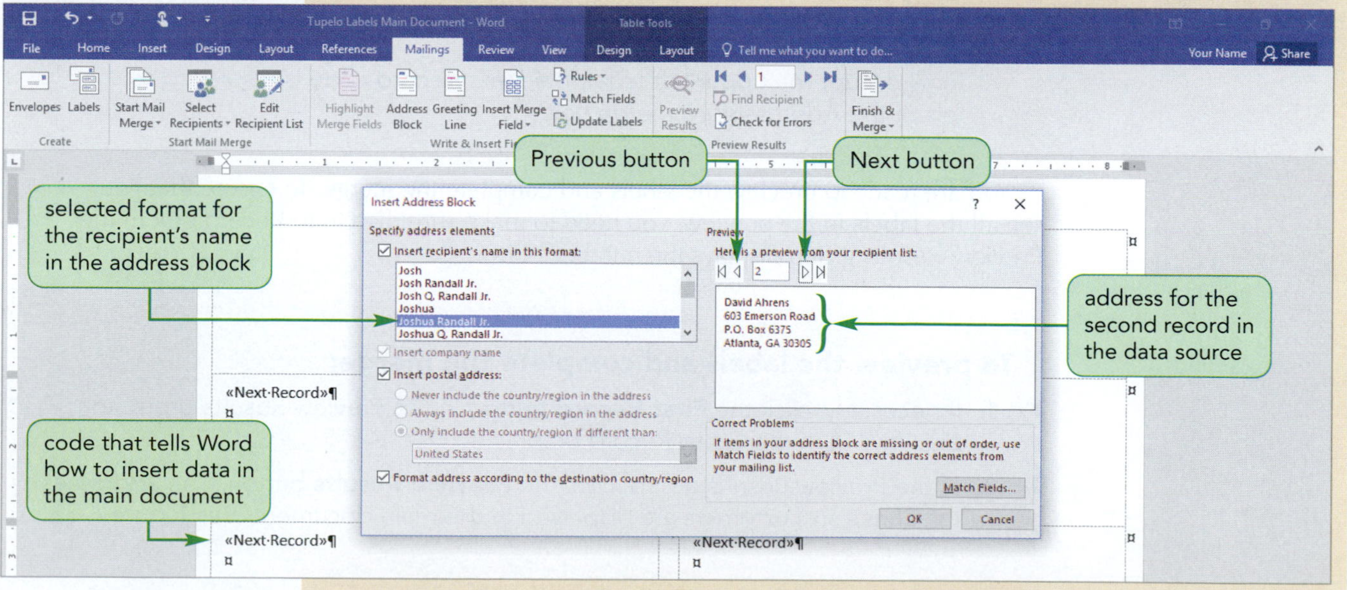

7. Click the **OK** button. The Insert Address Block dialog box closes, and an AddressBlock merge field is displayed in the upper-left label on the page. Next, you need to update the remaining labels to match the one containing the AddressBlock merge field.

8. In the Write & Insert Fields group, click the **Update Labels** button. The AddressBlock merge field is inserted into all the labels in the document, as shown in Figure 6-31.

Figure 6-31 Field codes inserted into document

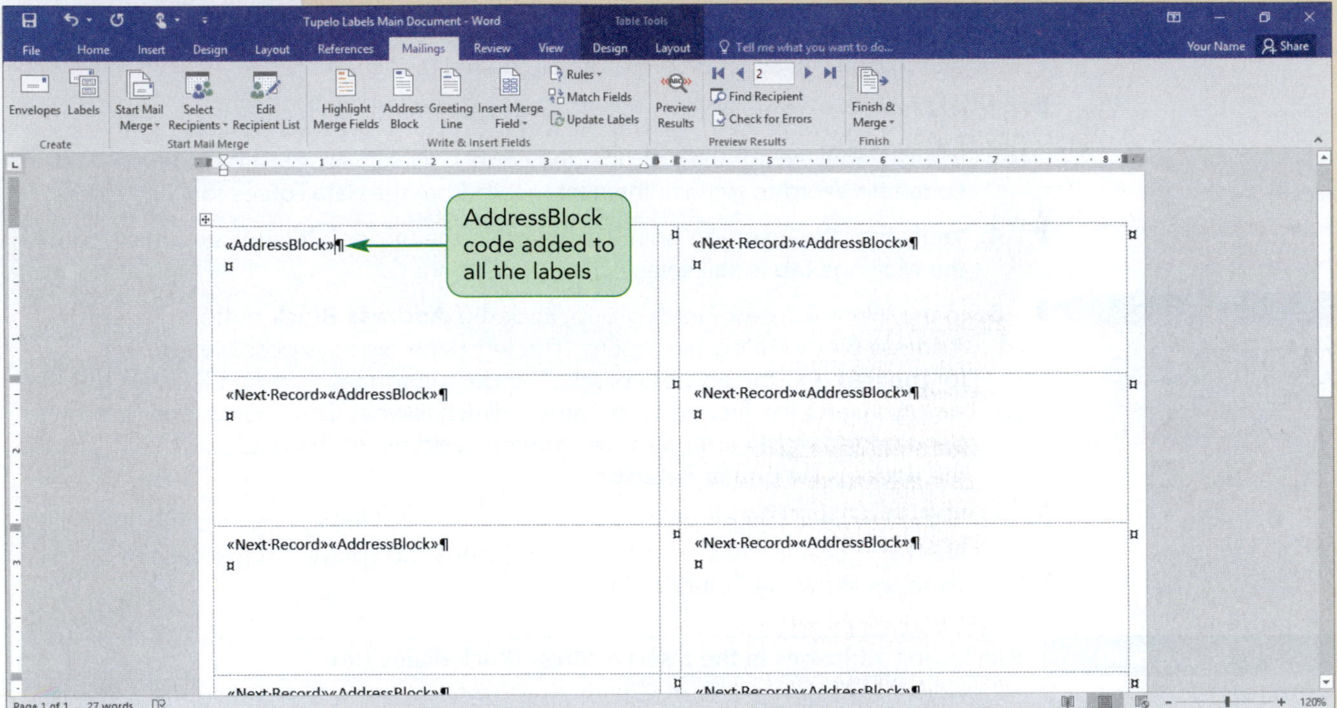

In all except the upper-left label, the Next Record code is displayed to the left of the AddressBlock merge field.

You are ready to preview the labels and complete the merge. To ensure that you see all the labels in the preview, you need to make sure the Go to Record box in the Preview Results group displays the number "1".

To preview the labels and complete the merge:

1. If necessary, click the **First Record** button in the Preview Results group to display "1" in the Go to Record box.

2. In the Preview Results group, click the **Preview Results** button. The addresses for Chris's six customers are displayed in the main document. See Figure 6-32.

Figure 6-32 Previewing addresses in labels

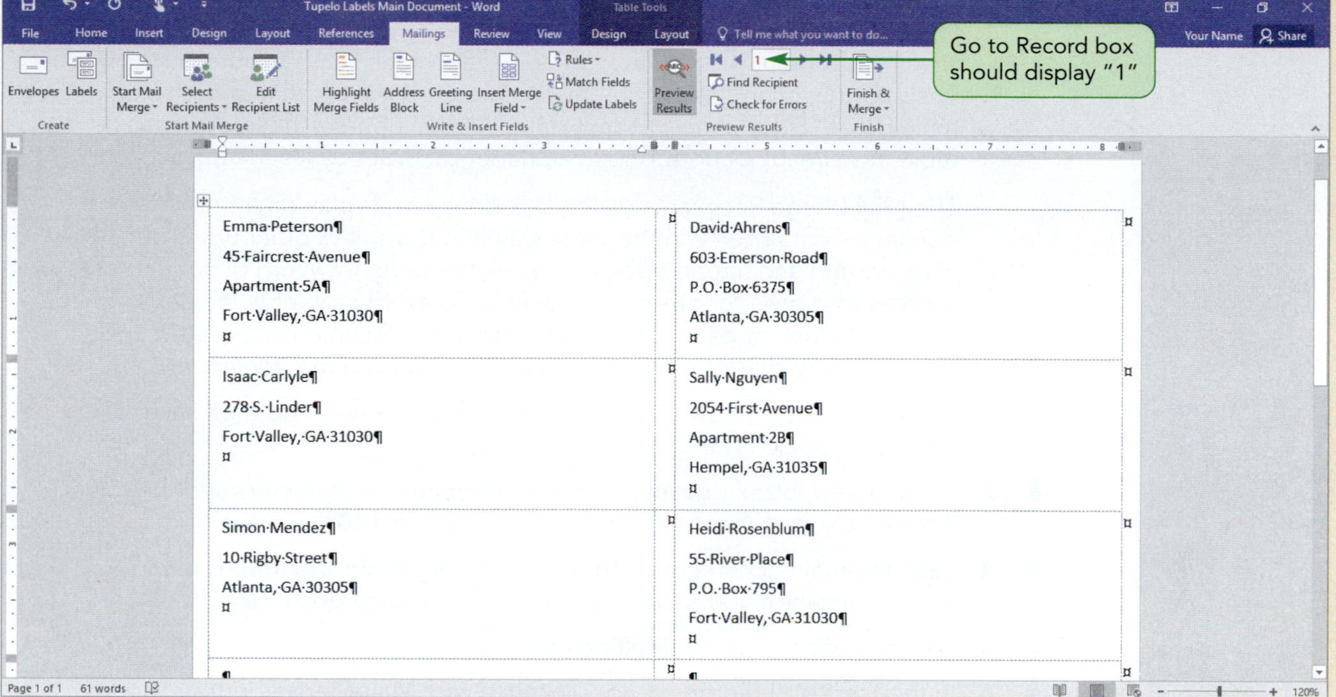

3. In the Finish group, click the **Finish & Merge** button, and then click **Edit Individual Documents**.
4. In the Merge to New Document dialog box, verify that the **All** option button is selected, and then click the **OK** button. The finished labels are inserted into a new document named Labels1.
5. Scroll through the document. The document contains space for 14 labels; but because the data source contains only six records, the new document only contains addresses for six labels.
6. In the upper-left label, change "Emma Peterson" to your first and last names, and then save the merged document as **Tupelo Merged Labels** in the location specified by your instructor.
7. Close the **Tupelo Merged Labels** document, then save and close the **Tupelo Labels Main Document** file.

Creating a Telephone Directory

Next, Chris wants you to create a telephone directory for all store employees. She has already created a Word document containing the phone numbers; you will use that document as the data source for the merge. You'll set up a mail merge as before, except this time you will select Directory as the main document type. Keep in mind that you should use a Word document as a data source only for a simple project like a directory. For letters, it's better to use an Access database, an Excel workbook, or a Microsoft Office Address Lists file. You'll start by examining the Word document that Chris wants you to use as the data source, and then you'll create the main document.

To review the data source and create the main document for the directory:

1. Open the document **Phone** from the Word6 > Module folder, and then save it as **Tupelo Phone Data** in the location specified by your instructor. The information in this document is arranged in a table with three column headings—"First Name," "Last Name," and "Phone." The information in the table has already been sorted in alphabetical order by last name.

   The Mail Merge Recipients dialog box does not display data from a Word document data source in the same way that it displays other types of data. Also, sorting and filtering does not work the same for Word document data sources as it does for other types of files. To avoid problems, it's easier to edit a Word document data source by opening the document separately, making any necessary changes, and then saving and closing the document.
2. Replace "Kiley Bradoff" with your first and last names, and then save and close the Tupelo Phone Data document.
3. Open a new, blank document, display nonprinting characters and the rulers, if necessary, and then change the Zoom level to **120%**.
4. Save the main document as **Tupelo Directory Main Document** in the location in which you saved the Tupelo Phone Data document.
5. On the ribbon, click the **Mailings** tab.
6. In the Start Mail Merge group, click the **Start Mail Merge** button, and then click **Directory**.
7. In the Start Mail Merge group, click the **Select Recipients** button, and then click **Use an Existing List** to open the Select Data Source dialog box.
8. Navigate to and select the Word document named **Tupelo Phone Data**, and then click the **Open** button.

You're ready to insert the fields in the main document. Chris wants the directory to include the names at the left margin of the page and the phone numbers at the right margin, with a dot leader in between. Recall that a dot leader is a dotted line that extends from the last letter of text on the left margin to the beginning of the nearest text aligned at a tab stop.

To set up the directory main document with dot leaders:

1. With the insertion point in the first line of the document, insert the **First_Name** merge field, insert a **space**, and then insert the **Last_Name** merge field.
2. In the Write & Insert Fields group, click the **Highlight Merge Fields** button. The First_Name and Last_Name merge fields are displayed on a gray background. Now you'll set a tab stop at the right margin (at the 5.5-inch mark on the horizontal ruler) with a dot leader.
3. On the ribbon, click the **Home** tab.
4. In the Paragraph group, click the **Dialog Box Launcher** to open the Paragraph dialog box, and then in the lower-left corner of the Indents and Spacing tab, click the **Tabs** button. The Tabs dialog box opens.
5. In the Tab stop position box, type **5.5** and then click the **Right** option button in the Alignment section.
6. Click the **2 ....** option button in the Leader section. See Figure 6-33.

TIP

You can click the Clear All button in the Tabs dialog box to delete all the tab stops in the document.

Figure 6-33 Creating a tab with a dot leader

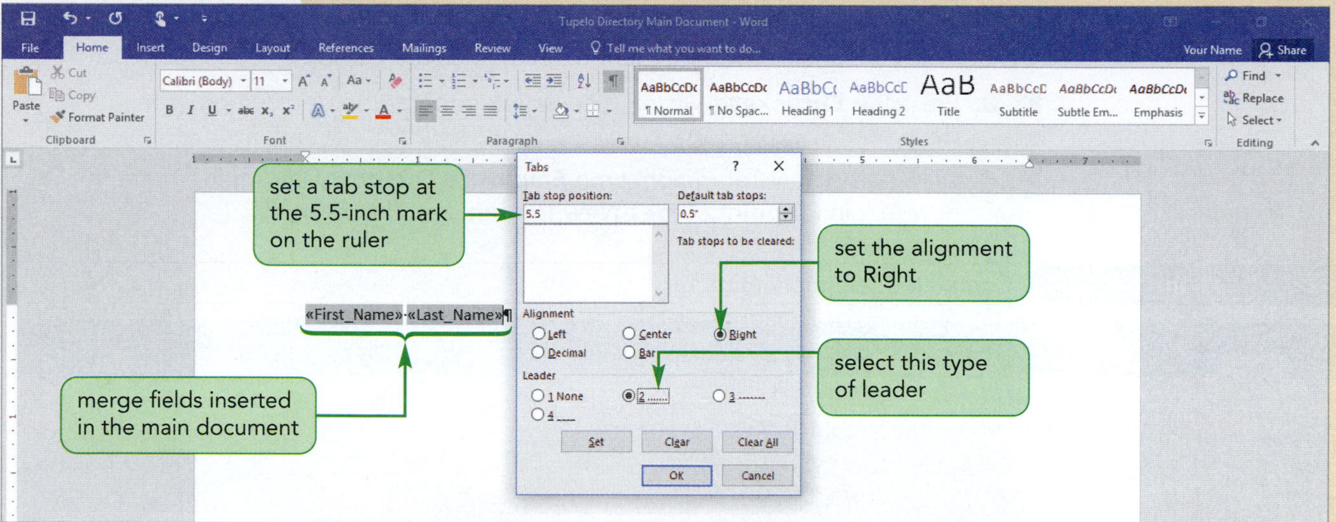

7. Click the **OK** button. Word clears the current tab stops and inserts a right-aligned tab stop at the 5.5-inch mark on the horizontal ruler.
8. Press the **Tab** key to move the insertion point to the new tab stop. A dotted line stretches from the Last_Name merge field to the right side of the page.
9. On the ribbon, click the **Mailings** tab.
10. Insert the **Phone** merge field at the insertion point. The dot leader shortens to accommodate the inserted merge fields.
11. Press the **Enter** key. The completed main document should look like the one shown in Figure 6-34.

Be sure to press the Enter key here to ensure that each name and telephone number is displayed on a separate line.

Figure 6-34 Completed main document for the telephone directory

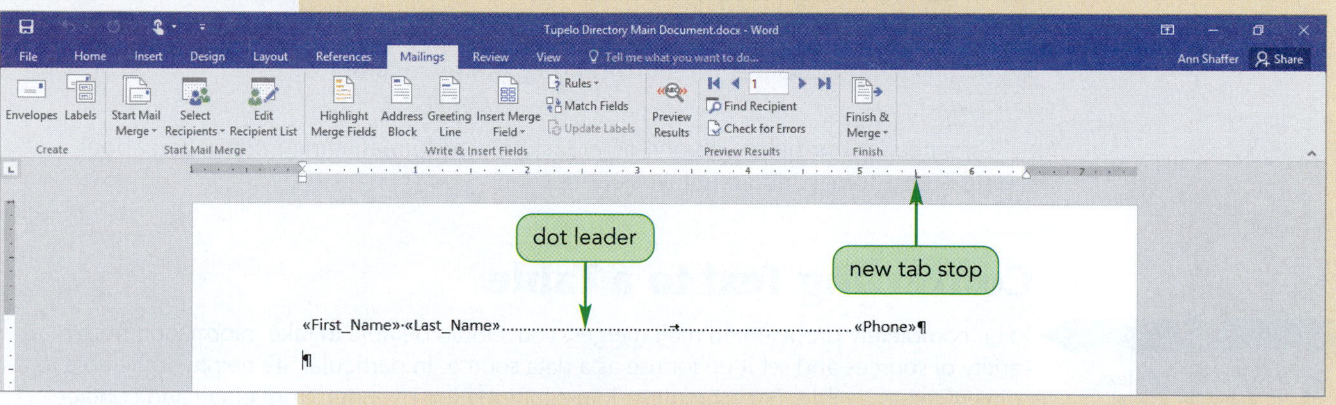

You are now ready to merge this file with the data source.

To finish the merge for the telephone directory:

1. In the Preview Results group, click the **Preview Results** button, and then review the data for the first record in the document.

2. In the Finish group, click the **Finish & Merge** button, and then click **Edit Individual Documents**. In the Merge to New Document dialog box, verify that the **All** option button is selected, and then click the **OK** button. Word creates a new document that contains the completed telephone list.
3. Press the **Enter** key to insert a new paragraph at the beginning of the document.
4. Click in the new paragraph, type **Employee Directory** and then format the new text in **22-point, Times New Roman**. See Figure 6-35.

Figure 6-35 Completed telephone directory

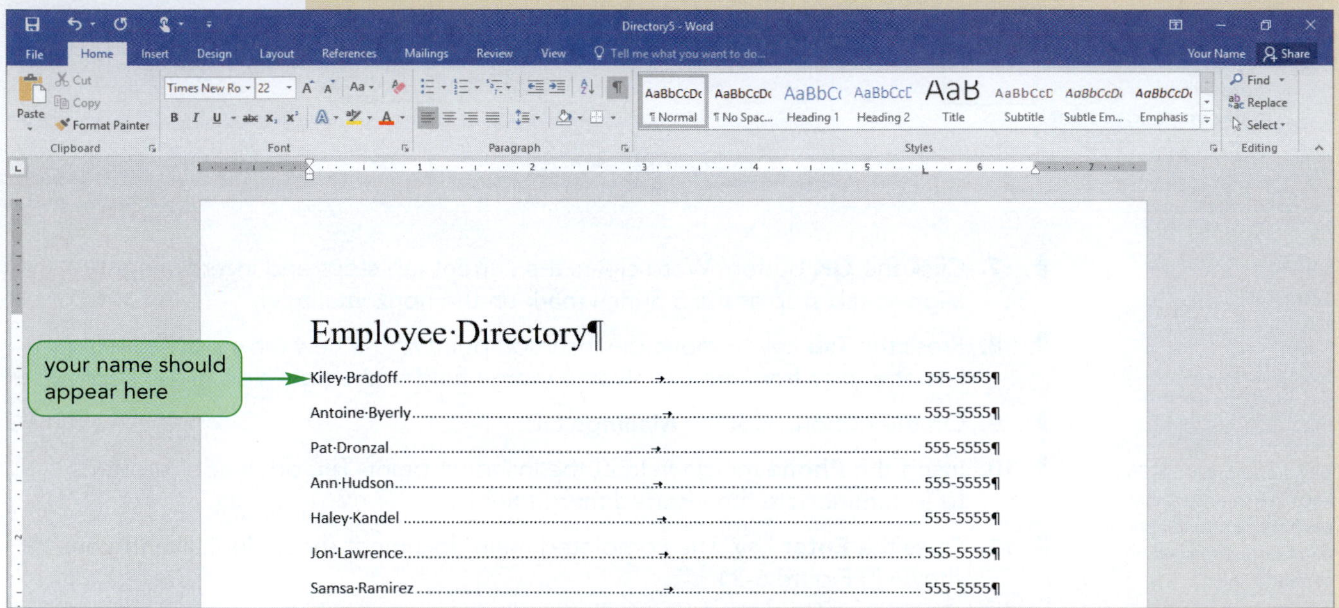

5. Save the document as **Tupelo Merged Directory** in the location in which you saved the main document, and then close it.
6. Save and close the **Tupelo Directory Main Document** file.

Chris needs your help with one other task related to managing information about the store's customers and employees.

Converting Text to a Table

> **TIP**
>
> To convert a table to text, click in the table, click the Table Tools Layout tab, click Convert to Text in the Data group, click the separator you prefer, and then click the OK button.

To be completely proficient in mail merges, you should be able to take information from a variety of sources and set it up for use as a data source. In particular, it's helpful to be able to convert text to a table. For example, address information exported from email and contact management programs often takes the form of a **CSV (comma-separated value) file**, a text file in which each paragraph contains one record, with the fields separated by commas. CSV files can have a .txt or .csv file extension. The commas in a CSV file are known as **separator characters**, or sometimes **delimiters**.

You can use the Convert Text to Table command on the Table menu to transform text from a Word document or a CSV file into a table. But first you need to make sure the text is set up correctly; that is, you need to make sure that separator characters are used consistently to divide the text into individual fields. In a CSV file, commas are used as separator characters, but you might encounter a Word document that uses tab characters, or other characters, as separator characters. After you verify that separator characters are used consistently within a document, you need to make sure each paragraph in the document contains the same number of fields.

Upon conversion, each field is formatted as a separate cell in a column, and each paragraph mark starts a new row, or record. Sometimes a conversion might not turn out the way you expect. In that case, undo it, and then review the text to make sure each paragraph contains the same number of data items, with the items divided by the same separator character.

Chris's assistant, who isn't familiar with Word tables, typed some information about new customers as text in a Word document. He forgot to include an email address and phone number for each customer. Chris wants to convert the text to a table and then add columns for the missing information. The next time the customers visit the store, one of the store clerks can ask for the missing information and then add it to the table.

To convert text into a table:

1. Open the document named **New** from the Word6 > Module folder, and then save it as **New Customers Table** in the location specified by your instructor.
2. Display nonprinting characters, if necessary, and then change the Zoom level to **120%**. See Figure 6-36.

Figure 6-36 **Text with inconsistent separator characters**

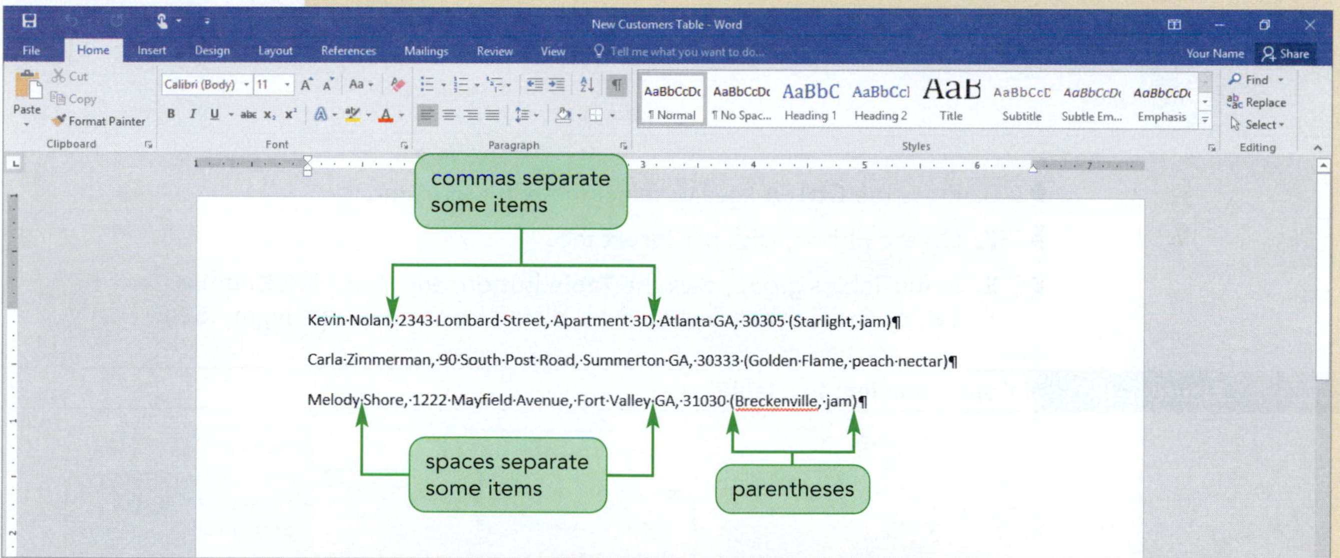

The document consists of three paragraphs, each of which contains a customer's name, address, city, state, ZIP code, favorite peach variety, and favorite other product. Some of the fields are separated by commas and spaces (for example, the address and the city), but some are separated only by spaces, with no punctuation character (for example, the first and last names). Also, the favorite peach variety and other product are enclosed in parentheses. You need to edit this information so that fields are separated by commas, with no parentheses enclosing the last two items.

3. Edit the document to insert a comma after each first name, city, and ZIP code, and then delete the parentheses in each paragraph.

Before you can convert the text into a table, you also need to make sure each paragraph includes the same fields. Currently, the first paragraph includes two pieces of address information—a street address and an apartment number, which is equivalent to an Address Line 1 field and an Address Line 2 field. However, the other paragraphs only include an Address Line 1 field.

4. In the second paragraph, click to the right of the comma after "Road," press the **spacebar**, and then type **,** (a comma).
5. In the third paragraph, click to the right of the comma after "Avenue," press the **spacebar**, and then type **,** (a comma). Now the second and third paragraphs each contain a blank field. See Figure 6-37.

Figure 6-37 Text set up for conversion to a table

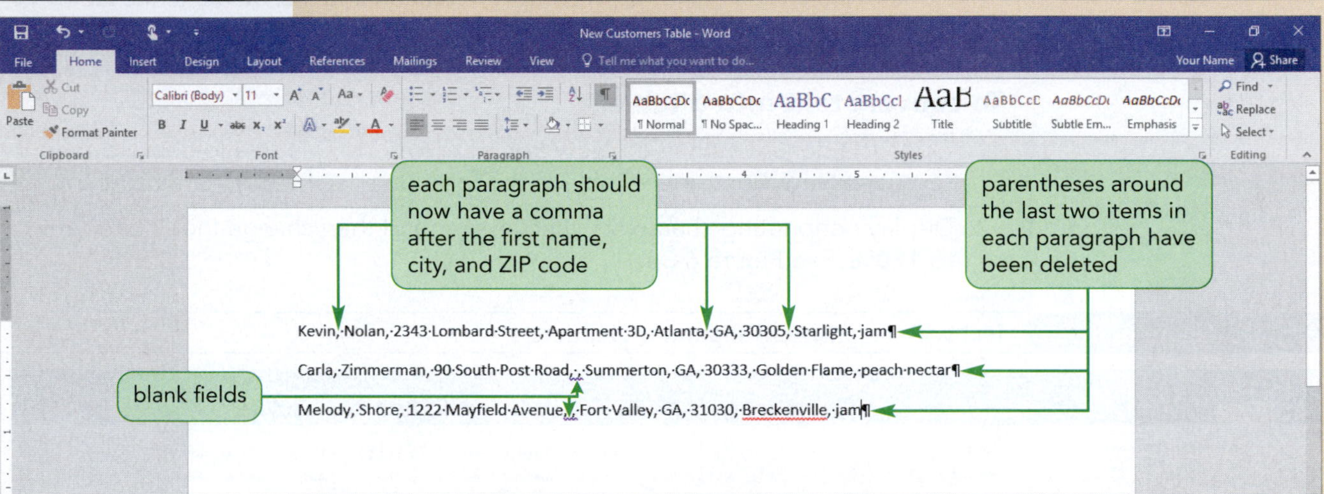

6. Press the **Ctrl+A** keys to select the entire document.
7. On the ribbon, click the **Insert** tab.
8. In the Tables group, click the **Table** button, and then click **Convert Text to Table**. The Convert Text to Table dialog box opens. See Figure 6-38.

Figure 6-38 Converting text to a table

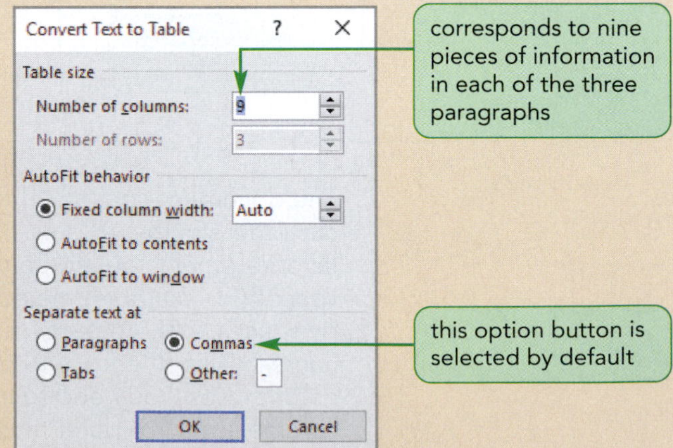

Note that the Number of columns setting is 9, and the Number of rows setting is 3. This corresponds to the nine fields in each of the three paragraphs.

In the Separate text at section of the dialog box, you can choose from three possible separator characters—paragraphs, commas, and tabs. If the text in your document was separated by a character other than paragraphs, commas, or tabs, you could type the character in the box to the right of the Other button. In this case, though, the default option, Commas, is the correct choice because the information in each paragraph is separated by commas.

9. Click the **OK** button. The Convert Text to Table dialog box closes, and the text in the document is converted into a table consisting of nine columns and three rows.
10. Save the document.

Now that you have converted the text to a table, you need to finish the table by adding the columns for the phone numbers and email addresses and adding a header row to identify the field names.

To finish the table by adding columns and a header row:

1. Switch to Landscape orientation, and then select the column containing the ZIP codes.
2. On the ribbon, click the **Table Tools Layout** tab.
3. In the Rows & Columns group, click the **Insert Right** button twice to add two blank columns to the right of the column containing ZIP codes.
4. Select the table's top row, and then in the Rows & Columns group, click the **Insert Above** button.
5. Enter the column headings shown in Figure 6-39, and format the column headings in bold.

Figure 6-39 Table with new columns and column headings

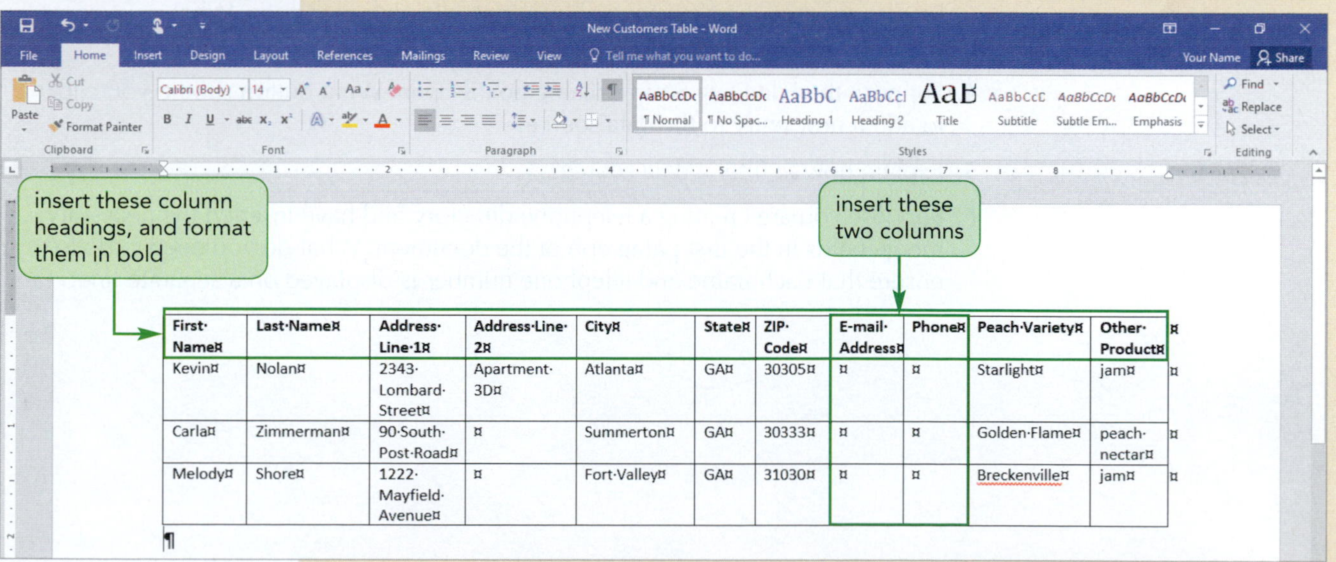
New Customers Table - Word
insert these column headings, and format them in bold
insert these two columns

First Name	Last Name	Address Line 1	Address Line 2	City	State	ZIP Code	E-mail Address	Phone	Peach Variety	Other Product
Kevin	Nolan	2343 Lombard Street	Apartment 3D	Atlanta	GA	30305			Starlight	jam
Carla	Zimmerman	90 South Post Road		Summerton	GA	30333			Golden Flame	peach nectar
Melody	Shore	1222 Mayfield Avenue		Fort Valley	GA	31030			Breckenville	jam

6. Save the **New Customers Table** document, and then close it.

You have finished converting text into a table. Chris can use the table later as the data source for another mail merge. As her business expands, she plans to continue to use Word's mail merge feature to inform her customers about new products and specials.

INSIGHT

Combining Data with a Microsoft Office Address Lists File

If you have data in a Word file that you want to combine with data in a Microsoft Office Address Lists file, or any other Microsoft Access file, start by setting up the Word document as a table. That way, you can be sure that each record includes the same fields. You can also review the table quickly to confirm that you have entered data in the various fields in a consistent format. Once you are confident that you have set up the table correctly, you can begin the process of combining it with the Microsoft Office Address Lists file.

First, delete the heading row, and then convert the table back to text by clicking the Table Tools Layout tab, clicking Convert to Text in the Data group, clicking the Commas button, and then clicking OK. Next, save the Word file as a Plain Text file with the .txt file extension. Finally, open the Microsoft Office Address Lists file in Access, click the External Data tab, and then click the Text File button in the Import & Link group to begin importing the text file into the Microsoft Office Address Lists file. In the Get External Data - Text File dialog box, click the Append a copy of the records to the table button, and then click the Browse button to select the plain text file.

REVIEW

Session 6.2 Quick Check

1. Does the connection between a main document and its data source persist after you close the main document, if you keep both files in their original locations?
2. What are two ways to edit a data source?
3. Suppose you want to edit a Microsoft Office Address Lists data source named Employees, and the Mail Merge Recipients dialog box is open. What must you do to begin editing the data source?
4. Suppose the Edit Data Source dialog box is open. What button should you click to add a new entry to the data source?
5. Explain how to filter a data source.
6. Suppose you are creating a telephone directory and have inserted the necessary merge fields in the first paragraph of the document. What do you need to do to ensure that each name and telephone number is displayed on a separate line?

PRACTICE

Review Assignments

Data Files needed for the Review Assignments: Ice.docx, More.docx, Suppliers.docx

The expanded Tupelo Family Market is a big hit. Chris has greatly expanded her customer base, and now she is adding a home delivery service. Customers who sign up for monthly peach deliveries also receive a free quart of homemade ice cream. On the home delivery sign-up form, customers can choose between vanilla peach or cinnamon peach ice cream. Now she wants to send a letter inviting weekly home delivery customers to reserve their free ice cream three days before they want it delivered. She also needs to create an email directory of suppliers she deals with regularly. Finally, she needs to convert some additional customer information into a table that she can use as a data source. Complete the following steps:

1. Open the document **Ice** from the Word6 > Review folder included with your Data Files, and then save the document as **Ice Cream Main Document** in the location specified by your instructor.
2. In the first paragraph, replace the placeholder text "[INSERT DATE FIELD]" with a Date field that displays the current month, day, and year—in the format March 11, 2017.
3. Begin the mail merge by selecting Letters as the type of main document.
4. Create a data source with the following fields in the following order: First Name, Last Name, Address Line 1, Address Line 2, City, State, ZIP Code, E-mail Address, Phone, and Ice Cream Type. Remove any extra fields, and rename fields as necessary.
5. Create four records using the information shown in Figure 6-40.

Figure 6-40 **Information for new data source**

First Name	Last Name	Address Line 1	Address Line 2	City	State	ZIP Code	E-mail Address	Phone	Ice Cream Type
Lara	Pushkin	821 Ruby Lane		Robbins	GA	31035	lara@sample.cengage.com	555-555-5555	cinnamon peach
Marcus	Hesse	933 Nakoma Way		Marigold	GA	31028	marcus@sample.cengage.com	555-555-5555	cinnamon peach
Derrick	Greely	52 Red Earth Road	P.O. Box 2233	Fort Valley	GA	31030	derrick@sample.cengage.com	555-555-5555	vanilla peach
Calista	Cutler	299 Eton Avenue	Apartment 4A	Fort Valley	GA	31030	calista@sample.cengage.com	555-555-5555	vanilla peach

6. Save the data source as **Ice Cream Data** in the location in which you saved the main document.
7. Edit the data source to replace "Marcus Hesse" with your first and last names.
8. Sort the data source in ascending order by ZIP code and then by last name.
9. Replace the placeholder text "[INSERT INSIDE ADDRESS]" with an inside address consisting of the necessary separate merge fields. Adjust the paragraph spacing in the inside address as necessary.
10. In the salutation, replace the placeholder text "[INSERT FIRST NAME]" with the First_Name merge field.
11. In the body of the letter, replace the placeholder text "[INSERT ICE CREAM TYPE]" with the Ice_Cream_Type merge field.
12. Save your changes to the main document, and then preview the merged document. Correct any formatting or spacing problems.
13. Merge to a new document, save the merged document as **Merged Free Ice Cream Letters** in the location in which you saved the main document, and then close the file.

14. Filter the data source to display only records for customers who requested a free cinnamon peach ice cream, and then complete a second merge. Save the new merged document as **Merged Cinnamon Peach Letters** in the location in which you saved the main document. Close all documents, saving all changes.
15. Open a new, blank document, and create a set of mailing labels using the vendor Avery US Letters and product number 5162. Save the main document as **Ice Cream Labels Main Document** in the location in which you saved the Ice Cream Data file.
16. Select the Ice Cream Data file you created earlier in this assignment as the data source.
17. Insert an AddressBlock merge field in the "Joshua Randall Jr." format, and then update the labels.
18. Preview the merged labels, merge to a new document, and then save the new document as **Merged Ice Cream Labels** in the location in which you saved the main document. Save and close all open documents.
19. Open the document **Suppliers** from the Word6 > Review folder, and then save it as **Suppliers Data** in the location specified by your instructor. Change "Carl Siska" to your first and last names, save the document, and close it.
20. Open a new, blank document, and then save it as **Suppliers Directory Main Document** in the location in which you saved the Suppliers Data file. Create a directory main document. Select the Suppliers Data file as the data source.
21. Set a right tab at 6 inches with a dot leader, and insert the necessary merge fields so that the directory shows a contact followed by a comma, followed by the contact's company name, and, on the right side of the page, the email address for each company. Merge to a new document, and then, at the top of the merged document, insert the heading **Supplier Contacts** formatted in 22-point, Times New Roman, with the Green, Accent 6 font color. Save the merged document as **Merged Suppliers Directory** in the location in which you saved the main document. Save and close all open documents.
22. Open the document **More** from the Word6 > Review folder, and then save it as **More Customer Data** in the location specified by your instructor. Convert the data in the document to a table with eight columns. Insert a header row with the following column headers formatted in bold—**First Name**, **Last Name**, **Address Line 1**, **Address Line 2**, **City**, **State**, **ZIP Code**, and **Ice Cream Type**. Replace "Jo Essenberg" with your first and last names. Save and close the document.

APPLY

Case Problem 1

Data File needed for this Case Problem: Newberry.docx

Newberry Glen School Yolanda Baird is the executive director of Newberry Glen School, an institution in Las Vegas, Nevada, devoted to helping adults earn high school degrees. As part of a new fund-raising campaign for the school, Yolanda plans to send out customized letters to last year's donors, asking them to consider donating the same amount or more this year. She asks you to help her create the letters and the envelopes for the campaign. Complete the following steps:

1. Open the document **Newberry** from the Word6 > Case1 folder, and then save it as **Newberry Glen Main Document** in the location specified by your instructor. In the closing, replace "Yolanda Baird" with your first and last names.
2. In the first paragraph, replace the placeholder text "[INSERT DATE FIELD]" with a Date field that displays the current month, day, and year—in the format March 11, 2017.
3. Begin the mail merge by selecting Letters as the type of main document.

4. Create a data source with the following field names, in the following order—**Title**, **First Name**, **Last Name**, **Address Line 1**, **Address Line 2**, **City**, **State**, **ZIP Code**, **E-mail Address**, and **Donation Amount**.
5. Enter the four records shown in Figure 6-41.

Figure 6-41 **Four records for new data source**

Title	First Name	Last Name	Address Line 1	Address Line 2	City	State	ZIP Code	E-mail Address	Donation Amount
Mr.	Tenzen	Sung	844 Sumerdale Way	Unit 6	Las Vegas	NV	89101	sung@sample.cengage.com	$2,000
Mr.	Jerome	Fuhrman	1577 Shanley Boulevard	Apartment 4C	Las Vegas	NV	89105	fuhrman@sample.cengage.com	$600
Ms.	Susannah	Royal	4424 Gatehouse Lane		New Mesa	NV	89099	royal@sample.cengage.com	$150
Mr.	Adriano	Borrego	633 Desert View		Las Vegas	NV	89105	borrego@sample.cengage.com	$325

6. Save the data source as **Newberry Glen Data** in the location in which you saved the main document.
7. Edit the data source to replace "Tenzen Sung" with your first and last names. Change the title to **Ms.** if necessary.
8. Sort the data source alphabetically by last name.
9. Build an inside address using separate merge fields. Adjust paragraph spacing as necessary.
10. Add a salutation using the Title and Last_Name merge fields, as indicated in the document. Verify that you deleted all placeholder text in the date paragraph, inside address, and the salutation.
11. In the paragraph that begins "In order to continue…," insert the Donation_Amount merge field where indicated. Delete the placeholder text.
12. Save your changes to the Newberry Glen Main Document file. Preview the merged document, and then merge to a new document.
13. Save the merged letters document as **Merged Newberry Glen Letters** in the location in which you saved the main document, and then close it.
14. Save the Newberry Glen Main Document file, and then close it.
15. Open a new, blank document, and then save it as **Newberry Glen Envelopes Main Document** in the location in which you saved the Newberry Glen Data file. The school has envelopes with a preprinted return address, so you don't need to type a return address. Begin the mail merge by selecting Envelopes as the type of main document, and then select Size 10 (4 1/8 × 9 1/2 in) as the envelope size in the Envelope Options dialog box.
16. Use the Newberry Glen Data file you created earlier as the data source. In the recipient address area of the envelope, insert an AddressBlock merge field in the format "Mr. Joshua Randall Jr.".
17. Filter the records in the Newberry Glen Data file so that only records with Las Vegas addresses are included in the merge.
18. Merge to a new document.
19. Save the merged document as **Merged Envelopes** in the location in which you saved the main document, and then close it. Save the main document, and close it.

TROUBLESHOOT

Case Problem 2

Data Files needed for this Case Problem: Concierge.docx, Directory.docx, Incomplete.docx, Residents.xlsx

Willow Bay Village Luxury Condominiums You are the director of concierge services at Willow Bay Village, a luxury condominium community in Gulf Shores, Alabama. You need to send letters to people around the country who have recently purchased newly built condominiums as winter getaway homes. Your data for the mail merge is saved as an Excel file. The data file includes names and addresses. It also includes the concierge service that most interests each new resident, as well as the name of the concierge at Willow Bay Village responsible for that service. To ensure that you can maintain the connection between the data source and the main document files, you will first start Excel and then save the data source file to the location specified by your instructor. Complete the following steps:

1. Start Excel, and on the Recent screen, click Open Other Workbooks. Navigate to the Word6 > Case2 folder included with your Data Files, and then open the Excel workbook **Residents**.
2. Click the File tab, click Save As, save the Excel workbook as **Residents Data** in the location specified by your instructor, and then close Excel.
3. Open the document **Concierge** from the Word6 > Case2 folder.
4. Save the Word document as **Concierge Services Main Document** in the location in which you saved the Client Data file.
5. In the letter's closing, replace "Student Name" with your first and last names.
6. Replace the field that displays the date and time with a Date field that displays the current month, day, and year—in the format March 11, 2017.
7. Begin the mail merge by selecting Letters as the type of main document.
8. For the data source, select the Excel workbook Residents Data that you just saved. Click the OK button in the Select Table dialog box.
9. From within Word, edit the data source to replace "StudentFirstName" and "StudentLastName" with your first and last names.
10. Delete the placeholder text for the inside address, and then insert an AddressBlock merge field for the inside address in the format "Joshua Randall Jr.".
11. In the salutation, insert the First_Name merge field where indicated.
12. In the body of the letter, replace the placeholders "[INSERT CONCIERGE SERVICE]" and "[INSERT CONCIERGE NAME]" with the appropriate merge fields.
13. Sort the records in the data source in ascending order by Concierge Service.

Troubleshoot 14. Preview the merged document, and note that the lines of the inside address (inserted by the AddressBlock merge field) are spaced too far apart. Make any changes necessary so the inside address and the salutation include the appropriate amount of paragraph and line spacing.

15. Preview all the records in the document.
16. Merge to a new document. Save the merged document as **Merged Concierge Services Letters** in the location in which you saved the main document.
17. Close all open documents, saving all changes.

Troubleshoot 18. Open the document **Incomplete** from the Word6 > Case2 folder, and save it as **Incomplete Labels** in the location specified by your instructor. Attach a comment to the ZIP code in the first label that explains what error in the main document would result in a set of labels that includes information for only one record. Save and close the document.

19. Create a main document for generating mailing labels on sheets of Avery US Letter Address labels, product number 5162, using the Residents Data file as your data source. Use the AddressBlock merge field in the format "Joshua Randall Jr.". Save the main document as **New Residents Labels Main Document** in the location in which you saved the Residents Data file.

20. Preview the merged document, merge to a new document, and then save the merged document as **Merged New Residents Labels** in the location in which you saved the main document. Close all open documents, saving any changes.
21. Re-open the **Concierge Services Main Document**, maintaining the connection to its data source, and then save it as **Concierge Services Main Document, Filtered** in the same folder. Filter out all records in the data source except records for clients interested in valet services, and then, if necessary, sort the filtered records so the one containing your name is displayed first.
22. Complete the merge to a new document. Save the merged document as **Merged Valet Letters** in the location in which you saved the main document.
23. Close all open documents, saving any changes.
24. **Troubleshoot** Open the document **Directory** from the Word6 > Case2 folder, and save it as **Incomplete Directory** in the location specified by your instructor. This directory is supposed to list each resident, along with the concierge service that most interests that resident. Attach a comment to the first name in the directory that explains what error in the main document would result in a directory formatted like the one in the Problem Directory file.
25. Save and close the document.

CHALLENGE

Case Problem 3

Data Files needed for this Case Problem: Des Moines Data.accdb, Des Moines.txt, Peterson.docx

Peterson Dental Health Meghan Dougherty is the patient services manager for Peterson Dental Health, a chain of dental clinics in Des Moines, Iowa. Meghan's company has just bought out a competitor, Des Moines Dentistry. Meghan needs to send a letter to patients of Des Moines Dentistry explaining that their records will be transferred to Peterson Dental Health. In the letter, she also wants to remind Des Moines Dentistry patients of the date of their next appointment. The patient data has been saved in a text file, with the data fields separated by commas. Meghan needs your help to convert the text file to a Word table. She will then ask one of her colleagues to import the Word table into an Access database, so that you can use it in the mail merge. Note that it is possible to import a simple text file into an Access database, but it's hard to tell if the data is set up properly. By converting the text file to a table in a Word document first, you can verify that the records all contain the same fields. Complete the following steps:

1. In Word, open the text file **Des Moines.txt** from the Word6 > Case3 folder included with your Data Files. (*Hint*: If the file is not listed in the Open dialog box, make sure All Files is selected in the box to the right of the File name box.)
2. Save the Des Moines.txt file as a Word document named **Des Moines Table** in the location specified by your instructor. (*Hint*: In the Save As dialog box, remember to select Word Document as the file type.)
3. Format the document text using the Normal style, and then switch to Landscape orientation.
4. Convert the text to a table with eight columns. Insert a header row with the following column headers formatted in bold—**First Name**, **Last Name**, **Address Line 1**, **Address Line 2**, **City**, **State**, **ZIP Code**, and **Appointment Date**. Save and close the document.
5. Open the document **Peterson** from the Word6 > Case3 folder, and then save it as **Peterson Main Document** in the location specified by your instructor.
6. In the first paragraph, replace the placeholder text "[INSERT DATE FIELD]" with a Date field that displays the current month, day, and year—in the format 3/11/17.
7. Start the mail merge by selecting Letters as the type of main document.
8. Select the Des Moines Data.accdb file as the data source. This Access database file contains all the data from the Des Moines Table document.
9. Replace the placeholder text "[INSERT INSIDE ADDRESS]" with an AddressBlock merge field in the format "Joshua Randall Jr.". Format the paragraph containing the AddressBlock merge field using the No Spacing style.

Explore 10. Delete the placeholder text "[INSERT SALUTATION]." Insert a salutation using the Greeting Line button in the Write & Insert Fields group on the Mailings tab. In the Insert Greeting Line dialog box, create a salutation that includes "Dear" and the customer's first name followed by a colon. For invalid recipient names (that is, recipients for which the First Name field in the data source is blank), select the "(none)" option. Add 12 points of paragraph spacing before the salutation paragraph.

11. In the body of the letter, replace the placeholder text"[INSERT APPOINTMENT DATE]" with the Appointment_Date merge field.

Explore 12. Use the Rules button in the Write & Insert Fields group on the Mailings tab to replace the placeholder text "[NEW CLINIC]" with a merge field that displays the message **We will soon complete construction on our new Pilot Plaza clinic, conveniently located near you.** if the value in the ZIP Code field is equal to 50305; otherwise, the field should display **We will soon complete construction on several new clinics.** (*Hint*: In the Rules menu, click If…Then…Else…, select ZIP_Code as the Field name, select Equal to as the Comparison, and type 50305 in the Compare to box. Insert the appropriate text in the Insert this text box and in the Otherwise insert this text box.)

Explore 13. In the Mail Merge Recipients dialog box, use the Filter command to display only the records that include either 5/1/2017 or 6/1/2017 in the Appointment Date field. (*Hint*: On the Filter Records tab of the Filter and Sort dialog box, you need to fill in two rows. Select Appointment Date in the Field box in both rows; in the first list box on the far left, select Or instead of And; select Equal to in the Comparison box for both rows; and type the correct dates in the Compare to boxes.)

14. In the Mail Merge Recipients dialog box, sort the displayed records in ascending order by ZIP code.
15. Preview the merged documents, adjust spacing around the merge fields as necessary, and then merge to a new document. Save the merged document as **Merged Peterson Letters** in the location in which you saved the main document.
16. Close all open documents, saving any changes.

RESEARCH

Case Problem 4

There are no Data Files needed for this Case Problem.

Population Research Associates Quinn Erickson is a senior scholar at Population Research Associates, a multidisciplinary center that conducts research in the field of human population growth. He is beginning research for an article on world population, but before he can get started, Quinn needs to organize a great deal of printed information into file folders. As his student intern, it's your job to create labels for the file folders, with one label for the top ten most populous countries in the world. You will retrieve a list of countries and their populations from the web, and then use it as the data source for a mail merge. Complete the following steps:

1. Open a new, blank document, and then save it as **Population Data** in the location specified by your instructor.
2. Open a browser, go to bing.com, and search for **population by country**. Explore the search results, looking for information arranged in a simple table format.
3. Click and drag the mouse to select information for the top ten most populous countries, and then copy it to the Clipboard.
4. Paste the information into the Population Data document, and then edit it as necessary to create a simple table with two columns, with the headings **Country** and **Population**. You might need to delete graphics, extra spaces, extra rows or columns, hyperlinks, or other elements. Format the text in the Normal style. If you can't remove special formatting from some of the text, try using the Format Painter to copy the Normal style where necessary. Remove any fill color. When you are finished, you should have a simple table with two columns, and the header row formatted in bold.
5. Save and close the Population Data file.

6. Open a new, blank document, and then save it as **Population Labels Main Document** in the location in which you saved the Population Data file.
7. Select Labels as the type of main document, using the Avery product 5966 Filing Labels.
8. Select the Population Data file as your data source.
9. In the first label, insert the Country merge field, type **,** (a comma), insert a space, and then insert the Population merge field.
10. Format the Country merge field in bold.
11. Update the labels, and preview the merge results.
12. In the "United States" label, type **,** (a comma) after the population, and then type your first and last names.
13. Merge to a new document, and then save the new document as **Merged Population Labels** in the location in which you saved the main document.
14. Close the Merged Population Labels document and any other open documents, saving any changes.

MODULE 7

Collaborating with Others and Integrating Data

Preparing an Information Sheet

OBJECTIVES

Session 7.1
- Track changes in a document
- Compare and combine documents
- Accept and reject tracked changes
- Embed an Excel worksheet
- Modify an embedded Excel worksheet

Session 7.2
- Link an Excel chart
- Modify and update a linked Excel chart
- Create bookmarks
- Insert and edit hyperlinks
- Optimize a document for online viewing
- Create and publish a blog post

Case | *Film Buff Trivia*

Rima Khouri is the marketing director for DBQ Games. The company is currently developing a new board game called Film Buff Trivia. Like many game companies, DBQ Games plans to use a crowdfunding website to raise the money required to finish developing and marketing its latest product. As part of her marketing effort, Rima also plans to email an information sheet about the fund-raising campaign to interested gamers she met at a recent gaming convention. Rima has asked James Benner, the company's development manager, to review a draft of the information sheet. While James is revising the document, Rima has asked you to work on another copy, making additional changes. When you are finished with your review, Rima wants you to merge James's edited version of the document with your most recent draft.

After you create a new version of the document for Rima, she wants you to add some fund-raising data from an Excel workbook. She also needs you to add a pie chart James created and optimize the information sheet for online viewing. Finally, Rima wants you to help her create a blog post in Word discussing the crowdfunding campaign.

STARTING DATA FILES

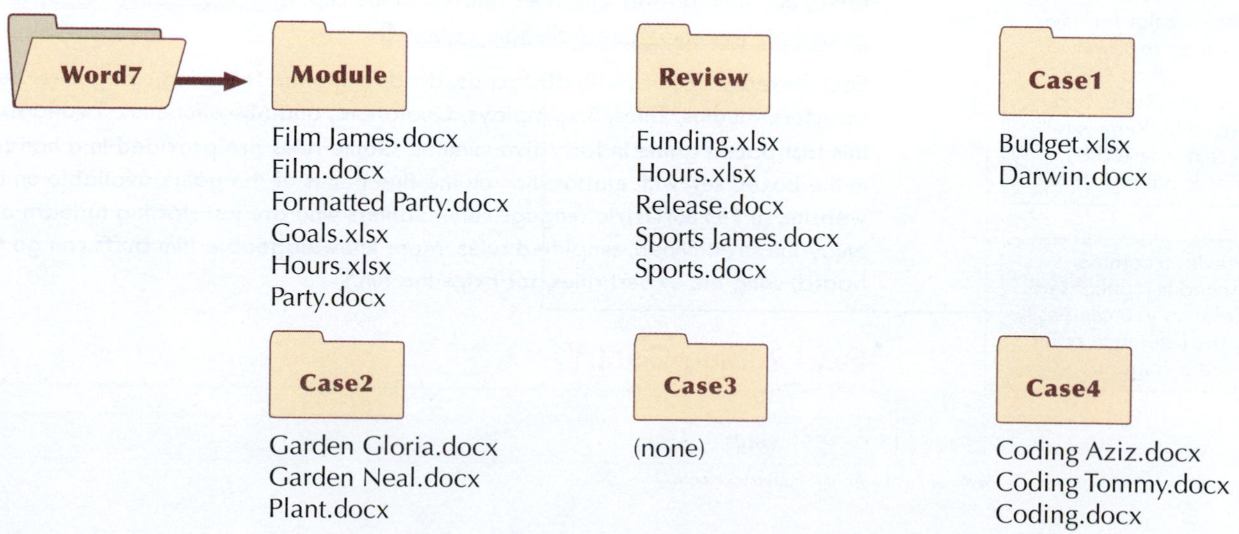

Session 7.1 Visual Overview:

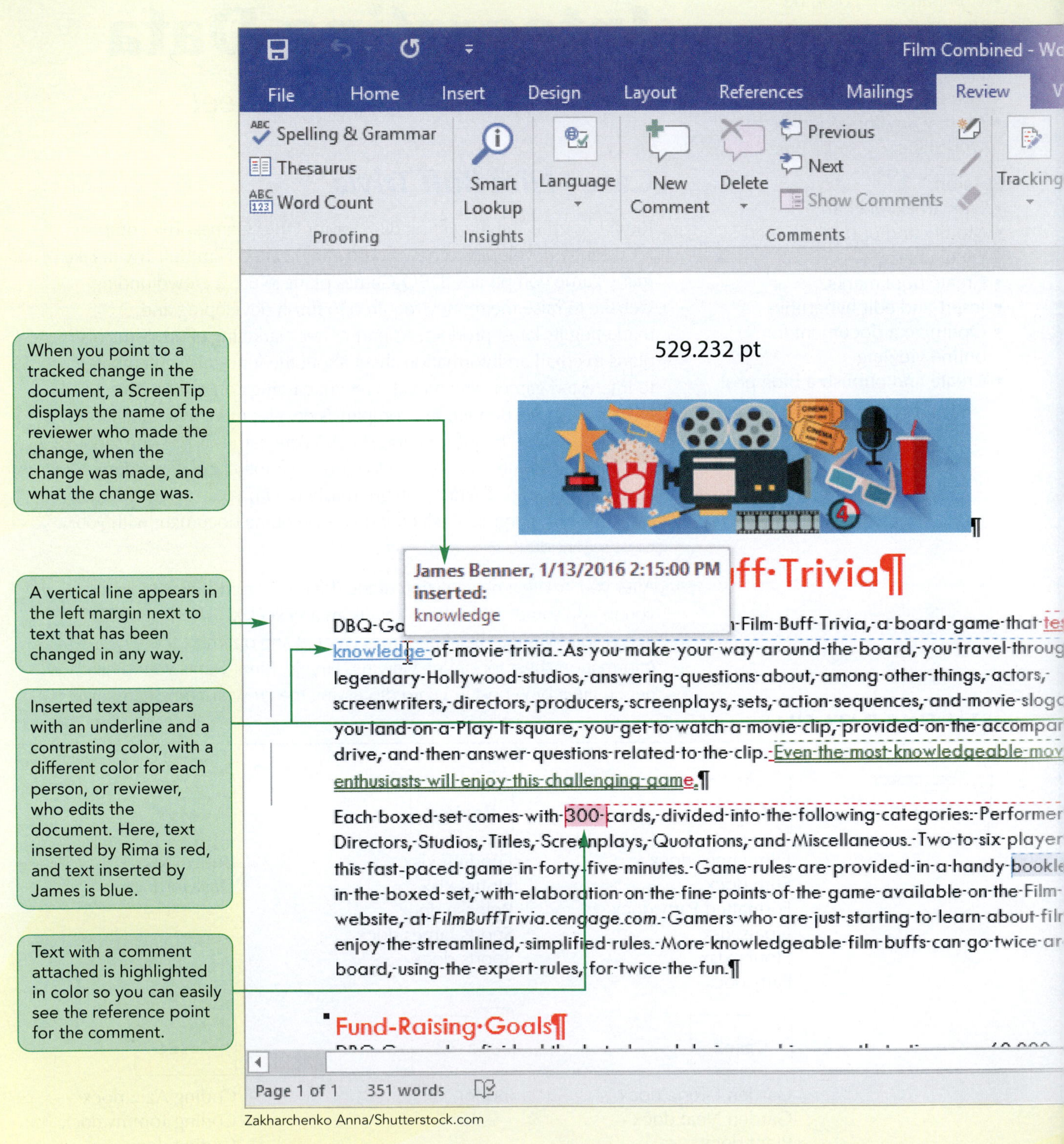

Film Combined - Wo
File
Home
Insert
Design
Layout
References
Mailings
Review
Spelling & Grammar
Thesaurus
Word Count
Proofing
Smart Lookup
Insights
Language
New Comment
Delete
Previous
Next
Show Comments
Comments
Tracking
529.232 pt
James Benner, 1/13/2016 2:15:00 PM
inserted:
knowledge
When you point to a tracked change in the document, a ScreenTip displays the name of the reviewer who made the change, when the change was made, and what the change was.
A vertical line appears in the left margin next to text that has been changed in any way.
Inserted text appears with an underline and a contrasting color, with a different color for each person, or reviewer, who edits the document. Here, text inserted by Rima is red, and text inserted by James is blue.
Text with a comment attached is highlighted in color so you can easily see the reference point for the comment.
Fund-Raising Goals
Page 1 of 1
351 words

Zakharchenko Anna/Shutterstock.com

Tracking Changes

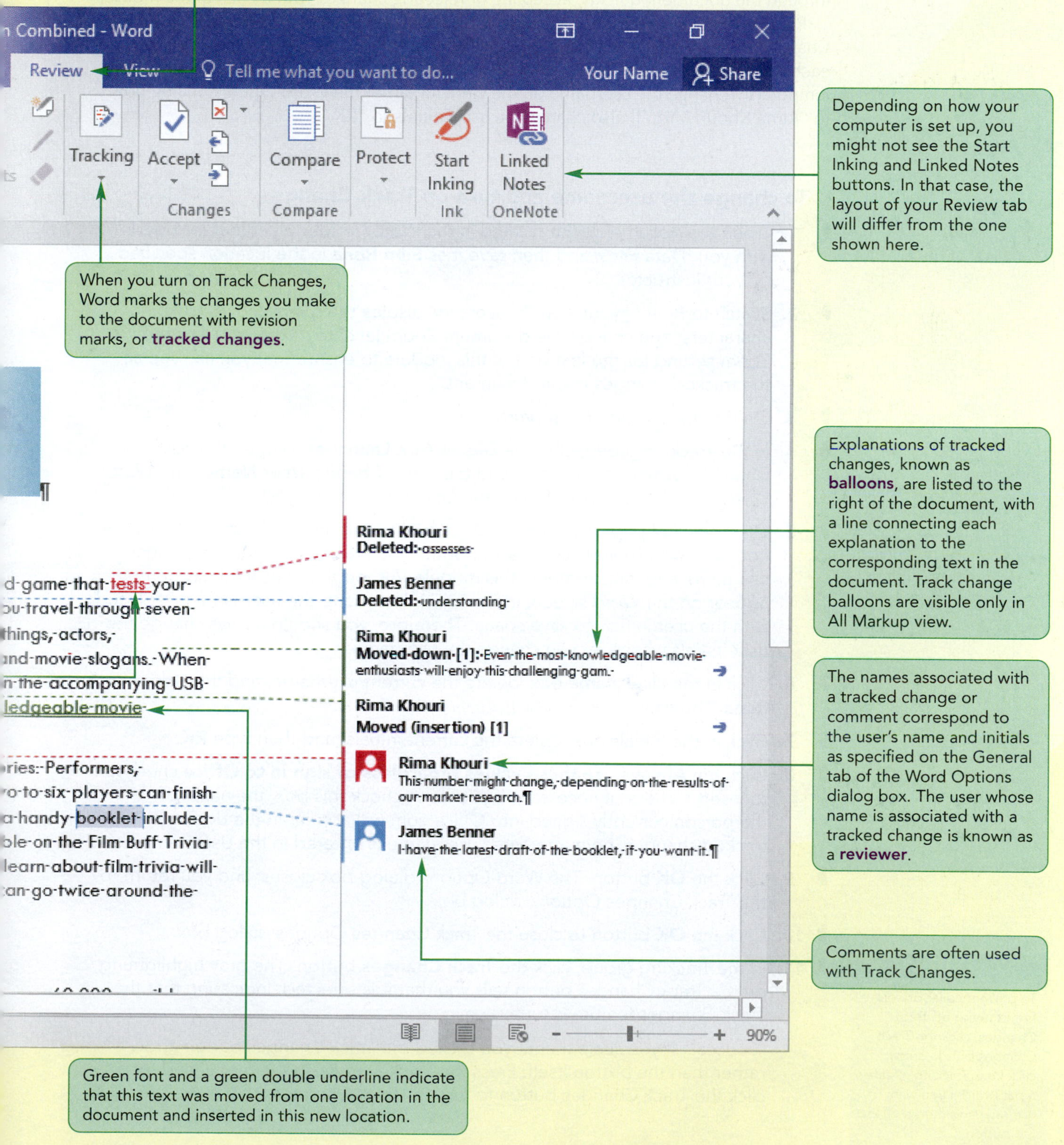

The Review tab contains all the options you need for editing a document using tracked changes and comments.
Depending on how your computer is set up, you might not see the Start Inking and Linked Notes buttons. In that case, the layout of your Review tab will differ from the one shown here.
When you turn on Track Changes, Word marks the changes you make to the document with revision marks, or tracked changes.
Explanations of tracked changes, known as balloons, are listed to the right of the document, with a line connecting each explanation to the corresponding text in the document. Track change balloons are visible only in All Markup view.
The names associated with a tracked change or comment correspond to the user's name and initials as specified on the General tab of the Word Options dialog box. The user whose name is associated with a tracked change is known as a reviewer.
Comments are often used with Track Changes.
Green font and a green double underline indicate that this text was moved from one location in the document and inserted in this new location.
Combined - Word
Review
View
Tell me what you want to do...
Your Name
Share
Tracking
Accept
Compare
Protect
Start Inking
Linked Notes
Changes
Compare
Ink
OneNote
Rima Khouri
Deleted: assesses
James Benner
Deleted: understanding
Rima Khouri
Moved down [1]: Even the most knowledgeable movie enthusiasts will enjoy this challenging gam.
Rima Khouri
Moved (insertion) [1]
Rima Khouri
This number might change, depending on the results of our market research.
James Benner
I have the latest draft of the booklet, if you want it.
90%

Editing a Document with Tracked Changes

The Track Changes feature in Word simulates the process of marking up a hard copy of a document with a colored pen, but offers many more advantages. Word keeps track of who makes each change, assigning a different color to each reviewer and providing ScreenTips indicating details of the change, such as the reviewer's name and the date and time the change was made. Using the buttons on the Review tab, you can move through the document quickly, accepting or rejecting changes with a click of the mouse.

Rima is ready to revise her first draft of the document. She asks you to turn on Track Changes before you make the edits for her. To ensure that her name is displayed for each tracked change, and that your screens match the figures in this module, you will temporarily change the username on the General tab of the Word Options dialog box to "Rima Khouri." You'll also change the user initials to "RK."

To change the username and turn on Track Changes:

1. Open the document **Film** located in the Word7 > Module folder included with your Data Files, and then save it as **Film Rima** in the location specified by your instructor.
2. Switch to Print Layout view if necessary, display the rulers and nonprinting characters, and change the document Zoom level to **110%**. You'll use this Zoom setting for the first part of this module to ensure that you can see all the tracked changes in the document.
3. On the ribbon, click the **Review** tab.
4. In the Tracking group, click the **Dialog Box Launcher** to open the Track Changes Options dialog box, and then click **Change User Name**. The Word Options dialog box opens, with the General tab displayed.
5. On a piece of paper, write down the current username and initials, if they are not your own, so you can refer to it when you need to restore the original username and initials later in this module. Although the user initials do not appear on the Word screen, in a printed document, the username is replaced with the user initials to save space. Therefore, you should always change the user initials whenever you change the username.
6. Click in the **User name** box, delete the current username, and then type **Rima Khouri**.
7. Click in the Initials box, delete the current initials, and then type **RK**.
8. Click the **Always use these values regardless of sign in to Office** checkbox to insert a check, if necessary. If you don't check this box, the name of the person currently signed into Office.com will appear in the document's tracked changes, no matter what user name is entered in the User name box.
9. Click the **OK** button. The Word Options dialog box closes, and you return to the Track Changes Options dialog box.
10. Click the **OK** button to close the Track Changes Options dialog box.
11. In the Tracking group, click the **Track Changes** button. The gray highlighting on the Track Changes button tells you that it is selected, indicating that the Track Changes feature is turned on.

    Trouble? If you see a menu, you clicked the Track Changes button arrow rather than the button itself. Press the Esc key to close the menu, and then click the Track Changes button to turn on Track Changes.

TIP

To prevent collaborators from turning off Track Changes, click the Track Changes button arrow, click Lock Tracking, create a password if you want to use one, and then click the OK button.

12. In the Tracking group, verify that the Display for Review box displays "All Markup." This setting ensures that tracked changes are displayed in the document as you edit it.

    Trouble? If the Display for Review box does not display "All Markup," click the Display for Review arrow, and then click All Markup.

13. In the Tracking group, click the **Show Markup** button, and then point to **Balloons**. See Figure 7-1.

Figure 7-1 Track Changes turned on

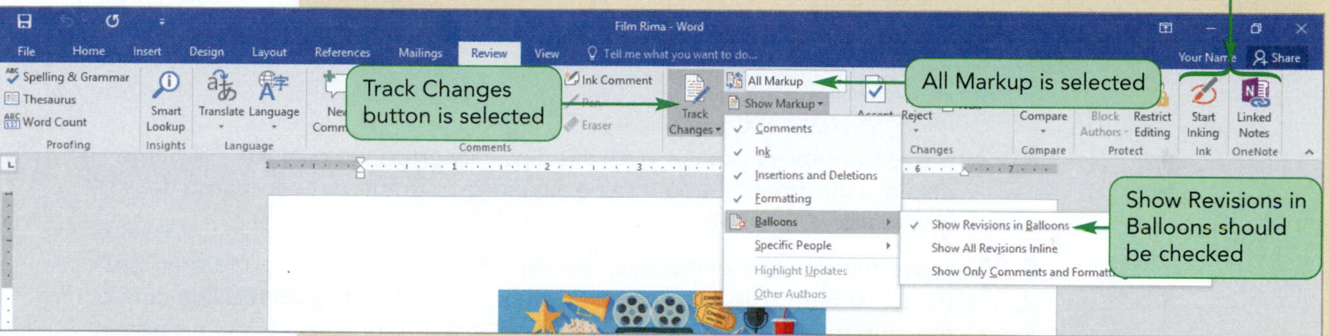

Zakharchenko Anna/Shutterstock.com

14. If you do not see a checkmark next to Show Revisions in Balloons, click **Show Revisions in Balloons** now to select it and close the menu. Otherwise, click anywhere in the document to close the menu.

Now that Track Changes is turned on, you can begin editing Rima's document. First, Rima needs to change the word "assesses" in the first sentence to "tests."

To edit Rima's document and view the tracked changes:

1. In the line below the "Film Buff Trivia" heading, select the word **assesses** and then type **tests**. The new word, "tests," is displayed in color, with an underline. A vertical line is displayed in the left margin, drawing attention to the change. To the right of the document, the username associated with the change (Rima Khouri) is displayed, along with an explanation of the change. See Figure 7-2.

Figure 7-2 Edit marked as tracked change

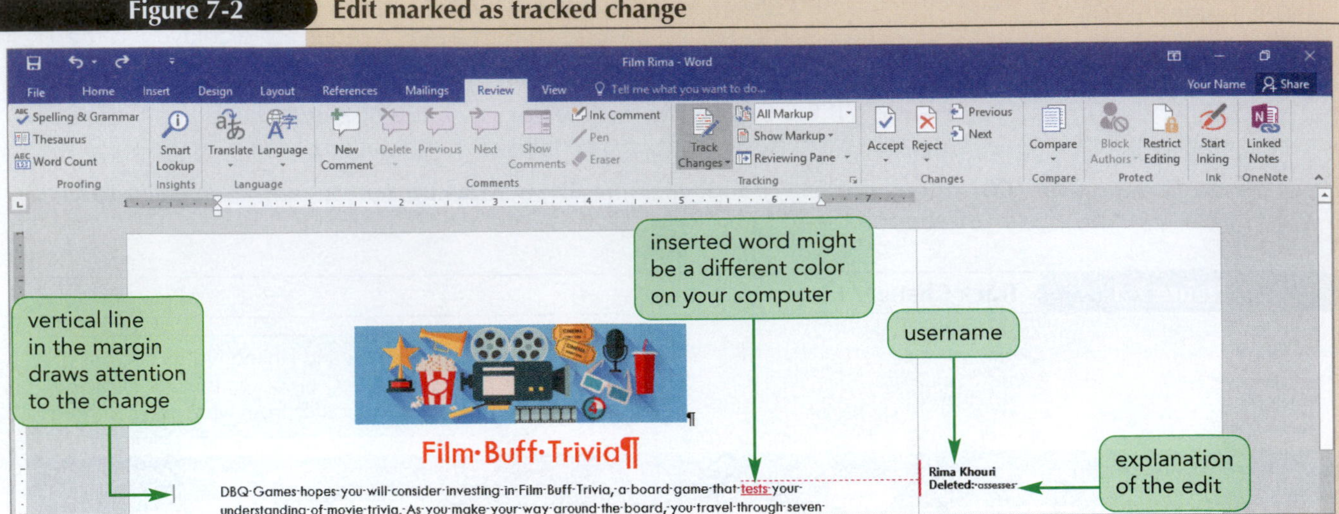

Zakharchenko Anna/Shutterstock.com

2. Move the mouse pointer over the newly inserted word "tests." A ScreenTip displays information about the edit, along with the date and time the edit was made.

3. Move the mouse pointer over the explanation of the change to the right of the document. The explanation is highlighted, and the dotted line connecting the change in the document to the explanation turns solid. In a document with many tracked changes, this makes it easier to see which explanation is associated with which tracked change.

   Next, Rima wants you to move the second-to-last sentence in this paragraph to the end of the paragraph.

4. Press the **Ctrl** key, and then click in the sentence that begins "Even the most knowledgeable…." The entire sentence is selected. Don't be concerned that the word "game," at the end of the sentence is misspelled. You'll correct that error shortly.

5. Drag the sentence to insert it at the end of the paragraph, and then click anywhere in the document to deselect it. See Figure 7-3.

Figure 7-3 Tracked changes showing text moved to a new location

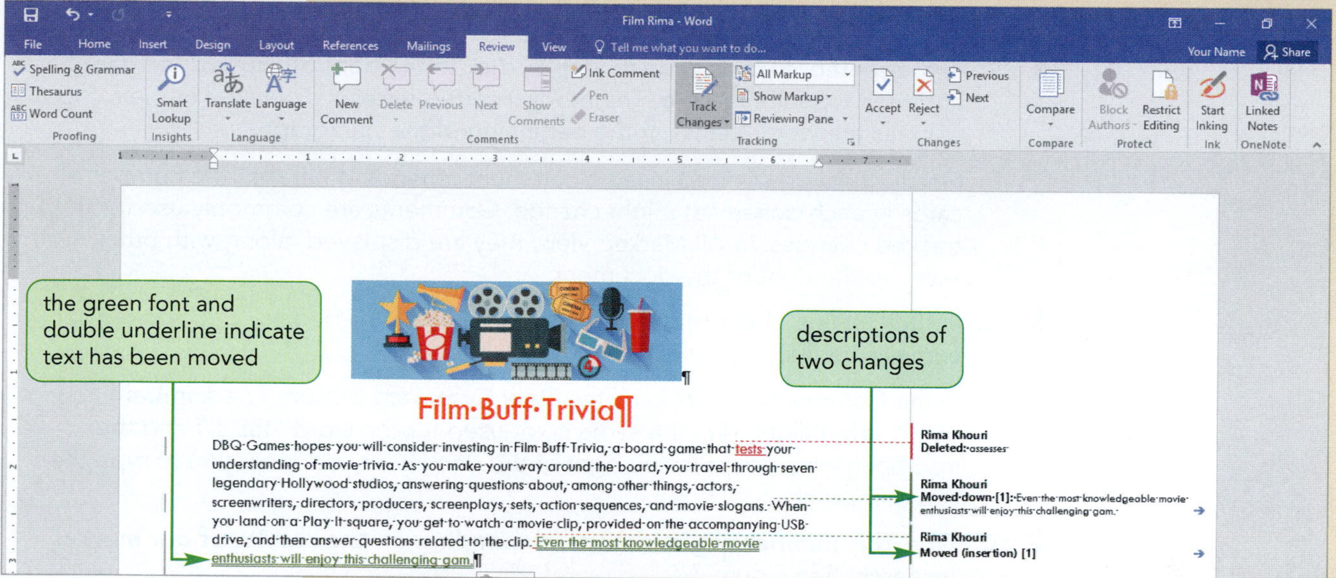

Zakharchenko Anna/Shutterstock.com

The sentence is inserted with a double underline in green, which is the color Word uses to denote moved text. Word also inserts a space before the inserted sentence and marks the nonprinting space character as a tracked change. A vertical bar in the left margin draws attention to the moved text.

To the right of the document, descriptions of two new changes are displayed. The "Moved down [1]" change shows the text of the sentence that was moved. The "Moved (insertion) [1]" change draws attention to the sentence in its new location at the end of the paragraph.

A blue, right-facing arrow next to a tracked change explanation indicates that the change is related to another change. You can click the arrow to select the related change.

6. Next to the "Moved (insertion) [1]" change, click the blue, right-facing arrow ➔ to select the moved sentence in the "Moved down [1]" balloon. See Figure 7-4.

Figure 7-4 Selecting a related change

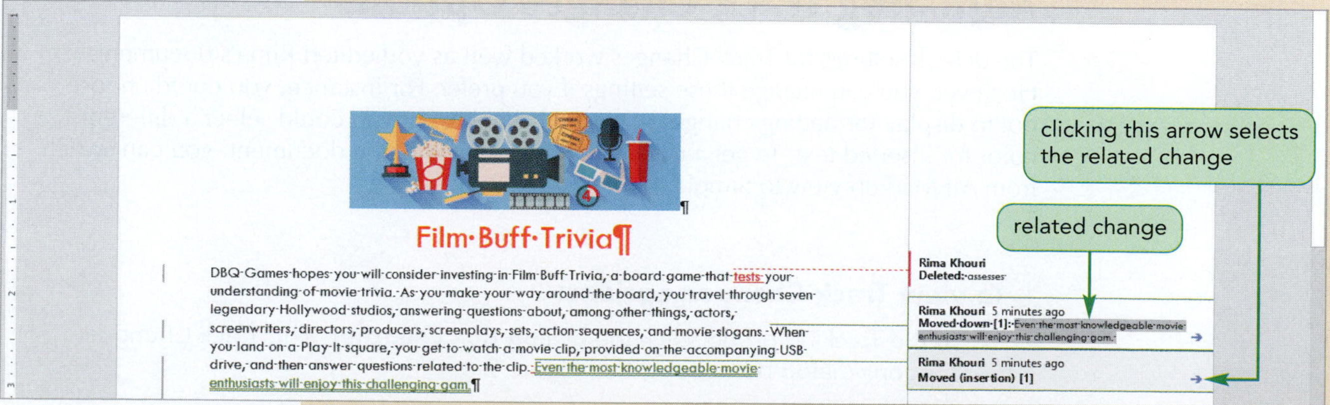

Zakharchenko Anna/Shutterstock.com

After reviewing the sentence in its new location at the end of the paragraph, Rima notices that she needs to add an "e" to the last word in the sentence so that it reads "...this challenging game."

7. In the sentence you moved in Step 5, click to the right of the "m" in "gam," and then type the letter **e**. The newly inserted letter is displayed in the same color as the word "tests" at the beginning of the paragraph.

Finally, Rima asks you to insert a comment reminding her that the number of cards in each boxed set might change. Comments are commonly used with tracked changes. In All Markup view, they are displayed, along with other edits, to the right of the document.

8. In the first line of the second main paragraph (which begins "Each boxed set comes with 300..."), select the number **300**.
9. In the Comments group, click the **New Comment** button. The number "300" is highlighted in the same color used for the word "tests," and the insertion point moves to the right of the document, ready for you to type the comment text.
10. Type **This number might change, depending on the results of our market research.** See Figure 7-5.

Figure 7-5 Comment added to document

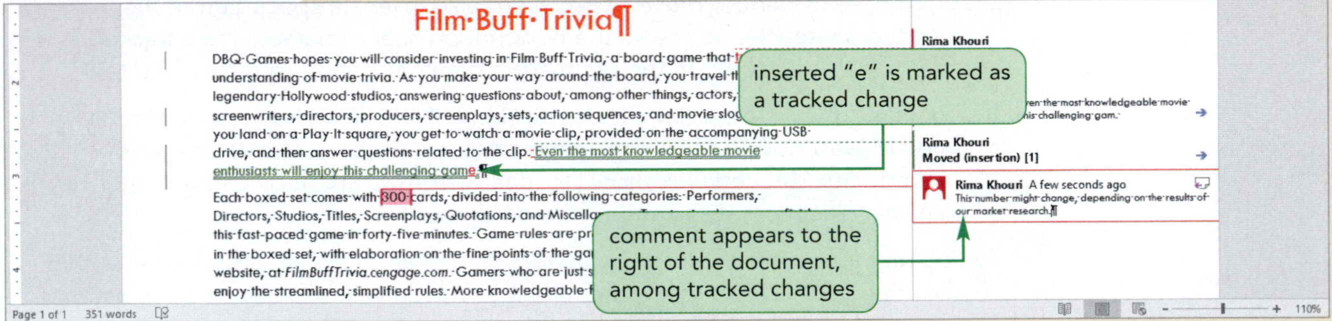

11. Save your document.

Adjusting Track Changes Options

The default settings for Track Changes worked well as you edited Rima's document. However, you can change these settings if you prefer. For instance, you could choose not to display formatting changes as tracked changes, or you could select a different color for inserted text. To get a more streamlined view of the document, you can switch from All Markup view to Simple Markup view.

To view Track Changes options:

1. In the Tracking group, click the **Dialog Box Launcher**. The Track Changes Options dialog box opens. See Figure 7-6.

Figure 7-6 **Track Changes Options dialog box**

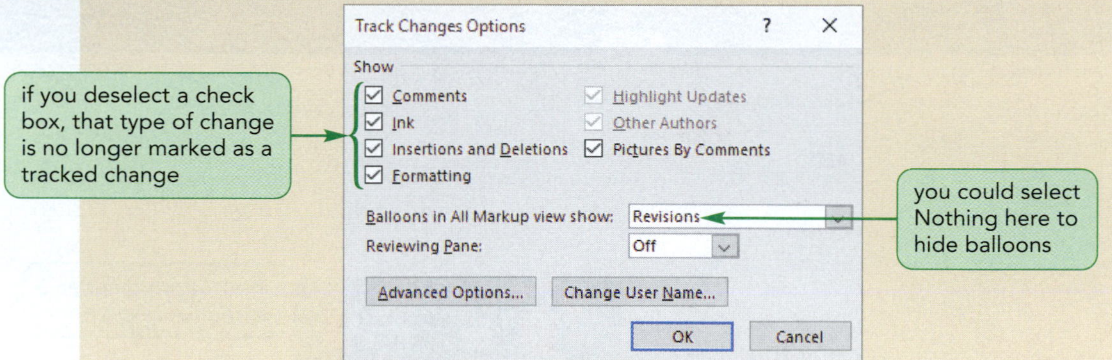

The check boxes in the Show section control which types of edits are marked as tracked changes. For example, the Formatting check box is currently selected. If you didn't want formatting changes to be marked as tracked changes, you could deselect the Formatting check box. Note that Revisions is currently selected in the "Balloons in All Markup view show" box. To turn off the balloon feature, so that no track changes or comment balloons are displayed to the right of the document in All Markup view, you could select Nothing instead.

2. Click **Advanced Options**. The Advanced Track Changes Options dialog box opens.

   The options in this dialog box allow you to select the colors you want to use for various types of edits. For example, you can use the Color box next to the Insertions box to select a color to use for inserted text. Note that the default setting for Insertions, Deletions, Comments, and Formatting is By author. This means that Word assigns one color to each person who edits the document. When you are working with multiple reviewers, you should always retain the By author settings to ensure that you can easily distinguish the edits made by each reviewer.

3. Click the **Cancel** button to close the Advanced Track Changes Options dialog box, and then click the **Cancel** button to close the Track Changes Options dialog box.

After reviewing the tracked changes with you, Rima decides the number of details shown in All Markup view makes the document too difficult to read. She wants you to switch to Simple Markup view instead.

To switch to Simple Markup view:

1. In the Tracking group, click the **Display for Review** arrow, and then click **Simple Markup**. See Figure 7-7.

Figure 7-7 Simple Markup view

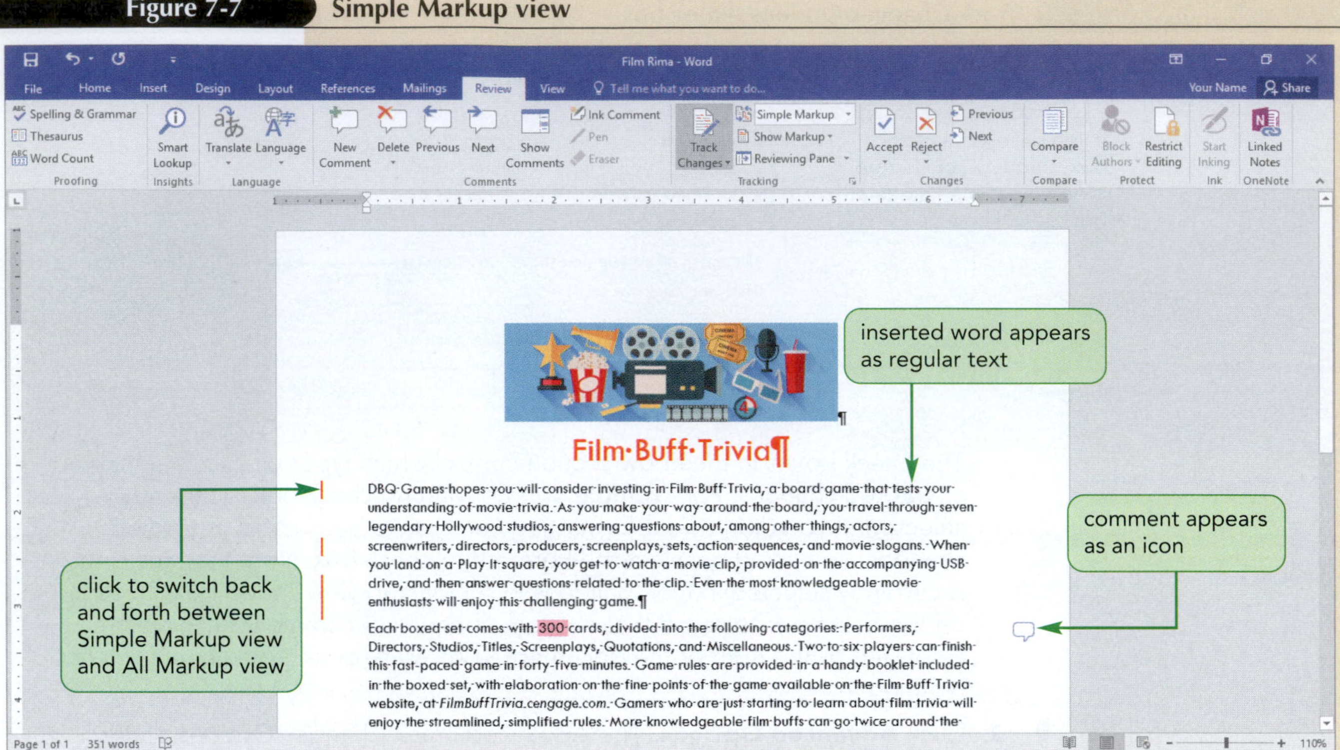

Zakharchenko Anna/Shutterstock.com

Trouble? If the comment balloon is still visible on your screen, click the Show Comments button in the Comments group on the Review tab to deselect it.

All of the tracked changes in the document are now hidden, and the comment balloon is replaced with an icon in the right margin. The inserted word "tests" is in black font, like the surrounding text, as is the sentence you moved to the end of the paragraph. The only signs that the document contains tracked changes is the red vertical bar in the left margin. You can click a vertical bar to switch back and forth between Simple Markup view and All Markup view.

2. Click the red vertical bar to the left of the paragraph that begins "DBQ Games hopes...." The document switches to All Markup view, with all the tracked changes and the comment visible. The vertical bar in the left margin changes from red to gray.

3. Click the gray vertical bar to the left of the paragraph that begins "DBQ Games hopes...." The document switches back to Simple Markup view.

Rima has received James's edited copy of the first draft via email, and now she'd like your help in combining her edited copy of the Film Rima document with James's copy.

Comparing and Combining Documents

When you work in a collaborative environment with multiple people contributing to the same document, Word's Compare and Combine features are essential tools. They allow you to see the difference between multiple versions of a document, with tracked changes highlighting the differences. The Compare and Combine features are similar, but they have different purposes.

The **Compare** feature, which is designed to help you quickly spot the differences between two copies of a document, is intended for documents that do not contain tracked changes. In a compared document, differences between the revised document and the original document are marked with tracked changes, with all the tracked changes assigned to the username associated with the revised document.

The **Combine** feature, which is designed for documents that do contain tracked changes, allows you to see which reviewers made which changes. In a combined document, each reviewer's tracked changes are displayed, with each tracked change assigned to the reviewer who made that change. The Combine feature works well when you want to combine, or **merge**, two documents to create a third, combined document, with which you can then combine additional documents, until you have incorporated all the tracked changes from all your reviewers. Because the Combine feature allows you to incorporate more than two documents into one, it's the option you'll use most when collaborating with a group.

When you compare or combine documents, you select one document as the original and one as the revised document. Together, these two documents are known as the **source documents**. By default, Word then creates a new, third document, which consists of the original document's text edited with tracked changes to show how the revised document differs. The source documents themselves are left unchanged. If Word detects a formatting conflict—that is, if identical text is formatted differently in the source documents—Word displays a dialog box allowing you to choose which formatting you want to keep. You can choose to keep the formatting of the original document or the revised document, but not both. Occasionally, Word will display this formatting conflict dialog box even if both source documents are formatted exactly the same. If so, keep the formatting for the original document, and continue with the process of combining the documents.

REFERENCE

Comparing and Combining Documents

- On the ribbon, click the Review tab.
- In the Compare group, click the Compare button.
- Click Compare to open the Compare Documents dialog box, or click Combine to open the Combine Documents dialog box.
- Next to the Original document box, click the Browse button, navigate to the location of the document, select the document, and then click the Open button.
- Next to the Revised document box, click the Browse button, navigate to the location of the document, select the document, and then click the Open button.
- Click the More button, if necessary, to display options that allow you to select which items you want marked with tracked changes, and then make any necessary changes.
- Click the OK button.

When you start combining or comparing documents, it's not necessary to have either the original document or the revised document open. In this case, however, the Film Rima document, which you will use as the original document, is open. You'll combine this document with James's edited copy.

To combine Rima's document with James's document:

1. Make sure you have saved your changes to the Film Rima document.
2. In the Compare group, click the **Compare** button. A menu opens with options for comparing or combining two versions of a document.
3. Click **Combine**. The Combine Documents dialog box opens.

4. Click the **More** button. The dialog box expands to display check boxes, which you can use to specify the items you want marked with tracked changes.

Trouble? If the dialog box has a Less button instead of a More button, the dialog box is already expanded to show the check boxes for selecting additional options. In this case, skip Step 4.

In the Show changes section at the bottom of the dialog box, the New document option button is selected by default, indicating that Word will create a new, combined document rather than importing the tracked changes from the original document into the revised document, or vice versa.

Now you need to specify the Film Rima document as the original document. Even though this document is currently open, you still need to select it.

5. Next to the Original document box, click the **Browse** button to open the Open dialog box.
6. If necessary, navigate to the location where you saved the Film Rima document, click **Film Rima** in the file list, and then click the **Open** button. You return to the Combine Documents dialog box, where the filename "Film Rima" is displayed in the Original document box.

Next, you need to select the document you want to use as the revised document.

7. Next to the Revised document box, click the **Browse** button, navigate to the Word7 > Module folder included with your Data Files if necessary, select the document **Film James**, and then click the **Open** button. The filename "Film James" is displayed in the Revised document box. See Figure 7-8.

Figure 7-8 Selecting the original and revised documents

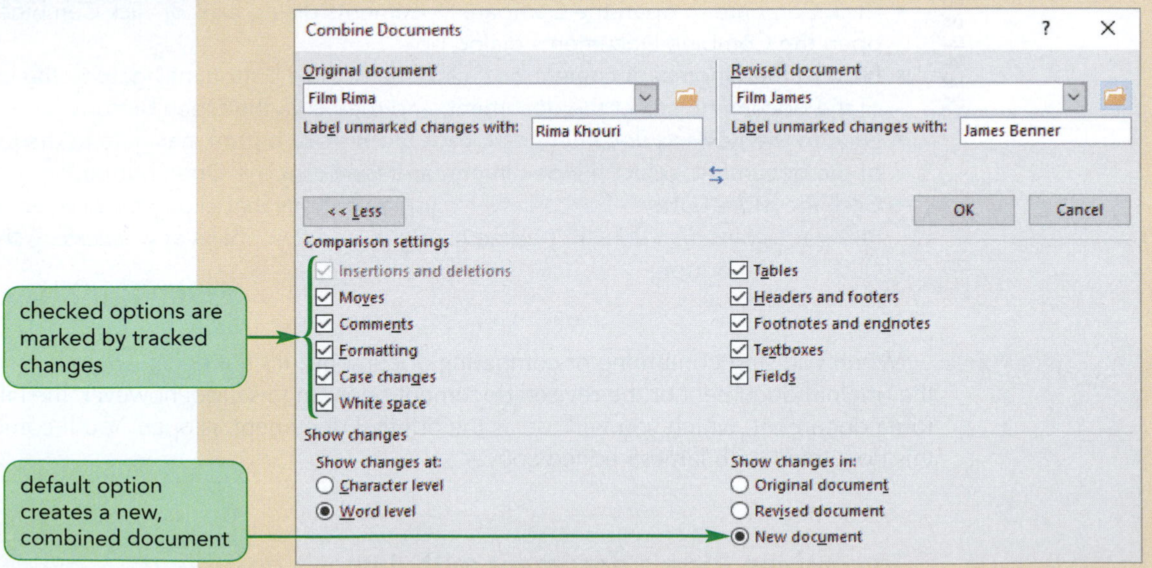

TIP

If you need to compare or combine a series of documents, use the Spelling and Grammar checker to look for errors resulting from missing spaces or misplaced letters in the final document.

8. Click the **OK** button. The Combine Documents dialog box closes.

   A new document opens. It contains the tracked changes from both the original document and the revised document.

   At this point, depending on the previous settings on your computer, you might see only the new, combined document, or you might also see the original and revised documents open in separate windows. You might also see the Reviewing pane, which includes a summary of the number of revisions in the combined document along with a list of all the changes, as shown in Figure 7-9.

Figure 7-9 Two documents combined

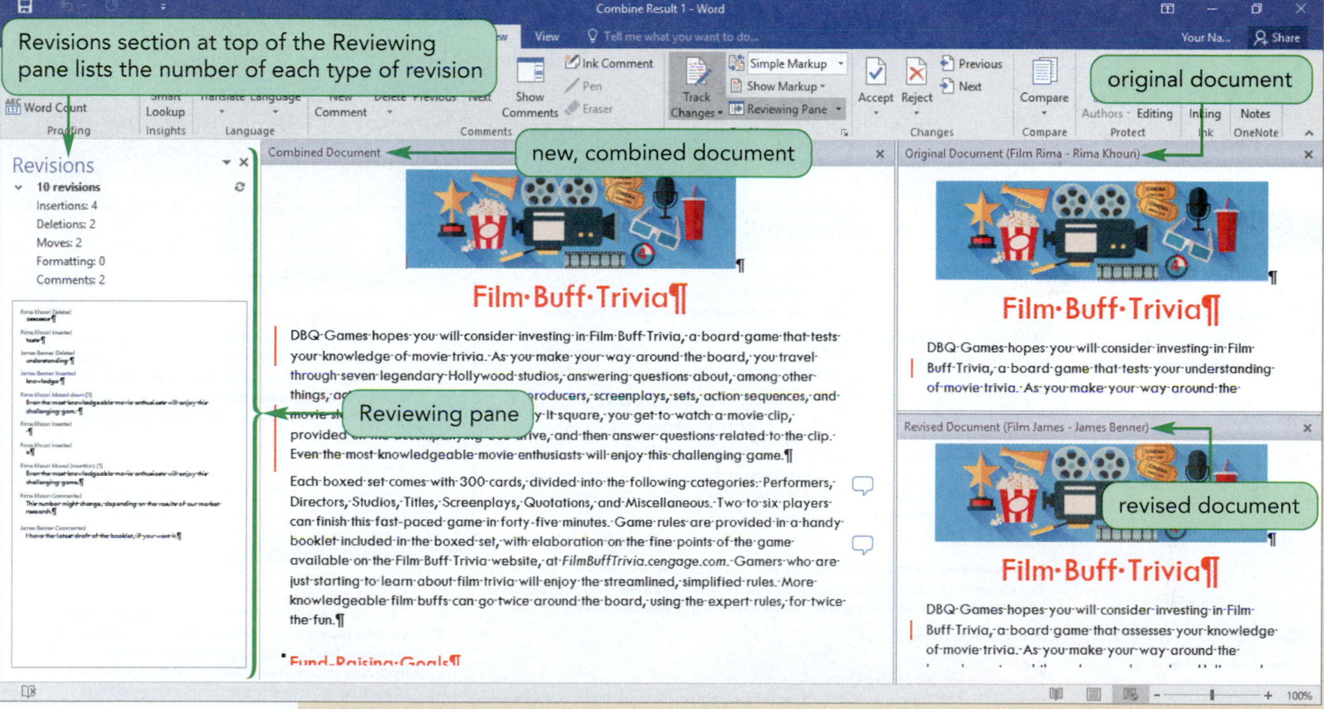

Zakharchenko Anna/Shutterstock.com

   Note that your combined document might have a different name than shown in Figure 7-9. For instance, it might be named "Document 1," instead of "Combine Result 1."

9. In the Compare group, click the **Compare** button, and then point to **Show Source Documents.**

10. If a checkmark appears next to Show Both, press the **Esc** key twice to close both menus; otherwise, click **Show Both.** Your screen should now match Figure 7-9.

    Trouble? If the Reviewing pane is still not displayed, click the Reviewing Pane button in the Tracking group to display the Reviewing pane.

    Trouble? If your Reviewing pane is displayed horizontally rather than vertically, as shown in Figure 7-9, click the Reviewing Pane button arrow in the Tracking group, and then click Reviewing Pane Vertical.

Note that the combined document and the two source documents are all displayed in Simple Markup. Also, instead of Print Layout view, which you typically use when working on documents, the three documents are displayed in Web Layout view. You'll learn more about Web Layout view later in this module. For now, all you need to know is that in Web Layout view, the line breaks change to suit the size of the document window, making it easier to read text in the small windows.

It's helpful to have the source documents displayed when you want to quickly compare the two documents. For example, right now Rima wants to scroll down the documents to see how they differ. When you scroll up or down in the Revised Document pane, the other documents scroll as well.

To scroll the document panes simultaneously:

1. Move the mouse pointer over the Revised Document (Film James - James Benner) pane to display its scroll bar, and then drag the scroll bar down to display the "Fund-Raising Goals" heading. The text in the Combined Document pane and in the Original Document (Film Rima - Rima Khouri) pane scrolls down to match the text in the Revised Document (Film James - James Benner) pane. See Figure 7-10.

Figure 7-10 Document panes scrolled to compare versions

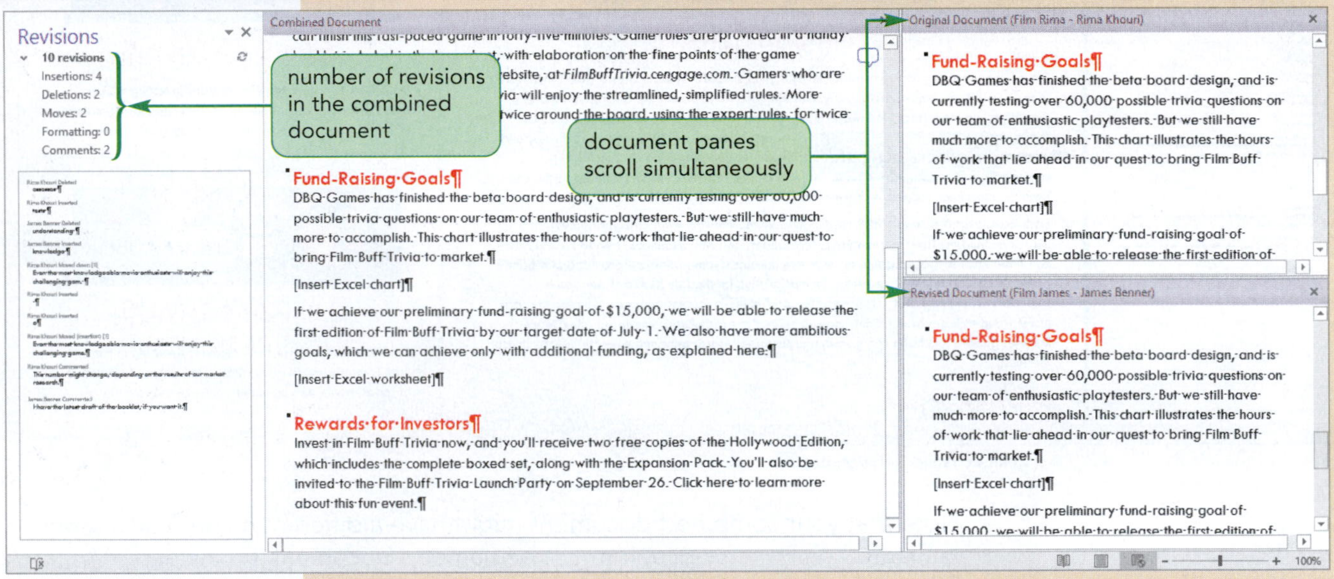

number of revisions in the combined document

document panes scroll simultaneously

Now that you've reviewed both documents, you can hide the source documents to make the combined document easier to read. After you hide the source documents, you can review the edits in the Reviewing pane.

To hide the source documents and review the edits in the Reviewing pane:

1. In the Compare group, click the **Compare** button, point to the **Show Source Documents** button, and then click **Hide Source Documents**. The panes displaying the original and revised documents close, and the combined document window switches to Print Layout view. Next, you will change the Zoom setting in the Reviewing pane to make its contents easier to read.

Trouble? If the combined window does not switch to Print Layout view, click the Print Layout view button on the status bar.

2. Click anywhere in the list of edits in the Reviewing pane, and then change the Zoom setting in the status bar to **100%**, if necessary.

TIP

To hide a reviewer's edits, click the Show Markup button in the Tracking group, point to Specific People, and then click the person's name.

3. Move the mouse pointer over the list of edits in the Reviewing pane to display the vertical scroll bar, and then scroll down and review the list of edits. Notice that the document contains the edits you made earlier (under Rima's name) as well as edits made by James Benner.

   Rima prefers to review changes using All Markup view instead of the Reviewing pane.

4. In the Tracking group, click the **Reviewing Pane** button to deselect it. The Reviewing pane closes.
5. In the Tracking group, click the **Display for Review** arrow, and then click **All Markup**.
6. In the Tracking group, click the **Show Markup** arrow, point to Balloons, and then make sure **Show Revisions in Balloons** is selected.
7. Save the document as **Film Combined** in the location specified by your instructor.
8. In the Tracking group, click the **Track Changes** button to turn off Track Changes. This ensures that you won't accidentally add any additional edit marks as you review the document.
9. Change the Zoom level to **120%**.

INSIGHT

Using Real-Time Co-Authoring to Collaborate with Others

Combining documents is a powerful way to incorporate the work of multiple people in one document. The only drawback to combining documents is that, typically, one person is charged with combining the documents, reviewing the tracked changes, and then making decisions about what to keep and what to delete. In some situations, it's more effective to give all team members the freedom to edit a document at the same time, with every person's changes showing up on everyone else's screen. You can accomplish this by saving a document to OneDrive and then sharing it using Word's co-authoring feature.

To get started, click Share in the upper-right corner of the Word window to open the Share pane, click Save to Cloud, and then save the document to OneDrive. Next, use the options in the Share pane to either: 1) share the document with specific people, in which case Microsoft will send an email to the people you specified, inviting them to work on the document; or 2) create a sharing link, which you can then email to your collaborators, and which they can then click to open the document in Office 365, the online version of Microsoft Office. After a delay of a few minutes or less, you and all of your collaborators can begin editing the document, while being able to see everyone else's changes to the document in real time.

Next, you will review the edits in the Film Combined document to accept and reject the changes as appropriate.

Accepting and Rejecting Changes

The document you just created contains all the edits from two different reviewers—Rima's changes made in the original document, and James's changes as they appeared in the revised document. In the combined document, each reviewer's edits are displayed in a different color, making it easy to see which reviewer made each change.

When you review tracked changes in a document, the best approach is to move the insertion point to the beginning of the document, and then navigate through the document one change at a time using the Next and Previous buttons in the Changes group on the Review tab. This ensures you won't miss any edits. As you review a tracked change, you can either accept the change or reject it.

REFERENCE

Accepting and Rejecting Changes

- Move the insertion point to the beginning of the document.
- On the ribbon, click the Review tab.
- In the Changes group, click the Next button to select the first edit or comment in the document.
- To accept a selected change, click the Accept button in the Changes group.
- To reject a selected change, click the Reject button in the Changes group.
- To accept all the changes in the document, click the Accept button arrow, and then click Accept All Changes.
- To reject all the changes in the document, click the Reject button arrow, and then click Reject All Changes.

To accept and reject changes in the Film Combined document:

1. Press the **Ctrl+Home** keys to move the insertion point to the beginning of the document.
2. In the Changes group, click the **Next** button. To the right of the document, in a tracked change balloon, the deleted word "assesses" is selected, as shown in Figure 7-11.

Figure 7-11 **First change in document selected**

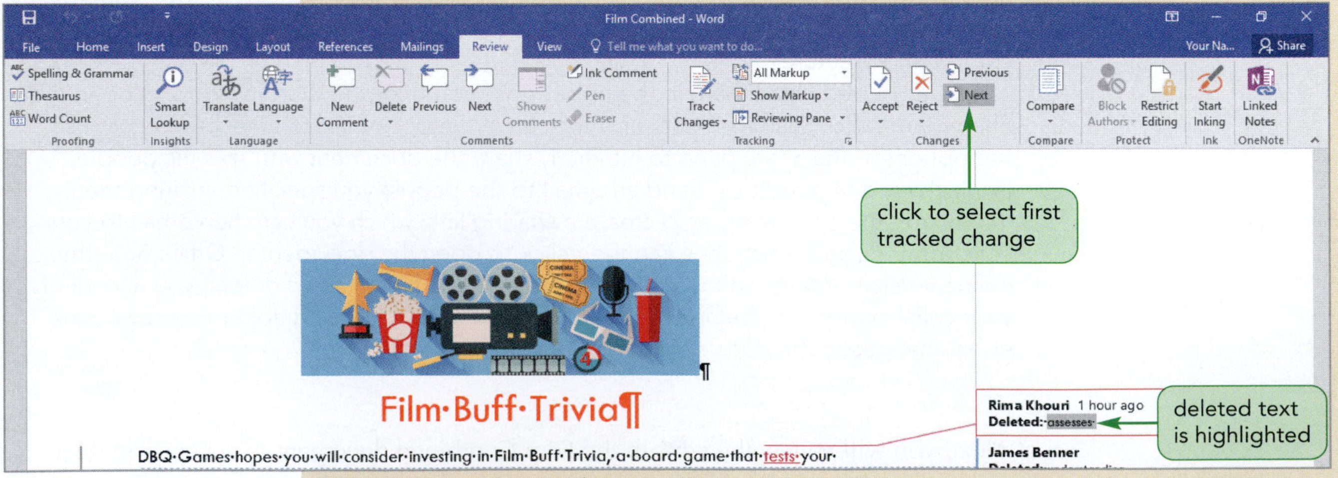

Zakharchenko Anna/Shutterstock.com

Trouble? If the insertion point moves to Rima's comment, you clicked the Next button in the Comments group instead of the Next button in the Changes group. Repeat Steps 1 and 2.

3. In the Changes group, click the **Accept** button. The tracked change balloon is no longer displayed, indicating that the change has been accepted. The inserted word "tests" is now selected in the document.

   Trouble? If you see a menu below the Accept button, you clicked the Accept button arrow by mistake. Press the Esc key to close the menu, and then click the Accept button.

4. Click the **Accept** button. In a tracked change balloon to the right of the document, James's deletion of the word "understanding" is selected. See Figure 7-12.

Figure 7-12 Reviewing James's changes

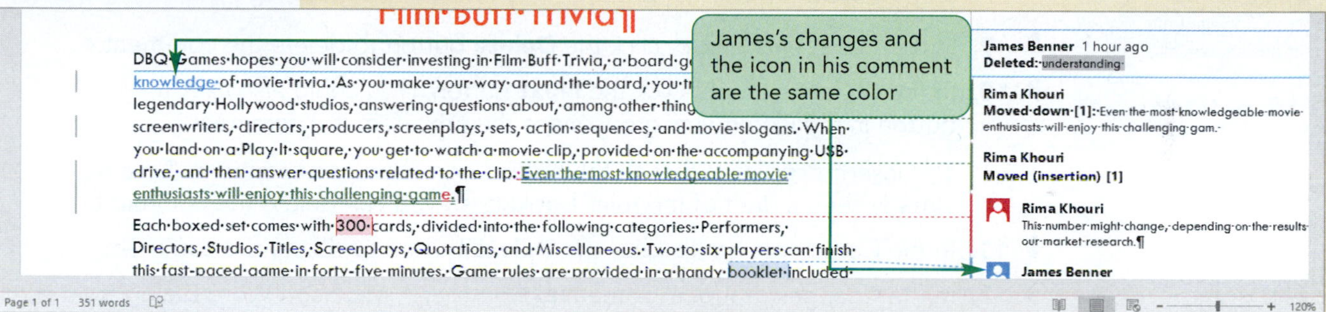

James deleted the word "understanding" and replaced it with the word "knowledge," which is displayed in the document as a tracked change. The inserted word, the tracked change balloon for the deleted word, and the icon in James's comment are all the same color.

Because the word "knowledgeable" is used later in this same paragraph, Rima prefers to keep the original word, "understanding," so you need to reject James's change.

5. In the Changes group, click the **Reject** button to reject the deletion of the word "understanding." The tracked change balloon is no longer displayed, and the word "understanding" is restored in the document, to the left of the inserted word "knowledge," which is now selected. See Figure 7-13.

Figure 7-13 Document after rejecting change

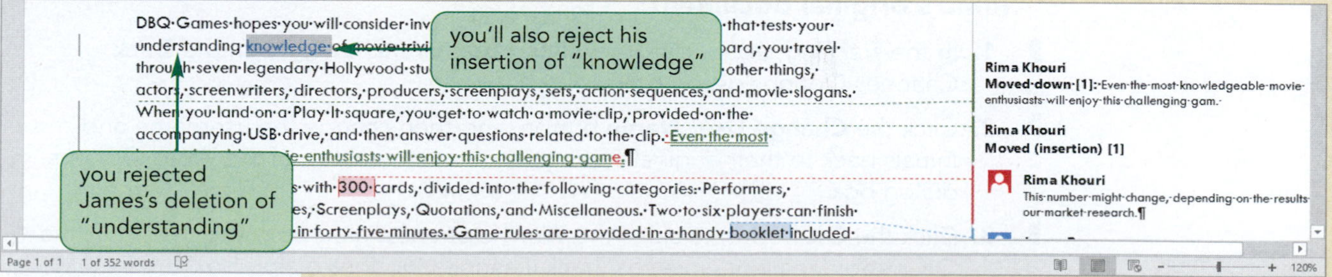

Next, you need to reject the insertion of the word "knowledge."

6. Click the **Reject** button. The inserted word "knowledge" is removed from the document. To the right of the document, in a tracked change balloon, the sentence that you moved is now selected.
7. Click the **Accept** button. The tracked change balloon containing the moved sentence and the related "Moved (insertion) [1]" tracked change balloon are no longer displayed. In the document, the sentence itself is displayed in black, like the surrounding text, indicating that the change has been accepted. Now the space before the moved sentence, which Word automatically inserted when you moved the sentence, is selected.
8. Click the **Accept** button to accept the insertion of the space, and then click the **Accept** button again to accept the insertion of the letter "e" at the end of "gam."

   The insertion point moves to the beginning of Rima's comment. Rima has received final confirmation that 300 is indeed the correct number of cards, so you can delete the comment.

TIP

To accept all changes currently displayed (not necessarily all the changes in the document), click the Accept button arrow, and click Accept All Changes Shown. To reject all changes shown, click the Reject button arrow, and click Reject All Changes Shown.

9. In the Comments group, click the **Delete** button to delete the comment.
10. In the Changes group, click the **Next** button. (You could also click the Next button in the Comments group since the next item is a comment.)

    The insertion point moves to the beginning of James's comment. Rima has already seen a draft of the rules booklet, so you can delete the comment.
11. In the Comments group, click the **Delete** button to delete the comment.
12. In the Changes group, click the **Next** button. A Microsoft Word dialog box opens with a message indicating that there are no more comments or tracked changes in the document.
13. Click the **OK** button to close the dialog box.
14. At the end of the last paragraph in the document, click to the left of the period, and type **, or contact *your name***, where *your name* is your first and last name. When you are finished, the text should read "about this fun event, or contact *your name*."

Now that you have finished editing and reviewing the document with tracked changes, you need to restore the original username and initials settings. Then you can close Rima's original document, which you no longer need.

To restore the original username and initials settings and close Rima's original document:

1. In the Tracking group, click the **Dialog Box Launcher** to open the Track Changes Options dialog box.
2. Click the **Change User Name** button, and then change the username and initials back to their original settings on the General tab of the Word Options dialog box.
3. Click the **OK** button to close the Word Options dialog box, and then click the **OK** button again to close the Track Changes Options dialog box.
4. On the taskbar, click the **Word** button, and then click the **Film Rima - Word** thumbnail to display the document.
5. Close the **Film Rima** document.

6. Save the **Film Combined** document, and then display the rulers.
7. On the ribbon, click the **Home** tab.

INSIGHT

Checking for Tracked Changes

Once a document is finished, you should make sure it does not contain any tracked changes or comments. This is especially important in situations where comments or tracked changes might reveal sensitive information that could jeopardize your privacy or the privacy of the organization you work for.

You can't always tell if a document contains comments or tracked changes just by looking at it because the comments or changes for some or all of the reviewers might be hidden. Also, the Display for Review box in the Tracking group on the Review tab might be set to No Markup, in which case all tracked changes would be hidden. To determine whether a document contains any tracked changes or comments, open the Reviewing pane and verify that the number of revisions for each type is 0. You can also use the Document Inspector to check for a variety of issues, including leftover comments and tracked changes. To use the Document Inspector, click the File tab, click Info, click Check for Issues, click Inspect Document, and then click the Inspect button.

Now that you have combined James's edits with Rima's, you are ready to add the Excel worksheet data and the pie chart to the document.

Embedding and Linking Objects from Other Programs

The programs in Office 2016 are designed to accomplish specific tasks. As you've seen with Word, you can use a word-processing program to create, edit, and format documents such as letters, reports, newsletters, and proposals. On the other hand, Microsoft Excel, a **spreadsheet program**, allows you to organize, calculate, and analyze numerical data in a grid of rows and columns and to illustrate data in the form of charts. A spreadsheet created in Microsoft Excel is known as a **worksheet**. Each Excel file—called a **workbook**—can contain multiple worksheets. Throughout this module, a portion of an Excel worksheet is referred to as a **worksheet object**, and a chart is referred to as a **chart object**.

Sometimes it is useful to combine information created in the different Office programs into one file. For her document, Rima wants to use fund-raising goals from an Excel worksheet. She also wants to include an Excel chart that shows the hours of work remaining on the project. You can incorporate the Excel data and chart into Rima's Word document by taking advantage of **object linking and embedding**, or **OLE**, a technology that allows you to share information among the Office programs. This process is commonly referred to as **integration**.

Before you start using OLE, you need to understand some important terms. Recall that in Word, an object is anything that can be selected and modified as a whole, such as a table, picture, or block of text. Another important term, **source program**, refers to the program used to create the original version of an object. The program into which the object is integrated is called the **destination program**. Similarly, the original file that contains the object you are integrating is called the **source file**, and the file into which you integrate the object is called the **destination file**.

You can integrate objects by either embedding or linking. **Embedding** is a technique that allows you to insert a copy of an object into a destination document. You can double-click an embedded object in the destination document to access the tools of the source program, allowing you to edit the object within the destination document using the source program's tools. Because the embedded object is a copy, any changes you make to it are not reflected in the original source file and vice versa. For instance, you could embed data from a worksheet named Itemized Expenses into a Word document named Travel Report. Later, if you change the Itemized Expenses file, those revisions would not be reflected in the Travel Report document. The opposite is also true; if you edit the embedded object from within the Travel Report file, those changes will not be reflected in the source file Itemized Expenses. The embedded object retains no connection to the source file.

Figure 7-14 illustrates the relationship between an embedded Excel worksheet object in Rima's Word document and the source file.

Figure 7-14 **Embedding an Excel worksheet object in a Word document**

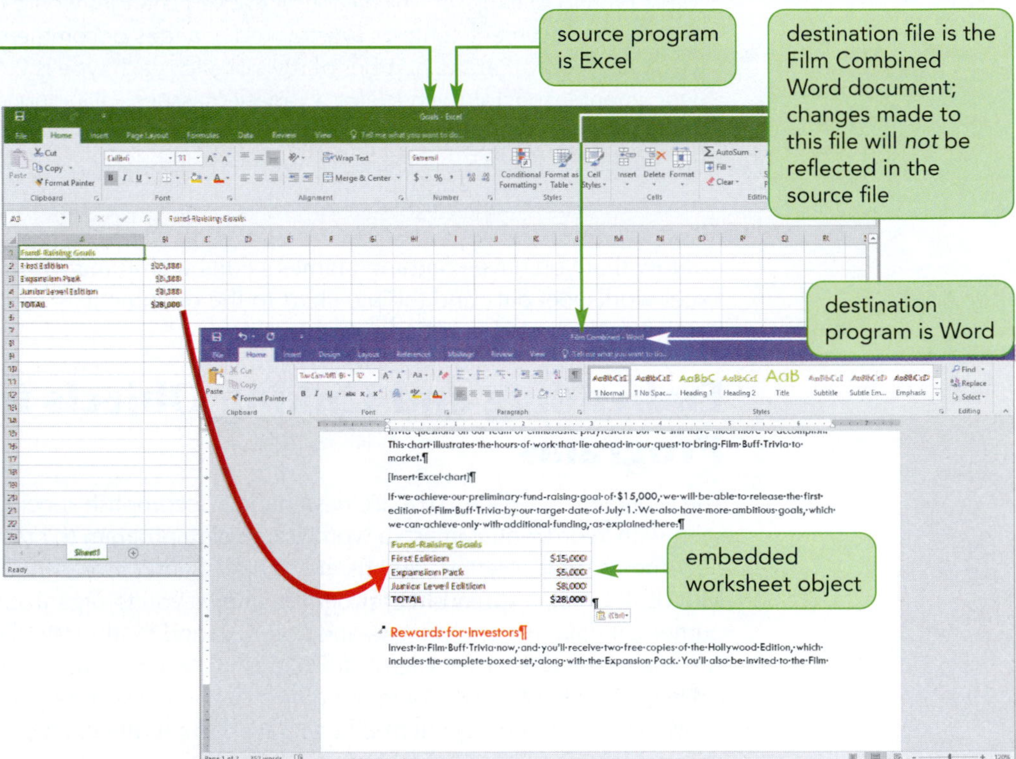
source file is an Excel workbook named Goals; changes made to this file will *not* be reflected in the destination file
source program is Excel
destination file is the Film Combined Word document; changes made to this file will *not* be reflected in the source file
destination program is Word
embedded worksheet object

Linking is similar to embedding, except that the object inserted into the destination file maintains a connection to the source file. Just as with an embedded object, you can double-click a linked object to access the tools of the source program. However, unlike with an embedded object, changes to a linked object show up in both the destination file and the source file. The linked object in the destination document is not a copy; it is a shortcut to the original object in the source file.

Figure 7-15 illustrates the relationship between the data in James's Excel chart and the linked object in Rima's Word document.

Figure 7-15 Linking an Excel chart object to a Word document

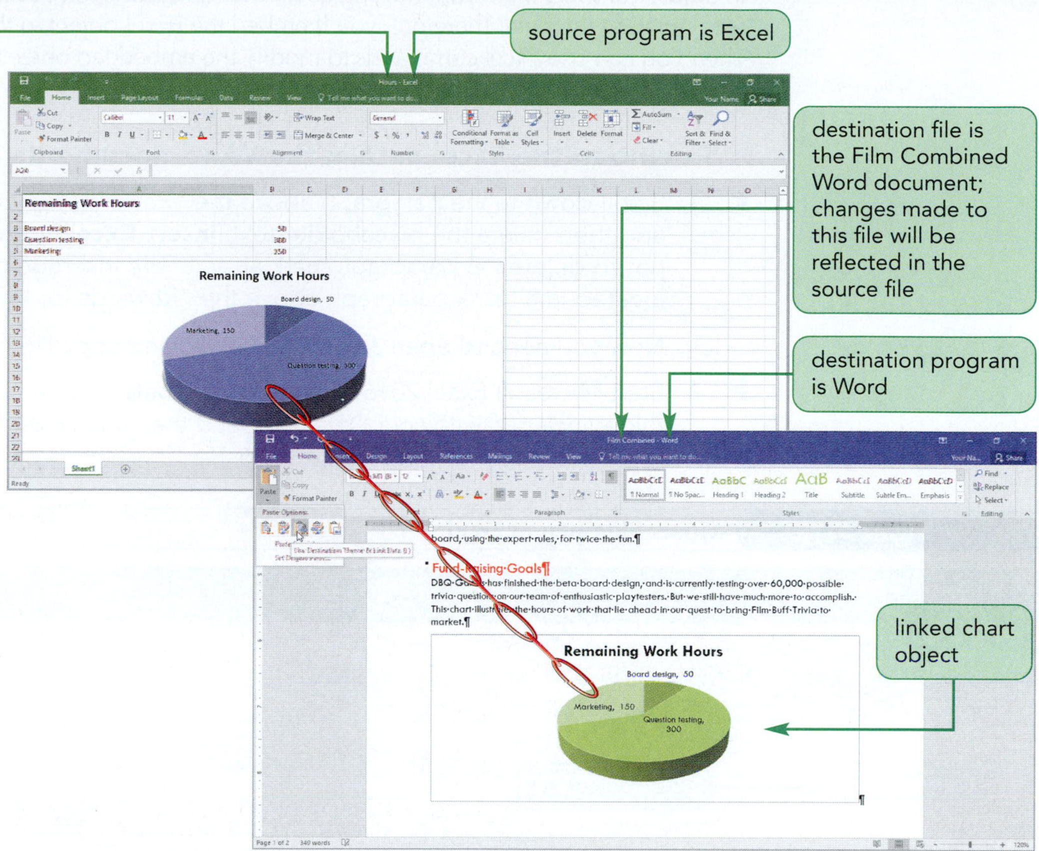
source file is an Excel workbook named Hours; changes made to this file will be reflected in the destination file
source program is Excel
destination file is the Film Combined Word document; changes made to this file will be reflected in the source file
destination program is Word
linked chart object
Remaining Work Hours
Board design, 50
Marketing, 150
Question testing, 300

PROSKILLS

Decision Making: Choosing Between Embedding and Linking

Embedding and linking are both useful when you know you'll want to edit an object after inserting it into Word. But how do you decide whether to embed or link the object? Create an embedded object if you won't have access to the original source file in the future, or if you don't need (or want) to maintain the connection between the source file and the document containing the linked object. Two advantages of embedding are that the source file is unaffected by any editing in the destination document, and the two files can be stored separately. You could even delete the source file from your disk without affecting the copy embedded in your Word document. A disadvantage is that the file size of a Word document containing an embedded object will be larger than the file size of a document containing a linked object.

Create a linked object whenever you have data that is likely to change over time and when you want to keep the object in your document up to date. In addition to the advantage of a smaller destination file size, both the source file and the destination file can reflect recent revisions when the files are linked. A disadvantage to linking is that you have to keep track of two files (the source file and the destination file) rather than just one.

Embedding an Excel Worksheet Object

To embed an object from an Excel worksheet into a Word document, you start by opening the Excel worksheet (the source file) and copying the Excel object to the Office Clipboard. Then, in the Word document (the destination file), you open the Paste Special dialog box. In this dialog box, you can choose to paste the copied Excel object in a number of different forms. To embed it, you select Microsoft Office Excel Worksheet Object.

Rima wants to include the company's fund-raising goals in her document. If she needs to adjust numbers in the fund-raising goals later, she will need access to the Excel tools for recalculating the data. Therefore, you'll embed the Excel object in the Word document. Then you can use Excel commands to modify the embedded object from within Word.

To embed the Excel data in the Word document:

1. Scroll down to the paragraph above the "Rewards for Investors" heading, and then delete the placeholder text [**Insert Excel worksheet**], taking care not to delete the paragraph mark after it. The insertion point should now be located in a blank paragraph above the "Rewards for Investors" heading.

   Now you need to open James's Excel file and copy the fund-raising data.

2. Start Microsoft Excel 2016, open the file **Goals** located in the Word7 > Module folder included with your Data Files, and then maximize the Excel program window if necessary. See Figure 7-16.

Figure 7-16 Goals file open in Excel

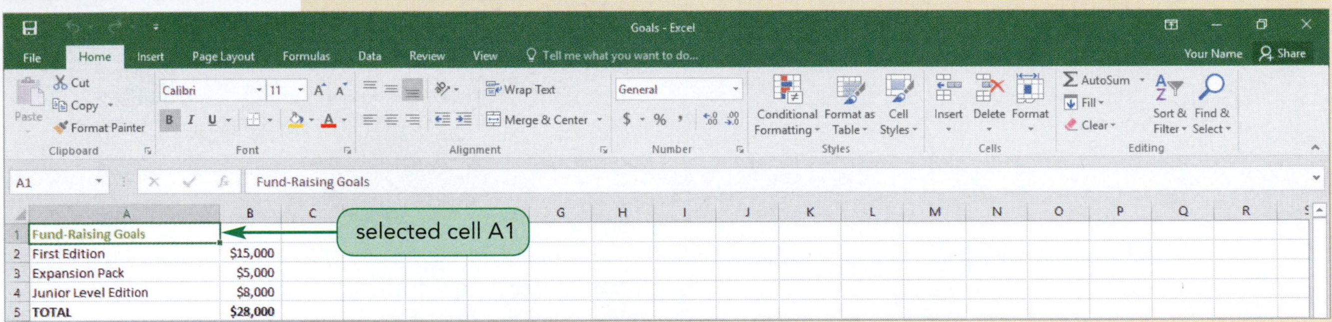

An Excel worksheet is arranged in rows and columns, just like a Word table. The intersection between a row and a column is called a **cell**; an individual cell takes its name from its column letter and row number. For example, the intersection of column A and row 1 in the upper-left corner of the worksheet is referred to as cell A1. Currently, cell A1 is selected, as indicated by its dark outline.

To copy the fund-raising data to the Office Clipboard, you need to select the entire block of cells containing the fund-raising data.

3. Click cell **A1** (the cell containing the text "Fund-Raising Goals"), if necessary, press and hold the **Shift** key, and then click cell **B5** (the cell containing "$28,000"). See Figure 7-17.

Figure 7-17 Fund-raising data selected in worksheet

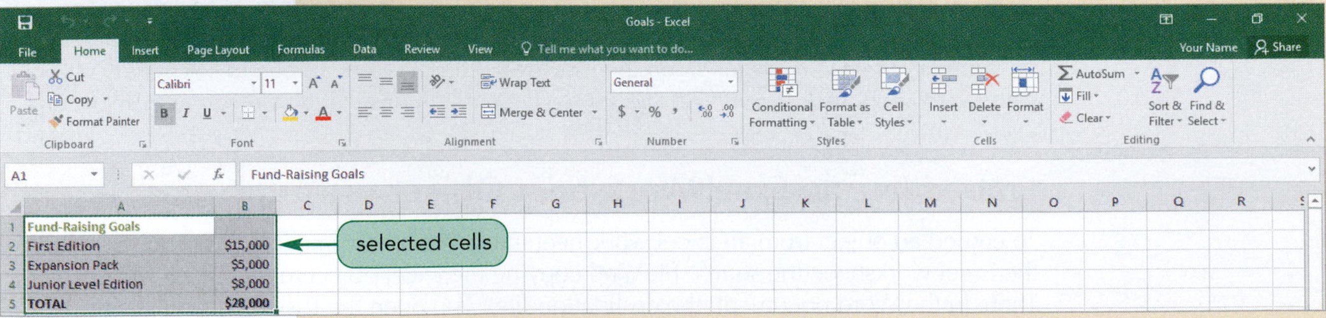

Now that the data is selected, you can copy it to the Office Clipboard.

Be sure to keep Excel open; otherwise, you won't have access to the commands for embedding the data in Word.

4. Press the **Ctrl+C** keys. The border around the selected cells is now flashing, indicating that you have copied the data in these cells to the Office Clipboard. Next, you will switch to Word without closing Excel.
5. On the taskbar, click the **Word** button to return to the Film Combined document. The insertion point is still located in the blank paragraph above the "Rewards for Investors" heading.
6. On the ribbon, click the **Home** tab, if necessary.
7. In the Clipboard group, click the **Paste button arrow**, and then click **Paste Special** to open the Paste Special dialog box.
8. In the As list, click **Microsoft Excel Worksheet Object**. See Figure 7-18.

Figure 7-18 Paste Special dialog box

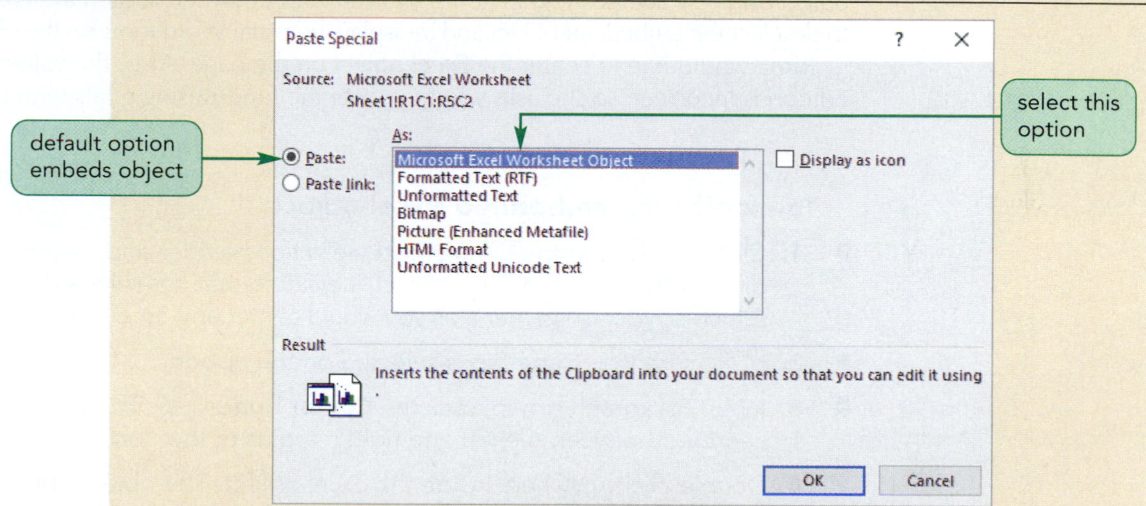

Next, you can choose to embed the Excel object or link it, depending on whether you select the Paste button (for embedding) or the Paste link button (for linking). The Paste button is selected by default, which is what you want in this case.

9. Click the **OK** button. The Excel worksheet object is inserted in the Word document, as shown in Figure 7-19.

Figure 7-19 Excel worksheet object embedded in Word document

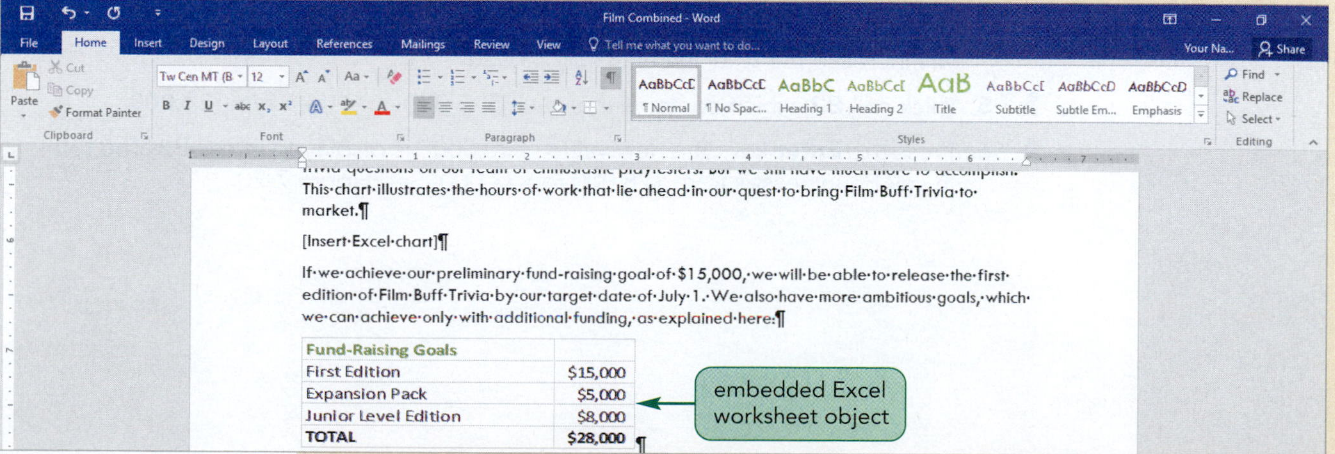

Trouble? If you don't see the top or bottom horizontal gridline in the embedded Excel object, don't be concerned. It won't affect the rest of the steps.

At this point, the Excel data looks like an ordinary table. But because you embedded it as an Excel worksheet object, you can modify it from within Word, using Excel tools and commands.

Modifying an Embedded Worksheet Object

After you embed an object in Word, you can modify it in two different ways. First, you can click the object to select it, and then move or resize it just as you would a graphic object. Second, you can double-click the object to display the tools of the source program on the Word ribbon and then edit the contents of the object. After you modify the embedded object using the source program tools, you can click anywhere else in the Word document to deselect the embedded object and redisplay the usual Word tools on the ribbon.

Rima would like to center the Excel object on the page. Also, the value for the First Edition is incorrect, so she asks you to update the fund-raising goals with the new data.

To modify the embedded Excel object:

1. Click anywhere in the Excel object. Selection handles and a dotted outline are displayed around the Excel object, indicating that it is selected. With the object selected, you can center it as you would center any other selected item.
2. Make sure the **Home** tab is selected on the ribbon.
3. In the Paragraph group, click the **Center** button. The Excel object is centered between the left and right margins of the document.
4. Double-click anywhere inside the Excel object. The object's border changes to resemble the borders of an Excel worksheet, with horizontal and vertical scroll bars, row numbers, and column letters. The Word tabs on the ribbon are replaced with Excel tabs.

   Trouble? If you don't see the Excel borders around the worksheet object, click outside the worksheet object to deselect it, and then repeat Step 4. If you still don't see the Excel borders, save the document, close it, reopen it, and then repeat Step 4.

   You need to change the value for the First Edition from $15,000 to $20,000. Although you can't see it, a formula automatically calculates and displays the total in cell B5. After you increase the value for the First Edition, the formula will increase the total in cell B5 by $5,000.
5. Click cell **B2**, which contains the value $15,000, and then type **20,000**.
6. Press the **Enter** key. The new value "$20,000" is displayed in cell B2. The total in cell B5 increases from $28,000 to $33,000. See Figure 7-20.

Figure 7-20 Revised data in embedded Excel object

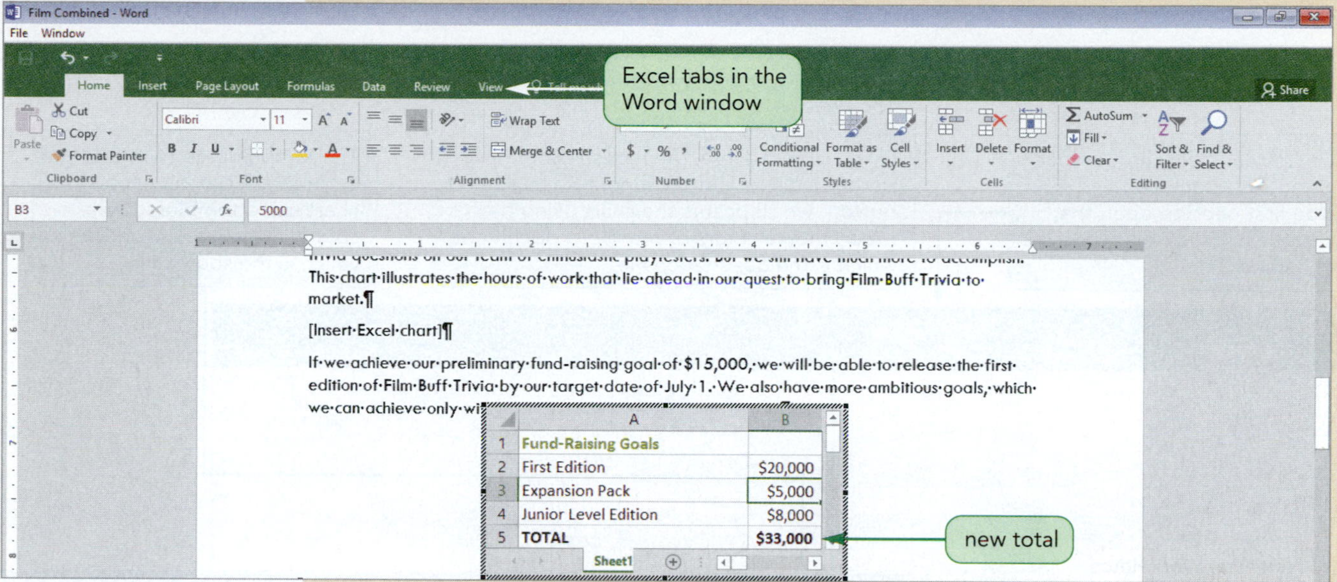

7. In the document, click outside the borders of the Excel object to deselect it. The Word tabs are now visible on the ribbon again.
8. On the taskbar, click the **Microsoft Excel** button to display the Excel window.

   Because you embedded the Excel object rather than linking it, the First Edition value of $15,000 and the Total of $28,000 remain unchanged.
9. On the ribbon, click the **File** tab, and then click **Close** in the navigation bar. The Goals workbook closes, but Excel remains open.

In this session, you worked with tracked changes in a document. You learned how to combine and compare documents, and you accepted and rejected tracked changes in a combined document. You also embedded an Excel Worksheet object in a Word document and modified the embedded worksheet object from within Word. In the next session, you'll learn how to link an object instead of embedding it. You'll also create bookmarks, insert and edit hyperlinks in a document, and optimize the document for online viewing. Finally, you'll learn how to create and publish a blog post.

REVIEW

Session 7.1 Quick Check

1. How can you ensure that your name is displayed for each tracked change?
2. Explain how to turn on Track Changes.
3. Which provides a more streamlined view of a document's tracked changes, All Markup view or Simple Markup view?
4. What should you do before using the Next and Previous buttons to review the tracked changes in a document?
5. Explain the difference between a linked object and an embedded object.
6. How do you start editing an embedded Excel object in Word?

Session 7.2 Visual Overview:

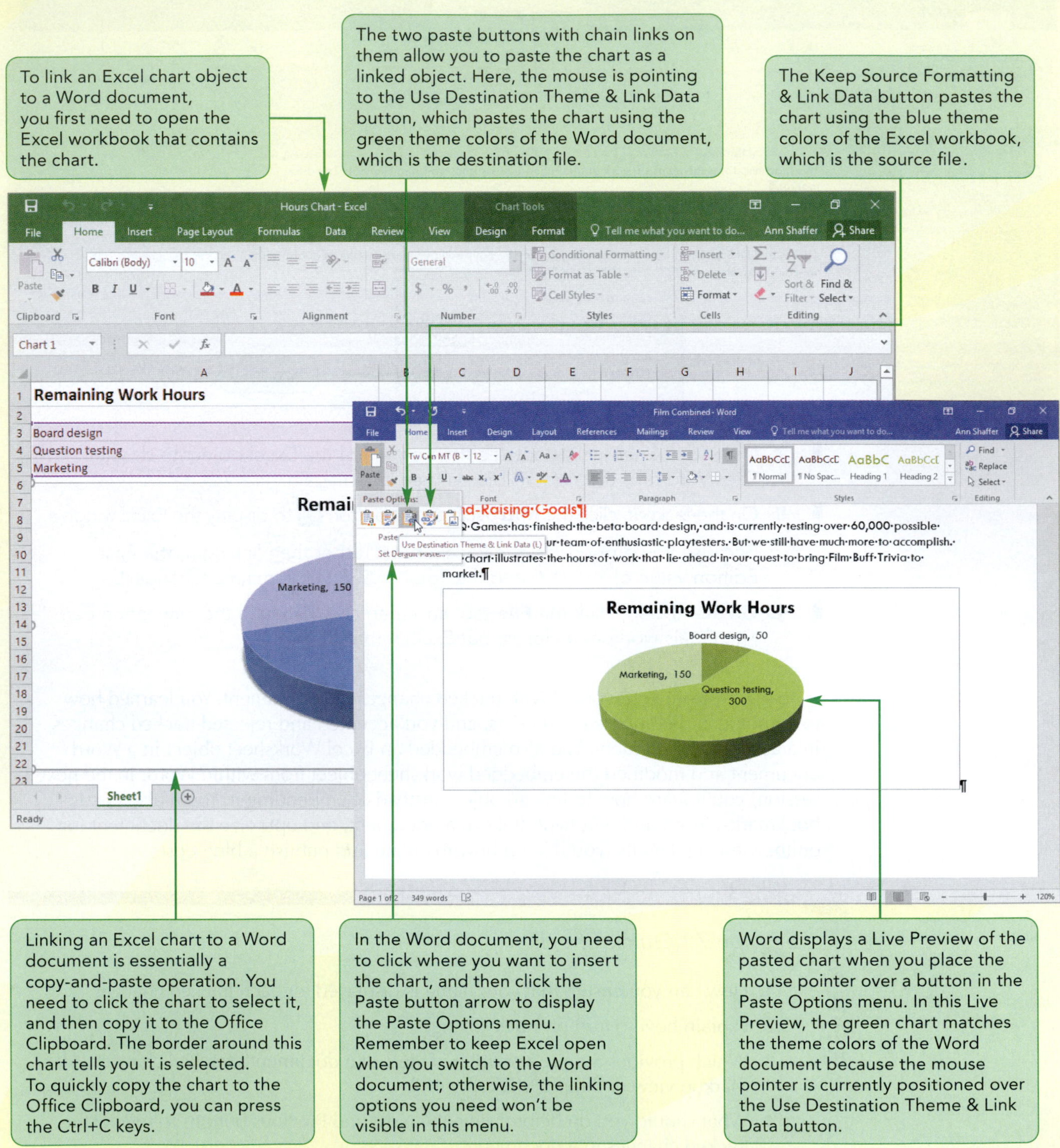

To link an Excel chart object to a Word document, you first need to open the Excel workbook that contains the chart.
The two paste buttons with chain links on them allow you to paste the chart as a linked object. Here, the mouse is pointing to the Use Destination Theme & Link Data button, which pastes the chart using the green theme colors of the Word document, which is the destination file.
The Keep Source Formatting & Link Data button pastes the chart using the blue theme colors of the Excel workbook, which is the source file.
Hours Chart - Excel
Remaining Work Hours
Board design
Question testing
Marketing
Film Combined - Word
Remaining Work Hours
Board design, 50
Marketing, 150
Question testing, 300
Linking an Excel chart to a Word document is essentially a copy-and-paste operation. You need to click the chart to select it, and then copy it to the Office Clipboard. The border around this chart tells you it is selected. To quickly copy the chart to the Office Clipboard, you can press the Ctrl+C keys.
In the Word document, you need to click where you want to insert the chart, and then click the Paste button arrow to display the Paste Options menu. Remember to keep Excel open when you switch to the Word document; otherwise, the linking options you need won't be visible in this menu.
Word displays a Live Preview of the pasted chart when you place the mouse pointer over a button in the Paste Options menu. In this Live Preview, the green chart matches the theme colors of the Word document because the mouse pointer is currently positioned over the Use Destination Theme & Link Data button.

Linking an Excel Chart Object

You can edit a linked chart object from within the Word document.

After you select the chart in the Word document, you click the Edit Data button on the Chart Tools Design tab. This opens a spreadsheet window with the Excel source file displayed.

If the chart in the Word window does not change to reflect changes made to data in the spreadsheet window, you can click the Refresh Data button to update the chart in the Word window.

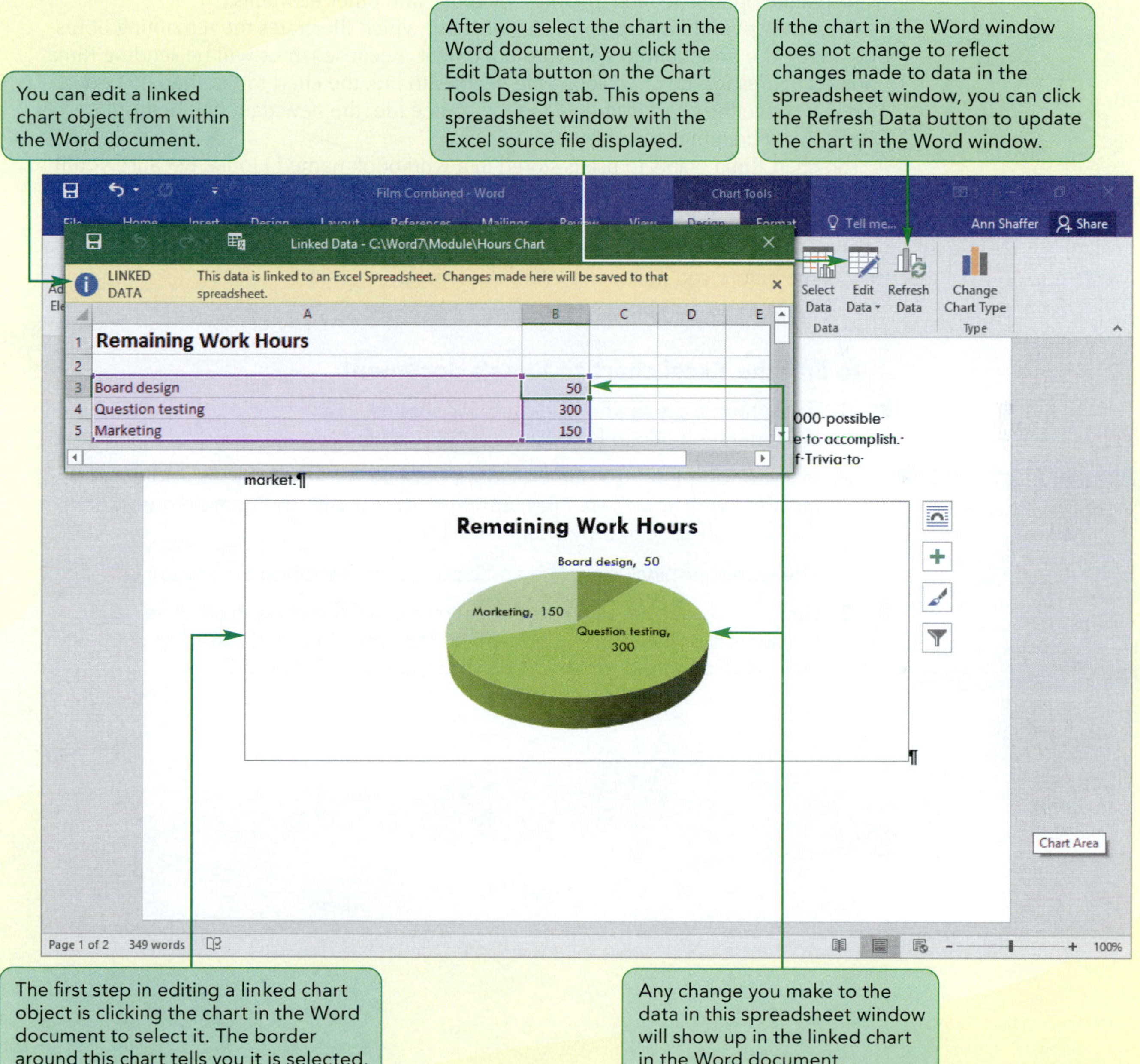

The first step in editing a linked chart object is clicking the chart in the Word document to select it. The border around this chart tells you it is selected.

Any change you make to the data in this spreadsheet window will show up in the linked chart in the Word document.

Linking an Excel Chart Object

When you link an object to a Word document, you start by selecting the object in the source program and copying it to the Office Clipboard. Then you return to Word and select one of the linking options from the Paste Options menu. The Paste Options menu displays different options depending on what you have copied to the Office Clipboard, with specific options related to tables, pictures, and other elements.

Rima wants you to insert James's Excel chart, which illustrates the remaining hours of work on the project, into her Word document. Because James will be sending Rima updated figures for the chart soon, she decides to link the chart rather than embed it. That way, once the chart is updated in the source file, the new data will be displayed in Rima's Word document as well.

The chart Rima wants to use is stored in a workbook named Hours. Because you'll make changes to the chart after you link it, you will save the workbook with a new name before you link it. This leaves the original workbook file unchanged in case you want to repeat the module steps later. Normally, you don't need to save a file with a new name before you link it to a Word document.

TIP

To link a Word file to the current document: on the Insert tab, click the Object button, click the Create from File tab, select the Link to file checkbox, click the Browse button, and select the file.

To link the Excel chart to Rima's document:

1. If you took a break after the previous session, make sure the **Film Combined** document is open in Print Layout view and that Excel is open.
2. In Excel, open the file named **Hours** from the Word7 > Module folder included with your Data Files, and then save it with the name **Hours Chart** in the location specified by your instructor.

   The worksheet includes data and a pie chart illustrating the data.
3. Click the chart border. Do not click any part of the chart itself. A selection border is displayed around the chart. The worksheet data used to create the chart is also highlighted in purple and blue. See Figure 7-21.

Figure 7-21 Pie chart selected in worksheet

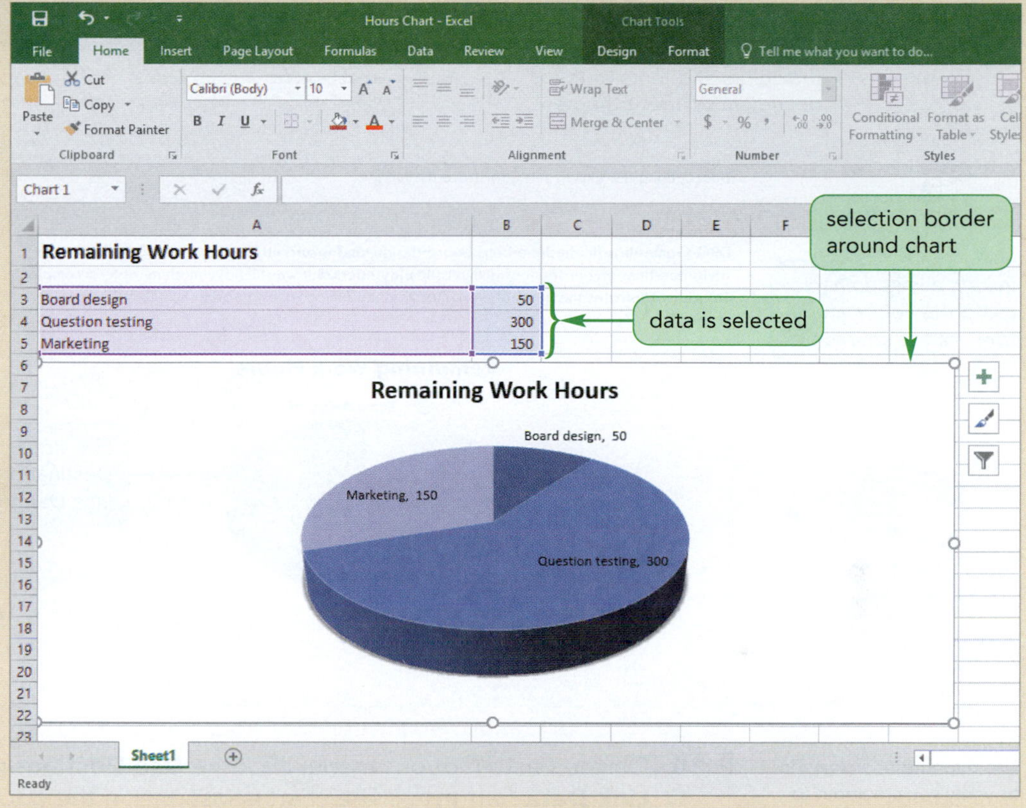

Trouble? If you see borders or handles around individual elements of the pie chart, you clicked the chart itself rather than the border. Click in the worksheet outside the chart border, and then repeat Step 3.

4. Press the **Ctrl+C** keys to copy the pie chart to the Office Clipboard.
5. On the taskbar, click the **Word button** to display the Word window with the Film Combined document.
6. On the ribbon, make sure the Home tab is selected.
7. In the second paragraph after the "Fund-Raising Goals" heading, delete the placeholder text **[Insert Excel chart]** but not the paragraph symbol after it, and then verify that the insertion point is located in a blank paragraph between two paragraphs of text.
8. In the Clipboard group, click the **Paste button arrow** to display the Paste Options menu.
9. Move the mouse pointer over the icons on the Paste Options menu, and notice the changing appearance of the chart's Live Preview, depending on which Paste Option you are previewing.

   For linking, you can choose between the Use Destination Theme & Link Data option, which formats the chart with the font and green colors of the Word document's current theme, and the Keep Source Formatting & Link Data option, which retains the font and blue colors of the Excel workbook. See Figure 7-22.

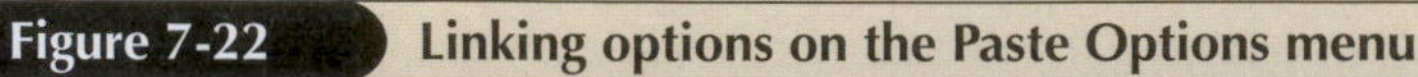

Figure 7-22 Linking options on the Paste Options menu

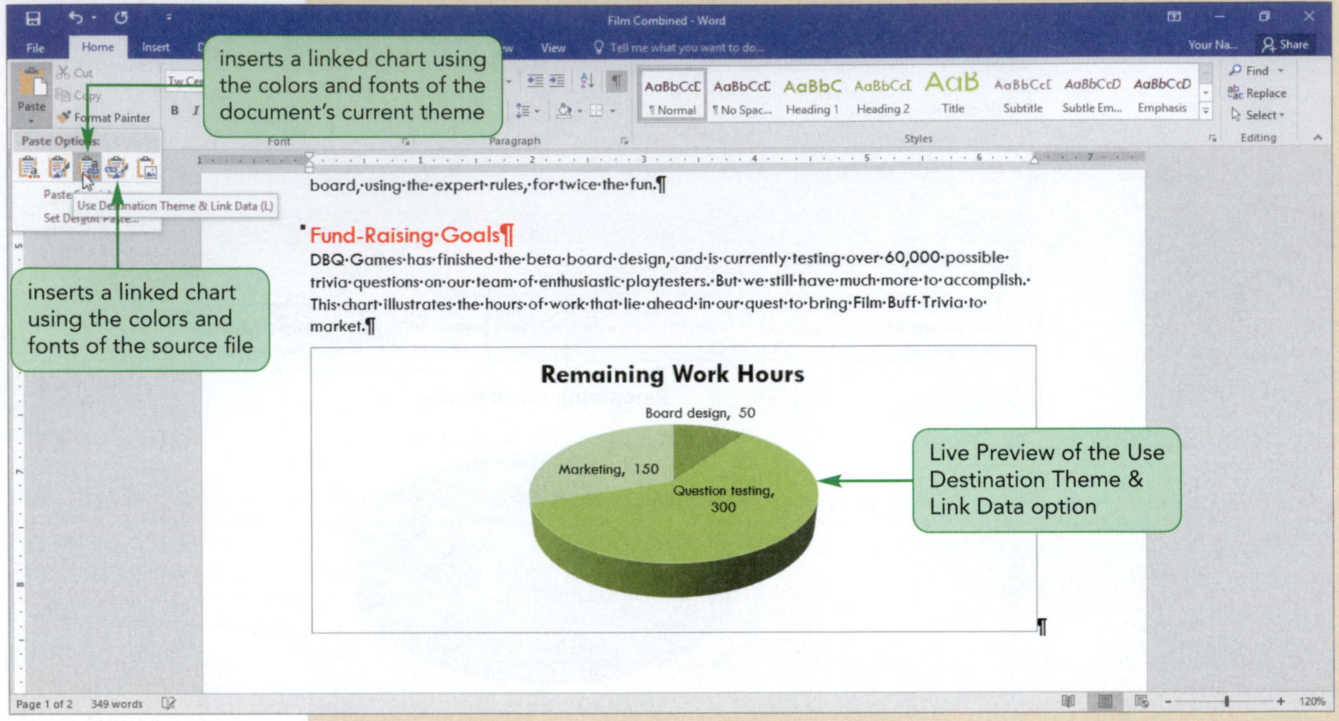

Use the button's ScreenTip to verify you are about to click the Use Destination Theme & Link Data button. It's easy to click the wrong button on the Paste Options menu.

10. On the Paste Options menu, click the **Use Destination Theme & Link Data** button. The chart is inserted in the document. It is formatted with the green colors and font of the Circuit theme used in the Word document.

INSIGHT

Storing Linked Files

When linking objects, it is important to keep the source and destination files in their original storage locations. If you move the files or the folders in which they are stored, you will disrupt the connection between the source file and the document containing the linked object because the shortcut in the destination file will no longer have a valid path to the source file.

For example, suppose you insert a linked Excel file into a Word document, and then later a colleague moves the Excel file to a different folder. The next time you open the Word document and try to update the linked object, you will see a dialog box explaining that the linked file is not available. At that point, you can make the link functional again by updating the path to the linked objects. To do so, click the File tab on the ribbon, and then click Info in the navigation bar, if necessary. On the Info screen, click Edit Links to Files. In the Links dialog box, click the link whose location has changed, click the Change Source button, and then navigate to the new location of the source file.

Modifying the Linked Chart Object

The advantage of linking compared to embedding is that you can change the data in the source file, and those changes will automatically be reflected in the destination file as well.

Rima has received James's updated data about the total hours remaining on the project, and she wants the chart in her document to reflect this new information. You will update the data in the source file. You'll start by closing Excel so you can clearly see the advantages of working with a linked object.

To modify the chart in the source file:

1. On the taskbar, click the **Microsoft Excel** button to display the Excel window, and then close Excel.
2. On the taskbar, click the **Word** button, if necessary, to display the Word window.
3. Click anywhere in the white area inside the chart border. The selection border is displayed around the chart, and the two Chart Tools contextual tabs are displayed on the ribbon.

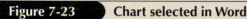

   Trouble? If you see a selection border around the pie chart itself, in addition to the selection border around the chart and the title, you can ignore it.
4. On the ribbon, click the **Chart Tools Design** tab. See Figure 7-23.

Figure 7-23 Chart selected in Word

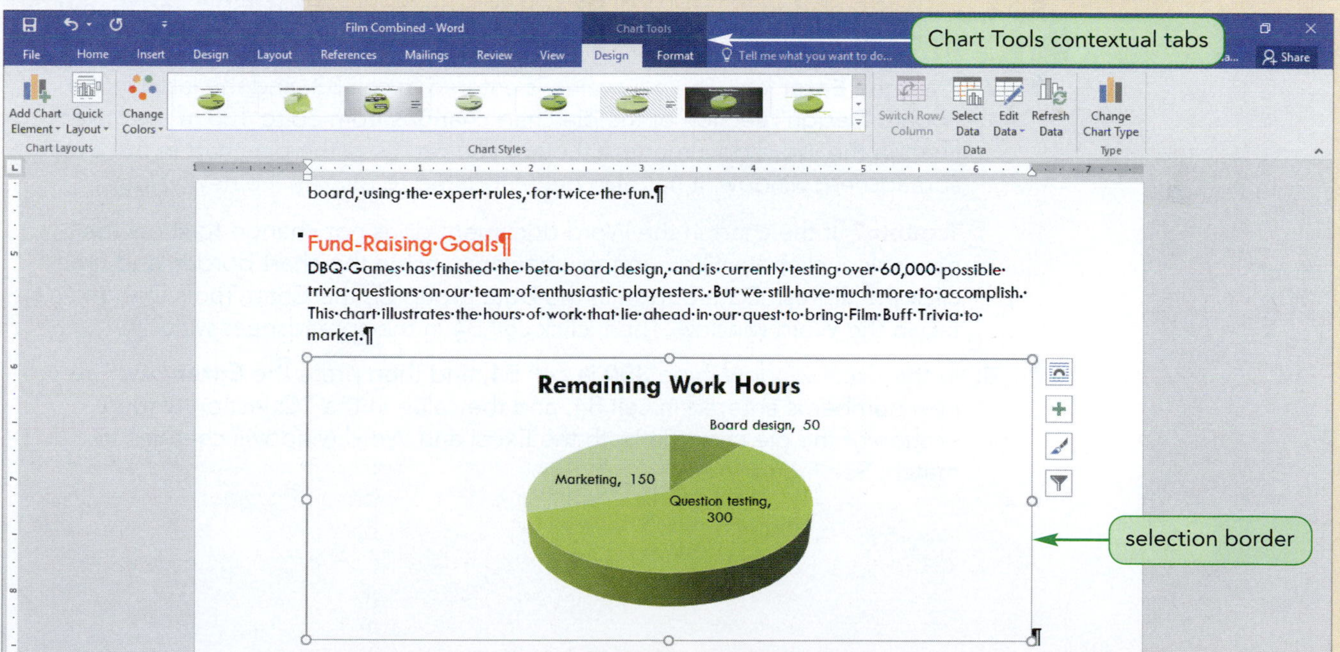

TIP

To edit the source file directly in Excel, click the Edit Data button arrow to display a menu, and then click Edit Data in Excel.

5. In the Data group, click the **Edit Data** button. A spreadsheet that contains the chart data opens on top of the Word document. Your spreadsheet might be larger or smaller than the one shown in Figure 7-24.

Figure 7-24 Spreadsheet window with chart data

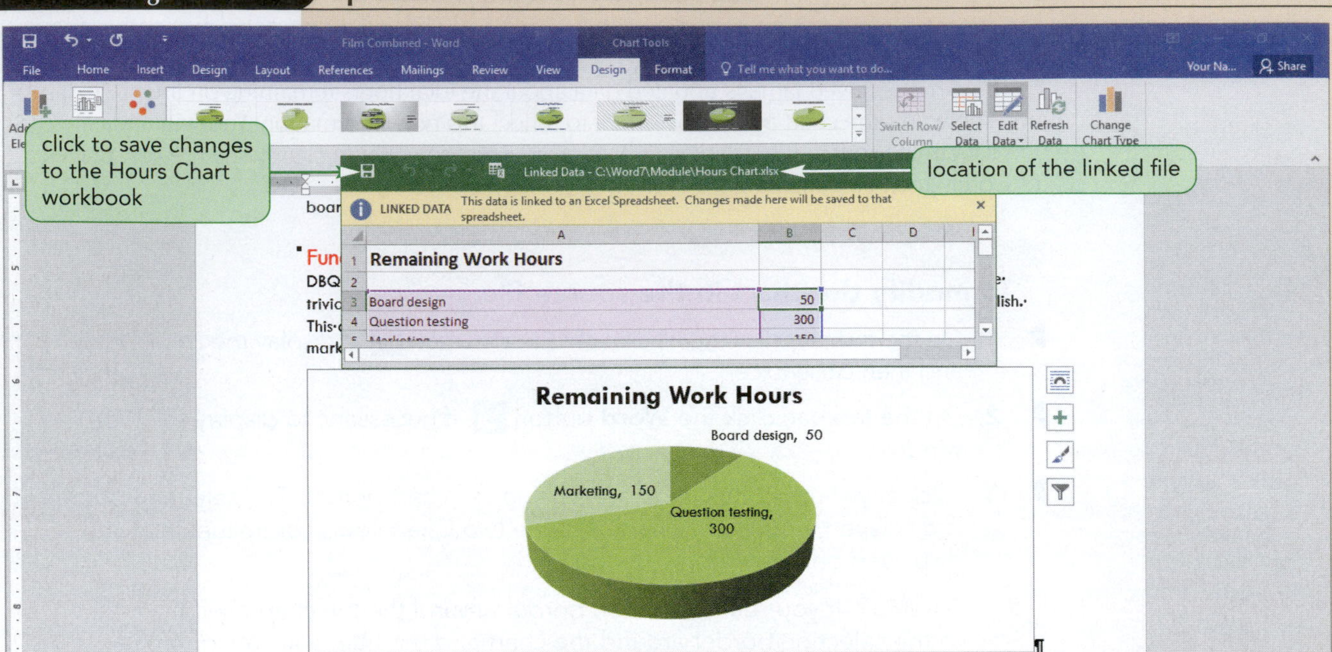

The file path at the top of the spreadsheet window shows the location of the linked file you are about to edit.

6. In the Excel window, click cell **B3**, which contains the value "50," and then type **100**.
7. Press the **Enter** key. The new value is entered in cell B3, and the label in the "Board Design" section of the pie chart changes from 50 to 100 in the linked chart in the Word document. Although you can't see the pie chart in the Excel spreadsheet window, it has also been updated to display the new value.

   Trouble? If the chart in the Word document does not change to show the new value, click anywhere in the white area inside the chart border, and then click the Refresh Data button in the Data group on the Chart Tools Design tab in the Word window. Then, click cell B4 in the spreadsheet window.

8. In the Excel window, type **350** in cell B4, and then press the **Enter** key. The new number is entered in cell B4, and the value in the "Question testing" section of the pie charts in both the Excel and Word windows changes to match. See Figure 7-25.

Figure 7-25 Modifying the linked chart data

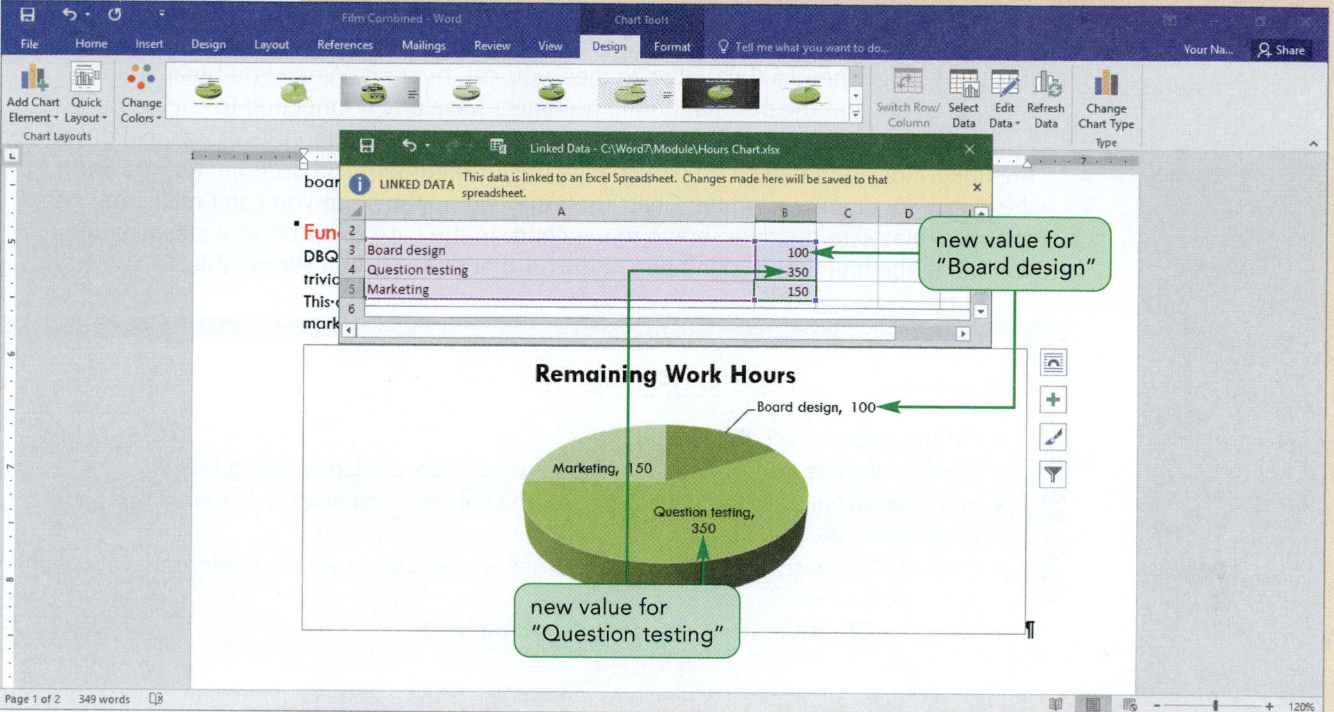

9. At the top of the spreadsheet window, click the **Save** button, and then click the **Close** button to close the spreadsheet window.
10. In the Word document, click anywhere outside the chart to deselect it, and then save the Film Combined document.

When you edited the data in the spreadsheet window, you were actually editing the Hours Chart workbook. If you wanted, you could start Excel and open the Hours Chart workbook to verify that it contains the new values.

INSIGHT

Editing a Linked Worksheet Object

The steps for editing a linked worksheet object are slightly different from the steps for editing a linked chart object. Instead of editing a linked worksheet object from within Word, you need to start Excel, open the workbook, and then edit the worksheet in Excel. You can quickly open the workbook in Excel by right-clicking the linked worksheet object in Word, pointing to Linked Worksheet Object on the shortcut menu, and then clicking Edit Link. This opens the workbook in Excel, where you can edit the data and save your changes. When you are finished, close the workbook, and then return to the Word document. Finally, to update the data within the Word document, right-click the linked worksheet object in the Word document to open a shortcut menu, and then click Update Link. When you open a Word document containing a linked worksheet object, you might see a dialog box asking if you want to update the document with the data from the linked files. Click Yes to continue.

Rima is finished with her work on the chart. She does not expect the data in it to change, so she wants to break the link between the Excel workbook and the Word document.

Breaking Links

If you no longer need a link between files, you can break it. When you break a link, the source file and the destination file no longer have any connection to each other, and changes made in the source file do not affect the destination file. After breaking the link to the source file, you can change the formatting of a chart object from within the Word document, using the Chart Tools contextual tabs, but you can't make any changes related to the data shown in the chart. In the case of an Excel worksheet, after you break the link to the source file, the worksheet turns into a Word table.

REFERENCE

Breaking a Link to a Source File

- On the ribbon, click the File tab.
- On the Info screen, click Edit Links to Files to open the Links dialog box.
- In the list of links in the document, click the link that you want to break.
- Click the Break Link button.
- Click the Yes button in the dialog box that opens, asking you to confirm that you want to break the link.
- Click the OK button to close the Links dialog box.

Now, you will break the link between Rima's document and the Hours Chart workbook.

To break the link between the Word document and the Excel workbook:

1. On the ribbon, click the **File** tab. Backstage view opens with the Info screen displayed.
2. In the lower-right corner of the Info screen, click **Edit Links to Files**. The Links dialog box opens with the only link in the document (the link to the Hours Chart workbook) selected. See Figure 7-26.

Figure 7-26 The Links dialog box

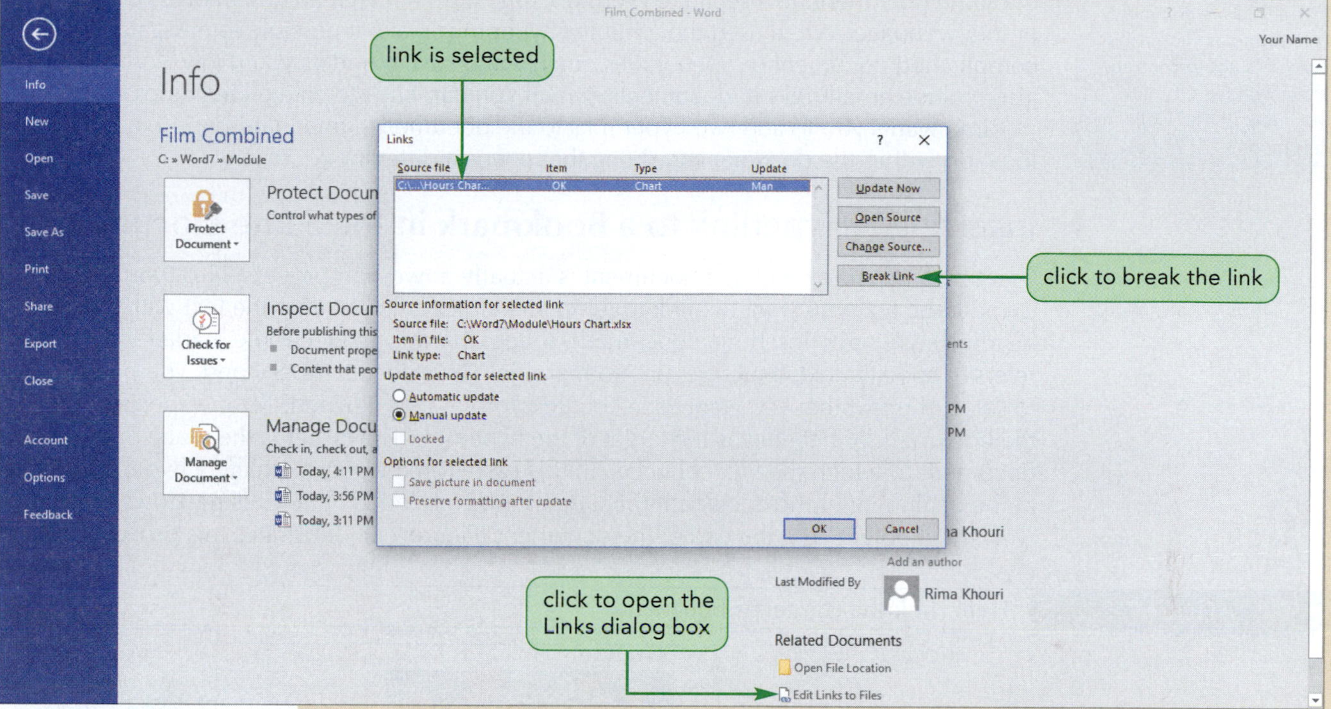

3. In the Links dialog box, click the **Break Link** button, and then click **Yes** in the dialog box that opens, asking if you are sure you want to break the link. The list in the Links dialog box now indicates there is no source file for the chart in the document.
4. Click the **OK** button to close the dialog box. You return to the Info screen in Backstage view.

   With the link broken, you can no longer edit the Excel data from within Word. You can verify this by looking at the Chart Tools Design tab.
5. At the top of the navigation bar, click the **Back** button to close Backstage view and return to the document.
6. Click anywhere inside the chart border to select the chart.
7. On the ribbon, click the **Chart Tools Design** tab, if necessary. Notice that the Edit Data button in the Data group is grayed out, indicating this option is no longer available.
8. Click anywhere outside the chart border to deselect it, and then save the document.

Next, Rima asks you to turn your attention to adding hyperlinks to her document. Although hyperlinks are widely used in webpages, you can also use them in ordinary Word documents.

Using Hyperlinks in Word

> **TIP**
>
> Hyperlinks are commonly referred to as "links," but take care not to confuse them with the OLE links you worked with earlier in this module.

A hyperlink is a word, phrase, or graphic that you can click to jump to another part of the same document, to a separate Word document, to a file created in another program, or to a webpage. When used thoughtfully, hyperlinks make it possible to navigate a complicated document or a set of files quickly and easily. And as you know, you can also include email links in documents, which you can click to create email messages.

Rima wants you to add two hyperlinks to the document—one that jumps to a location within the document, and one that opens a different document.

Inserting a Hyperlink to a Bookmark in the Same Document

Creating a hyperlink within a document is actually a two-part process. First, you need to mark the text you want the link to jump to—either by formatting the text with a heading style or by inserting a bookmark. A **bookmark** is an electronic marker that refers to specific text, a picture, or another object in a document. Second, you need to select the text that you want users to click, format it as a hyperlink, and specify the bookmark or heading as the target of the hyperlink. The **target** is the place in the document to which the link connects. In this case, Rima wants to create a hyperlink at the beginning of the document that targets the embedded Fund-Raising Goals Excel worksheet object near the end of the document. Figure 7-27 illustrates this process.

Figure 7-27 **Hyperlink that targets a bookmark**

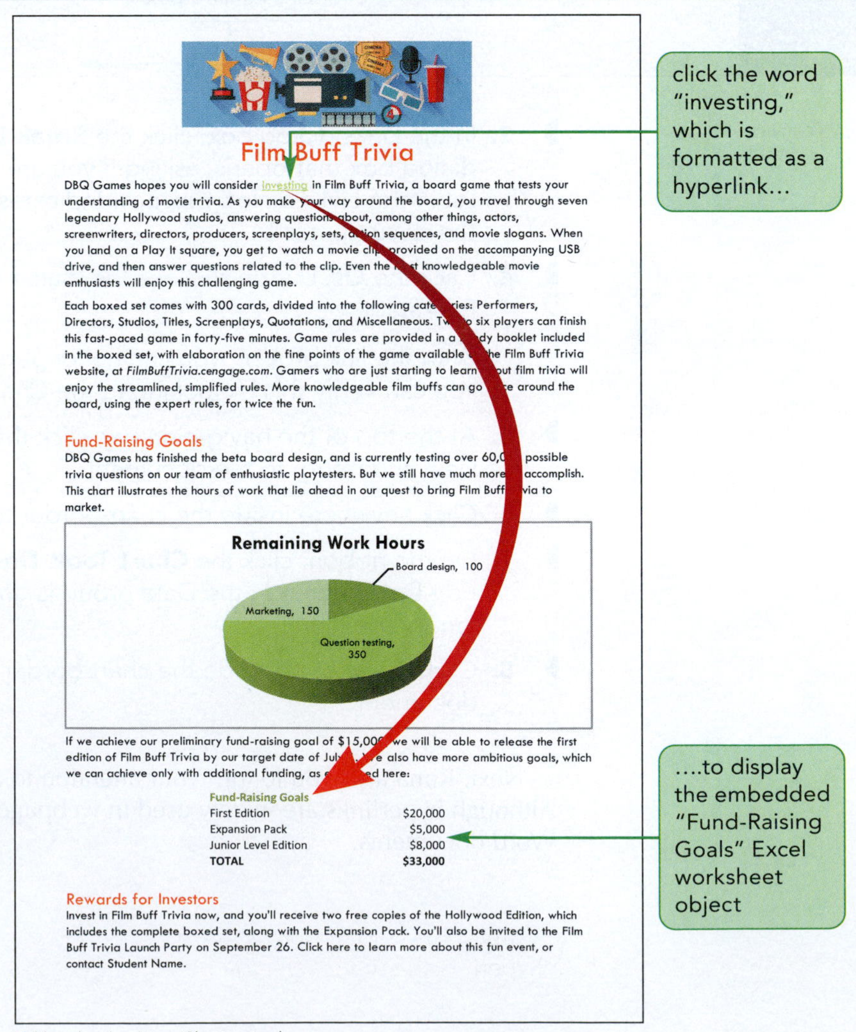
click the word "investing," which is formatted as a hyperlink...
....to display the embedded "Fund-Raising Goals" Excel worksheet object
Remaining Work Hours
Board design, 100
Marketing, 150
Question testing, 350

Film Buff Trivia

DBQ Games hopes you will consider investing in Film Buff Trivia, a board game that tests your understanding of movie trivia. As you make your way around the board, you travel through seven legendary Hollywood studios, answering questions about, among other things, actors, screenwriters, directors, producers, screenplays, sets, [illegible] sequences, and movie slogans. When you land on a Play It square, you get to watch a movie [illegible] provided on the accompanying USB drive, and then answer questions related to the clip. Even the [illegible] knowledgeable movie enthusiasts will enjoy this challenging game.

Each boxed set comes with 300 cards, divided into the following [illegible]: Performers, Directors, Studios, Titles, Screenplays, Quotations, and Miscellaneous. [illegible] six players can finish this fast-paced game in forty-five minutes. Game rules are provided in a [illegible] booklet included in the boxed set, with elaboration on the fine points of the game available [illegible] the Film Buff Trivia website, at *FilmBuffTrivia.cengage.com*. Gamers who are just starting to learn [illegible] film trivia will enjoy the streamlined, simplified rules. More knowledgeable film buffs can go [illegible] around the board, using the expert rules, for twice the fun.

Fund-Raising Goals

DBQ Games has finished the beta board design, and is currently testing over 60,[illegible] possible trivia questions on our team of enthusiastic playtesters. But we still have much more [illegible] accomplish. This chart illustrates the hours of work that lie ahead in our quest to bring Film Buff [illegible] to market.

If we achieve our preliminary fund-raising goal of $15,00[illegible] we will be able to release the first edition of Film Buff Trivia by our target date of Jul[illegible]. [illegible] also have more ambitious goals, which we can achieve only with additional funding, as [illegible] here:

Fund-Raising Goals	
First Edition	$20,000
Expansion Pack	$5,000
Junior Level Edition	$8,000
TOTAL	**$33,000**

Rewards for Investors

Invest in Film Buff Trivia now, and you'll receive two free copies of the Hollywood Edition, which includes the complete boxed set, along with the Expansion Pack. You'll also be invited to the Film Buff Trivia Launch Party on September 26. Click here to learn more about this fun event, or contact Student Name.

Zakharchenko Anna/Shutterstock.com

To create a hyperlink in Rima's document, you'll first need to designate the worksheet object as a bookmark.

To insert a bookmark:

1. Scroll down and click the "Fund-Raising Goals" worksheet object, on page 2. A dotted outline and handles are displayed around the worksheet object, indicating that it is selected.
2. On the ribbon, click the **Insert** tab.
3. In the Links group, click the **Bookmark** button. The Bookmark dialog box opens. You can now type the bookmark name, which cannot contain spaces.
4. In the Bookmark name box, type **Goals**. See Figure 7-28.

Figure 7-28 Creating a bookmark

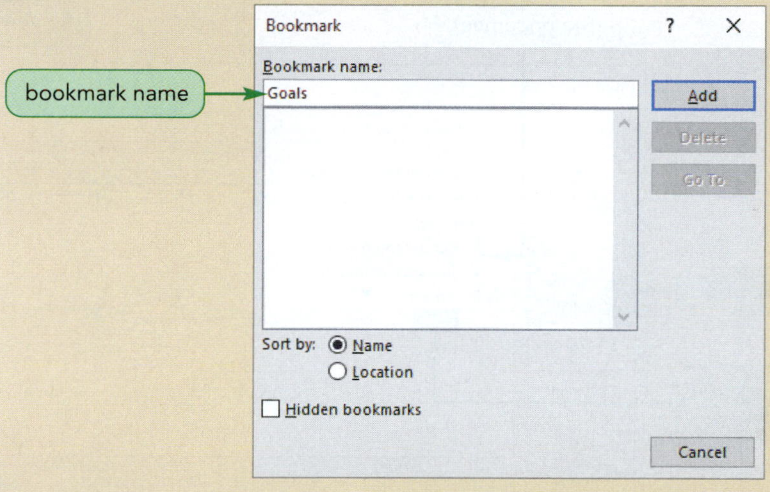

5. Click the **Add** button. The Bookmark dialog box closes. Although you can't see any change in the document, the "Fund-Raising Goals" worksheet object has been designated as a bookmark.

TIP
To delete a bookmark, click it in the Bookmark dialog box, and then click the Delete button.

The bookmark you just created will be the target of a hyperlink, which you will create next.

REFERENCE

Creating a Hyperlink to a Location in the Same Document

- Select the text, graphic, or other object that you want to format as a hyperlink.
- On the ribbon, click the Insert tab.
- In the Links group, click the Hyperlink button to open the Insert Hyperlink dialog box.
- In the Link to pane, click Place in This Document.
- In the Select a place in this document list, click the bookmark or heading you want to link to, and then click the OK button.

Rima wants you to format the word "investing" at the beginning of the document as a hyperlink that will target the bookmark you just created.

To create and test a hyperlink to the bookmark:

1. Scroll up to page 1, and then, in the first line under the "Film Buff Trivia" heading, select the word **investing**.
2. In the Links group, click the **Hyperlink** button. The Insert Hyperlink dialog box opens.
3. In the Link to pane, click **Place in This Document** to select it, if necessary. The "Select a place in this document" list shows the headings and bookmarks in the document. Here you can click the bookmark or heading you want as the target for the hyperlink.
4. Under Bookmarks, click **Goals**. See Figure 7-29.

Figure 7-29 Inserting a hyperlink to a location in the same document

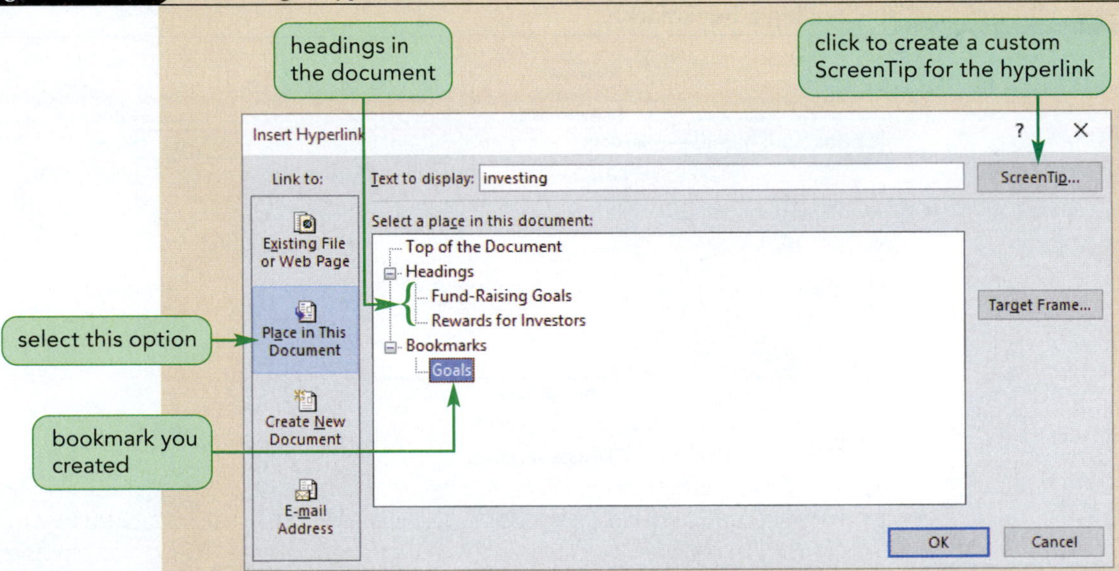

You can click the ScreenTip button to open the Set Hyperlink ScreenTip dialog box and type custom text for the hyperlink's ScreenTip, which appears when you place the mouse pointer over the hyperlink in the document. In this case, however, Rima prefers to use the default ScreenTip.

TIP

To change a hyperlink's font color, open the Styles pane and modify the Hyperlink style.

5. Click the **OK** button. The word "investing" is now formatted in the hyperlink style for the Circuit theme, which applies a green font color with an underline. The hyperlink targets the Goals bookmark that you created in the last set of steps. You can verify this by clicking the hyperlink.
6. Move the mouse pointer over the hyperlink **investing**. The default ScreenTip displays the name of the bookmark and instructions for following the link. See Figure 7-30.

Figure 7-30 Displaying the ScreenTip for a hyperlink

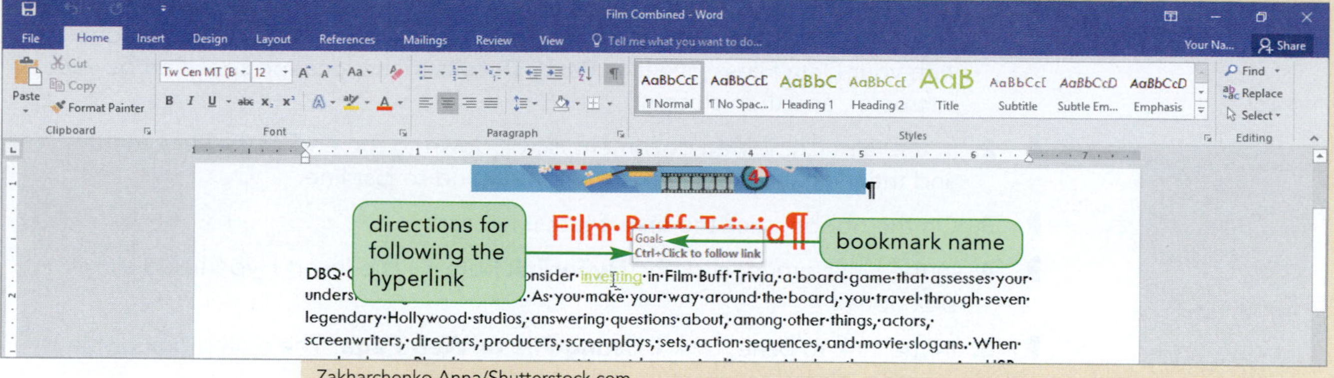

Zakharchenko Anna/Shutterstock.com

7. Press and hold the **Ctrl** key, and then click the **investing** hyperlink. The insertion point jumps to the "Fund-Raising Goals" worksheet object on page 2.
8. Scroll up to review the "investing" hyperlink. It is now turquoise, which is the color for clicked links in the Circuit theme.
9. Save your document.

Next, you will create a hyperlink that jumps to a different document.

Creating Hyperlinks to Other Documents

When you create a hyperlink to another document, you need to specify the document's filename and storage location as the hyperlink's target. The document can be stored on your computer or on a network; it can even be a webpage stored somewhere on the web. In that case, you need to specify the webpage's URL (web address) as the target. When you click a hyperlink to another document, the document opens on your computer, with the beginning of the document displayed. Keep in mind that if you move the document containing the hyperlink, or if you move the target document, the hyperlink will no longer work. However, if you create a hyperlink to a webpage on the Internet, the link will continue to work no matter where you store the document containing the hyperlink.

REFERENCE

Creating a Hyperlink to Another Document

- Select the text, graphic, or other object you want to format as a hyperlink.
- On the ribbon, click the Insert tab.
- In the Links group, click the Hyperlink button to open the Insert Hyperlink dialog box.
- In the Link to pane, click Existing File or Web Page.
- To target a specific file on your computer or network, click the Look in arrow, navigate to the folder containing the file, and then click the file in the file list.
- To target a webpage, type its URL in the Address box.
- Click the OK button.

Rima wants to insert a hyperlink that, when clicked, will open a Word document containing details about the Film Buff Trivia Launch Party. You'll start by opening the document containing the party details and saving it with a new name.

To create a hyperlink to a document with details about the Film Buff Trivia Launch Party:

1. Open the document **Party** located in the Word7 > Module folder included with your Data Files, save it as **Party Details** in the location specified by your instructor, and then close it.
2. In the Film Combined document, scroll down to the end of the document, and then select the word **here** in the second to last line.
3. On the ribbon, click the **Insert** tab, if necessary.
4. In the Links group, click the **Hyperlink** button. The Insert Hyperlink dialog box opens.
5. In the Link to pane, click **Existing File or Web Page**. The dialog box displays options related to selecting a file or a webpage.
6. Click the **Look in** arrow, navigate to the location where you stored the Party Details file, if necessary, and then click **Party Details** in the file list. See Figure 7-31.

Figure 7-31 **Inserting a hyperlink to a different document**

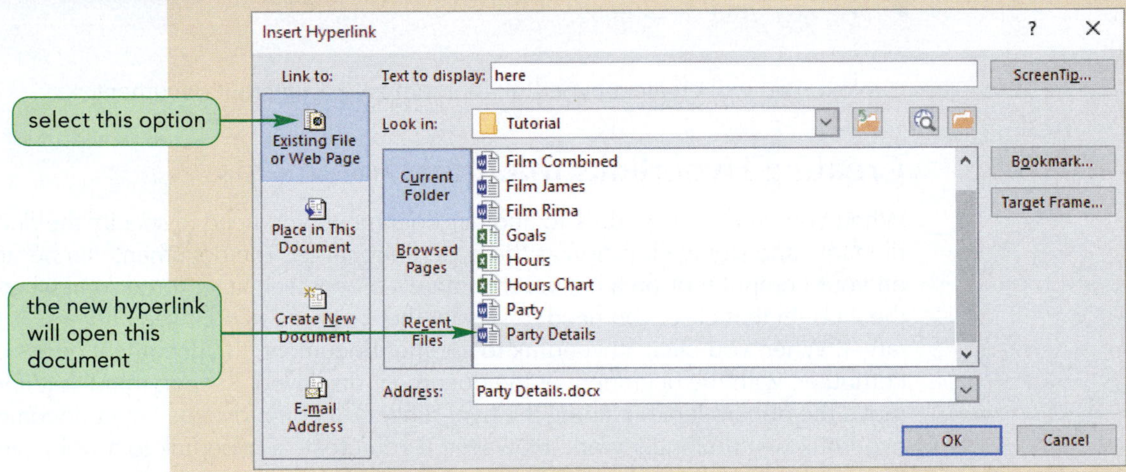

7. Click the **OK** button. The new "here" hyperlink is formatted in green with an underline. Now, you will test the hyperlink.
8. Press and hold the **Ctrl** key, and then click the **here** hyperlink. The Party Details document opens. See Figure 7-32.

Figure 7-32 Party Details document

Film·Buff·Trivia·
Launch·Party¶
Saturday,·September·26·at·8·p.m.¶

Page 1 of 1 52 words 120%

9. Close the Party Details document, and then return to the Film Combined document. The link is now turquoise because you clicked it.
10. Save your document.

Now that you have finalized the document and added the necessary hyperlinks, you will optimize the document for online viewing by switching to Web Layout view and adding some formatting that is useful for documents that will be viewed online.

Optimize a Document for Online Viewing

When preparing a document intended solely for online distribution, you can focus on how the page will look on the screen, without having to consider how it will look when printed. This means you can take advantage of some formatting options that are visible only on the screen, such as a background page color or a background fill effect. You can also switch to **Web Layout view**, which displays a document as it would look in a web browser.

TIP

Zooming in on text in Web Layout View is helpful when you have multiple panes open; the text wraps for easy reading.

In Web Layout view, the text spans the width of the screen, with no page breaks and without any margins or headers and footers. The advantage of Web Layout view is that it allows you to zoom in on the document text as close as you want, with the text rewrapping to accommodate the new Zoom setting. By contrast, in Print Layout view, if you increase the Zoom setting too far, you end up having to scroll from side-to-side to read an entire line of text. The only downside to Web Layout view is that graphics may shift position as the text wrapping changes. However, these changes are only visible in Web Layout view. When you switch back to Print Layout view, you will see the original page layout.

Rima wants to switch to Web Layout view before she continues formatting the document.

To switch to Web Layout view:

1. On the status bar, click the **Web Layout** button. The document text expands to span the entire Word screen.
2. Use the Zoom slider on the status bar to increase the Zoom setting to **160%**. The text rewraps to accommodate the new setting.
3. Scroll down and review the entire document, which no longer has any page breaks. See Figure 7-33.

Figure 7-33 Document displayed in Web Layout view, zoomed to 160%

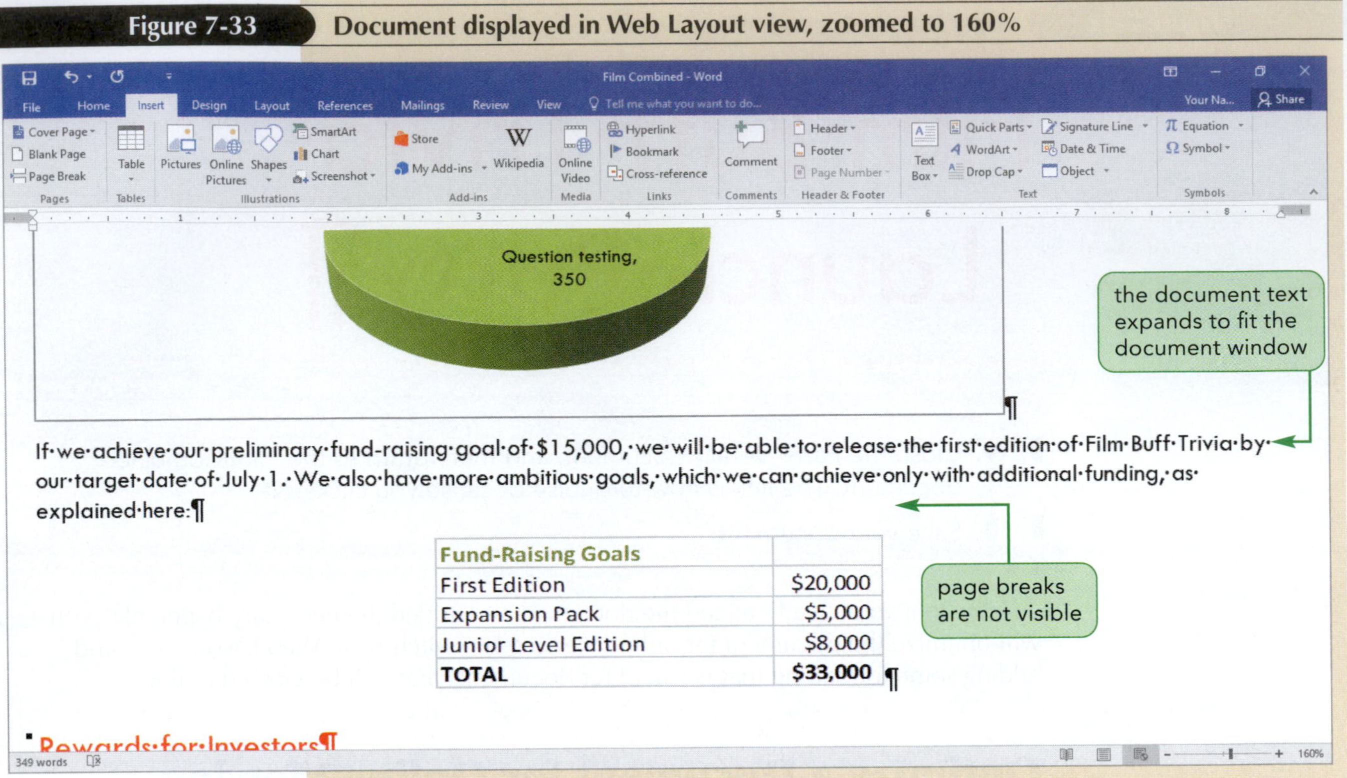

Applying a Background Fill Effect

To make the document more eye-catching when it's displayed on a screen, Rima wants to add a background fill effect. A **background fill effect** is a repeating graphic element, such as a texture, a photo, or a color gradient, that is visible only when a document is displayed online. It's essential to use fill effects judiciously. In the hands of a trained graphic designer, they can be striking; if used carelessly, they can be garish and distracting. As a general rule, you should avoid using photos and textures and instead stick with simple colors or color gradients.

Rima decides to use a gradient background in shades of blue.

To apply a background fill effect to the document:

1. On the ribbon, click the **Design** tab.
2. In the Page Background group, click the **Page Color** button. The Page Color gallery opens, with a menu at the bottom. You could click a color in the gallery to select it as a background color for the page. To select another type of background effect, you need to click Fill Effects.
3. Click **Fill Effects** to open the Fill Effects dialog box, and then click the **Gradient** tab, if necessary. Note that you could use other tabs in this dialog box to add a textured, patterned, or picture background.
4. In the Colors section, click the **Two colors** button. The Color 1 and Color 2 boxes and arrows are displayed.
5. Click the **Color 1** arrow, and then click **Blue, Accent 5**, the ninth color from the left in the first row of the Theme Colors section.

6. Click the **Color 2** arrow, and then click **Sky Blue, Background 2, Lighter 60%**, the third color from the left in the third row of the Theme Colors section.
7. In the Shading styles section, click the **Vertical** option button to change the gradient pattern so it stretches vertically up and down the page. Compare your dialog box to Figure 7-34.

Figure 7-34 Selecting a gradient background

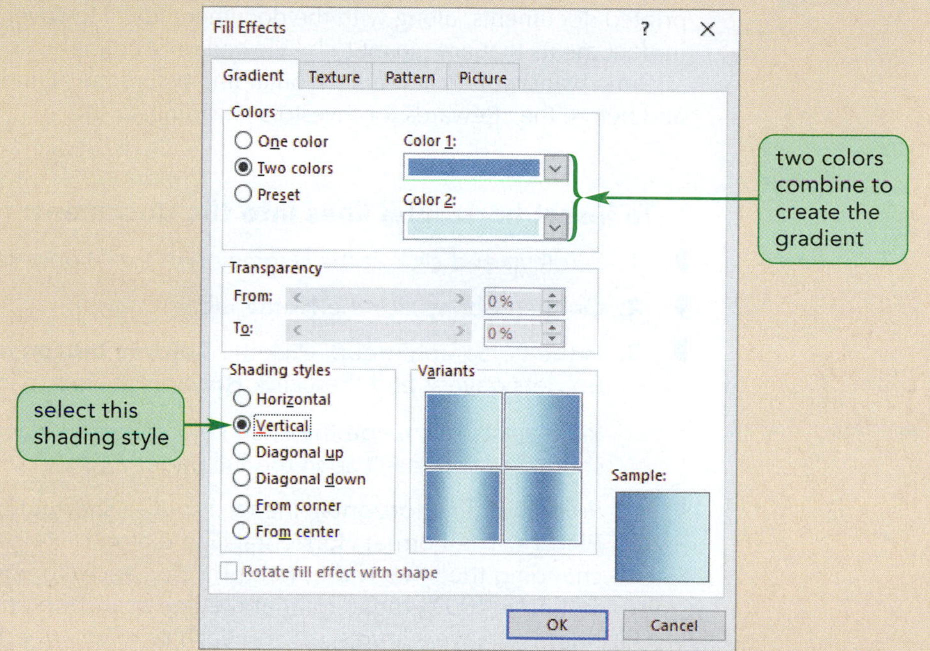

8. Click the **OK** button. The document's background is now a gradient that varies between light and dark blue.
9. Scroll down, if necessary, so you can see the Fund-Raising Goals worksheet object.

The gradient background is light enough to make the document text easy to read. However, it's now hard to see the gridlines of the worksheet object. You can fix that by changing the object's background color.

To change the background for the Fund-Raising Goals worksheet object:

1. Right-click the worksheet object to display a shortcut menu, and then click **Picture**. The Format Object dialog box opens, with the Picture tab displayed.
2. Click the **Colors and Lines** tab to display settings related to the colors used in the worksheet object. In the Fill section, the Color box currently displays "No Color," indicating that the object's background is the same as the document's background.
3. In the Fill section, click the **Color** arrow, and then click **White, Background 1**, the first square in the top row of the Theme Colors section.
4. Click the **OK** button to close the Format Object dialog box. The worksheet object now has a white background, which makes the gridlines easier to see.

5. Click outside the worksheet object to deselect it, and then save the document.

Next, you will add horizontal lines to separate the various sections of the document.

Inserting Horizontal Lines

Horizontal lines allow you to see at a glance where one part of a document ends and another begins. Unlike background colors and fill effects, horizontal lines do appear in printed documents, along with the document text. However, they are commonly used in documents that are meant to be viewed only online.

Rima wants you to add a horizontal line before the "Fund-Raising Goals" heading and before the "Rewards for Investors" heading.

To insert horizontal lines into the document:

1. Scroll up and click at the beginning of the "Fund-Raising Goals" heading.
2. On the ribbon, click the **Home** tab.
3. In the Paragraph group, click the **Borders button arrow** to open the Borders gallery, and then click **Horizontal Line** to insert a default gray line.

   Rima wants to change the line's color. She also wants to make the line shorter, so it doesn't span the full page.

4. Right-click the horizontal line to display a shortcut menu, and then click **Picture**. The Format Horizontal Line dialog box opens, with settings for changing the line's width, height, color, and alignment. The current Width setting is 100%, meaning that the line spans the entire page from left to right. To leave a little space on each side, you need to lower the percentage.
5. Triple-click the **Width** box, and then type **75**. Because the Center alignment option at the bottom of the dialog box is selected by default, the shorter line will be centered on the page, with space to its left and its right.
6. Click the **Color** arrow, and then click **Blue, Accent 5, Darker 50%**, the ninth square from the left in the sixth row of the Theme Colors section. The Color gallery closes, and the Use solid color (no shade) check box is now selected. See Figure 7-35.

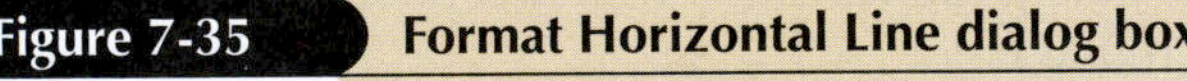
Figure 7-35 Format Horizontal Line dialog box

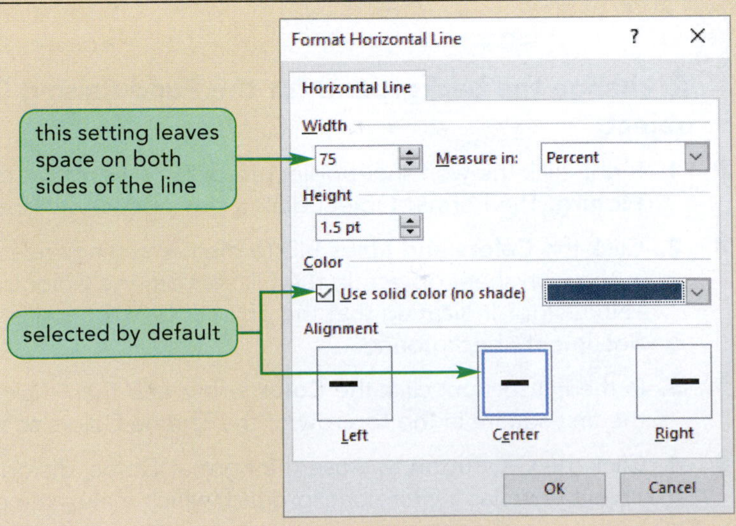

7. Click the **OK** button, and then click anywhere in the document to deselect the horizontal line. Your document should look similar to Figure 7-36.

Figure 7-36 Newly inserted horizontal line

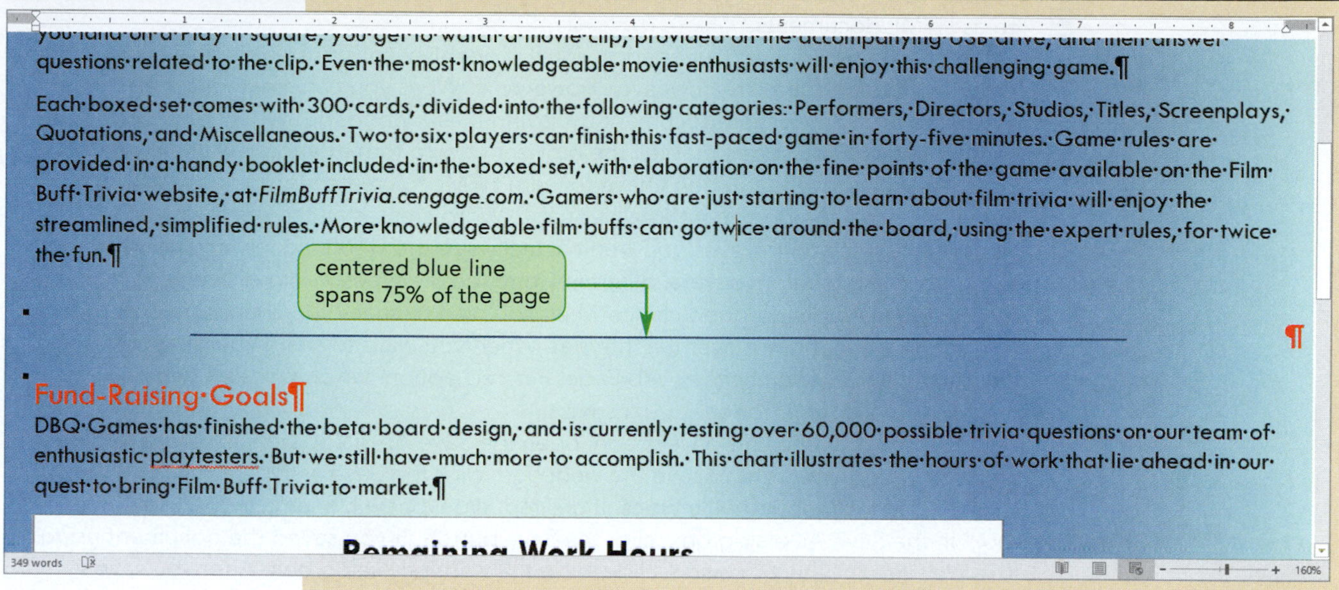

you·land·on·a·Play·It·square,·you·get·to·watch·a·movie·clip,·provided·on·the·accompanying·USB·drive,·and·then·answer· questions·related·to·the·clip.·Even·the·most·knowledgeable·movie·enthusiasts·will·enjoy·this·challenging·game.¶

Each·boxed·set·comes·with·300·cards,·divided·into·the·following·categories:·Performers,·Directors,·Studios,·Titles,·Screenplays,· Quotations,·and·Miscellaneous.·Two·to·six·players·can·finish·this·fast-paced·game·in·forty-five·minutes.·Game·rules·are· provided·in·a·handy·booklet·included·in·the·boxed·set,·with·elaboration·on·the·fine·points·of·the·game·available·on·the·Film· Buff·Trivia·website,·at·*FilmBuffTrivia.cengage.com*.·Gamers·who·are·just·starting·to·learn·about·film·trivia·will·enjoy·the· streamlined,·simplified·rules.·More·knowledgeable·film·buffs·can·go·twice·around·the·board,·using·the·expert·rules,·for·twice· the·fun.¶

centered blue line spans 75% of the page

¶

Fund-Raising·Goals¶

DBQ·Games·has·finished·the·beta·board·design,·and·is·currently·testing·over·60,000·possible·trivia·questions·on·our·team·of· enthusiastic·playtesters.·But·we·still·have·much·more·to·accomplish.·This·chart·illustrates·the·hours·of·work·that·lie·ahead·in·our· quest·to·bring·Film·Buff·Trivia·to·market.¶

Remaining Work Hours

349 words 160%

Now, you can copy the line, and then insert it before the other heading.

TIP

To remove a horizontal line, click the line to select it, and then press the Delete key.

8. Click the horizontal line to select it, and then press the **Ctrl+C** keys to copy it to the Clipboard.
9. Scroll down, click to the left of the "R" in the "Rewards for Investors" heading, and then press the **Ctrl+V** keys to insert the horizontal line before the heading.
10. Save the document.

You've finished formatting the Film Combined document. Next, Rima needs to edit the hyperlink that opens the document with information about the launch party.

INSIGHT

Saving a Word Document as a Webpage

Webpages are special documents designed to be viewed in a program called a **browser**. The browser included in Windows 10 is Microsoft Edge. Because webpages include code written in Hypertext Markup Language, or **HTML**, they are often referred to as HTML documents.

To create sophisticated webpages, you'll probably want to use a dedicated HTML editor, such as Adobe Dreamweaver. However, in Word you can create a simple webpage from an existing document by saving it as a webpage. When you do so, Word inserts HTML codes that tell the browser how to format and display the text and graphics. Fortunately, you don't have to learn HTML to create webpages with Word. When you save the document as a webpage, Word creates all the necessary HTML codes (called tags); however, you won't actually see the HTML codes in your webpage.

You can choose from several different webpage file types in Word. The Single File Web Page file type is a good choice when you plan to share your webpage only over a small network and not over the Internet. When you want to share your files over the Internet, it's better to use the Web Page, Filtered option, which breaks a webpage into multiple smaller files, for easier transmittal.

To save a document as a webpage, open the Save As dialog box, navigate to the location where you want to save the webpage, click the Save as type arrow, and then click one of the webpage file types. If desired, type a new filename in the File name box. In the Save As dialog box, click the Save button. If you saved the document using the Web Page, Filtered option, click Yes in the warning dialog box. After you save a document as a webpage, Word displays it in Web Layout view.

Editing Hyperlinks

Rima's document contains two hyperlinks—the "investing" link, which jumps to the Fund-Raising Goals worksheet object, and the "here" link, which jumps to the Party Details document. To give all the Film Buff Trivia documents a coherent look, Rima formatted the Party Details document with a fill effect. She saved the newly formatted document as file named "Formatted Party." Now she wants you to edit the "here" hyperlink, so it opens this new version of the document. To make it possible to repeat these steps later if you want, you'll start by saving the Formatted Party document with a new name.

To edit the "here" hyperlink:

1. Open the document **Formatted Party** located in the Word7 > Module folder included with your Data Files, and then switch to Web Layout view, if necessary, so you can see the two-color gradient background.
2. Save the document as **Formatted Party Details** in the location specified by your instructor, and then close it.
3. In the Film Combined document, scroll down to the end of the document, and then position the pointer over the **here** hyperlink near the end of the document to display a ScreenTip, which indicates that the link will jump to a document named Party Details.docx.

   Trouble? If you also see a ScreenTip that reads "Chart Area" you can ignore it.
4. Right-click the **here** hyperlink to open a shortcut menu, and then click **Edit Hyperlink**. The Edit Hyperlink dialog box opens. It looks just like the Insert Hyperlink dialog box, which you have already used. To edit the hyperlink, you simply select a different target file.

5. In the Link to pane, verify that the Existing File or Web Page option is selected.
6. Navigate to the location where you saved the Formatted Party Details document, if necessary, and then click **Formatted Party Details** in the file list.
7. Click the **OK** button. You return to the Film Combined document.
8. Place the mouse pointer over the list hyperlink to display a ScreenTip, which indicates that the link will now jump to a document named Formatted Party Details.docx.
9. Press and hold the **Ctrl** key, and then click the **here** hyperlink. The Formatted Party Details document opens.
10. Close the Formatted Party Details document, and then save and close the Film Combined document.

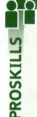

PROSKILLS

Teamwork: Emailing Word Documents

After you optimize a document for online viewing, you can share it with colleagues via email. To get started emailing a document, first make sure you have set up Microsoft Outlook as your email program. Then, in Word, open the document you want to email. On the ribbon, click the File tab, and then click Share in the navigation bar. On the Share screen, click Email, and then select the email option you want. When you email documents, keep in mind the following:

- Many email services have difficulty handling attachments larger than 4 MB. Consider storing large files in a compressed (or zipped) folder to reduce their size before emailing them.
- Other word-processing programs and early versions of Word might not be able to open files created in Word 2016. To avoid problems with conflicting versions, you have two options. You can save the Word document as a rich text file (using the Rich Text File document type in the Save As dialog box) before emailing it; all versions of Word can open rich text files. Another option is to save the document as a PDF.
- If you plan to email a document that contains links to other files, remember to email all the linked files.
- Attachments, including Word documents, are sometimes used maliciously to spread computer viruses. Remember to include an explanatory note with any email attachment so that the recipient can be certain the attachment is legitimate. Also, it's important to have a reliable virus checker program installed if you plan to receive and open email attachments.

The new documents are just one way to share information about Film Buff Trivia. Rima also wants to write a blog post discussing the game's development. She asks you to help her create a blog post in Word.

Creating and Publishing a Blog Post

Creating a blog post in Word is similar to creating a new Word document except that instead of clicking Blank document on the New screen in Backstage view, you click Blog post. Note that before you can publish your blog post using Word, you need to register a blog account with an Internet blog provider that is compatible with Microsoft Word 2016.

Rima asks you to help her create a blog post about the development of the Film Buff Trivia game.

To create and publish a blog post:

1. On the ribbon, click the **File** tab, and then click **New** in the navigation bar to display the icons for the various document templates.
2. Scroll down if necessary, and then click **Blog post**.
3. In the Blog post window, click the **Create** button. A blank blog post opens. Assuming you have not previously registered for a blog account, you also see the Register a Blog Account dialog box.

   To register a blog account, you could click the Register Now button to open the New Blog Account dialog box. From there, you could follow the prompts to register your blog account. Rima will register her blog account later, so you can skip the registration step for now.
4. Click the **Register Later** button to close the dialog box.
5. At the top of the blog post, click the **[Enter Post Title Here]** placeholder, and then type **Film Buff Trivia**.
6. Click in the blank paragraph below the blog title, and then type **Film Buff Trivia is a board game that tests your knowledge of film trivia.** See Figure 7-37.

Figure 7-37 Blog post

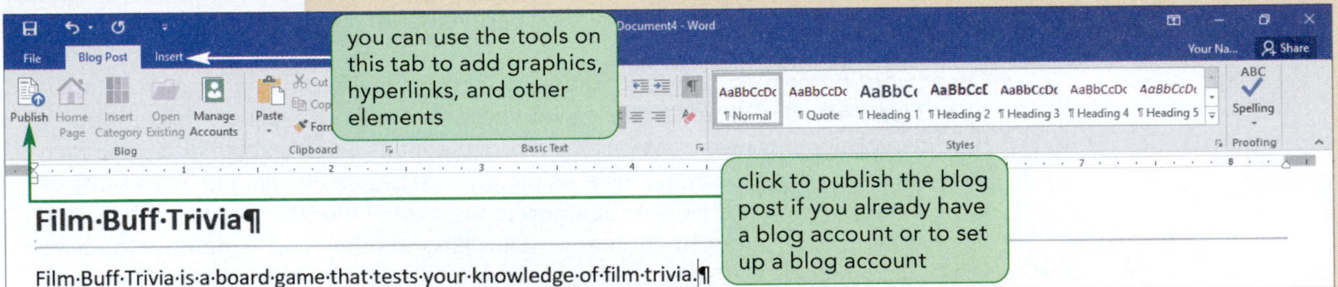

At this point, you could use the tools on the Insert tab to add hyperlinks, graphics, and other items to your blog post. Rima plans to add more text and some graphics to her blog post later. For now, you can save the post, and then explore options for publishing it.

7. Save the blog post as **Film Buff Trivia Blog Post** in the location specified by your instructor. Note that a blog post is a regular Word document file, with a .docx extension.
8. On the Blog Post tab, in the Blog group, click the **Publish** button.

   Assuming you have not previously registered for a blog account, you see the Register a Blog Account dialog box again. At this point, you could click the Register an Account button and then follow the on-screen instructions to register a blog account and publish your blog. Because Rima plans to do that later, you can close the blog post for now.

   Trouble? If you see a menu below the Publish button, you clicked the Publish button arrow instead of the Publish button. Press the Esc key, and then click the Publish button.

TIP

To add, remove, or change blog accounts, click the Manage Accounts button in the Blog group on the Blog Post tab.

9. Click the **Cancel** button to close the Register a Blog Account dialog box, and then click the **OK** button in the Microsoft Word dialog box.
10. Close the blog post.

Rima plans to write weekly blog posts describing the company's progress with the new game. Combined with the fact sheet, they will help generate interest in the company's crowd-sourcing effort.

INSIGHT

Working with Saved and Unsaved Document Versions

As you work on a document, versions of it are automatically saved every ten minutes. (To change how often a version is saved, click the File tab, click Options in the navigation bar, click Save in the navigation bar in the Word Options dialog box, and then change the number of minutes in the Save AutoRecover information every box.) If you want to open a version of a document that was autosaved, open the document, and click the File tab to display the Info screen. If autosaved versions of the document are available, they are listed in the Manage Document section, along with the date and time each version was saved. Click a version to open it in Read Mode as a read-only document with the AutoSaved Version bar below the title bar. To restore the version that you opened, click the Restore button in the AutoSaved Version bar. To compare the version you opened with the current version of the document before deciding whether to restore it, click the Compare button in the AutoSaved Version bar. When you do this, a Compare Result document opens, similar to the Compare Result document that opens when you use the Compare or Combine command. If you want to delete a saved version of a document, right-click the version in the Manage Document section of the Info screen, and then click Delete This Version.

If your computer is shut down unexpectedly while a document is open, the next time you start Word, the left pane of the Recent screen includes a Recovered section. To recover an unsaved version of a document, click Show Recovered Files in the Recovered section to create a new, blank document with the Document Recovery pane open. In the pane, click the unsaved version of the document that you want to open. You can also click the Manage Document button on the Info Screen, and then click Recover Unsaved Documents to display the Open dialog box to the folder that contains unsaved versions of files. If you want to delete all unsaved versions of all files, click Delete All Unsaved Documents on the Manage Document menu.

REVIEW

Session 7.2 Quick Check

1. Describe two options on the Paste Options menu that allow you to control the formatting applied to a linked Excel chart.
2. What is the first step in creating a hyperlink to a location in the same document?
3. Are horizontal lines displayed on a printed page?
4. What is the difference between the way text is displayed in Web Layout view and the way it is displayed in Print Layout view?
5. Explain how to edit a hyperlink.
6. What do you need to do before you can publish a blog post?

PRACTICE

Review Assignments

Data Files needed for the Review Assignments: Funding.xlsx, Hours.xlsx, Release.docx, Sports James.docx, Sports.docx

Rima is working on a document about a new game. She has written a draft of the document and has emailed it to James. While he reviews it, Rima asks you to turn on Track Changes and continue working on the document. Then, she can combine her edited version of the document with James's, accepting or rejecting changes as necessary. She also needs you to insert some data from an Excel worksheet as an embedded object and insert an Excel chart as a linked object. She then wants you to create a version of the document with hyperlinks, optimize the document for online viewing, and create a blog post. Complete the following steps:

1. Open the document **Sports** located in the Word7 > Review folder included with your Data Files. Save the file as **Sports Rima** in the location specified by your instructor.
2. Change the username to **Rima Khouri** and the user initials to **RK**, and then turn on Track Changes.
3. In the second paragraph, move the sentence that begins "When you land on a Ref It square..." to the end of the paragraph, and then add an **s** to the word "drive" in that sentence so the text reads "...USB drives...."
4. In the third paragraph, in the first line, attach a comment to the number "300" that reads **Should this be 325?**
5. Just before the period at the end of the document, add **or contact *your name*** (replacing *your name* with your first and last name) so that the sentence reads "Click here to learn more about this fun event, or contact *your name*."
6. Save your changes to the Sports Rima document.
7. Combine the Sports Rima document with James's edited version, which is named **Sports James**. Use the Sports Rima document as the original document.
8. Save the combined document as **Sports Combined** in the location specified by your instructor.
9. Turn off Track Changes, and then reject James's deletion of "chart" and his insertion of "graph." Accept all the other changes in the document. Delete all comments.
10. Change the username and initials back to their original settings, and then save the Sports Combined document. Close the Sports Rima document, saving changes if you didn't save them earlier.
11. In the Sports Combined document, replace the placeholder "[Insert Excel worksheet]" with the funding goals in the **Funding.xlsx file**. Include everything from cell A1 through cell B5. Insert the worksheet as an embedded object, and then close the Funding.xlsx file.
12. Center the embedded object, and then change the "Complete and Release Expansion Pack" value in the embedded worksheet object from $6,000 to **$7,000**.
13. Open the workbook **Hours.xlsx**, and then save it as **Hours Chart.xlsx** in the location specified by your instructor. Copy the pie chart to the Office Clipboard.
14. Return to the Sports Combined document, and then replace the placeholder "[Insert Excel chart]" with a linked copy of the chart using the destination theme. Save the Sports Combined document, and then close it.
15. Return to the Hours Chart workbook in Excel. Edit the data in the workbook by changing the hours for online test marketing to **100**, and the hours for trivia question development to **325**. Save the workbook, and then close Excel.

16. Open the **Sports Combined** document and review the chart. If it doesn't contain the new numbers, click the chart, and use the Refresh Data button to update the chart.
17. Save the Sports Combined document, and then save the document with the new name **Sports No Links** in the location specified by your instructor.
18. Break the link to the Excel workbook, and then save the document.
19. Format the Excel worksheet object as a bookmark named **Funding**. In the first line of the third paragraph below the page title, format the phrase "Sports Fan Trivia Expansion Pack" as a hyperlink that targets the "Funding" bookmark. Test the hyperlink to make sure it works. Save the document.
20. Open the document **Release** from the Word7 > Review folder included with your Data Files, and then save the file as **Release Party** in the location specified by your instructor. Close the Release Party document, and return to the Sports No Links document.
21. In the last paragraph of the document, format the word "here" as a hyperlink that targets the Release Party document. Test the hyperlink to make sure it works, and then close the Release Party document. Save the Sports No Links document.
22. Switch to Web Layout view, and add a two-color gradient page color using Dark Blue, Text 2, Lighter 80% as Color 1 and White, Background 1 as Color 2—with the shading style set to Diagonal up.
23. Change the background color for the worksheet object to white, and center the chart.
24. Insert a horizontal line before the "Our Goals" heading. Keep the default color, but change the width to 75%. Insert an identical horizontal line before the "Your Reward for Investing" heading.
25. Save and close the Sports No Links document.
26. Create a new blog post without attempting to register a blog account. Save the blog post as **Sports Blog Post** in the location specified by your instructor. Insert **Future Game Development** as the post title, and then type the following as the text of the blog post: **DBQ games has many exciting new sports games in development**.
27. Save and close the Sports Blog Post file.

APPLY

Case Problem 1

Data Files needed for this Case Problem: Budget.xlsx, Darwin.docx

Silver Day Wedding Planners You recently started working as a wedding planner at Silver Day Wedding Planners, in Raleigh, North Carolina. A client just called and asked you to send a copy of the wedding budget you discussed with her recently. The budget information is stored in an Excel workbook. You need to respond with a letter that contains the budget embedded as an Excel worksheet object. After you embed the worksheet object, you need to make some edits to the document using Track Changes. Finally, the company owner is considering using Word to create posts for the company's new wedding-planning blog, so she asks you to create a sample blog post. Complete the following steps:

1. Open the document **Darwin** from the Word7 > Case1 folder included with your Data Files. Save the file as **Darwin Letter** in the location specified by your instructor.
2. In the signature line, replace "Student Name" with your name.
3. Delete the placeholder "[Insert Excel worksheet]."
4. Start Excel, open the workbook **Budget** from the Word7 > Case1 folder included with your Data Files, and then save it as **Darwin Budget** in the location specified by your instructor.

5. Select the two-column list of items and amounts, from cell A6 through cell B10, and then copy the selection to the Clipboard.
6. Insert the worksheet data into the Word document in the blank paragraph that previously contained the placeholder text. Insert the data as a linked object that uses the destination styles.
7. Save the Word document, and then return to the Darwin Budget workbook and close Excel.
8. Starting from within the Word window, edit the linked worksheet object to change the amount for flowers to **700.00**. (*Hint*: Remember that the steps for editing a linked worksheet object are different from the steps for editing a linked chart. Also, note that you don't need to type the dollar sign. Excel adds that automatically.) Save the workbook, close Excel, and then update the link in Word.
9. Save the Darwin Letter document, and then save it again as **Darwin Letter No Links** in the location specified by your instructor.
10. Break the link in the Darwin Letter No Links document.
11. If necessary, change the username to your first and last names, change the initials to your initials, and then turn on Track Changes.
12. At the beginning of the letter, delete the date, and then type the current date using the format 1/1/17.
13. In the inside address, change "Road" to **Lane**.
14. At the end of the paragraph that reads "Please call if you have any questions." add the sentence **I will contact you next week to provide the username and password for your online account**.
15. Open the Reviewing pane and note the total number of revisions, the number of insertions, and the number of deletions in the document. Attach a comment to the word "Planners" in the first paragraph that reads **This document contains *x* insertions and *x* deletions. It contains a total of *x* revisions**. Replace the three instances of *x* with the correct numbers. (*Hint:* The total number of revisions will change when you insert the comment. The number that you type in the comment should reflect this updated total.)
16. Close the Reviewing pane, save your changes to the Darwin Letter No Links document, and then save it with the new name **Darwin Letter Changes Accepted** in the location specified by your instructor.
17. Turn off Track Changes, delete the comment, and then reject the replacement of "Lane" for "Road." Accept all the other changes in the document.
18. Return the username and initials to their original settings.
19. Save the Darwin Letter Changes Accepted document, and then close it.
20. Create a new blog post without attempting to register a blog account. Save the blog post as **Wedding Blog Post** in the location specified by your instructor. Insert **News from Silver Day Wedding Planners** as the post title, and then type the following as the text of the blog post: **We will be hosting a weekend wedding-planning seminar later this spring.**
21. Save and close the blog post.

TROUBLESHOOT

Case Problem 2

Data Files needed for this Case Problem: Garden Gloria.docx, Garden Neal.docx, Plant.docx

Bennington Park and Botanical Gardens You are an office assistant at Bennington Park and Botanical Gardens, located in Bennington, Oklahoma. Your supervisor, Neal Caves, is working on a set of documents about rain gardens, a type of garden designed to take advantage of rainwater runoff. He's already edited the main document using Track Changes. Now, he asks for your help in combining his copy of the edited file with a copy edited by his colleague, Gloria. Complete the following steps:

1. Open the document **Garden Gloria** from the Word7 > Case2 folder included with your Data Files, review its contents, and then close it.
2. Open the document **Garden Neal** from the Word7 > Case2 folder included with your Data Files, and then review its contents.
3. Combine the Garden Neal and Garden Gloria documents, using the Garden Neal file as the original document. Save the resulting new document as **Garden Combined** in the location specified by your instructor. Close the Garden Neal document.
4. In the Garden Combined document, review the tracked changes. Reject Gloria's deletion of "colorful." Accept the rest of the changes in the document, and then delete the comment.
5. Change the username and initials to yours, and then turn on Track Changes, if necessary.
6. Edit the title at the beginning of the document so it reads **Creating a Rain Garden**. Delete the extra space at the end of the second paragraph (after the phrase "and streams."), and then, in the last line of the document, replace "Neal Caves" with your first and last name.
7. Save the Garden Combined document, and then save it again as **Rain Garden Information** in the location specified by your instructor.
8. Accept all changes in the Rain Garden Information document, turn off Track Changes, and then change the username and initials back to their original settings.
9. Open the document **Plant** from the Word7 > Case2 folder included with your Data Files, and then save it as **Plant Information** in the location specified by your instructor.
10. **Troubleshoot** Because the Rain Garden Information and Plant Information documents will be emailed together, the overall look of the documents should match. Make any necessary changes to the page background, theme, and the style set in the Plant Information document to match the settings in the Rain Garden Information document.
11. **Troubleshoot** The Plant Information document contains an erroneous hyperlink that jumps to an unrelated external website. Remove that hyperlink from the document. Check the remaining hyperlink to make sure it jumps to the appropriate target in the current document. Make any necessary edits to the hyperlink to correct any errors.
12. In the last paragraph of the Plant Information document, format the word "here" as a hyperlink that jumps to the Rain Garden Information document.
13. In the last sentence of the Rain Garden Information document, format the word "list" as a hyperlink that jumps to the Plant Information document.
14. Test the links, save both documents, and then close them.

CREATE

Case Problem 3

There are no Data Files needed for this Case Problem.

J. Q. Whittier Foundation You have just started an internship in the communications department at the J. Q. Whittier Foundation, an organization that makes large donations to nonprofits around the country. As part of your job, you will eventually learn how to use a full-blown web design program. But first, your supervisor asks you to demonstrate your understanding of hyperlinks by creating a set of linked pages using Microsoft Word. The pages should focus on charitable organizations that you would like the foundation to consider funding. The charitable organizations you choose should all operate in a similar field—for example, you might choose healthcare charities that combat various diseases. On each page, include multiple graphics and links to live webpages accessible via the Internet. Your supervisor asks you to use all your formatting skills to create an attractive set of pages. Complete the following steps:

1. Select a field that interests you, such as health care, education, or the environment. Because you are creating sample pages for your work supervisor, choose a topic that is appropriate for a professional setting.
2. Open a new, blank Word document, and save it as **Main Page** in the location specified by your instructor.
3. Create two more new, blank documents named **Linked Page 1** and **Linked Page 2**, saving them in the location specified by your instructor.
4. In the Main Page file, add text and at least three pictures that introduce the reader to your chosen charitable field. The page should explain why the J.Q. Whittier Foundation should donate to charities in your chosen field. Use your own pictures or search for pictures online. Include at least three headings.
5. In the Linked Page 1 document, add text that provides details about a related nonprofit organization. For example, if your Main Page document discusses healthcare charities, then your Linked Page 1 document might contain information about the American Cancer Society. The text should mention one external webpage available via the Internet. Include at least one picture and at least one heading at the beginning of the page. Do the same in the Linked Page 2 document.
6. In the Linked Page 1 document, format the text that refers to an external webpage as a hyperlink that jumps to that page. Do the same in the Linked Page 2 file. (*Hint*: Use your browser to display the external webpage, right-click the URL in the box at the top of the browser window, and then click Copy. In the Insert Hyperlink dialog box, use the appropriate keyboard shortcut to paste the URL into the Address box.)
7. In the Main Page file, add hyperlinks that jump to the Linked Page 1 file and to the Linked Page 2 file.
8. In the Linked Page 1 and Linked Page 2 files, add hyperlinks that jump back to the Main Page file.
9. Format the three pages identically, using a theme, heading styles, and a style set of your choice. Use horizontal lines to separate the different sections on each page, and add a two-color gradient page background to all three documents.
10. Test the hyperlinks, and then close any open Word documents.

CHALLENGE

Case Problem 4

Data Files needed for this Case Problem: Coding Aziz.docx, Coding Tommy.docx, Coding.docx

123 Coding Academy Kendall Aihara is the marketing manager for 123 Coding Academy, a computer programming school that specializes in weekend coding camps and week-long classes on specific topics. She is creating a series of fact sheets that she can email to potential students. The fact sheets will summarize course offerings at the school. Each fact sheet will also include a link to an Internet video about learning to code. Kendall has already emailed a draft of her first fact sheet to her two colleagues, Aziz and Tommy, and she now needs to combine their versions with hers to create a final draft. However, because Aziz forgot to turn on Track Changes before he edited the document, Kendall will need to compare her draft with his so that she can see his changes marked as tracked changes.

After she finishes accepting and rejecting changes, Kendall wants you to show her how to add a video to the document. A video production company is preparing a series of videos that she will eventually incorporate into her fact sheets before distributing them; but for now, she asks you to show her how to insert any video from the Internet. Finally, after the fact sheet is finished, Kendall would like you to help her create a chart that illustrates the average distance each client travels to 123 Coding Academy. Complete the following steps:

1. Open the document **Coding** from the Word7 > Case4 folder included with your Data Files, save it as **Coding Kendall** in the location specified by your instructor, review the document to familiarize yourself with its contents, and then close it.
2. Open the document **Coding Aziz** from the Word7 > Case4 folder, review its contents, and then close it.
3. **Explore** Compare the Coding Kendall document with the Coding Aziz document, using Coding Kendall as the original document, and show the changes in a new document.
4. Review the new document to verify that Aziz's changes to Kendall's draft are now displayed as tracked changes, and then save the document as **Coding Aziz Tracked Changes** in the location specified by your instructor.
5. Combine the Coding Tommy document with the Coding Aziz Tracked Changes document, using the Coding Tommy file as the original document.
6. Save the new document as **Coding Academy Fact Sheet** in the location specified by your instructor.
7. Accept all changes in the document, turn off Track Changes, if necessary, and then use the Spelling and Grammar checker to correct any errors caused by missing spaces.
8. **Explore** Use Word Help to learn how to insert an Internet video in a document. In the blank paragraph at the end of the document, insert a video of a coding tutorial. Take care to choose a video that is appropriate for a professional setting. After you insert the video in the document, click the Play button on the video image to test it. Press the Esc button to close the video window when you are finished watching it.
9. **Explore** In the Word document, size the video image just as you would an ordinary picture so that it fits on the first page.
10. Save the Coding Academy Fact Sheet document, and close it and any other open documents.
11. Open a new, blank document, and then save it as **Student Travel Time Chart** in the location specified by your instructor.

Explore 12. Use Word Help to learn how to create a chart using Word's Chart tool. Create a bar chart using the 3-D Stacked Bar type. For the chart title, use **Miles Driven by Students for Weekend, Week-Long, and Month-Long Classes**. Use the Chart Elements button (which appears next to the chart when it is selected) to include the following elements: axes, chart title, gridlines, and legend. Include the data shown in Figure 7-38.

Figure 7-38 **Data for bar chart**

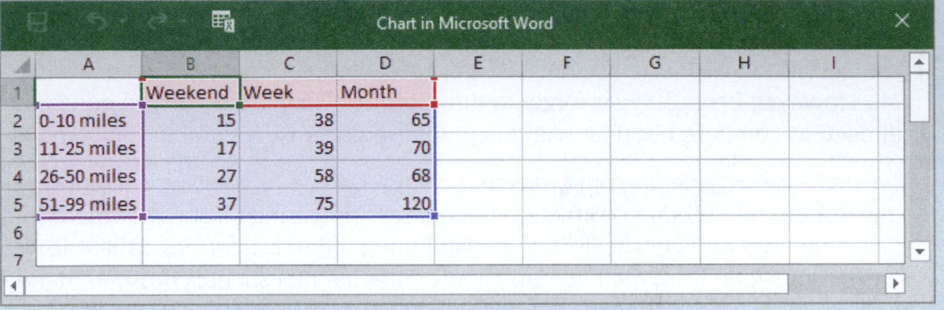

Chart in Microsoft Word

	A	B	C	D	E	F	G	H	I
1		Weekend	Week	Month					
2	0-10 miles	15	38	65					
3	11-25 miles	17	39	70					
4	26-50 miles	27	58	68					
5	51-99 miles	37	75	120					
6									
7									

Explore 13. Format the chart with the Style 2 chart style.

14. Change the document's theme to Facet.

15. Save and close all documents.

MODULE 5

Working with Excel Tables, PivotTables, and PivotCharts

Tracking Sales Data

EXCEL

OBJECTIVES

Session 5.1
- Explore a structured range of data
- Freeze rows and columns
- Plan and create an Excel table
- Rename and format an Excel table
- Add, edit, and delete records in an Excel table
- Sort data

Session 5.2
- Filter data using filter buttons
- Filter an Excel table with a slicer
- Insert a Total row to summarize an Excel table
- Split a worksheet into two panes
- Insert subtotals into a range of data
- Use the Outline buttons to show or hide details

Session 5.3
- Create and modify a PivotTable
- Apply PivotTable styles and formatting
- Filter a PivotTable
- Insert a slicer to filter a PivotTable
- Insert a recommended PivotTable
- Create a PivotChart

Case | *Victoria's Veggies*

Victoria Calderon has a very large backyard farm in Watertown, Wisconsin, and a passion for local, organic, fresh vegetables. Five years ago, she started selling organic vegetables harvested from her backyard farm at a roadside stand in front of her home. Over the years, she expanded from selling fresh vegetables to individual customers to supplying restaurants, group homes, and residential care facilities. As the stand has become more popular, Victoria has hired staff to help during the busy selling times. To better accommodate both her individual customers and business clients, six months ago, she opened Victoria's Veggies as a storefront. She stocks the store with vegetables grown in her own backyard farm and supplements her supply with fresh vegetables that she purchases from the year-round farmers market in Madison.

Victoria wants to use the June data to analyze the current state of Victoria's Veggies storefront operations. Victoria has entered the June sales data into an Excel workbook and wants you to help her analyze the data. You'll work with the data as an Excel table so you can easily edit, sort, and filter the data. You'll also summarize the data using the Subtotals command, a PivotTable, and a PivotChart.

STARTING DATA FILES

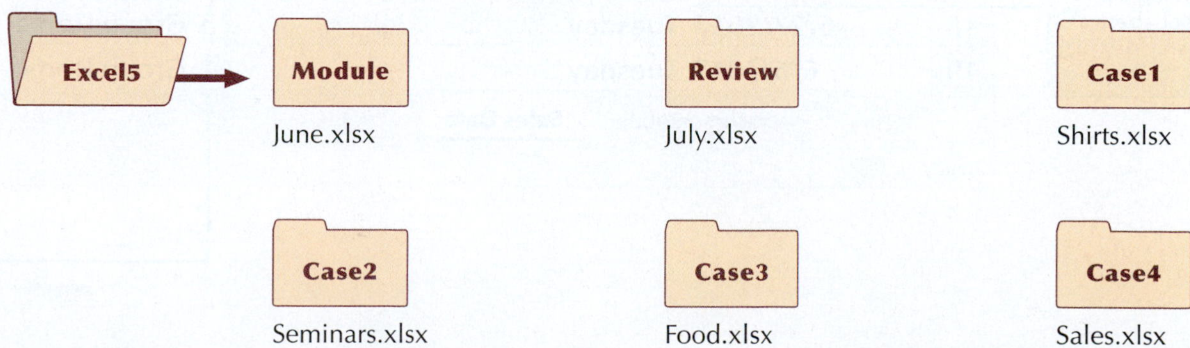

Session 5.1 Visual Overview:

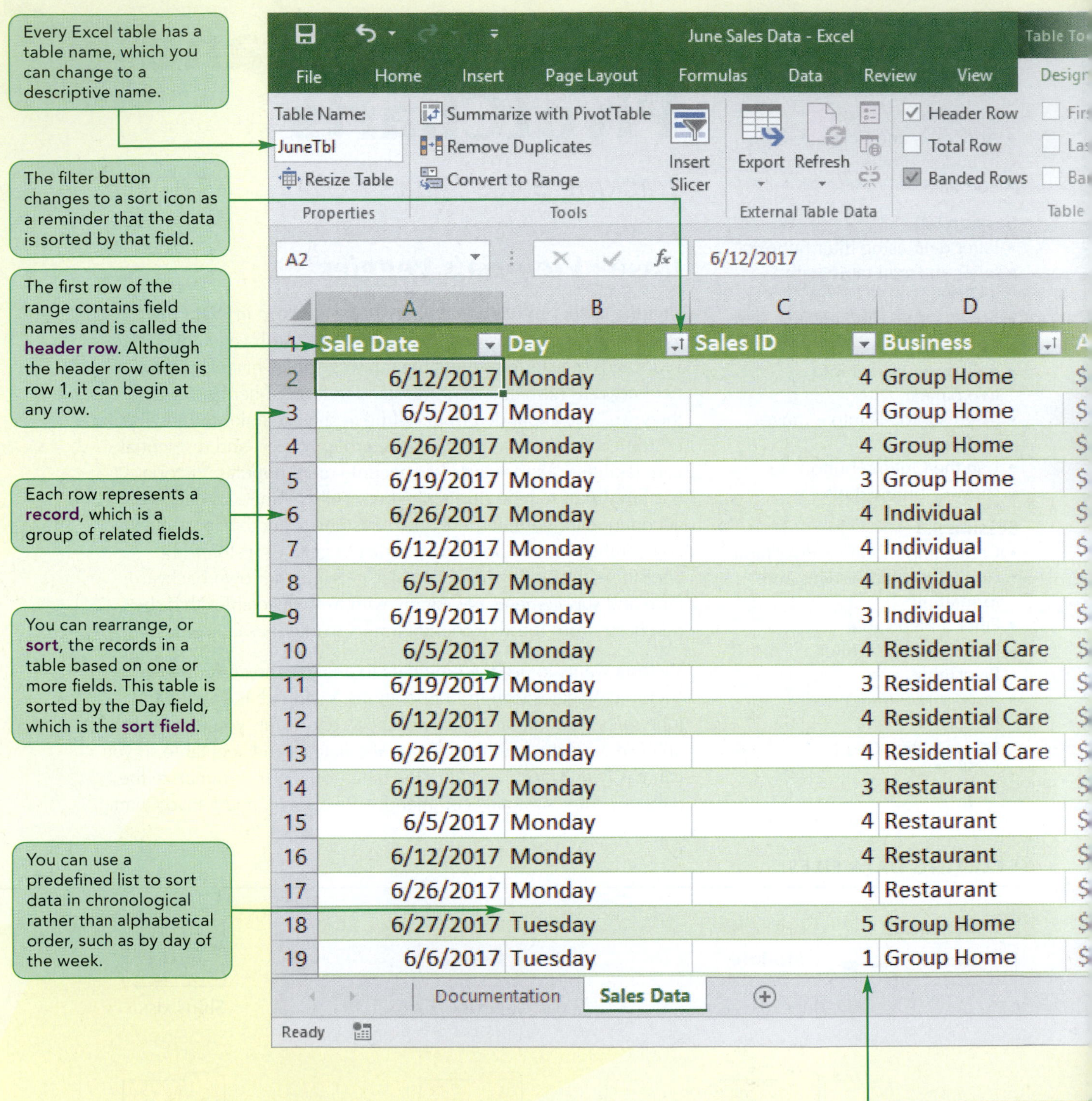
Every Excel table has a table name, which you can change to a descriptive name.
The filter button changes to a sort icon as a reminder that the data is sorted by that field.
The first row of the range contains field names and is called the header row. Although the header row often is row 1, it can begin at any row.
Each row represents a record, which is a group of related fields.
You can rearrange, or sort, the records in a table based on one or more fields. This table is sorted by the Day field, which is the sort field.
You can use a predefined list to sort data in chronological rather than alphabetical order, such as by day of the week.
June Sales Data - Excel
File
Home
Insert
Page Layout
Formulas
Data
Review
View
Table Name:
JuneTbl
Resize Table
Properties
Summarize with PivotTable
Remove Duplicates
Convert to Range
Tools
Insert Slicer
Export
Refresh
External Table Data
Header Row
Total Row
Banded Rows
A2
6/12/2017
Sale Date
Day
Sales ID
Business
Documentation
Sales Data
Ready

	A	B	C	D
1	Sale Date	Day	Sales ID	Business
2	6/12/2017	Monday	4	Group Home
3	6/5/2017	Monday	4	Group Home
4	6/26/2017	Monday	4	Group Home
5	6/19/2017	Monday	3	Group Home
6	6/26/2017	Monday	4	Individual
7	6/12/2017	Monday	4	Individual
8	6/5/2017	Monday	4	Individual
9	6/19/2017	Monday	3	Individual
10	6/5/2017	Monday	4	Residential Care
11	6/19/2017	Monday	3	Residential Care
12	6/12/2017	Monday	4	Residential Care
13	6/26/2017	Monday	4	Residential Care
14	6/19/2017	Monday	3	Restaurant
15	6/5/2017	Monday	4	Restaurant
16	6/12/2017	Monday	4	Restaurant
17	6/26/2017	Monday	4	Restaurant
18	6/27/2017	Tuesday	5	Group Home
19	6/6/2017	Tuesday	1	Group Home

Elements of an Excel Table

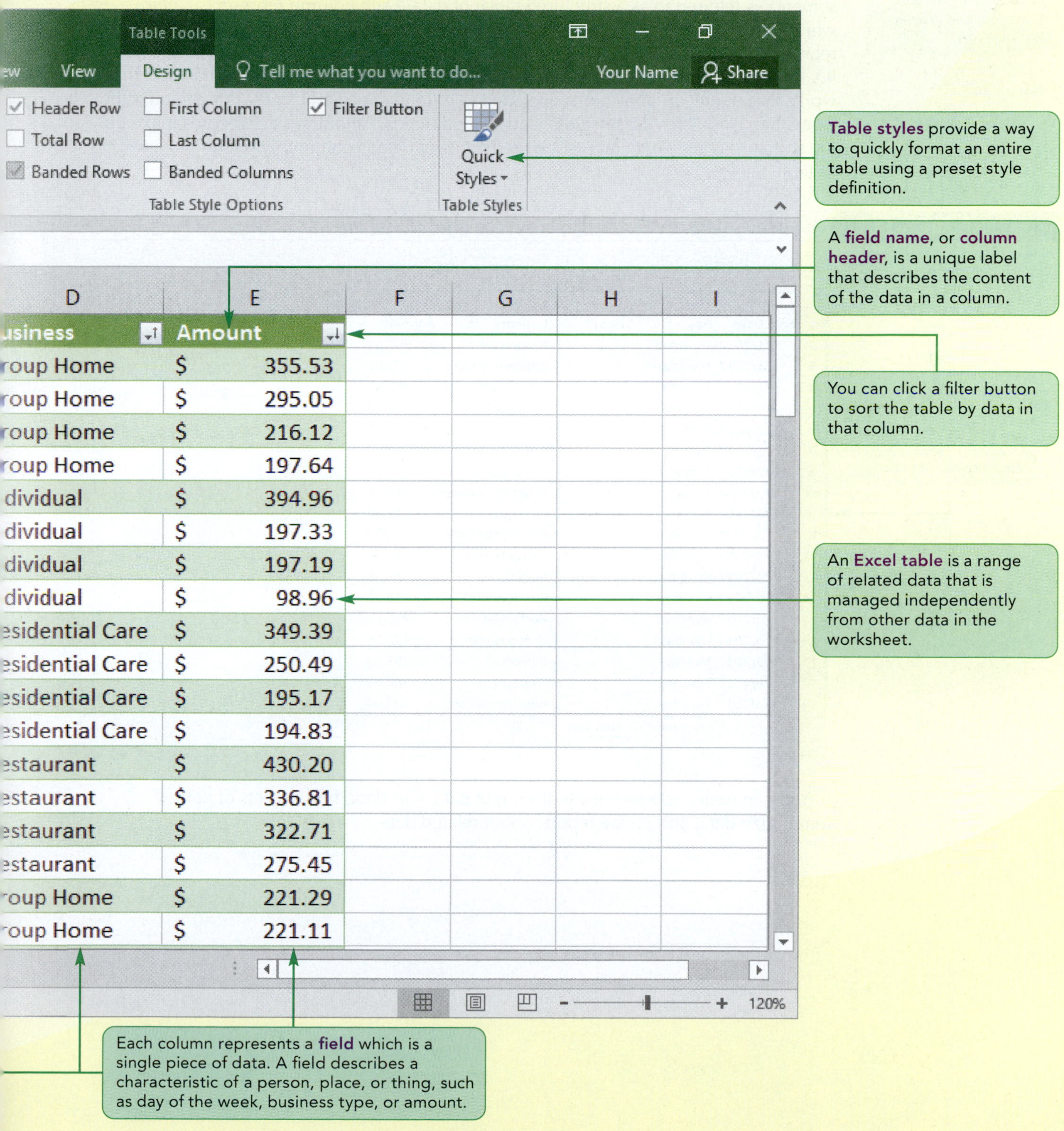
Table Tools
View
Design
Tell me what you want to do...
Your Name
Share
Header Row
First Column
Filter Button
Total Row
Last Column
Banded Rows
Banded Columns
Table Style Options
Quick Styles
Table Styles
D
E
F
G
H
I
usiness
Amount
roup Home $ 355.53
roup Home $ 295.05
roup Home $ 216.12
roup Home $ 197.64
dividual $ 394.96
dividual $ 197.33
dividual $ 197.19
dividual $ 98.96
esidential Care $ 349.39
esidential Care $ 250.49
esidential Care $ 195.17
esidential Care $ 194.83
estaurant $ 430.20
estaurant $ 336.81
estaurant $ 322.71
estaurant $ 275.45
roup Home $ 221.29
roup Home $ 221.11
120%
Table styles provide a way to quickly format an entire table using a preset style definition.
A **field name**, or **column header**, is a unique label that describes the content of the data in a column.
You can click a filter button to sort the table by data in that column.
An **Excel table** is a range of related data that is managed independently from other data in the worksheet.
Each column represents a **field** which is a single piece of data. A field describes a characteristic of a person, place, or thing, such as day of the week, business type, or amount.

Planning a Structured Range of Data

TIP

In Excel, a range of data is any block of cells, whereas a structured range of data has related records and fields organized in rows and columns.

A worksheet is often used to manage related data, such as lists of clients, products, or transactions. For example, the June sales for Victoria's Veggies that Victoria entered in the Sales Data worksheet, which is shown in Figure 5-1, are a collection of related data. Related data that is organized in columns and rows, such as the June sales, is sometimes referred to as a structured range of data. Each column represents a field, which is a single piece of data. Each row represents a record, which is a group of related fields. In the Sales Data worksheet, the columns labeled Sale Date, Day, Sales ID, Business, and Amount are fields that store different pieces of data. Each row in the worksheet is a record that stores one day's sales for a specific business that includes the Sale Date, Day, Sales ID, Business, and Amount fields. All of the sales records make up the structured range of data. A structured range of data is commonly referred to as a list or table.

Figure 5-1 June sales data

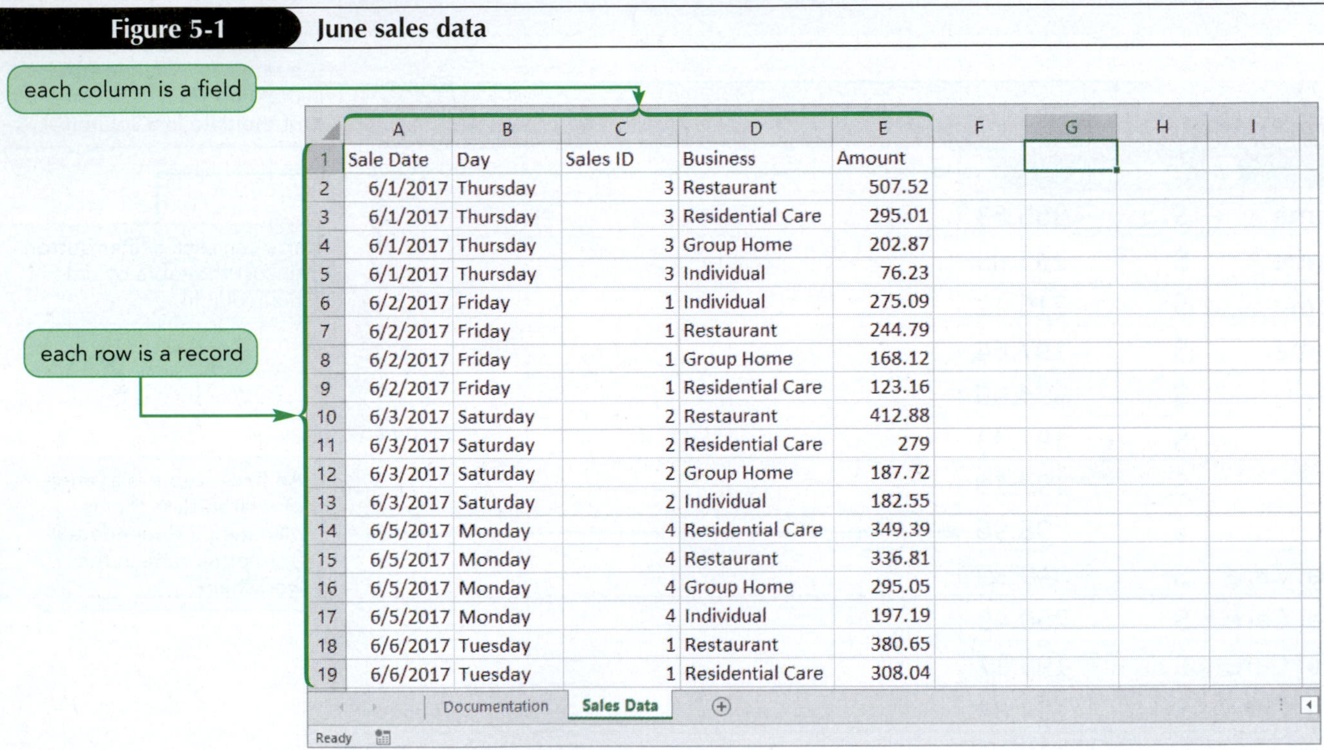

	A	B	C	D	E	F	G	H	I
1	Sale Date	Day	Sales ID	Business	Amount				
2	6/1/2017	Thursday	3	Restaurant	507.52				
3	6/1/2017	Thursday	3	Residential Care	295.01				
4	6/1/2017	Thursday	3	Group Home	202.87				
5	6/1/2017	Thursday	3	Individual	76.23				
6	6/2/2017	Friday	1	Individual	275.09				
7	6/2/2017	Friday	1	Restaurant	244.79				
8	6/2/2017	Friday	1	Group Home	168.12				
9	6/2/2017	Friday	1	Residential Care	123.16				
10	6/3/2017	Saturday	2	Restaurant	412.88				
11	6/3/2017	Saturday	2	Residential Care	279				
12	6/3/2017	Saturday	2	Group Home	187.72				
13	6/3/2017	Saturday	2	Individual	182.55				
14	6/5/2017	Monday	4	Residential Care	349.39				
15	6/5/2017	Monday	4	Restaurant	336.81				
16	6/5/2017	Monday	4	Group Home	295.05				
17	6/5/2017	Monday	4	Individual	197.19				
18	6/6/2017	Tuesday	1	Restaurant	380.65				
19	6/6/2017	Tuesday	1	Residential Care	308.04				

You can easily add and delete data, edit data, sort data, find subsets of data, summarize data, and create reports about related data.

PROSKILLS

Decision Making: The Importance of Planning

Before you create a structured range of data, you should create a plan. Planning involves gathering relevant information about the data and deciding your goals. The end results you want to achieve will help you determine the kind of data to include in each record and how to divide that data into fields. Specifically, you should do the following to create an effective plan:

- Spend time thinking about how you will use the data.
- Consider what reports you want to create for different audiences (supervisors, customers, directors, and so forth) and the fields needed to produce those reports.
- Think about the various questions, or queries, you want answered and the fields needed to create those results.

This information is often documented in a **data definition table**, which lists the fields to be maintained for each record, a description of the information each field will include, and the type of data (such as numbers, text, or dates) stored in each field. Careful and thorough planning will help you avoid having to redesign a structured range of data later.

Before creating the list of sales, Victoria carefully considered what information she needs and how she wants to use it. Victoria plans to use the data to track daily sales for each business type, which she has identified as group home, individual, residential care, and restaurant. She wants to be able to create reports that show specific lists of sales, such as all the sales for a specific date, day of the week, or Sales ID. Based on this information, Victoria developed the data definition table shown in Figure 5-2.

Figure 5-2 **Data definition table for the sales data**

Data Definition Table			
Field	**Description**	**Data Type**	**Notes**
Sale Date	Date of the sale	Date	Use the *mm/dd/yyyy* format
Day	Day of the week	Text	Monday, Tuesday, Wednesday, ...
Sales ID	Salesperson ID	Number	1=Victoria, 2=Miguel, 3=Michelle, 4=Sandy, 5=James
Business	Type of business for the sale	Text	Group Home, Individual, Residential Care, and Restaurant
Amount	Sales total for a specific transaction date and business type	Number	Use the Accounting format and show two decimal places

After you determine the fields and records you need, you can enter the data in a worksheet. You can then work with the data in many ways, including the following common operations:

- Add, edit, and delete data in the range.
- Sort the data range.
- Filter to display only rows that meet specified criteria.
- Insert formulas to calculate subtotals.
- Create summary tables based on the data in the range (usually with PivotTables).

You'll perform many of these operations on the sales data.

INSIGHT

Creating an Effective Structured Range of Data

For a range of data to be used effectively, it must have the same structure throughout. Keep in mind the following guidelines:

- **Enter field names in the top row of the range.** This clearly identifies each field.
- **Use short, descriptive field names.** Shorter field names are easier to remember and enable more fields to appear in the workbook window at once.
- **Format field names.** Use formatting to distinguish the header row from the data. For example, apply bold, color, and a different font size.
- **Enter the same kind of data in a field.** Each field should store the smallest bit of information and be consistent from record to record. For example, enter Los Angeles, Tucson, or Chicago in a City field, but do not include states, such as CA, AZ, or IL, in the same column of data.
- **Separate the data from the rest of the worksheet.** The data, which includes the header row, should be separated from other information in the worksheet by at least one blank row and one blank column. The blank row and column enable Excel to accurately determine the range of the data.

Victoria created a workbook and entered the sales data for June based on the plan outlined in the data definition table. You'll open this workbook and review its structure.

To open and review Victoria's workbook:

1. Open the **June** workbook located in the **Excel5 > Module** folder included with your Data Files, and then save the workbook as **June Sales Data** in the location specified by your instructor.
2. In the Documentation worksheet, enter your name in cell B3 and the date in cell B4.
3. In the range A7:D13, review the data definition table. This table, which is shown in Figure 5-2, describes the different fields that are used in the Sales Data worksheet.
4. Go to the **Sales Data** worksheet. This worksheet, which is shown in Figure 5-1, contains data about the vegetable store's sales. Currently, the worksheet includes 101 sales records. Each sale record is a separate row (rows 2 through 102) and contains five fields (columns A through E). Row 1, the header row, contains labels that describe the data in each column.
5. Scroll the worksheet to row **102**, which is the last record.

When you scroll the worksheet, the first column headers in row 1 are no longer visible. Without seeing the column headers, it is difficult to know what the data entered in each column represents.

Freezing Rows and Columns

You can select rows and columns to remain visible in the workbook window as you scroll the worksheet. **Freezing** a row or column lets you keep the headers visible as you work with the data in a large worksheet. You can freeze the top row, freeze the first column, or freeze the rows and columns above and to the left of the selected cell. If you freeze the top row, row 1 remains on the screen as you scroll, leaving column headers visible and making it easier to identify the data in each record.

Victoria wants to see the column headers as she scrolls the sales records. You'll freeze row 1, which contains the column headers.

To freeze row 1 of the worksheet:

TIP

To freeze the columns and rows above and to the left of the selected cell, click the Freeze Panes button, and then click Freeze Panes.

1. Press the **Ctrl+Home** keys to return to cell A1. You want to freeze row 1.
2. On the ribbon, click the **View** tab.
3. In the Window group, click the **Freeze Panes** button, and then click **Freeze Top Row**. A horizontal line appears below the column labels to indicate which row is frozen.
4. Scroll the worksheet to row **102**. This time, the column headers remain visible as you scroll. See Figure 5-3.

Figure 5-3 Top row of the worksheet is frozen

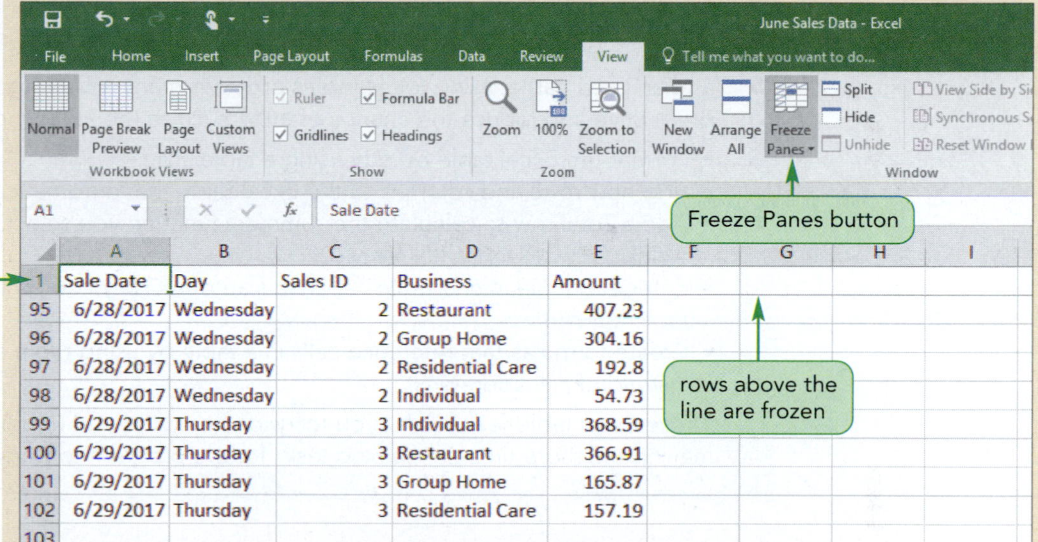

	A	B	C	D	E
1	Sale Date	Day	Sales ID	Business	Amount
95	6/28/2017	Wednesday	2	Restaurant	407.23
96	6/28/2017	Wednesday	2	Group Home	304.16
97	6/28/2017	Wednesday	2	Residential Care	192.8
98	6/28/2017	Wednesday	2	Individual	54.73
99	6/29/2017	Thursday	3	Individual	368.59
100	6/29/2017	Thursday	3	Restaurant	366.91
101	6/29/2017	Thursday	3	Group Home	165.87
102	6/29/2017	Thursday	3	Residential Care	157.19
103					

5. Press the **Ctrl+Home** keys. Cell A2, the cell directly below the frozen row, becomes the active cell.

After you freeze panes, the first option on the Freeze Panes button menu changes to Unfreeze Panes. This option releases the frozen panes so that all the columns and rows in the worksheet shift when you scroll. Victoria wants you to use a different method to keep the column headers visible, so you will unfreeze the top row of the worksheet.

To unfreeze the top row of the worksheet:

1. On the View tab, in the Window group, click the **Freeze Panes** button. The first Freeze Panes option is now Unfreeze Panes.
2. Click **Unfreeze Panes**. The headers are no longer frozen, and the horizontal line below the column headers is removed. You can now scroll all the rows and columns in the worksheet.

Creating an Excel Table

You can convert a structured range of data, such as the sales data in the range A1:E102, to an Excel table. An Excel table makes it easier to identify, manage, and analyze the groups of related data. When a structured range of data is converted into an Excel table, you see the following:

- A filter button in each cell of the header row
- The range formatted with a table style
- A sizing handle (a small triangle) in the lower-right corner of the last cell of the table
- The Table Tools Design tab on the ribbon

You can create more than one Excel table in a worksheet. Although you can leave the sales data as a structured range of data and still perform all of the tasks in this section, creating an Excel table helps you to be more efficient and accurate.

INSIGHT

Saving Time with Excel Tables

Although you can perform the same operations for both a structured range of data and an Excel table, using Excel tables provides many advantages to help you be more productive and reduce the chance of error, such as the following:

- Format the Excel table quickly using a table style.
- Add new rows and columns to the Excel table that automatically expand the range.
- Add a Total row to calculate the summary function you select, such as SUM, AVERAGE, COUNT, MIN, or MAX.
- Enter a formula in one table cell that is automatically copied to all other cells in that table column.
- Create formulas that reference cells in a table by using table and column names instead of cell addresses.

These Excel table features let you focus on analyzing and understanding the data, leaving the more time-consuming tasks for the program to perform.

Victoria wants you to create an Excel table from the sales data in the Sales Data worksheet. You'll be able to work with the Excel tables to analyze Victoria's data effectively.

To create an Excel table from the sales data:

1. If necessary, select any cell in the range of sales data to make it the active cell.
2. On the ribbon, click the **Insert** tab.
3. In the Tables group, click the **Table** button. The Create Table dialog box opens. The range of data you want to use for the table is selected in the worksheet, and a formula with its range reference, =$A$1:$E$102, is entered in the dialog box.
4. Verify that the **My table has headers** check box is selected. The headers are the field names entered in row 1. If the first row did not contain field names, the My table has headers check box would be unchecked, and Excel would insert a row of headers with the names Column1, Column2, and so on.

5. Click the **OK** button. The dialog box closes, and the range of data is converted to an Excel table, which is selected. Filter buttons appear in the header row, the sizing handle appears in the lower-right corner of the last cell of the table, the table is formatted with a predefined table style, and the Table Tools Design tab appears on the ribbon. See Figure 5-4.

Figure 5-4 Excel table with the sales data

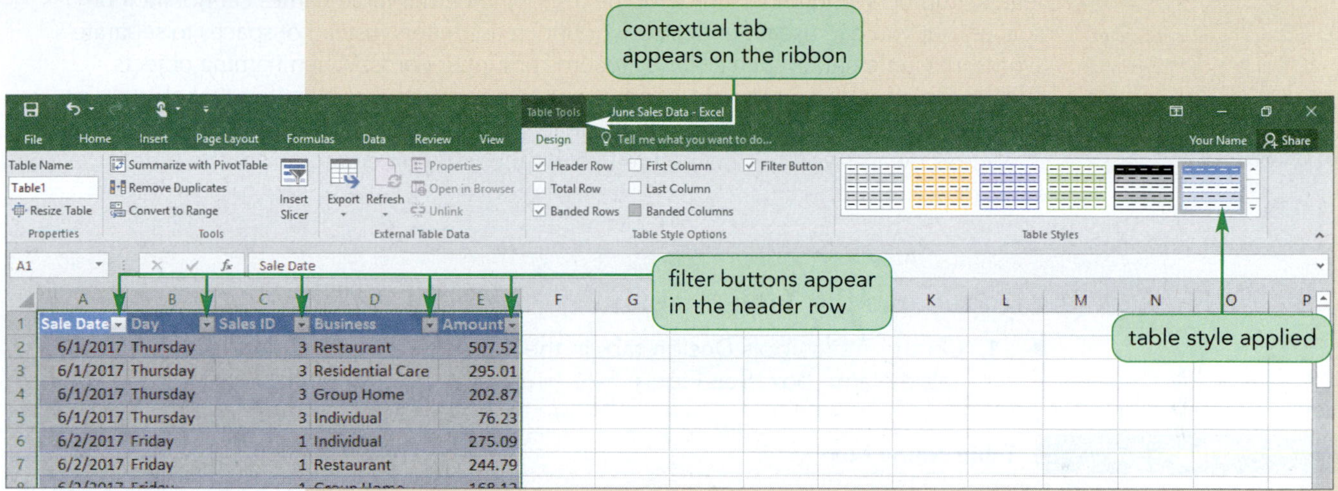

6. Select any cell in the table, and then scroll down the table. The field names in the header row replace the standard lettered column headings (A, B, C, and so on) as you scroll, so you don't need to freeze panes to keep the header row visible. See Figure 5-5.

Figure 5-5 Sales table scrolled

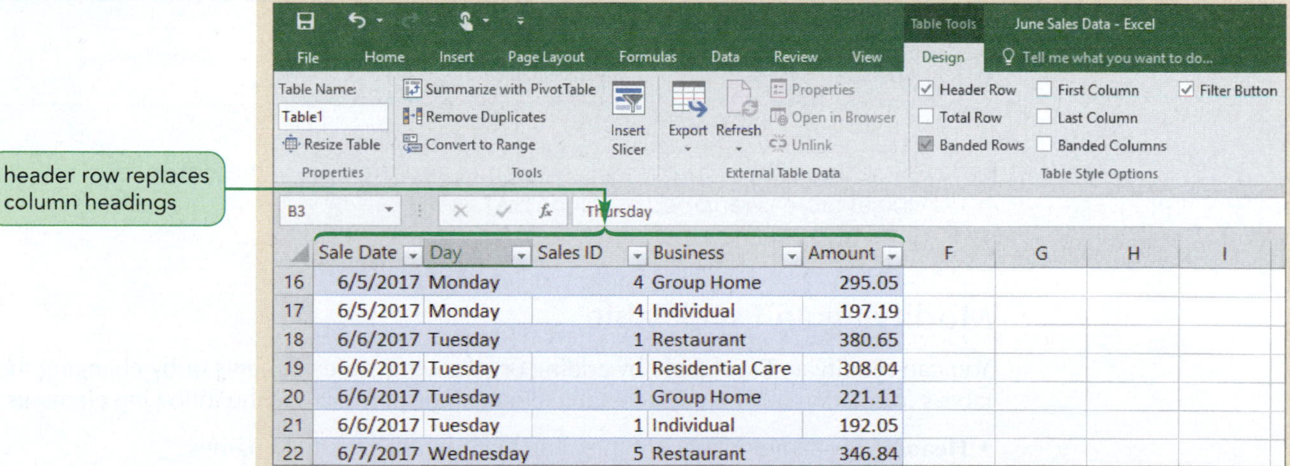

7. Press the **Ctrl+Home** keys to make cell A1 the active cell. The column headers return to the standard display, and the Excel table header row scrolls back into view as row 1.

Renaming an Excel Table

Each Excel table in a workbook must have a unique name. Excel assigns the name Table1 to the first Excel table created in a workbook. Any additional Excel tables you create in the workbook are named consecutively as Table2, Table3, and so forth. You can assign a more descriptive name to a table, making it easier to identify a particular table by its content. Descriptive names are especially useful when you create more than one Excel table in the same workbook because they make it easier to reference the different Excel tables.

TIP

If you copy a worksheet that contains a table, Excel adds the next consecutive number at the end of the table name to create a unique table name.

Table names must start with a letter or an underscore but can use any combination of letters, numbers, and underscores for the rest of the name. Table names cannot include spaces, but you can use an underscore or uppercase letters instead of spaces to separate words in a table name, such as June_Records or JuneRecords. When naming objects such as tables, a best practice is to include an abbreviation that identifies that object. For example, table names often end with the letters *Tbl*, such as June_Records_Tbl or JuneTbl.

Victoria wants you to rename the Excel table you just created from the June sales data.

To rename the Table1 table:

1. On the Table Tools Design tab, in the Properties group, select **Table1** in the Table Name box. See Figure 5-6.

Figure 5-6 **Table Name box**

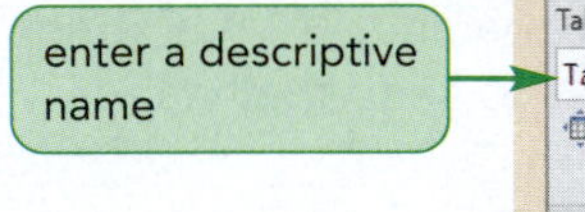

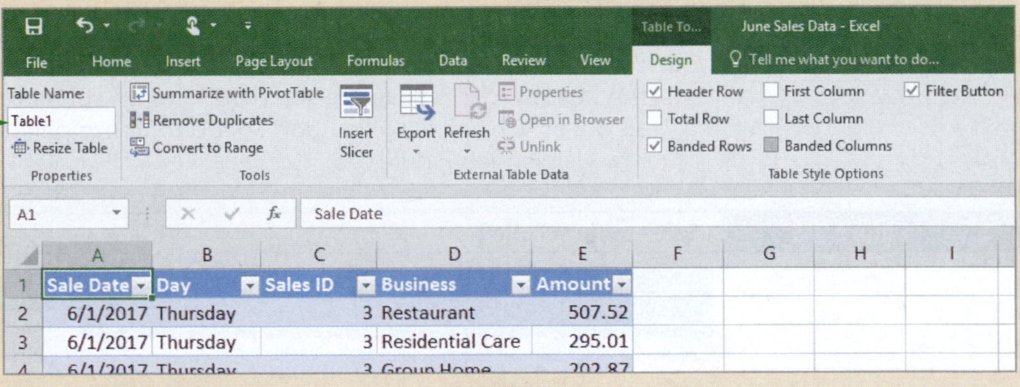

2. Type **JuneTbl** as the descriptive name, and then press the **Enter** key. The Excel table is renamed as "JuneTbl."

Modifying an Excel Table

You can modify an Excel table by adding or removing table elements or by changing the table's formatting. For every Excel table, you can display or hide the following elements:

- **Header row**—The first row of the table that includes the field names
- **Total row**—A row at the bottom of the table that applies a function to the column values
- **First column**—Formatting added to the leftmost column of the table
- **Last column**—Formatting added to the rightmost column of the table
- **Banded rows**—Formatting added to alternating rows so that even and odd rows are different colors, making it simpler to distinguish records
- **Banded columns**—Formatting added to alternating columns so they are different colors, making it simpler to distinguish fields
- **Filter buttons**—Buttons that appear in each column of the header row and open a menu with options for sorting and filtering the table data

You can also modify a table by applying a table style. As with other styles, a table style formats all of the selected table elements with a consistent, unified design. You can change the font, fill, alignment, number formats, column widths and row heights, and other formatting of selected cells in the table the same way you would for other cells in the worksheet.

Victoria wants the JuneTbl table to have a format that makes the table easier to read. You will apply a table style and make other formatting changes to the table.

To format the JuneTbl table:

1. On the Table Tools Design tab, in the Table Styles group, click the **More** button. A gallery of table styles opens.
2. In the Table Styles gallery, in the Medium section, click **Table Style Medium 7**. The table now has a green style.
3. In the Table Style Options group, click the **Banded Rows** check box. The alternating row colors disappear. The table is more challenging to read this way, so you will reapply the banded rows formatting.
4. In the Table Style Options group, click the **Banded Rows** check box to select it. The alternating row colors reappear.
5. Change the width of columns A through E to **15** characters. The entire column headers and all of the values are now visible.
6. Select the **Amount** column, and then change the values to the **Accounting** format. See Figure 5-7.

TIP

To display or hide alternating column colors, click the Banded Columns check box in the Table Style Options group.

Figure 5-7 Modified JuneTbl table

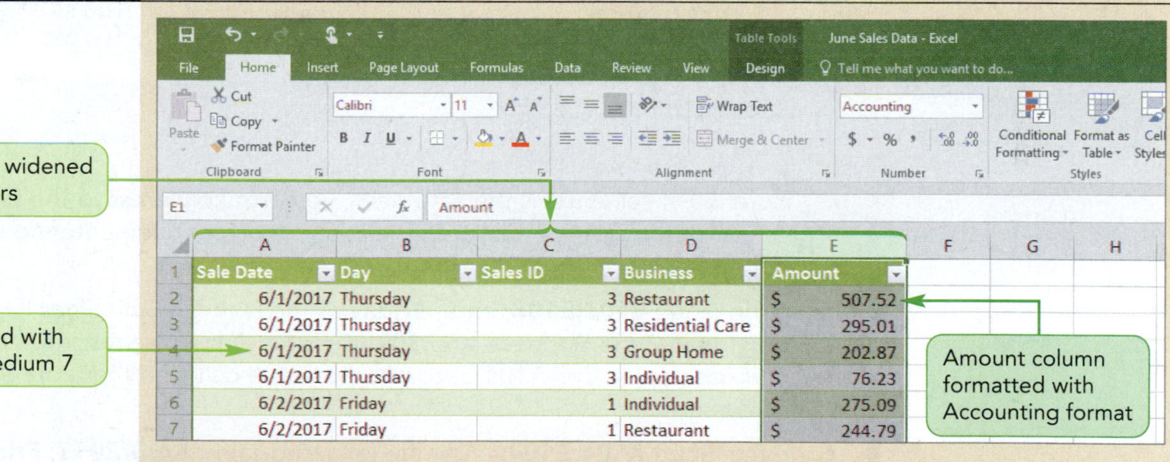

7. Select cell **A1** to make it the active cell.

Maintaining Data in an Excel Table

As you develop a worksheet with an Excel table, you may need to add new records to the table, find and edit existing records in the table, and delete records from the table. Victoria wants you to make several changes to the data in the JuneTbl table.

Adding Records

As you maintain data in an Excel table, you often need to add new records. You add a record to an Excel table in a blank row. The simplest and most convenient way to add a record to an Excel table is to enter the data in the first blank row below the last record. You can then sort the data to arrange the table in the order you want. If you want the record in a specific location, you can also insert a row within the table for the new record.

The sales records for June 30 are missing from the JuneTbl table. Victoria asks you to add to the table four new records that contain the missing data.

To add four records to the JuneTbl table:

1. Press the **End** key, and then press the ↓ key to make cell A102 the active cell. This cell is in the last row of the table.
2. Press the ↓ key to move the active cell to cell A103, which is in the first blank row below the table.
3. In cell A103, type **6/30/2017**, and then press the **Tab** key. Cell B103 in the Day column becomes the active cell. The table expands to include a new row with the same formatting as the rest of the table. The AutoCorrect Options button appears so you can undo the table formatting if you hadn't intended the new data to be part of the existing table. The sizing handle moves to the lower-right corner of cell E103, which is now the cell in the lower-right corner of the table. See Figure 5-8.

TIP

You can drag the sizing handle to add columns or rows to the Excel table or delete them from it.

Figure 5-8 New row added to the JuneTbl table

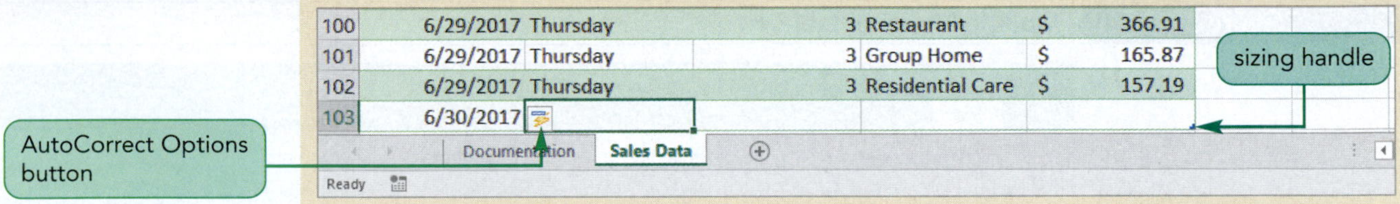
100
6/29/2017 Thursday
3 Restaurant
$
366.91
101
6/29/2017 Thursday
3 Group Home
$
165.87
102
6/29/2017 Thursday
3 Residential Care
$
157.19
103
6/30/2017
Documentation
Sales Data
Ready
sizing handle
AutoCorrect Options button

Trouble? If cell A104 is the active cell, you probably pressed the Enter key instead of the Tab key. Click cell B103, and then continue entering the data in Step 4.

4. In the range **B103:E103**, enter **Friday** as the Day, **1** as the Sales ID, **Individual** as the Business, and **309.00** as the Amount, pressing the **Tab** key after each entry. Cell A104 becomes the active cell, and the table expands to include row 104.
5. In the range **A104:E104**, enter the following sales: **6/30/2017**, **Friday**, **1**, **Restaurant**, and **464.12**.
6. In the range **A105:E105**, enter the following sales: **6/30/2017**, **Friday**, **1**, **Group Home**, and **431.12**.
7. In the range **A106:E106**, enter the following sales: **6/30/2017**, **Friday**, **1**, **Residential Care**, and **225.02**.
8. Press the **Enter** key. The records are added to the table. See Figure 5-9.

Figure 5-9 Records added to the JuneTbl table

Trouble? If a new row is added to the table, you probably pressed the Tab key instead of the Enter key after the last entry in the record. On the Quick Access Toolbar, click the Undo button to remove the extra row.

Finding and Editing Records

Although you can manually scroll through the table to find a specific record, often a quicker way to locate a record is to use the Find command. When using the Find or Replace command, it is best to start at the top of a worksheet to ensure that all cells in the table are searched. You edit the data in a table the same way as you edit data in a worksheet cell.

Victoria wants you to update the June 20 Residential Care sales amount. You'll use the Find command to locate the record, which is currently blank. Then, you'll edit the record in the table to change the amount to $309.00.

To find and edit the 6/20/2017 Residential Care record:

1. Press the **Ctrl+Home** keys to make cell A1 the active cell so that all cells in the table will be searched.
2. On the Home tab, in the Editing group, click the **Find & Select** button, and then click **Find** (or press the **Ctrl+F** keys). The Find and Replace dialog box opens.
3. In the Find what box, type **6/20/2017**, and then click the **Find Next** button. Cell A67, which contains the record for an Individual, is selected. This is not the record you want.
4. Click the **Find Next** button three times to display the record for Residential Care on 6/20/2017.
5. Click the **Close** button. The Find and Replace dialog box closes.
6. Press the **Tab** key four times to move the active cell to the Amount column, type **309**, and then press the **Enter** key. The record is updated to reflect the $309.00 amount.
7. Press the **Ctrl+Home** keys to make cell A1 the active cell.

Deleting a Record

As you work with the data in an Excel table, you might find records that are outdated or duplicated. In these instances, you can delete the records. To delete records that are incorrect, out of date, or no longer needed, select a cell in each record you want to delete, click the Delete button arrow in the Cells group on the Home tab, and then click Delete Table Rows. You can also delete a field by selecting a cell in the field you want to delete, clicking the Delete button arrow, and then clicking Delete Table Columns. In addition, you can use the Remove Duplicates dialog box to locate and remove records that have the same data in selected columns. The Remove Duplicates dialog box lists all columns in the table. Usually, all columns in a table are selected to identify duplicate records.

Victoria thinks that one sales record was entered twice. You'll use the Remove Duplicates dialog box to locate and delete the duplicate record from the table.

To find and delete the duplicate record from the JuneTbl table:

1. Scroll to row **56**, and observe that the entries in row 56 and row 57 are exactly the same. One of these records needs to be deleted.
2. On the ribbon, click the **Table Tools Design** tab.
3. In the Tools group, click the **Remove Duplicates** button. The Remove Duplicates dialog box opens, and all of the columns in the table are selected. Excel looks for repeated data in the selected columns to determine whether any duplicate records exist. If duplicates are found, all but one of the records are deleted. See Figure 5-10.

Figure 5-10 Remove Duplicates dialog box

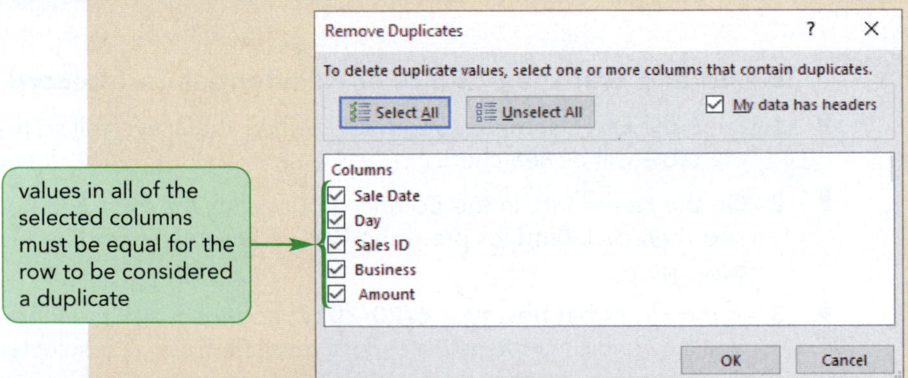

You want to search all of the columns in the table for duplicated data so that you don't inadvertently delete a record that has duplicate values in the selected fields but a unique value in the deselected field.

4. Click the **OK** button. A dialog box opens, reporting "1 duplicate values found and removed; 104 unique values remain."
5. Click the **OK** button.

   Trouble? If you deleted records you did not intend to delete, you can reverse the action. On the Quick Access Toolbar, click the Undo button, and then repeat Steps 3 through 5.
6. Press the **Ctrl+Home** keys to make cell A1 the active cell.

Sorting Data

The records in an Excel table initially appear in the order they were entered. As you work, however, you may want to view the same records in a different order. For example, Victoria might want to view the sales by business or day of the week. You can sort data in ascending or descending order. **Ascending order** arranges text alphabetically from A to Z, numbers from smallest to largest, and dates from oldest to newest. **Descending order** arranges text in reverse alphabetical order from Z to A, numbers from largest to smallest, and dates from newest to oldest. In both ascending and descending order, blank cells are placed at the end of the table.

Sorting One Column Using the Sort Buttons

You can quickly sort data with one sort field using the Sort A to Z button or the Sort Z to A button. Victoria wants you to sort the sales in ascending order by the Business column. This will rearrange the table data so that the records appear in alphabetical order by Business.

To sort the JuneTbl table in ascending order by the Business column:

1. Select any cell in the Business column. You do not need to select the entire JuneTbl table, which consists of the range A1:E105. Excel determines the table's range when you click any cell in the table.
2. On the ribbon, click the **Data** tab.
3. In the Sort & Filter group, click the **Sort A to Z** button. The data is sorted in ascending order by Business. The Business filter button changes to show that the data is sorted by that column. See Figure 5-11.

TIP

You can also use the Sort & Filter button in the Editing group on the Home tab.

Figure 5-11 JuneTbl table sorted by the Business field

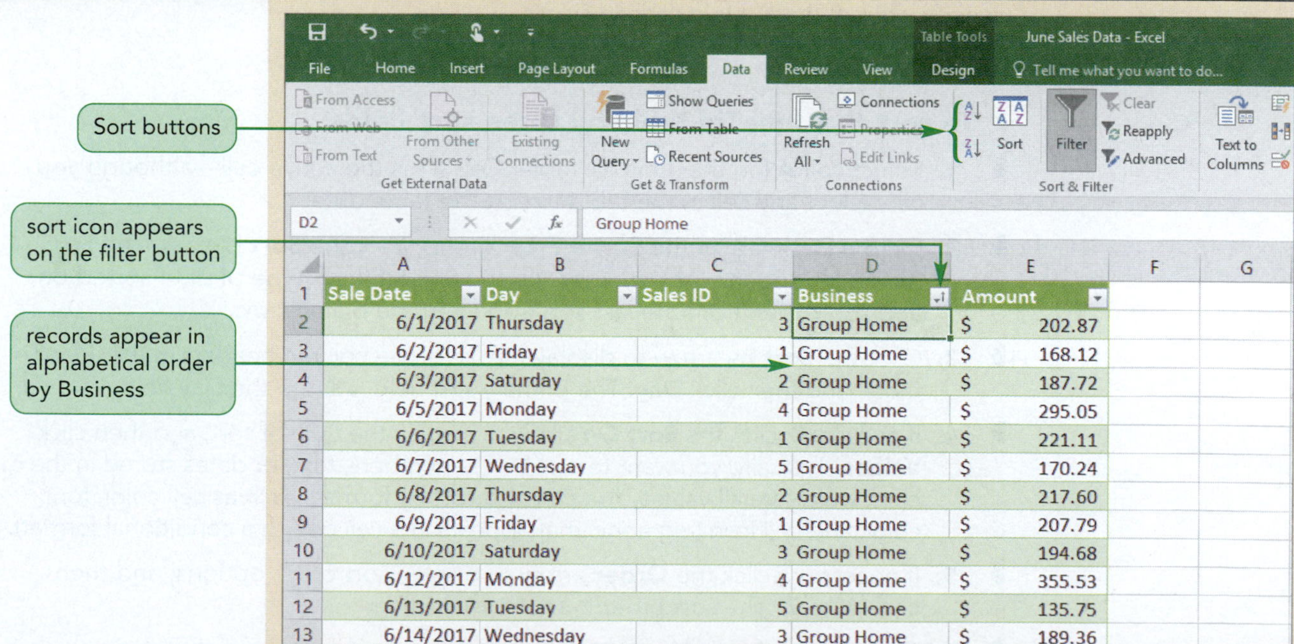

Trouble? If the data is sorted in the wrong order, you might have clicked in a different column than the Business column. Repeat Steps 1 through 3.

Sorting Multiple Columns Using the Sort Dialog Box

Sometimes one sort field is not adequate for your needs. For example, Victoria wants to arrange the JuneTbl table so that the sales are ordered first by Day (Monday, Tuesday, and so forth), then by Business for each day of the week, and then by Amount (highest to lowest). You must sort by more than one column to accomplish this. The first sort field is called the **primary sort field**, the second sort field is called the **secondary sort field**, and so forth. Although you can include up to 64 sort fields in a single sort, you typically will use one to three sort fields. In this case, the Day field is the primary sort field, the Business field is the secondary sort field, and the Amount field is the tertiary sort field. When you have more than one sort field, you should use the Sort dialog box to specify the sort criteria.

REFERENCE

Sorting Data Using Multiple Sort Fields

- Select any cell in a table or range.
- On the Data tab, in the Sort & Filter group, click the Sort button.
- If necessary, click the Add Level button to insert the Sort by row.
- Click the Sort by arrow, select the column heading for the primary sort field, click the Sort On arrow to select the type of data, and then click the Order arrow to select the sort order.
- For each additional column to sort, click the Add Level button, click the Then by arrow, select the column heading for the secondary sort field, click the Sort On arrow to select the type of data, and then click the Order arrow to select the sort order.
- Click the OK button.

Victoria wants to see the sales sorted by day, and then within day by business, and then within business by amount, with the highest amounts appearing before the smaller ones for each business. This will make it easier for Victoria to evaluate sales on specific days of the week in each business.

To sort the JuneTbl table by three sort fields:

1. Select cell **A1** in the JuneTbl table. Cell A1 is the active cell—although you can select any cell in the table to sort the table data.
2. On the Data tab, in the Sort & Filter group, click the **Sort** button. The Sort dialog box opens. Any sort specifications (sort field, type of data sorted on, and sort order) from the last sort appear in the dialog box.
3. Click the **Sort by** arrow to display the list of the column headers in the JuneTbl table, and then click **Day**. The primary sort field is set to the Day field.
4. If necessary, click the **Sort On** arrow to display the type of sort, and then click **Values**. Typically, you want to sort by the numbers, text, or dates stored in the cells, which are all values. You can also sort by formats such as cell color, font color, and cell icon (a graphic that appears in a cell due to a conditional format).
5. If necessary, click the **Order** arrow to display sort order options, and then click **A to Z**. The sort order is set to ascending.
6. Click the **Add Level** button. A Then by row is added below the primary sort field.
7. Click the **Then by** arrow and click **Business**, and then verify that **Values** appears in the Sort On box and **A to Z** appears in the Order box.

8. Click the **Add Level** button to add a second Then by row.
9. Click the second **Then by** arrow, click **Amount**, verify that **Values** appears in the Sort On box, click the **Order** arrow, and then click **Largest to Smallest** to specify a descending sort order for the Amount values. See Figure 5-12.

Figure 5-12 Sort dialog box with three sorted fields

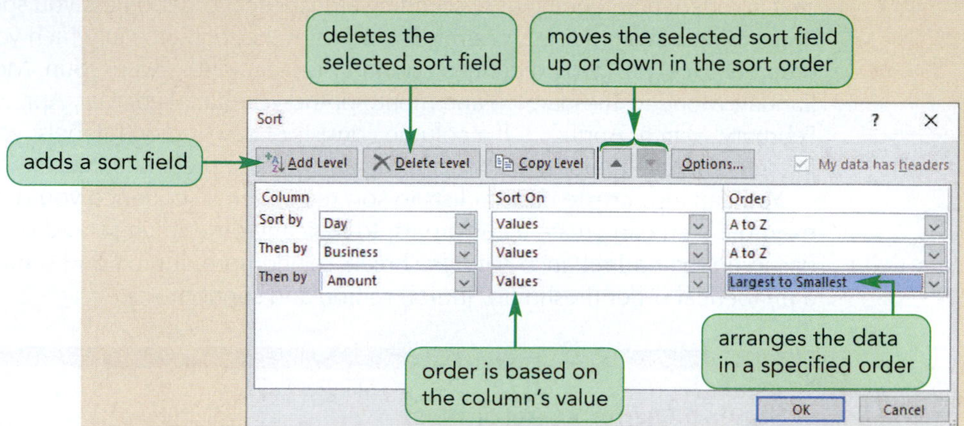

10. Click the **OK** button. Excel sorts the table records first in ascending order by the Day field, then within each Day in ascending order by the Business field, and then within each Business in descending order by the Amount field. For example, the first 20 records are Friday sales. Of these records, the first five are Group Home, the next five are Individual, and so on. Finally, the Friday Group Home sales are arranged from highest to lowest in the Amount column. See Figure 5-13.

Figure 5-13 Sales sorted by Day, then by Business, and then by Amount

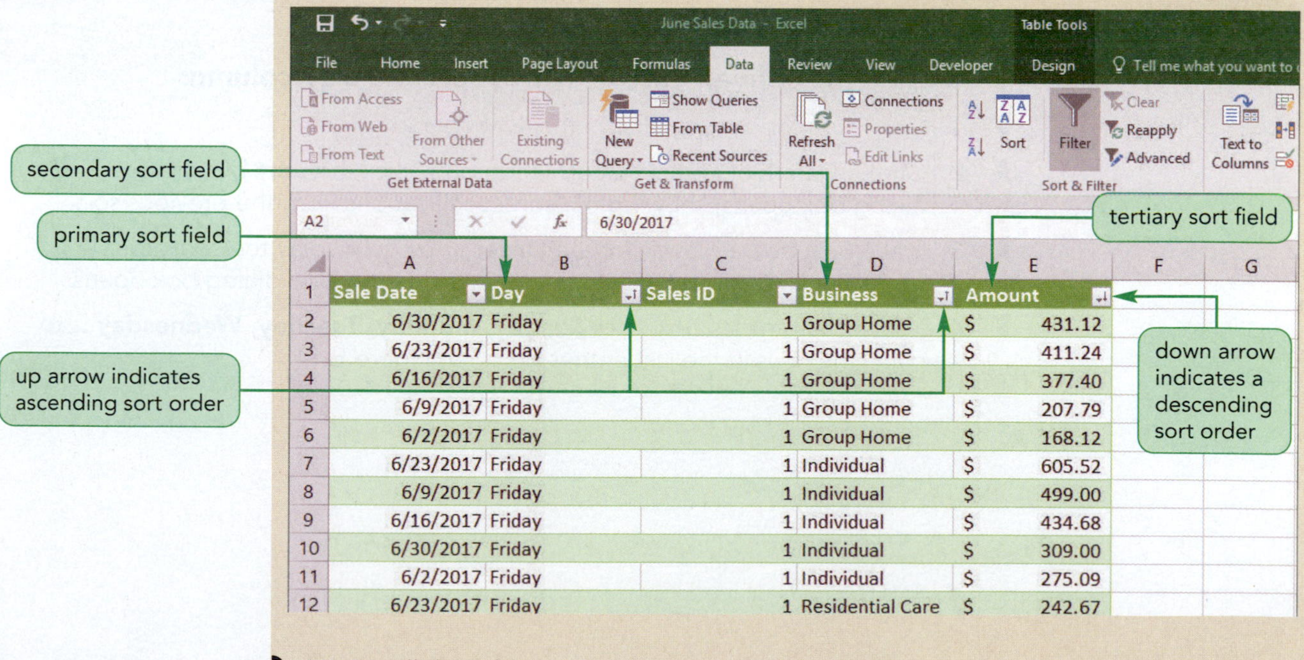

	A	B	C	D	E	F	G
1	Sale Date	Day	Sales ID	Business	Amount		
2	6/30/2017	Friday	1	Group Home	$ 431.12		
3	6/23/2017	Friday	1	Group Home	$ 411.24		
4	6/16/2017	Friday	1	Group Home	$ 377.40		
5	6/9/2017	Friday	1	Group Home	$ 207.79		
6	6/2/2017	Friday	1	Group Home	$ 168.12		
7	6/23/2017	Friday	1	Individual	$ 605.52		
8	6/9/2017	Friday	1	Individual	$ 499.00		
9	6/16/2017	Friday	1	Individual	$ 434.68		
10	6/30/2017	Friday	1	Individual	$ 309.00		
11	6/2/2017	Friday	1	Individual	$ 275.09		
12	6/23/2017	Friday	1	Residential Care	$ 242.67		

11. Scroll the table to view the sorted table data.

The table data is sorted in alphabetical order by the day of the week—Friday, Monday, Saturday, and so forth. This default sort order for fields with text values is not appropriate for days of the week. Instead, Victoria wants you to base the sort on chronological rather than alphabetical order. You'll use a custom sort list to set up the sort order Victoria wants.

Sorting Using a Custom List

Text is sorted in ascending or descending alphabetical order unless you specify a different order using a custom list. A **custom list** indicates the sequence in which you want data ordered. Excel has two predefined custom lists—day-of-the-week (Sun, Mon, Tues, ... and Sunday, Monday, Tuesday, ...) and month-of-the-year (Jan, Feb, Mar, Apr, ... and January, February, March, April, ...). If a column consists of day or month labels, you can sort them in their correct chronological order using one of these predefined custom lists.

You can also create custom lists to sort records in a sequence you define. For example, you can create a custom list to logically order high school or college students based on their admittance date (freshman, sophomore, junior, and senior) rather than alphabetical order (freshman, junior, senior, and sophomore).

REFERENCE

Sorting Using a Custom List

- On the Data tab, in the Sort & Filter group, click the Sort button.
- Click the Order arrow, and then click Custom List.
- If necessary, in the List entries box, type each entry for the custom list (in the desired order) and press the Enter key, and then click the Add button.
- In the Custom lists box, select the predefined custom list.
- Click the OK button.

You'll use a predefined custom list to sort the records by the Day column in chronological order rather than alphabetical order.

To use a predefined custom list to sort the Day column:

1. Make sure the active cell is in the JuneTbl table.
2. On the Data tab, in the Sort & Filter group, click the **Sort** button. The Sort dialog box opens, showing the sort specifications from the previous sort.
3. In the Sort by Day row, click the **Order** arrow to display the sort order options, and then click **Custom List**. The Custom Lists dialog box opens.
4. In the Custom lists box, click **Sunday**, **Monday**, **Tuesday**, **Wednesday**... to place the days in the List entries box. See Figure 5-14.

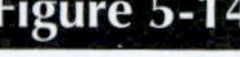

Figure 5-14 Custom Lists dialog box

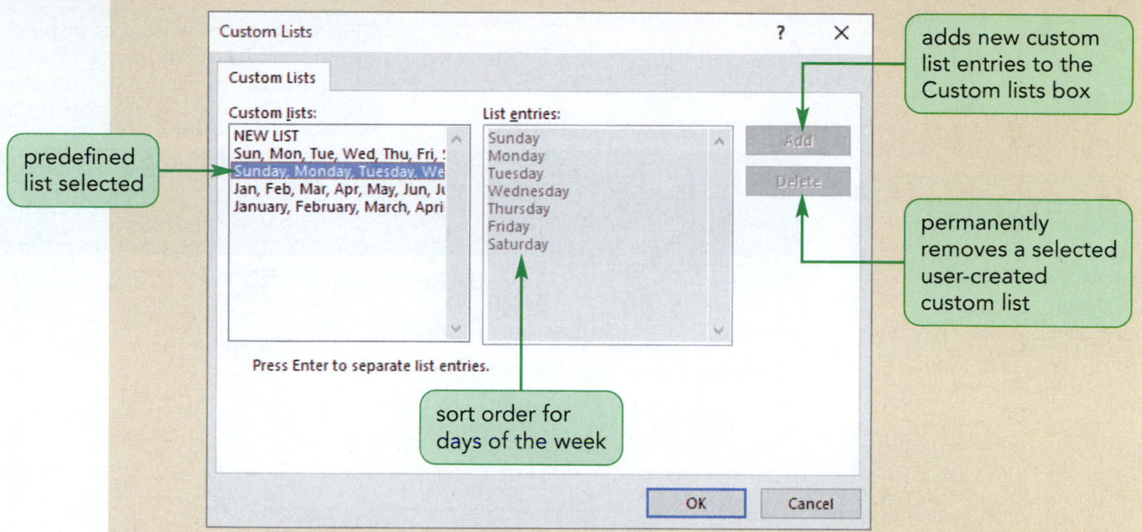

5. Click the **OK** button to return to the Sort dialog box. The custom sort list—Sunday, Monday, Tuesday, Wednesday…—appears in the Order box.
6. Click the **OK** button. The table is sorted based on the predefined custom list.
7. Scroll the sorted table to verify that the sales are sorted by their chronological day order—Sunday, Monday, Tuesday, Wednesday, Thursday, Friday, Saturday. No sales appear for Sundays because Victoria's Veggies is closed on that day.

So far, you created an Excel table for the sales and then named and formatted the table. You updated the table by adding, editing, and deleting records. You also sorted the records and used a predefined custom list to sort the Day field by its chronological order. In the next session, you will continue to work with the JuneTbl table.

REVIEW

Session 5.1 Quick Check

1. In Excel, what is the difference between a range of data and a structured range of data?
2. Explain the difference between a field and a record.
3. What is the purpose of the Freeze Panes button in the Window group on the View tab? Why is this feature helpful?
4. What three elements indicate that a range of data is an Excel table?
5. How can you quickly find and delete duplicate records from an Excel table?
6. If you sort table data from the most recent purchase date to the oldest purchase date, in what order have you sorted the data?
7. An Excel table of college students tracks each student's first name, last name, major, and year of graduation. How can you order the table so that students graduating in the same year appear together in alphabetical order by the students' last names?
8. An Excel table of sales data includes the Month field with the values Jan, Feb, Mar, … Dec. How can you sort the data so the sales data is sorted by Month in chronological order (Jan, Feb, Mar, … Dec)?

Session 5.2 Visual Overview:

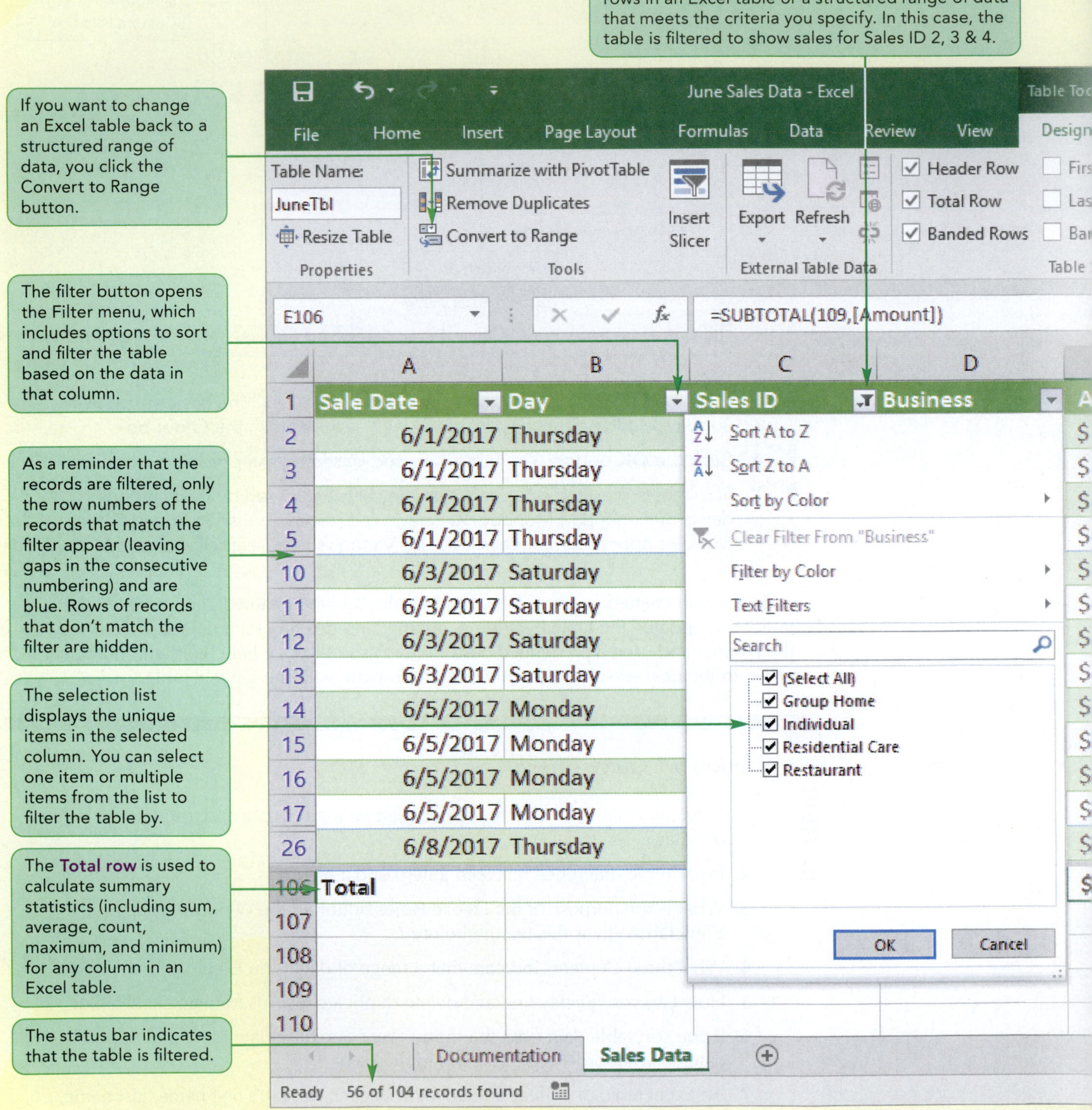

Filtering Table Data

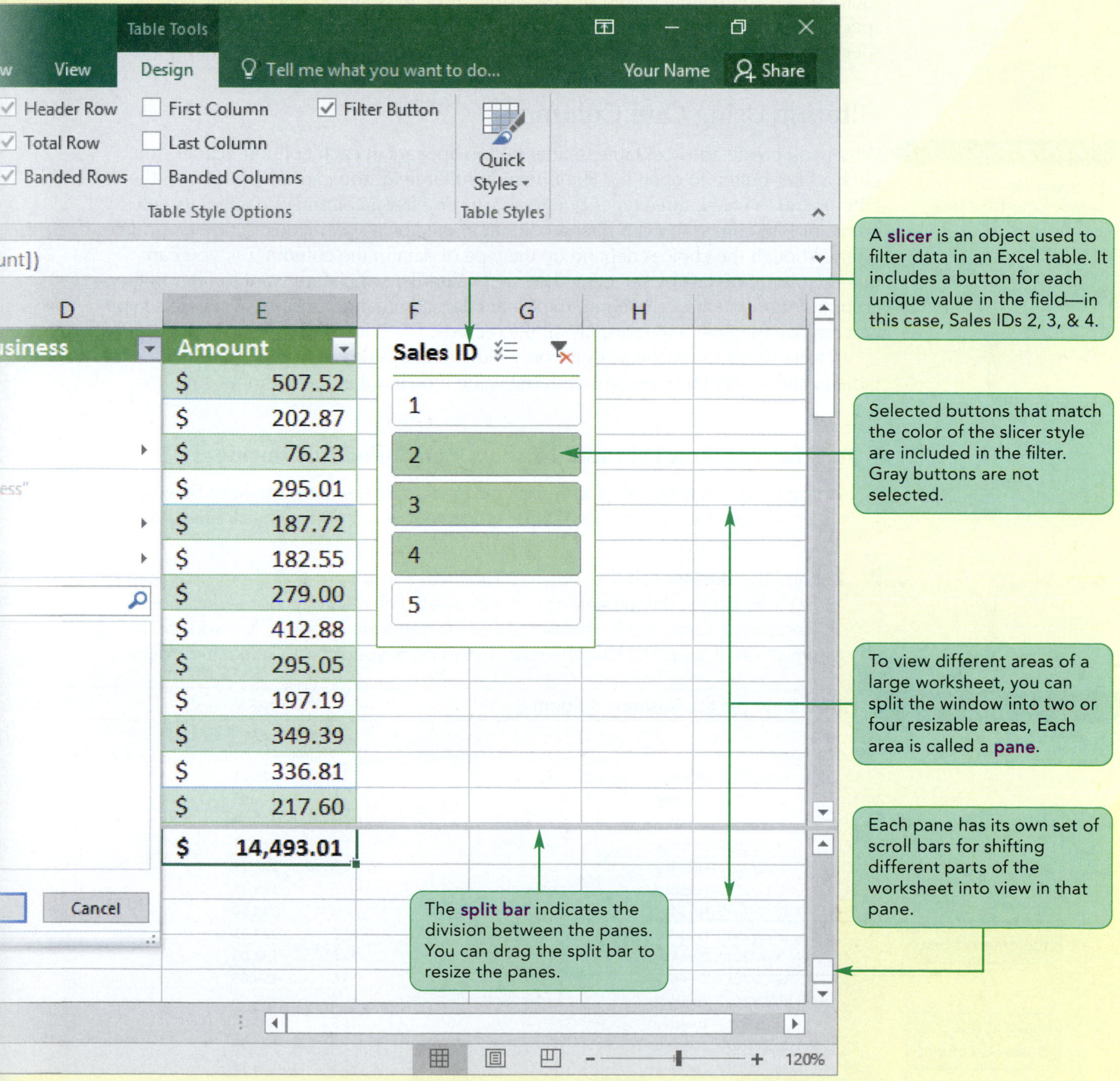

Table Tools
View
Design
Tell me what you want to do...
Your Name
Share
Header Row
First Column
Filter Button
Total Row
Last Column
Banded Rows
Banded Columns
Quick Styles
Table Style Options
Table Styles
D
E
F
G
H
I
Amount
Sales ID
1
2
3
4
5
$ 507.52
$ 202.87
$ 76.23
$ 295.01
$ 187.72
$ 182.55
$ 279.00
$ 412.88
$ 295.05
$ 197.19
$ 349.39
$ 336.81
$ 217.60
$ 14,493.01
Cancel
120%
A slicer is an object used to filter data in an Excel table. It includes a button for each unique value in the field—in this case, Sales IDs 2, 3, & 4.
Selected buttons that match the color of the slicer style are included in the filter. Gray buttons are not selected.
To view different areas of a large worksheet, you can split the window into two or four resizable areas, Each area is called a pane.
Each pane has its own set of scroll bars for shifting different parts of the worksheet into view in that pane.
The split bar indicates the division between the panes. You can drag the split bar to resize the panes.

Filtering Data

Victoria wants to analyze the sales data to determine if she could close Victoria's Veggies to individual customers one day during the week and use that time for buying and planning. She wants to see a list of all of the individual sales and then narrow that list to see only those days with sales less than or equal to $200. Although you could sort the sales by Business and Amount to group the records of interest to Victoria, the entire table would still be visible. A better solution is to display only the specific records you want. Filtering temporarily hides any records that do not meet the specified criteria. After data is filtered, you can sort, copy, format, chart, and print it.

Filtering Using One Column

TIP

To show or hide filter buttons for an Excel table or a structured range of data, click the Filter button in the Sort & Filter group on the Data tab.

When you create an Excel table, a filter button appears in each column header. You click a filter button to open the Filter menu for that field. You can use options on the Filter menu to create three types of filters. You can filter a column of data by its cell colors or font colors. You can filter a column of data by a specific text, number, or date filter, although the choices depend on the type of data in the column. Or, you can filter a column of data by selecting the exact values by which you want to filter in the column. After you filter a column, the Clear Filter command becomes available so you can remove the filter and redisplay all the records.

Victoria wants to see the sales for only individual customers. You'll filter the JuneTbl table to show only those records with the value Individual in the Business column.

To filter the JuneTbl table to show only individual business:

1. If you took a break after the previous session, make sure the June Sales Data workbook is open, the Sales Data worksheet is the active sheet, and the JuneTbl table is active.
2. Click the **Business** filter button. The Filter menu opens, as shown in Figure 5-15, listing the unique entries in the Business field—Group Home, Individual, Residential Care, and Restaurant. All of the items are selected, but you can set which items to use to filter the data. In this case, you want to select Individual.

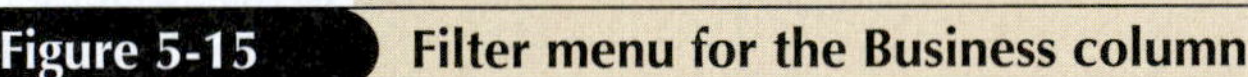

Figure 5-15 Filter menu for the Business column

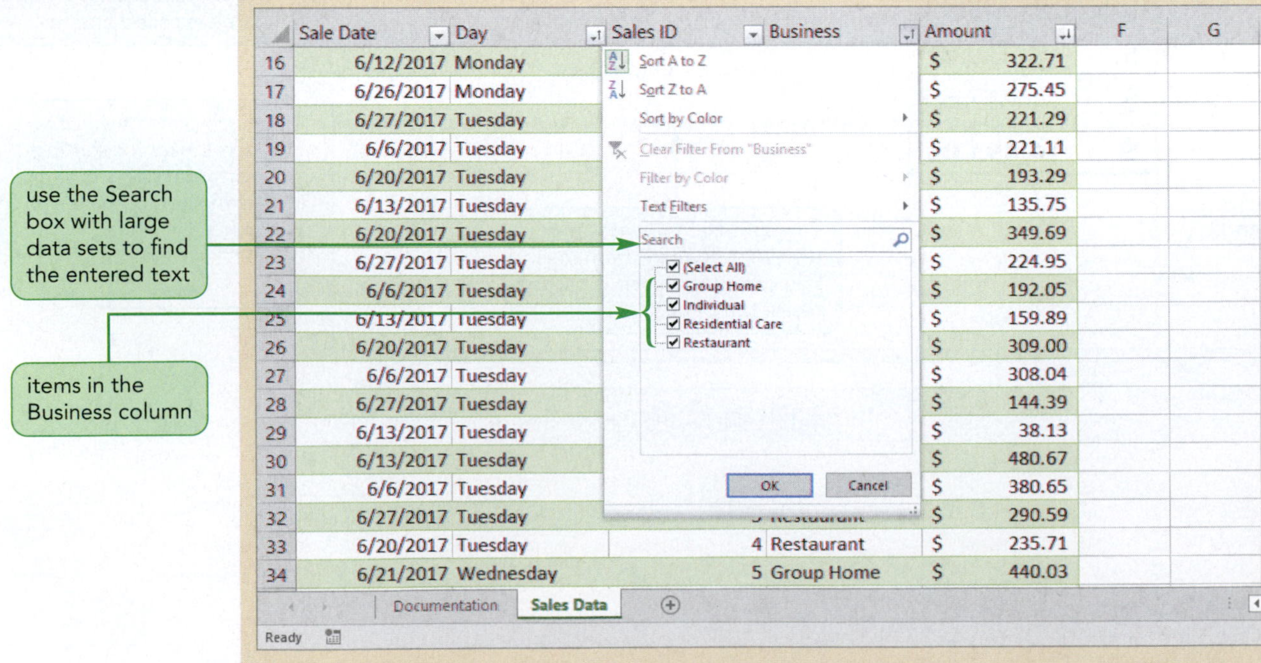

3. Click the **(Select All)** check box to remove the checkmarks from all of the Business items.
4. Click the **Individual** check box to select it. The filter will show only records that match the checked item and will hide records that contain the unchecked items.
5. Click the **OK** button. The filter is applied. The status bar lists the number of Individual rows found in the entire table—in this case, 26 of the 104 records in the table are displayed. See Figure 5-16.

Figure 5-16 JuneTbl table filtered to show only Individual business

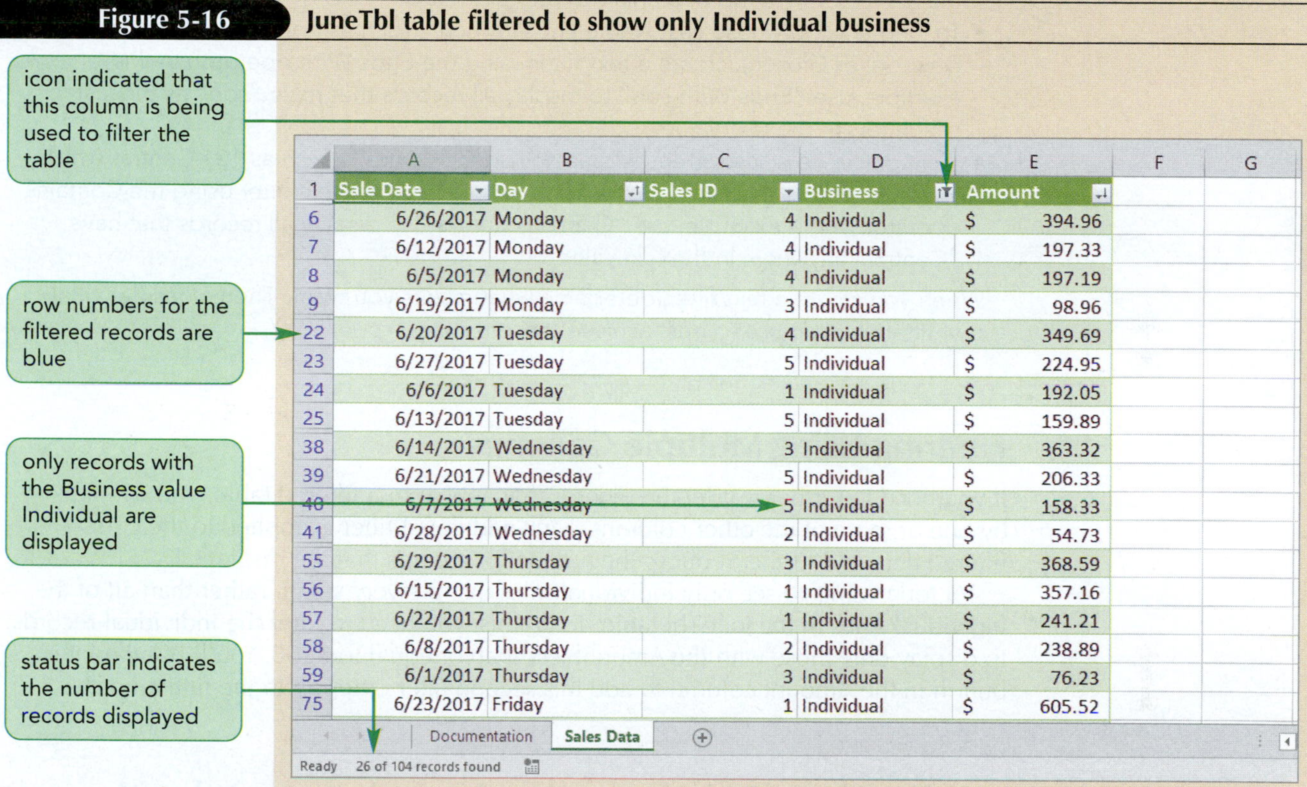
icon indicated that this column is being used to filter the table
row numbers for the filtered records are blue
only records with the Business value Individual are displayed
status bar indicates the number of records displayed
Documentation
Sales Data
Ready 26 of 104 records found

	A	B	C	D	E
1	Sale Date	Day	Sales ID	Business	Amount
6	6/26/2017	Monday	4	Individual	$ 394.96
7	6/12/2017	Monday	4	Individual	$ 197.33
8	6/5/2017	Monday	4	Individual	$ 197.19
9	6/19/2017	Monday	3	Individual	$ 98.96
22	6/20/2017	Tuesday	4	Individual	$ 349.69
23	6/27/2017	Tuesday	5	Individual	$ 224.95
24	6/6/2017	Tuesday	1	Individual	$ 192.05
25	6/13/2017	Tuesday	5	Individual	$ 159.89
38	6/14/2017	Wednesday	3	Individual	$ 363.32
39	6/21/2017	Wednesday	5	Individual	$ 206.33
40	6/7/2017	Wednesday	5	Individual	$ 158.33
41	6/28/2017	Wednesday	2	Individual	$ 54.73
55	6/29/2017	Thursday	3	Individual	$ 368.59
56	6/15/2017	Thursday	1	Individual	$ 357.16
57	6/22/2017	Thursday	1	Individual	$ 241.21
58	6/8/2017	Thursday	2	Individual	$ 238.89
59	6/1/2017	Thursday	3	Individual	$ 76.23
75	6/23/2017	Friday	1	Individual	$ 605.52

6. Review the records to verify that only records with Individual in the Business column are visible. All of the other records in this column are hidden, leaving gaps in the row numbers.
7. Point to the **Business** filter button. A ScreenTip—Business: Equals "Individual"—describes the filter applied to the column.

The Filter menu includes options to Sort by Color and Filter by Color. These options enable you to filter and sort data using color, one of many cell attributes. Victoria could use specific cell background colors for certain sales in the JuneTbl table. For example, she might want to highlight dates when the store could have used an additional employee. So cells in the Sale Date column for busy days would be formatted with yellow as a reminder. You could click the Sort by Color option to display a list of available colors by which to sort and then click the specific color so that all the records for the days when she needed more help in the store (formatted with yellow) would appear together. Similarly, you could click the Filter by Color option to display a submenu with the available colors by which to filter, and then click a color.

INSIGHT

Exploring Text Filters

You can use different text filters to display the records you want. If you know only part of a text value or if you want to match a certain pattern, you can use the Begins With, Ends With, and Contains operators to filter a text field to match the pattern you specify. The following examples are based on a student directory table that includes First Name, Last Name, Address, City, State, and Zip fields:

- To find a student named Smith, Smithe, or Smythe, create a text filter using the Begins With operator. In this example, use "Begins With Sm" to display all records that have "Sm" at the beginning of the text value.
- To Find anyone whose Last Name ends in "son" (such as Robertson, Anderson, Dawson, or Gibson), create a text filter using the Ends With operator. In this example, use "Ends With son" to display all records that have "son" as the last characters in the text value.
- To find anyone whose street address includes "Central" (such as 101 Central Ave., 1024 Central Road, or 457 SW Willow Central), create a text filter using the Contains operator. In this example, use "Contains Central" to display all records that have "Central" anywhere in the text value.

When you create a text filter, determine what results you want. Then, consider what text filter you can use to best achieve those results.

Filtering Using Multiple Columns

If you need to further restrict the records that appear in a filtered table, you can filter by one or more of the other columns. Each additional filter is applied to the currently filtered data and further reduces the number of records that are displayed.

Victoria wants to see only individual sales that are very small, rather than all of the individual sales in the JuneTbl table. To do this, you need to filter the Individual records to display only those with the Amount less than or equal to $200. You'll use the filter button in the Amount column to add this second filter criterion to the filtered data.

To filter the Individual records to show only Amounts less than or equal to $200:

1. Click the **Amount** filter button. The Filter menu opens.
2. Click the **(Select All)** check box to remove the checkmarks from all of the check boxes.
3. Click the check boxes for all of the amounts that are less than or equal to $200, starting with the **54.73** check box and ending with the **$197.33** check box. The ten check boxes are selected.
4. Click the **OK** button. The JuneTbl table is further filtered and shows the ten records in June for Individual sales that are less than or equal to $200. See Figure 5-17.

Figure 5-17 JuneTbl table filtered to show Individual business with amounts less than $200

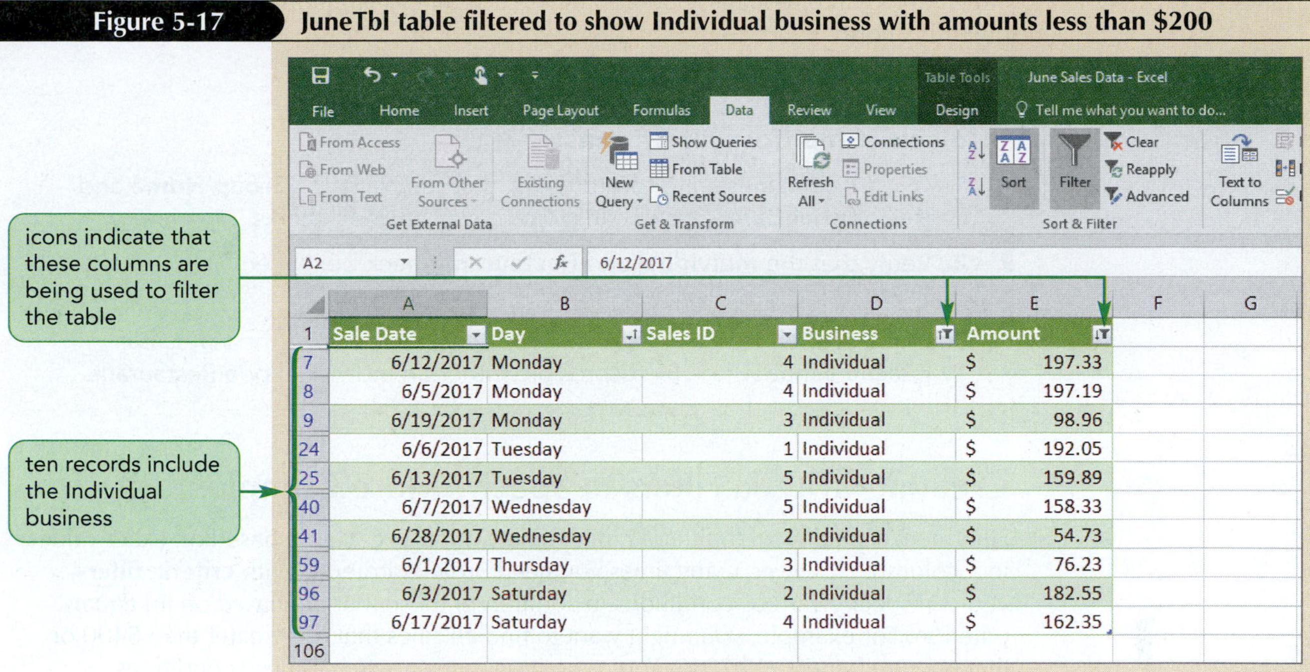

Clearing Filters

When you want to redisplay all of the data in a filtered table, you need to **clear** (or remove) the filters. When you clear a filter from a column, any other filters are still applied. For example, in the JuneTbl table, you would see all the Individual sales if you cleared the filter from the Amount field. To redisplay all of the sales in the table, you need to clear both the Amount filter and the Business filter. You will do this now to redisplay the entire table of sales.

To clear the filters to show all the records in the JuneTbl table:

1. Click the **Amount** filter button, and then click **Clear Filter From "Amount"**. The Amount filter is removed from the table. The table shows only Individual sales because the Business filter is still in effect.
2. Click the **Business** filter button, and then click **Clear Filter From "Business"**. The Business filter is removed, and all of the records in the JuneTbl table are displayed.

Selecting Multiple Filter Items

You can often find the information you need by selecting a single filter item from a list of filter items. Sometimes, however, you need to specify a more complex set of criteria to find the records you want. Earlier, you selected one filter item for the Business column and one filter item for the Amount column to display the records whose Business field value equals Individual *and* whose Amount field value equals less than or equal to $200. A record had to contain both values to be displayed. Now you want the Business column to display records whose Business field value equals Individual *or* Restaurant. The records must have one of these values to be displayed. You do this by selecting two filter items from the list of filter items. For example, checking the Individual and Restaurant check boxes in the Business filter items creates the filter "Business equals Individual" *or* "Business equals Restaurant."

Victoria wants a list of all Individual and Restaurant sales on days when their sales are greater than or equal to $400. You'll create a filter with multiple items selected to find this information.

To select multiple filter items:

1. Click the **Business** filter button, and then click the **Group Home** and **Residential Care** check boxes to remove the checkmarks.
2. Verify that the **Individual** and **Restaurant** check boxes remain checked. Selecting more than one item creates a multiselect filter.
3. Click the **OK** button. The JuneTbl table is filtered, and the status bar indicates that 52 of 104 records are either an Individual or a Restaurant.

Creating Criteria Filters to Specify More Complex Criteria

Filter items enable you to filter a range of data or an Excel table based on exact values in a column. However, many times you need broader criteria. With **criteria filters**, you can specify various conditions in addition to those that are based on an equals criterion. For example, you might want to find all sales that are greater than $400 or that occurred after 6/15/2017. You use criteria filters to create these conditions.

The types of criteria filters available change depending on whether the data in a column contains text, numbers, or dates. Figure 5-18 shows some of the options for text, number, and date criteria filters.

Figure 5-18 **Options for text, number, and date criteria filters**

Filter	Criteria	Records Displayed
Text	Equals	Exactly match the specified text
	Does Not Equal	Do not exactly match the specified text
	Begins With	Begin with the specified text
	Ends With	End with the specified text
	Contains	Have the specified text anywhere
	Does Not Contain	Do not have the specified text anywhere
Number	Equals	Exactly match the specified number
	Greater Than or Equal to	Are greater than or equal to the specified number
	Less Than	Are less than the specified number
	Between	Are greater than or equal to and less than or equal to the specified numbers
	Top 10	Are the top or bottom 10 (or the specified number)
	Above Average	Are greater than the average
Date	Today	Have the current date
	Last Week	Are in the prior week
	Next Month	Are in the month following the current month
	Last Quarter	Are in the previous quarter of the year (quarters defined as Jan, Feb, Mar; Apr, May, June; and so on)
	Year to Date	Are since January 1 of the current year to the current date
	Last Year	Are in the previous year (based on the current date)

You can use these criteria filters to find the answers to complex questions that you ask about data.

PROSKILLS

Problem Solving: Using Filters to Find Appropriate Data

Problem solving often requires finding information from a set of data to answer specific questions. When you're working with a range of data or an Excel table that contains hundreds or thousands of records, filters help you find that information without having to review each record in the table. For example, a human resources manager can use a filter to narrow the search for a specific employee out of the 2500 working at the company knowing only that the employee's first name is Elliot.

Filtering limits the data to display only the specific records that meet the criteria you set, enabling you to more effectively analyze the data. The following examples further illustrate how filtering can help people to quickly locate the data they need to answer a particular question:

- A customer service representative can use a filter to search a list of 10,000 products to find all products priced between $500 and $1000.
- A donations coordinator can use a filter to prepare a report that shows the donations received during the first quarter of the current year.
- An academic dean can use a filter to retrieve the names of all students with GPAs below 2.0 (probation) or above 3.5 (high honors).
- A professor who has 300 students in a psychology class can use a filter to develop a list of potential student assistants for next semester from the names the professor has highlighted in blue because their work was impressive. Filtering by the blue color generates a list of students to interview.
- The author of a guide to celebrity autographs can use a filter to determine whether an entry for a specific celebrity already exists in an Excel table and, if it does, determine whether the entry needs to be updated. If the entry does not exist, the author will know to add the autograph data to the table.

As these examples show, filtering is a useful tool for locating the answers to a wide variety of questions. You then can use this information to help you resolve problems.

Victoria wants you to display the records for sales to individuals or restaurants that are greater than $400. You'll modify the filtered JuneTbl table to add a criteria filter that includes records for Individual or Restaurant with Amounts greater than $400.

To add a number filter that shows sales amounts greater than $400:

1. Click the **Amount** filter button, and then point to **Number Filters**. A menu opens, displaying the comparison operators available for columns of numbers.
2. Click **Greater Than**. The Custom AutoFilter dialog box opens. The upper-left box displays *is greater than*, which is the comparison operator you want to use to filter the Amount column. You enter the value you want to use for the filter criteria in the upper-right box, which, in this case, is $400.
3. Type **400** in the upper-right box. See Figure 5-19. You use the lower set of boxes if you want the filter to meet a second condition. You click the And option button to display rows that meet both criteria. You click the Or option button to display rows that meet either of the two criteria. You only want to set one criterion for this filter, so you'll leave the lower boxes empty.

Figure 5-19 **Custom AutoFilter dialog box**

Custom AutoFilter

Show rows where:

Amount

is greater than | 400

(•) And ( ) Or

Use ? to represent any single character

Use * to represent any series of characters

OK | Cancel

column being filtered

operator for the first condition

criterion for the first condition

logical operators used when there are two conditions

boxes to specify a second condition

4. Click the **OK** button. The status bar indicates that 14 of 104 records were found. The 14 records that appear in the JuneTbl table are either Individual or Restaurant and have an Amount greater than $400.

Next, you'll sort the filtered data to show the largest Amount first. Although you can sort the data using Sort buttons, as you did earlier, these sort options are also available on the Filter menu. If you want to perform a more complex sort, you still need to use the Sort dialog box.

To sort the filtered table data:

1. Click the **Amount** filter button. The Filter menu opens. The sort options are at the top of the menu.
2. Click **Sort Largest to Smallest**. The filtered records are sorted in descending order. The filtered table now displays records for individuals and restaurants with daily sales greater than $400 sorted in descending order. See Figure 5-20.

Figure 5-20 **Filtered and sorted JuneTbl table**

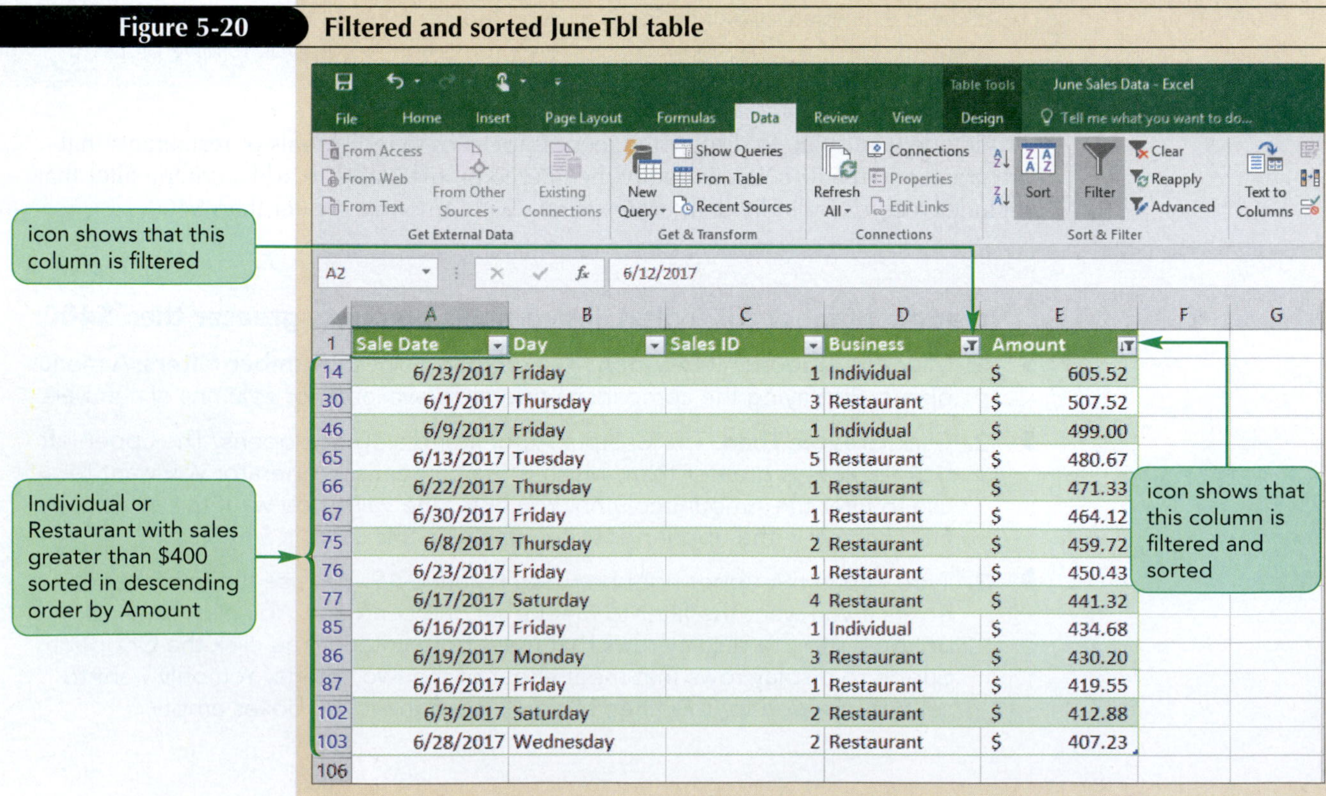

	Sale Date	Day	Sales ID	Business	Amount
14	6/23/2017	Friday	1	Individual	$ 605.52
30	6/1/2017	Thursday	3	Restaurant	$ 507.52
46	6/9/2017	Friday	1	Individual	$ 499.00
65	6/13/2017	Tuesday	5	Restaurant	$ 480.67
66	6/22/2017	Thursday	1	Restaurant	$ 471.33
67	6/30/2017	Friday	1	Restaurant	$ 464.12
75	6/8/2017	Thursday	2	Restaurant	$ 459.72
76	6/23/2017	Friday	1	Restaurant	$ 450.43
77	6/17/2017	Saturday	4	Restaurant	$ 441.32
85	6/16/2017	Friday	1	Individual	$ 434.68
86	6/19/2017	Monday	3	Restaurant	$ 430.20
87	6/16/2017	Friday	1	Restaurant	$ 419.55
102	6/3/2017	Saturday	2	Restaurant	$ 412.88
103	6/28/2017	Wednesday	2	Restaurant	$ 407.23
106					

Victoria will use this data to help her decide which days she may need to hire additional workers. You need to restore the entire table of JuneTbl, which you can do by clearing all the filters at one time.

To clear all the filters from the JuneTbl table:

1. On the ribbon, click the **Data** tab, if necessary.
2. In the Sort & Filter group, click the **Clear** button. All of the records are redisplayed in the table.

Creating a Slicer to Filter Data in an Excel Table

TIP

You can insert a Timeline to filter PivotTable data by time periods. On the PivotTable Tools Analyze tab, in the Filter group, click Insert Timeline, select the field, and then click the OK button. Use the scrollbar to select the time period.

Another way to filter an Excel table is with slicers. You can create a slicer for any field in the Excel table. You also can create more than one slicer for a table. Every slicer consists of an object that contains a button for each unique value in that field. For example, a slicer created for the Day field would include six buttons—one for each day of the week that Victoria's Veggies is open. One advantage of a slicer is that it clearly shows what filters are currently applied—the buttons for selected values are a different color. However, a slicer can take up a lot of space or hide data if there isn't a big enough blank area near the table. You can format the slicer and its buttons, changing its style, height, and width.

Victoria wants to be able to quickly filter the table to show sales for a specific Sales ID. You will add a slicer for the Sales ID field so she can do this.

To add the Sales ID slicer to the JuneTbl table:

1. On the ribbon, click the **Table Tools Design** tab.
2. In the Tools group, click the **Insert Slicer** button. The Insert Slicers dialog box opens, listing every available field in all tables in the workbook. You can select any or all of the fields.
3. Click the **Sales ID** check box to insert a checkmark, and then click the **OK** button. The Sales ID slicer appears on the worksheet. All of the slicer buttons are selected, indicating that every Sales ID is included in the table.
4. Drag the **Sales ID** slicer to the right of the JuneTbl table, placing its upper-left corner in cell G1.
5. If the Slicer Tools Options tab does not appear on the ribbon, click the **Sales ID** slicer to select it. The Slicer Tools Options tab appears on the ribbon and is selected.
6. In the Size group, enter **1.9"** in the Height box and **1.25"** in the Width box. The slicer is resized, eliminating the extra space below the buttons and to the right of the labels.
7. In the Slicer Styles group, click the **More** button, and then click **Slicer Style Dark 6**. The slicer colors now match the formatting of the Excel table. See Figure 5-21.

Figure 5-21 JuneTbl table with the Sales ID slicer

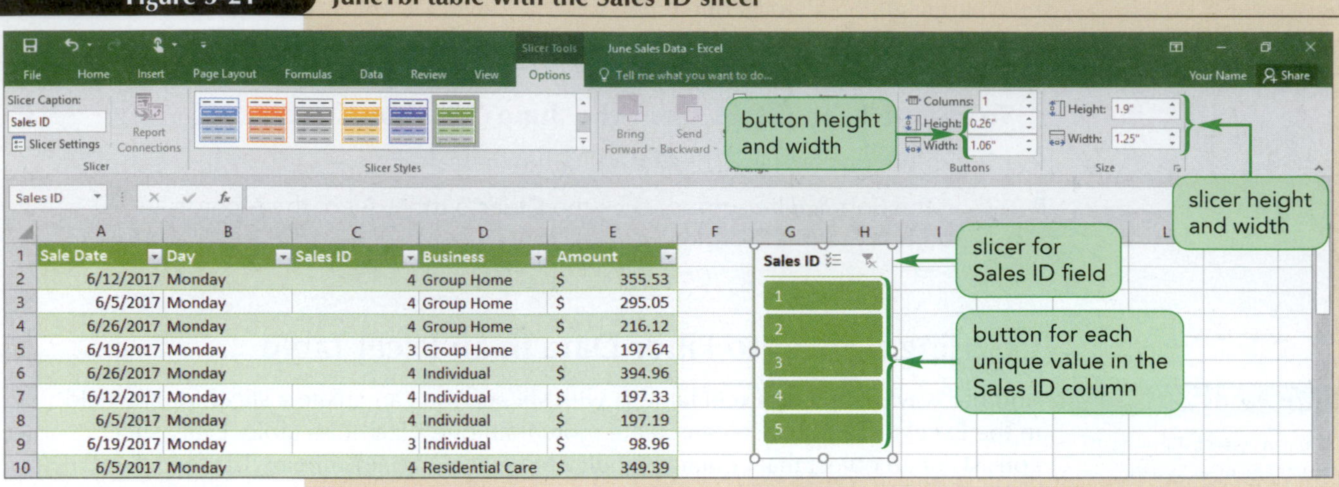

You can use the slicer to quickly filter records in an Excel table. Just click the slicer button corresponding to the data you want to display in the table. If you want to show more than one Sales ID, hold down the Ctrl key as you click the buttons that correspond to the additional data you want to show.

Victoria wants you to filter the JuneTbl table to display sales for Sales ID 1 and Sales ID 5. You will use the Sales ID slicer to do this.

To filter the JuneTbl table using the Sales ID slicer:

1. On the Sales ID slicer, click the **1** button. Only Sales ID 1 data appears in the JuneTbl table. All of the other buttons are gray, indicating that these Sales IDs are not included in the filtered data.
2. Press and hold the **Ctrl** key, click the **5** button, and then release the **Ctrl** key. Sales for Sales ID 5 are now added to the JuneTbl filtered table. See Figure 5-22.

Figure 5-22 **JuneTbl table filtered to show Sales IDs 1 and 5**

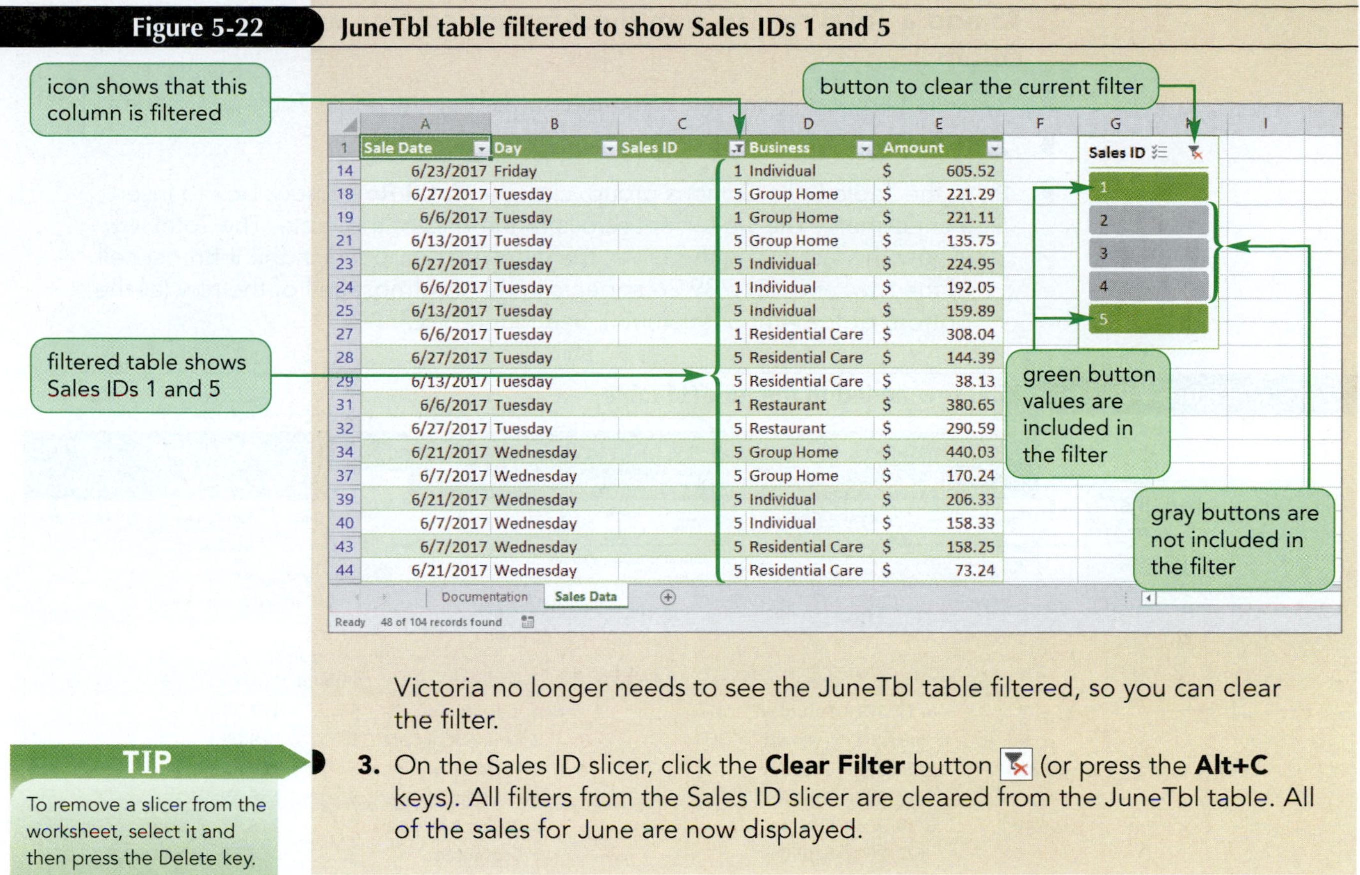
icon shows that this column is filtered
button to clear the current filter
filtered table shows Sales IDs 1 and 5
green button values are included in the filter
gray buttons are not included in the filter
Sales ID
1
2
3
4
5
Documentation
Sales Data
Ready 48 of 104 records found

	Sale Date	Day	Sales ID	Business	Amount
14	6/23/2017	Friday	1	Individual	$ 605.52
18	6/27/2017	Tuesday	5	Group Home	$ 221.29
19	6/6/2017	Tuesday	1	Group Home	$ 221.11
21	6/13/2017	Tuesday	5	Group Home	$ 135.75
23	6/27/2017	Tuesday	5	Individual	$ 224.95
24	6/6/2017	Tuesday	1	Individual	$ 192.05
25	6/13/2017	Tuesday	5	Individual	$ 159.89
27	6/6/2017	Tuesday	1	Residential Care	$ 308.04
28	6/27/2017	Tuesday	5	Residential Care	$ 144.39
29	6/13/2017	Tuesday	5	Residential Care	$ 38.13
31	6/6/2017	Tuesday	1	Restaurant	$ 380.65
32	6/27/2017	Tuesday	5	Restaurant	$ 290.59
34	6/21/2017	Wednesday	5	Group Home	$ 440.03
37	6/7/2017	Wednesday	5	Group Home	$ 170.24
39	6/21/2017	Wednesday	5	Individual	$ 206.33
40	6/7/2017	Wednesday	5	Individual	$ 158.33
43	6/7/2017	Wednesday	5	Residential Care	$ 158.25
44	6/21/2017	Wednesday	5	Residential Care	$ 73.24

Victoria no longer needs to see the JuneTbl table filtered, so you can clear the filter.

TIP

To remove a slicer from the worksheet, select it and then press the Delete key.

3. On the Sales ID slicer, click the **Clear Filter** button (or press the **Alt+C** keys). All filters from the Sales ID slicer are cleared from the JuneTbl table. All of the sales for June are now displayed.

Using the Total Row to Calculate Summary Statistics

The Total row is used to calculate summary statistics (including sum, average, count, maximum, and minimum) for any column in an Excel table. The Total row is inserted immediately after the last row of data in the table. A double-line border is inserted to indicate that the following row contains totals, and the label Total is added to the leftmost cell of the row. By default, the Total row adds the numbers in the last column of the Excel table or counts the number of records if the data in the last column contains text. When you click in each cell of the Total row, an arrow appears that you can click to open a list of the most commonly used functions. You can also select other functions by opening the Insert Functions dialog box.

Victoria wants to see the total amount of sales in June and the total number of records being displayed. You will add a Total row to the JuneTbl table and then use the SUM and COUNT functions to calculate these statistics for Victoria.

To add a Total row to sum the Amount column and count the Day column:

1. Select any cell in the JuneTbl table to display the Table Tools contextual tab.
2. On the ribbon, click the **Table Tools Design** tab.
3. In the Table Style Options group, click the **Total Row** check box to insert a checkmark. The worksheet scrolls to the end of the table. The Total row is now the last row in the table, the label Total appears in the leftmost cell of the row, and $27,739.26 appears in the rightmost cell of the row (at the bottom of the Amount column). See Figure 5-23.

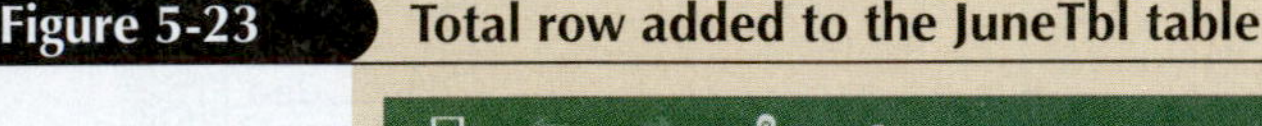
Figure 5-23 Total row added to the JuneTbl table

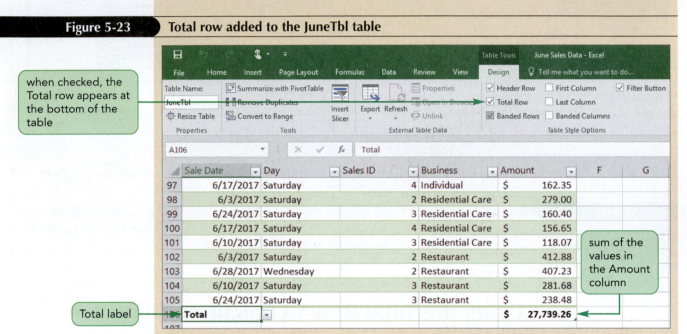

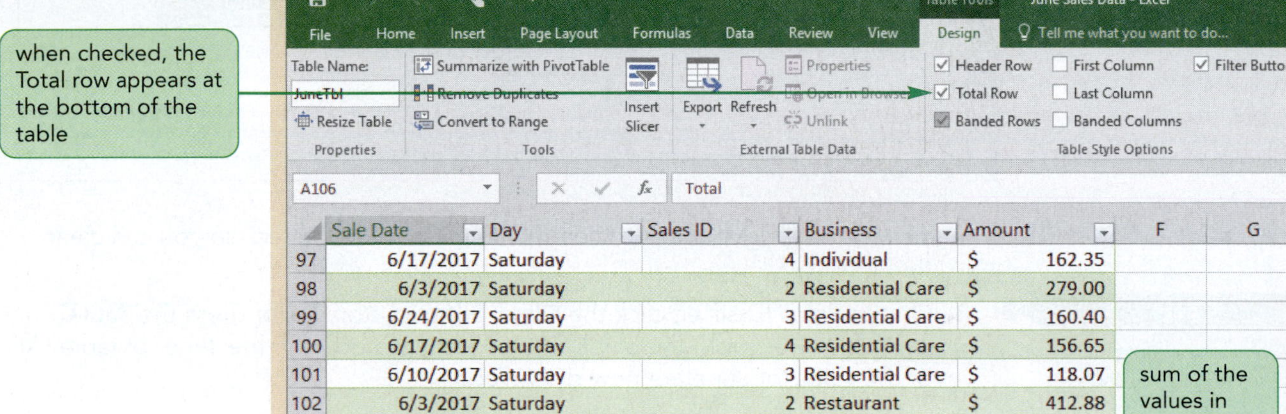

Next, you will use the COUNT function to add the number of records displayed.

4. Click cell **B106** (the Day cell in the Total row), and then click the **arrow** button [▼] to display a list of functions. None is the default function in all columns except the last column. See Figure 5-24.

Figure 5-24 Total row functions

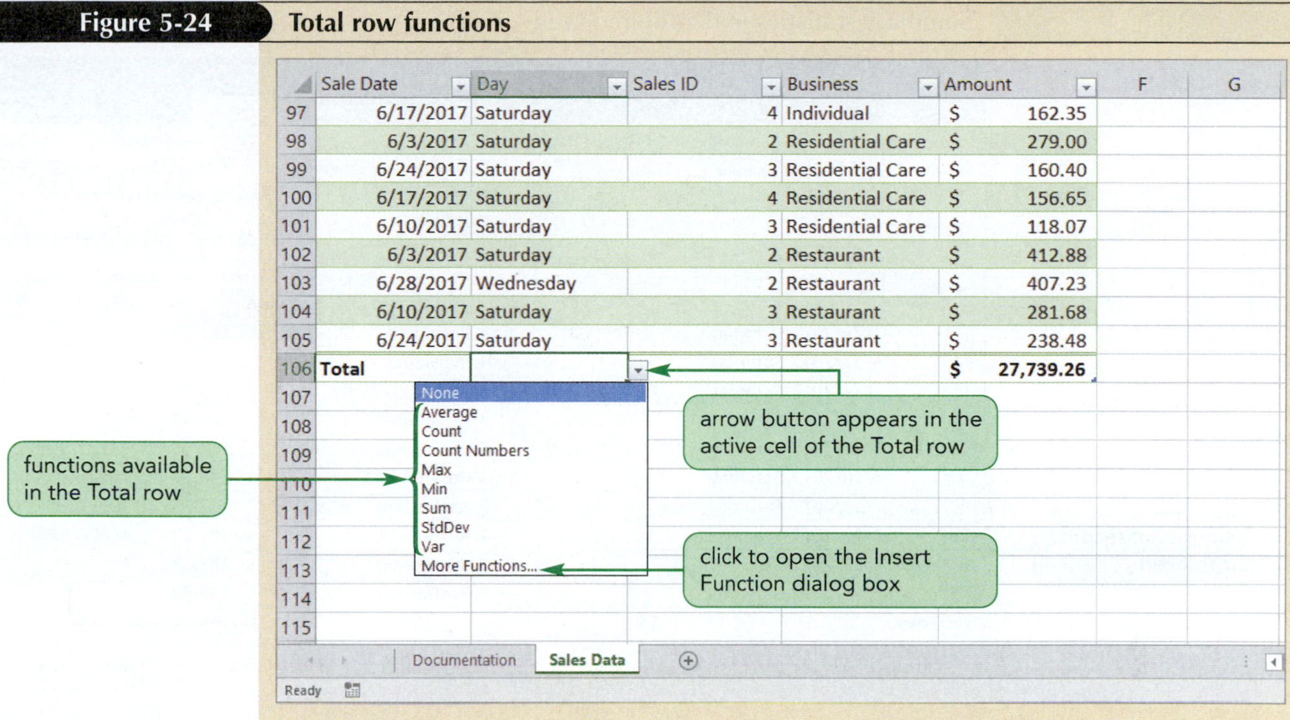

TIP

When you select Sum, Count, or Average, Excel uses the SUBTOTAL function to calculate the summary statistic in the Total row.

5. Click **Count**. The number 104, which is the number of records in the JuneTbl table, appears in the cell.

As you add, edit, or delete data in the table, the Total row values change. This also happens if you filter the table to show only some of the table data. Victoria wants the total sales to include sales from all seasonal employees (Sales IDs 2 through 4). You will filter the table to exclude Sales IDs 1 and 5, displaying the total Amount for Sales IDs 2 through 4 only. The COUNT function will also change to show only the number of transactions for the filtered data.

To filter sales by excluding sales from Sales ID 1 and Sales ID 5:

1. Press the **Ctrl+Home** keys to make cell A1 the active cell.
2. On the Sales ID slicer, click the **2** slicer button, press and hold the **Ctrl** key as you click the **3** and **4** slicer buttons, and then release the **Ctrl** key. The JuneTbl table is filtered to display sales for the seasonal employees in June.
3. Scroll to the end of the table. The Total row shows that the 56 records contain total sales of $14,393.01. See Figure 5-25.

Figure 5-25 Summary statistics in the filtered table

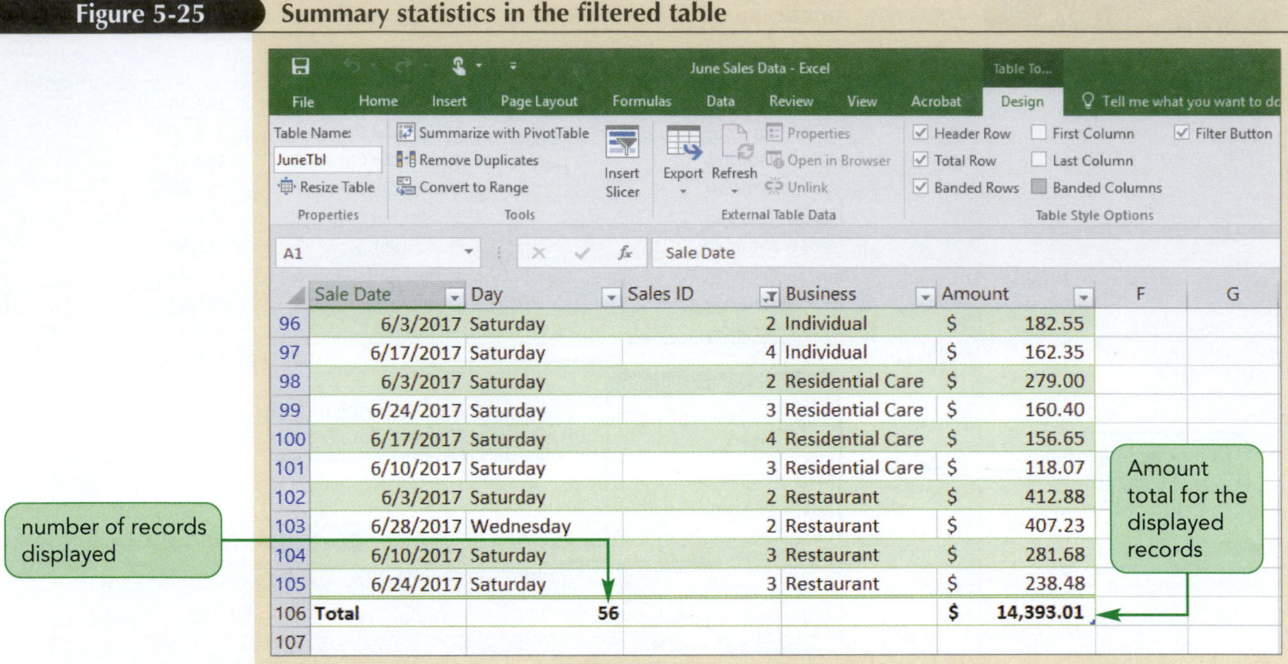

	Sale Date	Day	Sales ID	Business	Amount	F	G
96	6/3/2017	Saturday	2	Individual	$ 182.55		
97	6/17/2017	Saturday	4	Individual	$ 162.35		
98	6/3/2017	Saturday	2	Residential Care	$ 279.00		
99	6/24/2017	Saturday	3	Residential Care	$ 160.40		
100	6/17/2017	Saturday	4	Residential Care	$ 156.65		
101	6/10/2017	Saturday	3	Residential Care	$ 118.07		
102	6/3/2017	Saturday	2	Restaurant	$ 412.88		
103	6/28/2017	Wednesday	2	Restaurant	$ 407.23		
104	6/10/2017	Saturday	3	Restaurant	$ 281.68		
105	6/24/2017	Saturday	3	Restaurant	$ 238.48		
106	**Total**	**56**			**$ 14,393.01**		
107							

Splitting the Worksheet Window into Panes

You can split the worksheet window into two or four separate panes. This allows you to easily view data from several areas of the worksheet at the same time. Each pane has its own scroll bars so you can navigate easily within one pane or display different parts of the worksheet. You can move between panes using the mouse. To create two panes, select a cell in row 1 to split the worksheet vertically, or select a cell in column A to split the worksheet horizontally; to create four panes, select any other cell in the worksheet.

Victoria wants to view the JuneTbl summary totals at the same time she views the data on individual sales. You will divide the worksheet into two horizontal panes to view the sales records in the top pane and the totals in the bottom pane.

To split the Sales Data worksheet window into panes:

1. Press the **Ctrl+Home** keys to make cell A1 at the top of the table the active cell.
2. Select the cell in column A that is two rows above the last row visible on your screen.
3. On the ribbon, click the **View** tab.
4. In the Window group, click the **Split** button. The worksheet window splits into two panes. Each pane has its own set of scroll bars. The active cell is in the bottom pane below the split bar. See Figure 5-26.

Figure 5-26 Worksheet split into two panes

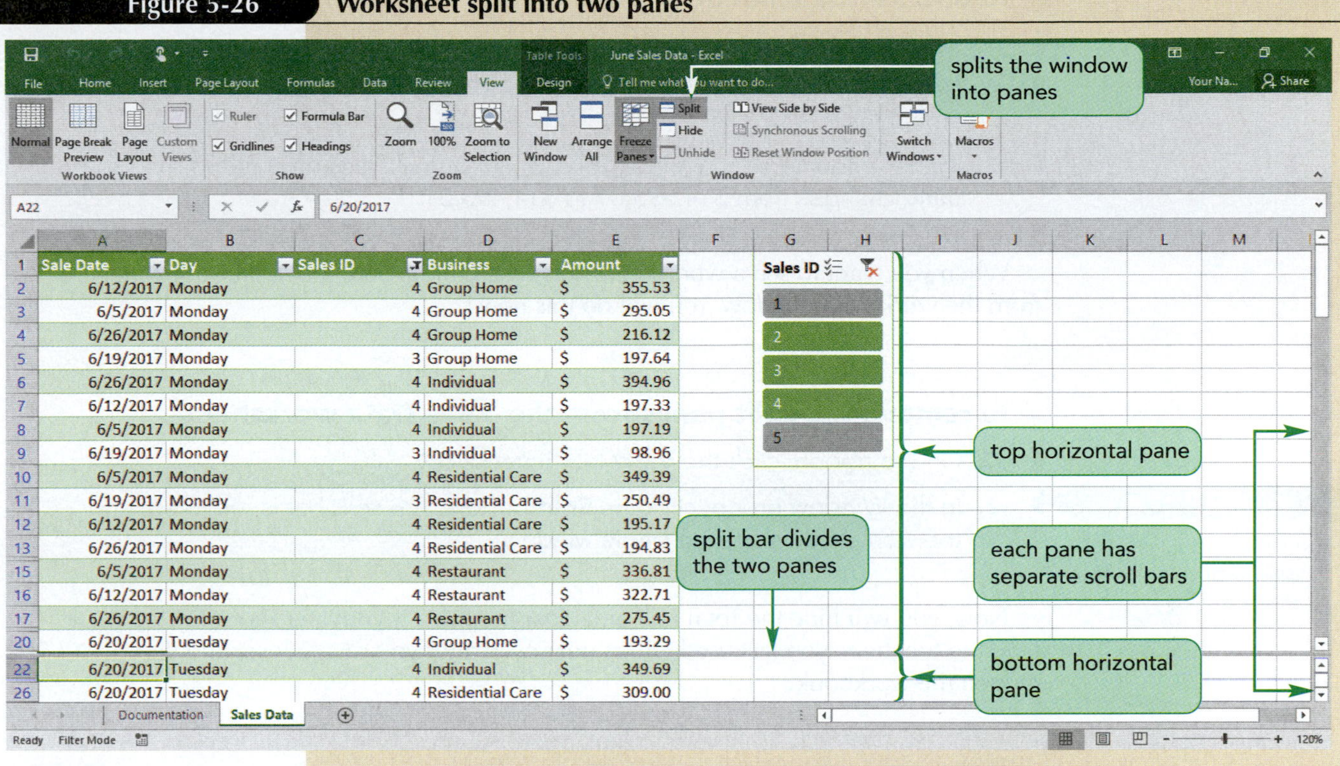

Trouble? If the window splits into four panes rather than two, click the Split button to remove all panes, and then repeat Step 1 through 4.

5. Using the lower scroll bar, scroll down until the Total row appears immediately below the split bar. See Figure 5-27.

Figure 5-27 Total row displayed in the bottom pane

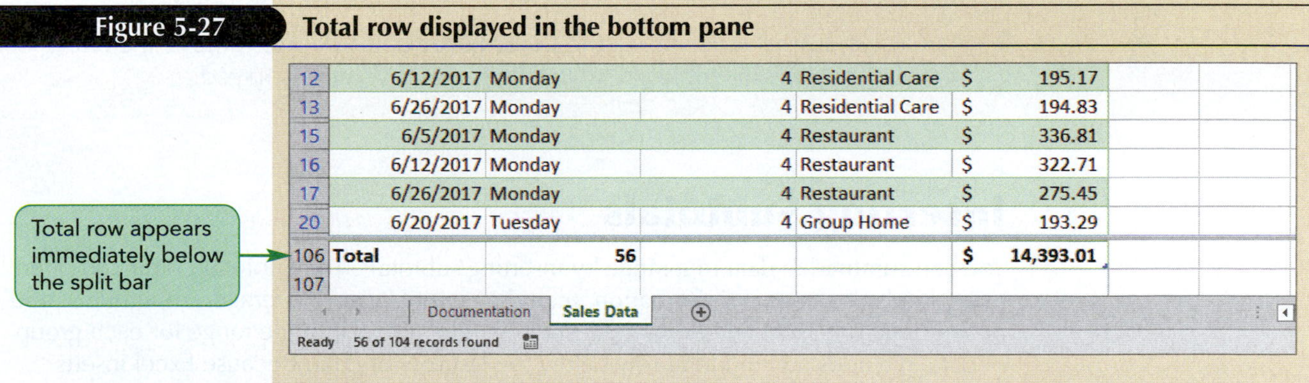

Victoria discovered a data entry error in the sales amount for Individual on 6/28/2017. It was entered as $54.73; the correct amount is $154.73. You will change the amount.

To update the amount of the Individual sales on 6/28/2017:

1. Select any cell in the top pane.
2. Use the Find command to locate the **6/28/2017** sales for **Individual**. The amount is $54.73.
3. In the Amount column, enter **154.73**. The total sales amount in the bottom pane changes from $14,393.01 to $14,493.01.

When you want to see a worksheet in a single pane, you remove the split panes from the worksheet window. You will do this now.

To remove the split panes from the Sales Data worksheet

1. On the ribbon, click the **View** tab, if necessary.
2. In the Window group, click the **Split** button. The split bar is removed, and the worksheet is again a single window.

TIP

You can also double-click the split bar to remove the panes.

Now, you will hide the Total row and clear the filter. If you later redisplay the Total row, the functions you last used will appear even after you save, close, and then reopen the workbook.

To hide the Total row and clear the filter from the JuneTbl table:

1. On the ribbon, click the **Table Tools Design** tab.
2. In the Table Style Options group, click the **Total Row** check box to remove the checkmark. The Total row is no longer visible.
3. Press the **Ctrl+Home** keys to make cell A1 the active cell.
4. On the Sales ID slicer, click the **Clear Filter** button to remove the filters from the JuneTbl table. All of the sales for June are displayed.

Inserting Subtotals

You can summarize data in a range by inserting subtotals. The Subtotal command offers many kinds of summary information, including counts, sums, averages, minimums, and maximums. The Subtotal command inserts a subtotal row into the range for each group of data and adds a grand total row below the last row of data. Because Excel inserts subtotals whenever the value in a specified field changes, you need to sort the data so that records with the same value in a specified field are grouped together *before* you use the Subtotal command. The Subtotal command cannot be used in an Excel table, so you must first convert the Excel table to a normal range.

REFERENCE

Calculating Subtotals for a Range of Data

- Sort the data by the column for which you want a subtotal.
- If the data is in an Excel table, on the Table Tools Design tab, in the Tools group, click the Convert to Range button, and then click the Yes button to convert the Excel table to a range.
- On the Data tab, in the Outline group, click the Subtotal button.
- Click the At each change in arrow, and then click the column that contains the group you want to subtotal.
- Click the Use function arrow, and then click the function you want to use to summarize the data.
- In the Add subtotal to box, click the check box for each column that contains the values you want to summarize.
- To calculate another category of subtotals, click the Replace current subtotals check box to remove the checkmark, and then repeat the previous three steps.
- Click the OK button.

Victoria wants to create a report that shows all the vegetable store's sales sorted by Sale Date with the total amount of the sales for each date. She also wants to see the total amount for each sale date after the last item of that date. The Subtotal command is a simple way to provide the information Victoria needs. First, you will sort the sales by Sale Date, then you will convert the Excel table to a normal range, and finally you will calculate subtotals in the Amount column for each Sale Date grouping to produce the results Victoria needs.

To sort the sales and convert the table to a range:

Be sure to sort the table and convert the table to a range before calculating subtotals.

1. Click the **Sale Date** filter button, and then click **Sort Oldest to Newest** on the Filter menu. The JuneTbl table is sorted in ascending order by the Sale Date field. This ensures one subtotal is created for each date.
2. On the Table Tools Design tab, in the Tools group, click the **Convert to Range** button. A dialog box opens, asking if you want to convert the table to a normal range.
3. Click the **Yes** button. The Excel table is converted to a range, and the Home tab is selected on the ribbon. You can tell the table data is now a normal range because the filter buttons, the Table Tools Design tab, and the slicer disappear.

Next, you'll calculate the subtotals.

To calculate the sales amount subtotals for each date:

1. On the ribbon, click the **Data** tab.
2. In the Outline group, click the **Subtotal** button. The Subtotal dialog box opens. See Figure 5-28.

Figure 5-28 Subtotal dialog box

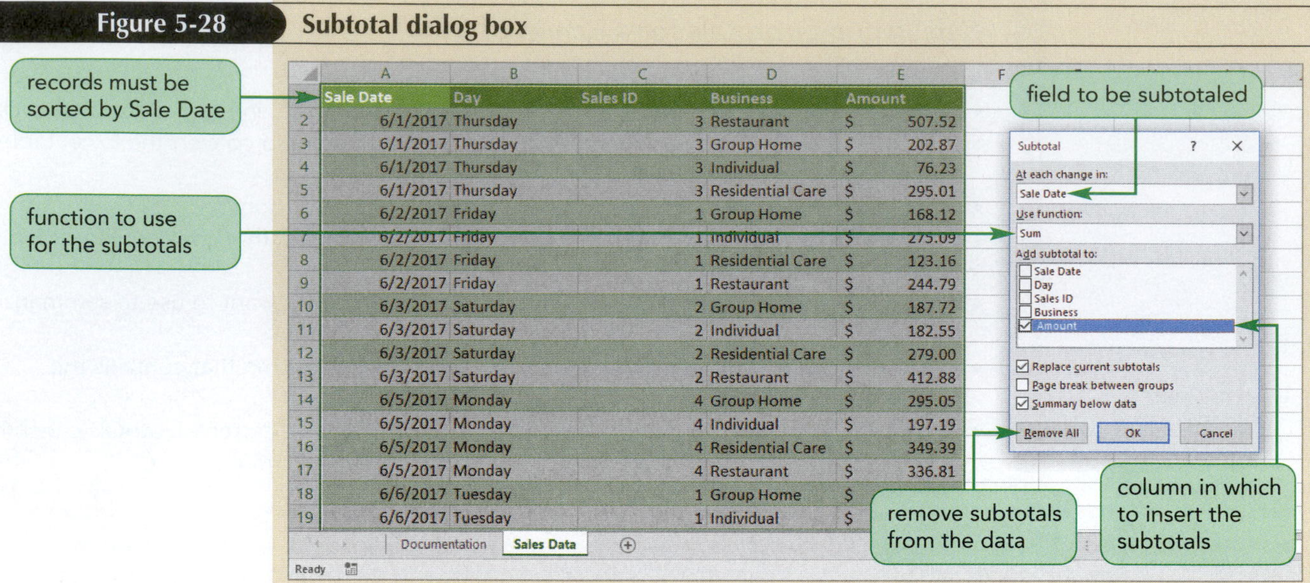

3. If necessary, click the **At each change in** arrow, and then click **Sale Date**. This is the column you want Excel to use to determine where to insert the subtotals; it is the column you sorted. A subtotal will be calculated at every change in the Sale Date value.

4. If necessary, click the **Use function** arrow, and then click **Sum**. The Use function list provides several options for subtotaling data, including counts, averages, minimums, maximums, and products.

5. In the Add subtotal to box, make sure only the **Amount** check box is checked. This specifies the Amount field as the field to be subtotaled.

   If the data already included subtotals, you would check the Replace current subtotals check box to replace the existing subtotals or uncheck the option to display the new subtotals on separate rows above the existing subtotals. Because the data has no subtotals, it makes no difference whether you select this option.

6. Make sure the **Summary below data** check box is checked. This option places the subtotals below each group of data instead of above the first entry in each group and places the grand total at the end of the data instead of at the top of the column just below the row of column headings.

7. Click the **OK** button. Excel inserts rows below each Sale Date group and displays the subtotals for the amount of each Sale Date in the Amount column. A series of Outline buttons appear to the left of the worksheet so you can display or hide the detail rows within each subtotal.

   Trouble? If each item has a subtotal following it, or repeating subtotals appear for the same item, you probably forgot to sort the data by Sale Date. Click the Undo button on the Quick Access Toolbar, sort the data by Sale Date, and then repeat Steps 1 through 7.

8. Scroll through the data to see the subtotals below each category and the grand total at the end of the data. See Figure 5-29.

Figure 5-29 Subtotals and grand total added to the sales data

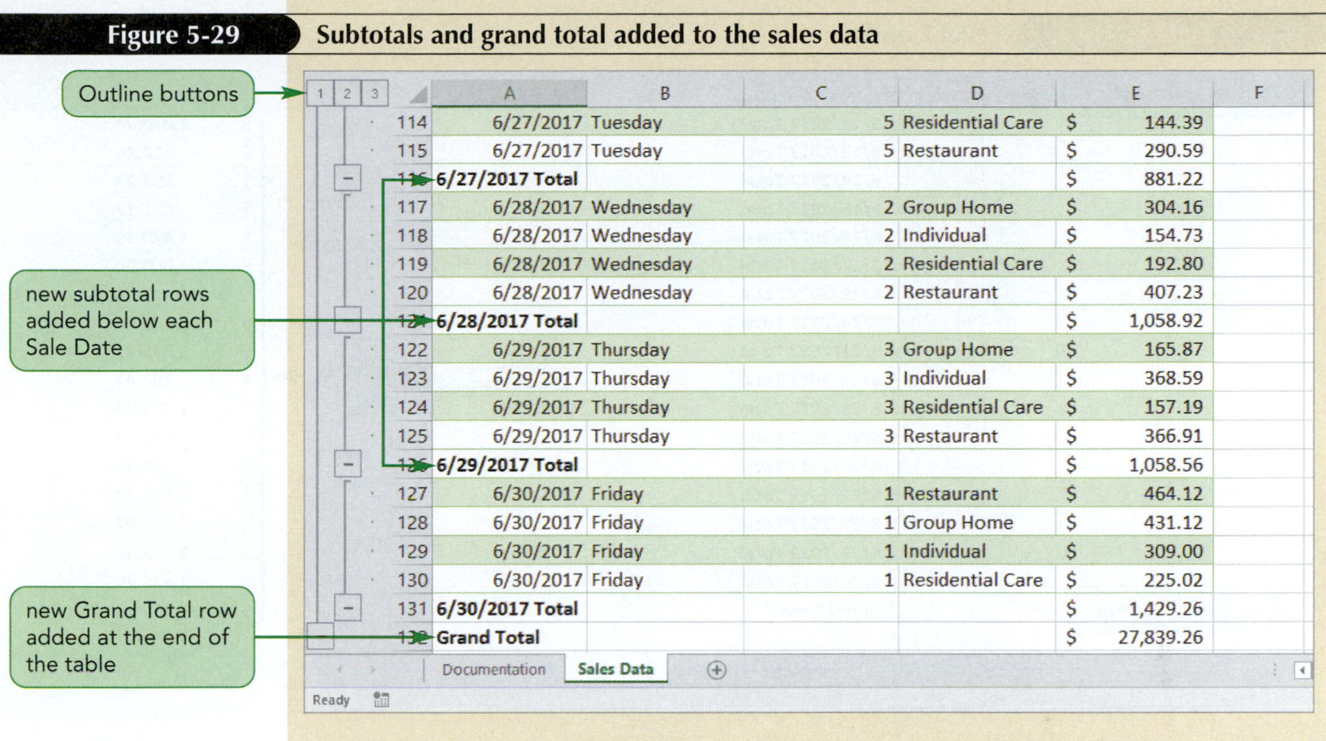

Outline buttons
new subtotal rows added below each Sale Date
new Grand Total row added at the end of the table
1 2 3
A B C D E F
114 6/27/2017 Tuesday 5 Residential Care $ 144.39
115 6/27/2017 Tuesday 5 Restaurant $ 290.59
116 6/27/2017 Total $ 881.22
117 6/28/2017 Wednesday 2 Group Home $ 304.16
118 6/28/2017 Wednesday 2 Individual $ 154.73
119 6/28/2017 Wednesday 2 Residential Care $ 192.80
120 6/28/2017 Wednesday 2 Restaurant $ 407.23
121 6/28/2017 Total $ 1,058.92
122 6/29/2017 Thursday 3 Group Home $ 165.87
123 6/29/2017 Thursday 3 Individual $ 368.59
124 6/29/2017 Thursday 3 Residential Care $ 157.19
125 6/29/2017 Thursday 3 Restaurant $ 366.91
126 6/29/2017 Total $ 1,058.56
127 6/30/2017 Friday 1 Restaurant $ 464.12
128 6/30/2017 Friday 1 Group Home $ 431.12
129 6/30/2017 Friday 1 Individual $ 309.00
130 6/30/2017 Friday 1 Residential Care $ 225.02
131 6/30/2017 Total $ 1,429.26
132 Grand Total $ 27,839.26
Documentation
Sales Data
Ready

Using the Subtotal Outline View

The Subtotal feature "outlines" the worksheet so you can control the level of detail that is displayed. The three Outline buttons at the top of the outline area, shown in Figure 5-29, allow you to show or hide different levels of detail in the worksheet. By default, the highest level is active; in this case, Level 3. Level 3 displays the most detail—the individual sales records, the subtotals, and the grand total. Level 2 displays the subtotals and the grand total but not the individual records. Level 1 displays only the grand total.

Victoria wants you to isolate the different subtotal sections so that she can focus on them individually. You will use the Outline buttons to prepare a report for Victoria that includes only subtotals and the grand total.

To use the Outline buttons to hide records:

1. Click the **Level 2 Outline** button [2], and then scroll to view the daily subtotals and grand total. The individual sales records are hidden; only the subtotals for each Sale Date and the grand total are displayed. See Figure 5-30.

Figure 5-30 Level 2 outline

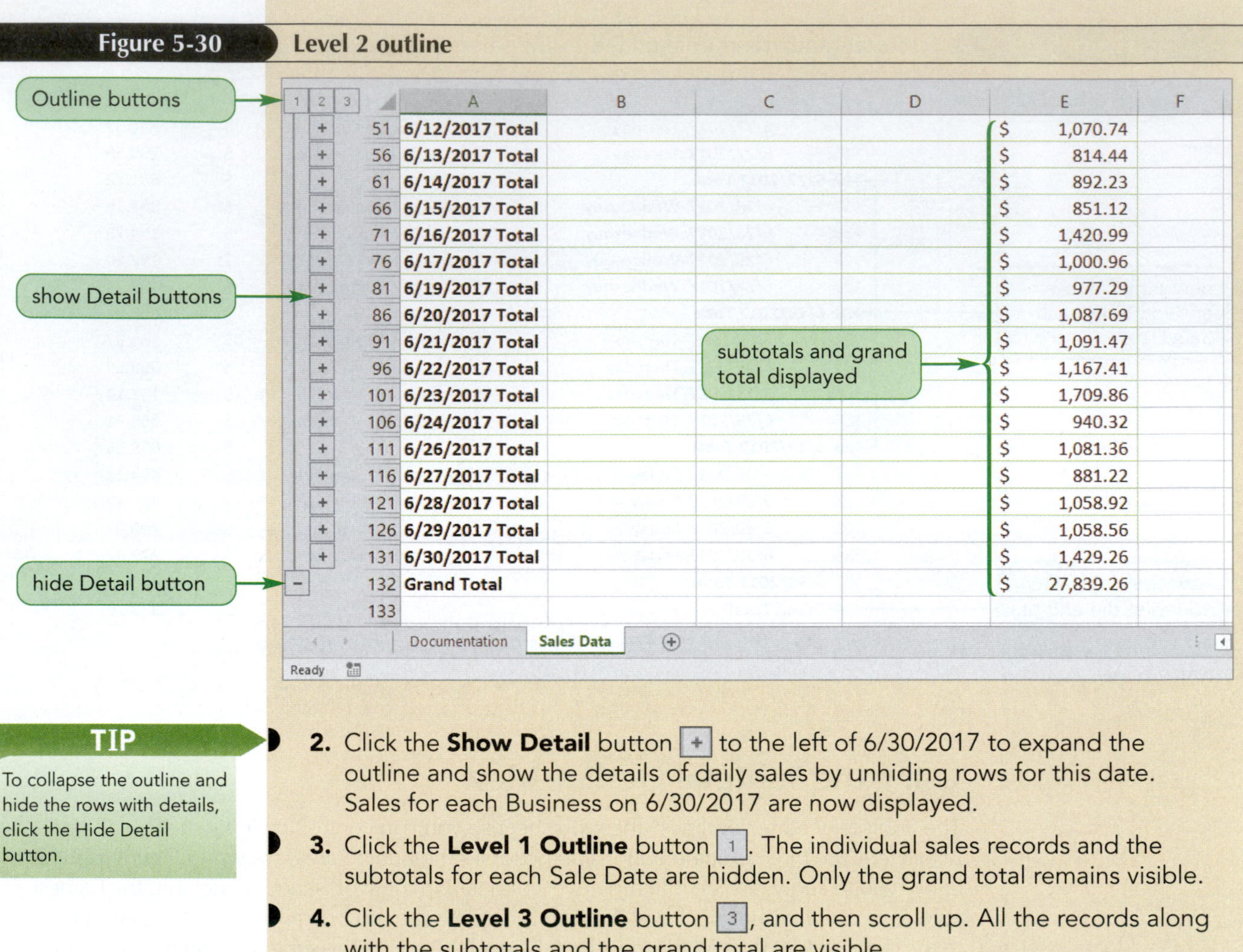

TIP

To collapse the outline and hide the rows with details, click the Hide Detail button.

2. Click the **Show Detail** button [+] to the left of 6/30/2017 to expand the outline and show the details of daily sales by unhiding rows for this date. Sales for each Business on 6/30/2017 are now displayed.
3. Click the **Level 1 Outline** button [1]. The individual sales records and the subtotals for each Sale Date are hidden. Only the grand total remains visible.
4. Click the **Level 3 Outline** button [3], and then scroll up. All the records along with the subtotals and the grand total are visible.

Victoria has completed her review of the daily sales report for June. She asks you to remove the subtotals from the data.

To remove the subtotals from the Sales Data worksheet:

1. On the Data tab, in the Outline group, click the **Subtotal** button. The Subtotal dialog box opens.
2. Click the **Remove All** button. The subtotals are removed from the data, and only the records appear in the worksheet.

   You'll reset the JuneTbl Excel table.
3. Make sure the active cell is a cell within the normal range of data.
4. On the ribbon, click the **Insert** tab.
5. In the Tables group, click the **Table** button. The Create Table dialog box opens.
6. Click the **OK** button to create the Excel table, and then click any cell in the table. The table structure is active.
7. On the Table Tools Design tab, in the Properties group, type **JuneTbl** in the Table Name box, and then press the **Enter** key. The Excel table is again named JuneTbl.

In this session, you filtered the table data, inserted a Total row, and determined totals and subtotals for the data. In the next session, you will work with PivotTables and PivotCharts to gather information to help Victoria with staffing and storefront opening decisions.

REVIEW

Session 5.2 Quick Check

1. Explain filtering.
2. How can you display a list of economics majors with a GPA less than 2.5 from an Excel table with records for 1000 students?
3. An Excel table includes records for 500 employees. What can you use to calculate the average salary of employees in the finance department?
4. What is a slicer, and how does it work?
5. If you have a list of employees that includes fields for gender and salary, among others, how can you determine the average salary for females using the Total row feature?
6. Explain the relationship between the Sort and Subtotal commands.
7. After you display subtotals, how can you use the Outline buttons?

Session 5.3 Visual Overview:

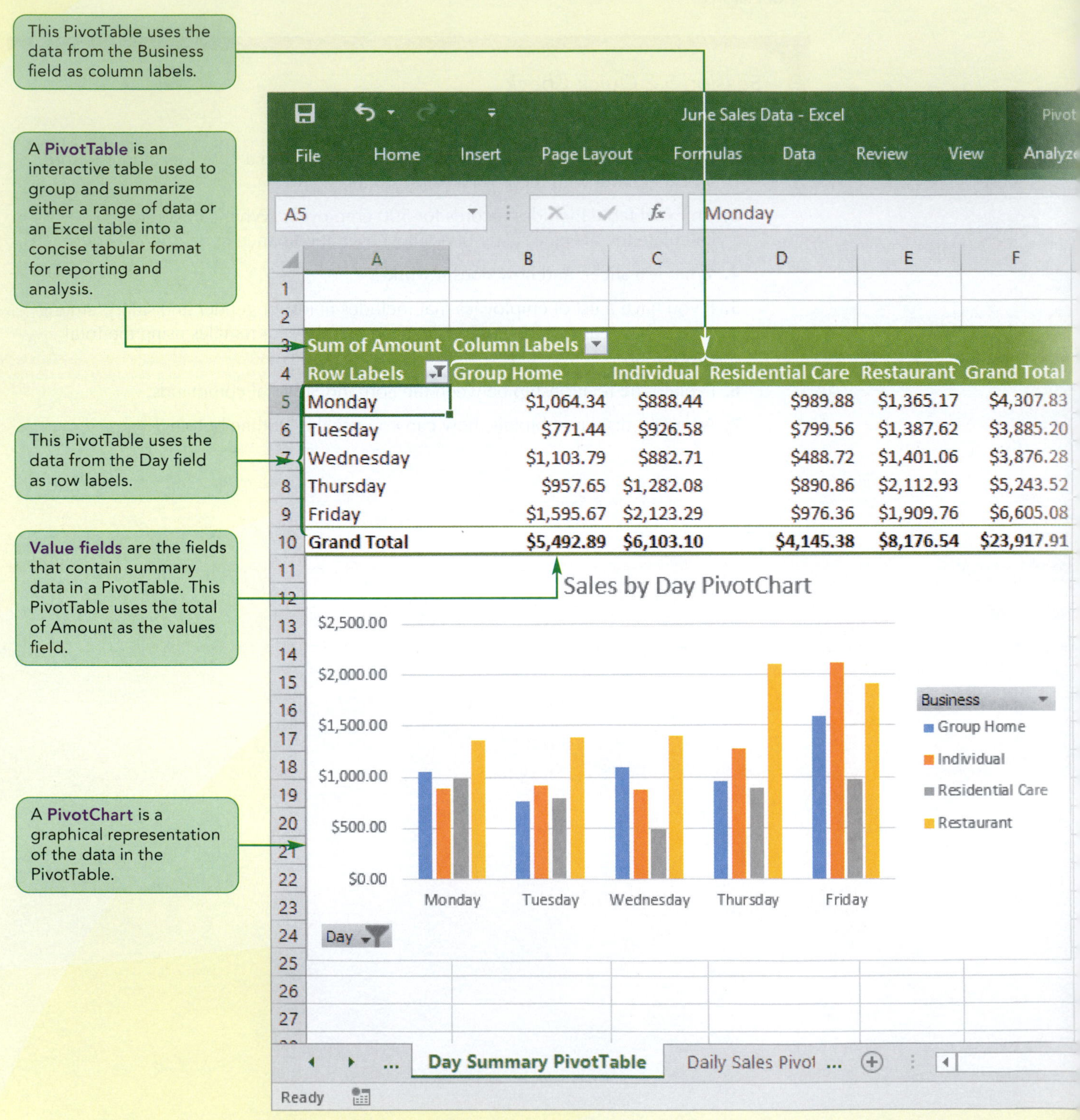

PivotTable and PivotChart

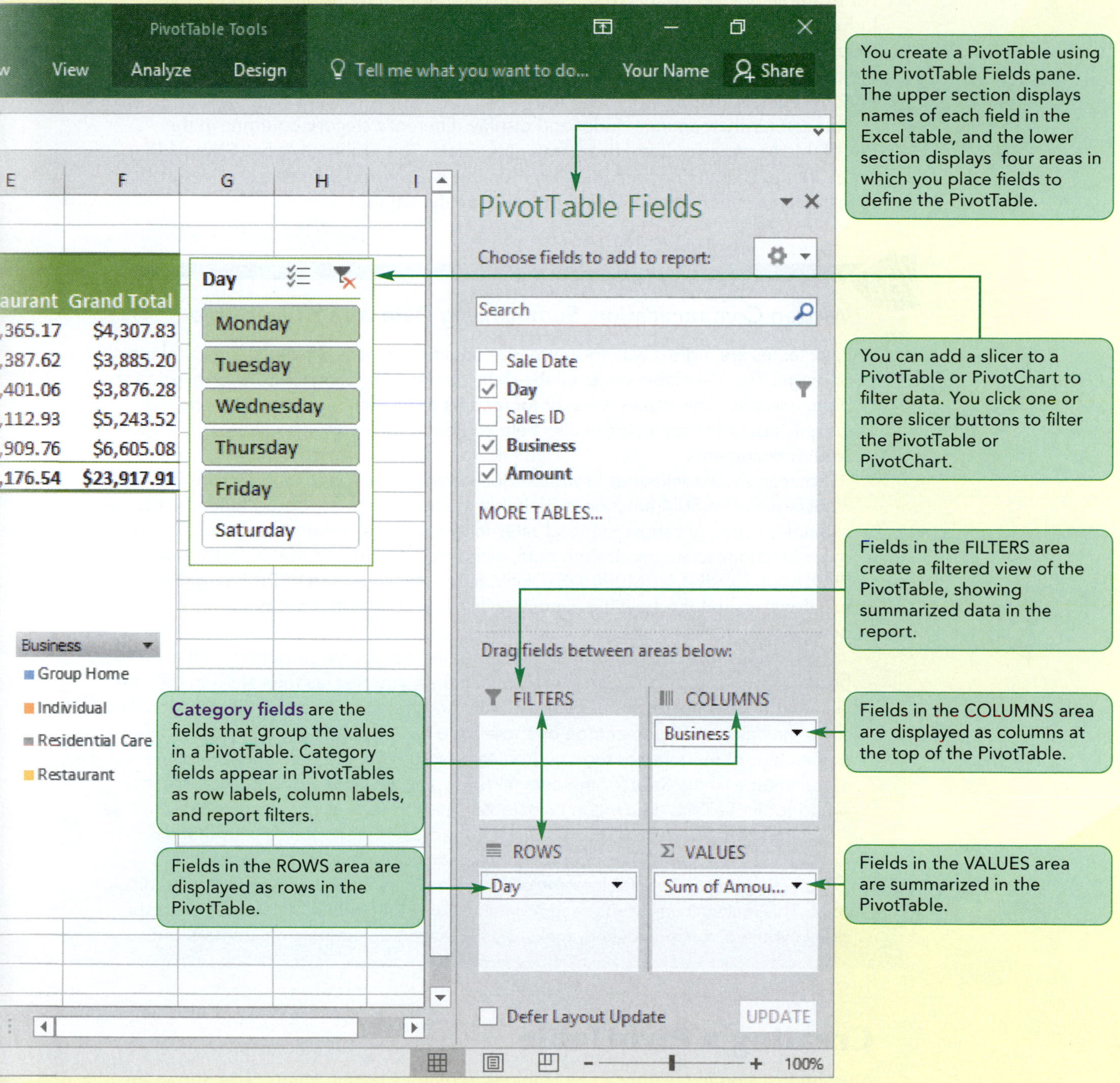
PivotTable Tools
View
Analyze
Design
Tell me what you want to do...
Your Name
Share
E
F
G
H
I
aurant
Grand Total
,365.17
$4,307.83
,387.62
$3,885.20
,401.06
$3,876.28
,112.93
$5,243.52
,909.76
$6,605.08
,176.54
$23,917.91
Day
Monday
Tuesday
Wednesday
Thursday
Friday
Saturday
Business
Group Home
Individual
Residential Care
Restaurant
PivotTable Fields
Choose fields to add to report:
Search
Sale Date
Day
Sales ID
Business
Amount
MORE TABLES...
Drag fields between areas below:
FILTERS
COLUMNS
Business
ROWS
Day
VALUES
Sum of Amou...
Defer Layout Update
UPDATE
100%
You create a PivotTable using the PivotTable Fields pane. The upper section displays names of each field in the Excel table, and the lower section displays four areas in which you place fields to define the PivotTable.
You can add a slicer to a PivotTable or PivotChart to filter data. You click one or more slicer buttons to filter the PivotTable or PivotChart.
Fields in the FILTERS area create a filtered view of the PivotTable, showing summarized data in the report.
Category fields are the fields that group the values in a PivotTable. Category fields appear in PivotTables as row labels, column labels, and report filters.
Fields in the COLUMNS area are displayed as columns at the top of the PivotTable.
Fields in the ROWS area are displayed as rows in the PivotTable.
Fields in the VALUES area are summarized in the PivotTable.

Analyzing Data with PivotTables

An Excel table can contain a wealth of information. However, when the table contains large amounts of detailed data, it often becomes more difficult to obtain a clear, overall view of that information. You can use a PivotTable to help organize the data into a meaningful summary. A PivotTable groups data into categories and then uses functions such as COUNT, SUM, AVERAGE, MAX, and MIN to summarize that data. For example, Victoria wants to see the daily sales for each business (Group Home, Individual, Residential Care, and Restaurant) grouped by week. Although there are several ways to generate the information Victoria needs, you can use a PivotTable like the one shown in the Session 5.3 Visual Overview to generate this information quickly and present it concisely.

You can easily rearrange, hide, and display different category columns in the PivotTable to provide alternative views of the data. This ability to "pivot" the table—for example, change row headings to column positions and vice versa—gives the PivotTable its name and makes it a powerful analytical tool.

PROSKILLS

Written Communication: Summarizing Data with a PivotTable

PivotTables are a great way to summarize data from selected fields of an Excel table or range. The PivotTable omits all the detailed data, enabling readers to focus on the bigger picture. This makes it easier for readers to understand the results and gain insights about the topic. It can also help you back up or support specific points in written documents.

You can show summaries in written documents based on function results in PivotTables. The SUM function is probably the most frequently used function. For example, you might show the total sales for a region. However, you can use many other functions to summarize the data, including COUNT, AVERAGE, MIN, MAX, PRODUCT, COUNT NUMBERS, STDDEV, STDDEVP, VAR, and VARP. Using these functions, you might show the average sales for a region, the minimum price of a product, or a count of the number of students by major.

When you write a report, you want supporting data to be presented in the way that best communicates your points. With PivotTables, you display the values in different views. For example, to compare one item to another item in the PivotTable, you can show the values as a percentage of a total. You can display the data in each row as a percentage of the total for the row. You can also display the data in each column as a percentage of the total for the column or display the data as a percentage of the grand total of all the data in the PivotTable. Viewing data as a percentage of the total is useful for analyses such as comparing product sales with total sales within a region or comparing expense categories to total expenses for the year.

As you can see, PivotTables provide great flexibility in how you analyze and display data. This makes it easier to present data in a way that highlights and supports the points you are communicating, making your written documents much more effective.

Creating a PivotTable

A useful first step in creating a PivotTable is to plan its layout. Figure 5-31 shows the PivotTable that Victoria wants you to create. As you can see in the figure, the PivotTable will show the total Amount of the sales organized by Sales ID, Sale Date, and Business.

Figure 5-31 PivotTable plan

Sales ID	XXXX					
Total Sales						
Sale Date		Group Home	Individual	Residential Care	Restaurant	Total
Total						

You are ready to create the PivotTable summarizing the total sales for Victoria.

REFERENCE

Creating a PivotTable

- Click in the Excel table (or select the range of data for the PivotTable).
- On the Insert tab, in the Tables group, click the PivotTable button.
- Click the Select a table or range option button, and then verify the reference in the Table/Range box.
- Click the New Worksheet option button, or click the Existing Worksheet option button and specify a cell.
- Click the OK button.
- Click the check boxes for the fields you want to add to the PivotTable (or drag fields to the appropriate box in the layout section).
- If needed, drag fields to different boxes in the layout section.

When you create a PivotTable, you need to specify where to find the data for the PivotTable. The data can be in an Excel table or range in the current workbook or an external data source such as an Access database file. You also must specify whether to place the PivotTable in a new or an existing worksheet. If you place the PivotTable in an existing worksheet, you must also specify the cell in which you want the upper-left corner of the PivotTable to appear.

To create the PivotTable that will provide the information Victoria needs, you will use the JuneTbl table and place the PivotTable in a new worksheet.

TIP

You can also click the Summarize with PivotTable button in the Tools group on the Table Tools Design tab.

To create a PivotTable using the JuneTbl table:

1. If you took a break after the previous session, make sure the June Sales Data workbook is open, the Sales Data worksheet is the active sheet, and the JuneTbl table is active.
2. On the ribbon, click the **Insert** tab.
3. In the Tables group, click the **PivotTable** button. The Create PivotTable dialog box opens. See Figure 5-32.

Figure 5-32 Create PivotTable dialog box

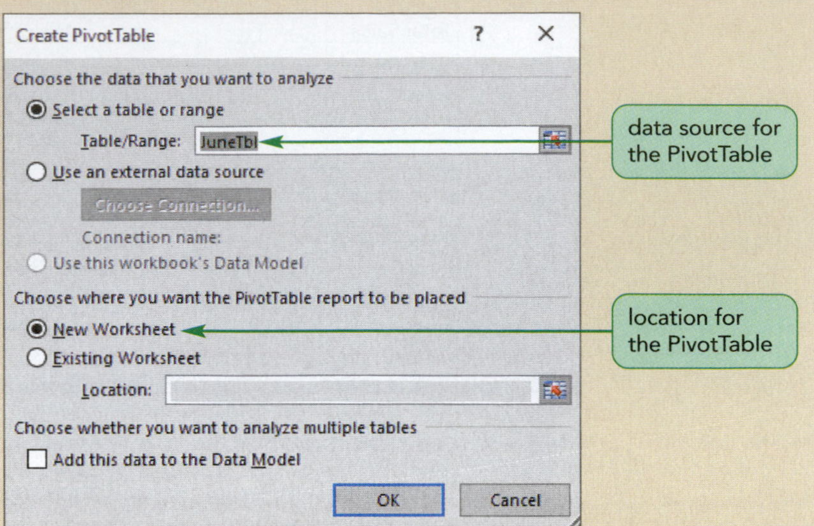

4. Make sure the **Select a table or range** option button is selected and **JuneTbl** appears in the Table/Range box.
5. Click the **New Worksheet** option button, if necessary. This sets the PivotTable report to be placed in a new worksheet.
6. Click the **OK** button. A new worksheet, Sheet1, is inserted to the left of the Sales Data worksheet. On the left is the empty PivotTable report area, where the finished PivotTable will be placed. On the right is the PivotTable Fields task pane, which you use to build the PivotTable. The PivotTable Tools tabs appear on the ribbon. See Figure 5-33.

Figure 5-33 Empty PivotTable report

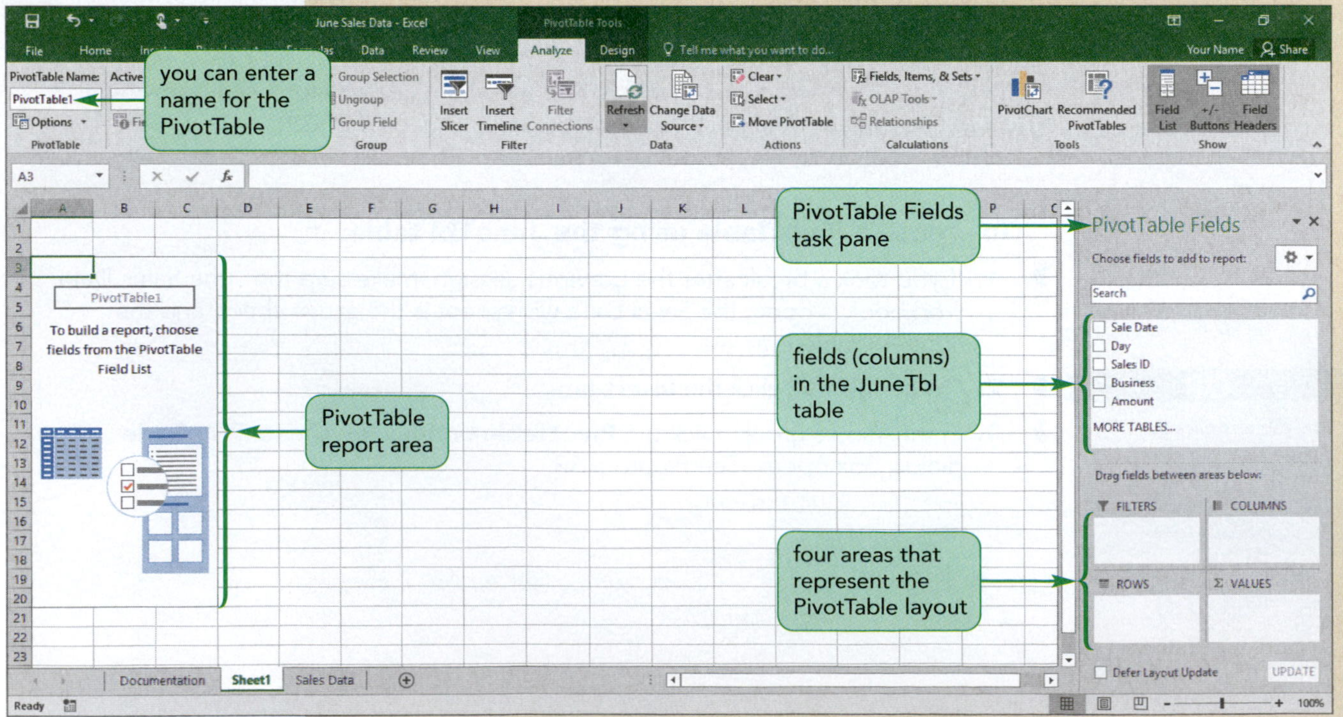

Trouble? If the PivotTable Fields task pane is not displayed, you need to display it. On the PivotTable Tools Analyze tab, in the Show group, click the Field List button.

Adding Fields to a PivotTable

To display data in a PivotTable, you add fields to the PivotTable. In PivotTable terminology, fields that contain summary data are Values fields, and fields that group the values in the PivotTable are Category fields. Category fields appear in PivotTables as row labels, column labels, and filters. You add fields to a PivotTable from the PivotTable Fields task pane, which is divided into two sections. The upper section lists the names of each field in the data source, which is the JuneTbl table, in this case. You select a field check box or drag the field into the lower section to add that field to the FILTERS, ROWS, COLUMNS, or VALUES area (described in Figure 5-34). The placement of fields in the area boxes determines the layout of the PivotTable.

Figure 5-34 **Layout areas for a PivotTable**

Area	Description
ROWS	Fields placed in this area appear as Row Labels on the left side of the PivotTable. Each unique item in this field is displayed in a separate row. Row fields can be nested.
COLUMNS	Fields placed in this area appear as Column Labels on the top of the PivotTable. Each unique item in this field is displayed in a separate column. Column fields can be nested.
FILTERS	Fields placed in this area appear as top-level filters above the PivotTable. These fields are used to select one or more items to display in the PivotTable.
VALUES	Fields placed in this area are numbers that are summarized in the PivotTable.

TIP

By default, Excel uses the COUNT function for nonnumeric fields placed in the VALUES area.

Typically, fields with text or nonnumeric data are placed in the ROWS area. Fields with numeric data are most often placed in the VALUES area and by default are summarized with the SUM function. If you want to use a different function, click the field button in the VALUES area, click Value Field Settings to open the Value Field Settings dialog box, select a different function such as AVERAGE, COUNT, MIN, MAX, and so on, and then click the OK button. You can move fields between the areas at any time to change how data is displayed in the PivotTable. You can also add the same field to the VALUES area more than once so you can calculate its sum, average, and count in one PivotTable.

Victoria wants to see the total value of sales by Sales ID. Then, within each Sales ID, she wants to see total sales for each Day. Finally, she wants each Day further divided to display sales for each Business. You'll add fields to the PivotTable so that the Sales ID, Sale Date, and Business fields are row labels, and the Amount field is the data to be summarized as the Values field.

To add fields to the PivotTable:

1. In the PivotTable Fields task pane, drag **Sales ID** from the upper section to the ROWS area in the lower section. The Sales ID field appears in the ROWS area, and the unique values in the Sales ID field—1, 2, 3, 4, and 5—appear in the PivotTable report area. See Figure 5-35.

Figure 5-35 PivotTable with the Sales ID field values as row labels

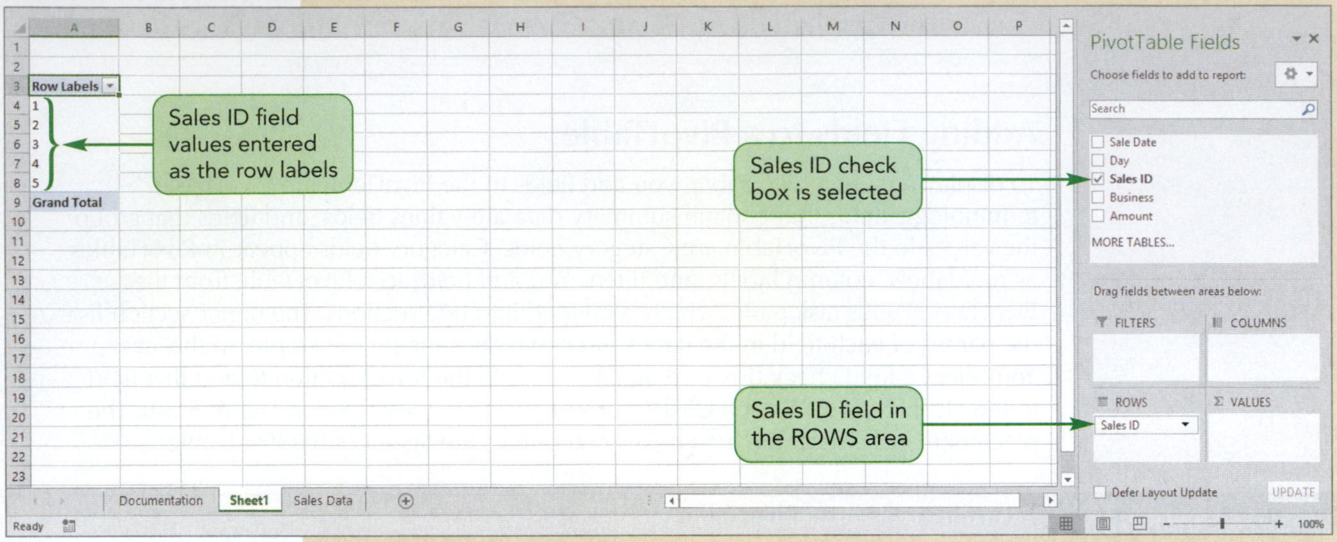

Trouble? If the Sales ID field appears in the VALUES area, you probably checked the Sales ID field, which places fields with numeric values in the VALUES area. Drag the Sales ID field from the VALUES area to the ROWS area.

2. In the PivotTable Fields task pane, click the **Amount** check box. The Sum of Amount button is placed in the VALUES box because the field contains numeric values. The PivotTable groups the items from the JuneTbl table by Sales ID and calculates the total Amount for each week. The grand total appears at the bottom of the PivotTable. See Figure 5-36.

Figure 5-36 PivotTable shows the sum of the Amounts field for each Sales ID

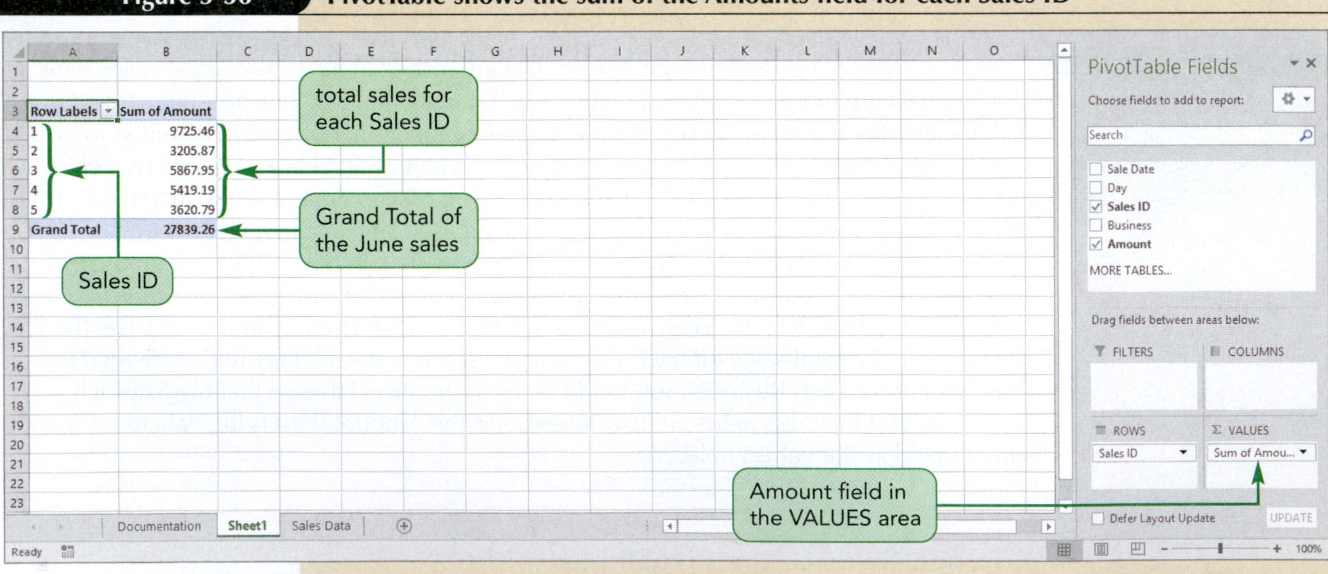

Next, you'll add the Sale Date and Business fields to the PivotTable.

3. In the PivotTable Fields task pane, click the **Sale Date** check box. The Sale Date field appears in the ROWS area box below the Sales ID field, and the unique items in the Sale Date field are indented below each Sales ID field item in the PivotTable report.

Trouble? If the PivotTable Fields task pane is not visible, the active cell is probably not in the PivotTable. Click any cell within the PivotTable to redisplay the PivotTable Fields task pane. If the PivotTable Fields task pane is still not visible, click the PivotTable Tools Analyze tab, and then click the Field List button in the Show group.

4. In the PivotTable Fields task pane, click the **Business** check box. The Business field appears in the ROWS area below the Sale Date field, and its unique items are indented below the Sales ID and Sale Date fields already in the PivotTable. See Figure 5-37.

Figure 5-37 PivotTable with Sales ID, Sale Date, and Business field items as row labels

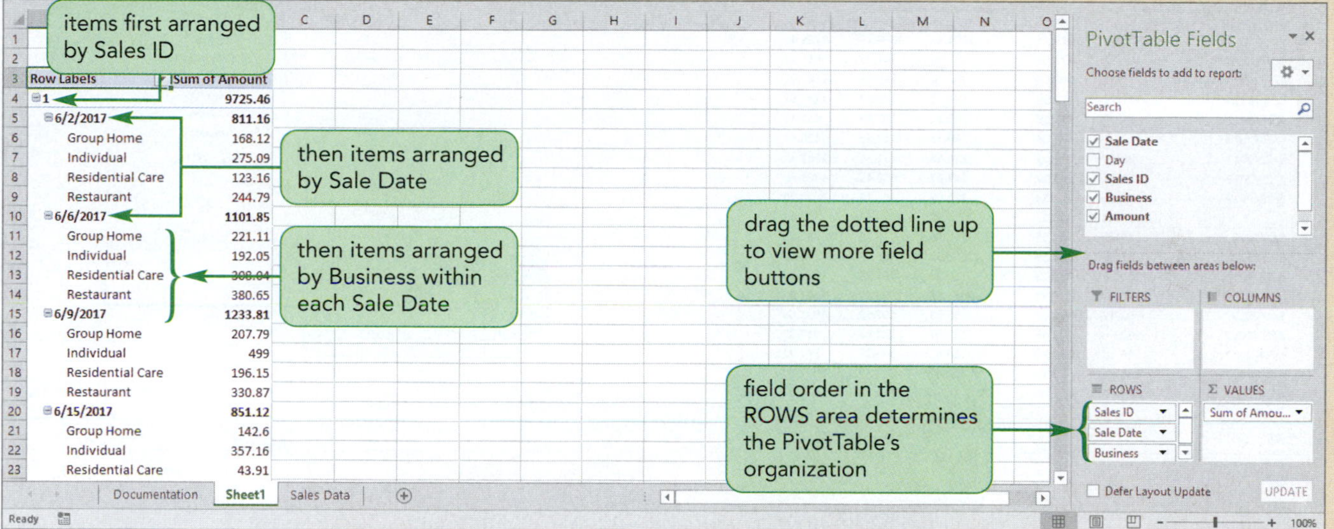

Trouble? If the Business field button is not visible in the ROWS area, drag the dotted line above the "Drag fields between areas below" label up until the Business field button is visible.

If a PivotTable becomes too detailed or confusing, you can always remove one of its fields. In the PivotTable Fields task pane, click the check box of the field you want to remove. The field is then deleted from the PivotTable and the area box.

Changing the Layout of a PivotTable

You can add, remove, and rearrange fields to change the PivotTable's layout. Recall that the benefit of a PivotTable is that it summarizes large amounts of data into a readable format. After you create a PivotTable, you can view the same data in different ways. Each time you make a change in the areas section of the PivotTable Fields task pane, the PivotTable layout is rearranged. This ability to "pivot" the table—for example, change row headings to column positions and vice versa—makes the PivotTable a powerful analytical tool.

Based on Victoria's PivotTable plan that is shown in Figure 5-31, the Business field items should be positioned as columns instead of rows in the PivotTable. You'll move the Business field now to produce the layout Victoria wants.

To move the Business field to the COLUMNS area:

1. In the PivotTable Fields task pane, locate the **Business** field button in the ROWS area.
2. Drag the **Business** field button from the ROWS area to the COLUMNS area. The PivotTable is rearranged so that the Business field is a column label instead of a row label. See Figure 5-38.

Figure 5-38 PivotTable rearranged with Business as a column label

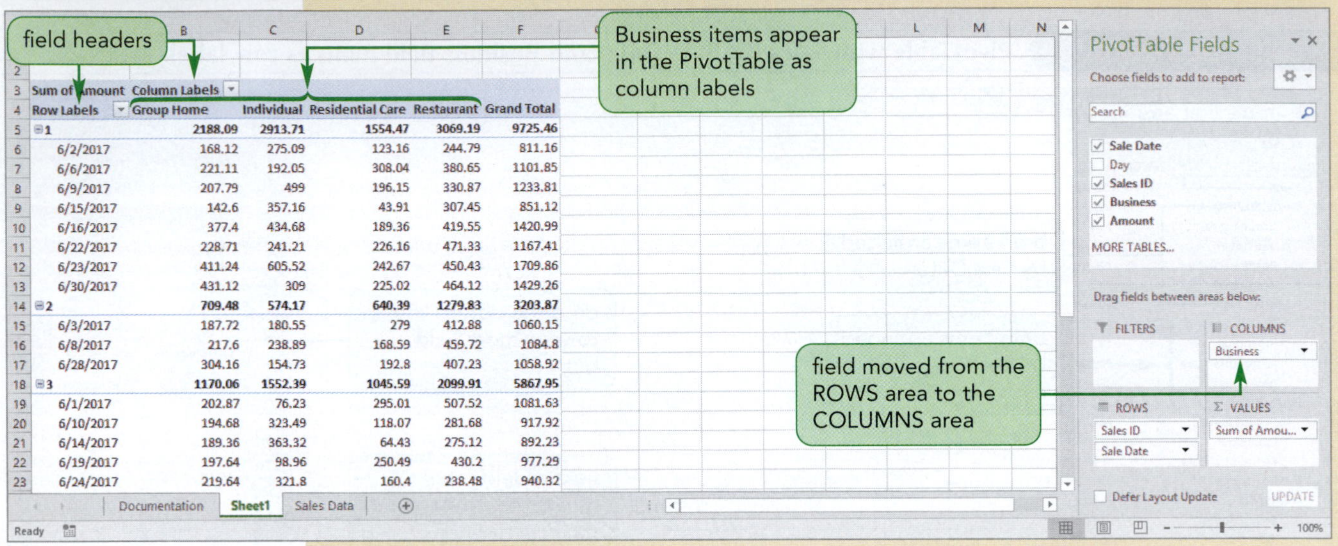

Sum of Amount	Column Labels				
Row Labels	Group Home	Individual	Residential Care	Restaurant	Grand Total
1	**2188.09**	**2913.71**	**1554.47**	**3069.19**	**9725.46**
6/2/2017	168.12	275.09	123.16	244.79	811.16
6/6/2017	221.11	192.05	308.04	380.65	1101.85
6/9/2017	207.79	499	196.15	330.87	1233.81
6/15/2017	142.6	357.16	43.91	307.45	851.12
6/16/2017	377.4	434.68	189.36	419.55	1420.99
6/22/2017	228.71	241.21	226.16	471.33	1167.41
6/23/2017	411.24	605.52	242.67	450.43	1709.86
6/30/2017	431.12	309	225.02	464.12	1429.26
2	**709.48**	**574.17**	**640.39**	**1279.83**	**3203.87**
6/3/2017	187.72	180.55	279	412.88	1060.15
6/8/2017	217.6	238.89	168.59	459.72	1084.8
6/28/2017	304.16	154.73	192.8	407.23	1058.92
3	**1170.06**	**1552.39**	**1045.59**	**2099.91**	**5867.95**
6/1/2017	202.87	76.23	295.01	507.52	1081.63
6/10/2017	194.68	323.49	118.07	281.68	917.92
6/14/2017	189.36	363.32	64.43	275.12	892.23
6/19/2017	197.64	98.96	250.49	430.2	977.29
6/24/2017	219.64	321.8	160.4	238.48	940.32

The PivotTable now has the layout that Victoria wants.

INSIGHT

Choosing a Report Layout

There are three different report layouts available for PivotTables. The report layout shown in Figure 5-38, which is referred to as the Compact Form, is the default layout. It places all fields from the ROWS area in a single column and indents the items from each field below the outer fields. In the Outline Form layout, each field in the ROWS area takes a column in the PivotTable. The subtotal for each group appears above every group. The Tabular Form layout displays one column for each field and leaves space for column headers. A total for each group appears below each group. To select a different report layout, click the Report Layout button in the Layout group on the PivotTable Tools Design tab.

Formatting a PivotTable

Like worksheet cells and Excel tables, you can quickly format a PivotTable report using one of the built-in styles available in the PivotTable Styles gallery. As with cell and table styles, you can point to any style in the gallery to see a Live Preview of the PivotTable with that style. You also can modify the appearance of PivotTables by adding or removing banded rows, banded columns, row headers, and column headers.

Victoria wants you to apply the Pivot Style Medium 14 style, which makes each group in the PivotTable stand out and makes subtotals in the report easier to find.

To apply the Pivot Style Medium 14 style to the PivotTable:

1. Make sure the active cell is in the PivotTable.
2. On the ribbon, click the **PivotTable Tools Design** tab.
3. In the PivotTable Styles group, click the **More** button to open the PivotTable Styles gallery.
4. Move the pointer over each style to see the Live Preview of the PivotTable report with that style.
5. Click the **Pivot Style Medium 14** style (the last style in the second row of the Medium section). The style is applied to the PivotTable.

You can format cells in a PivotTable the same way that you format cells in a worksheet. This enables you to further customize the look of the PivotTable by changing the font, color, alignment, and number formats of specific cells in the PivotTable. Victoria wants the numbers in the PivotTable to be quickly recognized as dollars. You'll change the total Amount values in the PivotTable to the Currency style.

To format the Amount field in the PivotTable as currency:

1. In the VALUES area of the PivotTable Fields task pane, click the **Sum of Amount** button. A shortcut menu opens with options related to that field.
2. Click the **Value Field Settings** button on the shortcut menu. The Value Field Settings dialog box opens. See Figure 5-39.

Figure 5-39 Value Field Settings dialog box

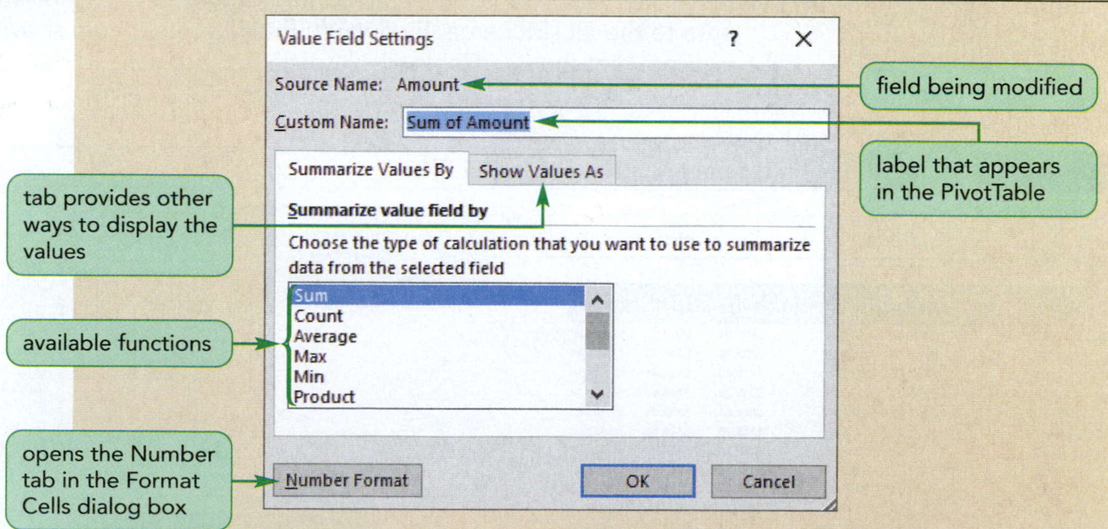

3. In the Custom Name box, type **Total Sales** as the label for the field. You will leave Sum as the summary function for the field; however, you could select a different function.
4. Click the **Number Format** button. The Format Cells dialog box opens. This is the same dialog box you have used before to format numbers in worksheet cells.

TIP

You can also right-click in the PivotTable data area and click Number Format or Format Cells to quickly format the PivotTable.

5. In the Category box, click **Currency**. You will use the default number of decimal places, currency symbol, and negative number format.
6. Click the **OK** button. The numbers in the PivotTable will be formatted as currency with two decimal places.
7. Click the **OK** button. The Value Field Settings dialog box closes. The PivotTable changes to reflect the label you entered, and the number format for the field changes to currency.

Filtering a PivotTable

As you analyze the data in a PivotTable, you might want to show only a portion of the total data. You can do this by filtering the PivotTable. Filtering a field lets you focus on a subset of items in that field.

Adding a Field to the FILTERS Area

You can drag one or more fields to the FILTERS area of the PivotTable Fields task pane to change what values are displayed in the PivotTable. A field placed in the FILTERS area provides a way to filter the PivotTable so that it displays summarized data for one or more items or all items in that field. For example, placing the Sales ID field in the FILTERS area allows you to view or print the total sales for all Sales IDs, a specific Sales ID such as 1, or multiple Sales IDs such as 2 through 5.

Victoria wants you to move the Sales ID field from the ROWS area to the FILTERS area so that she can focus on specific subsets of the sales.

To add the Sales ID field to the FILTERS area:

1. In the PivotTable Fields task pane, drag the **Sales ID** button from the ROWS area to the FILTERS area. By default, the Filter field item shows "(All)" to indicate that the PivotTable displays all the summarized data associated with the Sales ID field. See Figure 5-40.

Figure 5-40 PivotTable with the Sales ID filter

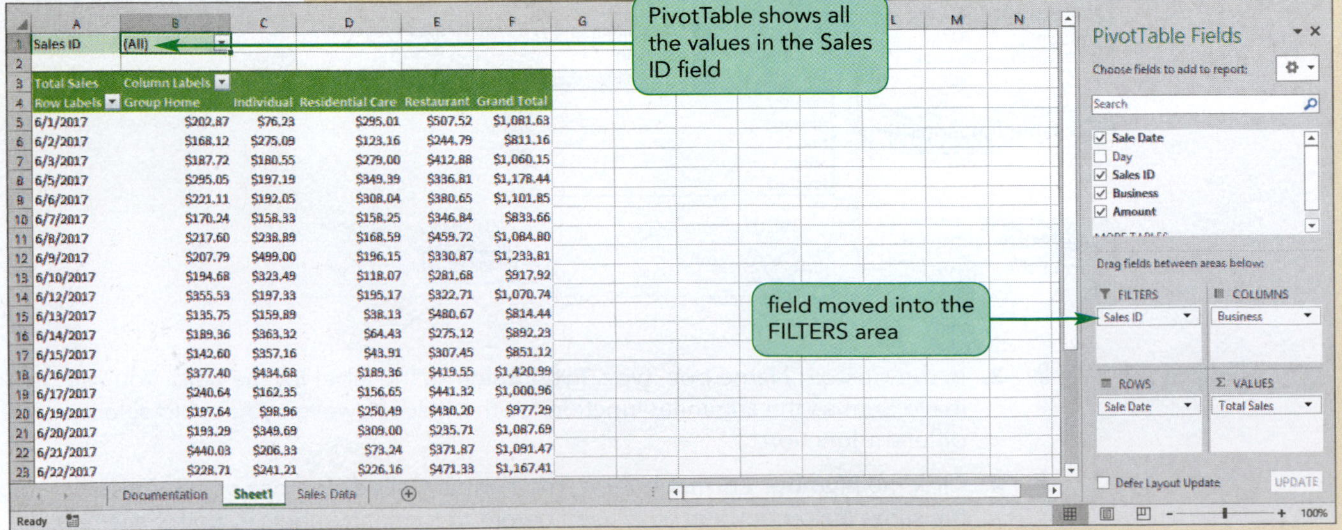

Sales ID	(All)				
Total Sales	Column Labels				
Row Labels	Group Home	Individual	Residential Care	Restaurant	Grand Total
6/1/2017	$202.87	$76.23	$295.01	$507.52	$1,081.63
6/2/2017	$168.12	$275.09	$123.16	$244.79	$811.16
6/3/2017	$187.72	$180.55	$279.00	$412.88	$1,060.15
6/5/2017	$295.05	$197.19	$349.39	$336.81	$1,178.44
6/6/2017	$221.11	$192.05	$308.04	$380.65	$1,101.85
6/7/2017	$170.24	$158.33	$158.25	$346.84	$833.66
6/8/2017	$217.60	$238.89	$168.59	$459.72	$1,084.80
6/9/2017	$207.79	$499.00	$196.15	$330.87	$1,233.81
6/10/2017	$194.68	$323.49	$118.07	$281.68	$917.92
6/12/2017	$355.53	$197.33	$195.17	$322.71	$1,070.74
6/13/2017	$135.75	$159.89	$38.13	$480.67	$814.44
6/14/2017	$189.36	$363.32	$64.43	$275.12	$892.23
6/15/2017	$142.60	$357.16	$43.91	$307.45	$851.12
6/16/2017	$377.40	$434.68	$189.36	$419.55	$1,420.99
6/17/2017	$240.64	$162.35	$156.65	$441.32	$1,000.96
6/19/2017	$197.64	$98.96	$250.49	$430.20	$977.29
6/20/2017	$193.29	$349.69	$309.00	$235.71	$1,087.69
6/21/2017	$440.03	$206.33	$73.24	$371.87	$1,091.47
6/22/2017	$228.71	$241.21	$226.16	$471.33	$1,167.41

Next, you'll filter the summarized report to show only sales for Sales ID 2.

2. In cell B1, click the **filter** button ▾. The Filter menu opens, showing the field items displayed.

3. In the Filter menu, click **2**, and then click the **OK** button. The PivotTable displays the total Amount of sales on dates associated with Sales ID 2. The filter button changes to indicate that the PivotTable is currently filtered. See Figure 5-41.

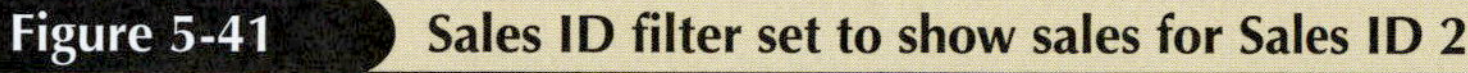
Figure 5-41 Sales ID filter set to show sales for Sales ID 2

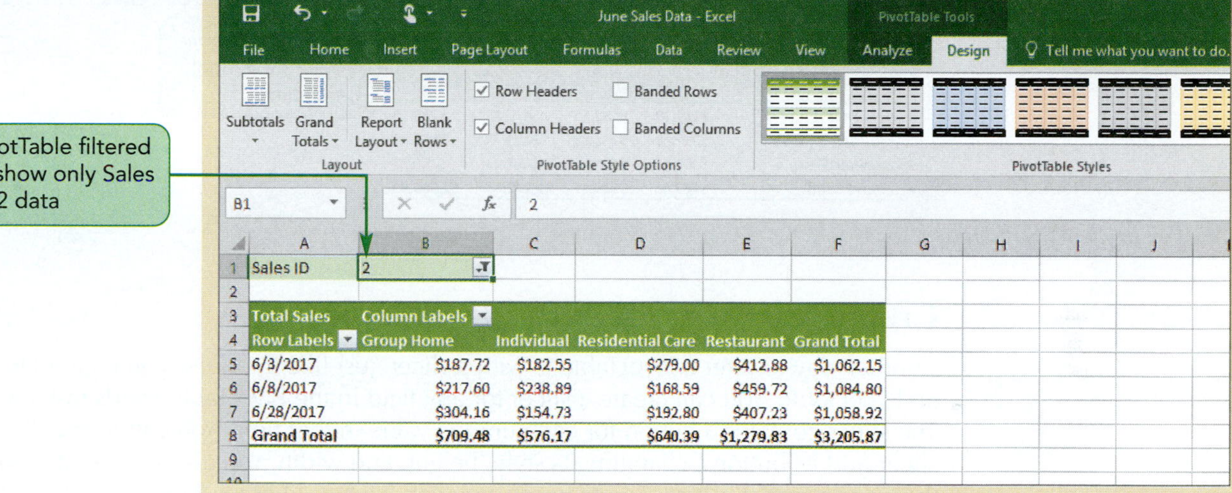

Filtering PivotTable Fields

Another way that you can filter field items in the PivotTable is by using the Filter menu, which you open by clicking the Row Labels filter button or the Column Labels filter button. You then check or uncheck items to show or hide them, respectively, in the PivotTable.

Victoria wants to exclude Residential Care from the analysis. She asks you to remove the Residential Care sales from the PivotTable.

To filter Residential Care from the Business column labels:

1. In the PivotTable, click the **Column Labels** filter button ▾. The Filter menu opens, listing the items in the Business field.

2. Click the **Residential Care** check box to remove the checkmark. The Select All check box is filled with black indicating that all items are not selected.

3. Click the **OK** button. The Residential Care column is removed from the PivotTable. The PivotTable includes sales from only Group Home, Individual, and Restaurant. See Figure 5-42. You can show the hidden objects by clicking the Column Labels filter button and checking the Residential Care check box.

Figure 5-42 PivotTable report filtered by Business

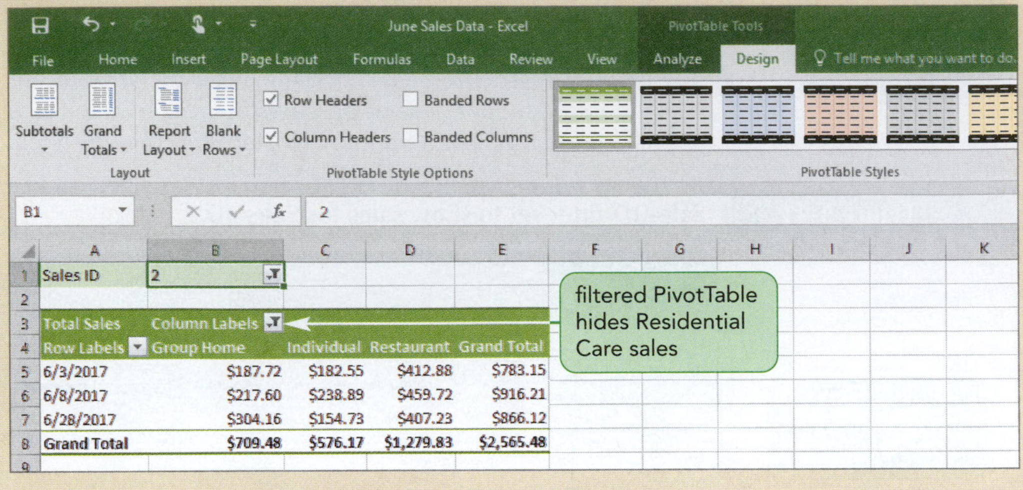

Creating a Slicer to Filter a PivotTable

Another way to filter a PivotTable is with a slicer, just like the slicer you created to filter an Excel table. You can create a slicer for any field in the PivotTable Fields task pane. The slicer contains a button for each unique value in that field. You can format the slicer and its buttons, changing its style, height, and width. You also can create more than one slicer at a time. For example, you can have a slicer for Sales ID that has a button for each unique Sales ID value and a second slicer for Business. This allows you to filter a PivotTable report so that it displays the sales amount for Sales ID 2, Group Home, Individual, and Restaurant by clicking the corresponding slicer buttons.

Victoria wants flexibility in how she views the data in the PivotTable, so she asks you to add a slicer for the Sales ID field to the current PivotTable.

To add the Sales ID slicer to the PivotTable:

1. On the ribbon, click the **PivotTable Tools Analyze** tab.
2. In the Filter group, click the **Insert Slicer** button. The Insert Slicers dialog box opens, displaying a list of available PivotTable fields. You can select any or all of the fields.
3. Click the **Sales ID** check box to insert a checkmark, and then click the **OK** button. The Sales ID slicer appears on the worksheet. Because the PivotTable is already filtered to display only the results for Sales ID 2, the 2 button is selected. The other slicer buttons are white because those weeks have been filtered and are not part of the PivotTable.
4. If the Slicer Tools Options tab does not appear on the ribbon, click the **Sales ID** slicer to select it.
5. On the Slicer Tools Options tab, in the Size group, change the height to **1.9"** and change the width to **1.25"**. The slicer object is resized, eliminating the extra space below the buttons and to the right of the labels.
6. In the Slicer Styles group, click the **More** button, and then click **Slicer Style Dark 6**. The slicer colors now match the PivotTable.
7. Drag the **Sales ID** slicer to the right of the PivotTable, placing its upper-left corner in cell G3. See Figure 5-43.

Figure 5-43 Sales ID slicer

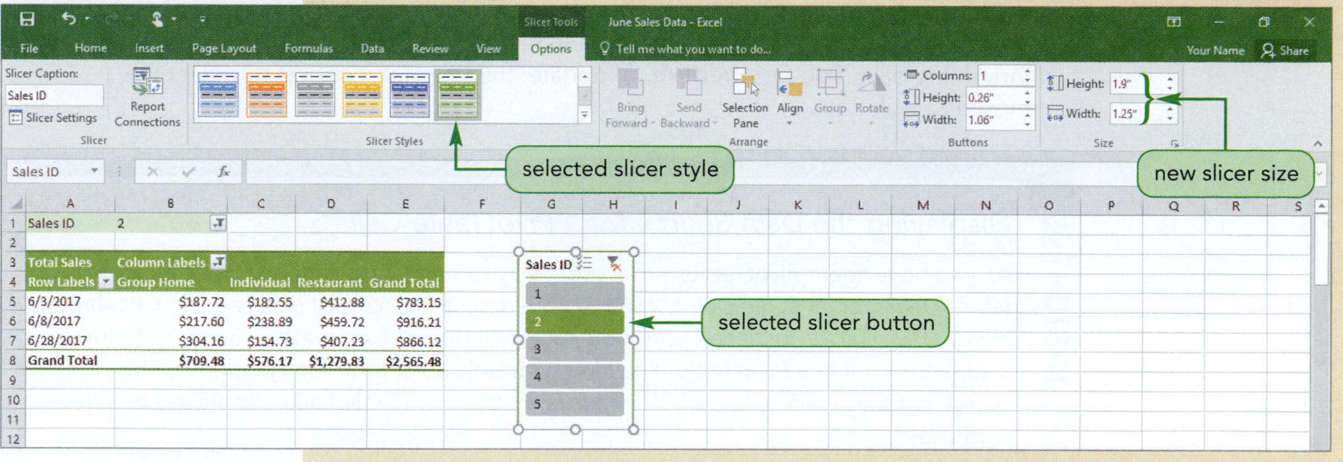

Victoria wants you to display the results of the PivotTable for all the seasonal employees in June—Sales IDs 2, 3, and 4. You can do this quickly using the Sales ID slicer.

To filter the PivotTable using the Sales ID slicer:

1. Press and hold the **Ctrl** key, click the **3** button, and then release the **Ctrl** key. Sales ID 3 data also appears on the PivotTable.
2. Press and hold the **Ctrl** key, click the **4** button, and then release the **Ctrl** key. Data for Sales ID 4 is added to the PivotTable.
3. Click the **Sales ID 2** slicer button. Only the sales for Sales ID 2 are displayed in the PivotTable.

TIP

To remove all filters from the PivotTable, click the Clear Filter button in the upper-right corner of the slicer.

After you have finished creating a PivotTable, you can hide the PivotTable Fields task pane so that it won't appear when a cell is selected in the PivotTable. You can also assign more descriptive names to the PivotTable as well as the worksheet that contains the PivotTable.

To hide the PivotTable Fields task pane and rename the PivotTable and worksheet:

1. Click in the PivotTable to display the PivotTable Tools contextual tabs on the ribbon.
2. Click the **PivotTable Tools Analyze** tab.
3. In the Show group, click the **Field List** button. The PivotTable Fields task pane is hidden and won't reappear when a cell in the PivotTable is selected.
4. In the PivotTable group, select the name in the PivotTable Name box, type **SalesIDSummary** as the descriptive PivotTable name, and then press the **Enter** key.
5. Rename the worksheet as **Sales ID Summary PivotTable**.

Refreshing a PivotTable

You cannot change data directly in a PivotTable. Instead, you must edit the data source on which the PivotTable is created. However, PivotTables are not updated automatically when the source data for the PivotTable is updated. After you edit the underlying data, you must **refresh**, or update, the PivotTable report to reflect the revised calculations.

INSIGHT

Displaying the Data Source for a PivotTable Cell

As you have seen, PivotTables are a great way to summarize the results of an Excel table. However, at some point, you may question the accuracy of a specific calculation in your PivotTable. In these cases, you can "drill down" to view the source data for a summary cell in a PivotTable. You simply double-click a summary cell, and the corresponding source data of the records for the PivotTable cell is displayed in a new worksheet.

The sales entry for Individual on 6/3/2017 should have been $180.55 (not $182.55 as currently listed). You'll edit the record in the JuneTbl table, which is the underlying data source for the PivotTable. This one change will affect the PivotTable in several locations—the Amount for Individual on 6/3/2017 (currently $182.55), the Grand Total for Individual (currently $576.17), the Grand Total for 6/3/2017 (currently $783.15), and the overall Grand Total for Sales ID 2 (currently $2,565.48).

To update the JuneTbl table and refresh the PivotTable:

1. Go to the **Sales Data** worksheet, and then find the Individual sales for 6/3/2017. The amount is $182.55.
2. Click the record's **Amount** cell, and then enter **180.55**. The sales Amount is updated in the table. You'll return to the PivotTable report to see the effect of this change.
3. Go to the **Sales ID Summary PivotTable** worksheet. The Amount for Individual on 6/3/2017 is still $182.55, the Grand Total for Individual is still $576.17, the Grand Total for 6/3/2017 is still $783.15, and the overall Grand Total is still $2,565.48.

   The PivotTable was not automatically updated when the data in its source table changed, so you need to refresh the PivotTable.
4. Click any cell in the PivotTable.
5. On the ribbon, click the **PivotTable Tools Analyze** tab.
6. In the Data group, click the **Refresh** button (or press the **Alt+F5** keys). The PivotTable report is updated. The totals are now $180.55, $574.17, $781.15, and $2,563.48. See Figure 5-44.

Figure 5-44 **Refreshed PivotTable**

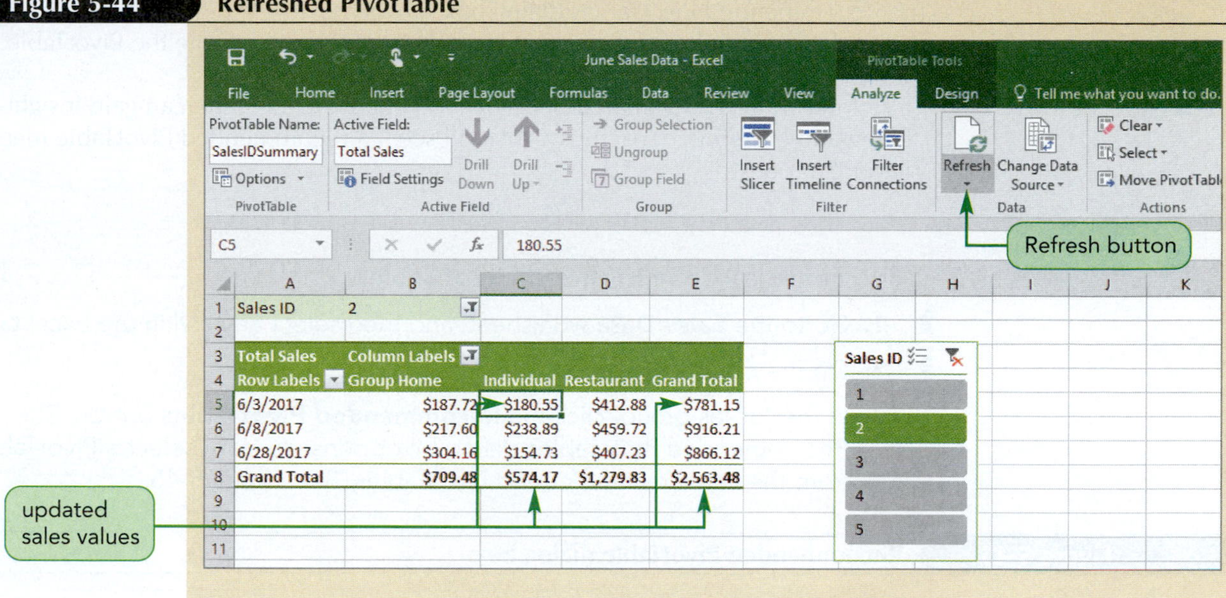

PivotTables provide an efficient way to display and analyze data. Like with charts, if a value displayed in the PivotTable is incorrect, you must update the data itself and then refresh the PivotTable to show that new data.

INSIGHT

Creating Different Types of PivotTables

This module only scratched the surface of the variety of PivotTables you can create. Here are a few more examples:

- Most PivotTable summaries are based on numeric data; Excel uses SUM as the default calculation. If your analysis requires a different calculation, you can select any of the 11 built-in summary calculations. For example, you could build a report that displays the minimum, maximum, and average sales for each week in June.
- You can use PivotTables to combine row label and column label items into groups. If items are numbers or dates, they can be grouped automatically using the Grouping dialog box, or they can be grouped manually using the Ctrl key to select items in a group and then clicking Group Selection from the shortcut menu. For example, you can manually combine Saturday and Sunday sales into a Weekend group, combine Monday through Friday sales into a Weekday group, and then display total sales by these groups within the PivotTable. Over time, you will also be able to group the Sale Date field to summarize daily sales by month, quarter, and year.
- You can develop PivotTables that use the percent of row, percent of column, or percent of total calculation to view each item in the PivotTable as a percent of the total in the current row, current column, or grand total. For example, you can display the total weekly sales as a percent of the total monthly sales.
- You can develop PivotTables that display how the current month/quarter/year compares to the previous month/quarter/year. For example, you can compare this month's sales for each Business to the corresponding sales for the previous month to display the difference between the two months.

Being able to enhance PivotTables by changing summary calculations, consolidating data into larger groups, and creating custom calculations based on other data in the VALUES area gives you flexibility in your analysis.

Creating a Recommended PivotTable

The Recommended PivotTables dialog box shows previews of PivotTables based on the source data, which lets you see different options for how to create the PivotTable. You can then choose the one that best meets your needs.

Victoria wants to summarize sales by days of the week so she can gain insights into staffing and ordering for each day. You will see if a recommended PivotTable meets Victoria's request.

To create a recommended PivotTable:

1. Go to the **Sales Data** worksheet, and then select any cell in the Excel table.
2. On the ribbon, click the **Insert** tab.
3. In the Tables group, click the **Recommended PivotTables** button. The Recommended PivotTables dialog box opens. You can select a PivotTable from the list of recommended PivotTables. See Figure 5-45.

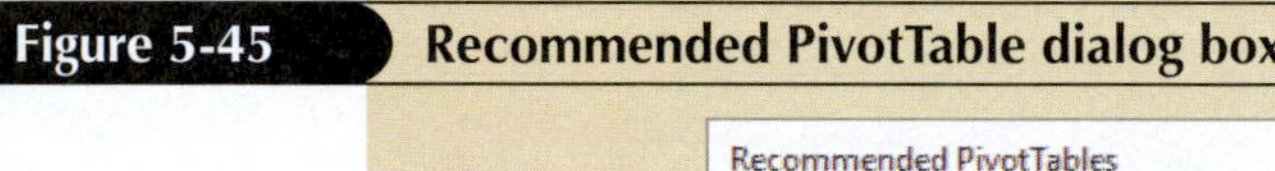

Figure 5-45 Recommended PivotTable dialog box

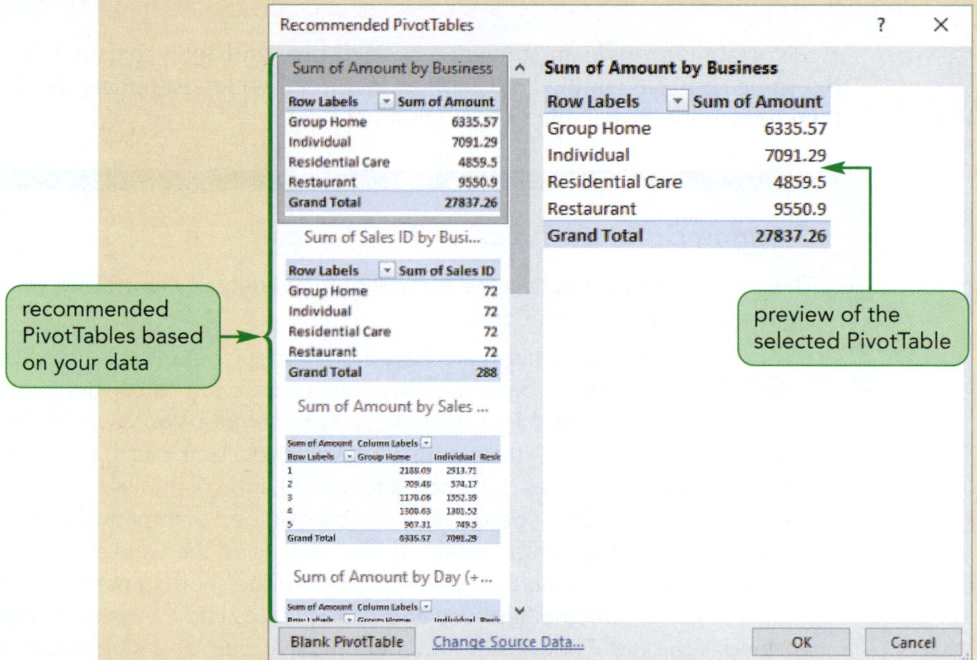

The Sum of Amount by Day PivotTable meets Victoria's request.

4. Click **Sum of Amount by Day** (the sixth PivotTable in the left pane). An enlarged version of the selected PivotTable is displayed in the right pane of the dialog box.
5. Click the **OK** button. A PivotTable of the sales by day appears in a new worksheet. See Figure 5-46.

Figure 5-46 PivotTable of sales by day

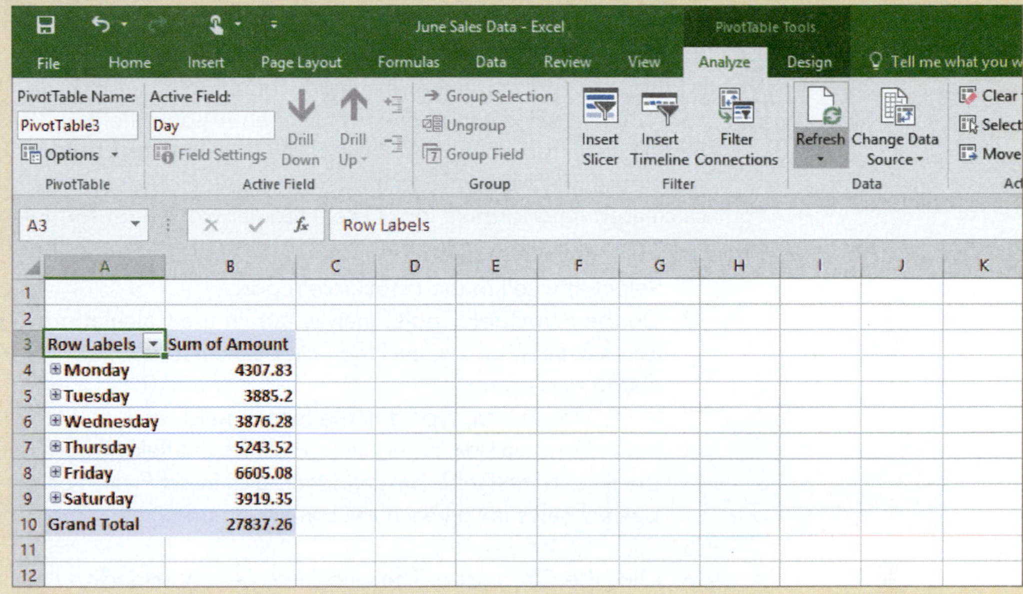

6. In the PivotTable Fields task pane, in the VALUES area, click the **Sum of Amount** button, and then click **Value Field Settings** on the shortcut menu. The Value Field Settings dialog box opens.
7. Click the **Number Format** button. The Format Cells dialog box opens.
8. In the Category box, click **Currency**, and then click the **OK** button.
9. In the Value Field Settings dialog box, click the **OK** button. The numbers in the PivotTable are formatted as currency with two decimal places.
10. On the ribbon, click the **PivotTable Tools Design** tab.
11. In the PivotTable Styles group, click the **More** button to open the PivotTable Styles gallery, and then click the **Pivot Style Medium 14** style. The style is applied to the PivotTable.
12. Rename the worksheet as **Daily Sales PivotTable**.

Victoria will use the summary of sales by days of the week in the Daily Sales PivotTable worksheet to evaluate staffing and ordering for each day.

INSIGHT

Adding a Calculated Field to a PivotTable Report

Occasionally, you might need to display more information than a PivotTable is designed to show, but it doesn't make sense to alter your data source to include this additional information. For example, you might want to include a field that shows an 8 percent sales tax on each value in an Amount field. In these instances, you can add a calculated field to the PivotTable. A **calculated field** is a formula you define to generate PivotTable values that otherwise would not appear in the PivotTable. The calculated field formula looks like a regular worksheet formula.

To add a calculated field to a PivotTable, complete the following steps:

1. Select any cell in the PivotTable report.
2. On the PivotTable Tools Analyze tab, in the Calculations group, click the Fields, Items & Sets button, and then click Calculated Field. The Insert Calculated Field dialog box opens.
3. In the Name box, type a name for the field, such as Sales Tax.
4. In the Formula box, enter the formula for the field. To use data from another field, click the field in the Fields box, and then click Insert Field. For example, to calculate an 8 percent sales tax on each value in the Amount field, enter =Amount*8%.
5. Click the Add button.
6. Click the OK button. The calculated field is added to the PivotTable's data area and to the PivotTable Fields task pane.

As you can see, you can use calculated fields to include additional information in a PivotTable.

Creating a PivotChart

A PivotChart is a graphical representation of the data in a PivotTable. You can create a PivotChart from a PivotTable. A PivotChart allows you to interactively add, remove, filter, and refresh data fields in the PivotChart similar to working with a PivotTable. PivotCharts can have all the same formatting as other charts, including layouts and styles. You can move and resize chart elements or change formatting of individual data points.

Victoria wants you to add a PivotChart next to the Sum of Amount by Day PivotTable. You will prepare a clustered column chart next to the PivotTable.

TIP

You can also create a PivotChart based directly on an Excel table, which creates both a PivotTable and a PivotChart.

To create and format the PivotChart:

1. In the Daily Sales PivotTable worksheet, select any cell in the PivotTable.
2. On the ribbon, click the **PivotTable Tools Analyze** tab.
3. In the Tools group, click the **PivotChart** button. The Insert Chart dialog box opens.
4. If necessary, click the **Clustered Column** chart (the first chart subtype for Column charts), and then click the **OK** button. A PivotChart appears next to the PivotTable, and the task pane changes to the PivotChart Fields task pane.

   Trouble? If you selected the wrong PivotChart, delete the PivotChart you just created, and then repeat Steps 1 through 4.
5. To the right of the PivotChart, click the **Chart Elements** button [+], and then click the **Legend** check box to remove the checkmark. The legend is removed from the PivotChart. You do not need a legend because the PivotChart has only one data series.

6. Click the PivotChart chart title, type **Sales by Day** as the new title, and then press the **Enter** key. The PivotChart displays the descriptive name.
7. To the right of the PivotChart, click the **Chart Styles** button, click **Color** at the top of the gallery, and then in the Colorful section, click **Color 4**. The columns change to green, the first color in that palette.
8. Drag the PivotChart so its upper-left corner is in cell **D3**. The PivotChart is aligned with the PivotTable. See Figure 5-47.

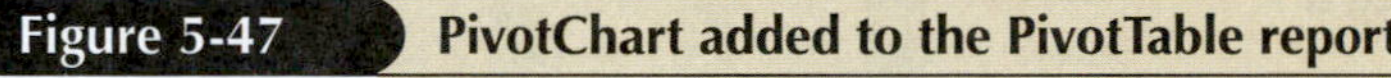
Figure 5-47 **PivotChart added to the PivotTable report**

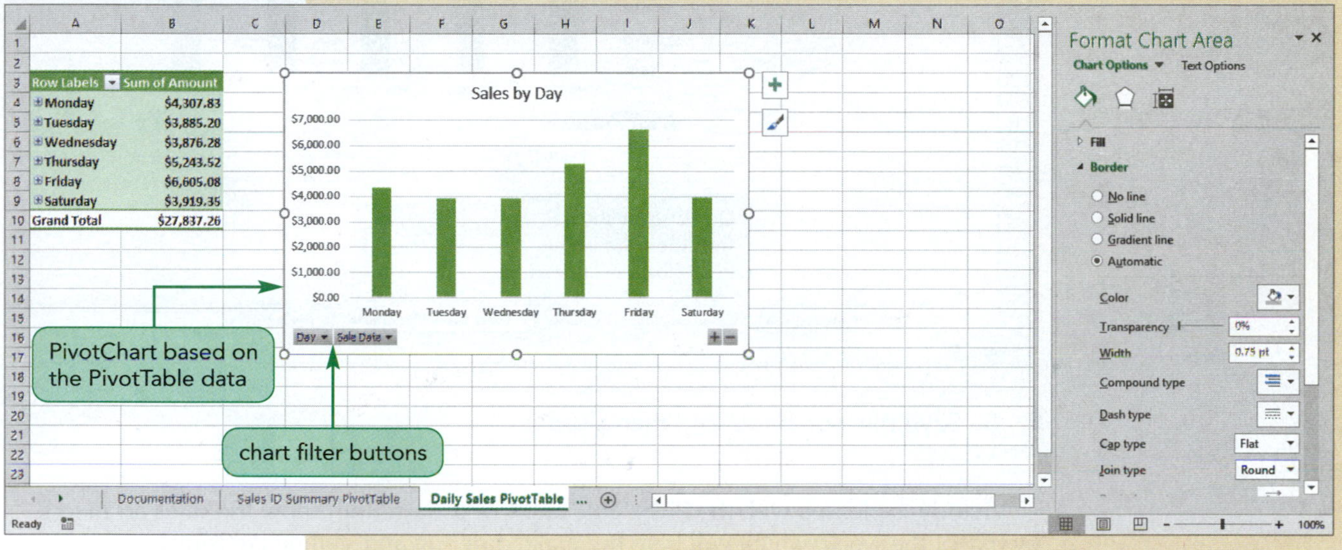

The PivotChart Tools contextual tabs enable you to work with and format the selected PivotChart the same way as an ordinary chart. A PivotChart and its associated PivotTable are linked. When you modify one, the other also changes. You can quickly display different views of the PivotChart by using the chart filter buttons on the PivotChart to filter the data.

Victoria wants you to display sales for only Monday through Friday. You will filter the PivotChart to display only those items.

To filter the PivotChart to display sales for Monday through Friday:

1. Make sure the PivotChart is selected, and then click the **Day** filter button in the lower-left corner of the PivotChart. The Filter menu opens.
2. Click the **Saturday** check box to remove its checkmark. Only the weekdays remain selected.
3. Click the **OK** button. The PivotChart updates to display only sales for weekdays. The PivotTable is automatically filtered to display the same results.
4. Select cell **A1**. See Figure 5-48.

Figure 5-48 **Filtered PivotChart**

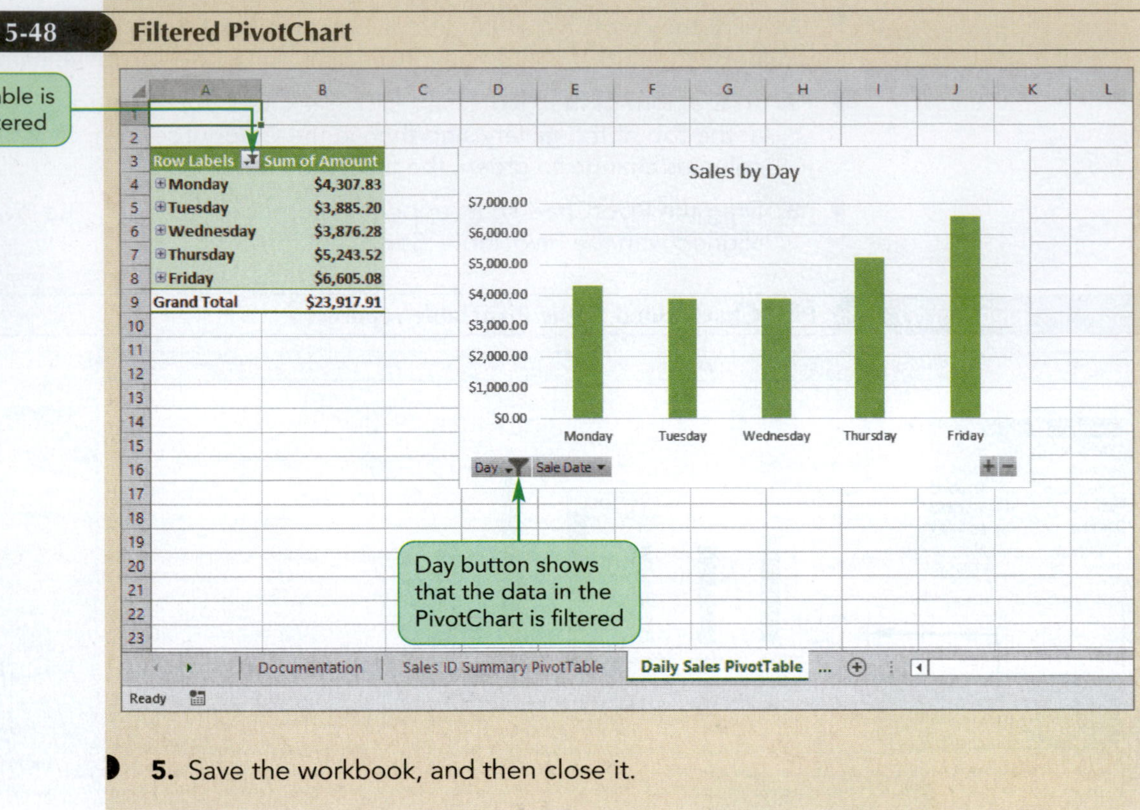

5. Save the workbook, and then close it.

Victoria is pleased with the PivotTable and PivotChart. Both show the sales arranged by day of the week, which will help her make ordering and staffing decisions.

REVIEW

Session 5.3 Quick Check

1. What is a PivotTable?
2. How do you add fields to a PivotTable?
3. How are fields such as region, state, and country most likely to appear in a PivotTable?
4. How are fields such as revenue, costs, and profits most likely to appear in a PivotTable?
5. A list of college students includes a code to indicate the student's gender (male or female) and a field to identify the student's major. Would you use a filter or a PivotTable to (a) create a list of all females majoring in history and (b) count the number of males and females in each major?
6. An Excel table of professional baseball player data consists of team name, player name, position, and salary. What area of a PivotTable report would be used for the Team name field if you wanted to display the average salaries by position for all teams or an individual team?
7. After you update data in an Excel table, what must you do to a PivotTable that is based on that Excel table?
8. What is a PivotChart?

Review Assignments

PRACTICE

Data File needed for the Review Assignments: July.xlsx

Victoria needs to analyze the sales for July. She entered this data into a new workbook and wants you to sort and filter the data, as well as create summary reports using the Subtotal command, PivotTables, and PivotCharts. Complete the following:

1. Open the **July** workbook located in the Excel5 > Review folder included with your Data Files, and then save the workbook as **July Sales Data** in the location specified by your instructor.
2. In the Documentation worksheet, enter your name and the date.
3. In the Sales Data worksheet, freeze the top row so that the headers remain on the screen as you scroll.
4. Make a copy of the Sales Data worksheet, and then rename the copied worksheet as **July Data**. (*Hint*: To make a copy of a worksheet, press and hold the Ctrl key as you drag the sheet tab to the right of the Sales Data sheet tab.)
5. In the July Data worksheet, unfreeze the top row.
6. Create an Excel table for the sales data in the July Data worksheet.
7. Format the Excel table with Table Style Medium 4, and then change the Amount field to the Accounting format with two decimal places.
8. Rename the Excel table as **JulyTbl**.
9. Make the following changes to the JulyTbl table:
   a. Add a record for 7/31/2017, Monday, 4, Group Home, 256.52.
   b. Edit the record for Individual on 7/27/2017 by changing the Amount from 462.74 to 492.05.
   c. Remove any duplicate records.
10. Make a copy of the July Data worksheet, and then rename the copied worksheet as **Sort by Sale Date**. In the Sort by Sale Date worksheet, sort the JulyTbl table by Sale Date, displaying the newest sales first, and then by Amount, displaying the largest amounts first.
11. Make a copy of the July Data worksheet, and then rename the copied worksheet as **Sort by Day**. In the Sort by Day worksheet, sort the sales data by Day (use the custom list order of Sunday, Monday,… for the chronological sort), then by Business (A to Z), and then by Amount (smallest to largest).
12. Make a copy of the July Data worksheet, and then rename the copied worksheet as **Filter to Omit Restaurant**. In the Filter to Omit Restaurant worksheet, filter the JulyTbl table to display the sales for all businesses except Restaurant.
13. In the Filter to Omit Restaurant worksheet, insert the Total row to calculate the average amount of sales for the filtered data. Change the label in the Total row to **Average**. Sort the filtered data by descending order by Amount.
14. Split the Filter to Omit Restaurant worksheet into two panes above the last row of the table. Display the sales records in the top pane, and display only the Total row in the bottom pane.
15. Make a copy of the July Data worksheet, and then rename the copied worksheet as **Filter by Sales ID**. In the Filter by Sales ID worksheet, insert a slicer for the Sales ID column. Move the slicer to row 1. Format the slicer with Slicer Style Light 3. Change the slicer's height to 1.9" and its width to 1.25". Use the slicer to display sales for Sales ID 3 and Sales ID 5.
16. Make a copy of the July Data worksheet, and then rename the copied worksheet as **July Subtotals**. In the July Subtotals worksheet, convert the JulyTbl Table to a range, and then sort the range by the Business column in ascending order.
17. In the July Subtotals worksheet, use the Subtotal command to calculate the total sales for each business in the Amount column. Display only the subtotal results. Widen columns as needed so that all of the data is visible.

18. Based on the JulyTbl table in the July Data worksheet, create a PivotTable in a new worksheet that shows the total sales Amount by Day. Format the data area with the Currency format. Rename the worksheet with the PivotTable as **PivotTableChart Sales by Day**.
19. In the PivotTableChart Sales by Day worksheet, insert a Clustered Column PivotChart based on the PivotTable you created. Move the PivotChart to row 3. Remove the legend. Change the PivotChart title to **Sales by Day of Week**.
20. Based on the JulyTbl table in the July Data worksheet, create a PivotTable in a new worksheet that shows Amount by Sale Date. Add the Business field to the FILTERS area. Format the PivotTable with Pivot Style Medium 4. Format the Amount field with the Accounting format with two decimal places. Rename that worksheet as **PivotTable by Sale Date**.
21. In the PivotTable by Sale Date worksheet, insert a slicer for the Business field of the PivotTable. Change the slicer height to 1.6" and the width to 1.5". Format the slicer with Slicer Style Dark 3. Move the slicer to row 3.
22. Use the slicer to filter the PivotTable to display only the Restaurant and Group Home sales.
23. Based on the JulyTbl table in the July Data worksheet, create the Recommended PivotTable Sum of Amount by Sales ID and Business. Rename the worksheet as **Recommended PivotTable**.
24. Save the workbook, and then close it.

APPLY

Case Problem 1

Data File needed for this Case Problem: Shirts.xlsx

Go Sports Anton Aliyev is the store manager for Go Sports, a sports clothing store in Middletown, Ohio. In addition to its clothing inventory, the store will print logos provided by local sports teams on T-shirts, jerseys, or sweatshirts purchased at the store. Anton uses Excel for a variety of tasks, including pricing and inventory. He wants you to create an Excel table from information about current products and then analyze this data. Complete the following:

1. Open the **Shirts** workbook located in the Excel5 > Case1 folder included with your Data Files, and then save the workbook as **Shirts Inventory** in the location specified by your instructor.
2. In the Documentation worksheet, enter your name and the date.
3. In the Shirts worksheet, create an Excel table using all of the data in the worksheet. Rename the table as **ShirtsTbl**. Format the table with Table Style Medium 9. Change the Price data to the Currency format showing no decimal places. Change the In Stock data to the Number format with no decimals.
4. Make a copy of the Shirts worksheet, and then rename the copied worksheet as **Sort by Style**. (*Hint*: Press the Ctrl key as you drag and drop the Shirts sheet tab to the right of the Shirts sheet tab to make a copy of the worksheet.)
5. In the Sort by Style worksheet, sort the data in ascending order by Style, and then in descending order by In Stock.
6. Filter the ShirtsTbl table by Size to remove the youth extra small (yxsm) and ladies extra small (lxsm) sizes.
7. Insert a Total row that shows the total shirts In Stock. Change the Total row label to **Total Shirts**.
8. Split the worksheet window into two horizontal panes. Place the split bar two rows above the bottom row of the worksheet. In the top pane, display the shirt data. In the bottom pane, display only the Total row.
9. Make a copy of the Shirts worksheet, and then rename the copied worksheet as **Filter by Color**. In the Filter by Color worksheet, filter the ShirtsTbl table to display only T-shirt style.

10. Insert a slicer for Color, position the slicer so its upper-left corner is in cell G1, resize the slicer's height to 1.8" and its width to 1.2", and then format the slicer with Slicer Style Dark 1.
11. Use the Color slicer to further filter the ShirtsTbl table to display only blue T-shirts and white T-shirts.
12. Filter the ShirtsTbl table so that it displays only blue and white T-shirts with a price greater than $10. Sort the filtered data in ascending order by Price and then in descending order by In Stock.
13. Make a copy of the Shirts worksheet, and then rename the copied worksheet as **Subtotals**. Convert the table to a range because the Subtotal command cannot be used with an Excel table. Sort the table in ascending order by Style. Use the Subtotal command to display the minimum In Stock for each Style.
14. Based on the ShirtsTbl table in the Shirts worksheet, insert a PivotTable in a new worksheet that calculates the total In Stock for each Style and Color. Display both Style and Color in rows. Use the Value Field Settings dialog box to rename Sum of In Stock as **Total Inventory**. Apply the Pivot Style Medium 9 style to the PivotTable. Rename the worksheet as **PivotTable by Style and Color**.
15. In the PivotTable by Style and Color worksheet, insert a PivotChart with the Clustered Column chart subtype. Place the PivotChart to the right of the PivotTable. Remove the legend. Filter the PivotChart to exclude any white shirts. Change the chart title to **Inventory by Style and Color**.
16. Based on the ShirtsTbl table in the Shirts worksheet, insert a PivotTable in a new worksheet that displays the total In Stock and count of Item IDs by Style and Color. Place Style in the FILTERS area. Rename the worksheet as **PivotTable by Style**.
17. In the PivotTable by Style worksheet, format the PivotTable with Pivot Style Medium 2 style. In the Value Field Settings dialog box, rename the Count of Item ID as **Number of Shirts** and change the Number format to Number with no decimal places. Change the Number format of the Sum of In Stock to the Number format with no decimal places.
18. In the PivotTable, change the Style filter to show only Jersey.
19. Save the workbook, and then close it.

APPLY

Case Problem 2

Data File needed for this Case Problem: Seminars.xlsx

Collegiate Seminars Phillip Cunningham is the new manager of Collegiate Seminars in McLean, Virginia. To help him better understand the current schedule, he created an Excel table that tracks the data he has collected about currently scheduled seminars, including topic, type, instructor, length, location, cost, and maximum enrollment. He asks you to analyze this data. Complete the following:

1. Open the **Seminars** workbook located in the Excel5 > Case2 folder included with your Data Files, and then save the workbook as **Seminar Bookings** in the location specified by your instructor.
2. In the Documentation worksheet, enter your name and the date.
3. In the Seminars worksheet, create an Excel table, and then name it **SeminarsTbl**. Format the Cost column with the Accounting format and no decimal places. Format the SeminarsTbl table with the table style of your choice.
4. Make a copy of the Seminars worksheet, and then rename the copied worksheet as **Sort by Type**. (*Hint*: Press the Ctrl key, and drag the Seminars sheet tab to the right of the Seminars sheet tab to make a copy of the worksheet.) Sort the SeminarsTbl table in ascending order by Type, then in descending order by Cost.

5. Use conditional formatting to highlight all Seminars with a cost greater than $950 with yellow fill with dark yellow text.
6. Make a copy of the Seminars worksheet, and then rename the copied worksheet as **Filter by Location**. Insert a slicer to filter by Location. Place the slicer to the right of the top of the SeminarsTbl table. Select a slicer style that matches the style you used to format the SeminarsTbl table. Resize the slicer's height and width to improve its appearance.
7. Use the slicer to filter the SeminarsTbl table to display only Seminars at the Downtown location.
8. Expand the filter to also display Beltway seminars in the SeminarsTbl table. Sort the filtered table in ascending order by cost.
9. Make a copy of the Seminars worksheet, and then rename the copied worksheet as **Filter Top 25%**. Filter the SeminarsTbl table to display Seminars whose Costs are in the top 25 percent. (*Hint*: Use the Top 10 number format.) Sort the data in descending order by Cost.
10. Use the Total row to include the average cost at the bottom of the table, and then change the Total row label to **Average**. Remove the entry in the Max column of the Total row.
11. Make a copy of the Seminars worksheet, and then rename the copied worksheet as **Subtotals**. Use the Subtotal command to display the total cost for each Topic in the Cost column. Make sure your table is sorted in the correct sequence for the required subtotals, and remember to convert the table to a range before subtotaling.
12. Based on the SeminarsTbl table in the Seminars worksheet, create a PivotTable in a new worksheet that totals cost by Type and Topic. Place the Type field in the COLUMNS area. Format the cost in the PivotTable with the Accounting format and no decimal places. Format the PivotTable with the style of your choice. Rename the worksheet as **PivotTable by Type**.
13. Insert a slicer to filter the PivotTable by Type. Resize the slicer object and buttons as needed, and then select a slicer style that matches the PivotTable. Use the slicer to filter the PivotTable to display totals for Graduate and Undergrad.
14. Based on the SeminarsTbl table in the Seminars worksheet, create a PivotTable in a new worksheet that calculates average Cost by Location and the count of Seminar IDs. Format the average cost to the Accounting format with no decimal places. Apply the same PivotTable style to this PivotTable. Rename the worksheet as **PivotTable for Average Cost**.
15. Save the workbook, and then close it.

TROUBLESHOOT

Case Problem 3

Data File needed for this Case Problem: Food.xlsx

Food for All Samuel Hamilton started Food for All in Lake Charles, Louisiana, three years ago in response to a growing number of residents who encountered unexpected challenges with being able to feed themselves and their families. The food bank has been very successful providing healthy food for the town residents. Samuel is considering expanding the food bank's reach to include several other towns in the area and needs to analyze current donations to see whether it can support the expansion. Samuel tracks donations in Excel. He has entered donation data for the first quarter of the year in a worksheet and wants you to analyze the data. Complete the following:

1. Open the **Food** workbook located in the Excel5 > Case3 folder included with your Data Files, and then save the workbook as **Food Bank** in the location specified by your instructor.
2. In the Documentation sheet, enter your name and the date.

Troubleshoot 3. Samuel wants to view donations with values that are either less than $10 or greater than $100. He tried filtering the donations in the Donation Amount Filter worksheet, but it's not working as expected. Review the custom Number filter in the worksheet, and fix the problems.

4. In the Donations worksheet, create an Excel table, and then rename the table as **DonationsTbl**. Format the DonationsTbl table using the table style of your choice.
5. In the DonationsTbl table, format the Value column so that it is clear that this field contains dollars.
6. Find the record that has a year of 3018. Correct the year so that it is **2017**.
7. Make a copy of the Donations worksheet, and then rename the copied worksheet as **Sorted Donations**. (*Hint*: Press the Ctrl key and drag the sheet tab to the right of the current sheet tab to make a copy of the worksheet.) In the Sorted Donations worksheet, sort the data in ascending order by Zip and then in ascending order by Date.
8. Using conditional formatting, highlight all of the records in the sorted table that are the type Food with the format of your choice.
9. Make a copy of the Donations worksheet, and then rename the copied worksheet as **Filtered Donations**. Filter the DonationsTbl table to display records that have not been sent a receipt. Sort the data by Zip in ascending order and then by Value in descending order.
10. Insert a Total row that calculates the total of the Value column for the filtered data and the count of the Receipt column. Remove any totals that appear for other columns. Make sure that the columns are wide enough to display the values.

Troubleshoot 11. In the Donation Type Subtotal worksheet, Samuel is trying to include subtotals that show the total Value for each donation Type. However, the subtotal for each type appears more than once. Fix this report so it shows only one subtotal for each type.

12. Based on the DonationsTbl table in the Donations worksheet, create a PivotTable in a new worksheet that displays the Count of Value and the average Value of the donations by Type. Place the Type field in the ROWS area of the PivotTable. Apply the PivotTable style that matches the DonationsTbl table style. Format the Average values using the Accounting format. Change the labels above the average donations to **Average**, and change the label above the count of donations to **Number**.
13. Insert a slicer to filter the PivotTable by Type, and then use the slicer to filter Food from the PivotTable. Format the slicer to match the PivotTable style. Resize and position the slicer appropriately. Rename the worksheet as **PivotTable by Type**.
14. Based on the DonationsTbl table in the Donations worksheet, create a PivotTable in a new worksheet that shows the Total Value by Zip. Format the Sum of Value so that it is more readable. Apply a PivotTable style to match the style of the DonationsTbl table. Rename the worksheet as **PivotTable Value by Zip**.
15. Based on the PivotTable in the PivotTable Value by Zip worksheet, create a PivotChart using the Clustered column chart type. Move the PivotChart to row 3. Change the chart title to **Donations by Zip**. Change the fill color of the bars to a color that matches the style in the PivotTable. Remove the legend.
16. Filter the PivotChart to hide the donations in the ZIP code 70611.
17. Save the workbook, and then close it.

CREATE

Case Problem 4

Data File needed for this Case Problem: Sales.xlsx

BePresent BePresent is a social networking consulting group in Yuma, Arizona, that plans, implements, and tracks social networking campaigns to help small-business owners create a strong presence on the Internet. Sales manager Alana Laidlaw regularly creates reports about the response rates for the social networking campaigns. She asks you to help her analyze data about the performance of the past year's introductory campaigns. Complete the following:

1. Open the **Sales** workbook located in the Excel5 > Case4 folder included with your Data Files, and then save the workbook as **Intro Sales** in the location specified by your instructor.
2. In the Documentation sheet, enter your name and the date.
3. In the Campaigns worksheet, create an Excel table. Rename the table as **CampaignsTbl**. Format the Responses column in the Number format with no decimal places using the comma separator. Apply a table style of your choice.
4. Make a copy of the Campaigns worksheet, and then rename the copied worksheet as **Sorted Campaigns**. (*Hint*: Press the Ctrl key, and drag the Campaigns sheet tab to the right of the Campaigns sheet tab to make a copy of the worksheet.) Sort the table in ascending order by Type of social media, then in chronological order by Month (January, February, March,...), and then in ascending order by Name.
5. Make a copy of the Campaigns worksheet, and then rename the copied worksheet as **Filter with Total Row**. Insert a slicer for the Type field. Move the slicer to row 1. Match the slicer style with the style you selected for the CampaignsTbl table. Resize the slicer height and width to eliminate any excess space.
6. Display the records for Facebook campaigns that occurred from January through June. Sort the filtered data in descending order of Responses.
7. Add a Total row to the table that calculates the average number of Responses for the filtered data. Change the label in the Total row to **Average**.
8. Make a copy of the Campaigns worksheet, and then rename the copied worksheet as **Campaign Subtotals**. Include subtotals that calculate the total Responses per Month and the total Responses per Type of Social Media. (*Hint*: Remember to sort the data, and then add two sets of subtotals. When you use the Subtotal command the second time, do not replace existing subtotals.)
9. Make a copy of the Campaigns worksheet, and then rename the copied worksheet as **Bottom 15 Campaigns**. Use the Top Number filter to display the 15 campaigns with the lowest Responses (each row represents a campaign). Sort the filtered table so that the lowest Responses appear first.
10. Based on the CampaignsTbl table in the Campaigns worksheet, create the PivotTable and the PivotChart shown in Figure 5-49 in a new worksheet to summarize the social media responses. Rename the worksheet as **PivotTableChart by Month**.

Figure 5-49 **PivotTable and PivotChart of social media responses**

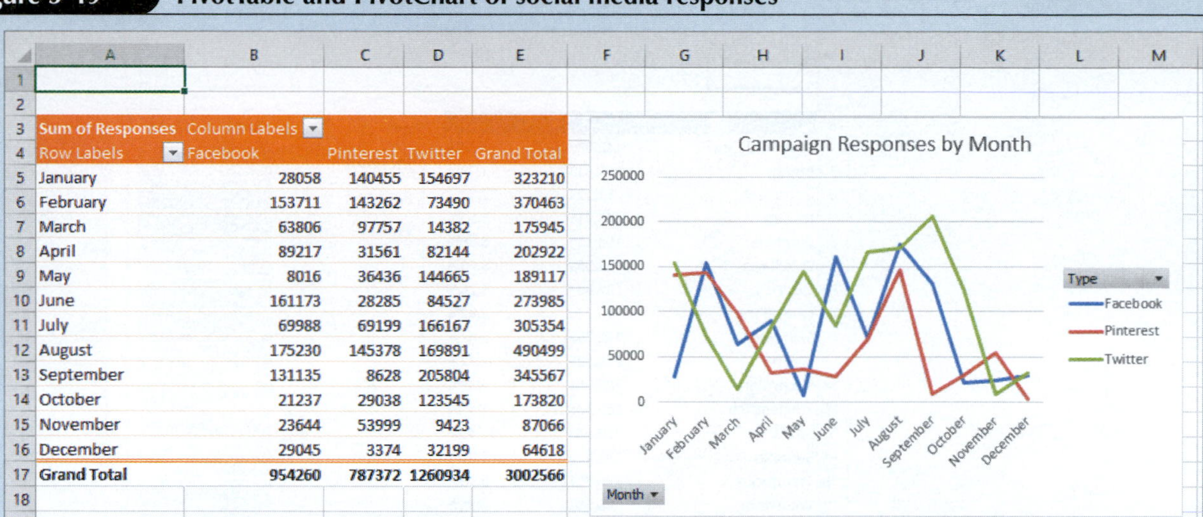

Sum of Responses	Column Labels			
Row Labels	Facebook	Pinterest	Twitter	Grand Total
January	28058	140455	154697	323210
February	153711	143262	73490	370463
March	63806	97757	14382	175945
April	89217	31561	82144	202922
May	8016	36436	144665	189117
June	161173	28285	84527	273985
July	69988	69199	166167	305354
August	175230	145378	169891	490499
September	131135	8628	205804	345567
October	21237	29038	123545	173820
November	23644	53999	9423	87066
December	29045	3374	32199	64618
Grand Total	**954260**	**787372**	**1260934**	**3002566**

11. Based on the CampaignsTbl table in the Campaigns worksheet, create the PivotTable shown in Figure 5-50 in a new worksheet to calculate the sum of Responses categorized by Description and Type using Month as a filter. Insert slicers for Type and Month. Format the slicers to coordinate with the PivotTable, resize the slicers as needed, and then position them next to the PivotTable. Rename the worksheet as **PivotTable Response Analysis**.

Figure 5-50 **PivotTable displaying sales analyzing social media responses**

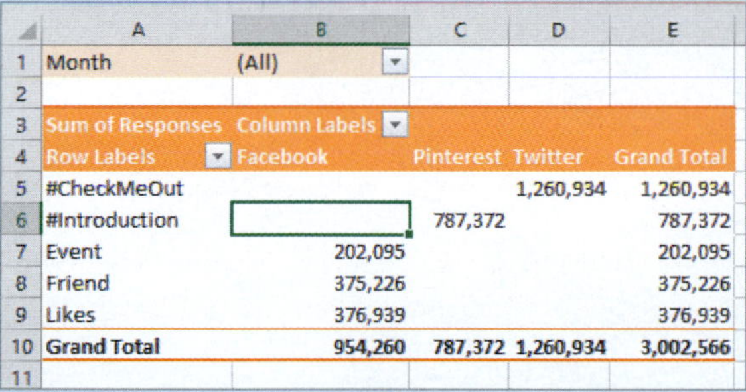

Month	(All)			
Sum of Responses	Column Labels			
Row Labels	Facebook	Pinterest	Twitter	Grand Total
#CheckMeOut			1,260,934	1,260,934
#Introduction		787,372		787,372
Event	202,095			202,095
Friend	375,226			375,226
Likes	376,939			376,939
Grand Total	**954,260**	**787,372**	**1,260,934**	**3,002,566**

12. Based on the CampaignsTbl table in the Campaigns worksheet, create the PivotTable and slicers shown in Figure 5-51 in a new worksheet, displaying total Responses, by Name with Month as a filter. Include a second calculation that displays each of the Reponses by Name as a percentage of the total Responses. (*Hint*: In the Value Field Settings dialog box, use the Show Values As tab to show values as a percentage of the column total.) Format the PivotTable and slicers with matching styles, and adjust the height and width of the slicers as needed to improve their appearance. Rename the worksheet as **PivotTable Response by Name**.

Figure 5-51 PivotTable displaying Responses by Name

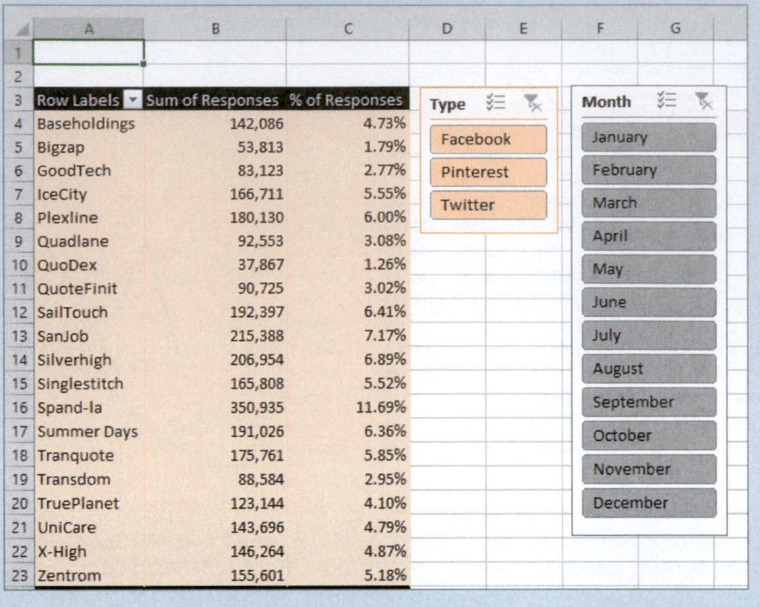

	A	B	C
1			
2			
3	Row Labels	Sum of Responses	% of Responses
4	Baseholdings	142,086	4.73%
5	Bigzap	53,813	1.79%
6	GoodTech	83,123	2.77%
7	IceCity	166,711	5.55%
8	Plexline	180,130	6.00%
9	Quadlane	92,553	3.08%
10	QuoDex	37,867	1.26%
11	QuoteFinit	90,725	3.02%
12	SailTouch	192,397	6.41%
13	SanJob	215,388	7.17%
14	Silverhigh	206,954	6.89%
15	Singlestitch	165,808	5.52%
16	Spand-la	350,935	11.69%
17	Summer Days	191,026	6.36%
18	Tranquote	175,761	5.85%
19	Transdom	88,584	2.95%
20	TruePlanet	123,144	4.10%
21	UniCare	143,696	4.79%
22	X-High	146,264	4.87%
23	Zentrom	155,601	5.18%

Type: Facebook, Pinterest, Twitter

Month: January, February, March, April, May, June, July, August, September, October, November, December

13. Save the workbook, and then close it.

MODULE 6

Managing Multiple Worksheets and Workbooks

Summarizing Rental Income Data

OBJECTIVES

Session 6.1
- Create a worksheet group
- Format and edit multiple worksheets at once
- Create cell references to other worksheets
- Consolidate information from multiple worksheets using 3-D references
- Create and print a worksheet group

Session 6.2
- Create a link to data in another workbook
- Create a workbook reference
- Learn how to edit links

Session 6.3
- Insert a hyperlink in a cell
- Create a workbook based on an existing template
- Create a custom workbook template

Case | *Reveries Urban Centers*

Reveries Urban Centers is a rental agency with three locations in Michigan—Jackson, Fint, and Petosky. The agency specializes in innovative leasing of empty retail spaces to meet other community needs, including child care centers, medical clinics, religious centers, and music practice rooms, in addition to retail stores. Timothy Root is the COO (chief operating officer). Aubrette Caron manages the Jackson rental center, Gordon Warren manages the Petosky rental center, and Tammy Hernandez manages the Flint rental center.

As COO, Timothy is responsible for analyzing rental income at all locations. Each rental center tracks the rental amounts and types for each quarter in a workbook, which is sent to Timothy to consolidate and analyze. Timothy has received the workbooks with the quarterly rental income data for the past year from all three locations. You will create a worksheet in each workbook that summarizes the rental income totals.

STARTING DATA FILES

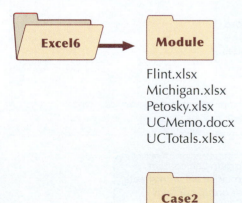

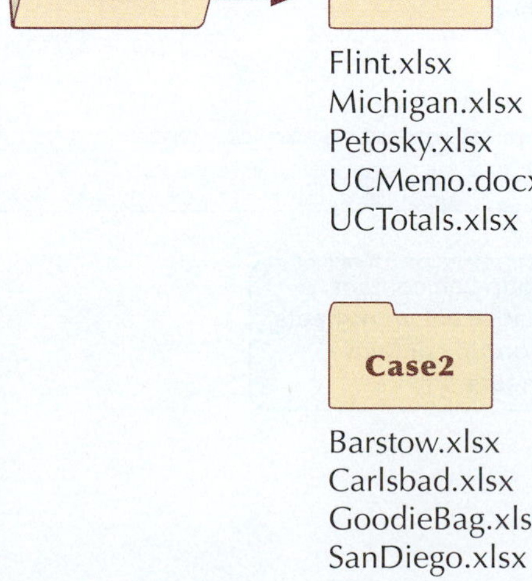

Module
Flint.xlsx
Michigan.xlsx
Petosky.xlsx
UCMemo.docx
UCTotals.xlsx

Review
FlintMI.xlsx
JacksonMI.xlsx
Midland.xlslx
NewUC.xlsx
NewUCMemo.docx
PetoskyMI.xlsx

Case1
Tea.xlsx

Case2
Barstow.xlsx
Carlsbad.xlsx
GoodieBag.xlsx
SanDiego.xlsx

Case3
RoomGroom.xlsx

Case4
Delaware.xlsx
ELSSummary.xlsx
ELSTemplate.xltx
Maryland.xlsx
NewMD.xlsx
Virginia.xlsx

Session 6.1 Visual Overview:

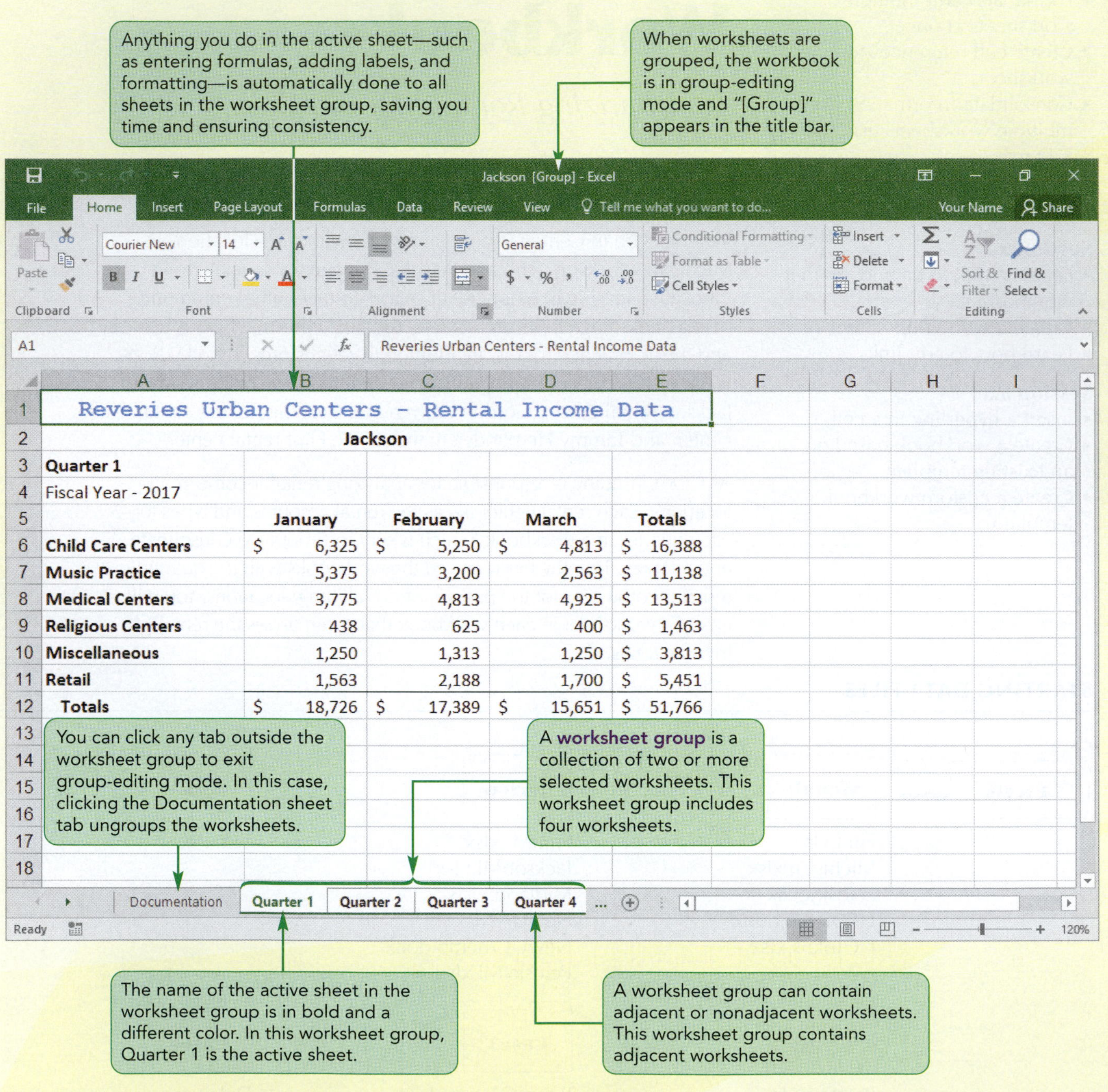
Anything you do in the active sheet—such as entering formulas, adding labels, and formatting—is automatically done to all sheets in the worksheet group, saving you time and ensuring consistency.
When worksheets are grouped, the workbook is in group-editing mode and "[Group]" appears in the title bar.
Jackson [Group] - Excel
Reveries Urban Centers - Rental Income Data
Jackson
Quarter 1
Fiscal Year - 2017
January February March Totals
Child Care Centers $ 6,325 $ 5,250 $ 4,813 $ 16,388
Music Practice 5,375 3,200 2,563 $ 11,138
Medical Centers 3,775 4,813 4,925 $ 13,513
Religious Centers 438 625 400 $ 1,463
Miscellaneous 1,250 1,313 1,250 $ 3,813
Retail 1,563 2,188 1,700 $ 5,451
Totals $ 18,726 $ 17,389 $ 15,651 $ 51,766
You can click any tab outside the worksheet group to exit group-editing mode. In this case, clicking the Documentation sheet tab ungroups the worksheets.
A worksheet group is a collection of two or more selected worksheets. This worksheet group includes four worksheets.
Documentation
Quarter 1
Quarter 2
Quarter 3
Quarter 4
The name of the active sheet in the worksheet group is in bold and a different color. In this worksheet group, Quarter 1 is the active sheet.
A worksheet group can contain adjacent or nonadjacent worksheets. This worksheet group contains adjacent worksheets.

Worksheet Groups and 3-D References

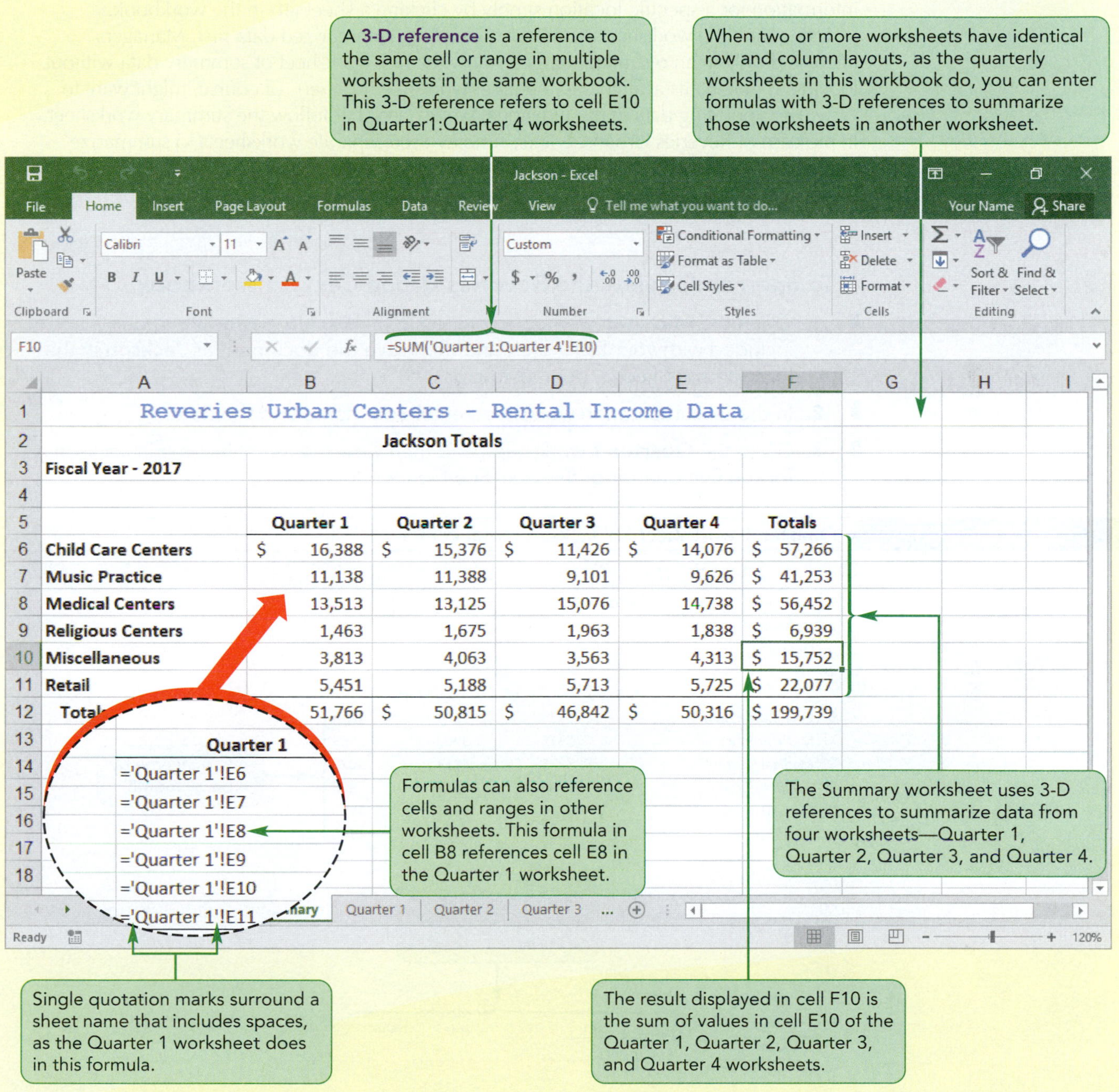
A 3-D reference is a reference to the same cell or range in multiple worksheets in the same workbook. This 3-D reference refers to cell E10 in Quarter1:Quarter 4 worksheets.
When two or more worksheets have identical row and column layouts, as the quarterly worksheets in this workbook do, you can enter formulas with 3-D references to summarize those worksheets in another worksheet.
Jackson - Excel
=SUM('Quarter 1:Quarter 4'!E10)
Reveries Urban Centers - Rental Income Data
Jackson Totals
Fiscal Year - 2017
Quarter 1
Quarter 2
Quarter 3
Quarter 4
Totals
Child Care Centers $ 16,388 $ 15,376 $ 11,426 $ 14,076 $ 57,266
Music Practice 11,138 11,388 9,101 9,626 $ 41,253
Medical Centers 13,513 13,125 15,076 14,738 $ 56,452
Religious Centers 1,463 1,675 1,963 1,838 $ 6,939
Miscellaneous 3,813 4,063 3,563 4,313 $ 15,752
Retail 5,451 5,188 5,713 5,725 $ 22,077
51,766 $ 50,815 $ 46,842 $ 50,316 $ 199,739
='Quarter 1'!E6
='Quarter 1'!E7
='Quarter 1'!E8
='Quarter 1'!E9
='Quarter 1'!E10
='Quarter 1'!E11
Formulas can also reference cells and ranges in other worksheets. This formula in cell B8 references cell E8 in the Quarter 1 worksheet.
The Summary worksheet uses 3-D references to summarize data from four worksheets—Quarter 1, Quarter 2, Quarter 3, and Quarter 4.
Single quotation marks surround a sheet name that includes spaces, as the Quarter 1 worksheet does in this formula.
The result displayed in cell F10 is the sum of values in cell E10 of the Quarter 1, Quarter 2, Quarter 3, and Quarter 4 worksheets.

Grouping Worksheets

Workbook data is often placed in several worksheets. Using multiple worksheets makes it easier to group and summarize data. For example, a company such as Reveries Urban Centers with locations in different cities within a geographic region can place income information for each site in a separate worksheet. Rather than scrolling through one large and complex worksheet that contains data for all locations, users can access collection information for a specific location simply by clicking a sheet tab in the workbook.

Using multiple worksheets enables you to place summarized data first. Managers interested only in an overall picture can view the first worksheet of summary data without looking at the details available in the other worksheets. Others, of course, might want to view the supporting data in the individual worksheets that follow the summary worksheet. In the case of Reveries Urban Centers, Timothy used separate worksheets to summarize the rental income for the Jackson location for each quarter of the 2017 fiscal year.

You will open Timothy's workbook and review the current information.

To open and review the Reveries Urban Centers workbook:

1. Open the **Michigan** workbook located in the **Excel6 > Module** folder included with your Data Files, and then save the document as **Jackson** in the location specified by your instructor.
2. In the Documentation worksheet, enter your name and the date.
3. Go to the **Quarter 1** worksheet, and then view the rental income in Jackson for the first quarter of the year. See Figure 6-1.

Figure 6-1 Quarter 1 worksheet for Jackson rental center

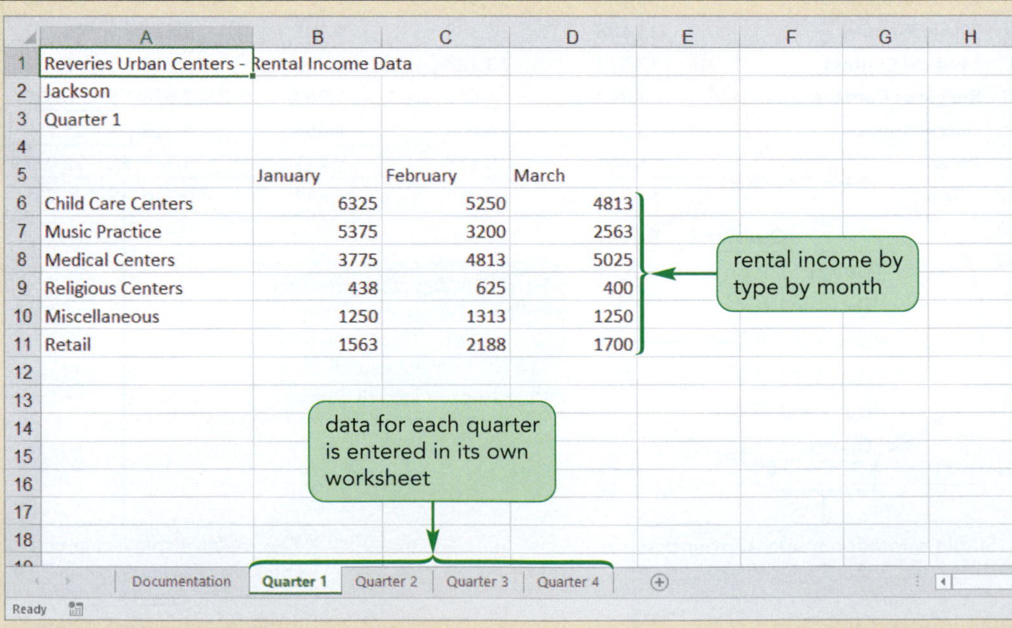

	A	B	C	D
1	Reveries Urban Centers - Rental Income Data			
2	Jackson			
3	Quarter 1			
4				
5		January	February	March
6	Child Care Centers	6325	5250	4813
7	Music Practice	5375	3200	2563
8	Medical Centers	3775	4813	5025
9	Religious Centers	438	625	400
10	Miscellaneous	1250	1313	1250
11	Retail	1563	2188	1700

Documentation | Quarter 1 | Quarter 2 | Quarter 3 | Quarter 4

Ready

4. Review the **Quarter 2**, **Quarter 3**, and **Quarter 4** worksheets. The layout for all four worksheets is identical.

Timothy didn't enter any formulas in the workbook. You need to enter formulas to calculate the total rental income for each column (columns B through D) and each row (rows 6 through 11) in all four worksheets. Rather than retyping the formulas in each worksheet, you can enter them all at once by creating a worksheet group.

A worksheet group, like a range, can contain adjacent or nonadjacent worksheets. In group-editing mode, most editing tasks that you complete in the active worksheet also affect the other worksheets in the group. By forming a worksheet group, you can:

- **Enter or edit data and formulas.** Changes made to content in the active worksheet are also made in the same cells in all the worksheets in the group. You can also use the Find and Replace commands with a worksheet group.
- **Apply formatting.** Changes made to formatting in the active worksheet are also made to all the worksheets in the group, including changing row heights or column widths and applying conditional formatting.
- **Insert or delete rows and columns.** Changes made to the worksheet structure in the active worksheet are also made to all the worksheets in the group.
- **Set the page layout options.** Changes made to the page layout settings in one worksheet also apply to all the worksheets in the group, such as changing the orientation, scaling to fit, and inserting headers and footers.
- **Apply view options.** Changes made to the worksheet view such as zooming, showing and hiding worksheets, and so forth are also made to all the worksheets in the group.
- **Print all the worksheets.** You can print all of the worksheets in the worksheet group at the same time.

Worksheet groups save you time and help improve consistency among the worksheets because you can perform an action once, yet affect multiple worksheets.

REFERENCE

Grouping and Ungrouping Worksheets

- To select an adjacent group, click the sheet tab of the first worksheet in the group, press and hold the Shift key, click the sheet tab of the last worksheet in the group, and then release the Shift key.
- To select a nonadjacent group, click the sheet tab of one worksheet in the group, press and hold the Ctrl key, click the sheet tabs of the remaining worksheets in the group, and then release the Ctrl key.
- To ungroup the worksheets, click the sheet tab of a worksheet that is not in the group (or right-click the sheet tab of one worksheet in the group, and then click Ungroup Sheets on the shortcut menu).

In the Jackson workbook, you'll group an adjacent range of worksheets—the Quarter 1 worksheet through the Quarter 4 worksheet.

To group the quarterly worksheets:

1. Click the **Quarter 1** sheet tab to make the worksheet active. This is the first worksheet you want to include in the group.
2. Press and hold the **Shift** key, and then click the **Quarter 4** sheet tab. This is the last worksheet you want to include in the group.
3. Release the **Shift** key. The four selected sheet tabs are white, the green border extends across the bottom of the four selected sheet tabs, and the sheet tab labels—Quarter 1 through Quarter 4—are in bold, indicating they are all selected. The text "[Group]" appears in the title bar to remind you that a worksheet group is selected in the workbook. See Figure 6-2.

TIP

If you cannot see the sheet tab of a worksheet you want to include in a group, use the sheet tab scroll buttons to display it.

Figure 6-2 Grouped worksheets

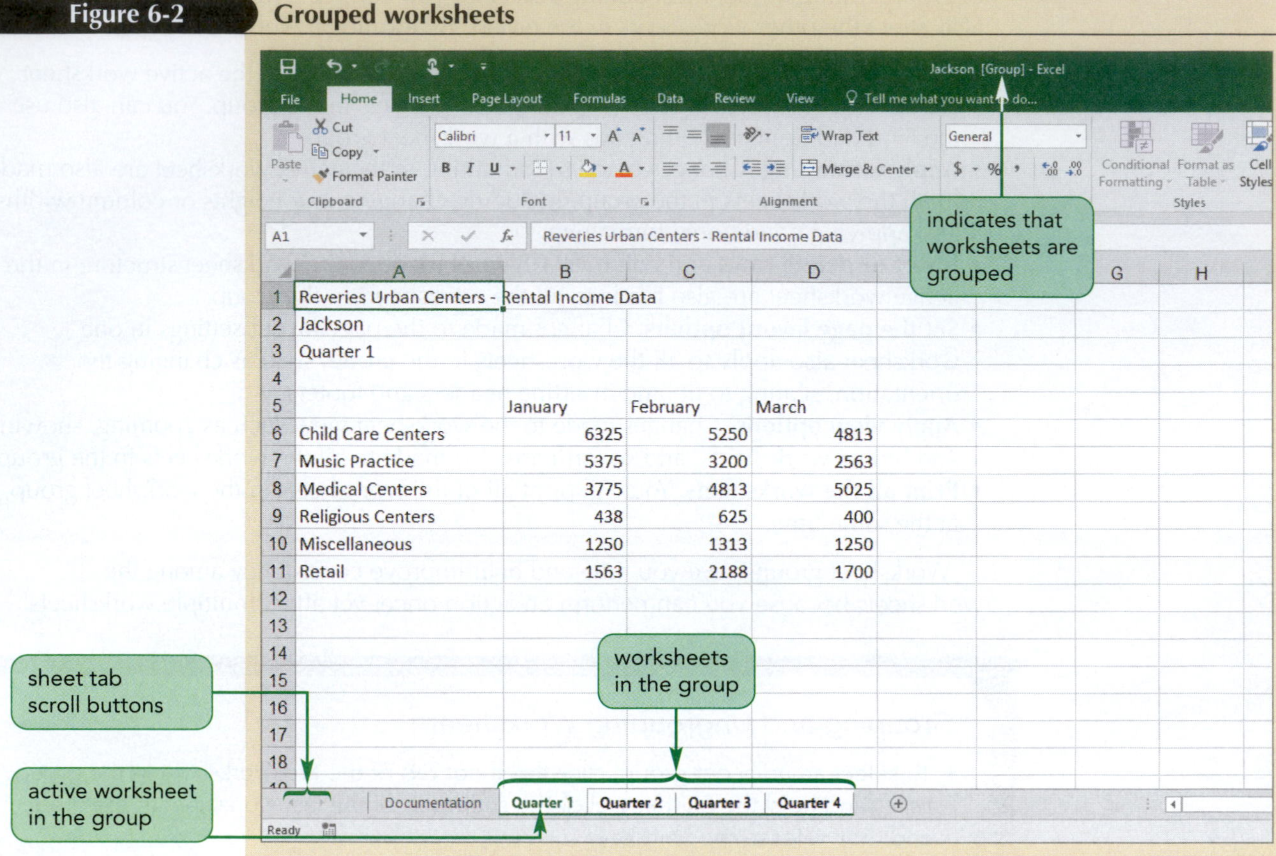

You can change which worksheet in a worksheet group is active. Just click the sheet tab of the worksheet you want to make active. If a worksheet group includes all the worksheets in a workbook, you cannot change which worksheet is the active sheet because clicking a sheet tab ungroups the worksheets.

To change the active sheet in the grouped quarterly worksheets:

1. Click the **Quarter 2** sheet tab to make the worksheet active. The Quarter 2 worksheet is now the active worksheet in the group.
2. Click the **Quarter 4** sheet tab. The Quarter 4 worksheet is now the active worksheet in the group.

Entering Headings and Formulas in a Worksheet Group

When you enter a formula in the active worksheet (in this case, the Quarter 4 worksheet), the formula is entered in the same cells in all the worksheets in the group. The grouped worksheets must have the exact same organization and layout (rows and columns) in order for this to work. Otherwise, any formulas you enter in the active worksheet will be incorrect in the other worksheets in the group and could overwrite existing data.

With the quarterly worksheets grouped, you will enter formulas to calculate the rental income totals for each month.

To enter formulas to calculate the rental income totals in the worksheet group:

1. Select cell **B12**. You want to enter the formula in cell B12 in each of the four worksheets in the group.
2. On the Home tab, in the Editing group, click the **AutoSum** button, and then press the **Enter** key. The formula =SUM(B6:B11) is entered in cell B12 in each worksheet, adding the total rental income at the Jackson rental center for the first month of each quarter. For Quarter 4, the October total of rental income shown in cell B12 is 15426.
3. Copy the formula in cell B12 to the range **C12:D12**. The formula calculates the rental income for the other months in each quarter. For Quarter 4, the rental incomes are 16427 in November and 18413 in December.
4. In cell **E6**, enter a formula with the SUM function to add the total rental income for Child Care Centers for each quarter at the Jackson rental center. The formula =SUM(B6:D6) adds the monthly rental income for Child Care Centers. In Quarter 4, the rental income was 14076.
5. Copy the formula in cell E6 to the range **E7:E12** to calculate the rental income for Music Practice, Medical Centers, Religious Centers, Miscellaneous, and Retail, as well as the grand total of rental income at the Jackson rental center for the quarter. For Quarter 4, the Jackson site had 9626 in rental income for Music Practice, 14738 for Medical Centers, 1838 for Religious Centers, 4313 for Miscellaneous, 5675 for Retail, and 50266 overall.
6. In cells **A12** and **E5**, enter **Totals** as the labels.
7. Click the **Quarter 3** sheet tab, and then click cell **B12** to make it the active cell. The formula =SUM(B6:B11), which adds the rental income for July, appears in the formula bar, and the formula result 15014 appears in the cell. See Figure 6-3.

Figure 6-3 Formulas entered in all worksheets in the group

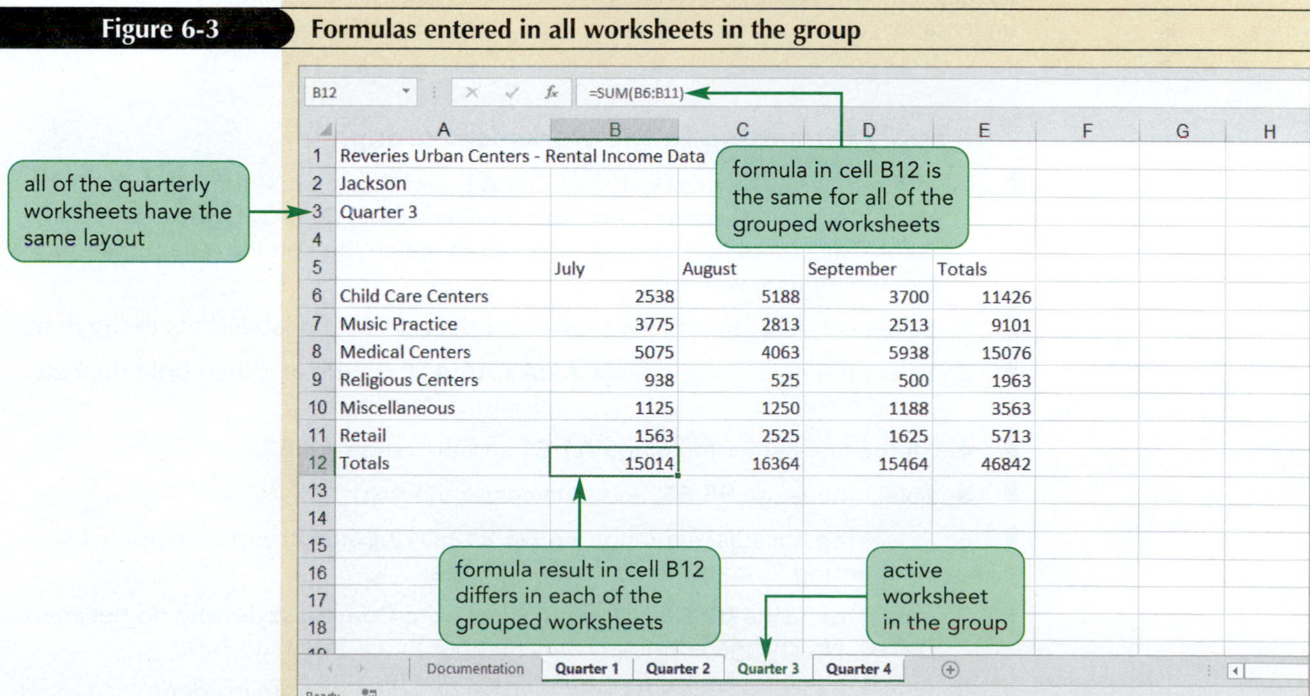

B12 =SUM(B6:B11)

	A	B	C	D	E
1	Reveries Urban Centers - Rental Income Data				
2	Jackson				
3	Quarter 3				
4					
5		July	August	September	Totals
6	Child Care Centers	2538	5188	3700	11426
7	Music Practice	3775	2813	2513	9101
8	Medical Centers	5075	4063	5938	15076
9	Religious Centers	938	525	500	1963
10	Miscellaneous	1125	1250	1188	3563
11	Retail	1563	2525	1625	5713
12	Totals	15014	16364	15464	46842

The formulas and labels you entered in the Quarter 4 worksheet were entered in the Quarter 1, 2, and 3 worksheets at the same time.

8. Click the **Quarter 2** sheet tab. Cell B12 is the active cell. The formula =SUM(B6:B11), which adds the rental income for April, appears in the formula bar, and the formula result 18938 appears in the cell.
9. Click the **Quarter 1** sheet tab. Cell B12 is the active cell. The formula =SUM(B6:B11), which adds the rental income for January, appears in the formula bar, and the formula result 18726 appears in the cell.

The grouped worksheets made it quick to enter the formulas needed to calculate the rental incomes for each quarter.

INSIGHT

Editing Grouped Worksheets

When you enter, edit, or format cells in a worksheet group, the changes you make to one worksheet are automatically applied to the other worksheets in the group. For example, if you delete a value from one cell, the content is also deleted from the same cell in all the worksheets in the group. Be cautious when editing a worksheet that is part of a group. If the layout and structure of the other grouped worksheets are not exactly the same, you might inadvertently overwrite data in some of the worksheets. Also, remember to ungroup the worksheet group after you finish entering data, formulas, and formatting. Otherwise, changes you intend to make in one worksheet will be made to all the worksheets in the group, potentially producing incorrect results.

Formatting a Worksheet Group

As when inserting formulas and text, any formatting changes you make to the active worksheet are applied to all worksheets in the group. Timothy wants you to format the quarterly worksheets, which are still grouped, so that they are easier to read and understand.

To apply formatting to the worksheet group:

1. In the Quarter 1 worksheet, click cell **A1**, and then format the cell with **bold**, **14**-point, **Courier New**, and the **Dark Blue, Text 2, Lighter 40%** font color. The company name is formatted to match the company name on the Documentation worksheet.
2. Select cell **A12**, and then increase its indent once. The label shifts to the right.
3. Select the nonadjacent range **A2:A3,A6:A12,B5:E5**, and then bold the text in the headings.
4. Merge and center the range **A1:E1** and the range **A2:E2**.
5. Select the range **B5:E5**, and then center the text.
6. Select the nonadjacent range **B6:D6,B12:D12,E6:E12**, and then apply the **Accounting** format with no decimal places.
7. Select the range **B7:D11**, and then apply the **Comma style** with no decimal places. No change is visible in any number that is less than 1000.
8. Select the range **B5:E5,B11:E11**, and then add a bottom border.
9. Select cell **A1**. All the worksheets in the group are formatted.

10. Go to each worksheet in the group and review the formatting changes, and then go to the **Quarter 1** worksheet. See Figure 6-4.

Figure 6-4 Formatting applied to the worksheet group

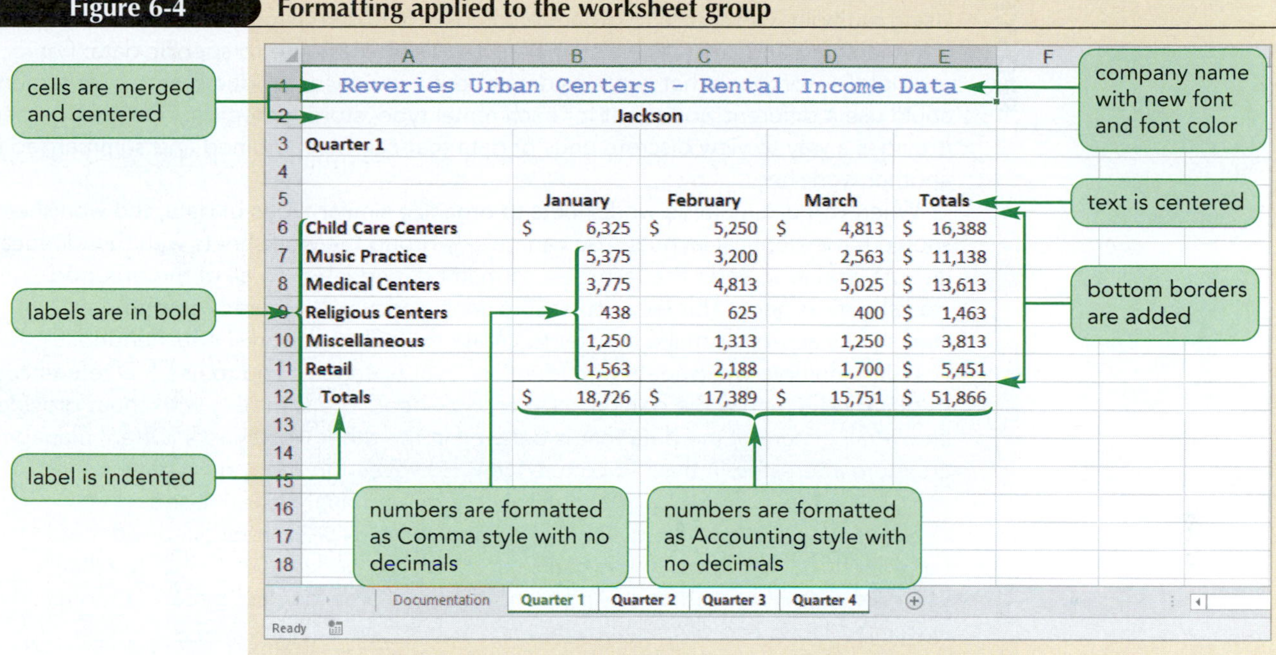

Ungrouping Worksheets

When you ungroup the worksheets, each worksheet functions independently again. If you forget to ungroup the worksheets, any changes you make in one worksheet will be applied to all the worksheets in the group. So be sure to ungroup worksheets when you are finished making changes that apply to multiple worksheets. To ungroup worksheets, click the sheet tab of a worksheet that is not part of the group. If a worksheet group includes all of the sheets in a workbook, click any of the sheet tabs to ungroup the worksheets.

You will ungroup the quarterly worksheets so you can work in each worksheet separately.

To ungroup the quarterly worksheets:

Be sure to ungroup the worksheets; otherwise, any changes you make will affect all worksheets in the group.

1. Click the **Documentation** sheet tab. The worksheets are ungrouped because the Documentation worksheet was not part of the worksheet group. The text "[Group]" no longer appears in the Excel title bar.
2. Verify that the worksheets are ungrouped and the word "[Group]" no longer appears in the title bar.

Timothy wants you to include a new Summary worksheet in the workbook. You'll start working on that next.

PROSKILLS

Written Communication: Using Multiple Worksheets with Identical Layouts

Using multiple worksheets to organize complex data can help make that data simpler to understand and analyze. It also makes it easier to navigate to specific data. For example, a workbook that contains data about a variety of products, stores, or regions could use a different worksheet for each rental type, store, or region. This arrangement provides a way to view discrete units of data that can be combined and summarized in another worksheet.

When you use multiple worksheets to organize similar types of data, the worksheets should have identical layouts. You can quickly group the worksheets with the identical layouts, and then enter the formulas, formatting, and labels in all of the grouped worksheets at once. This helps to ensure consistency and accuracy among the worksheets as well as make it faster to create the different worksheets needed.

Using multiple worksheets with identical layouts enables you to use 3-D references to quickly summarize the data in another worksheet. The summary worksheet provides an overall picture of the data that is detailed in the other worksheets. Often, managers are more interested in this big-picture view. However, the supporting data is still available in the individual worksheets when a deeper analysis is needed.

So, when you are working with a large and complex worksheet filled with data, consider the different ways to organize it in multiple worksheets. Not only will you save time when entering and finding data, but also the data becomes more understandable, and connections and results become clearer.

Working with Multiple Worksheets

As you develop a workbook, you might need to add a worksheet that has the same setup as an existing worksheet. Rather than starting from scratch, you can copy that worksheet as a starting point. For example, Timothy wants the workbook to include a Summary worksheet that adds the annual rental income from the quarterly worksheets. The formulas you create in the Summary worksheet will reference cells in each quarterly worksheet using 3-D references. You can then group the completed worksheets to develop a consistent page setup in all worksheets and then print them all at once.

Copying Worksheets

Often, after spending time developing a worksheet, you can use it as a starting point for creating another, saving you time and energy compared to developing a new worksheet from scratch. Copying a worksheet duplicates all the values, formulas, and formats into the new worksheet, leaving the original worksheet intact. You can then edit, reformat, and enter new content as needed to create the exact worksheet you need.

REFERENCE

Copying Worksheets

- Select the sheet tabs of the worksheets you want to copy.
- Right-click the sheet tabs, and then click Move or Copy on the shortcut menu.
- Click the To book arrow, and then click the name of an existing workbook or click (new book) to create a new workbook for the worksheets.
- In the Before sheet box, click the worksheet before which you want to insert the new worksheet.
- Click the Create a copy check box to insert a checkmark to copy the worksheets.
- Click the OK button.

or

- Select the sheet tabs of the worksheets you want to copy.
- Press and hold the Ctrl key as you drag the selected sheet tabs to a new location in the sheet tabs, and then release the Ctrl key.

Timothy wants you to create the Summary worksheet to provide an overall picture of the data in the detailed quarterly worksheets. The Summary worksheet needs the same formatting and structure as the quarterly worksheets. To ensure consistency among worksheets, you will copy the Quarter 1 worksheet to the beginning of the workbook and then modify its contents.

To copy the Quarter 1 worksheet and create the Summary worksheet:

1. Click the **Quarter 1** sheet tab, and then press and hold the **Ctrl** key as you drag the worksheet to the left of the Documentation worksheet. The pointer changes to and a triangle indicates the drop location.
2. Release the mouse button, and then release the **Ctrl** key. An identical copy of the Quarter 1 worksheet appears in the new location. The sheet tab shows "Quarter 1 (2)" to indicate that this is the copied sheet.
3. Rename the Quarter 1 (2) worksheet as **Summary**.
4. Drag the **Summary** worksheet between the Documentation worksheet and the Quarter 1 worksheet to make it the second worksheet in the workbook.

TIP

You can move or copy a worksheet group within a workbook by dragging one of the group's sheet tabs and dropping it in the new location.

Timothy wants the Summary worksheet to show the rental income for each rental type by quarter and the total rental income for each rental type and quarter. You will modify the Summary worksheet to do this now.

To modify the Summary worksheet:

1. Make sure the **Summary** worksheet is the active sheet.
2. In cell **A2**, enter **Jackson Totals**. The new title reflects this worksheet's content.
3. In cell **A3**, enter **2017**. This is the year to which the summary refers.
4. Clear the contents of the cells in the range **B6:E11**. You removed the rental incomes and the formulas in column E, though the formatting remains intact.
5. Insert a new column **C** into the worksheet. The column appears between the January and February labels and has the same formatting as the January column.

6. In the range **B5:E5**, enter **Quarter 1**, **Quarter 2**, **Quarter 3**, and **Quarter 4** as the new labels.
7. Copy the formula in cell B12 to cell **C12**. See Figure 6-5.

Figure 6-5 Summary Worksheet created from the Quarter 1 worksheet

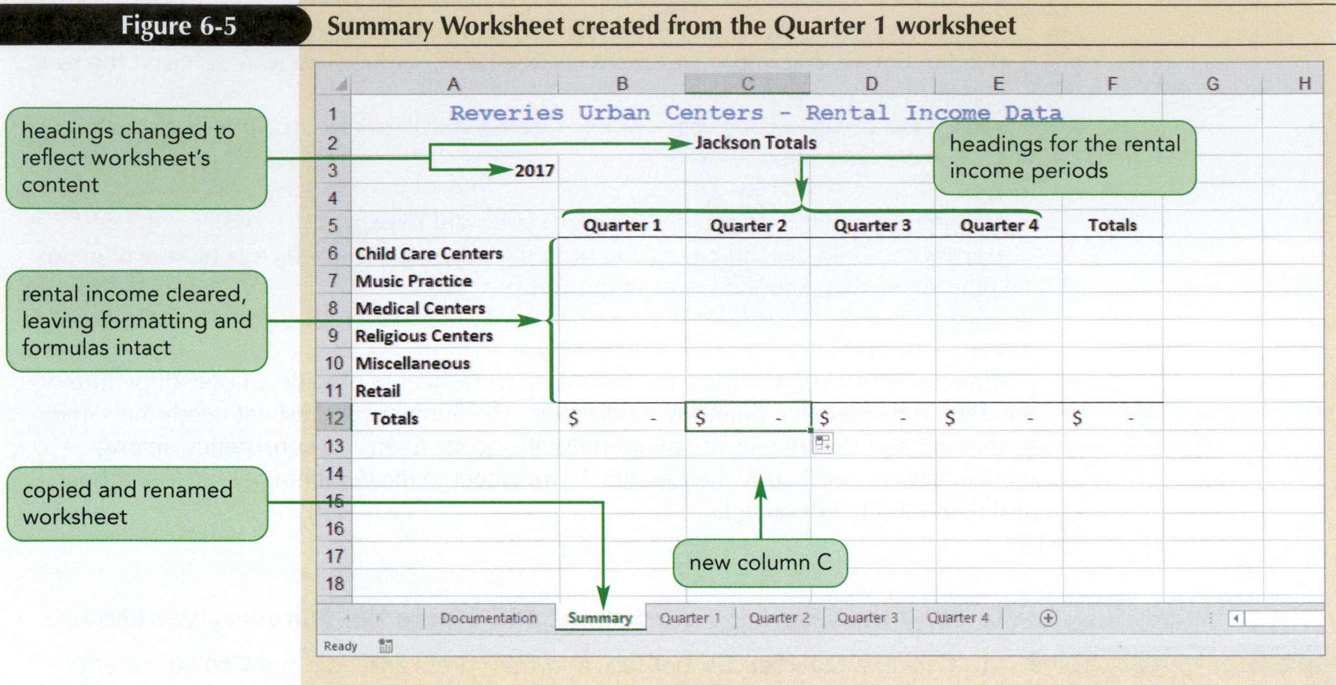

Referencing Cells and Ranges in Other Worksheets

When you use multiple worksheets to organize related data, you can reference a cell or a range in another worksheet in the same workbook. For example, the Summary worksheet references cells in the four quarterly worksheets to calculate the total rental income for the entire year. The syntax to reference a cell or a range in a different worksheet is

```
=SheetName!CellRange
```

where *SheetName* is the worksheet's name as listed on the sheet tab and *CellRange* is the reference for the cell or range in that worksheet. An exclamation mark (!) separates the worksheet reference from the cell or range reference. For example, you could enter the following formula in the Summary worksheet to reference cell D10 in the Quarter1 worksheet:

```
=Quarter1!D10
```

If the worksheet name contains spaces, you must enclose the name in single quotation marks. For example, the following formula references cell D10 in the Quarter 1 worksheet:

```
='Quarter 1'!D10
```

You can use these references to create formulas that reference cells in different locations in different worksheets. For example, to add rental income from two worksheets—cell C9 in the Quarter 1 worksheet and cell C9 in the Quarter 2 worksheet—you would enter the following formula:

```
='Quarter 1'! C9+'Quarter 2'!C9
```

You could type the formula directly in the cell, but it is faster and more accurate to use your mouse to select cells to enter their references to other worksheets.

REFERENCE

Entering a Formula with References to Another Worksheet

- Select the cell where you want to enter the formula.
- Type = and begin entering the formula.
- To insert a reference from another worksheet, click the sheet tab for the worksheet, and then click the cell or select the range you want to reference.
- When the formula is complete, press the Enter key.

Timothy wants you to enter a formula in cell A4 in each quarterly worksheet that displays the fiscal year entered in cell A3 in the Summary worksheet. All four quarterly worksheets will use the formula =Summary!A3 to reference the fiscal year in cell A3 of the Summary worksheet.

To enter the formula that references the Summary worksheet:

1. Click the **Quarter 1** sheet tab, press and hold the **Shift** key, and then click the **Quarter 4** sheet tab. The Quarter 1 through Quarter 4 worksheets are grouped.
2. Select cell **A4**. This is the cell in which you want to enter the formula to display the fiscal year.
3. Type = to begin the formula, click the **Summary** sheet tab, and then click cell **A3**. The reference to cell A3 in the Summary worksheet is added to the formula in cell A4 in the grouped worksheets.
4. On the formula bar, click the **Enter** button ✓. The formula =Summary!A3 is entered in cell A4 in each the worksheet in the group. The formula appears in the formula bar and 2017 appears in cell A4. See Figure 6-6.

Figure 6-6 **Formula with a worksheet reference**

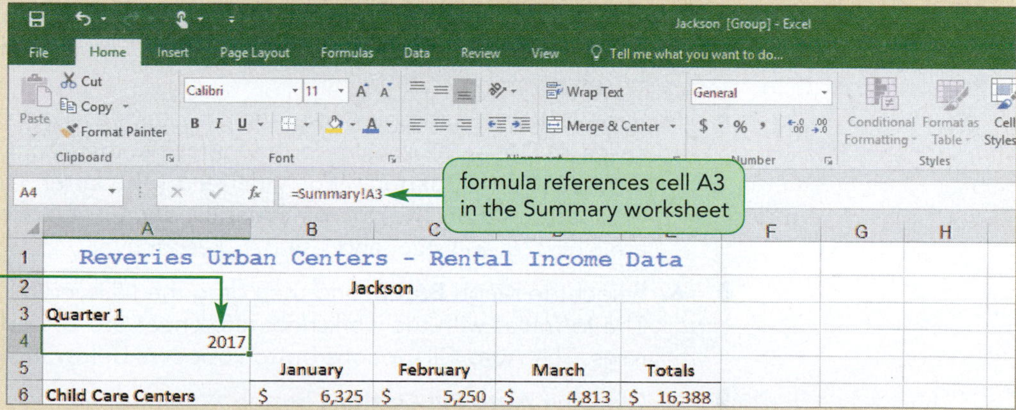

5. Go to each worksheet in the group and verify that the formula =Summary!A3 appears in the formula bar and 2017 appears in cell A4.
6. Go to the **Summary** worksheet. The quarterly worksheets are ungrouped.
7. In cell **A3**, enter **Fiscal Year - 2017**. The descriptive label in cell A3 is entered in the Summary worksheet and is also displayed in the quarterly worksheets because of the formula you entered.

8. Go to the **Quarter 1** through **Quarter 4** worksheets and verify that the label "Fiscal Year - 2017" appears in cell A4 in each worksheet. See Figure 6-7.

Figure 6-7 Edited content displayed in the cell with the worksheet reference

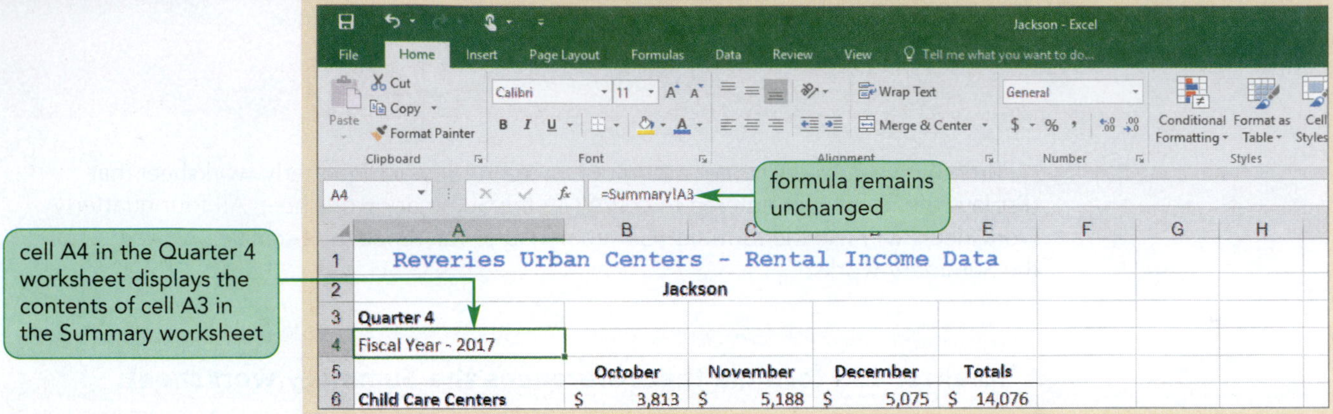

The Summary worksheet needs to include the quarterly totals for each category. You will use formulas that reference the totals in the quarterly worksheets to calculate those totals.

To enter worksheet references for the quarterly totals:

1. Go to the **Summary** worksheet, and then select cell **B6.**
2. Type **=** to begin the formula.
3. Click the **Quarter 1** sheet tab, and then click cell **E6**. The cell is selected and added to the formula.
4. Click the **Enter** button on the formula bar to complete the formula and return to the Summary worksheet. Cell B6 remains selected, and the formula ='Quarter 1'!E6 appears in the formula bar. The formula result showing the rental income from Child Care Centers in the first quarter of 2017—$16,388—appears in cell B6.
5. Repeat Steps 2 through 4 to enter formulas with worksheet references in cells **C6**, **D6**, and **E6** that add the rental income from Child Care Centers in Quarter 2 (='Quarter 2'!E6), Quarter 3 (='Quarter 3'!E6), and Quarter 4 (='Quarter 4'!E6). The quarterly rental income totals from Child Care Centers are $15,376, $11,426, and $14,076, respectively.
6. Select the range **B6:E6**, and then drag the fill handle over the range **B7:E11**. The formulas with the worksheet references are copied to the rest of the item rows. The Auto Fill Options button appears below the copied range.
7. Click the **Auto Fill Options** button, and then click the **Fill Without Formatting** option button. You didn't copy the formatting in this case because you want to keep the Accounting format in the range B7:E11 and the bottom border formatting in the range B11:E11. The total values for the year appear in the range.
8. Click cell **B6** to deselect the range. The Summary worksheet now shows the 2017 totals for each rental type in Jackson by quarter and for all rental income in 2017. See Figure 6-8.

Figure 6-8 Rental income totals for Jackson in 2017

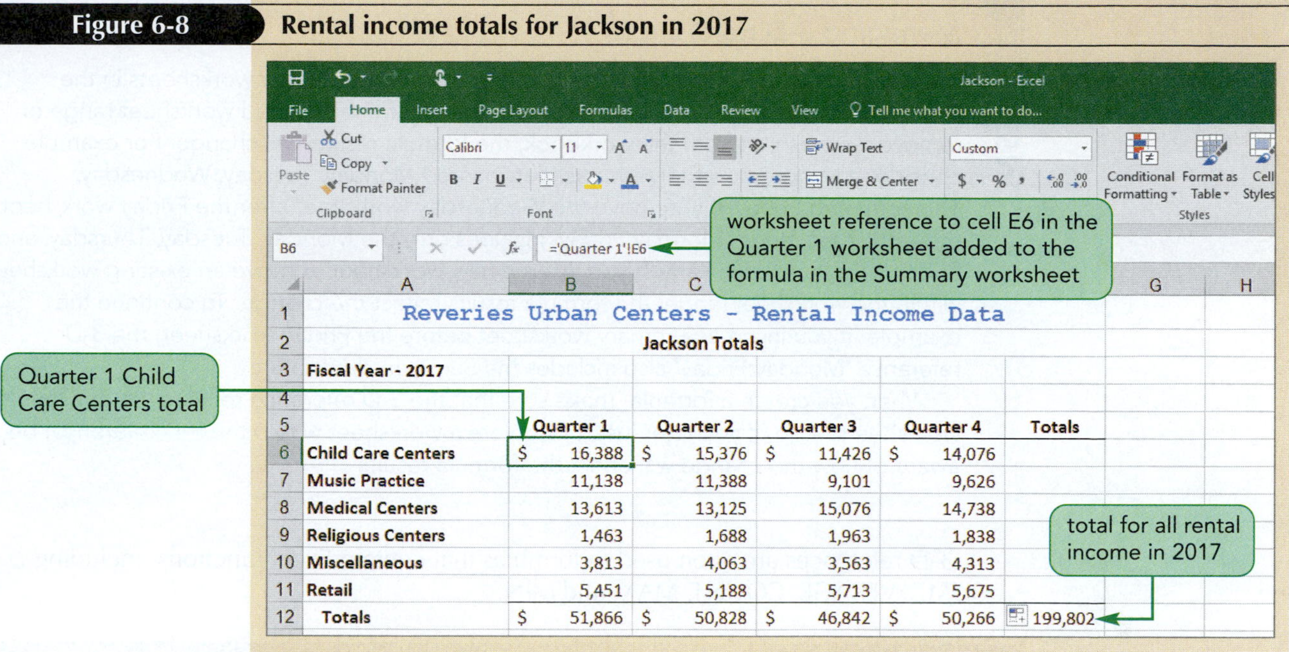

Using 3-D References to Add Values Across Worksheets

Timothy wants you to calculate the rental income for each type of rental for the year and display the totals for the fiscal year in the Summary worksheet. To calculate the totals for the year, you can add the results from each quarterly worksheet and place the sum in the Summary worksheet. For example, in cell B6 of the Summary worksheet, you can enter the following formula:

```
='Quarter 1'!E6+'Quarter 2'!E6+'Quarter 3'!E6+'Quarter 4'!E6
```

This formula calculates the total rental income for Child Care Centers by adding the values in cell E6 in each of the quarterly worksheets. Continuing this approach for the entire worksheet would be time consuming and error prone.

Instead, when two or more worksheets have *identical* row and column layouts, as the quarterly worksheets in the Jackson workbook do, you can enter formulas with 3-D references to summarize those worksheets in another worksheet. The 3-D reference specifies not only the range of rows and columns but also the range of worksheet names in which the cells appear. The general syntax of a 3-D reference is

```
WorksheetRange!CellRange
```

where *WorksheetRange* is the range of worksheets you want to reference and is entered as *FirstSheetName*:*LastSheetName* with a colon separating the first and last worksheets in the worksheet range. If the sheet names include spaces, they are surrounded by ' ' (single quotation marks). *CellRange* is the same cell or range in each of those worksheets that you want to reference. An exclamation mark (!) separates the worksheet range from the cell or range. For example, the following formula adds the values in cell D11 in the worksheets between Monday and Friday, including Monday and Friday:

```
=SUM(Monday:Friday!D11)
```

If worksheets named Monday, Tuesday, Wednesday, Thursday, and Friday are included in the workbook, the worksheet range Monday:Friday references all five worksheets. Although the Tuesday, Wednesday, and Thursday worksheets aren't specifically mentioned in this 3-D reference, all worksheets positioned within the starting and ending names are included in the calculation.

INSIGHT

Managing 3-D References

The results of a formula using a 3-D reference reflect the current worksheets in the worksheet range. If you move a worksheet outside the referenced worksheet range or remove a worksheet from the workbook, the formula results will change. For example, consider a workbook with five worksheets named Monday, Tuesday, Wednesday, Thursday, and Friday. If you move the Wednesday worksheet after the Friday worksheet, the worksheet range 'Monday:Friday' includes only the Monday, Tuesday, Thursday, and Friday worksheets. Similarly, if you insert a new worksheet or move an existing worksheet within the worksheet range, the formula results reflect the change. To continue the example, if you insert a Summary worksheet before the Friday worksheet, the 3-D reference 'Monday:Friday' also includes the Summary worksheet.

When you create a formula, make sure that the 3-D reference reflects the appropriate worksheets. Also, if you later insert or delete a worksheet within the 3-D reference, be aware of how the change will affect the formula results.

3-D references are often used in formulas that contain Excel functions, including SUM, AVERAGE, COUNT, MAX, and MIN.

REFERENCE

Entering a Function That Contains a 3-D Reference

- Select the cell where you want to enter the formula.
- Type = to begin the formula, type the name of the function, and then type (to indicate the beginning of the argument.
- Click the sheet tab for the first worksheet in the worksheet range, press and hold the Shift key, and then click the tab for the last worksheet in the worksheet range.
- Select the cell or range to reference, and then press the Enter key.

In the Jackson workbook, Timothy wants to use 3-D references in the Summary worksheet to add the total rental income for each type of rental for the year. You will begin by entering a formula to add the total rental income for Child Care Centers in the first quarter. Then, you'll copy this formula to calculate the total rental income for Music Practice, Medical Centers, Religious Centers, Miscellaneous, and Retail in the first quarter.

To use a 3-D reference to enter the total rental income for Child Care Centers:

1. In the Summary worksheet, select cell **F6**, and then type **=SUM(** to begin the formula.
2. Click the **Quarter 1** sheet tab, press and hold the **Shift** key, click the **Quarter 4** sheet tab, and then release the **Shift** key. The quarterly worksheets are grouped to create the worksheet range.
3. In the Quarter 1 worksheet, click cell **E6**. Cell E6 is selected in each quarterly worksheet and added to the function. Notice that the worksheet names are enclosed in single quotation marks because the worksheet names include spaces. See Figure 6-9.

Figure 6-9 3-D reference added to the SUM function

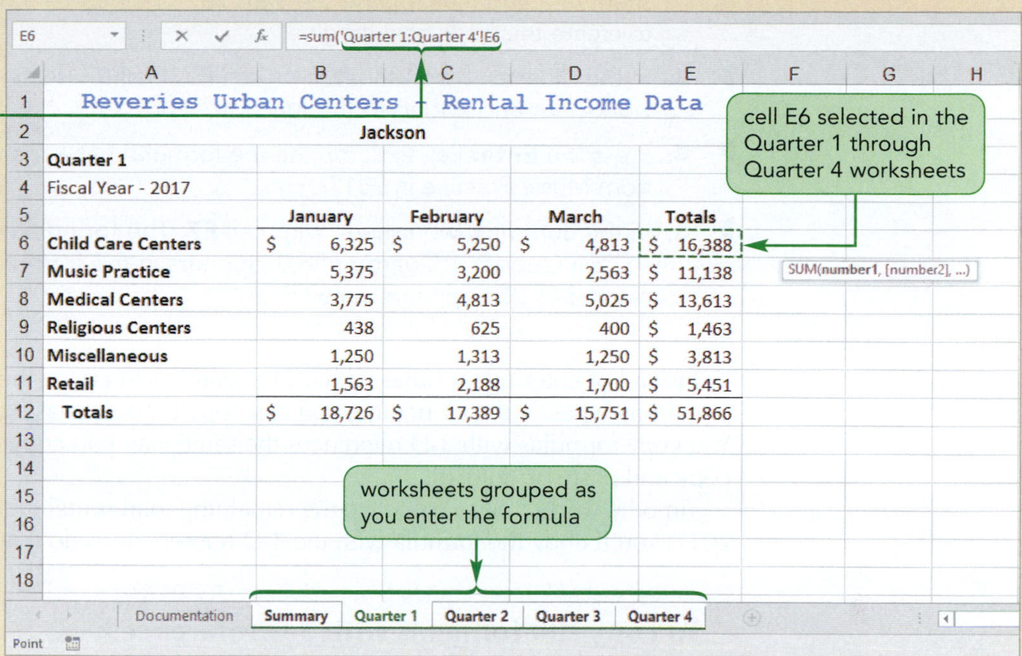

4. Press the **Enter** key. The completed formula in the Summary worksheet adds the total rental income for Child Care Centers in 2017.
5. In the Summary worksheet, select cell **F6**. The formula with the 3-D reference, =SUM('Quarter 1:Quarter 4'!E6), appears in the formula bar. The formula result—$57,266—appears in the cell. See Figure 6-10.

Figure 6-10 3-D reference used in the SUM function

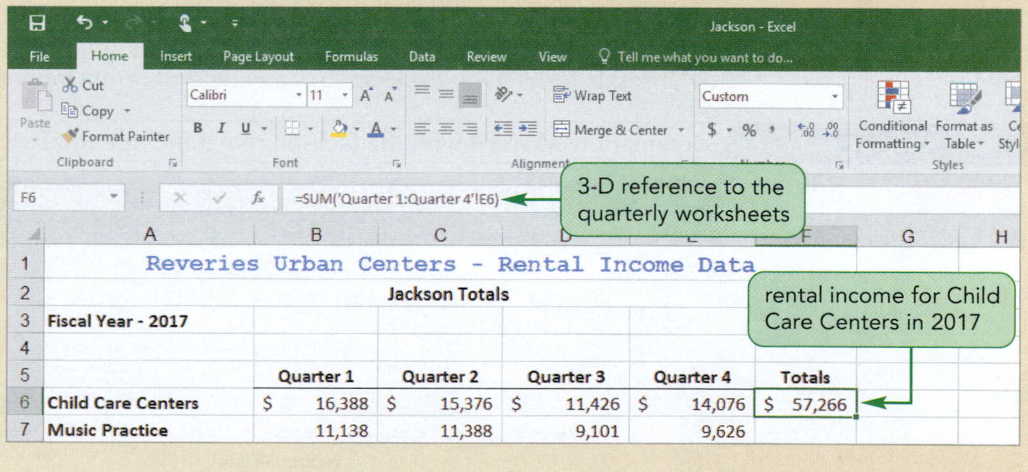

The next formula will add the total rental income for Music Practice in the first quarter.

To calculate the total rental income for Music Practice:

1. In the Summary worksheet, click cell **F7**, and then type **=SUM(** to begin the formula.

2. Click the **Quarter 1** sheet tab, press and hold the **Shift** key, click the **Quarter 4** sheet tab, and then release the **Shift** key. The quarterly worksheets are grouped to create the worksheet range.
3. In the Quarter 1 worksheet, click cell **E7**. Cell E7 is selected in each quarterly worksheet and added to the function.
4. Press the **Enter** key to complete the formula that adds the total rental income from Music Practice in 2017.
5. In the Summary worksheet, click cell **F7**. The formula with the 3-D reference, =SUM('Quarter 1:Quarter 4'!E7), appears in the formula bar, and the formula result $41,253 appears in cell F7.

Instead of entering formulas with 3-D references to create the totals for the remaining types of rental income, you can copy the formulas to the rest of the range. You copy formulas with 3-D references the same way you copy other formulas—using copy and paste or AutoFill.

Timothy wants you to calculate the remaining total rental incomes by rental type in 2017. You'll copy the formula with the 3-D references to do that.

To copy the formulas with 3-D references:

1. In the Summary worksheet, make sure cell **F7** is selected. This cell contains the formula with the 3-D reference you already entered.
2. Drag the fill handle over the range **F8:F11**. The formulas are copied for the rest of the rental income totals. The Auto Fill Options button appears below the copied range.
3. Click the **Auto Fill Options** button, and then click the **Fill Without Formatting** option button. You don't want to copy the formatting in this case because you want to keep the bottom border formatting in cell F11. The total values for the year appear in the range.
4. Select cell **B6** to deselect the range. The Summary worksheet now shows the totals for 2017 in Jackson for each type of rental income. See Figure 6-11.

Figure 6-11 Summary worksheet with the Jackson rental income totals

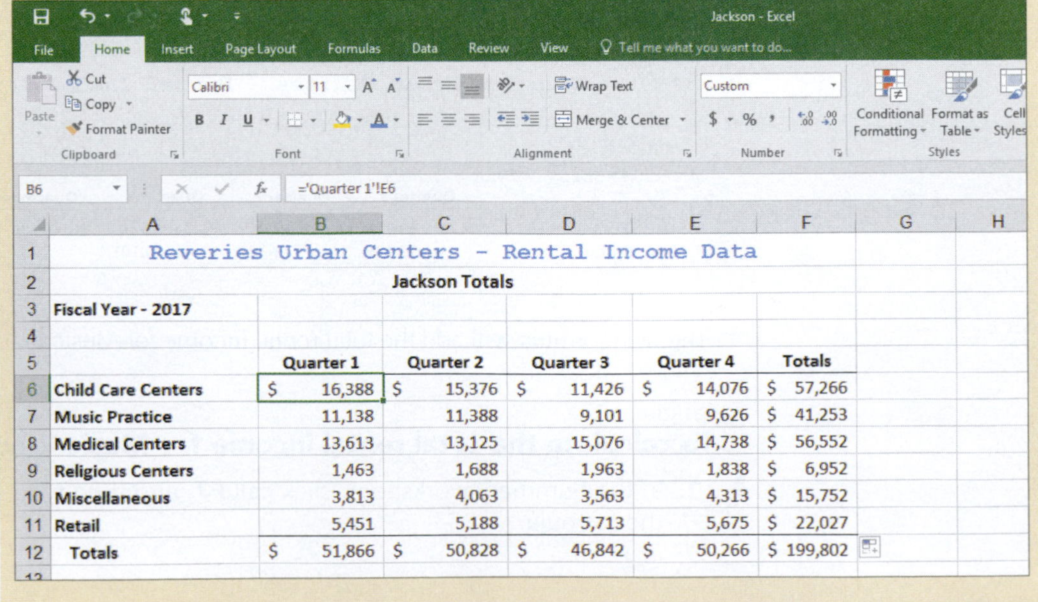

	Quarter 1	Quarter 2	Quarter 3	Quarter 4	Totals
Child Care Centers	$ 16,388	$ 15,376	$ 11,426	$ 14,076	$ 57,266
Music Practice	11,138	11,388	9,101	9,626	$ 41,253
Medical Centers	13,613	13,125	15,076	14,738	$ 56,552
Religious Centers	1,463	1,688	1,963	1,838	$ 6,952
Miscellaneous	3,813	4,063	3,563	4,313	$ 15,752
Retail	5,451	5,188	5,713	5,675	$ 22,027
Totals	$ 51,866	$ 50,828	$ 46,842	$ 50,266	$ 199,802

One benefit of summarizing data using formulas with 3-D references, like any other formula, is that if you change the value in one worksheet, the results of formulas that reference that cell reflect the change.

Timothy has discovered an error in the Jackson rental income data. In May, the rental income from Religious Centers was $425, not $438. You will correct the rental income.

To change the rental income in the Quarter 2 worksheet:

1. In the Summary worksheet, note that the rental income for Religious Centers in Quarter 2 is 1,688.
2. Go to the **Quarter 2** worksheet.
3. In cell **C9**, enter **425**. The total rental income for Religious Centers for Quarter 2 is now $1,675.

   The results in the Summary worksheet are also updated because of the 3-D references in the formulas.
4. Go to the **Summary** worksheet. The total rental income for Religious Centers in Quarter 2 is now 1,675. The Quarter 2 total is now $50,815, the 2017 total for Religious Centers is now $6,939, and the total rental income for 2017 is $199,789. See Figure 6-12.

Figure 6-12 Summary worksheet with updated Quarter 2 data

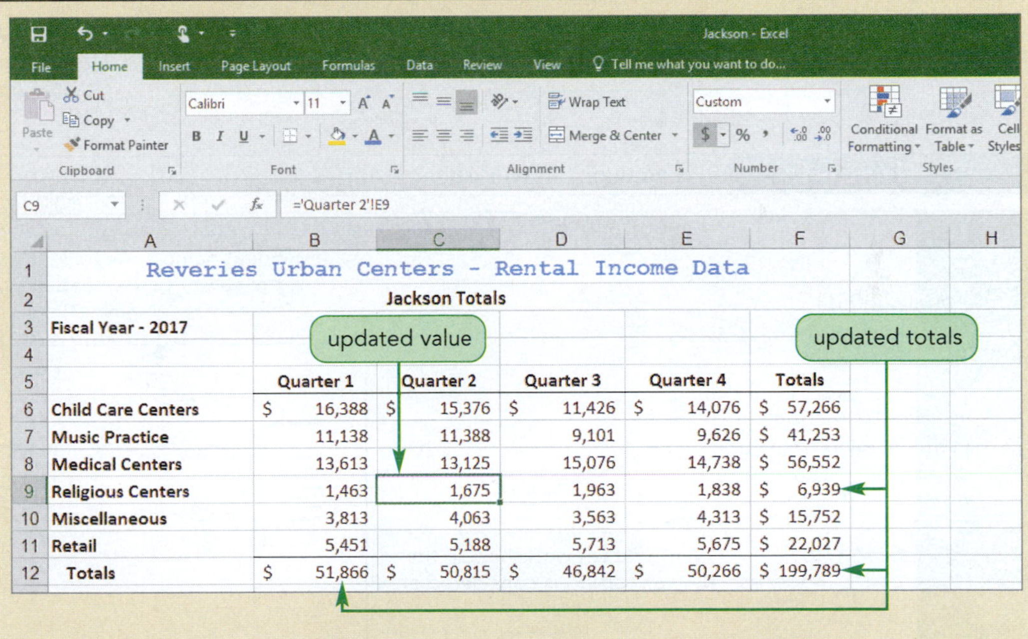

Reveries Urban Centers - Rental Income Data

Jackson Totals

Fiscal Year - 2017

	Quarter 1	Quarter 2	Quarter 3	Quarter 4	Totals
Child Care Centers	$ 16,388	$ 15,376	$ 11,426	$ 14,076	$ 57,266
Music Practice	11,138	11,388	9,101	9,626	$ 41,253
Medical Centers	13,613	13,125	15,076	14,738	$ 56,552
Religious Centers	1,463	1,675	1,963	1,838	$ 6,939
Miscellaneous	3,813	4,063	3,563	4,313	$ 15,752
Retail	5,451	5,188	5,713	5,675	$ 22,027
Totals	$ 51,866	$ 50,815	$ 46,842	$ 50,266	$ 199,789

Printing a Worksheet Group

When you create a worksheet group, you apply the same page layout settings to all of the worksheets in the group at the same time. You can also print all of the worksheets in the group at once. The process for printing a worksheet group is the same as for printing a single worksheet, except that you must first group the worksheets you want to print.

Timothy wants a printed copy of the five rental income worksheets to include in his report. Each page should have the same setup. Because the layout will be the same for all the quarterly worksheets in the Jackson workbook, you can speed the page layout setup by creating a worksheet group before selecting settings.

Be sure to include all five worksheets in the group so you can apply page layout settings and print the worksheets at once.

To preview the Summary and quarterly worksheets with a custom header and footer:

1. Group the **Summary, Quarter 1**, **Quarter 2**, **Quarter 3**, and **Quarter 4** worksheets. The five worksheets are grouped.
2. On the ribbon, click the **Page Layout** tab.
3. In the Page Setup group, click the **Dialog Box Launcher**. The Page Setup dialog box opens with the Page tab active.
4. Click the **Margins** tab, and then click the **Horizontally** check box in the Center on page section to insert a checkmark. The printed content will be centered horizontally on the page.
5. Click the **Header/Footer** tab, click the **Custom Header** button to open the Header dialog box, click in the **Center section** box, click the **Insert Sheet Name** button to add the &[Tab] code in the section box, and then click the **OK** button. A preview of the header appears in the upper portion of the dialog box.
6. Click the **Custom Footer** button to open the Footer dialog box, type your name in the Left section box, click in the Right section box, click the **Insert Date** button to add the &[Date] code in the section box, and then click the **OK** button. A preview of the footer appears in the center of the dialog box.
7. Click the **Print Preview** button. The preview of the Summary worksheet, the first worksheet in the group, appears on the Print screen in Backstage view. See Figure 6-13.

Figure 6-13 Preview of the worksheet group

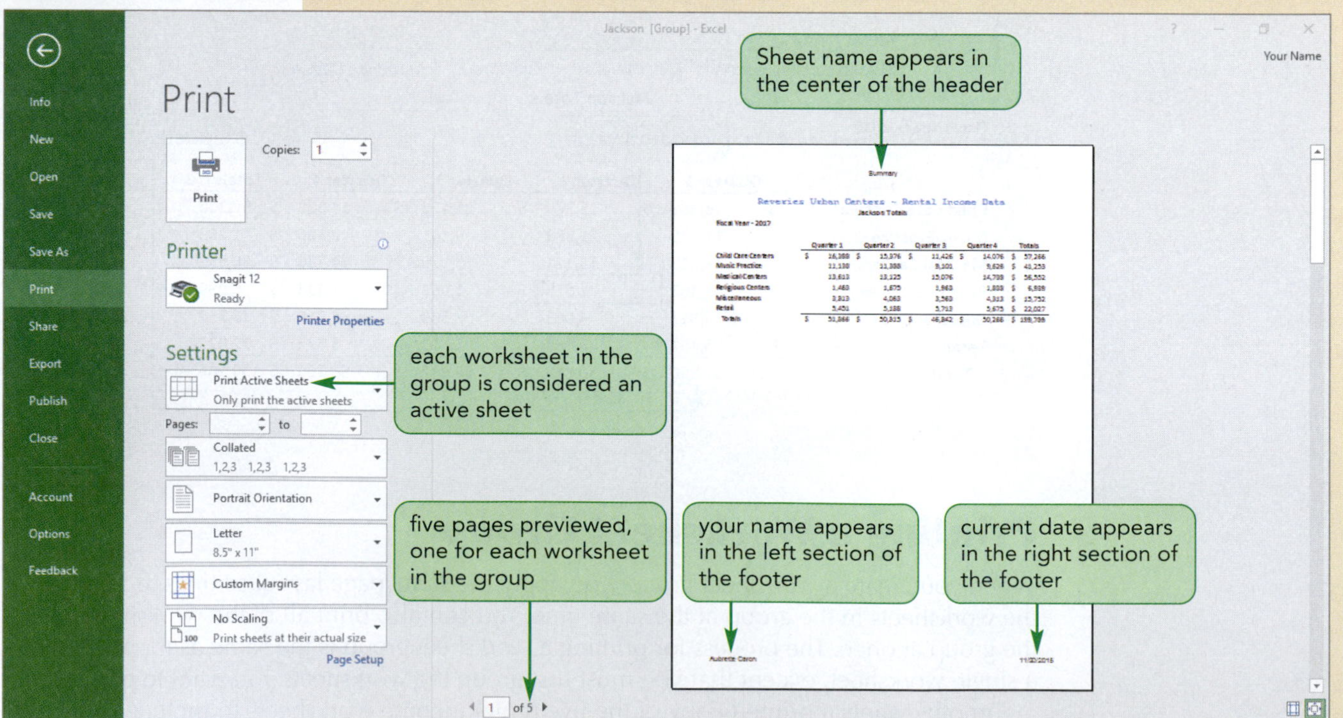

8. Below the preview, click the **Next Page** button four times to view the other worksheets in the group. Each page has the same page layout, but the header shows the sheet tab names.

   Trouble? If only one page appears in the preview, the worksheets are not grouped. Click the Back button to exit Backstage view, and then repeat Steps 1 through 8.

9. Click the **Back** button to exit Backstage view without printing the worksheet group.

10. Go to the **Documentation** worksheet to ungroup the worksheets, and then go to the **Summary** worksheet.

In this session, you consolidated the data in Reveries Urban Centers Jackson workbook into a Summary worksheet so that Timothy can quickly see the collection totals for the rental income totals for each rental type. In the next session, you will help Timothy determine the annual totals for the other Reveries Urban Centers—Flint and Petosky.

REVIEW

Session 6.1 Quick Check

1. What is a worksheet group?
2. How do you select an adjacent worksheet group? How do you select a nonadjacent worksheet group? How do you deselect a worksheet group?
3. What formula would you enter in the Summary worksheet to reference cell C8 in the Quarter 2 worksheet?
4. What is the 3-D reference to cell E6 in the adjacent Summary 1, Summary 2, and Summary 3 worksheets?
5. Explain what the formula =AVERAGE(Sheet1:Sheet4!B1) calculates.
6. If you insert a new worksheet named Sheet5 after Sheet4, how would you change the formula =MIN(Sheet1:Sheet4!B1) to include Sheet5 in the calculation?
7. If you insert a new worksheet named Sheet5 before Sheet4, how would you change the formula =SUM(Sheet1:Sheet4!B1) to include Sheet5 in the calculation?
8. How do you apply the same page layout to all of the worksheets in a workbook at one time?

Session 6.2 Visual Overview:

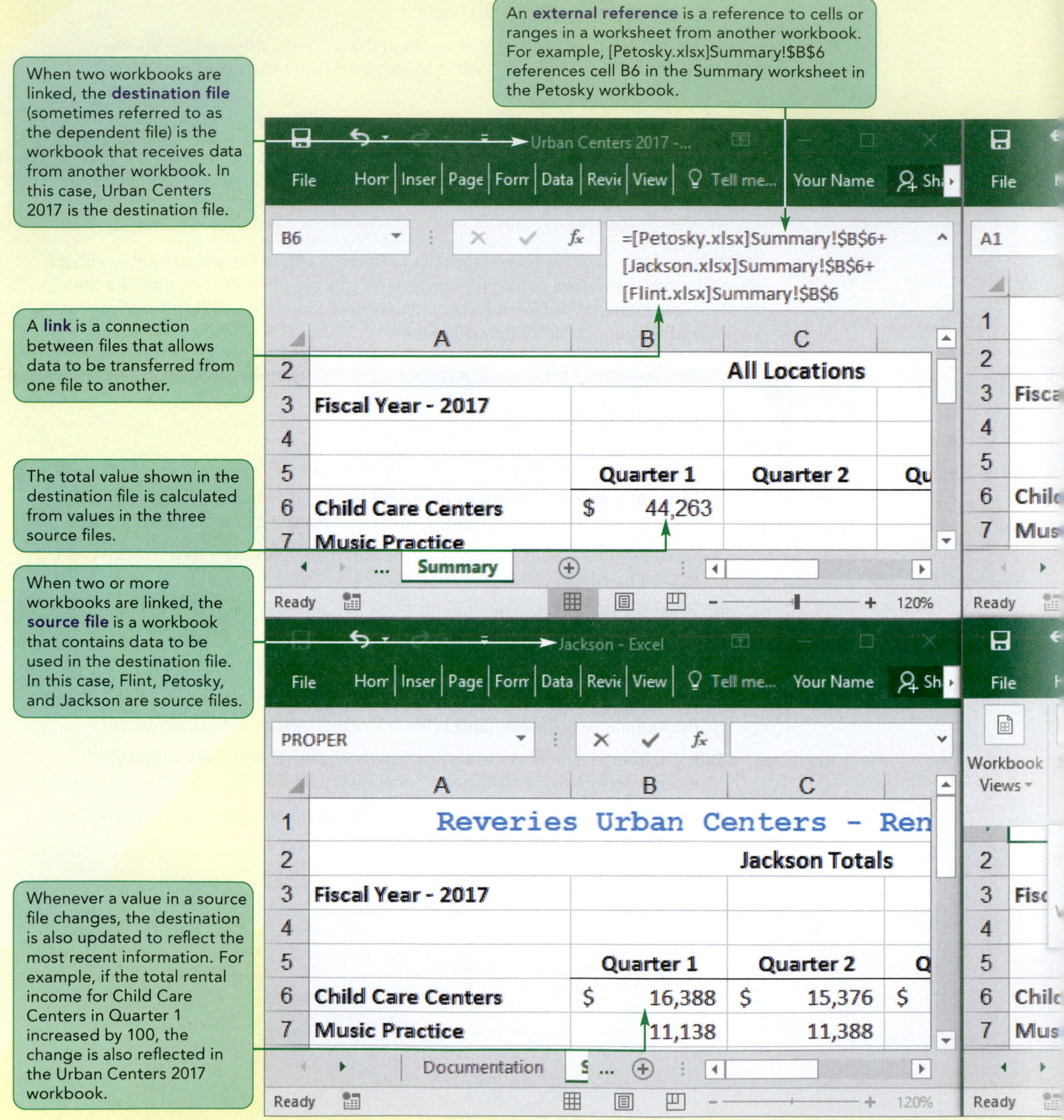
An **external reference** is a reference to cells or ranges in a worksheet from another workbook. For example, [Petosky.xlsx]Summary!$B$6 references cell B6 in the Summary worksheet in the Petosky workbook.
When two workbooks are linked, the **destination file** (sometimes referred to as the dependent file) is the workbook that receives data from another workbook. In this case, Urban Centers 2017 is the destination file.
A **link** is a connection between files that allows data to be transferred from one file to another.
The total value shown in the destination file is calculated from values in the three source files.
When two or more workbooks are linked, the **source file** is a workbook that contains data to be used in the destination file. In this case, Flint, Petosky, and Jackson are source files.
Whenever a value in a source file changes, the destination is also updated to reflect the most recent information. For example, if the total rental income for Child Care Centers in Quarter 1 increased by 100, the change is also reflected in the Urban Centers 2017 workbook.
Urban Centers 2017 -...
B6
=[Petosky.xlsx]Summary!$B$6+
[Jackson.xlsx]Summary!$B$6+
[Flint.xlsx]Summary!$B$6
All Locations
Fiscal Year - 2017
Quarter 1
Quarter 2
Child Care Centers
$ 44,263
Music Practice
Summary
Jackson - Excel
PROPER
Reveries Urban Centers - Ren
Jackson Totals
Fiscal Year - 2017
Quarter 1
Quarter 2
Child Care Centers
$ 16,388
$ 15,376
Music Practice
11,138
11,388
Documentation
Workbook Views

Links and External References

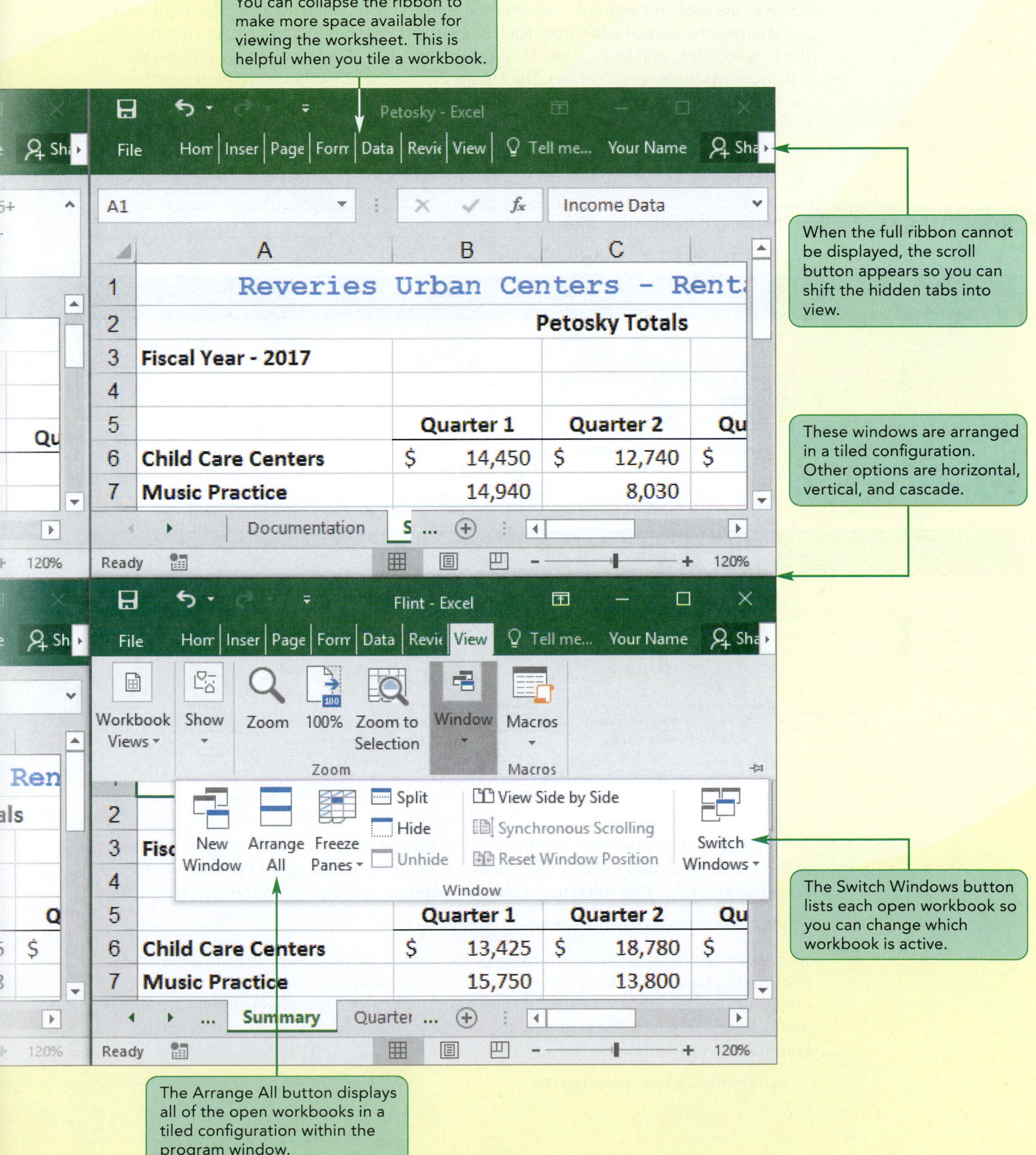
You can collapse the ribbon to make more space available for viewing the worksheet. This is helpful when you tile a workbook.
When the full ribbon cannot be displayed, the scroll button appears so you can shift the hidden tabs into view.
These windows are arranged in a tiled configuration. Other options are horizontal, vertical, and cascade.
The Switch Windows button lists each open workbook so you can change which workbook is active.
The Arrange All button displays all of the open workbooks in a tiled configuration within the program window.
Petosky - Excel
File
Data
View
Tell me...
Your Name
Income Data
Reveries Urban Centers - Rent
Petosky Totals
Fiscal Year - 2017
Quarter 1
Quarter 2
Child Care Centers
$ 14,450
$ 12,740
Music Practice
14,940
8,030
Documentation
Ready
120%
Flint - Excel
Workbook Views
Show
Zoom
100%
Zoom to Selection
Window
Macros
New Window
Arrange All
Freeze Panes
Split
Hide
Unhide
View Side by Side
Synchronous Scrolling
Reset Window Position
Switch Windows
$ 13,425
$ 18,780
15,750
13,800
Summary

Linking Workbooks

When creating formulas in a workbook, you can reference data in other workbooks. To do so, you must create a link between the workbooks. When two files are linked, the source file contains the data, and the destination file (sometimes called the dependent file) receives the data. For example, Timothy wants to create a company-wide workbook that summarizes the annual totals from each of the three Reveries Urban Centers. In this case, the Petosky, Flint, and Jackson workbooks are the source files because they contain the data from the three rental centers. The Urban Centers 2017 workbook is the destination file because it receives the data from the three rental center workbooks to calculate the company totals for 2017. The Urban Centers 2017 workbook will always have access to the most recent information in the rental center workbooks because it can be updated whenever any of the linked values change. See Figure 6-14.

Figure 6-14 Source and destination files

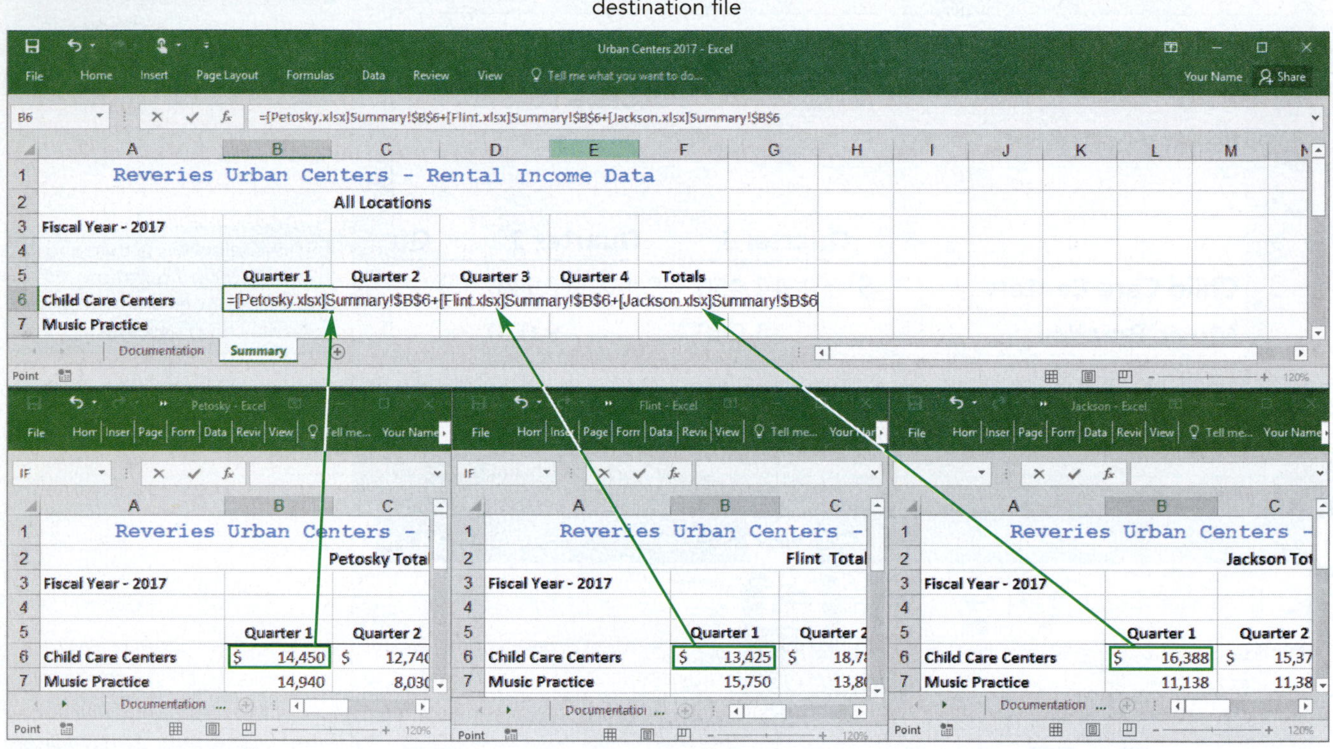

To create the link between destination and source files, you need to insert a formula in the UCTotals workbook that references a specific cell or range in the three rental center workbooks. That reference, called an external reference, has the syntax

`[WorkbookName]WorksheetName!CellRange`

where *WorkbookName* is the filename of the workbook (including the file extension) enclosed in square brackets; *WorksheetName* is the name of the worksheet that contains the data followed by an exclamation mark; and *CellRange* is the cell or range that contains the data. For example, the following formula references cell B6 in the Summary worksheet of the Jackson.xlsx workbook:

```
=[Jackson.xlsx]Summary!B6
```

TIP

When you click cells to include in formulas with external references, Excel enters all of the required punctuation, including quotation marks.

If the workbook name or the worksheet name contains one or more spaces, you must enclose the entire workbook name and worksheet name in single quotation marks. For example, the following formula references cell B6 in the Summary worksheet of the Flint 2017.xlsx workbook:

```
='[Flint 2017.xlsx]Summary'!B6
```

When the source and destination workbooks are stored in the same folder, you need to include only the workbook name in the external reference. However, when the source and destination workbooks are located in different folders, the workbook reference must include the file's complete location (also called the path). For example, if the destination file is stored in C:\Rental Income and the source file is stored in C:\Rental Income\Local Data, the complete reference in the destination file would be:

```
='C:\Rental Income\Local Data\[Flint.xlsx]Summary'!B6
```

The single quotation marks start at the beginning of the path and end immediately before the exclamation mark.

PROSKILLS

Decision Making: Understanding When to Link Workbooks

More than one person is usually involved in developing information that will be used in an organization's decision-making process. If each person has access to only part of the data, everyone's ability to see the whole picture and make good decisions is limited. Linking workbooks provides one way to pull together all of the data being compiled by different people or departments to support the decision-making process.

When deciding whether to link workbooks, consider the following questions:

- **Can separate workbooks have the same purpose and structure?** With linked workbooks, each workbook can focus on a different store, branch office, or department with the same products or expenditure types and reporting periods (such as weekly, monthly, and quarterly).
- **Is a large workbook too unwieldy to use?** A large workbook can be divided into smaller workbooks for each quarter, division, or product and then linked to provide the summary information.
- **Can information from different workbooks be summarized?** Linked workbooks provide a way to quickly and accurately consolidate information from multiple source workbooks, and the summary worksheet will always contain the most current information even when information is later updated.
- **Are source workbooks continually updated?** With linked workbooks, an outdated source workbook can be replaced and the destination workbook will then reflect the latest information.
- **Will the source workbooks be available to the destination workbook?** If the person who is working with the destination workbook cannot access the source workbooks, then the destination workbook cannot be updated.

If you can answer yes to these questions, then linked workbooks are the way to go. Creating linked workbooks can help you analyze data better, leading to better decision making. It also provides greater flexibility as data becomes more expansive and complex. However, keep in mind that workbooks with many links can take a long time to open and update.

Navigating Multiple Workbooks

When you create external reference formulas, you'll need to move between open workbooks. The Switch Windows button in the Window group on the View tab lists each open workbook so you can change which workbook is active. Another method is to click the Excel button on the taskbar and then click the thumbnail of the workbook you want to make active.

Timothy received workbooks from the Flint and Petosky managers that are similar to the one you helped prepare. These three rental income workbooks (named Petosky, Flint, and Jackson) contain the rental income for 2017. Timothy wants to create a company-wide workbook that summarizes the annual totals from each rental center workbook. You'll combine the three rental center workbooks into one rental center summary workbook. First you need to open the workbooks that you want to reference. Then you'll switch between them to make each Summary worksheet the active sheet in preparation for creating the external references.

To open the regional workbooks and switch between them:

1. If you took a break after the previous session, make sure the Jackson workbook is open and the Summary worksheet is active.
2. Open the **UCTotals** workbook located in the **Excel6 > Module** folder included with your Data Files, and then save the workbook as **Urban Centers 2017** in the location specified by your instructor.
3. In the Documentation worksheet of the Urban Centers 2017 workbook, enter your name and the date.
4. Open the **Petosky** workbook located in the **Excel6 > Module** folder included with your Data Files, and then go to the **Summary** worksheet.
5. Open the **Flint** workbook located in the **Excel6 > Module** folder included with your Data Files, and then go to the **Summary** worksheet. All three location workbooks have the same active sheet.
6. On the ribbon, click the **View** tab.
7. In the Window group, click the **Switch Windows** button. A menu lists the names of all the workbooks that are currently open.
8. Click **Urban Centers 2017** to make that the active workbook, and then go to the **Summary** worksheet. The Summary worksheet is the active sheet in each workbook.

Arranging Multiple Workbooks

Rather than continually switching between open workbooks, you can display all the open workbooks on your screen at the same time. This way, you can easily click among the open workbooks to create links as well as quickly compare the contents of worksheets in different workbooks. You can arrange workbooks in the following layouts:

- **Tiled**—divides the open workbooks evenly on the screen
- **Horizontal**—divides the open workbooks into horizontal bands
- **Vertical**—divides the open workbooks into vertical bands
- **Cascade**—layers the open workbooks on the screen

The layout you select will depend on the contents being displayed and your purpose.

REFERENCE

Arranging Workbooks

- On the View tab, in the Window group, click the Arrange All button.
- Select the layout in which you want to arrange the open workbooks.
- When arranging multiple workbooks, uncheck the Windows of active workbook option. When arranging multiple worksheets within one workbook, check this option.
- Click the OK button.

Currently, the four workbooks are open, but only one is visible. You'll make all the workbooks visible by displaying the workbooks in the tiled arrangement.

To tile the open workbooks:

1. On the ribbon, click the **View** tab.
2. In the Window group, click the **Arrange All** button. The Arrange Windows dialog box opens so you can select the layout arrangement you want.
3. Click the **Tiled** option button, if necessary. The Tiled option will arrange the four Reveries Urban Centers workbooks evenly on the screen.
4. Click the **OK** button. The four open workbooks appear in a tiled layout.
5. Click in the **Urban Centers 2017** workbook to make it the active workbook, if necessary. In the tiled layout, the active workbook contains the active cell.
6. In the Summary worksheet, click cell **B6** to make it the active cell.

   The ribbon appears in each window, taking up a lot of the workbook space. To see more of the worksheets, you will collapse the ribbon in each window to show only the ribbon tabs.
7. In each window, click the **Collapse the Ribbon** button in the lower-right corner of the ribbon (or press the **Ctrl+F1** keys). Only the ribbon tabs are visible in each window. If the ribbon includes more tabs than can be displayed, a ribbon scroll button appears to the right of the last visible tab, which you can click to display the other tabs. See Figure 6-15.

TIP

You can click the Windows of active workbook check box to tile the sheets in the current workbook on the screen.

Figure 6-15 Four workbooks arranged in a tiled layout

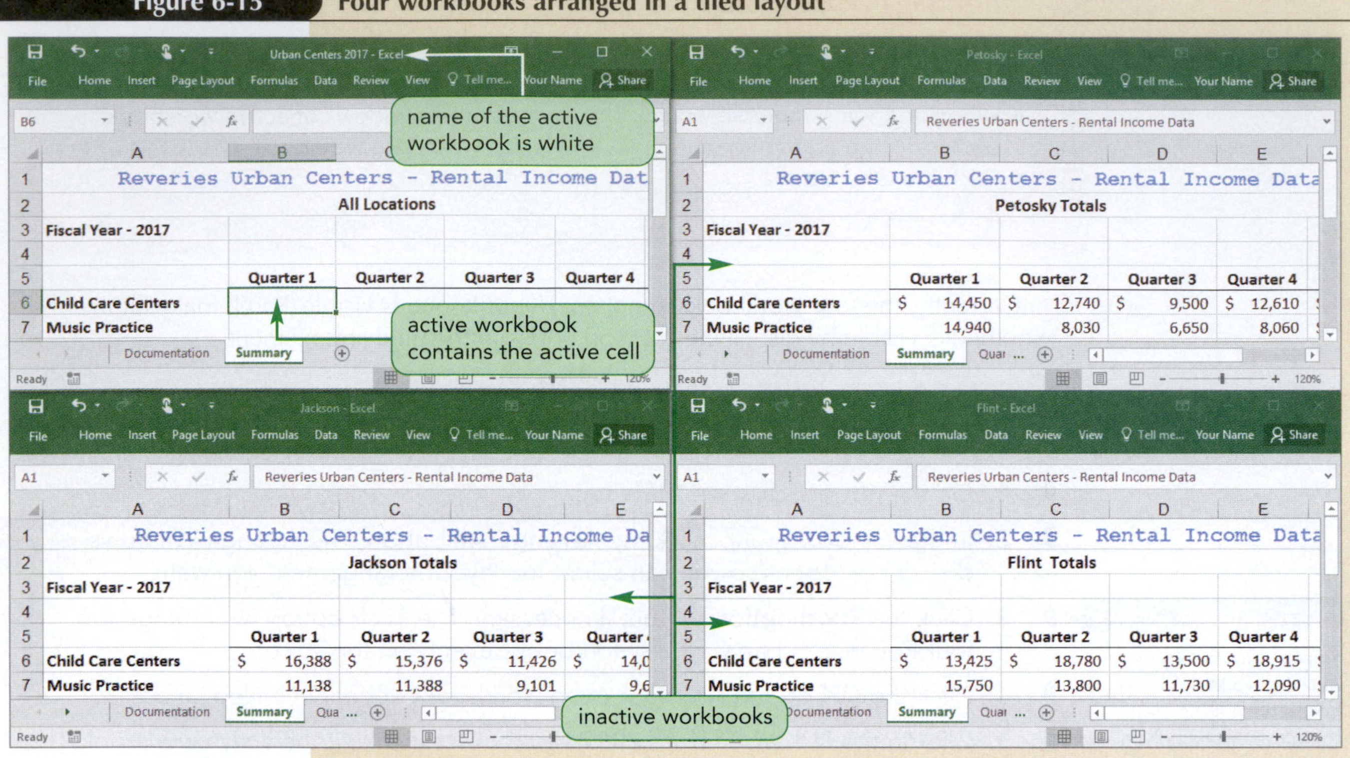

Creating Formulas with External References

A formula can include a reference to another workbook (called an external reference), which creates a set of linked workbooks. The process for entering a formula with an external reference is the same as for entering any other formula using references within the same worksheet or workbook. You can enter the formulas by typing them or using the point-and-click method. In most situations, you will use the point-and-click method to switch between the source files and the destination files so that Excel enters the references to the workbook, worksheet, and cell using the correct syntax.

You need to enter the external reference formulas in the Urban Centers 2017 workbook to summarize the rental center totals into one workbook for Timothy. You'll start by creating the formula that adds the total rental income for Child Care Centers in Petosky, Flint, and Jackson for Quarter 1 of 2017. You cannot use the SUM function with 3-D references here because you are referencing multiple workbooks, and 3-D references can be used only to reference multiple worksheets in the same workbook.

To create the formula with external references to add the total rental income for Child Care Centers:

1. In the Urban Centers 2017 workbook, in the Summary worksheet, make sure cell **B6** is the active cell, and then type **=** to begin the formula.
2. Click anywhere in the **Petosky** workbook to make the Petosky workbook active and place the formula in its formula bar, and then click cell **B6** in the Summary worksheet. The external reference to cell B6 in the Summary worksheet of the Petosky workbook—[Petosky.xlsx]Summary!$B$6—is added to the formula in the Urban Centers 2017 workbook. See Figure 6-16.

As you create the formula, be sure to verify each external reference before going to the next step.

Figure 6-16 Formula with an external cell reference

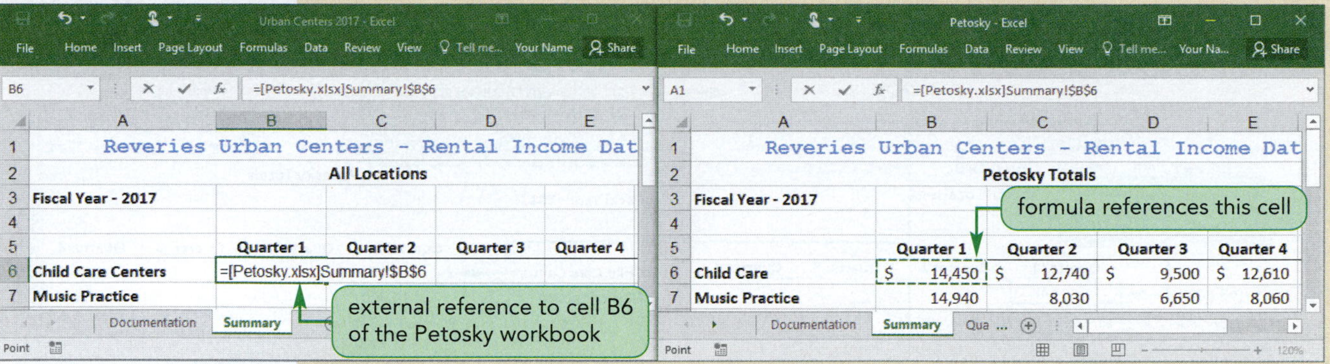

The reference created in a 3-D reference is an absolute cell reference, which does not change when the formula is copied. The formula remains in the formula bar of both the Urban Centers 2017 and Petosky workbooks until you make another workbook active. At that time, the formula will appear in the Urban Centers 2017 workbook and the active worksheet.

3. Type **+**. The Urban Centers 2017 workbook becomes active, and you can continue entering the formula. You need to create an external reference to the Flint workbook.
4. Click anywhere in the **Flint** workbook, click cell **B6** in the Summary worksheet, and then type **+**. The formula in the Urban Centers 2017 workbook includes the external reference to the cell that contains the total rental income for Child Care Centers in Flint during Quarter 1.
5. Click anywhere in the **Jackson** workbook, click cell **B6** in the Summary worksheet, and then press the **Enter** key. The formula with three external references is entered in the Summary worksheet in the Urban Centers 2017 workbook.
6. In the Urban Centers 2017 workbook, in the Summary worksheet, click cell **B6**. The complete formula is too long to appear in the formula bar of the tiled window. You will expand the formula bar so that it can display the full formula.
7. At the right edge of the formula bar, click the **Expand Formula Bar** button (or press the **Ctrl+Shift+U** keys). The complete formula is now visible in the formula bar, and the Collapse Formula Bar button appears at the right edge of the formula bar, which you can click to return the formula bar to a single line. The formula results in cell B6 show that the Child Care Centers had rental income of 44263 during Quarter 1 in the three rental centers—$14,450 in Petosky, $13,425 in Flint, and $16,388 in Jackson. See Figure 6-17.

Figure 6-17 Total rental income for Child Care Centers from Petosky, Flint, and Jackson in Quarter 1

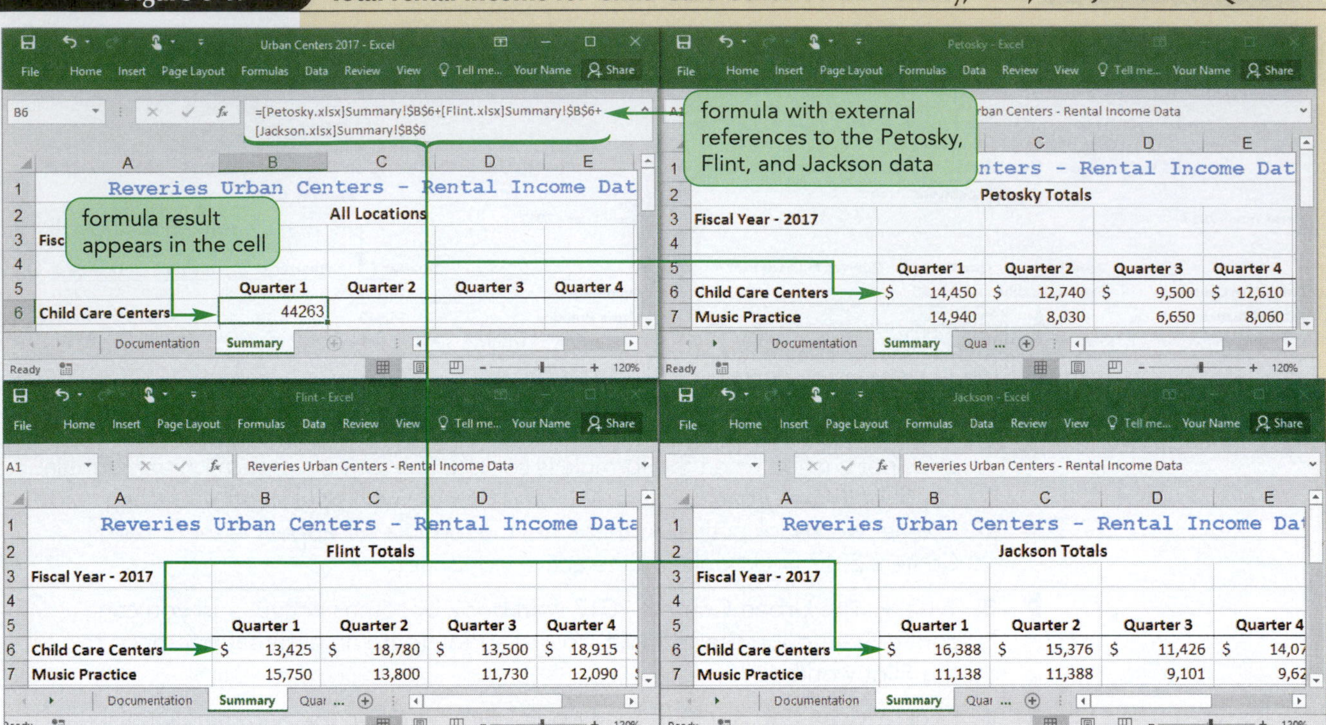

Trouble? If 44263 doesn't appear in cell B6 in the Summary worksheet in the Urban Centers 2017 workbook, you might have clicked an incorrect cell for an external reference in the formula. Repeat Steps 1 through 6 to correct the formula.

You'll use the same process to enter the external reference formula for cells C6, D6, and E6, which contain the total rental income for Child Care Centers in Quarter 2, Quarter 3, and Quarter 4, respectively. These formulas will calculate the total amounts from all three locations.

To create the remaining external reference formulas:

1. In the Urban Centers 2017 workbook, in the Summary worksheet, select cell **C6,** and then type **=** to begin the formula.
2. Click the **Petosky** workbook, click cell **C6** in the Summary worksheet, and then type **+**. The formula in the Urban Centers 2017 workbook includes the external reference to cell C6 in the Summary worksheet in the Petosky workbook.
3. Click the **Flint** workbook, click cell **C6** in the Summary worksheet, and then type **+**. The formula includes an external reference to cell C6 in the Summary worksheet in the Flint workbook.
4. Click the **Jackson** workbook, click cell **C6** in the Summary worksheet, and then press the **Enter** key. The external reference formula is complete.
5. In the Urban Centers 2017 workbook, in the Summary worksheet, click cell **C6**. Cell C6 displays 46896—the total rental income for Child Care Centers in Quarter 2 in Petosky, Flint, and Jackson, and the following formula appears in the formula bar: =[Petosky.xlsx]Summary!$C$6+[Flint.xlsx]Summary!$C$6 +[Jackson.xlsx]Summary!$C$6.

Next, you'll enter the external reference formulas in cells D6 and E6 to add the total rental income in Quarter 3 and Quarter 4.

6. Repeat Steps 1 through 4 to enter the formula from cell **D6** in the Summary worksheet in the Urban Centers 2017 workbook. The formula result displayed in cell D6 is 34426—the total rental income for Child Care Centers during Quarter 3 in Petosky, Flint, and Jackson.
7. Repeat Steps 1 through 4 to enter the formula from cell **E6** in the Summary worksheet in the Urban Centers 2017 workbook. The formula result displayed in cell E6 is 45601—the total rental income for Child Care Centers during Quarter 4 in Petosky, Flint, and Jackson.

You need to enter the remaining formulas for the other types of rental income. Rather than creating the rest of the external reference formulas manually, you can copy the formulas in row 6 and paste them in rows 7 through 11. The formulas created using the point-and-click method contain absolute references. Before you copy them to other cells, you need to change them to use mixed references because the rows in the formula need to change.

To edit the external reference formulas to use mixed references:

1. Maximize the Urban Centers 2017 workbook, click the **Ribbon Display Options** button in the title bar, and then click **Show Tabs and Commands** (or press the **Ctrl+F1** keys) to pin the ribbon to show both the tabs and the commands. The other workbooks are still open but are not visible.
2. At the right edge of the formula bar, click the **Collapse Formula Bar** button (or press the **Ctrl+Shift+U** keys) to reduce the formula bar to one line.
3. In the Summary worksheet, double-click cell **B6** to enter Edit mode and display the formula in the cell.
4. Click in the first absolute reference in the formula, and then press the **F4** key twice to change the absolute reference $B$6 to the mixed reference $B6.
5. Edit the other two absolute references in the formula to be mixed references with absolute column references and relative row references.
6. Press the **Enter** key, and then select cell **B6**. The formula is updated to include mixed references, but the formula results aren't affected. Cell B6 still displays 44263, which is correct. See Figure 6-18.

TIP

You can also create the mixed reference by deleting the $ symbol from the row references in the formula.

Figure 6-18 External reference formula with mixed references

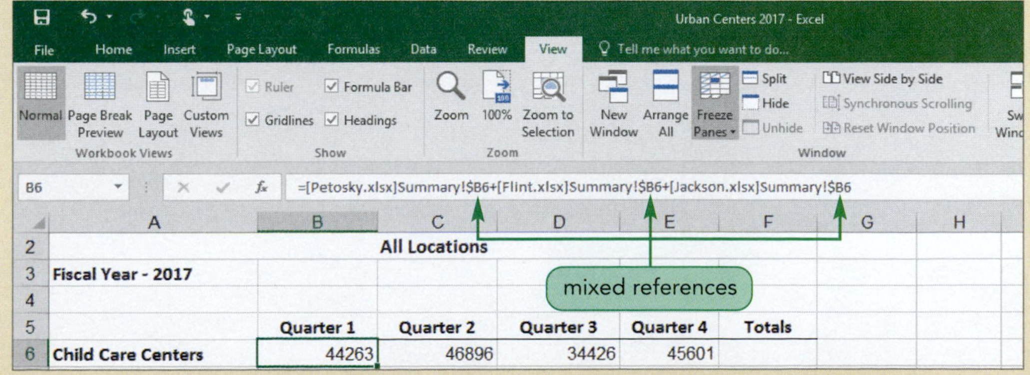

7. Edit the formulas in cells **C6**, **D6**, and **E6** to change the absolute references to the mixed references **$C6**, **$D6**, and **$E6**, respectively. The formulas are updated, but the cells in the range C6:E6 still correctly display 46896, 34426, and 45601, respectively.

With the formulas corrected to include mixed references, you can now copy the external reference formulas in the range B6:E6 to the other rows. Then you'll enter the SUM function to total the values in each row and column.

To copy and paste the external reference formulas:

1. Select the range **B6:E6**, and then drag the fill handle to select the range **B7:E11**. The formulas are copied to the range B7:E11, and the formula results appear in the cells. The Auto Fill Options button appears in the lower-right corner of the selected range, but you do not need to use it.

   Trouble? If all of the values in the range B7:E11 are the same as those in the range B6:E6, you didn't change the absolute cell references to mixed cell references in the formulas in the range B6:E6. Repeat Steps 3 through 7 in the previous set of steps, and then repeat Step 1 in this set of steps.

2. In cell **B12**, enter the SUM function to add the range **B6:B11**. The total rental income is 163016 in Quarter 1.
3. Copy the formula in cell **B12** to the range **C12:E12**. The total rental income is 152010 in Quarter 2, 144197 in Quarter 3, and 153921 in Quarter 4.
4. In cell **F6**, enter the SUM function to add the range B6:E6. The total rental income is 171186 for Child Care Centers at all rental centers in 2017.
5. Copy the formula in cell **F6** to the range **F7:F12**. The total for Music Practice is 132303, Medical Centers is 170087, Religious Centers is 20304, Miscellaneous is 44752, and Retail is 74512, with a grand total of 613144 for the year.
6. Format the nonadjacent range **B6:E6,F6:F11,** and **B12:F12** with the **Accounting** style and no decimal places.
7. Format the range **B7:E11** with the **Comma** style and no decimal places.
8. Format the range **B11:F11** with a bottom border, and then select cell **A1** to deselect the range. See Figure 6-19.

Figure 6-19 Completed summary of rental income data

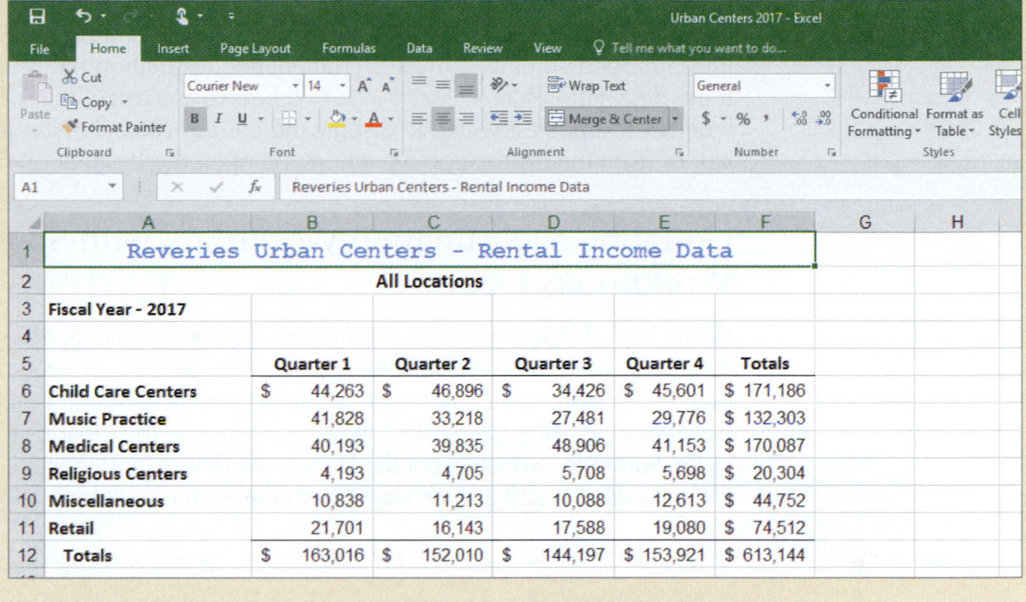

	A	B	C	D	E	F
1	Reveries Urban Centers - Rental Income Data					
2			All Locations			
3	Fiscal Year - 2017					
4						
5		Quarter 1	Quarter 2	Quarter 3	Quarter 4	Totals
6	Child Care Centers	$ 44,263	$ 46,896	$ 34,426	$ 45,601	$ 171,186
7	Music Practice	41,828	33,218	27,481	29,776	$ 132,303
8	Medical Centers	40,193	39,835	48,906	41,153	$ 170,087
9	Religious Centers	4,193	4,705	5,708	5,698	$ 20,304
10	Miscellaneous	10,838	11,213	10,088	12,613	$ 44,752
11	Retail	21,701	16,143	17,588	19,080	$ 74,512
12	Totals	$ 163,016	$ 152,010	$ 144,197	$ 153,921	$ 613,144

Timothy is pleased; the summary results match his expectations.

INSIGHT

Managing Linked Workbooks

As you work with a linked workbook, you might need to replace a source file or change where you stored the source and destination files. However, replacing or moving a file can affect the linked workbook. Keep in mind the following guidelines to manage your linked workbooks:

- If you rename a source file, the destination workbook won't be able to find it. A dialog box opens, indicating "This workbook contains one or more links that cannot be updated." Click the Continue button to open the workbook with the most recent values, or click the Change Source button in the Edit Links dialog box to specify the new name of that linked source file.
- If you move a source file to a different folder, the link breaks between the destination and source files. Click the Change Source button in the Edit Links dialog box to specify the new location of the linked workbook.
- If you receive a replacement source file, you can swap the original source file with the replacement file. No additional changes are needed.
- If you receive a destination workbook but the source files are not included, Excel will not be able to find the source files, and a dialog box opens with the message "This workbook contains one or more links that cannot be updated." Click the Continue button to open the workbook with the most recent values, or click the Break Link button in the Edit Links dialog box to replace the external references with the existing values.
- If you change the name of a destination file, you can open that renamed version destination file without affecting the source files or the original destination file.

Updating Linked Workbooks

When workbooks are linked, it is important that the data in the destination file accurately reflects the contents of the source file. When data in a source file changes, you want the destination file to reflect those changes. If both the source and destination files are open when you make a change, the destination file is updated automatically. If the destination file is closed when you make a change in a source file, you choose whether to update the link to display the current values or continue to display the older values from the destination file when you open the destination file.

Updating a Destination Workbook with Source Workbooks Open

When both the destination and source workbooks are open, any changes you make in a source workbook automatically appear in the destination workbook. Timothy tells you that the Jackson rental income for Medical Centers in March is actually $100 less than was recorded. After you correct the March value in the Quarter 1 worksheet, the amount in the Summary worksheet of the Jackson workbook and the total in the Urban Centers 2017 workbook will also change if both the source and destination files are open.

To update the source workbook with the destination file open:

1. Maximize the **Petosky**, **Flint**, and **Jackson** workbooks, and show the ribbon tabs and commands in each workbook.
2. Make the **Jackson** workbook active, and then go to the **Quarter 1** worksheet. You'll update the rental income for Medical Centers in March.
3. In cell **D8**, enter 4925. Jackson's rental income is updated, and the total rental income for March changes to $15,651.
4. Go to the **Summary** worksheet in the Jackson workbook, and then verify that the total rental income for Medical Centers in Quarter 1 (cell B8) is 13,513, the total rental income for Medical Centers in 2017 (cell F8) is $56,452, the total rental income in Quarter 1 (cell B12) is $51,766, and the total rental income in 2017 (cell F12) is $199,689. See Figure 6-20.

Figure 6-20 Summary worksheet in the Jackson workbook with revised Quarter 1 data

	A	B	C	D	E	F	G	H
1	Reveries Urban Centers - Rental Income Data							
2			Jackson Totals					
3	Fiscal Year - 2017							
4								
5		Quarter 1	Quarter 2	Quarter 3	Quarter 4	Totals		
6	Child Care Centers	$ 16,388	$ 15,376	$ 11,426	$ 14,076	$ 57,266		
7	Music Practice	11,138	11,388	9,101	9,626	$ 41,253		
8	Medical Centers	13,513	13,125	15,076	14,738	$ 56,452		
9	Religious Centers	1,463	1,675	1,963	1,838	$ 6,939		
10	Miscellaneous	3,813	4,063	3,563	4,313	$ 15,752		
11	Retail	5,451	5,188	5,713	5,675	$ 22,027		
12	Totals	$ 51,766	$ 50,815	$ 46,842	$ 50,266	$ 199,689		
13								
14								
15								

reflects the new value in the Quarter 1 worksheet

5. Make the **Urban Centers 2017** workbook active, and then verify in the Summary worksheet that the rental income for Medical Centers in Quarter 1 (cell B8) is 40,093, the total rental income for Medical centers in 2017 (cell F8) is $169,987, the total rental income in Quarter 1 (cell B12) is $162,916, and the total rental income in 2017 (cell F12) is $613,044, reflecting the new value you entered in the Jackson workbook. Because both the destination and source files are open, Excel updated the destination file automatically. See Figure 6-21.

Figure 6-21 Summary worksheet in the Urban Centers 2017 workbook with the revised Quarter 1 data

	A	B	C	D	E	F	G	H
1	Reveries Urban Centers - Rental Income Data							
2			All Locations					
3	Fiscal Year - 2017							
4								
5		Quarter 1	Quarter 2	Quarter 3	Quarter 4	Totals		
6	Child Care Centers	$ 44,263	$ 46,896	$ 34,426	$ 45,601	$ 171,186		
7	Music Practice	41,828	33,218	27,481	29,776	$ 132,303		
8	Medical Centers	40,093	39,835	48,906	41,153	$ 169,987		
9	Religious Centers	4,193	4,705	5,708	5,698	$ 20,304		
10	Miscellaneous	10,838	11,213	10,088	12,613	$ 44,752		
11	Retail	21,701	16,143	17,588	19,080	$ 74,512		
12	Totals	$ 162,916	$ 152,010	$ 144,197	$ 153,921	$ 613,044		
13								
14								
15								

reflects the new value in the Jackson worksheet

6. Save the Jackson and Urban Centers 2017 workbooks.

Updating a Destination Workbook with Source Workbooks Closed

When you save a workbook that contains external reference formulas, such as the Urban Centers 2017 workbook, Excel stores the most recent results of those formulas in the destination file. Source files, such as the Petosky, Flint, and Jackson workbooks, are often updated while the destination file is closed. In that case, the values in the destination file are not updated at the same time the source files are updated. The next time you open the destination file, the cells containing external reference formulas still display the old values. Therefore, some of the values in the edited source workbooks are different from the values in the destination workbook.

To update the destination workbook with the current data, you must specify that you want the update to occur. As part of the Excel security system that attempts to protect against malicious software, links to other workbooks are not updated without your permission. When you open a workbook with external reference formulas (the destination file), a dialog box appears, notifying you that the workbook contains links to an external source that could be unsafe. You then can choose to update the content, which allows the external reference formulas to function and updates the links in the destination workbook, or you can choose not to update the links, which lets you continue working with the data you have. The old values in the destination workbook are displayed and the links to the source files have an unknown status.

Timothy realizes that the Jackson workbook needs a second correction. In Quarter 4, the total rental income for Retail in December was $1,925 not $1,875 as currently entered in the Jackson workbook. He asks you to increase the rental income for Retail in December by $50. As a result, the totals in the Summary worksheet in the Jackson workbook and the rental income in the Urban Centers 2017 workbook will both increase by $50. You'll edit the source file, the Jackson workbook, while the destination file is closed.

To update the source workbook with the destination file closed:

1. Close the Petosky, Flint, and Urban Centers 2017 workbooks. The Jackson workbook remains open.
2. In the Jackson workbook, go to the **Quarter 4** worksheet.
3. In cell **D11**, enter 1,925. The rental income from Retail in Quarter 4 increases to $5,725.
4. Go to the **Summary** worksheet. The rental income from Retail for Quarter 4 (cell E11) is 5,725, the rental income from Retail for 2017 (cell F11) is $22,077, the total rental income for Quarter 4 (cell E12) is $50,316, and the total rental income in 2017 (cell F12) is $199,739. See Figure 6-22.

Figure 6-22 Revised Retail rental income for Quarter 4 in the Jackson workbook

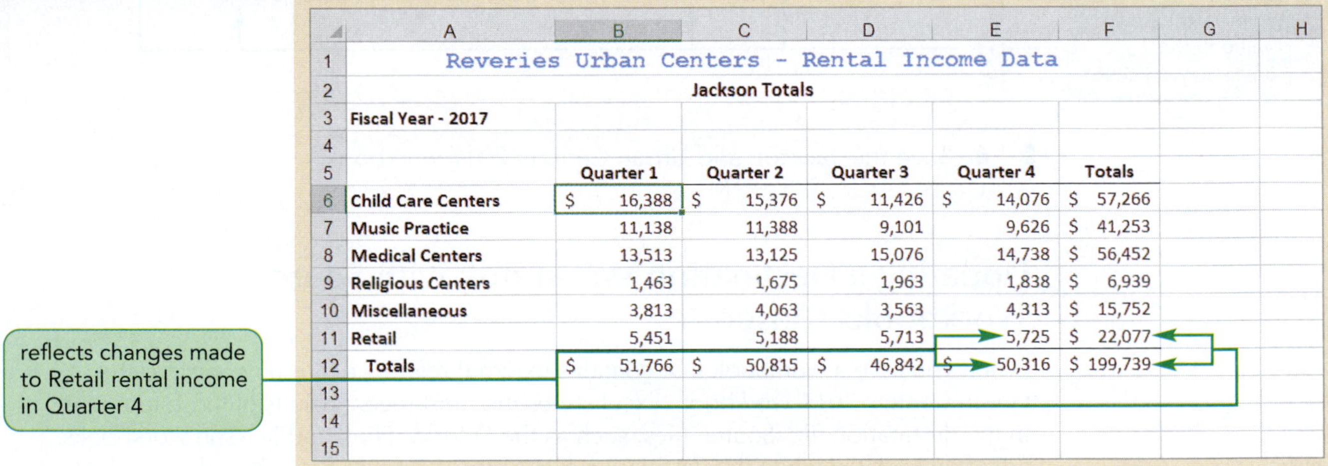

	A	B	C	D	E	F	G	H
1	Reveries Urban Centers - Rental Income Data							
2			Jackson Totals					
3	Fiscal Year - 2017							
4								
5		Quarter 1	Quarter 2	Quarter 3	Quarter 4	Totals		
6	Child Care Centers	$ 16,388	$ 15,376	$ 11,426	$ 14,076	$ 57,266		
7	Music Practice	11,138	11,388	9,101	9,626	$ 41,253		
8	Medical Centers	13,513	13,125	15,076	14,738	$ 56,452		
9	Religious Centers	1,463	1,675	1,963	1,838	$ 6,939		
10	Miscellaneous	3,813	4,063	3,563	4,313	$ 15,752		
11	Retail	5,451	5,188	5,713	5,725	$ 22,077		
12	Totals	$ 51,766	$ 50,815	$ 46,842	$ 50,316	$ 199,739		
13								
14								
15								

reflects changes made to Retail rental income in Quarter 4

5. Save the Jackson workbook, and then close it.

Now you'll open the destination file (the Urban Centers 2017 workbook). The rental income from the source workbooks won't be updated until you specify that it should. When the destination file is open and the source files are closed, the complete file path is included as part of the external reference formula that appears in the formula bar.

To open and update the destination workbook:

1. Open the **Urban Centers 2017** workbook, and then go to the **Summary** worksheet, if necessary. The value in cell E11 has *not* changed; it is still 19,080. A dialog box appears, indicating that the workbook contains links to one or more external sources that could be unsafe. See Figure 6-23.

Figure 6-23 Dialog box warning of possible unsafe links

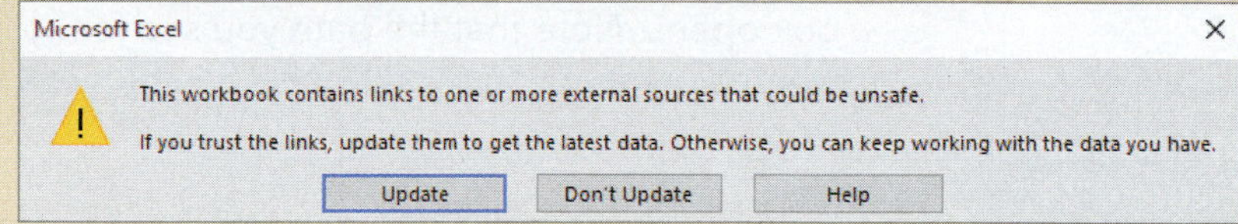

Trouble? If the Message Bar appears below the ribbon with "SECURITY WARNING Automatic update of links has been disabled," click the Enable Content button. The values in the destination workbook are updated. Continue with Step 3.

You want the current values in the source files to appear in the destination workbook.

2. In the dialog box, click the **Update** button. The values in the destination file are updated. The total rental income from Retail in Quarter 4, shown in cell E11 of the Urban Centers 2017 workbook, increased to 19,130, the rental income from Retail for 2017 (cell F11) is $74,562, the total Quarter 4 rental income (cell E12) is $153,971, and the grand total of all rental income in 2017 (cell F12) increased to $613,094.
3. Click cell **E11**, and then look at the complete file path for each external reference in the formula. The full path appears because the source workbooks are closed. Note that the path you see will match the location where you save your workbooks.
4. Save the workbook.

Managing Links

When workbooks are linked, the Edit Links dialog box provides ways to manage the links. You can review the status of the links and update the data in the files. You can repair **broken links**, which are references to files that have been moved since the link was created. Broken links appear in the dialog box as having an unknown status. You can also open the source file and break the links, which converts all external reference formulas to their most recent values.

After the fiscal year audit is completed and the source workbooks are final, Timothy will archive the summary workbook and move the files to an off-site storage location as part of his year-end backup process. You will save a copy of the Urban Centers 2017 workbook and then break the links to the source files in the copy.

To save a copy of the Urban Centers 2017 workbook and open the Edit Links dialog box:

1. Save the Urban Centers 2017 workbook as **Urban Centers Audited 2018** in the location specified by your instructor. The Urban Centers 2017 workbook closes, and the Urban Centers Audited 2018 workbook remains open.
2. On the ribbon, click the **Data** tab.
3. In the Connections group, click the **Edit Links** button. The Edit Links dialog box opens. Note that the path you see for source files will match the location where you save your workbooks. See Figure 6-24.

Figure 6-24 Edit Links dialog box

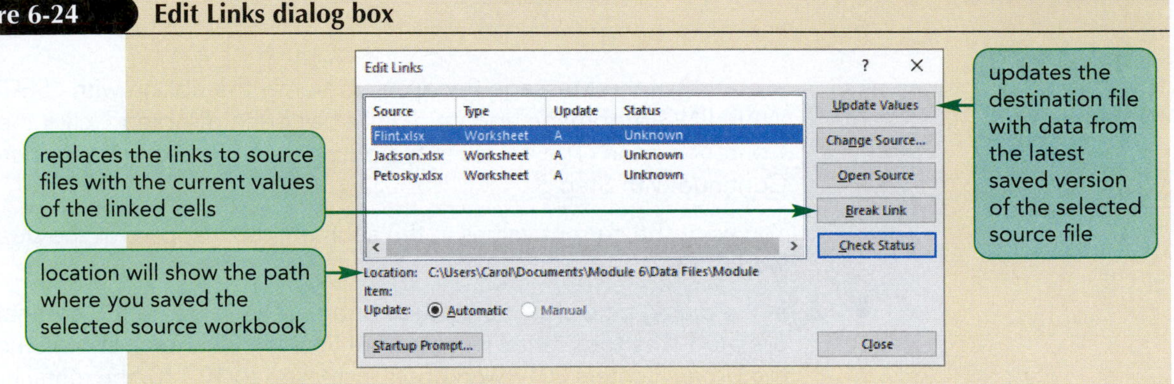

The Edit Links dialog box lists all of the files to which the destination workbook is linked so that you can update, change, open, or remove the links. You can see that the destination workbook—Urban Centers Audited 2018—has links to the Flint, Jackson, and Petosky workbooks. The dialog box shows the following information about each link:

- **Source**—indicates the file to which the link points. The Urban Centers Audited 2018 workbook contains three links pointing to the Flint.xlsx, Jackson.xlsx, and Petosky.xlsx workbooks.
- **Type**—identifies the type of each source file. In this case, the type is an Excel worksheet, but it could also be a Word document, a PowerPoint presentation, or some other type of file.
- **Update**—specifies the way values are updated from the source file. The letter *A* indicates the link is updated automatically when you open the workbook or when both the source and destination files are open simultaneously. The letter *M* indicates the link must be updated manually by the user, which is useful when you want to see the older data values before updating to the new data. To manually update the link and see the new data values, click the Update Values button.
- **Status**—shows whether Excel successfully accessed the link and updated the values from the source document (status is OK), or Excel has not attempted to update the links in this session (status is Unknown). The status of the three links in the Urban Centers Audited 2018 workbook is Unknown.

Timothy wants you to break the links so that the Urban Centers Audited 2018 workbook contains only the updated values (and is no longer affected by changes in the source files). Then he wants you to save the Urban Centers Audited 2018 workbook for him to archive. This allows Timothy to store a "snapshot" of the data at the end of the fiscal year.

To convert all external reference formulas to their current values:

1. In the Edit Links dialog box, click the **Break Link** button. A dialog box opens, alerting you that breaking links in the workbook permanently converts formulas and external references to their existing values.
2. Click the **Break Links** button. No links appear in the Edit Links dialog box.
3. Click the **Close** button. The Urban Centers Audited 2018 workbook now contains values instead of formulas with external references.
4. Select cell **B6**. The value $44,263 appears in the cell and the formula bar; the link (the external reference formula) was replaced with the data value. All of the cells in the range B6:E11 contain values rather than external reference formulas.
5. Save the Urban Centers Audited 2018 workbook, and then close it. The Urban Centers 2017 workbook contains external reference formulas, and the Urban Centers Audited 2018 workbook contains current values.

TIP

You cannot undo the break link action. To restore the links, you must reenter the external reference formulas.

In this session, you worked with multiple worksheets and workbooks, summarizing data and linking workbooks. This ensures that the data in the summary workbook is accurate and remains updated with the latest data in the source files. In the next session, you will create templates and hyperlinks.

REVIEW

Session 6.2 Quick Check

1. What is the external reference to the range B6:F6 in the Grades worksheet in the Grade Book workbook located in the Course folder on drive D?
2. What is a source file?
3. What is a destination file?
4. What are the layouts that you can use to arrange multiple workbooks?
5. How are linked workbooks updated when both the destination and source files are open?
6. How are linked workbooks updated when the source file is changed and the destination file is closed?
7. How would you determine what workbooks a destination file is linked to?
8. What happens to an external reference formula in a cell after you break the links in the worksheet?

Session 6.3 Visual Overview:

This Weekly Time Sheet workbook was created from one of the templates available from Office.com. Microsoft provides many templates that you can download.

A template is a workbook with labels, formats, and formulas already built into it with data removed. In other words, a template includes everything but the variable data.

A template can use any Excel feature, including formatting, formulas, and charts. The template used to create this workbook includes labels, formatting, and formulas.

Variable data is entered in the workbook created from the template. In this workbook, employee data was entered to fill out the weekly time record.

The formulas to calculate the total hours worked and total pay were included in the template.

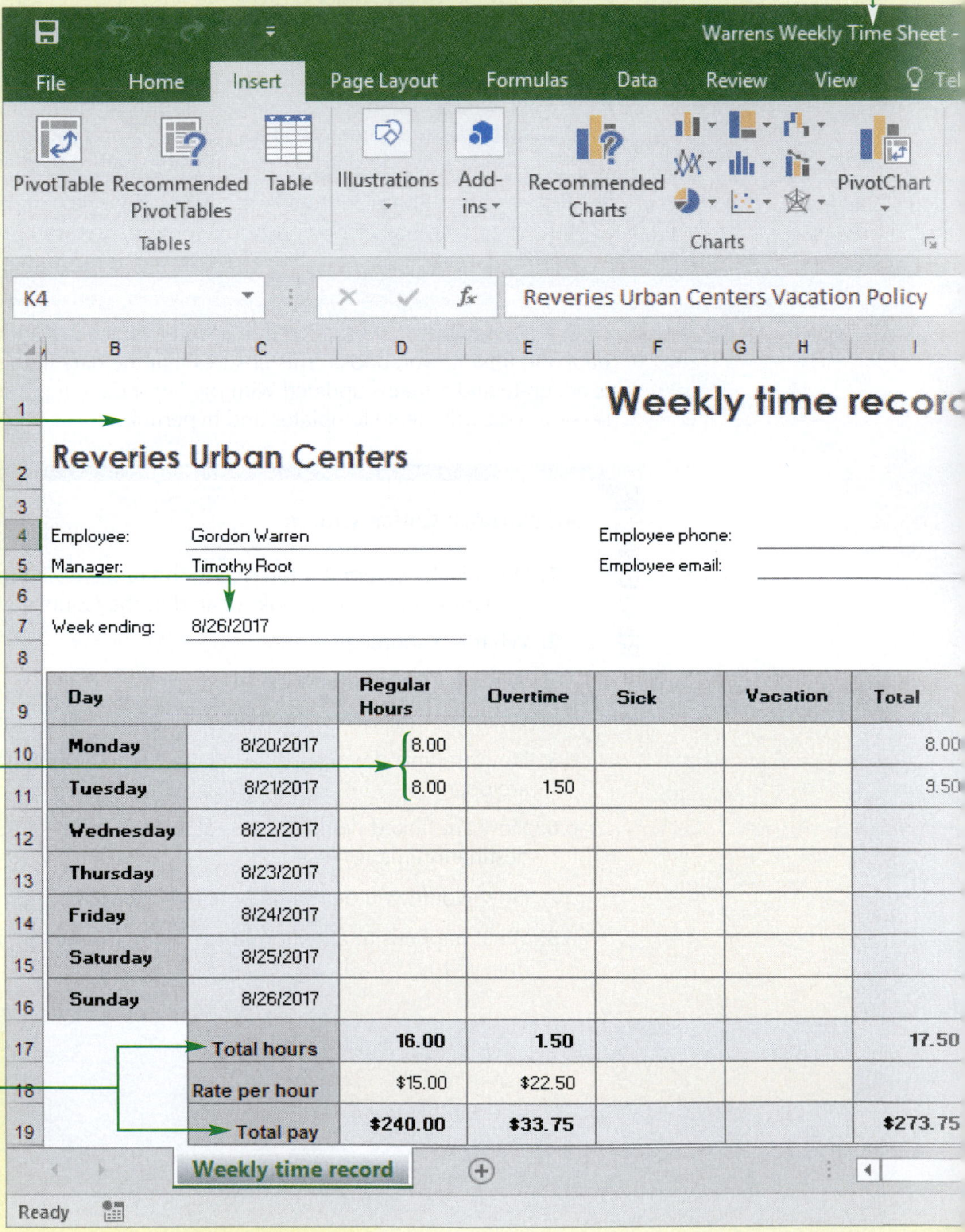

Templates and Hyperlinks

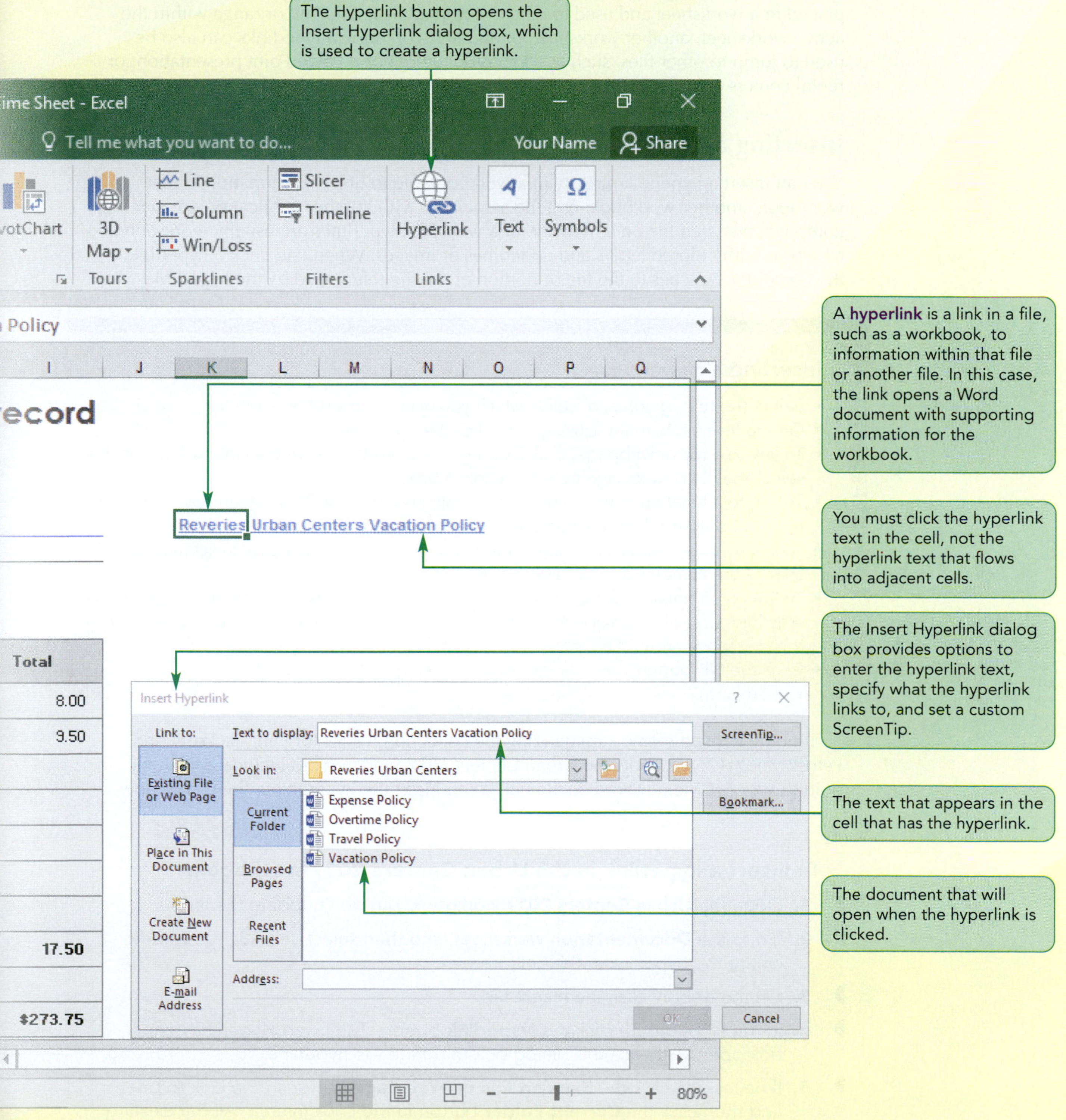
The Hyperlink button opens the Insert Hyperlink dialog box, which is used to create a hyperlink.
Time Sheet - Excel
Tell me what you want to do...
Your Name
Share
PivotChart
3D Map
Tours
Line
Column
Win/Loss
Sparklines
Slicer
Timeline
Filters
Hyperlink
Links
Text
Symbols
Policy
record
Reveries Urban Centers Vacation Policy
Total
8.00
9.50
17.50
$273.75
Insert Hyperlink
Link to:
Existing File or Web Page
Place in This Document
Create New Document
E-mail Address
Text to display: Reveries Urban Centers Vacation Policy
ScreenTip...
Look in: Reveries Urban Centers
Current Folder
Browsed Pages
Recent Files
Expense Policy
Overtime Policy
Travel Policy
Vacation Policy
Bookmark...
Address:
OK
Cancel
80%
A hyperlink is a link in a file, such as a workbook, to information within that file or another file. In this case, the link opens a Word document with supporting information for the workbook.
You must click the hyperlink text in the cell, not the hyperlink text that flows into adjacent cells.
The Insert Hyperlink dialog box provides options to enter the hyperlink text, specify what the hyperlink links to, and set a custom ScreenTip.
The text that appears in the cell that has the hyperlink.
The document that will open when the hyperlink is clicked.

Creating a Hyperlink

A hyperlink is a link in a file, such as a workbook, to information within that file or another file. Although hyperlinks are most often found on webpages, they can also be placed in a worksheet and used to quickly jump to a specific cell or range within the active worksheet, another worksheet, or another workbook. Hyperlinks can also be used to jump to other files, such as a Word document or a PowerPoint presentation, or rental centers on the web.

Inserting a Hyperlink

You can insert a hyperlink directly in a workbook file to link to information in that workbook, another workbook, or a file associated with another application on your computer, a shared file on a network, or a website. Hyperlinks are usually represented by words with colored letters and underlines or images. When you click a hyperlink, the computer switches to the file or portion of the file referenced by the hyperlink.

REFERENCE

Inserting a Hyperlink

- Select the text, graphic, or cell in which you want to insert the hyperlink.
- On the Insert tab, in the Links group, click the Hyperlink button.
- To link to a file or webpage, click Existing File or Web Page in the Link to list, and then select the file or webpage from the Look in box.
- To link to a location in the current workbook, click Place in This Document in the Link to list, and then select the worksheet, cell, or range in the current workbook.
- To link to a new document, click Create New Document in the Link to list, and then specify the filename and path of the new document.
- To link to an email address, click E-mail Address in the Link to list, and then enter the email address of the recipient (such as name@example.com) and a subject line for the message.
- Click the OK button.

Timothy wrote a memo summarizing the collection results for Flint, Jackson, and Petosky in 2017. He wants the Urban Centers 2017 workbook to include a link that points to the UCMemo Word document. You'll insert the hyperlink to the memo now.

To insert a hyperlink in the Urban Centers 2017 workbook:

1. Open the **Urban Centers 2017** workbook, but don't update the links.
2. Go to the **Documentation** worksheet, and then select cell **A8**. You want to create the hyperlink in this cell.
3. On the ribbon, click the **Insert** tab.
4. In the Links group, click the **Hyperlink** button. The Insert Hyperlink dialog box opens. You use this dialog box to define the hyperlink.
5. If necessary, click the **Existing File or Web Page** button in the Link to bar, and then click the **Current Folder** button in the Look in area. All the existing files and folders in the current folder are displayed. See Figure 6-25, which shows the Excel6 > Module folder included with your Data Files.

Figure 6-25 **Insert Hyperlink dialog box**

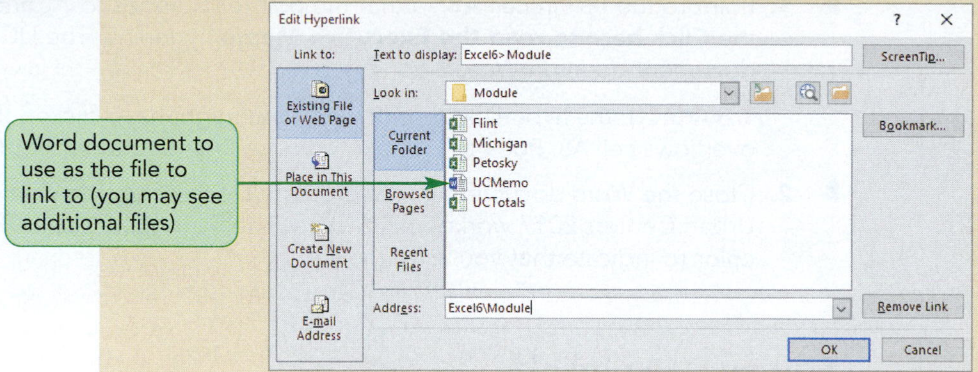

6. Click the **UCMemo** Word document in the list of files. This is the file you want to open when the hyperlink is clicked.
7. Click the **Text to display** box, select the filename in the box, and then type **Click here to read the Executive Memo** as the hyperlink text that will appear in cell A8 in the Documentation worksheet.
8. Click the **OK** button. The hyperlink text entered in cell A8 is underlined and in a blue font, indicating that the text within the cell is a hyperlink. See Figure 6-26.

Figure 6-26 **Hyperlink to the Reveries Urban Centers memo**

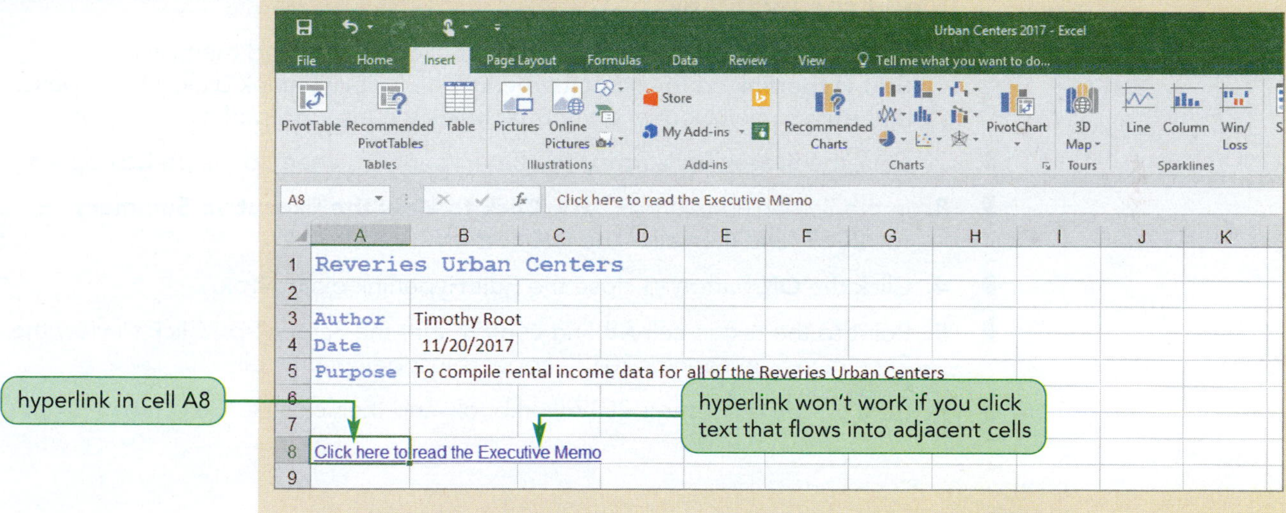

You will test the hyperlink that you just created to ensure it works correctly. To use a hyperlink in a worksheet, you must click the text inside the cell that contains the link. If you click white space in the cell or any text that flows into an adjacent cell, the hyperlink does not work.

To test the hyperlink to the UCMemo:

1. Point to the text in cell **A8** so that the pointer changes to the pointing hand, and then click the **Click here to read the Executive Memo** hyperlink. The UCMemo document opens in Word.

   Trouble? If the hyperlink doesn't work, you might have clicked the text that overflows cell A8. Point to the text within cell A8, and then click the hyperlink.

2. Close the Word document and Word. The Documentation worksheet in the Urban Centers 2017 workbook is active. The hyperlink in cell A8 changed color to indicate that you used the link.

Editing a Hyperlink

TIP

You can right-click a hyperlink cell and then click Clear Contents to delete a hyperlink or click Remove Hyperlink to delete the hyperlink but keep the text.

You can modify an existing hyperlink by changing its target file or webpage, modifying the text that is displayed, or changing the ScreenTip for the hyperlink. ScreenTips, which appear whenever you place the pointer over a hyperlink, provide additional information about the target of the link. The default ScreenTip is the folder location and filename of the file you will link to, which isn't very helpful. You can insert a more descriptive ScreenTip when you create a hyperlink or edit an existing hyperlink.

Timothy wants you to edit the hyperlink to the memo so that it has a more descriptive ScreenTip.

To edit the hyperlink:

1. In the Documentation worksheet, right-click cell **A8**, and then click **Edit Hyperlink** on the shortcut menu. The Edit Hyperlink dialog box opens; it has the same layout and information as the Insert Hyperlink dialog box.
2. Click the **ScreenTip** button. The Set Hyperlink ScreenTip dialog box opens.
3. In the ScreenTip text box, type **Click to view the Executive Summary for 2017**, and then click the **OK** button.
4. Click the **OK** button to close the Edit Hyperlink dialog box.
5. Point to the text in cell **A8** and confirm that the ScreenTip "Click to view the Executive Summary for 2017" appears just below the cell.
6. Save the Urban Centers 2017 workbook, and then close it. Excel remains open.

Using Templates

If you want to create a new workbook that has the same format as an existing workbook, you could save the existing workbook with a new name and replace the values with new data or blank cells. The potential drawback to this method is that you might forget to rename the original file and overwrite data you intended to keep. A better method is to create a template workbook that includes all the text (row and column labels), formatting, and formulas but does not contain any data. The template workbook is a model from which you create new workbooks. When you create a new workbook from a template, an unnamed copy of the template opens. You can then enter data as well as modify the existing content or structure as needed. Any changes or additions you make to the new workbook do not affect the template file; the next time you create a workbook based on the template, the original text, formatting, and formulas will be present.

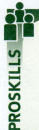

PROSKILLS

Teamwork: Using Excel Templates

A team working together will often need to create the same types of workbooks. Rather than each person or group designing a different workbook, each team member should create a workbook from the same template. The completed workbooks will then all have the same structure with identical formatting and formulas. Not only does this ensure consistency and accuracy, it also makes it easier to compile and summarize the results. Templates help teams work better together and avoid misunderstandings.

For example, a large organization may need to collect the same information from several regions. By creating and distributing a workbook template, each region knows what data to track and where to enter it. The template already includes the formulas, so the results are calculated consistently. If you want to review the formulas that are in the worksheet, you can display them using the Show Formula command in the Formula Auditing group on the Formulas tab or by pressing the Ctrl+` keys.

The following are just some of the advantages of using a template to create multiple workbooks with the same features:

- Templates save time and ensure consistency in the design and content of workbooks because all labels, formatting, and formulas are entered once.
- Templates ensure accuracy because formulas can be entered and verified once, and then used with confidence in all workbooks.
- Templates standardize the appearance and content of workbooks.
- Templates prevent data from being overwritten when an existing workbook is inadvertently saved with new data rather than saved as a new workbook.

If you are part of a team that needs to create the same type of workbook repeatedly, it's a good idea to use a template to both save time and ensure consistency in the design and content of the workbooks.

Creating a Workbook Based on an Existing Template

The Blank workbook template that you have used to create new, blank workbooks contains no text or formulas, but it includes formatting—General format applied to numbers, Calibri 11-point font, text left-aligned in cells, numbers and formula results right-aligned in cells, column widths set to 8.38 characters, one worksheet inserted in the workbook, and so forth.

Excel has many other templates available. Some are automatically installed on your hard drive when you install Excel. Other templates are available to download from the Office.com site or other sites that you can find by searching the web. These templates provide commonly used worksheet formats that can save you the time of creating the template yourself. Some of the task-specific templates available from the Office.com site include:

- **Family monthly budget planner**—builds projections and actual expenditures for items such as housing, transportation, and insurance
- **Inventory list**—tracks the cost and quantity reorder levels of inventory
- **Sports team roster**—organizes a list with each player's name, phone number, email address, and so forth
- **Employee time sheet**—creates an online time card to track employees' work hours
- **Expense report**—creates an expense report to track employee expenses for reimbursement

Using a template to create a new workbook lets you focus on the unique content for that workbook.

REFERENCE

Creating a Workbook Based on a Template

- On the ribbon, click the File tab, and then click New in the navigation bar.
- On the New screen, click a template category for the type of workbook you want to create (or type a keyword in the Search for online templates box, and then press the Enter key).
- Click the template you want to create, then click the Create button.
- Save the workbook based on the template with a new filename.

Gordon Warren, manager for the Petosky rental center, uses the Weekly time sheet template to submit his work hours to Timothy. You'll download this template and enter Gordon's most recent hours. *If you don't have an Internet connection, you should read but not complete the steps involving creating and using the online template.*

To create a workbook based on the Weekly time sheet template:

1. On the ribbon, click the **File** tab.
2. Click **New** in the navigation bar. The New screen in Backstage view shows the available templates on your computer and template categories on Office.com.
3. Click in the **Search for online templates** box, type **time sheets**, and then press the **Enter** key. All of the available time sheet templates are displayed. See Figure 6-27.

Figure 6-27 New screen with available time sheet templates

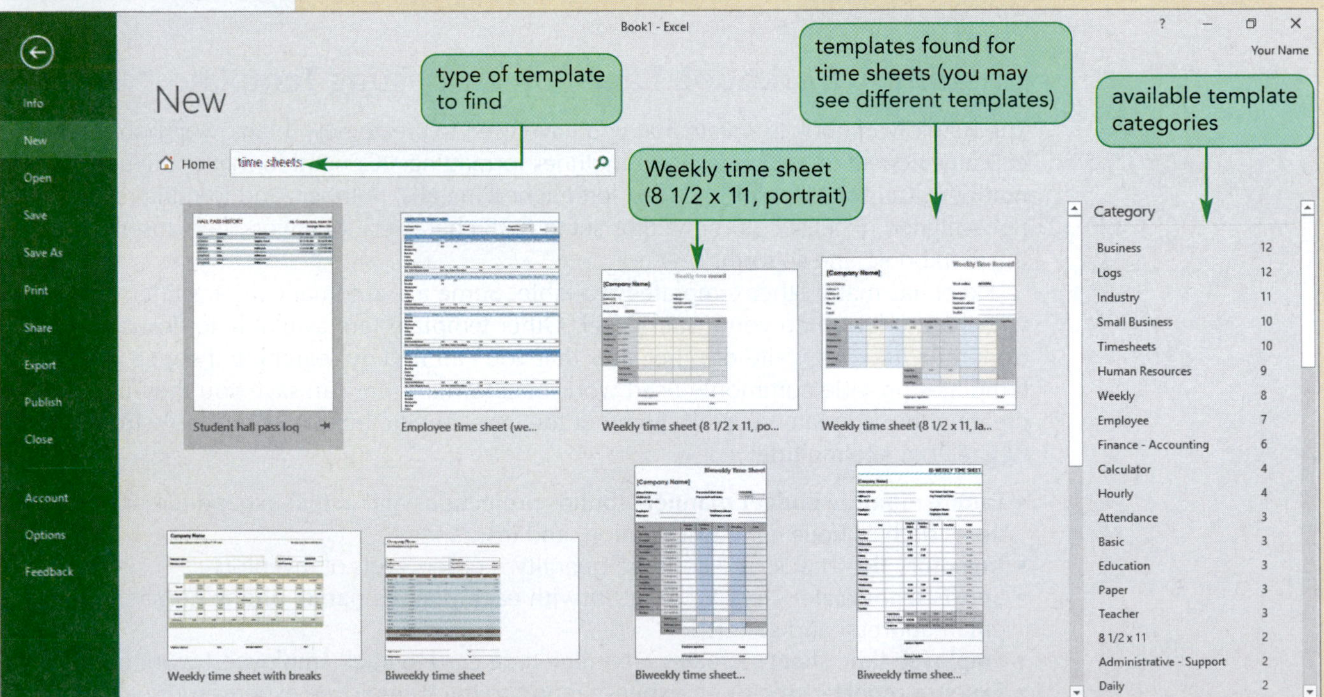

4. Click **Weekly time sheet (8 1/2 × 11, portrait)**. A preview of a worksheet based on the selected template appears in the center of the screen. If this is not the template you need, you can scroll through the time sheets by clicking the left or right arrow button. See Figure 6-28.

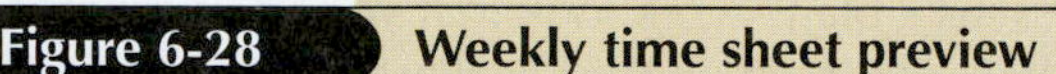

Figure 6-28 Weekly time sheet preview

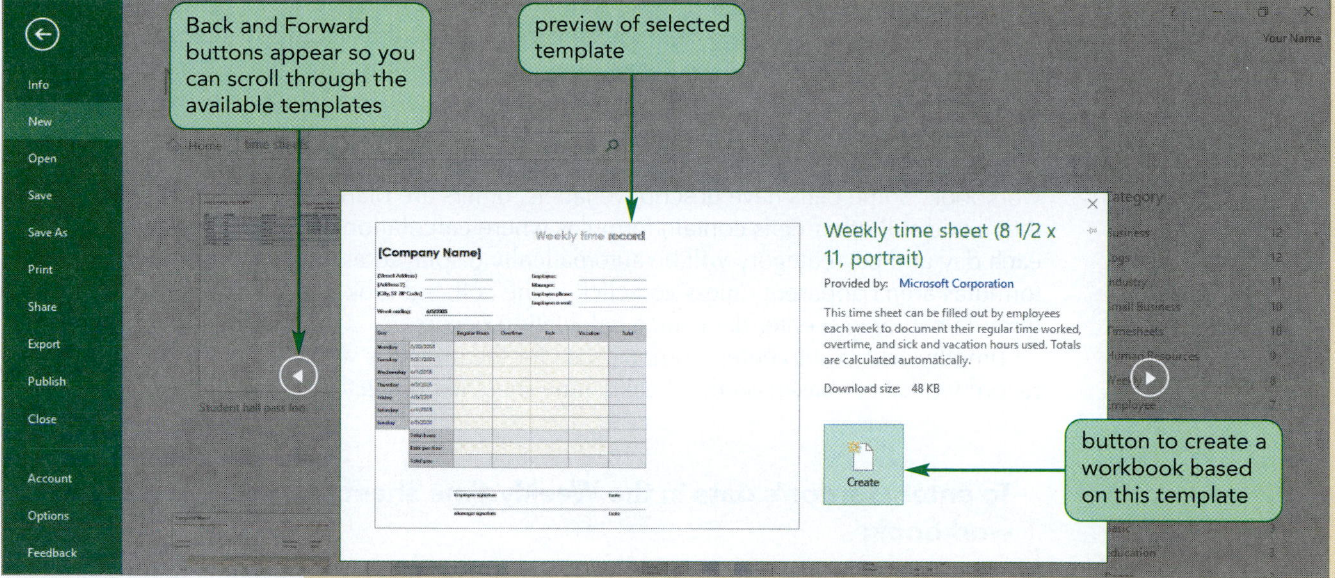
Back and Forward buttons appear so you can scroll through the available templates
preview of selected template
button to create a workbook based on this template
Weekly time sheet (8 1/2 x 11, portrait)
Provided by: Microsoft Corporation
This time sheet can be filled out by employees each week to document their regular time worked, overtime, and sick and vacation hours used. Totals are calculated automatically.
Download size: 48 KB
Create

5. Click the **Create** button. A new workbook based on the selected template opens. See Figure 6-29.

Figure 6-29 Workbook created from the Weekly time sheet template

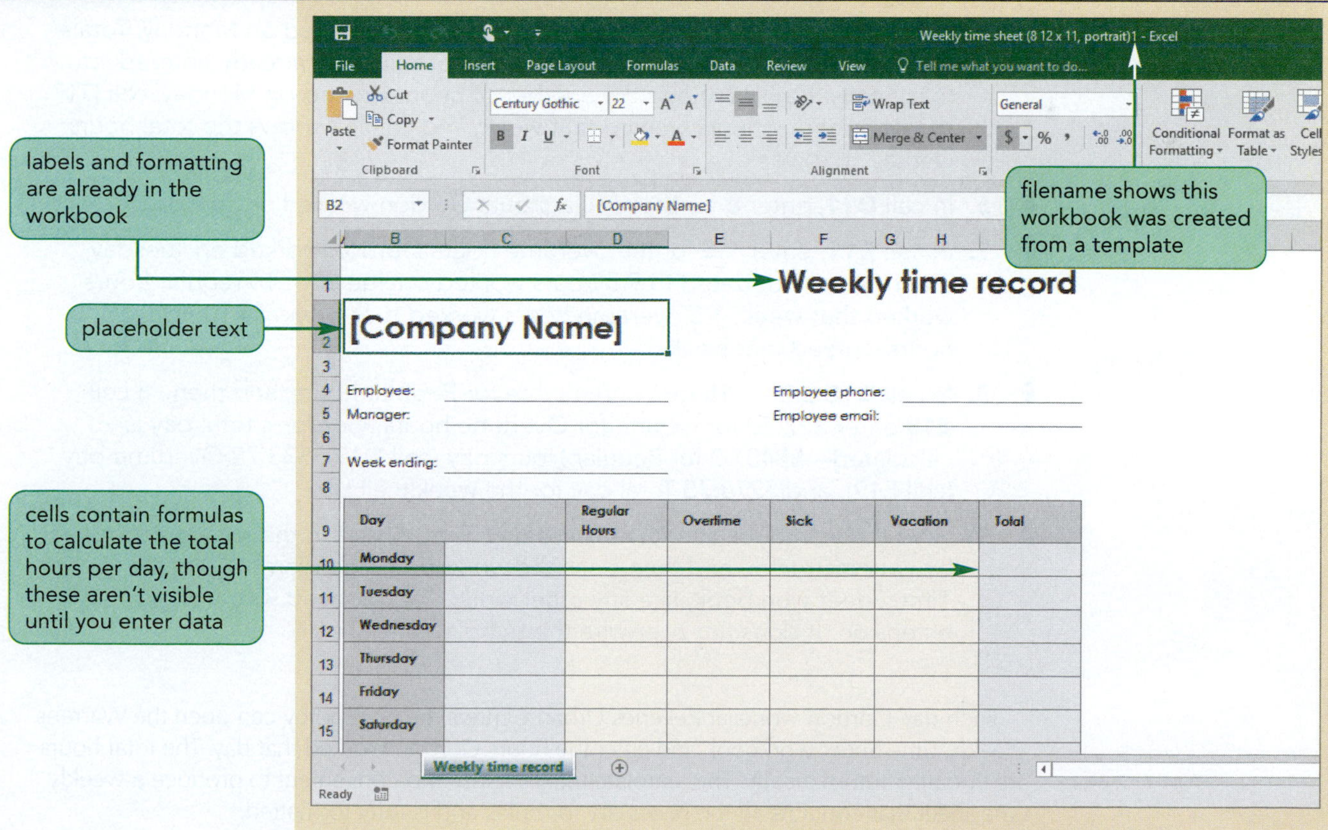
labels and formatting are already in the workbook
placeholder text
cells contain formulas to calculate the total hours per day, though these aren't visible until you enter data
filename shows this workbook was created from a template
Weekly time sheet (8 12 x 11, portrait)1 - Excel
Weekly time record
[Company Name]
Employee:
Manager:
Employee phone:
Employee email:
Week ending:
Day
Regular Hours
Overtime
Sick
Vacation
Total
Monday
Tuesday
Wednesday
Thursday
Friday
Saturday
Weekly time record

A workbook based on a specific template always displays the name of the template followed by a sequential number. Just as a blank workbook that you open is named Book1, Book2, and so forth, the workbook based on the Weekly time sheet template is named "Weekly time sheet (8 ½ x 11, portrait)1" in the title bar, not "Weekly time sheet." Any changes or additions to data, formatting, or formulas that you make affect only this workbook and not the template (in this case, the Weekly time sheet template). When you save the workbook, the Save As screen opens so you can save the workbook with a new name and to the location you specify.

Look at the labels and formatting already included in the Weekly time sheet workbook. Some cells have descriptive labels, others are blank so you can enter data in them, and still other cells contain formulas where calculations for total hours worked each day and pay category will be automatically displayed as data is entered. The formulas aren't apparent unless you click in the cell and look at the cell contents in the formula bar, or you enter data and a calculation occurs.

Timothy asks you to enter Gordon's data for the previous week in the Weekly time record worksheet based on the Weekly time sheet template.

To enter Gordon's data in the Weekly time sheet (8 ½ x 11, portrait)1 workbook:

1. In cell **B2,** enter **Reveries Urban Centers** as the company name, and then format the text in **18** point font size.
2. In cell **C4,** enter **Gordon Warren** as the employee.
3. In cell **C5,** enter **Timothy Root** as the manager.
4. In cell **C7**, enter **8/26/2017** as the week ending date.
5. In cell **D10**, enter **8** for the regular hours Gordon worked on Monday. Totals appear in cells I10, D17, and I17 because formulas are already entered into these cells. Cell I10 shows the number of hours worked on Monday, cell D17 shows 8 regular hours worked that week, and cell I17 shows the total hours worked that week.
6. In cell **D11**, enter **8** for the regular hours Gordon worked on Tuesday.
7. In cell **E11**, enter **1.5** for the overtime hours Gordon worked on Tuesday. The totals are updated to 9.5 hours worked on Tuesday, 16 regular hours worked that week, 1.5 overtime hours worked that week, and 17.5 total hours worked that week.
8. In cell **D18** enter $15 for Warren's rate for Regular hours, and then, in cell **E18** enter $22.50 for his rate for Overtime hours. Gordon's total pay is calculated—$240.00 for Regular Hours pay (cell D19), $33.75 Overtime pay (cell E19), and $273.75 Total pay for the week (cell I19).
9. Save the workbook as **Warrens Weekly Time Sheet** in the location specified by your instructor, and then close the workbook. The Warrens Weekly Time Sheet workbook, like any other workbook, is saved with the .xlsx file extension. It does not overwrite the template file.

Each day Gordon works at Reveries Urban Centers, he or Timothy can open the Warrens Weekly Time Sheet workbook and enter the hours Gordon worked that day. The total hours are updated automatically. The template makes it fast and convenient to produce a weekly time sheet that contains all the necessary formulas and is fully formatted.

Creating a Custom Workbook Template

A **custom template** is a workbook template you create that is ready to run with the formulas for all calculations included as well as all formatting and labels. A template can use any Excel feature, including formulas and charts. To create a custom template, you build the workbook with all the necessary labels, formatting, and data, and then you save the workbook as a template. The template includes everything but the variable data. You can also create a template from a chart or chart sheet.

When you save a workbook as an Excel template file, the save location in the Save As dialog box defaults to the Templates folder. Although template files are usually stored in the Templates folder, you can store template files in any folder. However, custom template files stored in the Templates folder are available on the New screen in Backstage view.

All template files have the .xltx file extension. This extension differentiates template files from workbook files, which have the .xlsx file extension. After you have saved a workbook in a template format, you can make the template accessible to other users.

REFERENCE

Creating a Custom Template

- Prepare the workbook—enter values, text, and formulas as needed; apply formatting; and replace data values with zeros or blank cells.
- On the ribbon, click the File tab, and then click Save As in the navigation bar.
- Click the Browse button to open the Save As dialog box.
- In the File name box, enter the template name.
- Click the Save as type button, and then click Excel Template.
- If you don't want to save the template in the Custom Office Templates folder, select another folder in which to save the template file.
- Click the Save button.

or

- Create the chart you want to use for the template.
- Right-click the chart, and then click Save as Template.
- In the Save Chart Template dialog box, enter a filename, then select a folder in which to save the template file if you don't want to store it in the Charts subfolder of the Templates folder.
- Click the Save button.

The three rental income workbooks for 2017 have the same format. Timothy wants to use this workbook format for rental income data and analysis for next year. He asks you to create a template from one of the rental center workbooks. You'll save the Jackson workbook as a template file to use as the basis for the custom template.

To save the Jackson workbook as a template:

1. Open the **Jackson** workbook you created in this Module.
2. On the ribbon, click the **File** tab to open Backstage view, and then in the navigation bar, click **Save As**. The Save As screen appears.
3. Select the location where you are saving the files for this Module.
4. In the File name box, type **Urban Centers Template** as the template name.

5. Click the **Save as type** button, and then click **Excel Template**. The save location changes to the Custom Office Templates folder on your computer. You want to save the template in the same location as the other files you created in this Module.
6. Navigate to the location where you are storing the files you create in this Module.
7. Click the **Save** button. The Urban Centers Template is saved in the location you specified.

Make sure you change the save location so you can easily find and use the template file later in the next set of steps.

TIP

You can use a fill color or cell style to differentiate input cells from other cells in the worksheet.

When you create a template from an existing workbook, you should remove any values and text that will change in each workbook created from the custom template. Be careful not to delete the formulas. Also, you should make sure that all of the formulas work as intended, the numbers and text are entered correctly, and the worksheet is formatted appropriately.

Next, you will clear the data from the template file, so that the input cells are ready for new data. You will leave the formulas that you already entered. You will also add placeholder text to the template to remind users what labels they need to enter.

To prepare a custom template from the Urban Centers Template:

1. With the Urban Centers Template open, group the **Quarter 1** through **Quarter 4** worksheets. The worksheet group includes the four quarterly worksheets but not the Summary and Documentation worksheets.
2. Select the range **B6:D11.** This range includes the rental income data. You want to delete these values.
3. Right-click the selected range, and then click **Clear Contents** on the shortcut menu. The data values are cleared from the selected range in each of the quarterly worksheets, but the formulas and formatting remain intact. The cleared cells are blank. The ranges E6:E12 and B12:D12 display dashes, representing zeros, where there are formulas.
4. Change the fill color of the selected range to the **Dark Blue, Text 2, Lighter 80%** theme color. The blue fill color indicates where users should enter data for rental income in the quarterly worksheets.
5. In cell **A2,** enter **[Center Name]** as the placeholder text to remind users to enter the correct rental center name.
6. Go to the **Summary** worksheet. The quarterly worksheets are ungrouped, and dashes, representing zeros, appear in the cells in the ranges B6:F12, which contain formulas.
7. In cell **A2**, enter **[Center Name]** as the placeholder text to remind users to enter the correct rental center name.
8. In cell **A3,** enter **[Enter Fiscal Year - yyyy]**. This text will remind users to enter the year.
9. Group the **Summary** through **Quarter 4** worksheets, and then make sure column A is wide enough to see the entire contents of cell A3. See Figure 6-30.

Figure 6-30 Worksheet modified to be used as a custom template

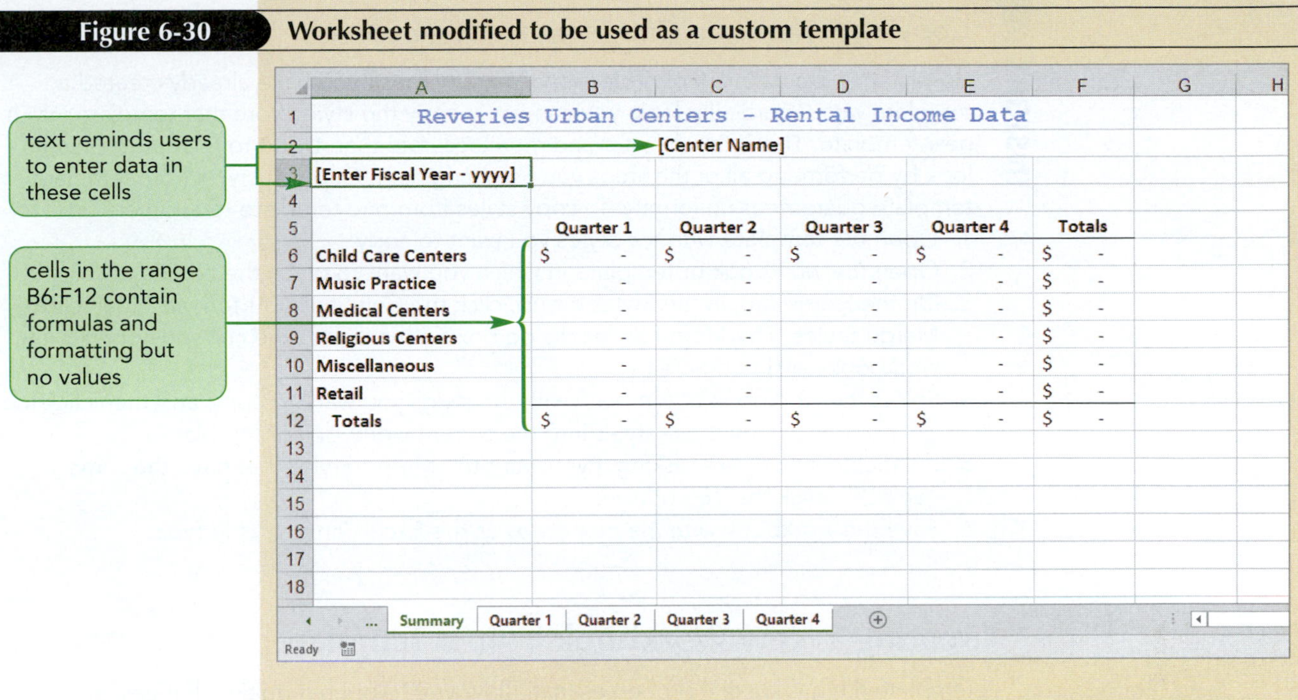

10. Go to the **Documentation** worksheet, and then delete your name and the date from the range B3:B4.
11. In cell **B5**, enter **To compile the rental income for [Center Name]**. The Documentation worksheet is updated to reflect the purpose of the workbook.
12. Save the Urban Centers Template, and then close it.

Timothy will use the Urban Centers Template file to create the workbooks to track next year's rental income for each rental center and then distribute the workbooks to each rental center manager. By basing these new workbooks on the template file, Timothy has a standard workbook with identical formatting and formulas for each manager to use. He also avoids the risk of accidentally changing the workbook containing the 2017 data when preparing for 2018.

INSIGHT

Copying Styles from One Template to Another

Consistency is a hallmark of professional documents. If you have already created a template with a particular look, you can easily copy the styles from that template into a new template. This is much faster and more accurate than trying to recreate the same look by performing all of the steps you used originally. Copying styles from template to template guarantees uniformity. To copy styles from one template to another:

1. Open the template with the styles you want to copy.
2. Open the workbook or template in which you want to place the copied styles.
3. On the Home tab, in the Styles group, click the Cell Styles button, and then click Merge Styles. The Merge Styles dialog box opens, listing the currently open workbooks and templates.
4. Select the workbook or template with the styles you want to copy, and then click the OK button to copy those styles into the current workbook or template.
5. If a dialog box opens, asking if you want to "Merge Styles that have the same names?", click the YES button.
6. Save the workbook with the new styles as the Excel Template file type.

Creating a New Workbook from a Template

A template file has special properties that allow you to open it, make changes, and save it in a new location. Only the data must be entered because the formulas are already in the template file. The original template file is not changed by this process. After you have saved a template, you can access the template from the New screen in Backstage view or in the location you saved it.

Timothy wants all Reveries Urban Centers locations to collect rental income data in the same format and submit the workbooks to the central office for analysis. He wants you to create a workbook for fiscal year 2018 based on the Urban Centers Template file. You will enter Jackson as the rental center name where indicated on all of the worksheets and then enter test data for January.

TIP

To create a copy of workbook based on a template stored in the Custom Office Templates folder, click the File tab, click New in the navigation bar, click Personal below the Search for online templates box, and then click the template.

To create a new workbook based on the Reveries Urban Centers Template file:

1. On the taskbar, click the **File Explorer** button. The File Explorer window opens.
2. Navigate to the location where you stored the template file.
3. Double-click the **Urban Centers Template** file. A new workbook opens named "Urban Centers Template1" to indicate this is the first copy of the Urban Centers workbook created during the current Excel session.
4. Go to the **Summary** worksheet, in cell **A2** replace [Center Name] with **Jackson Total**, and then, in cell **A3**, enter **Fiscal Year – 2018**.
5. Group the **Quarter 1** through **Quarter 4** worksheets, and then in cell **A2**, replace [Center Name] with **Jackson**.
6. Go to the **Documentation** worksheet to ungroup the worksheets.
7. In cell **B5**, replace [Center Name] with **Jackson.**
8. Go to the **Quarter 1** worksheet. The text "Fiscal Year - 2018" appears in cell A4.
9. In each cell in the range **B6:B11**, which has the blue fill color, enter **100**.
10. Review the totals in the range E6:E11 (the cells that contain formulas to sum each column). See Figure 6-31.

Figure 6-31 New workbook based on the Reveries Urban Centers template file

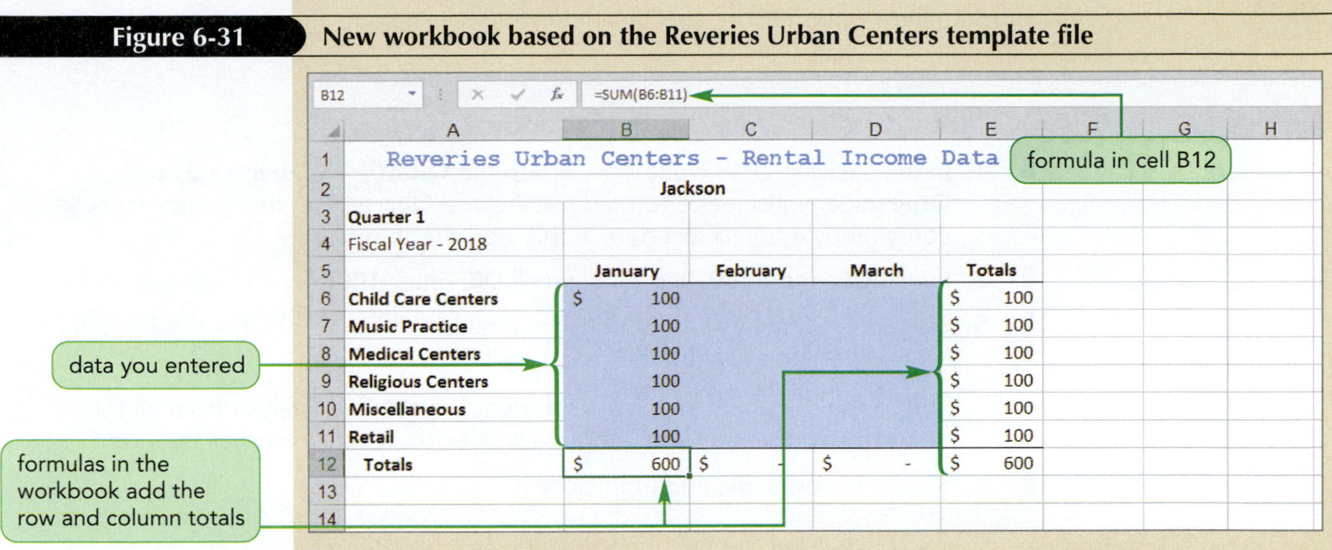

11. Go to the **Summary** worksheet. Totals appear in the ranges B6:B12 and F6:F12 as a result of the formulas in this worksheet. See Figure 6-32.

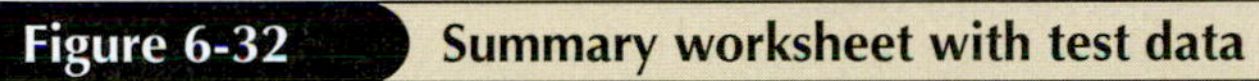

Figure 6-32 Summary worksheet with test data

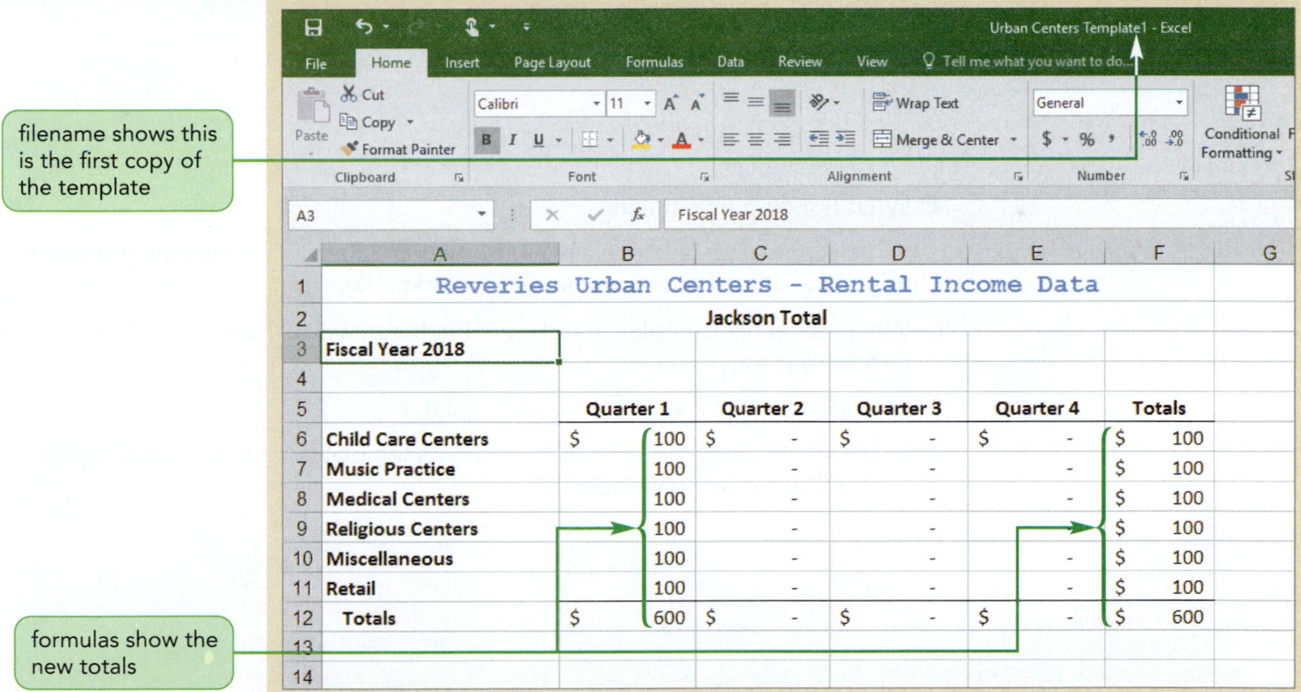

Make sure the Save as type box shows Excel Workbook so that you create a new workbook file without overwriting the template.

12. Save the workbook as **Jackson 2018** in the location specified by your instructor. The workbook is saved with the .xlsx file extension. The original template file is not changed.

You'll add data to the Quarter 2, Quarter 3, and Quarter 4 worksheets to verify that the Summary worksheet is correctly adding numbers from the four worksheets.

To test the Jackson 2018 workbook:

1. In the Jackson 2018 workbook, group the **Quarter 2, Quarter 3**, and **Quarter 4** worksheets. You did not include Quarter 1 in this group because you already entered test data in this worksheet.
2. In cell **C6**, enter **100**, and then in cell **D8**, enter **100**.
3. Go to the **Summary** worksheet. The total in cell F6 is $400, the total in cell F8 is $400, and the total for the year in cell F12 is $1,200.

   The formulas in the Summary worksheet correctly add values from all the quarterly worksheets. The template workbook is functioning as intended.
4. Save the workbook, and then close it.

The templates you created will ensure that all rental center managers enter data consistently, making it simpler for Timothy to add the rental income by rental type and time period for Reveries Urban Centers.

REVIEW

Session 6.3 Quick Check

1. How do you insert a hyperlink into a worksheet cell?
2. Why would you insert a hyperlink in a worksheet?
3. What is a template?
4. What is a custom template?
5. What is one advantage of using a custom template rather than simply using the original workbook file to create a new workbook?
6. What are some examples of task-specific templates available from the Office.com site?
7. How do you save a workbook as a template?
8. How do you create a workbook based on a template that is not saved in the Custom Office Templates folder?

PRACTICE

Review Assignment

Data Files needed for the Review Assignments: Midland.xlsx, NewUCMemo.docx, NewUC.xlsx, JacksonMI.xlsx, PetoskyMI.xlsx, FlintMI.xlsx.

Reveries Urban Centers opened a new rental center in Midland, Michigan, on January 1, 2017. Michael Verhallen, the manager of the Midland rental center, collected the year's rental income in a workbook provided by Timothy Root at the central office. Before Michael can send the completed workbook to Timothy for the year-end reporting, he needs you to summarize the results and format the worksheets. Complete the following:

1. Open the **Midland** workbook located in the Excel6 > Review folder included with your Data Files, and then save the workbook as **Midland MI** in the location specified by your instructor.
2. In the Documentation worksheet, enter your name and the date, and then review the worksheets in the workbook.
3. Create a worksheet group that contains the Quarter 1 through Quarter 4 worksheets.
4. In the worksheet group, in the range B12:D12, enter formulas that sum the values in each column, and then in the range E6:E12, enter formulas that sum the values in each row.
5. Format the quarterly worksheets as specified below:
   a. In cell E5 and cell A12, enter the label **Totals**.
   b. Increase the indent of cell A12 by one.
   c. In the range A2:A3, A6:A12;B5:E5, bold the text.
   d. Merge and center the range A1:E1 and the range A2:E2.
   e. In the range B5:E5, center the text.
   f. Add a bottom border to the range B5:E5 and the range B11:E11.
   g. Format the range B6:D6,B12:D12,E6:E12 with the Accounting style and no decimal places.
   h. Format the range B7:E11 with the Comma style and no decimal places.
6. Ungroup the worksheets, make a copy of the Quarter 1 worksheet, rename it as **Summary**, and then place it after the Documentation worksheet.
7. In the Summary worksheet, make the following changes:
   a. In cell A2, change the heading to **Midland Total**.
   b. Change cell A3 to **Fiscal Year - 2017**.
   c. Insert a column between columns B and C.
   d. In the range B5:E5, change the headings to **Quarter 1**, **Quarter 2**, **Quarter 3**, and **Quarter 4**, respectively.
   e. Make sure that the text in the range B5:F5 is centered.
   f. Clear the contents of the range B6:F11.
8. Complete the formulas in the Summary worksheet, as follows, using the Fill Without Formatting paste option so that you can keep the bottom border on the range B11:F11.
   a. In the range B6:E11, create formulas that reference cells in other worksheets to display the quarterly totals for the rental income by type. For example, the formula in cell B6 will reference cell E6 in the Quarter 1 worksheet.
   b. In the range F6:F11, create formulas that use 3-D cell references to calculate the total for each type of rental income.
   c. Copy the formula from cell B12 to cell C12.
9. Change the March rental income for medical centers to **1976**, and then verify that the total rental income for Medical Centers in Quarter 1 in the Summary worksheet is $5,214, the total rental income in Quarter 1 is $19,538, the total rental income for medical centers in 2017 is $22,186, and the total rental income for 2017 is $82,286.
10. Group the Quarter 1 through Quarter 4 worksheets, and then enter a formula in cell A4 that references cell A3 in the Summary worksheet.

11. In cell A8 of the Documentation worksheet, insert a hyperlink that points to the **NewUCMemo** located in the Module6 > Review folder included with your Data Files. Make sure the text to display is **Click here to read Midland Executive Memo**.
12. Edit the hyperlink to use the ScreenTip **Midland Rental Center Summary for 2017**.
13. Save the Midland MI workbook, and leave it open.
14. Open the **NewUC** workbook located in the Excel6 > Review folder included with your Data Files, and then save the workbook as **New Urban Centers** in the location specified by your instructor. In the Documentation worksheet enter your name and the date. Open the **JacksonMI**, **PetoskyMI**, and **FlintMI** workbooks located in the Excel6 > Review folder included with your Data Files.
15. Make the New Urban Centers the active workbook, and then arrange the workbooks in a tiled layout. The New Urban Centers is the full height of the screen on the left with the remaining four taking the rest the screen. In each workbook, hide the ribbon so you can see as much data in the Summary worksheet as possible.
16. In the Summary worksheet of the New Urban Centers workbook, enter external reference formulas to create a set of linked workbooks to summarize the totals for JacksonMI, PetoskyMI, Midland MI, and FlintMI. Format the Summary worksheet in the New UC Totals workbook so that the numbers are readable and the range B11:F11 has a bottom border.
17. Maximize the New Urban Centers and Midland MI worksheets, making sure that the ribbon is displayed. Save the New Urban Centers workbook, and leave it open. Close the JacksonMI, PetoskyMI, and FlintMI workbooks.
18. In the New Urban Centers workbook, break the links. Select a cell, and notice that the formula has been replaced with a value. Save the workbook as **New UC Audited 2018**.
19. Create headers and footers for the Summary worksheet. Display the name of the workbook and the name of the worksheet on separate lines in the right section of the header. Display your name and the date on separate lines in the right section of the footer. Save the New UC Audited 2018 workbook, and then close it.
20. Use the Midland MI workbook to create an Excel template with the filename **Midland MI Template** in the location specified by your instructor.
21. Create a new workbook based on the Midland MI Template file, and then save the workbook as **Midland MI 2018** in the location specified by your instructor. In the Documentation worksheet, enter your name and the date.
22. In the Summary worksheet, enter **2018** as the fiscal year in cell A3. The Center Name should be Midland in all worksheets. In the Quarter 1 worksheet, enter **500** in each cell in the range B6:D11. In the Quarter 2 worksheet, enter **1000** in each cell in the range B6:D11. Confirm that the values entered in this step are correctly totaled in the Summary worksheet.
23. Save the Midland MI 2018 workbook, and then close it.

APPLY

Case Problem 1

Data File needed for this Case Problem: Tea.xlsx

Paige's Tea Room Paige's Tea Room has three locations: Atlanta, Georgia; Naples, Florida; and New Orleans, Louisiana. Paige Sapienza is the chief of operations and supervises the ongoing business operations of the three tea rooms. She uses Excel to summarize annual sales data from each location in separate workbooks. She wants you to total the sales by type of tea and location for each quarter and then format each worksheet. Paige also wants you to calculate sales for all of the locations and types of tea. Complete the following:

1. Open the **Tea** workbook located in the Excel6 > Case1 folder included with your Data Files, and then save the document as **Tea Room** in the location specified by your instructor.
2. In the Documentation worksheet, enter your name and the date.
3. Group the Atlanta, Naples, and New Orleans worksheets.

4. In the grouped worksheets, calculate the quarterly totals in the range B12:E12 and the types of tea totals in the range F4:F12.
5. In cells A12 and F3, enter **Totals** as the labels.
6. Improve the look of the quarterly worksheets using the formatting of your choice. Ungroup the worksheets.
7. Place a copy of one of the location worksheets between the Documentation and Atlanta worksheets, and then rename the new worksheet as **Summary Sales**.
8. In the Summary Sales worksheet, delete the values in the range B4:E11, and then change the label in cell A2 to **Summary Sales**.
9. In the range B4:E11, enter formulas that add the sales in the corresponding cells of the four quarterly worksheets. Use 3-D references to calculate the sum of each tea type per quarter.
10. Set up the Summary Sales and the three location worksheets for printing. Each worksheet should be centered horizontally, display the name of the worksheet centered in the header, and display your name and the current date on separate lines in the right section of the footer.
11. Make sure that any grouped worksheets have been ungrouped, and then save the Tea Room workbook.
12. Save the workbook as an Excel template with the name **Tea Room Template** in the location specified by your instructor.
13. In the Documentation worksheet, clear your name and date. In each of the location worksheets, clear the sales data but not the formulas. Save and close the Tea Room Template.
14. Create a new workbook based on the **Tea Room Template** file, and then save the workbook as **Tea Room 2017** in the location specified by your instructor.
15. In the Documentation worksheet, enter your name and the date.
16. In the three location worksheets, in the range B4:E11, enter **10**. Verify that the formulas in the three location worksheets and the Summary Sales worksheet summarize the data accurately.
17. Save the workbook, and then close it.

TROUBLESHOOT

Case Problem 2

Data Files needed for this Case Problem: Barstow.xlsx, SanDiego.xlsx, Carlsbad.xlsx, GoodieBag.xlsx

Clara's Goodie Bags Clara Perry founded Clara's Goodie Bags to create unique party favor packages for private and corporate events. The first retail location opened on July 1, 2016, in Barstow, California. The San Diego location opened in 2017, and recently the Carlsbad location was added. Each location uses an Excel workbook to track the number of goodie bags sold in major categories—wedding, birthday, holiday, graduation, retirement, and custom. Clara wants you to use the workbooks to prepare a report showing the number of goodie bags sold by quarter and location for each category. Complete the following:

1. Open the **Barstow** workbook located in the Excel6 > Case2 folder included with your Data Files, and then save the workbook as **Barstow 2017** in the location specified by your instructor.
2. In the Documentation worksheet, enter your name and the date.
3. In the Barstow worksheet, calculate the total number of goodie bags sold in each category in the range B8:G8, and the total number sold each quarter in the range H4:H8.
4. Improve the look of the worksheet by using the formatting of your choice including a bottom border in the range A7:H7 and appropriate number formats for the total numbers of grab bags sold.
5. Save the Barstow 2017 workbook, and leave it open.
6. Repeat Steps 1 through 5 for the **SanDiego** and **Carlsbad** workbooks, naming them **San Diego 2017** and **Carlsbad 2017**, respectively.
7. Open the **GoodieBag** workbook located in the Excel6 > Case2 folder included with your Data Files, and then save the workbook as **Goodie Bags 2017** in the location specified by your instructor.

8. In the Documentation worksheet, enter your name and the date.
9. Rename Sheet1 as **Summary**. In cell A2, enter **Summary Sales** as the label.

Troubleshoot 10. The quarterly totals in the Goodie Bag 2017 Summary worksheet are not displaying the correct results. Make any necessary corrections to the formulas so that they add the correct cells from the Barstow 2017, San Diego 2017, and Carlsbad 2017 workbooks.

11. Insert formulas to calculate the totals for the range B8:G8 and the range H4:H8.

Troubleshoot 12. The Documentation worksheet in the Goodie Bag 2017 workbook includes hyperlinks in the range A9:A11 for each city's corresponding workbook (Barstow 2017, San Diego 2017, and Carlsbad 2017 located in the folder where you saved the workbooks). The text displayed for each hyperlink does not match its source file. Edit the hyperlinks so that each hyperlink points to its corresponding location workbook.

13. Add appropriate text for the ScreenTip to each hyperlink. Test each hyperlink.
14. Prepare each workbook for printing. For all worksheets except the Documentation worksheet, display the workbook name and the worksheet name on separate lines in the right section of the header and display your name and the current date on separate lines in the right section of the footer. Change the orientation so that each workbook will print on one page.
15. Save and close all of the workbooks.

APPLY

Case Problem 3

Data File needed for this Case Problem: RoomGroom.xlsx

Room and Groom Room and Groom has been kenneling and grooming small, medium, and large cats and dogs in Topeka, Kansas, since June 2010. The standard kennel program includes access to the outside fenced play area, healthy meals, and private rooms. With the deluxe kennel program, the animal also has a daily playtime with a kennel employee, daily treats, and music or video playing in its room. Grooming services can occur during a kennel stay or as a standalone service. Samuel Wooten, the manager of Room and Groom, has been tracking the kennel and grooming services by month for the past year. Samuel wants you to analyze the data he has collected and create some preliminary charts. Complete the following:

1. Open the **RoomGroom** workbook located in the Excel6 > Case3 folder included with your Data Files, and then save the workbook as **RoomGroom 2017** in the location specified by your instructor.
2. In the Documentation worksheet, enter your name and the date.
3. Group the 12 monthly worksheets to ensure consistency in headings and for ease in entering formulas. Enter the heading **Total** in cells A11 and E4. For each month (January through December), enter formulas to calculate the total for each type of visit (the range B11:D11) and the total for each type of animal (the range E5:E11).
4. Improve the formatting of the monthly worksheets using the formatting of your choice. Be sure to include a bottom border in the ranges A4:E4 and A10:E10. Ungroup the worksheets.
5. In the Service by Month worksheet, in the range B5:B16, enter formulas with worksheet references to display the total grooming services for each month (the formulas will range from =January!B11 through =December!B11). Copy these formulas to the range C5:C16 (Room-Standard) and the range D5:D16 (Room-Deluxe).
6. In cells A17 and E4, enter the label **Total**. In the range B17:D17, enter formulas to add the total for each type of service, and then in the range E5:E17, enter formulas to add the total services each month by animal type.
7. Add a bottom border to the ranges A4:E4 and A16:E16. Improve the formatting of the Service by Month worksheet using the formatting of your choice.

8. Create a bar chart or a column chart that compares the types of services by month (the range A4:D16). Include an appropriate chart title and a legend. Format the chart so that it is attractive and effective. Position the chart below the data.
9. In the Service by Animal worksheet, in the range B5:D10, enter formulas using 3-D cell references to sum the services for the year for each animal. For example, in cell B5, the formulas for Small Dog Groom would be =SUM(January:December!B5).
10. In cells A11 and E4, enter the label **Total**. In the range B11:D11, enter formulas to add the total by type of service, and then in the range E5:E11, enter formulas to add the total services and total services by animal type.
11. Add a bottom border to the ranges A4:E4 and A10:E10. Improve the formatting of the Service by Animal worksheet using the formatting of your choice.
12. Create a pie chart based on the annual total for each animal type. Include an appropriate chart title and a legend. Format the chart so that it is attractive and effective. Position the pie chart below the data in the Service by Animal worksheet.
13. Group all of the worksheets except Documentation. Prepare the workbook for printing by displaying the workbook name and the worksheet name on separate lines in the right section of the header. Display your name and the current date on separate lines in the right section of the footer.
14. Save the workbook, and then close it.

Case Problem 4

Data Files needed for this Case Problem: Maryland.xlsx, Delaware.xlsx, Virginia.xlsx, ELSSummary.xlsx, NewMD.xlsx, ELSTemplate.xltx

Economic Landscape Supplies Economic Landscape Supplies (ELS), a distributor of landscaping supplies, has offices in Delaware, Virginia, and Maryland. In December, each office submits a workbook that contains worksheets for all salespersons in that state. Each salesperson's worksheet contains the current year's sales by month and the projected increase that they will need to meet. Kyle Walker, the chief financial officer (CFO), wants you to calculate each salesperson's projected monthly sales based on the current sales and the projected increase. After you have added this information to each workbook, Kyle wants you to consolidate the information from the three workbooks into a single workbook. Complete the following:

1. Open the **Maryland** workbook located in the Excel6 > Case4 folder included with your Data Files, and then save the workbook as **ELS Maryland** in the location specified by your instructor.
2. In the Documentation worksheet, enter your name and the date.
3. Repeat Steps 1 and 2, opening the **Delaware** and **Virginia** workbooks and saving them as **ELS Delaware** and **ELS Virginia**, respectively.
4. Complete each salesperson worksheets in workbooks by doing the following:
   a. Group the Salesperson worksheets.
   b. Calculate the 2018 Projected Sales for each month by multiplying the 2017 Gross Sales by the Projected Increase. (*Hint*: Remember to use absolute cell references to the Project Increase cell.)
   c. Enter **Total** in cell A16, and then enter formulas to sum the totals of the 2017 Gross Sales and 2018 Projected Sales.
   d. Display all of the monthly sales numbers (the range B4:C15) with a comma and no decimal places. Display the total row values (the range B16:C16) with a dollar sign. Leave the Projected Increase value in cell B19 as formatted.
   e. Bold the ranges A4:A16 and B3:C3. Wrap the text and center the range B3:C3. Make sure all of the data and the headings are visible.
   f. Ungroup the worksheets.

5. In each of the state workbooks, do the following:
   a. Make a copy of the first salesperson's worksheet, rename it as **Summary**, and then place it after the Documentation worksheet.
   b. In cell A2, change the salesperson name to **Summary** and then clear the 2017 Gross Sales and 2018 Projected Sales data, leaving the formulas for the totals.
   c. Clear the label and data from the range A19:B19.
   d. In the range B4:C15, create 3-D reference formulas to calculate the total of each month's 2017 Gross Sales and 2018 Projected Sales. Widen columns as needed so you can see the totals.
   e. Group all worksheets except the Documentation worksheet. Prepare the workbook for printing by displaying the workbook name and the worksheet name on separate lines in the right section of the header. Display your name and the current date on separate lines in the right section of the footer.
   f. Ungroup the worksheets, and then save the workbook.
6. Open the **ELSSummary** workbook located in the Excel6 > Case4 folder included with your Data Files, and then save the workbook as **ELS Summary 2017** in the location specified by your instructor. Enter your name and date in the Documentation worksheet.
7. Make sure the three ELS state workbooks are open with the Summary worksheet active.
8. In the range B4:C15, enter external reference formulas to create a set of linked workbooks to summarize the 2017 Gross Sales and 2018 Projected Sales.
9. In cell A16, enter **Total**. In the range B16:C16, enter formulas to total the 2017 Gross Sales and 2018 Projected Sales.
10. Bold the range A4:A16. Bold, wrap text, and center the range B3:C3. Display all the monthly sales numbers with a comma and no decimal places. Display the total values (the range B16:C16) with a dollar sign and no decimal places.
11. Prepare the Summary worksheet for printing with the workbook name and the worksheet name on separate lines in the right section of the header. Display your name and the date on separate lines in the right section of the footer.
12. Save the Summary workbook.

Explore 13. The office manager for the Maryland ELS location found a newer workbook for that location's sales and commissions and has submitted it to you. Close the ELS Maryland workbook that you have been working with, open the **New MD** workbook located in the Excel6 > Case4 folder included with your Data Files, and then save the workbook as **New ELS Maryland** in the location specified by your instructor. Use Update Links to update the totals on the Summary worksheet in the ELS Summary 2017 workbook. The Totals before the update are 2017 Gross Sales $5,323,750 and 2018 Projected Sales $5,730,424. The totals after the update are 2017 Gross Sales $5,406,750 and 2018 Projected Sales $5,682,700.

14. Save and close all of the open workbooks.

Explore 15. Open the template named **ELSTemplate** located in the Excel6 > Case4 folder included with your Data Files, save the template as **ELS Template Revised** in the location specified by your instructor, and then change the company name in cell A1 of all the worksheets to **ELS**. Change the font for the company name to Bookman Old Style. Save the template.

16. Create a new workbook from the ELS Template Revised template. In the Documentation worksheet, enter your name and date.
17. In the Salesperson worksheet, enter **10,000** for each month's 2017 Gross Sales and Projected Increase of 1.20. Verify that the formulas are working correctly.
18. Save the workbook as **ELS Test** in a location specified by your instructor, and then close it.

MODULE 7

Developing an Excel Application

Creating a Registration Receipt

EXCEL

OBJECTIVES

Session 7.1
- Create an application
- Create, edit, and delete defined names for cells and ranges
- Paste a list of defined names as documentation
- Use defined names in formulas
- Add defined names to existing formulas

Session 7.2
- Create validation rules for data entry
- Protect the contents of worksheets and workbooks
- Add, edit, and delete comments

Session 7.3
- Learn about macro viruses and Excel security features
- Add the Developer tab to the ribbon
- Create and run a macro
- Edit a macro using the Visual Basic Editor
- Assign a macro to a keyboard shortcut and a button
- Save and open a workbook in macro-enabled format

Case | *Rockport Youth Center*

The Rockport Youth Center in Rockport, Indiana, offers classes and activities to school-age children. Each fall, the Center mails a brochure with the upcoming winter activities to households with students in grades 3 through 6 in the Rockport area. This winter's weekly activities include First Friday (games, pizza, and drinks), Kids Game Night (board games, video games, and snacks), Kids in the Kitchen (hands-on cooking), and Modern Manners (more than please and thank you). The brochure includes a registration form that guardians complete and return with their payment. The manager, Stephen Maynard, wants to automate the registration process, which will include capturing the data, calculating the charges, printing a receipt, and collecting the data for the shirts that participants will receive.

Many of these tasks can be accomplished in Excel. But without validating data entry, protecting cells with formulas from accidental deletion, and reducing repetitious keystrokes and mouse clicks, too many opportunities for errors exist. The Center relies on volunteers to assist with registration. To accommodate the volunteers' varying skill levels and reduce errors, Stephen wants to create a custom interface for this project that does not rely exclusively on the ribbon, galleries, and so forth. You will help Stephen create a unique Excel application to resolve these issues and help ensure accurate data entry.

STARTING DATA FILES

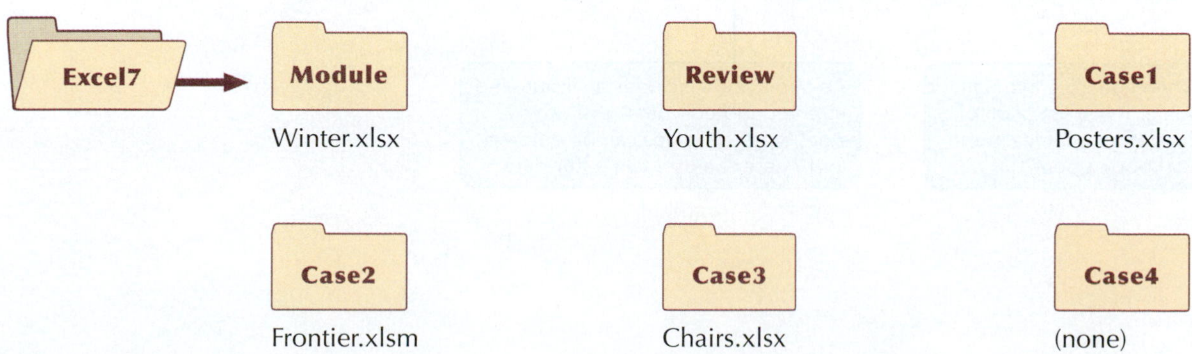

Winter.xlsx

Youth.xlsx

Posters.xlsx

Frontier.xlsm

Chairs.xlsx

(none)

Session 7.1 Visual Overview:

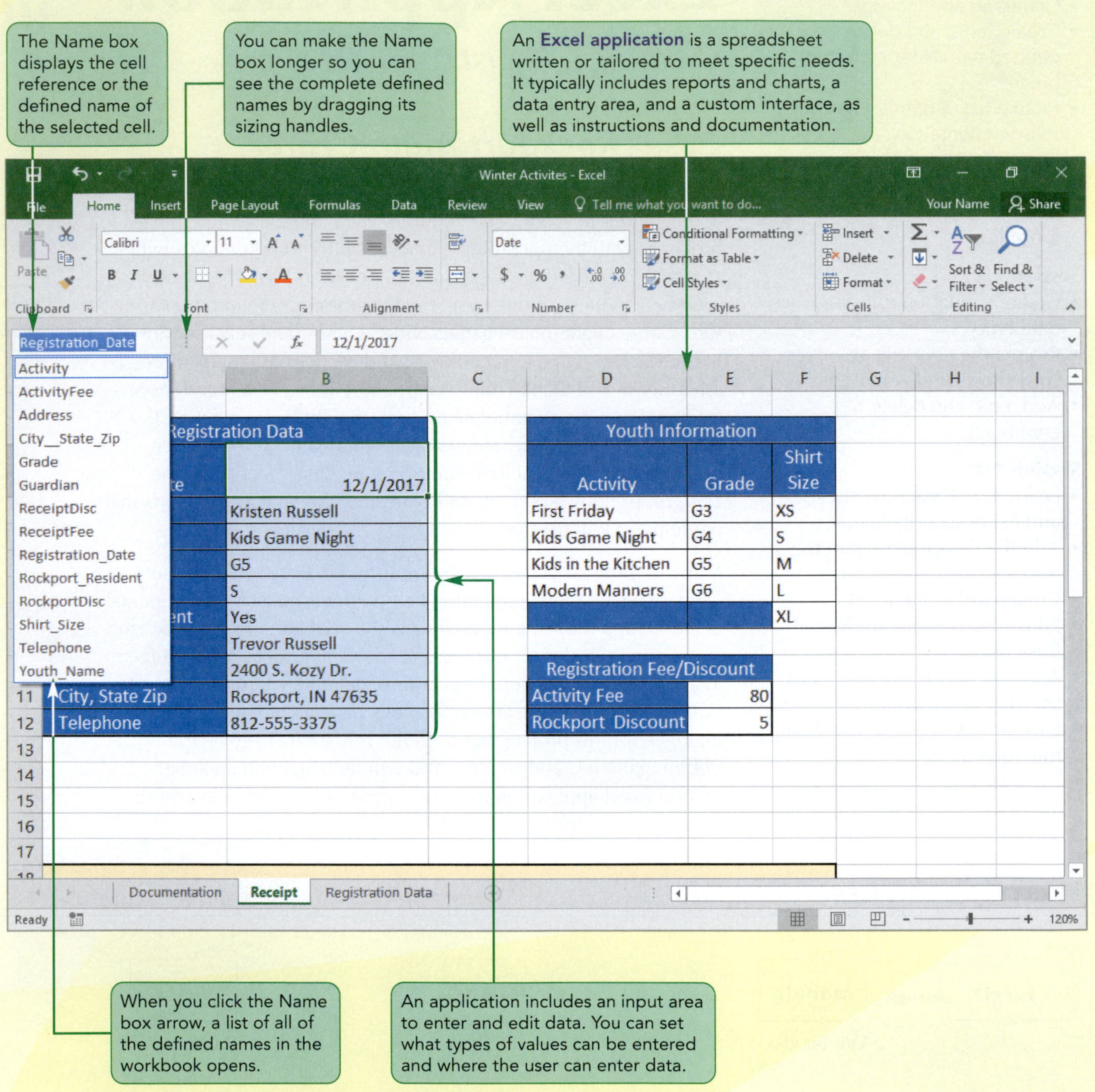

Excel Application and Defined Names

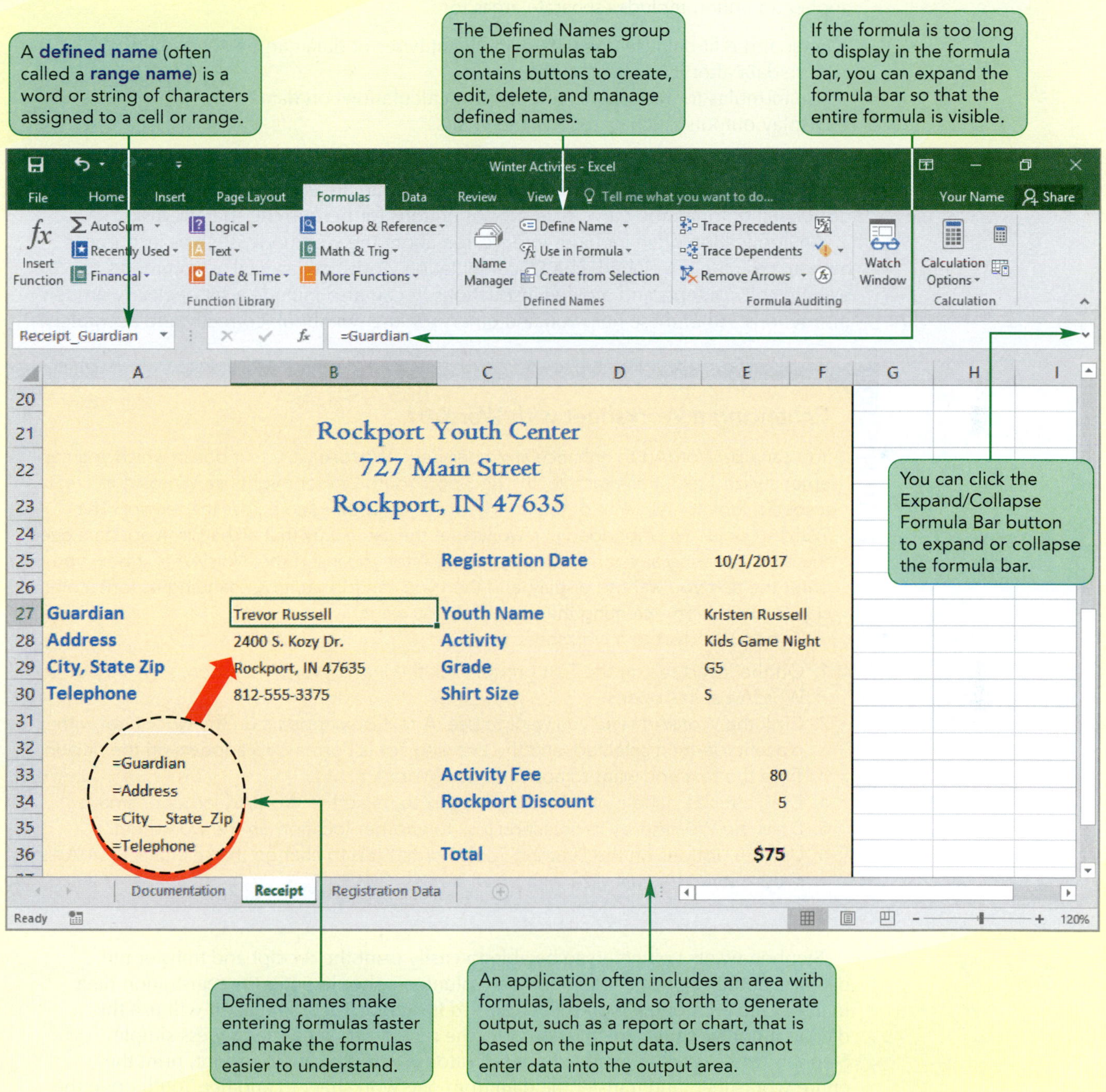
A **defined name** (often called a **range name**) is a word or string of characters assigned to a cell or range.
The Defined Names group on the Formulas tab contains buttons to create, edit, delete, and manage defined names.
If the formula is too long to display in the formula bar, you can expand the formula bar so that the entire formula is visible.
Winter Activities - Excel
Receipt_Guardian
=Guardian
Rockport Youth Center
727 Main Street
Rockport, IN 47635
Registration Date
10/1/2017
Guardian
Trevor Russell
Youth Name
Kristen Russell
Address
2400 S. Kozy Dr.
Activity
Kids Game Night
City, State Zip
Rockport, IN 47635
Grade
G5
Telephone
812-555-3375
Shirt Size
S
=Guardian
=Address
=City__State_Zip
=Telephone
Activity Fee
80
Rockport Discount
5
Total
$75
You can click the Expand/Collapse Formula Bar button to expand or collapse the formula bar.
Defined names make entering formulas faster and make the formulas easier to understand.
An application often includes an area with formulas, labels, and so forth to generate output, such as a report or chart, that is based on the input data. Users cannot enter data into the output area.

Planning an Excel Application

An Excel application is a spreadsheet written or tailored to meet specific needs, such as creating a receipt for winter activities registrations. Planning an Excel application includes designing how the worksheet(s) will be organized. You can include different areas for each function, depending on the complexity of the project. For example, an application often includes separate areas to:

- Enter and edit data (setting where and what types of data can be entered).
- Store data after it has been entered.
- Use formulas to manipulate and perform calculations on data.
- Display outputs, such as reports and charts.

Excel applications can be set up to help users understand how they will interact with the project. For example, you can have separate areas for inputting data and displaying outputs. You can create special buttons for performing specific tasks.

An application often includes information about the workbook, such as its purpose, author, and date developed, in a Documentation worksheet as well as comments to explain cell contents and provide instructions. It can also include a set of clearly written instructions. All of these help you and others use the workbook correctly and accurately.

INSIGHT

Enhancing a Worksheet with WordArt

You can use WordArt to enhance any worksheet. **WordArt** is a text box in which you can enter stylized text. For example, the Rockport Youth Center might use WordArt to create a special look for its name or to add the word "PAID" angled across the receipt. The WordArt object is embedded in a worksheet the same way that a chart is; it appears over the cells, covering any content they contain. After you insert the WordArt text box, you enter the text you want to display, and then you can format it by changing its font, color, size, and position—creating the exact look you want.

To add WordArt to a worksheet:

1. On the Insert tab, in the Text group, click the Insert WordArt button. A gallery of WordArt styles opens.
2. Click the WordArt style you want to use. A text box appears on the worksheet with placeholder text selected, and the Drawing Tools Format tab appears on the ribbon.
3. Type the text you want to appear in the WordArt.
4. Drag a resize handle on the selection box to make the WordArt larger or smaller.
5. Drag the WordArt by its selection box to another location on the worksheet.
6. Use the options on the Drawing Tools Format tab to change the selected WordArt's shape, style, text, fill, size, and position.

Stephen wants volunteers to be able to easily print the receipt and transfer the data to another worksheet. In addition, volunteers should enter the registration data in a specific area of the worksheet reserved for input. The application will use this data to automatically generate and print the receipt. To keep the process simple, Stephen wants users to be able to click buttons to print a single receipt, print the entire worksheet, and transfer the data from one worksheet to another. You'll open the workbook Stephen created.

To open and review the Winter workbook:

1. Open the **Winter** workbook located in the **Excel7 > Module** folder included with your Data Files, and then save the workbook as **Winter Activities** in the location specified by your instructor.
2. In the Documentation worksheet, enter your name and the date.
3. Review the contents of each worksheet, and then go to the **Receipt** worksheet. See Figure 7-1.

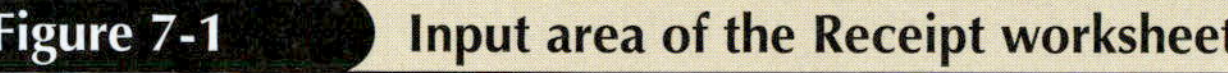

Figure 7-1 Input area of the Receipt worksheet

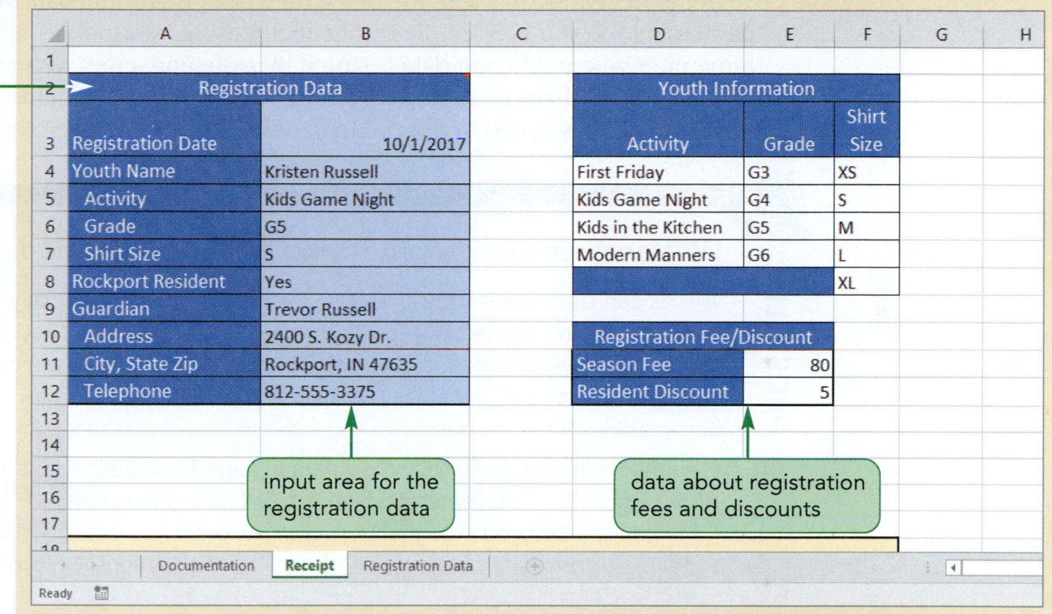

TIP

Larger and more complex applications often place the input and output areas in separate worksheets.

In addition to the Documentation worksheet, the Winter Activities workbook includes two other worksheets—Receipt and Registration Data. The Receipt worksheet contains input, output, and transfer areas. The input area is divided into the following three parts:

- Registration Data includes items that change for each registration, such as youth name, activity, grade, shirt size, guardian name, address, telephone, and whether the student is a Rockport resident.
- Youth Information is the list of codes for the different activities, grades, and shirt sizes.
- Registration Fee/Discount includes costs that will not change, such as activity fee ($80/youth) and Rockport resident discount ($5/youth).

The output section contains formulas and labels used to generate the receipt based on data in the input section. The receipt in the output section will be printed. The transfer section gathers selected data from the receipt in one area before the data is transferred to the Registration Data worksheet for storage. The transfer section makes it simpler and easier to identify the data to be moved to the Registration Data worksheet for storage and future analysis.

Naming Cells and Ranges

So far, you have referred to a cell or range by its column and row location except when you entered formulas in an Excel table. Cell and range references do not indicate what data is stored in those cells. Instead, you can use a defined name to assign a meaningful, descriptive name to a cell or range. For example, if the range D1:D100 contains sales data for 100 transactions, you can use the defined name Sales to refer to the range of sales data.

A defined name enables you to quickly navigate within a workbook to the cell or range with the defined name. You can also use defined names to create more descriptive formulas. However, keep in mind that the defined name includes only the specified range. Any cells you insert within that range are then included with the defined name, but any cells you insert outside the range with the defined name are not included in the defined name.

In the Receipt worksheet, the range B3:B12 contains the data values for each participant. As you can see, this range includes many variables. It will be simpler to remember where different data is stored by assigning a descriptive name to each cell or range rather than using its cell address. For example, the name YouthName better identifies what is stored in the cell than cell B4.

PROSKILLS

Written Communication: Saving Time with Defined Names

Words can be more descriptive than numbers. This is especially true in cell references. Instead of using the letter and number references for cells, you can create defined names to provide more intuitive references. Defined names have several advantages over cell references, especially as a worksheet becomes longer and more complex. Some advantages include:

- Names, such as TaxRate and TotalSales, are more descriptive than cell references, making it easier to remember what a cell or range contains.
- Names can be used in formulas, making it easier for users to understand the calculations being performed. For example, =GrossPay−Deductions is more understandable than =C15−C16.
- When you move a named cell or range within a worksheet, its name moves with it. Any formulas that contain the name automatically reference the new location.
- In a formula, referencing a named cell or range is the same as referencing the cell or range's absolute reference. So, if you move a formula that includes a defined name, the reference remains pointed to the correct cell or range.

By using defined names, you'll often save time, and everyone reviewing the worksheet will have a clearer understanding of what a formula is calculating.

Creating defined names for cells or ranges makes it easier to create and understand the formulas in a workbook. When you define a name for a cell or range, keep in mind the following rules:

- The name must begin with a letter or _ (an underscore).
- The name can include letters and numbers as well as periods and underscores but not other symbols or spaces. To distinguish multiword names, use an underscore between the words or capitalize the first letter of each word. For example, the names Net_Income and NetIncome are valid, but Net Income and Net-Income are not.
- The name cannot be a valid cell address (such as FY2017), a function name (such as Average), or a reserved word (such as Print_Area).
- The name can include as many as 255 characters, although short, meaningful names of 5 to 15 characters are more practical.
- The name is not case sensitive. For example, both Sales and SALES refer to the same cell or range.

REFERENCE

Creating a Defined Name for a Cell or Range

- Select the cell or range to which you want to assign a name.
- Click in the Name box, type the name, and then press the Enter key (or on the Formulas tab, in the Defined Names group, click the Define Name button, type a name in the Name box, and then click the OK button).

or

- Select the range with labels to which you want to assign a name.
- On the Formulas tab, in the Defined Names group, click the Create from Selection button.
- Specify whether to create the ranges based on the top row, bottom row, left column, or right column in the list.
- Click the OK button.

Using the Name Box to Create Defined Names

The Name box is a quick way to create a defined name for a selected cell or range. Stephen wants you to create defined names for cells and ranges in the Receipt worksheet. You'll start by using the Name box to define some of these names.

To create defined names for the input area using the Name box:

1. Select cell **E11**, and then click the **Name box** to the left of the formula bar. The cell reference for the active cell, E11 is selected in the Name box.
2. Type **ActivityFee** and then press the **Enter** key. Cell E11 remains active, and ActivityFee appears in the Name box instead of the cell reference. See Figure 7-2.

Figure 7-2 Defined name for cell E11

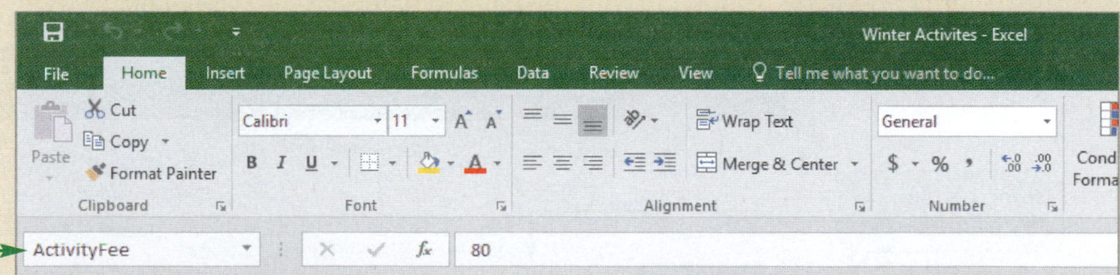

Trouble? If ActivityFee appears in cell E11, you did not click the Name box before typing the name. On the Quick Access Toolbar, click the Undo button, and then repeat Steps 1 and 2.

3. Select cell **E12**, click the **Name box** to select the cell reference, type **RockportDisc** and then press the **Enter** key. Cell E12 remains active, and RockportDisc appears in the Name box instead of the cell reference.
4. Select the range **D2:F8**. The cell reference for the active cell in the range appears in the Name box.
5. Click the **Name box**, type **YouthInfo** and then press the **Enter** key. The name YouthInfo is assigned to the range D2:F8.
6. Select the range **A40:F40**, click the **Name box**, type **TransferArea** and then press the **Enter** key. The name TransferArea is assigned to the range A40:F40.

7. Select cell **E33**, click the **Name box** to select the cell reference, type **RecActivityFee** and then press the **Enter** key. Cell E33 remains active, and RecActivityFee appears in the Name box instead of the cell reference.
8. Select cell **E34**, click the **Name box** to select the cell reference, type **RecRockportDisc** and then press the **Enter** key. Cell E34 remains active, and RecRockportDisc appears in the Name box instead of the cell reference.

Selecting Cells and Ranges by Their Defined Names

The Name box displays all of the defined names in a workbook. You can click a name in the Name box list to quickly select the cell or range referenced by that name. Stephen wants you to verify that defined names are associated with the correct cell or range. You'll view the defined names you added to the workbook, and then use them to select cells and ranges.

To select cells and ranges with the Name box:

1. Click the **Name box arrow** to open a list of defined names in the workbook. Six names appear in the list.

   If the names are longer than the Name box, you can make the Name box wider so that the full names are visible by performing Steps 2 and 3. Otherwise, skip to Step 4.
2. Press the **Esc key** to close the Name box.
3. On the right side of the Name box, drag the sizing handle (the three vertical dots) to the right until you can see the full names.
4. Click the **Name box arrow** to display the list of defined names. See Figure 7-3.

Figure 7-3 Name box with the defined names in the workbook

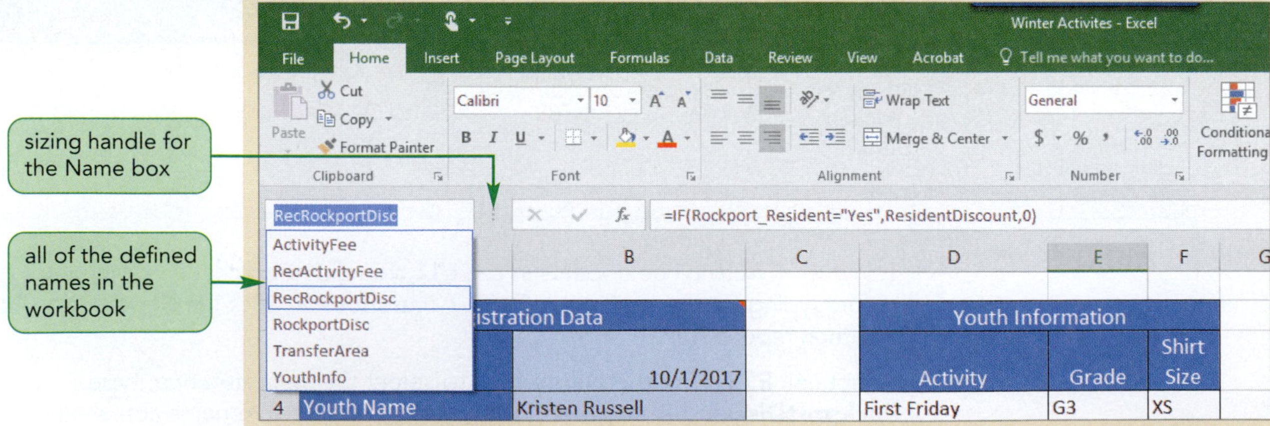

5. Click **ActivityFee**. Cell E11 becomes the active cell.
6. Click the **Name box arrow**, and then click **YouthInfo**. The range D2:F8 is selected in the worksheet.
7. Repeat Step 6 to select the **RockportDisc**, **RecRockportDisc**, **RecActivityFee**, and **TransferArea** defined names in the Name box to confirm that they select their associated cell or range.

Creating Defined Names by Selection

You can quickly define names without typing them if the data is organized as a structured range of data with labels in the first or last column or in the top or bottom row. The defined names are based on the row or column labels. For example, the Registration Data area contains labels in column A that can be used as the defined names for the corresponding cells in column B. Any blank space or parenthesis in a label is changed to an underscore (_) in the defined name.

Stephen wants you to create names for each cell in the Registration Data area using the labels in the range A3:A12 to name the cells in the range B3:B12.

To create defined names by selection for the registration data:

Select only the range A3:B12; otherwise, formulas you create later in this module will not work.

1. Select the range **A3:B12**. Column A contains the labels you want to use as the defined names, and column B contains the cells you want to name.
2. On the ribbon, click the **Formulas** tab.
3. In the Defined Names group, click the **Create from Selection** button. The Create Names from Selection dialog box opens.
4. Make sure only the **Left column** check box contains a checkmark. The labels in the left column will be used to create the defined names. See Figure 7-4.

Figure 7-4 Create Names from Selection dialog box

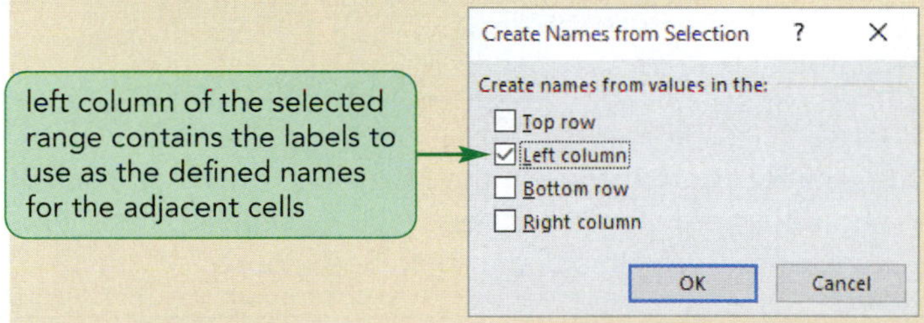

5. Click the **OK** button. Each cell in the range B3:B12 is named based on its corresponding label in column A. For example, cell B3 is named Registration_Date based on the Registration Date label in cell A3.
6. Click the **Name box arrow** to see the 16 defined names in the list. Notice that underscores have replaced spaces in the names.
7. Press the **Esc** key to close the list of defined names.

Editing and Deleting Defined Names

Although you can use the Name box to verify that the names were created, the Name Manager dialog box lists all of the names currently defined in the workbook, including Excel table names. In addition to the name, it identifies the current value for that name as well as the worksheet and cell or range it references. You can use the Name Manager dialog box to create a new name, edit or delete existing names, and filter the list of names.

The names RecActivityFee and RecRockportDisc define the location of these two cells on the worksheet. Although the names are descriptive, they are also fairly long. Stephen wants you to use the shorter names ReceiptFee and ReceiptDisc, respectively, which still reflect the stored data in each cell. Stephen also decides that the TransferArea and YouthInfo defined names are not needed, so you will delete them.

To edit and delete defined names with the Name Manager dialog box:

1. On the Formulas tab, in the Defined Names group, click the **Name Manager** button (or press the **Ctrl+F3** keys). The Name Manager dialog box opens, listing the 16 defined names in the workbook. See Figure 7-5.

Figure 7-5 Name Manager dialog box

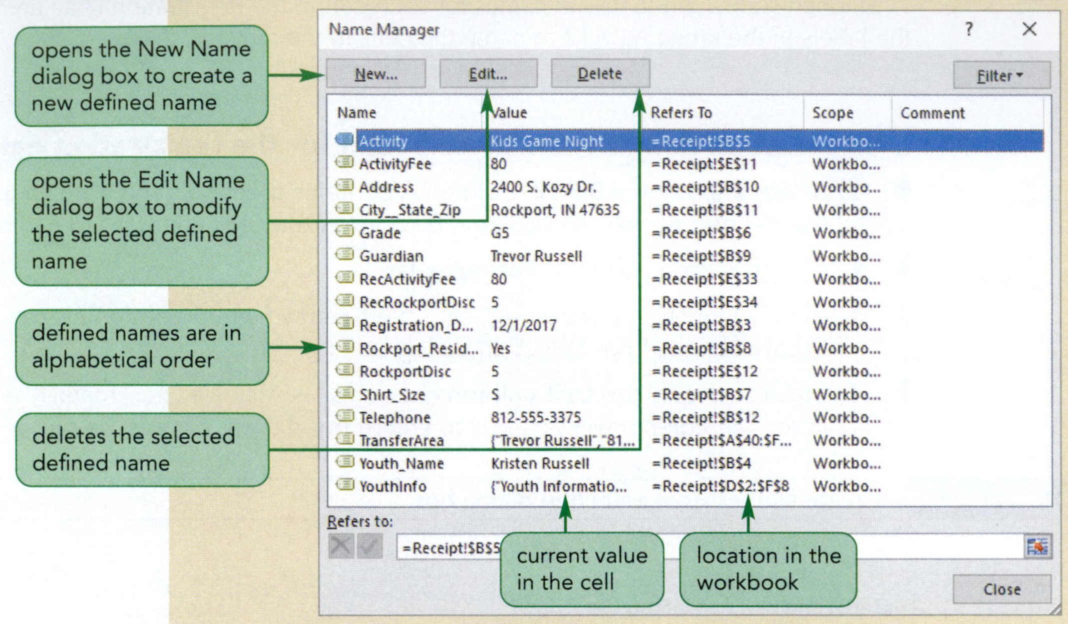

2. Click **RecActivityFee** in the Name list, and then click the **Edit** button. The Edit Name dialog box opens. You can change the name and its referenced cell or range in this dialog box. See Figure 7-6.

Figure 7-6 Edit Name dialog box

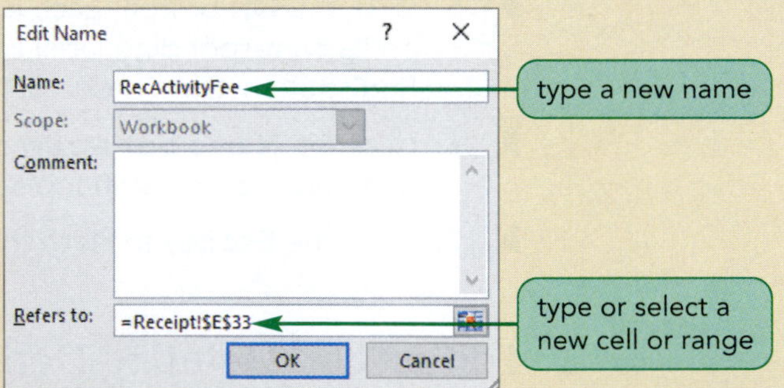

3. In the Name box, type **ReceiptFee** to create a shorter defined name, and then click the **OK** button. The edited name appears in the list in the Name Manager dialog box.
4. Repeat Steps 2 and 3 to rename the RecRockportDisc defined name as **ReceiptDisc**.
5. Click **TransferArea**, and then click the **Delete** button. A dialog box opens to confirm that you want to delete the selected defined name.
6. Click the **OK** button. The name is removed from the list.

7. Repeat Steps 5 and 6 to delete the **YouthInfo** name.
8. Click the **Close** button. The Name Manager dialog box closes.

Using the Paste Names Command

When a workbook contains many defined names, it can be helpful to list all of the defined names and their corresponding cell addresses in the workbook's documentation. You can generate a list of names using the Paste Names command.

To create a list of the defined names in the Documentation worksheet:

1. Go to the **Documentation** worksheet.
2. In cell **B10**, enter **Defined Names**, and then format the label with bold.
3. Select cell **B11**. This is the upper-left cell of the range where you want to paste the list of defined names.
4. On the Formulas tab, in the Defined Names group, click the **Use in Formula** button, and then click **Paste Names** (or press the **F3** key). The Paste Name dialog box opens. You can paste any selected name, or you can paste the entire list of names.
5. Click the **Paste List** button. The defined names and their associated cell references are pasted into the range B11:C24.
6. Click cell **A10** to deselect the range. See Figure 7-7. Only some names in the pasted list of defined names include underscores in place of spaces. The names with underscores were created using the Create from Selection button; you entered the names without underscores in the Name box.

Figure 7-7 Defined names in the Winter Activities workbook

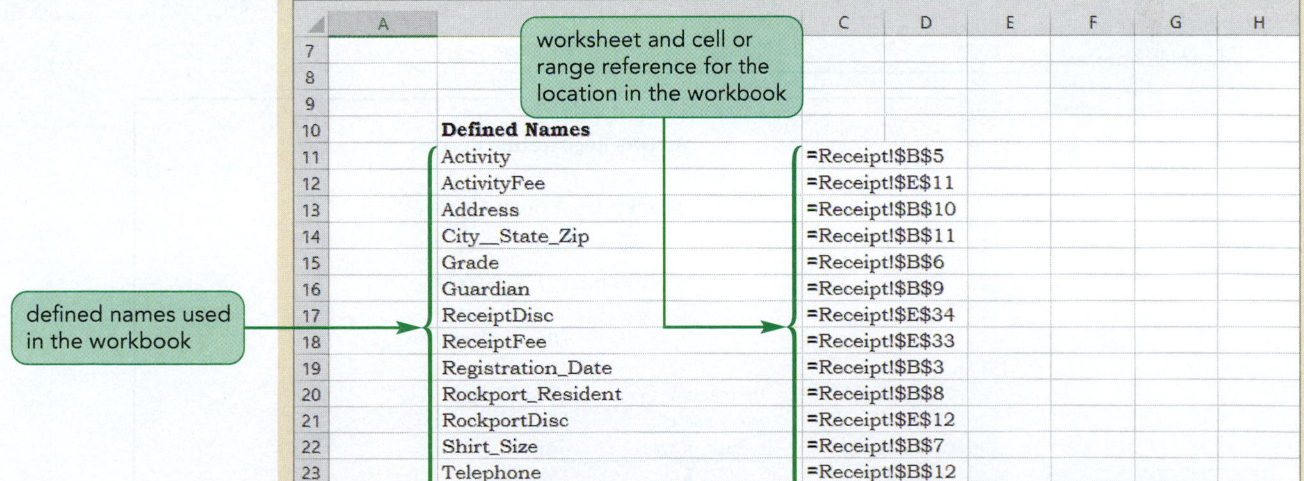

If you edit a defined name or add a new defined name, the list of defined names and their addresses in the Documentation worksheet is not updated. You must paste the list again to update the names and locations. Usually, it is a good idea to wait until the workbook is complete before pasting defined names in the Documentation worksheet.

Using Defined Names in Formulas

You can create more descriptive formulas by using defined names instead of cell or range references in formulas. For example, in the following formulas, the defined name Sales replaces the range reference D1:D100 in a formula to calculate average sales:

Range reference =AVERAGE(D1:D100)
Defined name =AVERAGE(Sales)

Keep in mind that range references in formulas are not updated with their defined names. So, if you enter a range reference in a formula, its corresponding defined name does *not* automatically replace the range reference in the formula.

Stephen wants you to enter the formulas required to generate the receipt. You'll start by entering formulas to display the registration date, the guardian's name, and the guardian's address entered in the Registration Data area in the receipt.

To enter formulas to display the guardian's name and address on the receipt:

1. Go to the **Receipt** worksheet.
2. In cell **B27**, enter **=B9**. Trevor Russell, the guardian's name, appears in the cell.
3. In cell **B28**, enter **=B10**. 2400 S. Kozy Dr., the guardian's street address, appears in the cell.
4. In cell **B29**, enter **=B11**. The guardian's city, state, and Zip code—Rockport, IN 47635—appear in the cell.
5. Select cell **B29**. The formula =B11 appears in the formula bar. See Figure 7-8.

Figure 7-8 Formula to display the City, State and Zip data

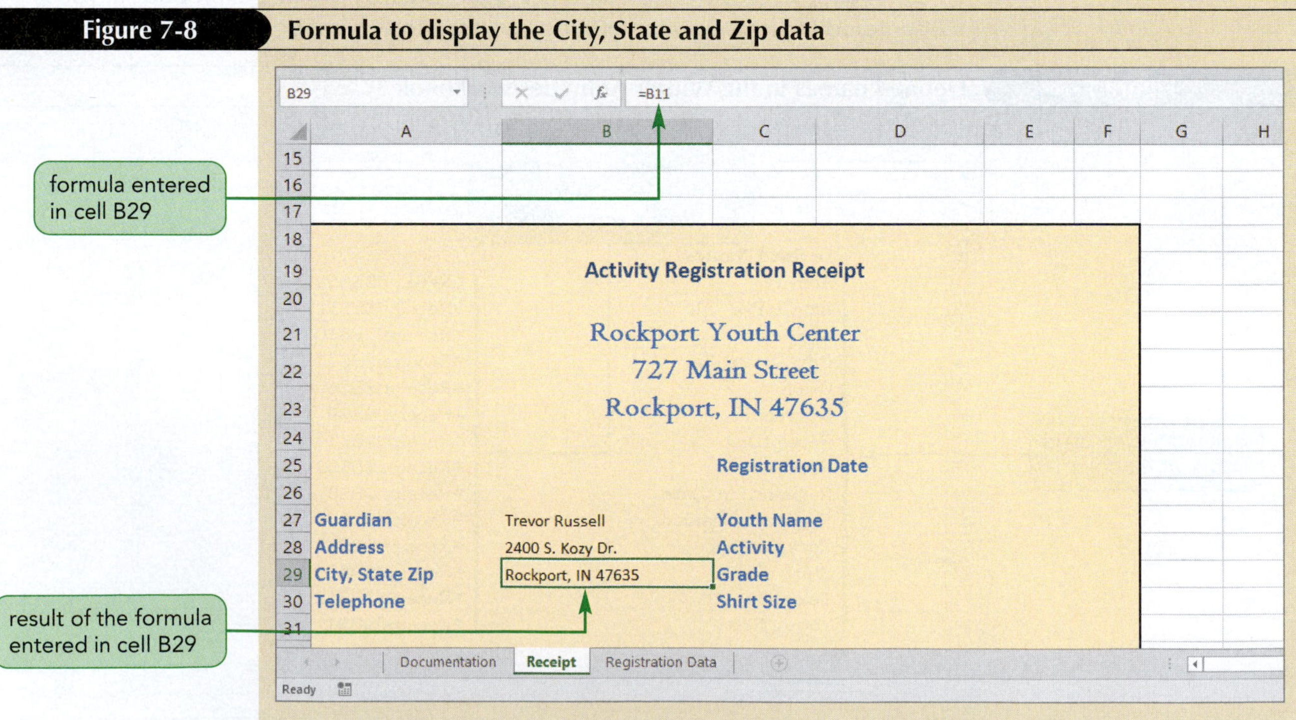

You entered these formulas using cell addresses rather than defined names. Although you defined names for cells B9, B10, and B11, the names do not automatically replace the cell addresses in the formula when you type the cell addresses.

Entering Formulas with Defined Names

Defined names make formulas simpler to enter and understand. To use a defined name in a formula, you enter the formula as usual. As you type a defined name in a formula, the Formula AutoComplete box appears, listing functions and defined names that begin with the letters you typed. As you type additional letters, the list narrows. You can double-click the name you want in the Formula AutoComplete box or press the Tab key to enter the selected name. You can also just continue to type the rest of the name.

Stephen wants you to use named cells and ranges in the remaining formulas. You'll enter these now.

To enter defined names in formulas:

1. In cell **B30**, type **=T** to display a list of functions and defined names that begin with the letter T.
2. Type **el** to narrow the list to the defined name =Telephone.
3. Press the **Tab** key to enter the defined name in the formula, and then press the **Enter** key. The guardian's telephone number appears in the cell.
4. Select cell **B30**. The data from cell B12 appears in the cell, and the formula with the defined name =Telephone appears in the formula bar.
5. In cell **E25**, enter **=Reg** to list the defined name =Registration_Date, press the **Tab** key to insert the defined name in the formula, and then press the **Enter** key.
6. Select cell **E25**. The data from cell B3, 10/1/2017, appears in the cell, and the formula with the defined name =Registration_Date appears in the formula bar. See Figure 7-9.

Figure 7-9 **Formula with a defined name**

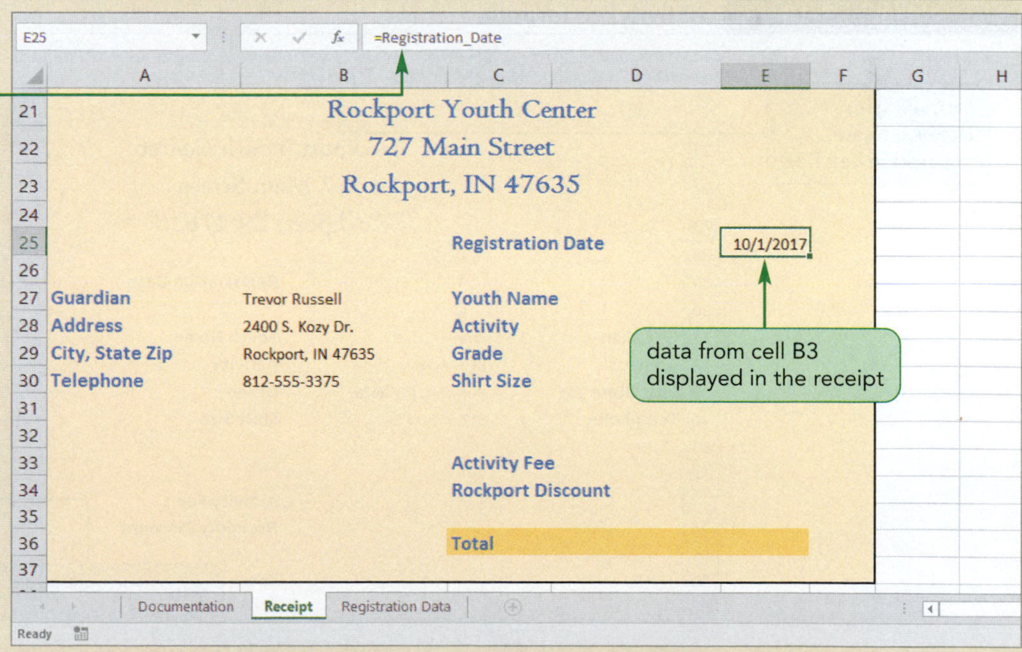

Trouble? If the date is displayed as an integer, you need to reformat the cell as a date. On the ribbon, click the Home tab. In the Number group, click the Number Format box arrow, and then click Short Date. AutoFit column E so that the date is displayed.

You can also use the point-and-click method to create a formula with defined names. When you click a cell or select a range, Excel substitutes the defined name for the cell reference in the formula. You'll use this method to enter formulas that display the youth name, activity, grade, and shirt size from the Registration Data area in the Activity Registration Receipt area.

To enter formulas with defined names using the point-and-click method:

1. Select cell **E27**, type **=**, and then click cell **B4**. The formula uses the defined name Youth_Name rather than the cell reference B4.
2. Press the **Enter** key. Kristen Russell, which is the name of the participant, appears in cell E27.
3. In cell **E28**, type **=**, and then click cell **B5**. The formula uses the defined name Activity rather than the cell reference B5.
4. Press the **Enter** key. Kids Game Night appears in cell E28.
5. In cell **E29**, type **=**, click cell **B6**, and then press the **Enter** key. The grade code, G5, appears in cell E29, and the formula with the defined name =Grade appears in the formula bar.
6. In cell **E30**, type **=**, click cell **B7**, and then press the **Enter** key. The participant's shirt size, S for small, appears in cell E30, and the formula with the defined name =Shirt_Size appears in the formula bar.
7. In cell **E33**, type **=**, click cell **E11**, and then click the **Enter** button ✓ on the formula bar. The activity fee, 80, appears in cell E33 and the formula with the defined name =ActivityFee appears in the formula bar. See Figure 7-10.

Figure 7-10 ActivityFee formula

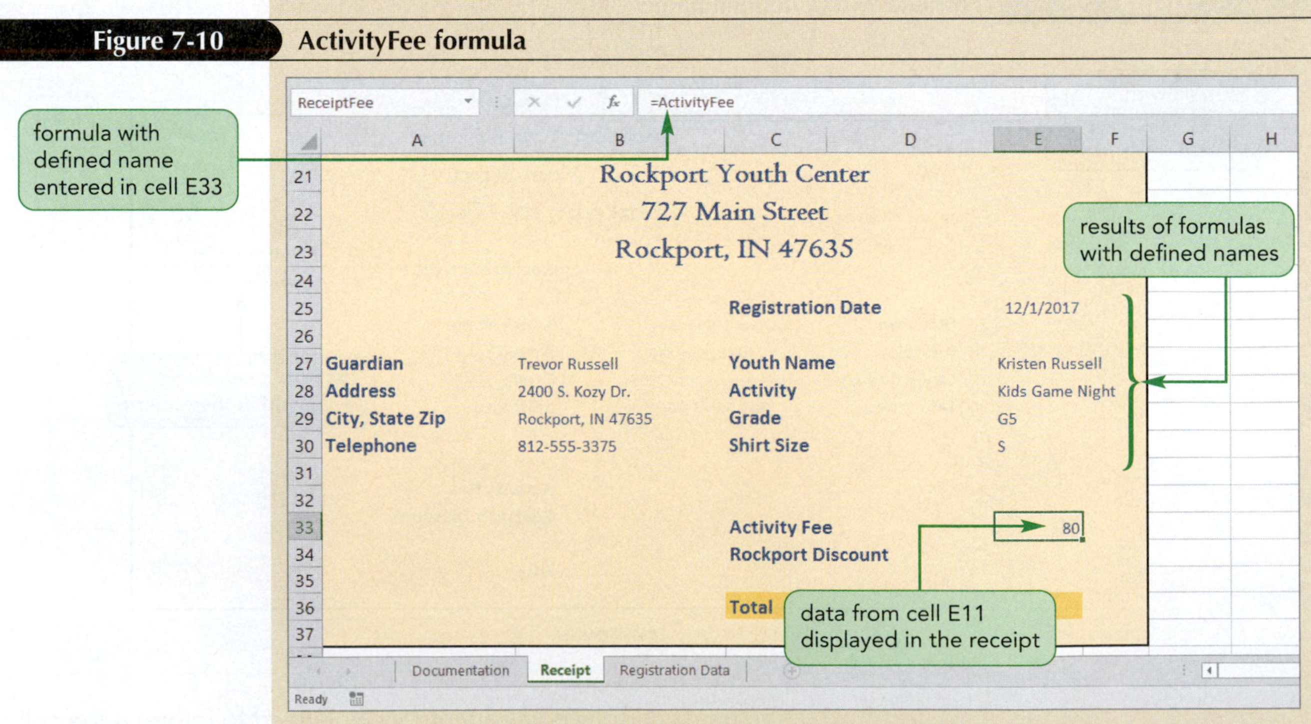

Next, Stephen wants you to enter the formula to calculate the total registration paid based on the data in the Registration Fee/Discount area. All participants pay the activity fee ($80). Rockport residents receive a $5 discount. You will need to use an IF function to determine whether the participant will receive the $5 discount.

To enter the IF function to calculate the registration total:

1. Select cell **E34**. The defined name ReceiptDisc appears in the Name box.
2. On the Formulas tab, in the Function Library group, click the **Logical** button, and then click **IF**. The Function Arguments dialog box opens.
3. In the Logical_test box, type **Rockport_Resident="Yes"**. This logical test evaluates whether the youth qualifies for the Rockport resident discount. If the value in cell B8 equals Yes, then the condition is true. TRUE appears to the right of the Logical_test box, indicating that this youth qualifies for the Rockport resident discount of $5.

   Trouble? If an error value appears to the right of the Logical_test box, you probably mistyped the formula. If the error value is #NAME?, you mistyped the defined name or didn't include quotation marks around the word "Yes." If the error value is Invalid, you used single quotation marks (') around the word "Yes." Edit the content in the Logical_test box as needed.

TIP

You must use quotation marks around text in the IF function.

4. In the Value_if_true box, type **RockportDisc**—the defined name for cell E12, which has the value 5. This discount amount will be added to the receipt if the logical test is true.
5. In the Value_if_false box, type **0** to indicate that no discount will be applied if the value in cell B8 does not equal Yes. See Figure 7-11.

Figure 7-11 Completed IF Function Arguments dialog box

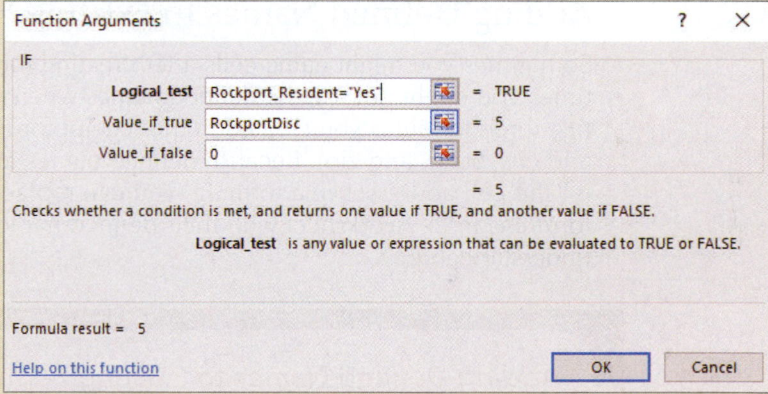

6. Click the **OK** button to enter the IF function in cell E34. In this case, cell E34 displays 5 because the participant is a Rockport resident.
7. In cell **E36**, enter the formula **=ReceiptFee-ReceiptDisc** to calculate the registration total, which is $75. See Figure 7-12.

Figure 7-12 Receipt with all formulas entered

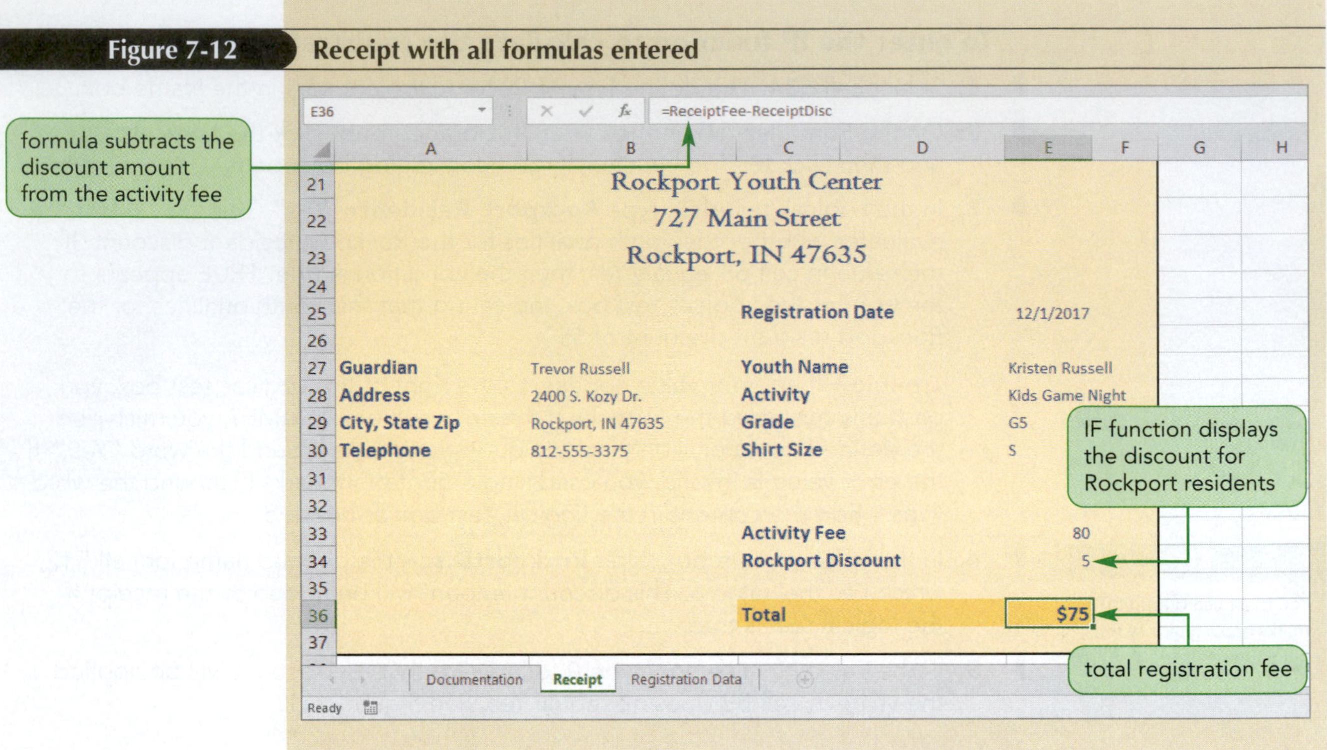

Adding Defined Names to Existing Formulas

Sometimes you might name cells after creating formulas in the worksheet. Other times you might not use the defined names when you create formulas (as with the first three formulas you created in the receipt for the guardian; guardian address; and city, state, and zip). Because defined names are not automatically substituted for the cell addresses in a formula, you can replace cell addresses in existing formulas in the worksheet with their defined names to make the formulas more understandable.

REFERENCE

Adding Defined Names to Existing Formulas

- On the Formulas tab, in the Defined Names group, click the Define Name button arrow, and then click Apply Names (if the cell reference and defined name are in the same worksheet).
- In the Apply Names dialog box, select the names you want to apply.
- Click the OK button.

or

- Edit the formula by selecting the cell reference and typing the defined name or clicking the appropriate cell.

In the formulas you created to display the guardian's name, address, and city state zip in the receipt, Stephen wants you to use defined names instead of cell references. This will make the formulas much clearer to anyone who looks at the worksheet.

To add defined names to existing formulas in the receipt:

1. On the Formulas tab, in the Defined Names group, click the **Define Name button arrow**, and then click **Apply Names**. The Apply Names dialog box opens. See Figure 7-13.

Figure 7-13 Apply Names dialog box

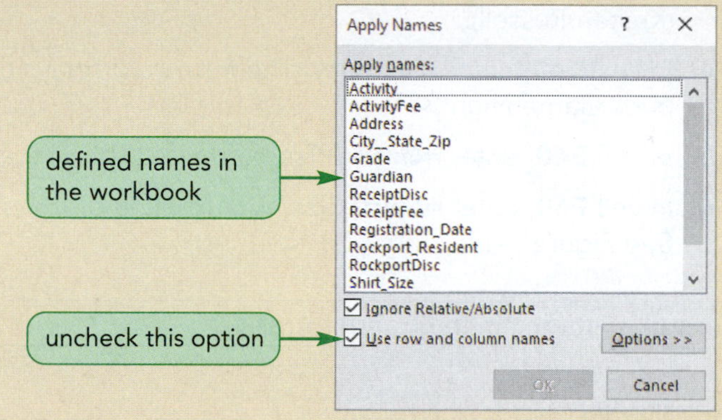

You want to select only the names you need for the existing formulas with cell references.

TIP

You can also select a cell that contains a formula, click the Use in Formula button in the Defined Names group, click the name to replace the cell reference, and then press the Enter key.

2. If any name is selected in the Apply names list, click that name to deselect it.
3. In the Apply names list, click **Address, City_State_Zip**, and **Guardian**. The three names you want to apply to the formulas are selected.
4. Make sure that the **Use row and column names** check box is unchecked. If you leave this checked, the formula will contain too many characters and return an error.
5. Click the **OK** button. The three selected names are applied to the formulas.
6. Click cell **B27** and verify that the formula changed to =Guardian.
7. Click cell **B28** and verify that the formula changed to =Address.
8. Click cell **B29** and verify that the formula changed to =City__State_Zip. The formulas now use the defined names in the files.

Stephen wants to store the following items in the Registration Data worksheet—guardian, telephone, youth name, activity, grade, and shirt size. Displaying this data in the Transfer Area enables you to copy and paste all of these items to the Registration Data worksheet at once. You'll enter formulas to display the appropriate items in this section of the worksheet.

To enter formulas to display data in the Transfer Area:

1. In cell **A40**, enter **=Guardian**. The formula displays the guardian name (Trevor Russell).
2. In cell **B40**, enter **=Telephone**. The formula displays the telephone number (812-555-3375).
3. In cell **C40**, enter **=Youth_Name**. The formula displays the name of the youth (Kristen Russell).
4. In cell **D40**, enter **=Activity**. The formula displays the Activity of the youth (Kids Game Night).
5. In cell **E40**, enter **=Grade**. The formula displays the youth Grade (G5).
6. In cell **F40**, enter **=Shirt_Size**. The formula displays the Shirt Size (S). See Figure 7-14.

Figure 7-14 Formulas entered in the Transfer Area

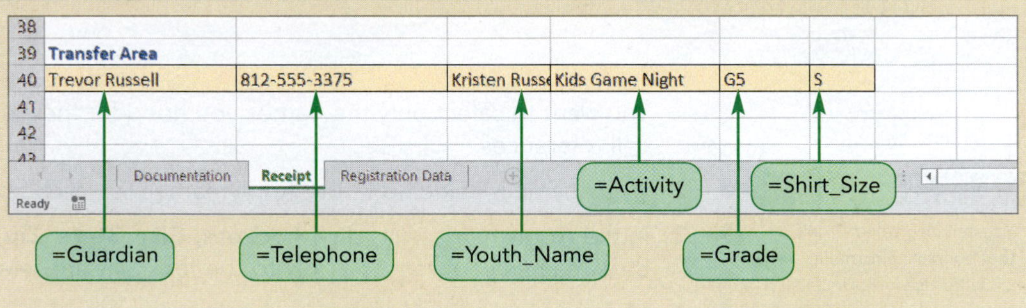

The worksheet contains all of the formulas required to create the receipt based on the registration data. Because Stephen relies on volunteers to enter registration data into the worksheet and print receipts, he wants to be sure the values entered are correct. You will continue to work on Stephen's application by creating validation checks, which are designed to prevent users from inserting incorrect data values. You will also protect cells so that volunteers cannot accidentally overwrite or delete the formulas. You'll complete both of these tasks in the next session.

REVIEW

Session 7.1 Quick Check

1. What is an Excel application?
2. What areas of a worksheet should you consider including in an Excel application?
3. What are two advantages of using defined names in workbooks?
4. What are three ways to create a defined name?
5. Is Annual Sales a valid defined name? Explain why or why not.
6. How do you select a cell or range using its defined name?
7. In the Report workbook, the defined name "Expenses" refers to a list of expenses in the range D2:D100. Currently, the total expenses are calculated by the formula =SUM(D2:D100). Change this formula to use the defined name.
8. How do you add defined names to existing formulas?

Session 7.2 Visual Overview:

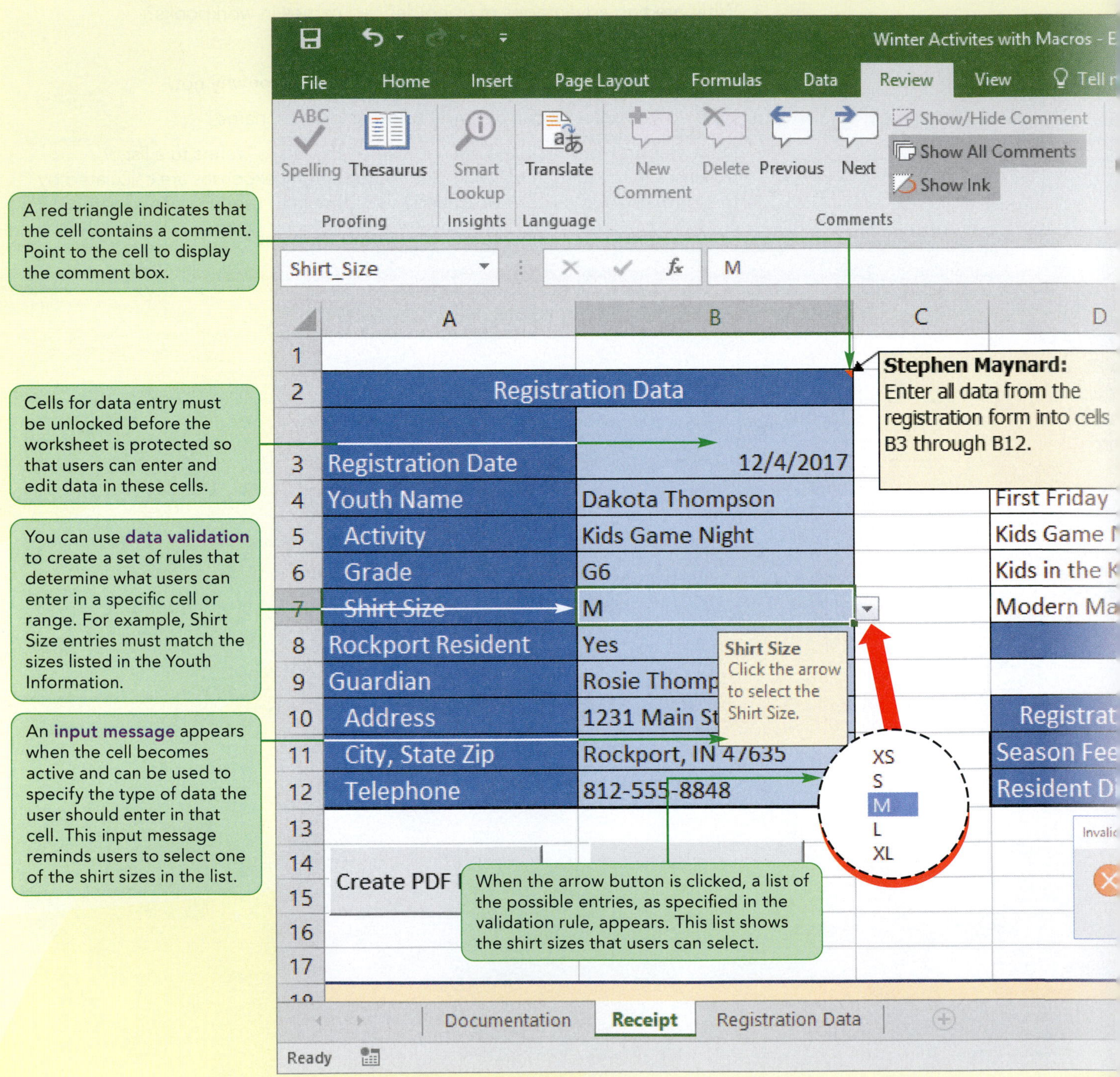

Winter Activites with Macros - E
File
Home
Insert
Page Layout
Formulas
Data
Review
View
Tell
Spelling
Thesaurus
Smart Lookup
Translate
New Comment
Delete
Previous
Next
Show/Hide Comment
Show All Comments
Show Ink
Proofing
Insights
Language
Comments
Shirt_Size
M
A red triangle indicates that the cell contains a comment. Point to the cell to display the comment box.
Cells for data entry must be unlocked before the worksheet is protected so that users can enter and edit data in these cells.
You can use data validation to create a set of rules that determine what users can enter in a specific cell or range. For example, Shirt Size entries must match the sizes listed in the Youth Information.
An input message appears when the cell becomes active and can be used to specify the type of data the user should enter in that cell. This input message reminds users to select one of the shirt sizes in the list.
Registration Data
Registration Date
12/4/2017
Youth Name
Dakota Thompson
Activity
Kids Game Night
Grade
G6
Shirt Size
M
Rockport Resident
Yes
Guardian
Rosie Thomp
Address
1231 Main St
City, State Zip
Rockport, IN 47635
Telephone
812-555-8848
Create PDF
Stephen Maynard:
Enter all data from the registration form into cells B3 through B12.
Shirt Size
Click the arrow to select the Shirt Size.
XS
S
M
L
XL
First Friday
Kids Game
Kids in the
Modern Ma
Registrat
Season Fee
Resident D
When the arrow button is clicked, a list of the possible entries, as specified in the validation rule, appears. This list shows the shirt sizes that users can select.
Documentation
Receipt
Registration Data
Ready

Data Validation and Protection

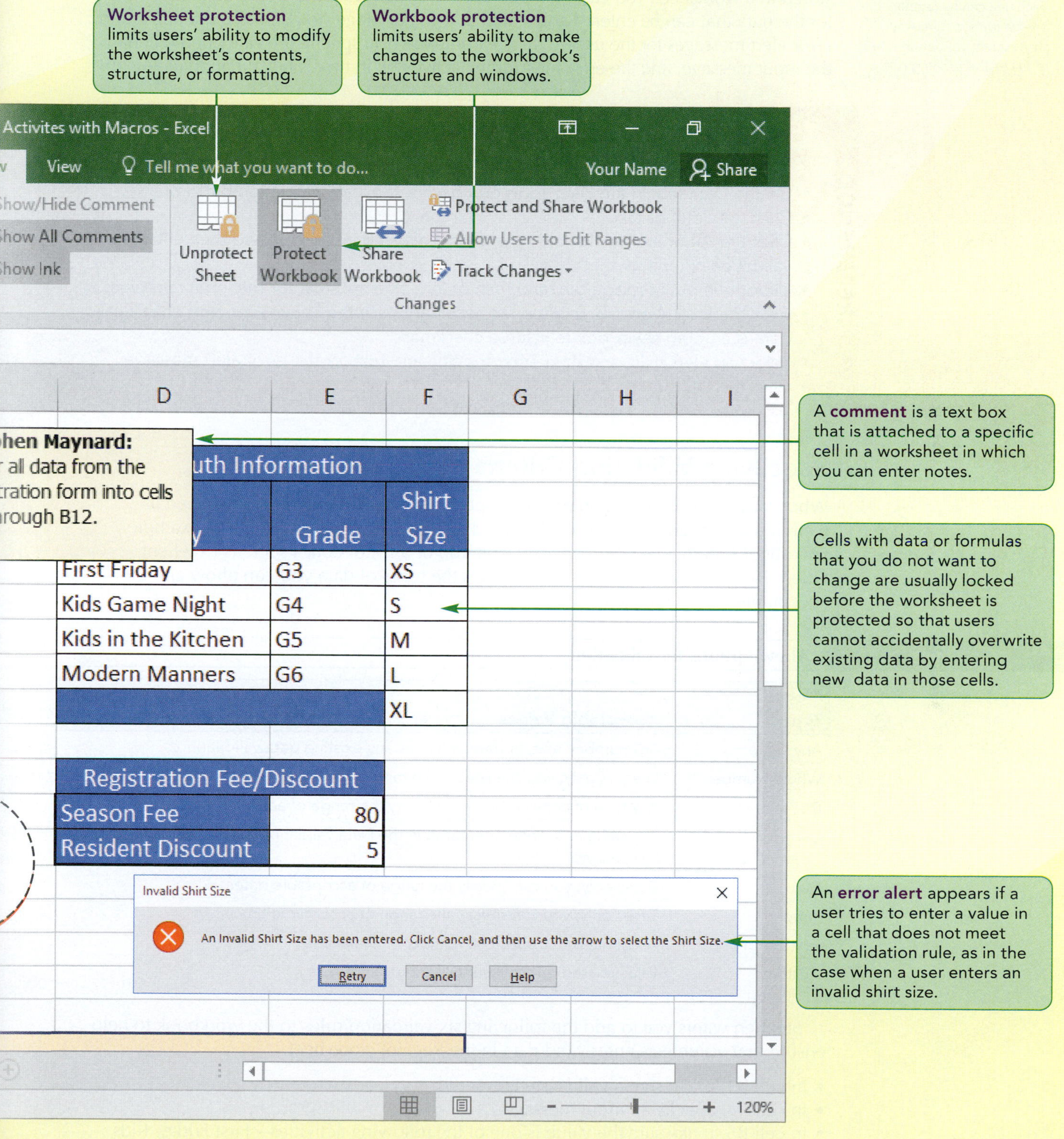
Worksheet protection limits users' ability to modify the worksheet's contents, structure, or formatting.
Workbook protection limits users' ability to make changes to the workbook's structure and windows.
Activites with Macros - Excel
View
Tell me what you want to do...
Your Name
Share
Show/Hide Comment
Show All Comments
Show Ink
Unprotect Sheet
Protect Workbook
Share Workbook
Protect and Share Workbook
Allow Users to Edit Ranges
Track Changes
Changes
D
E
F
G
H
I
phen Maynard:
r all data from the
tration form into cells
hrough B12.
uth Information
Grade
Shirt Size
First Friday
G3
XS
Kids Game Night
G4
S
Kids in the Kitchen
G5
M
Modern Manners
G6
L
XL
Registration Fee/Discount
Season Fee
80
Resident Discount
5
Invalid Shirt Size
An Invalid Shirt Size has been entered. Click Cancel, and then use the arrow to select the Shirt Size.
Retry
Cancel
Help
120%
A **comment** is a text box that is attached to a specific cell in a worksheet in which you can enter notes.
Cells with data or formulas that you do not want to change are usually locked before the worksheet is protected so that users cannot accidentally overwrite existing data by entering new data in those cells.
An **error alert** appears if a user tries to enter a value in a cell that does not meet the validation rule, as in the case when a user enters an invalid shirt size.

Validating Data Entry

TIP

Each cell can have only one validation rule. Any subsequent validation rule replaces the existing rule.

When collecting data, accuracy is important. To ensure that correct data is entered and stored in a worksheet, you can use data validation. Each **validation rule** defines criteria for the data that can be entered and stored in a cell or range. You can also add input and error alert messages for the user to that cell or range. You specify the validation criteria, the input message, and the error alert for the active cell in the Data Validation dialog box.

REFERENCE

Validating Data

- On the Data tab, in the Data Tools group, click the Data Validation button.
- Click the Settings tab.
- Click the Allow arrow, click the type of data allowed in the cell, and then enter the validation criteria for that data.
- Click the Input Message tab, and then enter a title and text for the input message.
- Click the Error Alert tab, and then, if necessary, click the Show error alert after invalid data is entered check box to insert a checkmark.
- Select an alert style, and then enter the title and text for the error alert message.
- Click the OK button.

Specifying Validation Criteria

When you create a validation rule, you specify the type of data that is allowed as well as a list or range of acceptable values (called **validation criteria**). For example, you might specify integers between 1 and 100 or a list of codes such as Excellent, Good, Fair, and Poor. Figure 7-15 describes the types of data you can allow and the acceptable values for each type.

Figure 7-15 **Allow options for validation**

Type	Acceptable Values
Any value	Any number, text, or date; removes any existing data validation
Whole Number	Integers only; you can specify the range of acceptable integers
Decimal	Any type of number; you can specify the range of acceptable numbers
List	Any value in a range or entered in the Data validation dialog box separated by commas
Date	Dates only; you can specify the range of acceptable dates
Time	Times only; you can specify the range of acceptable times
Text Length	Text limited to a specified number of characters
Custom	Values based on the results of a logical formula

Stephen wants you to add the following six validation rules to the workbook to help ensure that volunteers enter valid data in the Receipt worksheet:

- In cell B3, make sure a valid date is entered.
- In cell B4, specify an input message.
- In cell B5, make sure the value is one of the following activities—First Friday, Kids Game Night, Kids in the Kitchen, or Modern Manners.
- In cell B6, make sure the value is one of the following grades—G3, G4, G5, or G6.
- In cell B7, make sure the value is one of the following shirt sizes—XS, S, M, L, or XL.
- In cell B8, make sure the Rockport resident value is Yes or No.

Cell B3, which contains the Registration Date, requires the date that the registration was submitted, which is not necessary the date the registration is entered in the system. Stephen wants to be sure everyone enters a valid date in this cell. You will define the validation rule for the Registration Date.

To create the validation rule for the Registration Date cell:

1. If you took a break after the previous session, make sure the Winter Activities workbook is open and the Receipt worksheet is active.
2. Select cell **B3**. You will enter a date validation rule to ensure that a valid date is entered in this cell.
3. On the ribbon, click the **Data** tab.
4. In the Data Tools group, click the **Data Validation** button. The Data Validation dialog box opens with the Settings tab displayed. You use the Settings tab to enter the validation rule for the active cell.
5. On the Settings tab, click the **Allow arrow**, and then click **Date**. The Data Validation dialog box expands to display the options specific to dates.
6. Click the **Ignore blank** check box to deselect it. You want to ensure that cell B3 is not left blank and require users to enter a date value in the cell.
7. If necessary, click the **Data arrow**, and then click **greater than or equal to.** The dialog box reflects the selected criteria.
8. Enter **1/1/2017** in the Start date box to provide an example of what to look for when checking the cell. You cannot use data validation to simply check for the presence of data. You must provide an example for checking. See Figure 7-16.

TIP

To apply a validation rule to multiple cells, select the range and then create the validation rule.

Figure 7-16 Settings tab in the Data Validation dialog box

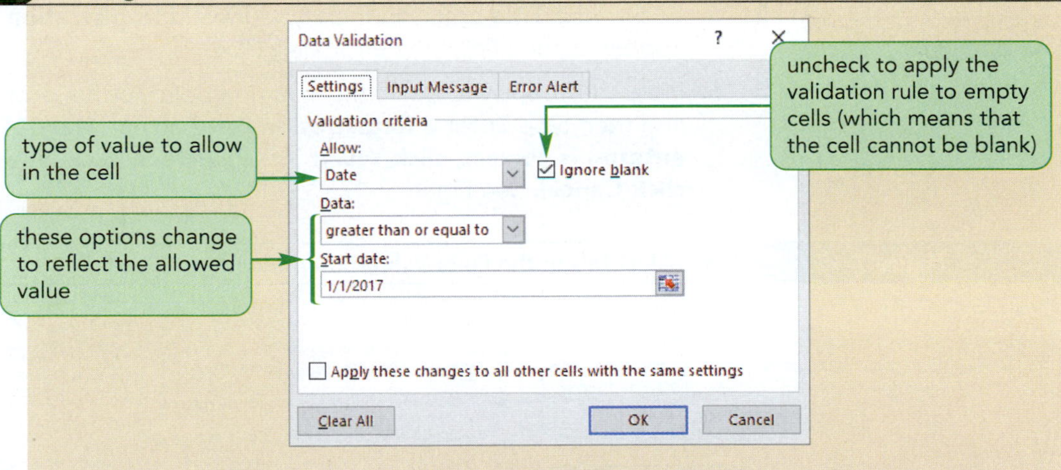

If you wanted to create a validation rule that checks if the date is the current date, you would select "equal to" in the Data list and then enter =TODAY() in the Date box. Then, a user cannot enter any date other than the current date. Stephen wants to check only for the presence of a date because sometimes the registration form is submitted on a different day than its data is entered.

Creating an Error Alert Style and Message

An error alert determines what happens after a user tries to make an invalid entry in a cell that has a validation rule defined. The three error alert styles are Stop, Warning, and Information. The Stop alert prevents the entry from being stored in the cell. The Warning alert prevents the entry from being stored in the cell unless the user overrides the rejection and decides to continue using the data. The Information alert accepts the data value entered but allows the user to choose to cancel the data entry.

Stephen wants to display an error alert if a volunteer enters data that violates the validation rule. Although the registration date is usually equal to the current date, a user might forget to enter the date. To account for this possibility, Stephen wants you to create a Warning error alert that appears when a user does not enter a registration date or enters a date prior to 1/1/2017. The user can then verify the date entered. If the entry is correct, the user can accept the entry. If the entry is incorrect, the user can reenter the correct date.

You'll create the Warning error alert for the Registration Date cell.

To create the Warning error alert for the Registration Date cell:

1. Make sure cell **B3** is still the active cell and the Data Validation dialog box is still open.
2. In the Data Validation dialog box, click the **Error Alert** tab. You use this tab to select the type of error alert and enter the message you want to appear.
3. Make sure that the **Show error alert after invalid data is entered** check box is selected. If unchecked, the error alert won't appear when an invalid value is entered in the cell.

TIP

You can change between showing and hiding the input and error alert messages as needed for new and experienced users.

4. Click the **Style arrow**, and then click **Warning**. This style allows the user to accept the invalid value, return to the cell and reenter a valid value, or cancel the data entry and restore the previous value to the cell.
5. Click in the **Title** box, and then type **Invalid Registration Date**. This text will appear as the title of the error alert box.
6. Press the **Tab** key to move the insertion point to the Error message box, and then type **Enter a Registration Date after 1/1/2017. If the date you entered is correct, click Yes. If it is incorrect, click No. If you are not sure, click Cancel.** See Figure 7-17.

Figure 7-17 Error Alert tab in the Data Validation dialog box

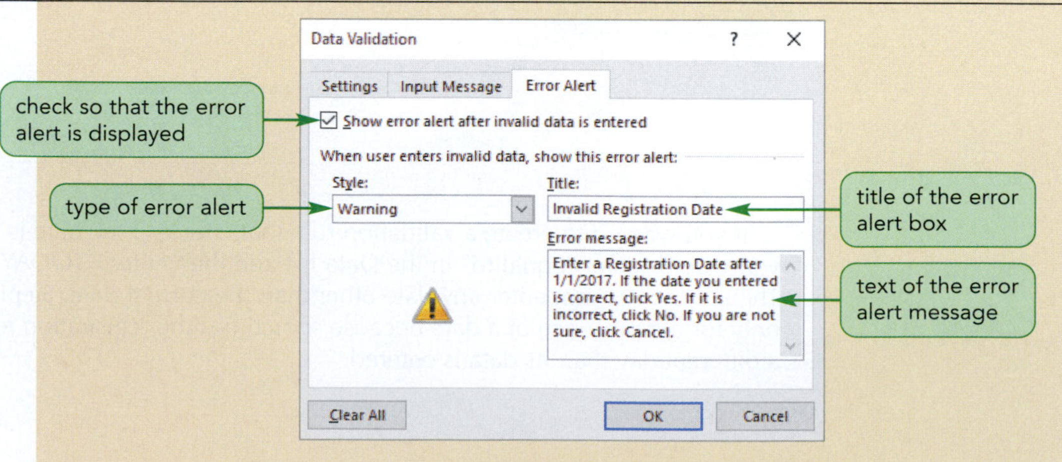

7. Click the **OK** button. The Data Validation dialog box closes.

Creating an Input Message

One way to reduce the chance of a data-entry error is to display an input message when a user makes the cell active. An input message provides additional information about the type of data allowed for that cell. Input messages appear as ScreenTips next to the cell when the cell is selected. You can add an input message to a cell even if you don't set up a rule to validate the data in that cell.

Stephen wants volunteers to see that they must enter a value for the Youth Name in cell B4. An input message will minimize the chance of a volunteer skipping this cell, so you will create an input message for cell B4.

To create an input message for the Youth Name cell:

1. Select cell **B4**. You will create an input message for this cell.
2. On the Data tab, in the Data Tools group, click the **Data Validation** button. The Data Validation dialog box opens.
3. Click the **Input Message** tab. You enter the input message title and text on this tab.
4. Verify that the **Show input message when cell is selected** check box contains a checkmark. If you uncheck this option, you cannot enter a new input message, and any existing input message will not be displayed when the selected cell becomes active.
5. Click in the **Title** box, and then type **Youth Name**. This title will appear in bold at the top of the ScreenTip above the text of the input message.
6. Press the **Tab** key to move the insertion point to the Input message box, and then type **Enter the youth's first and last name**. See Figure 7-18.

TIP

The maximum number of characters allowed in the Title box is 32.

Figure 7-18 Input Message tab in the Data Validation dialog box

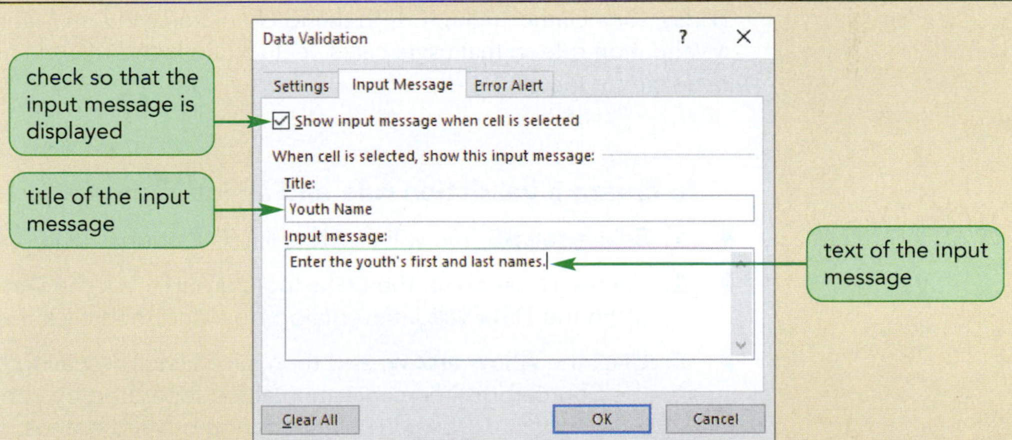

7. Click the **OK** button. The Data Validation dialog box closes. The input message appears in a ScreenTip because the cell is active. See Figure 7-19.

Figure 7-19 Input message for the Youth Name cell

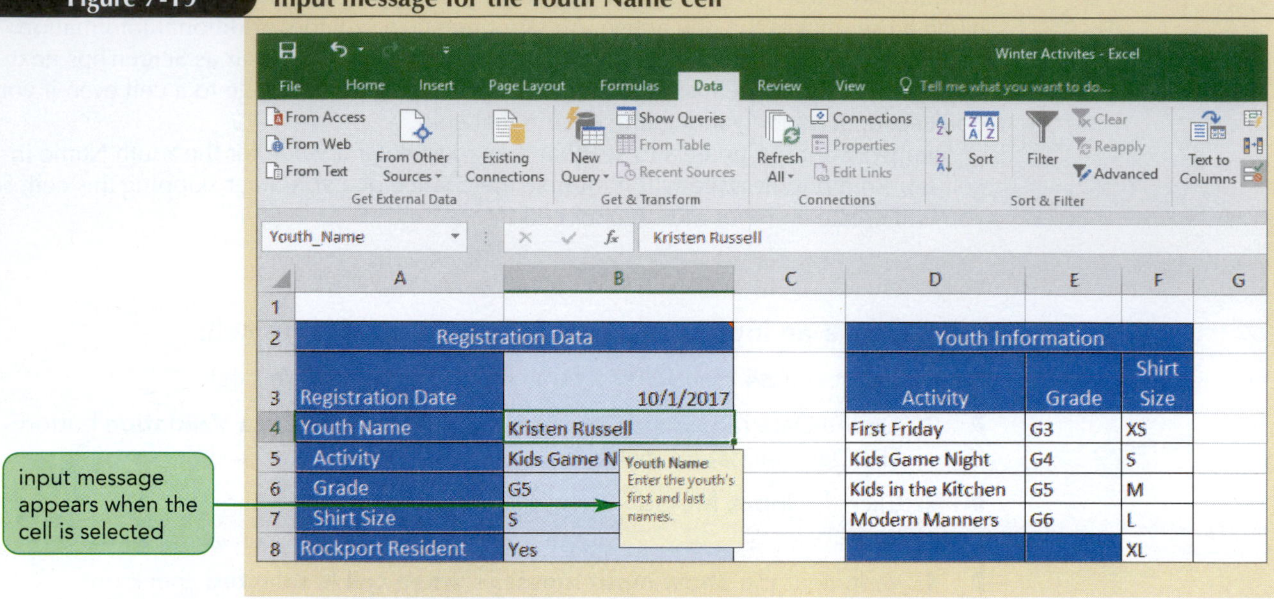

Creating a List Validation Rule

You can use the data validation feature to restrict a cell to accept only entries that are on a list you create. You can create the list of valid entries in the Data Validation dialog box, or you can use a list of valid entries in a single column or row. Once you create a list validation rule for a cell, a list box with the possible values appears when the user selects the cell.

Stephen wants you to use list validation rules for the Activity, Grade, and Shirt Size cells to ensure that users select a valid entry. The Activity has four possible values—First Friday, Kids Game Night, Kids in the Kitchen, and Modern Manners. You will create a validation rule so that users can select a valid entry. You will also create an input message for the cell.

To create a validation rule and an input message for the Activity cell:

1. Select cell **B5**. You will create a list validation rule for this cell.
2. On the Data tab, in the Data Tools group, click the **Data Validation** button to open the Data Validation dialog box, and then click the **Settings** tab.
3. Click the **Allow arrow**, and then click **List**. The dialog box expands to display the Source box. You can enter values separated by commas directly in the Source box, or you can select a range of valid entries in the worksheet.
4. Next to the Source box, click the **Collapse** button so you can see the entire worksheet.
5. Select the range **D4:D7**, which contains the four valid entry values, and then click the **Expand** button. The Data Validation dialog box returns to its full size, and =$D$4:$D$7 appears in the Source box. See Figure 7-20.

Figure 7-20 Activity List validation rule settings

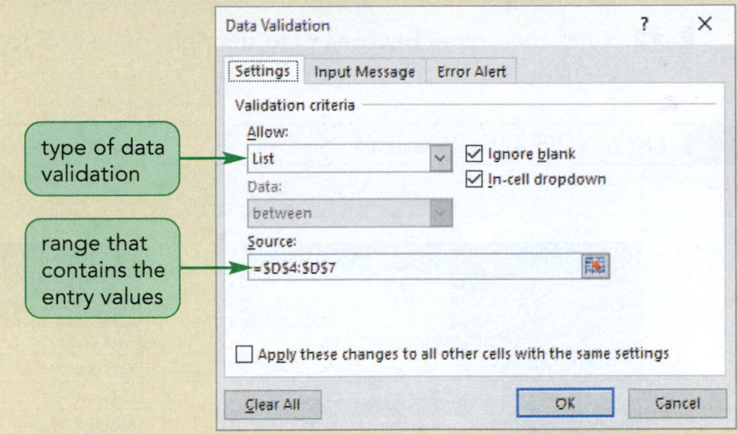

Next, you'll create an input message and an error alert.

6. Click the **Input Message** tab, click in the **Title** box, and then type **Activity** to enter the title of the input message.
7. Click in the **Input message** box, and then type **Click the arrow to select the Activity.** to enter the text of the input message.
8. Click the **Error Alert** tab, and then make sure that **Stop** appears in the Style box. You want to prevent a user from entering a value that is not included in the list of values you specified.
9. In the Title text box, type **Invalid Activity** to enter the title of the error alert.
10. In the Error message box, type **An invalid Activity has been entered. Click Cancel, and then use the arrow to select a valid Activity.** as the error message. See Figure 7-21.

Figure 7-21 Stop error alert for the Activity cell

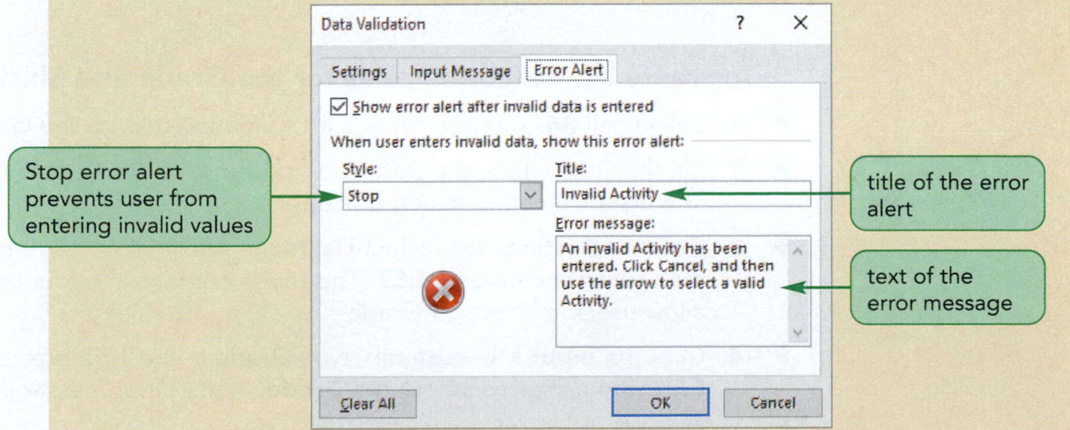

11. Click the **OK** button. The Data Validation dialog box closes, an arrow appears to the right of cell B5, and the input message appears in a ScreenTip.
12. Click the **arrow button** [▾] to the right of cell B5 to view the list of valid Activity entries. See Figure 7-22.

Figure 7-22 List of valid Activity entries

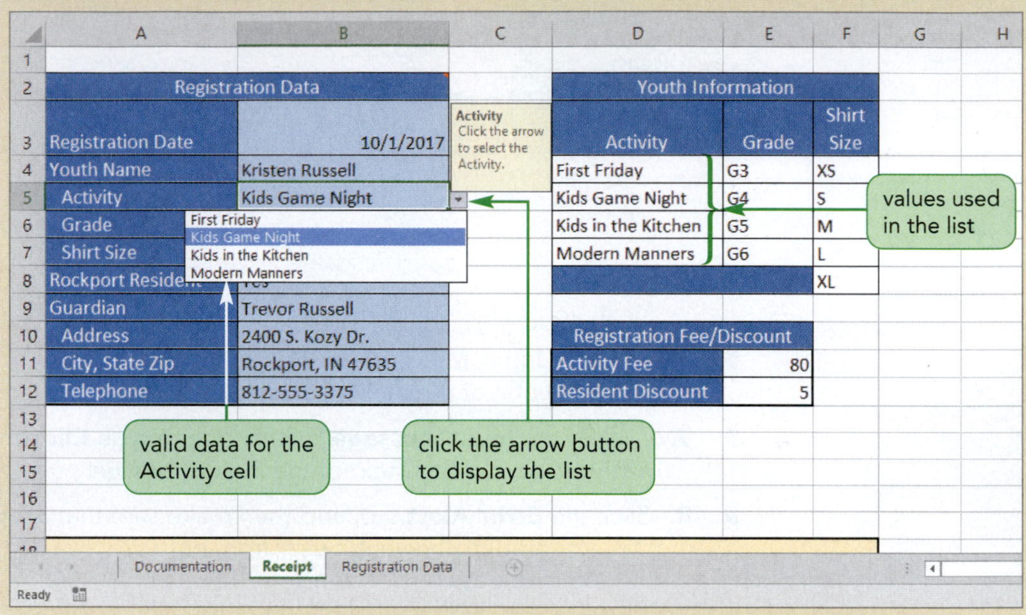

13. Press the **Esc** key to close the list.

Next, Stephen wants you to enter a list validation rule for cells B6 and B7, which specify the participant's Grade (G3, G4, G5, or G6) and Shirt Size (XS, S, M, L, or XL), respectively. Both rules will include an error alert.

To create list validation rules for the Grade and Shirt Size cells:

1. Select cell **B6**. You will create a list validation rule for the Grade cell.
2. On the Data tab, in the Data Tools group, click the **Data Validation** button. The Data Validation dialog box opens.
3. Click the **Settings** tab, select **List** in the Allow box, click the **Source** box, and then select the range **E4:E7**. This range contains the four values you want to allow users to select for Grade.
4. Click the **Input Message** tab, type **Grade** in the Title box, and then type **Click the arrow to select the Grade.** in the Input message box.
5. Click the **Error Alert** tab, verify that **Stop** appears in the Style box, type **Invalid Grade** in the Title box, and then type **An invalid Grade has been entered. Click Cancel, and then use the arrow to select the Grade.** in the Error message box.
6. Click the **OK** button. The dialog box closes, an arrow button appears to the right of cell B6, and the input message appears in a ScreenTip.
7. Select cell **B7** so you can create the validation rule for the Shirt Size cell.

8. In the Data Tools group, click the **Data Validation** button to open the Data Validation dialog box, and then click the **Settings** tab.
9. Select **List** in the Allow box, click the **Source** box, and then select the range **F4:F8**. This range contains the five values you want to allow users to select for the Shirt Size.
10. Click the **Input Message** tab, type **Shirt Size** in the Title box, and then type **Click the arrow to select the Shirt Size**. in the Input message box.
11. Click the **Error Alert** tab, make sure that **Stop** appears in the Style box, type **Invalid Shirt Size** in the Title box, and then type **An invalid Shirt Size has been entered. Click Cancel, and then use the arrow to select the Shirt Size.** in the Error message box.
12. Click the **OK** button. An arrow button appears to the right of cell B7, and the input message appears in a ScreenTip.

Stephen also wants you to enter a validation rule for cell B8 to limit the Rockport Resident cell to either Yes or No. This rule will also include an input message and an error alert. To specify the entries that the list includes, you will type each entry separated by commas in the Source box on the Settings tab in the Data Validation dialog box.

To create a list validation rule for the Rockport Resident cell:

1. Select cell **B8** so you can create a validation rule for the Rockport Resident cell.
2. On the Data tab, in the Data Tools group, click the **Data Validation** button. The Data Validation dialog box opens.
3. Click the **Settings** tab, select **List** in the Allow box, click the **Source** box, and then type **Yes, No** in the Source box. You typed the items for the list because they are not already entered in any range of the worksheet. See Figure 7-23.

Figure 7-23 List validation rule for the Rockport Resident cell

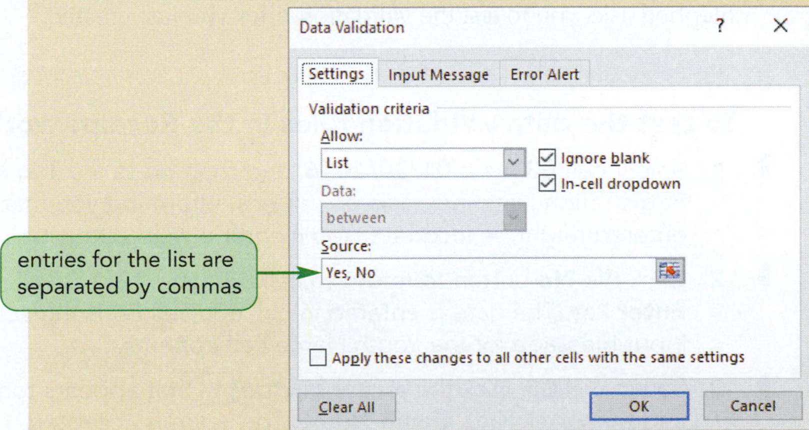

4. Click the **Input Message** tab, type **Rockport Resident** in the Title box, and then type **Click the arrow to select the correct response.** in the Input message box.

5. Click the **Error Alert** tab, make sure that **Stop** appears in the Style box, type **Invalid Rockport Resident** in the Title box, and then type **An invalid response for Rockport Resident has been entered. Click Cancel, and then use the arrow to select the response.** in the Error message box.
6. Click the **OK** button. An arrow button appears to the right of cell B8, and the input message appears in a ScreenTip.

You can edit an existing validation rule, input message, or error alert at any time by selecting the cell with the current validation rule and then opening the Data Validation dialog box. You can also add or remove an input message or error alert to an existing validation rule. Stephen notices that the Registration Date cell does not have an input message. For consistency, he wants you to add one now.

To create an input message for the Registration Date cell:

1. Select cell **B3**.
2. On the Data tab, in the Data Tools group, click the **Data Validation** button.
3. Click the **Settings** tab. The validation rule you created earlier is displayed.
4. Click the **Input Message** tab, type **Registration Date** in the Title box, and then type **Enter the date listed on the registration form.** in the Input message box.
5. Click the **OK** button. The input message is added to the Registration Date cell.

Testing Data Validation Rules

After you create validation rules, you should test them. You do this by entering incorrect values that violate the validation rules. Keep in mind that the only way an error occurs in cells that have a list validation is if an incorrect entry is typed or pasted in the cell. Entering invalid data will ensure that validation rules work as expected.

Stephen asks you to test the validation rules you just created.

To test the data validation rules in the Receipt worksheet:

1. Select cell **B3**, type **01/30/2016**, and then press the **Tab** key. The Invalid Registration Date message box opens, informing you that the value you entered might be incorrect. You'll enter a valid date.
2. Click the **No** button to return to cell B3, type **12/1/2017**, and then press the **Enter** key. The date is entered in cell B3. Cell B4 is the active cell, and the input message for the Youth Name cell appears.
3. Select cell **B5**, click the **arrow button** ▾ that appears to the right of cell B5, and then click **Kids Game Night**. The value is accepted.

   The only way an error occurs in cells that have a list validation is if an incorrect entry is typed or copied in the cell. You will try typing in cell B6.
4. In cell **B6**, type **5** and then press the **Enter** key. The Invalid Grade message box opens.
5. Click the **Cancel** button to close the message box and return to the original value in the cell.

6. Click the **arrow** button to the right of cell B6, and then click **G5**. The Grade is entered correctly as fifth grade.
7. In cell **B7**, type **M** and then press the **Enter** key. An error alert does not appear because M for medium is a valid entry.
8. In cell **B7**, type **SM** for small and then press the **Enter** key. The Invalid Shirt Size message appears.
9. Click the **Cancel** button, click the **arrow** button to the right of cell B7, and then click **S** in the validation list. The Shirt Size cell is entered as S for small.
10. Select cell **B8**, click the **arrow** button to the right of cell B8, and then click **Yes** for Rockport Resident.

TIP

If you click the Retry button in the error alert dialog box, you must press the Esc key to return to the original cell value.

The validation rules that you entered for cells B3 through B8 work as intended.

INSIGHT

Using the Circle Invalid Data Command

Validation rules come into play only during data entry. If you add validation rules to a workbook that already contains data with erroneous values, Excel does not determine if any existing data is invalid.

To ensure the entire workbook contains valid data, you need to also verify any data previously entered in the workbook. You can use the Circle Invalid Data command to find and mark cells that contain invalid data. Red circles appear around any data that does not meet the validation criteria, making it simple to scan a worksheet for errors. After you correct the data in a cell, the circle disappears.

To display circles around invalid data, perform the following steps:

1. Apply validation rules to an existing cell range, a worksheet, or a workbook.
2. On the Data tab, in the Data Tools group, click the Data Validation button arrow, and then click Circle Invalid Data. Red circles appear around cells that contain invalid data.
3. To remove the circle from a single cell, enter valid data in the cell.
4. To hide all circles, on the Data tab, in the Data Tools group, click the Data Validation button arrow, and then click Clear Validation Circles.

To ensure an error-free workbook, you should use the Circle Invalid Data command to verify data entered before you set up the validation criteria or to verify data in a workbook you inherited from someone else, such as a coworker.

Protecting a Worksheet and a Workbook

Another way to minimize data-entry errors is to limit access to certain parts of the workbook. Worksheet protection prevents users from changing cell contents, such as editing formulas in a worksheet. Workbook protection also prevents users from changing the workbook's association, such as inserting or deleting worksheets in the workbook. You can even keep users from viewing the formulas used in the workbook.

Stephen wants to protect the contents of the Receipt and Registration Data worksheets. He wants volunteers to have access only to the range B3:B12 in the Receipt worksheet, where new receipt data is entered. He also wants to prevent volunteers from editing the contents of any cells in the Registration Data worksheet.

Locking and Unlocking Cells

Every cell in a workbook has a **locked property** that determines whether changes can be made to that cell. The locked property has no impact as long as the worksheet is unprotected. However, after you protect a worksheet, the locked property controls whether the cell can be edited. You unlock a cell by turning off the locked property. By default, the locked property is turned on for each cell, and worksheet protection is turned off.

So, unless you unlock cells in a worksheet *before* protecting the worksheet, all of the cells in the worksheet will be locked, and you won't be able to make any changes in the worksheet. Usually, you will want to protect the worksheet but leave some cells unlocked. For example, you might want to lock cells that contain formulas and formatting so they cannot be changed, but unlock cells in which you want to enter data.

To protect some—but not all—cells in a worksheet, you first turn off the locked property of cells in which data can be entered. Then, you protect the worksheet to activate the locked property for the remaining cells.

In the Receipt worksheet, Stephen wants users to be able to enter data in the range B3:B12 but not in any other cell. To do this, you must unlock the cells in the range B3:B12.

To unlock the cells in the range B3:B12:

1. In the Receipt worksheet, select the range **B3:B12**. You want to unlock the cells in this range before you protect the worksheet.
2. On the ribbon, click the **Home** tab.
3. In the Cells group, click the **Format** button, and then click **Format Cells** (or press the **Ctrl+1** keys). The Format Cells dialog box opens. The locked property is on the Protection tab.
4. Click the **Protection** tab, and then click the **Locked** check box to remove the checkmark. See Figure 7-24.

TIP

Click the Format button in the Cells group, then click Lock Cell to add or remove the locked property for selected cells.

Figure 7-24 Protection tab in the Format Cells dialog box

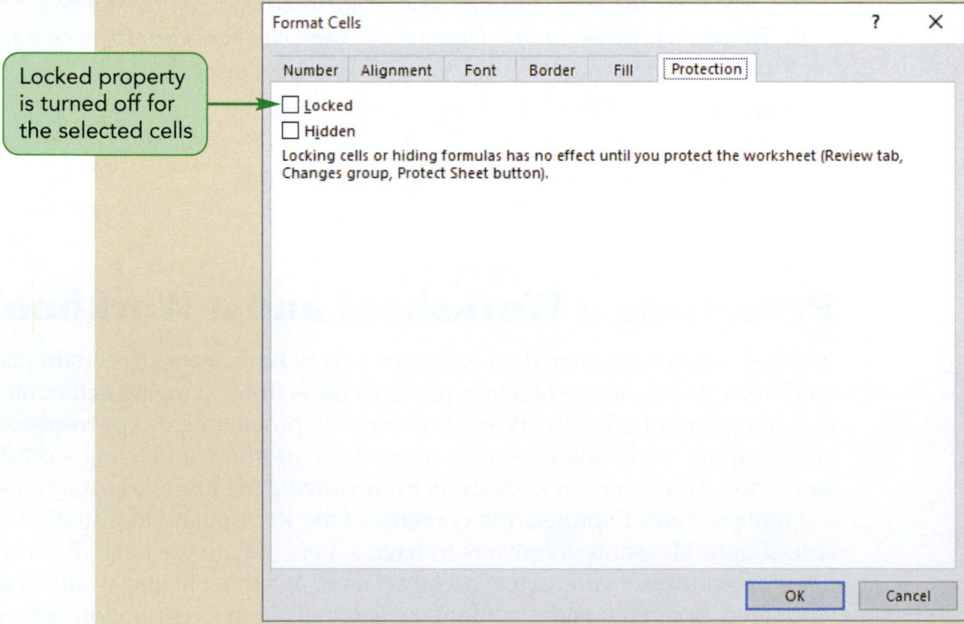

5. Click the **OK** button. The cells in the range B3:B12 are unlocked.
6. Select cell **A1** to deselect the range.

Protecting a Worksheet

When you set up worksheet protection, you specify which actions are still available to users in the protected worksheet. For example, you can choose to allow users to insert new rows or columns or to delete rows and columns. You can limit the user to selecting only unlocked cells or allow the user to select any cell in the worksheet. These choices remain active as long as the worksheet is protected.

A protected worksheet can always be unprotected. You can also add a password to the protected worksheet that users must enter in order to turn off the protection. Passwords are case sensitive, which means the uppercase and lowercase letters are considered different letters. If you are concerned that users will turn off protection and make changes to formulas, you should use a password; otherwise, it is probably best to not specify a password. Keep in mind that if you forget the password, it is very difficult to remove the worksheet protection.

REFERENCE

Protecting a Worksheet

- Select the cells and ranges to unlock so that users can enter data in them.
- On the Home tab, in the Cells group, click the Format button, and then click Format Cells (or press the Ctrl+1 keys).
- In the Format Cells dialog box, click the Protection tab.
- Click the Locked check box to remove the checkmark, and then click the OK button.
- On the Review tab, in the Changes group, click the Protect Sheet button.
- Enter a password (optional).
- Select all of the actions you want to allow users to take when the worksheet is protected.
- Click the OK button.

Stephen wants to protect the Receipt and Registration Data worksheets, but he doesn't want a password specified. You will enable worksheet protection that will allow users to select any cell in the worksheets but enter data only in the unlocked cells.

To protect the Receipt worksheet:

1. On the ribbon, click the **Review** tab.
2. In the Changes group, click the **Protect Sheet** button. The Protect Sheet dialog box opens. See Figure 7-25.

Figure 7-25 Protect Sheet dialog box

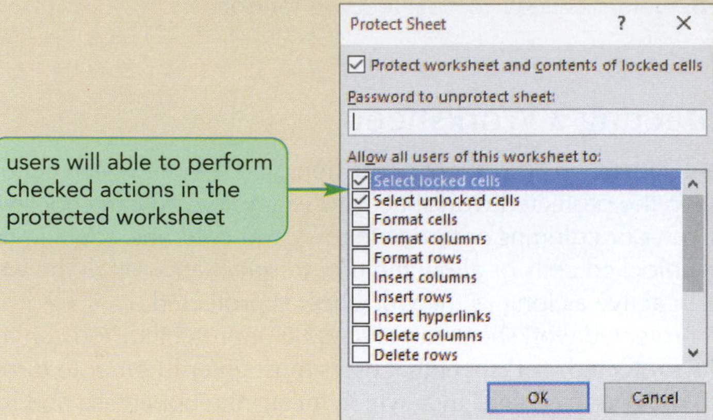

TIP

Keep passwords in a safe place. Remember, passwords are case sensitive. If you forget the password, it is very difficult to remove the worksheet protection.

You will leave the Password to unprotect sheet box blank because you do not want to use a password. By default, users can select both locked and unlocked cells, which constitute all of the cells in the worksheet, but they can enter or edit values only in unlocked cells.

3. Click the **OK** button. The Protect Sheet dialog box closes, and the Protect Sheet button changes to the Unprotect Sheet button.

Any time you modify a worksheet, you should test the worksheet to ensure that changes work as intended. You'll test the protection you added to the Receipt worksheet by trying to edit a locked cell and then trying to edit an unlocked cell.

To test the Receipt worksheet protection:

1. Select cell **B14**, and then type **1**. As soon as you press any key, a dialog box opens, indicating that the cell is protected and cannot be modified. See Figure 7-26.

Figure 7-26 Cell protection error message

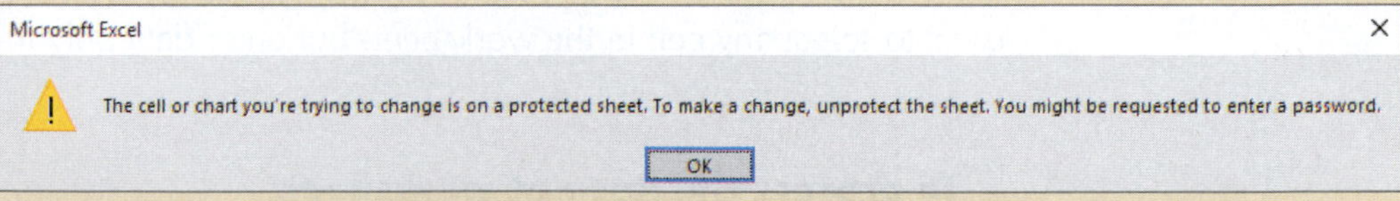

2. Click the **OK** button.
3. Click cell **B8**, type **No**, and then press the **Enter** key. The Rockport Resident cell is updated because you allowed editing in the range B3:B12.

   A user can enter and edit values in any cell in the range B3:B12. Although users can select any cell in the worksheet, they cannot make an entry in any other cell outside of that range.

4. On the Quick Access Toolbar, click the **Undo** button to return the Rockport Resident cell to Yes.

You will repeat this process to protect all of the cells in the Registration Data worksheet. Then you will test to see what would happen if someone tried to edit one of the cells. Because you did not unlock any cells in the Registration Data worksheet, no cells may be edited.

To protect and test the Registration Data worksheet:

1. Go to the **Registration Data** worksheet.
2. On the Review tab, in the Changes group, click the **Protect Sheet** button. The Protect Sheet dialog box opens.
3. Click the **OK** button to accept the default set of user actions.
4. Select cell **A2**, and then type **B**. A dialog box opens, indicating that the cell is protected and cannot be modified. All of the cells in this worksheet are protected because no cells have been unlocked.
5. Click the **OK** button to close the dialog box.

Protecting a Workbook

Worksheet protection applies only to the contents of a worksheet, not to the worksheet itself. To keep a worksheet from being modified, you need to protect the workbook. You can protect both the structure and the windows of a workbook. Protecting the structure prevents users from renaming, deleting, hiding, or inserting worksheets. Protecting the windows prevents users from moving, resizing, closing, or hiding parts of the Excel window. The default is to protect only the structure of the workbook, not the windows used to display it.

You can also add a password to the workbook protection. However, the same guidelines apply as for protecting worksheets. Add a password only if you are concerned that others might unprotect the workbook and modify it. If you add a password, keep in mind that it is case sensitive and you cannot unprotect the workbook without it.

REFERENCE

Protecting a Workbook

- On the Review tab, in the Changes group, click the Protect Workbook button.
- Click the check boxes to indicate whether you want to protect the workbook's structure, windows, or both.
- Enter a password (optional).
- Click the OK button.

The contents of the Receipt and Registration Data worksheets, with the exception of the range B3:B12 in the Receipt worksheet, cannot be changed. However, a volunteer could inadvertently rename or delete the protected worksheet. To keep the worksheets themselves from being modified, you will protect the workbook. Stephen doesn't want users to be able to change the structure of the workbook, so you will set workbook protection for the structure but not the window.

To protect the Winter Activities workbook:

1. On the Review tab, in the Changes group, click the **Protect Workbook** button. The Protect Structure and Windows dialog box opens. See Figure 7-27.

Figure 7-27 Protect Structure and Windows dialog box

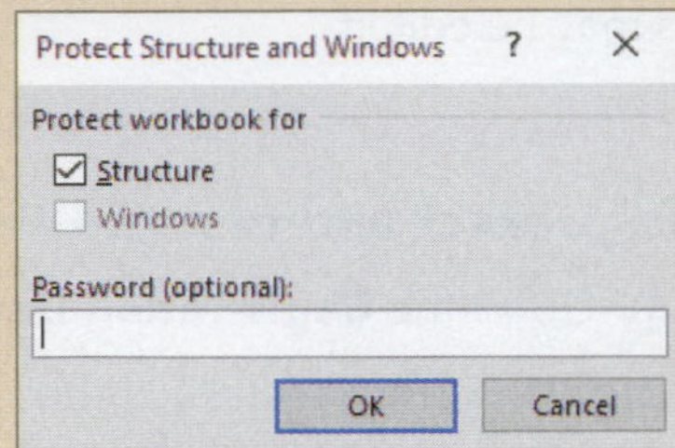

2. Make sure the **Structure** check box is checked and the **Password** box is blank. The Windows check box is unavailable and unchecked.
3. Click the **OK** button to protect the workbook without specifying a password.
4. Right-click the **Registration Data** sheet tab. On the shortcut menu, notice that the Insert, Delete, Rename, Move or Copy, Tab Color, Hide, and Unhide commands are gray. This indicates that the options for modifying the worksheets are no longer available for the Registration Data worksheet.
5. Press the **Esc** key to close the shortcut menu.

Unprotecting a Worksheet and a Workbook

You can turn off worksheet protection at any time. This is often referred to as *unprotecting* the worksheet. You must unprotect a worksheet to edit its contents. If you assigned a password when you protected the worksheet, you would need to enter the password to remove worksheet protection. Likewise, you can unprotect the workbook. If you need to insert a new worksheet or rename an existing worksheet, you can unprotect the protected workbook, make the changes to the structure, and then reapply workbook protection.

At this point, Stephen wants you to make additional changes to the Receipt worksheet, so you'll turn off worksheet protection in that worksheet. Later, when the worksheet is complete, Stephen can turn worksheet protection back on.

TIP

To remove workbook protection, click the Protect Workbook button in the Changes group on the Review tab.

To turn off worksheet protection for the Receipt worksheet:

1. Go to the **Receipt** worksheet.
2. On the Review tab, in the Changes group, click the **Unprotect Sheet** button. Worksheet protection is removed from the Receipt worksheet. The button changes back to the Protect Sheet button.

Inserting Comments

Comments are often used in workbooks to: (a) explain the contents of a particular cell, such as a complex formula; (b) provide instructions to users; and (c) share ideas and notes from several users collaborating on a project. The username for your installation of Excel appears in bold at the top of the comments box. If you collaborate on a workbook, the top of the comment boxes would show the name of each user who created that comment. A small red triangle appears in the upper-right corner of a cell with a comment. The comment box appears when you point to a cell with a comment.

REFERENCE

Inserting a Comment

- Select the cell to which you want to attach a comment.
- Right-click the selected cell, and then click Insert Comment on the shortcut menu (or press the Shift+F2 keys; or on the Review tab, in the Comments group, click the New Comment button).
- Type the comment into the box.
- Click a cell to hide the comment.

Stephen wants you to insert a note in cell A2 about entering data from the order form into the input section.

To insert a comment in cell A2:

1. In the Receipt worksheet, select cell **A2**.
2. On the Review tab, in the Comments group, click the **New Comment** button (or press the **Shift+F2** keys). A comment box opens to the right of cell A2. The username for your installation of Excel appears in bold at the top of the box. An arrow points from the box to the small red triangle that appears in the upper-right corner of the cell.
3. Type **Enter all data from the Registration form into cells B3 through B11.** in the comment box. A selection box with sizing handles appears around the comment box. If the box is too small or too large for the comment, you can drag a sizing handle to increase or decrease the size of the box. See Figure 7-28.

TIP

You can also add a comment by right-clicking the cell and then clicking Insert Comment on the shortcut menu.

Figure 7-28 Comment added to cell A2

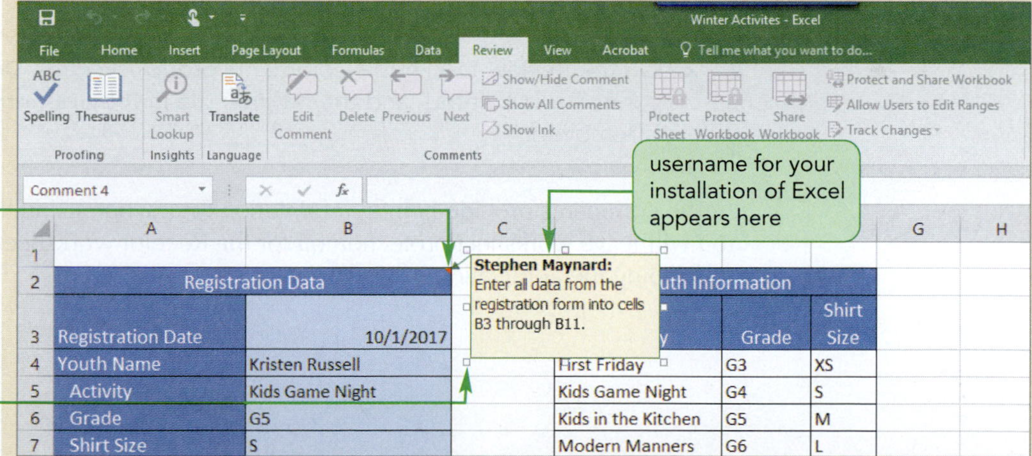

4. Click cell **B12** to hide the comment. The comment disappears. A small red triangle remains in the upper-right corner of cell A2 to indicate this cell contains a comment.

   Trouble? If the comment box did not disappear, comments are set to be displayed in the worksheet. On the Review tab, in the Comments group, click the Show All Comments button to deselect it.

5. Point to cell **A2**. The comment appears.

You can now edit your comments and enter a note in cell E34 explaining how the IF functions are used to determine whether to give the discount for Rockport Resident.

To edit comments in the input area:

1. Click cell **A2**.
2. On the Review tab, in the Comments group, click the **Edit Comment** button. The comment appears with the insertion point at the end of the comment text, so you can edit the incorrect cell reference.
3. Select **B11** in the comment box, and then type **B12**. The comment in cell A2 now correctly references the range B3:B12.
4. Select any other cell to hide the comment, and then point to cell **A2** to view the edited comment.
5. Click cell **E34**, and then on the Review tab, in the Comments group, click the **New Comment** button. A comment box opens to the right of cell E34.
6. In the comment box, type **This IF function determines whether to allow the Rockport Resident discount.**
7. Select cell **E35** to hide the comment. A small red triangle remains in the upper-right corner of cell E34 to indicate it contains a comment.
8. Point to cell **E34** to see the comment.

TIP

To keep an active cell's comment displayed, click the Show/Hide Comment button in the Comments group on the Review tab. Click the button again to hide the active cell's comment.

Stephen decides that the volunteers don't need to know how the Rockport Resident discount is calculated. You'll delete the comment in cell E34.

To edit and delete comments:

1. Select cell **E34**.
2. On the Review tab, in the Comments group, click the **Delete** button. The comment is deleted, and the red triangle in the upper-right corner of cell E34 is removed.

The comments provide helpful information for anyone using the Receipt worksheet. You will leave worksheet protection off for the Receipt worksheet while you finish developing the application for Stephen.

PROSKILLS

Written Communication: Documenting a Spreadsheet

Providing documentation for a spreadsheet is important because it provides instructions on the spreadsheet's use, defines technical terms, explains complex formulas, and identifies assumptions. By documenting a spreadsheet, you help users work more effectively. In addition, documentation helps you recall what is in the spreadsheet that might otherwise be forgotten months or years from now. Furthermore, when someone else becomes responsible for modifying the spreadsheet in the future, the documentation will help that person get up to speed quickly.

You can create a Documentation worksheet to provide an overview, definitions, assumptions, and instructions on how to use various parts of a workbook. Excel also offers a variety of tools to help you document spreadsheets, including:

- Defined names and structured references to make formulas easier to create and understand
- Data validation, including input messages specifying what to enter in a cell and error messages providing instructions on what to do if the data entered is incorrect
- Cell comments to explain complex formulas, give reminders, and so on
- Formula mode to view all formulas in a worksheet at one time

Providing documentation will help users better understand the application, which will save time and minimize frustration.

In this session, you used data validation to help ensure that all values entered in the Receipt worksheet are valid. You created validation rules that included input messages and error alert messages. You learned how to protect and unprotect both the worksheet and the workbook. In addition, you used comments to add notes to specific cells. In the next session, you'll automate some of the steps in the application by recording macros.

REVIEW

Session 7.2 Quick Check

1. Why would you want to validate data?
2. What is the purpose of the input message in the Data Validation command?
3. Describe the three types of error alert messages Excel can display when a user violates a validation rule.
4. What is a locked cell? What are unlocked cells?
5. What is the difference between worksheet protection and workbook protection?
6. Can you rename a protected worksheet? Explain why or why not.
7. Give two reasons for adding a comment to a worksheet cell.

Session 7.3 Visual Overview:

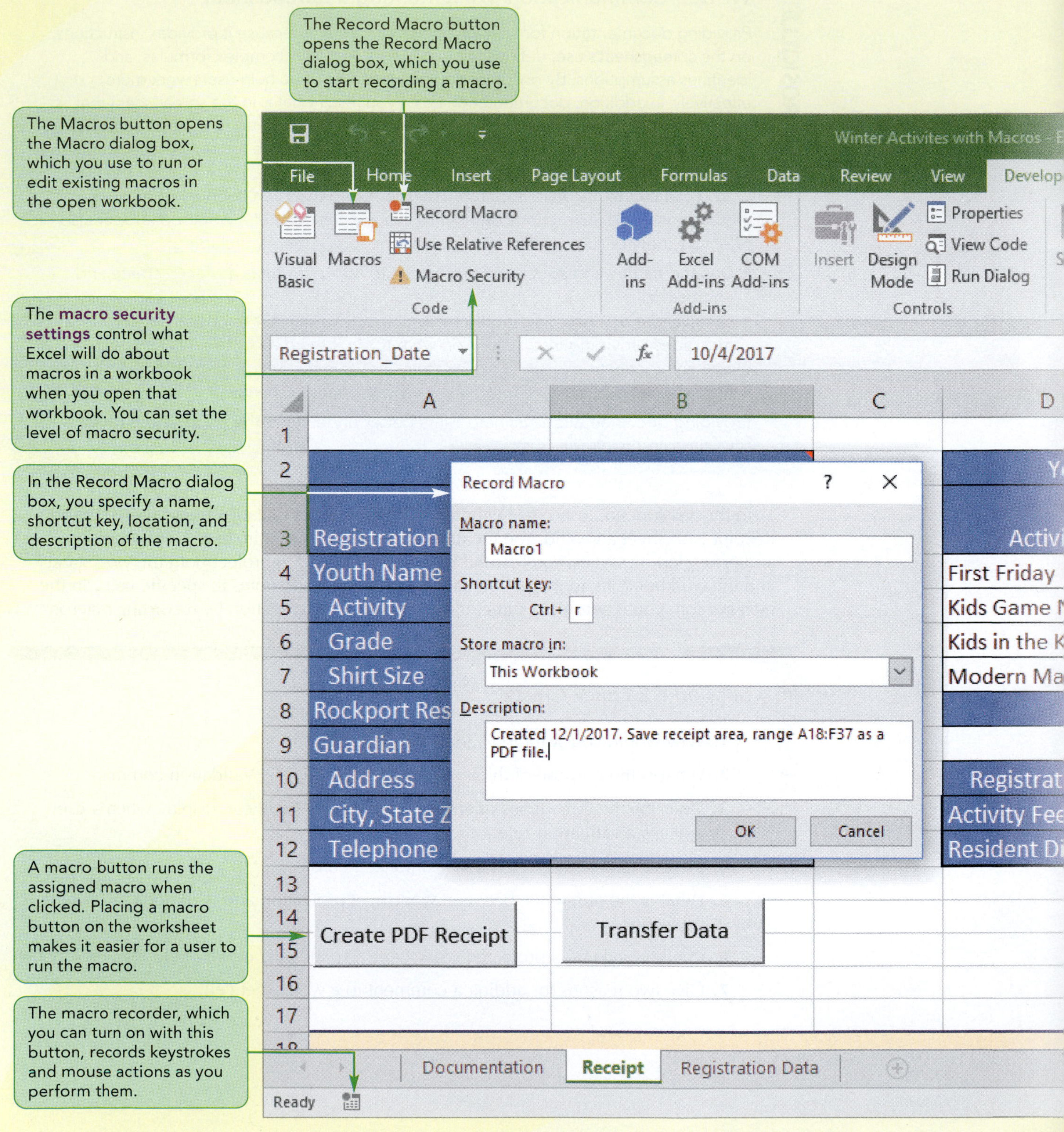
The Record Macro button opens the Record Macro dialog box, which you use to start recording a macro.
The Macros button opens the Macro dialog box, which you use to run or edit existing macros in the open workbook.
The macro security settings control what Excel will do about macros in a workbook when you open that workbook. You can set the level of macro security.
In the Record Macro dialog box, you specify a name, shortcut key, location, and description of the macro.
A macro button runs the assigned macro when clicked. Placing a macro button on the worksheet makes it easier for a user to run the macro.
The macro recorder, which you can turn on with this button, records keystrokes and mouse actions as you perform them.
Winter Activites with Macros
File
Home
Insert
Page Layout
Formulas
Data
Review
View
Visual Basic
Macros
Record Macro
Use Relative References
Macro Security
Code
Add-ins
Excel Add-ins
COM Add-ins
Insert
Design Mode
Properties
View Code
Run Dialog
Controls
Registration_Date
10/4/2017
Registration
Youth Name
Activity
Grade
Shirt Size
Guardian
Address
Telephone
First Friday
Activity Fee
Record Macro
Macro name:
Macro1
Shortcut key:
Ctrl+ r
Store macro in:
This Workbook
Description:
Created 12/1/2017. Save receipt area, range A18:F37 as a PDF file.
OK
Cancel
Create PDF Receipt
Transfer Data
Documentation
Receipt
Registration Data
Ready

Working with Macros

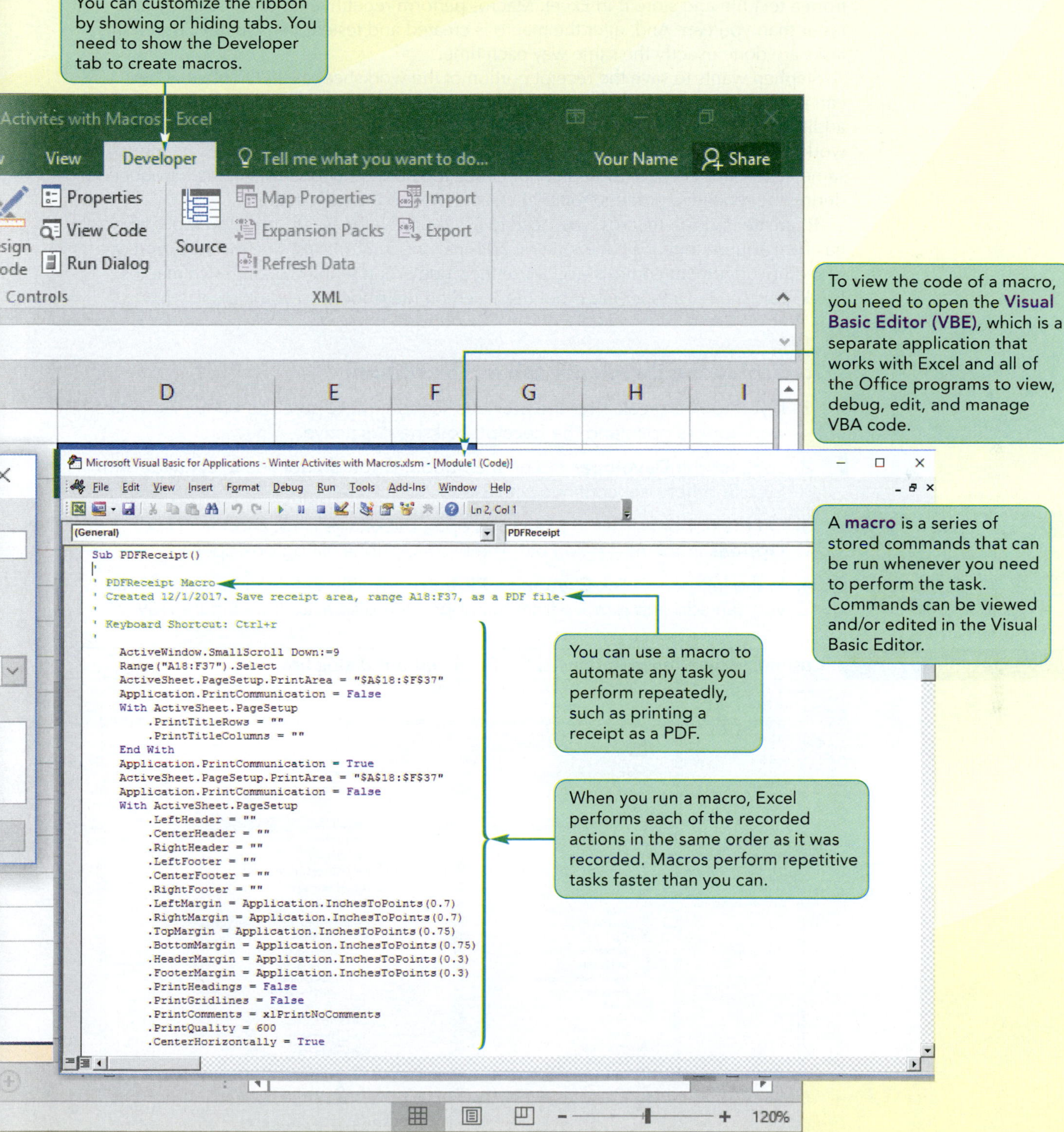

Automating Tasks with Macros

Using a macro, you can automate any task you perform repeatedly. For example, you can create a macro to print a worksheet, insert a set of dates and values, or import data from a text file and store it in Excel. Macros perform repetitive tasks consistently and faster than you can. And, after the macro is created and tested, you can be assured the tasks are done exactly the same way each time.

Stephen wants to save the receipt portion of the worksheet as a PDF file that he can send as an attachment to the guardian in an email confirming the registration. In addition, Stephen wants data from the receipt to be transferred to the Registration Data worksheet. He wants to simplify these tasks so volunteers don't need to repeat the same actions for each registration and reduce the possibility of errors being introduced during the repetitive process. You will create a macro for each action.

To create and run macros, you need to use the Developer tab. The Developer tab has five groups—one for code, one for add-ins, one for controls, one for XML, and one to modify document controls. You'll use the Code group when working with macros. By default, the Developer tab is not displayed on the ribbon, so you'll display it.

To display the Developer tab on the ribbon:

1. If you took a break after the previous session, make sure the Winter Activities workbook is open and the Receipt worksheet is active.
2. Look for the **Developer** tab on the ribbon. If you do not see it, continue with Step 3; otherwise, continue with Step 7.
3. On the ribbon, click the **File** tab to open Backstage view, and then click **Options** in the navigation bar. The Excel Options dialog box opens.
4. In the left pane, click **Customize Ribbon**. The different commands and tabs you can add and remove from the ribbon are displayed. See Figure 7-29.

TIP

You can also right-click the ribbon and click Customize the Ribbon to add a tab.

Figure 7-29 Customize the Ribbon options in the Excel Options dialog box

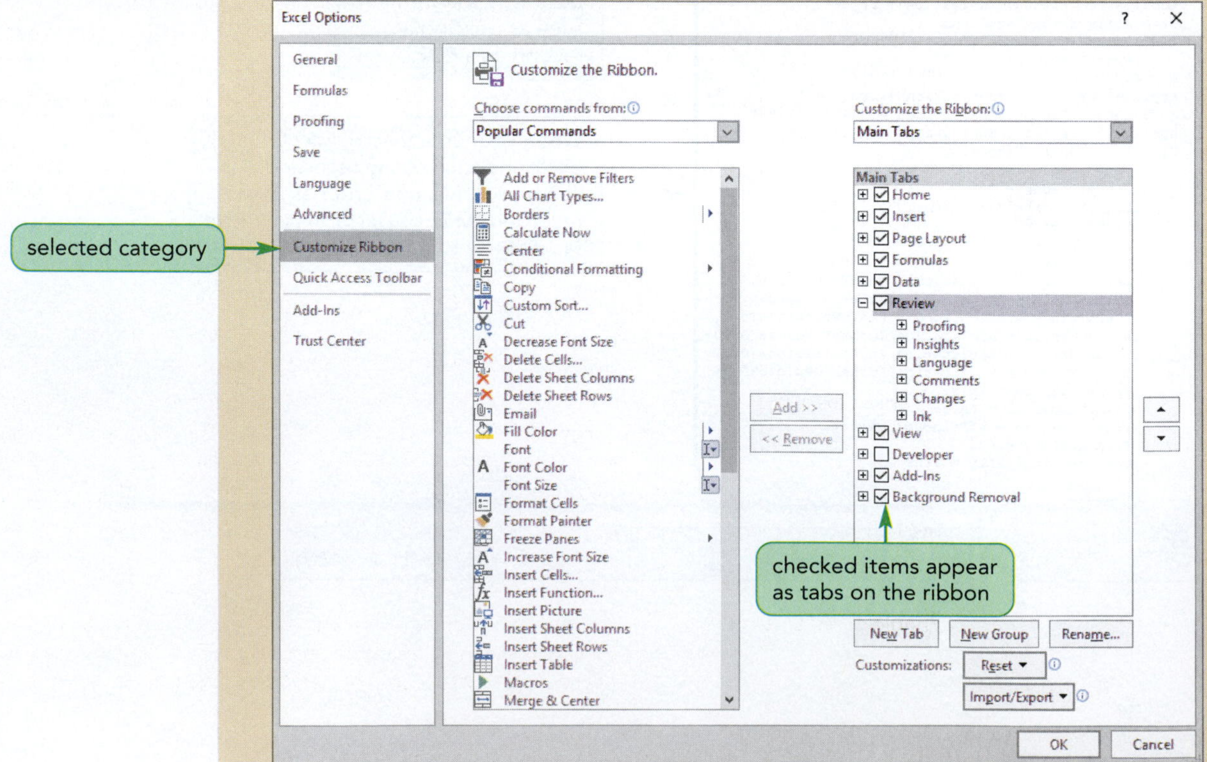

5. In the right pane, click the **Developer** check box to insert a checkmark.
6. Click the **OK** button. The Developer tab appears on the ribbon.
7. On the ribbon, click the **Developer** tab. See Figure 7-30.

Figure 7-30 Developer tab on the ribbon

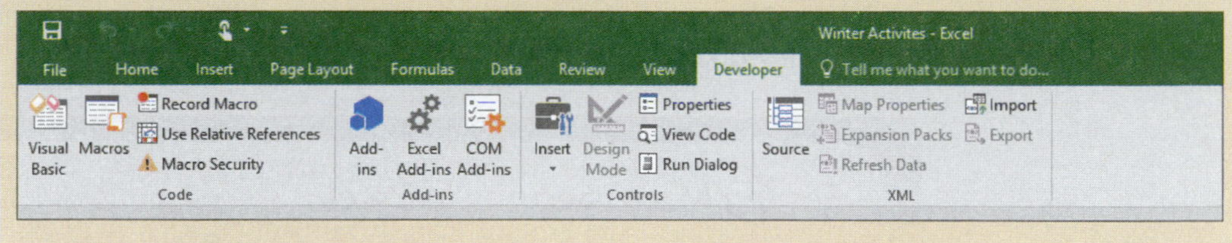

Protecting Against Macro Viruses

Viruses can be and have been attached as macros to files created in Excel and other Office programs. A **virus** is a computer program designed to copy itself into other programs with the intention of causing mischief or harm. When unsuspecting users open these infected workbooks, Excel automatically runs the attached virus-infected macro. **Macro viruses** are a type of virus that uses a program's own macro programming language to distribute the virus. Macro viruses can be destructive and can modify or delete files that may not be recoverable. Because it is possible for a macro to contain a virus, Microsoft Office 2016 provides several options from which you can choose to set a security level you feel comfortable with.

Macro Security Settings

The macro security settings control what Excel will do about macros in a workbook when you open that workbook. For example, one user may choose to run macros only if they are "digitally signed" by a developer who is on a list of trusted sources. Another user might want to disable all macros in workbooks and see a notification when a workbook contains macros. The user can then elect to enable the macros. Excel has four macro security settings, which are described in Figure 7-31.

Figure 7-31 Macro security settings

Setting	Description
Disable all macros without notification	All macros in all workbooks are disabled and no security alerts about macros are displayed. Use this setting if you don't want macros to run.
Disable all macros with notification	All macros in all workbooks are disabled, but security alerts appear when the workbook contains a macro. Use this default setting to choose on a case-by-case basis whether to run a macro.
Disable all macros except digitally signed macros	The same as the "Disable all macros with notification" setting except any macro signed by a trusted publisher runs if you have already trusted the publisher. Otherwise, security alerts appear when a workbook contains a macro.
Enable all macros	All macros in all workbooks run. Use this setting temporarily in such cases as when developing an application that contains macros. This setting is not recommended for regular use.

You set macro security in the Trust Center. The **Trust Center** is a central location for all of the security settings in Office. By default, all potentially dangerous content, such as macros and workbooks with external links, is blocked without warning. If content is blocked, the Message Bar (also called the trust bar) opens below the ribbon, notifying you that some content was disabled. You can click the Message Bar to enable that content.

You can place files you consider trustworthy in locations you specify; the file paths of these locations are stored as Trusted Locations in the Trust Center. Any workbook opened from a trusted location is considered safe, and content such as macros will work without the user having to respond to additional security questions in order to use the workbook.

REFERENCE

Setting Macro Security in Excel

- On the Developer tab, in the Code group, click the Macro Security button.
- Click the option button for the macro setting you want.
- Click the OK button.

or

- Click the File tab, and then click Options in the navigation bar (or right-click the ribbon, and then click Customize the Ribbon on the shortcut menu).
- Click the Trust Center category, and then click the Trust Center Settings button.
- Click the Macro Settings category, and then click the option button for a macro setting.
- Click the OK button.

Stephen wants the workbook to have some protection against macro viruses, so he asks you to set the security level to "Disable all macros with notification." When you open a file with macros, this macro security level disables the macros and displays a security alert, allowing you to enable the macros if you believe the workbook comes from a trusted source. After the macros are enabled, you can run them.

To set the macro security level:

1. On the Developer tab, in the Code group, click the **Macro Security** button. The Trust Center dialog box opens with the Macro Settings category displayed.
2. In the Macro Settings section, click the **Disable all macros with notification** option button if it is not already selected. See Figure 7-32.

Figure 7-32 Macro Settings in the Trust Center dialog box

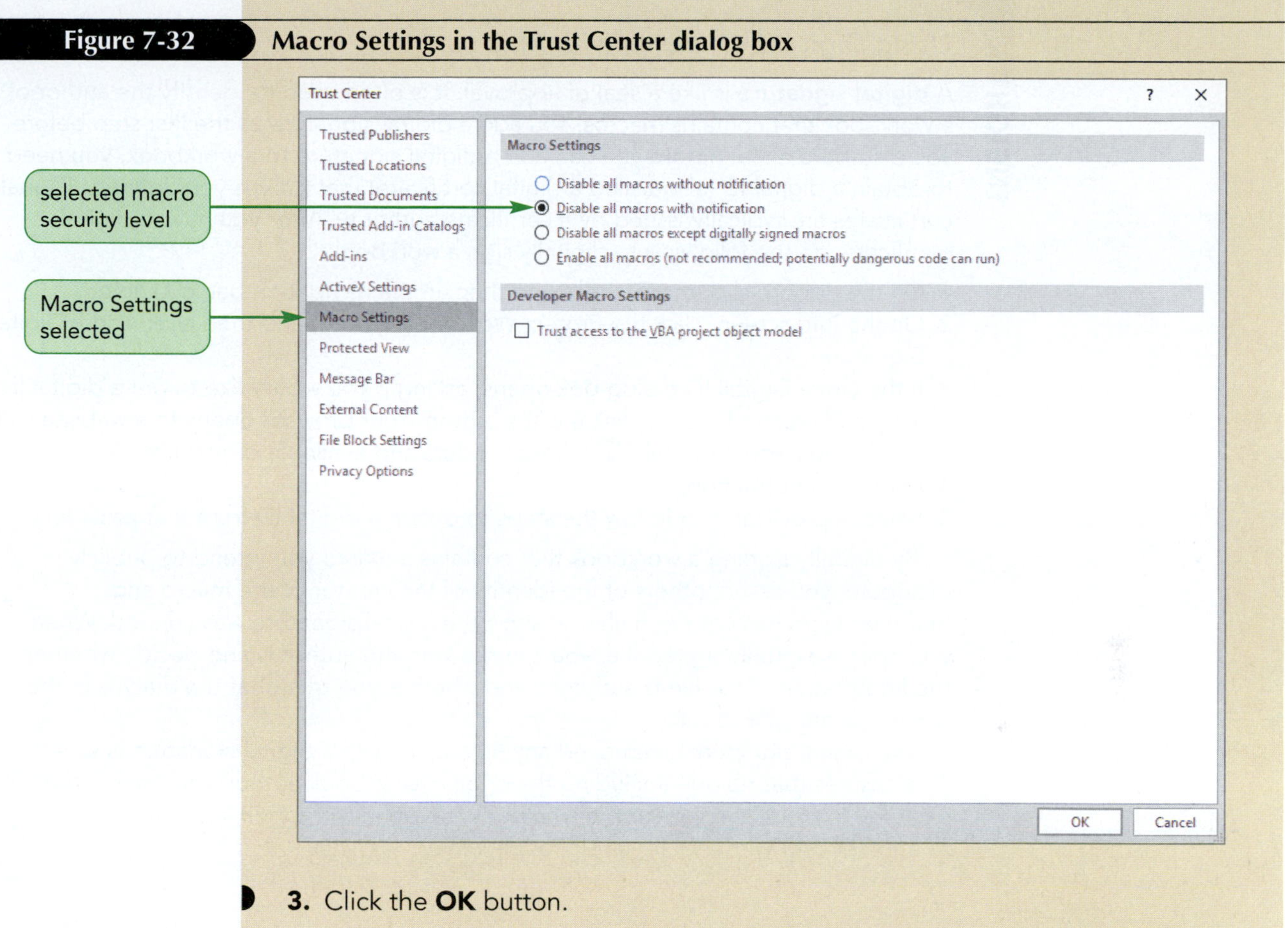

3. Click the **OK** button.

Each time you open a workbook that contains a macro detected by the Trust Center, the macro is disabled, and a Message Bar containing the SECURITY WARNING that macros have been disabled appears below the ribbon. If you developed the workbook or trust the person who sent you the workbook, click the Enable Content button to run the macros in the workbook. If you do not click the Enable Content button, you cannot run the macros in the workbook, but you can use the rest of the workbook.

INSIGHT

Using Digital Signatures with Macros

A **digital signature** is like a seal of approval. It is often used to identify the author of a workbook that contains macros. You add a digital signature as the last step before you distribute a file. Before you can add a digital signature to a workbook, you need to obtain a digital ID (also called a digital certificate) that proves your identity. Digital certificates are typically issued by a certificate authority. After you have a digital certificate, do the following to digitally sign a workbook:

1. On the ribbon, click the File tab, and then, in the navigation bar, click Info.
2. On the Info screen, click the Protect Workbook button, and then click Add a Digital Signature.
3. If the Get a Digital ID dialog box opens, asking if you would like to get a digital ID from a Microsoft Partner, click the Yes button. Your browser opens to a website with information about digital signature providers and available digital IDs.
4. Read the information.
5. Select a provider, and follow the steps to obtain a digital ID from that provider.

By digitally signing a workbook that contains a macro you intend to publicly distribute, you assure others of the identity of the creator of the macro and that the macro has not been altered since the digital signature was created. When you open a digitally signed file, you can see who the author is and decide whether the information in the file is authentic and whether you trust that the macros in the workbook are safe to run.

The digital signature is removed any time a file with a digital signature is saved. This ensures that no one (including the original workbook author) can open a digitally signed file, make changes to the workbook, save the workbook, and then send the file to another user with the digital signature intact.

Recording a Macro

You can create an Excel macro in one of two ways: You can use the macro recorder to record keystrokes and mouse actions as you perform them, or you can enter a series of commands in the **Visual Basic for Applications (VBA)** programming language. The macro recorder can record only those actions you perform with the keyboard or mouse. The macro recorder is a good choice for creating simple macros. For more sophisticated macros, you might need to write VBA code directly in the Visual Basic Editor (VBE).

For Stephen's application, the actions you need to perform can all be done with the keyboard and the mouse, so you will use the macro recorder to record the two macros. One macro will save the receipt as a PDF file, which is a file format created by Adobe Systems for document exchange. The second macro will transfer data from the Receipt worksheet to the Registration Data worksheet.

PROSKILLS

Decision Making: Planning and Recording a Macro

Planning and practice help to ensure you create an error-free macro. First, decide what you want to accomplish. Then, consider the best way to achieve those results. Next, practice the keystrokes and mouse actions before you actually record the macro. This may seem like extra work, but it reduces the chance of error when you actually record the macro. As you set up the macro, consider the following:

- Choose a descriptive name that helps you recognize the macro's purpose.
- Weigh the benefits of selecting a shortcut key against its drawbacks. Although a shortcut key is an easy way to run a macro, you are limited to one-letter shortcuts, which can make it difficult to remember the purpose of each shortcut key. In addition, the macro shortcut keys will override the standard Office shortcuts for the workbook.
- Store the macro with the current workbook unless the macro can be used with other workbooks.
- Include a description that provides an overview of the macro and perhaps your name and contact information.

Good decision making includes thinking about what to do and what not to do as you progress to your goals. This is true when developing a macro as well.

Each macro must have a unique name that begins with a letter. The macro name can contain up to 255 characters, including letters, numbers, and the underscore symbol. The macro name cannot include spaces or special characters. It is helpful to use a descriptive name that describes the macro's purpose.

Macro shortcut keys are used to run a macro directly from the keyboard. You can assign a shortcut key to run the macro by selecting the Ctrl key plus a letter or the Ctrl+Shift keys plus a letter. If you use the same set of shortcut keys that are already assigned to a default Excel shortcut, the new shortcut you create overrides the default Excel shortcut for the open workbook. For example, using the Ctrl+p keys to run a macro overrides the default Excel 2016 shortcut for opening the Print screen while the workbook containing the macro is open. Some people find macro shortcut keys a quick way to run a macro; others dislike them because they override the original function of the shortcut key. It's a personal preference.

A macro needs to be stored somewhere. By default, the macro is stored in the current workbook, making the macro available in only that workbook when it is open. Another option is to store the macro in the **Personal Macro workbook**, a hidden workbook named Personal.xlsb that opens whenever you start Excel, making the macro available any time you use Excel. The Personal Macro workbook stores commonly used macros that apply to many workbooks. It is most convenient for users on stand-alone computers. Finally, you can store the macro in a new workbook. Keep in mind that the new workbook must be open in order to use the macro. For example, an accountant might store a set of macros that help with end-of-the-month tasks in a separate workbook.

You can also add a description of the macro to briefly explain what it does. The description can also include the name of the person to contact and the date it was created.

REFERENCE

Recording a Macro

- On the Developer tab, in the Code group, click the Record Macro button.
- Enter a name for the macro.
- Specify a shortcut key (optional).
- Specify the location to store the macro.
- Enter a description of the macro (optional).
- Click the OK button to start the macro recorder.
- Perform the tasks you want to automate.
- Click the Stop Recording button.

Stephen provided you with the following outline of the actions needed for the macro to save the receipt as a PDF file:

1. Set the range A18:F37 as the print area for the Activity Registration Receipt range.
2. Create the PDF file, and name it "Receipt."
3. Remove the horizontal centering from the page.
4. Remove the print area.
5. Make cell A1 the active cell.

You'll record the steps for this macro using a macro named PDFReceipt that is assigned a keyboard shortcut, has a description, and is stored in the Winter Activities workbook. Practice these steps before recording the macro. Once you feel comfortable with the steps, you can start the macro recorder.

To start the macro recorder:

Save the workbook before recording a macro in case you make a mistake and need to restart.

1. Save the **Winter Activities** workbook. If you make a mistake when recording the macro, you can close the workbook without saving, reopen the workbook, and then record the macro again.
2. On the Developer tab, in the Code group, click the **Record Macro** button. The Record Macro dialog box opens. The Macro name box displays a default name for the macro that consists of the word "Macro" followed by a number that is one greater than the number of macros already recorded in the workbook during the current Excel session. See Figure 7-33.

Figure 7-33 Record Macro dialog box

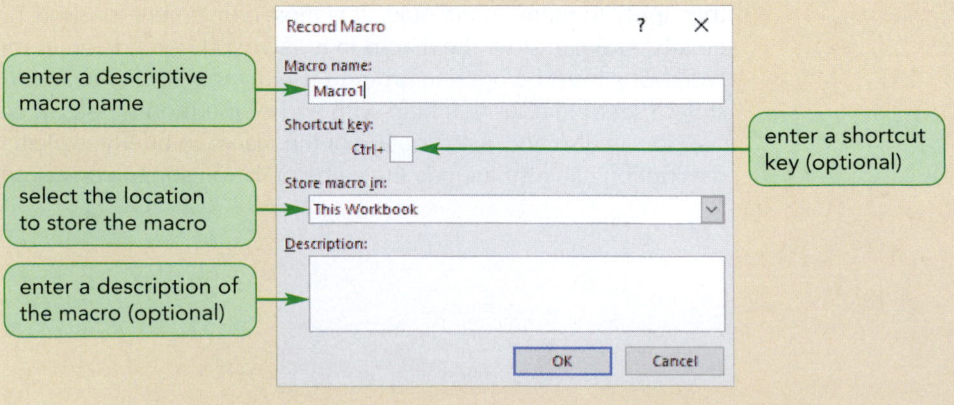

3. In the Macro name box, type **PDFReceipt** to change the selected default name to a more descriptive one, and then press the **Tab** key.
4. In the Shortcut key box, type **r** to set the Ctrl+r keys as the shortcut to run the macro from the keyboard, and then press the **Tab** key.
5. Verify that the Store macro in box is set to **This Workbook** to store the macro in the Winter Activities workbook, and then press the **Tab** key.
6. In the Description box, type **Created 12/1/2017. Save receipt area, range A18:F37, as a PDF file.** to enter notes about the macro.
7. Click the **OK** button. The workbook enters macro record mode. The Record Macro button changes to the Stop Recording button, which also appears on the status bar.

From this point on, *every* mouse click and keystroke you perform will be recorded and stored as part of the PDFReceipt macro. For that reason, it is very important to follow the instructions in the next steps precisely. Take your time as you perform each step, reading the entire step carefully first. After you finish recording the keystrokes, click the Stop Recording button to turn off the macro recorder.

To record the PDFReceipt macro:

1. Select the range **A18:F37**. This range contains the receipt that you want to print.
2. On the ribbon, click the **Page Layout** tab.
3. In the Page Setup group, click the **Print Area** button, and then click **Set Print Area**. The receipt is set as the print area.
4. In the Page Setup group, click the **Dialog Box Launcher** to open the Page Setup dialog box.
5. In the Page Setup dialog box, click the **Margins** tab, click the **Horizontally** check box to select it, and then click the **OK** button. The receipt is centered on the page.
6. On the ribbon, click the **File** tab to open Backstage view, and then click **Export** in the navigation bar.
7. On the Export screen, make sure **Create PDF/XPS Document** is selected in the left pane, and then click the **Create PDF/XPS** button in the right pane. The Publish as PDF or XPS dialog box opens, which is similar to the Save As dialog box.
8. In the File name box, type **Receipt** to replace the suggested filename.
9. Make sure the folder is set to the location specified by your instructor.
10. Click the **Publish** button. The receipt is saved as a PDF file, and automatically opens in a PDF reader, such as Windows Reader, Adobe Reader, or Adobe Acrobat, depending on which program is installed on your computer.

    Trouble? If the receipt doesn't open, you probably don't have a PDF reader installed on your computer. Continue with Step 14.

    Trouble? If a dialog box asking how you want to open this file opens, you need to specify an app to use. Select an app, and then click the OK button. Continue with Step 11.

11. Close the PDF file. You should now see the Receipt worksheet in the Winter Activities workbook.
12. On the Page Layout tab, in the Page Setup group, click the **Print Area** button, and then click **Clear Print Area**.
13. In the Page Setup group, click the Dialog Box Launcher to open the Page Setup dialog box, click the **Margins** tab, click the **Horizontally** check box so that the printout is no longer centered on the page, and then click the **OK** button.
14. In the Receipt worksheet, click cell **A1**.

    You have completed all of the steps in the PDFReceipt macro. You'll turn off the macro recorder.

15. Click the **Stop Recording** button on the status bar. The macro recorder turns off, and the button changes to the Record Macro button.

    Trouble? If you made a mistake while recording the macro, close the Winter Activities workbook without saving. If you created the Receipt file, delete the Receipt PDF file that you created. Reopen the workbook, and then repeat all of the steps beginning with the "To start the macro recorder" steps.

Be sure to turn off the macro recorder; otherwise, you'll continue to record your keystrokes and mouse clicks, leading to unintended consequences.

The process for saving a workbook that contains a macro is different from saving one that does not contain a macro. If you need to save the workbook before you complete this session, refer to the "Saving a Workbook with Macros" section later in this session.

Running a Macro

After you record a macro, you should run it to test whether it works as intended. Running a macro means Excel performs each of the steps in the same order as when it was recorded. To run the macro you created, you can either use the shortcut key you specified or select the macro in the Macro dialog box. The Macro dialog box lists all of the macros in the open workbooks. From this dialog box, you can select and run a macro, edit the macro with VBA, run the macro one step at a time so you can determine in which step an error occurs, or delete it.

REFERENCE

Running a Macro

- Press the shortcut key assigned to the macro.

or

- On the Developer tab, in the Code group, click the Macros button.
- Select the macro from the list of macros.
- Click the Run button.

You will test the PDFReceipt macro by running it.

To run the PDFReceipt macro:

1. On the ribbon, click the **Developer** tab.
2. In the Code group, click the **Macros** button. The Macro dialog box opens, listing all of the macros in the open workbooks. See Figure 7-34.

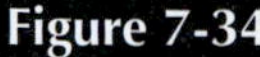

Figure 7-34 Macro dialog box

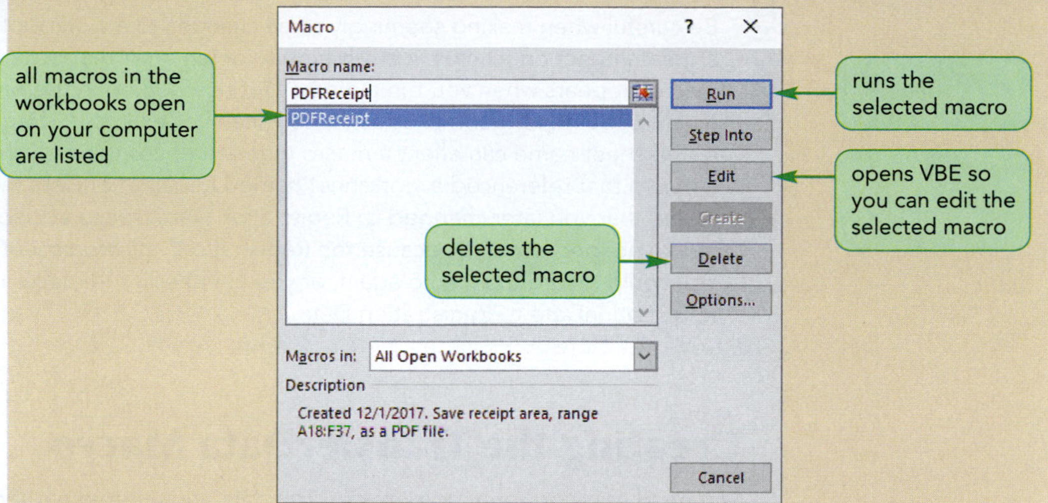

3. Verify that **PDFReceipt** is selected in the Macro name box, and then click the **Run** button. The PDFReceipt macro runs. The receipt is saved as a PDF file, and the file is opened in the PDF reader installed on your computer.
4. Close the PDF reader installed on your computer. No print area is selected, and cell A1 is the active cell in the Receipt worksheet.

   Trouble? If the PDFReceipt macro did not run properly, you might have made a mistake in the steps while recording the macro. On the Developer tab, in the Code group, click the Macros button. Select the PDFReceipt macro, and then click the Delete button. Click the OK button to confirm the deletion, and then repeat all of the steps beginning with the "To start the macro recorder" steps.

   Next, you will test the shortcut keys you used for the PDFReceipt macro.

5. Press the **Ctrl+r** keys. The PDFReceipt macro runs. The receipt is saved as a PDF file. No print area is selected, and cell A1 in the Receipt worksheet is the active cell.
6. Close the PDF reader installed on your computer.

   Trouble? If your macro doesn't end on its own, you need to end it. Press the Ctrl+Break keys to stop the macro from running.

The macro works as expected, printing the receipt as a PDF file.

INSIGHT

How Edits Can Affect Macros

Be careful when making seemingly small changes to a workbook, as these can have a great impact on macros. If a run-time error (an error that occurs while running a macro) appears when you run a macro that has worked in the past, some part of the macro code no longer makes sense to Excel. For example, simply adding a space to a worksheet name can affect a macro that references the worksheet. If you recorded a macro that referenced a worksheet named RegistrationData (no spaces in the name) that you later changed to Registration Data (space added to the name), the macro no longer works because the RegistrationData worksheet no longer exists. You could record the macro again, or you could edit the macro in VBA by changing RegistrationData to Registration Data.

Creating the TransferData Macro

You need to record one more macro. The data you entered earlier in the input section of the Receipt worksheet was never added to the Registration Data worksheet. Stephen wants to add this data to the next available blank row in the Registration Data worksheet. You'll record another macro to do this. You may want to practice the following steps before recording the macro:

1. Go to the Registration Data worksheet.
2. Turn off worksheet protection in the Registration Data worksheet.
3. Switch to the Receipt worksheet.
4. Select and copy the Transfer Area to the Clipboard.
5. Go to the Registration Data worksheet.
6. Go to cell A1, and then go to the last row in the Registration Data area.
7. Turn on Use Relative References. The Use Relative Reference button controls how Excel records the act of selecting a range in the worksheet. By default, the macro will select the same cells regardless of which cell is first selected because the macro records a selection using absolute cell references. If you want a macro to select cells regardless of the position of the active cell when you run the macro, set the macro recorder to record relative cell references.
8. Move down one row.
9. Turn off Use Relative References.
10. Paste values to the Registration Data worksheet.
11. Go to cell A1.
12. Turn on worksheet protection.
13. Switch to the Receipt worksheet, and then make cell B3 the active cell.

You may want to practice these steps before recording the macro. Stephen wants you to name this new macro "TransferData" and assign the Ctrl+t keys as the shortcut.

To record the TransferData macro:

1. Click the **Record Macro** button on the status bar to open the Record Macro dialog box, type **TransferData** in the Macro name box, type **t** in the Shortcut key box, store the macro in this workbook, type **Created 12/1/2017. Copy values in the Transfer Area in the Receipt worksheet to the Registration Data worksheet.** in the Description box, and then click the **OK** button. The macro recorder is on.
2. Go to the **Registration Data** worksheet.
3. Click the **Review** tab on the ribbon, and then click the **Unprotect Sheet** button in the Changes group to turn off protection.
4. Go to the **Receipt** worksheet, and then select the range **A40:F40** in the Transfer Area.
5. Click the **Home** tab on the ribbon, and then click the **Copy** button in the Clipboard group.
6. Click the **Registration Data** sheet tab, click cell **A1**, and then press the **Ctrl+↓** keys to go to the last row with values.
7. Click the **Developer** tab on the ribbon.
8. In the Code group, click the **Use Relative References** button. Relative references ensure that the receipt data being transferred is inserted in the next blank row (in this case, row 3) and not always in row 3 in the Registration Data worksheet.
9. Press the ↓ key to move to the first blank cell in the worksheet.
10. On the Developer tab, in the Code group, click the **Use Relative References** button. The Use Relative References button is toggled off.
11. On the ribbon, click the **Home** tab.
12. In the Clipboard group, click the **Paste button arrow**, and then click the **Values** button in the Paste Values section. This option pastes the values rather than the formulas from the Transfer Area.

    Trouble? If #REF! appears in row 3 of the Registration Data worksheet, you clicked the Paste button instead of the Paste Values button. Stop the macro recorder. Delete the macro, and begin recording the macro again.
13. Click cell **A1**, and then click the **Review** tab on the ribbon.
14. In the Changes group, click the **Protect Sheet** button. The Protect Sheet dialog box opens.
15. In the Protect Sheet dialog box, click the **OK** button.
16. Click the **Receipt** sheet tab, and then click cell **B3**.
17. Click the **Stop Recording** button on the status bar. The macro recorder turns off, and the button changes to the Record Macro button.

TIP

You can also turn off the macro recorder by clicking the Stop Recording button in the Code group on the Developer tab.

You have completed recording the TransferData macro. Next, you'll test whether it works. Stephen has a new registration to add to the worksheet. You'll enter this data as you test the TransferData macro.

To test the TransferData macro:

1. In the range **B3:B12**, enter the following data, pressing the **Enter** key after each entry:

   12/5/2017

   Will Lang

   First Friday

   G5

   L

   No

   Sandy Lang

   115 N. 7th St.

   Chrisney, IN 47611

   812-555–3444

2. Press the **Ctrl+t** keys. The TransferData macro runs, and the data transfers to the Registration Data worksheet.
3. Go to the **Registration Data** worksheet, and then verify that the data for Sandy Lang appears in row 4.
4. Go to the **Receipt** worksheet.

The TransferData macro makes it easy for the entered data to be transferred to the Registration Data worksheet.

Fixing Macro Errors

If a macro does not work correctly, you can fix it. Sometimes you'll find a mistake when you test a macro you just created. Other times you might not discover that error until later. No matter when you find an error in a macro, you have the following options:

- Rerecord the macro using the same macro name.
- Delete the recorded macro, and then record the macro again.
- Run the macro one step at a time to locate the problem, and then use one of the previous methods to correct the problem.

You can delete or edit a macro by opening the Macro dialog box (shown earlier in Figure 7-34), selecting the macro from the list, and then clicking the appropriate button. To rerecord the macro, simply restart the macro recorder, and enter the same macro name you used earlier. Excel overwrites the previous version of the macro.

Working with the Visual Basic Editor

To view the code of a macro, you need to open the Visual Basic Editor, which is a separate application that works with Excel and all of the Office programs to view, debug, edit, and manage VBA code. The VBE consists of several components, including the Code window that contains the VBA code, the Project Explorer window that displays a treelike diagram consisting of every open workbook, and a menu bar with menus of commands you use to edit, debug, and run VBA statements. You can access the Visual Basic Editor through the Macro dialog box or the Visual Basic button in the Code group on the Developer tab.

REFERENCE

Editing a Macro

- On the Developer tab, in the Code group, click the Macros button, select the macro in the Macro name list, and then click the Edit button (or on the Developer tab, in the Code group, click the Visual Basic button).
- Use the Visual Basic Editor to edit the macro code.
- Click File on the menu bar, and then click Close and Return to Microsoft Excel.

You can also use the Visual Basic Editor to copy a macro from one workbook to another. Do the following:

1. Set the security level on your computer to enable all macros.
2. Open both the workbook that contains the module you want to copy and the workbook that you want to copy the module to.
3. On the ribbon, click the Developer tab, and then in the Code group, click the Visual Basic button (or press the Alt+F11 keys) to open the Visual Basic Editor.
4. In the Visual Basic Editor, on the Standard toolbar, click the Project Explorer button (or press the Ctrl+R keys) to open the Project pane.
5. In the Project pane, drag the module that you want to copy to the destination workbook.
6. Close the Visual Basic Editor, and save the workbook with the copied module.
7. Return the security level to its original setting.

Stephen wants the PDFReceipt macro to stop in cell B3 of the Receipt worksheet. Right now, the macro stops with cell A1 selected. Although you can delete the PDFReceipt macro and record it again, it is simpler to edit the existing macro. You will edit the VBA command in the macro.

To view the code for the PDFReceipt macro:

1. On the ribbon, click the **Developer** tab.
2. In the Code group, click the **Macros** button. The Macro dialog box opens.
3. Click **PDFReceipt** in the Macro name list, and then click the **Edit** button. The Visual Basic Editor opens as a separate program, consisting of three windows—the Project Explorer, Properties, and the Code window.
4. If the Code window is not maximized, click the **Maximize** button on the Code window title bar. The Code window contains the VBA code generated by the macro recorder. You will see the beginning of the PDFReceipt sub. See Figure 7-35 (your window may differ).

Figure 7-35 Visual Basic for Applications Editor window

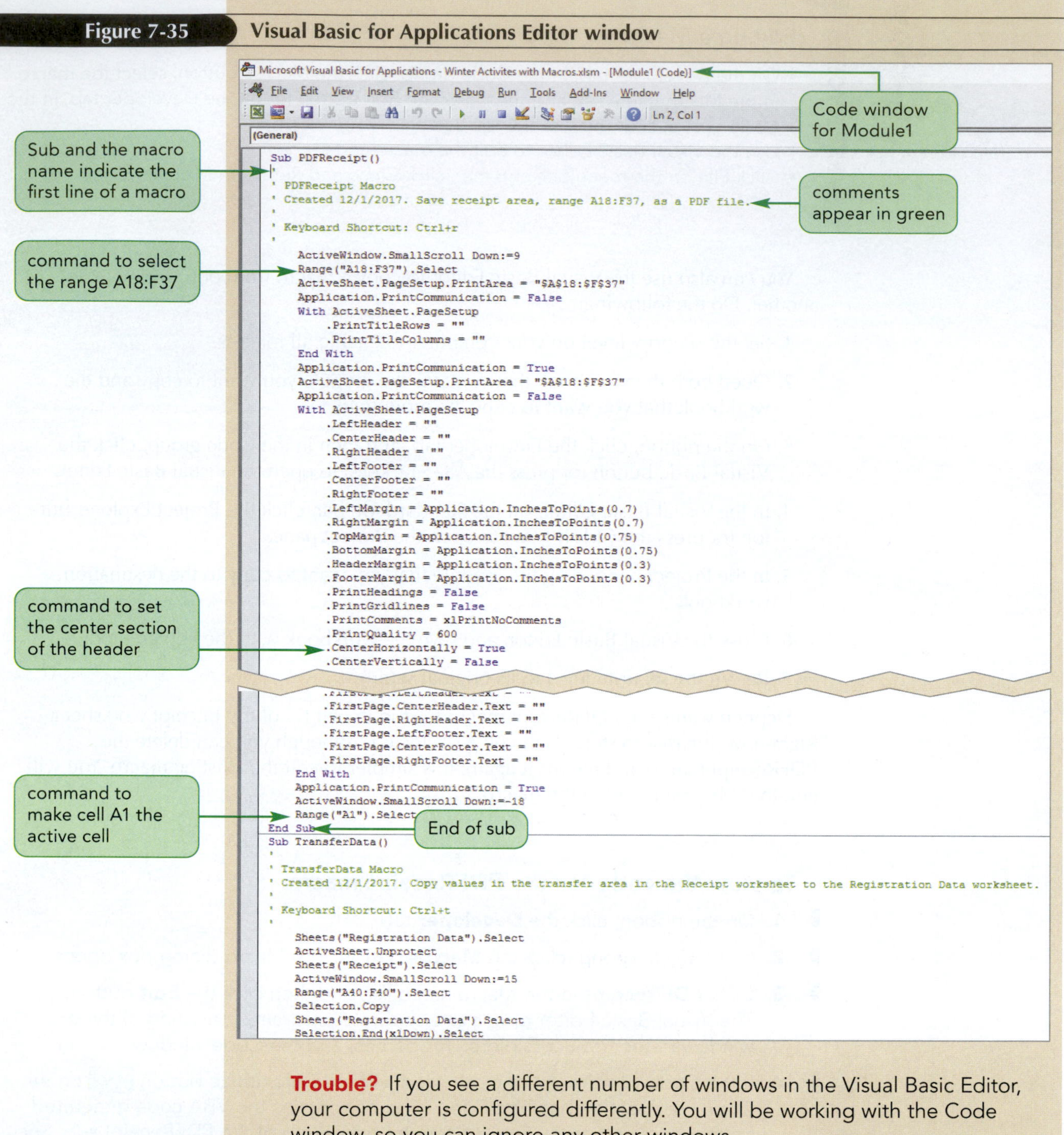

Trouble? If you see a different number of windows in the Visual Basic Editor, your computer is configured differently. You will be working with the Code window, so you can ignore any other windows.

Understanding the Structure of Macros

The VBA code in the Code window lists all of the actions you performed when recording the PDFReceipt macro. In VBA, macros are called **sub procedures**. Each sub procedure begins with the keyword *Sub* followed by the name of the sub procedure and a set of parentheses. In the example in Figure 7-35, the code begins with

```
Sub PDFReceipt()
```

which provides the name of this sub procedure—PDFReceipt—the name you gave the macro. The parentheses are used to include any arguments in the procedure. These arguments pass information to the sub procedure and have roughly the same purpose as the arguments in an Excel function. If you write your own VBA code, sub procedure arguments are an important part of the programming process. However, they are not used when you create macros with the macro recorder.

Following the `Sub PDFReceipt()` statement are comments about the macro taken from the macro name, shortcut key, and description you entered in the Record Macro dialog box. Each line appears in green and is preceded by an apostrophe ('). The apostrophe indicates that the line is a comment and does not include any actions Excel needs to perform.

After the comments is the body of the macro, a listing of all of the commands performed by the PDFReceipt macro as written in the VBA language. Your list of commands might look slightly different, depending on the exact actions you performed when recording the macro. Even though you might not know VBA, some of the commands are easy to interpret. For example, near the top of the PDFReceipt macro, you should see the command:

```
Range("A18:F37").Select
```

which tells Excel to select the range A18:F37. Several lines below this command you see the following command, which centers the worksheet horizontally on the page:

```
.CenterHorizontally = True
```

At the bottom of the macro is the following statement, which indicates the end of the PDFReceipt sub procedure:

```
End Sub
```

A Code window can contain several sub procedures, with each procedure separated from the others by the `Sub` *`ProcedureName`*`()` statement at the beginning, and the `End Sub` statement at the end. Sub procedures are organized into **modules**. As was shown in Figure 7-35, all of the macros that have been recorded are stored in the Module1 module.

Editing a Macro Using the Visual Basic Editor

The Visual Basic Editor provides tools to assist you in writing error-free code. As you type a command, the editor will provide pop-up windows and text to help you insert the correct code.

Stephen wants you to edit the following command in the PDFReceipt sub procedure, which sets the active cell to cell A1:

```
Range("A1").Select
```

You'll change the command to

```
Range("B3").Select
```

to change the active cell from cell A1 to cell B3.

To edit a command in the macro:

1. Scroll down the Code window to the line immediately before `End Sub` in the PDFReceipt macro.
2. In the line with the command `Range("A1").Select`, select **A1**, and then type **B3**. The command in the macro is edited to select a different cell. See Figure 7-36.

Figure 7-36 **Edited Macro**

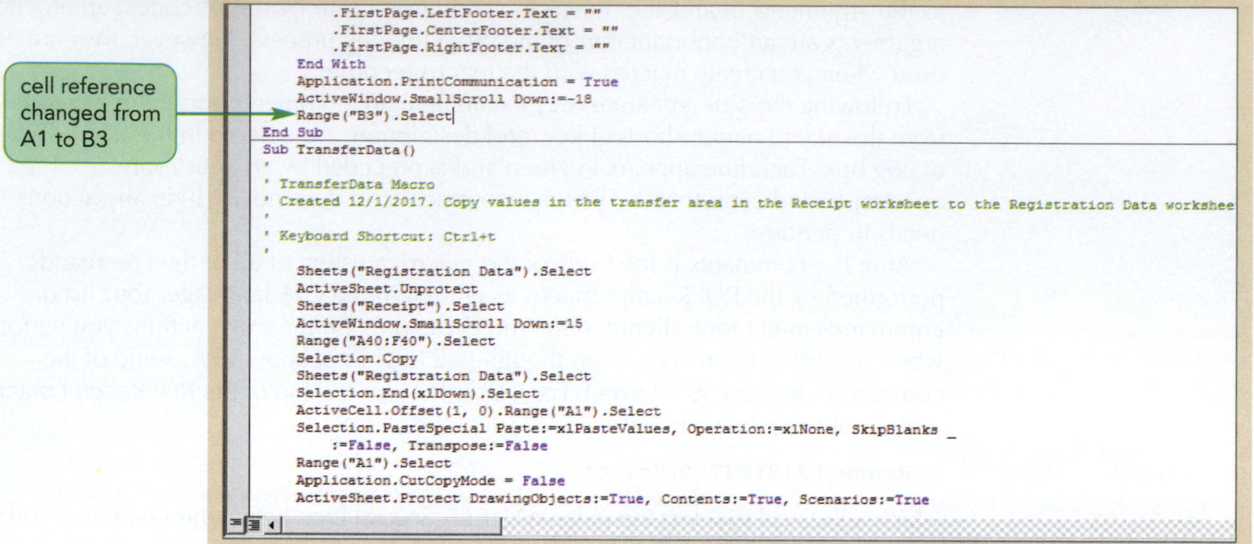

```
            .FirstPage.LeftFooter.Text = ""
            .FirstPage.CenterFooter.Text = ""
            .FirstPage.RightFooter.Text = ""
        End With
        Application.PrintCommunication = True
        ActiveWindow.SmallScroll Down:=-18
        Range("B3").Select
    End Sub
    Sub TransferData()
    '
    ' TransferData Macro
    ' Created 12/1/2017. Copy values in the transfer area in the Receipt worksheet to the Registration Data workshee
    '
    ' Keyboard Shortcut: Ctrl+t
    '
        Sheets("Registration Data").Select
        ActiveSheet.Unprotect
        Sheets("Receipt").Select
        ActiveWindow.SmallScroll Down:=15
        Range("A40:F40").Select
        Selection.Copy
        Sheets("Registration Data").Select
        Selection.End(xlDown).Select
        ActiveCell.Offset(1, 0).Range("A1").Select
        Selection.PasteSpecial Paste:=xlPasteValues, Operation:=xlNone, SkipBlanks _
            :=False, Transpose:=False
        Range("A1").Select
        Application.CutCopyMode = False
        ActiveSheet.Protect DrawingObjects:=True, Contents:=True, Scenarios:=True
```

cell reference changed from A1 to B3

3. On the menu bar, click **File**, and then click **Close and Return to Microsoft Excel** (or press the **Alt+Q** keys). The Visual Basic Editor closes, and the Winter Activities workbook is displayed.

Stephen wants you to test the macro. You'll check to see whether cell B3 is the active cell once the macro has run.

To test the edited PDFReceipt macro:

1. Press the **Ctrl+r** keys. The PDFReceipt macro runs.

   Trouble? If a Microsoft Visual Basic message box appears with a run-time error, click the End button, click the Macros button, click PDFReceipt in the Macro name box, and then click the Edit button. In the Code window, find the line you edited (one line above `End Sub`), and then change it to `Range("B3").Select`. On the menu bar, click File, and then click Close and Return to Microsoft Excel.

2. Close your PDF reader. Cell B3 is the active cell in the Receipt worksheet.

Creating Macro Buttons

Another way to run a macro is to assign it to a button placed directly in the worksheet. A macro button is often a better way to run a macro than shortcut keys. Clicking a button (with a descriptive label) is often more intuitive and simpler for users than trying to remember different combinations of keystrokes.

REFERENCE

Creating a Macro Button

- On the Developer tab, in the Controls group, click the Insert button.
- In the Form Controls section, click the Button (Form Control) button.
- Click the worksheet where you want the macro button to be located, drag the pointer until the button is the size and shape you want, and then release the mouse button.
- In the Assign Macro dialog box, select the macro you want to assign to the button.
- With the button still selected, type a new label.

Stephen wants you to add two macro buttons to the Receipt worksheet—one for each of the macros you've created. You will create the macro buttons in the blank range A14:A16 so they don't cover any existing data.

To insert a macro button in the worksheet:

1. Scroll until the range **A14:A16** of the Receipt worksheet is completely visible.
2. On the Developer tab, in the Controls group, click the **Insert** button. The Form Controls appear, with a variety of objects that can be placed in the worksheet. You'll insert the Button form control. See Figure 7-37.

Figure 7-37 Form Controls

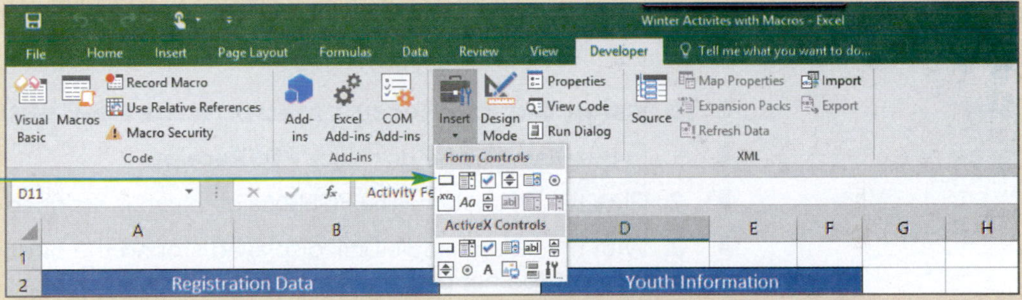

Trouble? If the Insert button is unavailable, the worksheet is protected. Click the Review tab. In the Changes group, click the Unprotect Sheet button to unprotect the Receipt worksheet, and then repeat Step 2.

3. In the Form Controls section, click the **Button (Form Control)** button, and then point to cell **A14**. The pointer changes to +.
4. Click and drag the pointer over the range **A14:A16**, and then release the mouse button. The Assign Macro dialog box opens with the button's default name in the Macro name box. See Figure 7-38.

Figure 7-38 Assign Macro dialog box

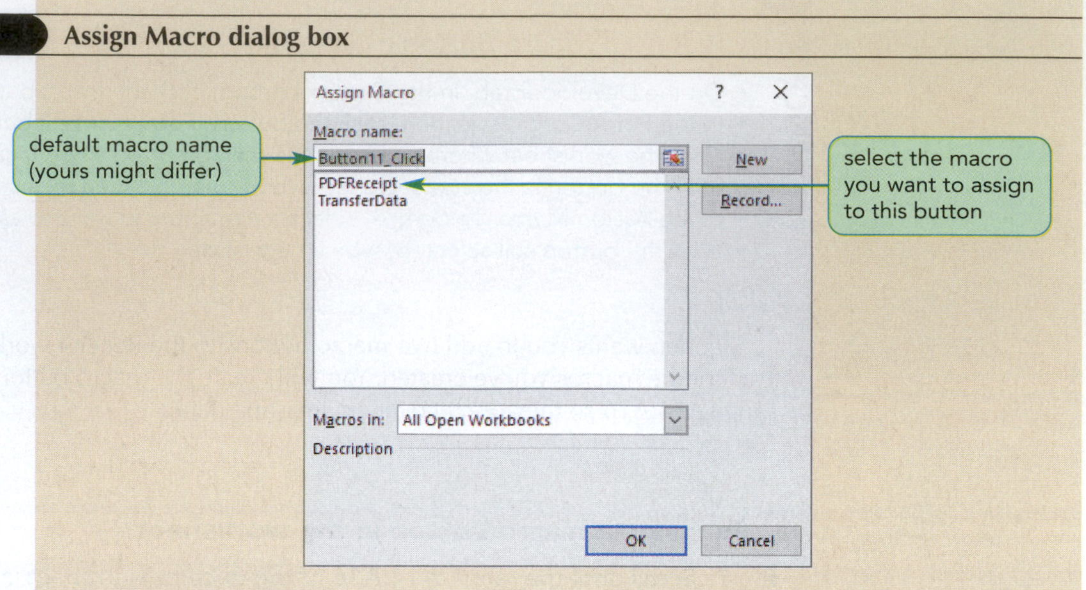

From the Assign Macro dialog box, you can assign a macro to the button. After you assign a macro to the button, the button appears with a default label. You can change the default label to a descriptive one that will indicate which macro will run when the button is clicked.

Stephen wants you to assign the PDFReceipt macro to this new button and then rename the button with a label that reflects the PDFReceipt macro.

To assign the PDFReceipt macro to the new button:

1. In the Macro name box, click **PDFReceipt**.
2. Click the **OK** button. The PDFReceipt macro is assigned to the selected button.
3. With the sizing handles still displayed around the button, type **Create PDF Receipt** (do not press the Enter key). The new label replaces the default label.

   Trouble? If no sizing handles appear around the button, the button is not selected. Right-click the button, click Edit Text to place the insertion point within the button, and then repeat Step 3.

   Trouble? If a new line appeared in the button, you pressed the Enter key after entering the label. Press the Backspace key to delete the line, and then continue with Step 4.
4. Click any cell in the worksheet to deselect the macro button.

At this point, if you click the Create PDF Receipt button, the PDFReceipt macro will run. Before you test the Create PDF Receipt button, you will add the other button.

To add a Transfer Data macro button to the Receipt worksheet:

1. On the Developer tab, in the Controls group, click the **Insert** button, and then click the **Button (Form Control)** button.
2. Drag the pointer over the range **B14:B16**.
3. In the Assign Macro dialog box, click **TransferData** in the Macro name box, and then click the **OK** button.
4. Type **Transfer Data** as the button label, and then click any cell in the worksheet to deselect the button. See Figure 7-39.

TIP

To move or resize a macro button, right-click it, press the Esc key, and then drag a sizing handle or the selection box.

Figure 7-39 Macro buttons on the Receipt worksheet

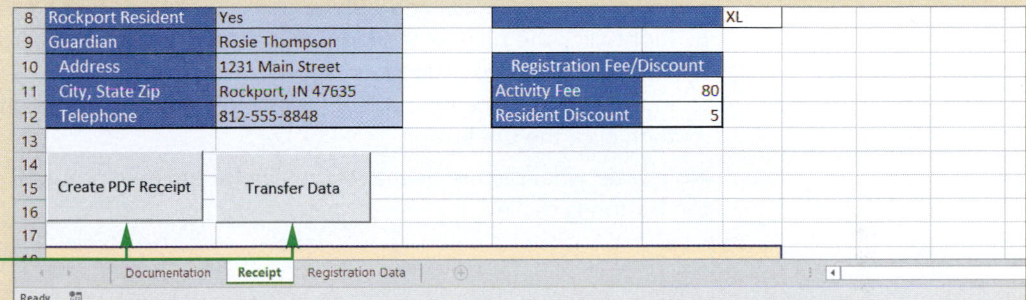

Trouble? If the macro buttons on your screen do not match the size and location of the buttons shown in the figure, right-click a button to select it, press the Esc key to close the shortcut menu, and then resize or reposition the button on the worksheet as needed.

You have completed the application, so you will reset worksheet protection.

5. On the ribbon, click the **Review** tab.
6. In the Changes group, click the **Protect Sheet** button. The Protect Sheet dialog box opens.
7. Click the **OK** button to turn on worksheet protection.

You have completed the Create PDF Receipt and Transfer Data macro buttons.

INSIGHT

Creating a Macro Button with Pictures or Shapes

You are not restricted to using the control buttons on the Developer tab for macro buttons. A macro can also be assigned to a picture or shape. For example, sometimes you might want to assign to an arrow a macro that takes you to another worksheet.

1. On the Insert tab, in the Illustrations group, click the button for the picture, online picture, or shape you want to use for a macro button.
2. Drag the pointer over the range where you want to insert the picture or shape on the worksheet.
3. Resize and position the picture or shape as needed.
4. Right-click the picture or shape, and then click Edit Text on the shortcut menu to add a name to the button.
5. Change the style, fill, and outline of the picture or shape as needed.
6. Right-click the picture or shape, and then click Assign Macro on the shortcut menu. The Assign Macro dialog box opens.
7. In the Macro name box, select the macro you want to assign to the button, and then click the OK button.

No matter what picture or shape you use for the macro button, the macro runs when the button is clicked.

Stephen has a new activity registration to add to the worksheet. You'll enter this data and then test the Create PDF Receipt and TransferData macro buttons.

To test the macro buttons:

1. In the range **B3:B12**, enter the following subscriber order:

   12/4/2017

   Dakota Thompson

   Kids Game Night

   G6

   M

   Yes

   Rosie Thompson

   1231 Main St.

   Rockport, IN 47635

   812-555-8848

2. Click the **Create PDF Receipt** button to save the current receipt as a PDF file. See Figure 7-40.

Figure 7-40 PDF file created from the PDFReceipt macro

Activity Registration Receipt

Rockport Youth Center
727 Main Street
Rockport, IN 47635

		Registration Date	10/4/2017
Guardian	Rosie Thompson	Youth Name	Dakota Thompson
Address	1231 Main Street	Activity	Kids Game Night
City, State Zip	Rockport, IN 47635	Grade	G6
Telephone	812-555-8848	Shirt Size	M
		Season Fee	80
		Resident Discount	5
		Total	$75

3. Close your PDF reader to return to the Receipt worksheet.
4. Click the **Transfer Data** button to transfer data to the Registration Data worksheet. Excel inserts the new transaction in the table.
5. Go to the **Registration Data** worksheet and make sure the data was transferred. See Figure 7-41.

Figure 7-41 Data transferred to the Registration Data worksheet with the TransferData macro

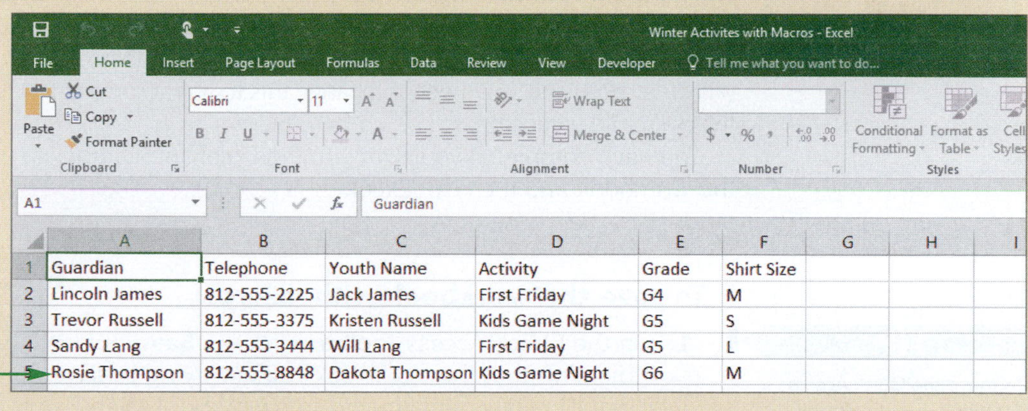

	A	B	C	D	E	F	G	H	I
1	Guardian	Telephone	Youth Name	Activity	Grade	Shirt Size			
2	Lincoln James	812-555-2225	Jack James	First Friday	G4	M			
3	Trevor Russell	812-555-3375	Kristen Russell	Kids Game Night	G5	S			
4	Sandy Lang	812-555-3444	Will Lang	First Friday	G5	L			
5	Rosie Thompson	812-555-8848	Dakota Thompson	Kids Game Night	G6	M			

new record inserted

The macro buttons make it simpler to create the receipt and transfer the data from the Receipt worksheet into the Registration Data worksheet.

INSIGHT

Making Data Entry Easier with a Data Form

When a lot of data needs to be entered, consider creating a data form. A data form is a dialog box that lists the labels and entry boxes from an Excel table or structured range of data in a worksheet. Data forms can be helpful when people who are unfamiliar with Excel need to enter the data. They can also be useful when a worksheet is very wide and requires repeated horizontal scrolling.

To create a data form, do the following:

1. Make sure each column in the structured range of data or the Excel table has column headers. These headers become the labels for each field on the form.
2. Add the Form button to the Quick Access Toolbar. Click the Customize Quick Access Toolbar button, and then click More Commands. In the Quick Access Toolbars options, click the Choose commands from arrow, click Commands Not in the Ribbon, click the Form button in the box, click the Add button, and then click the OK button. The Form button appears on the Quick Access Toolbar.
3. Select the range or table for which you want to create the data form.
4. On the Quick Access Toolbar, click the Form button. The data form opens with the selected fields ready for data entry.
5. Enter data in each box, and then click the New button to add the complete record to end of the range or table and create a new record.
6. Click the Close button to close the data form.

Saving a Workbook with Macros

When you save a workbook that contains macros, a dialog box opens indicating that the workbook you are trying to save contains features that cannot be saved in a macro-free workbook. The default Excel workbook does not allow macros to be stored as part of the file. If you want to save the workbook without the macros, click the Yes button. The workbook will be saved as a macro-free workbook, which means the macros you created will be lost. If you want to save the workbook with the macros, click the No button, and then save the workbook as a new file—one that allows macros to be saved as part of the file. The default Excel Workbook format, which is a macro-free workbook, has the .xlsx file extension. You need to change this to a macro-enabled workbook, which has the .xlsm file extension.

You have completed your work on the Excel application, so you will save and close the workbook and then exit Excel.

TIP

To move the Quick Access Toolbar below the ribbon, click the Customize Quick Access Toolbar button, and then click Show Below the Ribbon.

To save the workbook with macros:

1. On the Quick Access Toolbar, click the **Save** button. A dialog box opens indicating that the workbook you are trying to save contains features that cannot be saved in a macro-free workbook. See Figure 7-42.

Figure 7-42 Macro warning dialog box

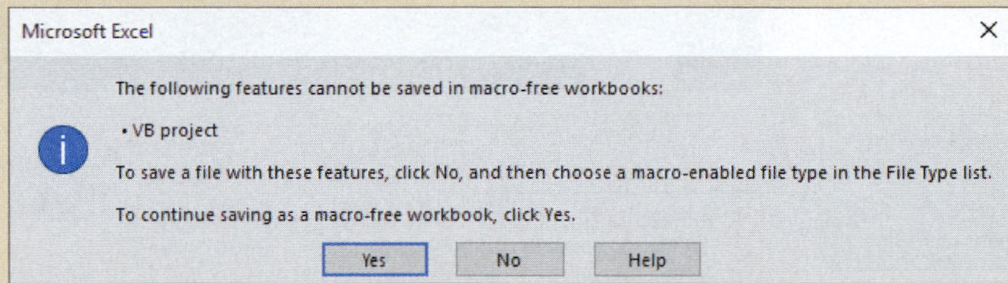
Microsoft Excel

The following features cannot be saved in macro-free workbooks:

• VB project

To save a file with these features, click No, and then choose a macro-enabled file type in the File Type list.

To continue saving as a macro-free workbook, click Yes.

Yes	No	Help

2. Click the **No** button. The Save As dialog box opens so you can save the workbook as a macro-enabled workbook.
3. Navigate to the location where you saved the files you created in this module.
4. In the File name box, type **Winter Activities with Macros** so you can easily determine which workbook contains macros.
5. Click the **Save as type** button, and then click **Excel Macro-Enabled Workbook**.
6. Click the **Save** button. The workbook is saved with the macros.
7. Close the workbook.

Opening a Workbook with Macros

TIP

After you enable the content, the filename is added to a list of trusted files and the SECURITY WARNING will not reappear as long as the workbook name or location is not changed

When you open a file with macros, Excel checks the opening workbook to see if it contains any macros. The response you see is based on the security level set on the computer. Earlier, you disabled all macros with notification. Therefore, all of the macros will be disabled when the workbook opens. When the workbook opens the first time, a SECURITY WARNING appears in the Message Bar providing the option to enable the macros so they can be run, or to open the workbook with the macros disabled. If you know a workbook contains macros that you or a coworker created, you can enable them, which adds the filename to a list of trusted files so that you won't see the SECURITY WARNING when you open this file again. If you do not click the Enable Content button, the macros remain disabled and unavailable during the current session, but the other features of the workbook are still available.

You'll open the Winter Activities with Macros workbook and enable the macros.

To open the Winter Activities with Macros workbook and enable the macros:

1. Open the **Winter Activities with Macros** workbook. The workbook opens, and "SECURITY WARNING Macros have been disabled." appears in the Message Bar below the ribbon. See Figure 7-43.

Figure 7-43 SECURITY WARNING in the Message Bar

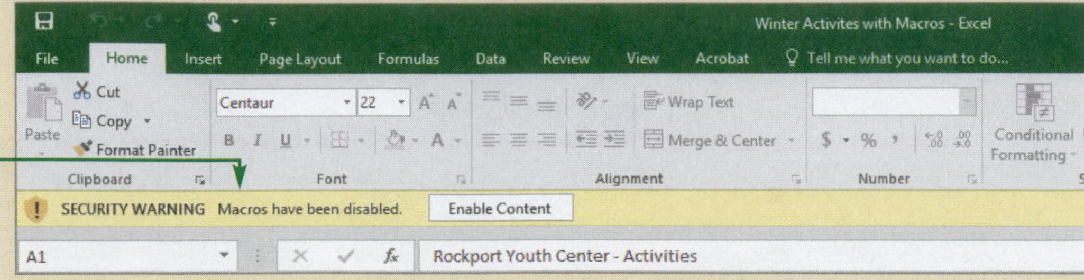

2. In the Message Bar, click the **Enable Content** button. The macros in the workbook are available for use.
3. Go to the **Receipt** worksheet.

Removing a Tab from the Ribbon

If you decide you don't want a tab displayed on the ribbon, you can remove it. Now that the macros are completed, Stephen doesn't need the Developer tab to appear on the ribbon. You will remove it.

To remove the Developer tab from the ribbon:

1. Right-click any tab on the ribbon, and then click **Customize the Ribbon** on the shortcut menu. The Excel Options dialog box opens with the Customize Ribbon options displayed.
2. In the right box listing the Main Tabs, click the **Developer** check box to remove the checkmark.
3. Click the **OK** button. The Developer tab is removed from the ribbon.
4. Save the workbook, and then close it.

Stephen is pleased with your work on the Winter Activities workbook. The workbook protection and macros will streamline the data-entry process for volunteers.

REVIEW

Session 7.3 Quick Check

1. Which tab must be displayed on the ribbon in order to record a macro?
2. What types of actions should you record as a macro?
3. Describe two ways of creating a macro.
4. What are the three places in which you can store a macro?
5. Identify two ways to run a macro.
6. What are the steps to edit a macro?
7. How do you insert a macro button into a worksheet?
8. What happens when you save a workbook with the .xlsx extension and it contains a macro?

PRACTICE

Review Assignments

Data File needed for the Review Assignments: Youth.xlsx

The Rockport Youth Center also runs half-day Winter Youth Events, Hip-Hop Dance, Secret Agent Day, and Zombietron Workshop, for boys and girls in grades 1 through 5. Stephen wants you to automate the registration process for the Winter Youth Events so it is similar to the process you created for the Winter Activities registration. Complete the following:

1. Open the **Youth** workbook located in the Excel7 > Review folder included with your Data Files, and then save the workbook as **Youth Events** in the location specified by your instructor.
2. In the Documentation worksheet, enter your name and the date.
3. In the Receipt worksheet, define names as follows:
   a. Create defined names from selection using the range A3:B11 to name all of the input cells.
   b. Change the defined name Address to **Street_Address**.
   c. Use the Name box to create the defined name **Youth_Info** for the range D2:E8 and the defined name **Events** for the range A13:B16.
4. In the Documentation worksheet, in the range B9:B19, paste the list of defined names.
5. In the Receipt worksheet, in the range B3:B11, create the data validation rules, input messages, and error alerts shown in Figure 7-44.

Figure 7-44 Validation rules for the range B3:B11

Cell(s)	Settings	Input Message	Error Alert
B3	Registration Date must be >=1/1/2017	Title: Registration Date Message: Enter the date on the registration form.	Style: Stop Title: Invalid Registration Date Message: The registration date must be present and >=1/1/2017.
B4	Any value	Title: Youth Name Message: Please enter the full name of the youth participant.	
B5	List Source (range A14:A16 in the Receipt worksheet)	Title: Event Message: Click the arrow to select the Event.	Style: Stop Title: Invalid Event Message: Use the arrow to select the Event.
B6	List Source (range D4:D8 in the Receipt worksheet)	Title: Grade Message: Click the arrow to select the Grade.	Style: Stop Title: Invalid Grade Message: Use the arrow to select the Grade.
B7	List Source (range E4:E8 in the Receipt worksheet)	Title: Shirt Size Message: Click the arrow to select the Shirt Size.	Style: Stop Title: Invalid Shirt Size Message: Use the arrow to select the Shirt Size.
B8:B11	Any value	Title: Guardian contact information Message: Please enter the Guardian contact information.	

6. In the range B3:B11, enter the data shown in Figure 7-45.

Figure 7-45 Registration data

Registration Date	10/1/2017
Youth Name	Henry Boardman
Event	Zombietron Workshop
Grade	G5
Shirt Size	L
Guardian	Sharon Boardman
Address	3642 Washington Ave.
City State Zip	Rockport, IN 47635
Telephone	812-555-1234

7. Enter the following formulas for the transfer area in the specified cells using the defined names you created earlier:
   a. Cell A40: **=Guardian**
   b. Cell B40: **=Telephone**
   c. Cell C40: **=Youth_Name**
   d. Cell D40: **=Event**
   e. Cell E40: **=Grade**
   f. Cell F40: **=Shirt_Size**
8. Enter the following formulas in the specified cells to add information to the registration receipt:
   a. Cell B27: **=Guardian**
   b. Cell B28: **=Street_Address**
   c. Cell B29: **=City_State_Zip**
   d. Cell B30: **=Telephone**
   e. Cell E25: **=Registration_Date**
   f. Cell E27: **=Youth_Name**
   g. Cell E28: **=Event**
   h. Cell E29: **=Grade**
   i. Cell E30: **=Shirt_Size**
9. Make sure that column E displays the date in the short date format and is wide enough to see the entire date.
10. In cell E36, enter a formula with a nested IF function. If the event is Hip-Hop Dance, the fee will be the value in cell B14; otherwise, if the event is Secret Agent Day, the fee will be the value in B15; otherwise, it will be the value in cell B16.
11. Unlock the input cells on the Receipt worksheet so that the user can enter data only in the range B3:B11.
12. Protect the Documentation and Registration Data worksheets so that the user cannot enter data. Do not use a password. The Receipt worksheet remains unprotected.
13. Add the Developer tab to the ribbon.
14. Save the workbook. If you have any trouble as you record the macros, you can close the workbook without saving, open the workbook that you saved, and start with Step 15.
15. Create a macro named **PDFEvent** with **Ctrl+e** as the shortcut key. Store the macro in the current workbook. Type **Created 12/7/2017. Save receipt area, range A18:F37, as a PDF file.** as the description. Record the following steps to create the PDFEvent macro:
    a. Make the Receipt worksheet the active sheet.
    b. Select the range A18:F37, and then set the selected range as the print area.
    c. Open the Page Setup dialog box. On the Margins tab make sure that the print area is centered horizontally on the page.

d. Export the worksheet to create a PDF/XPS document with the filename **Event Receipt** saved in the location specified by your instructor.
e. Close the PDF file.
f. Clear the print area.
g. Open the Page Setup dialog box. On the Margins tab, uncheck the Horizontally check box.
h. In the Receipt worksheet, make cell A1 the active cell.

16. Create a macro named **TransferData** with **Ctrl+d** as the shortcut key. Store the macro in the current workbook. Type **Created 12/7/2017. Copy values in the transfer area of the Receipt worksheet to the Registration Data worksheet.** in the macro description. Record the following steps to create the TransferData macro:
    a. Remove worksheet protection from the Registration Data worksheet.
    b. Make the Receipt worksheet the active worksheet.
    c. Select the range A40:F40 and then copy it to the Clipboard.
    d. Go to the Registration Data worksheet.
    e. Click cell A1, and then press the Ctrl+↓ keys to go to the last row with values.
    f. On the Developer tab, in the Code group, click the Use Relative References button.
    g. Move down one row.
    h. On the Developer tab, in the Code group, click the Use Relative References button.
    i. Paste the values you copied in the Registration Data worksheet.
    j. Click cell A1.
    k. Turn on worksheet protection for the Registration Data worksheet.
    l. Go to the Receipt worksheet, and then make cell B3 the active cell.
17. Test each macro using the shortcut keys you assigned to it.
18. In the Receipt worksheet, create the following macro buttons:
    a. For the PDFEvent macro, create a macro button over the range D10:D11 with the label **Print PDF Receipt**.
    b. For the TransferData macro, create a macro button over the range D12:D13 with the label **Transfer Data**.
19. Turn on cell protection for the Receipt worksheet.
20. Test the PDFEvent and TransferData macro buttons.
21. Edit the PDFEvent macro. Scroll to the last lines of the macro and in the line with the command `Range("A1").select`, change A1 to B3.
22. Remove the Developer tab from the ribbon.
23. Save the workbook as **Youth Events with Macros**, a macro-enabled workbook, and then close the workbook.

APPLY

Case Problem 1

Data File needed for this Case Problem: Posters.xlsx

Vintage Posters Ernest Loden collects vintage posters. He started his collection with circus posters but has since expanded his collection to include posters of cars, movies, and music. Ernest needs to keep track of his collection for insurance purposes. He has started to design a worksheet to enter this information, but he needs your help to set up data validation rules and record macros to update his inventory with the new posters. Complete the following:

1. Open the **Posters** workbook located in the Excel7 > Case1 folder included with your Data Files, and then save the workbook as **Vintage Posters** in the location specified by your instructor.
2. In the Documentation worksheet, enter your name and the date.

3. In the Input worksheet, create defined names from selection using the range A2:B9 to name all of the input cells.
4. In the Data Tables worksheet, paste the list of defined names in the range A9:B16.
5. In the Input worksheet, create the validation rules for cells B2, B4, B7, B8, and B9, as shown in Figure 7-46.

Figure 7-46 Validation rules for the cells B2, B4, B7, B8, and B9

Cell	Validation	Input Message	Error Alert
B2	Date Date Purchased >=1/1/2017	Title: Date Purchased Message: Enter the date purchased.	Stop Title: Invalid Date Purchased Message: You must enter a date >= 1/1/2017
B4	List Source (range A2:A5 in the Data Tables worksheet)	Title: Category Message: Click the arrow to select the Category.	Type: Stop Title: Invalid Category Message: Use the arrow to select the Category.
B7	List Source (Antique, Collectable, Print)	Title: Classification Message: Click the arrow to select the Classification.	Type: Stop Title: Invalid Classification Message: Use the arrow to select the Classification.
B8	List Source (range C2:C6 in the Data Tables worksheet)	Title: Location Message: Click the arrow to select the Location.	Type: Stop Title: Invalid Location Message: Use the arrow to select the Location.
B9	Text length Data between 0 and 100	Title: Comments Message: Enter additional comments about the poster here. Comments are restricted to 100 characters.	Type: Warning Title: Invalid Comments Message: You have exceeded 100 characters.

6. In the range B2:B9, enter the following data:
   - Cell B2: **12/5/2017**
   - Cell B3: **Frank Sinatra Pop Music Star**
   - Cell B4: **Music**
   - Cell B5: **28″ x 24″**
   - Cell B6: **9.99**
   - Cell B7: **Print**
   - Cell B8: **Loft**
   - Cell B9: **Fabric Poster**
7. Enter the following formulas for the specified cells in the transfer area:
   - Cell A12: **=Date_Purchased**
   - Cell B12: **=Brief_Description**
   - Cell C12: **=Category**
   - Cell D12: **=Size**
   - Cell E12: **=Purchase_Price**
   - Cell F12: **=Classification**
   - Cell G12: **=Location**
   - Cell H12: **=Comments**

8. Unlock the input cells in the Input worksheet so that a user can enter data only in the range B2:B9.
9. Protect the Documentation, Data, and Data Tables worksheets so that the user cannot enter data. Do not use a password. The Input worksheet will remain unprotected.
10. Add the Developer tab to the ribbon.
11. Save the workbook so that you can return to Step 12 and rerecord the macros if you have trouble.
12. Create a macro named **TransferData** with **Ctrl+t** as the shortcut key. Store the macro in the current workbook. Type **Created 12/1/2017. Copy values in the transfer area of the Input worksheet to the Data worksheet.** as the description. Record the following steps to create the TransferData macro:
    a. Go to the Data worksheet, and turn off the worksheet protection.
    b. Make the Input worksheet the active worksheet.
    c. Select the transfer area, and then copy it to the Clipboard.
    d. Go to the Data worksheet, select cell A1, and then go to the last row with values. (*Hint*: Press the Ctrl+down arrow keys.)
    e. On the Developer tab, turn on Use Relative References.
    f. Move down one row.
    g. Turn off Use Relative References.
    h. Paste the contents the Clipboard to the Data worksheet using the Values option.
    i. Go to cell A1.
    j. Turn on the worksheet protection.
    k. Go to the Input worksheet, and then make cell B2 the active cell.
13. Create a macro named **ClearInput** with **Ctrl+i** as the shortcut key. Store the macro in the current workbook. Type **Created 12/1/2017. Clear the values in the input area, range B2:B9, of the Input worksheet.** in the macro description. Record the following steps to create the ClearInput macro:
    a. In the Input worksheet, select the range B2:B9.
    b. Delete the data from the selected cells.
    c. Make cell B2 the active cell.
14. Test the macros using the shortcut keys you assigned to each of them. The Transfer Area will show zeros after the ClearInput macro has been run.
15. In the Input worksheet, create a macro button for each macro to the right of the Vintage Poster Input form. Enter labels that describe the corresponding macro. Protect the Input worksheet. Do not use a password.
16. Remove the Developer tab from the ribbon.
17. Re-enter the data from Step 6, and then test the macro buttons.
18. Save your workbook as **Vintage Posters with Macros**, a macro-enabled workbook, and then close the workbook.

TROUBLESHOOT

Case Problem 2

Data File needed for this Case Problem: Frontier.xlsm

Frontier School's Out Event Frontier School in Pineville, Missouri, is being sold to developers who plan to convert the 1949 building into a boutique shopping center. Originally serving kindergarten through 12th grade, changing demographics and more schooling options have led to the school district plan to close the school and sell the building and surrounding property. Lourdes Dreyer, president of the school's alumni association, is planning a School's Out Event at the old school. The event will include Building Tours, Breakfast with Principal Sanderson (the school principal for the past 30 years), Lunch with the Teachers and Staff who are still in the area, and a silent auction of school memorabilia. Lourdes has created a workbook to record the breakfast and lunch reservations for. She asks you to finish creating the application that will enable volunteers to enter the reservations for the event and tally a final count of attendees for the caterer. Complete the following:

1. Open the macro-enabled **Frontier** workbook located in the Excel7 > Case2 folder included with your Data Files, and then save the macro-enabled workbook as **Frontier School** in the location specified by your instructor.
2. In the Documentation worksheet, enter your name and the date. Review the formulas, defined names, and data validation information in the Reservation Input worksheet and the Catering worksheet.
3. **Troubleshoot** In the Reservation Input worksheet, the Amount to Pay calculation, which multiplies the number of guests by the charge, is incorrect. Identify the error and correct it.
4. Once you have corrected the error, run the Transfer Data macro to make sure the data is calculated correctly and that the macro is transferring the correct data.
5. **Troubleshoot** In the Documentation worksheet, Lourdes pasted a list of defined names used in the workbook, but then she continued to modify the worksheet. Make sure all of the defined names are included in the list and are accurate. Fix any errors you find or replace the list.
6. Unlock the ranges B2:B10 in the Reservation Input worksheet so that the user can enter data only in those cells. Cell B11 is a formula, so it should remain locked.
7. Protect the Reservation Input worksheet. Do not use a password.
8. Make sure that the Developer tab is on the ribbon.
9. Save the workbook to back it up in case you have problems as you work with the ClearInput macro in the next step.
10. **Troubleshoot** In the Reservation Input worksheet, use the Clear Input button to run the ClearInput macro. The macro is not working correctly. Use the Visual Basic for Applications editor to edit the macro as needed so that it performs the following tasks:
    - Select the range B2:B10.
    - Clear the contents of the selected range.
    - Make cell B2 the active cell.

    Test the macro. If the macro still does not run correctly, close the workbook without saving your changes, reopen the workbook, and then edit the macro again.
11. **Troubleshoot** In the Catering worksheet, the PivotTable should show the total number of guests who have registered for each event. The numbers in the Sum of Guests column are incorrect. Update the PivotTable so that it shows the current counts.
12. Save the workbook as **New Frontier School with Macros**, a macro-enabled workbook, to back it up before recording the CateringCounts macro in the next step.

13. Create a macro named **CateringCounts** with the **Ctrl+n** shortcut key and an appropriate macro description that performs the following actions:
    - Select the Catering worksheet.
    - Filter the PivotTable to show only breakfast and lunch events.
    - Export the PivotTable worksheet to a PDF named **Catering Counts** in the location specified by your instructor.
    - Remove the filters from the PivotTable to show all events.
    - In the Reservation Input worksheet, make cell B2 the active cell.
14. Test the CateringCounts macro using the shortcut key. If the macro doesn't work, close the workbook without saving your changes, reopen the workbook, and record the macro again.
15. Create a button below the Transfer Data button on the Reservation Input worksheet, and then assign the CateringCounts macro to the button. Change the default label to a more descriptive one. (*Hint*: Remove cell protection while creating the macro button, and then reapply cell protection.)
16. Run the CateringCounts and ClearInput macros to test the buttons. Revise the macros, if necessary.
17. Remove the Developer tab from the ribbon.
18. Save the workbook as **Final Frontier School with Macros**, a macro-enabled workbook, and then close the workbook.

CHALLENGE

Case Problem 3

Data File needed for this Case Problem: Chairs.xlsx

The Chair Guy During the long winters at Castle Rock Lake, Wisconsin, Alexander Wilson handcrafts wooden Adirondack chairs. In the spring and summer, he sells this stock at local craft fairs and specialty stores. Alexander wants to create an order form to enter and print customer orders. He also wants to save the basic sale information (chair name, style, wood, and color) so he can analyze the chair sales. Alexander started a workbook to enter information about his customer orders. He asks you to finish it by incorporating input validation, cell protection, and macros to help ensure that the collected information is accurate. Complete the following:

1. Open the **Chairs** workbook located in the Excel7 > Case3 folder included with your Data Files, and then save the workbook as **Chair Orders** in the location specified by your instructor.
2. In the Documentation worksheet, enter your name and the date, and then review all of the worksheets in the workbook.
3. In the Order Form worksheet, create appropriate defined names for each cell in the range A5:B13.
4. Create the following validation rules:
    a. Style (cell B10): The list of styles is in the range E2:E8. Enter an appropriate input message and error alert.
    b. Wood (cell B11): The list of woods is in the range E11:E12. Enter an appropriate input message and error alert.
    c. Color (cell B12): The list of colors is in the range G2:G12 Enter an appropriate input message and error alert.
5. Test the validation rules for cells you created in the range B10:B12, making corrections as needed.
6. Create the following input messages:
    a. Customer contact information (range B5:B8): Prompt the user to enter the customer contact information, such as name, address, city, state, Zip, and telephone number or email address.
    b. Chair Name (cell B9): Prompt the user to name the chair.
7. In cell B13, create a comment that explains the pricing for chairs. All pine chairs are $100 and oak chairs are $150.
8. In cell B13, enter a formula to compute the pricing based on the wood selected in cell B11. (*Hint:* You will need to use the IF function for this formula.)

Explore 9. In the Order Form worksheet, insert a WordArt text box, and then enter **The Chair Guy** as the text. Rotate the WordArt so that it is vertical in column C. Change the text fill to a color that complements the other colors used in the worksheet. (*Hint*: On the Insert tab, in the Text group, click the Insert WordArt button, and then select a WordArt style. Use the Drawing Tools Format tab to format the WordArt.)

10. Create the following formulas for the specified cells in the Chair Sale Transfer Area:
    - Cell A22: **=Chair_Name**
    - Cell B22: **=Style**
    - Cell C22: **=Wood**
    - Cell D22: **=Color**
11. In the Order Form worksheet, unlock the input cells, which are in the range B5:B12. Cell B13 has a formula and will be locked.
12. Protect the Documentation, Order Form, and Chair Sales worksheets.
13. In the Order Form worksheet, enter the following data:
    - Customer Name: **Glenn Cole**
    - Address: **1044 Sycamore Lake Road**
    - City, State, Zip: **Castle Rock Lake, WI 43573**
    - Telephone/e-mail: **glenncole@example.com**
    - Chair Name: **Amanda**
    - Style: **Rocking - Child**
    - Wood: **Oak**
    - Color: **Purple**
14. Save the workbook to back it up before you record the macros.
15. Create a macro named **PrintOrder** with the shortcut key **Ctrl+o** that does the following:
    - Set the Order Form print area to the range A1:C20.
    - Set the orientation to landscape and center the print area horizontally.
    - Export to a PDF file.
    - Return the worksheet to its original state.
16. Create a macro named **AddSale** with the shortcut key **Ctrl+s** that does the following:
    - Go to the Chair Sales worksheet, and then remove the cell protection.
    - Make the Order Form worksheet the active sheet.
    - Select the Chair Sale Transfer Area, and copy it to the Clipboard.
    - Return to the Chair Sales worksheet. Select cell A1, and then press the Ctrl+↓ keys to go to the last row with values.
    - On the Developer tab, turn on Use Relative References.
    - Move down one row.
    - Turn off Use Relative References
    - Paste the values in the Clipboard to the Chair Sales worksheet using the Values option.
    - Go to cell A1.
    - Turn on the worksheet protection.
    - Go to the Order Form worksheet, and then make cell B5 the active cell.
17. Record a macro named **ClearOrderInput** with no shortcut key that clears the range B5:B12, which is the Order Form input area, and then make cell B5 the active cell.
18. Test all of the macros by selecting and running the macros.

Explore 19. Remove the cell protection from the Order Form worksheet. Create macro buttons for all three macros using either clip art or shapes. (*Hint*: On the Insert tab, in the Illustrations group, click the button for the picture, shape, or online picture and place on the worksheet. Right-click the object to edit the text or style of the button and assign the macro to the button). Use descriptive labels for each macro button. Place the buttons in the blank area of columns D through G so they will not show up on the printed order.

20. Reset cell protection for the Order Form worksheet.
21. Test all of the macro buttons. Check the Chair Sales worksheet to see how and where new records were added.
22. Save the workbook as **Chair Orders with Macros**, a macro-enabled workbook, and then close the workbook.

CREATE

Case Problem 4

There are no Data Files needed for this Case Problem.

Resale Shoppe Debbie Oboyle opened a resale shop in Anacortes, Washington, in 2015. She sells everything from children's toys to clothes to jewelry to books. She wants to develop an electronic billing/invoicing system for organizing sales by their type (for example, coat) and the intended user (for example, adult). She asks you to follow her plan to create an Excel application that does these tasks. Complete the following:

1. Open a new, blank workbook, and then save it as **Resale** in the location specified by your instructor.
2. Rename the worksheet as **Documentation**, and then enter the company name, your name, the date, and a purpose statement.
3. Insert two additional worksheets, and then rename them as **Invoice** and **Item Information**.
4. In the Item Information worksheet, enter the data for the types of items and the age groups shown in Figure 7-47.

Figure 7-47 **Input data for the Resale Shoppe**

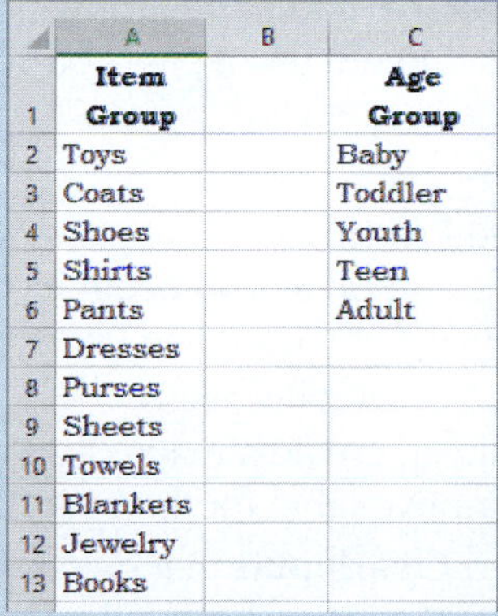

	A	B	C
1	**Item Group**		**Age Group**
2	Toys		Baby
3	Coats		Toddler
4	Shoes		Youth
5	Shirts		Teen
6	Pants		Adult
7	Dresses		
8	Purses		
9	Sheets		
10	Towels		
11	Blankets		
12	Jewelry		
13	Books		

5. In the Invoice worksheet, create the invoice shown in Figure 7-48. Use defined names for the Customer Name, Street Address, City, Associate, Subtotal, Sales Tax, and Total to assist in creating formulas. (*Hint*: Review the steps below before you begin to create the invoice.)
   a. Enter the labels as shown in Figure 7-48.
   b. Change the column widths, and format the labels appropriately.
   c. Use a function to insert the current date.
   d. Insert an input message in the Customer cells with a reminder about what data should be entered in cells C10, C11, and C12.
   e. For each of the four item lines (rows 17–20), use data validation rules to create lists of the different item groups and age groups that you entered in the Item Information worksheet. Use appropriate input messages and error alerts.
   f. In each item's description, insert an input message with a reminder to enter a brief description of the item.
   g. In the Subtotal cell, enter a formula to add the price from each of the four items.
   h. In the Sales Tax cell, enter a formula that uses a defined name to calculate 8.5 percent of the subtotal.
   i. In the Total cell, enter a formula that sums the Subtotal, and the Sales Tax cells.

Figure 7-48 **Finished invoice for the Resale Shoppe**

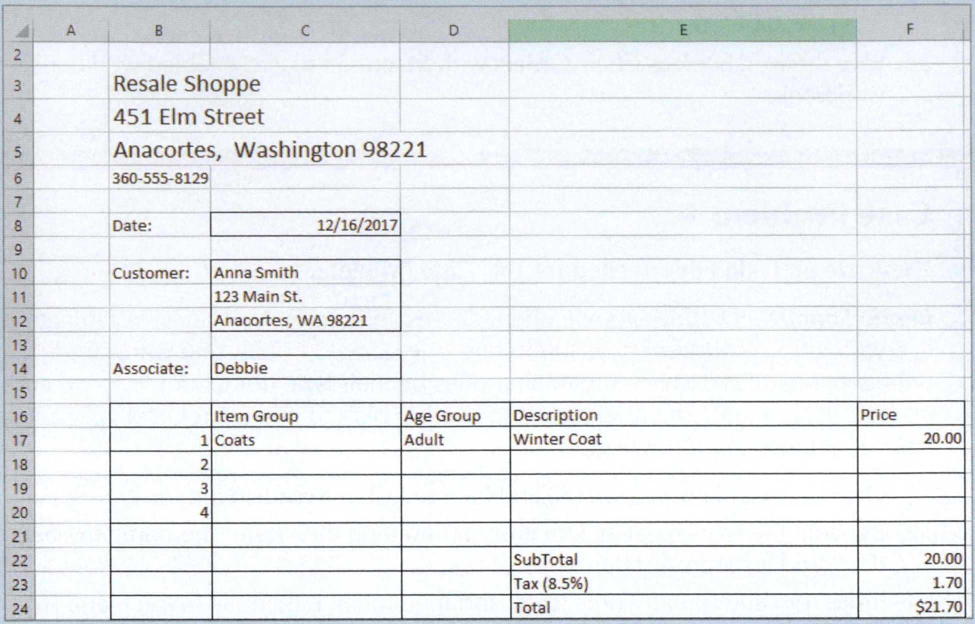

	A	B	C	D	E	F
2						
3		Resale Shoppe				
4		451 Elm Street				
5		Anacortes, Washington 98221				
6		360-555-8129				
7						
8		Date:	12/16/2017			
9						
10		Customer:	Anna Smith			
11			123 Main St.			
12			Anacortes, WA 98221			
13						
14		Associate:	Debbie			
15						
16			Item Group	Age Group	Description	Price
17		1	Coats	Adult	Winter Coat	20.00
18		2				
19		3				
20		4				
21						
22					SubTotal	20.00
23					Tax (8.5%)	1.70
24					Total	$21.70

6. Format the worksheet with fonts, font sizes, font colors, cell styles borders, and shading to make the invoice attractive and easy to read.
7. Protect the worksheet so a user can enter the Customer data in cells C10, C11, and C12, the Associate name in cell C14, and item information in the range C17:F20 data but cannot enter data in any other cells. Do not use a password. Protect Documentation and Item Information worksheets. Do not use a password.
8. Save the workbook.
9. Create a macro named **PrintInvoice** that prints the invoice. Assign a shortcut key, and type an appropriate macro description as you begin recording this macro. Set the print area to the range A1:G25 with landscape orientation, and center the worksheet horizontally. Export to a PDF, and return the worksheet to its original state.
10. On the Invoice worksheet, create a macro button, assign the PrintInvoice macro to the button, and then enter a descriptive label for the button.
11. Create a macro named **ClearInputs** that deletes the values from the range C10:C12,C14,C17:F20. Assign a shortcut key, and type an appropriate macro description as you begin recording this macro. (*Hint*: Use the Delete key to clear a value from a cell.)
12. On the Invoice worksheet, create a macro button, assign the ClearInputs macro to the button, and then enter a descriptive label for the button.
13. Remove the cell protection from the Item Information worksheet. In the Item Information worksheet, paste a list of the defined names with their locations. Below this entry, type a list of the macro names and their shortcut keys. Reapply cell protection to the Item Information worksheet.
14. Apply worksheet protection to the Invoice worksheet.
15. Test the worksheet by entering the data shown in Figure 7-48.
16. Use the PrintInvoice macro button to print the invoice for the data you entered, and then use the ClearInputs macro button to remove the input data.
17. Save the workbook as **Resale with Macros**, a macro-enabled workbook, and then close the workbook.

MODULE 8

Working with Advanced Functions

Analyzing Employee and Product Data

OBJECTIVES

Session 8.1
- Use the IF function
- Use the AND function
- Use the OR function
- Use structured references in formulas

Session 8.2
- Nest the IF function
- Use the VLOOKUP function
- Use the HLOOKUP function
- Use the IFERROR function

Session 8.3
- Use conditional formatting to highlight duplicate values
- Summarize data using the COUNTIF, SUMIF, and AVERAGEIF functions

Case | *MB Hobbies & Crafts*

Vanessa Beals is the managing director for MB Hobbies & Crafts (MBHC), a Texas-based craft and hobby supplier. MBHC has nearly 100 employees employed at its four stores, which are located in Bonham, Bowie, Garland, and Graham. The MBHC product list includes more than 10,000 items for dressmaking, floral crafting, jewelry making, model ship or boat building, quilting, or yarn crafting. Each store has a focus on specific crafts, although all of the stores stock a large selection of supplies for all crafts. For example, Garland stocks a wide range of items from the product list, but its main focus is on quilting supplies.

Vanessa has an Excel worksheet that she uses to track basic employee information, including each employee's ID, name, hire date, birth date, job status, and current salary. She wants to analyze this data in different ways. For example, she wants to send each employee a birthday greeting during their birthday month, create name badges that are color-coded by years of employment, identify part-time employees who are eligible for comp days, and calculate salary increases and bonuses. Vanessa is also developing a product data worksheet for analyzing the store suppliers. So far, the worksheet includes basic data such as part number, category, and description. Vanessa wants to expand the data to include the supplier name for each product and which store specializes in that product. To provide Vanessa with all this information, you'll use a variety of logical and lookup functions.

STARTING DATA FILES

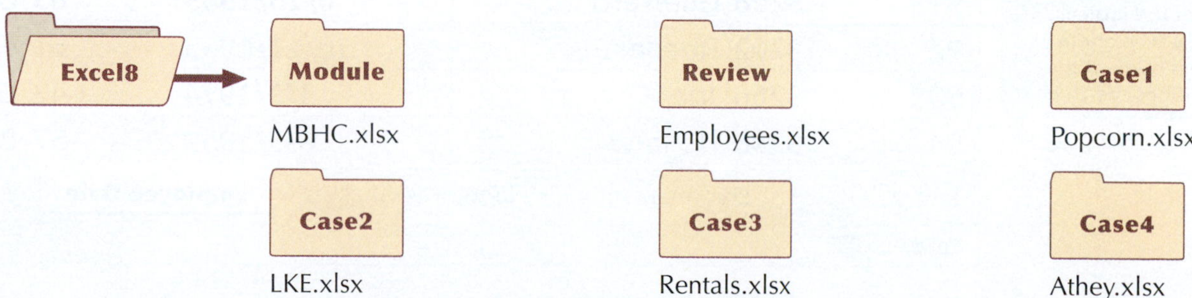

Session 8.1 Visual Overview:

When you create a formula that references all or parts of an Excel table, you can replace a specific cell or range address with a **structured reference**, which is the actual table name or column header.

The IF function is a logical function that evaluates a condition, and then returns one value if the condition is true and a different value if the condition is false.

A **logical condition** is an expression such as I80="PT" that returns either a TRUE or FALSE value.

The **AND function** is a logical function that returns a TRUE value if all of the logical conditions are true and a FALSE value if any of the logical conditions are false.

The **OR function** is a logical function that returns a TRUE value if any of the logical conditions are true and a FALSE value if none of the logical conditions are true.

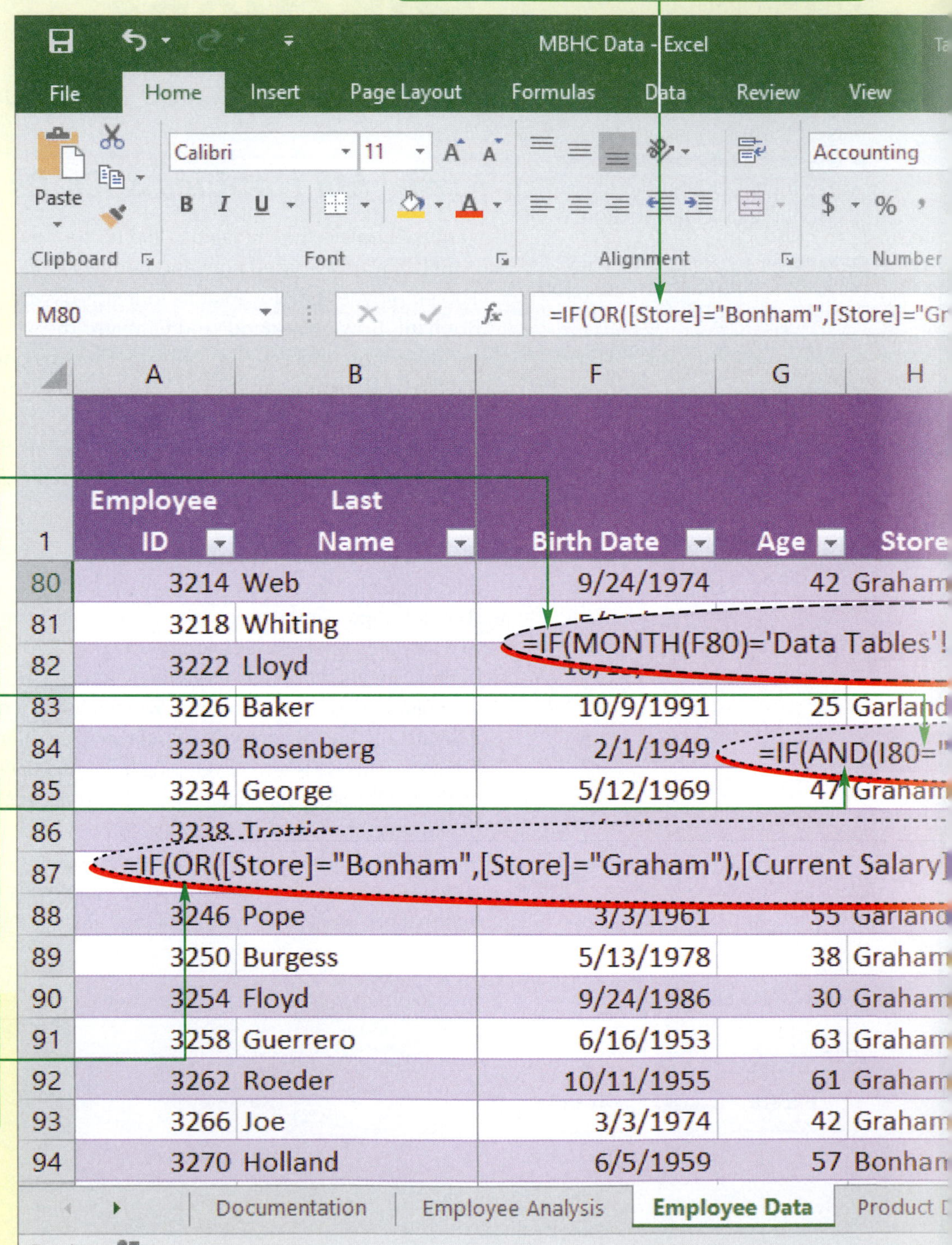

Logical Functions

In this formula, the structured reference [Current Salary] references the cells in column J of the EmployeeTbl table.

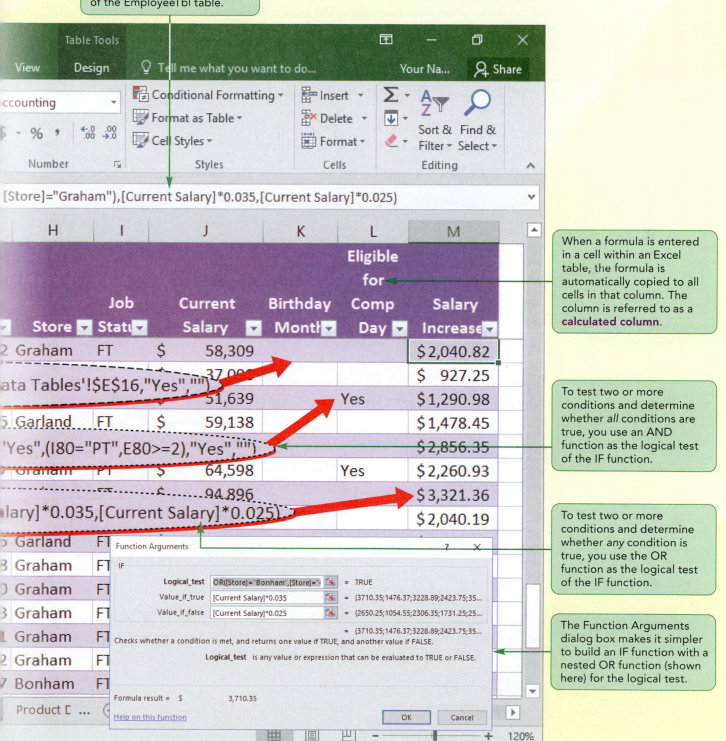

When a formula is entered in a cell within an Excel table, the formula is automatically copied to all cells in that column. The column is referred to as a **calculated column**.

To test two or more conditions and determine whether *all* conditions are true, you use an AND function as the logical test of the IF function.

To test two or more conditions and determine whether *any* condition is true, you use the OR function as the logical test of the IF function.

The Function Arguments dialog box makes it simpler to build an IF function with a nested OR function (shown here) for the logical test.

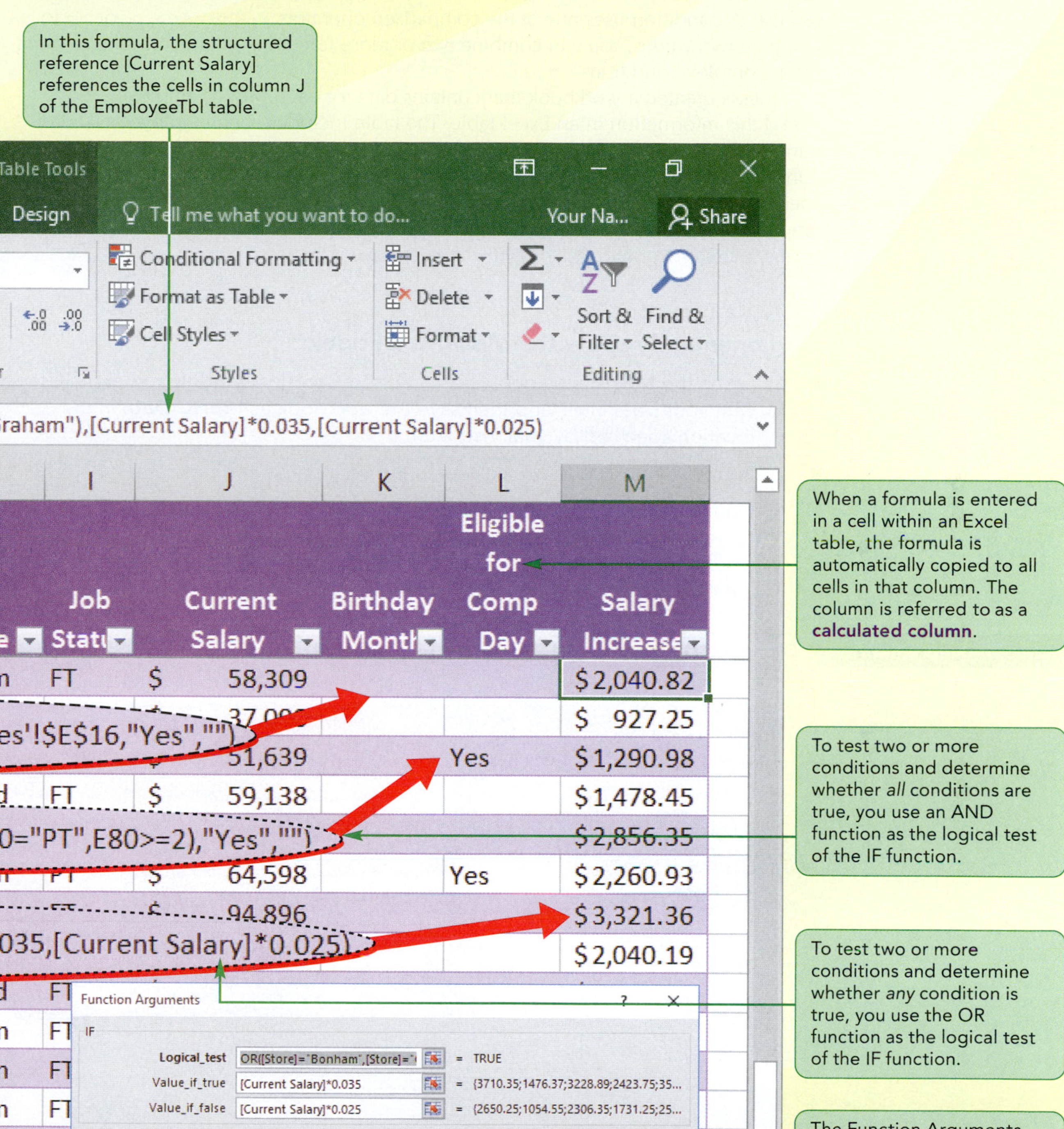

Working with Logical Functions

Logical functions such as IF, AND, and OR determine whether a condition is true or false. A condition uses one of the comparison operators <, <=, =, <>, >, or >= to compare two values. You can combine two or more functions in one formula, creating more complex conditions.

Vanessa created a workbook that contains data for each MBHC employee. She stored this information in an Excel table. The table includes each employee's ID, last name, first name, hire date, years of service, birth date, age, store, job status, and current salary. Vanessa wants you to determine if employee birth dates occur in a specified month, determine comp day eligibility of part-time employees, and compute employee salary increases. You will use IF, AND, and OR functions to do this after you open Vanessa's workbook and review the employee data.

To open and review the MBHC workbook:

1. Open the **MBHC** workbook located in the **Excel8 > Module** folder included with your Data Files, and then save the workbook as **MBHC Data** in the location specified by your instructor.
2. In the Documentation worksheet, enter your name and the date.
3. Go to the **Employee Data** worksheet. The worksheet contains an Excel table named EmployeeTbl, which includes each employee's ID, last name, first name, hire date, years of service, birth date, age, store, job status, and current salary. See Figure 8-1.

Figure 8-1 Employee Data worksheet

	A	B	C	D	E	F	G	H	I	J
1	Employee ID	Last Name	First Name	Hire Date	Years of Servic	Birth Date	Age	Store	Job Stat	Current Salary
2	1102	Delosreyes	Lori	7/10/2014	3.5	4/11/1961	55	Bonham	FT	$ 106,010
3	1106	Goode	Bari	11/6/2015	2.2	11/23/1991	25	Graham	FT	$ 42,182
4	1110	Reams	Linda	12/4/2015	2.1	10/15/1966	50	Bonham	FT	$ 92,254
5	1114	Rodriguez	Richard	3/24/2003	14.8	12/8/1964	52	Graham	FT	$ 69,250
6	1118	Peters	Jessica	5/23/2011	6.6	2/15/1962	54	Bonham	FT	$ 102,567
7	1122	Cortez	Nick	8/12/2002	15.4	10/15/1968	48	Bowie	FT	$ 94,517
8	1126	Millard	Melissa	11/6/2015	2.2	3/20/1973	43	Garland	FT	$ 51,791
9	1130	Burns	Brenda	6/10/2010	7.6	4/20/1966	50	Garland	FT	$ 32,530
10	1134	Kimball	Susan	1/20/2016	1.9	3/21/1957	59	Graham	FT	$ 94,502
11	1138	Ford	Charles	5/4/2012	5.7	6/28/1967	49	Bonham	PT	$ 45,671
12	1142	Vazquez	Johnny	7/16/2011	6.5	2/8/1986	30	Graham	FT	$ 70,346
13	1146	Whetstone	William	4/12/2008	9.7	7/13/1986	30	Garland	FT	$ 34,685
14	1150	Arnold	Leroy	3/13/2012	5.8	7/8/1949	67	Bonham	FT	$ 96,944
15	1154	Basile	Santos	8/8/2015	2.4	12/1/1956	60	Bonham	FT	$ 92,091
16	1158	Loftis	Robert	7/17/2015	2.5	7/12/1959	57	Garland	FT	$ 30,150
17	1162	Olson	Ruth	1/8/2015	3.0	3/6/1970	46	Bonham	FT	$ 81,536
18	1166	Gridley	Marjorie	10/4/2013	4.2	10/25/1959	57	Bowie	FT	$ 96,021

Documentation | Employee Analysis | Employee Data | Product Data | Data Tables

Ready

4. Scroll down and to the right. Although the column headers remain visible as you scroll down, the employee ID and last name disappear as you scroll to the right.
5. Select cell **C2**, and then freeze the panes so columns A and B remain on the screen as you scroll across the screen.

Inserting Calculated Columns in an Excel Table

TIP

Calculated columns work only in Excel tables. In a range of data, you must copy and paste the formula or use the AutoFill feature.

An Excel table does not have a fixed structure. When you add a column to an Excel table, the table expands, and the new column has the same table formatting style as the other columns. If you enter a formula in one cell of a column, the formula is automatically copied to all cells in that column. These calculated columns are helpful as you add formulas to an Excel table.

If you need to modify the formula in a calculated column, you edit the formula in any cell in the column, and the formulas in all of the cells in that table column are also modified. If you want to edit only one cell in a calculated column, you need to enter a value or a formula that is different from all the others in that column. A green triangle appears in the upper-left corner of the cell with the custom formula in the calculated column, making the inconsistency easy to find. After a calculated column contains one inconsistent formula or value, any other edits you make to that column are no longer automatically copied to the rest of the cells in that column. Excel does not overwrite custom values.

PROSKILLS

Written Communication: Creating Excel Table Fields

Excel tables should be both easy to use and easy to understand. This requires labeling and entering data in a way that effectively communicates a table's content or purpose. If a field is entered in a way that is difficult to use and understand, it becomes more difficult to find and present data in a meaningful way.

To effectively communicate a table's function, keep the following guidelines in mind when creating fields in an Excel table:

- **Create fields that require the least maintenance.** For example, hire date and birth date require no maintenance after they are entered, unlike age and years of service, whose values change each year. If you need to know the specific age or years of service, use calculations to determine them based on values in the Hire Date and Birth Date columns.
- **Store the smallest unit of data possible in a field.** For example, use three separate fields for city, state, and zip code rather than one field. Using separate fields for each unit of data enables you to sort or filter each field. If you want to display data from two or more fields in one column, you can use a formula to reference the City, State, and zip Code columns. For example, you can use the & operator to combine the city, state, and zip code in one cell as follows: =C2&D2&E2
- **Apply a text format to fields with numerical text data.** For example, formatting fields such as zip codes and Social Security numbers as text ensures that leading zeros are stored as part of the data. Otherwise, the zip code 02892 is stored as a number and displayed as 2892.

Using these guidelines means that you and others will spend less time interpreting data and more time analyzing results. This lets you more effectively communicate the data in an Excel table.

Using the IF Function

In many situations, the value you store in a cell depends on certain conditions. Consider the following examples:

- An employee's gross pay depends on whether that employee worked overtime.
- A sales tax depends on the sales tax rate and the value of the purchase.
- A shipping charge depends on the dollar amount of an order.

To evaluate these types of conditions, you use the IF function. Recall that the IF function is a logical function that evaluates a condition and then returns one value if the condition is true and another value if the condition is false. The value can be text, numbers, cell references, formulas, or functions. The IF function has the syntax

```
IF(logical_test,value_if_true,value_if_false)
```

where `logical_test` is a condition that is either true or false, `value_if_true` is the value returned by the function if the condition is true, and `value_if_false` is the value returned by the function if the condition is false. The IF function results in only one value—either the `value_if_true` or the `value_if_false`.

You will use an IF function to alert Vanessa that an employee has a birth date during a specified month. MBHC employees who have an upcoming birthday receive a birthday card with a gift card to MBHC. A Yes value in the Birthday Month column will indicate that an employee has a birthday during the specified month, and a blank cell will indicate that an employee does not have a birthday during the specified month.

The flowchart shown in Figure 8-2 illustrates Vanessa's logic for determining whether an employee's birthday occurs in a specified month. The flowchart shows that if an employee's birthday month occurs in the specified month (*birthday month = specified month* is True), "Yes" is entered in the cell. If the employee does not have a birthday in the specified month, the cell is left blank.

Figure 8-2 Flowchart with logic to determine if an employee's birthday is in the specified month

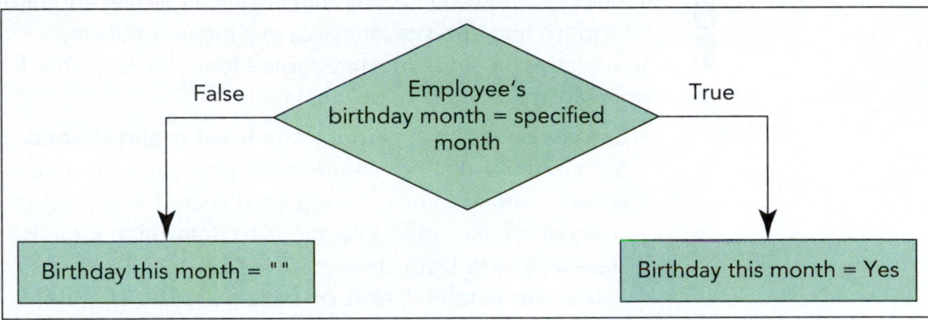

The EmployeeTbl table doesn't include a column that lists only the birthday month; this information is included as part of the employee's complete birth date, which is stored in column F. To extract the month portion of the employee's birth date, you will use the MONTH function. This function is a Date function that returns the month as a number from 1 (January) to 12 (December). The MONTH function has the syntax

```
MONTH(date)
```

where `date` is a date that includes the month you want to extract. Recall that Excel stores dates as a number equal to the number of days between January 1, 1900 and the specified date so they can be used in calculations. For example, January 1, 2017 is stored as the serial number 42736 because it occurs 42,736 days since the start of the Excel calendar. The MONTH function determines the month number from the stored serial number. For example, the birth date of the employee in row 2 of the EmployeeTbl table is 4/11/1961, which is stored in cell F2. The following MONTH function extracts the month portion of this stored date, which is 4:

```
=MONTH(F2)
```

You'll use the MONTH function in the logical test of the IF function, which will check whether the employee's birth month matches the month number entered in cell E16 of the Data Tables worksheet. Vanessa wants to know which employees have birthdays in April, so she entered 4 as the month number in cell E16. The following formula includes the complete IF function to determine if an employee has a birthday in April:

```
=IF(MONTH(F2)='Data Tables'$E$16,"Yes","")
```

The logical test `MONTH(F2)='Data Tables'$E$16` determines if the employee's birth month is equal to the birthday month stored in cell E16 of the Data Tables worksheet. If the condition is TRUE, Yes is displayed in the Birthday Month column; otherwise, the cell is left blank.

You'll add a column to the EmployeeTbl table to display the results of the IF function that determines if an employee's birthday occurs in the specified month.

To determine which employees have birthdays in the specified month:

1. In cell **K1**, enter **Birthday Month** as the column header. The Excel table expands to include this column and applies the table formatting to all the rows in the new column.
2. Make sure cell **K2** is the active cell, and then click the **Insert Function** button next to the formula bar. The Insert Function dialog box opens.
3. Click **Logical** in the Or select a category list, click **IF** in the Select a function box, and then click the **OK** button. The Function Arguments dialog box for the IF function opens.
4. In the Logical_test box, type **MONTH(F2)='Data Tables'!$E$16** and then press the **Tab** key. This condition tests whether the employee's birth month is equal to the month specified in cell E16 of the Data Tables worksheet. The function MONTH returns the month number of the date specified in cell F2. TRUE appears to the right of the Logical_test argument box, indicating this employee has a birthday in the specified month.
5. In the Value_if_true box, type **Yes** and then press the **Tab** key. This argument specifies that if the condition is true (the employee's birth month matches the value in cell E16 of the Data Tables worksheet), display Yes as the formula result. The value to the right of the Value_if_true argument box is Yes because the condition is true. Notice that Excel inserts quotation marks around the text value because you did not include them.
6. In the Value_if_false box, type **""**. This argument specifies that if the condition is false (the employee's birth month does not match the value in cell E16 of the Data Tables worksheet), display nothing in cell K2. The value to the right of the Value_if_false argument box is "", which indicates that cell K2 appears blank if the condition is false. See Figure 8-3.

Figure 8-3 Function Arguments dialog box for the IF function

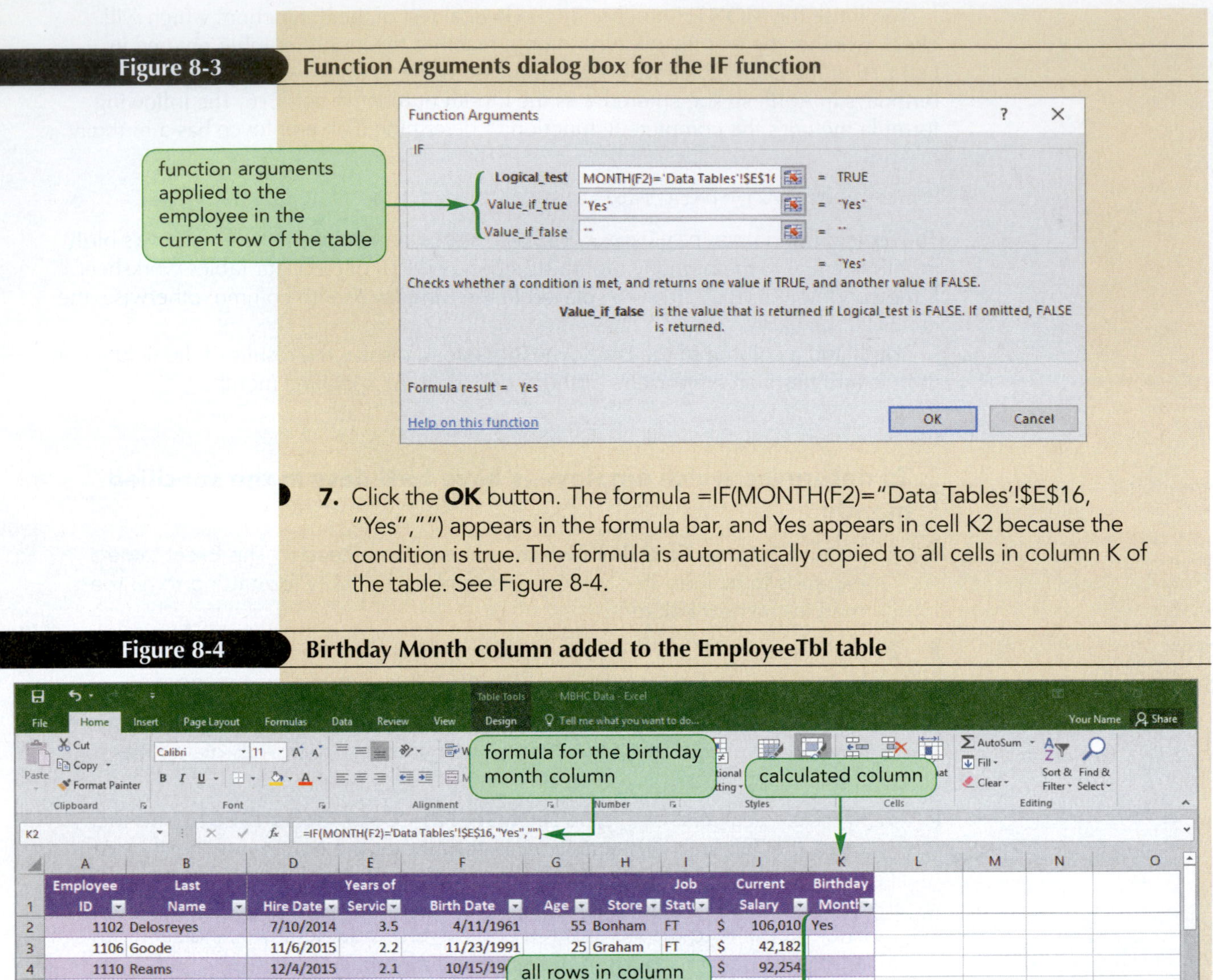

7. Click the **OK** button. The formula =IF(MONTH(F2)="Data Tables'!$E$16, "Yes","") appears in the formula bar, and Yes appears in cell K2 because the condition is true. The formula is automatically copied to all cells in column K of the table. See Figure 8-4.

Figure 8-4 Birthday Month column added to the EmployeeTbl table

Employee ID	Last Name	Hire Date	Years of Servic	Birth Date	Age	Store	Job Statu	Current Salary	Birthday Month
1102	Delosreyes	7/10/2014	3.5	4/11/1961	55	Bonham	FT	$ 106,010	Yes
1106	Goode	11/6/2015	2.2	11/23/1991	25	Graham	FT	$ 42,182	
1110	Reams	12/4/2015	2.1	10/15/19				$ 92,254	
1114	Rodriguez	3/24/2003	14.8	12/8/19				$ 69,250	
1118	Peters	5/23/2011	6.6	2/15/19				$ 102,567	
1122	Cortez	8/12/2002	15.4	10/15/19				$ 94,517	
1126	Millard	11/6/2015	2.2	3/20/1973	43	Garland	FT	$ 51,791	
1130	Burns	6/10/2010	7.6	4/20/1966	50	Garland	FT	$ 32,530	Yes
1134	Kimball	1/20/2016	1.9	3/21/1957	59	Graham	FT	$ 94,502	

Using the AND Function

The IF function evaluates a single condition. However, you often need to test two or more conditions and determine whether *all* conditions are true. You can do this with the AND function. The AND function is a logical function that returns the value TRUE if all of the logical conditions are true and returns the value FALSE if any or all of the logical conditions are false. The syntax of the AND function is

```
AND(logical1[,logical2]...)
```

where `logical1` and `logical2` are conditions that can be either true or false. If all of the logical conditions are true, the AND function returns the logical value TRUE; otherwise, the function returns the logical value FALSE. You can include up to 255 logical conditions in an AND function. However, keep in mind that *all* of the logical conditions listed in the AND function must be true for the AND function to return a TRUE value.

Figure 8-5 illustrates how the AND function is used to determine student eligibility for the dean's list. In this scenario, when students have 12 or more credits (stored in cell B1) *and* their GPA is greater than 3.5 (stored in cell B2), they are placed on the dean's list. Both conditions must be true for the AND function to return the logical value TRUE.

Figure 8-5 **AND function example**

Purpose: To determine dean's list requirements

Logic Scenario: 12 or more semester credits and GPA above 3.5

Formula: AND function with two conditions
`=AND(B1>=12,B2>3.5)`

Data: cell B1 stores number of credits
cell B2 stores student's GPA

Example:

Data		Condition1	Condition2	Results
Cell B1	**Cell B2**	**B1>=12**	**B2>3.5**	**(Dean's List?)**
15	3.6	True	True	True
12	3.25	True	False	False
6	3.8	False	True	False
10	3.0	False	False	False

Vanessa wants you to use an AND function to determine part-time employees' eligibility for comp days. MBHC part-time employees are eligible for comp days if they are part-time employees (PT in Job Status) *and* have worked for the company for two or more years (equal to or greater than 2 in Years of Service). As long as *both* conditions are true, the employee is eligible for comp days. If neither condition is true or if only one condition is true, the employee is not eligible for comp days. Vanessa outlined these eligibility conditions in the flowchart shown in Figure 8-6.

Figure 8-6 **Flowchart illustrating AND logic for the comp day eligibility**

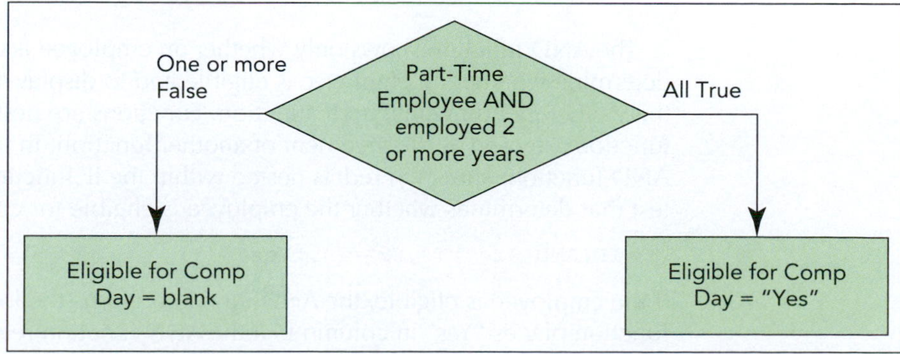

To calculate eligibility of each part-time employee, you need to use the AND function with the IF function. You use the AND function shown in the following formula as the logical test to evaluate whether each employee in the EmployeeTbl table fulfills the eligibility requirements:

```
=AND(I2="PT",E2>=2)
```

This formula tests whether the value in cell I2 (the job status for the first employee) is equal to PT (an abbreviation for part time), and whether the value in cell E2 (the years of service for the first employee) is greater than or equal to 2 (indicating two or more years of employment at MBHC). When an employee is a part-time employee (I2="PT") *and* has worked two or more years at MBHC (E2>=2), the AND function returns the value TRUE; otherwise, the AND function returns the value FALSE. Figure 8-7 shows the result returned by the AND function for four different sets of employee values for job status and years of service.

Figure 8-7 **AND function results for comp day eligibility**

Purpose: To determine eligibility for comp days

Logic Scenario: A part-time employee is eligible for comp days if the employee has part-time (PT) job status and has two or more years of service.

Formula: AND function with two conditions
`=AND(I2="PT",E2>=2)`

Data: cell I2 stores Job Status
cell E2 stores Years of Service

Example:

Data		Condition1	Condition2	Results
Cell I2	Cell E2	I2="PT"	E2>=2	(Comp Day?)
FT	2.5	False	True	False
FT	1.5	False	False	False
PT	2.5	True	True	True
PT	1.5	True	False	False

The AND function shows only whether an employee is eligible for comp days. To determine whether an employee is eligible *and* to display "Yes" in column L, you nest this AND function within an IF function. Functions are nested when the results of one function are used as the argument of another function. In the following formula, the AND function (shown in red) is nested within the IF function and is used as the logical test that determines whether the employee is eligible for comp days:

```
=IF(AND(I2="PT",E2>=2),"Yes","")
```

If the employee is eligible, the AND function returns the logical value TRUE and the IF function places "Yes" in column L. If the AND function returns the logical value FALSE, the IF function displays nothing in the cell.

You'll insert a new column in the EmployeeTbl table, and then enter the formula to determine whether the employee is qualified for comp days.

To determine if part-time employees are eligible for comp days:

1. In cell **L1**, enter **Eligible for Comp Day** as the column header. The Excel table expands to include the new column, and cell L2 is the active cell.
2. AutoFit column L so that the entire heading is visible.
3. Make sure cell **L2** is the active cell, and then click the **Insert Function** button fx next to the formula bar. The Insert Function dialog box opens.
4. Click **IF** in the Select a function box, and then click the **OK** button. The Function Arguments dialog box opens.
5. In the Logical_test box, type **AND(I2="PT",E2>=2)** and then press the **Tab** key. This logical test evaluates whether the employee is part time, indicated by PT in cell I2, *and* has worked at MBHC for two years or more. FALSE appears to the right of the Logical_test box, indicating that this condition for the employee in row 2 is false. This employee's job status is full time, so one of the conditions is not true.
6. In the Value_if_true box, type **Yes** and then press the **Tab** key. This argument specifies that if the condition is true (the employee is eligible for comp time as determined by the AND function), the word Yes appears to the right of the Value_if_true box.
7. In the Value_if_false box, type **""**. This argument specifies that if the condition is false (the employee is not eligible for comp time as determined by the AND function), nothing is displayed in cell L2, as specified by "" to the right of the Value_if_false box. See Figure 8-8.

Figure 8-8 Function Arguments dialog box for the IF function with nested AND function

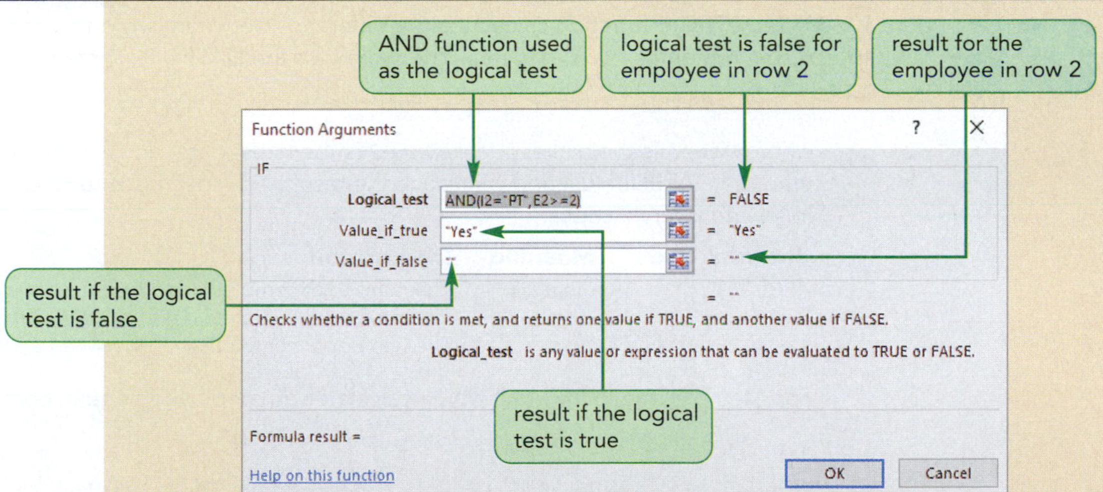

8. Click the **OK** button. The formula with the IF function that you just created is entered in cell L2 and copied to all rows in column L of the table.
9. Select cell **L2**. The formula =IF(AND(I2="PT",E2>=2),"Yes","") appears in the formula bar and nothing appears in cell L2 because the condition is false. See Figure 8-9.

Figure 8-9 IF function with the AND function to determine comp day eligibility

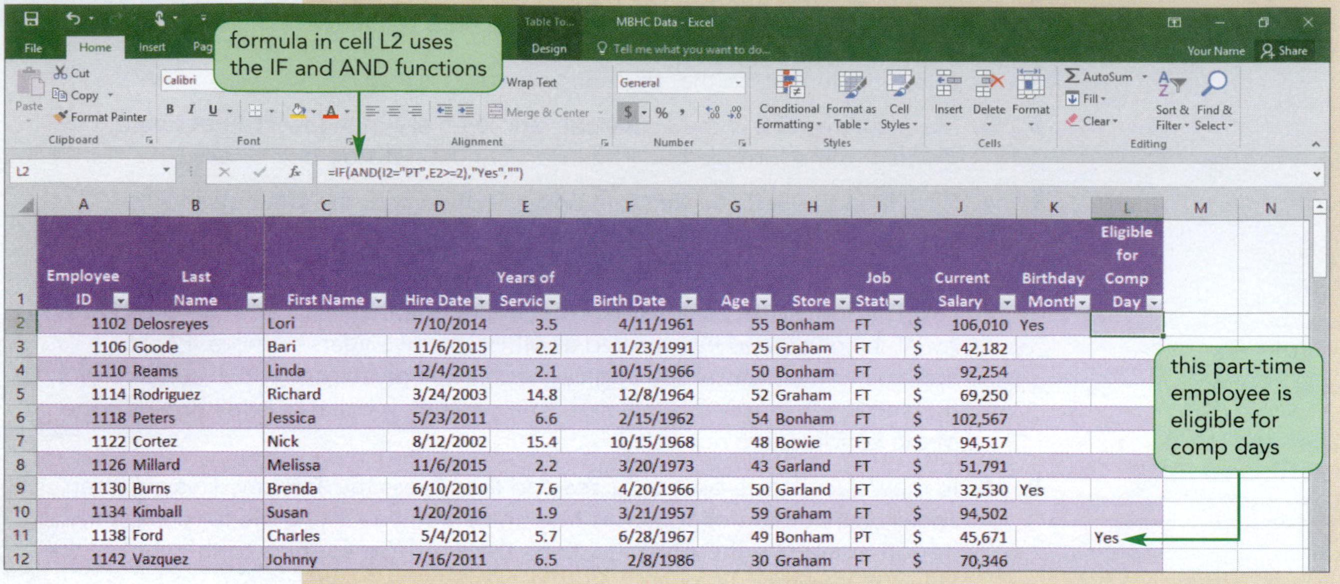

	A	B	C	D	E	F	G	H	I	J	K	L
1	Employee ID	Last Name	First Name	Hire Date	Years of Service	Birth Date	Age	Store	Job Status	Current Salary	Birthday Month	Eligible for Comp Day
2	1102	Delosreyes	Lori	7/10/2014	3.5	4/11/1961	55	Bonham	FT	$ 106,010	Yes	
3	1106	Goode	Bari	11/6/2015	2.2	11/23/1991	25	Graham	FT	$ 42,182		
4	1110	Reams	Linda	12/4/2015	2.1	10/15/1966	50	Bonham	FT	$ 92,254		
5	1114	Rodriguez	Richard	3/24/2003	14.8	12/8/1964	52	Graham	FT	$ 69,250		
6	1118	Peters	Jessica	5/23/2011	6.6	2/15/1962	54	Bonham	FT	$ 102,567		
7	1122	Cortez	Nick	8/12/2002	15.4	10/15/1968	48	Bowie	FT	$ 94,517		
8	1126	Millard	Melissa	11/6/2015	2.2	3/20/1973	43	Garland	FT	$ 51,791		
9	1130	Burns	Brenda	6/10/2010	7.6	4/20/1966	50	Garland	FT	$ 32,530	Yes	
10	1134	Kimball	Susan	1/20/2016	1.9	3/21/1957	59	Graham	FT	$ 94,502		
11	1138	Ford	Charles	5/4/2012	5.7	6/28/1967	49	Bonham	PT	$ 45,671		Yes
12	1142	Vazquez	Johnny	7/16/2011	6.5	2/8/1986	30	Graham	FT	$ 70,346		

All part-time employees who qualify for comp days have been identified.

INSIGHT

Using the DATEDIF Function to Calculate Employee Age

In the EmployeeTbl table, the Age column was calculated using the DATEDIF function. The **DATEDIF function** calculates the difference between two dates and shows the result in months, days, or years. The syntax for the DATEDIF function is

```
DATEDIF(Date1,Date2,Interval)
```

where `Date1` is the earliest date, `Date2` is the latest date, and `Interval` is the unit of time the DATEDIF function will use in the result. You specify `Interval` with one of the following interval codes:

Interval Code	Meaning	Description
"m"	Months	The number of complete months between *Date1* and *Date2*
"d"	Days	The number of complete days between *Date1* and *Date2*
"y"	Years	The number of complete years between *Date1* and *Date2*

For example, the following formula calculates an employee's age in complete years:

```
=DATEDIF(F2,'Data Tables'!$E$17,"y")
```

The earliest date is located in cell F2, the birth date. The latest date is in cell E17 in the Data Tables worksheet, which shows the date used to compare against the birth date—as of a cut-off date. The interval "y" indicates that you want to display the number of complete years between these two dates.

The DATEDIF function is undocumented in Excel, but it has been available since Excel 97. To learn more about this function, search the web using "DATEDIF function in Excel" as the search text in your favorite search engine.

Using the OR Function

The OR function is a logical function that returns a TRUE value if any of the logical conditions are true, and returns a FALSE value if all of the logical conditions are false. The syntax of the OR function is

```
OR(logical1[,logical2]...)
```

where `logical1` and `logical2` are conditions that can be either true or false. If any of the logical conditions are true, the OR function returns the logical value TRUE; otherwise, the function returns the logical value FALSE. You can include up to 255 logical conditions in the OR function. However, keep in mind that if any logical condition listed in the OR function is true, the OR function returns a TRUE value.

Figure 8-10 illustrates how the OR function is used to determine eligibility for a 10 percent discount. In this scenario, anyone who is 65 years or older (stored in cell B1) or anyone who is a college student (stored in cell B2) receives a 10 percent discount. At least one condition must be true for the OR function to return the logical value TRUE.

Figure 8-10 **Example of the OR function**

Purpose: To determine who is eligible for a discount

Logic Scenario: Discount is 10 percent for seniors (65 or older) or college students (Status =STU)

Formula: OR function with two conditions
`=OR(B1>=65,B2="STU")`

Data: cell B1 stores Age
cell B2 stores Status (STU, FAC, STF)

Example:

Data		Condition1	Condition2	Results
Cell B1	**Cell B2**	**B1>=65**	**B2="STU"**	**(Discount?)**
22	STU	False	True	True
67	FAC	True	False	True
65	STU	True	True	True
45	STF	False	False	False

MBHC is considering awarding a 3.5 percent raise to employees working in the original stores (Bonham or Graham) and a 2.5 percent raise for all other employees. The criteria for awarding a salary increase are based on location. If the employee is working in either Bonham or Graham, the employee will receive the 3.5 percent raise. In other words, if either Store equals Bonham or Store equals Graham is True, the condition is true, and the employee will receive the 3.5 percent raise. If the condition is false—meaning the employee works at a store other than Bonham or Graham—the employee receives a 2.5 percent raise. Vanessa outlined the salary increase criteria in the flowchart shown in Figure 8-11.

Figure 8-11 Flowchart of the OR function to calculate salary increase

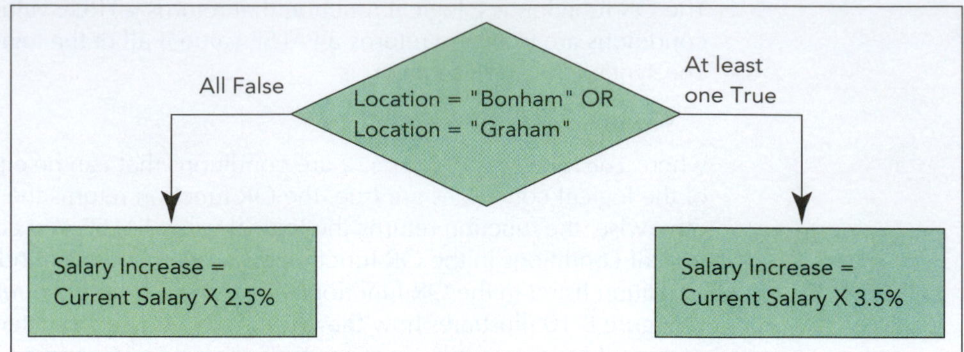

You need to use the OR function to test whether an employee meets the criteria for the 3.5 percent or 2.5 percent salary increase. The following formula uses the OR function to test whether the value in cell H2 (the store for the first employee) is equal to Bonham *or* whether the value in cell H2 is equal to Graham:

```
=OR(H2="Bonham",H2="Graham")
```

If the employee works in the Bonham store *or* the employee works in the Graham store, the OR function returns the value TRUE; otherwise, the OR function returns the value FALSE.

Figure 8-12 shows the results returned using the OR function for four different employee work locations—Bonham, Bowie, Garland, and Graham.

Figure 8-12 OR function results for four employee work locations

Purpose: To determine an employee's salary increase percentage

Logic Scenario: Proposed 3.5 percent salary increase to full-time (FT) employees located in Graham or Bonham

Formula: OR function with two conditions
`=OR(F2="Graham",F2="Bonham")`

Data: cell F2 stores Location

Example:

Data	Condition1	Condition2	Results
<u>Cell F2</u>	<u>F2="Graham"</u>	<u>B2="Bonham"</u>	<u>(OR function)</u>
Graham	True	False	True
Bonham	False	True	True
Garland	False	False	False
Bowie	False	False	False

The OR function only determines which raise an employee is eligible for. It does not calculate the amount of the salary increase. To determine the amount of the salary increase, the OR function must be nested within an IF function. In the formula

```
=IF(OR(H2="Bonham",H2="Graham"),J2*0.035,J2*0.025)
```

the logical test of the IF function uses the OR function (shown in red) to determine whether an employee is either working in the Bonham store *or* working in the Graham store. If the OR function returns a TRUE value, the IF function multiplies the Current Salary by 3.5 percent. If the OR function returns a FALSE value, the IF function multiplies the Current Salary by 2.5 percent.

Using Structured References to Create Formulas in Excel Tables

When you create a formula that references all or parts of an Excel table, you can replace the specific cell or range address with a structured reference, the actual table name, or a column header. This makes the formula easier to create and understand. The default Excel table name is Table1, Table2, and so forth unless you enter a more descriptive table name, as Vanessa did for the EmployeeTbl table. Column headers provide a description of the data entered in each column. Structured references make it easier to create formulas that use portions or all of an Excel table because the names or headers are usually simpler to identify than cell addresses. For example, in the EmployeeTbl table, the table name EmployeeTbl refers to the range A2:L101, which is the range of data in the table excluding the header row and the Total row. When you want to reference an entire column of data in a table, you create a column qualifier, which has the syntax

```
Tablename[qualifier]
```

where *Tablename* is the name entered in the Table Name box in the Properties group on the Table Tools Design tab, and *qualifier* is the column header enclosed in square brackets. For example, the following structured reference references the Current Salary data in the range J2:J101 of the EmployeeTbl table (excluding the column header and total row, if any):

```
EmployeeTbl[Current Salary]
```

You can use structured references in formulas. The following formula adds the Current Salary data in the range J2:J101 of the EmployeeTbl table; in this case, [Current Salary] is the column qualifier:

```
=SUM(EmployeeTbl[Current Salary])
```

When you create a calculated column you can use structured references in the formula. A formula that includes a structured reference can be fully qualified or unqualified. In a fully qualified structured reference, the table name precedes the column qualifier. In an unqualified structured reference, only the column qualifier (column header enclosed in square brackets) appears in the reference.

If you are creating a calculated column or formula within an Excel table, you can use either the fully qualified structured reference or the unqualified structured reference in the formula. If you use a structured reference outside the table or in another worksheet to reference an Excel table or portion of the table, you must use a fully qualified reference.

You'll use structured references to calculate the salary increases for MBHC Employees.

Be sure to type square brackets and use the exact spelling and location shown. Otherwise, the formula will return an error.

To calculate the salary increases using the IF and OR functions:

1. In cell **M1**, enter **Salary Increase** as the column header. The Excel table expands to include the new column, and cell M2 is the active cell.
2. Make sure cell **M2** is the active cell, and then click the **Insert Function** button next to the formula bar. The Insert Function dialog box opens.
3. Click **IF** in the Select a function box, and then click the **OK** button. The Function Arguments dialog box opens.
4. In the Logical_test box, type **OR([Store]="Bonham",[Store]="Graham")** to enter the OR function with structured references. This logical test evaluates whether the employee works in the Bonham store or works in the Graham.
5. Click the **Collapse dialog box** button so you can see the entire function in the Logical_test box. See Figure 8-13.

Figure 8-13 Logical_test argument for the OR function

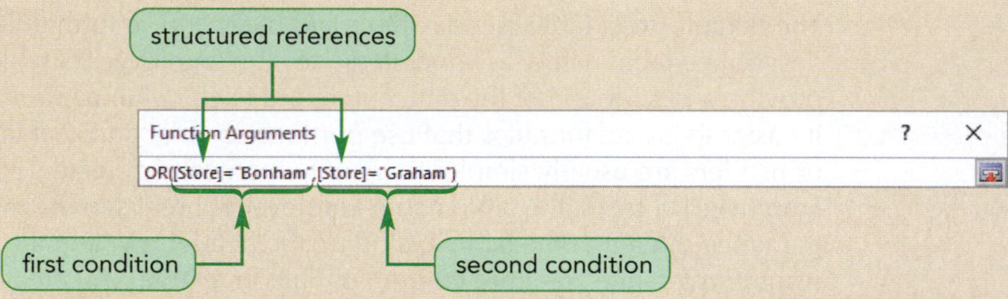

6. Click the **Expand dialog box** button, and then press the **Tab** key. TRUE appears to the right of the Logical_test box because the employee in the active row, row 2, is eligible for the 3.5 percent salary increase.

   Trouble? If Invalid appears instead of TRUE as the logical test results, you probably mistyped the logical test. Compare the function in your Logical_test box to the one shown in Figure 8-13, confirming that you used square brackets around the structured reference [Store] and typed all the text correctly.
7. In the Value_if_true box, type **[Current Salary]*0.035** and then press the **Tab** key. This argument specifies that if the logical test is true (the employee is eligible for the 3.5 percent increase), the amount in the employee's salary cell is multiplied by 3.5 percent. The salary increases for all employees, beginning in row 2, whose logical test is true appear to the right of the Value_if_true box.

8. In the Value_if_false box, type **[Current Salary]*0.025**. This argument specifies that if the logical test is false (the employee is not eligible for the 3.5 percent salary increase), the amount in the employee's salary cell is multiplied by 2.5 percent. The salary increases for all employees, beginning in row 2, whose logical test is false appear to the right of the Value_if_false box. See Figure 8-14.

Figure 8-14 **Function Arguments dialog box for the IF function with an OR function**

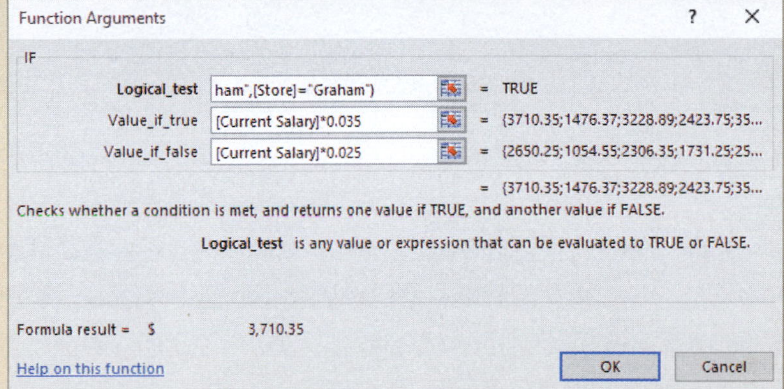

9. Click the **OK** button. The formula =IF(OR([Store]="Bonham",[Store]="Bonham"), [Current Salary]*0.035,[Current Salary]*0.025) appears in the formula bar, and the value 3710.35 appears in cell M2 because the condition is true. The formula is automatically copied to all rows in column M of the table.

TIP

Double-click above the header row to select the column header and data.

10. Position the pointer at the top of cell **M1** until the pointer changes to ⬇, and then click the left mouse button to select the Salary Increase data values.

11. Format the range with the **Accounting** style with two decimal places, and then increase the column width to display all values, if necessary.

12. Select cell **M2** to deselect the column. See Figure 8-15.

Figure 8-15 IF function with the OR function calculates salary increase

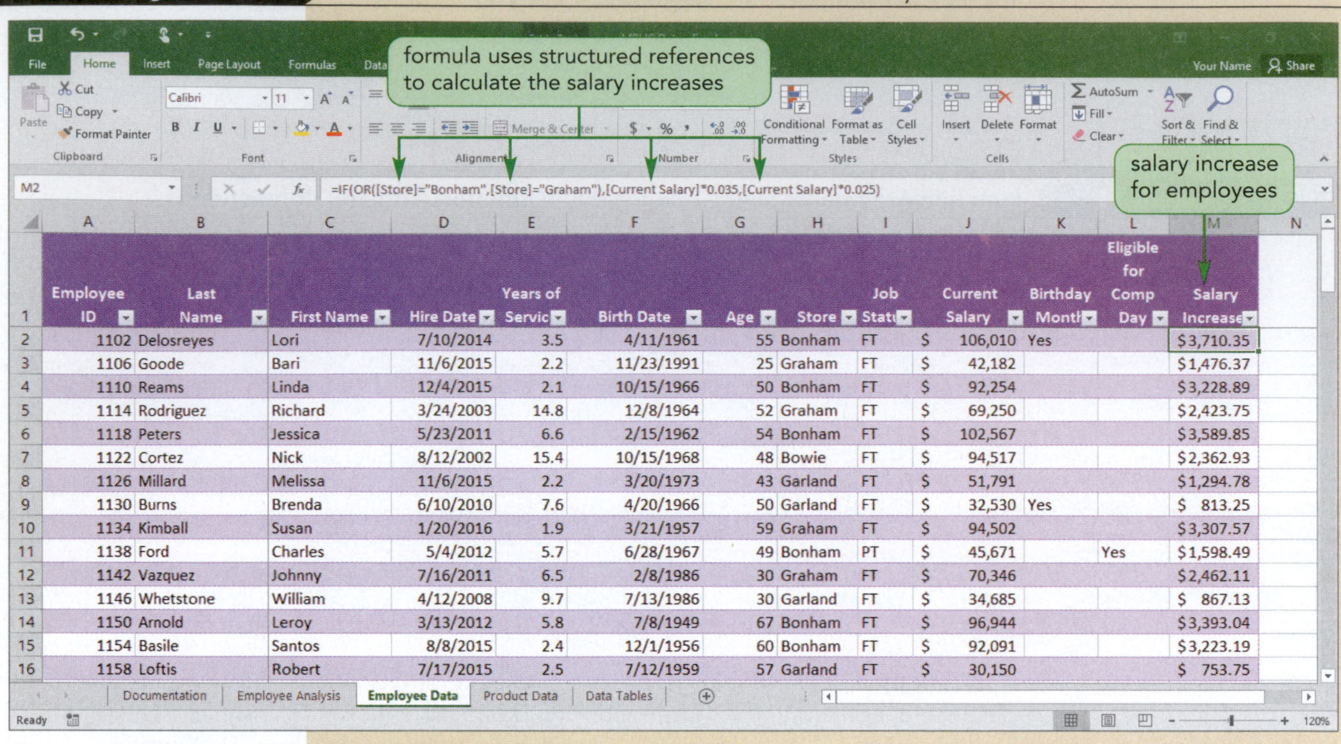

Employee ID	Last Name	First Name	Hire Date	Years of Servic	Birth Date	Age	Store	Job Statu	Current Salary	Birthday Month	Eligible for Comp Day	Salary Increase
1102	Delosreyes	Lori	7/10/2014	3.5	4/11/1961	55	Bonham	FT	$ 106,010	Yes		$3,710.35
1106	Goode	Bari	11/6/2015	2.2	11/23/1991	25	Graham	FT	$ 42,182			$1,476.37
1110	Reams	Linda	12/4/2015	2.1	10/15/1966	50	Bonham	FT	$ 92,254			$3,228.89
1114	Rodriguez	Richard	3/24/2003	14.8	12/8/1964	52	Graham	FT	$ 69,250			$2,423.75
1118	Peters	Jessica	5/23/2011	6.6	2/15/1962	54	Bonham	FT	$ 102,567			$3,589.85
1122	Cortez	Nick	8/12/2002	15.4	10/15/1968	48	Bowie	FT	$ 94,517			$2,362.93
1126	Millard	Melissa	11/6/2015	2.2	3/20/1973	43	Garland	FT	$ 51,791			$1,294.78
1130	Burns	Brenda	6/10/2010	7.6	4/20/1966	50	Garland	FT	$ 32,530	Yes		$ 813.25
1134	Kimball	Susan	1/20/2016	1.9	3/21/1957	59	Graham	FT	$ 94,502			$3,307.57
1138	Ford	Charles	5/4/2012	5.7	6/28/1967	49	Bonham	PT	$ 45,671		Yes	$1,598.49
1142	Vazquez	Johnny	7/16/2011	6.5	2/8/1986	30	Graham	FT	$ 70,346			$2,462.11
1146	Whetstone	William	4/12/2008	9.7	7/13/1986	30	Garland	FT	$ 34,685			$ 867.13
1150	Arnold	Leroy	3/13/2012	5.8	7/8/1949	67	Bonham	FT	$ 96,944			$3,393.04
1154	Basile	Santos	8/8/2015	2.4	12/1/1956	60	Bonham	FT	$ 92,091			$3,223.19
1158	Loftis	Robert	7/17/2015	2.5	7/12/1959	57	Garland	FT	$ 30,150			$ 753.75

In this session, you used the IF, AND, and OR functions to determine if employees' birth dates occur in a specified month, to determine if part-time employees are eligible for comp days, and to calculate employees' salary increases for next year. Vanessa still needs to calculate the employee bonuses and complete the product data worksheet with the product supplier and specialty store for each product. In the next session, you will create formulas with functions to perform these calculations.

REVIEW

Session 8.1 Quick Check

1. What changes occur in the appearance and size of an Excel table after you enter a new column header named "Phone"?
2. Whenever you enter a formula in an empty column of an Excel table, Excel automatically fills the column with the same formula. What is this called?
3. If an Excel worksheet stores the cost per meal in cell Q5, the number of attendees in cell Q6, and the total cost of meals in cell Q7, what IF function would you enter in cell Q7 to calculate the total cost of meals (cost per meal times the number of attendees) with a minimum cost of $10,000?
4. When does the AND function return a TRUE value?
5. Write the formula that displays the label "Outstanding" in cell Y5 if the amount owed (cell X5) is greater than 0 and the transaction date (cell R5) is after 3/1/2016 (stored in cell R1) but otherwise leaves the cell blank.
6. When you create a formula that references all or parts of an Excel table, what can you use to replace the specific cell or range addresses with the actual table or column header names?
7. If the formula `=IF(OR(B25="NY",B25="CA",B25="TX"),"Select","Ignore")` is entered in cell B26, and `"PA"` is entered in cell B25, what is displayed in cell B26?
8. Write the OR function that represents the following rule—"A potential enlistee in the army is not eligible to enlist if younger than 17 or older than 42." The age is stored in cell B25. Display "Eligible" if the potential enlistee can enlist, and display "Not Eligible" if the potential enlistee cannot enlist.

Session 8.2 Visual Overview:

When the lookup value matches the first row of the lookup table, the corresponding value from the second row of the lookup table is returned to the cell with the HLOOKUP function.

The exact match **HLOOKUP function** (horizontal lookup) searches across the first row of the lookup table until the lookup value exactly matches a value in the first row, and then retrieves the corresponding value from the second row of the lookup table.

When the lookup value matches the first column of the lookup table, the corresponding value from the second column of the lookup table is returned to the cell with the VLOOKUP function.

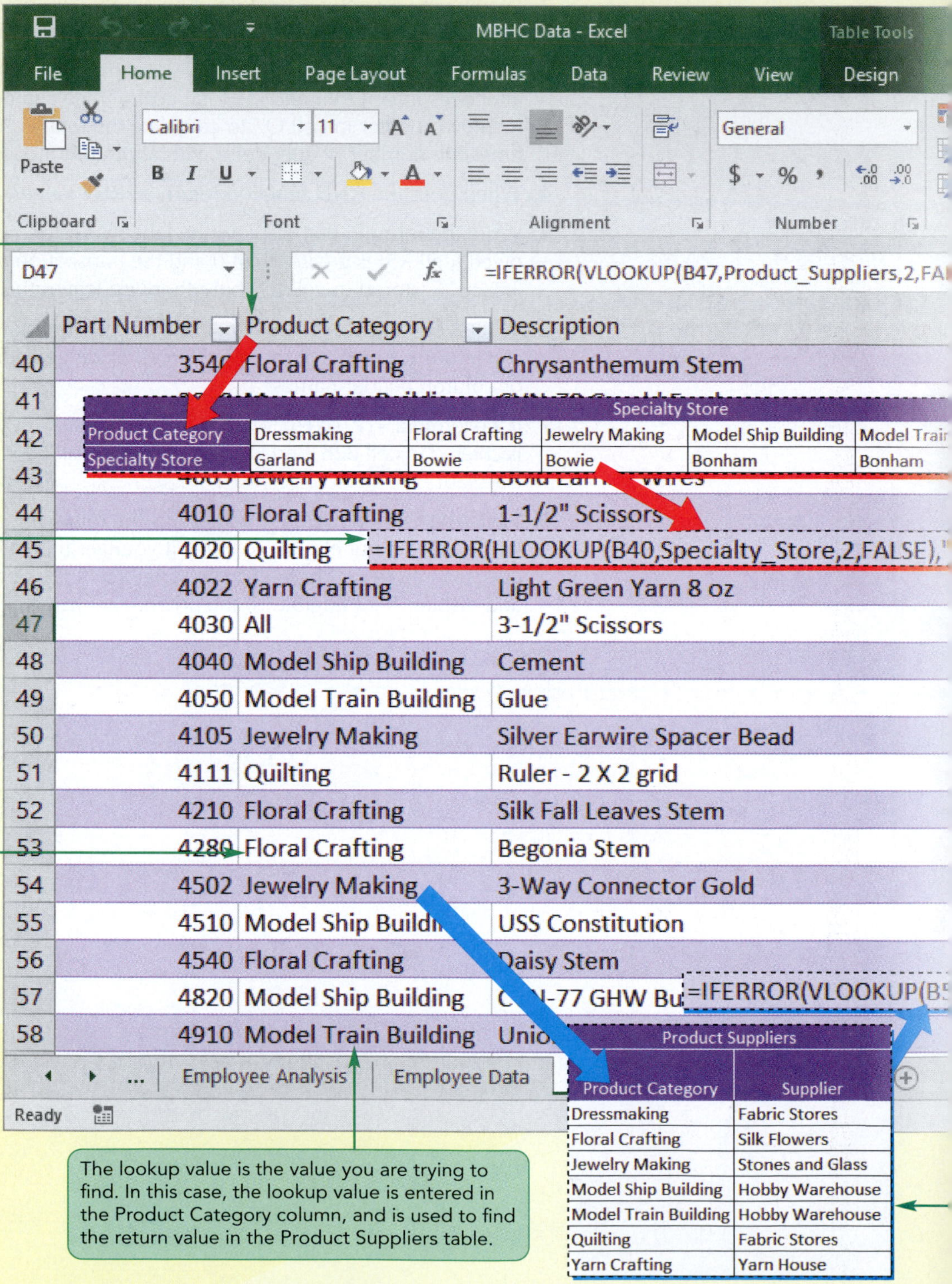

The lookup value is the value you are trying to find. In this case, the lookup value is entered in the Product Category column, and is used to find the return value in the Product Suppliers table.

	Part Number	Product Category	Description
40	3540	Floral Crafting	Chrysanthemum Stem
41			
42			
43			
44	4010	Floral Crafting	1-1/2" Scissors
45	4020	Quilting	=IFERROR(HLOOKUP(B40,Specialty_Store,2,FALSE),"
46	4022	Yarn Crafting	Light Green Yarn 8 oz
47	4030	All	3-1/2" Scissors
48	4040	Model Ship Building	Cement
49	4050	Model Train Building	Glue
50	4105	Jewelry Making	Silver Earwire Spacer Bead
51	4111	Quilting	Ruler - 2 X 2 grid
52	4210	Floral Crafting	Silk Fall Leaves Stem
53	4280	Floral Crafting	Begonia Stem
54	4502	Jewelry Making	3-Way Connector Gold
55	4510	Model Ship Buildi	USS Constitution
56	4540	Floral Crafting	Daisy Stem
57	4820	Model Ship Building	C -77 GHW Bu =IFERROR(VLOOKUP(B5
58	4910	Model Train Building	Unio

Specialty Store

Product Category	Dressmaking	Floral Crafting	Jewelry Making	Model Ship Building	Model Trai
Specialty Store	Garland	Bowie	Bowie	Bonham	Bonham

Product Suppliers

Product Category	Supplier
Dressmaking	Fabric Stores
Floral Crafting	Silk Flowers
Jewelry Making	Stones and Glass
Model Ship Building	Hobby Warehouse
Model Train Building	Hobby Warehouse
Quilting	Fabric Stores
Yarn Crafting	Yarn House

Lookup Tables and the IFERROR Function

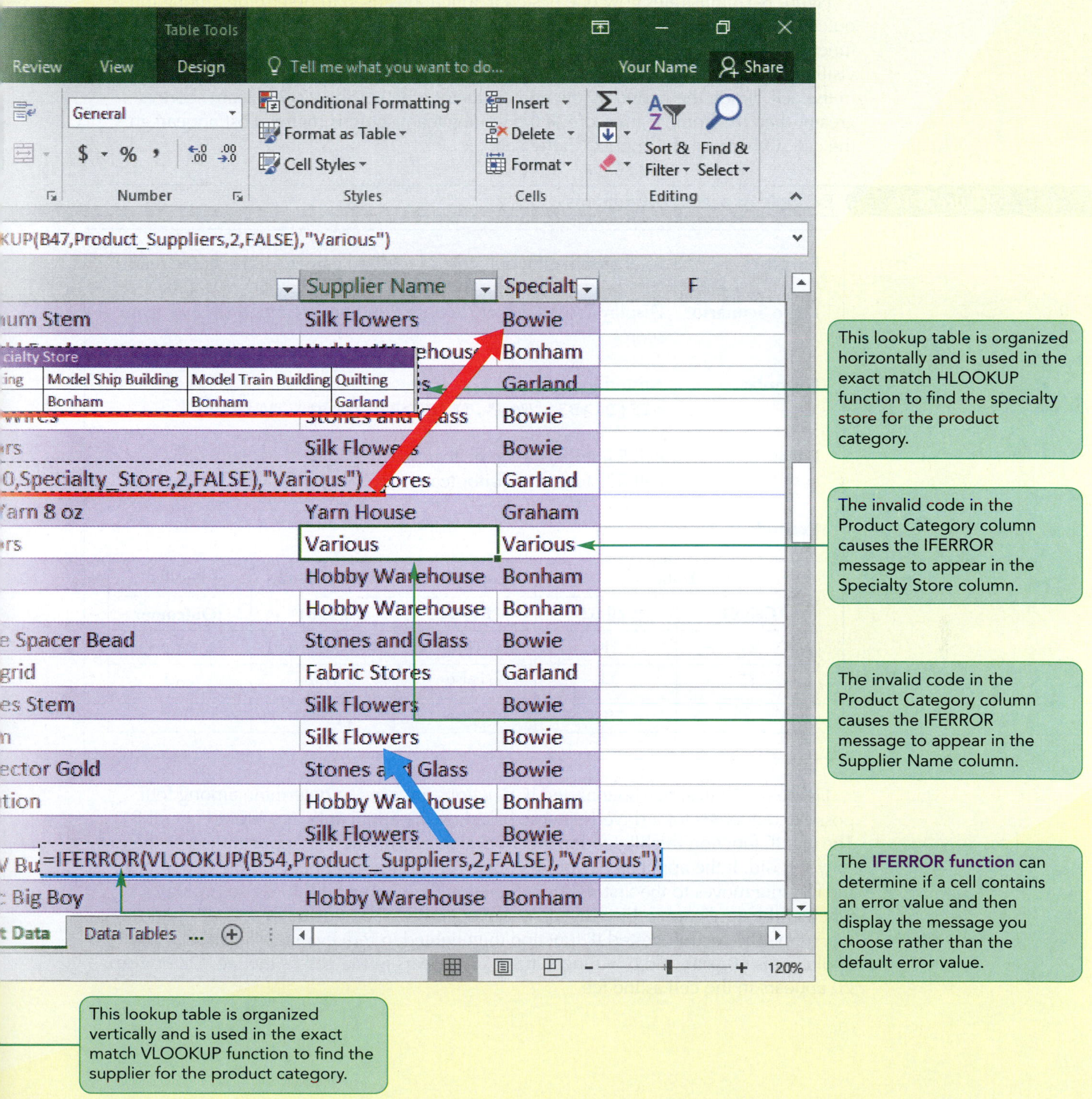

Table Tools
Review
View
Design
Tell me what you want to do...
Your Name
Share
General
Conditional Formatting
Format as Table
Cell Styles
Insert
Delete
Format
Sort & Filter
Find & Select
Number
Styles
Cells
Editing
KUP(B47,Product_Suppliers,2,FALSE),"Various")
Supplier Name
Specialt
F
cialty Store
Model Ship Building
Model Train Building
Quilting
Bonham
Bonham
Garland
0,Specialty_Store,2,FALSE),"Various")
=IFERROR(VLOOKUP(B54,Product_Suppliers,2,FALSE),"Various")
Data Tables
120%
This lookup table is organized horizontally and is used in the exact match HLOOKUP function to find the specialty store for the product category.
The invalid code in the Product Category column causes the IFERROR message to appear in the Specialty Store column.
The invalid code in the Product Category column causes the IFERROR message to appear in the Supplier Name column.
The IFERROR function can determine if a cell contains an error value and then display the message you choose rather than the default error value.
This lookup table is organized vertically and is used in the exact match VLOOKUP function to find the supplier for the product category.

Creating Nested IFs

The IF function can choose between only two outcomes. When you want the function to choose from three or more outcomes, you can nest IF functions. A **nested IF function** is when one IF function is placed inside another IF function to test an additional condition. You can nest more than one IF function to test for multiple outcomes.

Figure 8-16 illustrates how one nested IF function is used to determine among three outcomes—whether the home football team won, lost, or tied a game. The first IF function evaluates whether the home team score (stored in cell B1) is greater than the visiting team score (stored in cell B2). If the home team score is higher, Won appears in the cell. If not, the nested IF function evaluates whether the visiting team score is greater than the home team score. If the visiting team score is higher, Lost appears in the cell. Otherwise, Tie appears in the cell.

Figure 8-16 **Example of nested IF functions**

Purpose: To determine the outcome of football games for the home team

Logic Scenario: Display Won, Lost, or Tie based on home team and visitor team scores

Formula: Nested IF functions

```
=IF(B1>B2,"Won",IF(B2>B1,"Lost","Tie"))
```

Data: cell B1 stores the home team score
cell B2 stores the visitor team score

Example:

Data		Condition1	Condition2	Results
Cell B1	Cell B2	B1>B2	B2>B1	(Outcome)
21	18	True	Not evaluated	Won
17	24	False	True	Lost
9	9	False	False	Tie

Figure 8-17 illustrates how nested IF functions are used to determine among four possible outcomes for a driver's license based on the applicant's age (stored in cell B1). The first IF function (highlighted in green) evaluates whether the applicant is less than 16 years old. If the applicant is younger than 16, Too Young appears in the cell. If not, the formula moves to the first nested IF function (highlighted in blue) and evaluates whether the applicant is 45 years old or younger. If so, 30 appears in the cell as the fee. If not, the second nested IF function (highlighted in red) evaluates whether the applicant is 60 years old or younger. If so, 25 appears in the cell as the fee. Otherwise, 20 appears in the cell as the fee.

Figure 8-17 **Additional example of nested IF functions**

Purpose: To determine the fee for a driver's license

Logic Scenario: Driver's license fee varies by age

Below 16	"Too Young"
16–45	$30
46–60	$25
61 and older	$20

Formula: Nested IF functions

```
=IF(B1<16,"Too Young",IF(B1<=45,30,IF(B1<=60,25,20)))
```

Data: cell B1 stores the driver's age

Example:

Data	Condition1	Condition2	Condition3	Results
Cell B1	B1<16	B1<=45	B1<=60	(Fee)
15	True	Not evaluated	Not evaluated	Too Young
25	False	True	Not evaluated	30
55	False	False	True	25
65	False	False	False	20

You need to use nested IF functions to determine MBHC employee bonus amounts. MBHC pays employee bonuses based on each employee's years of service. MBHC has three bonus amounts. Employees who have been at the company for 10 or more years will receive a bonus of $500. Employees who have been at the company for 5 years to less than 10 years will receive $250. Employees who have been at the company less than 5 years will receive $100. In this case, you need to nest IF functions to calculate the different series of outcomes for the employee bonuses.

Vanessa created the flowchart shown in Figure 8-18 to illustrate the logic for determining bonus awards. She used different colors to identify each IF function. The flowchart shows that if an employee's years of service is >=10, the bonus amount equals $500 and the IF function (shown in green) is finished. If the employee's years of service is >=5, then the second IF function (shown in blue) is evaluated. If the employee's years of service is >=5, then the bonus amount equals $250 and the IF function is finished. All other employees (years of service is less than 5 years) will receive a bonus of $100.

Figure 8-18 **Flowchart of nested IF functions to determine the bonus amount**

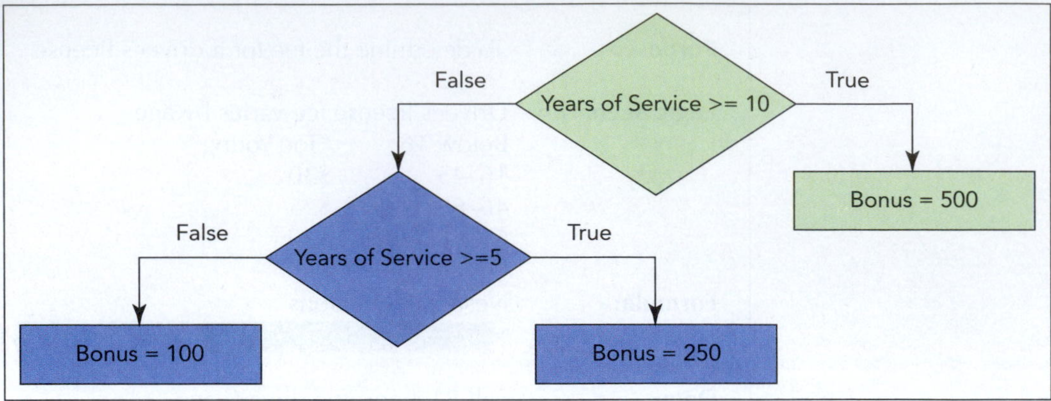

The following formula converts Vanessa's flowchart into a formula with nested IF functions:

```
=IF([Years of Service]>=10,500,IF([Years of Service]>=5,250,100))
```

The first IF function (shown in green) tests whether the value in the Years of Service is greater than or equal to 10. If this condition ([Years of Service]>=10) is true, the formula returns 500 in the Bonus cell. If this condition is false (the Years of Service is < 10), the second IF function (shown in blue) is evaluated. The second IF function tests whether the value in the Years of Service cell is greater than or equal to 5. If this condition ([Years of Service]>=5) is true, the formula returns 250 in the Bonus cell. If this condition is false (the value in the Years of Service cell is less than 5), the formula returns 100 in the Bonus cell.

PROSKILLS

Problem Solving: Finding and Fixing Errors in Formulas

If formulas in a worksheet are returning errors or not working as expected, you need to find and fix the problems. Two common categories of formula errors in Excel are syntax errors and logic errors. A syntax error is an error in a statement that violates the rules of Excel. A syntax error might occur due to unmatched parentheses or a required argument that is omitted in a function. Logic errors occur in formulas that work but return an incorrect result. Logic errors are often detected by the user because the results seem out of line. A logic error could occur because the formula uses the wrong calculation, the formula references the wrong cell, or the formula uses faulty reasoning, leading to incorrect results.

Some problem-solving approaches can help resolve these types of errors. First, examine the formulas in worksheet cells instead of the results by pressing the Ctrl+~ keys to display the formulas in each cell. Or, you can use the Formula Auditing tools on the Formulas tab to visually identify and trace cells used in a formula. This can help you locate and fix inaccurate cell references and faulty logic.

By carefully evaluating formulas and fixing any problems, you help to ensure that a worksheet is error-free and returns accurate results.

Vanessa wants the EmployeeTbl table to include a column that contains a formula to calculate the bonus amount. Vanessa stored the three bonus amounts (0, 250, and 500) in the Data Tables worksheet cells B17, B18, and B19. You will reference these cells in the formula to calculate the employee bonus. This approach enables you to quickly update the calculated bonus amounts in the Data Tables worksheet without having to edit the bonus formula.

To enter nested IFs to calculate employee bonuses:

1. If you took a break at the end of the previous session, make sure the MBHC Data workbook is open and the Employee Data worksheet is active.
2. In cell **N1**, enter **Bonus Amount** as the column header. The Excel table expands to include the new column, and cell N2 is the active cell.
3. Make sure cell **N2** is the active cell, and then click the **Insert Function** button next to the formula bar. The Insert Function dialog box opens.
4. Click **IF** in the Select a function box, and then click the **OK** button. The Function Arguments dialog box opens.
5. In the Logical_test box, type **[Years of Service]>=10** and then press the **Tab** key to enter the logical test using a structured reference. This logical test evaluates whether the employee's years of service is greater than or equal to 10. The FALSE values to the right of the Logical_test box indicate that the years of service for the first few employees is not greater than or equal to 10.

   Trouble? If the value to the right of the Logical_test box is Invalid, you probably mistyped the logical test. Select the text in the Logical_test box, and then repeat Step 5, typing the logical test exactly as shown, being sure to use square brackets around the structured reference.

TIP

If you type a formula directly in a cell, the available structured references appear after you type the opening bracket. Double-click the structured reference to add it to the formula, and then type the closing bracket.

6. In the Value_if_true box, type **'Data Tables'!$B$19** and then press the **Tab** key. The value to the right of the Value_if_true argument box is 500, which is the value in cell B19 of the Data Tables worksheet. This argument specifies that if the logical test is true (the years of service is greater than or equal to 10), display the value stored in cell B19 of the Data Tables worksheet (500 bonus amount). The absolute reference ensures that the formula in each row will refer to cell B19 of the Data Tables worksheet, which contains the bonus amount. Note that values that change, such as the Bonus Amount, are stored in a separate worksheet.
7. In the Value_if_false box, type **IF([Years of Service]>=5,'Data Tables'!$B$18,'Data Tables'!$B$17)** and then press the **Tab** key. This argument is a nested IF function that specifies if the logical condition is true (years of service are greater than or equal to 5), display the value stored in cell B18 of the Data Tables worksheet (250 bonus amount); otherwise, display the value stored in cell B17 of the Data Tables worksheet (100 bonus amount). Again, you used absolute references to ensure that the formula will always refer to cell B18 and cell B17 of the Data Tables worksheet. The values to the right of the Value_if_false box indicate the bonus amounts for the employees in the first few rows. See Figure 8-19.

Figure 8-19 **Function Arguments dialog box with a nested IF**

structured references make the formula easier to write and understand

use an absolute reference because this value is the same for all rows

use a nested IF function to calculate the value_if_false

Function Arguments

IF

Logical_test [Years of Service]>=10 = {FALSE;FALSE;FALSE;TRUE;FALSE;TR...

Value_if_true 'Data Tables'!$B$19 = 500

Value_if_false IF([Years of Service]>=5,'Data Ta = {100;100;100;250;250;250;100;250;10...

= {100;100;100;500;250;500;100;250;10...

Checks whether a condition is met, and returns one value if TRUE, and another value if FALSE.

Logical_test is any value or expression that can be evaluated to TRUE or FALSE.

Formula result = $ 100

Help on this function

OK Cancel

8. Click the **OK** button. The formula =IF([Years of Service]>=10,'Data Tables'!$B$19,IF([Years of Service]>=5,'Data Tables'!$B$18,'Data Tables!$B$17)) appears in the formula bar, and the value 100 appears in cell N2 because this employee has 3.5 years of service. The bonus formula is automatically copied to all other rows in the Bonus Amount column. The references to cells B19, B18, and B17 of the Data Tables worksheet are absolute references and do not change from cell to cell in the Bonus Amount column.
9. Select the Bonus values, and then format the selected range using the **Accounting** format with no decimal places.
10. Select cell **N2** to deselect the column. See Figure 8-20.

Figure 8-20 **Nested IF function calculating the employee bonus amounts**

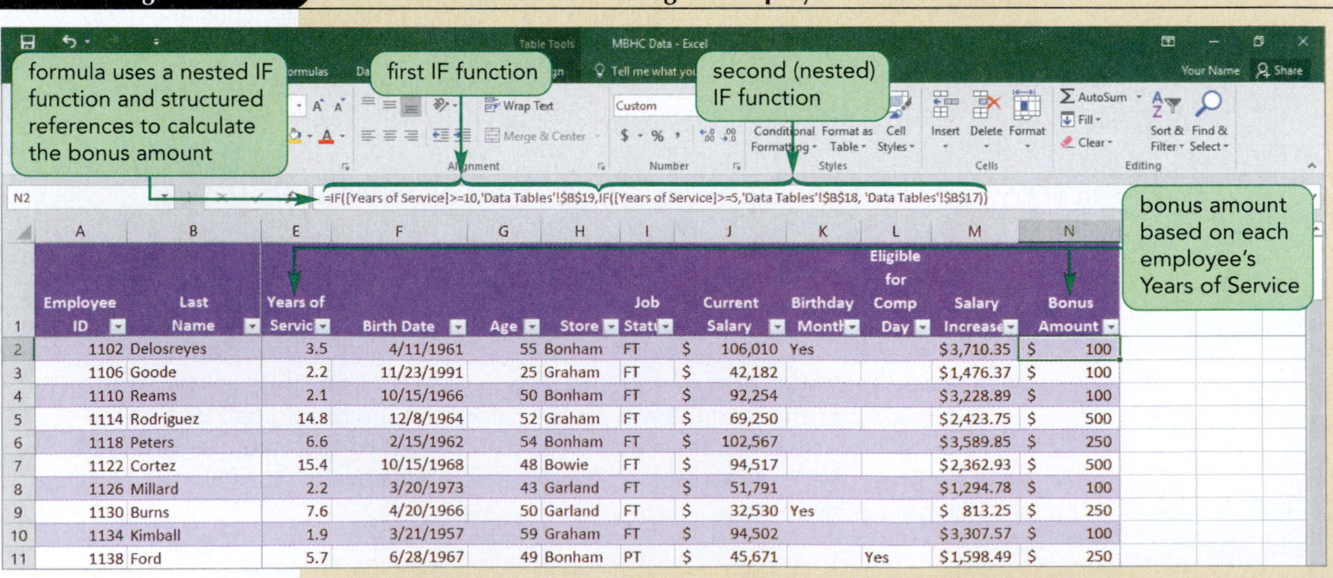

	Employee ID	Last Name	Years of Servic	Birth Date	Age	Store	Job Statu	Current Salary	Birthday Month	Eligible for Comp Day	Salary Increase	Bonus Amount
2	1102	Delosreyes	3.5	4/11/1961	55	Bonham	FT	$ 106,010	Yes		$3,710.35	$ 100
3	1106	Goode	2.2	11/23/1991	25	Graham	FT	$ 42,182			$1,476.37	$ 100
4	1110	Reams	2.1	10/15/1966	50	Bonham	FT	$ 92,254			$3,228.89	$ 100
5	1114	Rodriguez	14.8	12/8/1964	52	Graham	FT	$ 69,250			$2,423.75	$ 500
6	1118	Peters	6.6	2/15/1962	54	Bonham	FT	$ 102,567			$3,589.85	$ 250
7	1122	Cortez	15.4	10/15/1968	48	Bowie	FT	$ 94,517			$2,362.93	$ 500
8	1126	Millard	2.2	3/20/1973	43	Garland	FT	$ 51,791			$1,294.78	$ 100
9	1130	Burns	7.6	4/20/1966	50	Garland	FT	$ 32,530	Yes		$ 813.25	$ 250
10	1134	Kimball	1.9	3/21/1957	59	Graham	FT	$ 94,502			$3,307.57	$ 100
11	1138	Ford	5.7	6/28/1967	49	Bonham	PT	$ 45,671		Yes	$1,598.49	$ 250

The Bonus Amount column shows the bonuses for each employee.

INSIGHT

Checking Formulas for Matching Parentheses

A common problem when creating formulas is mismatched parentheses. As you write a formula, you should verify that you enclosed the correct argument, function, or term within the parentheses of the formula you are creating. This is especially important when you develop a complex formula that includes many parentheses, such as a nested IF function. Excel color-codes the parentheses as you build a formula so you can quickly determine whether the formula includes complete pairs of them. You can also verify that the formula includes matching pairs of parentheses by selecting the cell with the formula and then clicking in the formula bar. Press the right arrow key to move the insertion point through the formula one character at a time. When the insertion point moves across one parenthesis, its matching parenthesis is also highlighted briefly. This color-coding helps you ensure that all parentheses in a formula are paired (opening and closing parentheses).

By using cell references to input values rather than including constants in formulas, you make a worksheet more flexible and easier to update. The executive team has increased the bonus for employees with 10 or more years of service from $500 to $750. Vanessa asks you to update this bonus amount so the employee bonuses will be current.

To update the bonus amount for years of service >=10:

1. Go to the **Data Tables** worksheet.
2. In cell **B19**, enter **750**. The new bonus amount is entered in the data table.
3. Go to the **Employee Data** worksheet.
4. In the Bonus Amount column, observe that the bonus amount for all employees who have 10 or more years of service is now $750.

Using LOOKUP Functions

Recall that lookup functions allow you to find values in a table of data and insert them in another worksheet location. For example, you might enter a product table in a worksheet that includes the product ID, product name, and price of all products a company sells. You could then use this product table to build an invoice in another worksheet by entering a product ID and having Excel look up the product name and price, and insert these values in the invoice. The table that stores the data you want to retrieve is called a lookup table.

Both the VLOOKUP and HLOOKUP functions are used to return a value from a lookup table. The VLOOKUP function always searches for a value in the first column of the lookup table. The HLOOKUP function always searches for a value in the first row of the lookup table. Both these functions can retrieve a value from lookup tables designed for *exact match* or *approximate match* lookups. Recall that an exact match lookup occurs when the lookup value must match one of the values in the first column (or row) of the lookup table. An approximate match lookup occurs when the lookup value is found within a range of numbers in the first column (or row) of the lookup table. Which function you use depends on how the data is arranged in the lookup table. If the first column of the lookup table is searched, then use VLOOKUP; if the first row of the lookup table is searched, then use HLOOKUP.

At MBHC, all products have a supplier based on the product category. The supplier for dressmaking and quilting is Fabric Stores, the supplier for floral crafting is Silk Flowers, the supplier for jewelry making is Stones and Glass, the supplier for model ship and train building is Hobby Warehouse, and the supplier for yarn crafting is Yarn House. If a product can be supplied by many sources and is located in all stores it will have a product category of All. You could determine the supplier for a product by using several nested IF functions. However, a simpler approach is to use a lookup function.

You can use the Product Suppliers data shown in Figure 8-21 as an exact match lookup table. The lookup table includes the product categories and their corresponding suppliers. To retrieve the product supplier, Excel moves down the first column in the Product Suppliers lookup table until it finds the category that matches the product category of the product. Then it moves to the second column in the lookup table to locate the supplier, which is then displayed in the cell where the lookup formula is entered or used as part of a calculation. If the product category code doesn't match one of the values in the first column of the Product Suppliers table (spelling or spaces are different), the #N/A error value is displayed. For example, to find the return value for the Floral Crafting lookup value, Excel searches the first column of the lookup table until the Floral Crafting entry is found. Then, Excel moves to the second column of the lookup table to locate the corresponding return value, which is Silk Flowers, in this case.

Figure 8-21 Product Suppliers lookup table used for an exact match lookup

Lookup Value = Floral Crafting

search down the first column until the lookup value exactly matches the value in the first column

Product Suppliers	
Product Category	Supplier
Dressmaking	Fabric Stores
Floral Crafting	Silk Flowers
Jewelry Making	Stones and Glass
Model Ship Building	Hobby Warehouse
Model Train Building	Hobby Warehouse
Quilting	Fabric Stores
Yarn Crafting	Yarn House

return the corresponding value from the second column of the lookup table

Return Value = Silk Flowers

Lookup tables can also be constructed as approximate match lookups. A discount based on the quantity of items purchased where each discount covers a range of units purchased is an example of an approximate match lookup. Figure 8-22 shows the approximate match lookup table for these quantity discounts. In this example, purchases of fewer than 25 units receive no discount, purchases of between 25 and 99 units receive a 2 percent discount, purchases of between 100 and 499 units receive a 3 percent discount, and purchases of 500 or more units receive a 4 percent discount. For example, to find the quantity discount for a purchase of 55 units, Excel searches the first column of the lookup table until it finds the largest value that is less than or equal to 55 (the lookup value), which is 25 in this example. Then, Excel moves to the second column of the lookup table and returns 2 percent as the quantity discount.

Figure 8-22 Approximate match lookup table

Lookup Value = 55
search down the first column until the largest value less than or equal to the lookup value is found
return the corresponding value from the second column of the lookup table
Return Value = 2%

Quantity	Discount Rate
0	0%
25	2%
100	3%
500	4%

Using the VLOOKUP Function to Find an Exact Match

To retrieve the correct value from the lookup table, you use the VLOOKUP function. Recall that the VLOOKUP function searches vertically down the first column of the lookup table for the value you entered and then retrieves the corresponding value from another column of the table. The VLOOKUP function has the syntax

```
VLOOKUP(lookup_value,table_array,col_index_num[,range_lookup])
```

where `lookup_value` is the value, cell reference, defined name, or structured reference you want to search for in the first column of the lookup table; `table_array` is a range reference, a defined name, or the name of an Excel table that is the lookup table; `col_index_num` is the number of the column in the lookup table that contains the value you want to return; and `range_lookup` indicates whether the lookup table is an exact match (FALSE) or an approximate match (TRUE). The `range_lookup` argument is optional; if you don't include a `range_lookup` value, the value is considered TRUE (an approximate match).

You'll use the VLOOKUP function to identify the product supplier because you can search the values in the first column of the lookup table. You can use the range reference (the range A8:B14 on the Data Tables worksheet) or the defined name Product_Suppliers when you reference the lookup table in the VLOOKUP formula to determine the product supplier for a product on the Product Data worksheet:

Range reference `=VLOOKUP(B2,'Data Tables'!$A$8:$B$14,2,FALSE)`

Defined name `=VLOOKUP(B2,Product_Suppliers,2,FALSE)`

Both of these formulas use the VLOOKUP function to search for the product's supplier using the product category, column B in the Product Data worksheet, and the Product Suppliers lookup table in the Data Tables worksheet. The lookup uses the value in column B of the Product Data worksheet to find the matching product category in first column of the Product Suppliers lookup table (the range A8:B14 in the Data Tables worksheet) and then return the corresponding value from the second column of the lookup table, which shows the supplier. The formulas use FALSE as the *range_lookup* argument because you want the lookup value to exactly match a value in the first column of the lookup table.

Vanessa wants you to enter the VLOOKUP function using the defined name to reference the lookup table in the VLOOKUP function so she can easily determine what's included in the function. This is also simpler than entering range references, and you don't need to change the reference to an absolute reference.

To find an exact match in the Product Suppliers table using the VLOOKUP function:

1. Go to the **Product Data** worksheet.
2. In cell **D1**, enter **Supplier Name**. The table expands to include the new column.

3. Make sure cell **D2** is the active cell, and then click the **Insert Function** button next to the formula bar. The Insert Function dialog box opens.
4. Click the **Or select a category** arrow, click **Lookup & Reference**, and then double-click **VLOOKUP** in the Select a function box. The Function Arguments dialog box opens.
5. Drag the Function Arguments dialog box below row 2, if necessary, so you can see the column headers.
6. In the Lookup_value box, type **B2** and then press the **Tab** key. The lookup value is the product category, which is located in column B.
7. In the Table_array box, type **Product_Suppliers** and then press the **Tab** key. Product_Suppliers is the defined name assigned to the range A8:B14 in the Data Tables worksheet. If the Product Suppliers data was entered as a range rather than a defined name, the table_array argument would be entered as 'Data Tables'!A8:B14, and you would need to change the range to absolute references ('Data Tables'!$A$8:$B$14) so the formula would copy correctly to other cells.

For the col_index_num value, be sure to enter the number of the column's position in the table, not its column letter, to avoid receiving #NAME? or #VALUE! as the result.

8. In the Col_index_num box, type **2** and then press the **Tab** key. The number 2 indicates the product supplier is stored in the second column of the Product_Suppliers lookup table.
9. In the Range_lookup box, type **FALSE**. This sets the function to find an exact match in the lookup table. See Figure 8-23.

Figure 8-23 **Function Arguments dialog box for VLOOKUP function**

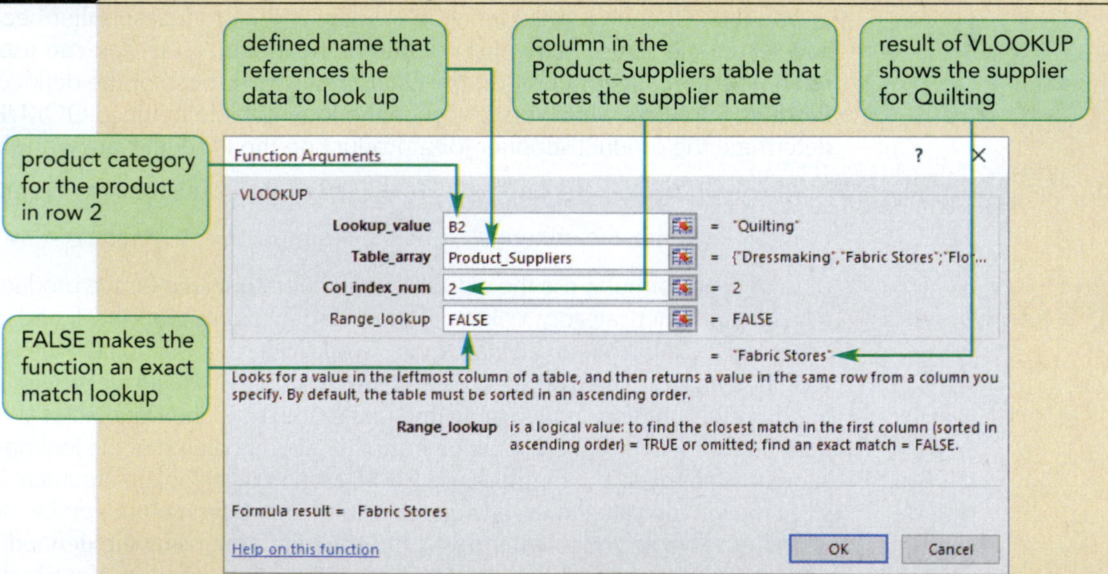
defined name that references the data to look up
column in the Product_Suppliers table that stores the supplier name
result of VLOOKUP shows the supplier for Quilting
product category for the product in row 2
FALSE makes the function an exact match lookup
Function Arguments
VLOOKUP
Lookup_value B2 = "Quilting"
Table_array Product_Suppliers = {"Dressmaking","Fabric Stores";"Flo...
Col_index_num 2 = 2
Range_lookup FALSE = FALSE
= "Fabric Stores"
Looks for a value in the leftmost column of a table, and then returns a value in the same row from a column you specify. By default, the table must be sorted in an ascending order.
Range_lookup is a logical value: to find the closest match in the first column (sorted in ascending order) = TRUE or omitted; find an exact match = FALSE.
Formula result = Fabric Stores
Help on this function
OK
Cancel

10. Click the **OK** button. The dialog box closes, Fabric Stores appears in cell D2, and the formula =VLOOKUP(B2,Product_Suppliers,2,FALSE) appears in the formula bar. The remaining rows in the Supplier Name column are filled with the VLOOKUP function. If the value in column D does not match a value in the first column of the Product_Suppliers table, an exact match does not exist, and the function returns #N/A in the cell.
11. AutoFit the contents of column D so you can see the full Supplier Name.
12. Select cell **D2** to deselect the column. See Figure 8-24.

Figure 8-24 Exact match VLOOKUP function to locate the supplier for a product group

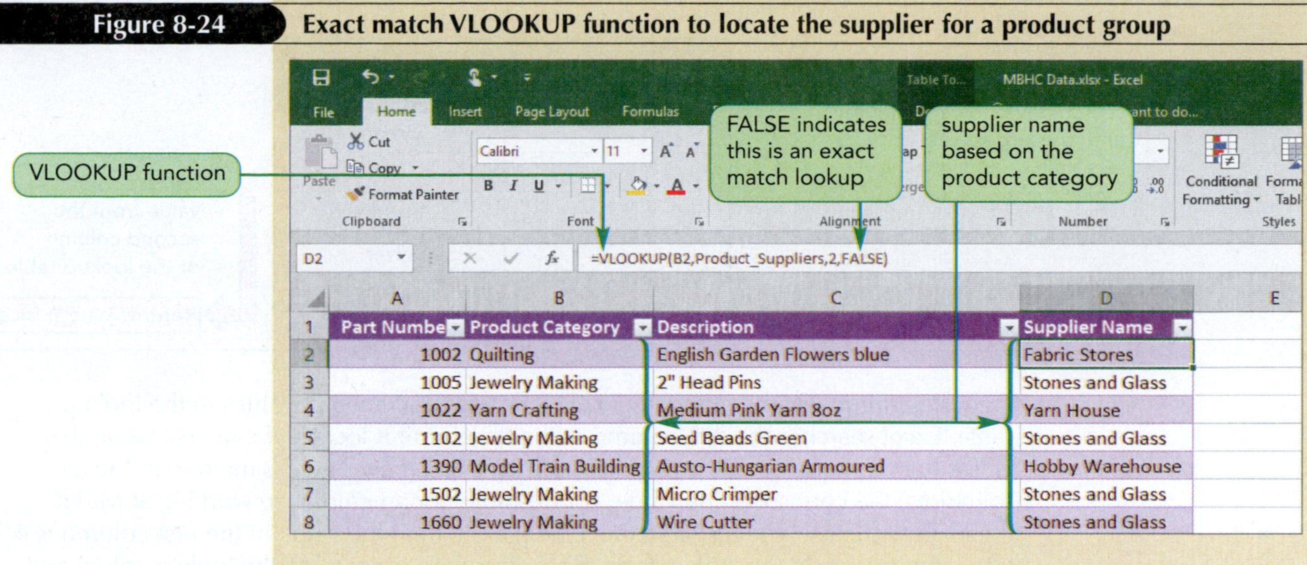

Using the VLOOKUP Function to Find an Approximate Match

You can also use a VLOOKUP function to return a value from a lookup table that is based on an approximate match lookup. The previous lookup used the Product_Suppliers table to return a value only if Excel found an exact match in the first column of the lookup table. The values in the first column or row of a lookup table can also represent a range of values. Quantity discounts, shipping charges, and income tax rates are a few examples of approximate match lookups.

MBHC's management wants all employee name badges to identify employees' years of service by color. Vanessa developed the criteria shown in Figure 8-25 to summarize the colors planned for the name badges.

Figure 8-25 Criteria for the Name Badge Color lookup table

Years of Service	Name Badge Color
>=0 and <1	Green
>=1 and <4	Blue
>=4 and <7	Purple
>=7 and <10	Silver
>=10	Gold

In the Name Badge table, you are not looking for an exact match for the lookup value. Instead, you need to use an approximate match lookup to determine which range of values the lookup value falls within. You want to use the lookup table to determine an employee's years of service range and then return the badge color based on the appropriate row. To accomplish this, you must rearrange the first column of the lookup table so that each row in the table represents the *low end* of the years of service range, as shown in Figure 8-26.

Figure 8-26 Name Badge lookup table for an approximate match lookup

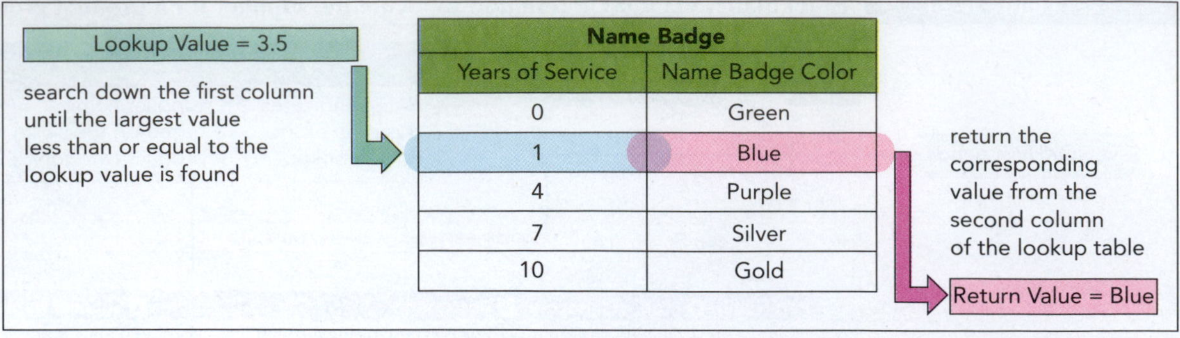

To determine whether a lookup value falls within a range of values in the lookup table, Excel searches the first column of the table until it locates the largest value that is less than or equal to the lookup value. Then Excel moves across the row in the table to retrieve the corresponding value. For example, for an employee working at MBHC for six years, Excel would search the lookup table until the value in the first column is 4 (the largest value in the lookup table that is less than or equal to the lookup value) and retrieve Purple from the second column of that row.

When a lookup table is used with a range of values (approximate match), the values in the first column must be sorted in low-to-high order. When the first column's values are arranged in a different order, Excel may not retrieve the correct value, leading to incorrect results. The setup of the lookup table in an approximate match is critical for a VLOOKUP formula to work properly.

INSIGHT

Setting Up an Approximate Match Lookup Table

Approximate lookup tables are commonly used to find a taxpayer's tax rate in a tax table, find a shipping charge based on the weight of a package in a shipping charges table, or determine a student's letter grade from a table of grading criteria. Setting up the lookup tables for an approximate match lookup can be tricky. Consider the following example, in which an instructor uses Excel to calculate grades. The instructor assigns final grades based on the following grading policy table:

Score	Grade
90–100	A
80–89	B
70–79	C
60–69	D
0–59	F

To set up the lookup table so it works in Excel, the leftmost column in the lookup table must (1) represent the lower end of the range for each category, and (2) be sorted in ascending order based on the value in the first column. Otherwise, Excel cannot retrieve the correct result. Following this structure, the lookup table for the instructor's grading policy would be arranged as follows:

Score	Grade
0	F
60	D
70	C
80	B
90	A

In the EmployeeTbl table, you will create the formula

```
=VLOOKUP([Years of Service],Name_Badge,2)
```

to determine the color for each employee's name badge, where `[Years of Service]` is the structured reference for the employee's years of service (the lookup value), `Name_Badge` is the defined name that references the lookup table, and `2` specifies the column in the lookup table in which to find the badge color. The fourth argument is not needed because this is an approximate match lookup. You will use an approximate match VLOOKUP formula because each cell in the Years of Service column in the lookup table represents a range of values.

To insert the approximate match VLOOKUP formula:

1. Go to the **Employee Data** worksheet. You will enter this VLOOKUP function in the EmployeeTbl.
2. In cell **O1**, enter **Name Badge Color** as the column heading. A new column is added to the table, and cell O2 is the active cell.
3. AutoFit the contents of column O so you can view the entire column heading in cell O1.
4. Click the **Insert Function** button next to the formula bar. The Insert Function dialog box opens with the Lookup & Reference category active.
5. In the Select a function box, double-click **VLOOKUP**. The Function Arguments dialog box opens.
6. In the Lookup_value box, type **[Years of Service]** and then press the **Tab** key. The lookup value is entered using the column header (structured reference) for the employee's years of service. The value 3.479452055 appears as the lookup value for the current row.
7. In the Table_array box, type **Name_Badge** and then press the **Tab** key. Name_Badge is the defined name assigned to the range D8:E12 in the Data Tables worksheet. If the Name_Badge data was entered as a range reference, the *table_array* argument would be entered as 'Data Tables'!D8:E12, and you would need to change the range to absolute references ('Data Tables'!$D$8:$E$12) so that the formula would copy correctly to other cells.
8. In the Col_index_num box, type **2**. The number 2 indicates the column where the name badge color is stored—the second column of the Name_Badge table. You do not need to enter the optional fourth argument in the VLOOKUP formula because Excel assumes the value to be TRUE and will use an approximate match table lookup. See Figure 8-27.

Figure 8-27 Function Arguments dialog box for the VLOOKUP function

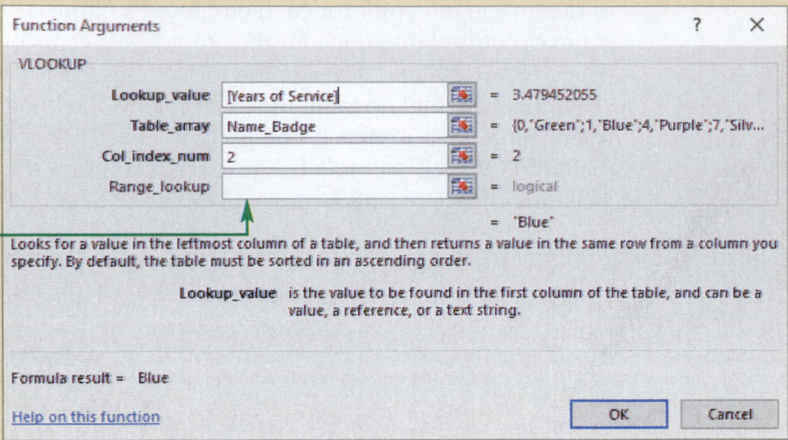
Function Arguments
VLOOKUP
Lookup_value [Years of Service] = 3.479452055
Table_array Name_Badge = {0,"Green";1,"Blue";4,"Purple";7,"Silv...
Col_index_num 2 = 2
Range_lookup = logical
= "Blue"
Looks for a value in the leftmost column of a table, and then returns a value in the same row from a column you specify. By default, the table must be sorted in an ascending order.
Lookup_value is the value to be found in the first column of the table, and can be a value, a reference, or a text string.
Formula result = Blue
Help on this function
OK
Cancel
omitting the Range_lookup entry is the same as entering TRUE and creates an approximate match lookup

9. Click the **OK** button. All of the cells in the Name Badge Color calculated column are filled with the VLOOKUP formula and display a color. The employee in row 2 has 3.5 years of service and will have a Blue badge. This is a good illustration of the approximate match lookup because 3.5 does not equal a value in the first column of the lookup table. Instead, it falls between two values in the table.
10. Select cell **O2** to deselect the column. See Figure 8-28.

Figure 8-28 Approximate match VLOOKUP function for determining Name Badge Color

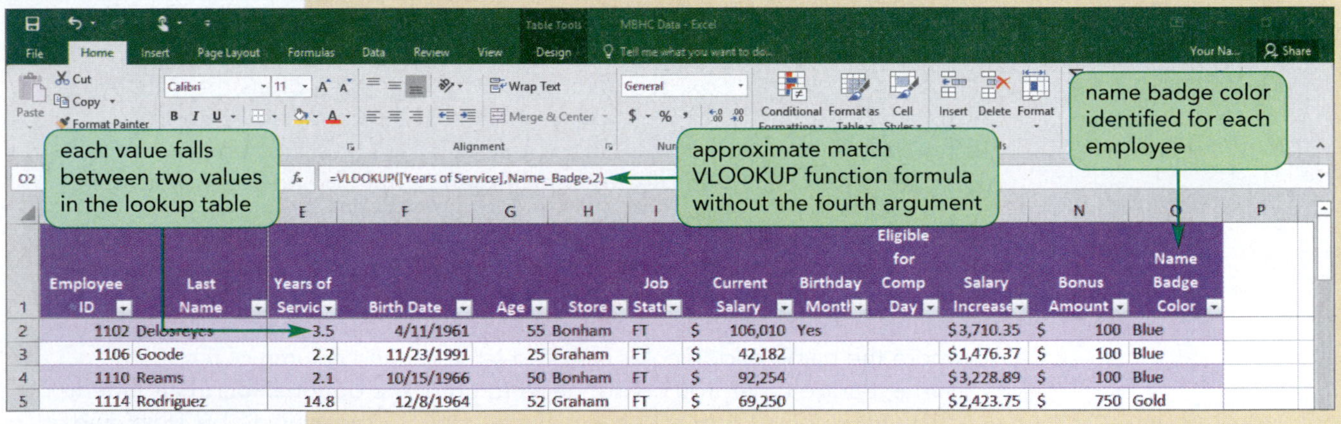
=VLOOKUP([Years of Service],Name_Badge,2)
each value falls between two values in the lookup table
approximate match VLOOKUP function formula without the fourth argument
name badge color identified for each employee

	Employee ID	Last Name	Years of Servic	Birth Date	Age	Store	Job Statu	Current Salary	Birthday Month	Eligible for Comp Day	Salary Increase	Bonus Amount	Name Badge Color
2	1102	Delosreyes	3.5	4/11/1961	55	Bonham	FT	$ 106,010	Yes		$3,710.35	$ 100	Blue
3	1106	Goode	2.2	11/23/1991	25	Graham	FT	$ 42,182			$1,476.37	$ 100	Blue
4	1110	Reams	2.1	10/15/1966	50	Bonham	FT	$ 92,254			$3,228.89	$ 100	Blue
5	1114	Rodriguez	14.8	12/8/1964	52	Graham	FT	$ 69,250			$2,423.75	$ 750	Gold

Using the HLOOKUP Function to Find an Exact Match

The HLOOKUP function is very similar to the VLOOKUP function. The HLOOKUP function (horizontal lookup function) searches across the top row of the lookup table until the lookup value is found and then retrieves the value from the same column in the lookup table. The HLOOKUP function has the syntax

```
HLOOKUP(lookup_value,table_array,row_index_num[,range_lookup])
```

where `lookup_value` is the value, cell reference, defined name, or structured reference you want to search for in the first row of the lookup table; `table_array` is the range reference, defined name, or Excel table name of the lookup table; `row_index_num` is the number of the row in the lookup table that contains the value you want to return;

and *range_lookup* indicates whether the lookup table is an exact match (FALSE) or an approximate match (TRUE). The *range_lookup* argument is optional; if you don't include a *range_lookup* value, the value is considered TRUE (an approximate match).

The major difference between the HLOOKUP and VLOOKUP functions is the way the lookup tables are organized. Figure 8-29 shows how the Product Suppliers and Name Badge tables would be arranged for a lookup using the HLOOKUP function.

Figure 8-29 **Lookup tables for the HLOOKUP function**

Product Suppliers							
Product Category	Dress Making	Floral Crafting	Jewelry Making	Model Ship Building	Model Train Building	Quilting	Yarn Crafting
Supplier	Fabric Stores	Silk Flowers	Stones and Glass	Hobby Warehouse	Hobby Warehouse	Fabric Stores	Yarn House

Name Badge					
Years of Service	0	1	4	7	10
Name Badge Color	Green	Blue	Purple	Silver	Gold

With the lookup tables arranged as shown in Figure 8-29, the exact match formula to identify the Supplier on the Product Data worksheet is

```
=HLOOKUP(B2,Product_Suppliers,2,FALSE)
```

and the approximate match formula to calculate the name badge color on the Employee Data worksheet is

```
=HLOOKUP(E2,Name_Badge,2)
```

Vanessa wants you to use the HLOOKUP function to identify the specialty store for each product. Figure 8-30 shows the Specialty Store table in the Data Tables worksheet, which includes the specialty store for each product category. The values in the first row of the horizontal lookup table are compared to the product category that you want to find (lookup value). When the match is found, the corresponding value in one of the rows in the lookup table is returned. For example, to find the return value for product with Jewelry Making as the product category, Excel searches across the first row of the lookup table until it finds the Jewelry Making entry. Then Excel moves down to the second row to locate the corresponding return value, which is Bowie in this case. The table in Figure 8-30 is an exact match lookup because if the product category does not match one of the values in the first row of the lookup table, the #N/A error value is returned.

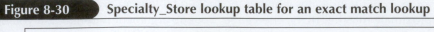

Figure 8-30 Specialty_Store lookup table for an exact match lookup

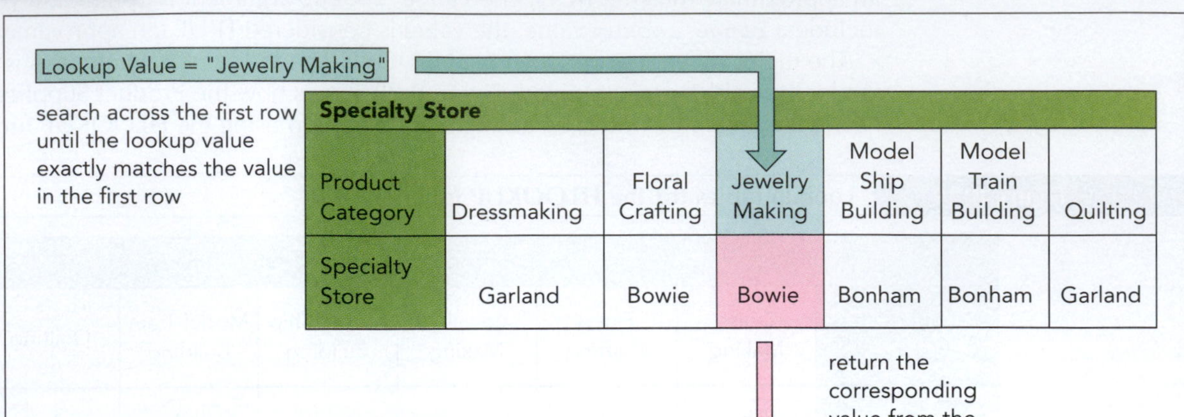

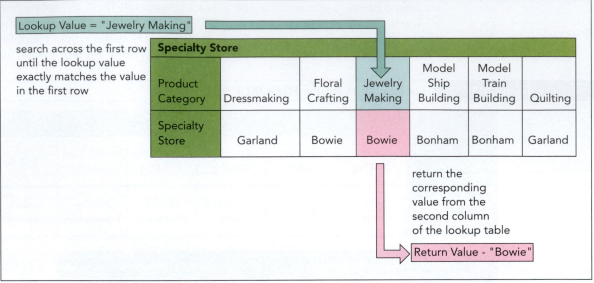

The following formula uses the product category and the Specialty_Store table to determine the specialty store for the product:

```
=HLOOKUP(B2,Specialty_Store,2,FALSE)
```

In this formula, B2 is the cell that stores the product category in the Product Data worksheet, Specialty_Store is the defined name that references the lookup table, 2 specifies the row to find the specialty store, and FALSE indicates that this is an exact match lookup. You will enter this formula to identify the Specialty Store for each product in the ProductTbl table.

To find an exact match in the Specialty_Store table using the HLOOKUP function:

1. Go to the **Product Data** worksheet.
2. In cell **E1**, enter **Specialty Store**. The table expands to include the new column.
3. Make sure cell **E2** is the active cell, and then click the **Insert Function** button next to the formula bar. The Insert Function dialog box opens.
4. Click the **Or select a category** arrow and click **Lookup & Reference**, if necessary, and then double-click **HLOOKUP** in the Select a function box. The Function Arguments dialog box opens.
5. If necessary, drag the Function Arguments dialog box below row 2 so you can see the column headers.
6. In the Lookup_value box, enter **B2** and then press the **Tab** key. The lookup value is the product category, which is located in column B.
7. In the Table_array box, type the defined name **Specialty_Store** and then press the **Tab** key. Specialty_Store references the range B3:H4 in the Data Tables worksheet. If the defined name Specialty_Store was not defined, the table_array argument would be entered as 'Data Tables'!B3:H4, and you would need to change the range to absolute references ('Data Tables'!$B$3:$H$4) so the formula would copy correctly to other cells.

8. In the Row_index_num box, type **2** and then press the **Tab** key. The number 2 indicates that the specialty store location is stored in the second row of the Specialty_Store lookup table.
9. In the Range_lookup box, type **FALSE**. This sets the function to find an exact match in the lookup table. See Figure 8-31.

Figure 8-31 Function Arguments dialog box for HLOOKUP function

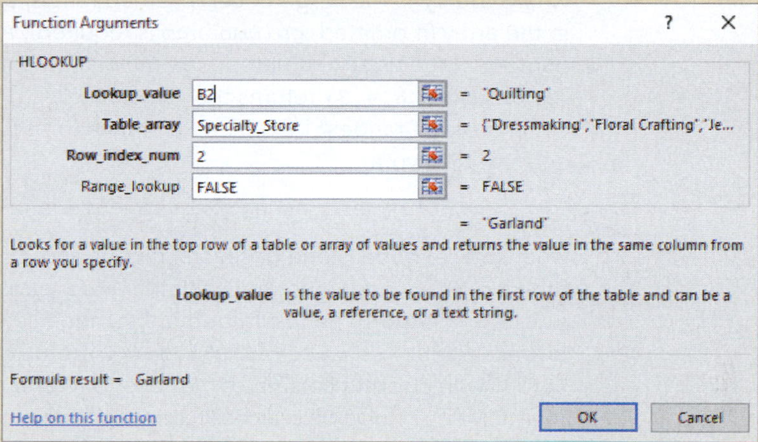

10. Click the **OK** button. The dialog box closes, Garland appears in cell E2, and the formula =HLOOKUP(B2,Specialty_Store,2,FALSE) appears in the formula bar. The remaining rows in the Specialty Store column are filled with the HLOOKUP function.

    Trouble? If #N/A appears in the Specialty Store column, you may have used a VLOOKUP function. If necessary, edit the formula in cell E2 to use HLOOKUP instead of VLOOKUP.

11. Select cell **E2** to deselect the column. See Figure 8-32.

Figure 8-32 Exact match HLOOKUP function for identifying the Specialty Store for each product

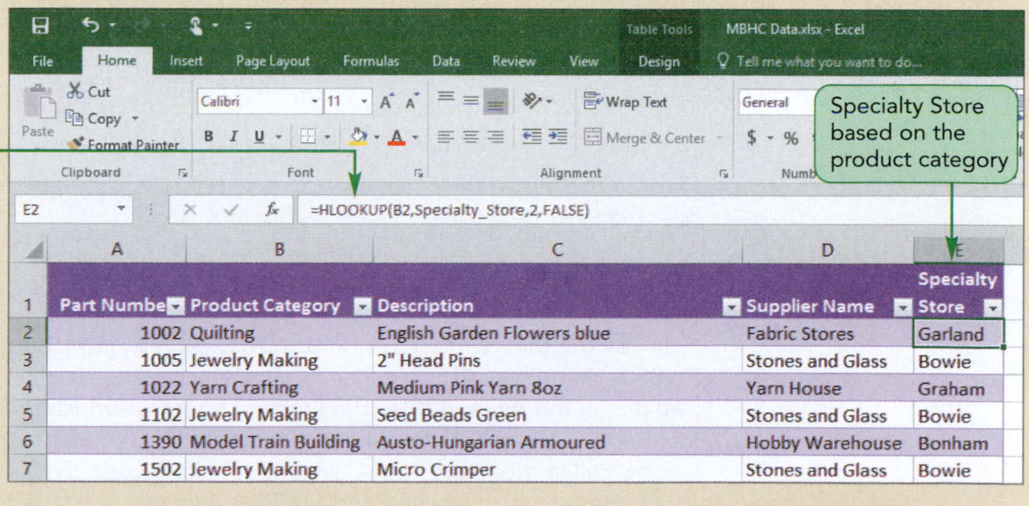

	A	B	C	D	E
1	Part Numbe	Product Category	Description	Supplier Name	Specialty Store
2	1002	Quilting	English Garden Flowers blue	Fabric Stores	Garland
3	1005	Jewelry Making	2" Head Pins	Stones and Glass	Bowie
4	1022	Yarn Crafting	Medium Pink Yarn 8oz	Yarn House	Graham
5	1102	Jewelry Making	Seed Beads Green	Stones and Glass	Bowie
6	1390	Model Train Building	Austo-Hungarian Armoured	Hobby Warehouse	Bonham
7	1502	Jewelry Making	Micro Crimper	Stones and Glass	Bowie

The specialty store for each part is entered in the worksheet.

INSIGHT

Using the INDEX and MATCH Functions to Perform a Lookup

The INDEX function returns a value or the reference to a value from within a table or range. For example, you would use the INDEX function when you know (or can calculate) the position of a cell in a range and you want to return the actual value. The Array form returns the value of a specified cell or array of cells, and has the syntax

`INDEX(array,row_num,column_num)`

where ***array*** is the range of cells, named range, or table; ***row_num*** is the row number in the array (if omitted, ***column_num*** is required); and ***column_num*** is the column number in the array (if omitted, ***row_num*** is required). For example, the formula `=INDEX(A1:D6,4,3)` returns the value in cell C4, the cell in the fourth row and third column of the range A1:D6. The Reference form returns a reference to specified cells, and has the syntax

`INDEX(reference,row_num,column_num,area_num)`

where ***reference*** is one or several ranges and ***area_num*** specifies which range from the ***reference*** argument to use. If the ***area_num*** argument is omitted, the INDEX function will return the result for the first range listed in the reference. For example, the formula `=INDEX((A2:D3,A5:D7),3,4,2)` returns the value in cell D7, the cell in the third row and fourth column of the second reference.

The MATCH function searches for a specified number or text in a range of cells, and then returns the relative position of that data in the range. The MATCH function has the syntax

`MATCH(lookup_value,lookup_array,[match_type])`

where ***lookup_value*** is the number or text you are looking for, ***lookup_array*** is the range of cells being searched, and the optional argument ***match_type*** specifies whether you want to return an exact match or the nearest match. The ***match_type*** argument can be 1, 0, or –1. You enter 1 to find the largest value less than or equal to the ***lookup_value*** (the list must be in ascending order), 0 to find the value exactly equal to the ***lookup_value*** (the list can be in any order), or–1 to find the smallest value greater than or equal to the ***lookup_value*** (the list must be in descending order). If the ***match_type*** argument is omitted, it is assumed to be 1.

You can use the Array form of the INDEX function to return the value of the cell identified by the MATCH function in the ***lookup_array*** argument. For example, consider the following item codes and items entered in the range A1:B6:

	A	**B**
1	*Item Code*	*Item*
2	SH001	Shirt
3	SW050	Sweater
4	CO200	Coat
5		
6	Sweater	

In cell B6, the `=INDEX(A2:A4,MATCH(A6,B2:B4,0))` formula returns the value SW050. First, the MATCH function looks for an exact match for data in cell A6, which is Sweater, in the range B2:B4. The function returns 2, which is the position of Sweater in the range B2:B4. Then, the Array form of the INDEX function returns the value of the second cell in the range A2:A4, which is the item code SW050.

When you use the INDEX and MATCH functions, the lookup value can be any column in the array. In the VLOOKUP function, it must be in the first column.

Using the IFERROR Function

Error values indicate that some element in a formula or a cell referenced in a formula is preventing Excel from returning a calculated value. Recall that an error value begins with a number sign (#) followed by an error name that indicates the type of error. For instance, the error value #N/A appears in a Product Supplier cell when the VLOOKUP function cannot find the product supplier in the Product_Suppliers lookup table. This error value message is not particularly descriptive or helpful.

You can use the IFERROR function to display a more descriptive message that helps users fix the problem. The IFERROR function can determine if a cell contains an error value and then display the message you choose rather than the default error value; or if no error value exists in the formula, display the result of the formula. The IFERROR function has the syntax

```
IFERROR(expression,valueIfError)
```

where *expression* is the formula you want to check for an error, and *valueIfError* is the message you want displayed if Excel detects an error in the formula you are checking. If Excel does not detect an error, the result of the *expression* is displayed.

You can use the IFERROR function to find and handle formula errors. For example, you can enter the following formula to determine whether an invalid code was entered in the Product Category of the Product Data worksheet and then display a more descriptive message if Excel detects an error:

```
=IFERROR(VLOOKUP(B2,Product_Suppliers,2,FALSE),"Various")
```

Based on this formula, if the value in cell B2 is Quilting, the result of the VLOOKUP formula is Fabric Stores (the corresponding value from the Product_Suppliers table), the first argument in the IFERROR function (shown in red) is executed, and the product supplier is displayed. On the other hand, if cell B2 has an invalid product category, such as All, the VLOOKUP function returns the error value #N/A, the second argument in the IFERROR function (shown in blue) is executed, and Various is displayed.

Vanessa wants to verify that all products in the product data worksheet have a valid product category in the Product Category column. You will check whether any cell in the Product Category column contains an error value.

To check for an error value in the Supplier Name column:

1. In the Product Data worksheet, scroll to row **47**. Notice the error value #N/A in cells D47 and E47, the supplier name and specialty store, respectively.
2. Select cell **D47**. See Figure 8-33.

Figure 8-33 Error value in the Supplier Name and Specialty Store columns

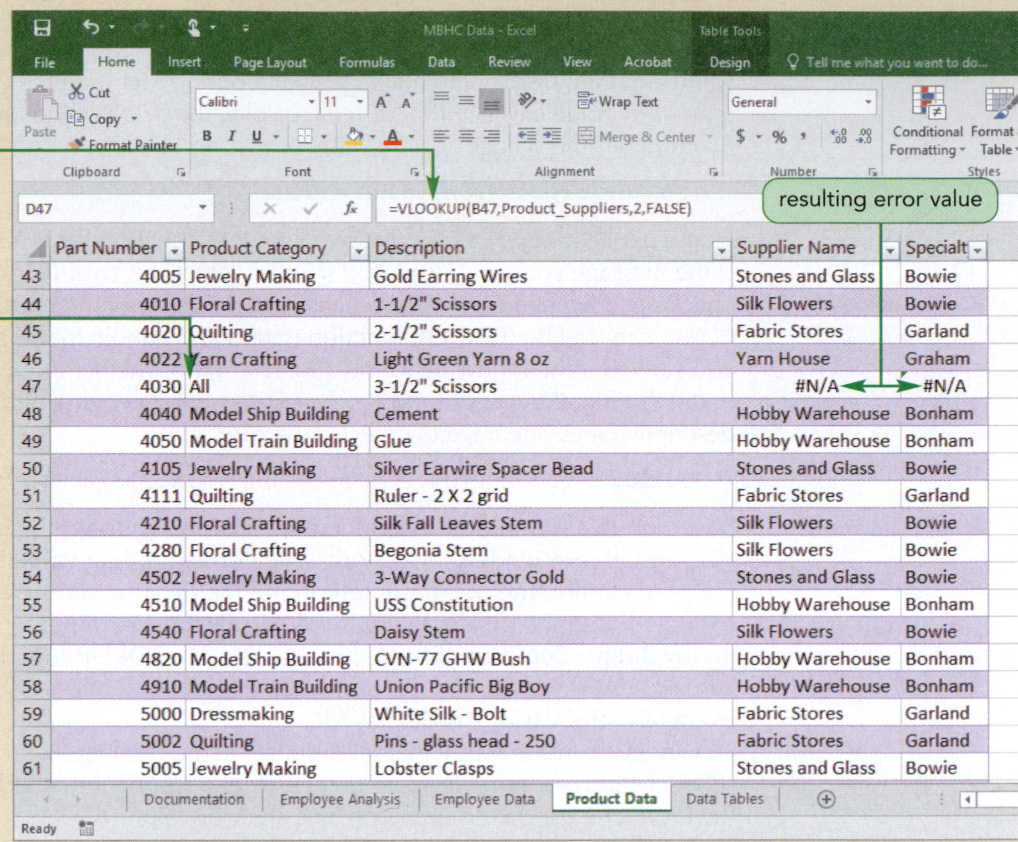

3. In row 47, observe that the Product Category is All. This invalid code causes the error messages #N/A because the lookup table does not have a corresponding value.

Vanessa asks you to modify the formulas in the Supplier Name and the Specialty Store columns so that the descriptive error message "Various" appears rather than the error value. The IFERROR function will check for errors in the formula and display the error message you create rather than the error value if it finds an error.

You'll nest the VLOOKUP function within the IFERROR function to display "Various" in the Supplier Name and Special Store columns if Excel detects an error value.

Be sure to type a comma before the error message.

To nest the VLOOKUP function within the IFERROR function:

1. Double-click cell **D47** to enter Edit mode. The formula =VLOOKUP(B47,Product_Suppliers,2,FALSE) appears in the cell and the formula bar. You'll nest this formula within the IFERROR function.
2. Click to the right of = (the equal sign), and then type **IFERROR(** to begin entering the IFERROR function. The first argument in the IFERROR function is the formula you want to use if no error value is found; this is the VLOOKUP function already entered in the cell.
3. Move the insertion point to the right of the entire formula, and then type **,"Various")** to add the text you want to display if an error is found.
4. Press the **Enter** key. The error message "Various" appears in cell D47, and the revised formula is automatically copied to all cells in the column.
5. Double-click cell **E47** to enter Edit mode. The formula =HLOOKUP(B47,Specialty_Store,2,FALSE) appears in the cell and the formula bar. You'll nest this formula within the IFERROR function.
6. Click to the right of = (the equal sign), and then type **IFERROR(** to begin entering the IFERROR function. The first argument in the IFERROR function is the formula you want to use if no error value is found; this is the VLOOKUP function already entered in the cell.
7. Move the insertion point to the right of the entire formula, and then type **,"Various")** to add the text you want to display if an error is found.
8. Press the **Enter** key. The error message "Various" appears in cell E47, and the revised formula is automatically copied to all cells in the column. See Figure 8-34.

Figure 8-34 Various message in the Supplier Name and Specialty Store columns

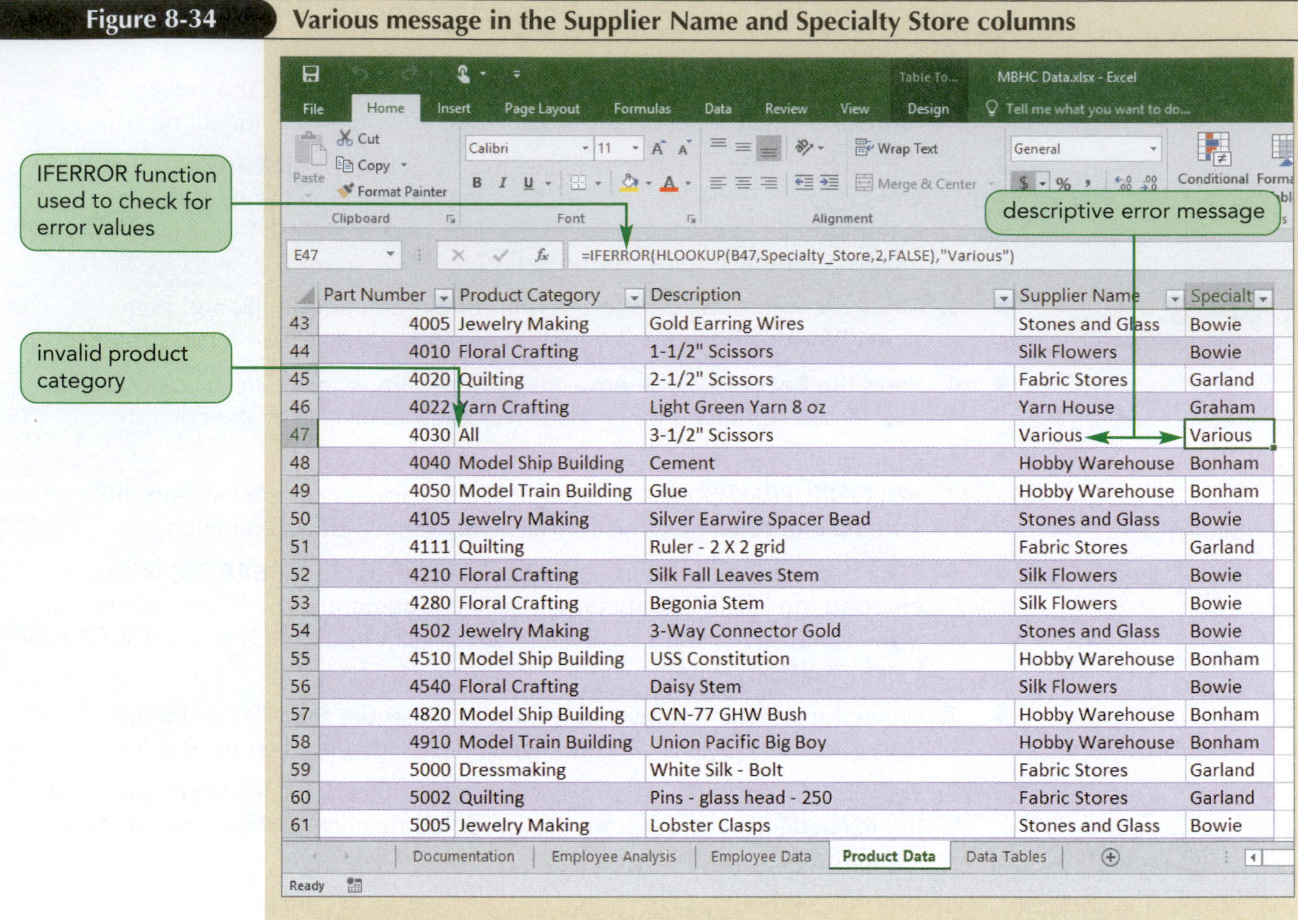

	Part Number	Product Category	Description	Supplier Name	Specialt
43	4005	Jewelry Making	Gold Earring Wires	Stones and Glass	Bowie
44	4010	Floral Crafting	1-1/2" Scissors	Silk Flowers	Bowie
45	4020	Quilting	2-1/2" Scissors	Fabric Stores	Garland
46	4022	Yarn Crafting	Light Green Yarn 8 oz	Yarn House	Graham
47	4030	All	3-1/2" Scissors	Various	Various
48	4040	Model Ship Building	Cement	Hobby Warehouse	Bonham
49	4050	Model Train Building	Glue	Hobby Warehouse	Bonham
50	4105	Jewelry Making	Silver Earwire Spacer Bead	Stones and Glass	Bowie
51	4111	Quilting	Ruler - 2 X 2 grid	Fabric Stores	Garland
52	4210	Floral Crafting	Silk Fall Leaves Stem	Silk Flowers	Bowie
53	4280	Floral Crafting	Begonia Stem	Silk Flowers	Bowie
54	4502	Jewelry Making	3-Way Connector Gold	Stones and Glass	Bowie
55	4510	Model Ship Building	USS Constitution	Hobby Warehouse	Bonham
56	4540	Floral Crafting	Daisy Stem	Silk Flowers	Bowie
57	4820	Model Ship Building	CVN-77 GHW Bush	Hobby Warehouse	Bonham
58	4910	Model Train Building	Union Pacific Big Boy	Hobby Warehouse	Bonham
59	5000	Dressmaking	White Silk - Bolt	Fabric Stores	Garland
60	5002	Quilting	Pins - glass head - 250	Fabric Stores	Garland
61	5005	Jewelry Making	Lobster Clasps	Stones and Glass	Bowie

Trouble? If the error #NAME? appears in cell D47, you may have omitted quotation marks around the "Various" error message. Correct the formula, and then continue with Step 9.

9. Scroll to the top of the table, select cell **D2**, and then observe in the formula bar that the IFERROR formula was copied to this cell.

In this session, you used nested IF functions to determine employee bonuses, you used the VLOOKUP function to calculate the product suppliers and name badge color, and you used the HLOOKUP function to identify the specialty store. You also used the IFERROR function to display a descriptive message in cells where invalid product categories are entered in the ProductTbl table. In the next session, you will use conditional formatting to identify duplicate records, and use the COUNTIF, SUMIF, and AVERAGEIF functions to report on employee salaries.

REVIEW

Session 8.2 Quick Check

1. What is a nested IF function?
2. If cell Y5 displays the value 35, cell Y6 displays the value 42, and cell Y7 contains the following formula, what is displayed in cell Y7?

```
=IF(Y5>Y6,"Older",IF(Y5<Y6,"Younger","Same Age"))
```

3. Explain the difference between an exact match lookup and an approximate match lookup.
4. A customer table includes columns for name, street address, city, state abbreviation, and zip code. A second table includes state abbreviations and state names from all 50 states (one state per row). You need to add a new column to the customer table with the state name. What is the most appropriate function to use to display the state name in this new column?
5. Convert the following criteria used to determine a student's level to a table that can be used in a VLOOKUP function to display the level of each student:

Earned Credits	Level
>=0 and <=30	Freshman
>=31 and <=60	Sophomore
>=61 and <=90	Junior
>=91	Senior

6. In cell X5, the error value #DIV/0! appears when you divide by 0. What IFERROR function can you use with the formula =W5/W25 so that instead of the error value #DIV/0! being displayed, the message "Dividing by zero" appears in the cell?
7. In cell X5, the formula =W5/W25 results in the error value #DIV/0! when W25 stores the value 0. Use the IF function to modify the formula =W5/W25 so that instead of the error value #DIV/0! being displayed when W25 stores 0, the message "Dividing by zero" appears in the cell.
8. Which function could be used with the following Sales Tax Rate table to display the sales tax rate for a customer in one of these four states?

State	CO	NM	OK	TX
Sales Tax Rate	10%	7%	9%	9.5%

Session 8.3 Visual Overview:

Highlighting duplicate values adds formatting to cells that have the same entry. In this instance, duplicate values with a gold fill highlights cells with the same Employee ID.

The Conditional Formatting button provides access to the Duplicate Values conditional format and the Manage Rule option, which opens the Conditional Formatting Rules Manager dialog box.

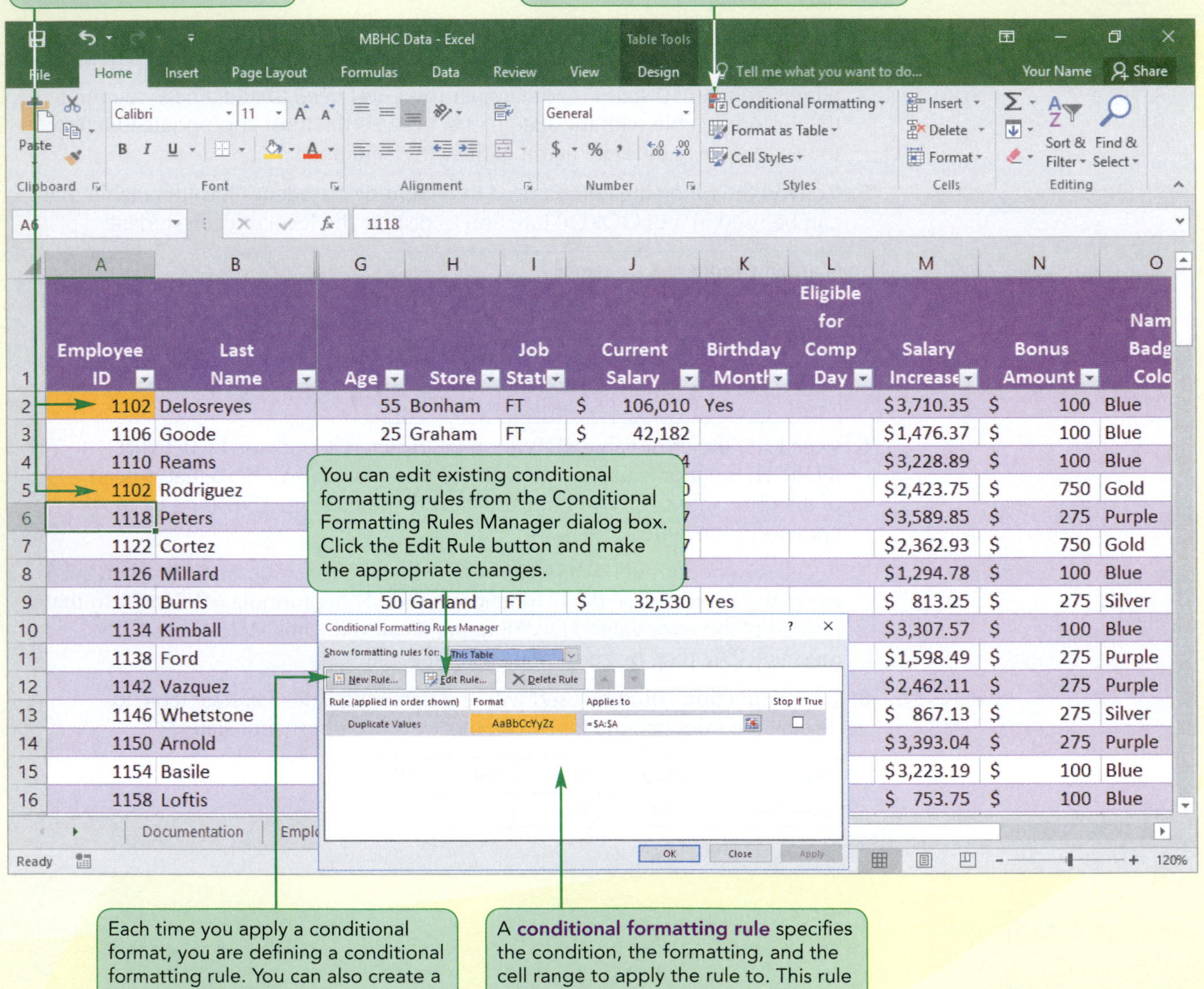

You can edit existing conditional formatting rules from the Conditional Formatting Rules Manager dialog box. Click the Edit Rule button and make the appropriate changes.

Each time you apply a conditional format, you are defining a conditional formatting rule. You can also create a new rule from this dialog box by clicking the New Rule button.

A **conditional formatting rule** specifies the condition, the formatting, and the cell range to apply the rule to. This rule highlights duplicate values with a gold fill in the range A1:A102.

Conditional Formatting and Functions

This formula uses fully qualified structured references to make it easier to create and understand.

The **AVERAGEIF** function calculates the average of values in a range that match criteria you specify, such as calculating the average salary paid to employees in each of the four stores.

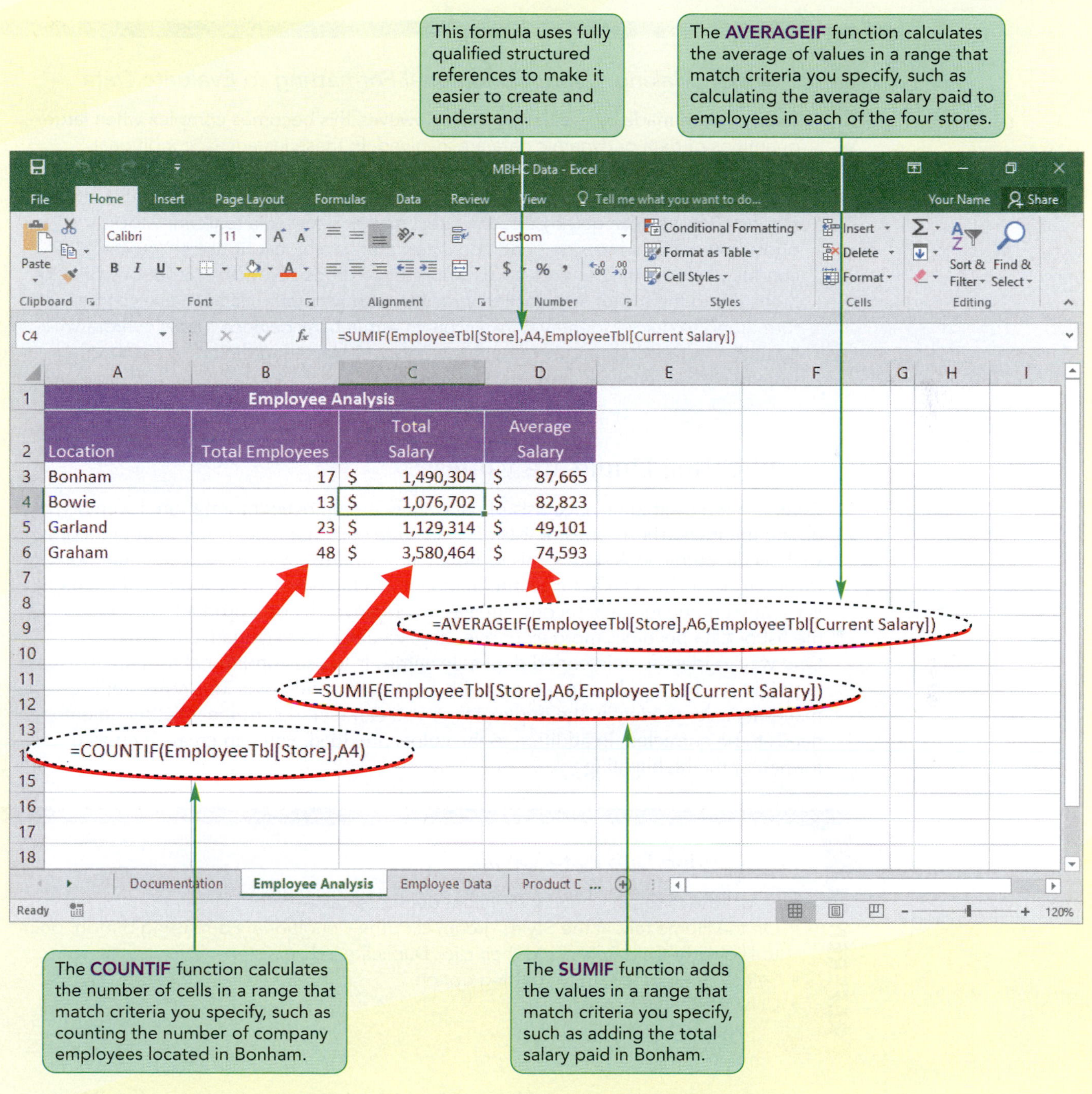

The **COUNTIF** function calculates the number of cells in a range that match criteria you specify, such as counting the number of company employees located in Bonham.

The **SUMIF** function adds the values in a range that match criteria you specify, such as adding the total salary paid in Bonham.

Applying Conditional Formatting

Conditional formatting changes a cell's formatting when its contents match a specified condition. You have already used conditional formatting to highlight cells based on their values and to add data bars that graph the relative values in a range. You can also use conditional formatting to highlight duplicate values in a column of data.

PROSKILLS

Decision Making: Using Conditional Formatting to Evaluate Data

Decisions are made by evaluating data. However, this becomes complex when large quantities of data or dynamic data are involved. In these instances, conditional formatting can be a useful tool to help with your decision making. Conditional formatting is designed to make searching a data range both simple and efficient. For instance, you can quickly find the latest market prices in a real-time stock quote spreadsheet by using conditional formatting to highlight them. You can use conditional formatting to find stocks whose price drops below the target buy price by highlighting the row of any stock that meets the buy criteria. You can use conditional formatting to quickly identify bank accounts with a bank balance that is overdrawn by highlighting accounts with a negative balance. Mastering the art of conditional formatting can help you make better decisions.

Highlighting Duplicate Values

Excel is often used to manage lists of data, such as employee information, inventory, or phone numbers. These types of lists often include data that repeats in different records, such as the employee's state in his or her mailing address, a warehouse location for inventory, or an area code for phone numbers. On the other hand, some of the data is usually unique for each record, such as an employee ID or a product number. As the list of data becomes more extensive, duplicate entries may inadvertently occur. One way to identify unintended duplicate entries is to use conditional formatting to highlight duplicate values in a range with a font and/or fill color. This color coding makes it easier to identify the duplicates so you can then determine whether an entry needs to be corrected. In addition to the colors provided, you can create a custom format for the highlighting.

REFERENCE

Highlighting Duplicate Values

- Select the range in which to highlight duplicate values.
- On the Home tab, in the Styles group, click the Conditional Formatting button, point to Highlight Cells Rules, and then click Duplicate Values.
- Select the appropriate formatting option.
- Click the OK button

Vanessa wants you to use duplicate value highlighting to verify that each cell in the employee ID column has a unique entry. She believes the current employee ID data in the EmployeeTbl table is accurate but wants you to use conditional formatting to ensure that there are no duplicate entries.

To highlight duplicate employee IDs using conditional formatting:

1. If you took a break at the end of the previous session, make sure the MBHC Data workbook is open.
2. Go to the **Employee Data** worksheet, and then select the data in column **A**. Rows 2 through 101 in the Employee ID column are selected.
3. On the Home tab, in the Styles group, click the **Conditional Formatting** button, point to **Highlight Cells Rules**, and then click **Duplicate Values**. The Duplicate Values dialog box opens.
4. Click the **values with** arrow to display a list of formatting options, and then click **Custom Format**. The Format Cells dialog box opens so you can create a format that is not in the list. You'll change the background fill color to red.
5. Click the **Fill** tab, and then, in the Background Color palette, click **red** (the second color in the last row).
6. Click the **OK** button in the Format Cells dialog box, and then click the **OK** button in the Duplicate Values dialog box. Any duplicate values in the ID column appear in a red cell.
7. Scroll the table to ensure that no duplicate values are found.

After you enter a formula, you should test all situations to verify how the formula performs in each case. In this case, you should test the column both with duplicate values and without duplicate values. No duplicate records appear in the EmployeeTbl table, so you'll change the Employee ID of the fourth record from 1114 to 1102, which is the Employee ID of the first employee. The backgrounds of the cells with the duplicate Employee IDs should turn red, which will confirm that the conditional formatting is working as intended. Then, you will return the ID to its original value and confirm that the duplicate value highlighting disappears.

To test the duplicate value conditional formatting:

1. Click cell **A2**, and observe that the employee ID in that cell is 1102.
2. Select cell **A5** in the EmployeeTbl table. Notice that this employee ID is 1114.
3. In cell A5, enter **1102**. The Employee ID changes from 1114 to 1102, and cells A2 and A5 are filled with red because they contain a duplicate Employee ID. See Figure 8-35.

Figure 8-35 Duplicate values highlighted

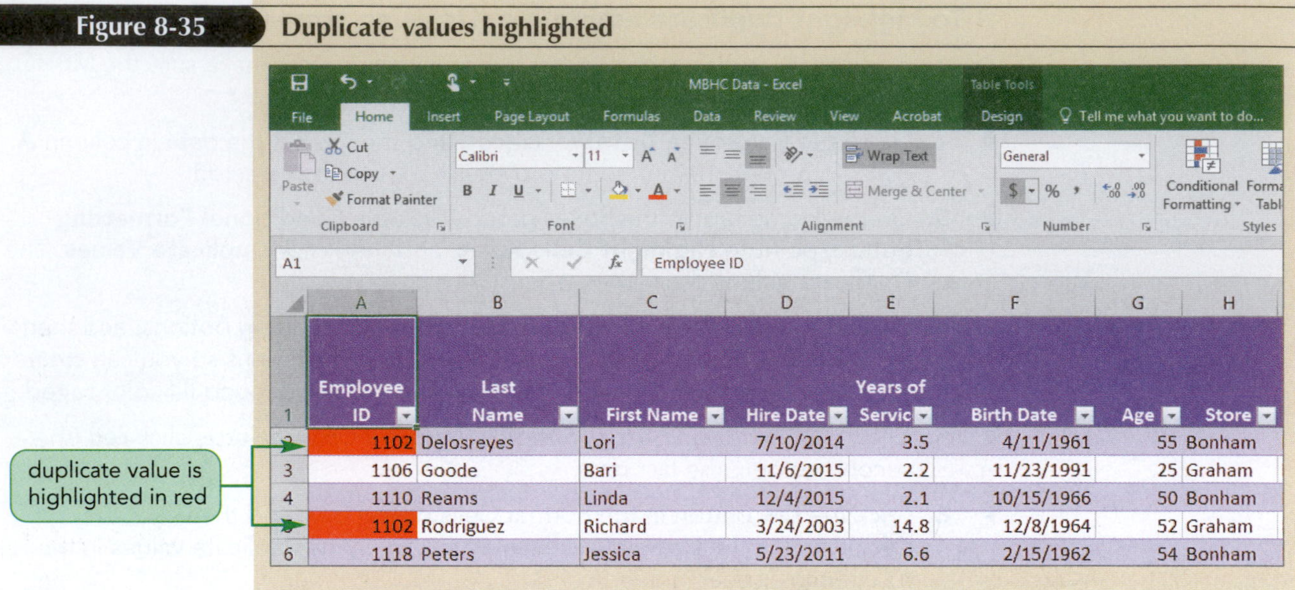

The conditional formatting correctly identified the duplicate values.

Using the Conditional Formatting Rules Manager

Each time you apply a conditional format, you are defining a conditional formatting rule. A rule specifies the type of condition (such as formatting cells greater than a specified value), the type of formatting when that condition occurs (such as light red fill with dark red text), and the cell or range the formatting is applied to. You can edit existing conditional formatting rules from the Conditional Formatting Rules Manager dialog box.

REFERENCE

Editing a Conditional Formatting Rule

- Select the range with the conditional formatting you want to edit.
- On the Home tab, in the Styles group, click the Conditional Formatting button, and then click Manage Rules.
- Select the rule you want to edit, and then click the Edit Rule button.
- In the Select a Rule Type box, click a rule type, and then make the appropriate changes in the Edit the Rule Description section.
- Click the OK button in each dialog box.

The red background fill makes the cell content difficult to read. Vanessa asks you to use a gold fill color to better contrast with the black text. You'll use the Conditional Formatting Rules Manager dialog box to edit the rule that specifies the formatting applied to duplicate values in the Employee ID column.

To change the duplicate values fill color using the Conditional Formatting Rules Manager:

1. On the Home tab, in the Styles group, click the **Conditional Formatting** button, and then click **Manage Rules**. The Conditional Formatting Rules Manager dialog box opens, listing all the formatting rules for the current selection, which, in this case, is the EmployeeTbl table.
2. Verify that the Show formatting rules for box shows **This Table**. All of the rules currently in effect in the EmployeeTbl table are displayed. You can add new rules and edit or delete existing rules. You also can control which formatting rules are displayed in the dialog box, such as all rules in a specific worksheet or table. See Figure 8-36.

Figure 8-36 Conditional Formatting Rules Manager dialog box

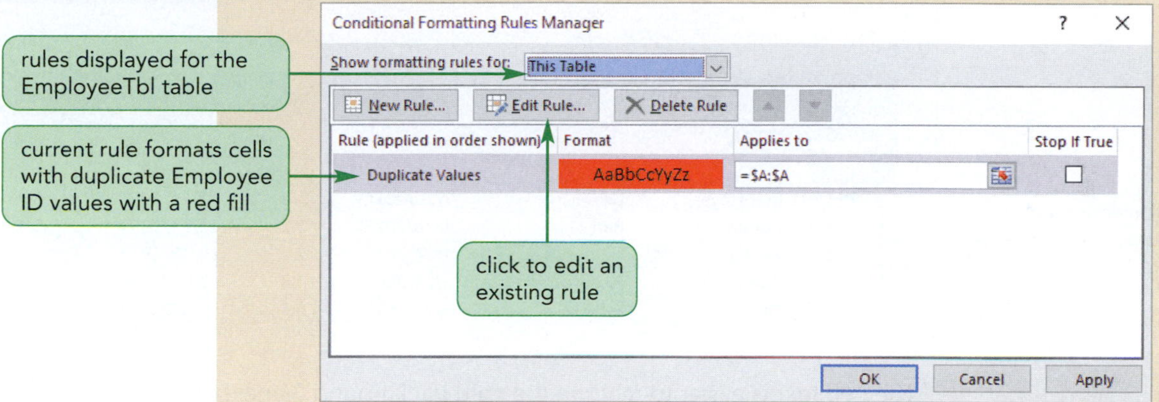

3. Click the **Edit Rule** button. The Edit Formatting Rule dialog box opens. See Figure 8-37.

Figure 8-37 Edit Formatting Rule dialog box

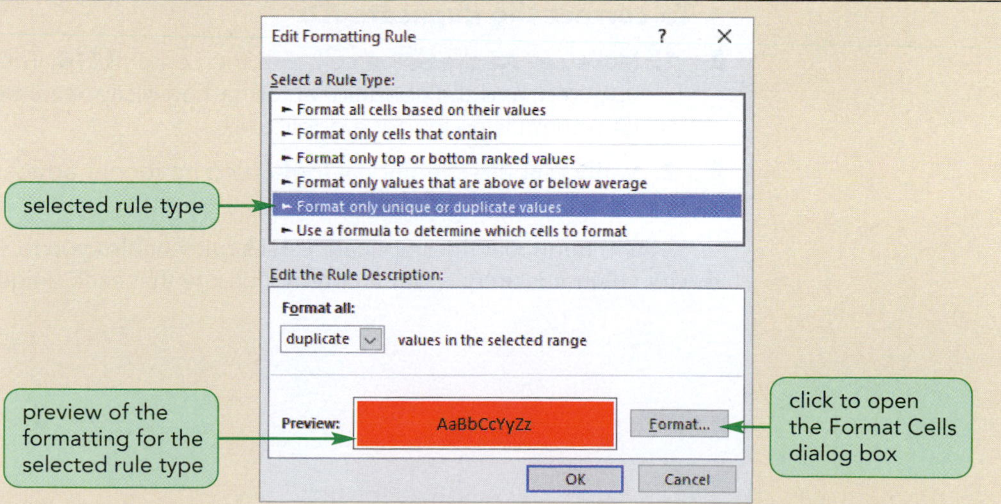

4. Click the **Format** button. The Format Cells dialog box opens.
5. Click the **Fill** tab, if necessary, and then, in the Background Color palette, click **gold** (the third color in the last row).
6. Click the **OK** button in each of the three dialog boxes. The duplicate records in the table are formatted with a gold background color. See Figure 8-38.

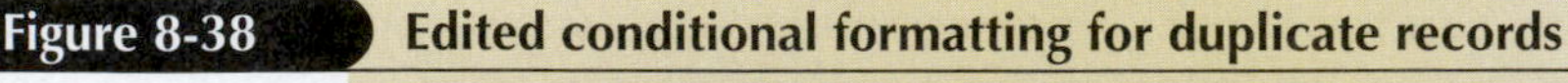

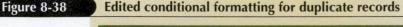

Figure 8-38 Edited conditional formatting for duplicate records

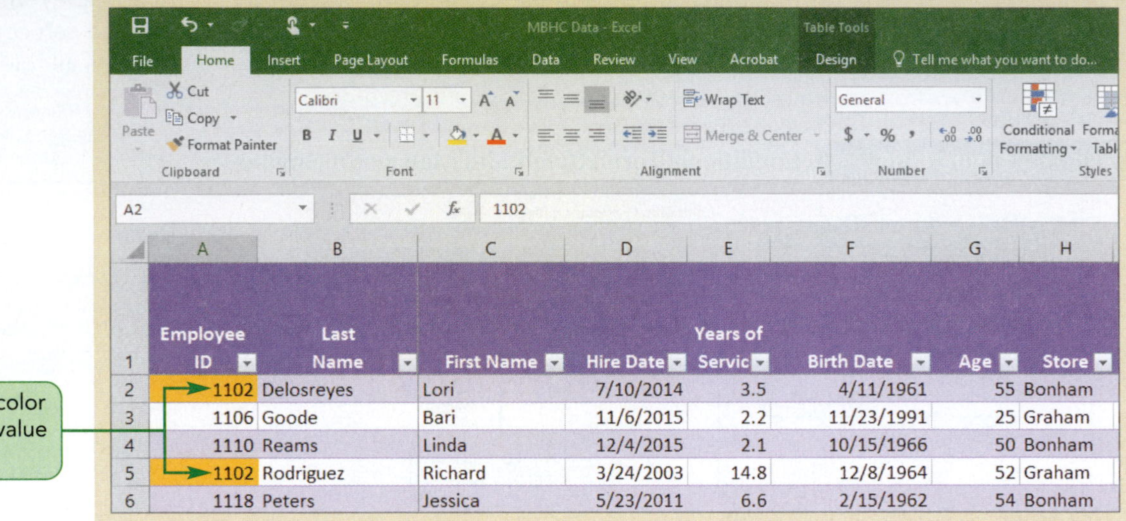

	A	B	C	D	E	F	G	H
1	Employee ID	Last Name	First Name	Hire Date	Years of Servic	Birth Date	Age	Store
2	1102	Delosreyes	Lori	7/10/2014	3.5	4/11/1961	55	Bonham
3	1106	Goode	Bari	11/6/2015	2.2	11/23/1991	25	Graham
4	1110	Reams	Linda	12/4/2015	2.1	10/15/1966	50	Bonham
5	1102	Rodriguez	Richard	3/24/2003	14.8	12/8/1964	52	Graham
6	1118	Peters	Jessica	5/23/2011	6.6	2/15/1962	54	Bonham

The cell text is easier to read on the gold background. Vanessa wants you to correct the duplicate ID in cell A5 by entering the employee's actual ID number. The conditional format will remain active and apply to any new records that Vanessa adds to the EmployeeTbl table.

To correct the duplicate ID:

1. Make cell **A5** the active cell, and then enter **1114**. The employee's ID is updated, and the conditional formatting disappears because the value in the ID column is no longer a duplicate.
2. Verify that the conditional formatting no longer appears in cell A2.

Keep in mind that the Duplicate Values rule enables you to verify that each entry in the ID column is unique, but it does not ensure that each unique value is accurate.

INSIGHT

Creating a Formula to Conditionally Format Cells

Sometimes the built-in conditional formatting rules do not apply the formatting you need. In these instances, you may be able to create a conditional formatting rule based on a formula that uses a logical expression to describe the condition you want. For example, you can create a formula that uses conditional formatting to compare cells in different columns or to highlight an entire row.

When you create the formula, keep in mind the following guidelines:

- The formula must start with an equal sign.
- The formula must be in the form of a logical test that results in a True or False value.
- In most cases, the formula should use relative references and point to the first row of data in the table. If the formula references a cell or range outside the table, use an absolute reference.
- After you create the formula, enter test values to ensure the conditional formatting works in all situations that you intended.

For example, to use conditional formatting to highlight whether the hire date entered in column D is less than the birth date entered in column F, you need to enter a formula that applies conditional formatting and compares cells in different columns of a table. The following steps describe how to create this formula:

1. Select the range you want to format (in this case, the Hire Date column).
2. On the Home tab, in the Styles group, click the Conditional Formatting button, and then click New Rule.
3. In the Select a Rule Type box, click the "Use a formula to determine which cells to format" rule.
4. In the "Format values where this formula is true" box, enter the appropriate formula (in this case, =D2<F2).
5. Click the Format button to open the Format Cells dialog box, and then select the formatting you want to apply.
6. Click the OK button in each dialog box.

Another example is to highlight the entire row if an employee has 10 or more years of service. In this case, you would select the range of data, such as A2:O101, and then enter =E$2>=10 in the "Format values where this formula is true" box. The other steps remain the same.

Using Functions to Summarize Data Conditionally

The COUNT function tallies the number of data values in a range, the SUM function adds the values in a range, and the AVERAGE function calculates the average of the values in a range. However, sometimes you need to calculate a conditional count, sum, or average using only those cells that meet a particular condition. In those cases, you need to use the COUNTIF, SUMIF, and AVERAGEIF functions. For example, Vanessa wants to create a report that shows the number, total, and average salaries for employees in each store. You will use the COUNTIF, SUMIF, and AVERAGEIF functions to do this.

Using the COUNTIF Function

You can calculate the number of cells in a range that match criteria you specify by using the COUNTIF function, which is sometimes referred to as a **conditional count**. The COUNTIF function has the syntax

```
COUNTIF(range, criteria)
```

where *range* is the range of cells you want to count, and *criteria* is a number, an expression, a cell reference, or text that defines which cells to count.

There are many ways to express the criteria in a COUNTIF function, as shown in Figure 8-39.

Figure 8-39 Examples of COUNTIF function criteria

Formula	Explanation of Formula	Result
=COUNTIF(H2:H101,"Bonham")	Number of employees in Bonham	17
=COUNTIF(H2:H101,H3)	Number of employees in cell H3 (Graham)	48
=COUNTIF(J2:J101,<50000)	Number of employees with salary <50000	22
=COUNTIF(J2:J101, ">=" &J2)	Number of employees with salary >= value in cell J2 (106010)	7

TIP

You can use structured references or cell and range addresses to reference cells within an Excel table.

Vanessa wants to know how many employees are located in Bonham. You can use the COUNTIF function to find this answer because you want a conditional count (a count of employees who meet a specified criterion; in this case, employees located in Bonham). The location information is stored in column H of the EmployeeTbl table. To count the number of employees in Bonham you can use either one of the following formulas:

Range reference `=COUNTIF('Employee Data'!H2:H101,"=Bonham")`

Fully qualified structured reference `=COUNTIF(EmployeeTbl[Store],"=Bonham")`

With either formula, Excel counts all of the cells in the Store column of the EmployeeTbl table that contain the text equal to Bonham. Because Bonham is text, you must enclose it within quotation marks. It is not necessary to enclose numbers in quotation marks.

You will enter this formula using the COUNTIF function in the Employee Analysis worksheet. You will use the Insert Function dialog box to help you build the formula using worksheet and range references to calculate the number of employees who work in Bonham.

To count employees located in Bonham using the COUNTIF function:

1. Go to the **Employee Analysis** worksheet.
2. Select cell **B3**, and then click the **Insert Function** button *fx* next to the formula bar. The Insert Function dialog box opens.
3. Click the **Or select a category** arrow, and then click **Statistical**.
4. In the Select a function box, double-click **COUNTIF**. The Function Arguments dialog box opens.
5. In the Range box, type **'Employee Data'!H2:H101** to enter the range to search, and then press the **Tab** key. The range 'Employee Data'!H2:H101 refers to all data values in the range H2:H101 (Store column) in the Employee Data worksheet.

6. In the Criteria box, type **A3**. Cell A3 in this worksheet contains Bonham, which is the criterion you want Excel to use to determine which employee records to count. You could also have typed "=Bonham" or "Bonham" in the criteria box. See Figure 8-40.

Figure 8-40 Function Arguments dialog box for the COUNTIF function

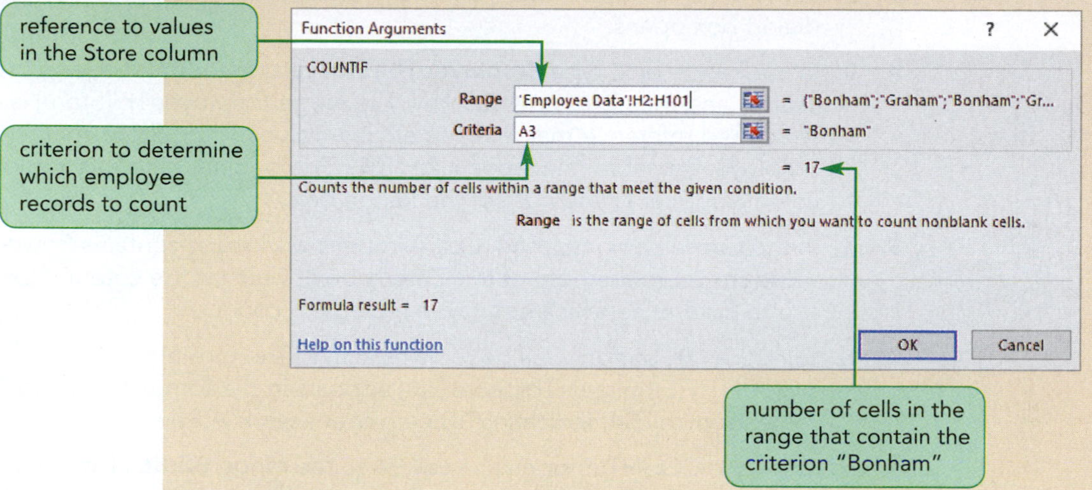

7. Click the **OK** button. Cell B3 remains active. The formula =COUNTIF('Employee Data'!H2:H101,A3) appears in the formula bar, and 17 appears in cell B3, indicating that the company has 17 employees in Bonham. See Figure 8-41.

Figure 8-41 Location summary for Bonham employees

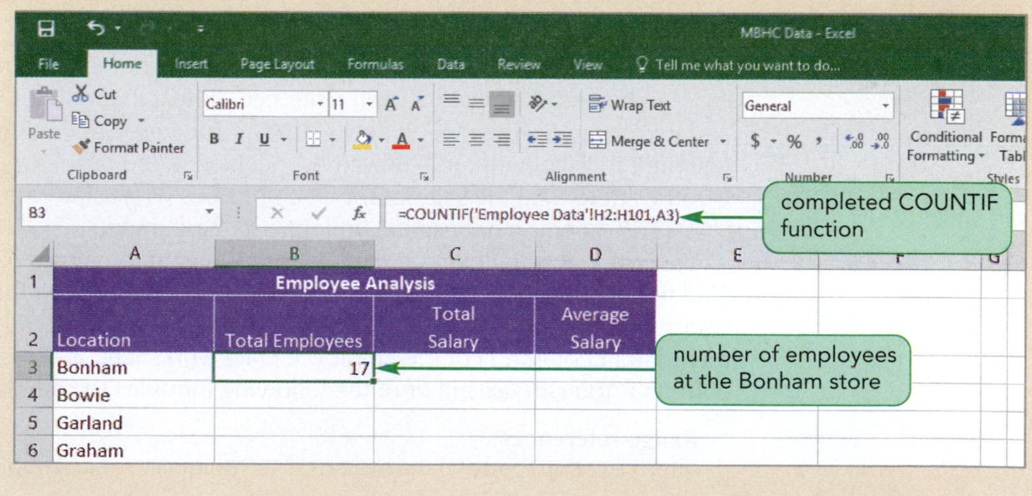

You will enter a similar formula to calculate the number of employees who work in Bowie, Garland, and Graham. This time, however, you will use structured references to specify the range to search.

To count the number of employees who work in Bowie, Garland, and Graham:

1. Select cell **B4**, and then click the **Insert Function** button *fx* next to the formula bar. The Insert Function dialog box opens with the Statistical category still selected.
2. In the Select a function box, double-click **COUNTIF**. The Function Arguments dialog box opens.
3. In the Range box, type **EmployeeTbl[Store]** to enter the range to search, and then press the **Tab** key. The range EmployeeTbl[Store] is a structured reference that refers to all data values in the Store column in the EmployeeTbl table (the range H2:H101). The beginning values in the Store column appear to the right of the Range box.
4. In the Criteria box, type **A4**. Cell A4 in this worksheet contains Bowie (the value shown to the right of the Criteria box), which is the criterion Excel will use to determine which employee records to count.
5. Click the **OK** button. Cell B4 remains active. The formula =COUNTIF(EmployeeTbl[Store],A4) appears in the formula bar, and 13 appears in cell B4, indicating 13 employees work in Bowie.
6. Copy the COUNTIF formula in cell B4 to the range **B5:B6**. The total employees for Garland is 22 and Graham is 48.

Using the SUMIF Function

The SUMIF function adds the values in a range that meet criteria you specify. The SUMIF function is also called a **conditional sum**. The syntax of the SUMIF function is

```
SUMIF(range,criteria[,sum_range])
```

where *range* is the range of cells you want to filter before calculating a sum; *criteria* is a number, an expression, a cell reference, or text that defines which cells to count; and *sum_range* is the range of cells to total. The *sum_range* argument is optional; if you omit it, Excel will total the values specified in the *range* argument. For example, if you want to total the salaries for all employees with salaries greater than $50,000 (">50000"), you do not use the optional third argument.

Vanessa wants to compare the total salaries paid to employees in Bonham, Bowie, Garland, and Graham. You can use the SUMIF function to do this because Vanessa wants to conditionally add salaries of employees at a specified location. Store is recorded in column H of the Employee Data worksheet, and the salary data is stored in column J. You can use either of the following formulas to calculate this value:

Range references

```
=SUMIF('Employee Data'!H2:H101,"Bonham",'Employee Data'!J2:J101)
```

Fully qualified structured references

```
=SUMIF(EmployeeTbl[Store],"Bonham",EmployeeTbl[Current Salary])
```

Both of these formulas state that the salary of any employee whose store is Bonham will be added to the total. Using the SUMIF function, you will insert the formula with structured references into the Employee Analysis worksheet.

To sum employee salaries in the Bonham, Bowie, Garland, and Graham stores using the SUMIF function:

1. Select cell **C3**, and then click the **Insert Function** button next to the formula bar. The Insert Function dialog box opens.
2. Click the **Or select a category** arrow, and then click **Math & Trig**.
3. In the Select a function box, double-click **SUMIF**. The Function Arguments dialog box opens.
4. In the Range box, type **EmployeeTbl[Store]** to specify the range of data to filter, and then press the **Tab** key. The range EmployeeTbl[Store] is a structured reference that refers to all data values in the Store column in the EmployeeTbl table (the range H2:H101).
5. In the Criteria box, type **A3** and then press the **Tab** key. Cell A3 in this worksheet contains "Bonham" (shown to the right of the Criteria box), which is the criterion Excel will use to determine which employee records to sum.
6. In the Sum_range box, type **EmployeeTbl[Current Salary]** to indicate that the Current Salary column in the EmployeeTbl table contains the data to sum in the filtered rows. The values to the right of the Sum_range box are the amounts in the filtered Current Salary column. See Figure 8-42.

Figure 8-42 Function Arguments dialog box for the SUMIF function

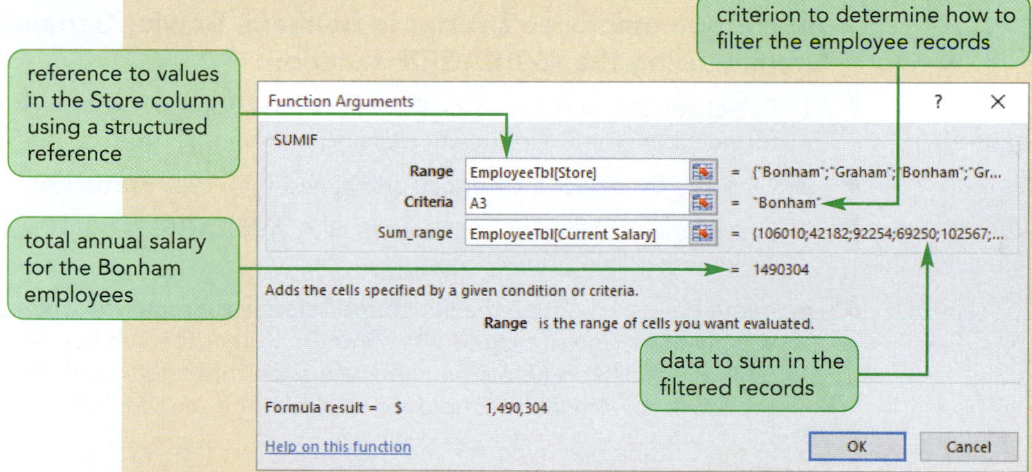

7. Click the **OK** button. Cell C3 is active. The formula =SUMIF(EmployeeTbl[Store],A3,EmployeeTbl[Current Salary]) appears in the formula bar and $1,490,304 appears in cell C3, indicating the total annual salaries paid to Bonham employees.

   Trouble? If Invalid appears in the cell or an error message appears, you probably mistyped some part of the formula. Review the SUMIF formula you entered, and make sure it matches the formula =SUMIF(EmployeeTbl[Store],A3,EmployeeTbl[Current Salary]).

8. Copy the SUMIF formula in cell C3 to the range **C4:C6**. The total Current Salary for employees working in Bowie is $1,076,702, Garland is $1,106,314, and Graham is $3,580,464.

Using the AVERAGEIF Function

The AVERAGEIF function is similar to the SUMIF function. You use the AVERAGEIF function to calculate the average of values in a range that meet criteria you specify. The syntax of the AVERAGEIF function is

```
AVERAGEIF(range,criteria[,average_range])
```

where *range* is the range of cells you want to filter before calculating the average, *criteria* is the condition used to filter the range, and *average_range* is the range of cells to average. The *average_range* argument is optional; if you omit it, Excel will average the values specified in the *range* argument.

Vanessa also wants to compare the average salaries paid to employees in Bonham, Bowie, Garland, and Graham. Store is recorded in column H of the Employee Data worksheet, and the current salary data is stored in column J. The formulas to calculate this value are:

Range references

```
=AVERAGEIF('Employee Data'!H2:H101,"Bonham",'Employee Data'!J2:J101)
```

Fully qualified structured references

```
=AVERAGEIF(EmployeeTbl[Store],"Bonham",EmployeeTbl[Current Salary])
```

Both of these formulas state that the current salary of any employee whose store is Bonham will be included in the average. You will enter the formula into the Employee Analysis worksheet using the AVERAGEIF function with structured references.

To average employee salaries in Bonham, Bowie, Garland and Graham using the AVERAGEIF function:

1. Select cell **D3**, and then click the **Insert Function** button next to the formula bar. The Insert Function dialog box opens.
2. Click the **Or select a category** arrow, and then click **Statistical**.
3. In the Select a function box, double-click **AVERAGEIF**. The Function Arguments dialog box opens.
4. In the Range box, type the structured reference **EmployeeTbl[Store]** to specify the range of data to filter, and then press the **Tab** key. The range EmployeeTbl[Store] is a structured reference that refers to all data values in the Store column in the EmployeeTbl table (the range H2:H101).
5. In the Criteria box, type **A3** and then press the **Tab** key. Cell A3 in this worksheet contains "Bonham" (shown to the right of the Criteria box), which is the criterion Excel will use to determine which employee records to average.
6. In the Average_range box, type **EmployeeTbl[Current Salary]** to indicate that the Current Salary column in the EmployeeTbl table contains the data to average in the filtered rows. See Figure 8-43.

Figure 8-43 Function Arguments dialog box for the AVERAGEIF function

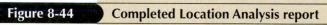

criterion to determine how to filter the employee records

reference to values in the Store column using a structured reference

total average salary for the Bonham employees

data to average in the filtered records

Function Arguments ? X

AVERAGEIF

Range EmployeeTbl[Store] = {"Bonham";"Graham";"Bonham";"Gr...

Criteria A3 = "Bonham"

Average_range EmployeeTbl[Current Salary] = {106010;42182;92254;69250;102567;...

= 87664.94118

Finds average(arithmetic mean) for the cells specified by a given condition or criteria.

Range is the range of cells you want evaluated.

Formula result = $ 87,665

Help on this function OK Cancel

7. Click the **OK** button. Cell D3 remains active. The formula =AVERAGEIF(EmployeeTbl[Store],A3,EmployeeTbl[Current Salary]) appears in the formula bar and $87,665 appears in cell E3, indicating the average current salary paid to Bonham employees.

8. Copy the formula in cell D3 to cell **D4:D6**. MBHC pays an average of $87,665 to employees working in Bonham, $82,823 in Bowie, $50,287 in Garland, and $74,593 in Graham. See Figure 8-44.

Figure 8-44 Completed Location Analysis report

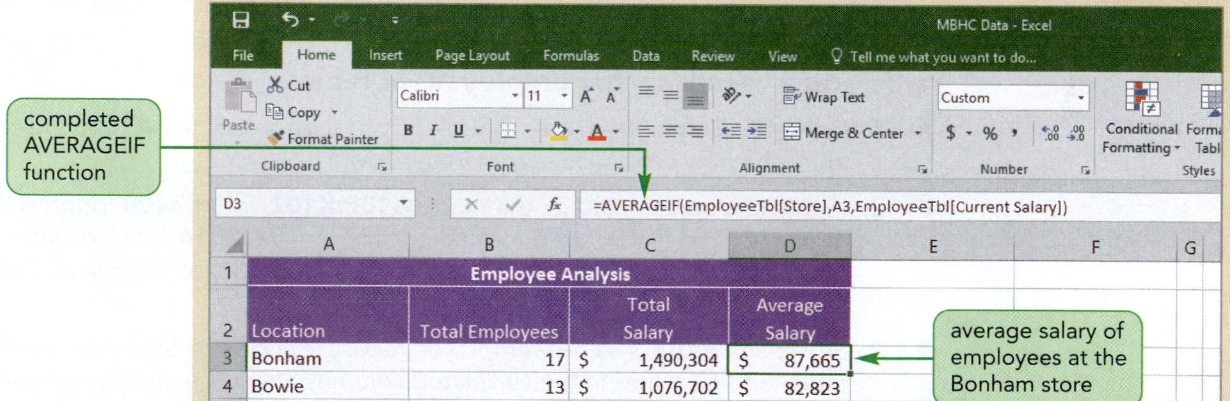

As Vanessa enters new employees or edits the location or current salary values of current employees, the values in the Employee Analysis worksheet will be automatically updated because the formulas reference the EmployeeTbl table.

INSIGHT

Using the TRANSPOSE Function

The **TRANSPOSE function** is used to change the orientation of a range—that is, return a vertical range of cells as a horizontal range, or vice versa. The TRANSPOSE function has the syntax

```
TRANSPOSE(array)
```

where `array` is the range you want to convert from row data to column data (or vice versa). To use the TRANSPOSE function, complete the following steps:

1. Select the range where you want to place the transposed data. Be sure to select the opposite number of rows and columns as the original data. For example, if the range has five rows and three columns, you would select a range that has three rows and five columns.
2. In the first cell of the selected range, type =TRANSPOSE(to begin the function.
3. Type the range reference of the original range of data.
4. Type) to complete the function.
5. Press the Ctrl+Shift+Enter keys to enter the function. (Note that pressing only the Enter key would create incorrect formula results.) Excel places curly brackets { } around the array formula and enters the formula in every cell of the selected range.

Keep in mind that the TRANSPOSE function only copies the data from the cells in the initial range. Any formatting applied to the original range must be reapplied to the new range. However, any changes made to the data in the original range are automatically made to the data in the transposed range. To delete the transposed range, select the entire range, and then press the Delete key.

Vanessa recently hired a new employee, and she asks you to add the new record to the Excel table.

To add a record to the EmployeeTbl table:

1. Go to the **Employee Data** worksheet, and then select cell **A102**. You will enter the new employee record in this row.
2. In the appropriate cells in the range **A102:K102**, enter **3400** for Emp ID, **Joplin** for Last Name, **Jodi** for the First Name, **4/1/2016** for Hire Date, **11/15/1970** for Birth Date, **Garland** for Store, **PT** for Job Status, and **23000** for Current Salary.
3. Select cell **A103**. The new employee record is added to the EmployeeTbl table, and all values in the calculated columns are automatically updated.
4. Go to the **Employee Analysis** worksheet, and then select cell **B5**, if necessary. The Employee Analysis report has been updated to reflect the new employee. The number of employees in Garland is 23, the total salary is $1,129,314, and the average salary is $49,101. See Figure 8-45.

Figure 8-45 Updated Location Analysis report

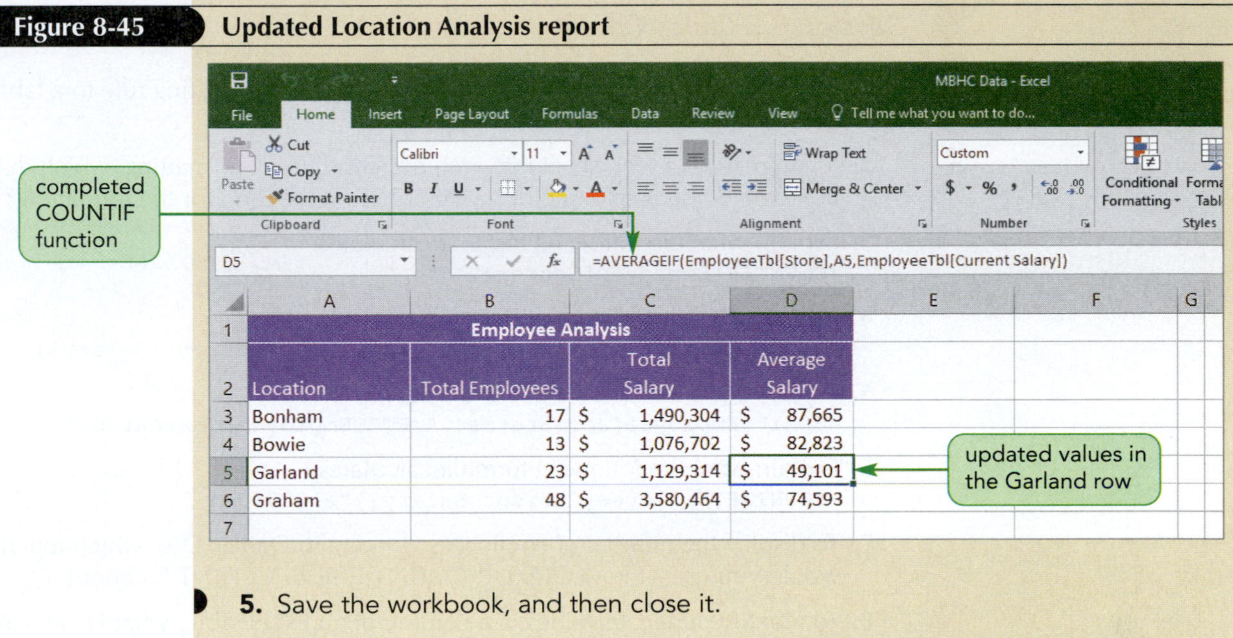

Employee Analysis			
Location	Total Employees	Total Salary	Average Salary
Bonham	17	$ 1,490,304	$ 87,665
Bowie	13	$ 1,076,702	$ 82,823
Garland	23	$ 1,129,314	$ 49,101
Graham	48	$ 3,580,464	$ 74,593

5. Save the workbook, and then close it.

If the employee data had been stored as a range of data instead of an Excel table, the Employee Analysis report would not have automatically updated. Instead, you would have had to modify all the formulas in the report to reflect the expanded range of employee data. Vanessa is pleased with the formulas you added to the Employee Analysis, Employee Data, and Product Data worksheets.

REVIEW

Session 8.3 Quick Check

1. Would you apply the duplicate value conditional formatting rule to a table column of last names? Why or why not?
2. If you receive a worksheet that includes conditional formatting, which dialog box would you use to find out what criteria were used for the formatting?
3. Explain what the following formula calculates:
   `=COUNTIF(Employee[Gender],"F")`
4. Explain what the following formula calculates:
   `=AVERAGEIF(Employee[Age],">50",Employee[Current Salary])`
5. Explain what the following formula calculates:
   `=SUMIF(Employee[Job Status],"=FT",Employee[Current Salary])`
6. Explain what the following formula calculates:
   `=COUNTIF(Employee[Current Salary],">100000")`
7. To display the number of employees working in Dallas (DA), which function would you use—the VLOOKUP, COUNTIF, IF, or COUNT function?
8. To identify duplicate values in a column of an Excel table, what Excel feature would you use?

PRACTICE

Review Assignments

Data File needed for the Review Assignments: Employees.xlsx

Vanessa wants you to analyze the MBHC employee data to determine each employee's work anniversary, available comp days, and bonus eligibility. She also wants you to calculate the bonus amount for eligible employees. Complete the following:

1. Open the **Employees** workbook located in the Excel8 > Review folder included with your Data Files, and then save the workbook as **MBHC Employees** in the location specified by your instructor.
2. In the Documentation worksheet, enter your name and the date.
3. In the Employee Data worksheet, rename the Excel table as **EmployeeTbl**.
4. In the Work Anniversary column, enter an IF function. If the month in the employee's hire date matches the month in the Data Tables worksheet (cell B4), **Yes** should appear in the work anniversary column; otherwise, the cell should remain blank. (*Hint*: Remember to use an absolute cell reference to cell B4 because the formula will be copied to the rest of the column.) All employees receive a card on their work anniversary.
5. In the Eligible for Bonus column, enter a formula with IF and OR functions to display the text **No** if the employee's pay grade is **D** or the employee's job status is a part time (**PT**). Leave the cell blank if the employee is eligible for a bonus.
6. In the Comp Days column, enter a formula with nested IFs to display the number of comp days that an employee will receive based on their years of service. The table for Comp Days is on the Data Tables worksheet. (*Hint*: Remember to use absolute references to the cells in the Data Tables worksheet because the formula will be copied to the entire column.)
7. In the Bonus column, enter an IF function with a nested VLOOKUP function to calculate the bonus for each employee based on whether the employee is eligible for a bonus (column M) and his or her Pay Grade. The bonus information for qualifying employees is in a table named Bonus_Table in the Data Tables worksheet. Format the Bonus column with the Accounting format with no decimal places.
8. In the Years of Service column, modify the formula to include the IFERROR function and display the message **Invalid hire date** if an error value occurs. Test the modified formula by changing the date in cell E2 from 7/10/2014 to **17/10/2014**. AutoFit the column.
9. In the Work Anniversary column, which also uses the Hire Date, modify the formula to include the IFERROR function and display the message **Invalid hire date** if an error value occurs. AutoFit the column.
10. Edit the Duplicate Values conditional formatting rule applied to the Employee ID column so that the fill color of the duplicate value is formatted as light blue (the seventh color in the bottom row of the Background Color palette). Test this change by typing **3226** in cell A101.
11. In the Employee Analysis worksheet, enter the COUNTIF function in cells B3 and B4 to count the number of part-time and full-time employees, respectively. (*Hint*: Count the Job Status column in the EmployeeTbl table.)
12. In cells C3 and C4, enter the SUMIF function to calculate the total salaries of part-time employees and the total salaries of full-time employees, respectively. Format the Total Salary column with the Accounting format and no decimal places.
13. In cells D3 and D4, enter the AVERAGEIF function to calculate the average salary of part-time employees and the average salary of full-time employees, respectively. Format the Average Salary column with the Accounting format and no decimal places.
14. Save the workbook, and then close it.

APPLY

Case Problem 1

Data File needed for this Case Problem: Popcorn.xlsx

Ricky's Popcorn Ricky Nolan established Ricky's Popcorn in Hawthorne, Nevada, in 2000. He ships flavored popcorn in standard flavors such as plain and kettle corn and gourmet flavors such as grape and orange. Customers place their orders via the company website and then receive their popcorn in one to three days, depending on the shipping option they choose. Ricky wants to create a professional-looking invoice he can use for each customer transaction. Ricky used Excel to create the invoice layout and wants you to add formulas to calculate the price per item, sales tax, shipping, and invoice total based on existing tables for pricing and shipping. Complete the following:

1. Open the **Popcorn** workbook located in the Excel8 > Case1 folder included with your Data Files, and then save the workbook as **Rickys Popcorn** in the location specified by your instructor.
2. In the Documentation worksheet, enter your name and the date.
3. In the Pricing and Shipping worksheet, assign the defined name **ShippingCost** to the data in the range D3:E7, which can be used for an approximate match lookup. (*Hint*: The lookup table includes only the values, not the descriptive labels.)
4. In the Customer Invoice worksheet, in the Item column (range B16:B26), use data validation to create a list of the items in the Product Pricing table in the Pricing and Shipping worksheet. (*Hint*: Select the entire range before setting the validation rule.)
5. In the Flavor column (range E16:E26), use data validation to create an input message indicating that the popcorn flavor should be entered. The flavors are located below the invoice.
6. In the Price cell (cell G16), use a VLOOKUP function to retrieve the price of the ordered item listed in the Product Pricing table in the Pricing and Shipping worksheet. (*Hint*: Use the defined name ProductPrice that was assigned to the Product Pricing table.) When no item is selected, this cell will display an error message.
7. Modify the formula in the cell G16 by combining the IFERROR function with the VLOOKUP function to display either the price or a blank cell if an error value occurs. Copy the formula down the range G16:G26.
8. In the Total column (range H16:H26), enter a formula to calculate the total charge for that row (Qty × Price). Use the IFERROR function to display either the total charge or a blank cell if an error value occurs.
9. In the Subtotal cell (cell H27), add a formula to sum the Total column. Use the IFERROR function to display either the subtotal or a blank cell if an error value occurs.
10. In the Sales Tax cell (cell H28), enter a formula with an IF function so if the customer's state (cell C12) is **NV**, then calculate 6.85 percent of the subtotal (cell H27); otherwise, use 0 for the sales tax. (*Hint*: The defined name State is assigned to cell C12, and the defined name Sub_Total is assigned to cell H27. Note that the defined name "Sub_Total" is intentionally not spelled as "Subtotal," which is the name of an Excel function.)
11. In the Shipping cell (cell H29), enter a formula that nests the VLOOKUP function in an IF function to look up the shipping cost from the Shipping Cost table in the Pricing and Shipping worksheet based on the subtotal in cell H27. If the subtotal is 0, the shipping cost should display 0. (*Hint*: Use the defined name you created for the Shipping Cost table data.)
12. In the Total Due cell (cell H30), calculate the invoice total by entering a formula that adds the values in the Subtotal, Sales Tax, and Shipping cells.

13. Test the worksheet by using the following order data:
    - Sold to: **Lauri Bradford**
    - Street: **3226 South Street**
    - City, State Zip: **Hawthorne, NV 89415**
    - Date: **12/1/2017**
    - Item 1: **Gourmet (2) 1g**
    - Flavor: **Nacho Cheese**
    - Quantity **2**
    - Item 2: **Plain Tin 1g**
    - Quantity: **1**
14. Save the workbook, and then close it.

TROUBLESHOOT

Case Problem 2

Data File needed for this Case Problem: LKE.xlsx

LKE Distribution LKE Distribution in North Platte, Nebraska, sells everything needed to outfit an office from basic office supplies to high-end office equipment and technology to furniture. Laura Easterling manages the Accounts Receivable (the amount customers owe LKE Distribution). She has entered the billing information in an Excel workbook. She wants you to enter formulas that will help her to analyze the data. Complete the following:

1. Open the **LKE** workbook located in the Excel8 > Case2 folder included with your Data Files, and then save the workbook as **LKE Receivables** in the location specified by your instructor.
2. In the Documentation worksheet, enter your name and the date.
3. In the Invoices worksheet, in cell B1, enter **7/1/2017** as the current date. Note the defined name CurrentDate has been assigned to cell B1.

Troubleshoot 4. The sales rep commission rate varies for each sales rep. In column E, Laura used a VLOOKUP function to look up the commission rate for each sales rep and then multiplied the commission rate by the invoice amount to calculate the commission. Although the first row in column E of the Excel table named Aging displays the correct commission, all the other cells display a number, "-", or #N/A. Find the problem with the formulas in the Commission column and fix it.

5. In column G, enter a formula with an IF function to calculate the days past due. If the number of days since the invoice was sent (CurrentDate – Invoice Date) is greater than 30, calculate the days past due (Current Date – Invoice Date – 30); otherwise, enter 0.
6. Create the following formulas to assign the value in the Invoice Amount column to one of five columns—Current, 1–30 days, 31–60 days, 61–90 days, and Over 90 days:
   a. In Current (column H), if the Days Past Due equals 0, display the invoice amount (column F); otherwise, display a blank cell.
   b. In 1–30 days (column I), if the days past due is greater than or equal to 1 and less than or equal to 30, display the invoice amount (column F); otherwise, display a blank cell.
   c. In 31–60 days (column J), if the number of days past due is greater than or equal to 31 and less than or equal to 60, display the invoice amount (column F); otherwise, display a blank cell.
   d. In 61–90 days (column K), if the number of days past due is greater than or equal to 61 and less than or equal to 90, display the invoice amount (column F); otherwise, display a blank cell.
   e. In Over 90 days (column L), if the number of days past due is greater than or equal to 91 days, display the invoice amount (column F); otherwise, display a blank cell.

7. Copy the Invoices worksheet, and then rename the copied worksheet as **Overdue Accounts**. In the Overdue Accounts worksheet, do the following:
   a. Filter the records so only invoices whose balance is past due are displayed. These are all records with an amount in 1–30 days (column I), 31–60 days (column J), 61–90 days (column K), or Over 90 days (column L).
   b. Sort the filtered data by invoice date (oldest first).
   c. Include a Total row in this table, and display sums for columns I through L.
   d. Hide columns D, E, F, G, and H.
   e. Remove the filter buttons and gridlines from the table. (*Hint*: Use options on View tab and the Table Tools Design tab.)

Troubleshoot 8. In the Invoice Reports worksheet, Laura used the COUNTIF function to count the number of invoices for each sales rep. The formulas she created display only zeros. Fix the formulas in the range B3:B6 so that they display the number of invoices processed by each sales rep.

9. In the Invoice Reports worksheet, complete the Sales Rep Analysis report. In the Commission and Total Amount columns (columns C and D), use the SUMIF function to summarize sales commissions (column E in the Aging table in the Invoices worksheet) and the invoice amount (column F in the Aging table) for each sales rep.
10. In the range B7:D7, enter a formula to calculate the totals. Format these columns appropriately.
11. In the Invoice Reports worksheet, complete the Accounts Receivable Aging report. In the Number of Invoices column, create formulas that count the number of invoices for each group in the Invoices worksheet. (*Hint*: A cell with a zero, not blank as specified in Step 6, will be counted).
12. In the Total Amount column, sum the total amounts for those invoices.
13. Save the workbook, and then close it.

CHALLENGE

Case Problem 3

Data File needed for this Case Problem: Rentals.xlsx

Barrett Furniture Rentals Barrett Furniture Rentals leases furniture by the room to corporations outfitting apartments for temporary stays as well as to homeowners and realtors for staging a house for sale. They offer a variety of grouping for living rooms, dining rooms, bedrooms, and game rooms. Elise Williams, the manager, maintains an Excel worksheet to track furniture rentals. She wants to know the number of rentals and the total rental income for July, August, and September. Elise also wants to know the total number of 6- and 12-month rentals along with the total income for each type of rental. Complete the following:

1. Open the **Rentals** workbook located in the Excel8 > Case3 folder included with your Data Files, and then save the workbook as **Furniture Rentals** in the location specified by your instructor.
2. In the Documentation worksheet, enter your name and the date. In the range A10:D22, review the data definition table. This table describes the different fields used in the Rental Data worksheet.
3. In the Rental Data worksheet, in column G, create a formula that uses the HLOOKUP function to assign a group code (A, B, C, D, or E) from the FurnitureGroups range in the Rental Information worksheet to the furniture listed in column B.
4. In column H, create a formula using the IF and VLOOKUP functions to calculate the rental charges for each set of furniture based on the furniture's group code, the rental period, and the Furniture Rental Charges table. (*Hint*: For the IF function arguments, use one VLOOKUP function for 3 months and another for 9 months. The defined name RentalCharges has been assigned to the Furniture Rental Charges table.)

5. In column I, enter a formula to calculate the insurance charge if the renter has elected insurance coverage (Yes in column E). Use the furniture's group code and the Monthly Insurance column in the RentalCharges table to look up the insurance charge. Remember to multiply the monthly insurance charge by the rental period. If the renter has not elected insurance, the cost is 0.
6. In column J, enter the formula with an IF function to determine the shipping charge for each set of furniture. Use the shipping code (column F) and the shipping charge options Pickup (0) and Truck ($50) to assign shipping costs to rental furniture.
7. In column K, enter a formula to calculate the total cost, which is the sum of the rental charges, the insurance cost, and the shipping cost.
8. Format columns H through K with the Accounting format with no decimal places.
9. In the Rental Report worksheet, complete the Rental Summary report by creating formulas in the range C4:D5 using the COUNTIF and SUMIF functions.
10. In the Rental Data worksheet, enter the following new record:
    - Renter: **Allen**
    - Furniture: **LR-3pc**
    - Rental Date: **9/15/2017**
    - Rental Period: **12**
    - Insurance: **Yes**
    - Shipping Code: **Truck**

Explore 11. Create a PivotTable to display the number of rentals and rental $ by rental month. Rename the worksheet as **Monthly Rentals**. (*Hint*: Select any Rental Date in the PivotTable, and then on the PivotTable Tools Analyze tab, in the Group group, click the Group Field button to open the Grouping dialog box. Use Months as the grouping field.)

12. Save the workbook, and then close it.

CREATE

Case Problem 4

Data File needed for this Case Problem: Athey.xlsx

Athey Department Store Athey Department Store in Fort Dodge, Iowa, has always accepted returns of any product purchased in its store. Mitchell Athey wants to develop a system for handling the returns. A routing slip will allow him to monitor who handled the return at each step. He will also be able to collect the returns data in a worksheet for count of returns in each category. Mitchell has started developing the routing slip, and he wants you to finish creating it. Complete the following:

1. Open the **Athey** workbook located in the Excel8 > Case4 folder included with your Data Files, and then save the workbook as **Athey Routing Slip** in the location specified by your instructor.
2. In the Documentation worksheet, enter your name and the date.
3. Create a defined name for the table on the Return Data worksheet to help you when you create formulas with VLOOKUP functions. (*Hint*: Use a name other than ReturnTbl because this name is already used as the defined name for the table on the Return Data worksheet.)
4. In the Return Routing worksheet, do the following:
    a. In cell B9, use a date function to display the current date.
    b. In cell B11, use an input message to inform the user to enter a product description in this cell.
    c. In cell B14, use a list validation for the Department located on the Return Data worksheet.
    d. In cell B16, use a list validation for the Resolution located on the Return Table worksheet (the range B1:E1).
    e. In cell B20, use an input message to inform the person entering the information to enter their name, initials, or Employee ID in this area.

5. In cell B18, create a formula using nested IF functions and VLOOKUP functions to determine what to do with the returns. Use the lookup table in the Return Data worksheet. Refer to Figure 8-46 for some hints on how to create the formula.

Figure 8-46 **Formula for return resolution**

If the value in B16 is:	The lookup_ value is:	The table_ array is:	The col_ index_num is:	The range_ lookup is:	Nested IF Function
Destroy	B14	Dept_Returns	2	FALSE	IF(B16="Destroy",VLOOKUP(B14, Dept_Returns,2,FALSE),
Return to Mfg	B14	Dept_Returns	3	FALSE	IF(B16="Return to Mfg",VLOOKUP (B14,Dept_Returns,3,FALSE),
Repack	B14	Dept_Returns	4	FALSE	IF(B16="Repack",VLOOKUP(B14, Dept_Returns,4,FALSE),
Restock	B14	Dept_Returns	5	FALSE	IF(B16="Restock",VLOOKUP(B14, Dept_Returns,5,FALSE),"None"))))

6. Test your routing slip by entering the following information:
   - Product Name: **Deluxe Vacuum**
   - Department: **Electronics**
   - Resolution: **Return to Mfg**
   - Customer Assistant: **01265**
7. Protect all cells in the Return Routing worksheet except those in which you enter data.
8. In the Return Analysis worksheet, complete the following analysis of the Return Data worksheet using COUNTIF:
   a. Compute the total Returns by Department.
   b. Compute the total Returns by Resolution.
9. Save the workbook, and then close it.

MODULE 5

Creating Advanced Queries and Enhancing Table Design

Making the CareCenter Database Easier to Use

ACCESS

OBJECTIVES

Session 5.1
- Review object naming standards
- Use the Like, In, Not, and & operators in queries
- Filter data using an AutoFilter
- Use the IIf function to assign a conditional value to a calculated field in a query
- Create a parameter query

Session 5.2
- Use query wizards to create a crosstab query, a find duplicates query, and a find unmatched query
- Create a top values query

Session 5.3
- Modify table designs using lookup fields, input masks, and data validation rules
- Identify object dependencies
- Review a Long Text field's properties
- Designate a trusted folder

Case | *Riverview Veterinary Care Center*

Riverview Veterinary Care Center, a veterinary care center in Cody, Wyoming, provides a range of medical services for pets and livestock in the greater Cody area. In addition to caring for household pets, such as dogs and cats, the center specializes in serving the needs of livestock on ranches in the surrounding area. Kimberly Johnson, the office manager for Riverview Veterinary Care Center, oversees a small staff and is responsible for maintaining the medical records for all of the animals the care center serves.

Kimberly and her staff rely on Microsoft Access 2016 to manage electronic medical records for owner and animal information, billing, inventory control, purchasing, and accounts payable. The Riverview staff developed the CareCenter database, which contains tables, queries, forms, and reports that Kimberly and other staff members use to track animal, owner, visit, and billing information.

Kimberly is interested in taking better advantage of the power of Access to make the database easier to use and to create more sophisticated queries. For example, Kimberly wants to obtain lists of owners in certain cities. She also needs a summarized list of invoice amounts by city. In this module, you'll modify and customize the CareCenter database to satisfy these and other requirements.

STARTING DATA FILES

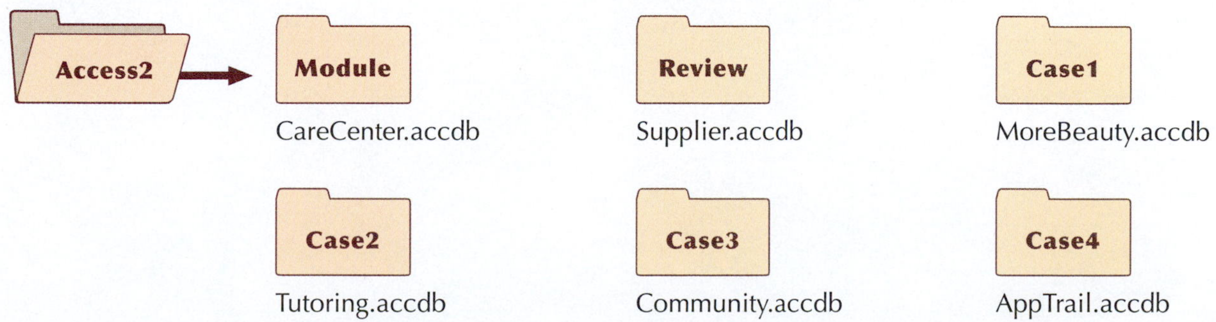

Session 5.1 Visual Overview:

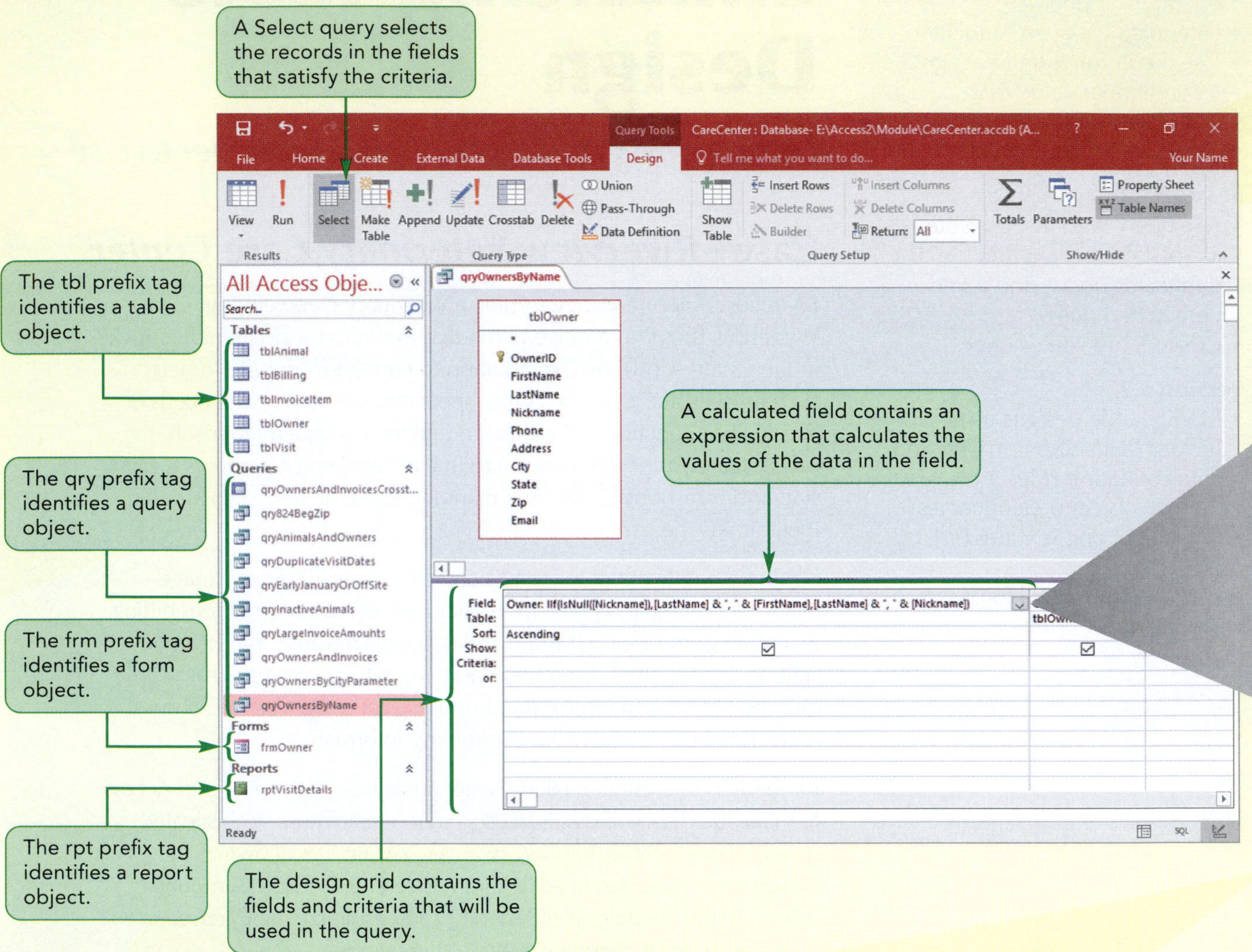

Calculated Field

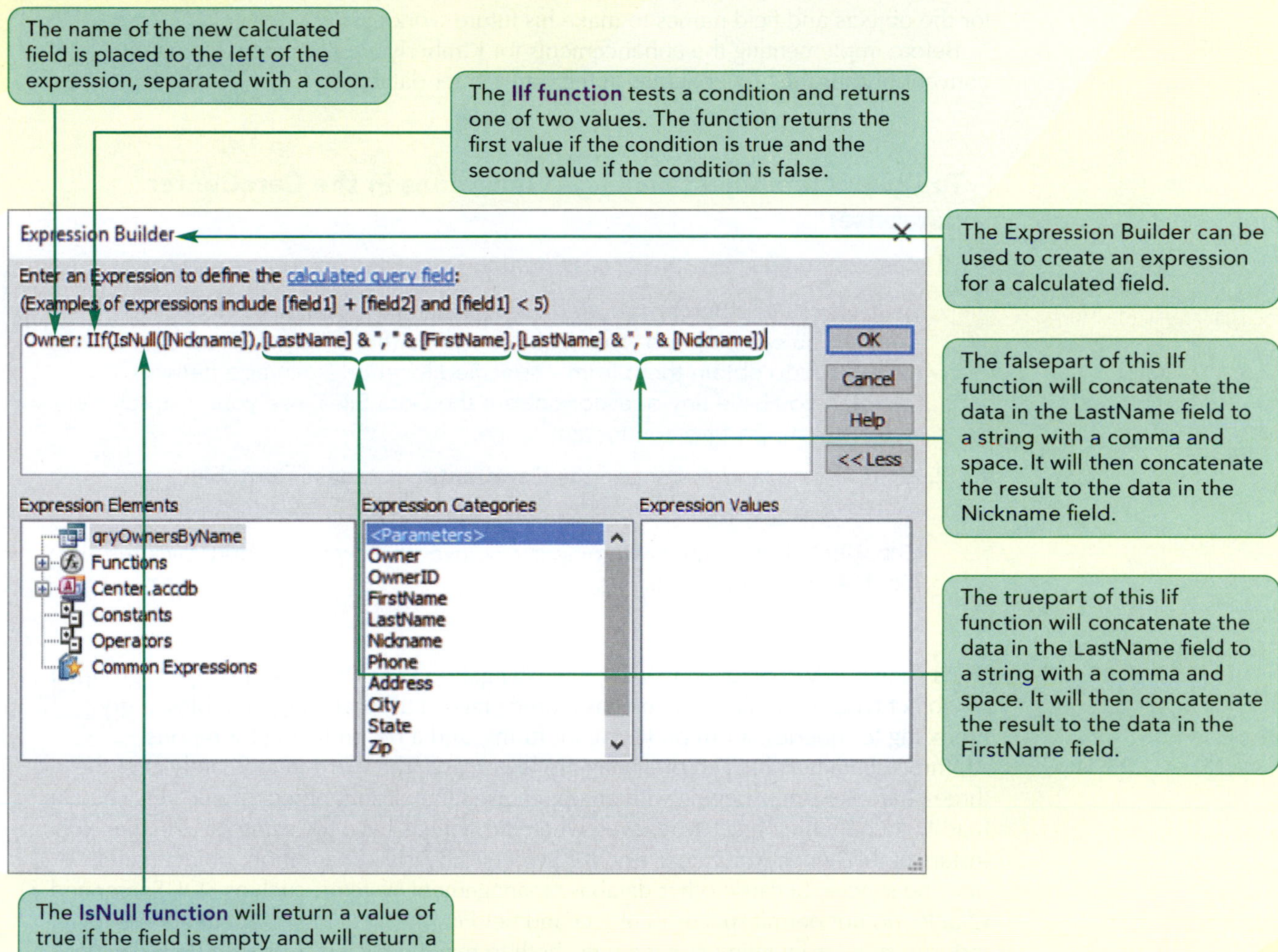
The name of the new calculated field is placed to the left of the expression, separated with a colon.
The IIf function tests a condition and returns one of two values. The function returns the first value if the condition is true and the second value if the condition is false.
Expression Builder
Enter an Expression to define the calculated query field:
(Examples of expressions include [field1] + [field2] and [field1] < 5)
Owner: IIf(IsNull([Nickname]),[LastName] & ", " & [FirstName],[LastName] & ", " & [Nickname])
OK
Cancel
Help
<< Less
Expression Elements
qryOwnersByName
Functions
Center.accdb
Constants
Operators
Common Expressions
Expression Categories
<Parameters>
Owner
OwnerID
FirstName
LastName
Nickname
Phone
Address
City
State
Zip
Expression Values
The Expression Builder can be used to create an expression for a calculated field.
The falsepart of this IIf function will concatenate the data in the LastName field to a string with a comma and space. It will then concatenate the result to the data in the Nickname field.
The truepart of this Iif function will concatenate the data in the LastName field to a string with a comma and space. It will then concatenate the result to the data in the FirstName field.
The IsNull function will return a value of true if the field is empty and will return a value of false if the field is not empty.

Reviewing the CareCenter Database

Kimberly and her staff had no previous database experience when they created the CareCenter database; they simply used the wizards and other easy-to-use Access tools. As business continued to grow at Riverview Veterinary Care Center, Kimberly realized she needed a database expert to further enhance the CareCenter database. She hired Daksha Yatawara, who has a business information systems degree and nine years of experience developing database systems. Daksha spent a few days reviewing the CareCenter database, making sure the database adhered to simple naming standards for the objects and field names to make his future work easier.

Before implementing the enhancements for Kimberly, you'll review the naming conventions for the object names in the CareCenter database.

To review the object naming conventions in the CareCenter database:

1. Make sure you have the Access starting Data Files on your computer.

   Trouble? If you don't have the Access Data Files, you need to get them before you can proceed. Your instructor will either give you the Data Files or ask you to obtain them from a specified location (such as a network drive). If you have any questions about the Data Files, see your instructor or technical support person for assistance.

2. Start Access, and then open the **CareCenter** database from the Access2 > Module folder where your starting Data Files are stored.

   Trouble? If the security warning is displayed below the ribbon, click the Enable Content button.

As shown in Visual Overview 5.1, the Navigation Pane displays the objects grouped by object type. Each object name has a prefix tag—a tbl prefix tag for tables, a qry prefix tag for queries, a frm prefix tag for forms, and a rpt prefix tag for reports. All three characters in each prefix tag are lowercase. The word immediately after the three-character prefix begins with an uppercase letter. Using object prefix tags, you can readily identify the object type, even when the objects have the same base name—for instance, tblOwner, frmOwner, and rptOwnersAndVisits. In addition, object names have no spaces, because other database management systems, such as SQL Server and Oracle, do not permit spaces in object and field names. It is important to adhere to industry standard naming conventions, both to make it easier to convert your database to another DBMS in the future, if necessary, and to develop personal habits that enable you to work seamlessly with other major DBMSs. If Riverview Veterinary Care Center needs to upscale to one of these other systems in the future, using standard naming conventions means that Daksha will have to do less work to make the transition.

PROSKILLS

Teamwork: Following Naming Conventions

Most Access databases have hundreds of fields, objects, and controls. You'll find it easier to identify the type and purpose of these database items when you use a naming convention or standard. Most companies adopt a standard naming convention, such as the one used for the CareCenter database, so that multiple people can develop a database, troubleshoot database problems, and enhance and improve existing databases. When working on a database, a team's tasks are difficult, if not impossible, to perform if a standard naming convention isn't used. In addition, most databases and database samples on websites and in training books use standard naming conventions that are similar to the ones used for the CareCenter database. By following the standard naming convention established by your company or organization, you'll help to ensure smooth collaboration among all team members.

Now you'll create the queries that Kimberly needs.

Using a Pattern Match in a Query

You are already familiar with queries that use an exact match or a range of values (for example, queries that use the > or < comparison operators) to select records. Many other operators are available for creating select queries. These operators let you build more complicated queries that are difficult or impossible to create with exact-match or range-of-values selection criteria.

Kimberly created a list of questions she wants to answer using the CareCenter database:

- Which owners have a zip code beginning with 824?
- What is the owner information for owners located in Cody, Ralston, or Powell?
- What is the owner information for all owners except those located in Cody, Ralston, or Powell?
- What is the owner and visit information for owners in Cody or Powell whose animals were seen offsite or visited during early January?
- What are the first and last names of Riverview Veterinary Care Center owners? Nicknames should be used where listed.
- What is the owner information for owners in a particular city? This query needs to be flexible to allow the user to specify the city.

Next, you will create the queries necessary to answer these questions. Kimberly wants to view the records for all owners whose zip code begins with 824. To answer Kimberly's question, you can create a query that uses a pattern match. A **pattern match** selects records with a value for the designated field that matches the pattern of a simple condition value—in this case, owners with a zip code beginning with 824. You do this using the Like comparison operator.

The **Like comparison operator** selects records by matching field values to a specific pattern that includes one or more of these wildcard characters: asterisk (*), question mark (?), and number symbol (#). The asterisk represents any string of characters, the question mark represents any single character, and the number symbol represents any single digit. Using a pattern match is similar to using an exact match, except that a pattern match includes wildcard characters.

To create the new query, you must first place the tblOwner table field list in the Query window in Design view.

To create the new query in Design view:

1. If necessary, click the **Shutter Bar Open/Close Button** « at the top of the Navigation Pane to close it.
2. On the ribbon, click the **Create** tab.
3. In the Queries group, click the **Query Design** button. The Show Table dialog box opens in front of the Query window in Design view.
4. Click **tblOwner** in the Tables box, click the **Add** button, and then click the **Close** button. The tblOwner table field list is added to the Query window, and the Show Table dialog box closes.
5. Drag the bottom border of the tblOwner window down until you can see the full list of fields.
6. Double-click the **title bar** of the tblOwner field list to highlight all the fields, and then drag the highlighted fields to the first column's Field box in the design grid. Each field is placed in a separate column in the design grid, in the same order that the fields appear in the table. See Figure 5-1.

TIP

You can also double-click a table name to add the table's field list to the Query window.

Figure 5-1 Adding the fields for the pattern match query

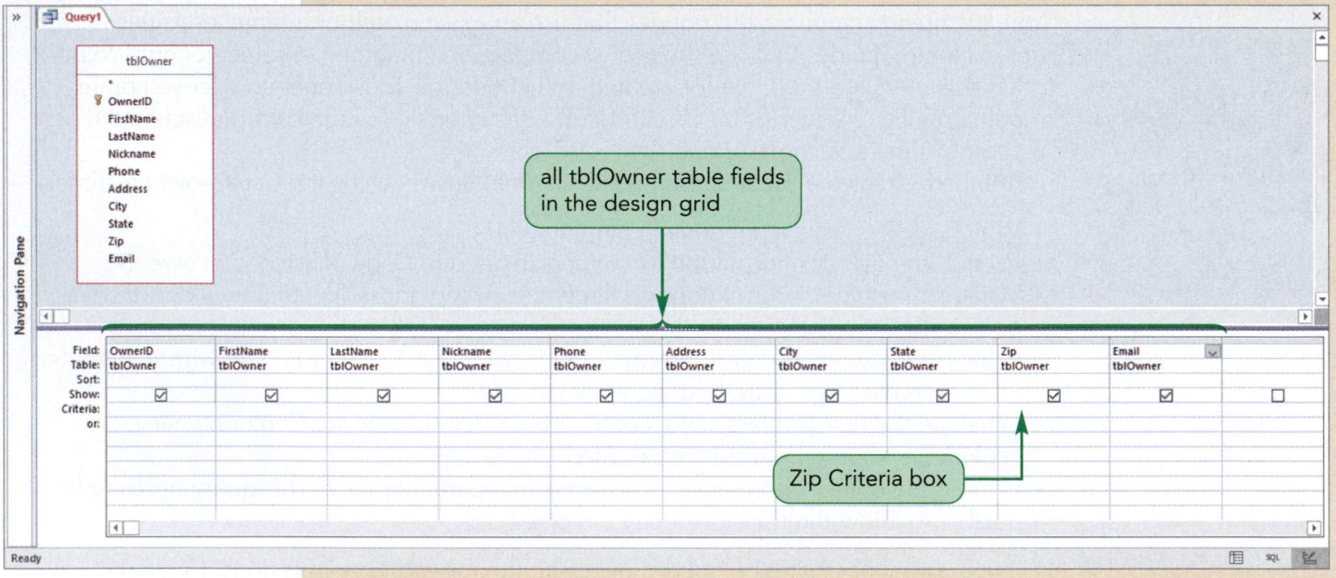

Trouble? If tblOwner.* appears in the first column's Field box, you dragged the * from the field list instead of the highlighted fields. Press the Delete key, and then repeat Step 6.

Now you will enter the pattern match condition Like "824*" for the Zip field. The query will select records with a Zip field value of 824 in positions one through three. The asterisk wildcard character specifies that any characters can appear in the remaining positions of the field value.

To specify records that match the indicated pattern:

TIP

If you omit the Like operator, it is automatically added when you run the query.

1. Click the **Zip Criteria** box, and then type **L**. The Formula AutoComplete menu displays a list of functions beginning with the letter L, but the Like operator is not one of the choices in the list. You'll finish typing the condition.
2. Type **ike "824*"**. See Figure 5-2.

Figure 5-2 Record selection based on matching a specific pattern

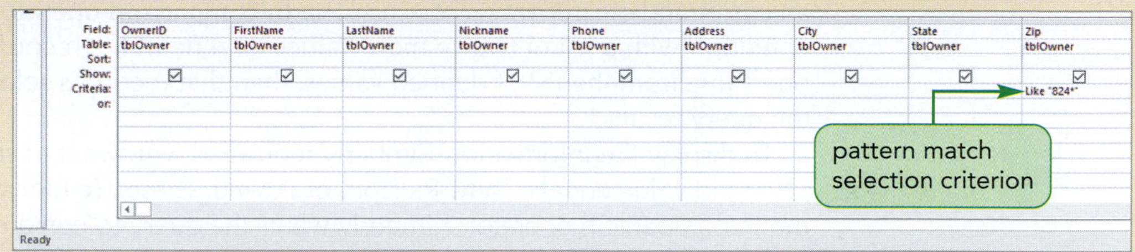

3. Click the **Save** button on the Quick Access Toolbar to open the Save As dialog box.
4. Type **qry824BegZip** in the Query Name box, and then press the **Enter** key. The query is saved, and the name is displayed on the object tab.
5. On the Query Tools Design tab, in the Results group, click the **Run** button. The query results are displayed in the query window. Twenty-three records have zip codes beginning with 824. See Figure 5-3.

Figure 5-3 tblOwner table records for zip codes starting with 824

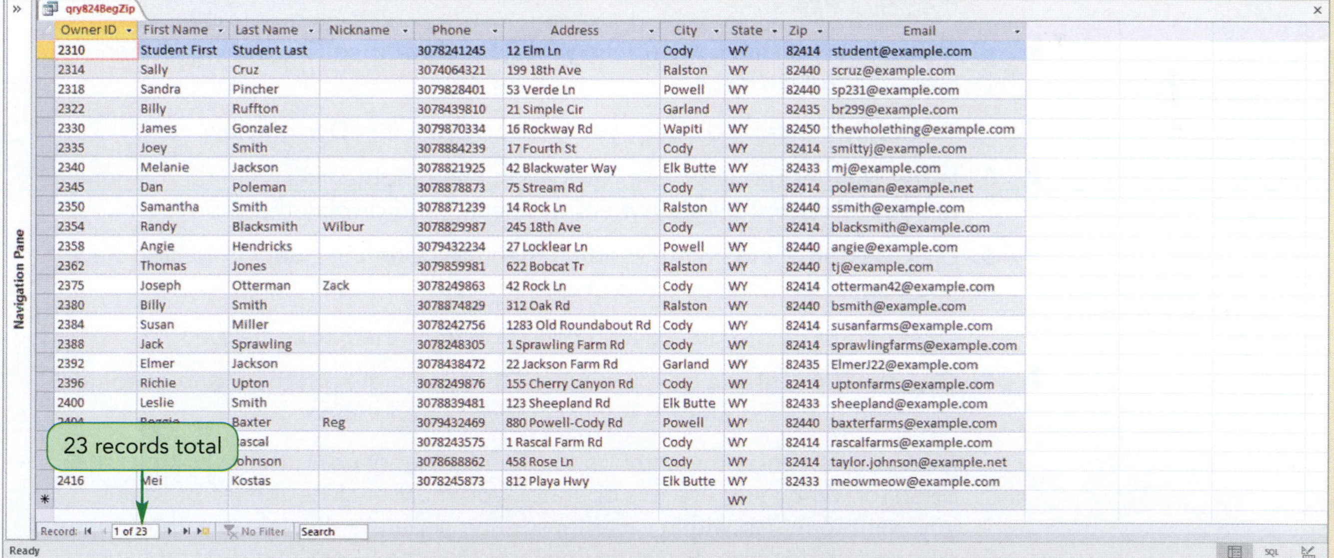

Owner ID	First Name	Last Name	Nickname	Phone	Address	City	State	Zip	Email
2310	Student First	Student Last		3078241245	12 Elm Ln	Cody	WY	82414	student@example.com
2314	Sally	Cruz		3074064321	199 18th Ave	Ralston	WY	82440	scruz@example.com
2318	Sandra	Pincher		3079828401	53 Verde Ln	Powell	WY	82440	sp231@example.com
2322	Billy	Ruffton		3078439810	21 Simple Cir	Garland	WY	82435	br299@example.com
2330	James	Gonzalez		3079870334	16 Rockway Rd	Wapiti	WY	82450	thewholething@example.com
2335	Joey	Smith		3078884239	17 Fourth St	Cody	WY	82414	smittyj@example.com
2340	Melanie	Jackson		3078821925	42 Blackwater Way	Elk Butte	WY	82433	mj@example.com
2345	Dan	Poleman		3078878873	75 Stream Rd	Cody	WY	82414	poleman@example.net
2350	Samantha	Smith		3078871239	14 Rock Ln	Ralston	WY	82440	ssmith@example.com
2354	Randy	Blacksmith	Wilbur	3078829987	245 18th Ave	Cody	WY	82414	blacksmith@example.com
2358	Angie	Hendricks		3079432234	27 Locklear Ln	Powell	WY	82440	angie@example.com
2362	Thomas	Jones		3079859981	622 Bobcat Tr	Ralston	WY	82440	tj@example.com
2375	Joseph	Otterman	Zack	3078249863	42 Rock Ln	Cody	WY	82414	otterman42@example.com
2380	Billy	Smith		3078874829	312 Oak Rd	Ralston	WY	82440	bsmith@example.com
2384	Susan	Miller		3078242756	1283 Old Roundabout Rd	Cody	WY	82414	susanfarms@example.com
2388	Jack	Sprawling		3078248305	1 Sprawling Farm Rd	Cody	WY	82414	sprawlingfarms@example.com
2392	Elmer	Jackson		3078438472	22 Jackson Farm Rd	Garland	WY	82435	ElmerJ22@example.com
2396	Richie	Upton		3078249876	155 Cherry Canyon Rd	Cody	WY	82414	uptonfarms@example.com
2400	Leslie	Smith		3078839481	123 Sheepland Rd	Elk Butte	WY	82433	sheepland@example.com
[illegible]	[illegible]	Baxter	Reg	3079432469	880 Powell-Cody Rd	Powell	WY	82440	baxterfarms@example.com
[illegible]	[illegible]	ascal		3078243575	1 Rascal Farm Rd	Cody	WY	82414	rascalfarms@example.com
[illegible]	[illegible]	ohnson		3078688862	458 Rose Ln	Cody	WY	82414	taylor.johnson@example.net
2416	Mei	Kostas		3078245873	812 Playa Hwy	Elk Butte	WY	82433	meowmeow@example.com
*							WY		

Note that Daksha removed the hyphens from the Phone field values; for example, 3078241245 in the first record used to be 307-824-1245. You'll modify the Phone field later in this module to format its values with hyphens.

6. Change the first record in the table, with Owner ID 2310, so the Last Name and First Name columns contain your last and first names, respectively.
7. Close the qry824BegZip query.

Next, Kimberly asks you to create a query that displays information about owners who live in Cody, Ralston, or Powell. To produce the results Kimberly wants, you'll create a query using a list-of-values match.

Using a List-of-Values Match in a Query

A **list-of-values match** selects records whose value for the designated field matches one of two or more simple condition values. You could accomplish this by including several Or conditions in the design grid, but the In comparison operator provides an easier and clearer way to do this. The **In comparison operator** lets you define a condition with a list of two or more values for a field. If a record's field value matches one value from the list of defined values, then that record is selected and included in the query results.

To display the information Kimberly requested, you want to select records if their City field value equals Cody, Ralston, or Powell. These are the values you will use with the In comparison operator. Kimberly wants the query to contain the same fields as the qry824BegZip query, so you'll make a copy of that query and modify it.

To create the query using a list-of-values match:

1. Open the Navigation Pane.
2. In the Queries group on the Navigation Pane, right-click **qry824BegZip**, and then click **Copy** on the shortcut menu.

   Trouble? If you don't see the qry824BegZip query in the Queries group, press the F5 function key to refresh the object listings in the Navigation pane.
3. Right-click in the empty area in the Navigation Pane below the report and then click **Paste**.
4. In the Query Name box, type **qryCodyRalstonPowellOwners**, and then press the **Enter** key.

   To modify the copied query, you need to open it in Design view.
5. In the Queries group on the Navigation Pane, right-click **qryCodyRalstonPowellOwners** to select it and display the shortcut menu.
6. Click **Design View** on the shortcut menu to open the query in Design view, and then close the Navigation Pane.

   You need to delete the existing condition from the Phone field.
7. Click the **Zip Criteria** box, press the **F2** key to highlight the entire condition, and then press the **Delete** key to remove the condition.

   Now you can enter the criterion for the new query using the In comparison operator. When you use this operator, you must enclose the list of values you want to match within parentheses and separate the values with commas. In addition, for fields defined using the Short Text data type, you enclose each value in quotation marks, although the quotation marks are automatically added if you omit them. For fields defined using the Number or Currency data type, you don't enclose the values in quotation marks.

8. Right-click the **City Criteria** box to open the shortcut menu, click **Zoom** to open the Zoom dialog box, and then type **In ("Cody","Ralston","Powell")**, as shown in Figure 5-4.

Figure 5-4 **Record selection based on matching field values to a list of values**

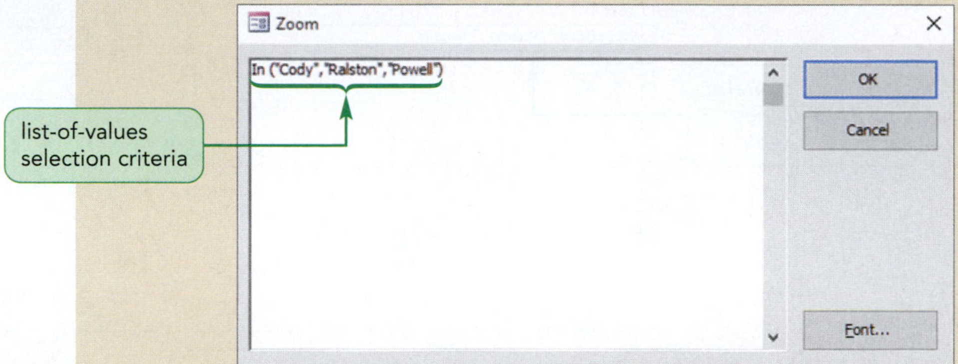

> **TIP**
> After clicking in a box, you can also open its Zoom dialog box by holding down the Shift key and pressing the F2 key.

9. Click the **OK** button to close the Zoom dialog box, and then save and run the query. The recordset is displayed, which shows the 17 records with Cody, Ralston, or Powell in the City field.
10. Close the query.

Kimberly would also like a list of owners who do not live in Cody, Ralston, or Powell. You can provide Kimberly with this information by creating a query with the Not logical operator.

Using the Not Logical Operator in a Query

The **Not logical operator** negates a criterion or selects records for which the designated field does not match the criterion. For example, if you enter *Not "Cody"* in the Criteria box for the City field, the query results show records that do not have the City field value Cody—that is, records of all owners not located in Cody.

To create Kimberly's query, you will combine the Not logical operator with the In comparison operator to select owners whose City field value is not in the list *("Cody","Ralston","Powell")*. The qryCodyRalstonPowellOwners query has the fields that Kimberly needs to see in the query results. Kimberly doesn't need to keep the qryCodyRalstonPowellOwners query, so you'll rename and then modify the query.

To create the query using the Not logical operator:

> **TIP**
> You can rename any type of object, including a table, in the Navigation Pane using the Rename command on the shortcut menu.

1. Open the Navigation Pane.
2. In the Queries group, right-click **qryCodyRalstonPowellOwners**, and then on the shortcut menu click **Rename**.
3. Position the insertion point after "qry," type **Non**, and then press the **Enter** key. The query name is now qryNonCodyRalstonPowellOwners.
4. Open the **qryNonCodyRalstonPowellOwners** query in Design view, and then close the Navigation Pane.

   You need to change the existing condition in the City field to add the Not logical operator.

5. Click the **City Criteria** box, open the Zoom dialog box, click at the beginning of the expression, type **Not**, and then press the **spacebar**. See Figure 5-5.

Figure 5-5 Record selection based on not matching a list of values

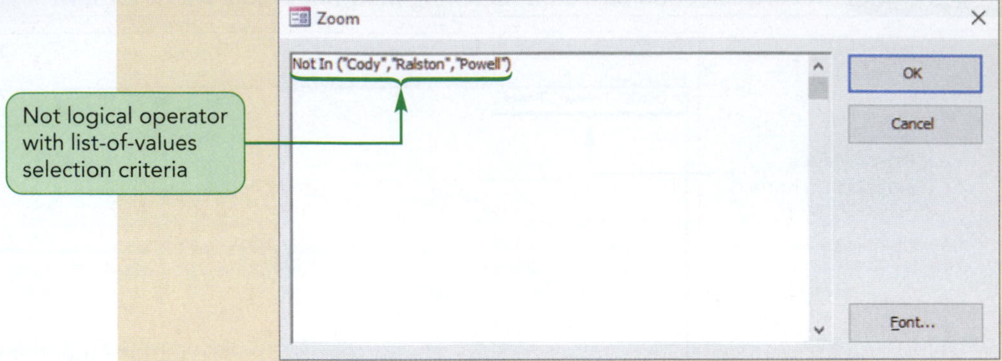

6. Click the **OK** button, and then save and run the query. The recordset displays only those records with a City field value that is not Cody, Ralston, or Powell. The recordset includes a total of nine owner records.
7. Scroll down the datasheet if necessary to make sure that no Cody, Ralston, or Powell owners appear in your results.

   Now you can close and delete the query, because Kimberly does not need to run this query again.
8. Close the query, and then open the Navigation Pane.
9. Right-click **qryNonCodyRalstonPowellOwners**, click **Delete** on the shortcut menu, and then click **Yes** in the dialog box warning that deleting this object will remove it from all groups.

TIP

You can delete any type of object, including a table, in the Navigation Pane using the Delete command on the shortcut menu.

You now are ready to answer Kimberly's question about owners in Cody or Powell who have invoice amounts for less than $75 or who visited during the first week of January.

Using an AutoFilter to Filter Data

Kimberly wants to view the owner first and last names, cities, animal names, visit dates, offsite statuses, and visit reasons for owners in Cody or Powell whose animals either were seen offsite or visited during the first week in January. The qryEarlyJanuaryOrOffSite query contains the same fields Kimberly wants to view. This query also uses the Or logical operator to select records if the OffSite field has a value of true or if the VisitDate field value is between 1/1/2017 and 1/7/2017. These are two of the conditions needed to answer Kimberly's question. You could modify the qryEarlyJanuaryOrOffSite query in Design view to further restrict the records selected to Owners located only in Cody or Powell. However, you can use the AutoFilter feature to choose the city restrictions faster and with more flexibility. You previously used the AutoFilter feature to sort records, and you previously used Filter By Selection to filter records. Now you'll use the AutoFilter feature to filter records.

To filter the records using an AutoFilter:

1. Open the **qryEarlyJanuaryOrOffSite** query in Design view, and then close the Navigation Pane.

   The true condition for the OffSite field selects records for owners whose animals were seen offsite, and the Between #1/1/2017# And #1/7/2017# condition for the VisitDate field selects records for animals whose visit date was in the first week of January 2017. Although the OffSite field is a yes/no field, these values are represented by true (yes) and false (no). Because the conditions are in two different rows, the query uses the Or logical operator. If you wanted to answer Kimberly's question in Design view, you would add a condition for the City field, using either the Or logical operator—"Cody" Or "Powell"—or the In comparison operator—In ("Cody","Powell"). You'd place the condition for the City field in both the Criteria row and in the Or row. The query recordset would include a record only if both conditions in either row are satisfied. Instead of changing the conditions in Design view, though, you'll choose the information Kimberly wants using an AutoFilter.

2. Run the query, and then click the **arrow** on the City column heading to display the AutoFilter menu. See Figure 5-6.

Figure 5-6 Using an AutoFilter to filter records in the query recordset

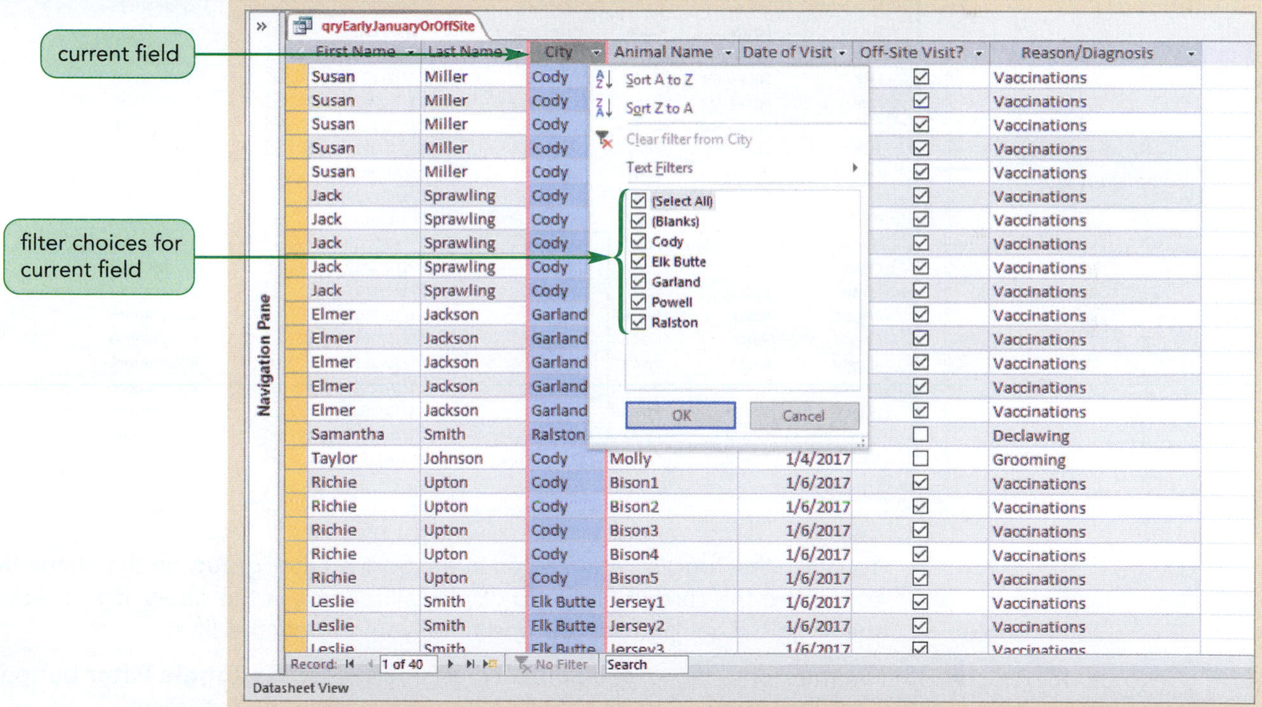

current field

filter choices for current field

The AutoFilter menu lists all City field values that appear in the recordset. A checkmark next to an entry indicates that records with that City field value appear in the recordset. To filter for selected City field values, you uncheck the cities you don't want selected and leave checked the cities you do want selected. You can click the "(Select All)" check box to select or deselect all field values. The "(Blanks)" option includes null values when checked and excludes null values when unchecked. (Recall that a null field value is the absence of a value for the field.)

3. Click the **(Select All)** check box to deselect all check boxes, click the **Cody** check box, and then click the **Powell** check box.

   The two check boxes indicate that the AutoFilter will include only Cody and Powell City field values.

4. Click the **OK** button. The AutoFilter displays the 28 records for owners in Cody and Powell whose animals were seen offsite or who had a visit in the first week in January. See Figure 5-7.

Figure 5-7 Recordset showing results of an AutoFilter

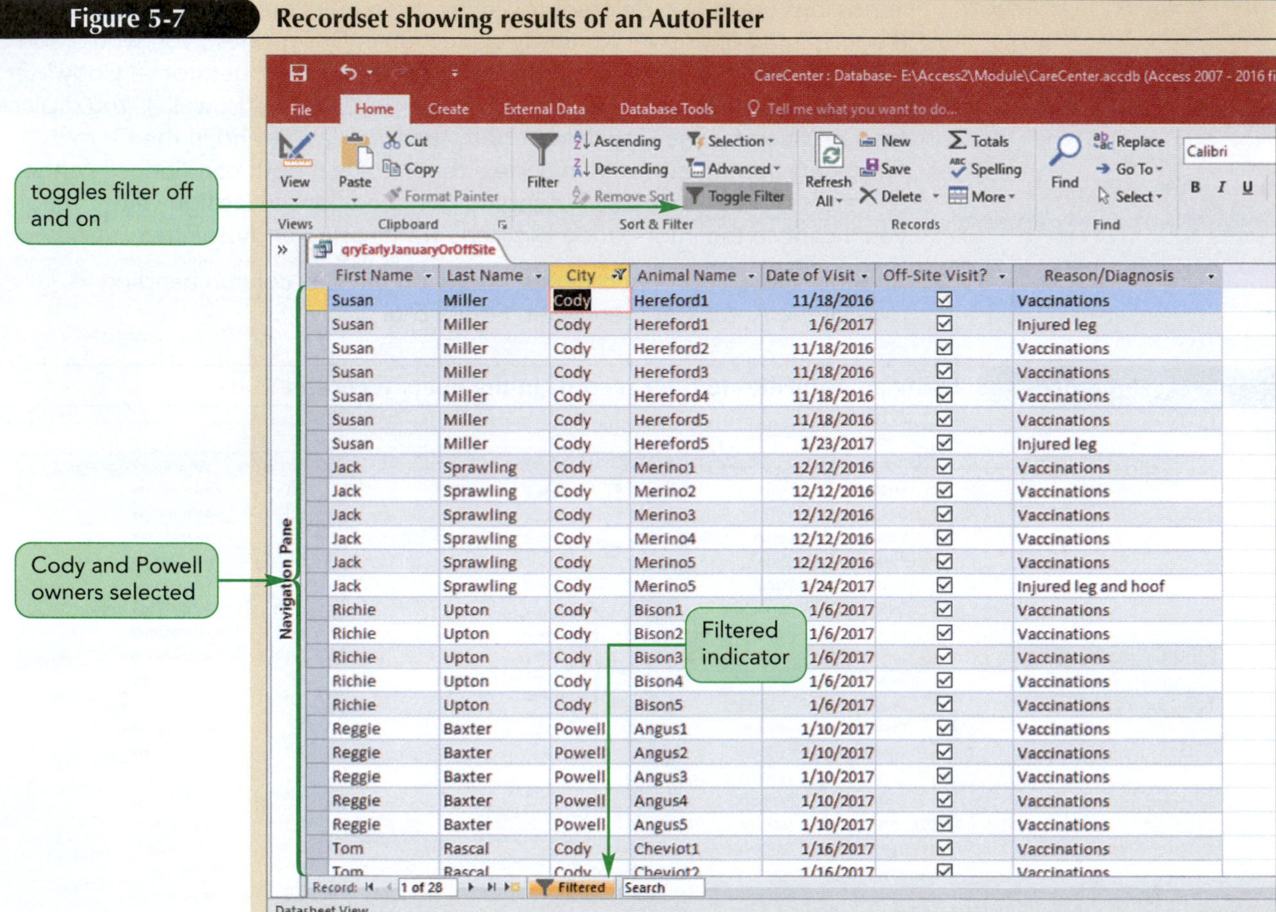

You click the Toggle Filter button in the Sort & Filter group on the Home tab to remove the current filter and display all records in the query. If you click the Toggle Filter button a second time, you reapply the filter.

5. On the Home tab, in the Sort & Filter group, click the **Toggle Filter** button. The filter is removed, and all 40 records appear in the recordset.

6. Click the **Toggle Filter** button. The City filter is applied, displaying the 28 records for owners in Cody and Powell.

7. Save the query and close it.

Next, Kimberly wants to view all fields from the tblOwner table, along with the owner name. If a nickname is available, she would like it to be used in place of the proper first name of the owner.

Assigning a Conditional Value to a Calculated Field

If a field in a record does not contain any information at all, it has a null value. Such a field is also referred to as a null field. A field in a record that contains any data at all—even a single space—is nonnull. Records for owners have nonnull FirstName and LastName field values in the tblOwner table. If an owner does not have a requested nickname, the owner has a null Nickname field value. Kimberly wants to view records from the tblOwner table in order by last name. She wants the owner's nickname to be shown in place of the first name if the Nickname field is nonnull; otherwise, if the Nickname field is null, she wants the FirstName field value to be shown. To produce this information for Kimberly, you need to create a query that includes all fields from the tblOwner table and then add a calculated field that will display the owner name, including either the Nickname field value, if present, or the FirstName field value. The LastName field and either the Nickname or FirstName fields will be separated by a comma and a space.

To combine the LastName and FirstName fields, you'll use the expression *LastName & ", " & FirstName*. The **& (ampersand) operator** is a concatenation operator that joins text expressions. **Concatenation** refers to joining two or more text fields or characters encapsulated in quotes. When you join the LastName field value to the string that contains the comma and space, you are concatenating these two strings. If the LastName field value is Vasquez and the FirstName field value is Katrina, for example, the result of the expression *LastName & ", " & FirstName* is *Vasquez & ", " & Katrina* which results in *Vasquez, Katrina*.

INSIGHT

Using Concatenation

IT professionals generally refer to a piece of text data as a string. Most programming languages include the ability to join two or more strings using concatenation.

Imagine you're working with a database table that contains Title, FirstName, and LastName values for people who have made donations, and you've been asked to add their names to a report. You could add each individual field separately, but the data would look awkward, with each field in a separate column. Alternatively, you could create a calculated field with an expression that combines the fields with spaces into a more readable format, such as "Mr. Jim Sullivan". To do this, you would concatenate the fields with a space separator. The expression to perform this task might look like *=Title & " " & FirstName & " " & LastName.*

To display the correct owner value, you'll use the IIf function. The IIf (Immediate If) function assigns one value to a calculated field or control if a condition is true and a second value if the condition is false. The IIf function has three parts: a condition that is true or false, the result when the condition is true, and the result when the condition is false. Each part of the IIf function is separated by a comma. The condition you'll use is *IsNull(Nickname)*. The IsNull function tests a field value or an expression for a null value; if the field value or expression is null, the result is true; otherwise, the result is false. The expression *IsNull(Nickname)* is true when the Nickname field value is null and is false when the Nickname field value is not null.

For the calculated field, you'll enter *IIf(IsNull(Nickname),LastName & ", " & FirstName,LastName & ", " & Nickname)*. You interpret this expression as follows: If the Nickname field value is null, then set the calculated field value to the concatenation of the LastName field value and the text string ", " and the FirstName field value. If the Nickname field value is not null, then set the calculated field value to the concatenation of the LastName field value and the text string ", " and the Nickname field value.

Now you're ready to create Kimberly's query to display the owner name.

To create the query to display the owner name:

1. Click the **Create** tab, and then in the Queries group, click the **Query Design** button. The Show Table dialog box opens on top of the Query window in Design View.
2. Click **tblOwner** in the Tables box, click the **Add** button, and then click the **Close** button. The tblOwner table field list is placed in the Query window, and the Show Table dialog box closes.

   Kimberly wants all fields from the tblOwner table to appear in the query recordset, with the new calculated field in the first column.
3. Drag the bottom border of the tblOwner field list down until all fields are visible, double-click the title bar of the tblOwner field list to highlight all the fields, and then drag the highlighted fields to the second column's Field box in the design grid. Each field is placed in a separate column in the design grid starting with the second column, in the same order that the fields appear in the table.

   Trouble? If you accidentally drag the highlighted fields to the first column in the design grid, click the OwnerID Field box, and then in the Query Setup group, click the Insert Columns button. Continue with Step 4.

TIP

After clicking in a box, you can also open its Expression Builder dialog box by holding down the Ctrl key and pressing the F2 key.

4. Right-click the blank Field box to the left of the OwnerID field, and then click **Build** on the shortcut menu. The Expression Builder dialog box opens.

   Kimberly wants to use "Owner" as the name of the calculated field, so you'll type that name, followed by a colon, and then you'll choose the IIf function.
5. Type **Owner:** and then press the **spacebar**.
6. Double-click **Functions** in the Expression Elements (left) column, and then click **Built-In Functions**.

Make sure you double-click instead of single-click the IIf function.

7. Scroll down the Expression Categories (middle) column, click **Program Flow**, and then in the Expression Values (right) column, double-click **IIf**. The IIf function is added with four placeholders to the right of the calculated field name in the expression box. See Figure 5-8.

Figure 5-8 IIf function inserted for the calculated field

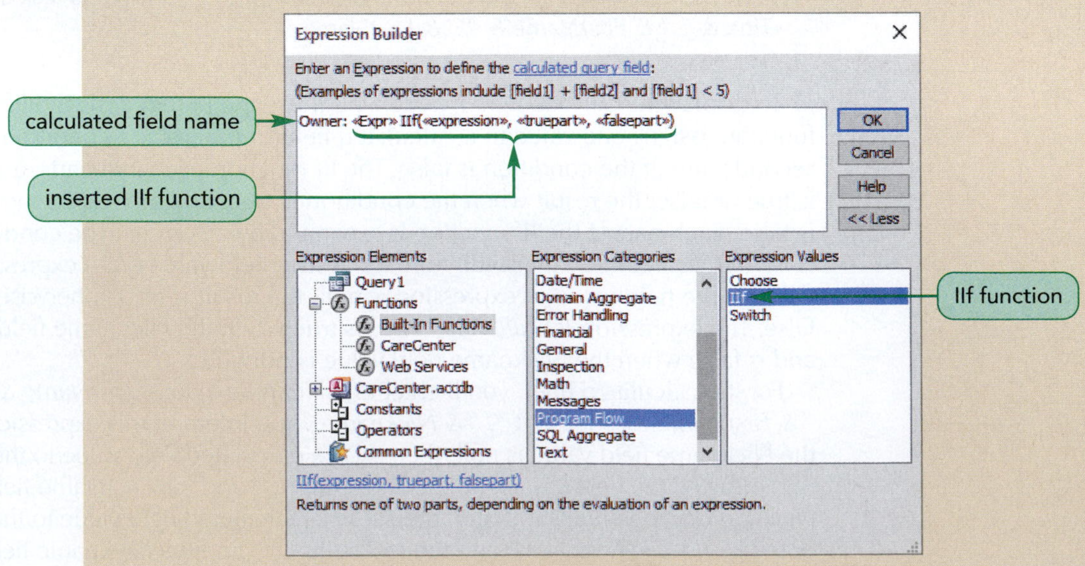

The expression you will create does not need the leftmost placeholder (<<Expr>>), so you'll delete it. You'll replace the second placeholder (<<expression>>) with the condition using the IsNull function, the third placeholder (<<truepart>>) with the expression using the & operator and the FirstName and LastName fields, and the fourth placeholder (<<falsepart>>) with the expression using the & operator and the Nickname and LastName fields.

8. Click **<<Expr>>** in the expression box, and then press the **Delete** key. The first placeholder is deleted.
9. Click **<<expression>>** in the expression box, and then click **Inspection** in the Expression Categories (middle) column.
10. Double-click **IsNull** in the Expression Values (right) column, click **<<expression>>** in the expression box, and then type **Nickname**. You've completed the entry of the condition in the IIf function. See Figure 5-9.

Figure 5-9 After entering the condition for the calculated field's IIf function

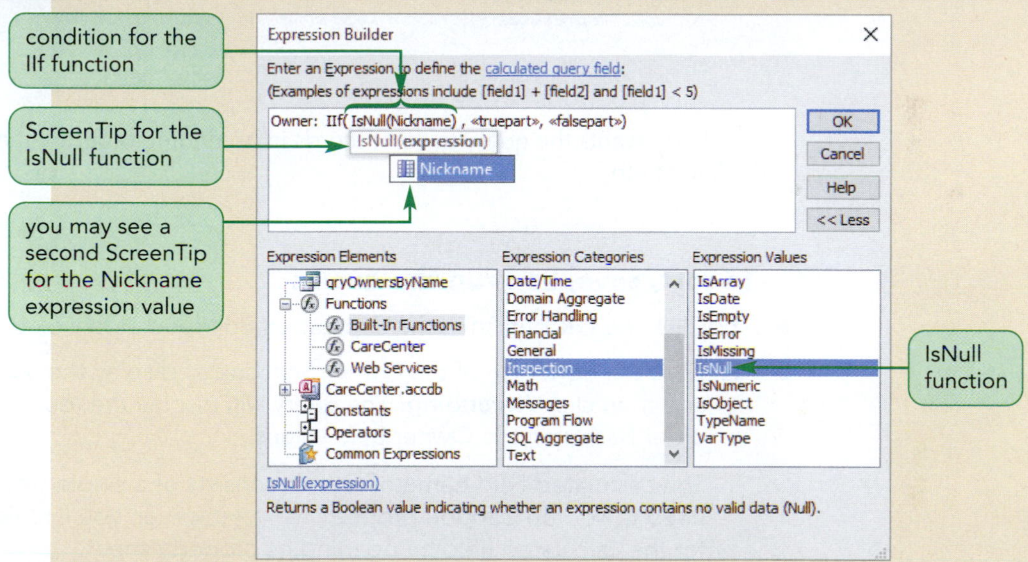

After you typed the first letter of "Nickname," the Formula AutoComplete box displayed a list of functions beginning with the letter N, and a ScreenTip for the IsNull function was displayed above the box. The box closed after you typed the third letter, but the ScreenTip remains on the screen.

Instead of typing the field name of Nickname in the previous step, you could have double-clicked CareCenter.accdb in the Expression Elements column, double-clicked Tables in the Expression Elements column, clicked tblOwner in the Expression Elements column, and then double-clicked Nickname in the Expression Categories column.

Now you'll replace the third placeholder and then the fourth placeholder.

11. Click **<<truepart>>**, and then type **LastName & ", " & FirstName**. Be sure you type a space after the comma within the quotation marks.
12. Click **<<falsepart>>**, and then type **LastName & ", " & Nickname**. Be sure you type a space after the comma within the quotation marks. See Figure 5-10.

Figure 5-10 Completed calculated field

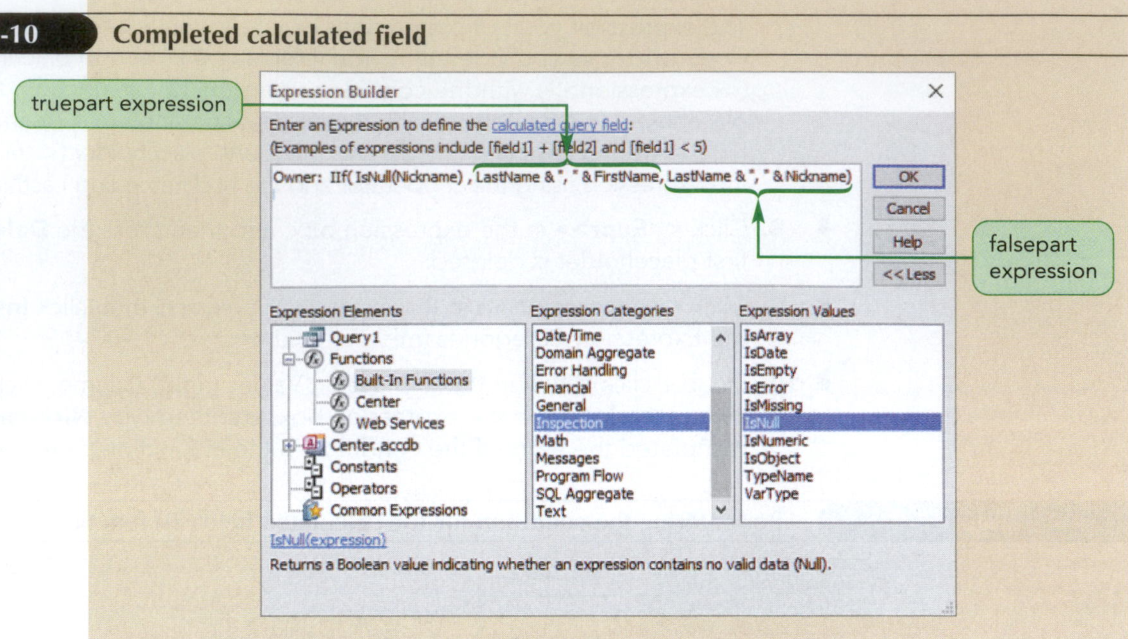

Kimberly wants the query to sort records in ascending order by the Owner calculated field.

To sort, save, and run the query:

1. Click the **OK** button in the Expression Builder dialog box to close it.
2. Click the right side of the Owner Sort box to display the sort order options, and then click **Ascending**. The query will display the records in alphabetical order based on the Owner field values.

   The calculated field name of Owner consists of a single word, so you do not need to set the Caption property for it. However, you'll review the properties for the calculated field by opening its property sheet.
3. On the Query Tools Design tab, in the Show/Hide group, click the **Property Sheet** button. The property sheet opens and displays the properties for the Owner calculated field. See Figure 5-11.

Figure 5-11 Property sheet for the Owner calculated field

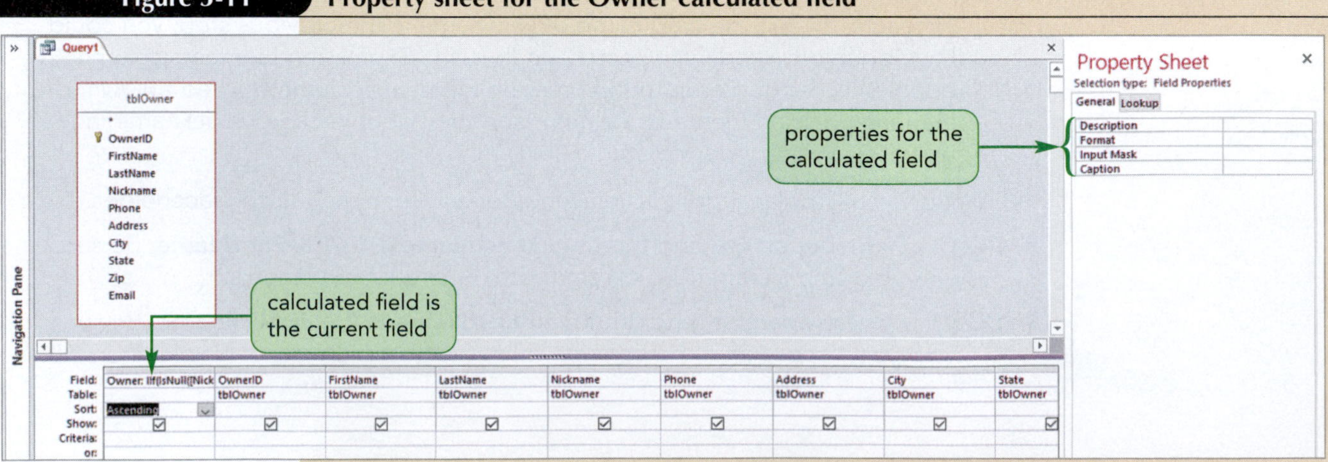

Among the properties for the calculated field, which is the current field, is the Caption property. Leaving the Caption property set to null means that the column name for the calculated field in the query recordset will be Owner, which is the calculated field name. The Property Sheet button is a toggle, so you'll click it again to close the property sheet.

4. Click the **Property Sheet** button again to close the property sheet.
5. Save the query as **qryOwnersByName**, run the query, and then resize the Owner column to its best fit. All records from the tblOwner table are displayed in alphabetical order by the Owner field. See Figure 5-12.

Figure 5-12 **Completed query displaying the Owner calculated field**

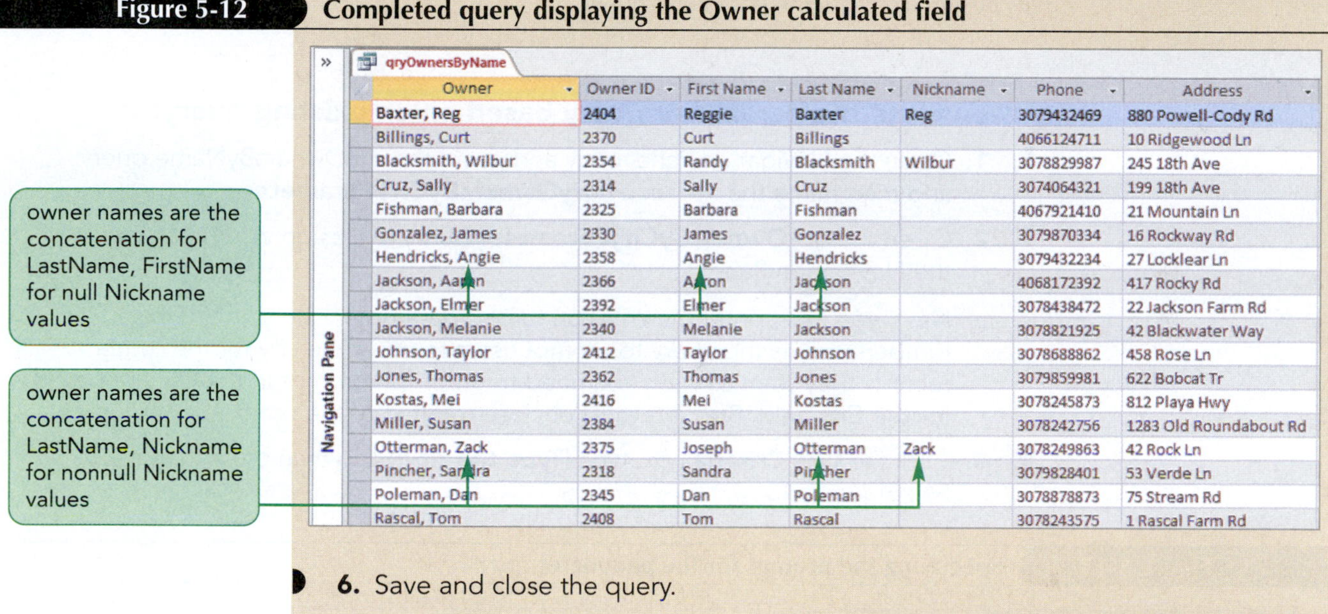

Owner	Owner ID	First Name	Last Name	Nickname	Phone	Address
Baxter, Reg	2404	Reggie	Baxter	Reg	3079432469	880 Powell-Cody Rd
Billings, Curt	2370	Curt	Billings		4066124711	10 Ridgewood Ln
Blacksmith, Wilbur	2354	Randy	Blacksmith	Wilbur	3078829987	245 18th Ave
Cruz, Sally	2314	Sally	Cruz		3074064321	199 18th Ave
Fishman, Barbara	2325	Barbara	Fishman		4067921410	21 Mountain Ln
Gonzalez, James	2330	James	Gonzalez		3079870334	16 Rockway Rd
Hendricks, Angie	2358	Angie	Hendricks		3079432234	27 Locklear Ln
Jackson, Aaron	2366	Aaron	Jackson		4068172392	417 Rocky Rd
Jackson, Elmer	2392	Elmer	Jackson		3078438472	22 Jackson Farm Rd
Jackson, Melanie	2340	Melanie	Jackson		3078821925	42 Blackwater Way
Johnson, Taylor	2412	Taylor	Johnson		3078688862	458 Rose Ln
Jones, Thomas	2362	Thomas	Jones		3079859981	622 Bobcat Tr
Kostas, Mei	2416	Mei	Kostas		3078245873	812 Playa Hwy
Miller, Susan	2384	Susan	Miller		3078242756	1283 Old Roundabout Rd
Otterman, Zack	2375	Joseph	Otterman	Zack	3078249863	42 Rock Ln
Pincher, Sandra	2318	Sandra	Pincher		3079828401	53 Verde Ln
Poleman, Dan	2345	Dan	Poleman		3078878873	75 Stream Rd
Rascal, Tom	2408	Tom	Rascal		3078243575	1 Rascal Farm Rd

6. Save and close the query.

You're now ready to create the query to satisfy Kimberly's request for information about owners in a particular city.

Creating a Parameter Query

Kimberly's next request is for records in the qryOwnersByName query for owners in a particular city. For this query, she wants to specify a city, such as Cody or Garland, each time she runs the query.

To create this query, you will copy, rename, and modify the qryOwnersByName query. You could create a simple condition using an exact match for the City field, but you would need to change it in Design view every time you run the query. Alternatively, Kimberly or a member of her staff could filter the qryOwnersByName query for the city records they want to view. Instead, you will create a parameter query. A **parameter query** displays a dialog box that prompts the user to enter one or more criteria values when the query is run. In this case, you want to create a query that prompts for the city and selects only those owner records with that City field value from the table. You will enter the prompt in the Criteria box for the City field. When the query runs, it will open a dialog box and prompt you to enter the city. The query results will then be created, just as if you had changed the criteria in Design view.

REFERENCE

Creating a Parameter Query

- Create a select query that includes all fields to appear in the query results.
- Choose the sort fields, and set the criteria that do not change when you run the query.
- Decide which fields to use as prompts when the query runs. In the Criteria box for each of these fields, type the prompt you want to appear in a dialog box when you run the query, and enclose the prompt in brackets.

You'll copy and rename the qryOwnersByName query now, and then you'll change its design to create the parameter query.

To create the parameter query based on an existing query:

1. Open the Navigation Pane, copy and paste the qryOwnersByName query, and then name the new copy **qryOwnersByCityParameter**.
2. Open the **qryOwnersByCityParameter** query in Design view, and then close the Navigation Pane.

   Next, you must enter the criterion for the parameter query. In this case, Kimberly wants the query to prompt users to enter the city for the owner records they want to view. You need to enter the prompt in the Criteria box for the City field. Brackets must enclose the text of the prompt.
3. Click the **City Criteria** box, type **[Type the city:]** and then press the **Enter** key. See Figure 5-13.

Figure 5-13 Specifying the prompt for the parameter query

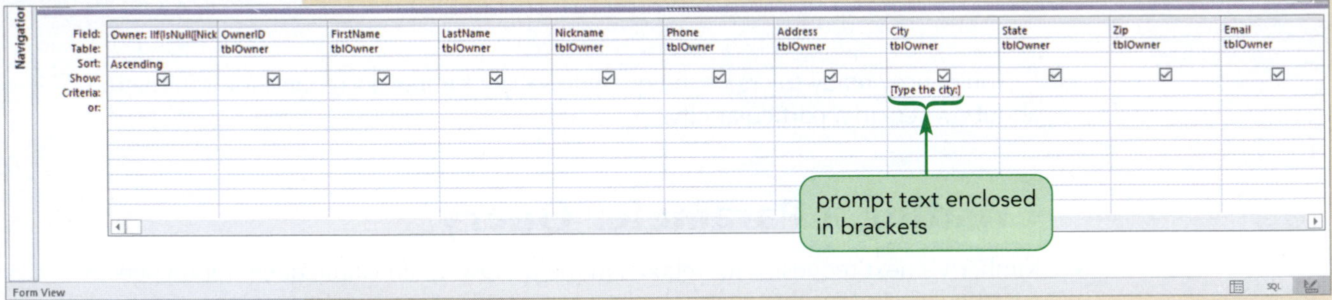

4. Save and run the query. A dialog box is displayed, prompting you for the name of the city. See Figure 5-14.

Figure 5-14 Enter Parameter Value dialog box

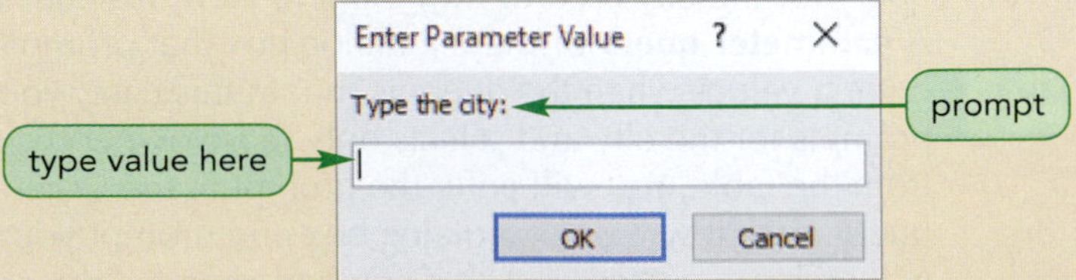

TIP

You must enter a value that matches the spelling of a City field value, but you can use either lowercase or uppercase letters.

The bracketed text you specified in the Criteria box of the City field appears above a box, in which you must type a City field value. Kimberly wants to see all owners in Cody.

5. Type **Cody**, press the **Enter** key, and then scroll the datasheet to the right, if necessary, to display the City field values. The recordset displays the data for the 10 owners in Cody. See Figure 5-15.

Figure 5-15 Results of the parameter query

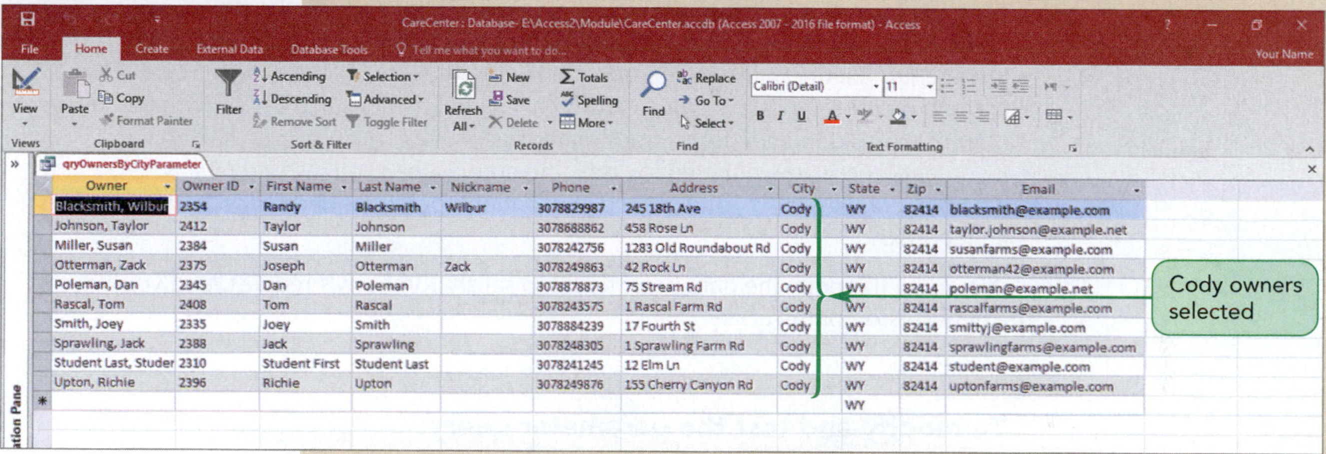

Owner	Owner ID	First Name	Last Name	Nickname	Phone	Address	City	State	Zip	Email
Blacksmith, Wilbur	2354	Randy	Blacksmith	Wilbur	3078829987	245 18th Ave	Cody	WY	82414	blacksmith@example.com
Johnson, Taylor	2412	Taylor	Johnson		3078688862	458 Rose Ln	Cody	WY	82414	taylor.johnson@example.net
Miller, Susan	2384	Susan	Miller		3078242756	1283 Old Roundabout Rd	Cody	WY	82414	susanfarms@example.com
Otterman, Zack	2375	Joseph	Otterman	Zack	3078249863	42 Rock Ln	Cody	WY	82414	otterman42@example.com
Poleman, Dan	2345	Dan	Poleman		3078878873	75 Stream Rd	Cody	WY	82414	poleman@example.net
Rascal, Tom	2408	Tom	Rascal		3078243575	1 Rascal Farm Rd	Cody	WY	82414	rascalfarms@example.com
Smith, Joey	2335	Joey	Smith		3078884239	17 Fourth St	Cody	WY	82414	smittyj@example.com
Sprawling, Jack	2388	Jack	Sprawling		3078248305	1 Sprawling Farm Rd	Cody	WY	82414	sprawlingfarms@example.com
Student Last, Studer	2310	Student First	Student Last		3078241245	12 Elm Ln	Cody	WY	82414	student@example.com
Upton, Richie	2396	Richie	Upton		3078249876	155 Cherry Canyon Rd	Cody	WY	82414	uptonfarms@example.com

Kimberly asks what happens if she doesn't enter a value in the dialog box when she runs the qryOwnersByCityParameter query. You can run the query again to show Kimberly the answer to her question.

6. Switch to Design view, and then run the query. The Enter Parameter Value dialog box opens.

   If you click the OK button or press the Enter key, you'll run the parameter query without entering a value for the City field criterion.

7. Click the **OK** button. No records are displayed in the query results.

When you run the parameter query and enter "Cody" in the dialog box, the query runs just as if you had entered "Cody" in the City Criteria box in the design grid and displays all Cody owner records. When you do not enter a value in the dialog box, the query runs as if you had entered "null" in the City Criteria box. Because none of the records has a null City field value, no records are displayed. Kimberly asks if there's a way to display records for a selected City field value when she enters its value in the dialog box and to display all records when she doesn't enter a value.

Creating a More Flexible Parameter Query

Most users want a parameter query to display the records that match the parameter value the user enters or to display all records when the user doesn't enter a parameter value. To provide this functionality, you can change the value in the Criteria box in the design grid for the specified column. For example, you could change an entry for a City field from *[Type the city:]* to *Like [Type the city:] & "*"*. That is, you can prefix the Like operator to the original criterion and concatenate the criterion to a wildcard character. When you run the parameter query with this new entry, one of the following recordsets will be displayed:

- If you enter a specific City field value in the dialog box, such as *Belfry*, the entry is the same as *Like "Belfry" & "*"*, which becomes *Like "Belfry*"* after the concatenation operation. That is, all records are selected whose City field values have Belfry in the first six positions and any characters in the remaining positions. If the table on which the query is based contains records with City field values of Belfry, only those records are displayed. However, if the table on which the query is based also contains records with City field values of Belfry City, then both the Belfry and the Belfry City records would be displayed.
- If you enter a letter in the dialog box, such as *B*, the entry is the same as *Like "B*"*, and the recordset displays all records with City field values that begin with the letter B, which would include Belfry and Bearcreek.
- If you enter no value in the dialog box, the entry is the same as *Like Null & "*"*, which becomes *Like "*"* after the concatenation operation, and the recordset displays all records.

Now you'll modify the parameter query to satisfy Kimberly's request, and you'll test the new version of the query.

To modify and test the parameter query:

1. Switch to Design view.
2. Click the **City Criteria** box, and then open the **Zoom** dialog box.

   You'll use the Zoom dialog box to modify the value in the City Criteria box.
3. Click to the left of the expression in the Zoom dialog box, type **Like**, press the **spacebar**, and then press the **End** key.
4. Press the **spacebar**, type **&**, press the **spacebar**, and then type **"*"** as shown in Figure 5-16.

   Be sure you type "*" at the end of the expression.

Figure 5-16 **Modified City Criteria value in the Zoom dialog box**

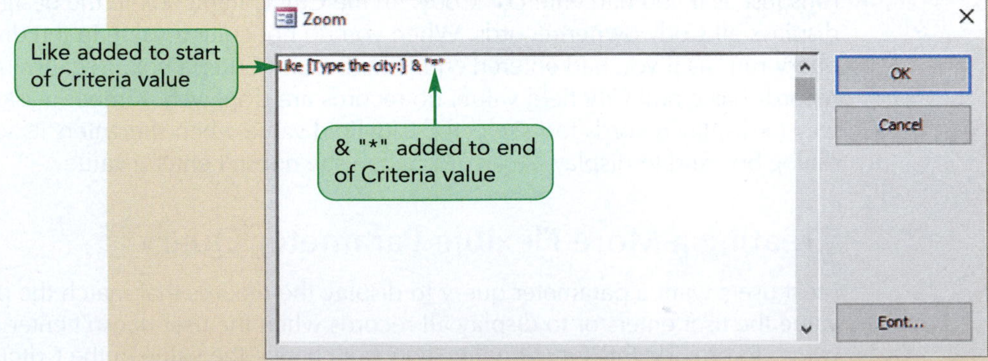

Now you can test the modified parameter query.

5. Click the **OK** button to close the Zoom dialog box, save your query design changes, and then run the query.

   First, you'll test the query to display owners in Powell.

6. Type **Powell**, and then press the **Enter** key. The recordset displays the data for the three owners in Powell.

   Now you'll test the query without entering a value when prompted.

7. Switch to Design view, run the query, and then click the **OK** button. The recordset displays all 26 original records from the tblOwner table.

   Finally, you'll test how the query performs when you enter B in the dialog box.

8. On the Home tab, in the Records group, click the **Refresh All** button to open the Enter Parameter Value dialog box.

9. Type **B**, press the **Enter** key, and then scroll to the right, if necessary, to display the City field values. The recordset displays the two records for owners in Belfry and Bearcreek.

10. Close the query.

11. If you are not continuing on to the next session, close the CareCenter database, and then click the **Yes** button if necessary to empty the Clipboard.

The queries you created will make the CareCenter database easier to use. In the next session, you'll use query wizards to create three different types of queries, and you'll use Design view to create a top values query.

REVIEW

Session 5.1 Quick Check

1. According to the naming conventions used in this session, you use the ______________ prefix tag to identify queries.
2. Which comparison operator selects records based on a specific pattern?
3. What is the purpose of the asterisk (*) in a pattern match query?
4. When do you use the In comparison operator?
5. How do you negate a selection criterion?
6. The ______________ function returns one of two values based on whether the condition being tested is true or false.
7. When do you use a parameter query?

Session 5.2 Visual Overview:

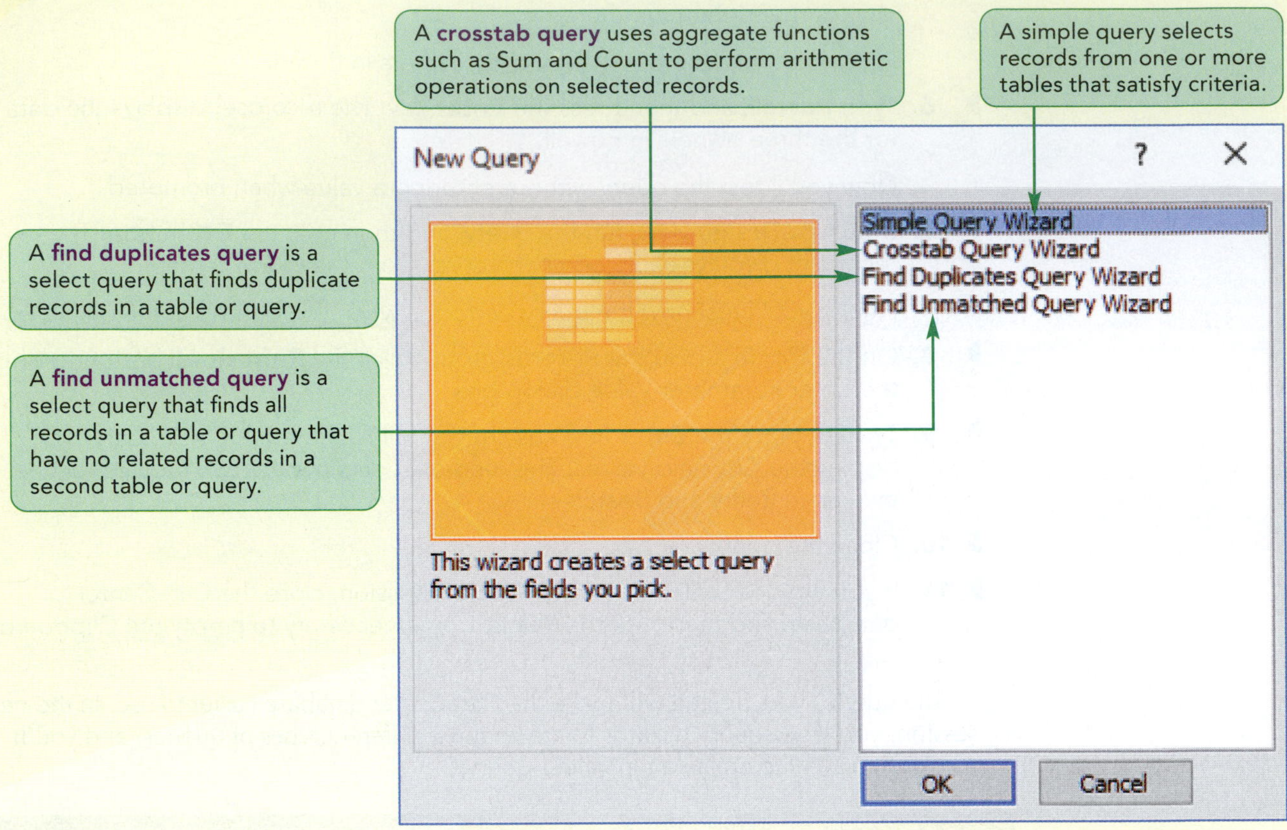

A crosstab query uses aggregate functions such as Sum and Count to perform arithmetic operations on selected records.
A simple query selects records from one or more tables that satisfy criteria.
A find duplicates query is a select query that finds duplicate records in a table or query.
A find unmatched query is a select query that finds all records in a table or query that have no related records in a second table or query.
New Query
Simple Query Wizard
Crosstab Query Wizard
Find Duplicates Query Wizard
Find Unmatched Query Wizard
This wizard creates a select query from the fields you pick.
OK
Cancel

Each column and row intersection will display the sum of the InvoiceAmt values.

The selected field (InvoiceAmt) is used in the calculations for each column and row intersection.

This option determines whether to display an overall totals column in the crosstab query.

The crosstab query will display one column for the paid invoices and a second column for the unpaid invoices.

The crosstab query will display one row for each unique City field value.

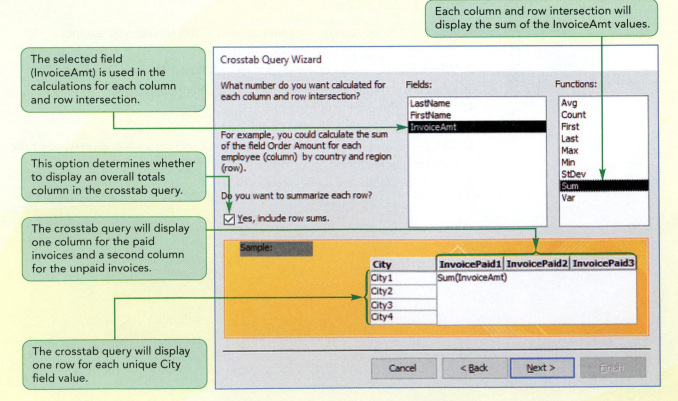

Crosstab Query Wizard

What number do you want calculated for each column and row intersection?

Fields:
LastName
FirstName
InvoiceAmt

Functions:
Avg
Count
First
Last
Max
Min
StDev
Sum
Var

For example, you could calculate the sum of the field Order Amount for each employee (column) by country and region (row).

Do you want to summarize each row?

Yes, include row sums.

Sample:

City	InvoicePaid1	InvoicePaid2	InvoicePaid3
City1	Sum(InvoiceAmt)		
City2			
City3			
City4			

Cancel | < Back | Next > | Finish

Advanced Query Wizards

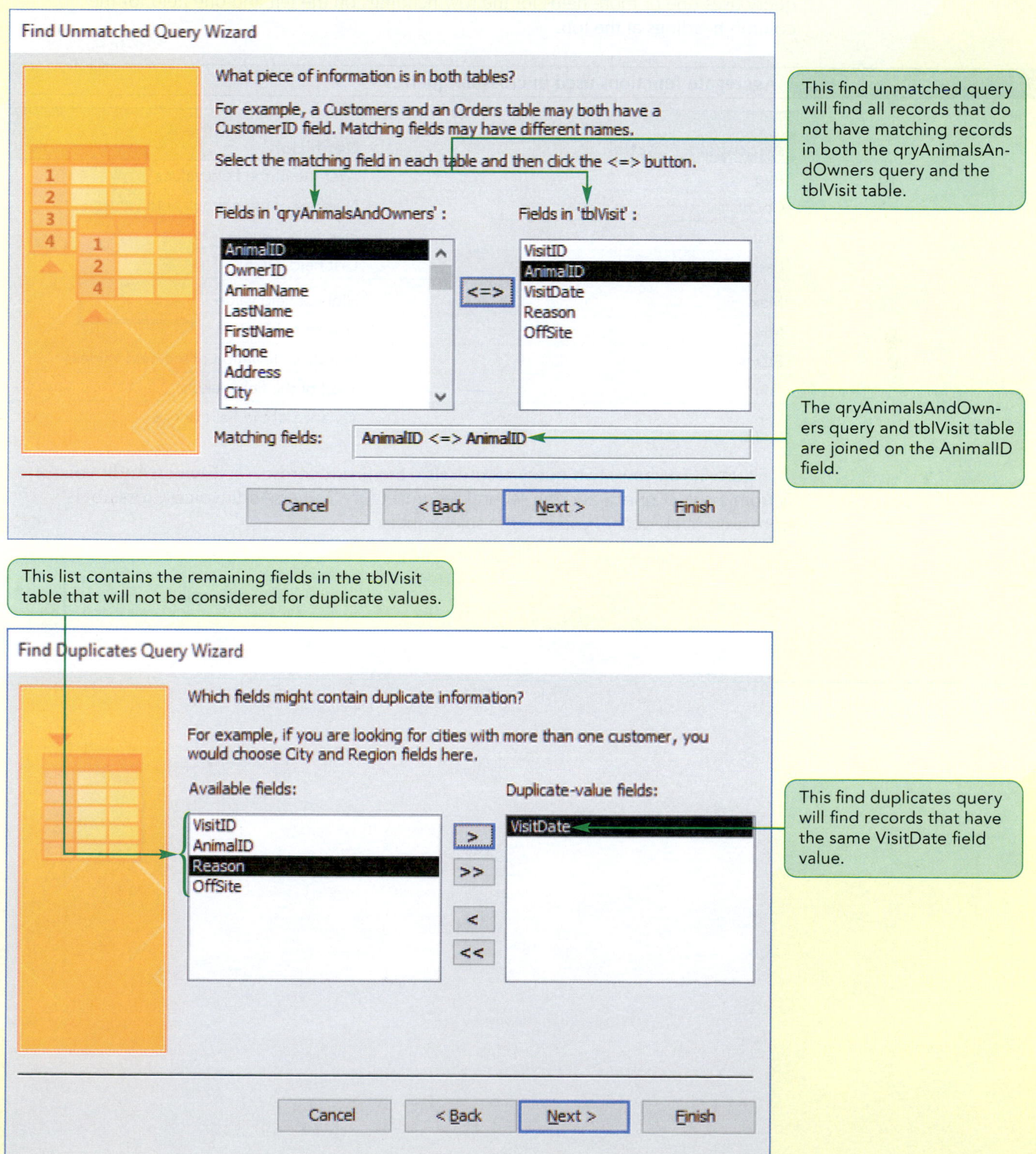

Creating a Crosstab Query

Kimberly wants to analyze the Riverview Veterinary Care Center invoices by city, so she can view the paid and unpaid invoice amounts for all owners located in each city. Crosstab queries use the aggregate functions shown in Figure 5-17 to perform arithmetic operations on selected records. A crosstab query can also display one additional aggregate function value that summarizes the set of values in each row. The crosstab query uses one or more fields for the row headings on the left and one field for the column headings at the top.

Figure 5-17 **Aggregate functions used in crosstab queries**

Aggregate Function	Definition
Avg	Average of the field values
Count	Number of the nonnull field values
First	First field value
Last	Last field value
Max	Highest field value
Min	Lowest field value
StDev	Standard deviation of the field values
Sum	Total of the field values
Var	Variance of the field values

Figure 5-18 shows two query recordsets—the first recordset (qryOwnersAndInvoices) is from a select query, and the second recordset (qryOwnersAndInvoicesCrosstab) is from a crosstab query based on the select query.

Figure 5-18 Comparing a select query to a crosstab query

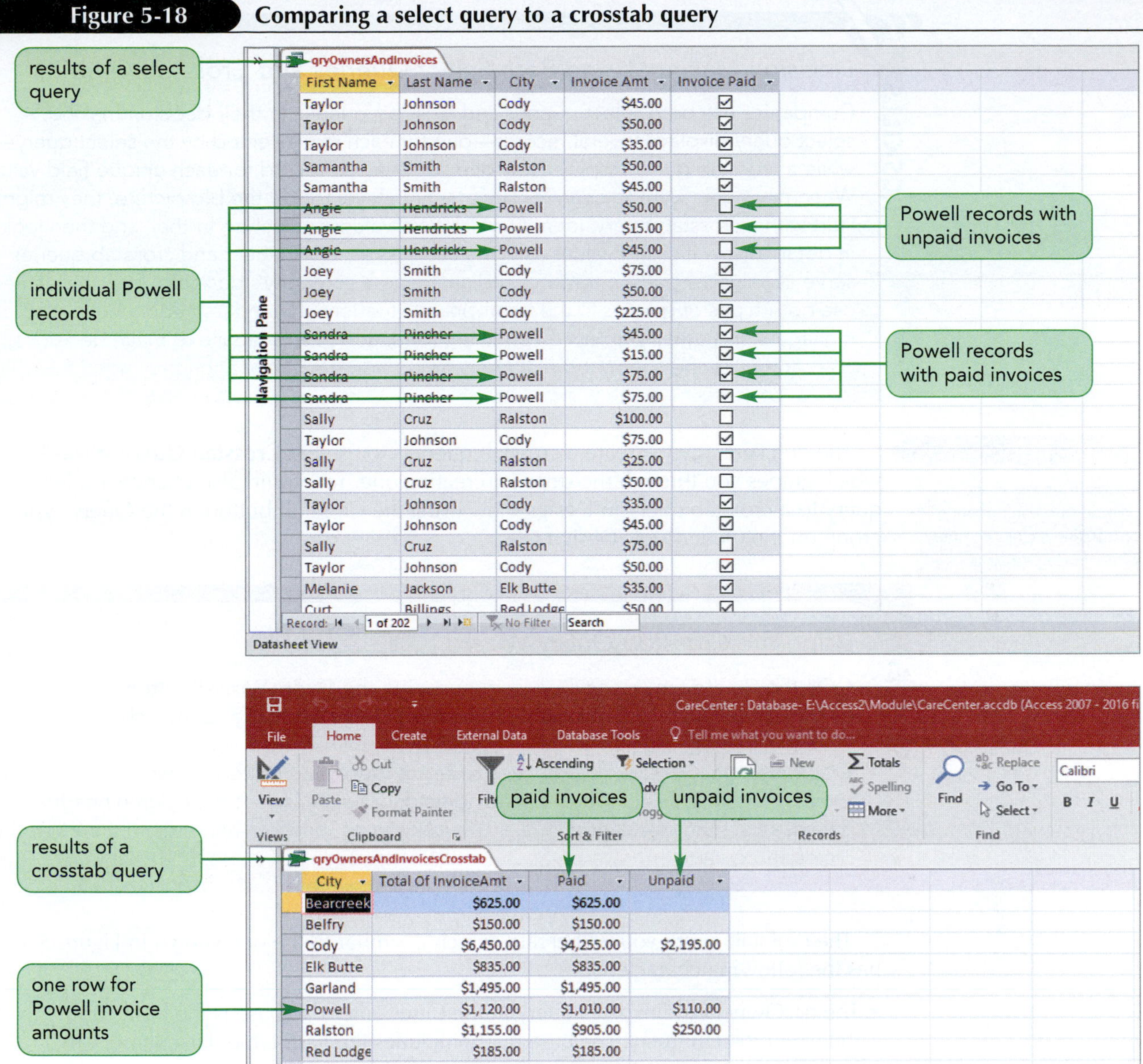

First Name	Last Name	City	Invoice Amt	Invoice Paid
Taylor	Johnson	Cody	$45.00	☑
Taylor	Johnson	Cody	$50.00	☑
Taylor	Johnson	Cody	$35.00	☑
Samantha	Smith	Ralston	$50.00	☑
Samantha	Smith	Ralston	$45.00	☑
Angie	Hendricks	Powell	$50.00	☐
Angie	Hendricks	Powell	$15.00	☐
Angie	Hendricks	Powell	$45.00	☐
Joey	Smith	Cody	$75.00	☑
Joey	Smith	Cody	$50.00	☑
Joey	Smith	Cody	$225.00	☑
Sandra	Pincher	Powell	$45.00	☑
Sandra	Pincher	Powell	$15.00	☑
Sandra	Pincher	Powell	$75.00	☑
Sandra	Pincher	Powell	$75.00	☑
Sally	Cruz	Ralston	$100.00	☐
Taylor	Johnson	Cody	$75.00	☑
Sally	Cruz	Ralston	$25.00	☐
Sally	Cruz	Ralston	$50.00	☐
Taylor	Johnson	Cody	$35.00	☑
Taylor	Johnson	Cody	$45.00	☑
Sally	Cruz	Ralston	$75.00	☐
Taylor	Johnson	Cody	$50.00	☑
Melanie	Jackson	Elk Butte	$35.00	☑
Curt	Billings	Red Lodge	$50.00	☑

City	Total Of InvoiceAmt	Paid	Unpaid
Bearcreek	$625.00	$625.00	
Belfry	$150.00	$150.00	
Cody	$6,450.00	$4,255.00	$2,195.00
Elk Butte	$835.00	$835.00	
Garland	$1,495.00	$1,495.00	
Powell	$1,120.00	$1,010.00	$110.00
Ralston	$1,155.00	$905.00	$250.00
Red Lodge	$185.00	$185.00	

The qryOwnersAndInvoices query, a select query, joins the tblOwner, tblVisit, and tblBilling tables to display selected data from those tables for all invoices. The qryOwnersAndInvoicesCrosstab query, a crosstab query, uses the qryOwnersAndInvoices query as its source query and displays one row for each unique City field value. The City column in the crosstab query identifies each row. The crosstab query uses the Sum aggregate function on the InvoiceAmt field to produce the displayed values in the Paid and Unpaid columns for each City row. An entry in the Total Of InvoiceAmt column represents the sum of the Paid and Unpaid values for the City field value in that row.

PROSKILLS

Decision Making: Using Both Select Queries and Crosstab Queries

Companies use both select queries and crosstab queries in their decision making. A select query displays several records—one for each row selected by the select query—while a crosstab query displays only one summarized record for each unique field value. When managers want to analyze data at a high level to see the big picture, they might start with a crosstab query, identify which field values to analyze further, and then look in detail at specific field values using select queries. Both select and crosstab queries serve as valuable tools in tracking and analyzing a company's business, and companies use both types of queries in the appropriate situations. By understanding how managers and other employees use the information in a database to make decisions, you can create the correct type of query to provide the information they need.

TIP

Microsoft Access Help provides more information on creating a crosstab query without using a wizard.

The quickest way to create a crosstab query is to use the **Crosstab Query Wizard**, which guides you through the steps for creating one. You could also change a select query to a crosstab query in Design view using the Crosstab button in the Query Type group on the Query Tools Design tab.

REFERENCE

Using the Crosstab Query Wizard

- On the Create tab, in the Queries group, click the Query Wizard button.
- In the New Query dialog box, click Crosstab Query Wizard, and then click the OK button.
- Complete the Wizard dialog boxes to select the table or query on which to base the crosstab query, select the row heading field (or fields), select the column heading field, select the calculation field and its aggregate function, and enter a name for the crosstab query.

The crosstab query you will create, which is similar to the one shown in Figure 5-18, has the following characteristics:

- The qryOwnersAndInvoices query in the CareCenter database is the basis for the new crosstab query. The base query includes the LastName, FirstName, City, InvoiceAmt, and InvoicePaid fields.
- The City field is the leftmost column in the crosstab query and identifies each crosstab query row.
- The values from the InvoicePaid field, which is a Yes/No field, identify the rightmost columns of the crosstab query.
- The crosstab query applies the Sum aggregate function to the InvoiceAmt field values and displays the resulting total values in the Paid and Unpaid columns of the query results.
- The grand total of the InvoiceAmt field values appears for each row in a column with the heading Total Of InvoiceAmt.

Next you will create the crosstab query based on the qryOwnersAndInvoices query.

To start the Crosstab Query Wizard:

1. If you took a break after the previous session, make sure that the CareCenter database is open and the Navigation Pane is closed.

   Trouble? If the security warning is displayed below the ribbon, click the Enable Content button next to the security warning.

2. Click the **Create** tab on the ribbon.
3. In the Queries group, click the **Query Wizard** button. The New Query dialog box opens.
4. Click **Crosstab Query Wizard**, and then click the **OK** button. The first Crosstab Query Wizard dialog box opens.

You'll now use the Crosstab Query Wizard to create the crosstab query for Kimberly.

To finish the Crosstab Query Wizard:

1. In the View section, click the **Queries** option button to display the list of queries in the CareCenter database, and then click **Query: qryOwnersAndInvoices**. See Figure 5-19.

Figure 5-19 Choosing the query for the crosstab query

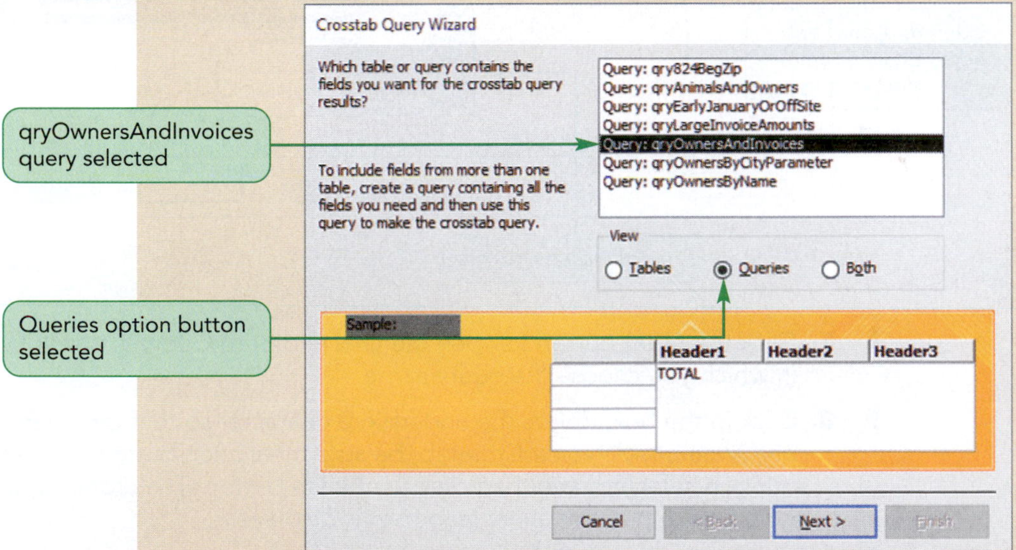

2. Click the **Next** button to open the next Crosstab Query Wizard dialog box. This is the dialog box where you choose the field (or fields) for the *row* headings. Because Kimberly wants the crosstab query to display one row for each unique City field value, you will select that field for the row headings.
3. In the Available Fields box, click **City**, and then click the > button to move the City field to the Selected Fields box.
4. Click the **Next** button to open the next Crosstab Query Wizard dialog box, in which you select the field values that will serve as column headings. Kimberly wants to see the paid and unpaid total invoice amounts, so you need to select the InvoicePaid field for the column headings.

TIP

When you select a field, the sample crosstab query in the dialog box changes to illustrate your choice.

5. Click **InvoicePaid** in the box, and then click the **Next** button.

   In the next Crosstab Query Wizard dialog box, you choose the field that will be calculated for each row and column intersection and the function to use for the calculation. The results of the calculation will appear in the row and column intersections in the query results. Kimberly needs to calculate the sum of the InvoiceAmt field value for each row and column intersection.

6. Click **InvoiceAmt** in the Fields box, click **Sum** in the Functions box, and then make sure that the "Yes, include row sums" check box is checked. The "Yes, include row sums" option creates a column showing the overall totals for the values in each row of the query recordset. See Figure 5-20.

Figure 5-20 Completed crosstab query design

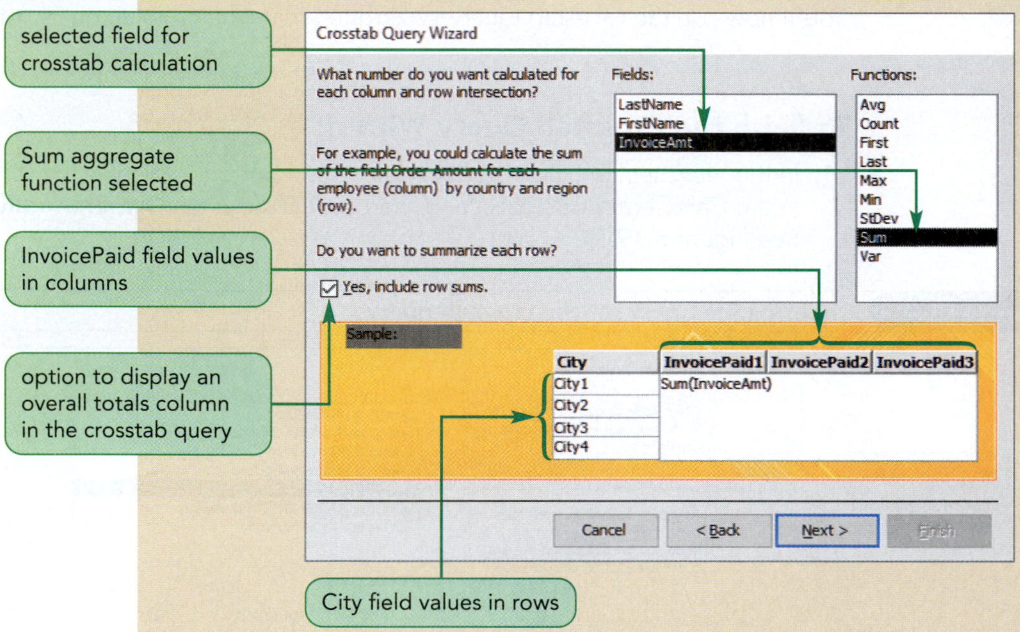

7. Click the **Next** button to open the final Crosstab Query Wizard dialog box, in which you choose the query name.

8. Click in the box, delete the underscore character so that the query name is qryOwnersAndInvoicesCrosstab, be sure the option button for viewing the query is selected, and then click the **Finish** button. The crosstab query is saved, and then the query recordset is displayed.

9. Resize all the columns in the query recordset to their best fit, and then click the City field value in the first row (**Bearcreek**). See Figure 5-21.

Figure 5-21 Crosstab query recordset

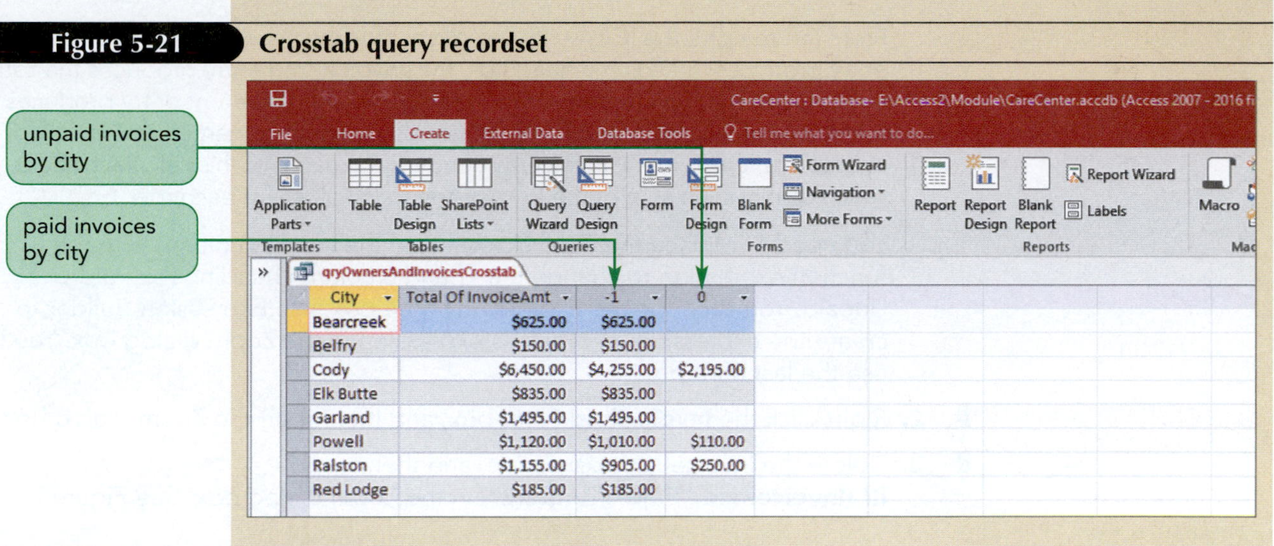

City	Total Of InvoiceAmt	-1	0
Bearcreek	$625.00	$625.00	
Belfry	$150.00	$150.00	
Cody	$6,450.00	$4,255.00	$2,195.00
Elk Butte	$835.00	$835.00	
Garland	$1,495.00	$1,495.00	
Powell	$1,120.00	$1,010.00	$110.00
Ralston	$1,155.00	$905.00	$250.00
Red Lodge	$185.00	$185.00	

The query recordset contains only one row for each City field value. The Total Of InvoiceAmt column shows the total invoice amount for the owners in each city. The columns labeled -1 and 0 show the sum total paid (-1 column) and sum total unpaid (0 column) invoice amounts for owners in each city. Because the InvoicePaid field is a Yes/No field, by default, field values in datasheets, forms, and reports are displayed in a check box (either checked or unchecked), but a checked value is stored in the database as a -1 and an unchecked value as a 0. Instead of displaying check boxes, the crosstab query displays the stored values as column headings.

Kimberly wants you to change the column headings of -1 to Paid and 0 to Unpaid. You'll use the IIf function to change the column headings, using the expression *IIf (InvoicePaid,"Paid","Unpaid")*—if the InvoicePaid field value is true (because it's a Yes/No field or a True/False field), or is checked, use "Paid" as the column heading; otherwise, use "Unpaid" as the column heading. Because the InvoicePaid field is a Yes/No field, the condition *InvoicePaid* is the same as the condition *InvoicePaid = -1*, which uses a comparison operator and a value. For all data types except Yes/No fields, you must use a comparison operator in a condition.

To change the crosstab query column headings:

1. Click the **Home** tab on the ribbon, and then switch to Design view. The design grid has four entries. See Figure 5-22.

Figure 5-22 Crosstab query in the design grid

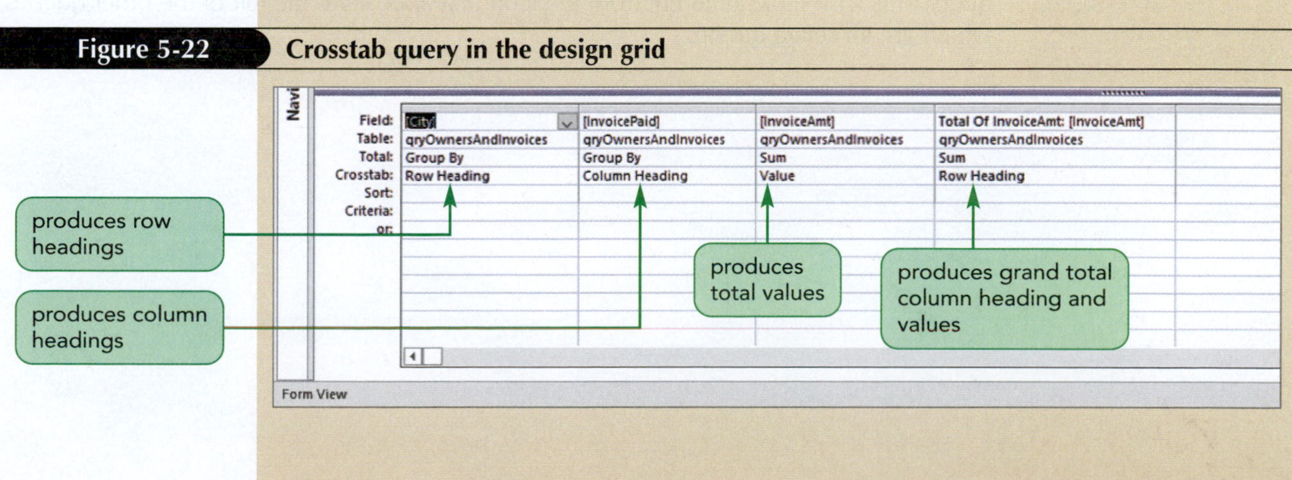

From left to right, the [City] entry produces the row headings, the [InvoicePaid] entry produces the column headings, the [InvoiceAmt] entry produces the totals in each row/column intersection, and the Total Of InvoiceAmt entry produces the row total column heading and total values. The field names are enclosed in brackets; the Total Of InvoiceAmt entry is the name of this calculated field, which displays the sum of the InvoiceAmt field values for each row.

You need to replace the Field box value in the second column with the IIf function expression to change the -1 and 0 column headings to Paid and Unpaid. You can type the expression in the box, use Expression Builder to create the expression, or type the expression in the Zoom dialog box. You'll use the last method.

2. Right-click the **InvoicePaid Field** box, and then open the Zoom dialog box.
3. Delete the InvoicePaid expression, and then type **IIf (InvoicePaid,"Paid","Unpaid")** in the Zoom dialog box. See Figure 5-23.

Figure 5-23 IIf function for the crosstab query column headings

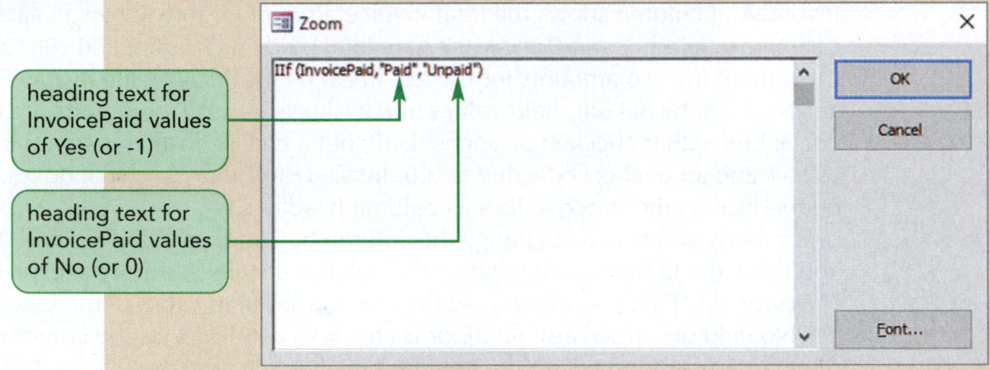

4. Click the **OK** button, and then save and run the query. The completed crosstab query is displayed with Paid and Unpaid as the last two column headings, in alphabetical order, as shown in Figure 5-18.
5. Close the query, and then open the Navigation Pane.

TIP

Point to an object in the Navigation Pane to display the full object name in a ScreenTip.

In the Navigation Pane, unique icons represent different types of queries. The crosstab query icon appears in the Queries list to the left of the qryOwnersAndInvoicesCrosstab query. This icon looks different from the icon that appears to the left of the other queries, which are all select queries.

INSIGHT

Using Special Database Features Cautiously

When you create a query in Design view or with a wizard, an equivalent SQL statement is constructed, and only the SQL statement version of the query is saved. **SQL (Structured Query Language)** is a standard language used in querying, updating, and managing relational databases. If you learn SQL for one relational DBMS, it's a relatively easy task to begin using SQL for other relational DBMSs. However, differences exist between DBMSs in their versions of SQL—somewhat like having different dialects in English—and in what additions they make to SQL. The SQL-equivalent statement created for a crosstab query in Access is one such SQL-language addition. If you need to convert an Access database to SQL Server, Oracle, or another DBMS, crosstab queries created in Access will not work in these other DBMSs. You'd have to construct a set of SQL statements in the other DBMS to replace the SQL statement automatically created by Access. Constructing this replacement set of statements is a highly technical process that only an experienced programmer can complete, so you should use special features of a DBMS judiciously.

Next, Kimberly wants to identify any visit dates that have the same visit dates as other owners because these are the ones that might have potential scheduling difficulties. To find the information Kimberly needs, you'll create a find duplicates query.

Creating a Find Duplicates Query

A find duplicates query is a select query that finds duplicate records in a table or query. You can create this type of query using the **Find Duplicates Query Wizard**. A find duplicates query searches for duplicate values based on the fields you select when answering the Wizard's questions. For example, you might want to display all employers that have the same name, all students who have the same phone number, or all products that have the same description. Using this type of query, you can locate duplicates to avert potential problems (for example, you might have inadvertently assigned two different numbers to the same product), or you can eliminate duplicates that cost money (for example, you could send just one advertising brochure to all owners having the same address).

REFERENCE

Using the Find Duplicates Query Wizard

- On the Create tab, in the Queries group, click the Query Wizard button.
- In the New Query dialog box, click Find Duplicates Query Wizard, and then click the OK button.
- Complete the Wizard dialog boxes to select the table or query on which to base the query, select the field (or fields) to check for duplicate values, select the additional fields to include in the query results, enter a name for the query, and then click the Finish button.

You'll use the Find Duplicates Query Wizard to create and run a new query to display duplicate visit dates in the tblVisit table.

To create the query using the Find Duplicates Query Wizard:

1. Close the Navigation Pane, click the **Create** tab on the ribbon, and then, in the Queries group, click the **Query Wizard** button to open the New Query dialog box.
2. Click **Find Duplicates Query Wizard**, and then click the **OK** button. The first Find Duplicates Query Wizard dialog box opens. In this dialog box, you select the table or query on which to base the new query. You'll use the tblVisit table.
3. Click **Table: tblVisit** (if necessary), and then click the **Next** button. The next Find Duplicates Query Wizard dialog box opens, in which you choose the fields you want to check for duplicate values.
4. In the Available fields box, click **VisitDate**, click the > button to select the VisitDate field as the field to check for duplicate values, and then click the **Next** button. In the next Find Duplicates Query Wizard dialog box, you select the additional fields you want displayed in the query results.

   Kimberly wants all remaining fields to be included in the query results.
5. Click the >> button to move all fields from the Available fields box to the Additional query fields box, and then click the **Next** button. The final Find Duplicates Query Wizard dialog box opens, in which you enter a name for the query. You'll use qryDuplicateVisitDates as the query name.
6. Type **qryDuplicateVisitDates** in the box, be sure the option button for viewing the results is selected, and then click the **Finish** button. The query is saved, and then the 51 records for visits with duplicate visit dates are displayed. See Figure 5-24.

Figure 5-24 Query recordset for duplicate visit dates

all records returned by the query share a visit date with other records

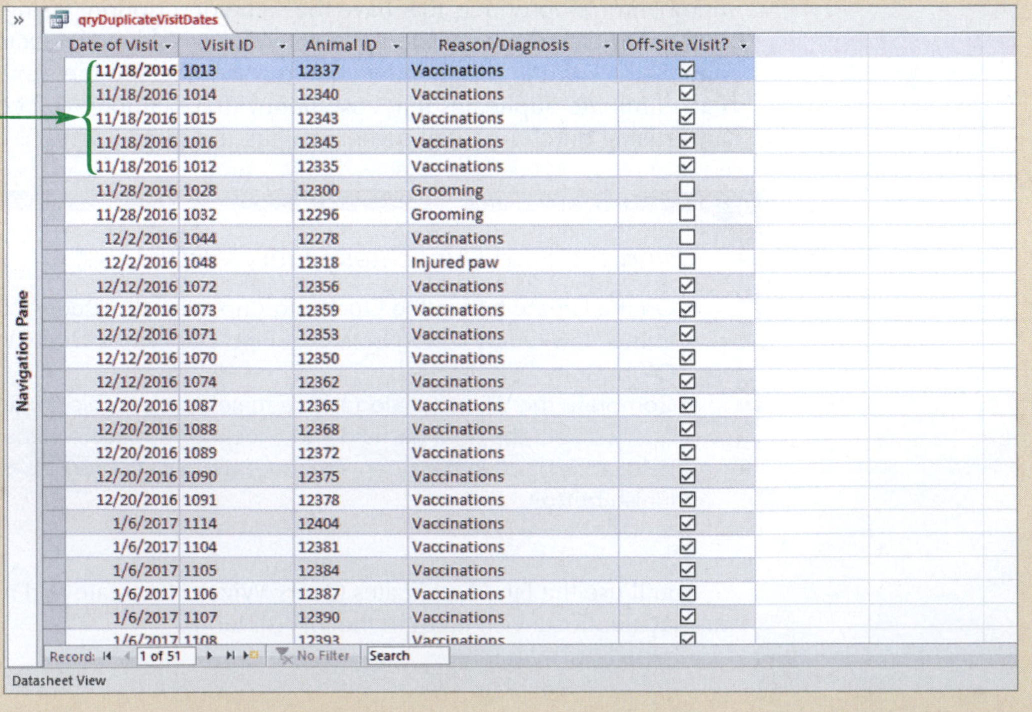

qryDuplicateVisitDates

Date of Visit	Visit ID	Animal ID	Reason/Diagnosis	Off-Site Visit?
11/18/2016	1013	12337	Vaccinations	☑
11/18/2016	1014	12340	Vaccinations	☑
11/18/2016	1015	12343	Vaccinations	☑
11/18/2016	1016	12345	Vaccinations	☑
11/18/2016	1012	12335	Vaccinations	☑
11/28/2016	1028	12300	Grooming	☐
11/28/2016	1032	12296	Grooming	☐
12/2/2016	1044	12278	Vaccinations	☐
12/2/2016	1048	12318	Injured paw	☐
12/12/2016	1072	12356	Vaccinations	☑
12/12/2016	1073	12359	Vaccinations	☑
12/12/2016	1071	12353	Vaccinations	☑
12/12/2016	1070	12350	Vaccinations	☑
12/12/2016	1074	12362	Vaccinations	☑
12/20/2016	1087	12365	Vaccinations	☑
12/20/2016	1088	12368	Vaccinations	☑
12/20/2016	1089	12372	Vaccinations	☑
12/20/2016	1090	12375	Vaccinations	☑
12/20/2016	1091	12378	Vaccinations	☑
1/6/2017	1114	12404	Vaccinations	☑
1/6/2017	1104	12381	Vaccinations	☑
1/6/2017	1105	12384	Vaccinations	☑
1/6/2017	1106	12387	Vaccinations	☑
1/6/2017	1107	12390	Vaccinations	☑
1/6/2017	1108	12393	Vaccinations	☑

Navigation Pane

Record: 1 of 51 No Filter Search

Datasheet View

7. Close the query.

Kimberly now asks you to find the records for animals with no visits. These are animals whose owners have contacted the center and have given the center information about themselves and their animals; however, the animals have not had a first visit. Kimberly wants to contact the owners of these animals to see if they would like to book initial appointments. To provide Kimberly with this information, you need to create a find unmatched query.

Creating a Find Unmatched Query

A find unmatched query is a select query that finds all records in a table or query that have no related records in a second table or query. For example, you could display all owners who have had an appointment but have never been invoiced or all students who are not currently enrolled in classes. Such a query provides information for a veterinary care center to ensure all owners who have received services have also been billed for those services and for a school administrator to contact the students to find out their future educational plans. You can use the **Find Unmatched Query Wizard** to create this type of query.

REFERENCE

Using the Find Unmatched Query Wizard

- On the Create tab, in the Queries group, click the Query Wizard button.
- In the New Query dialog box, click Find Unmatched Query Wizard, and then click the OK button.
- Complete the Wizard dialog boxes to select the table or query on which to base the new query, select the table or query that contains the related records, specify the common field in each table or query, select the additional fields to include in the query results, enter a name for the query, and then click the Finish button.

Kimberly wants to know which animals have no visits. She will contact their owners to determine if they will be visiting Riverview Veterinary Care Center or whether they are receiving their veterinary care elsewhere. To create a list of animals who have not had a visit to the Center, you'll use the Find Unmatched Query Wizard to display only those records from the tblAnimal table with no matching AnimalID field value in the related tblVisit table.

To create the query using the Find Unmatched Query Wizard:

1. On the Create tab, in the Queries group, click the **Query Wizard** button to open the New Query dialog box.
2. Click **Find Unmatched Query Wizard**, and then click the **OK** button. The first Find Unmatched Query Wizard dialog box opens. In this dialog box, you select the table or query on which to base the new query. You'll use the qryAnimalsAndOwners query.
3. In the View section, click the **Queries** option button to display the list of queries, click **Query: qryAnimalsAndOwners** in the box to select this query, and then click the **Next** button. The next Find Unmatched Query Wizard dialog box opens, in which you choose the table that contains the related records. You'll select the tblVisit table.
4. Click **Table: tblVisit** in the box (if necessary), and then click the **Next** button. The next dialog box opens, in which you choose the common field for both tables. See Figure 5-25.

Figure 5-25 Selecting the common field

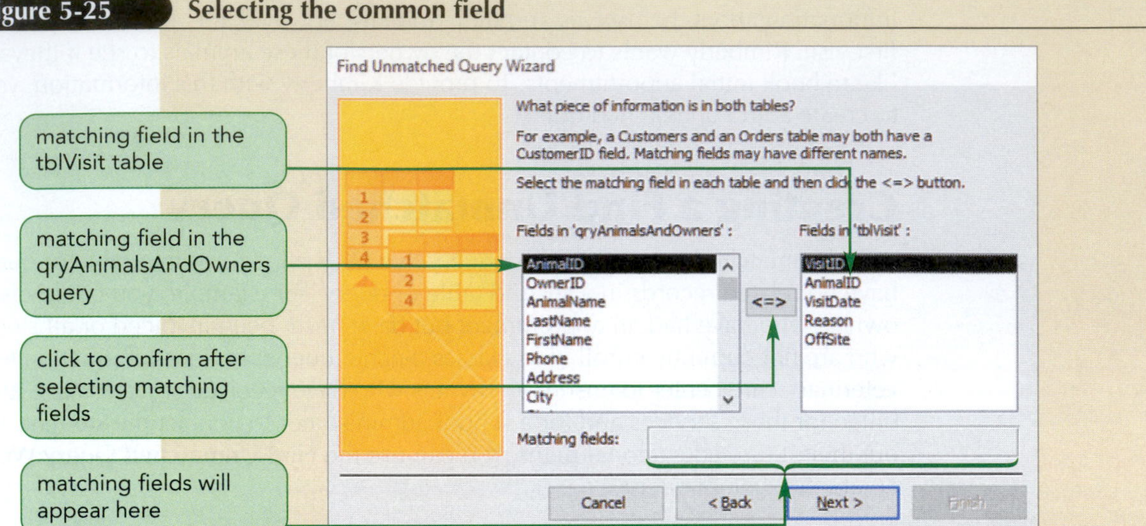

The common field between the query and the table is the AnimalID field. You need to click the common field in each box and then click the <=> button between the two boxes to join the two objects. The Matching fields box then will display AnimalID <=> AnimalID to indicate the joining of the two matching fields. If the two selected objects already have a one-to-many relationship defined in the Relationships window, the Matching fields box will join the correct fields automatically.

Be sure you click the AnimalID field in both boxes.

5. In the Fields in 'qryAnimalsAndOwners' box click **AnimalID**, in the Fields in 'tblVisit' box click **AnimalID**, click the <=> button to connect the two selected fields, and then click the **Next** button. The next Find Unmatched Query Wizard dialog box opens, in which you choose the fields you want to see in the query recordset. Kimberly wants the query recordset to display all available fields.
6. Click the >> button to move all fields from the Available fields box to the Selected fields box, and then click the **Next** button. The final dialog box opens, in which you enter the query name.
7. Type **qryInactiveAnimals**, be sure the option button for viewing the results is selected, and then click the **Finish** button. The query is saved, and then two records are displayed in the query recordset. See Figure 5-26.

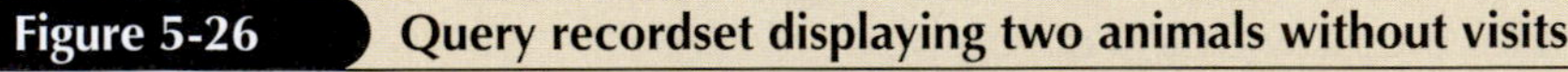

Figure 5-26 Query recordset displaying two animals without visits

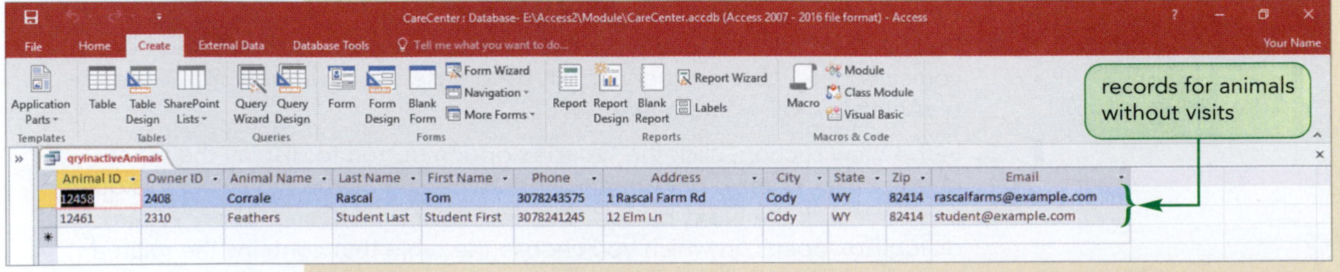

Animal ID	Owner ID	Animal Name	Last Name	First Name	Phone	Address	City	State	Zip	Email
12458	2408	Corrale	Rascal	Tom	3078243575	1 Rascal Farm Rd	Cody	WY	82414	rascalfarms@example.com
12461	2310	Feathers	Student Last	Student First	3078241245	12 Elm Ln	Cody	WY	82414	student@example.com

8. Close the query.

Next, Kimberly wants to contact those owners who have the highest invoice amounts to make sure that Riverview Veterinary Care Center is providing satisfactory service. To display the information Kimberly needs, you will create a top values query.

Creating a Top Values Query

Whenever a query displays a large group of records, you might want to limit the number to a more manageable size by displaying, for example, just the first 10 records. The **Top Values property** for a query lets you limit the number of records in the query results. To find a limited number of records using the Top Values property, you can click one of the preset values from a list or enter either an integer (such as 15, to display the first 15 records) or a percentage (such as 20%, to display the first fifth of the records).

For instance, suppose you have a select query that displays 45 records. If you want the query recordset to show only the first five records, you can change the query by entering a Top Values property value of either 5 or 10%. If the query contains a sort, and the last record that can be displayed is one of two or more records with the same value for the primary sort field, all records with that matching key value are displayed.

Kimberly wants to view the same data that appears in the qryLargeInvoiceAmounts query for owners with the highest 25 percent invoice amounts. Based on the number or percentage you enter, a top values query selects that number or percentage of records starting from the top of the recordset. Thus, you usually include a sort in a top values query to display the records with the highest or lowest values for the sorted field. You will modify the query and then use the Top Values property to produce this information for Kimberly.

To set the Top Values property for the query:

1. Open the Navigation Pane, open the **qryLargeInvoiceAmounts** query in Datasheet view, and then close the Navigation Pane. Ten records are displayed, all with InvoiceAmt field values greater than $75, in descending order by InvoiceAmt.
2. Switch to Design view.
3. On the Query Tools Design tab, in the Query Setup group, click the **Return** arrow (with the ScreenTip "Top Values"), and then click **25%**. See Figure 5-27.

Figure 5-27 Creating the top values query

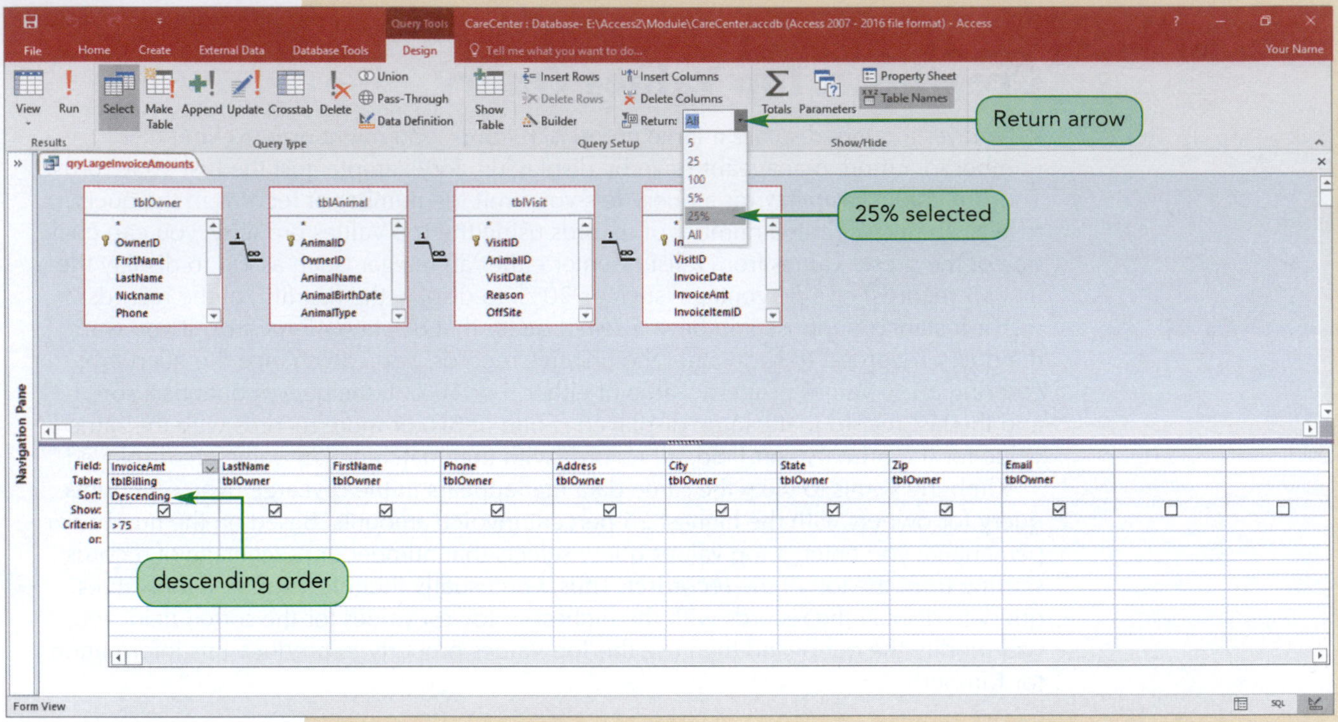

If the number or percentage of records you want to select, such as 15 or 20%, doesn't appear in the Top Values list, you can type the number or percentage in the Return box.

4. Run the query. Three records are displayed in the query recordset; these records represent the owners with the highest 25 percent of the invoice amounts (25 percent of the original 10 records). See Figure 5-28.

Figure 5-28 Top values query recordset

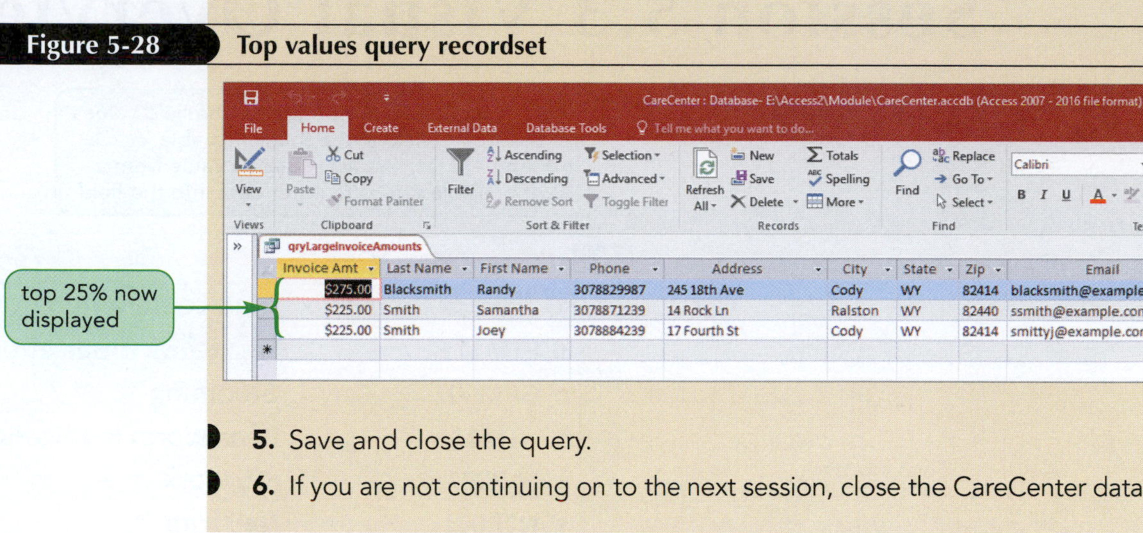

5. Save and close the query.
6. If you are not continuing on to the next session, close the CareCenter database.

Kimberly will use the information provided by the queries you created to analyze the Riverview Veterinary Care Center business and to contact owners. In the next session, you will enhance the tblOwner and tblVisit tables.

REVIEW

Session 5.2 Quick Check

1. What is the purpose of a crosstab query?
2. What are the four query wizards you can use to create a new query?
3. What is a find duplicates query?
4. What does a find unmatched query do?
5. What happens when you set a query's Top Values property?
6. What happens if you set a query's Top Values property to 2, and the first five records have the same value for the primary sort field?

Session 5.3 Visual Overview:

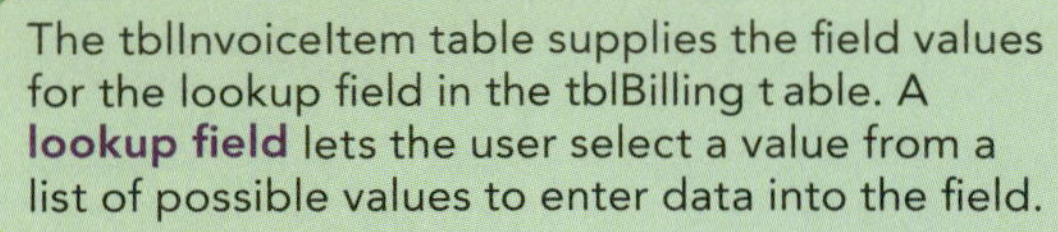

The tblInvoiceItem table supplies the field values for the lookup field in the tblBilling t able. A **lookup field** lets the user select a value from a list of possible values to enter data into the field.

tblInvoiceItem

Invoice Item ID	Invoice Item Description
FTM111	Flea & tick medications
GRM001	Grooming
HTM111	Heartworm medication
LAB001	Lab work
NTR001	Nail trim
OSV001	Off-site visit
PHA111	Pharmacy
SUP001	Supplies
SUR001	Minor surgery

The InvoiceItemID and InvoiceItemDesc fields from the tblInvoiceItem table are used to look up InvoiceItemID values in the tblBilling table.

The tblBilling table contains the lookup field.

tblBilling

Invoice Num	Visit ID	Invoice Date	Invoice Amt	Invoice Item ID	Invoice Paid
42098	1002	11/09/2016	$50.00	Lab work	☑
42099	1002	11/09/2016	$75.00		
42100	1002	11/09/2016	$45.00		
42110	1006	11/14/2016	$35.00		
42111	1006	11/14/2016	$65.00		
42112	1006	11/14/2016	$50.00		
42118	1009	11/16/2016	$50.00		
42119	1009	11/16/2016	$15.00		
42125	1012	11/21/2016	$50.00		
42126	1012	11/21/2016	$75.00		
42127	1012	11/21/2016	$75.00		
42128	1013	11/21/2016	$75.00		
42129	1013	11/21/2016	$75.00		
42130	1014	11/21/2016	$75.00		
42131	1014	11/21/2016	$75.00	Lab work	☑
42132	1015	11/21/2016	$75.00	Vaccinations	☑

Flea & tick medicati	FTM111
Grooming	GRM001
Heartworm medicat	HTM111
Lab work	LAB001
Nail trim	NTR001
Off-site visit	OSV001
Pharmacy	PHA111
Supplies	SUP001
Minor surgery	SUR001
Major surgery	SUR002
Spaying - surgery	SUR111
Neutering - surgery	SUR222
Declawing - surgery	SUR333
Vaccinations	VAC111

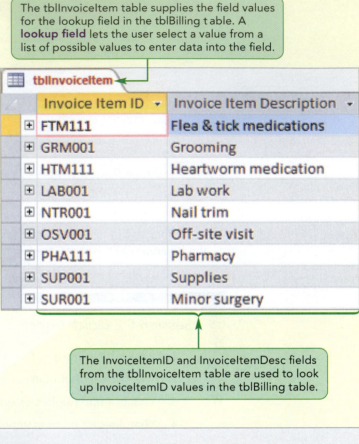

Values in the lookup field appear in alphabetical order, sorted by Invoice Item ID.

Only the InvoiceItemID values are stored in the InvoiceItemID field in the tblBilling table even though the user also sees the InvoiceItemDesc values in the datasheet.

Lookup Fields and Input Masks

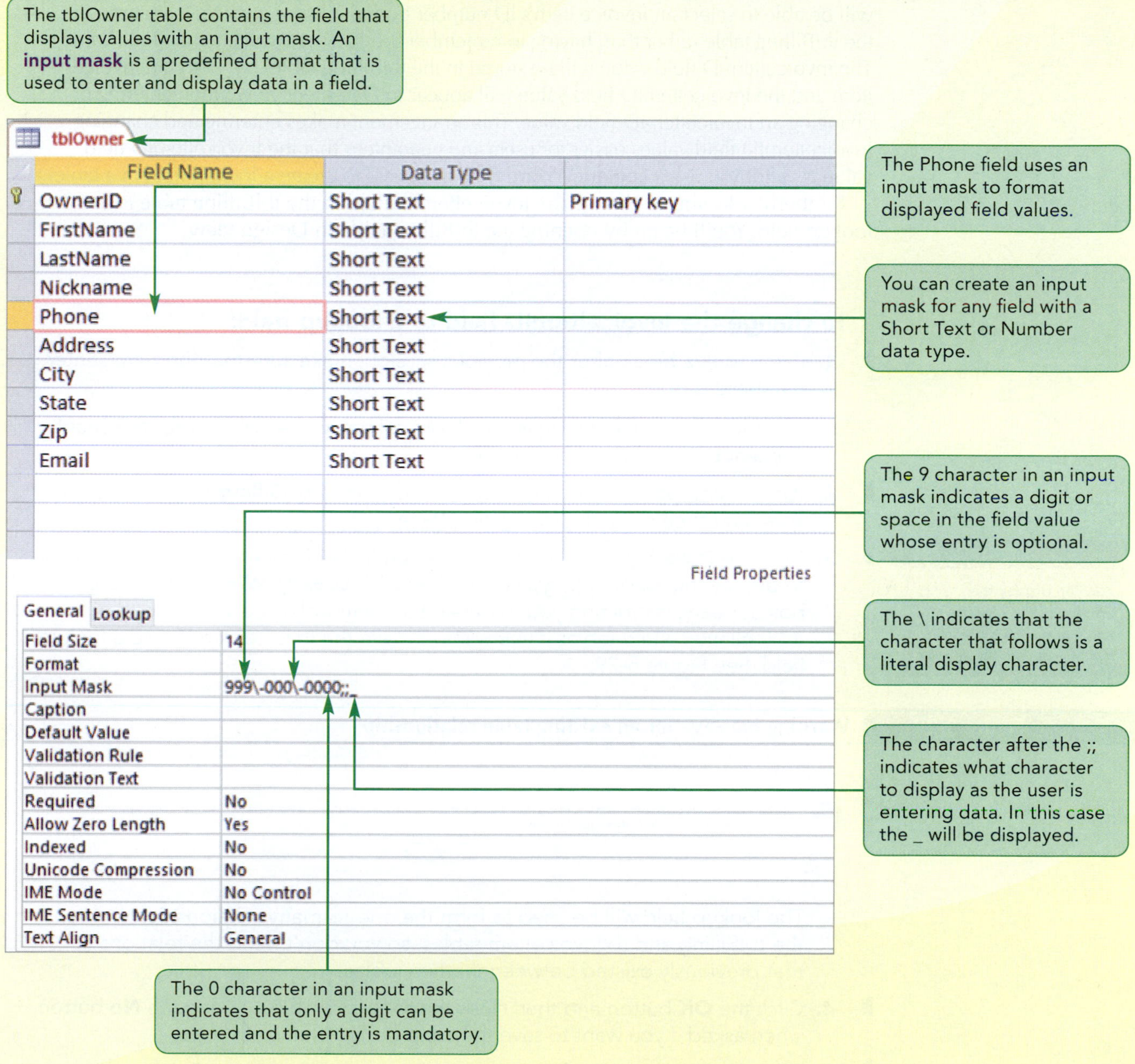

The tblOwner table contains the field that displays values with an input mask. An **input mask** is a predefined format that is used to enter and display data in a field.
tblOwner
Field Name
Data Type
OwnerID
Short Text
Primary key
FirstName
Short Text
LastName
Short Text
Nickname
Short Text
Phone
Short Text
Address
Short Text
City
Short Text
State
Short Text
Zip
Short Text
Email
Short Text
The Phone field uses an input mask to format displayed field values.
You can create an input mask for any field with a Short Text or Number data type.
The 9 character in an input mask indicates a digit or space in the field value whose entry is optional.
Field Properties
General
Lookup
Field Size
14
Format
Input Mask
999\-000\-0000;;_
Caption
Default Value
Validation Rule
Validation Text
Required
No
Allow Zero Length
Yes
Indexed
No
Unicode Compression
No
IME Mode
No Control
IME Sentence Mode
None
Text Align
General
The \ indicates that the character that follows is a literal display character.
The character after the ;; indicates what character to display as the user is entering data. In this case the _ will be displayed.
The 0 character in an input mask indicates that only a digit can be entered and the entry is mandatory.

Creating a Lookup Field

The tblBilling table in the CareCenter database contains information about owner invoices. Kimberly wants to make entering data in the table easier for her staff. In particular, data entry is easier if they do not need to remember the correct InvoiceItemID field value for each treatment. Because the tblInvoiceItem and tblBilling tables have a one-to-many relationship, Kimberly asks you to change the tblBilling table's InvoiceItemID field, which is a foreign key to the tblInvoiceItem table, to a lookup field. A lookup field lets the user select a value from a list of possible values. For the InvoiceItemID field, a user will be able to select an invoice item's ID number from the list of invoice item names in the tblBilling table rather than having to remember the correct InvoiceItemID field value. The InvoiceItemID field value will be stored in the tblBilling table, but both the invoice item and the InvoiceItemID field value will appear in Datasheet view when entering or changing an InvoiceItemID field value. This arrangement makes entering and changing InvoiceItemID field values easier for users and guarantees that the InvoiceItemID field value is valid. You use a **Lookup Wizard field** in Access to create a lookup field in a table.

Kimberly asks you to change the InvoiceItemID field in the tblBilling table to a lookup field. You'll begin by opening the tblBilling table in Design view.

To change the InvoiceItemID field to a lookup field:

1. If you took a break after the previous session, make sure that the CareCenter database is open.

   Trouble? If the security warning is displayed below the ribbon, click the Enable Content button next to the warning.

2. If necessary, open the Navigation Pane, open the **tblBilling** table in Design view, and then close the Navigation Pane.

3. Click the **Data Type** box for the InvoiceItemID field, click the drop-down arrow to display the list of data types, and then click **Lookup Wizard**. A message box appears, instructing you to delete the relationship between the tblBilling and tblInvoiceItem tables if you want to make the InvoiceItemID field a lookup field. See Figure 5-29.

TIP

You can display the arrow and the menu simultaneously if you click the box near its right side.

Figure 5-29 Warning message for an existing table relationship

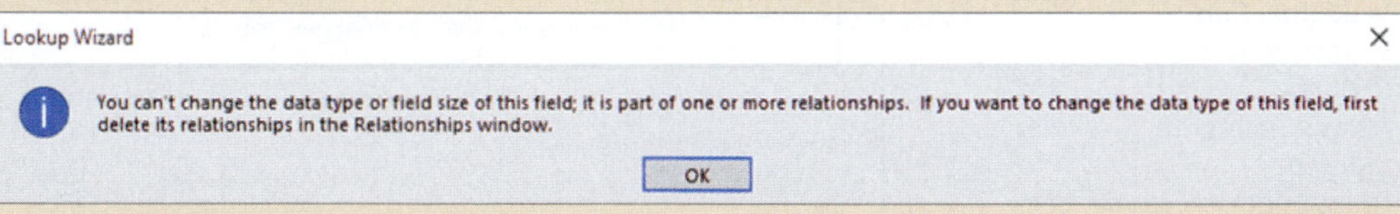

The lookup field will be used to form the one-to-many relationship between the tblBilling and tblInvoiceItem tables, so you don't need the relationship that previously existed between the two tables.

4. Click the **OK** button and then close the tblBilling table, clicking the **No** button when asked if you want to save the table design changes.

5. Click the **Database Tools** tab on the ribbon, and then in the Relationships group, click the **Relationships** button to open the Relationships window.

6. Right-click the join line between the tblBilling and tblInvoiceItem tables, click **Delete**, and then click the **Yes** button to confirm the deletion.

   Trouble? If the Delete command does not appear on the shortcut menu, click a blank area in the Relationships window to close the shortcut menu, and then repeat Step 6, ensuring you right-click on the relationship line.

7. Close the Relationships window.

Now you can resume changing the InvoiceItemID field to a lookup field.

To finish changing the InvoiceItemID field to a lookup field:

1. Open the **tblBilling** table in Design view, and then close the Navigation Pane.
2. Click the right side of the **Data Type** box for the InvoiceItemID field, if necessary click the drop-down arrow, and then click **Lookup Wizard**. The first Lookup Wizard dialog box opens.

   This dialog box lets you specify a list of allowed values for the InvoiceItemID field in a record in the tblBilling table. You can specify a table or query from which users select the value, or you can enter a new list of values. You want the InvoiceItemID values to come from the tblInvoiceItem table.

3. Make sure the option for "I want the lookup field to get the values from another table or query" is selected, and then click the **Next** button to display the next Lookup Wizard dialog box.
4. In the View section, click the **Tables** option button, if necessary, to display the list of tables, click **Table: tblInvoiceItem**, and then click the **Next** button to display the next Lookup Wizard dialog box. See Figure 5-30.

Figure 5-30 Selecting the lookup fields

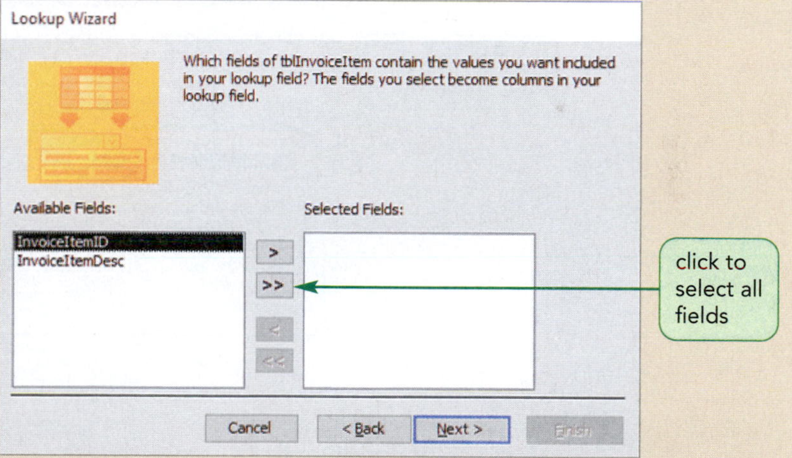

This dialog box lets you select the lookup fields from the tblInvoiceItem table. You need to select the InvoiceItemID field because it's the common field that links the tblInvoiceItem table and the tblBilling table. You must also select the InvoiceItemDesc field because Kimberly wants the user to be able to select from a list of invoice item names when entering a new contract record or changing an existing InvoiceItemID field value.

5. Click the >> button to move the InvoiceItemID and InvoiceItemDesc fields to the Selected Fields box, and then click the **Next** button to display the next Lookup Wizard dialog box. This dialog box lets you choose a sort order for the box entries. Kimberly wants the entries to appear in ascending Invoice Item Description order. Note that ascending is the default sort order.

6. Click the **arrow** for the first box, click **InvoiceItemDesc**, and then click the **Next** button to open the next dialog box.

   In this dialog box, you can adjust the widths of the lookup columns. Note that when you resize a column to its best fit, the column is resized so that the widest column heading and the visible field values fit the column width. However, some field values that aren't visible in this dialog box might be wider than the column width, so you must scroll down the column to make sure you don't have to repeat the column resizing.

7. Click the **Hide key column** check box to remove the checkmark and display the InvoiceItemID field.
8. Click the Invoice Item ID column heading to select it. With the mouse pointer on the Invoice Item ID heading, drag it to the right of the Invoice Item Description column to reposition it.
9. Place the pointer on the right edge of the Invoice Item Description field column heading, and then when the pointer changes to ↔, double-click to resize the column to its best fit.
10. Scroll down the columns, and repeat Step 9 as necessary until the Invoice Item Description column accommodates all contents, and then press **Ctrl + Home** to scroll back to the top of the columns. See Figure 5-31.

Figure 5-31 **Adjusting the width of the lookup column**

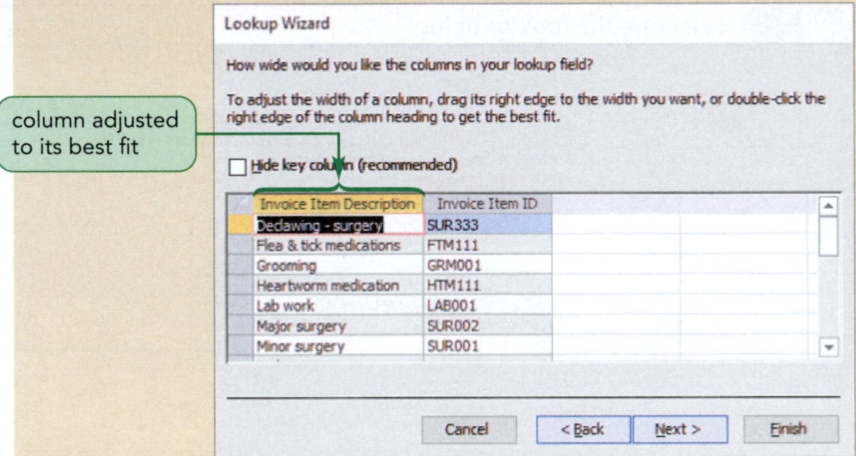

11. Click the **Next** button.

    In the next dialog box, you select the field you want to store in the table. You'll store the InvoiceItemID field in the tblBilling table because it's the foreign key to the tblInvoiceItem table.

12. Click **InvoiceItemID** in the Available Fields box if it's not already selected, and then click the **Next** button.

    In the next dialog box, you specify the field name for the lookup field. Because you'll be storing the InvoiceItemID field in the table, you'll accept the default field name, InvoiceItemID.

13. Click the **Finish** button, and then click **Yes** to save the table.

The Data Type value for the InvoiceItemID field is still Short Text because this field contains text data. However, when you update the field, the InvoiceItemID field value will be used to look up and display in the tblBilling table datasheet both the InvoiceItemDesc and InvoiceItemID field values from the tblInvoiceItem table.

In reviewing animal visits recently, Kimberly noticed that the InvoiceItemID field value stored in the tblBilling table for visit number 42112 is incorrect. She asks you to test the new lookup field to select the correct field value. To do so, you need to switch to Datasheet view.

To change the InvoiceItemID field value:

1. Switch to Datasheet view, and then resize the Invoice Item ID column to its best fit.

   Notice that the Invoice Item ID column displays InvoiceItem field values, even though the InvoiceItemID field values are stored in the table.

2. For Invoice Num 42112, click **Lab work** in the Invoice Item ID column, and then click the **arrow** to display the list of InvoiceItemDesc and InvoiceItemID field values from the tblInvoiceItems table. See Figure 5-32.

Figure 5-32 List of InvoiceItemDesc and InvoiceItemID field values

tblBilling

Invoice Num	Visit ID	Invoice Date	Invoice Amt	Invoice Item ID	Invoice Paid	Click to Add
42098	1002	11/09/2016	$50.00	Lab work	☑	
42099	1002	11/09/2016	$75.00	Vaccinations	☐	
42100	1002	11/09/2016	$45.00	Flea & tick medications	☐	
42110	1006	11/14/2016	$35.00	Heartworm medication	☑	
42111	1006	11/14/2016	$65.00	Vaccinations	☑	
42112	1006	11/14/2016	$50.00	Lab work	☑	
42118	1009	11/16/2016	$50.00			
42119	1009	11/16/2016	$15.00			
42125	1012	11/21/2016	$50.00			
42126	1012	11/21/2016	$75.00			
42127	1012	11/21/2016	$75.00			
42128	1013	11/21/2016	$75.00			
42129	1013	11/21/2016	$75.00			
42130	1014	11/21/2016	$75.00			
42131	1014	11/21/2016	$75.00			
42132	1015	11/21/2016	$75.00			
42133	1015	11/21/2016	$75.00			
42134	1016	11/21/2016	$75.00			
42135	1016	11/21/2016	$75.00			
42145	1020	11/22/2016	$275.00	Major surgery	☑	
42146	1020	11/22/2016	$50.00	Pharmacy	☑	
42147	1020	11/22/2016	$75.00	Lab work	☑	
42155	1024	11/23/2016	$50.00	Lab work	☑	
42156	1024	11/23/2016	$75.00	Vaccinations	☑	
42157	1024	11/23/2016	$45.00	Flea & tick medications	☑	

Flea & tick medicati	FTM111
Grooming	GRM001
Heartworm medicat	HTM111
Lab work	LAB001
Nail trim	NTR001
Off-site visit	OSV001
Pharmacy	PHA111
Supplies	SUP001
Minor surgery	SUR001
Major surgery	SUR002
Spaying - surgery	SUR111
Neutering - surgery	SUR222
Declawing - surgery	SUR333
Vaccinations	VAC111

Record: 6 of 202 No Filter Search

Navigation Pane

Datasheet View

scrollable list of values for the lookup table

   Note that the column displaying InvoiceItemDesc values in your list may be narrower than the values themselves, even though you resized the column. This bug should be fixed in a future version of Access.

   The invoice item for visit 42112 should be Pharmacy, so you need to select this entry in the list to change the InvoiceItemID field value.

3. Scroll through the list if necessary, and then click **Pharmacy** to select that value to display in the datasheet and to store the InvoiceItemID field value of PHA111 in the table. The list closes, and "Pharmacy" appears in the Invoice Item ID column.
4. Save and close the tblBilling table.

Next, Kimberly asks you to change the appearance of the Phone field in the tblOwner table to a standard telephone number format.

Using the Input Mask Wizard

The Phone field in the tblOwner table is a 10-digit number that's difficult to read because it appears with none of the special formatting characters usually associated with a telephone number. For example, the Phone field value for Sally Cruz, which appears as 3074064321, would be more readable in any of the following formats: 307-406-4321, 307.406.4321, 307/406-4321, or (307) 406-4321. Kimberly asks you to use the (307) 406-4321 style for the Phone field.

Kimberly wants the parentheses and hyphens to appear as literal display characters whenever users enter Phone field values. A literal display character is a special character that automatically appears in specific positions of a field value; users don't need to type literal display characters. To include these characters, you need to create an input mask, which is a predefined format used to enter and display data in a field. An easy way to create an input mask is to use the **Input Mask Wizard**, an Access tool that guides you in creating a predefined format for a field. You must be in Design view to use the Input Mask Wizard.

To use the Input Mask Wizard for the Phone field:

1. Open the **tblOwner** table, close the Navigation Pane, and then, if necessary, switch to Design view.
2. Click the **Phone Field Name** box to make that row the current row and to display its Field Properties options.
3. Click the **Input Mask** box in the Field Properties pane. The Build button ... appears at the right edge of the Input Mask box.
4. Click the **Build** button ... in the Input Mask box. The first Input Mask Wizard dialog box opens. See Figure 5-33.

Figure 5-33 Input Mask Wizard dialog box

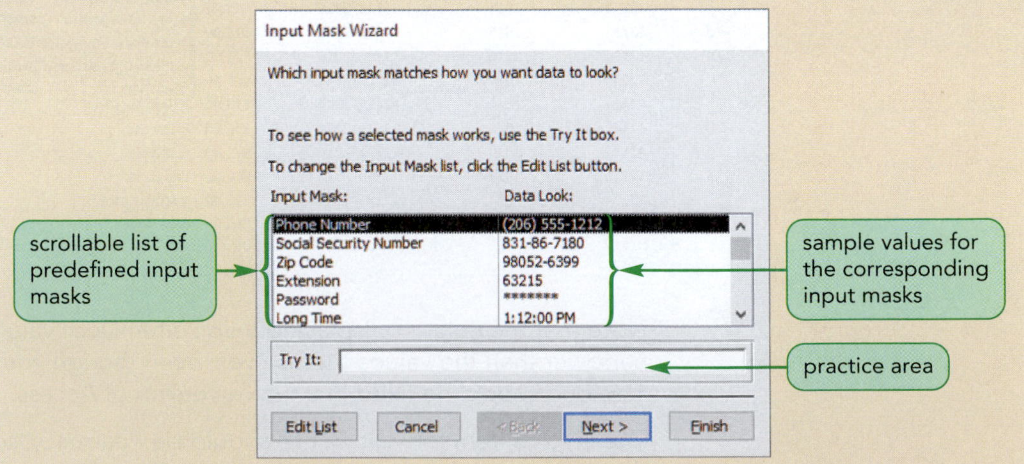

You can scroll the Input Mask box, select the input mask you want, and then enter representative values to practice using the input mask.

5. If necessary, click **Phone Number** in the Input Mask box to select it.

6. Click the far left side of the **Try It** box. (___) ___-____ appears in the Try It box. As you type a phone number, the underscores, which are placeholder characters, are replaced.

   Trouble? If your insertion point is not immediately to the right of the left parenthesis, press the ← key until it is.

7. Type **3074064321** to practice entering a sample phone number. The input mask formats the typed value as (307) 406-4321.

8. Click the **Next** button. The next Input Mask Wizard dialog box opens. In it, you can change the input mask and the placeholder character. Because you can change an input mask easily after the Input Mask Wizard finishes, you'll accept all wizard defaults.

9. Click the **Finish** button, and then click to the right of the value in the Input Mask box to deselect the characters. The Input Mask Wizard creates the phone number input mask, placing it in the Input Mask box for the Phone field. See Figure 5-34.

Figure 5-34 Phone number input mask created by the Input Mask Wizard

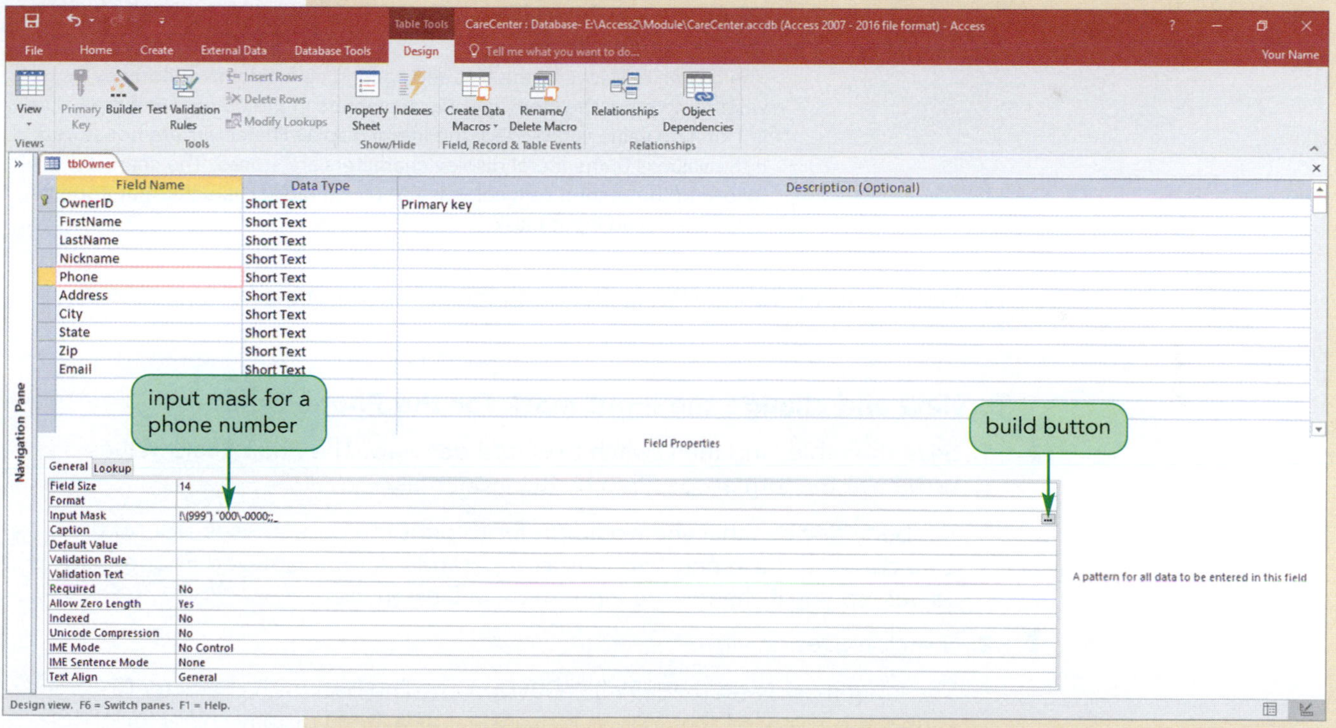

The characters used in a field's input mask restrict the data you can enter in the field, as shown in Figure 5-35. Other characters that appear in an input mask, such as the left and right parentheses in the phone number input mask, are literal display characters.

Figure 5-35 Input mask characters

Input Mask Character	Description
0	Digit only must be entered. Entry is required.
9	Digit or space can be entered. Entry is optional.
#	Digit, space, or a plus or minus sign can be entered. Entry is optional.
L	Letter only must be entered. Entry is required.
?	Letter only can be entered. Entry is optional.
A	Letter or digit must be entered. Entry is required.
a	Letter or digit can be entered. Entry is optional.
&	Any character or a space must be entered. Entry is required.
C	Any character or a space can be entered. Entry is optional.
>	All characters that follow are displayed in uppercase.
<	All characters that follow are displayed in lowercase.
"	Enclosed characters treated as literal display characters.
\	Following character treated as a literal display character. This is the same as enclosing a single character in quotation marks.
!	Input mask is displayed from right to left, rather than the default of left to right. Characters typed into the mask always fill in from left to right.
;;	The character between the first and second semicolons determines whether to store the literal display characters in the database. If the value is 1 or if no value is provided, the literal display characters are not stored. If the value is 0, the literal display characters are stored. The character following the second semicolon is the placeholder character that appears in the displayed input mask.

Kimberly wants to view the Phone field with the default input mask.

To view and change the input mask for the Phone field:

1. Save the table, and then switch to Datasheet view. The Phone field values now have the format specified by the input mask.

   Kimberly decides that she would prefer to omit the parentheses around the area codes and use only hyphens as separators in the displayed Phone field values, so you'll change the input mask in Design view.

2. Switch to Design view.

   The input mask is set to !\(999") "000\-0000;;_. The backslash character (\) causes the character that follows it to appear as a literal display character. Characters enclosed in quotation marks also appear as literal display characters. (See Figure 5-35.) The exclamation mark (!) forces the existing data to fill the input mask from right to left instead of left to right. This does not affect new data. This applies only to the situation when data already exists in the table and a new input mask is applied. For instance, if the existing data is 5551234 and the input mask fills from left to right, the data with the input mask would look like (555) 123-4. If the input mask fills from right to left, the data with the input mask applied would look like ( ) 555-1234.

   If you omit the backslashes preceding the hyphens, they will automatically be inserted when you press the Tab key. However, backslashes are not added automatically for other literal display characters, such as periods and slashes, so it's best to always type the backslashes. Since all of the existing data includes the area code, it will not make a difference whether the input mask applied to the data fills the data from left to right or from right to left, so you'll omit the ! symbol.

3. In the Input Mask box for the Phone field, change the input mask to **999\-000\-0000;;_** and then press the **Tab** key.

   Because you've modified a field property, the Property Update Options button appears to the left of the Input Mask property.

4. Click the **Property Update Options** button. A menu opens below the button, as shown in Figure 5-36.

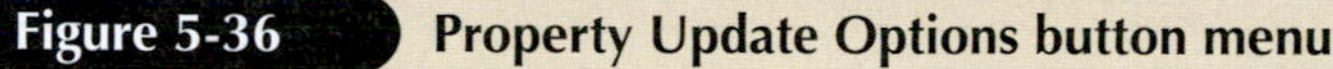

Figure 5-36 Property Update Options button menu

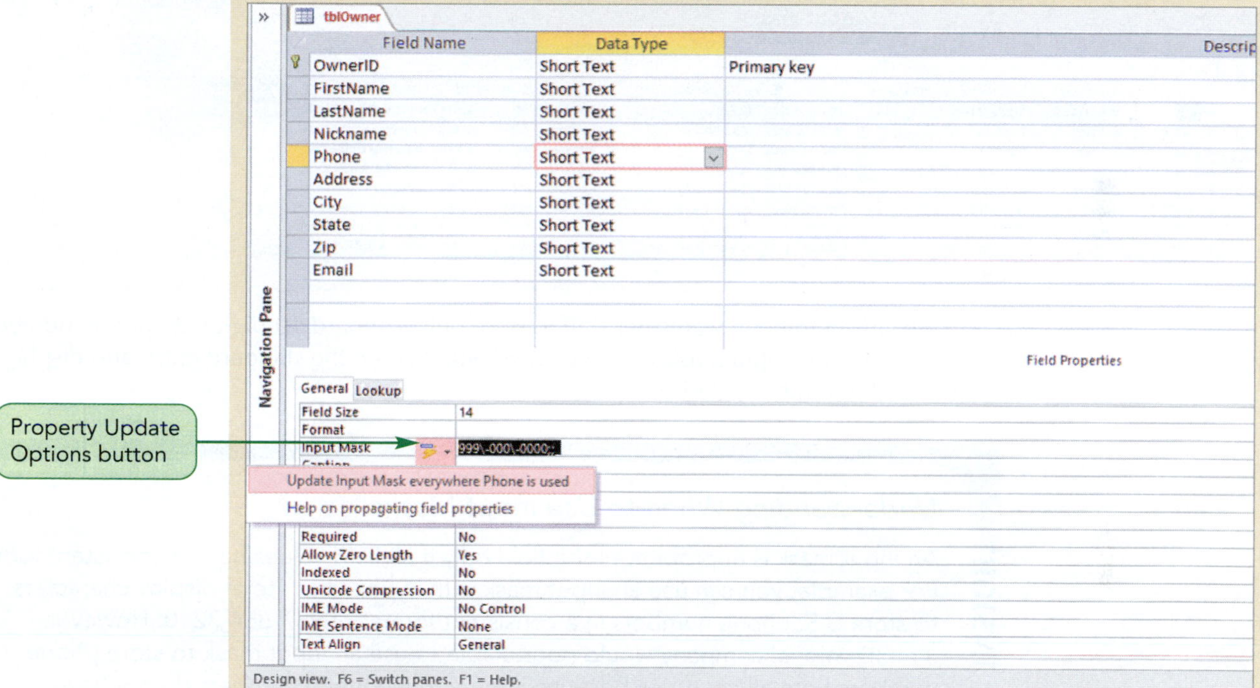

5. Click **Update Input Mask everywhere Phone is used**. The Update Properties dialog box opens. See Figure 5-37.

Figure 5-37 Update Properties dialog box

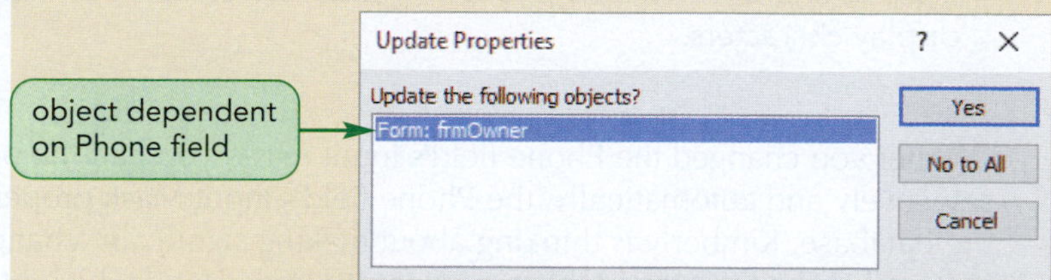

Because the frmOwner form displays the Phone field values from the tblOwner table, the Phone field's Input Mask property in this object will automatically be changed to your new input mask. If other form objects included the Phone field from the tblOwner table, they would be included in this dialog box as well. This capability to update field properties in objects automatically when you modify a table field property is called **property propagation**. Although the Update Properties dialog box displays no queries, property propagation also occurs with queries automatically. Property propagation is limited to field properties such as the Decimal Places, Description, Format, and Input Mask properties.

6. Click the **Yes** button, save the table, switch to Datasheet view, and then resize the Phone column to its best fit. The Phone field values now have the format Kimberly requested. See Figure 5-38.

Figure 5-38 After changing the Phone field input mask

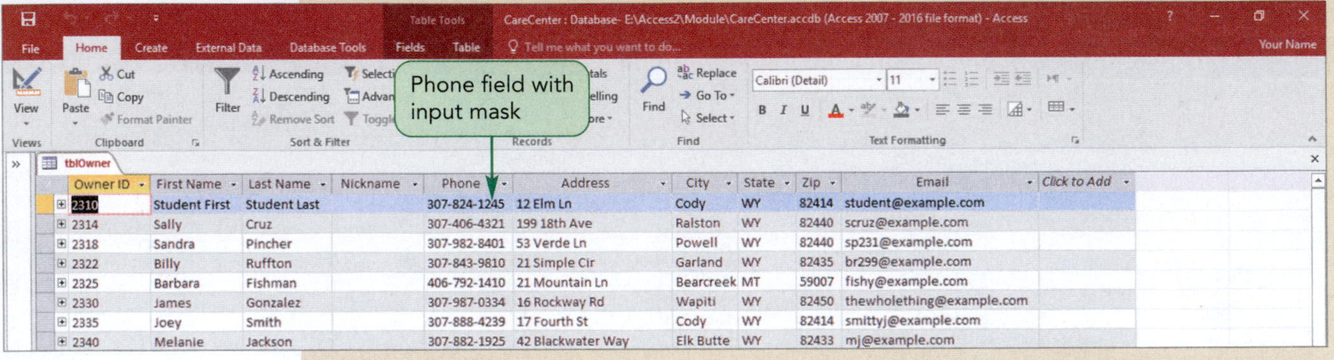

Because Kimberly wants her staff to store only standard 10-digit U.S. phone numbers for owners, the input mask you've created will enforce the standard entry and display format that Kimberly desires.

INSIGHT

Understanding When to Use Input Masks

An input mask is appropriate for a field only if all field values have a consistent format. For example, you can use an input mask with hyphens as literal display characters to store U.S. phone numbers in a consistent format of 987-654-3210. However, a multinational company would not be able to use an input mask to store phone numbers from all countries because international phone numbers do not have a consistent format. In the same way, U.S. zip codes have a consistent format, and you could use an input mask of 00000#9999 to enter and display U.S. zip codes such as 98765 and 98765-4321, but you could not use an input mask if you need to store and display foreign postal codes in the same field. If you need to store and display phone numbers, zip/postal codes, and other fields in a variety of formats, it's best to define them as Short Text fields without an input mask so users can enter the correct literal display characters.

After you changed the Phone field's input mask, you had the option to update, selectively and automatically, the Phone field's Input Mask property in other objects in the database. Kimberly is thinking about making significant changes to the way data is stored in the tblOwner table and wants to understand which other elements those changes might impact. To determine the dependencies among objects in an Access database, you'll open the Object Dependencies pane.

Identifying Object Dependencies

An **object dependency** exists between two objects when a change to the properties of data in one object affects the properties of data in the other object. Dependencies between Access objects, such as tables, queries, and forms, can occur in various ways. For example, the tblVisit and tblBilling tables are dependent on each other because they have a one-to-many relationship. In the same way, the tblOwner table uses the qryOwnersByName query to obtain the Owner field to display along with the OwnerID field, and this creates a dependency between these two objects. Any query, form, or other object that uses fields from a given table is dependent on that table. Any form or report that uses fields from a query is directly dependent on the query and is indirectly dependent on the tables that provide the data to the query. Large databases contain hundreds of objects, so it is useful to have a way to easily view the dependencies among objects before you attempt to delete or modify an object. The **Object Dependencies pane** displays a collapsible list of the dependencies among the objects in an Access database; you click the list's expand indicators to show or hide different levels of dependencies. Next, you'll open the Object Dependencies pane to examine the object dependencies in the CareCenter database.

To open and use the Object Dependencies pane:

1. Click the **Database Tools** tab on the ribbon.
2. In the Relationships group, click the **Object Dependencies** button to open the Object Dependencies pane, and then drag the left edge of the pane to the left until none of the items in the list are cut off.
3. If necessary, click the **Objects that depend on me** option button to select it, then click the **Refresh** link to display the list of objects. See Figure 5-39.

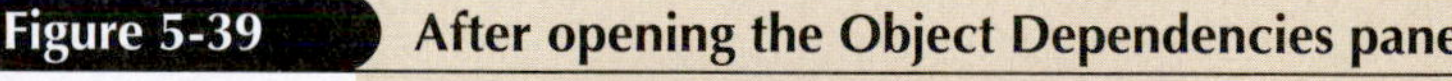

Figure 5-39 After opening the Object Dependencies pane

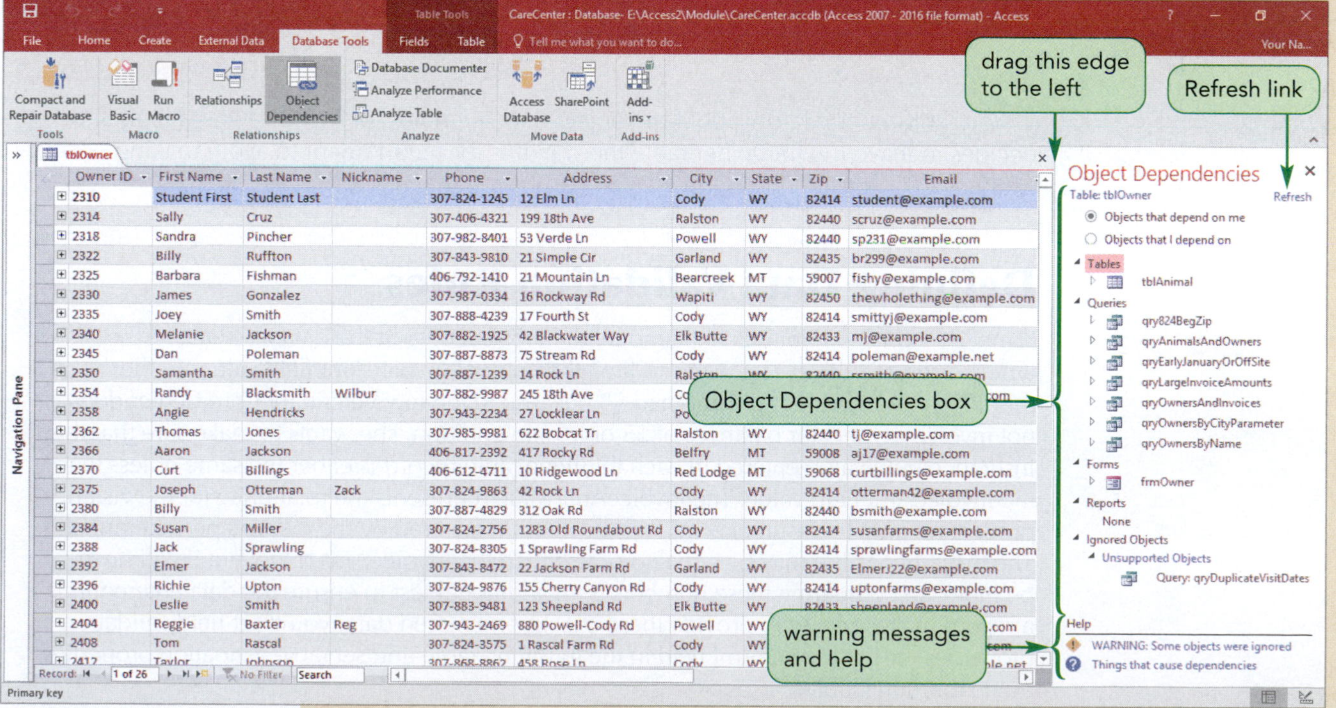

The Object Dependencies pane displays the objects that depend on the tblOwner table, the object name that appears at the top of the pane. If you change the design of the tblOwner table, the change might affect objects in the pane. Changing a property for a field in the tblOwner table that's also used by a listed object affects that listed object. If a listed object does not use the field you are changing, that listed object is not affected.

Objects listed in the Ignored Objects section of the box might have an object dependency with the tblOwner table, and you'd have to review them individually to determine if a dependency exists. The Help section at the bottom of the pane displays links for further information about object dependencies.

4. Click the **frmOwner** link in the Object Dependencies pane. The frmOwner form opens in Design view. All the fields in the form are fields from the tblOwner table, which is why the form has an object dependency with the table.
5. Switch to Form view for the frmOwner form. Note that the Phone field value is displayed using the input mask you applied to the field in the tblOwner table. This change was propagated from the table to the form.
6. Close the frmOwner form, open the Navigation Pane, open the **tblAnimal** table in Datasheet view, and then click the **Refresh** link near the top of the Object Dependencies pane. The Object Dependencies box now displays the objects that depend on the tblAnimal table.
7. Click the **Objects that I depend on** option button near the top of the pane to view the objects that affect the tblAnimal table.
8. Click the **Objects that depend on me** option button, and then click the **expand indicator** ▷ for the qryAnimalsAndOwners query in the Object Dependencies pane. The list expands to display the qryInactiveAnimals query, which is another query that the qryAnimalsAndOwners query depends upon.
9. Close the tblAnimal table, close the Object Dependencies pane, and then save and close the tblOwner table.

You let Kimberly know about the object dependencies for the tblOwner table. She decides to leave the tblOwner table the way it is for the moment to avoid making changes to forms and/or queries.

Defining Data Validation Rules

Kimberly wants to minimize the amount of incorrect data in the database caused by typing errors. To do so, she wants to limit the entry of InvoiceAmt field values in the tblBilling table to values greater than $5 because Riverview Veterinary Care Center does not invoice owners for balances of $5 or less. In addition, she wants to make sure that the Insurance field value entered in each tblBilling table record is either the same or less than the InvoiceAmt field value. The InvoiceAmt value represents the total price for the visit or procedure, and the Insurance value is the amount covered by the owner's pet insurance. The Insurance value may be equal to or less than the InvoiceAmt value, but it will never be more, so comparing these numbers is an additional test to ensure the data entered in a record makes sense. To provide these checks on entered data, you'll set field validation properties for the InvoiceAmt field in the tblBilling table and set table validation properties in the tblBilling table.

Defining Field Validation Rules

To prevent a user from entering an unacceptable value in the InvoiceAmt field, you can create a **field validation rule** that verifies a field value by comparing it to a constant or to a set of constants. You create a field validation rule by setting the Validation Rule and the Validation Text field properties. The **Validation Rule property** value specifies the valid values that users can enter in a field. The **Validation Text property** value will be displayed in a dialog box if a user enters an invalid value (in this case, an InvoiceAmt field value of $5 or less). After you set these two InvoiceAmt field properties in the tblBilling table, users will be prevented from entering an invalid InvoiceAmt field value in the tblBilling table and in all current and future queries and future forms that include the InvoiceAmt field.

You'll now set the Validation Rule and Validation Text properties for the InvoiceAmt field in the tblBilling table.

To create and test a field validation rule for the InvoiceAmt field:

1. Open the **tblBilling** table in Design view, close the Navigation Pane, and then click the **InvoiceAmt Field Name** box to make that row the current row.

   To make sure that all values entered in the InvoiceAmt field are greater than 5, you'll use the > comparison operator in the Validation Rule box.

2. In the Field Properties pane, click the **Validation Rule** box, type **>5**, and then press the **Tab** key.

   You can set the Validation Text property to a value that appears in a dialog box that opens if a user enters a value not listed in the Validation Rule box.

3. In the Validation Text box, type **Invoice amounts must be greater than 5.** See Figure 5-40.

Figure 5-40 Validation properties for the InvoiceAmt field

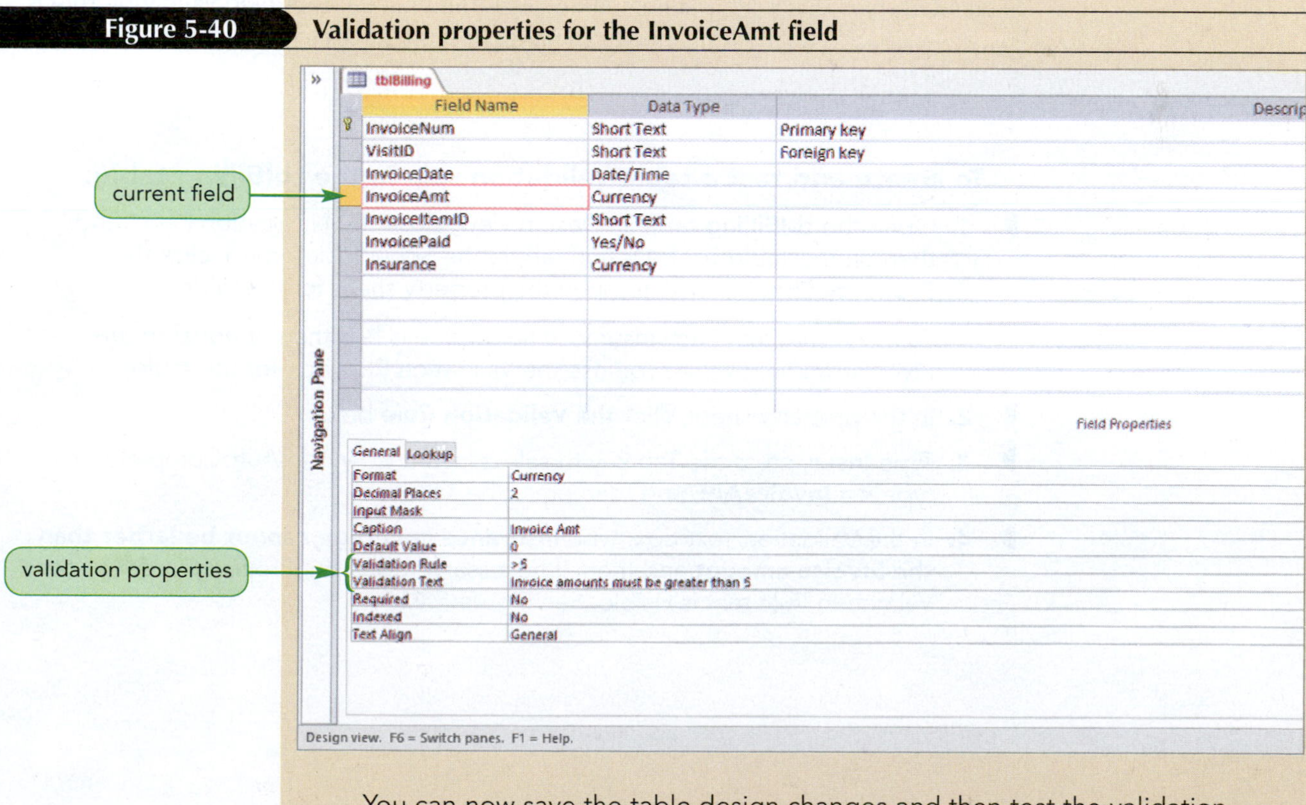

You can now save the table design changes and then test the validation properties.

4. Save the table, and then click the **Yes** button when asked if you want to test the existing InvoiceAmt field values in the tblBilling table against the new validation rule.

   The existing records in the tblBilling table are tested against the validation rule. If any existing record violated the rule, you would be prompted to continue testing or to revert to the previous Validation Rule property setting. Next, you'll test the validation rule.

5. Switch to Datasheet view, select **$50.00** in the first row's InvoiceAmt field box, type **3**, and then press the **Tab** key. A dialog box opens containing the message "Invoice amounts must be greater than 5," which is the Validation Text property setting you created in Step 3.

6. Click the **OK** button, and then press the **Esc** key. The first row's InvoiceAmt field reverts to its original value, $50.00.

7. Close the tblBilling table.

Now that you've finished entering the field validation rule for the InvoiceAmt field in the tblBilling table, you'll enter the table validation rule for the date fields in the tblVisit table.

Defining Table Validation Rules

To make sure that the Insurance field value that a user enters in the tblBilling table is not larger than the InvoiceAmt field value, you can create a **table validation rule**. Once again, you'll use the Validation Rule and Validation Text properties, but this time you'll set these properties for the table instead of for an individual field. You'll use a table validation rule because this validation involves multiple fields. A field validation rule is used when the validation involves a restriction for only the selected field and does not depend on other fields.

Be sure "Table Properties" is listed as the selection type in the property sheet.

To create and test a table validation rule in the tblBilling table:

1. Open the **tblBilling** table in Design view, close the Navigation Pane, and then on the Table Tools Design tab, in the Show/Hide group, click the **Property Sheet** button to open the property sheet for the table.

   To make sure that each Insurance field value is less than or equal to the InvoiceAmt field value, you use the Validation Rule box for the table.

2. In the property sheet, click the **Validation Rule** box.

3. Type **Insur**, press the **Tab** key to select Insurance in the AutoComplete box, type **<= InvoiceAm**, and then press the **Tab** key.

4. In the Validation Text box, type **Insurance coverage cannot be larger than the invoice amount** and then, if necessary, widen the Property Sheet so the Validation Rule text is visible. See Figure 5-41.

Figure 5-41 Setting table validation properties

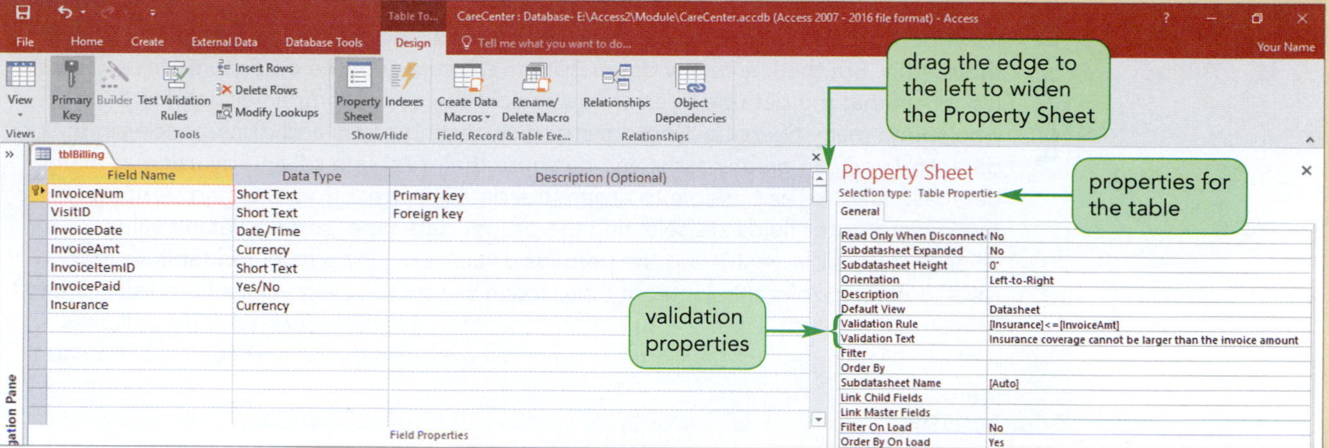

You can now test the validation properties.

5. Close the property sheet, save the table, and then click the **Yes** button when asked if you want to test the existing dates in the tblBilling table against the new validation rule.
6. Switch to Datasheet view, and then click the Insurance column value in the first record.
7. Edit the Insurance value to change it to $150.00, and then press the **Tab** key to complete your changes to the record. A dialog box opens containing the message "Insurance coverage cannot be larger than the invoice amount," which is the Validation Text property setting you entered in Step 4.

   Unlike field validation rule violations, which are detected immediately after you finish a field entry and advance to another field, table validation rule violations are detected only when you finish all changes to the current record and advance to another record.

8. Click the **OK** button, and then press the **Esc** key to undo your change to the Insurance column value.
9. Close the tblBilling table.

PROSKILLS

Problem Solving: Perfecting Data Quality

It's important that you design useful queries, forms, and reports and that you test them thoroughly. But the key to any database is the accuracy of the data stored in its tables. It's critical that the data be as error-free as possible. Most companies employ people who spend many hours tracking down and correcting errors and discrepancies in their data, and you can greatly assist and minimize their problem solving by using as many database features as possible to ensure the data is correct from the start. Among these features for fields are selecting the proper data type, setting default values whenever possible, restricting the permitted values by using field and table validation rules, enforcing referential integrity, and forcing users to select values from lists instead of typing the values. Likewise, having an arsenal of queries—such as find duplicates and top values queries—available to users will expedite the work they do to find and correct data errors.

Based on a request from Kimberly, Daksha added a Long Text field to the tblVisit table. Next you'll review Daksha's work.

Working with Long Text Fields

You use a Long Text field to store long comments and explanations. Short Text fields are limited to 255 characters, but Long Text fields can hold up to 65,535 characters. In addition, Short Text fields limit you to plain text with no special formatting, but you can define Long Text fields to store plain text similar to Short Text fields or to store rich text, which you can selectively format with options such as bold, italic, and different fonts and colors.

You'll review the Long Text field, named Comments, that Daksha added to the tblVisit table.

To review the Long Text field in the tblVisit table:

1. Open the Navigation Pane, open the **tblVisit** table in Datasheet view, and then close the Navigation Pane.
2. Increase the width of the Comments field so most of the comments fit in the column.

   Although everything fits on the screen when using a screen of average size and resolution, on some computer systems freezing panes is necessary to be able to view everything at once. On a smaller screen, if you scroll to the right to view the Comments field, you'll no longer be able to identify which animal applies to a row because the Animal ID column will be hidden. You may also see this effect if you shrink the size of the Access window. You'll freeze the Visit ID, Animal ID, and Date of Visit columns so they remain visible in the datasheet as you scroll to the right.
3. Click the **Visit ID column** selector, press and hold down the **Shift** key, click the **Date of Visit** column selector, and then release the **Shift** key. The Visit ID, Animal ID, and Date of Visit columns are selected.
4. On the Home tab, in the Records group, click the **More** button, and then click **Freeze Fields**.

5. If necessary, reduce the size of the Access window so not all columns are visible, and then scroll to the right until you see the Comments column. Notice that the Visit ID, Animal ID, and Date of Visit columns, the three leftmost columns, remain visible when you scroll. See Figure 5-42.

Figure 5-42 Freezing three datasheet columns

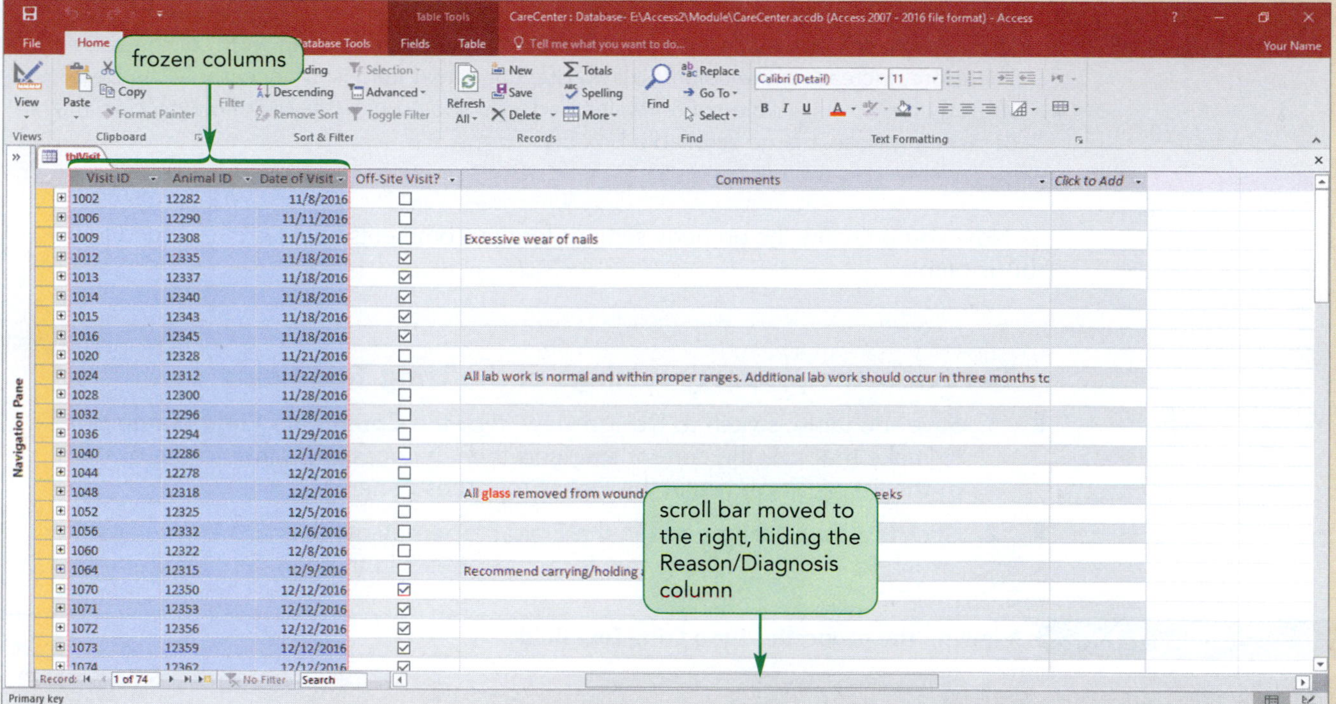

The Comments column is a Long Text field that Riverview Veterinary Care Center clinicians use to store observations and other commentary about each animal visit. Note that the Comment for Visit ID 1048 displays rich text using a bold and red font. Comments field values are partially hidden because the datasheet column is not wide enough. You'll view a record's Comments field value in the Zoom dialog box.

6. Click the **Comments** box for the record for Visit ID 1024, hold down the **Shift** key, press the **F2** key, and then release the **Shift** key. The Zoom dialog box displays the entire Comments field value.
7. Click the **OK** button to close the Zoom dialog box.

INSIGHT

Viewing Long Text Fields with Large Contents in Datasheet View

For a Long Text field that contains many characters, you can widen the field's column to view more of its contents by dragging the right edge of the field's column selector to the right or by using the Field Width command when you click the More button in the Records group on the Home tab. However, increasing the column width reduces the number of other columns you can view at the same time. Further, for Long Text fields containing thousands of characters, you can't widen the column enough to be able to view the entire contents of the field at one time across the width of the screen. Therefore, increasing the column width of a Long Text field isn't necessarily the best strategy for viewing table contents. Instead, you should use the Zoom dialog box in a datasheet or use a large scrollable box on a form.

Now you'll review the property settings for the Comments field Daksha added to the tblVisit table.

To review the property settings of the Long Text field:

1. Save the table, switch to Design view, click the **Comments Field Name** box to make that row the current row, and then, if necessary, scroll to the bottom of the list of properties in the Field Properties pane.
2. Click the **Text Format** box in the Field Properties pane, and then click its arrow. The list of available text formats appears in the box. See Figure 5-43.

Figure 5-43 Viewing the properties for a Long Text field

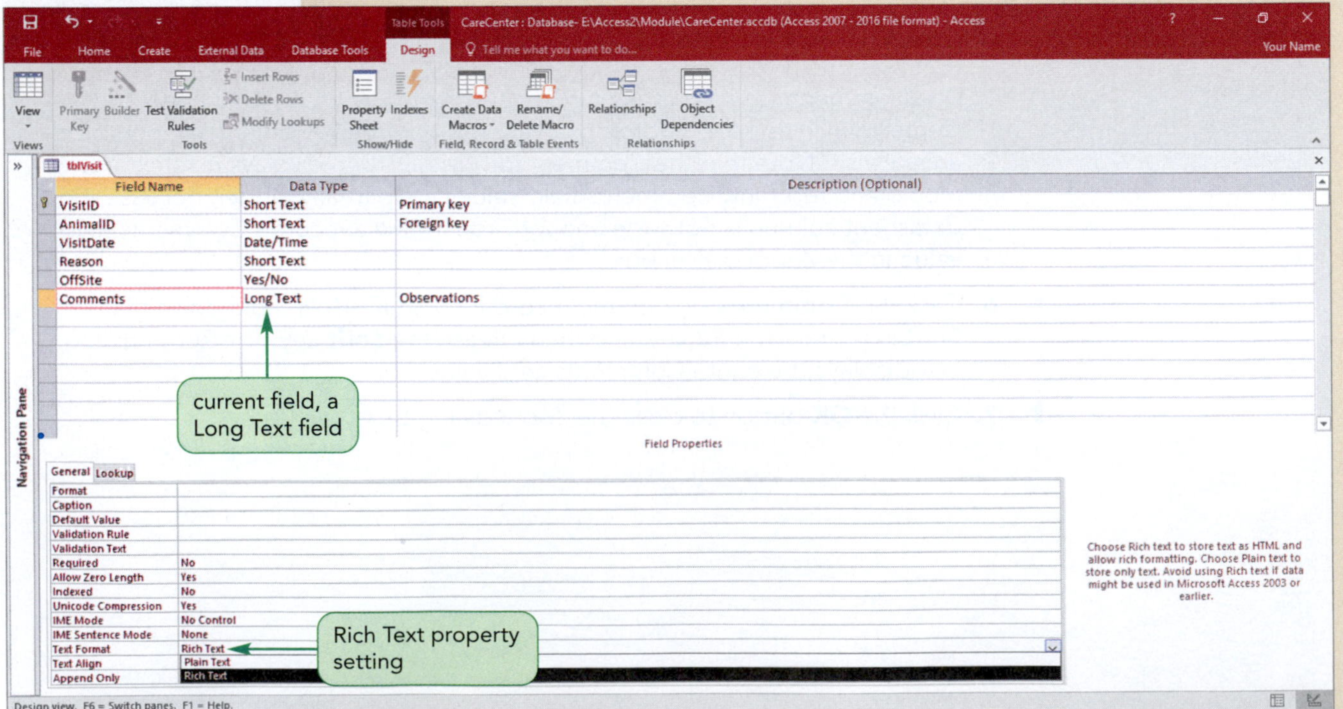

Daksha set the **Text Format property** for the Comments field to Rich Text, which lets you format the field contents using the options in the Font group on the Home tab. The default Text Format property setting for a Long Text field is Plain Text, which doesn't allow text formatting.

3. Click the **arrow** on the Text Format box to close the list, and then click the **Append Only** box.

   The **Append Only property**, which appears at the bottom of the list of properties, enables you to track the changes that you make to a Long Text field. Setting this property to Yes causes a historical record of all versions of the Long Text field value to be maintained. You can view each version of the field value, along with a date and time stamp of when each version change occurred.

   You've finished your review of the Long Text field, so you can close the table.

4. Close the tblVisit table.

When employees at Riverview Veterinary Care Center open the CareCenter database, a security warning might appear below the ribbon, and they must enable the content of the database before beginning their work. Kimberly asks if you can eliminate this extra step when employees open the database.

Designating a Trusted Folder

A database is a file, and files can contain malicious instructions that can damage other files on your computer or files on other computers on your network. Unless you take special steps, every database is treated as a potential threat to your computer. One special step that you can take is to designate a folder as a trusted folder. A **trusted folder** is a folder on a drive or network that you designate as trusted and where you place databases you know are safe. When you open a database located in a trusted folder, it is treated as a safe file, and a security warning is no longer displayed. You can also place files used with other Microsoft Office programs, such as Word documents and Excel workbooks, in a trusted folder to eliminate warnings when you open them.

Because the CareCenter database is from a trusted source, you'll specify its location as a trusted folder to eliminate the security warning when a user opens the database.

To designate a trusted folder:

1. Click the **File** tab, and then click **Options** in the navigation bar. The Access Options dialog box opens.
2. In the left section of the dialog box, click **Trust Center**. The Trust Center options are displayed in the dialog box.
3. In the right section of the dialog box, click the **Trust Center Settings** button to open the Trust Center dialog box.
4. In the left section of the Trust Center dialog box, click **Trusted Locations**. The trusted locations for your installation of Access and other trust options are displayed on the right. See Figure 5-44.

Figure 5-44 Designating a trusted folder

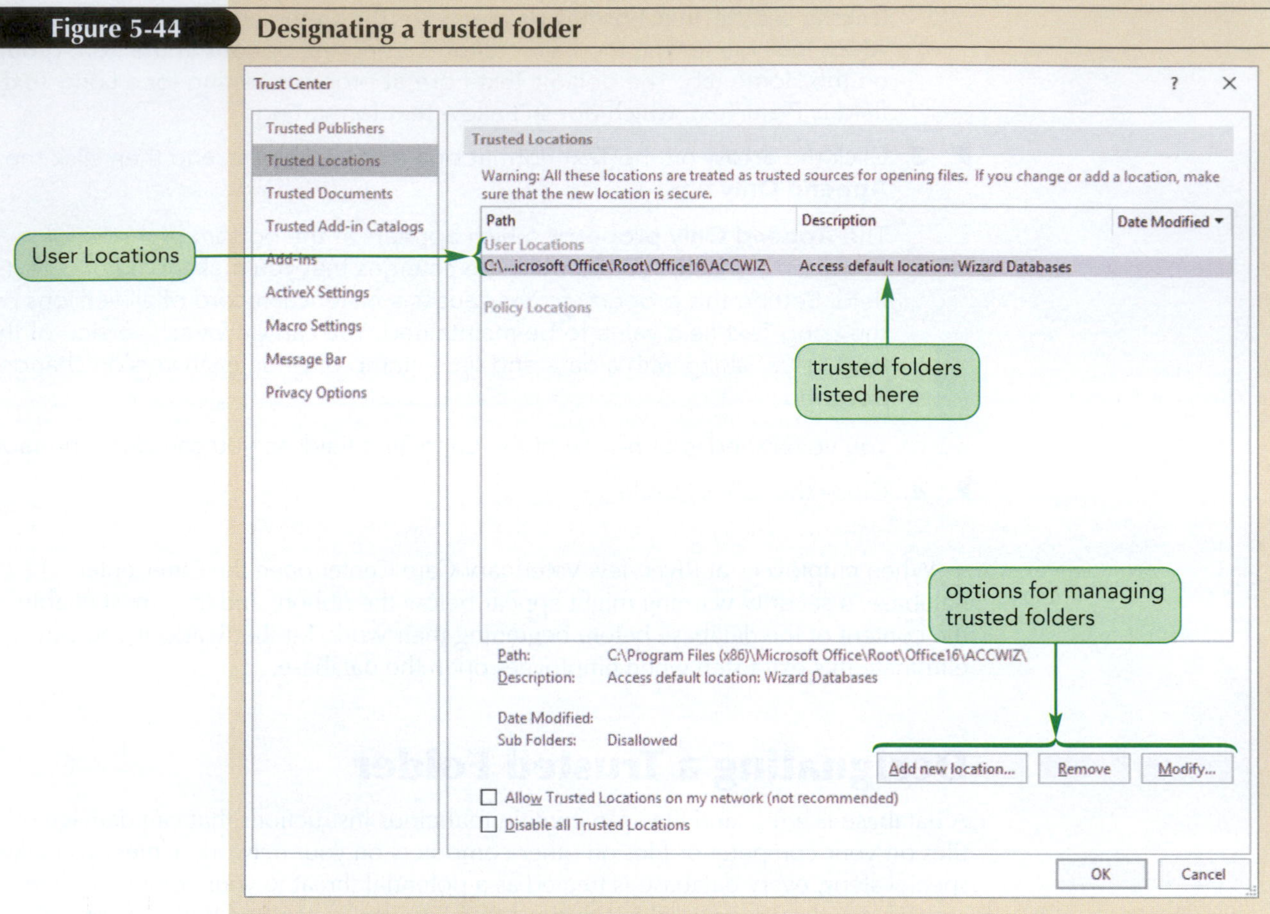

Existing trusted locations appear in the list at the top, and options to add, remove, and modify trusted locations appear at the bottom.

Trouble? Check with your instructor before adding a new trusted location. If your instructor tells you not to create a new trusted location, skip to Step 8.

5. Click the **Add new location** button to open the Microsoft Office Trusted Location dialog box.
6. In the Microsoft Office Trusted Location dialog box, click the **Browse** button, navigate to the Access2 > Module folder where your Data Files are stored, and then click the **OK** button.

   You can also choose to designate subfolders of the selected location as trusted locations, but you won't select this option. By default, files in subfolders are not trusted.
7. Click the **OK** button. The Access2 > Module folder is added to the list of trusted locations.
8. Click the **OK** button to close the Trust Center dialog box, and then click the **OK** button to close the Access Options dialog box.

You've created several queries and completed several table design changes, so you should compact and repair the CareCenter database. Daksha doesn't use the Compact on Close option with the CareCenter database because it's possible to lose the database if there's a computer malfunction when the Compact on Close operation runs.

As a precaution, you'll make a backup copy of the database before you compact and repair it. Making frequent backup copies of your critical files safeguards your data from hardware and software malfunctions, which can occur at any time.

To back up, compact, and repair the CareCenter database:

1. Click the **File** tab on the ribbon, and then click the **Save As** menu item.
2. Click the **Back Up Database** option, and then click the **Save As** button. The Save As dialog box opens with a suggested filename of CareCenter_date in the File name box, where date is the current date in the format year-month-day. For instance, if you made a backup on February 15, 2017, the suggested filename would be CareCenter_2017-02-15.
3. Navigate to the location of a USB drive or other external medium, if available, and then click the **Save** button to save the backup file.

   Next, you'll verify that the trusted location is working.
4. Click the **File** tab on the ribbon, and then click the **Close** command to close the CareCenter database.
5. Click the **File** tab on the ribbon, click **Open** on the navigation bar, and then click **CareCenter.accdb** in the Recent list. The database opens, and no security warning appears below the ribbon because the database is located in the trusted location you designated.

   Next, you'll compact and repair the database.
6. Click the **File** tab on the ribbon, and then click the **Compact & Repair Database** button.
7. Close the CareCenter database.

You've completed the table design changes to the CareCenter database, which will make working with it easier and more accurate.

REVIEW

Session 5.3 Quick Check

1. What is a lookup field?
2. A(n) ______________ is a predefined format you use to enter and display data in a field.
3. What is property propagation?
4. Define the Validation Rule property, and give an example of when you would use it.
5. Define the Validation Text property, and give an example of when you would use it.
6. Setting a Long Text field's Text Format property to ______________ lets you format its contents.
7. A(n) ______________ folder is a location where you can place databases that you know are safe.

PRACTICE

Review Assignments

Data File needed for the Review Assignments: Supplier.accdb

Kimberly asks you to create several new queries and enhance the table design for the Vendor database. This database contains information about the vendors that Riverview Veterinary Care Center works with to obtain medical supplies and equipment for the center, as well as the vendors who service and maintain the equipment. Complete the following steps:

1. Open the **Supplier** database located in the Access2 > Review folder provided with your Data Files.
2. Modify the first record in the **tblSupplier** table datasheet by changing the Contact First Name and Contact Last Name field values to your first and last names. Close the table.
3. Create a query called **qrySupplierNameAndAddress** that lists the following fields from the tblSupplier table: SupplierID, Company, City, State, and Zip. After you have created the query, use the Autofilter feature of Access to list on the suppliers in NC, SC, and VA only. Use the Toggle Filter button to remove and reapply the filter. Save and close the query.
4. Create a query to find all records in the tblSupplier table in which the City field value starts with the letter A. Display all fields in the query recordset, and sort in ascending order by the Company Name. Save the query as **qryASelectedCities**, run the query, and then close it.
5. Make a copy of the qryASelectedCities query using the new name **qryOtherSelectedCities**. Modify the new query to find all records in the tblSupplier table in which the City field values are not Boston, Charlotte, or Billings. Save and run the query, and then close it.
6. Create a query to find all records from the tblSupplier table in which the State value is GA, MA, or NC. Use a list-of-values match for the selection criteria. Display all fields in the query recordset, and sort in descending order by the company name. Save the query as **qrySelectedStates**, run the query, and then close it.
7. Create a query to display all records from the tblSupplier table, selecting the Company, City, and Phone fields, and sorting in ascending order by Company. Add a calculated field named **ContactName** as the last column that concatenates the ContactFirst value, a space, and the ContactLast value. If the contact has a nickname, use the nickname in place of the first name in the calculated field. Set the Caption property for the ContactName field to **Contact Name**. Save the query as **qryCompanyContacts**, run the query, resize the Contact Name column to its best fit, and then save and close the query.
8. Create a parameter query to select the tblSupplier table records for a State field value that the user specifies. If the user doesn't enter a State field value, select all records from the table. Display the Company, Category, City, State, ContactFirst, ContactLast, and Phone fields in the query recordset, sorting in ascending order by City. Save the query as **qryStateParameter**. Run the query and enter no value as the State field value, and then run the query again and enter **NC** as the State field value. Close the query.
9. Create a find duplicates query based on the tblProduct table. Select ProductName as the field that might contain duplicates, and select the ProductID, SupplierID, Price, and Units fields as additional fields in the query recordset. Save the query as **qryDuplicateProductTypes**, run the query, and then close it. Because the tblProduct table does not have any duplicate ProductName values, running this query should show that no duplicate records are found.
10. Create a find unmatched query that finds all records in the tblSupplier table for which there is no matching record in the tblProduct table. Display the SupplierID, Company, City, State, Phone, ContactFirst, and ContactLast fields from the tblSupplier table in the query recordset. Save the query as **qrySuppliersWithoutMatchingProducts**, run the query, and then close it. Because the tblSupplier and tblProduct tables do not have unmatched records, running this query should show that no unmatched records are found.

11. Create a query to display all records from the tblProduct table, selecting the ProductID, SupplierID, ProductName, and Price fields, and sorting in descending order by Price. Use the Top Values property to select the top 25 percent of records. Save the query as **qryTop25Price**, run the query, and then close it.
12. In the tblProduct table, change the SupplierID field to a lookup field. Select the Company field and then the SupplierID field from the tblSupplier table. Sort in ascending order by the Company field, do not hide the key column, make sure the Company Name column is the leftmost column, resize the lookup columns to their best fit, select SupplierID as the field to store in the table, and accept the default label for the lookup column. View the tblProduct table datasheet, resize the Supplier ID column to its best fit, test the lookup field without changing a value permanently, and then save and close the table.
13. Use the Input Mask Wizard to add an input mask to the Phone field in the tblSupplier table. The ending input mask should use periods as separators, as in 987.654.3210 with only the last seven digits required; do not store the literal display characters, if you are asked to do so. Update the Input Mask property everywhere the Phone field is used. Resize all columns in the datasheet to their best fit, and then test the input mask by typing over an existing Phone field value, being sure not to change the value by pressing the Esc key after you type the last digit in the Phone field.
14. Create a crosstab query based on the tblSupplier table. Use the Category field values for the row headings, the SupplierID field values for the column headings, and the count of the Company field values as the summarized value, and include row sums. Save the query as **qrySupplierCategoryCrosstab**. Change the column heading for the total of each category to **Total of Companies**. Resize the Total of Companies column in the query recordset to its best fit, and then save and close the query.
15. Open the tblProduct table, and then open the Object Dependencies pane for the tblProduct object. Click on the Objects that depend on me option button, then click the Refresh link if necessary to see the list of objects that depend upon the tblProduct table. Verify that the following objects depend upon the tblProduct table: tblSupplier table, qrySuppliersWithoutMatchingProducts query, and qryTop25Price query. Close the Object Dependencies pane.
16. Set a field validation rule on the Price field in the tblProduct table. Ensure that each product entered will have a price greater than zero. Should a user attempt to enter a value of zero, or less than zero, the following message should be displayed: "All prices must be greater than zero." Test the field validation rule by modifying the price of the first item in the recordset to 0, and verify that the error message is displayed. Reset the value of the record to its original value. Save and close the tblProduct table.
17. Open the tblSupplier table, and then set a table validation rule on the tblSupplier table to ensure the initial contact date is prior to, or equal to, the latest contact date. If an invalid value is entered, the following message should be displayed: "Latest contact date cannot be prior to the initial contact date." Test the table validation rule by changing the latest contact date prior to the initial contact date in the first record. Advance to the next record, then verify that the error message is displayed. Reset the values of the first record to their original values. Save your changes to the tblSupplier table.
18. In the tblSupplier table, examine the field properties pane for the Notes field. Verify that the Text Format property is set to Rich Text, and that the Append Only property is set to Yes. Close the tblSupplier table without saving changes.
19. Designate the Access2 > Review folder as a trusted folder. (*Note:* Check with your instructor before adding a new trusted location.)
20. Make a backup copy of the database, compact and repair the database, and then close it.

APPLY

Case Problem 1

Data File needed for this Case Problem: MoreBeauty.accdb

Beauty To Go Sue Miller, an owner of a nail and hair salon in Orlando, Florida, regularly checks in on her grandmother, who resides in a retirement community. On some of her visits, Sue does her grandmother's hair and nails. Her grandmother told Sue that some of her friends would be glad to pay her and have regularly scheduled services if she could do their hair and nails also. Sue expanded her business to include the services to friends of her grandmother in local retirement communities to meet the needs of these ladies. Sue created an Access database named MoreBeauty to store data about members, plans, and contracts. She wants to create several new queries and make design changes to the tables. Complete the following steps:

1. Open the **MoreBeauty** database located in the Access2 > Case1 folder provided with your Data Files.
2. Modify the first record in the tblMember table datasheet by changing the First Name and Last Name column values to your first and last names. Close the table.
3. Create a query to find all records in the tblOption table in which the OptionCost field is 70, 125, 140, or 250. Use a list-of-values match for the selection criterion, and include all fields from the table in the query recordset. Sort the query in descending order by the OptionID field. Save the query as **qryLowVolumePlans**, run the query, and then close it.
4. Make a copy of the qryLowVolumePlans query using the new name **qryHighVolumePlans**. Modify the new query to find all records in the tblPlan table in which the PlanCost field is not 70, 125, 140, or 250. Save and run the query, and then close it.
5. Create a query to display all records from the tblMember table, selecting the LastName, FirstName, Street, and Phone fields, and sorting in ascending order by LastName and then in ascending order by FirstName. Add a calculated field named **MemberName** as the first column that concatenates FirstName, a space, and LastName. Set the Caption property for the MemberName field to **Member Name**. Do not display the LastName and FirstName fields in the query recordset. Create a second calculated field named **CityLine**, inserting it between the Street and Phone fields. The CityLine field concatenates City, a space, State, two spaces, and Zip. Set the Caption property for the CityLine field to **City Line**. Save the query as **qryMemberNames**, run the query, resize all columns to their best fit, and then save and close the query.
6. Create a query to display all matching records from the tblOption and tblMember tables, selecting the LastName and FirstName fields from the tblMember table and the OptionDescription and OptionCost fields from the tblOption table. Add a calculated field named **FeeStatus** as the last column that equals *Fee Waived* if the FeeWaived field is equal to *yes*, and that equals *Fee Not Waived* otherwise. Set the Caption property for the calculated field to **Fee Status**. Sort the list in ascending order on the LastName field. Save the query as **qryFeeStatus**, run the query, resize all columns to their best fit, and then save and close the query.
7. Create a query based on the tblOption and tblMember tables, selecting the LastName, FirstName, and City fields from the tblMember table and the FeeWaived, OptionDescription, and OptionCost fields from the tblOption table. The query should find the records in which the City field value is Orlando or Celebration and the FeeWaived field value is *Yes*. Save the query as **qryOrlandoAndCelebrationFeeWaived**. Save and run the query, and then close the query.

8. Create a parameter query to select the tblMember table records for a City field value that the user specifies. If the user doesn't enter a City field value, select all records from the table. Display all fields from the tblMember table in the query recordset. Save the query as **qryMemberCityParameter**. Run the query and enter no value as the City field value, and then run the query again and enter **Celebration** as the City field value. Close the query.
9. Create a find duplicates query based on the tblMember table. Select OptionEnd as the field that might contain duplicates, and select all other fields in the table as additional fields in the query recordset. Save the query as **qryDuplicateMemberExpirationDates**, run the query, and then close it.
10. Create a find unmatched query that finds all records in the tblMember table for which there is no matching record in the tblOption table. Select FirstName, LastName, and Phone fields from the tblMembers table. Save the query as **qryMembersWithoutPlans**, run the query, and then close it. Because the tblMember and tblOption tables do not have unmatched records, running this query should show that no unmatched records are found.
11. Create a new query based on the tblMember table. Display the FirstName, LastName, Phone, OptionEnd, and OptionID fields, in this order, in the query recordset. Sort in ascending order by the OptionEnd field, and then use the Top Values property to select the top 25 percent of records. Save the query as **qryUpcomingExpirations**, run the query, and then close it.
12. Use the Input Mask Wizard to add an input mask to the Phone field in the tblMember table. Create the input mask such that the phone number is displayed with a dot separating each part of the phone number. For instance, if the phone number is (303) 123-4567 it should be displayed as 303.123.4567 for new entries. Test the input mask by typing over an existing Phone column value, being certain not to change the value by pressing the Esc key after you type the last digit in the Phone column, and then save and close the table.
13. Define a field validation rule for the OptionCost field in the tblOption table. Acceptable field values for the OptionCost field are values greater than or equal to 70. Enter the message **Value must be greater than or equal to 70** so it appears if a user enters an invalid OptionCost field value. Save your table changes, and then test the field validation rule for the OptionCost field; be certain the field values are the same as they were before your testing, and then close the table.
14. Define a table validation rule for the tblMember table to verify that OptionBegin field values precede OptionEnd field values in time. Use an appropriate validation message. Save your table changes, and then test the table validation rule, making sure any tested field values are the same as they were before your testing.
15. Add a Long Text field named **MemberComments** as the last field in the tblMember table. Set the Caption property to **Member Comments** and the Text Format property to Rich Text. In the table datasheet, resize the new column to its best fit, and then add a comment in the Member Comments column in the first record about special instructions for this member, formatting part of the text with blue, italic font. Save your table changes, and then close the table.
16. Designate the Access2 > Case1 folder as a trusted folder. (*Note:* Check with your instructor before adding a new trusted location.)
17. Make a backup copy of the database, compact and repair the database, and then close it.

APPLY

Case Problem 2

Data File needed for this Case Problem: Tutoring.accdb

Programming Pros While in college obtaining his bachelor's degree in Raleigh, North Carolina, Brent Hovis majored in computer science. Prior to graduating, Brent began tutoring freshman and sophomore students in programming to make some extra money. When Brent entered graduate school, he started Programming Pros, a company offering expanded tutoring services for high school and college students through group, private, and semiprivate tutoring sessions. Brent created an Access database to maintain information about the tutors who work for him, the students who sign up for tutoring, and the contracts they sign. To make the database easier to use, Brent wants you to create several queries and modify its table design. Complete the following steps:

1. Open the **Tutoring** database located in the Access2 > Case2 folder provided with your Data Files.
2. Change the last record in the tblTutor table datasheet so the FirstName and LastName field values contain your first and last names. Close the table.
3. Create a query to find all records in the tblStudent table in which the LastName field value begins with L. Display the FirstName, LastName, City, and HomePhone fields in the query recordset, and sort in ascending order by LastName. Save the query as **qryLastNameL**, run the query, and then close it.
4. Create a query that finds all records in the tblTutor table in which the YearInSchool field value is either Senior or Graduate. Use a list-of-values criterion, and include the fields First Name, Last Name, and YearInSchool in the recordset, sorted in ascending order on the LastName field. Save the query using the name **qrySelectedYearInSchool**. Run the query, and then close it.
5. Create a query to find all records in the tblStudent table in which the City field value is not equal to Raleigh. Display the FirstName, LastName, City, and HomePhone fields in the query recordset, and sort in ascending order by City. Save the query as **qryNonRaleigh**, run the query, and then close it.
6. Create a query to display all records from the tblTutor table, selecting all fields, and sorting in ascending order by LastName and then in ascending order by FirstName. Add a calculated field named **TutorName** as the second column that concatenates FirstName, a space, and LastName for each teacher. Set the Caption property for the TutorName field to **Tutor Name**. Do not display the FirstName and LastName fields in the query recordset. Save the query as **qryTutorNames**, run the query, resize the Tutor Name column to its best fit, and then save and close the query.
7. Create a parameter query to select the tblContract table records for a SessionType field value that the user specifies. If the user doesn't enter a SessionType field value, select all records from the table. Include all fields from the tblContract table in the query recordset. Save the query as **qrySessionTypeParameter**. Run the query and enter no value as the SessionType field value, and then run the query again and enter **Group** as the SessionType field value. Close the query.
8. Create a crosstab query based on the tblContract table. Use the SessionType field values for the row headings, the Length field values for the column headings, and the count of the ContractID field values as the summarized value, and include row sums. Save the query as **qrySessionTypeCrosstab**. Change the column heading for the row sum column, which represents the total of each type of session, to **Total Number of Sessions**. Resize the columns in the query recordset to their best fit, and then save and close the query.
9. Create a find duplicates query based on the tblContract table. Select StudentID and SessionType as the fields that might contain duplicates, and select all other fields in the table as additional fields in the query recordset. Save the query as **qryMultipleSessionsForStudents**, run the query, and then close it.

10. Create a find unmatched query that finds all records in the tblStudent table for which there is no matching record in the tblContract table. Display all fields from the tblStudent table in the query recordset. Save the query as **qryStudentsWithoutContracts**, run the query, and then close it.
11. In the tblContract table, change the TutorID field data type to Lookup Wizard. Select the FirstName, LastName, and TutorID fields from the tblTutor table, sort in ascending order by LastName, resize the lookup columns to their best fit, select TutorID as the field to store in the table, and accept the default label for the lookup column. In datasheet view, change the TutorID value for the first record to verify that the lookup functions correctly, then restore the original TutorID value for the first record. Save and close the table.
12. Use the Input Mask Wizard to add an input mask to the HomePhone and CellPhone fields in the tblStudent table. The ending input mask should use periods as separators, as in 987.654.3210, with only the last seven digits required; do not store the literal display characters, if you are asked to do so. Resize the Home Phone and Cell Phone columns to their best fit, and then test the input mask by typing over an existing Phone field value, being sure not to change the value permanently by pressing the Esc key after you type the last digit in the Phone field.
13. Define a field validation rule for the Gender field in the tblStudent table. Acceptable field values for the Gender field are F or M. Use the message "Gender value must be F or M" to notify a user who enters an invalid Gender field value. Save your table changes, test the field validation rule for the Gender field, making sure any tested field values are the same as they were before your testing, and then close the table.
14. Designate the Access2 > Case2 folder as a trusted folder. (*Note:* Check with your instructor before adding a new trusted location.)
15. Make a backup copy of the database, compact and repair the database, and then close it.

CHALLENGE

Case Problem 3

Data File needed for this Case Problem: Community.accdb

Diane's Community Center Diane Coleman is a successful businesswoman in Dallas, Georgia, but things were not always that way. Diane experienced trying times and fortunately had people in the community come into her life to assist her and her children when times were difficult. To give back to her community and support those in need, Diane has created a community center in Dallas where those in need can come in for goods and services. She has also opened a thrift store to sell and auction donated items to support the center. Diane has created an Access database to manage information about the center's patrons and donations. Diane now wants to create several queries and to make changes to the table design of the database. You'll help Diane by completing the following steps:

1. Open the **Community** database located in the Access2 > Case3 folder provided with your Data Files.
2. Modify the first record in the tblPatron table datasheet by changing the Title, FirstName, and LastName column values to your title and name. Close the table.
3. Create a query to find all records in the tblDonation table that were cash donations. Display the DonationID, PatronID, DonationDate, and DonationValue fields in the query recordset. Sort by descending order by DonationValue. Save the query as **qryCashDonations**, run the query, and then close it.
4. Create a query to find all records in the tblDonation table in which the item donated is a potential auction item. Display the DonationID, PatronID, DonationDate, Description, and DonationValue fields from the tblDonation table. Sort in ascending order by DonationDate. Save the query as **qryPotentialAuctionItems**, run the query, and then close it.

5. Create a query called **qryDonationsSeptemberOrLater** that will contain all fields from the tblDonation and tblPatron tables except for PatronID and DonationID, for all donations that are on or after September 1, 2017. Sort this query by DonationValue in descending order. Save and run the query, and then close it.
6. Create a query to display all records from the tblPatron table, selecting the Title and Phone fields. Add a calculated field named **PatronName** that concatenates FirstName, a space, and LastName. Position this column as the second column, and sort the recordset in ascending order by LastName. Set the Caption property for the PatronName field to **Patron Name**. Save the query as **qryPatronNames**, run the query, resize the new column to its best fit, and then save and close the query.
7. Create a parameter query to select the tblDonation table records for a Description field value that contains a phrase the user specifies. If the user doesn't enter a Description field phrase value, select all records from the table. Display all fields from the tblDonation table in the query recordset, and sort in ascending order by Description. Save the query as **qryDonationParameter**. Run the query and enter no value as the Description phrase field value, and then run the query again and enter **clothes** as the Description field phrase value. Close the query.

Explore 8. Create a crosstab query based on the qryDonationsSeptemberOrLater query. Use the DonationDate field values for the row headings, the CashDonation field values for the column headings, and the sum of the DonationValue field values as the summarized value, and include row sums. Save the query as **qryDonationsSeptemberOrLaterCrosstab**. Change the format of the displayed values to Fixed. Change the column headings to Cash and NonCash. Resize the columns in the query recordset to their best fit, and then save and close the query.

Explore 9. Create a find duplicates query based on the qryDonationsSeptemberOrLater query. Select FirstName and LastName as the fields that might contain duplicates, and select the CashDonation and DonationValue fields in the query as additional fields in the query recordset. Save the query as **qryMultipleDonorDonations**, run the query, and then close it.

10. Create a find unmatched query that finds all records in the tblPatron table for which there is no matching record in the tblDonation table. Include all fields from the tblPatron table, except for PatronID, in the query recordset. Save the query as **qryPatronsWithoutDonations**, run the query, and then close it.

Explore 11. Make a copy of the qryDonationsSeptemberOrLater query using the new name **qryTopDonations**. (*Hint:* Be sure to copy the correct query and not the qryDonationsSeptemberOrLaterCrosstab query.) Modify the new query by using the Top Values property to select the top 40 percent of the records. Save and run the query, and then close the query.

12. Use the Input Mask Wizard to add an input mask to the Phone field in the tblPatron table. The ending input mask should use hyphens as separators, as in 987-654-3210, with only the last seven digits required; do not store the literal display characters, if you are asked to do so. Test the input mask by typing over an existing Phone field value, being sure not to change the value permanently by pressing the Esc key after you type the last digit in the Phone field. Close the table.
13. Designate the Access2 > Case3 folder as a trusted folder. (*Note:* Check with your instructor before adding a new trusted location.)
14. Make a backup copy of the database, compact and repair the database, and then close it.

CHALLENGE

Case Problem 4

Data File needed for this Case Problem: AppTrail.accdb

Hike Appalachia Molly and Bailey Johnson own Hike Appalachia, a business in which they guide clients on hikes in the Blue Ridge Mountains of North Carolina. They advertise in local and regional outdoor magazines and field requests from people all around the region. Molly and Bailey have created an Access database for their business and now want you to create several queries and modify the table design. To do so, you'll complete the following steps:

1. Open the **AppTrail** database located in the Access2 > Case4 folder provided with your Data Files.
2. Modify the first record in the tblHiker table datasheet by changing the Hiker First Name and Hiker Last Name column values to your first and last names, and then close the table.
3. Create a query to find all records in the tbHiker table in which the HikerLast field value starts with the letter S, sorted in ascending order by HikerLast. Display all fields except the HikerID field in the query recordset. Save the query as **qryHikerLastNameS**, run the query, and then close it.
4. Create a query to find all records in the tblTour table where the tour type is not hiking. Name this query **qryNonHikingTours**. Display all fields, sorting by TourName. Save and run the query, and then close it.
5. Create a query to find all records in the tblHiker table in which the State field value is NC, SC, or GA and display all fields from the tblHiker table in the query recordset, sorted by HikerLast in ascending order. Save the query as **qrySelectedStates**, run the query, and then close it.
6. Create a query to select all records from the tblTour table with a price per person of $100 or less, where the TourType is Hiking. Display all fields in the query recordset, sorted by PricePerPerson in descending order. Save the query as **qryInexpensiveHikingTours**, run the query, and then close it.
7. Create a parameter query to select the tblTour table records for a TourType field phrase value that the user specifies. If the user doesn't enter a phrase field value, select all records from the table. Display all fields from the tblTour table in the query recordset, and sort in ascending order by TourName. Save the query as **qryTourParameter**. Run the query and enter no value as the phrase field value, and then run the query again and enter **Van** as the TourType phrase field value. Close the query.
8. Create a query that contains all records from the tblHiker table and all matching records from the tblReservation table. Display all fields from the tblHiker table and all fields except HikerID from the tblReservation table. Save the query as **qryHikersAndReservations**, run the query, and then close it.

Explore 9. Create a crosstab query based on the qryHikersAndReservations query. Use the TourID field values for the row headings, the HikerID field values for the column headings, and the sum of the People field as the summarized value, and include row sums. Save the query as **qryReservationsCrosstab**, resize the columns in the query recordset to their best fit, and then save and close the query.

Explore 10. Create a find duplicates query based on the qryHikersAndReservations query. Select HikerID as the field that might contain duplicates, and select the fields HikerFirst, HikerLast, TourID, TourDate, and People in the table as additional fields in the query recordset. Save the query as **qryMultipleReservations**, run the query, and then close it.

11. Create a find unmatched query that finds all records in the tblHiker table for which there is no matching record in the tblReservation table. Display the HikerFirst, HikerLast, City, State, and Phone fields from the tblHiker table in the query recordset. Save the query as **qryHikersWithoutReservations**, run the query, and then close it.

12. Copy the qryInexpensiveHikingTours query, and save it as **qryTopInexpensiveHikingTours**. Use the Top Values property to select the top 50 percent of the records. Save and run the query, and then close it.
13. In the tblReservation table, change the TourID field data type to Lookup Wizard. Select all of the fields from the tblTour table, sort in ascending order by TourName, do not show the key column, resize the lookup columns to their best fit, select TourID as the field to store in the table, and accept the default label for the lookup column. View the tblReservation datasheet, resize the TourID column to its best fit, test the lookup field without changing a field value permanently, and then close the table.
14. Define a field validation rule for the People field in the tblReservation table. Acceptable field values for the People field are values less than or equal to 6. Display the message **Please book a custom tour for large groups.** when a user enters an invalid People field value. Save your table changes, and then test the field validation rule for the People field; be certain the field values are the same as they were before your testing.
15. Designate the Access2 > Case4 folder as a trusted folder. (*Note:* Check with your instructor before adding a new trusted location.)
16. Make a backup copy of the database, compact and repair the database, and then close it.

MODULE 6

Using Form Tools and Creating Custom Forms

Creating Forms for Riverview Veterinary Care Center

OBJECTIVES

Session 6.1
- Change a lookup field to a Short Text field
- View and print database documentation
- Create datasheet, multiple item, and split forms
- Modify a form and anchor form controls in Layout view

Session 6.2
- Plan, design, and create a custom form in Design view and in Layout view
- Select, move, align, resize, delete, and rename controls in a form
- Add a combo box to a form
- Add headers and footers to a form

Session 6.3
- Use a combo box in a form to find records
- Add a subform to a form
- Add calculated controls to a form and a subform
- Change the tab order in a form
- Improve the appearance of a form

Case | *Riverview Veterinary Care Center*

Kimberly Johnson hired Daksha Yatawara to enhance the CareCenter database, and he initially concentrated on standardizing the table design and creating queries for Riverview Veterinary Care Center. Kimberly and her staff created a few forms before Daksha came onboard, and Daksha's next priority is to work with Kimberly to create new forms that will be more functional and easier to use.

In this module, you will create new forms for Riverview Veterinary Care Center. In creating the forms, you will use many Access form customization features, such as adding controls and a subform to a form, using combo boxes and calculated controls, and adding color and special effects. These features make it easier for database users like Kimberly and her staff to interact with a database.

STARTING DATA FILES

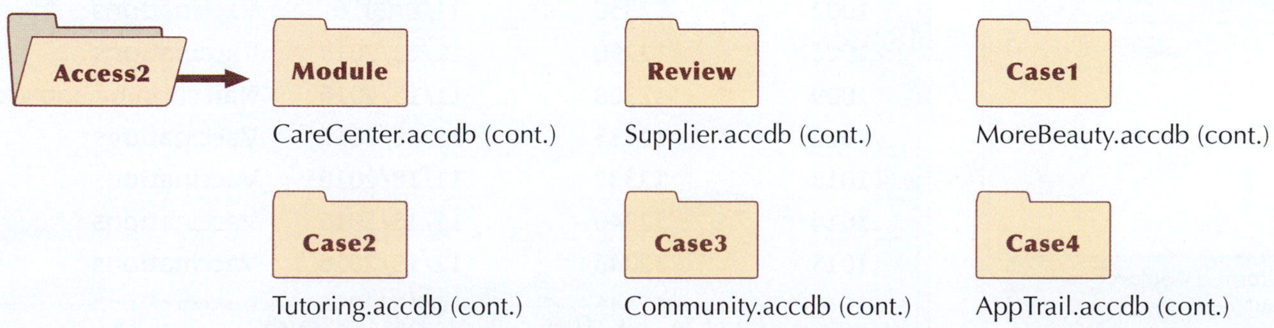

Session 6.1 Visual Overview:

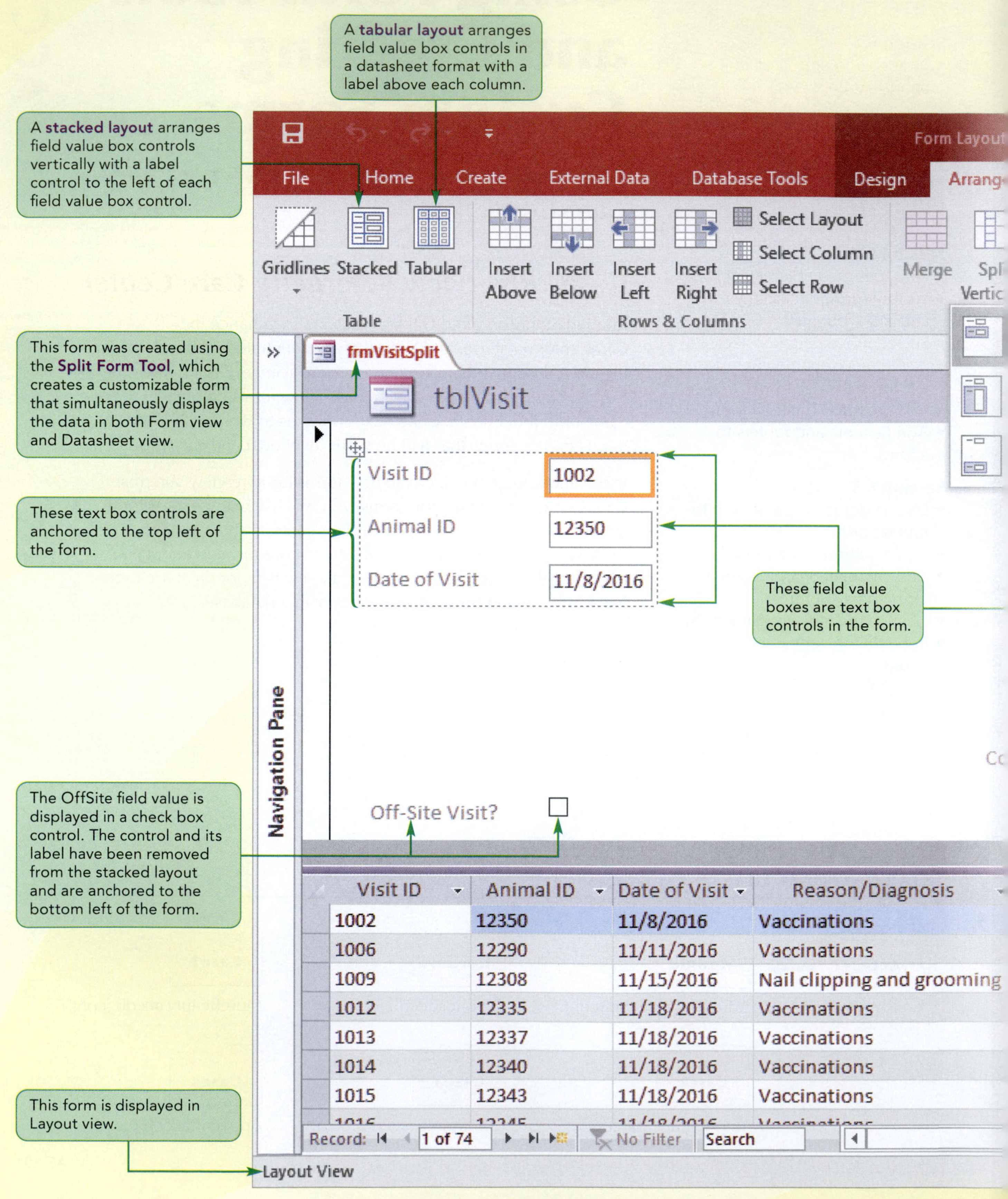
A **tabular layout** arranges field value box controls in a datasheet format with a label above each column.
A **stacked layout** arranges field value box controls vertically with a label control to the left of each field value box control.
This form was created using the **Split Form Tool**, which creates a customizable form that simultaneously displays the data in both Form view and Datasheet view.
These text box controls are anchored to the top left of the form.
These field value boxes are text box controls in the form.
The OffSite field value is displayed in a check box control. The control and its label have been removed from the stacked layout and are anchored to the bottom left of the form.
This form is displayed in Layout view.
Form Layout
File
Home
Create
External Data
Database Tools
Design
Gridlines
Stacked
Tabular
Table
Insert Above
Insert Below
Insert Left
Insert Right
Select Layout
Select Column
Select Row
Rows & Columns
Merge
frmVisitSplit
tblVisit
Navigation Pane
Visit ID
1002
Animal ID
12350
Date of Visit
11/8/2016
Off-Site Visit?
Visit ID
Animal ID
Date of Visit
Reason/Diagnosis
1002 12350 11/8/2016 Vaccinations
1006 12290 11/11/2016 Vaccinations
1009 12308 11/15/2016 Nail clipping and grooming
1012 12335 11/18/2016 Vaccinations
1013 12337 11/18/2016 Vaccinations
1014 12340 11/18/2016 Vaccinations
1015 12343 11/18/2016 Vaccinations
Record: 1 of 74
No Filter
Search
Layout View

Anchoring Controls

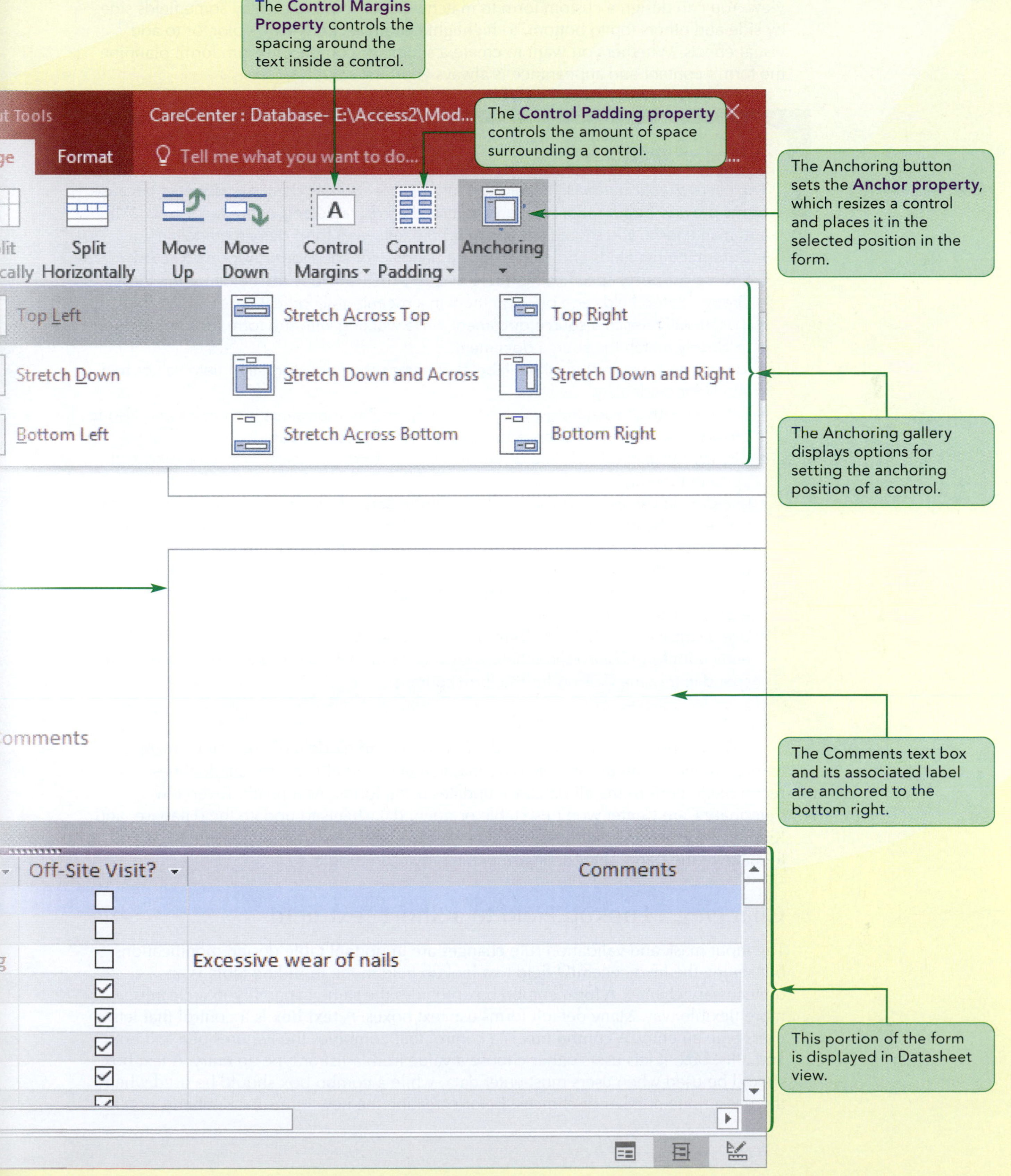
The Control Margins Property controls the spacing around the text inside a control.
The Control Padding property controls the amount of space surrounding a control.
The Anchoring button sets the Anchor property, which resizes a control and places it in the selected position in the form.
The Anchoring gallery displays options for setting the anchoring position of a control.
The Comments text box and its associated label are anchored to the bottom right.
This portion of the form is displayed in Datasheet view.
CareCenter : Database- E:\Access2\Mod...
Format
Tell me what you want to do...
Split Horizontally
Move Up
Move Down
Control Margins
Control Padding
Anchoring
Top Left
Stretch Across Top
Top Right
Stretch Down
Stretch Down and Across
Stretch Down and Right
Bottom Left
Stretch Across Bottom
Bottom Right
Off-Site Visit?
Comments
Excessive wear of nails

Designing Forms

To create a **custom form**, you can modify an existing form in Layout view or in Design view, or you can design and create a form from scratch in Layout view or in Design view. You can design a custom form to match a paper form, to display some fields side by side and others top to bottom, to highlight certain sections with color, or to add visual effects. Whether you want to create a simple or complex custom form, planning the form's content and appearance is always your first step.

INSIGHT

Form Design Guidelines

The users of your database should use forms to perform all database updates because forms provide better readability and control than do table and query recordsets. When you plan a form, you should keep in mind the following form design guidelines:

- Determine the fields and record source needed for each form. A form's **Record Source property** specifies the table or query that provides the fields for the form.
- Group related fields and position them in a meaningful, logical order.
- If users will refer to a source document while working with the form, design the form to closely match the source document.
- Identify each field value with a label that names the field, and align field values and labels for readability.
- Set the width of each field value box to fully display the values it contains and also to provide a visual cue to users about the length of those values.
- Display calculated fields in a distinctive way, and prevent users from changing and updating them.
- Use default values, list boxes, and other form controls whenever possible to reduce user errors by minimizing keystrokes and limiting entries. A control is an item, such as a text box or command button, that you place in a form or report.
- Use colors, fonts, and graphics sparingly to keep the form uncluttered and to keep the focus on the data. Use white space to separate the form controls so that they are easier to find and read.
- Use a consistent style for all forms in a database. When forms are formatted differently, with form controls in different locations from one form to another, users must spend extra time looking for the form controls.

Kimberly and her staff had created a few forms and made table design changes before implementing proper database maintenance guidelines. These guidelines recommend performing all database updates using forms. As a result, Riverview Veterinary Care Center won't use table or query datasheets to update the database, and Kimberly asks if she should reconsider any of the table design changes she asked you to make to the CareCenter database in the previous module.

Changing a Lookup Field to a Short Text field

The input mask and validation rule changes are important table design modifications, but setting the InvoiceItemID field to a lookup field in the tblBilling table is an unnecessary change. A form combo box provides the same capability in a clearer, more flexible way. Many default forms use text boxes. A **text box** is a control that lets users type an entry. A **combo box** is a control that combines the features of a text box and a list box; it lets users either choose a value from a list or type an entry. A text box should be used when users must enter data, while a combo box should be used when there is a finite number of choices. Before creating the new forms for Kimberly, you'll change the data type of the InvoiceItemID field in the tblBilling table from a Lookup Wizard field to a Short Text field, so that you can create the relationship with referential integrity between the tblBilling and tblInvoiceItems tables.

To change the data type of the InvoiceItemID field:

1. Start Access, and then open the **CareCenter** database you worked with in the previous module.

   Trouble? If the security warning is displayed below the ribbon, click the Enable Content button.

TIP

You can press the F11 key to open or close the Navigation Pane.

2. Open the Navigation Pane, if necessary, open the **tblBilling table** in Design view, and then close the Navigation Pane.
3. Click the **InvoiceItemID** Field Name box, and then in the Field Properties pane, click the **Lookup** tab. The Field Properties pane displays the lookup properties for the InvoiceItemID field. See Figure 6-1.

Figure 6-1 Lookup properties for the InvoiceItemID field

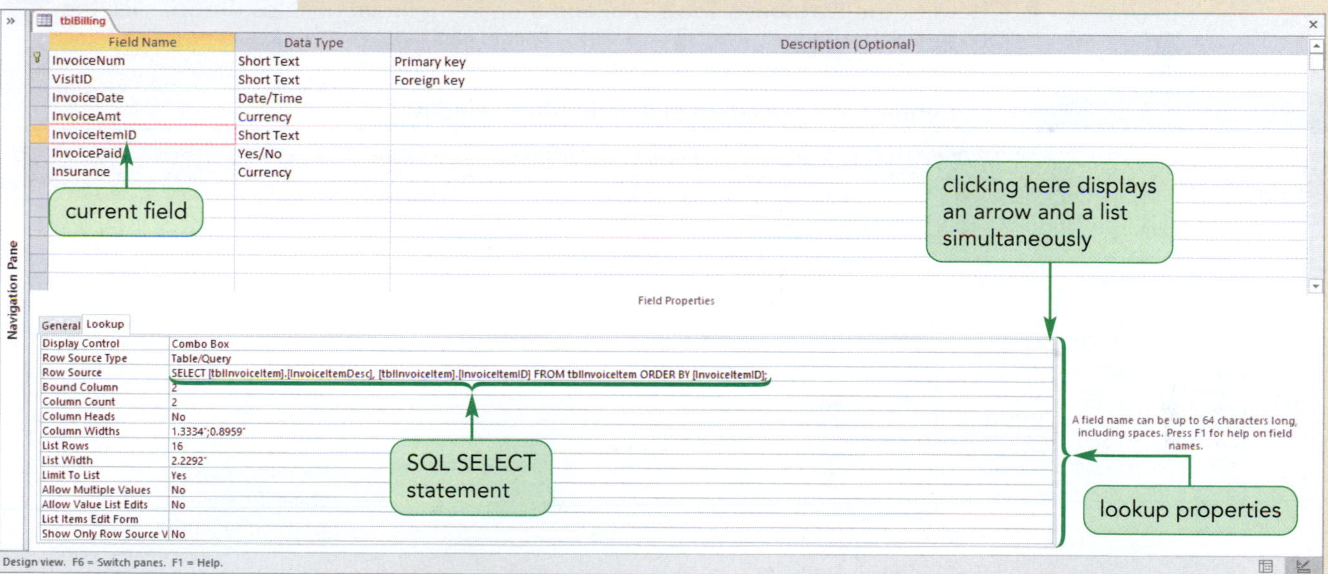

Notice the **Row Source property**, which specifies the data source for a control in a form or report or for a field in a table or query. The Row Source property is usually set to a table name, a query name, or an SQL statement. For the InvoiceItemID field, the Row Source property is set to an SQL SELECT statement. You'll learn more about SQL later in this text.

To remove the lookup feature for the InvoiceItemID field, you need to change the **Display Control property**, which specifies the default control used to display a field, from Combo Box to Text Box.

4. Click the right end of the **Display Control** box, and then click **Text Box** in the list. All the lookup properties in the Field Properties pane disappear, and the InvoiceItemID field changes back to a standard Short Text field without lookup properties.

5. Click the **General** tab in the Field Properties pane, and notice that the properties for a Short Text field still apply to the InvoiceItemID field.
6. Save the table, switch to Datasheet view, resize the Invoice Item ID column to its best fit, and then click one of the Invoice Item ID boxes. An arrow does not appear in the Invoice Item ID box because the InvoiceItemID field is no longer a lookup field.
7. Save the table, and then close the tblBilling table.

Before you could change the InvoiceItemID field in the tblBilling table to a lookup field in the previous module, you had to delete the one-to-many relationship between the tblInvoiceItem and tblBilling tables. Now that you've changed the data type of the InvoiceItemID field back to a Short Text field, you'll view the table relationships to make sure that the tables in the CareCenter database are related correctly.

To view the table relationships in the Relationships window:

1. Click the **Database Tools** tab, and then in the Relationships group, click the **Relationships** button to open the Relationships window. See Figure 6-2.

Figure 6-2 CareCenter database tables in Relationships window

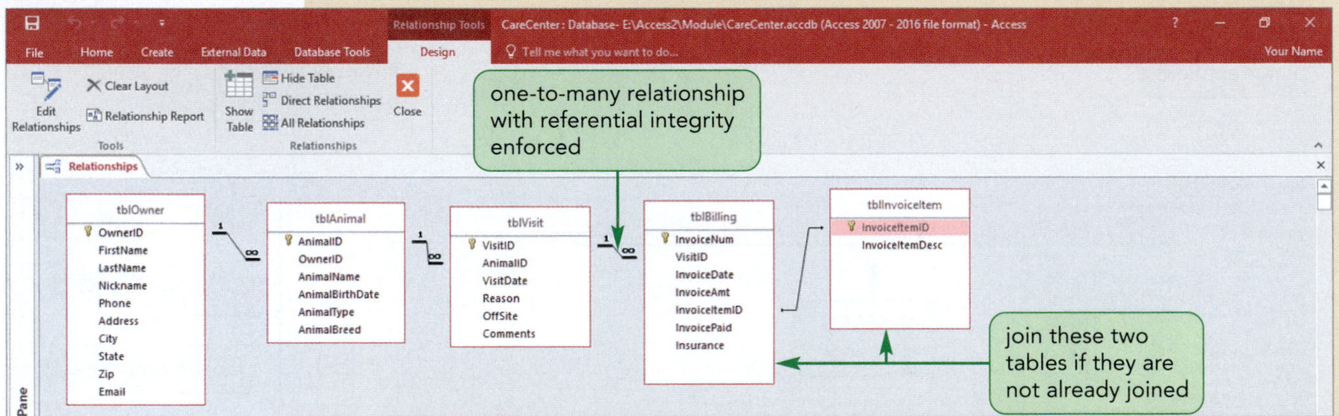

Trouble? If the order of the table field lists in your Relationships window do not match Figure 6-2, simply drag the table field lists to rearrange them so that they appear in the same left to right order shown in the figure.

The tblVisit table and the related tblBilling table have a one-to-many relationship with referential integrity enforced. You need to establish a similar one-to-many relationship between the tblInvoiceItem and tblBilling tables.

2. Double-click the **relationship line** between the tblBilling and tblInvoiceItem tables to open the Edit Relationships dialog box.
3. Click the **Enforce Referential Integrity** check box, click the **Cascade Update Related Fields** check box, and then click the **OK** button to close the dialog box. The join line connecting the tblInvoiceItem and tblBilling tables now indicates a one-to-many relationship with referential integrity enforced.

Kimberly is interested in documenting information on the objects and relationships between objects in the database she and her staff can use as a reference. In Access, you can create a report of the database relationships. You can also give Kimberly information on all the objects in the database using the Documenter.

Creating a Relationship Report and Using the Documenter

From the Relationships window, you can create a Relationship report to document the fields, tables, and relationships in a database. You can also use the **Documenter**, another Access tool, to create detailed documentation of all, or selected, objects in a database. For each selected object, the Documenter lets you print documentation, such as the object's properties and relationships, and the names and properties of fields used by the object. You can use the documentation on an object, referred to as an Object Definition Report, to help you understand an object and to help you plan changes to that object.

PROSKILLS

Written Communication: Satisfying User Documentation Requirements

The Documenter produces object documentation that is useful to the technical designers, analysts, and programmers who develop and maintain Access databases and who need to understand the intricate details of a database's design. However, users who interact with databases generally have little interest in the documentation produced by the Documenter. Users need to know how to enter and maintain data using forms and how to obtain information using forms and reports, so they require special documentation that matches these needs; this documentation isn't produced by the Documenter, though. Many companies assign one or more users the task of creating the documentation needed by users based on the idea that users themselves are the most familiar with their company's procedures and understand most clearly the specific documentation that they and other users require. Databases with dozens of tables and with hundreds of other objects are complicated structures, so be sure you provide documentation that satisfies the needs of users separate from the documentation for database developers.

Next, you will create a Relationship report and use the Documenter to create documentation for the tblVisit table.

To create the Relationship report:

1. On the Relationship Tools Design tab, in the Tools group, click the **Relationship Report** button to open the Relationships for CareCenter report in Print Preview.
2. In the Page Layout group, click the **Landscape** button to change the report to landscape orientation and display the entire relationship structure. See Figure 6-3.

Figure 6-3 **Relationships for CareCenter report**

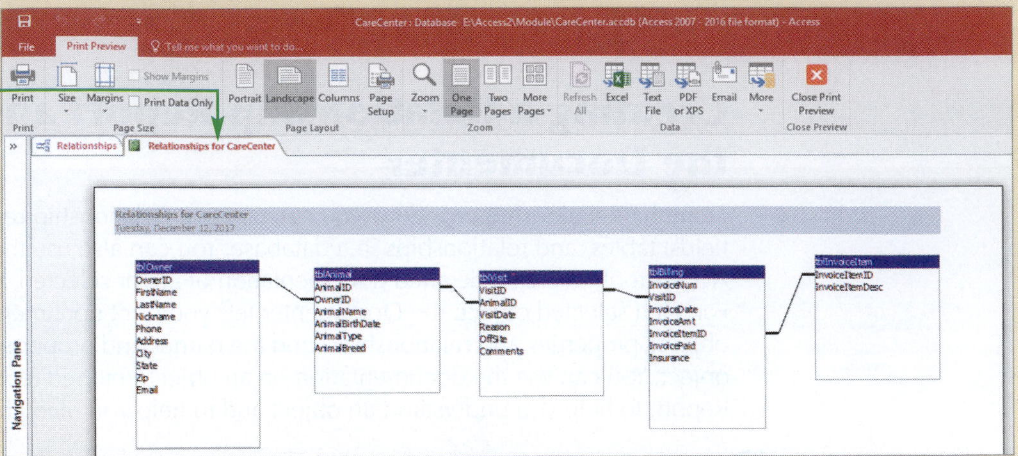

Trouble? If the order of the table field lists in your Relationships window do not match Figure 6-3, simply drag the table field lists to rearrange them so that they appear in the same left-to-right order shown in the figure.

3. Right-click the **Relationships for CareCenter** tab, and then click **Close** to close the tab. A dialog box opens and asks if you want to save the design of the report.
4. Click the **Yes** button to save the report, click the **OK** button to use the default report name Relationships for CareCenter, and then close the Relationships window.

Kimberly wants to show her staff a sample of the information the Documenter provides.

REFERENCE

Using the Documenter

- In the Analyze group on the Database Tools tab, click the Database Documenter button.
- In the Documenter dialog box, select the object(s) you want to document.
- If necessary, click the Options button to open the Print Table Definition dialog box, select specific documentation options for the selected object(s), and then click the OK button.
- Click the OK button to close the Documenter dialog box and open the Object Definition window in Print Preview.
- Print the documentation if desired, and then close the Object Definition window.

You will use the Documenter to create an Object Definition Report on the tblVisit table.

To use the Documenter to create, save, and print an Object Definition report:

1. On the ribbon, click the **Database Tools** tab.
2. In the Analyze group, click the **Database Documenter** button to open the Documenter dialog box, and then click the **Tables** tab (if necessary). See Figure 6-4.

Figure 6-4 Documenter dialog box

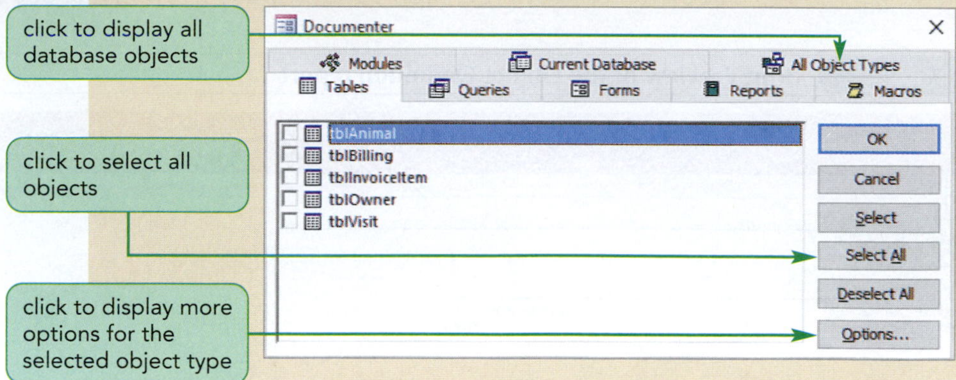

3. Click the **tblVisit** check box, and then click the **Options** button. The Print Table Definition dialog box opens. In this dialog box, you select which documentation you want the Documenter to include for the selected table, its fields, and its indexes.
4. Make sure the **Properties**, **Relationships**, and **Permissions by User and Group** check boxes are all checked in the Include for Table section.
5. In the Include for Fields section, click the **Names, Data Types, and Sizes** option button (if necessary), then click the **Names and Fields** option button in the Include for Indexes section (if necessary). See Figure 6-5.

Figure 6-5 Print Table Definition dialog box

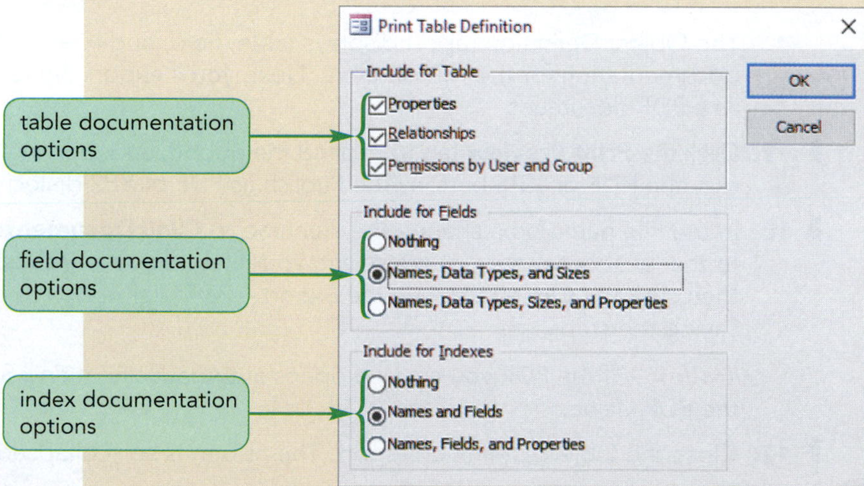

TIP

The Print Preview tab in the Print Preview window provides options for setting various printing options, such as page margins, page orientation, and number of columns to print for a form or report.

6. Click the **OK** button to close the Print Table Definition dialog box, and then click the **OK** button to close the Documenter dialog box. The Object Definition report opens in Print Preview.
7. On the Print Preview tab, in the Zoom group, click the **Zoom button arrow**, and then click **Zoom 100%**. To display more of the report, you will collapse the ribbon.

8. On the right end of the ribbon, click the **Collapse the Ribbon** button, and then scroll down the report and examine its contents. See Figure 6-6.

Figure 6-6 Print Preview of the Object Definition report

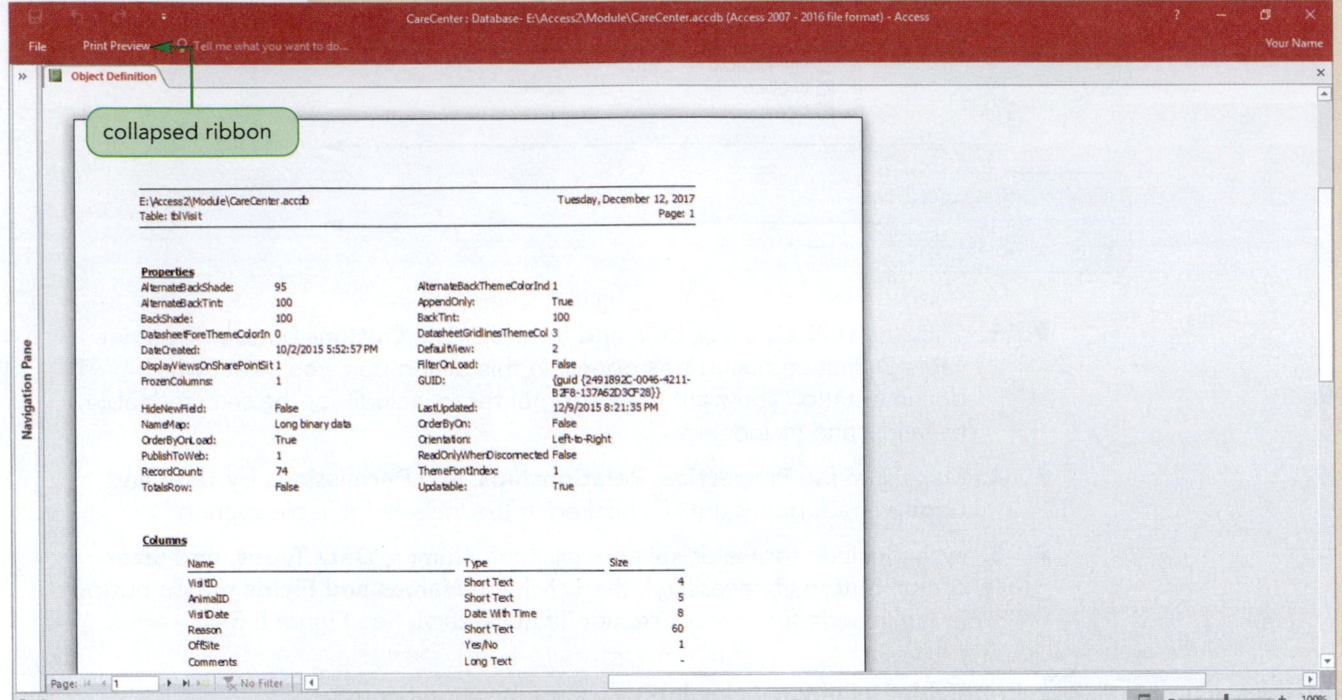

The Object Definition report displays table, field, and relationship documentation for the tblVisit table. Next, you'll export the report and save it as a PDF document.

9. Click the **Print Preview** tab to expand the ribbon, and then in the Data group, click the **PDF or XPS** button. The Publish as PDF or XPS dialog box opens.

10. In the File name box, change the filename to **ClinicDocumenter**, navigate to the location where you are saving your files, click the **Publish** button, and then click the **Close** button in the Export – PDF dialog box to close without saving the steps.

Trouble? If the PDF you created opens automatically during Step 10, close the PDF viewer.

11. Close the Object Definition report. The ribbon is still collapsed.

12. On the ribbon, click the **Home** tab, and then, on the right end of the ribbon, click the **Pin the ribbon** button to expand and pin the ribbon again.

TIP

You can also collapse the ribbon by double-clicking any ribbon tab or by right-clicking a blank area of the ribbon and clicking Collapse the Ribbon on the shortcut menu.

The CareCenter database currently contains the frmOwner form. The frmOwner form was created using the Form Wizard with some design changes that were made in Layout view including changing the theme, changing the form title color and line type, adding a picture, and moving a field. Next Kimberly would like you to create a form that allows her and her staff to see and modify the relevant data for animal visits. You will create this form using other form tools.

Creating Forms Using Form Tools

In earlier modules you created forms with and without subforms using the Form Wizard. You can create other types of forms using different form tools, namely the Datasheet tool, the Multiple Items tool, and the Split Form tool.

PROSKILLS

Decision Making: Creating Multiple Forms and Reports

When developing a larger database application, it's not uncommon for the users of the database to be unsure as to what they want with respect to forms and reports. You may obtain some sample data and sample reports during the requirements-gathering phase that give you some ideas, but in the end, it is a good idea to have the users approve the final versions.

While you are actively developing the application, you might design different versions of forms and reports that you think will meet users' needs; later in the process, you might narrow the selection to a few forms and reports. Ultimately, you should ask the users to make the final choices of which forms and reports to incorporate into the database. By involving the users in the planning phase for forms and reports, the database is more likely to meet everyone's needs.

Kimberly has requested a form that her staff can use to work with information from the tblVisit table. Because her requirements at this point are vague, you'll create a selection of form designs for Kimberly to choose from. You'll create two simple forms that show the contents of the tblVisit in a layout that resembles a table, and you'll create a custom form that Kimberly's staff may find a bit more user-friendly. First, you'll create the simple forms for Kimberly and her staff.

Creating a Form Using the Datasheet Tool

You can create a simple form using the Datasheet Tool. The **Datasheet tool** creates a form in a datasheet format that contains all the fields in the source table or query. Kimberly might prefer this if she and her staff are very comfortable entering data in an Access table in Datasheet view. You'll use the Datasheet tool to create a form based on the tblVisit table. When you use the Datasheet tool, the record source (either a table or query) for the form must either be open or selected in the Navigation Pane.

To create the form using the Datasheet tool:

1. Open the Navigation Pane, and then click **tblVisit**.
2. On the ribbon, click the **Create** tab.
3. In the Forms group, click the **More Forms** button, click **Datasheet**, and then, if necessary, close the Property Sheet. The Datasheet tool creates a form showing every field in the tblVisit table in a datasheet format. See Figure 6-7.

Figure 6-7 Form created with the Datasheet tool

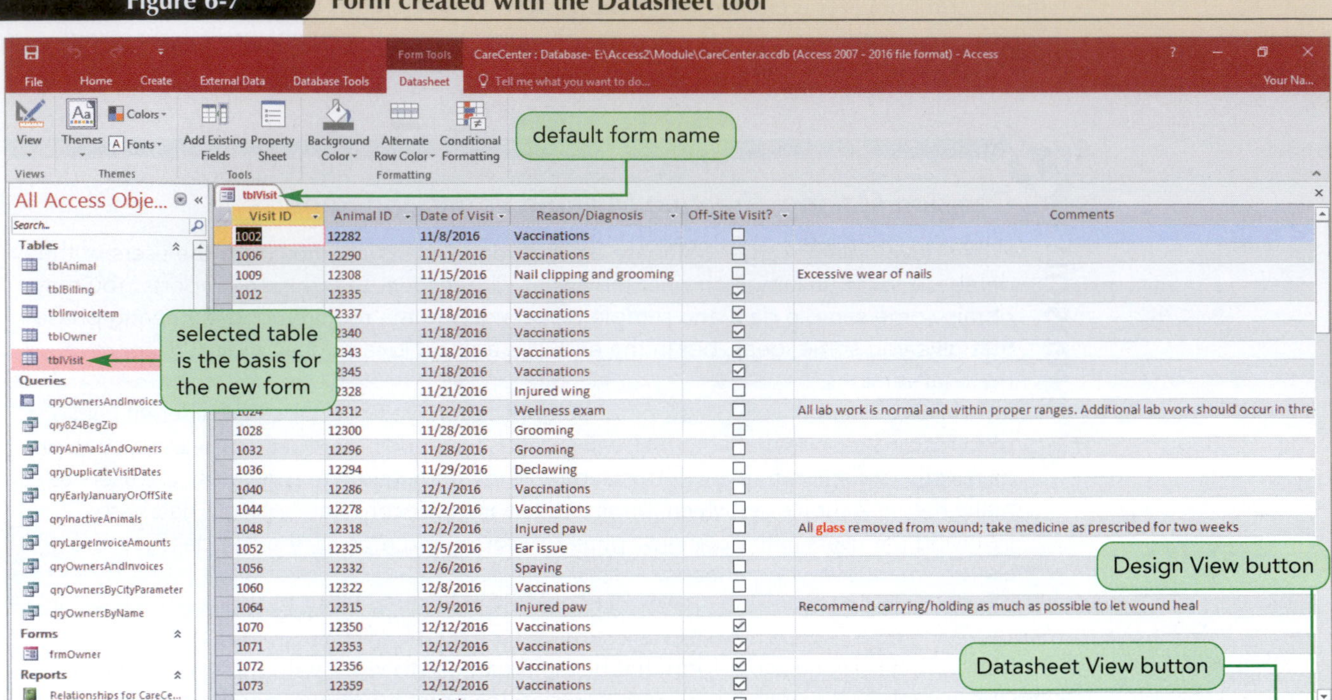

The form resembles the Datasheet view for the table except that it does not include the expand buttons at the beginning of each row. The form name, tblVisit, is the same name as the table used as the basis for the form. Recall that each table and query in a database must have a unique name. Although you could give a form or report the same name as a table or query, doing so would likely cause confusion. Fortunately, using object name prefixes prevents this confusing practice, and you will change the name when you save the form.

As you know, when working with forms, you view and update data in Form view, you view and make simple design changes in Layout view, and you make simple and complex design changes in Design view. However, not all of these views are available for every type of form. For the form created with the Datasheet tool, you'll check the available view options.

4. On the Form Tools Datasheet tab, in the Views group, click the **View button arrow**. See Figure 6-8.

Figure 6-8 View options for a form created with the Datasheet tool

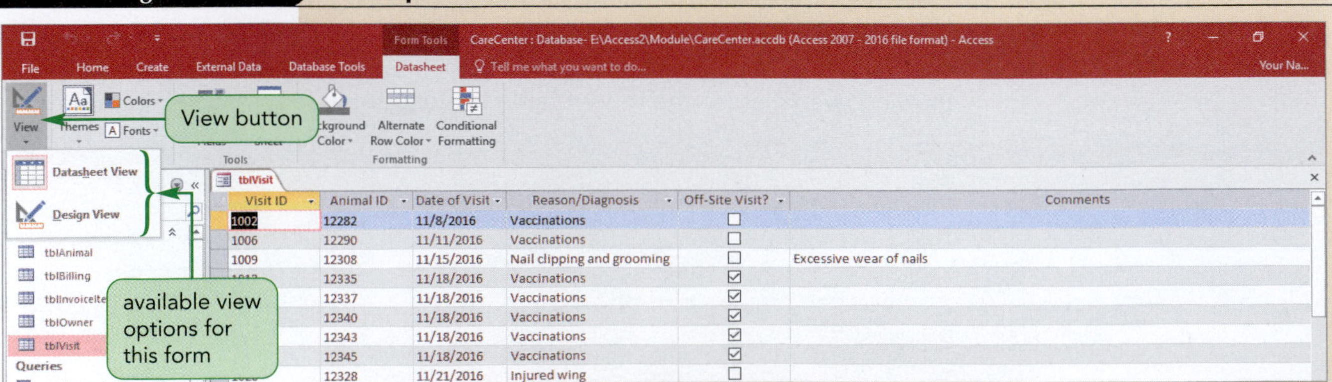

Notice Form view and Layout view are not options on the menu, which means that they are unavailable for this form type. Datasheet view allows you to view and update data, and Design view allows you to modify the form's layout and design. The buttons for accessing these two available views are also on the status bar.

You'll save this form to show Kimberly as one of the options for the forms for animal visits.

5. Save the form as **frmVisitDatasheet**, and close the form.

Kimberly might prefer a form created using the Multiple Items tool because it will provide a form with larger text boxes for displaying a record's field values.

Creating a Form Using the Multiple Items Tool

The **Multiple Items tool** creates a customizable form that displays multiple records from a source table or query in a datasheet format. You'll use the Multiple Items tool to create a form based on the tblVisit table.

To create the form using the Multiple Items tool:

1. Make sure that the tblVisit table is selected in the Navigation Pane, and then click the **Create** tab.
2. In the Forms group, click the **More Forms** button, and then click **Multiple Items**. The Multiple Items tool creates a form showing every field in the tblVisit table and opens the form in Layout view. See Figure 6-9.

Figure 6-9 **Form created with the Multiple Items tool**

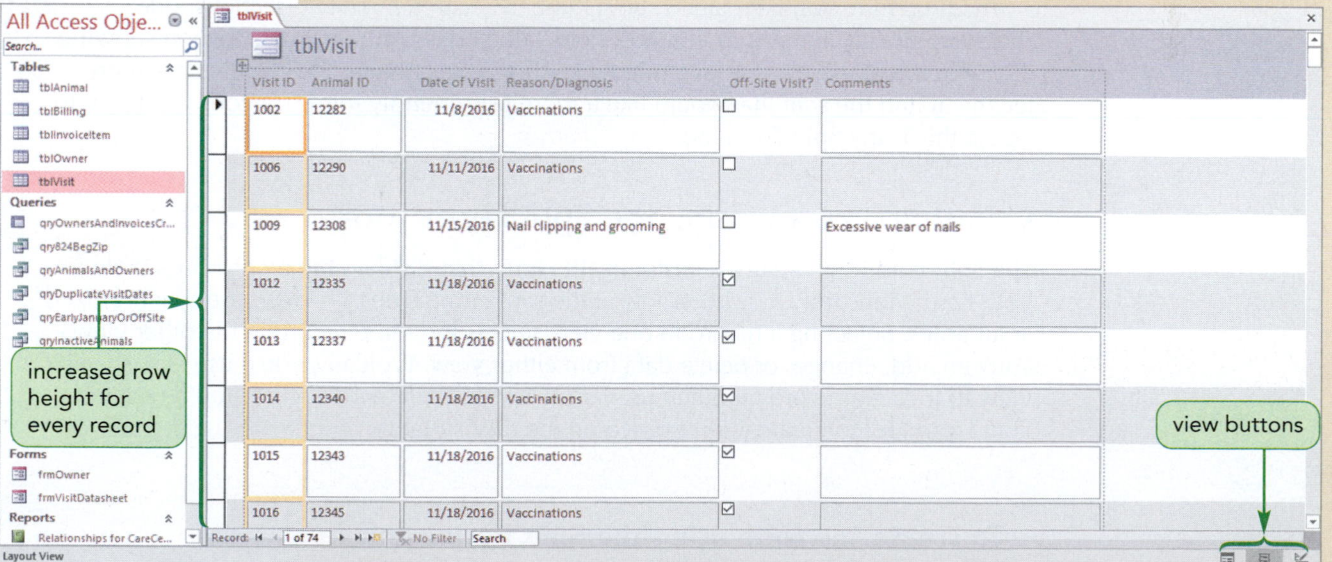

The new form displays all the records and fields from the tblVisit table in a format similar to a datasheet, but the row height for every record is increased compared to a standard datasheet. Unlike a form created with the Datasheet tool, which has only Datasheet view and Design view available, a Multiple Items form is a standard form that can be displayed in Form view, Layout view, and Design view, as indicated by the buttons on the right end of the status bar. You can also access these views for the forms created with the Multiple Items tool from the ribbon.

3. On the Form Layout Tools Design tab, in the Views group, click the **View button arrow**. See Figure 6-10.

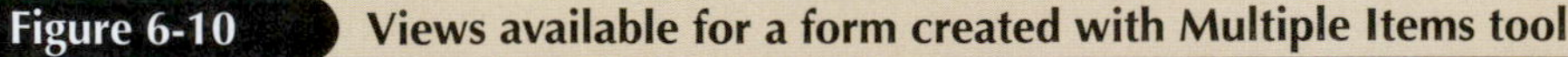

Figure 6-10 Views available for a form created with Multiple Items tool

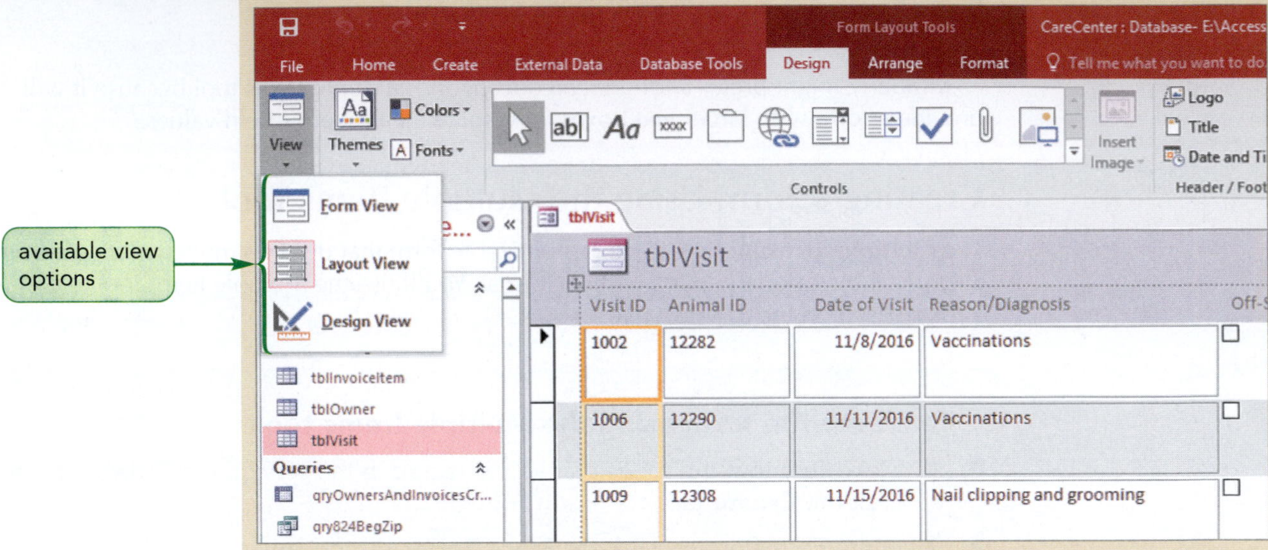

You'll want to show this form to Kimberly as one of the options, so you'll save it.

4. Save the form as **frmVisitMultipleItems**, and then close the form.

The final form you'll create to show Kimberly will include two sections, one providing the standard form inputs of field value boxes and the other section showing the table in datasheet view. She might like this to satisfy both the staff that are more technical and the staff that would like a more user-friendly form. The tool you'll use to create this is the Split Form tool.

Creating a Form Using the Split Form Tool

The Split Form tool creates a customizable form that displays the records in a table in both Form view and Datasheet view at the same time. The two views are synchronized at all times. Selecting a record in one view selects the same record in the other view. You can add, change, or delete data from either view. Typically, you'd use Datasheet view to locate a record and then use Form view to update the record. You'll use the Split Form tool to create a form based on the tblVisit table.

To create the form using the Split Form tool:

1. Make sure that the tblVisit table is selected in the Navigation Pane, and then click the **Create** tab.

2. In the Forms group, click the **More Forms** button, click **Split Form**, and then close the Navigation Pane. The Split Form tool creates a split form that opens in Layout view and displays a form with the contents of the first record in the tblVisit table in the top section and a datasheet showing the first several records in the tblVisit table in the bottom section. In Layout view, the form on top will present a record's fields either in either a single column or in two columns, depending on the size of the Access window when the form was created. If you have a two-column layout, that won't affect your ability to complete the steps that follow. Figure 6-11 shows the single-column layout.

Figure 6-11 **Form created with the Split Form tool**

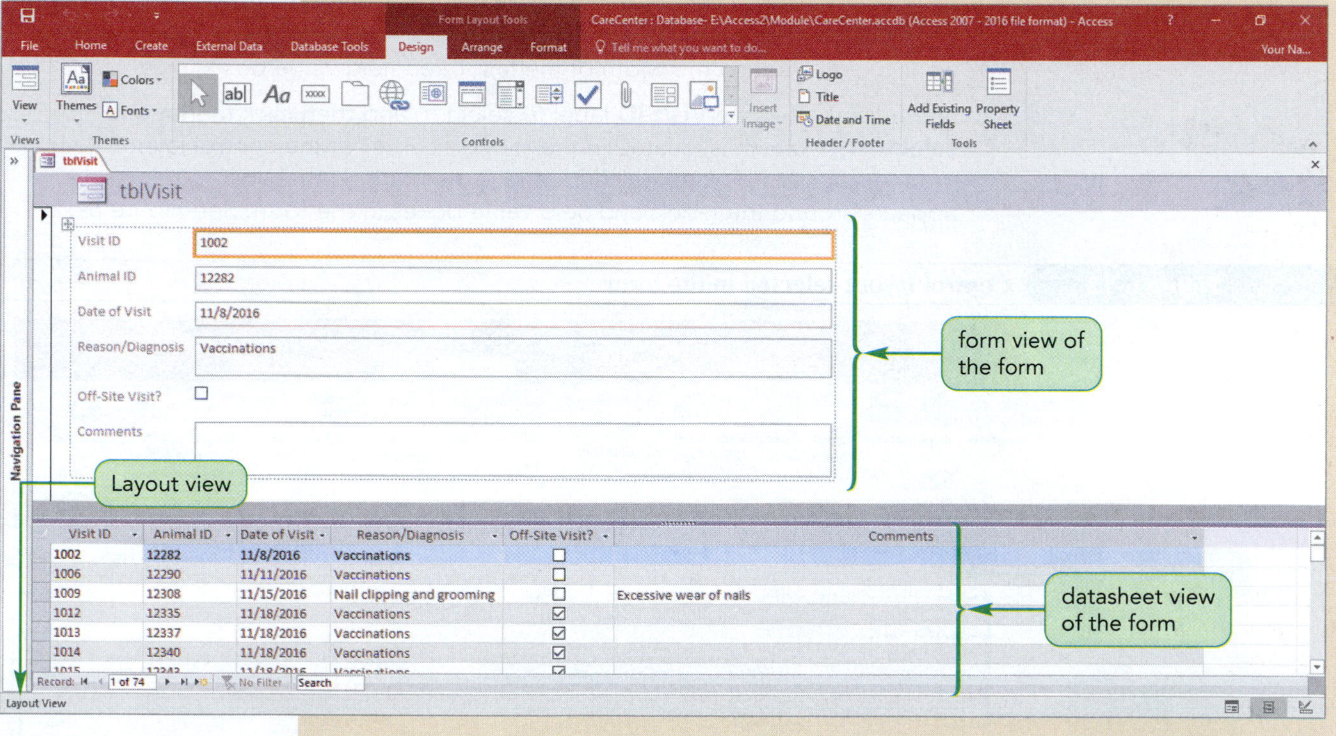

In Layout view, you can make layout and design changes to the form section and layout changes to the datasheet section of the split form.

Modifying a Split Form in Layout View

In previous modules, you've modified forms using options on the Form Layout Tools Format tab. Additional options for modifying forms are available on the Form Layout Tools Arrange tab. When working with a split form, you use the options on the Form Layout Tools Design tab to add controls and make other modifications to the form section but not to the datasheet section. Also in this case, the options on the Arrange tab apply only to the form section and do not apply to the datasheet section.

Kimberly notices that first three field value boxes in the form, Visit ID, Animal ID, and Date of Visit, are much wider than necessary. You will resize these field value boxes, and you will also move and resize the Reason/Diagnosis field label and field value box.

To resize field value boxes in the split form in Layout view:

1. On the ribbon, click the **Form Layout Tools Arrange** tab.

   The form's field label and field value boxes from the tblVisit table are grouped in a control layout. Recall that a control layout is a set of controls grouped together in a form or report so that you can manipulate the set as a single control. The control layout is a stacked layout, which arranges field value box controls vertically with a label control to the left of each field value box control in one or more vertical columns. You can also choose a tabular layout, which arranges field value box controls in a datasheet format with labels above each column.

   As you know, if you reduce the width of any field value box in a control layout, all the value boxes in the control layout are also resized. Kimberly wants you to reduce the width of the first three field value boxes only.

2. In the form, click the **Visit ID** label to select it, and then click the **layout selector** ⊞, which is located in the top-left corner of the control layout. An orange selection border, which identifies the controls that you've selected, appears around the labels and field value boxes in the form. See Figure 6-12.

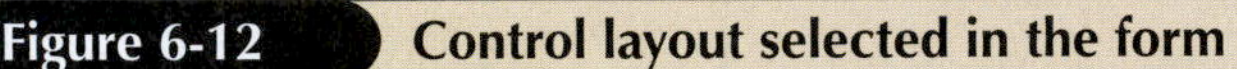

Figure 6-12 Control layout selected in the form

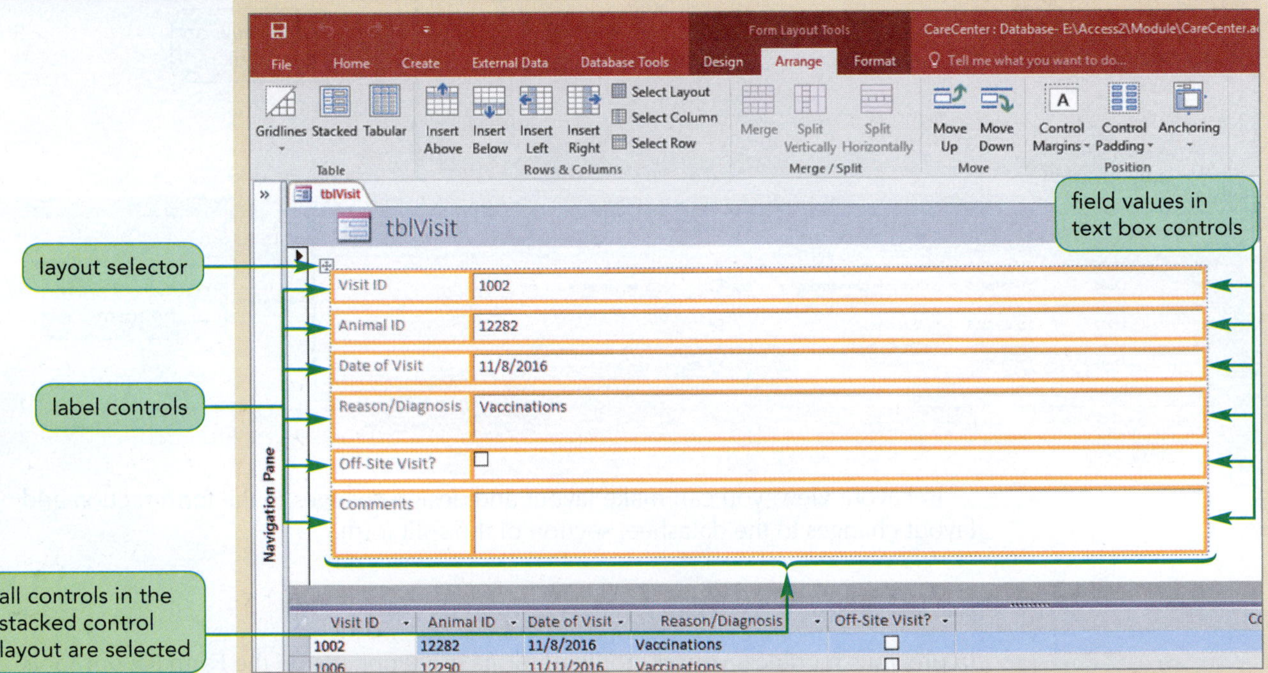

Next, you'll resize the field value boxes in the control layout.

3. Click the **VisitDate** field value box (containing the value 11/8/2016) to deselect the control layout and select just the **VisitDate** field value box.

4. Position the pointer on the right border of the VisitDate field value box until the pointer changes to ↔, click and drag to the left until the right edge is just to the right of the VisitDate field value, and then release the mouse button. If you have a one-column layout, you've resized all five field value boxes. If you have a two-column layout, you've resized the three field value boxes on the left. Figure 6-13 shows the single-column layout.

Figure 6-13 Resizing field value boxes in the control layout

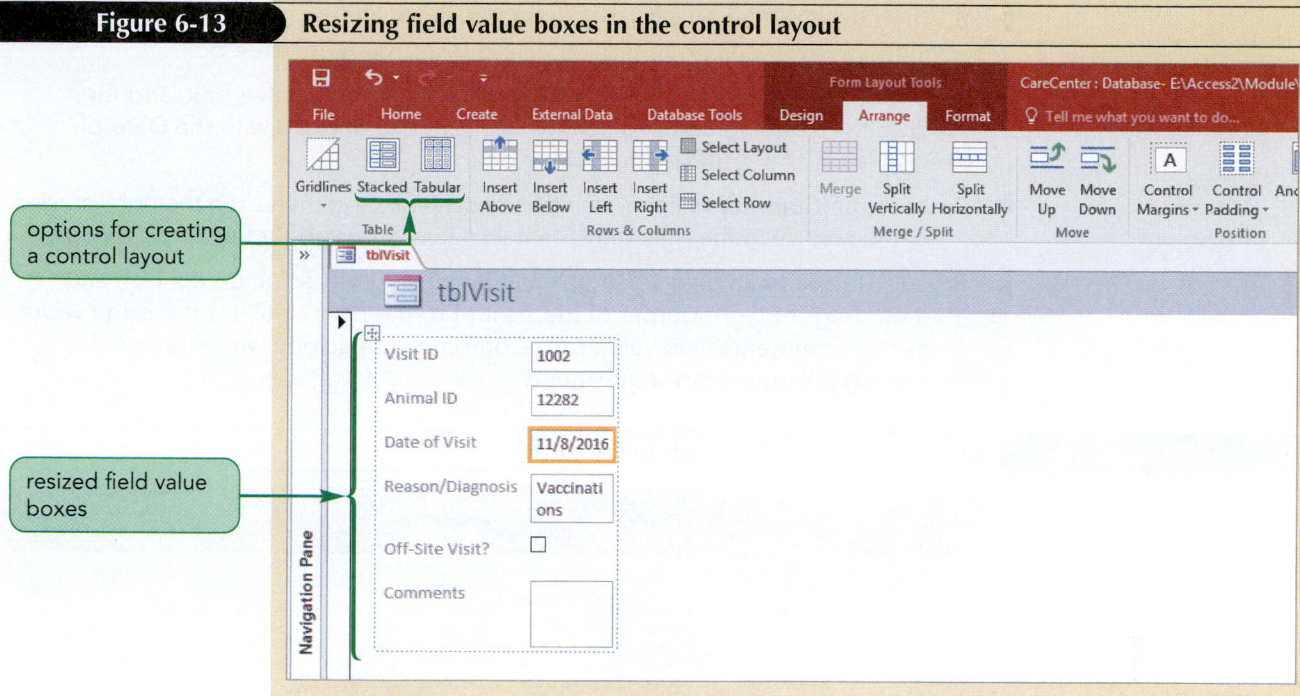

Trouble? If you resize the field value boxes too far to the left, number signs appear inside the field value boxes, indicating the boxes are too small to display the full values. Repeat Step 4, this time dragging the right border of the field value box to the right until the date values are visible inside the boxes.

With the one-column layout shown in Figure 6-13, the form has too much white space. To better balance the elements in the form, Kimberly suggests you move and resize the Reason/Diagnosis, Off-Site Visit?, and Comments labels and field value boxes to a second column so that they fill this available space. To do this, you first need to remove these items from the stacked layout control.

To remove field value labels and boxes from the layout control, and move, and resize them on the form:

1. Click the **Reason/Diagnosis** label, press and hold the **Ctrl** key, click the **Reason** field value box, click the **Off-Site Visit?** label, click the **OffSite** check box, click the **Comments** label, and then click the **Comments** field value box to select all six controls, and then release the **Ctrl** key.
2. Right-click the **Reason** field value box, point to **Layout** on the shortcut menu, and then click **Remove Layout**. You've removed the six selected controls from the stacked layout.
3. If your form has the single-column layout shown in Figure 6-13, make sure that the six controls are still selected, and then use the pointer to drag them up and to the right until the tops of the Reason label and field value box align with the tops of the VisitID label and field value box.

   Trouble? If your form already has a two-column layout, skip Step 3.
4. Click the **Off-Site Visit?** label, press and hold the **Ctrl** key, click the **OffSite** check box, and then release the **Ctrl** key. The Off-Site Visit? label and the OffSite check box are selected.

5. Drag the **Off-Site Visit?** label and **OffSite** check box to the left and position them below the Date of Visit label and VisitDate field value box.
6. Select the **Comments** label and the **Comments** field value box, and then drag the selected controls up until they are top-aligned with the Date of Visit label and VisitDate field value box.
7. Click the **Comments** field value box to select it, and then drag the right border of the control to the right until the field value box is about four inches wide.
8. Click the **Reason** field value box so that it's the only selected control, and then drag the right border of the control to the right until it is the same width as the Comments field value box. Compare your screen with Figure 6-14, making any necessary adjustments.

Figure 6-14 Moved and resized controls in the form

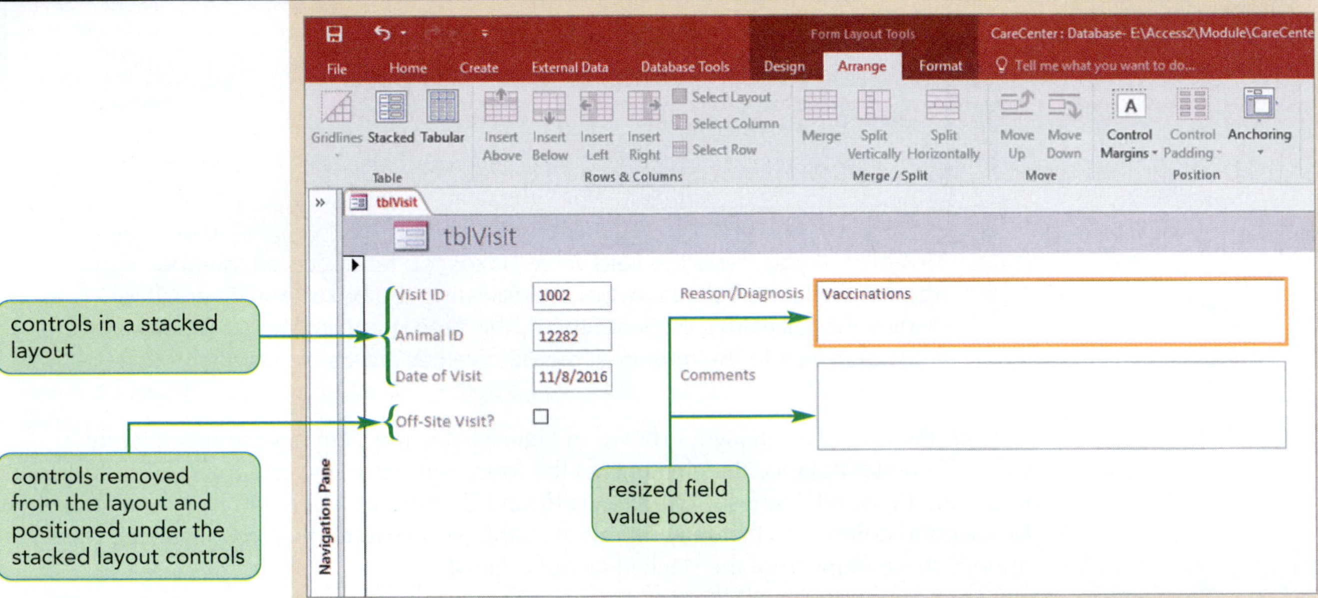

Trouble? It won't cause any problems if the controls on your screen are in slightly different positions than the ones shown in the figure.

You do not usually need to change the default settings for the Control Margins property, which controls the spacing around the text inside a control, or the Control Padding property, which controls the spacing around the outside of a control. However, you'll explore the effects of changing these properties.

9. In the form, click the **Visit ID** label to select it, and then click the **layout selector** ⊞ to select the six controls that are still grouped in the stacked layout.
10. On the Arrange tab, in the Position group, click the **Control Margins** button, and then click **Medium**. The text inside the stacked layout controls moves down slightly.
11. Click the **Control Margins** button, click **Wide**, and observe the effect of this setting on the text inside the controls.
12. Click the **Control Margins** button again, and then click **Narrow**. Narrow is the default setting for the Control Margins property. Narrow is also the default setting for the Control Padding property.

Now that the form is complete and the controls are sized appropriately, you will save the form.

13. Save the form as **frmVisitSplit**.

Next, you'll anchor the controls on the form.

Anchoring Controls in a Form

You can design forms that use the screen dimensions effectively when all the users of a database have the same-sized monitors and use the same screen resolution. How do you design forms when users have a variety of monitor sizes and screen resolutions? If you design a form to fit on large monitors using high screen resolutions, then only a portion of the controls in the form fit on smaller monitors with lower resolutions, forcing users to scroll the form. If you design a form to fit on smaller monitors with low screen resolutions, then the form displays on larger monitors in a small area in the upper-left corner of the screen, making the form look unattractively cramped. As a compromise, you can anchor the controls in the form. As shown in the Visual Overview for this session, as the screen size and resolution change, the Anchor property for a control automatically resizes the control and places it in the same relative position on the screen. Unfortunately, when you use the Anchor property, the control's font size is not scaled to match the screen size and resolution. Sometimes the results of anchoring controls work well, but sometimes the controls are spaced across a large screen, and the form may seem unorganized with controls moved to the corners of the screen.

Next, you'll anchor controls in the frmVisitSplit form. You can't anchor individual controls in a control layout; you can only anchor the entire control layout as a group. You've already removed the Reason/Diagnosis, Off-Site Visit?, and Comments controls from the stacked layout so that you can anchor them separately from the stacked layout. Therefore, you'll have four sets of controls to anchor—the stacked layout is one set, the Reason/Diagnosis controls are the second set, the Comments controls are the third set, and the Off-Site Visit? controls make up the fourth set.

To anchor controls in the form:

1. Click the **Off-Site Visit?** label, press and hold the **Ctrl** key, and then click the **OffSite** check box.
2. On the Arrange tab, in the Position group, click the **Anchoring** button to open the Anchoring gallery. See Figure 6-15.

Figure 6-15 The Anchoring gallery

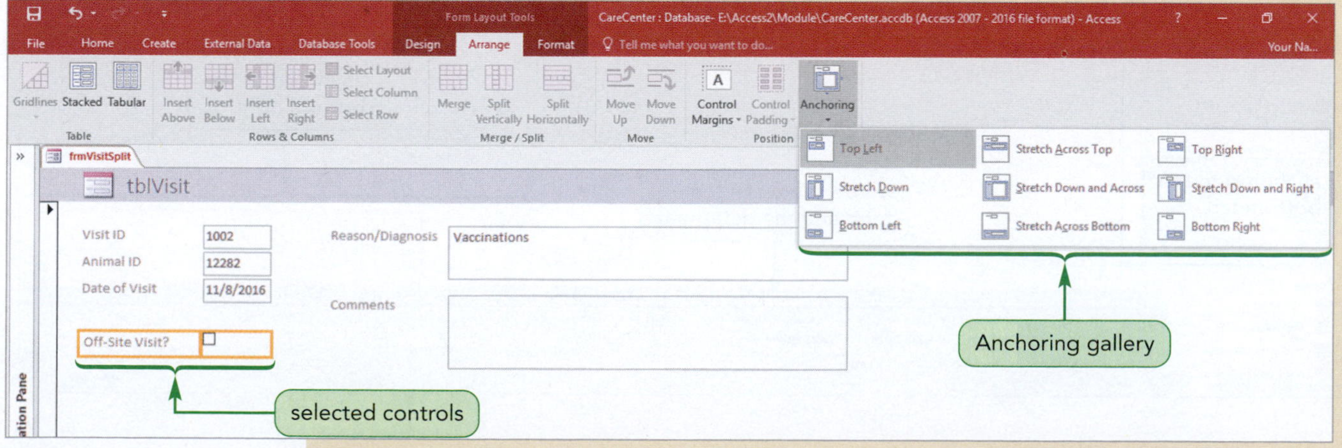

Four of the nine options in the Anchoring gallery fix the position of the selected controls in the top-left (the default setting), bottom-left, top right, or bottom-right positions in the form. If other controls block the corner positions for controls you're anchoring for the first time, the new controls are positioned in relation to the blocking controls. The other five anchoring options resize (or stretch) and position the selected controls.

You'll anchor the Off-Site Visit? controls in the bottom left, the Reason/Diagnosis controls in the top right, and the Comments controls in the bottom right.

3. Click **Bottom Left** in the Anchoring gallery. The gallery closes, and the Off-Site Visit? label and field value box move to the bottom-left corner of the form.
4. Click the **Reason** field value box, in the Position group, click the **Anchoring** button, and then click **Top Right**. The Reason label and field value box move to the upper-right corner of the form.
5. Anchor the Comments label and field value box to the Bottom Right.

Next, you'll increase the height of the form to simulate the effect of a larger screen for the form.

6. Open the Navigation Pane. The four sets of controls on the left shift to the right because the horizontal dimensions of the form decreased from the left, and these four sets of controls are anchored to the left in the form. The Reason and Comments controls remain in the same position in the form.
7. Position the pointer on the border between the form and the datasheet until the pointer changes to ╋, and then drag down until only the column headings and the first row in the datasheet are visible. The bottom sets of controls shift down, because they are anchored to the bottom of the form, and the two sets of controls at the top remain in the same positions in the form. See Figure 6-16.

Figure 6-16 Anchored controls in a resized form

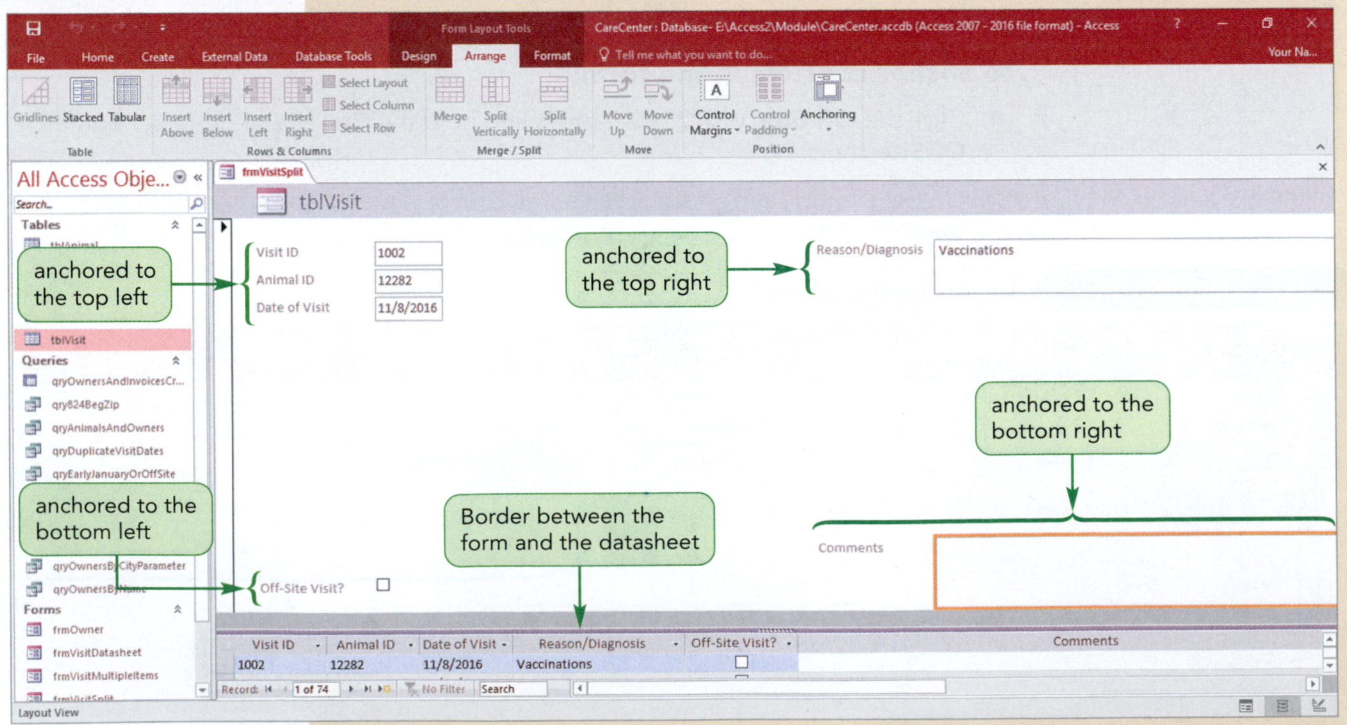

Finally, you'll use another anchoring option to resize the Comments text box as the form dimensions change.

8. Click the **Comments** field value box (if necessary), in the Position group, click the **Anchoring** button, and then click **Stretch Down and Right**. Because the Comments field value box is already anchored to the bottom right, it can't stretch any more to the right, but it does stretch up while leaving the label in place, to increase the height of the box.
9. Position the pointer on the border between the form and the datasheet until the pointer changes to ✢, and then drag up to display several rows in the datasheet. The bottom set of controls shifts up, and the bottom edge of the Comments field value box shifts up, and its height is reduced.

Kimberly and her staff have the same computer monitors and screen resolutions, so the controls do not need to be anchored. Therefore, you can close the form without saving the anchoring changes.

10. Close the form without saving the anchoring changes you've made to the form's design, and then, if you are not continuing on to the next session, close the CareCenter database.

You've used form tools to create forms, and you've modified forms in Layout view. In the next session, you will continue your work with forms.

REVIEW

Session 6.1 Quick Check

1. Which object(s) should you use to perform all database updates?
2. The ______________ property specifies the data source for a control in a form or report or for a field in a table or query.
3. What is the Documenter?
4. What is the Multiple Items tool?
5. What is a split form?
6. As the screen's size and resolution change, the ______________ property for a control automatically resizes the control.

Session 6.2 Visual Overview:

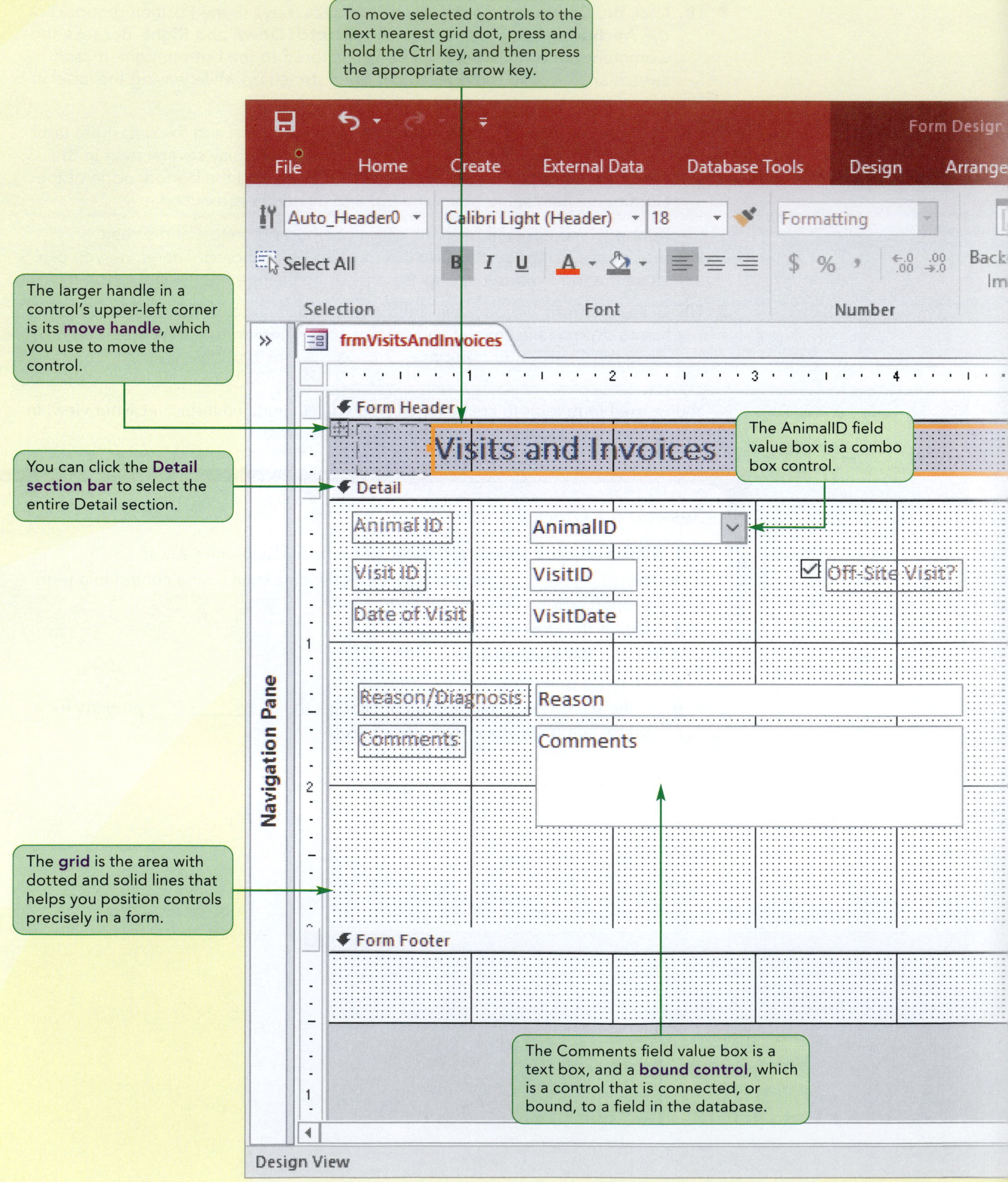

To move selected controls to the next nearest grid dot, press and hold the Ctrl key, and then press the appropriate arrow key.
The larger handle in a control's upper-left corner is its move handle, which you use to move the control.
You can click the Detail section bar to select the entire Detail section.
The AnimalID field value box is a combo box control.
The grid is the area with dotted and solid lines that helps you position controls precisely in a form.
The Comments field value box is a text box, and a bound control, which is a control that is connected, or bound, to a field in the database.
Form Design
File
Home
Create
External Data
Database Tools
Design
Arrange
Auto_Header0
Calibri Light (Header)
18
Formatting
Select All
Selection
Font
Number
frmVisitsAndInvoices
Form Header
Visits and Invoices
Detail
Animal ID
AnimalID
Visit ID
VisitID
Off-Site Visit?
Date of Visit
VisitDate
Reason/Diagnosis
Reason
Comments
Comments
Form Footer
Navigation Pane
Design View

Custom Form in Design View

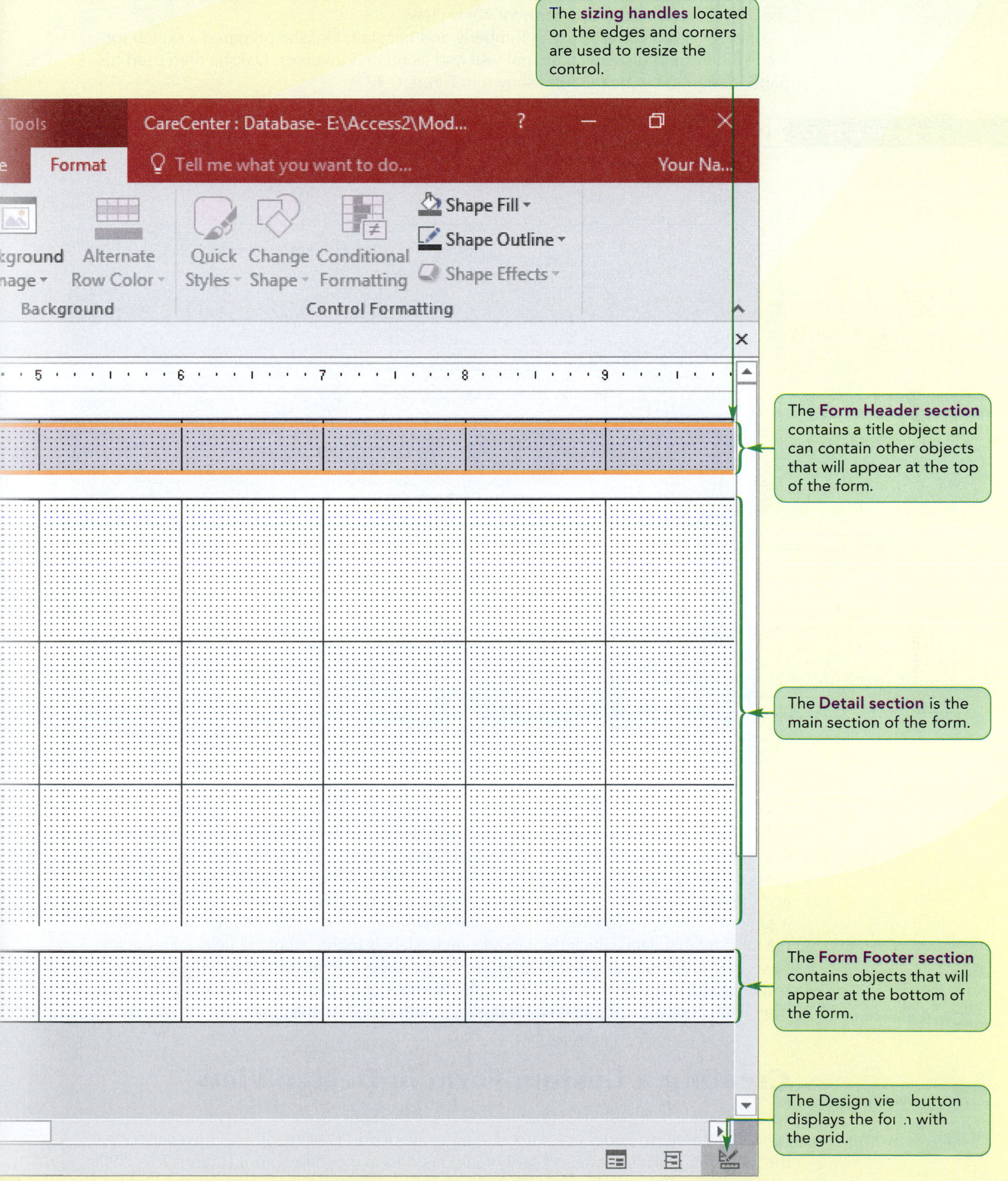
The **sizing handles** located on the edges and corners are used to resize the control.
Tools
CareCenter : Database- E:\Access2\Mod...
Format
Tell me what you want to do...
Your Na...
kground nage
Alternate Row Color
Quick Styles
Change Shape
Conditional Formatting
Shape Fill
Shape Outline
Shape Effects
Background
Control Formatting
The **Form Header section** contains a title object and can contain other objects that will appear at the top of the form.
The **Detail section** is the main section of the form.
The **Form Footer section** contains objects that will appear at the bottom of the form.
The Design vie button displays the fo with the grid.

Planning and Designing a Custom Form

Kimberly needs a form to enter and view information about Riverview Veterinary Care Center visits and their related invoices. She wants the information in a single form, and she asks Daksha to design a form for her review.

After several discussions with Kimberly and her staff, Daksha prepared a sketch for a custom form to display an animal visit and its related invoices. Daksha then used his paper design to create the form shown in Figure 6-17.

Figure 6-17 **Daksha's design for the custom form**

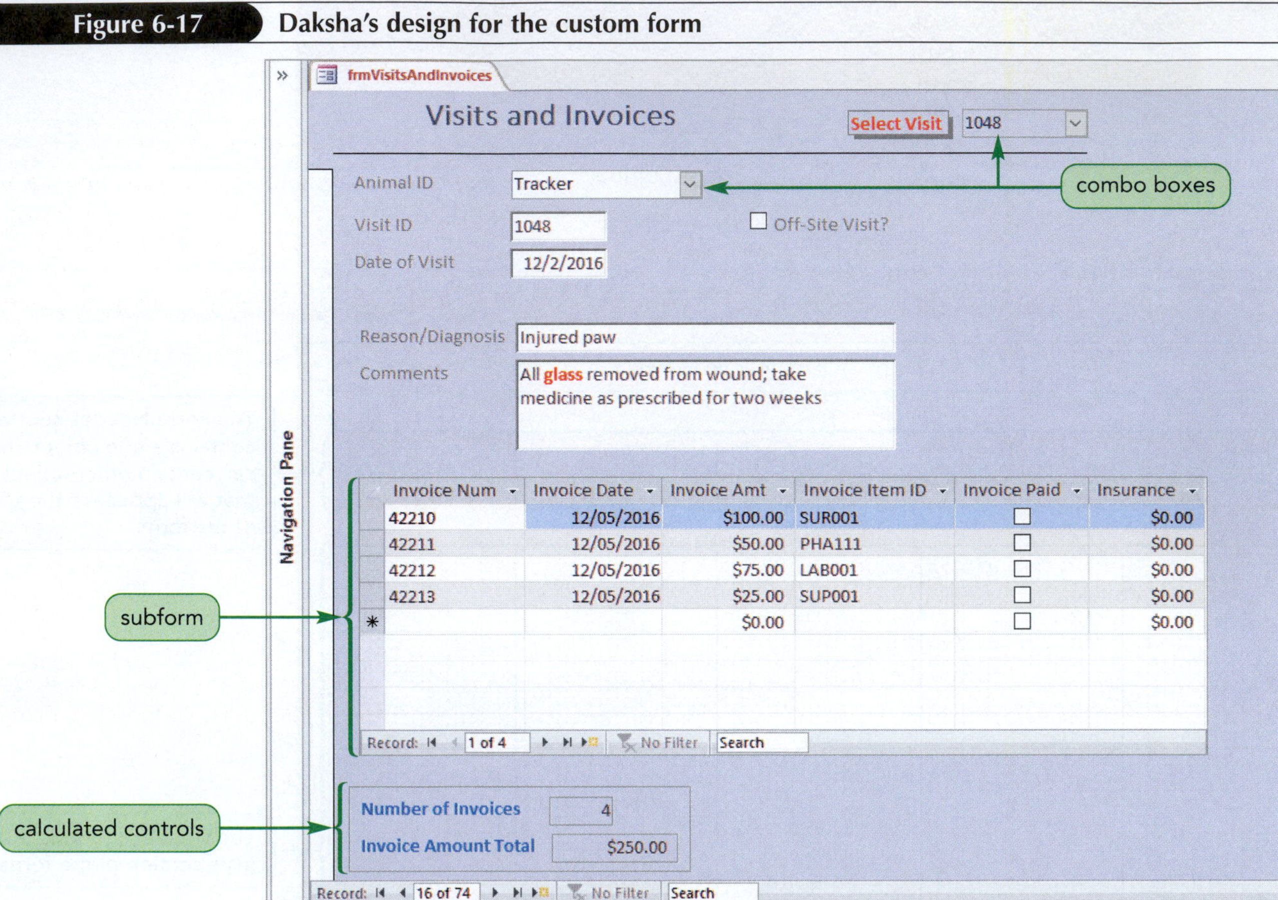

Notice that the top of the form displays a title and a combo box to select a visit record. Below these items are six field values with identifying labels from the tblVisit table; these fields are the AnimalID, VisitID, OffSite, VisitDate, Reason, and Comments fields. The AnimalID field is displayed in a combo box, the OffSite field is displayed as a check box, and the other field values are displayed in text boxes. The tblBilling table fields appear in a subform, which, as you know, is a separate form contained within another form. Unlike the tblVisit table data, which displays identifying labels to the left of the field values in text boxes, the tblBilling table data is displayed in datasheet format with identifying column headings above the field values. Finally, the Number of Invoices and Invoice Amount Total calculated controls in the main form display values based on the content of the subform.

Creating a Custom Form in Design View

To create Daksha's custom form, you could use the Form Wizard to create a basic version of the form and then customize it in Layout and Design views. However, for the form that Daksha designed, you would need to make many modifications to a basic form created by a wizard. You can instead build the form in a more straightforward manner by creating it directly in Design view. Creating forms in Design view allows you more control and precision and provides more options than creating forms in Layout view. You'll also find that you'll create forms more productively if you switch between Design view and Layout view because some design modifications are easier to make in one of the two views than in the other view.

Working in the Form Window in Design View

You can use the Form window in Design view to create and modify forms. To create the custom form based on Daksha's design, you'll create a blank form, add the fields from the tblVisit and tblBilling tables, and then add other controls and make other modifications to the form.

The form you'll create will be a bound form. A **bound form** is a form that has a table or query as its record source. You use bound forms for maintaining and displaying table data. **Unbound forms** are forms that do not have a record source and are usually forms that help users navigate among the objects in a database.

REFERENCE

Creating a Form in Design View

- On the ribbon, click the Create tab.
- In the Forms group, click the Blank Form button to open the Form window in Layout view.
- Click the Design View button on the status bar to switch to Design view.
- Make sure the Field List pane is open, and then add the required fields to the form.
- Add other required controls to the form.
- Modify the size, position, and other properties as necessary for the fields and other controls in the form.
- Save the form.

Now you'll create a blank bound form based on the tblVisit table.

To create a blank bound form in Design view:

1. If you took a break after the previous session, make sure that the CareCenter database is open and the Navigation Pane is open.
2. On the ribbon, click the **Create** tab, and then, in the Forms group, click the **Blank Form** button. The Form window opens in Layout view.
3. Click the **Design View** button on the status bar to switch to Design view, and then close the Navigation Pane. See Figure 6-18.

Figure 6-18 Blank form in Design view

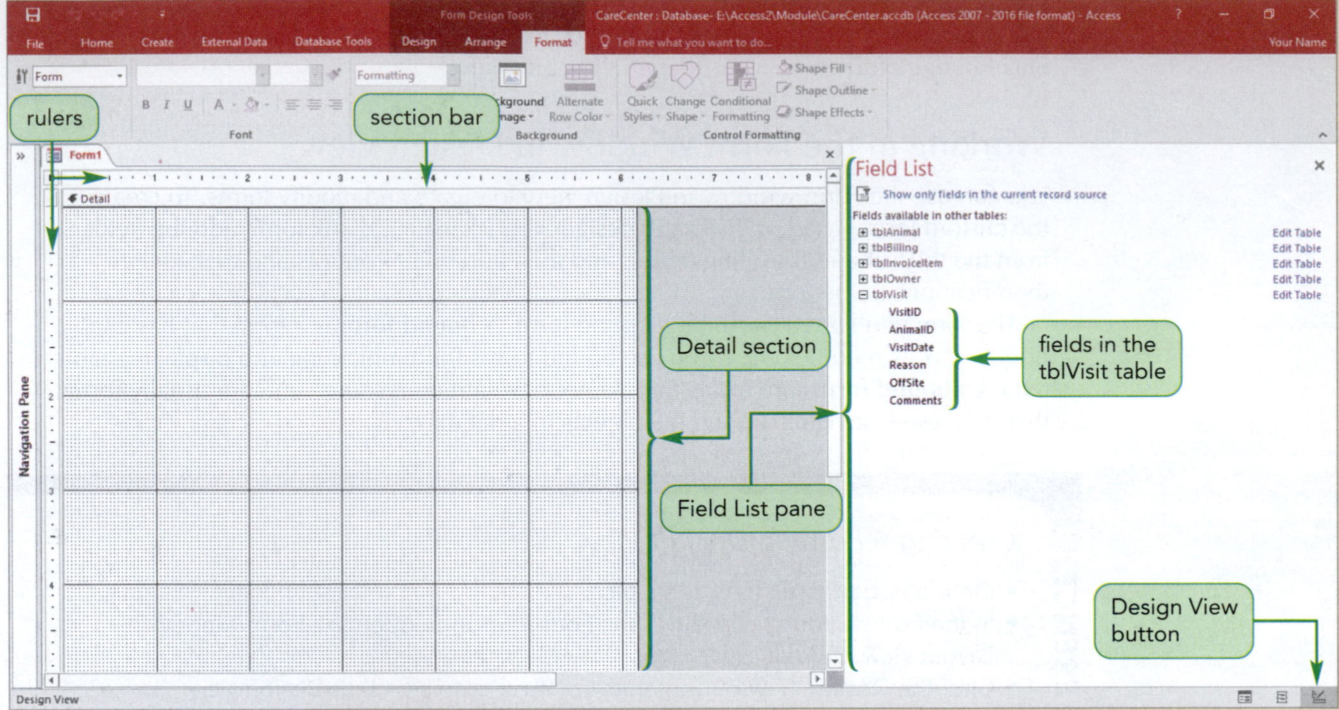

Trouble? If the Field List pane displays the "No fields available to be added to the current view" message, click the "Show all tables" link to display the tables in the CareCenter database, and then click the plus sign next to tblVisit in the Field List pane to display the fields in the tblVisit table.

Trouble? If the tblVisit table in the Field List pane is not expanded to show the fields in the table, click the plus sign next to tblVisit to display the fields.

Design view contains the tools necessary to create a custom form. You create the form by placing controls in the blank form. You can place three kinds of controls in a form:

- A **bound control** is connected, or bound, to a field in the database. The field could be selected from the fields in a table or query that are used as the record source. You use bound controls to display and maintain table field values.
- An **unbound control** is not connected to a field in the database. You use unbound controls to display text, such as a form title or instructions; to display lines, rectangles, and other objects; or to display graphics and pictures created using other software programs. An unbound control that displays text is called a **label**.
- A **calculated control** displays a value that is the result of an expression. The expression usually contains one or more fields, and the calculated control is recalculated each time any value in the expression changes.

To create a bound control, you add fields from the Field List pane to the Form window, and then position the bound controls where you want them to appear in the form. To place other controls in a form or a report, you use the tools in the Controls and Header/Footer groups on the Form Design Tools Design tab. The tools in the Controls group let you add controls such as lines, rectangles, images, buttons, check boxes, and list boxes to a form.

Design view for a form contains a Detail section, which is a rectangular area consisting of a grid with a section bar above the grid. You click the section bar to select the section in preparation for setting properties for the entire section. Some forms use Header, Detail, and Footer sections, but a simple form might have only a Detail section. The grid consists of dotted and solid lines that you use to position controls precisely in a form. In the Detail section, you place bound controls, unbound controls, and calculated controls in your form. You can change the size of the Detail section by dragging its borders. Rulers at the top and left edges of the Detail section define the horizontal and vertical dimensions of the form and serve as guides for placing controls in a form.

Your first task is to add bound controls to the Detail section for the six fields from the tblVisit table.

Adding Fields to a Form

When you add a bound control to a form, Access adds a field value box and, to its left, an attached label. The field value box displays a field value from the record source. The attached label displays either the Caption property value for the field, if the Caption property value has been set, or the field name. To create a bound control, you first display the Field List pane by clicking the Add Existing Fields button in the Tools group on the Form Design Tools Design tab. Then you double-click a field in the Field List pane to add the bound control to the Detail section. You can also drag a field from the Field List pane to the Detail section.

The Field List pane displays the five tables in the CareCenter database and the six fields in the tblVisit table. Next, you'll add bound controls to the Detail section for the tblVisit table's six fields.

To add bound controls from the tblVisit table to the Detail section:

1. Double-click **VisitID** in the Field List pane. A bound text box control appears in the Detail section of the form, and the Field List pane lists the tblVisit table in the "Fields available for this view" section and lists the tblAnimal and tblBilling and tables in the "Fields available in related tables" section.
2. Repeat Step 1 for the **VisitDate**, **AnimalID**, **Reason**, **Comments**, and **OffSite** fields, in this order, in the Field List pane. Six bound controls—one for each of the six fields in the Field List pane—are added in the Detail section of the form. See Figure 6-19.

Figure 6-19 Bound controls added to the form

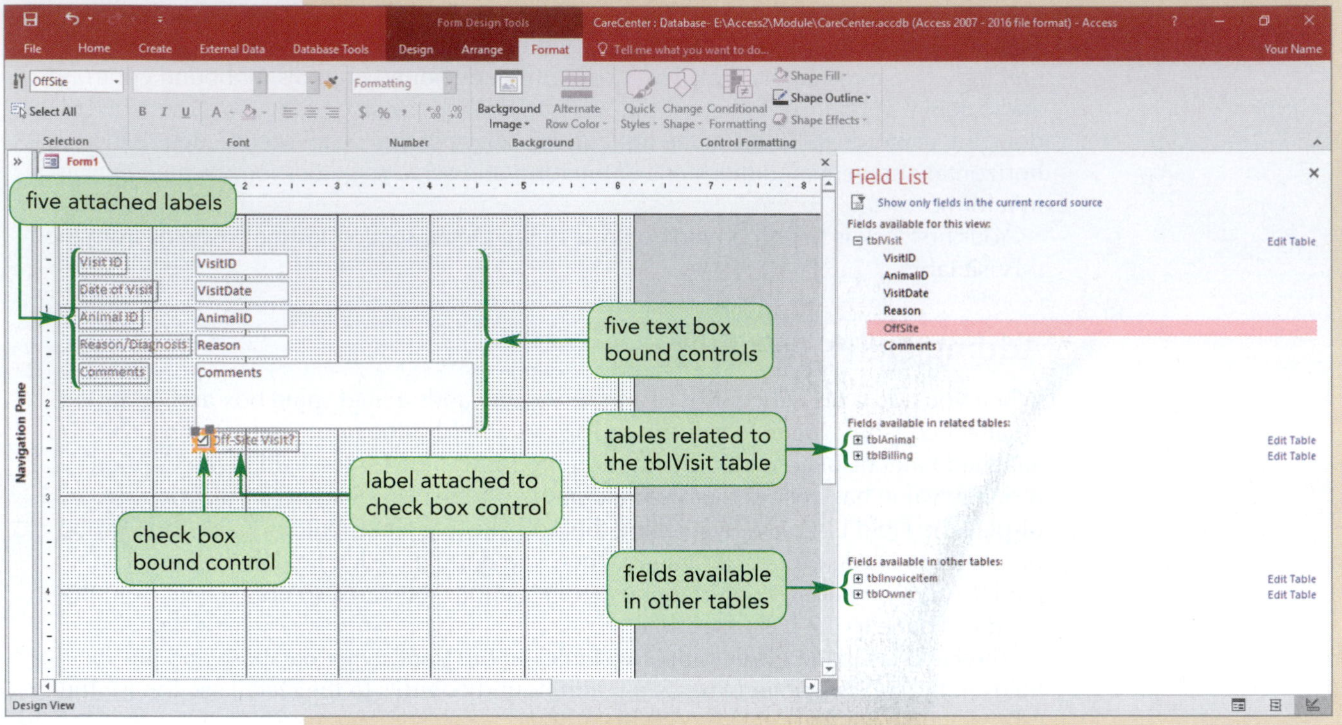

You should periodically save your work as you create a form, so you'll save the form now.

3. Click the **Save** button on the Quick Access Toolbar. The Save As dialog box opens.
4. With the default name selected in the Form Name box, type **frmVisitsAndInvoices**, and then press the **Enter** key. The tab for the form now displays the form name, and the form design is saved in the CareCenter database.

   You've added the fields you need to the grid, so you can close the Field List pane.

5. Click the **Form Design Tools Design** tab, and then, in the Tools group, click the **Add Existing Fields** button to close the Field List pane.

INSIGHT

Strategies for Building Forms

To help prevent common problems and more easily recover from errors while building forms, you should keep in mind the following suggestions:

- You can click the Undo button one or more times immediately after you make one or more errors or make form adjustments you don't wish to keep.
- You should back up your database frequently, especially before you create new objects or customize existing objects. If you run into difficulty, you can revert to your most recent backup copy of the database.
- You should save your form after you've completed a portion of your work successfully and before you need to perform steps you've never done before. If you're not satisfied with subsequent steps, close the form without saving the changes you made since your last save, and then open the form and perform the steps again.
- You can always close the form, make a copy of the form in the Navigation Pane, and practice with the copy.
- Adding controls, setting properties, and performing other tasks correctly in Access should work all the time with consistent results, but in rare instances, you might find a feature doesn't work properly. If a feature you've previously used successfully suddenly doesn't work, you should save your work, close the database, make a backup copy of the database, open the database, and then compact and repair the database. Performing a compact and repair resolves most of these types of problems.

To make your form's Detail section match Daksha's design (Figure 6-17), you need to move the OffSite bound control up and to the right. To do so, you must start by selecting the bound control.

Selecting, Moving, and Aligning Form Controls

Six field value boxes now appear in the form's Detail section, one below the other. Each field value box is a bound control connected to a field in the underlying table, with an attached label to its left. Each field value box and each label is a control in the form; in addition, each pairing of a field value box and its associated label is itself a control. When you select a control, an orange selection border appears around the control, and eight squares, called handles, appear on the selection border's four corners and at the midpoints of its four edges. The larger handle in a control's upper-left corner is its move handle, which you use to move the control. You use the other seven handles, called sizing handles, to resize the control. When you work in Design view, controls you place in the form do not become part of a control layout, so you can individually select, move, resize, and otherwise manipulate one control without also changing the other controls. However, at any time you can select a group of controls and place them in a control layout—either a stacked layout or a tabular layout.

Based on Daksha's design for the custom form, shown in Figure 6-17, you need to move the OffSite bound control up and to the right in the Detail section. The OffSite bound control consists of a check box and an attached label, displaying the text "Off-Site Visit?" to its right.

You can move a field value box and its attached label together. To move them, you place the pointer anywhere on the selection border of the field value box, but not on a move handle or a sizing handle. When the pointer changes to ✥, you drag the field value box and its attached label to the new location. As you move a control, an outline of the control moves on the rulers to indicate the current position of the control as you drag it. To move a group of selected controls, point to any selected control until the pointer changes to ✥, and then drag the group of selected controls to the new position. As you know, you can move controls with more precision by pressing the appropriate arrow key on the keyboard to move the selected control in small increments. To move selected controls to the next nearest grid dot, press and hold the Ctrl key and then press the appropriate arrow key on the keyboard.

You can also move either a field value box or its label individually. If you want to move the field value box but not its label, for example, place the pointer on the field value box's move handle. When the pointer changes to ✥, drag the field value box to the new location. You use the label's move handle in a similar way to move only the label.

You'll now arrange the controls in the form to match Daksha's design.

To move the OffSite bound control:

1. If necessary, click the **Off-Site Visit?** label box to select it. Move handles, which are the larger handles, appear on the upper-left corners of the selected label box and its associated bound control. Sizing handles also appear but only on the label box. See Figure 6-20.

Figure 6-20 **Selected OffSite bound control and label**

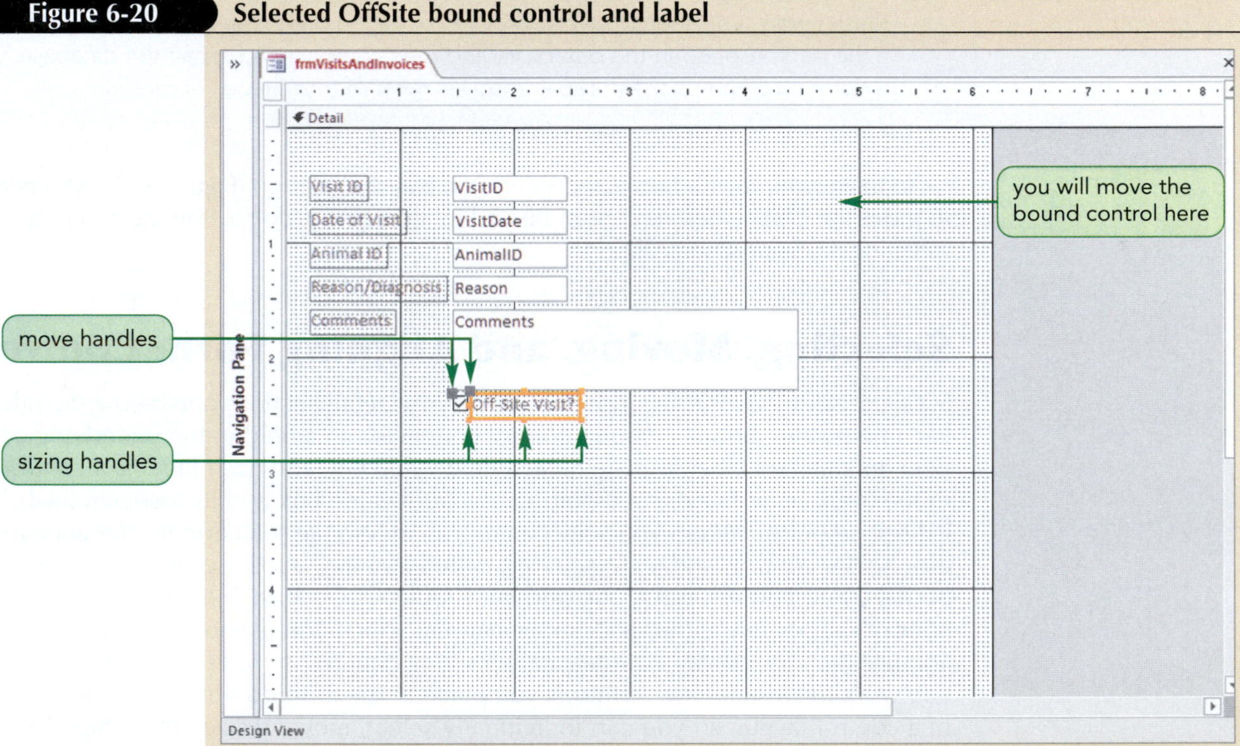

Be sure to position the pointer on one of the edges but not on a move handle or a sizing handle.

2. Position the pointer on the Off-Site Visit? label box's orange selection border, but not on a move handle or a sizing handle, until the pointer changes to a ✥, drag the control up and to the right of the VisitID field value box, as shown in Figure 6-21, and then release the mouse button.

Figure 6-21 Repositioned Off-Site Visit? label and associated bound control

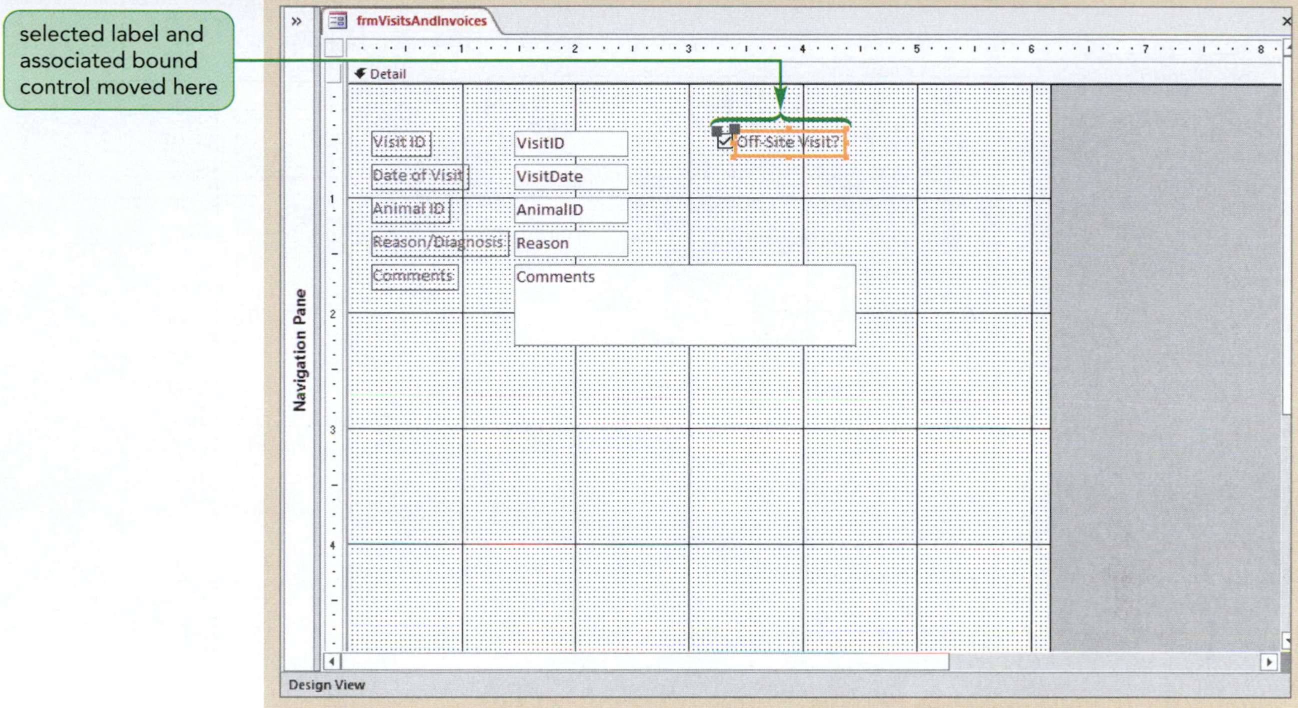

Trouble? If you need to make major adjustments to the placement of the OffSite bound control, click the Undo button on the Quick Access Toolbar one or more times until the bound control is back to its starting position, and then repeat Step 2. If you need to make minor adjustments to the placement of the OffSite bound control, use the arrow keys on the keyboard.

Now you need to top-align the OffSite and VisitID bound controls (meaning their top borders are aligned with one another). When you select a column of controls, you can align the controls along their left or their right borders (left-align or right-align). When you select a row of controls, you can top-align or bottom-align the controls. You can also align To Grid, which aligns the selected controls with the dots in the grid. You access these five alignment options on the Form Design Tools Arrange tab or on the shortcut menu for the selected controls.

You'll use the shortcut menu to align the two bound controls. Then you'll save the modified form and review your work in Form view.

To align the OffSite and VisitID bound controls:

1. Make sure the Off-Site Visit? label box is selected.
2. Press and hold the **Shift** key, click the **OffSite** check box, click the **VisitID** field value box, click the **Visit ID** label, and then release the **Shift** key. The four controls are selected, and each selected control has an orange selection border.
3. Right-click one of the selected controls, point to **Align** on the shortcut menu, and then click **Top**. The four selected controls are top-aligned. See Figure 6-22.

Figure 6-22 Aligned controls in the Detail section

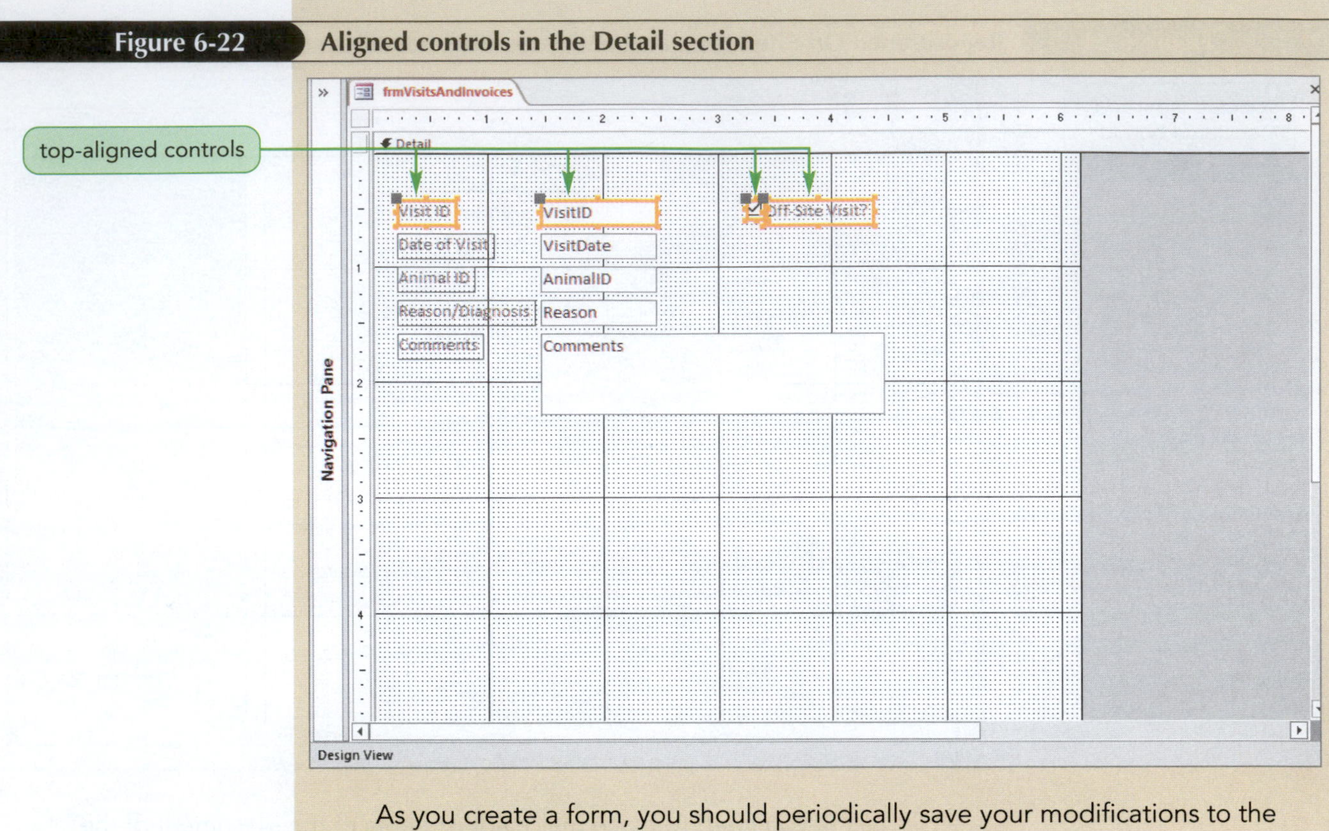

As you create a form, you should periodically save your modifications to the form and review your progress in Form view.

4. Save your form design changes, and then switch to Form view.
5. Click the **Next record** button twice to display the third record in the dataset (Visit ID #1009) in the form. See Figure 6-23.

Figure 6-23 Form displayed in Form view

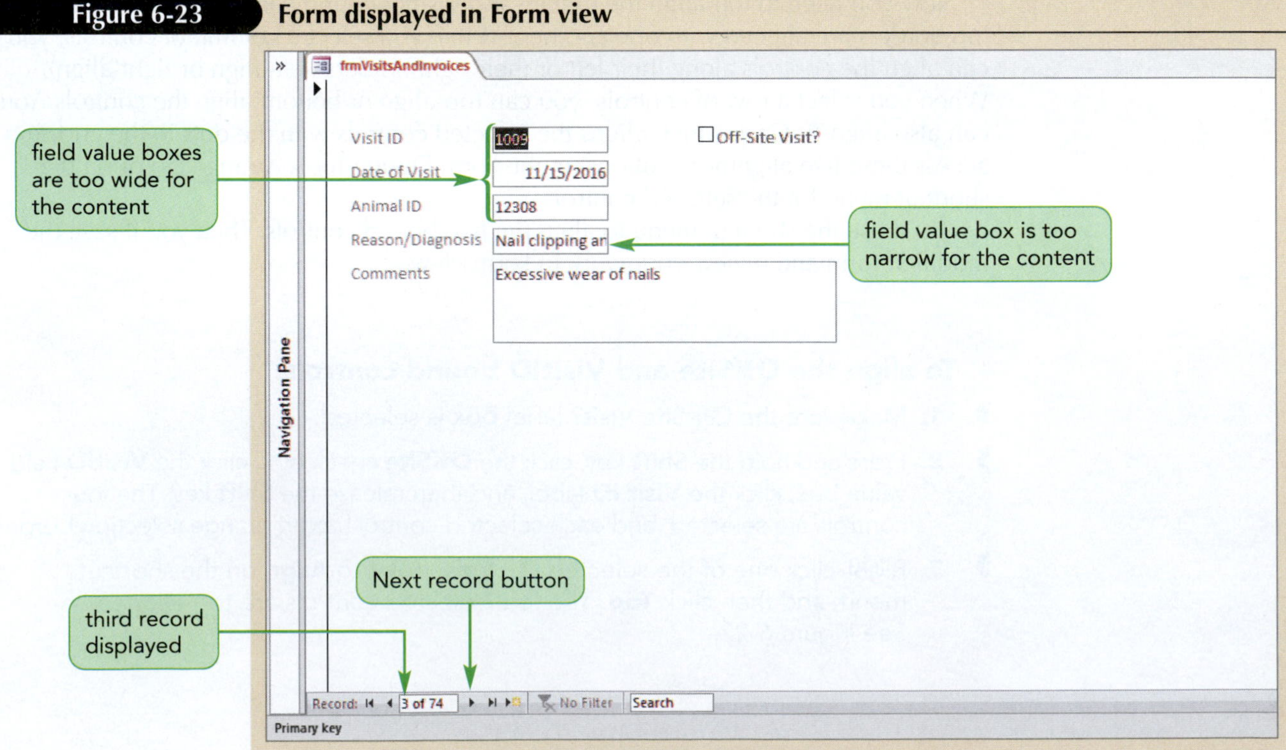

The value in the Reason field value box is not fully displayed, so you need to increase the width of the text box control. The widths of the VisitID and VisitDate text boxes are wider than necessary, so you'll reduce their widths. Also, the AnimalID bound control consists of a label and a text box, but the plan for the form shows a combo box for the AnimalID positioned below the OffSite bound control. You'll delete the AnimalID bound control, and then add it to the form, this time as a combo box.

Resizing and Deleting Controls

As you have seen, a selected control displays seven sizing handles: four at the midpoints on each edge of the control and one at each corner except the upper-left corner. Recall that the upper-left corner displays the move handle. Positioning the pointer over a sizing handle changes the pointer to a two-headed arrow; the directions in which the arrows point indicate in which direction you can resize the selected control. When you drag a sizing handle, you resize the control. As you resize the control, a thin line appears alongside the sizing handle to guide you in completing the task accurately, along with outlines that appear on the horizontal and vertical rulers.

You'll begin by deleting the AnimalD bound control. Then you'll resize the Reason text box, which is too narrow and too short to display Reason field values. Next you'll resize the VisitID and VisitDate text boxes to reduce their widths.

To delete a bound control and resize field value boxes:

1. Switch to Design view, click a blank area of the screen to deselect all controls, and then click the **AnimalID** text box control to select it.

TIP

If you want to delete a label but not its associated field value box, right-click the label, and then click Delete on the shortcut menu.

2. Right-click the **AnimalID** text box to open the shortcut menu, and then click **Delete**. The label and the bound text box control for the AnimalID field are deleted.
3. Click the **Reason** text box to select it.
4. Place the pointer on the middle-right handle of the Reason text box until it changes to ↔, drag the right border to the right until it is approximately the same width as the Comments text box. See Figure 6-24.

Figure 6-24 **Resized Reason text box**

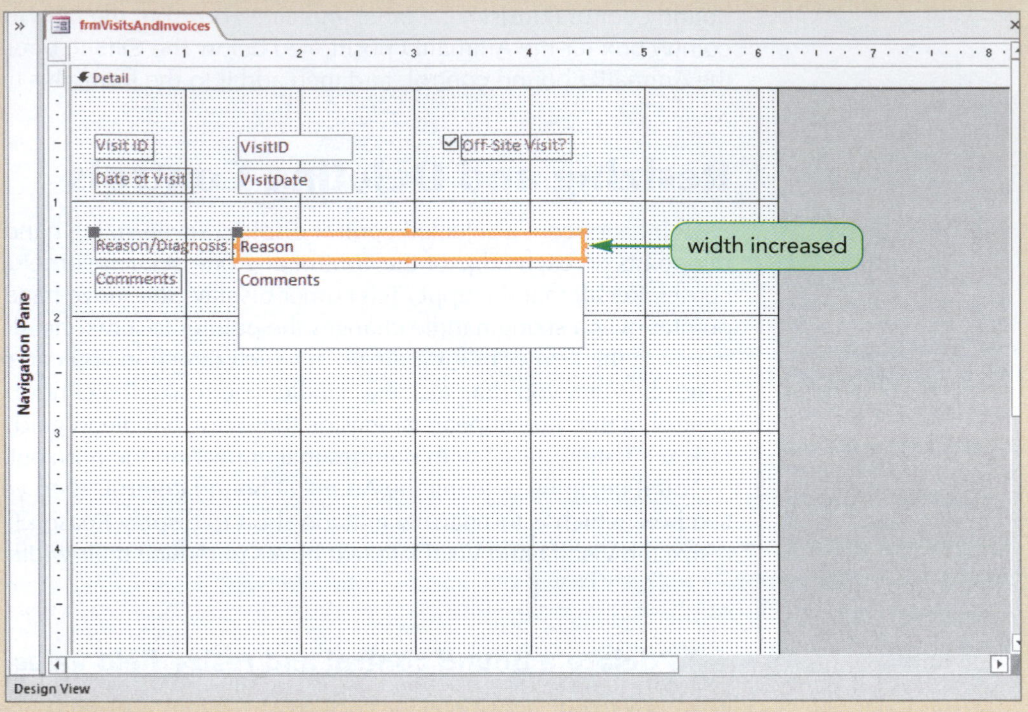

Resizing controls in Design view is a trial-and-error process, in which you resize a control in Design view, switch to Form view to observe the effect of the resizing, switch back to Design view to make further refinements to the control's size, and continue until the control is sized correctly. It's easier to resize controls in Layout view because you can see actual field values while you resize the controls. You'll resize the other two text box controls in Layout view. The sizes of the VisitID and VisitDate controls will look fine if you reduce them to have the same widths, so you'll select both boxes and resize them with one action.

5. Switch to Layout view, and then click the **VisitID** field value box (if necessary) to select it.
6. Press and hold the **Shift** key, click the **VisitDate** field value box (next to the label "Date of Visit") to select it, and then release the mouse button.
7. Position the pointer on the right border of the **VisitID** field value box until the pointer changes to ↔, drag the border to the left until the field box is slightly wider than the field value it contains, and the date in the VisitID field is also visible, and then release the mouse button. See Figure 6-25.

Figure 6-25 Resized field value boxes in Layout view

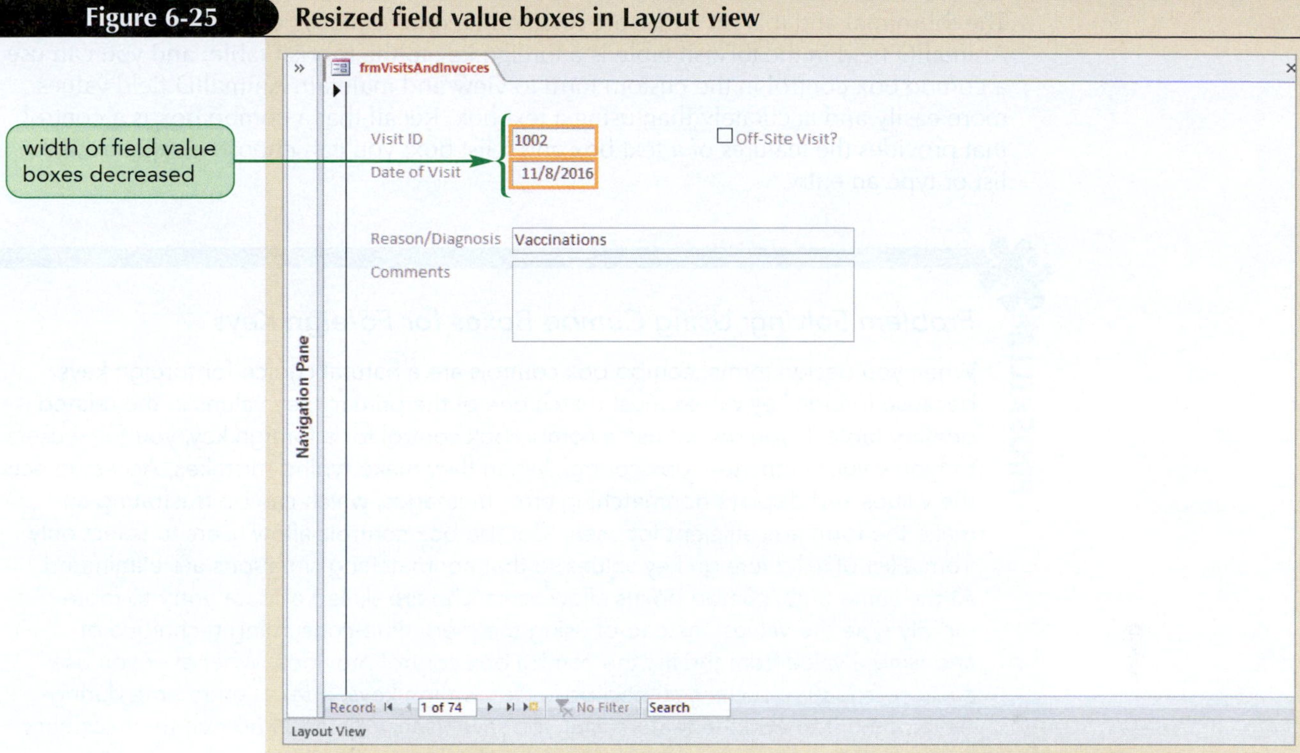

Trouble? If you resized the field value boxes too far to the left, number signs will be displayed inside the VisitDate field value box. Drag the right border to the right slightly until the date value is visible.

8. Navigate through the first several records to make sure the three field value boxes are sized properly and display the full field values. If any field value box is too small, select it, and then resize it as appropriate.
9. Save your form design changes, switch to Design view, and then deselect all controls by clicking a blank area of the screen.

INSIGHT

Making Form Design Modifications

When you design forms and other objects, you'll find it helpful to switch frequently between Design view and Layout view. Some form modifications are easier to make in Layout view, other form modifications are easier to make in Design view, and still other form modifications can be made only in Design view. You should check your progress frequently in either Layout view or Form view, and you should save your modifications after completing a set of changes successfully.

Recall that you removed the lookup feature from the AnimalID field because a combo box provides the same lookup capability in a form. Next, you'll add a combo box control for the AnimalID field to the custom form.

Adding a Combo Box Control to a Form

The tblAnimal and tblVisit tables are related in a one-to-many relationship. The AnimalID field in the tblVisit table is a foreign key to the tblVisit table, and you can use a combo box control in the custom form to view and maintain AnimalID field values more easily and accurately than using a text box. Recall that a combo box is a control that provides the features of a text box and a list box; you can choose a value from the list or type an entry.

PROSKILLS

Problem Solving: Using Combo Boxes for Foreign Keys

When you design forms, combo box controls are a natural choice for foreign keys because foreign key values must match one of the primary key values in the related primary table. If you do not use a combo box control for a foreign key, you force users to type values in the text box control. When they make typing mistakes, Access rejects the values and displays nonmatching error messages, which can be frustrating and make the form less efficient for users. Combo box controls allow users to select only from a list of valid foreign key values so that nonmatching situations are eliminated. At the same time, combo boxes allow users who are skilled at data entry to more rapidly type the values, instead of using the more time-consuming technique of choosing a value from the list the combo box control provides. Whenever you use an Access feature such as combo boxes for foreign keys, it takes extra time during development to add the feature, but you save users time and improve their accuracy for the many months or years they use the database.

You use the **Combo Box tool** in Design view to add a combo box control to a form. If you want help when adding the combo box, you can select one of the Control Wizards. A **Control Wizard** asks a series of questions and then, based on your answers, creates a control in a form or report. Access offers Control Wizards for the Combo Box, List Box, Option Group, Command Button, Subform/Subreport, and other control tools.

You will use the Combo Box Wizard to add a combo box control to the form for the AnimalID field.

To add a combo box control to the form:

1. Click the **Form Design Tools Design** tab, and then in the Controls group, click the **More** button to open the Controls gallery. See Figure 6-26.

Figure 6-26 Controls gallery

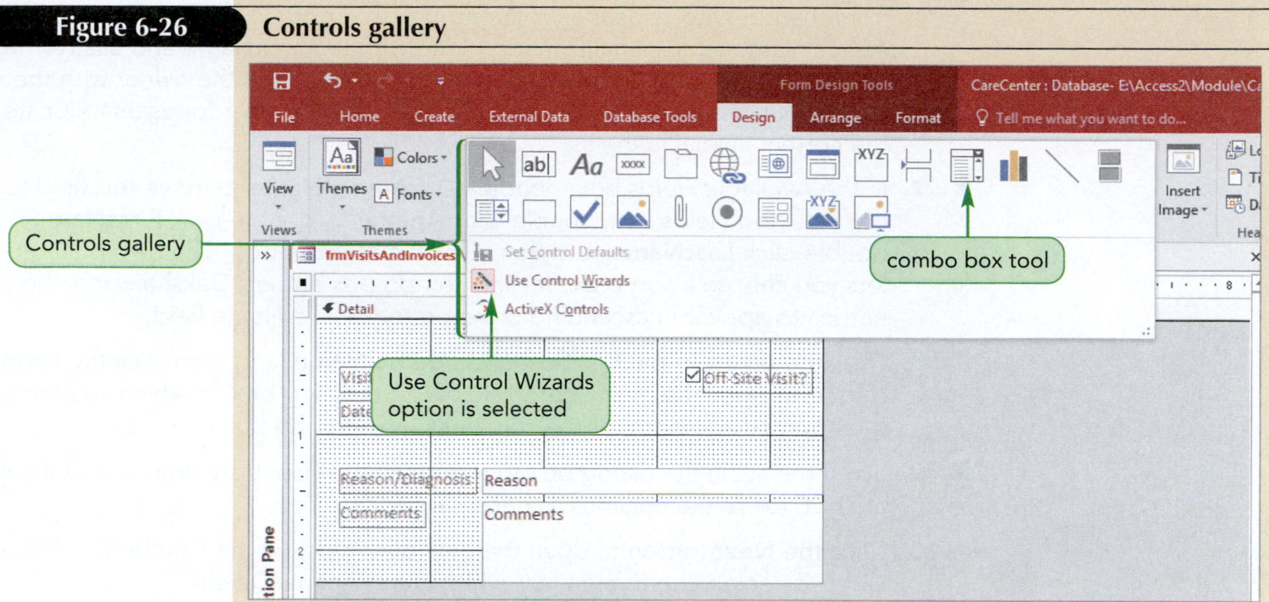

The Controls gallery contains tools that allow you to add controls (such as text boxes, lines, charts, and labels) to a form. You drag a control from the Controls gallery and place it in position in the grid. If you want to use the Combo Box Wizard to add a control, you need to select that option below the gallery.

2. In the gallery, make sure the Use Control Wizards option is selected (its icon should appear with an orange background) at the bottom of the Controls gallery, and if it is not selected, click **Use Control Wizards** to select it, and then click the **More** button again to open the Controls gallery.

3. In the Controls gallery, click the **Combo Box** tool. The Controls gallery closes.

   Once you select the Combo Box tool (or most other tools in the Controls gallery) and move the mouse pointer into the Detail section of the form, the pointer changes to a shape that is unique for the control with a plus symbol in its upper-left corner. You position the plus symbol in the location where you want to place the upper-left corner of the control.

   You'll place the combo box near the top of the form, below the OffSite bound control, and then position it more precisely after you've completed the steps in the wizard.

4. Position the plus symbol of the pointer shape below the OffSite bound control and at the 3.5 inch mark on the horizontal ruler, and then click the mouse button. A combo box control appears in the form, and the first Combo Box Wizard dialog box opens.

   You can use an existing table or query as the source for a new combo box or type the values for the combo box. In this case, you'll use the qryAnimalsAndOwners query as the basis for the new combo box.

5. Click the **I want the combo box to get the values from another table or query** option button (if necessary), then click the **Next** button to open the next Combo Box Wizard dialog box, in which you will specify the source of information for the combo box.

6. In the View section of the dialog box, click the **Queries** option button, click **Query: qryAnimalsAndOwners** in the list, and then click the **Next** button. The next dialog box in the Combo Box Wizard lets you select the fields

from the query to appear as columns in the combo box. You will select the AnimalName and AnimalID fields, along with the FirstName and LastName fields corresponding to the owner. Having the name of the owner with the Animal Name and Animal ID values might make it easier for users to locate the correct animal in the list.

7. In the Available Fields box, double-click **AnimalName** to move this field to the Selected Fields box, double-click **AnimalID**, double-click **FirstName**, double-click **LastName**, and then click the **Next** button. The next dialog box lets you choose a sort order for the combo box entries. Daksha wants the entries to appear in ascending order on the AnimalName field.

8. Click the **arrow** in the first box, click **AnimalName**, and then click the **Next** button to open the next Combo Box Wizard dialog box, in which you specify the appropriate width for the columns in the combo box control.

9. Scroll the list in the dialog box to ensure all the values are visible, and if any are not, resize the columns as necessary.

10. Click the **Next** button to open the next dialog box in the Combo Box Wizard. Here you select the foreign key, which is the AnimalID field.

11. In the Available Fields list, click **AnimalID**, and then click the **Next** button.

    In this dialog box, you specify the field in the tblVisit table where to store the selected AnimalID value from the combo box. You'll store the value in the AnimalID field in the tblVisit table.

12. Click the **Store that value in this field** option button, click the arrow to display a list of fields, click **AnimalID**, and then click the **Next** button.

    Trouble? If AnimalID doesn't appear in the list, click the Cancel button, press the Delete key to delete the combo box, click the Add Existing Fields button in the Tools group on the Form Design Tools Design tab, double-click AnimalID in the Field List pane, press the Delete key to delete AnimalID, close the Field List pane, and then repeat Steps 1–12.

    In the final Combo Box Wizard dialog box, you specify the name for the combo box control. You'll use the field name of AnimalID.

13. With the current text selected in the "What label would you like for your combo box?" box, type **AnimalID** and then click the **Finish** button. The completed AnimalID combo box control appears in the form.

You need to position and resize the combo box control, but first you will change the caption property for the AnimalID combo box label control so that it matches the format used by the other label controls in the form.

REFERENCE

Changing a Label's Caption

- Right-click the label to select it and to display the shortcut menu, and then click Properties to display the Property Sheet.
- If necessary, click the All tab to display the All page in the Property Sheet.
- Edit the existing text in the Caption box; or click the Caption box, press the F2 key to select the current value, and then type a new caption.

You want the label control attached to the combo box control to display "Animal ID" instead of "AnimalID". You will change the Caption property for the label control next.

To set the Caption property for the AnimalID combo box's label control:

TIP

After selecting a control, you can press the F4 key to open and close the Property Sheet for the control.

1. Right-click the **AnimalID** label, which is the control to the left of the AnimalID combo box control, and then click **Properties** on the shortcut menu. The Property Sheet for the AnimalID label control opens.

   Trouble? If the Selection type entry below the Property Sheet title bar is not "Label," then you selected the wrong control in Step 1. Click the AnimalID label in the form to change to the Property Sheet for this control.

2. If necessary, in the Property Sheet, click the **All** tab to display all properties for the selected AnimalID label control.

   The Selection type entry, which appears below the Property Sheet title bar, displays the control type (Label in this case) for the selected control. Below the Selection type entry in the Property Sheet is the Control box, which you can use to select another control in the form and list its properties in the Property Sheet. Alternately, you can simply click a control in the form and modify its properties in the Property Sheet. The first property in the Property Sheet, the **Name property**, specifies the name of a control, section, or object (AnimalID_Label in this case). The Name property value is the same as the value displayed in the Control box, unless the Caption property has been set. For bound controls, the Name property value matches the field name. For unbound controls, an underscore and a suffix of the control type (for example, Label) is added to the Name property setting. For unbound controls, you can set the Name property to another, more meaningful value at any time.

3. In the Caption box, click before "ID", press the **spacebar**, and then press the **Tab** key to move to the next property in the Property Sheet. The Caption property value changes to Animal ID, and the label for the AnimalID bound label control displays Animal ID. See Figure 6-27.

Figure 6-27 AnimalID combo box and updated label added to the form

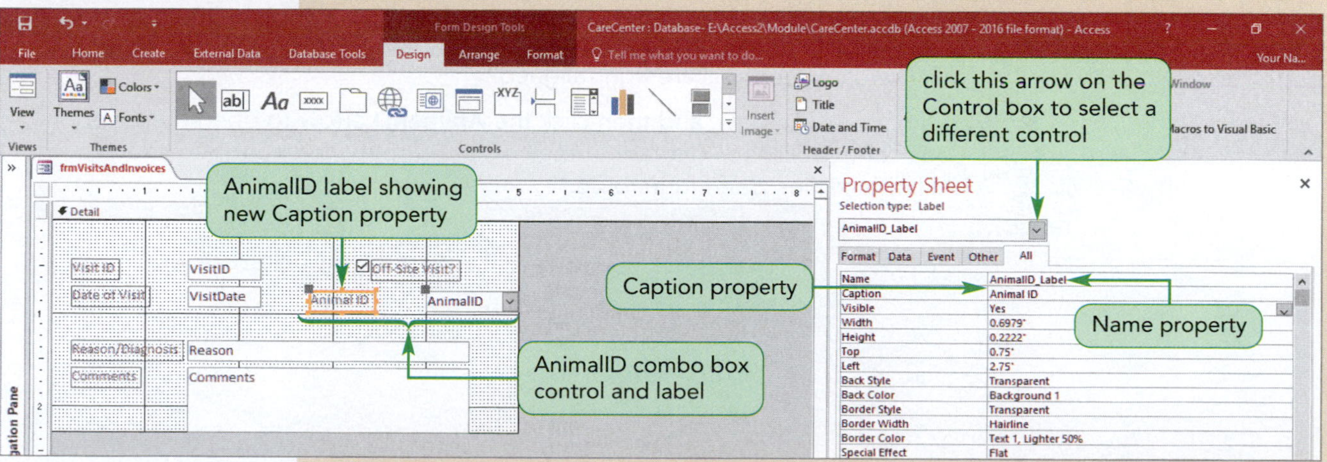

Trouble? Some property values in your Property Sheet, such as the Width and Top property values, might differ if your label's position slightly differs from the label position used as the basis for Figure 6-27. These differences cause no problems.

TIP

You won't see the effects of the new property setting until you select another property, select another control, or close the Property Sheet.

4. Close the Property Sheet, and then save your design changes to the form.

Now that you've added the combo box control to the form, you can position and resize it appropriately. You'll need to view the form in Form view to determine any fine-tuning necessary for the width of the combo box.

To modify the combo box in Design and Layout views:

1. Click the **AnimalID** combo box control, press and hold the **Shift** key, click the **Animal ID** label control, and then release the **Shift** key to select both controls.

   First, you'll move the selected controls above the VisitID controls. Then you'll left-align the AnimalID, VisitID, VisitDate, Reason, and Comments labels; left-align the AnimalID combo box control with the VisitID, VisitDate, Reason, and Comments text box controls; and then right-align the OffSite label and check box control with the right edges of the Reason and Comments text box controls.

2. Drag the selected controls to a position above the VisitID controls. Do not try to align them.
3. Click in a blank area of the screen to deselect the selected controls.
4. Press and hold the **Shift** key while you click the **Animal ID** label, the **Visit ID** label, **Date of Visit** label, **Reason/Diagnosis** label, and the **Comments** label, and then release the **Shift** key.
5. Click the **Form Design Tools Arrange** tab, in the Sizing & Ordering group, click the **Align** button, and then click **Left**. The selected controls are left-aligned.
6. Repeat Steps 4 and 5 to left-align the AnimalID combo box, VisitID text box, VisitDate text box, Reason text box, and the Comments text box.
7. Click the **Off-Site Visit?** label, press and hold the **Shift** key, click the **OffSite** check box, the **Reason** text box, and **Comments** text box, and then release the **Shift** key.
8. In the Sizing & Ordering group, click the **Align** button, and then click **Right**. The selected controls are right-aligned.
9. Switch to Form view, and then click the **AnimalID** arrow to open the combo box control's list box. Note that the column is not wide enough to show the full data values. See Figure 6-28.

Figure 6-28 AnimalID combo box and updated label in Form view

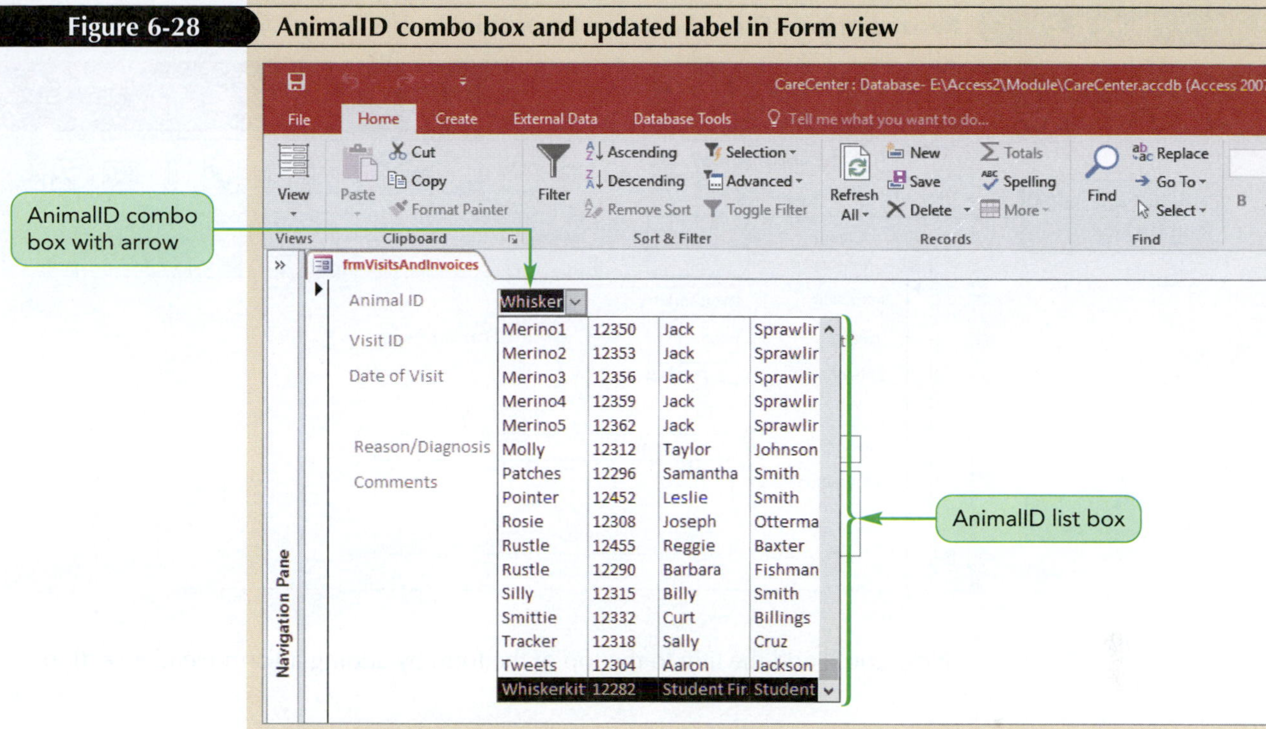

You need to widen the AnimalID combo box so that that the widest value in the list is displayed in the combo box. You can widen the combo box in Layout view or in Design view. Because Form view and Layout view display actual data from the table rather than placeholder text in each bound control, these views let you immediately see the effects of your layout changes. You'll use Layout view instead of Design view to make this change because you can determine the proper width more accurately in Layout view.

10. Switch to Layout view, and then navigate to record 1 (if necessary). Whiskerkitty, which is the animal name for this record, is one of the widest values that is displayed in the combo box. You want to widen the combo box so that it is a little bit wider than the value in record 1.

11. Make sure that only the combo box is selected, and then drag the right border to widen the combo box until the entire name of the animal is visible. See Figure 6-29.

Figure 6-29 **Resized AnimalID combo box in Layout view**

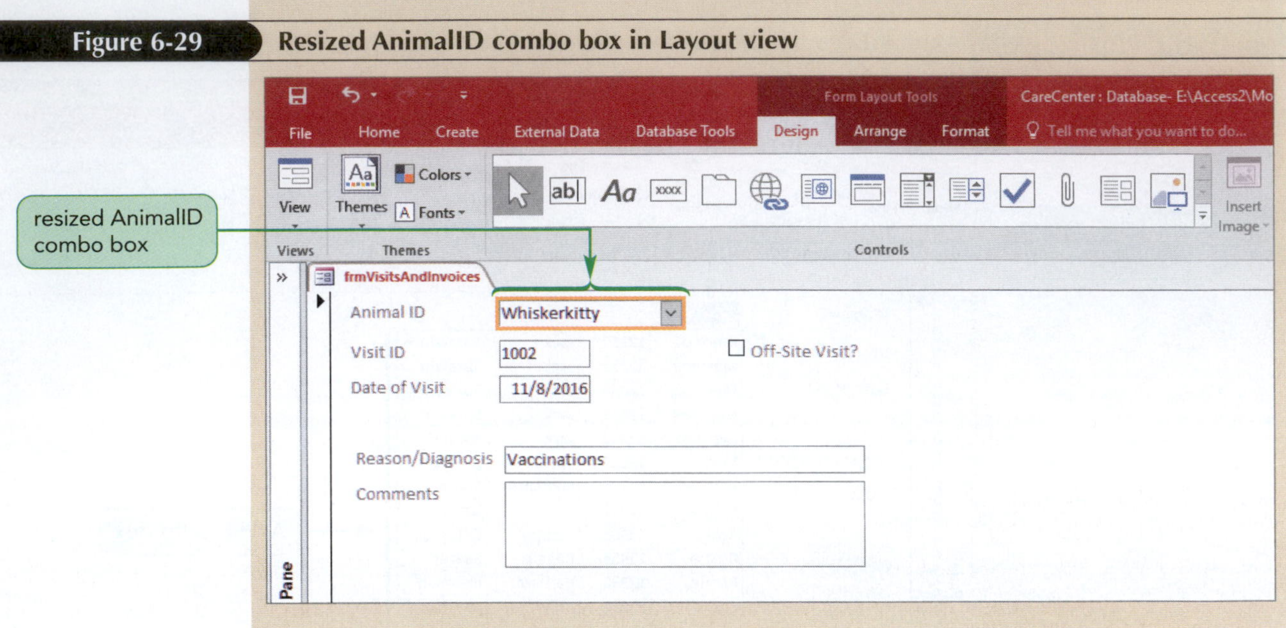

Now you'll add the title to the top of the form by adding a Form Header section.

Using Form Headers and Form Footers

The **Form Header** and **Form Footer sections** let you add titles, instructions, command buttons, and other controls to the top and bottom of your form, respectively. Controls placed in the Form Header or Form Footer sections remain on the screen whenever the form is displayed in Form view or Layout view; they do not change when the contents of the Detail section change as you navigate from one record to another record.

To add either a form header or footer to your form, you must first add both the Form Header and Form Footer sections as a pair to the form. If your form needs one of these sections but not the other, you can remove a section by setting its height to zero, which is the same method you would use to remove any form section. You can also prevent a section from appearing in Form view or in Print Preview by setting its Visible property to "No." The **Visible property** determines if a control or section appears in Form view, in Print Preview, or when printed. You set the Visible property to Yes to display the control or section, and set the Visible property to No to hide it.

If you've set the Form Footer section's height to zero or set its Visible property to No and a future form design change makes adding controls to the Form Footer section necessary, you can restore the section by using the pointer to drag its bottom border back down or by setting its Visible property to Yes.

In Design view, you can add the Form Header and Form Footer sections as a pair to a form by right-clicking the Detail section selector, and then clicking Form Header/Footer. You also can click the Logo button, the Title button, or the Date and Time button in the Header/Footer group on the Form Design Tools Design tab or the Form Layout Tools Design tab. Clicking any of these three buttons adds the Form Header and Form Footer sections to the form and places an appropriate control in the Form Header section only. A footer section is added to the form, but with a height set to zero to one-quarter inch.

Daksha's design includes a title at the top of the form. Because the title will not change as you navigate through the form records, you will add the title to the Form Header section in the form.

Adding a Title to a Form

You'll add the title to Daksha's form in Layout view. When you add a title to a form in Layout view, a Form Header section is added to the form and contains the form title. At the same time, a Page Footer section with a height setting of zero is added to the form.

To add a title to the form:

1. On the Form Layout Tools Design tab, in the Header/Footer group, click the **Title** button. A title consisting of the form name is added to the form and is selected.

   You need to change the title.

2. Type **Visits and Invoices** to replace the selected default title text. See Figure 6-30.

Figure 6-30 Title added to the form in the Form Header section

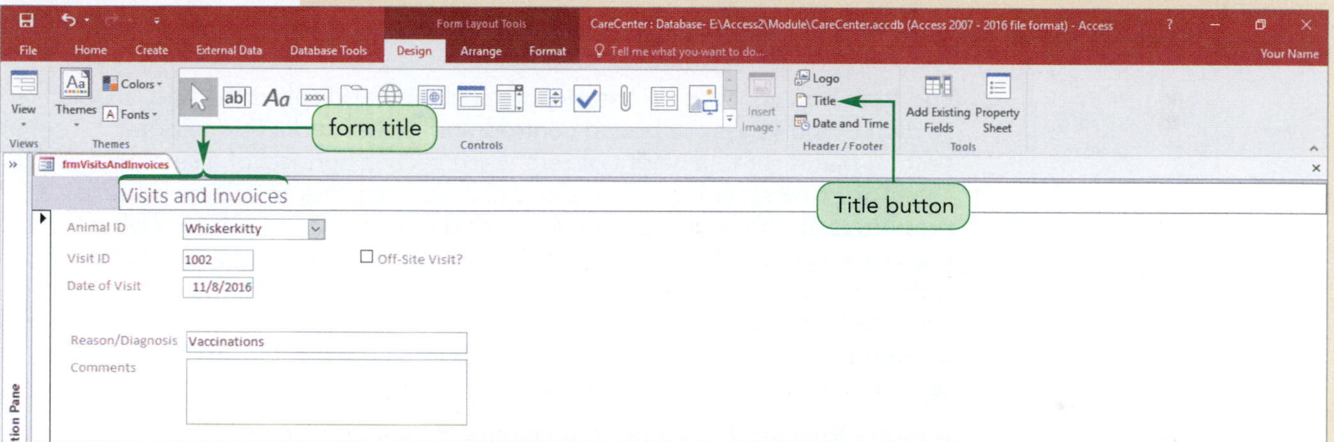

The title is a larger font size than the font used for the form's labels and field value boxes, but Daksha would like you to apply bold to increase its prominence.

3. Select the title control, click the **Form Layout Tools Format** tab, and then in the Font group, click the **Bold** button B. The title is displayed in 18-point, bold text.

   It is not obvious in Layout view that the title is displayed in the Form Header section, so you'll view the form design in Design view.

4. Switch to Design view, click a blank area of the screen to deselect all controls. The title is displayed in the Form Header section. See Figure 6-31.

Figure 6-31 Form Header and Form Footer sections in Design view

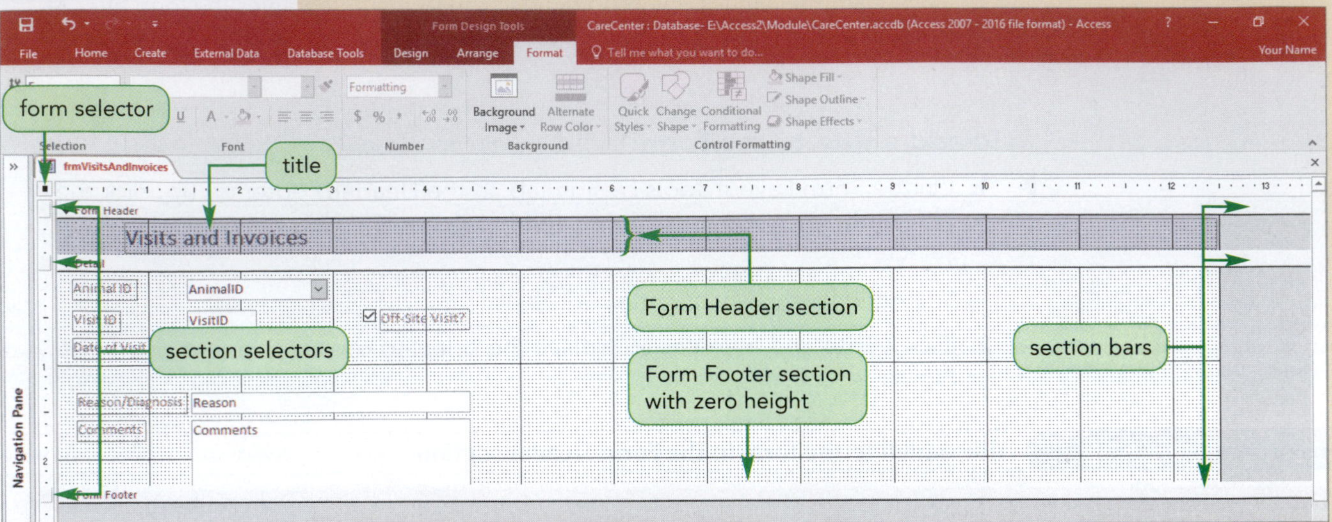

The form now contains a Form Header section that displays the title, a Detail section that displays the bound controls and labels, and a Form Footer section that is set to a height of zero. Each section consists of a **section selector** and a section bar, either of which you can click to select and set properties for the entire section, and a grid or background, which is where you place controls that you want to display in the form. The **form selector** is the selector at the intersection of the horizontal and vertical rulers; you click the form selector when you want to select the entire form and set its properties. The vertical ruler is segmented into sections for the Form Header section, the Detail section, and the Form Footer section.

A form's total height includes the heights of the Form Header, Detail, and Form Footer sections. If you set a form's total height to more than the screen size, users will need to use scroll bars to view the content of your form, which is less productive for users and isn't good form design.

5. Save the design changes to the form, and then, if you are not continuing on to the next session, close the CareCenter database.

So far, you've added controls to the form and modified the controls by selecting, moving, aligning, resizing, and deleting them. You've added and modified a combo box and added a title in the Form Header section. In the next session, you will continue your work with the custom form by adding a combo box control for use in finding records, adding a subform, adding calculated controls, changing form and section properties, and changing control properties.

REVIEW

Session 6.2 Quick Check

1. What is a bound form, and when do you use bound forms?
2. What is the difference between a bound control and an unbound control?
3. The ______________ consists of the dotted and solid lines that appear in the Header, Detail, and Footer sections in Design view to help you position controls precisely in a form.
4. The larger handle in a selected object's upper-left corner is the ______________ handle.
5. How do you move a selected field value box and its label at the same time?
6. How do you resize a control?
7. A(n) ______________ control provides the features of a text box and a list box.
8. How do you change a label's caption?
9. What is the purpose of the Form Header section?

Session 6.3 Visual Overview:

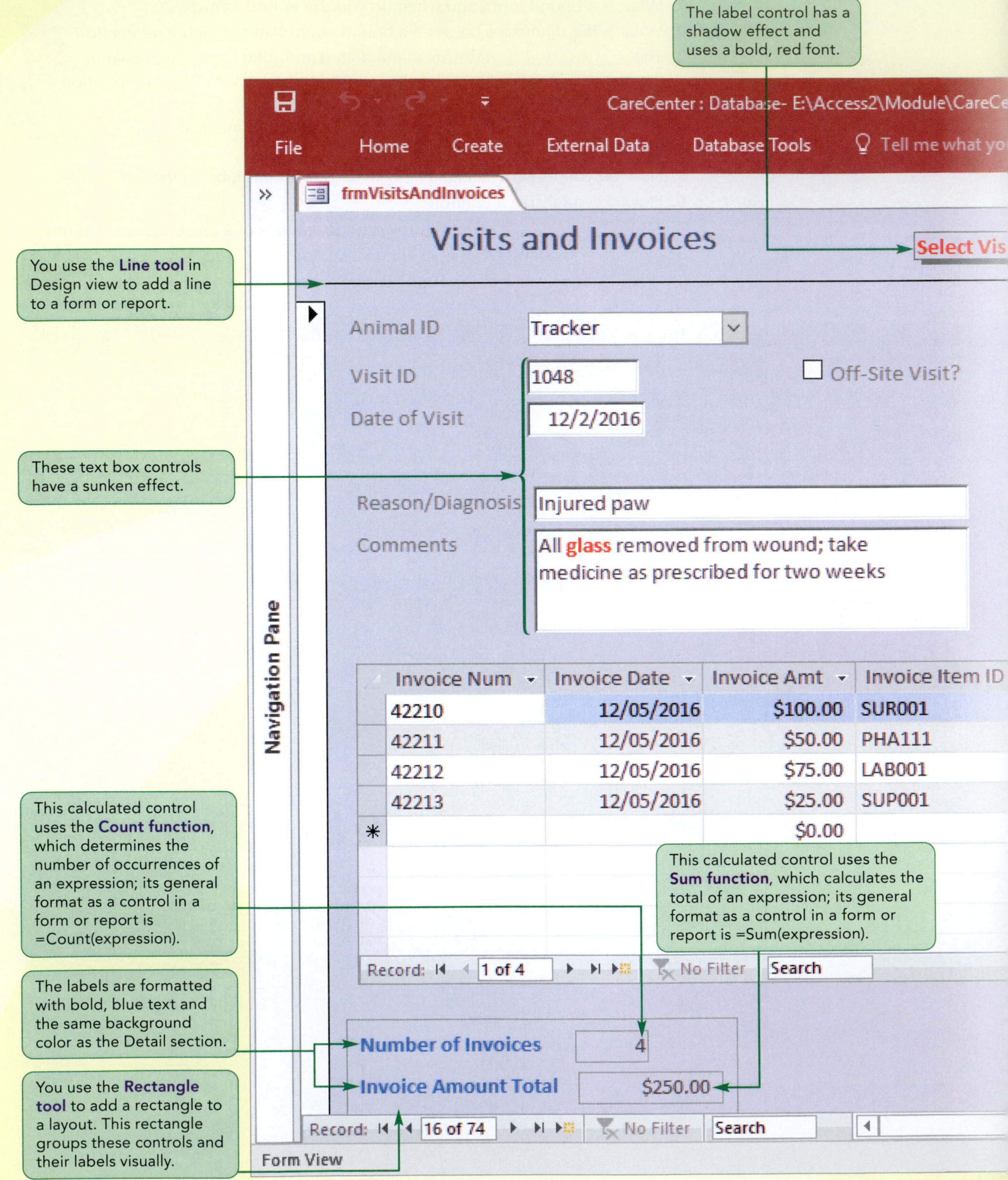
The label control has a shadow effect and uses a bold, red font.
CareCenter : Database- E:\Access2\Module\CareCe
File
Home
Create
External Data
Database Tools
Tell me what yo
frmVisitsAndInvoices
Visits and Invoices
Select Vis
You use the Line tool in Design view to add a line to a form or report.
Animal ID
Tracker
Visit ID
1048
Off-Site Visit?
Date of Visit
12/2/2016
These text box controls have a sunken effect.
Reason/Diagnosis
Injured paw
Comments
All glass removed from wound; take medicine as prescribed for two weeks
Navigation Pane
Invoice Num
Invoice Date
Invoice Amt
Invoice Item ID
42210 12/05/2016 $100.00 SUR001
42211 12/05/2016 $50.00 PHA111
42212 12/05/2016 $75.00 LAB001
42213 12/05/2016 $25.00 SUP001
$0.00
This calculated control uses the Count function, which determines the number of occurrences of an expression; its general format as a control in a form or report is =Count(expression).
This calculated control uses the Sum function, which calculates the total of an expression; its general format as a control in a form or report is =Sum(expression).
Record: 1 of 4
No Filter
Search
The labels are formatted with bold, blue text and the same background color as the Detail section.
Number of Invoices
4
Invoice Amount Total
$250.00
You use the Rectangle tool to add a rectangle to a layout. This rectangle groups these controls and their labels visually.
Record: 16 of 74
No Filter
Search
Form View

Custom Form in Form View

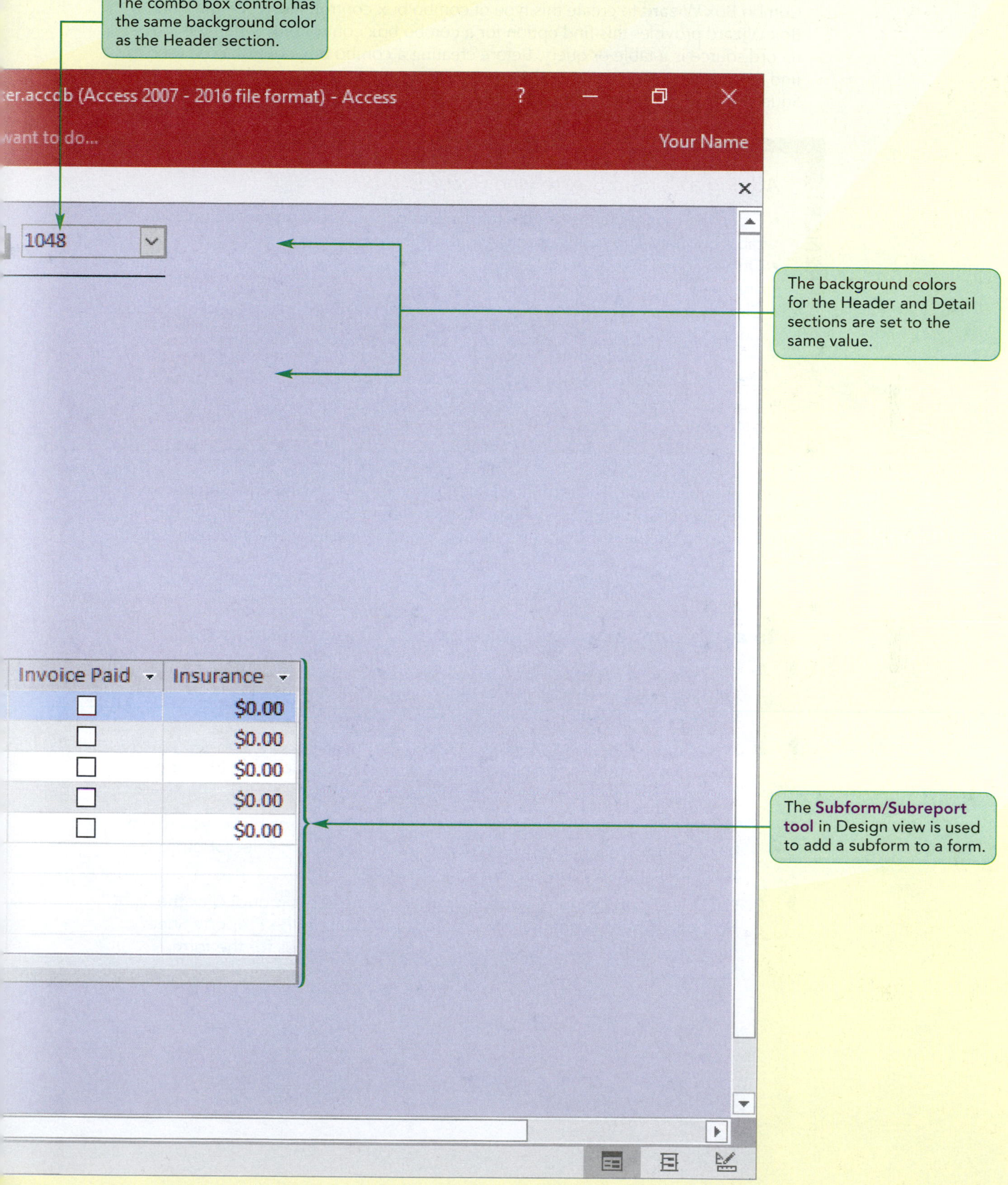

The combo box control has the same background color as the Header section.
er.accdb (Access 2007 - 2016 file format) - Access
want to do...
Your Name
1048
The background colors for the Header and Detail sections are set to the same value.
Invoice Paid
Insurance
$0.00
$0.00
$0.00
$0.00
$0.00
The Subform/Subreport tool in Design view is used to add a subform to a form.

Adding a Combo Box to Find Records

As you know, a combo box control is used to display and update data in a form. You can also use a combo box control to allow users to find records. You can use the Combo Box Wizard to create this type of combo box control. However, the Combo Box Wizard provides this find option for a combo box control only when the form's record source is a table or query. Before creating a combo box control to be used to find records, you should view the Property Sheet for the form to confirm the Record Source property is set to a table or query.

REFERENCE

Adding a Combo Box to Find Records

- Open the Property Sheet for the form in Design view, confirm the record source is a table or query, and then close the Property Sheet.
- On the Form Design Tools Design tab, in the Controls group, click the More button, and then click the Combo Box tool.
- Click the location in the form where you want to place the control, and open the Combo Box Wizard.
- In the first dialog box of the Combo Box Wizard, click the "Find a record on my form based on the value I selected in my combo box" option button.
- Complete the remaining Combo Box Wizard dialog boxes to finish creating the combo box control.

To continue creating the form that Daksha sketched, you will add a combo box to the Form Header section that will allow users to find a specific record in the tblVisit table to display in the form. But first you will view the Property Sheet to make sure the Record Source property is set to the tblVisit table.

To add a combo box to find records to display in the form:

1. If you took a break after the previous session, make sure that the CareCenter database is open, the frmVisitsAndInvoices form is open in Design view, and the Navigation Pane is closed.
2. To the left of the horizontal ruler, click the form selector ☐ to select the form, if necessary. The form selector changes to ▣, indicating that the form is selected.

   Trouble? If the Form Header section head instead turns black, you might have clicked the header selector button. Click the form selector button, which is just above the header selector button.
3. Click the **Form Design Tools Design** tab, in the Tools group, click the **Property Sheet** button, and then click the **All** tab in the Property Sheet, if necessary. The Property Sheet displays the properties for the form. See Figure 6-32.

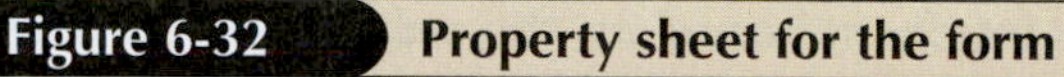

Figure 6-32 Property sheet for the form

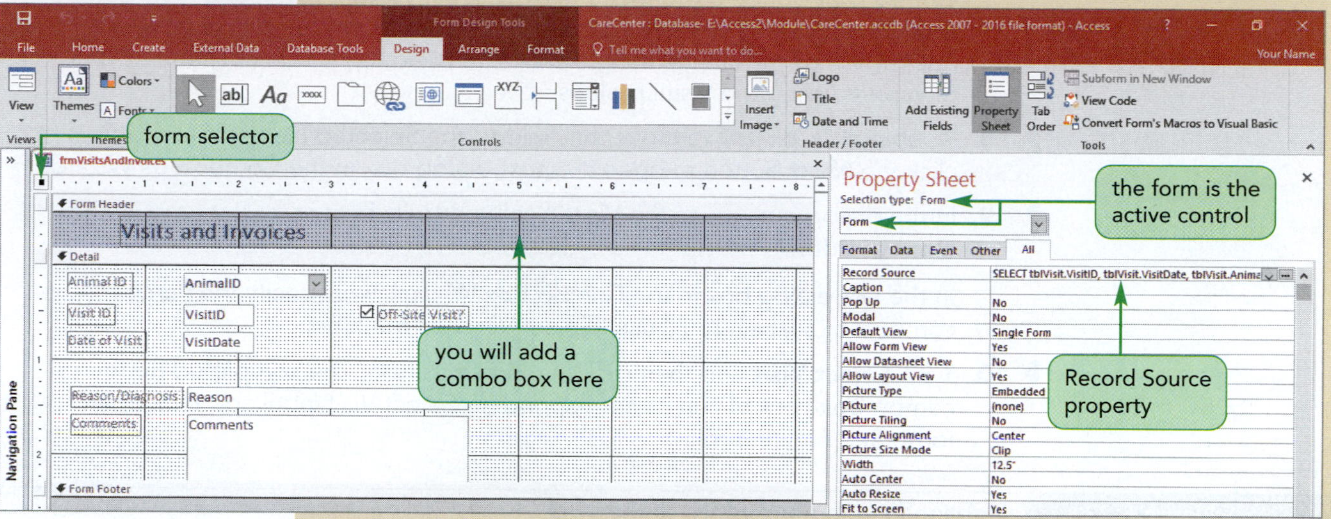

The Record Source property is set to an SQL SELECT statement, which is code that references a table. You need to change the Record Source property to a table or query, or the Combo Box Wizard will not present you with the option to find records in a form. You'll change the Record Source property to the tblVisit table because this table is the record source for all the bound controls you have added to the Detail section of the form.

4. In the Record Source box, click the **Record Source** arrow, click **tblVisit** in the list, and then close the Property Sheet.

   You'll now use the Combo Box Wizard to add a combo box to the form's Form Header section, which will enable a user to find a record in the tblVisit table to display in the form.

5. On the Form Design Tools Design tab, in the Controls group, click the **More** button to open the Controls gallery, and then click the **Combo Box** tool.

6. Position the plus symbol pointer at the top of the Form Header section at the 5-inch mark on the horizontal ruler (see Figure 6-32), and then click the mouse button. A combo box control appears in the Form Header section of the form, and the first Combo Box Wizard dialog box opens.

   Trouble? If the Combo Box Wizard dialog box does not open, delete the new controls and try again, ensuring the plus symbol pointer is very near the top of the Form Header grid.

   You will recall seeing this dialog box when you used the Combo Box Wizard in the previous session. The first dialog box in the Combo Box Wizard this time displays an additional option than what was available previously. This additional option, "Find a record on my form based on the value I selected in my combo box," is what you need to use for this combo box. (Recall in the last session you selected the first option, "I want the combo box to get the values from another table or query" when you used the Combo Box Wizard to create the AnimalID combo box, allowing the user to select a value from a list of foreign key values from an existing table or query.) You would choose the second option if you wanted users to select a value from a short fixed list of values that don't change. For example, if Riverview Veterinary Care Center wanted to include a field in the tblAnimal table to identify the state in which the animal resides, you could use a combo box with this second option to display a list of states.

7. Click the **Find a record on my form based on the value I selected in my combo box** option button, and then click the **Next** button. The next Combo Box Wizard dialog box lets you select the fields from the tblVisit table to appear as columns in the combo box. You need to include only one column of values, listing the VisitID values.
8. Double-click **VisitID** to move this field to the Selected Fields box, and then click the **Next** button to open the next dialog box in the Combo Box Wizard.
9. In the dialog box, resize the VisitID column to its best fit, and then click the **Next** button.

   In the last dialog box in the Combo Box Wizard, you specify the name for the combo box's label. You'll use "Select Visit" as the label.
10. Type **Select Visit** and then click the **Finish** button. The completed unbound combo box control and its corresponding Select Visit label appear in the form. See Figure 6-33.

Figure 6-33 **Unbound combo box added to the form**

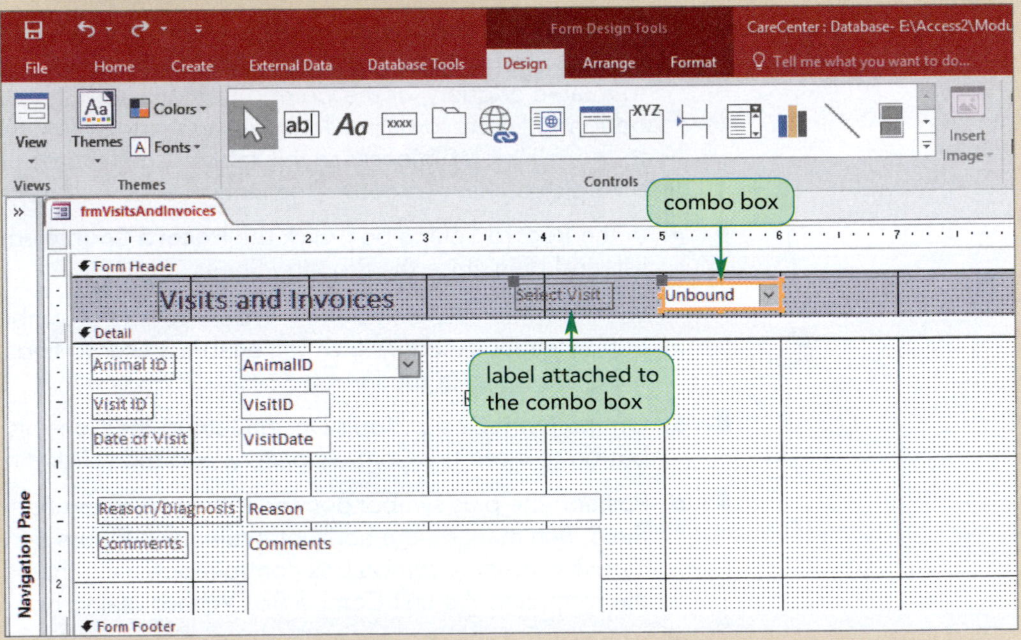

You'll move the attached label closer to the combo box control, and then you'll align the bottoms of the combo box control and its attached label with the bottom of the title in the Form Header section.

11. Click the **Select Visit** label, point to the label's move handle on the upper-left corner of the orange selection border, and then drag the label to the right until its right edge is two grid dots to the left of the combo box.
12. With the Select Visit label still selected, press and hold the **Shift** key, click the **combo box**, and then click the **Visit and Invoices** form title.
13. Right-click the selected controls, point to **Align** on the shortcut menu, and then click **Bottom**. The three selected controls are bottom-aligned. See Figure 6-34.

Figure 6-34 Aligned combo box control and form title

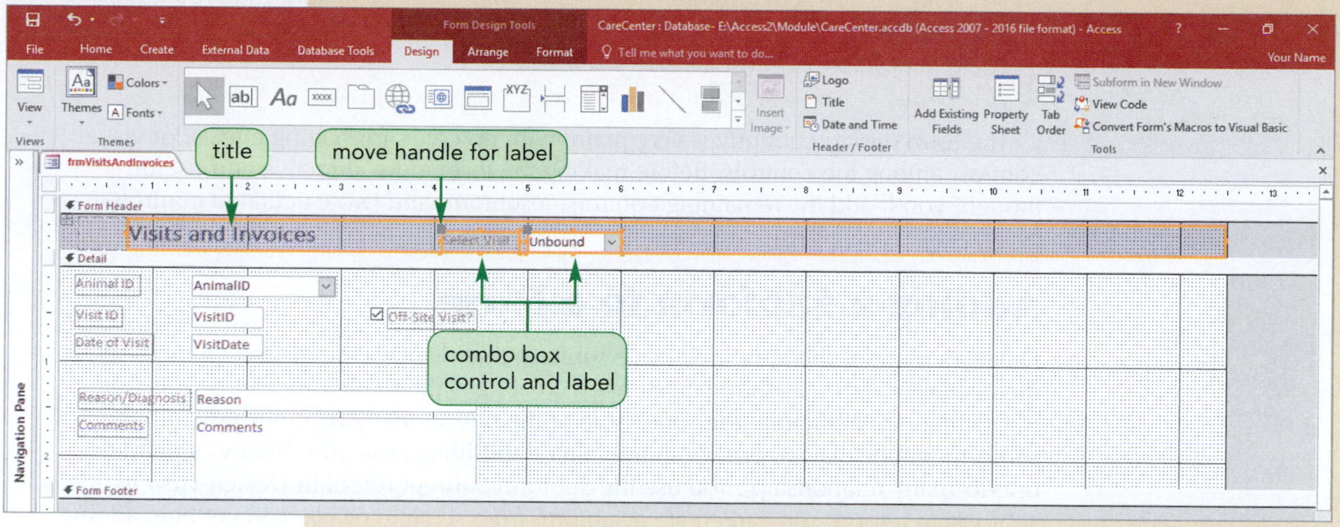

You'll save your form changes and view the new combo box control in Form view.

To save the form and view the Select Visit combo box control:

1. Save the form design changes, and then switch to Form view.
2. Click the **Select Visit** arrow to display the list of Visit ID numbers. See Figure 6-35.

Figure 6-35 List of Visit IDs in the combo box

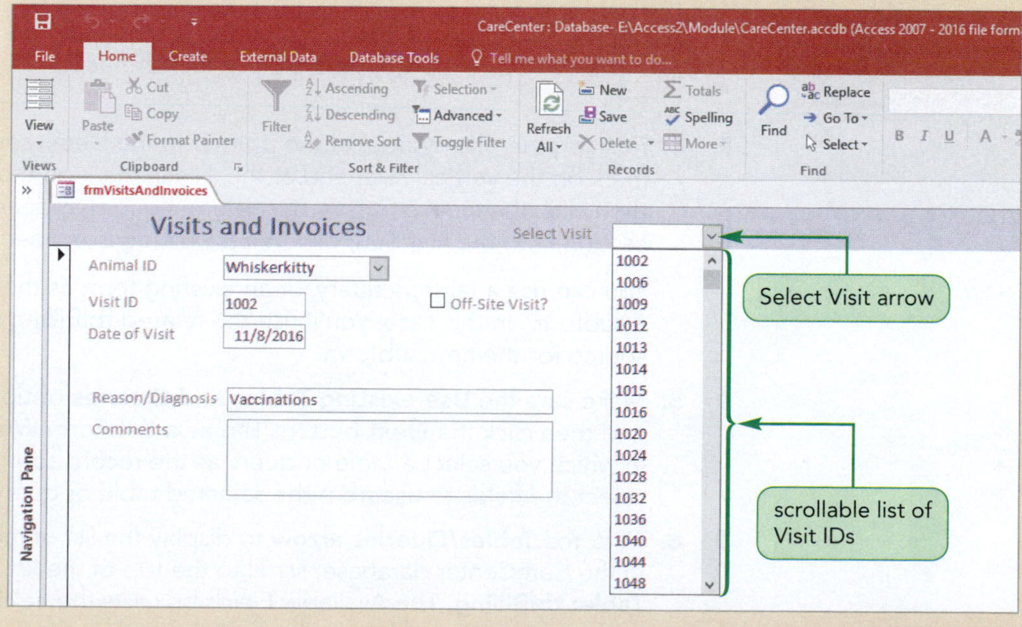

3. Scroll down the list, and then click **1048**. The current record changes from record 1 to record 16, which is the record for visit ID 1048.

Trouble? If you see the data for record 1, the navigation combo box is not working correctly. Delete the combo box, check to ensure that you have set the Record Source for the form object correctly, and repeat the previous set of steps to re-create the combo box.

The form design currently is very plain, with no color, formatting effects, or visual contrast among the controls. Before making the form more attractive and useful, though, you'll add the remaining controls: a subform and two calculated controls.

Adding a Subform to a Form

Daksha's plan for the form includes a subform that displays the related invoices for the displayed visit. The form you've been creating is the main form for records from the primary tblVisit table (the "one" side of the one-to-many relationship), and the subform will display records from the related tblBilling table (the "many" side of the one-to-many relationship). You use the Subform/Subreport tool in Design view to add a subform to a form. You can create a subform from scratch, or you can get help adding the subform by using the SubForm Wizard.

You will use the SubForm Wizard to add the subform for displaying tblBilling table records to the bottom of the form. First, you'll increase the height of the Detail section to make room for the subform.

TIP

Drag slightly beyond the desired ending position to expose the vertical ruler measurement, and then decrease the height back to the correct position.

To add the subform to the form:

1. Switch to Design view.
2. Position the pointer on the bottom border of the Detail section until the pointer changes to ✛, and then drag the border down to the 5-inch mark on the vertical ruler.
3. On the Form Design Tools Design tab, in the Controls group, click the **More** button to open the Controls gallery, and then click the **Subform/Subreport** tool.
4. Position the plus symbol of the pointer in the Detail section at the 2.5-inch mark on the vertical ruler and at the 1-inch mark on the horizontal ruler, and then click the mouse button. A subform control appears in the form's Detail section, and the first SubForm Wizard dialog box opens.

   You can use a table, a query, or an existing form as the record source for a subform. In this case, you'll use the related tblBilling table as the record source for the new subform.
5. Make sure the **Use existing Tables and Queries** option button is selected, and then click the **Next** button. The next SubForm Wizard dialog box opens, in which you select a table or query as the record source for the subform and select the fields to use from the selected table or query.
6. Click the **Tables/Queries arrow** to display the list of tables and queries in the CareCenter database, scroll to the top of the list, and then click **Table: tblBilling**. The Available Fields box lists the fields in the tblBilling table.

   Daksha's form design includes all fields from the tblBilling table in the subform, except for the VisitID field, which you already placed in the Detail section of the form from the tblVisit table.

7. Click the >> button to move all available fields to the Selected Fields box, click **VisitID** in the Selected Fields box, click the < button, and then click the **Next** button to open the next SubForm Wizard dialog box. See Figure 6-36.

Figure 6-36 Selecting the linking field

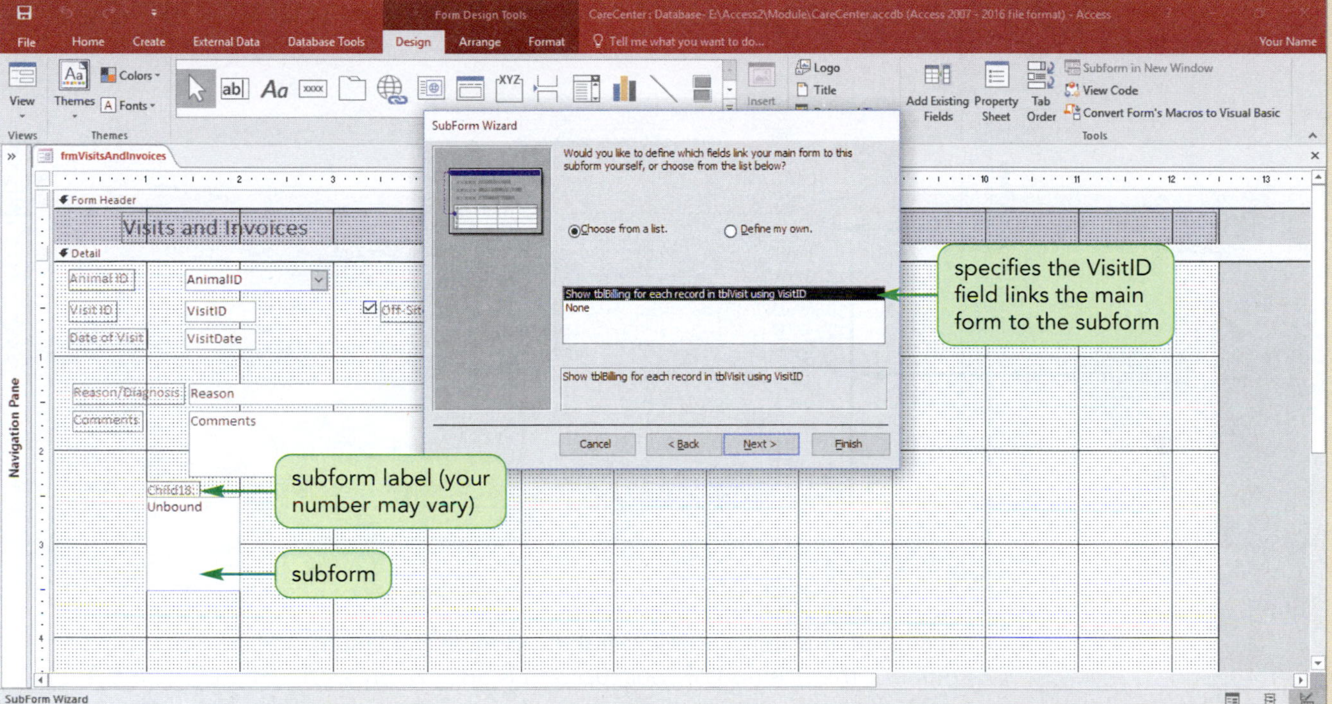

In this dialog box, you select the link between the primary tblVisit table and the related tblBilling table. The common field in the two tables, VisitID, links the tables. The form will use the VisitID field to display a record in the main form, which displays data from the primary tblVisit table, and to select and display the related records for that contract in the subform, which displays data from the related tblBilling table.

8. Make sure the **Choose from a list** option button is selected, make sure **"Show tblBilling for each record in tblVisit using VisitID"** is selected in the list, and then click the **Next** button. In the last SubForm Wizard dialog box, you specify a name for the subform.

9. Type **frmBillingSubform** and then click the **Finish** button. The completed subform appears in the Details section of the Form window; its label appears above the subform and displays the subform name.

10. Click a blank area of the screen, and then save the form.

11. Switch to Form view, click the **Select Visit** arrow, and then click **1048**. The subform displays the four invoices related to visit ID 1048. See Figure 6-37.

Figure 6-37 The subform in Form view

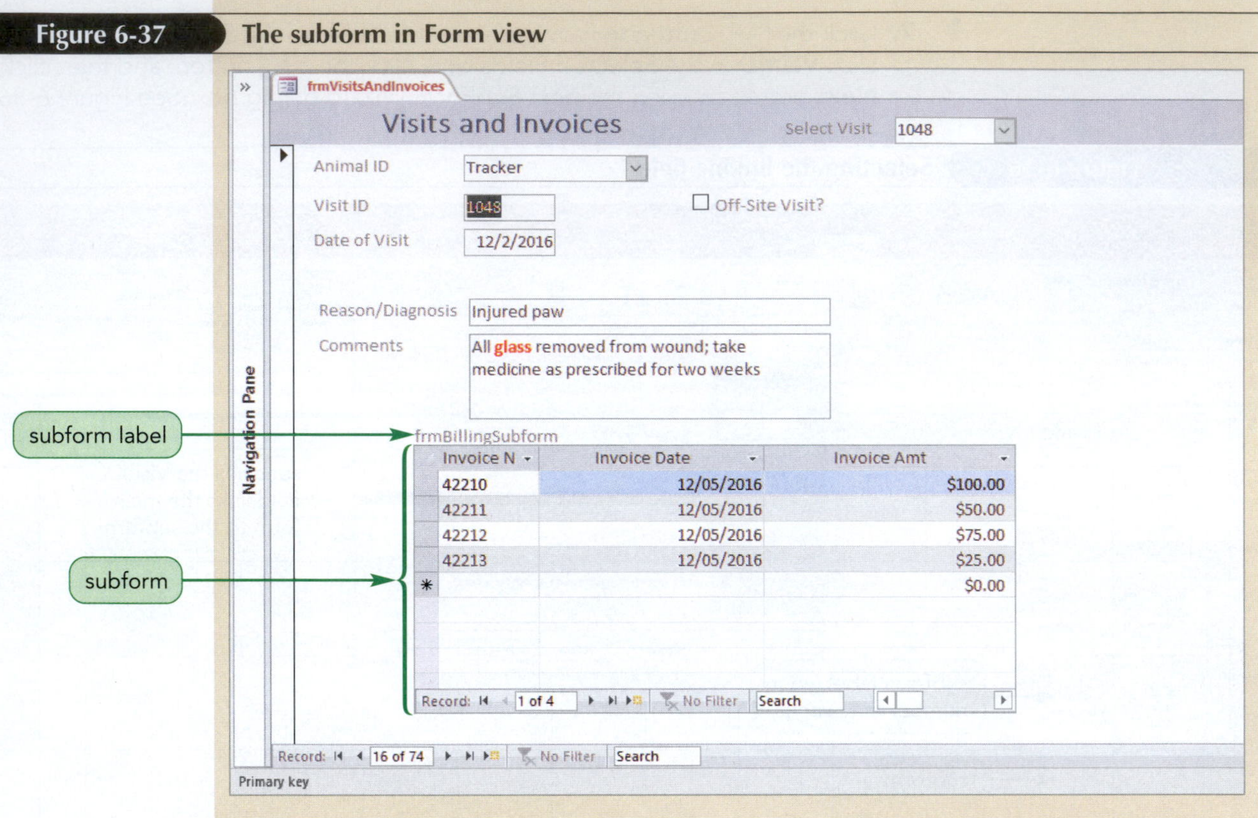

Trouble? It is not a problem if the widths of the columns in your datasheet differ or the position of your subform is not exactly as shown in Figure 6-37. You will resize columns and position the subform in the next set of steps.

After viewing the form, Daksha identifies some modifications he wants you to make. He wants you to resize the subform and its columns so that all columns in the subform are entirely visible and the columns are sized to best fit. Also, he asks you to delete the subform label, because the label is unnecessary for identifying the subform contents. You'll use Design view and Layout view to make these changes.

To modify the subform's design and adjust its position in the form:

1. Switch to Design view. Notice that in Design view, the data in the subform control does not appear in a datasheet format as it does in Form view. That difference causes no problem; you can ignore it.

   First, you'll delete the subform label control.

2. Deselect all controls (if necessary), right-click the **frmBillingSubform** subform label control to open the shortcut menu, and then click **Delete**.

   Next, you'll align the subform control with the Comments label control.

3. Click the border of the subform control to select it, press and hold the **Shift** key, click the **Comments** label control, and then release the **Shift** key. The subform control and the Comments label control are selected. Next you'll left-align the two controls.

4. Right-click the **Comments** label control, point to **Align** on the shortcut menu, and then click **Left**. The two controls are left-aligned. Next, you'll resize the subform control in Layout view so that you can observe the effects of your changes as you make them.
5. Switch to Layout view, click the border of the subform to select it, and then drag the right border of the subform to the right until the Insurance column arrow is fully visible.

   Before resizing the columns in the subform to best fit, you'll display record 16 in the main form. The subform for this record contains the related records in the tblBilling table with one of the longest field values.
6. Use the record navigation bar for the main form (at the bottom left of the form window) to display record 16, for visit number 1048, and then resize each column in the subform to its best fit.

   Next, you'll resize the subform again so that its width matches the width of the five resized columns.
7. Resize the subform so that its right border is aligned with the right border of the Insurance column. See Figure 6-38.

Figure 6-38 Moved and resized subform

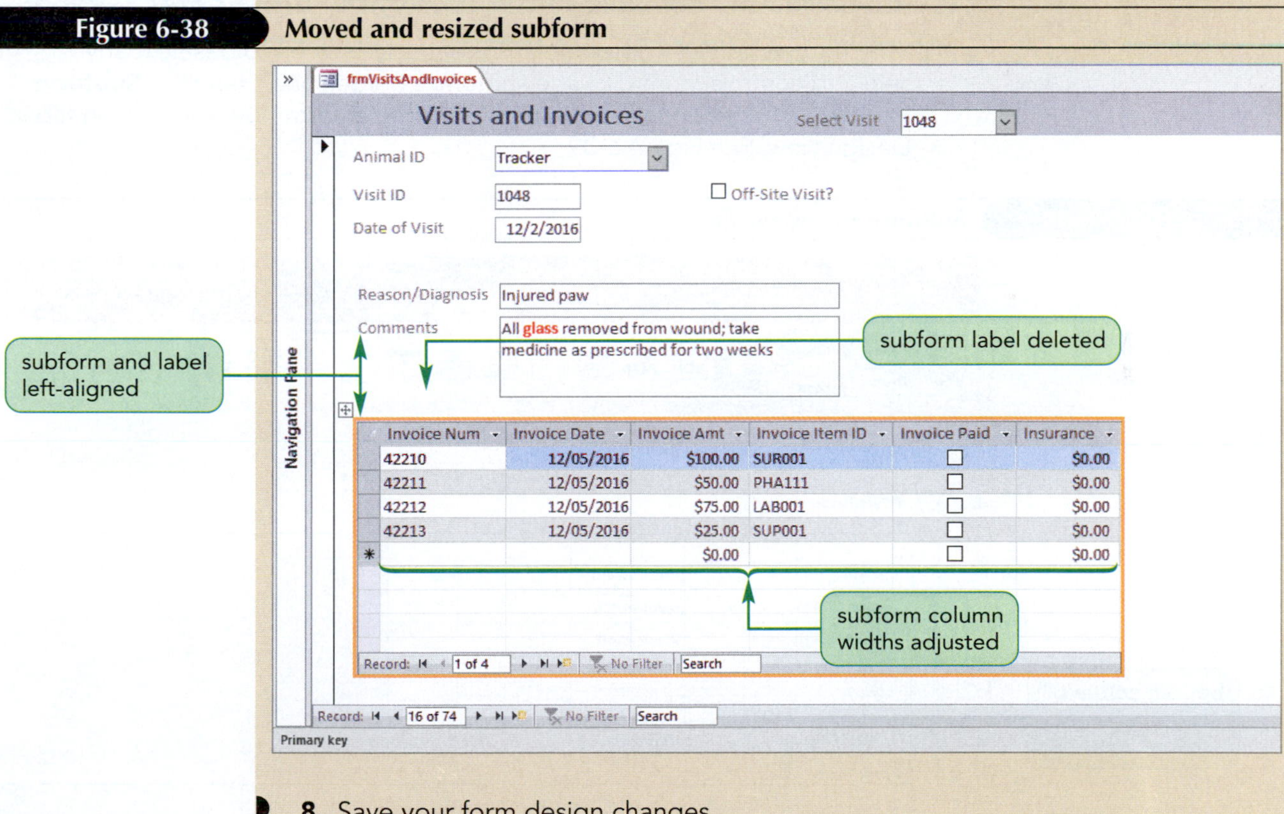

8. Save your form design changes.

You've finished your work with the subform. Now you need to add two calculated controls to the main form.

Displaying a Subform's Calculated Controls in the Main Form

TIP

You precede expressions with an equal sign to distinguish them from field names, which do not have an equal sign.

Daksha's form design includes the display of calculated controls in the main form that tally the number of invoices and the total of the invoice amounts for the related records displayed in the subform. To display these calculated controls in a form or report, you use the Count and Sum functions. The Count function determines the number of occurrences of an expression; its general format as a control in a form or report is =Count(*expression*). The Sum function calculates the total of an expression, and its general format as a control in a form or report is =Sum(*expression*). The number of invoices and total of invoice amounts are displayed in the subform's Detail section, so you'll need to place the calculated controls in the subform's Form Footer section.

Adding Calculated Controls to a Subform's Form Footer Section

First, you'll open the subform in Design view in another window and add the calculated controls to the subform's Form Footer section.

To add calculated controls to the subform's Form Footer section:

1. Switch to Design view, click a blank area of the screen to deselect any selected controls, right-click the subform's border, and then click **Subform in New Window** on the shortcut menu. The subform opens in its own tab in Design view. See Figure 6-39.

Figure 6-39 Subform in Design view

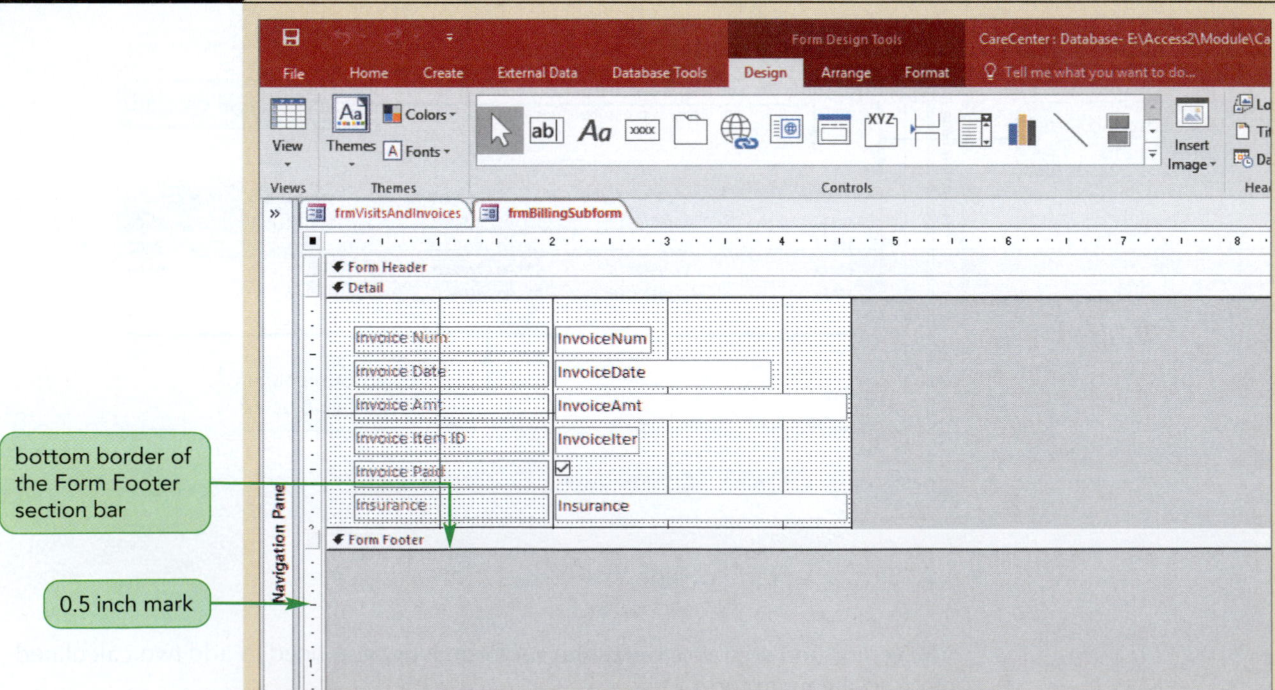

The subform's Detail section contains the tblBilling table fields. As a subform in the main form, the fields appear in a datasheet even though the fields do not appear that way in Design view. The heights of the subform's Form

Header and Form Footer sections are zero, meaning that these sections have been removed from the subform. You'll increase the height of the Form Footer section so that you can add the two calculated controls to the section.

2. Click the **Form Footer** section bar, position the pointer on the bottom border of the Form Footer section bar until the pointer changes to ✛, and then drag the bottom border of the section down to the 0.5-inch mark on the vertical ruler.

Now you'll add the first calculated control to the Form Footer section. To create the text box for the calculated control, you use the Text Box tool in the Controls group on the Form Design Tools Design tab. Because the Form Footer section is not displayed in a datasheet, you do not need to position the control precisely.

3. On the Form Design Tools Design tab, in the Controls group, click the **Text Box** tool [ab|].

4. Position the plus symbol of the pointer near the top of the Form Footer section and aligned with the 1-inch mark on the horizontal ruler, and then click the mouse button. A text box control and an attached label control appear in the Form Footer section. The text "Unbound" appears in the text box, indicating it is an unbound control.

Next, you'll set the Name and Control Source properties for the text box. Recall that the Name property specifies the name of an object or control. Later, when you add the calculated control in the main form, you'll reference the subform's calculated control value by using its Name property value. The **Control Source property** specifies the source of the data that appears in the control; the Control Source property setting can be either a field name or an expression.

5. Open the Property Sheet for the text box in the Form Footer section, click the **All** tab (if necessary), select the value in the Name box, type **txtInvoiceAmtSum** in the Name box, and then press the **Tab** key to move to the Control Source box.

6. In the Control Source box, type **=Sum(Inv**, press the **Tab** key to accept the rest of the field name of InvoiceAmt suggested by Formula AutoComplete, type **)** (a right parenthesis), and then press the **Tab** key. InvoiceAmt is enclosed in brackets in the expression because it's a field name. See Figure 6-40.

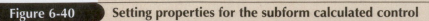

Figure 6-40 Setting properties for the subform calculated control

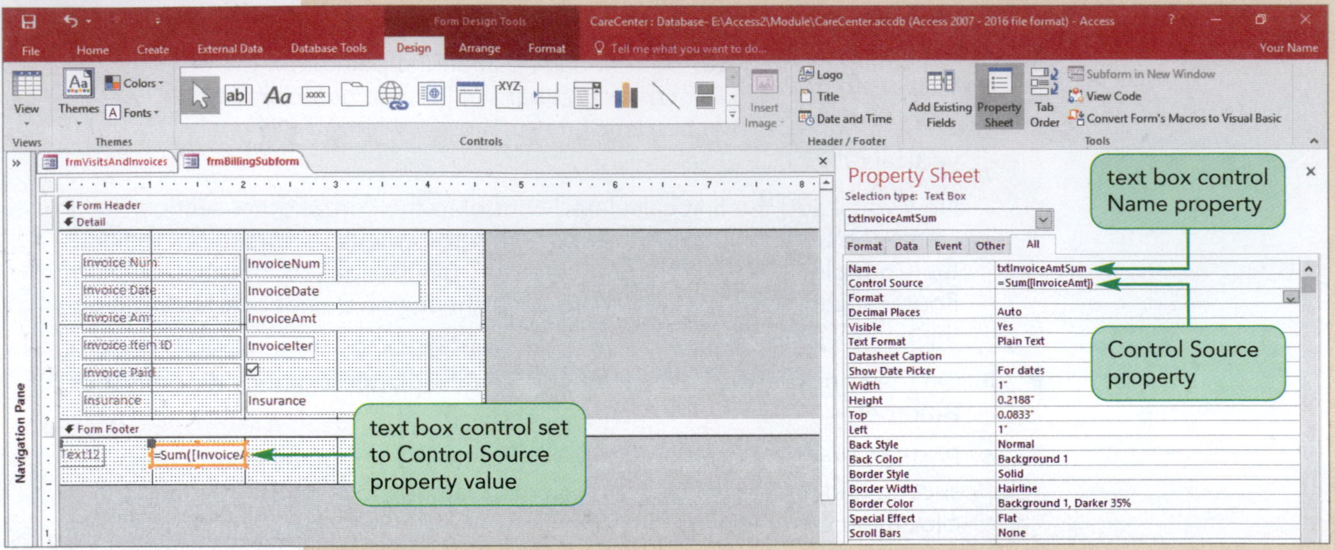

You've finished creating the first calculated control; now you'll create the other calculated control.

TIP

In the Name property, txtInvoiceNumCount, txt identifies the control type (a text box), InvoiceNum is the related field name, and Count identifies the control as a count control.

7. Repeat Steps 3 through 6, positioning the calculated field text box near the top of the Form Footer section aligned to the 3.5-inch mark on the horizontal ruler, setting the Name property value to **txtInvoiceNumCount**, and setting the Control Source property value to **=Count([InvoiceNum])**.

   When you use the Count function, you are counting the number of displayed records—in this case, the number of records displayed in the subform. Instead of using InvoiceNum as the expression for the Count function, you could use any of the other fields displayed in the subform.

   You've finished creating the subform's calculated controls.

8. Close the Property Sheet, save your subform changes, and then close the subform. The active object is now the main form in Design view.

   Trouble? The subform in the frmContractsAndInvoices form might appear to be blank after you close the frmInvoiceSubform form. This is a temporary effect; the subform's controls do still exist. Switch to Form view and then back to Design view to display the subform's controls.

9. Switch to Form view. The calculated controls you added in the subform's Form Footer section are *not* displayed in the subform.

10. Switch to Design view.

Next, you'll add two calculated controls in the main form to display the two calculated controls from the subform.

Adding Calculated Controls to a Main Form

The subform's calculated controls now contain a count of the number of invoices and a total of the invoice amounts. However, notice that Daksha's design has the two calculated controls displayed in the main form, *not* in the subform. You need to add two calculated controls in the main form that reference the values in the subform's calculated controls. Because it's easy to make a typing mistake with these references, you'll use Expression Builder to set the Control Source property for the two main form calculated controls.

To add a calculated control to the main form's Detail section:

1. Adjust the length of the Detail section if necessary so that there is approximately 0.5 inch below the frmBillingSubform control. The Detail section should be approximately 5.5 inches.
2. On the Form Design Tools Design tab, in the Controls group, click the **Text Box** tool [ab].
3. Position the pointer's plus symbol below the frmBillingSubform at the 5-inch mark on the vertical ruler and aligned with the 1-inch mark on the horizontal ruler, and then click to insert the text box control and label in the form. Don't be concerned about positioning the control precisely because you'll resize and move the label and text box later.
4. Open the Property Sheet, click the label control for the text box, set its Caption property to **Number of Invoices**, right-click the border of the label control, point to **Size** on the shortcut menu, and then click **To Fit**. Don't worry if the label control now overlaps the text box control.

   You'll use Expression Builder to set Control Source property for the text box control.
5. Click the unbound text box control to select it, click the **Control Source** box in the Property Sheet, and then click the property's **Build** button [...] to open Expression Builder.
6. In the Expression Elements box, click the **expand indicator** [+] next to frmVisitsAndInvoices, and then click **frmBillingSubform** in the Expression Elements box.
7. Scroll down the Expression Categories box, and then double-click **txtInvoiceNumCount** in the Expression Categories box. See Figure 6-41.

Figure 6-41 Text box control's expression in the Expression Builder dialog box

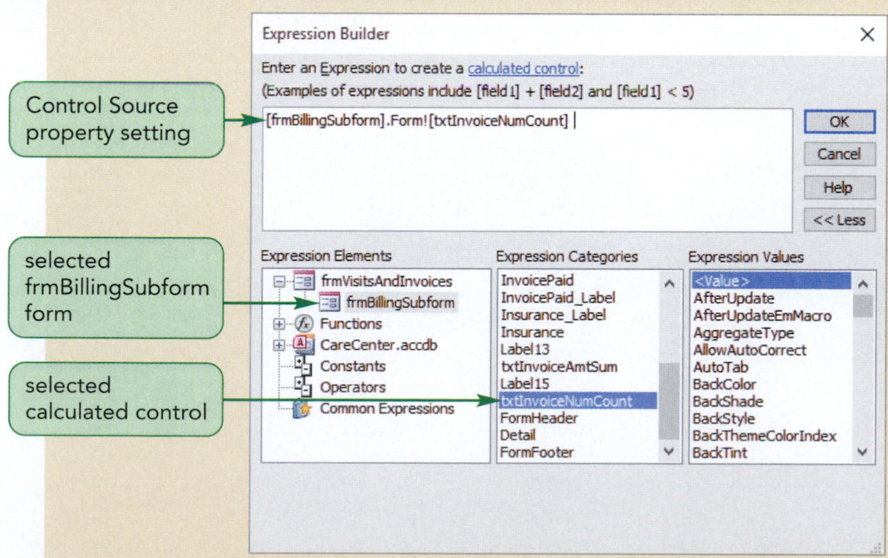

Instead of adding txtInvoiceNumCount to the expression box at the top, the Expression Builder changed it to [frmBillingSubform].Form![txtInvoiceNumCount]. This expression displays the value of the txtInvoiceNumCount control that is located in the frmBillingSubform form, which is a form object.

You need to add an equal sign to the beginning of the expression.

8. Press the **Home** key, type **=** (an equal sign), and then click the **OK** button. The Expression Builder dialog box closes, and the Control Source property is set.

Next, you'll add a second text box control to the main form, set the Caption property for the label control, and use Expression Builder to set the text box's Control Source property.

Be sure you resize the label to its best fit.

9. Repeat Steps 2 through 4 to add a text box to the main form, positioning the text box at the 3.5-inch mark on the horizontal ruler and approximately the 5-inch mark on the vertical ruler, and setting the label's Caption property to **Invoice Amount Total**.
10. Click the unbound text box control to select it, click the **Control Source** box in the Property Sheet, and then click the property's **Build** button [...] to open Expression Builder.
11. In the Expression Builder dialog box, type **=** (an equal sign), in the Expression Elements box, click the **expand indicator** [+] next to frmVisitsAndInvoices, click **frmBillingSubform** in the Expression Elements box, scroll down the Expression Categories box, and then double-click **txtInvoiceAmtSum** in the Expression Categories box.
12. Click the **OK** button to accept the expression and close the Expression Builder dialog box, close the Property Sheet, and save the form.
13. Click the **Collapse the Ribbon** button [^], switch to Form view, and then display the record for VisitID 1048. See Figure 6-42.

Figure 6-42 Form with calculated controls

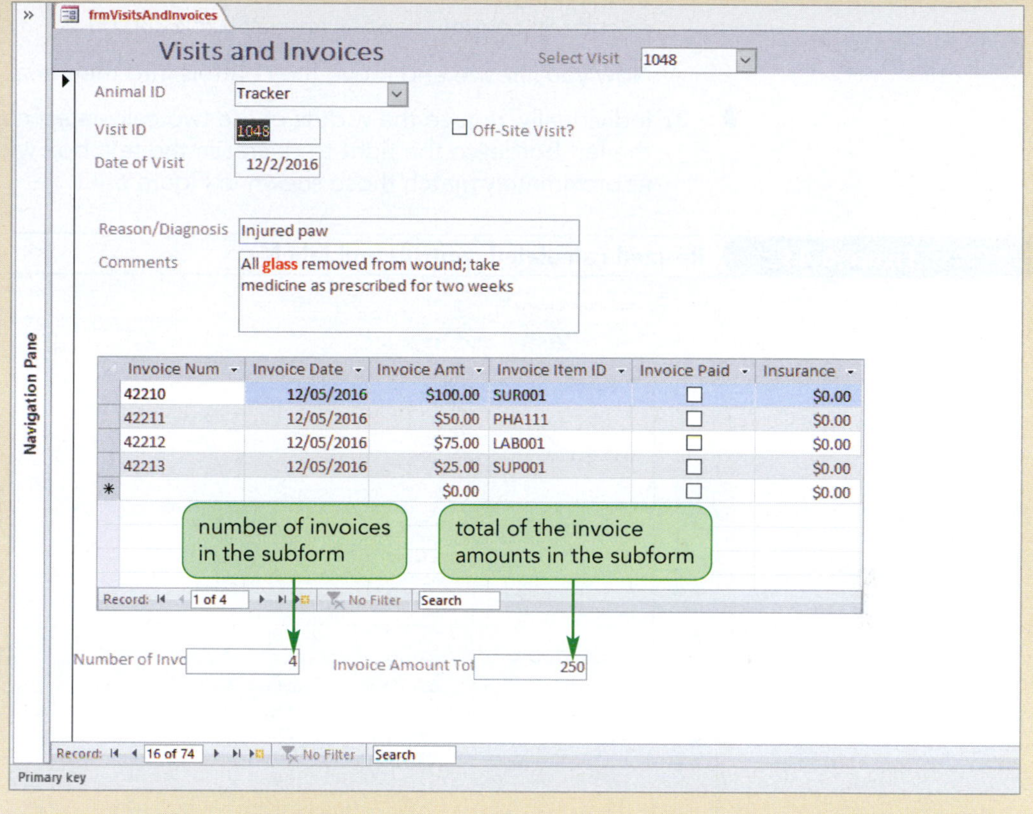

Now that the calculated controls are in the form, you will modify their appearance. You also will set additional properties for the calculated controls.

Resizing, Moving, and Formatting Calculated Controls

In addition to resizing and repositioning the two calculated controls and their attached labels, you need to change the format of the rightmost calculated control to Currency and to set the following properties for both calculated controls.

- Set the Tab Stop property to a value of No. The **Tab Stop property** specifies whether users can use the Tab key to navigate to a control on a form. If the Tab Stop property is set to No, users can't tab to the control.
- Set the ControlTip Text property to a value of "Calculated total number of invoices for this animal visit" for the calculated control on the left and "Calculated invoice total for this animal visit" for the calculated control on the right. The **ControlTip Text property** specifies the text that appears in a ScreenTip when users position the mouse pointer over a control in a form.

Now you'll resize, move, and format the calculated controls and their attached labels.

To size, move, and format the calculated controls and their attached labels:

1. Switch to Layout view, right-click the **Invoice Amount Total** calculated control, and then click **Properties** on the shortcut menu to open the Property Sheet.

2. Click the **All** tab in the Property Sheet (if necessary), set the Format property to **Currency**, and then close the Property Sheet. The value displayed in the calculated control changes from 250 to $250.00.

   Now you'll resize and move the controls into their final positions in the form.

3. Individually, reduce the widths of the two calculated controls by dragging the left border to the right to decrease the text box width so that they approximately match those shown in Figure 6-43.

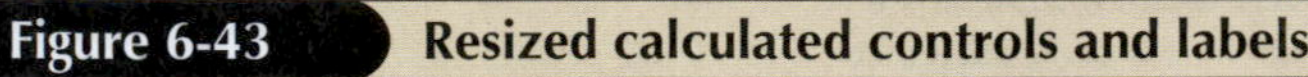

Figure 6-43 Resized calculated controls and labels

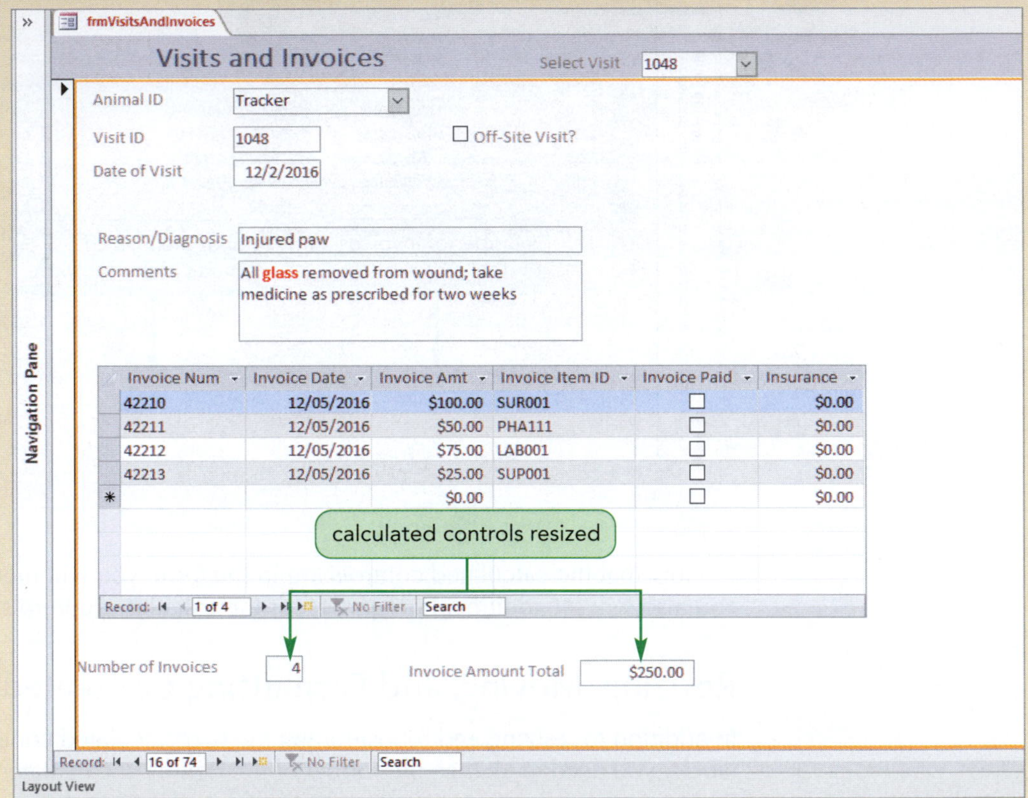

4. Switch to Design view, select the **Number of Invoices** label and its related calculated control, and then use the → key to move the label and its related text box to the right, aligning the left edge of the label with the left edge of the Comments label as closely as possible.

5. Press the ↑ key four times to move the selected calculated control and its label until it is two grid dots from the bottom of the subform control.

6. Lengthen the Detail section to approximately the 6-inch marker on the vertical ruler.

7. Click the **Invoice Amount Total** label control, press the **Shift** key, click the corresponding calculated control text box, release the **Shift** key, and then drag the selected calculated control and its label to position them below and left-aligned with the Number of Invoices label control and its calculated control.

TIP

In Design view you must use the move handle to move only a text box or its label, while in Layout view you can use either the move handle or the arrow keys.

8. Switch to Layout view.
9. Click the **Invoice Amount Total** label control, and use the arrow keys to left-align the label control with the Number of Invoices label, select the **Invoice Amount Total** text box, and then use the arrows to left-align the calculated control text box with the Number of Invoices calculated control text box.
10. Deselect all controls, switch to Form view, and then select record 1048. See Figure 6-44.

Figure 6-44 Calculated controls and labels aligned

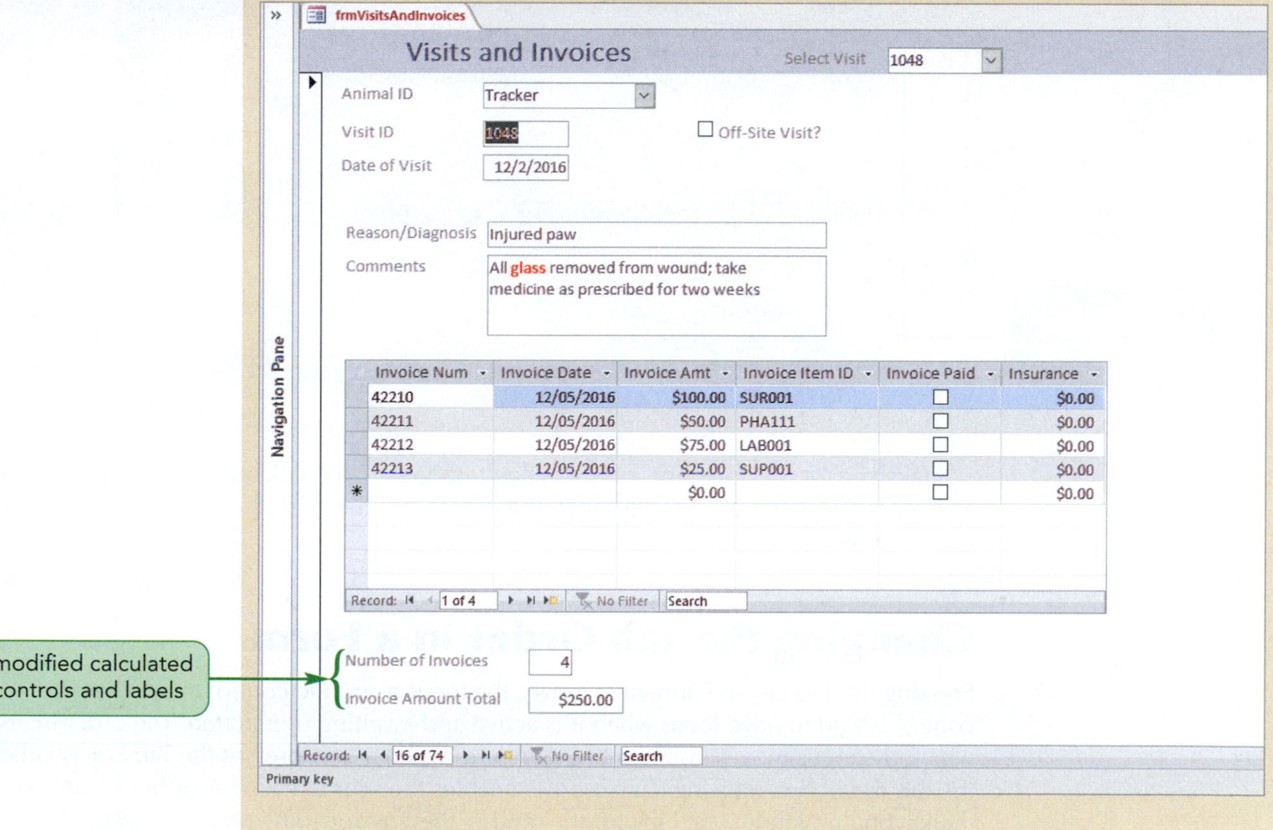

The calculated controls and their labels are properly placed in the form. Next you will set the Tab Stop Property and the ControlTip Text property for both controls, which you can do on the Other tab in the control's Property Sheet.

To set the Tab Stop Property and the ControlTipText property for the calculated controls:

1. Switch to Layout view, right-click the **Invoice Amount Total** calculated control, click **Properties** on the shortcut menu, and then click the **Other** tab in the Property Sheet.
2. Set the Tab Stop property to **No**, and then set the ControlTip Text property to **Calculated invoice total for this animal visit**.
3. Click the **Number of Invoices** calculated control to display this control's properties in the Property Sheet, set the Tab Stop property to **No**, and then set the ControlTip Text property to **Calculated total number of invoices for this animal visit**.

4. Close the Property Sheet, save your form design changes, switch to Form view, and then display visit 1048.

5. Position the pointer on the **Number of Invoices** box to display its ScreenTip, and then position the pointer on the **Invoice Amount Total** box to display its ScreenTip. You may have to pause while you position the pointer over the box, until the ScreenTip appears. See Figure 6-45.

Figure 6-45 ScreenTip for the calculated control

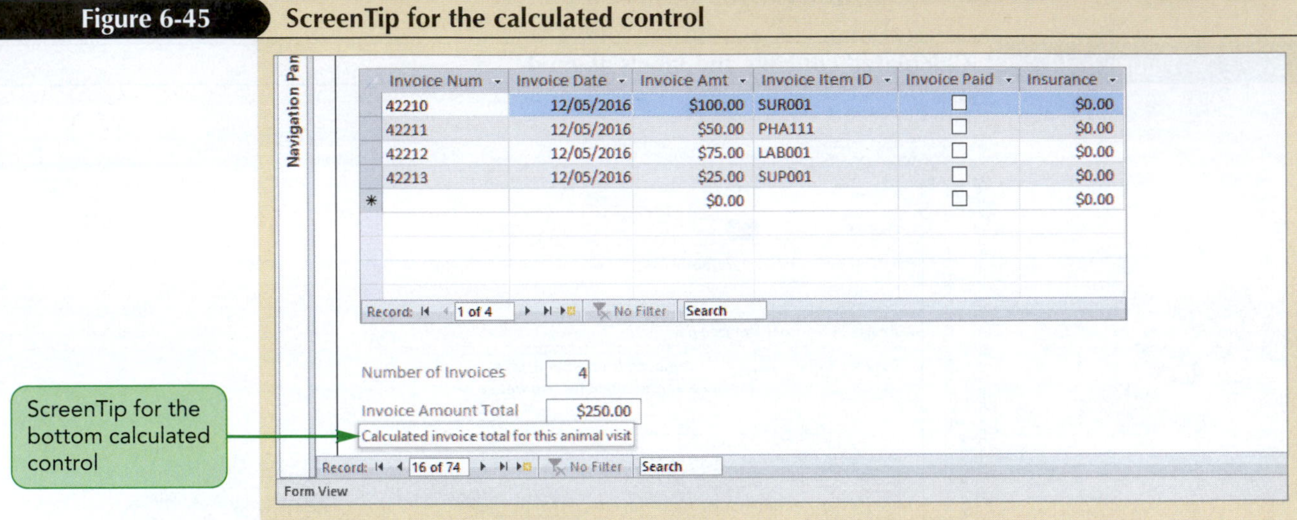

Daksha asks you to verify that users can't update the calculated controls in the main form and that when users tab through the controls in the form, the controls are selected in the correct order.

Changing the Tab Order in a Form

Pressing the Tab key in Form view moves the focus from one control to another. A control is said to have **focus** when it is active and awaiting user action. The order in which the focus moves from control to control when a user presses the Tab key is called the **tab order**. Setting a logical tab order enables the user to keep his or her hands on the keyboard without reaching for the mouse, thereby speeding up the process of data entry in a form. Daksha wants to verify that the tab order in the main form is top-to-bottom, left-to-right. First, you'll verify that users can't update the calculated controls.

To test the calculated controls and modify the tab order:

1. Select the value in the Number of Invoices box, and then type **8**. The Number of Invoices value remains unchanged, and the message "Control can't be edited; it's bound to the expression '[frmBillingSubform].[Form]![txtInvoiceNumCount]'" is displayed on the status bar. The status bar message warns you that you can't update, or edit, the calculated control because it's bound to an expression. The calculated control in the main form changes in value only when the value of the expression changes in the subform.

2. Click the Invoice Amount Total box, and then type **8**. The value remains unchanged, and a message again displays on the status bar because you cannot edit a calculated control.

Next, you'll determine the tab order of the fields in the main form. Daksha wants the tab order to be down and then across.

3. Select the value in the Visit ID box, press the **Tab** key to advance to the Date of Visit box, and then press the **Tab** key five more times to advance to the Reason/Diagnosis box, Comments text box, OffSite check box, and AnimalID combo box, in order, and then to the subform.

Access sets the tab order in the same order in which you add controls to a form, so you should always check the form's tab order when you create a custom form in Layout or Design view. In this form you can see that the tab order is set such that the user will tab through the field value boxes in the main form before tabbing through the fields in the subform. In the main form, tabbing bypasses the two calculated controls because you set their Tab Stop properties to No, and you bypass the Select Visit combo box because it's an unbound control. Also, you tab through only the field value boxes in a form, not the labels.

The tab order Daksha wants for the field value boxes in the main form (top-to-bottom, left-to-right) should be the following: AnimalID, VisitID, OffSite, VisitDate, Reason, Comments, and then the subform. The default tab order doesn't match the order Daksha wants, so you'll change the tab order. You can change the tab order only in Design view.

4. Double-click the **Home** tab to restore the ribbon, switch to Design view, and then on the Form Design Tools Design tab, in the Tools group, click the **Tab Order** button. The Tab Order dialog box opens. See Figure 6-46.

Figure 6-46 Tab Order dialog box

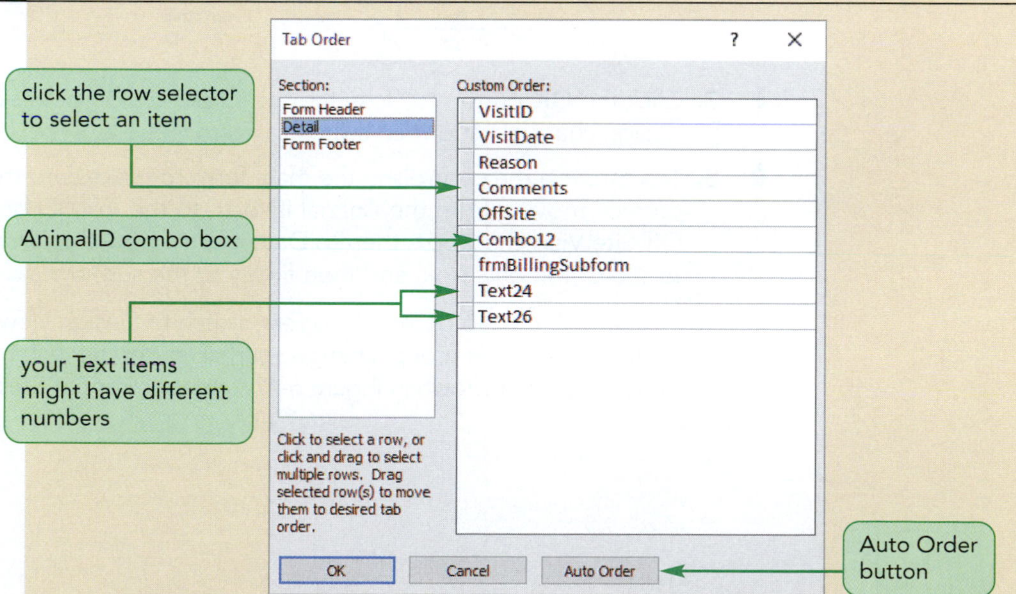

Because you did not set the Name property for the combo box control and the calculated controls, Access assigned them names that consist of the type of control and number; for example Combo12 for the AnimalID combo box, Text24 for the Number of Invoices calculated control, and Text26 for the Invoice Amount Total calculated control as shown in Figure 6-46. (The numbers assigned to your controls might differ.) The Auto Order button lets you create a left-to-right, top-to-bottom tab order automatically, which is not the order Daksha wants. You need to move the Combo12 entry above the VisitID entry.

TIP

Setting the Name property for all your controls to meaningful names avoids having to guess which control a name references in this and similar situations.

5. Click the **row selector** to the left of the Combo12 item (your number might differ), and then drag the row selector up to position it above the VisitID entry.
6. Click the row selector to the left of the OffSite item, and then drag the row selector up to position it above VisitDate. The entries are now correct and in the correct order. See Figure 6-47.

Figure 6-47 **Tab Order dialog box with corrected order**

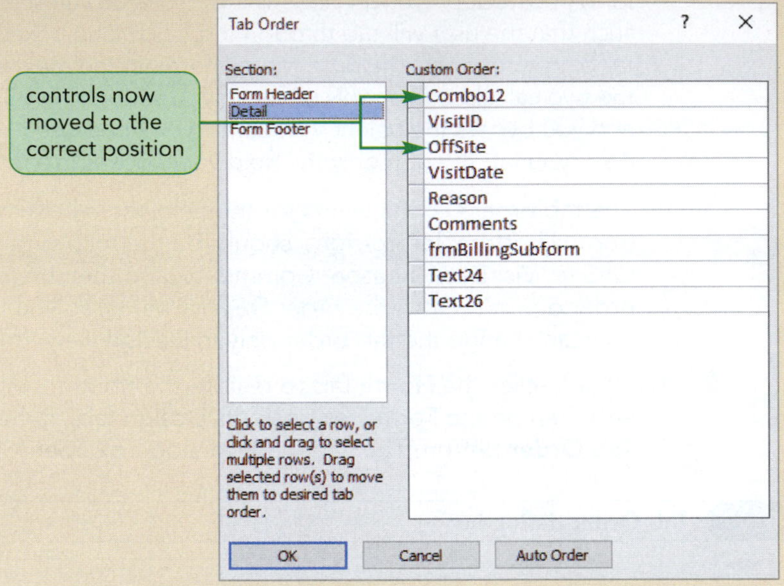

7. Click the **OK** button to close the Tab Order dialog box, save your form design changes, and then switch to Form view.
8. Tab through the controls in the main form to make sure the tab order is correct, moving from the Animal ID box, to the Visit ID box, then to the Off-Site Visit checkbox, then to Date of Visit box, the Reason/Diagnosis box, to the Comments box, and then finally to the subform.

Trouble? If the tab order is incorrect, switch to Design view, click the Tab Order button in the Tools group, change your tab order in the Tab Order dialog box to match the order shown in Figure 6-47, and then repeat Steps 7 and 8.

PROSKILLS

Written Communication: Enhancing Information Using Calculated Controls

For a small number of records in a subform, it's easy for users to quickly count the number of records and to calculate numeric total amounts when the form doesn't display calculated controls. For instance, when students have completed few courses or when people have made few tax payments, it's easy for users to count the courses and calculate the student's GPA or to count and total the tax payments. But for subforms with dozens or hundreds of records—for instance, students with many courses, or people with many tax payments—displaying summary calculated controls is mandatory. By adding a few simple calculated controls to forms and reports, you can increase the usefulness of the information presented and improve the ability of users to process the information, spot trends, and be more productive in their jobs.

You've finished adding controls to the form, but the form is plain looking and lacks visual clues organizing the controls in the form. You'll complete the form by making it more attractive and easier for Kimberly and her staff to use.

Improving a Form's Appearance

The frmVisitsAndInvoices form has four distinct areas: the Form Header section containing the title and the Select Visit combo box, the six bound controls in the Detail section, the subform in the Detail section, and the two calculated controls in the Detail section. To visually separate these four areas, you'll increase the height of the Form Header section, add a horizontal line at the bottom of the Form Header section, and draw a rectangle around the calculated controls.

Adding a Line to a Form

You can use lines in a form to improve the form's readability, to group related information, or to underline important values. You use the Line tool in Design view to add a line to a form or report.

REFERENCE

Adding a Line to a Form or Report

- Display the form or report in Design view.
- On the Form Design Tools Design tab, in the Controls group, click the More button, and then click the Line tool.
- Position the pointer where you want the line to begin.
- Drag the pointer to the position for the end of the line, and then release the mouse button. If you want to ensure that you draw a straight horizontal or vertical line, press and hold the Shift key as you drag the pointer to draw the line.

You will add a horizontal line to the Form Header section to separate the controls in this section from the controls in the Detail section.

To add a line to the form:

1. Switch to Design view, and then drag the bottom border of the Form Header section down to the 1-inch mark on the vertical ruler to make room to draw a horizontal line at the bottom of the Form Header section.
2. On the Form Design Tools Design tab, in the Controls group, click the **Line** tool.
3. Position the pointer's plus symbol at the left edge of the Form Header section just below the title.
4. Press and hold the **Shift** key, drag right to the 6-inch mark on the vertical ruler, release the mouse button, and then release the **Shift** key. See Figure 6-48.

Figure 6-48 Line added to the form

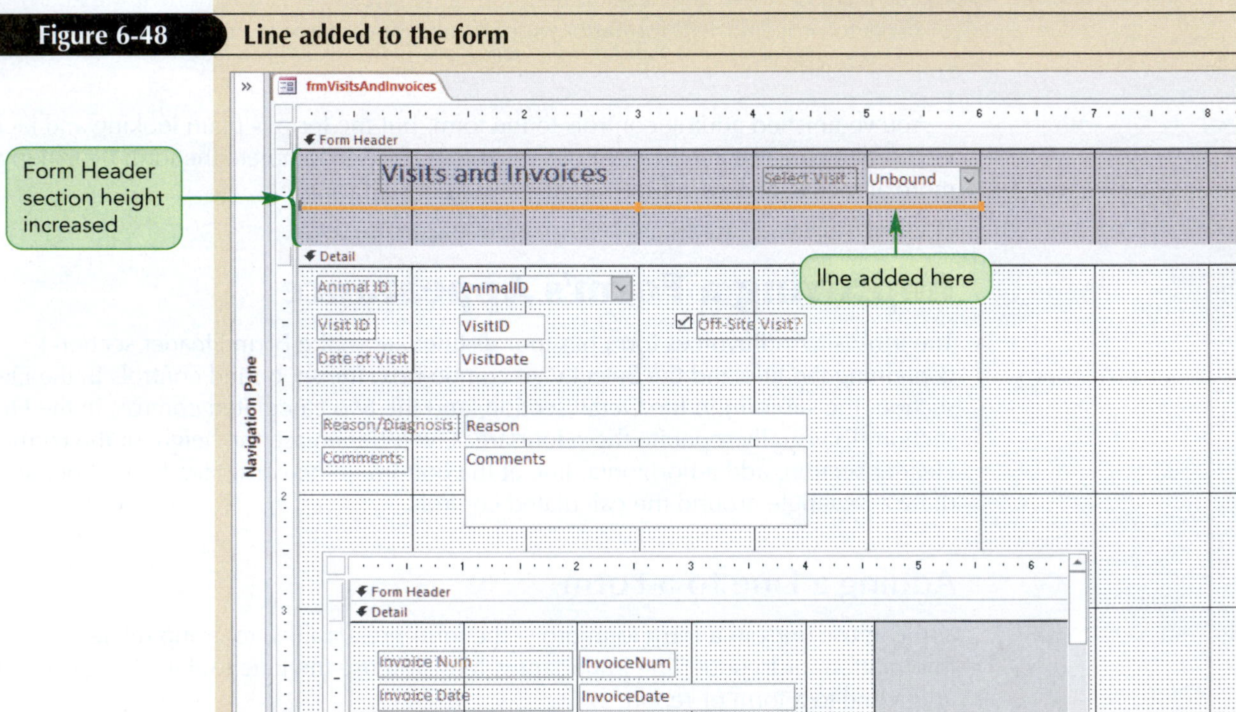

Trouble? If the line is not straight or not positioned correctly, click the Undo button on the Quick Access Toolbar, and then repeat Steps 2 through 4. If the line is not the correct length, be sure the line is selected, press and hold the Shift key, and press the left or right arrow key until the line's length is the same as that of the line shown in Figure 6-48.

5. Drag the bottom border of the Form Header section up to just below the line.
6. Save your form design changes.

Next, you'll add a rectangle around the calculated controls in the Detail section.

Adding a Rectangle to a Form

You can use a rectangle in a form to group related controls and to visually separate the group from other controls. You use the **Rectangle tool** in Design view to add a rectangle to a form or report.

REFERENCE

Adding a Rectangle to a Form or Report

- Display the form or report in Design view.
- On the Form Design Tools Design tab, in the Controls group, click the More button, and then click the Rectangle tool.
- Click in the form or report to create a default-sized rectangle, or drag a rectangle in the position and size you want.

You will add a rectangle around the calculated controls and their labels to separate them from the subform and from the other controls in the Detail section.

To add a rectangle to the form:

1. On the Form Design Tools Design tab, in the Controls group, click the **More** button to open the Controls gallery, and then click the **Rectangle** tool.
2. Position the pointer's plus symbol approximately two grid dots above and two grid dots to the left of the Number of Invoices label.
3. Drag the pointer down and to the right to create a rectangle that that has all four sides approximately two grid dots from the two calculated controls and their labels. See Figure 6-49.

Figure 6-49 **Rectangle added to the form**

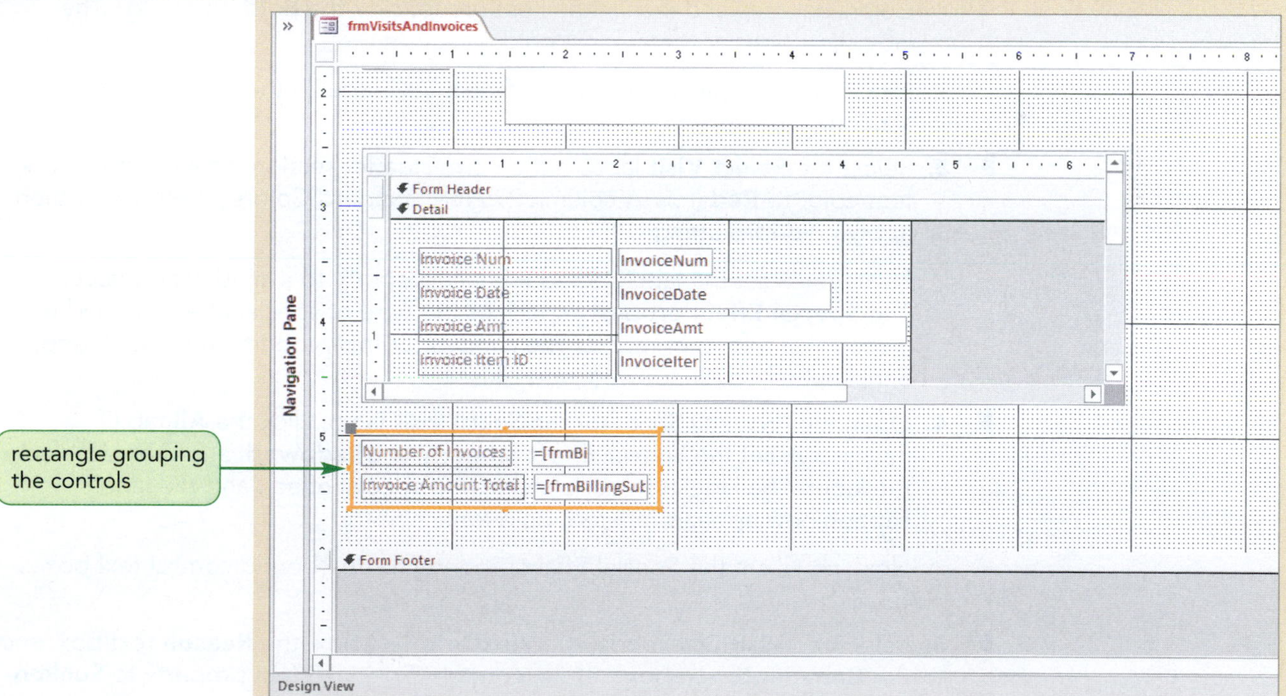

Trouble? If the rectangle is not sized or positioned correctly, use the sizing handles on its selection border to adjust its size and the move handle to adjust its position.

Next, you'll set the thickness of the rectangle's lines.

4. Click the **Form Design Tools Format** tab.
5. In the Control Formatting group, click the **Shape Outline button arrow**, point to **Line Thickness** at the bottom of the gallery, and then click **1 pt** line (second line from the top).
6. Click a blank area of the Form window to deselect the control.

Next, you'll add color and visual effects to the form's controls.

Modifying the Visual Effects of the Controls in a Form

TIP

Using a theme can improve a form's appearance, but a theme doesn't provide the control you can achieve by setting individual properties in Design or Layout view.

Distinguishing one group of controls in a form from other groups is an important visual cue to the users of the form. For example, users should be able to distinguish the bound controls in the form from the calculated controls and from the Select Visit control in the Form Header section. You'll now modify the controls in the form to provide these visual cues. You'll start by setting font properties for the calculated control's labels.

To modify the format of the controls in the form:

1. Select the **Number of Invoices** label and the **Invoice Amount Total** label, using the Shift key to select multiple controls.
2. On the Form Design Tools Format tab, in the Font group, click the **Font Color button arrow** [A], click the **Blue** color (row 7, column 8 in the Standard Colors palette), and then in the Font group, click the **Bold** button [B]. The labels' captions now appear in bold, blue font.

   Next, you'll set properties for the Select Visit label in the Form Header section.
3. Select the **Select Visit** label in the Form Header section, change the label's font color to **Red** (row 7, column 2 in the Standard Colors palette), and then apply bold formatting.

   Next, you'll set the label's Special Effect property to a shadowed effect. The **Special Effect property** specifies the type of special effect applied to a control in a form or report. The choices for this property are Flat, Raised, Sunken, Etched, Shadowed, and Chiseled.
4. Open the Property Sheet for the Select Visit label, click the **All** tab (if necessary), set the Special Effect property to **Shadowed**, and then deselect the label. The label now has a shadowed special effect, and the label's caption now appears in a red, bold font.

   Next, you'll set the Special Effect property for the bound control text boxes to a sunken effect.
5. Select the **VisitID** text box, the **VisitDate** text box, the **Reason** text box, and the **Comments** text box, set the controls' Special Effect property to **Sunken**, close the Property Sheet, and then deselect the controls.

   Finally, you'll set the background color of the Form Header section, the Detail section, the Select Visit combo box, and the two calculated controls. You can use the **Background Color button** in the Font group on the Form Design Tools Format tab to change the background color of a control, section, or object (form or report).

TIP

To set a background image instead of a background color, click the Background Image button in the Background group on the Form Design Tools Format tab.

6. Click the **Form Header** section bar.
7. On the Form Design Tools Format tab, in the Font group, click the **Background Color button arrow**, and then click the **Light Blue 2** color (row 3, column 5 in the Standard Colors palette). The Form Header's background color changes to the Light Blue 2 color.
8. Click the **Detail** section bar, and then in the Font Group, click the **Background Color** button to change the Detail section's background color to the **Light Blue 2** color.
9. Select the **Select Visit** combo box, **Number of Invoices** calculated control box, and the **Invoice Amount Total** calculated control box, set the selected controls' background color to the **Light Blue 2** color, and then deselect all controls by clicking to the right of the Detail section's grid.
10. Save your form design changes, switch to Form view, click the **Select Visit** arrow, and then click **1048** in the list to display this visit record in the form. See Figure 6-50.

Figure 6-50 Completed custom form in Form view

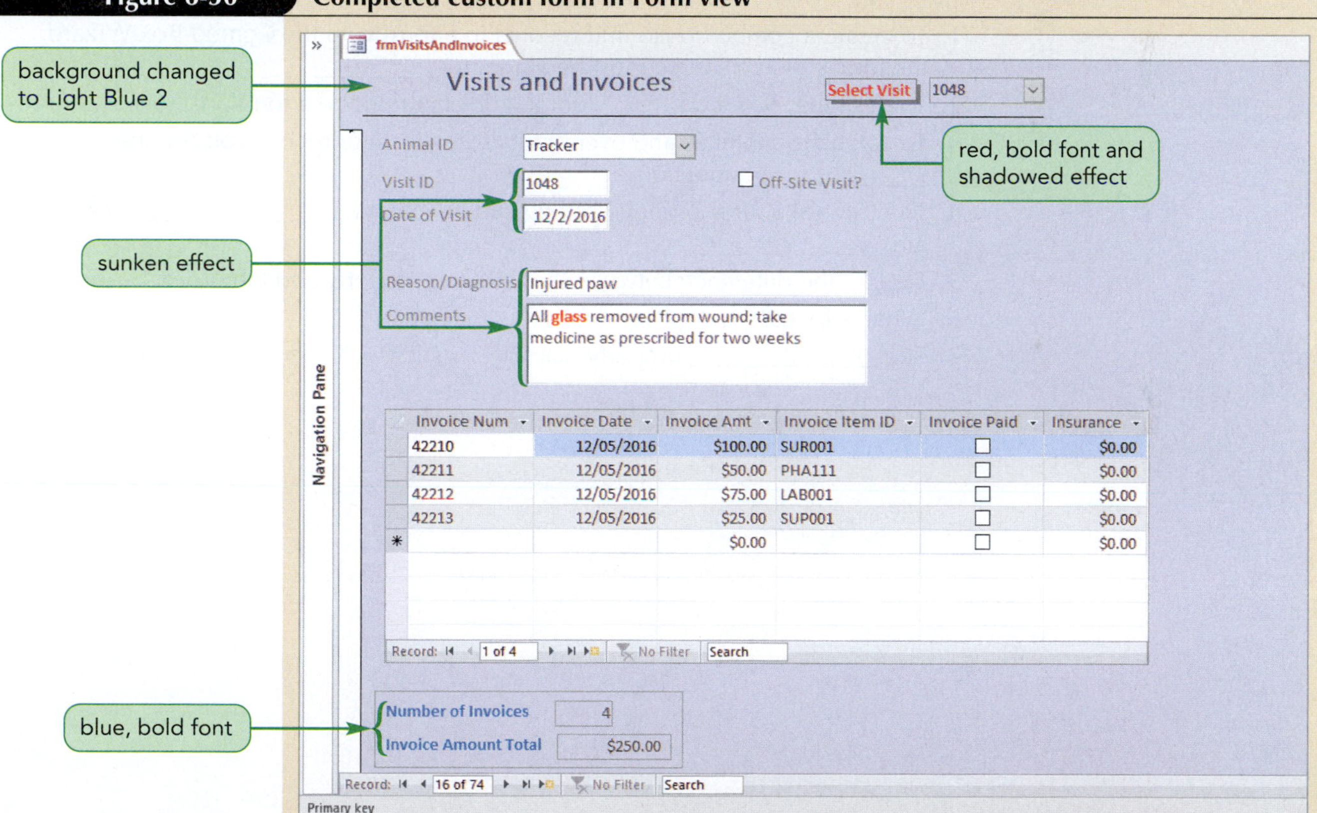

11. Test the form by tabbing between fields, navigating between records, and using the Select Visit combo box to find records, making sure you don't change any field values and observing that the calculated controls display the correct values.
12. Close the form, make a backup copy of the database, compact and repair the database, and then close the database.

INSIGHT

Applying Styles to Form and Report Controls

You can use the Quick Styles gallery to apply a built-in style reflecting a combination of several formatting options to a control in a form or report. To do this, select the control in either Layout or Design view, and then, on the Form or Report Design Tools Format tab, click the Quick Styles button in the Control Formatting group to display the Quick Styles gallery. Click a style in the gallery to apply it to the selected control.

You can also change the shape of a control in a form or report by clicking the Change Shape button in the Control Formatting group to display the Change Shape gallery, and then clicking a shape to apply it to the selected control.

Kimberly is pleased with the forms you have created. She will show these to her staff, and determine which of the forms will be most effective for using and managing the CareCenter database.

REVIEW

Session 6.3 Quick Check

1. To create a combo box to find records in a form with the Combo Box Wizard, the form's record source must be a(n) ______________.
2. You use the ______________ tool to add a subform to a form.
3. To calculate subtotals and overall totals in a form or report, you use the ______________ function.
4. The Control Source property setting can be either a(n) ______________ or a(n) ______________.
5. Explain the difference between the Tab Stop property and tab order.
6. What is focus?
7. The ______________ property has settings such as Raised and Sunken.

PRACTICE

Review Assignments

Data File needed for the Review Assignments: Supplier.accdb (cont. from Module 5)

Kimberly wants you to create several forms, including a custom form that displays and updates companies and the products they offer. Complete the following steps:

1. Open the **Supplier** database you worked with in the previous module.
2. In the **tblProduct** table, remove the lookup feature from the SupplierID field, and then resize the Supplier ID column in the datasheet to its best fit. Save and close the table.
3. Edit the relationship between the primary tblSupplier and related tblProduct tables to enforce referential integrity and to cascade-update related fields. Create the relationship report, save the report as **rptRelationshipsForProducts**, and then close it.
4. Use the Documenter to document the qryCompanyContacts query. Select all query options; use the Names, Data Types, and Sizes option for fields; and use the Names and Fields option for indexes. Print the report produced by the Documenter, and then close it.
5. Use the Datasheet tool to create a form based on the tblProduct table, save the form as **frmProductDatasheet**, and then close it.
6. Use the Multiple Items tool to create a form based on the qryDuplicateProduct Types query, save the form as **frmProductTypeMultipleItems**, and then close it.
7. Use the Split Form tool to create a split form based on the tblProduct table, and then make the following changes to the form in Layout view:
   a. Remove the two Units controls from the stacked layout, reduce the width of the Units field value box by about half, and then anchor the two Units controls to the bottom left. Depending on the size of your window, the two Units controls may be positioned at the bottom left of the right column.
   b. Remove the four control pairs in the right column from the stacked layout, and then anchor the group to the bottom right. You may see a dotted border outlining the location of the previously removed controls. This may be automatically selected as well.
   c. Remove the ProductName control pair from the stacked layout, move them to the top right, and then anchor them to the top right.
   d. Reduce the widths of the ProductID and SupplierID field value boxes to a reasonable size.
   e. Change the title to **Product**, save the modified form as **frmProductSplitForm**, and then close it.
8. Use Figure 6-51 and the following steps to create a custom form named **frmSuppliersWithProducts** based on the tblSupplier and tblProduct tables.

Figure 6-51 **Supplier database custom form design**

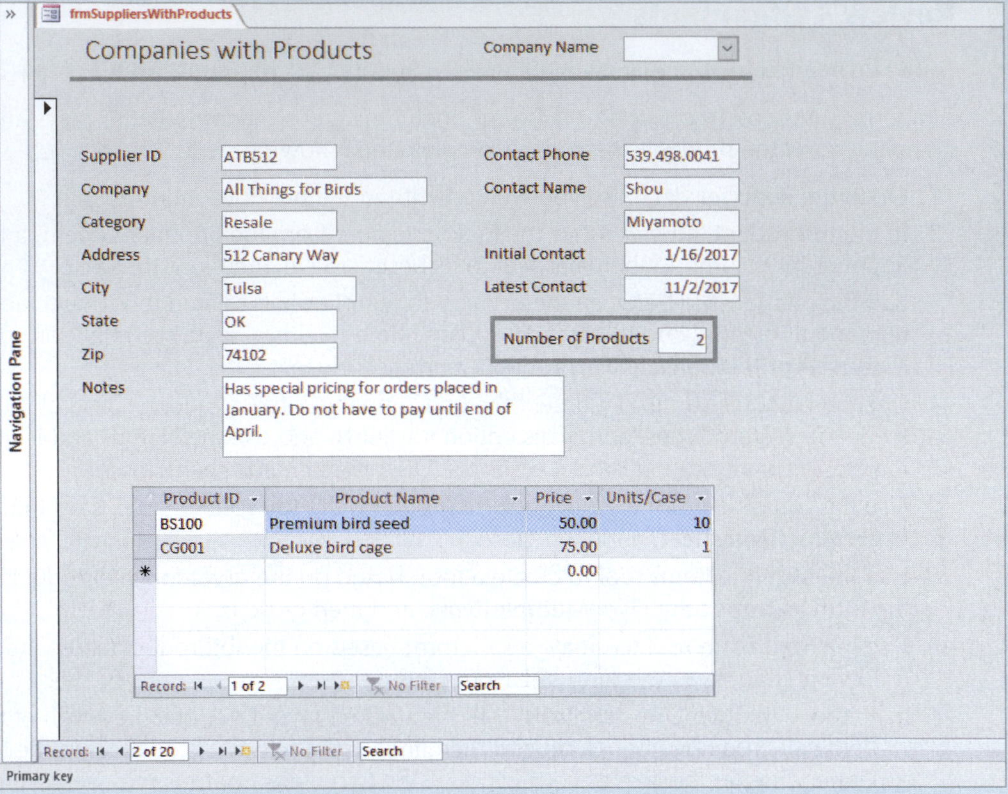

a. Place the fields from the tblSupplier table at the top of the Detail section. Delete the Contact Last Name label, and change the caption for the Contact First Name label to Contact Name.

b. Move the fields into two columns in the Detail section, as shown in Figure 6-51, resizing and aligning controls, as necessary, and increasing the width of the form.

c. Add the title in the Form Header section.

d. Make sure the form's Record Source property is set to tblSupplier, and then add a combo box in the Form Header section to find Company field values. In the Combo Box Wizard steps, select the Company and SupplierID fields, and hide the key column. Resize and move the control. Ensure the label displays the text "Company Name". Make sure the size of the Company Name field value box can accommodate the largest company name.

e. Add a subform based on the tblProduct table, include only the fields shown in Figure 6-51, link with SupplierID, name the subform **frmPartialProductSubform**, delete the subform label, resize the columns in the subform to their best fit, and resize and position the subform.

f. Add a calculated control that displays the number of products displayed in the subform. Set the calculated control's Tab Stop property to No, and the ControlTip Text property to Calculated number of products.

g. Add a line in the Form Header section, and add a rectangle around the calculated control and its label, setting the line thickness of both controls to 3 pt. Set the rectangle's color the same as the line's color.

h. In the main form, use the Light Gray 1 fill color (row 2, column 1 in the Standard Colors palette) for all form sections, and use the Black font color (row 1, column 2 in the Standard Colors palette) for all the label text, the calculated control, Company Name combo box, and the Title.

i. Make sure the tab order is top-to-bottom, left-to-right for the main form text boxes.

9. Make a backup copy of the database, compact and repair the database, and then close the database.

APPLY

Case Problem 1

Data File needed for this Case Problem: MoreBeauty.accdb (cont. from Module 5)

Beauty To Go Sue Miller wants you to create several forms, including two custom forms that display and update data in the database. Complete the following steps:

1. Open the **MoreBeauty** database you worked with in the previous module.
2. Use the Documenter to document the qryMemberNames query. Select all query options; use the Names, Data Types, and Sizes option for fields; and use the Names and Fields option for indexes. Print the first page of the report produced by the Documenter.
3. Use the Datasheet tool to create a form based on the tblOption table, and then save the form as **frmOptionDatasheet**.
4. Create a custom form based on the qryUpcomingExpirations query. Display all fields from the query in the form. Create your own design for the form. Add a label to the bottom of the Detail section that contains your first and last names. Change the label's font so that your name appears in bold, red font. Change the OptionEnd text box format so that the field value displays in bold, red font. Save the form as **frmUpcomingExpirations**.
5. Use Figure 6-52 and the following steps to create a custom form named **frmPlansWithMembers** based on the tblOption and tblMember tables.

Figure 6-52 **Plans custom form design**

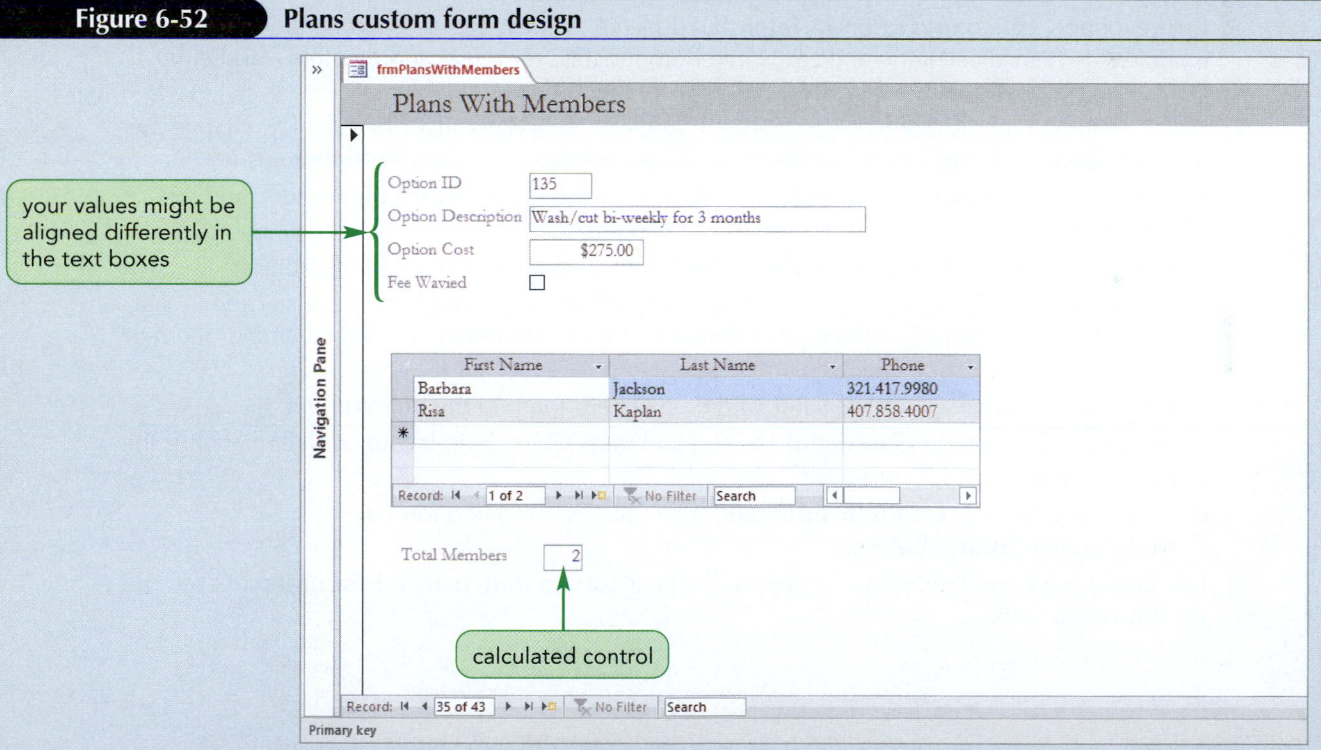

   a. Place the fields from the tblOption table at the top of the Detail section, and edit the captions in the associated label controls as shown.
   b. Selected fields from the tblMember table appear in a subform named **frmPlansWithMembersSubform**.
   c. The calculated control displays the total number of records that appear in the subform. Set the calculated control's ControlTip Text property to Total number of members in this plan. Set the calculated control's Tab Stop property to No.

   d. Apply the Organic theme to the frmPlansWithMembers form only.
   e. Save and close the form.
6. Make a backup copy of the database, compact and repair the database, and then close the database.

APPLY

Case Problem 2

Data File needed for this Case Problem: Tutoring.accdb (cont. from Module 5)

Programming Pros Brent Hovis wants you to create several forms, including a custom form that displays and updates the tutoring service's contracts with students. Complete the following steps:

1. Open the **Tutoring** database you worked with in the previous module.
2. Remove the lookup feature from the TutorID field in the tblContract table, and then resize the Tutor ID column to its best fit. Save and close the table.
3. Define a one-to-many relationship between the primary tblTutor table and the related tblContract table. Select the referential integrity option and the cascade updates option for this relationship.
4. Use the Documenter to document the tblContract table. Select all table options; use the Names, Data Types, and Sizes option for fields; and use the Names and Fields option for indexes. Print the report produced by the Documenter.
5. Create a query called **qryLessonsByTutor** that uses the tblTutor and tblContract tables and includes the fields FirstName and LastName from the tblTutor table, and the fields StudentID, ContractDate, SessionType, Length, and Cost from the tblContract table.
6. Use the Multiple Items tool to create a form based on the qryLessonsByTutor query, change the title to **Lessons by Tutor**, and then save the form as **frmLessonsByTutorMultipleItems**.
7. Use the Split Form tool to create a split form based on the qryLessonsByTutor query, and then make the following changes to the form in Layout view.
   a. Size the field value boxes in variable lengths to fit a reasonable amount of data.
   b. Remove the SessionType, Length, and Cost controls and their labels from the stacked layout, move these six controls to the right and then to the top of the form, and then anchor them to the top right.
   c. Select the Cost control and its label, and then anchor them to the bottom right.
   d. Remove the Contract Date control and its label from the stacked layout, and then anchor the pair of controls to the bottom left.
   e. Change the title to **Lessons by Tutor**, and then save the modified form as **frmLessonsByTutorSplitForm**.
8. Use Figure 6-53 and the following steps to create a custom form named **frmContract** based on the tblContract table.

Figure 6-53 Tutoring database custom form design

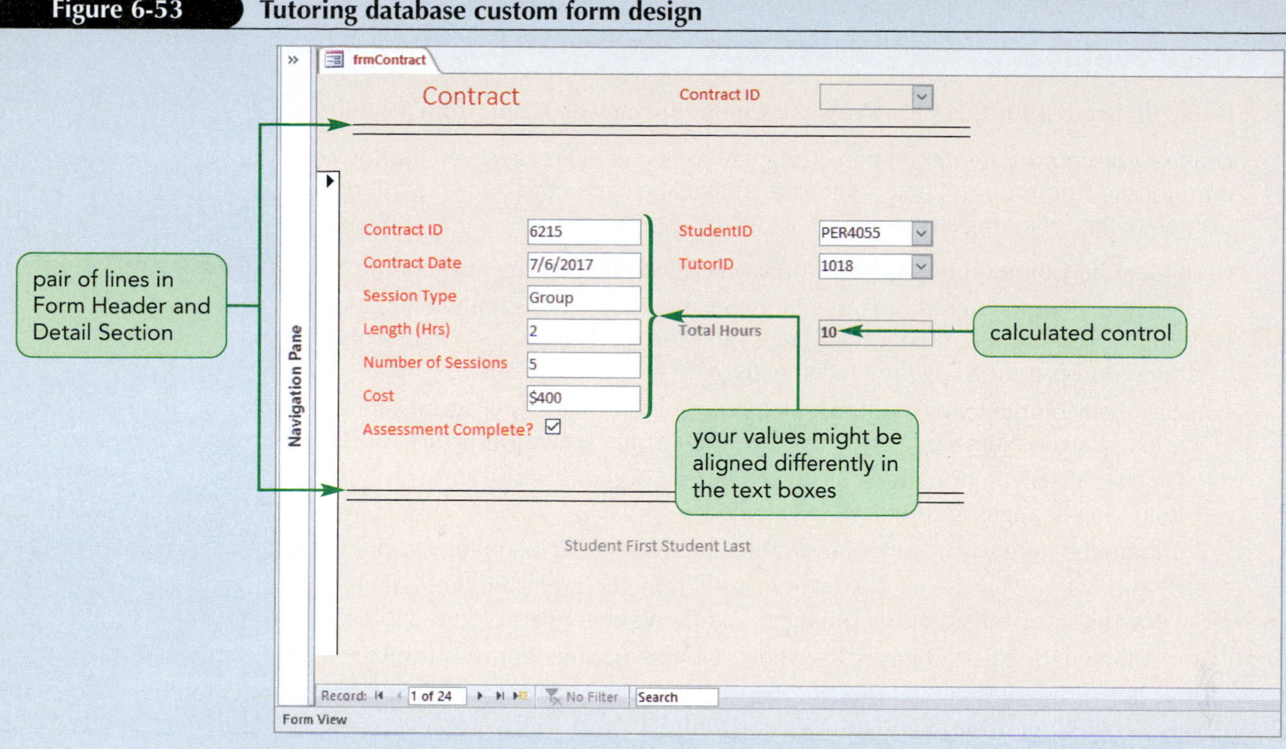

a. For the StudentID combo box, select the LastName, FirstName, and StudentID fields from the tblStudent table, in order, and sort in ascending order by the LastName field and then by the FirstName field.

b. For the TutorID combo box, select the LastName, FirstName, and TutorID fields from the tblTutor table, in order, and sort in ascending order by the LastName field and then by the FirstName field.

c. Make sure the form's Record Source property is set to tblContract, and then add a combo box in the Form Header section to find ContractID field values.

d. Add a calculated control that displays the total number of hours (length multiplied by sessions). *Hint*: Use the * symbol for multiplication. Set the calculated control's Tab Stop property to No, and set the number of decimal places to Auto.

e. Add a line in the Form Header section, add a second line below it, and then add a second pair of lines near the bottom of the Detail section. Set the line thickness of all lines to 1 pt.

f. Use the Label tool to add your name below the pair of lines at the bottom of the Detail section.

g. For the labels in the Detail section, except for the Total Hours label and the label displaying your name, use the Red font color (row 7, column 2 in the Standard Colors palette).

h. For the title and Contract ID label, use the Dark Red font color (row 7, column 1 in the Standard Colors palette).

i. Apply bold to the calculated control and its label.

j. For the background fill color of the sections, the calculated control, and the Contract ID combo box, apply the Medium Gray color (row 1, column 3 in the Standard Colors palette).

k. Make sure the tab order is top-to-bottom, left-to-right for the main form field value boxes.

9. Make a backup copy of the database, compact and repair the database, and then close the database.

CREATE

Case Problem 3

Data File needed for this Case Problem: Community.accdb (cont. from Module 5)

Diane's Community Center Diane Coleman asks you to create several forms, including a custom form for the Community Center database so that she can better track donations made to the center. Complete the following steps:

1. Open the **Community** database you worked with in the previous module.
2. Use the Documenter to document the tblPatron table. Select all table options; use the Names, Data Types, and Sizes option for fields; and use the Names and Fields option for indexes. Print the report produced by the Documenter.
3. Use the Multiple Items tool to create a form based on the qryPatronNames query, change the title to **Patron Name List**, and then save the form as **frmPatronNamesMultipleItems**.
4. Use the Split Form tool to create a split form based on the tblPatron table, and then make the following changes to the form in Layout view.
   a. Size the field value boxes in variable lengths to fit a reasonable amount of data.
   b. Remove the FirstName, LastName, and Phone controls and their labels from the stacked layout, move them to the top right, and then anchor them to the top right.
   c. Change the title to **Patron**, and then save the modified form as **frmPatronSplitForm**.
5. Use Figure 6-54 and the following steps to create a custom form named **frmPatronDonations** based on the tblPatron and tblDonation tables.

Figure 6-54 Community database custom form design

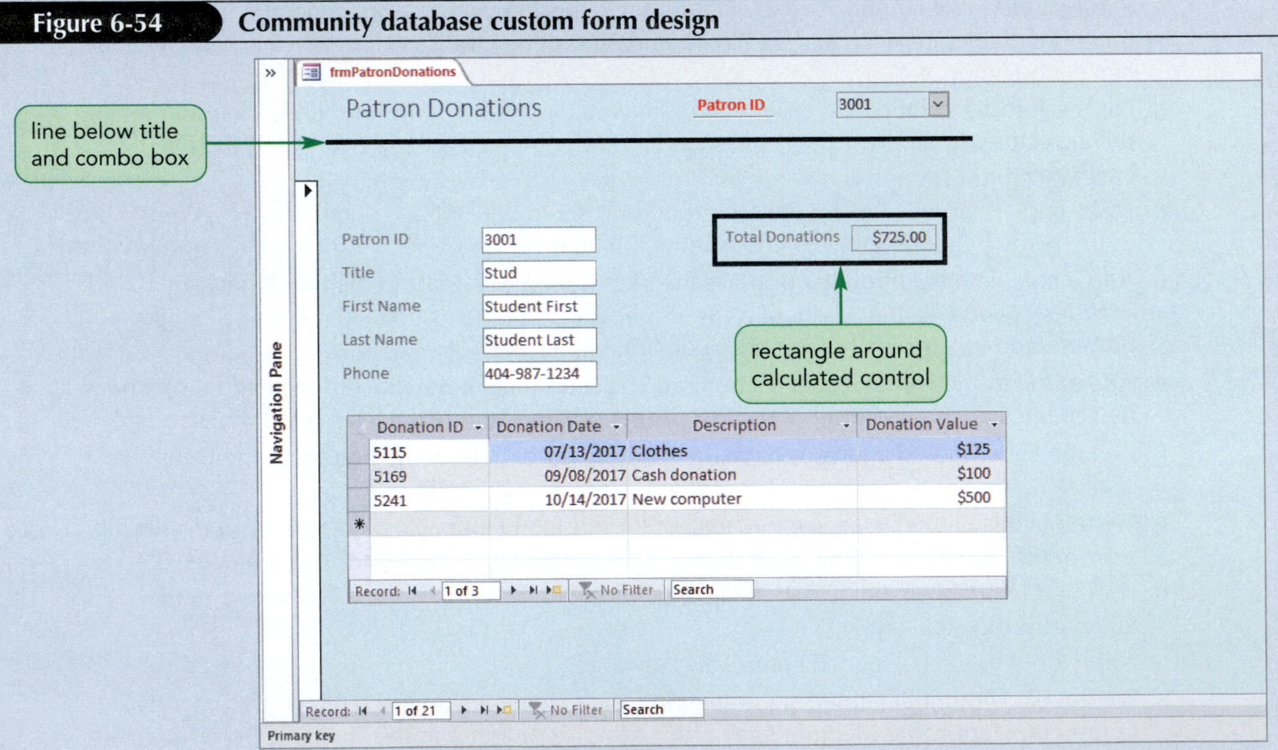

   a. Add the title Patron Donations in the Form Header section.
   b. Make sure the form's Record Source property is set to tblPatron, and then add a combo box in the Form Header section to find PatronID field values. In the Combo Box Wizard steps, select the PatronID field. Format the label using the Red font (row 7, column 2 in the Standard Colors palette), bold, and the Chiseled special effect.

c. Add a subform based on the tblDonation table, name the subform **frmPatronDonationsSubform**, delete the subform label, and resize the columns in the subform to their best fit, and resize and position the subform.
d. Add a calculated control that displays the total of the DonationValue field displayed in the subform with the Currency format. Set the calculated control's Tab Stop property to No and the Border Style property to Transparent.
e. Add a line in the Form Header section, and add a rectangle around the calculated control and its label, setting the line thickness of both controls to 3 pt. Set the rectangle color to Black (row 1, column 2 in the Standard Colors section) using the Shape Outline button in the Control Formatting group on the Form Design Tools Format tab.
f. Use the background color Aqua Blue 2 (row 3, column 9 in the Standard Colors palette) for the sections, the calculated control, and the Patron ID combo box.
g. Make sure the tab order is top-to-bottom for the main form text boxes.

6. Make a backup copy of the database, compact and repair the database, and then close the database.

CREATE

Case Problem 4

Data File needed for this Case Problem: AppTrail.accdb (cont. from Module 5)

Hike Apalachia Molly and Bailey Johnson want you to create several forms, including a custom form that displays and updates guest and reservation data in the AppTrail database. Complete the following steps:

1. Open the **AppTrail** database you worked with in the previous module.
2. Remove the lookup feature from the TourID field in the tblReservation table. Size the TourID field, and save and close the table.
3. Edit the relationship between the primary tblTour and related tblReservation tables to enforce referential integrity and to cascade-update related fields. Create the relationship report, and then save the report as **rptRelationshipsForAppTrail.pdf**, without exporting steps.
4. Use the Documenter to document the qrySelectedStates query. Select all query options; use the Names, Data Types, and Sizes option for fields; and use the Nothing option for indexes. Print the report produced by the Documenter.
5. Use the Datasheet tool to create a form based on the qryHikerLastNameS query, and then save the form as **frmHikerLastNameS**.
6. Create a custom form based on the qryNonHikingTours query. Display all fields in the form. Use your own design for the form, but use the title **Tours with No Hiking** in the Form Header section, and use the Label tool to add your name to the Form Header section. Save the form as **frmNonHikingTours**.
7. Use Figure 6-55 and the following steps to create a custom form named **frmHikersWithReservations** based on the tblHiker and tblReservation tables.

Figure 6-55 AppTrail database custom form design

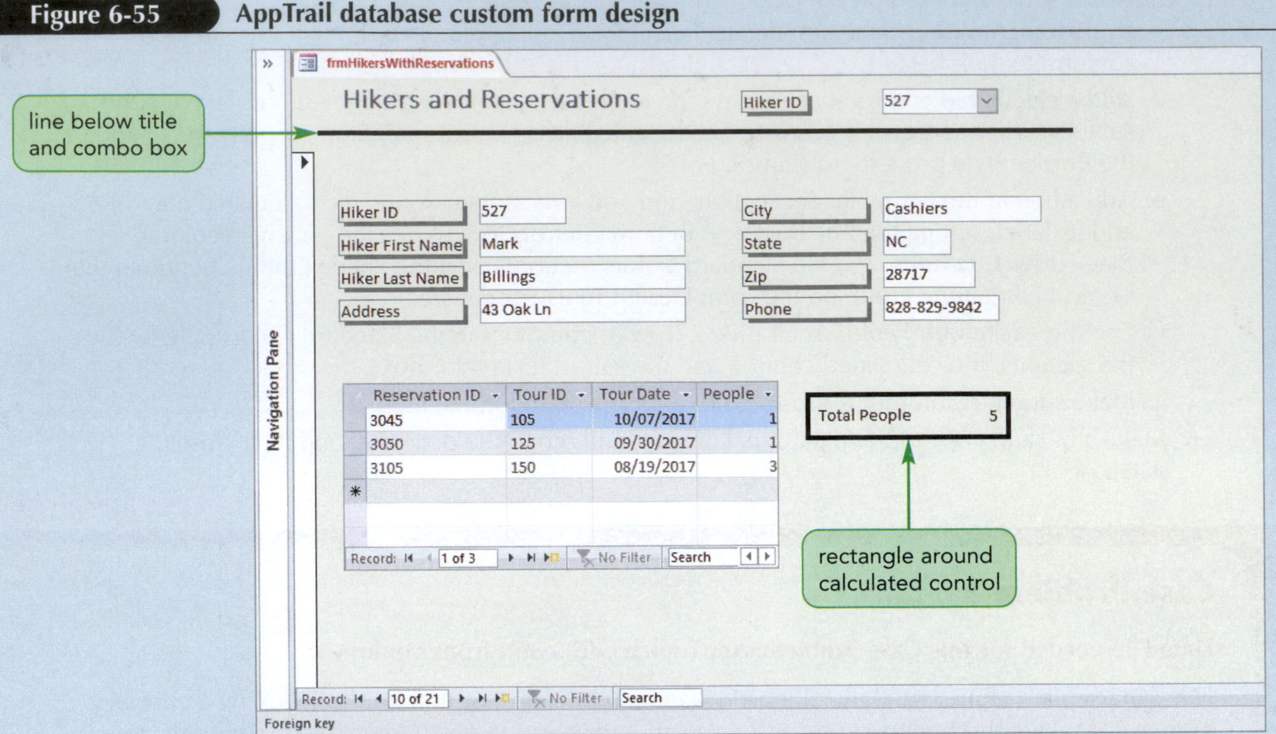

a. Add the title Hikers and Reservations in the Form Header section, and apply bold formatting.

b. Add the fields from the tblHiker table. Size the associated labels so that they're all the same length. Size the field value boxes in variable lengths to fit a reasonable amount of data, as shown in Figure 6-55.

c. Make sure the form's Record Source property is set to tblHiker, and then add a combo box in the Form Header section to find HikerID field values.

d. Add a subform based on the tblReservation table, name the subform **frmHikersWithReservationsSubform**, delete the subform label, resize the columns in the subform to their best fit, and then resize and position the subform.

e. Add a calculated control that displays the total of the People field displayed in the subform. Set the calculated control's Tab Stop property to No, and set the calculated control's Border Style property to Transparent.

f. Add a line in the Form Header section, and add a rectangle around the calculated control and its label, setting the line thickness of both controls to 3 pt. Set the rectangle color to Black (row 1, column 2 in the Standard Colors section) using the Shape Outline button in the Control Formatting group on the Form Design Tools Format tab.

g. Apply the black font color for all controls, including the controls in the subform.

h. Apply the Green 1 fill color (row 2, column 7 in the Standard Colors palette) for the sections and the calculated control.

i. Use the Shadowed special effect for the labels in the Detail section, except for the calculated control label, and the Form Header section, except for the title.

j. Make sure the tab order is top-to-bottom and left-to-right for the main form field value boxes.

8. Make a backup copy of the database, compact and repair the database, and then close the database.

MODULE 7

Creating Custom Reports

Creating Custom Reports for Riverview Veterinary Care Center

ACCESS

OBJECTIVES

Session 7.1
- View and filter a report in Report view
- Copy information from a report into a Word document
- Modify a report in Layout view
- Modify a report in Design view

Session 7.2
- Design and create a custom report
- Sort and group data in a report
- Add, move, resize, and align controls in a report
- Hide duplicate values in a report

Session 7.3
- Add the date and page numbers to a report's Footer section
- Add and format report titles
- Create and modify mailing labels

Case | *Riverview Veterinary Care Center*

At a recent staff meeting, Kimberly Johnson, the office manager, indicated that she would like to make some changes to an existing report in the database. She also requested a new report that she can use to produce a printed list of all invoices for all visits.

In this module, you will modify an existing report and create the new report for Kimberly. In modifying and building these reports, you will use many Access features for customizing reports, including grouping data, calculating totals, and adding lines to separate report sections. These features will enhance the reports and make them easier for Kimberly and her staff to work with.

STARTING DATA FILES

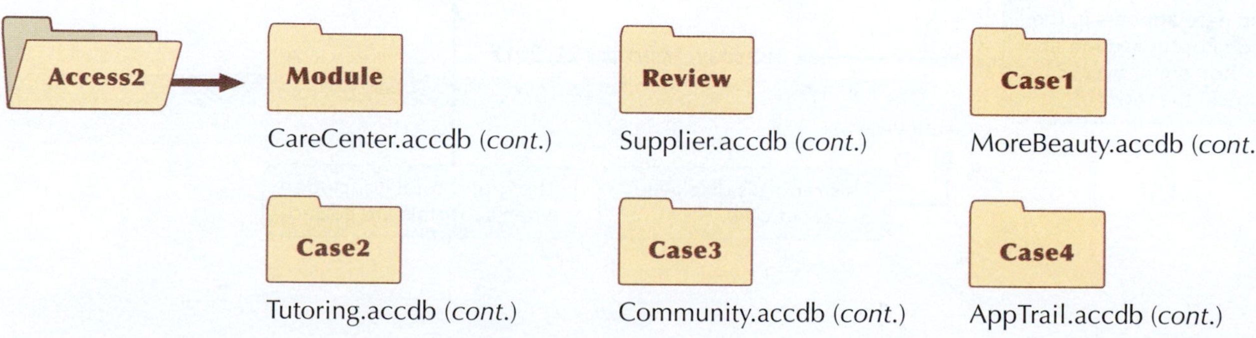

Session 7.1 Visual Overview:

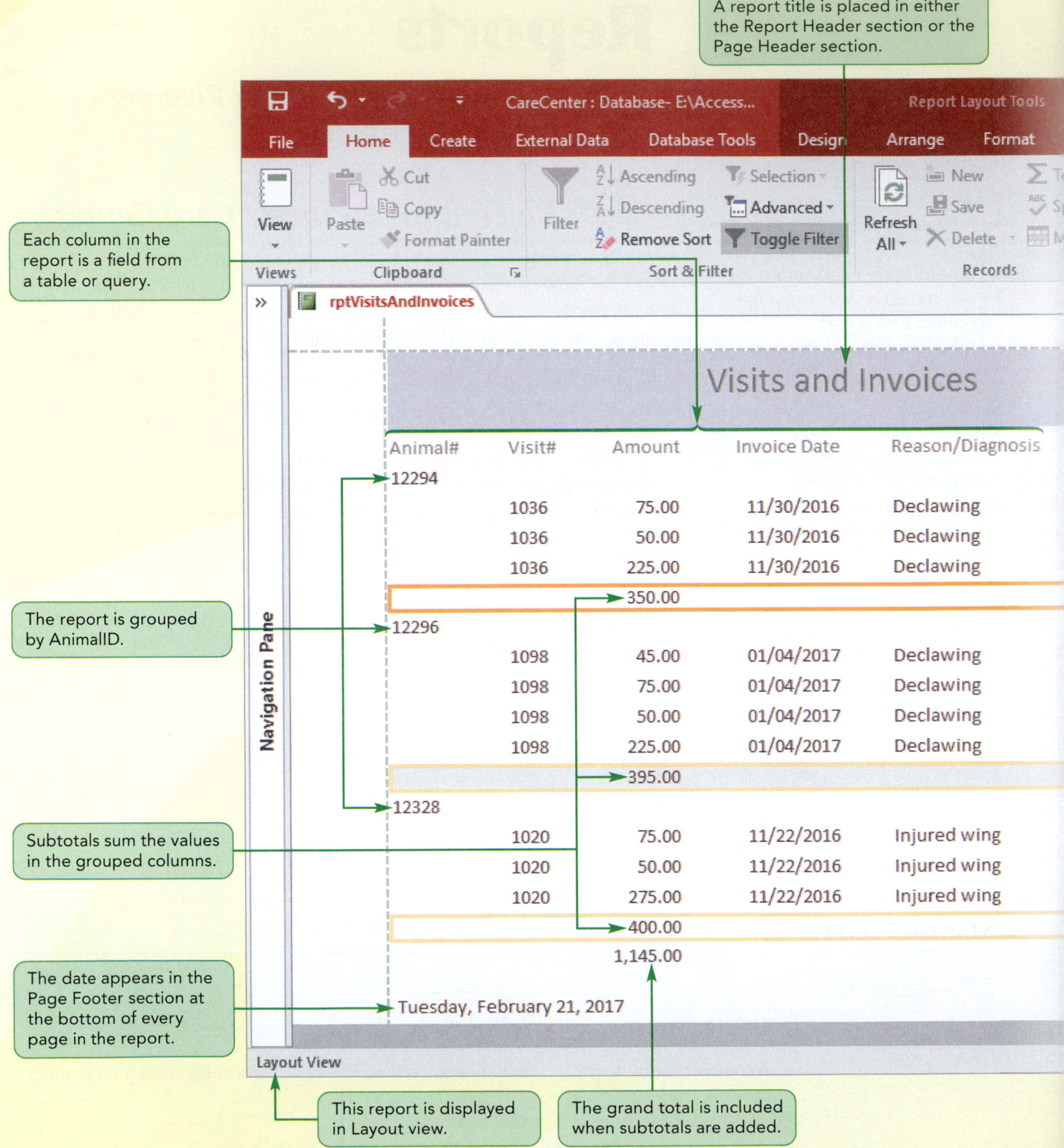

Custom Report in Layout View

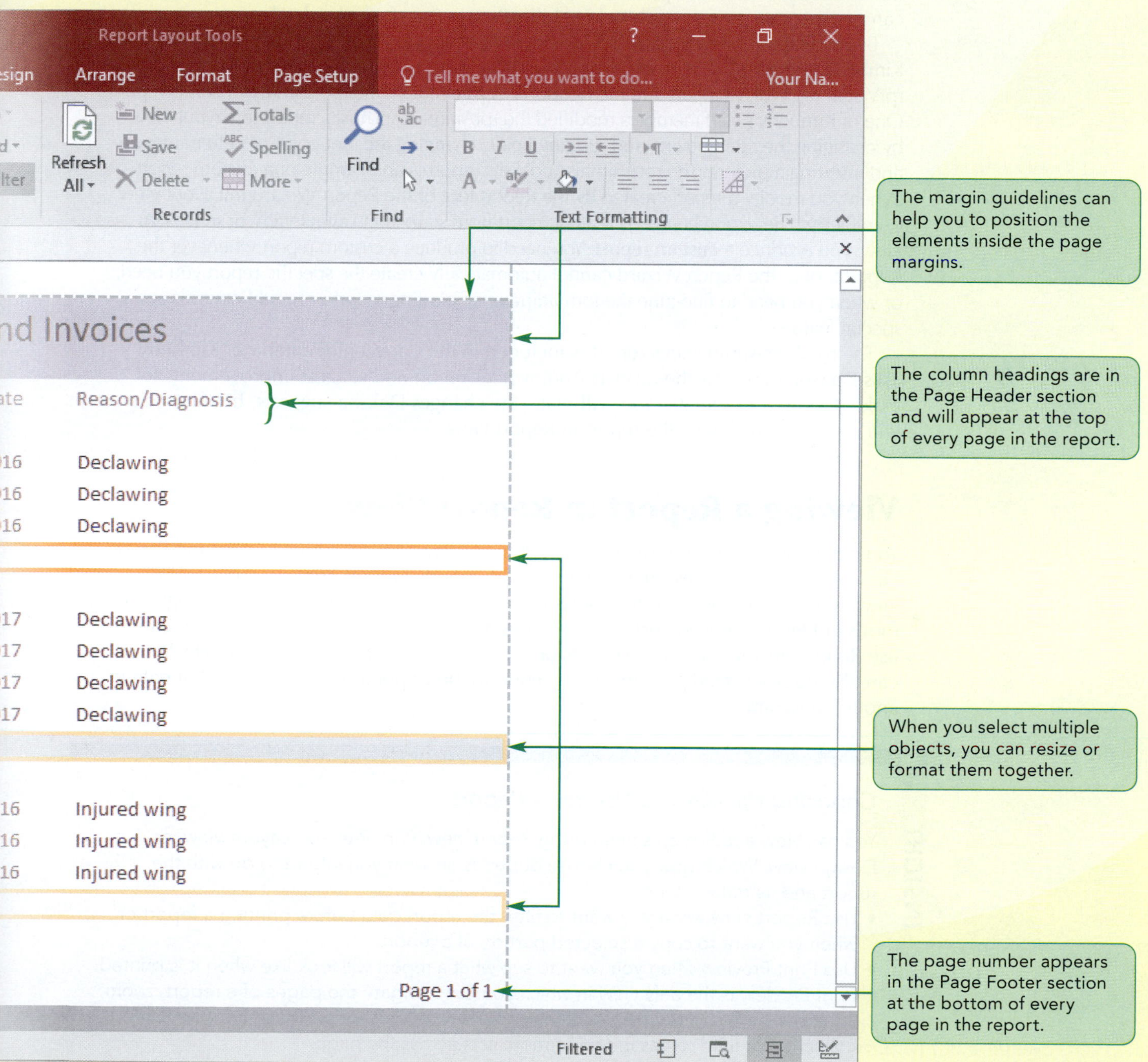

Customizing Existing Reports

As you know, a report is a formatted output (screen display or printout) of the contents of one or more tables in a database. Although you can format and print data using datasheets, queries, and forms, reports offer greater flexibility and provide a more professional, readable appearance. For example, a billing statement created using a datasheet would not look professional, but the staff at Riverview Veterinary Care Center can easily create professional-looking billing statements from the database using reports.

Before Daksha Yatawara was tasked with enhancing the CareCenter database, Kimberly and her staff created two reports. Kimberly used the Report tool to create the rptVisitsAndInvoices report and the Report Wizard to create the rptAnimalsAndVisits report. One of Kimberly's staff members modified the rptAnimalsAndVisits report in Layout view by changing the title, moving and resizing fields, changing the font color of field names, and inserting a picture. The rptAnimalsAndVisits report is an example of a custom report. When you modify a report created by the Report tool or the Report Wizard in Layout view or in Design view, or when you create a report from scratch in Layout view or in Design view, you produce a **custom report**. You need to produce a custom report whenever the Report tool or the Report Wizard cannot automatically create the specific report you need, or when you need to fine-tune the formatting of an existing report or to add controls and special features.

The rptVisitsAndInvoices report is included in the CareCenter database. Kimberly asks Daksha to review the rptVisitsAndInvoices report and suggest improvements to make it more user friendly. You will make the changes Daksha suggests, but first, you will view and work with the report in Report view.

Viewing a Report in Report View

You can view reports on screen in Print Preview, Layout view, Design view, and Report view. You've already viewed and worked with reports in Print Preview and Layout view. Making modifications to reports in Design view is similar to making changes to forms in Design view. **Report view** provides an interactive view of a report. You can use Report view to view the contents of a report and to apply a filter to its data. You can also copy selected portions of the report to the Clipboard and then use that data in another program.

INSIGHT

Choosing the View to Use for a Report

You can view a report on screen using Report view, Print Preview, Layout view, or Design view. Which view you choose depends on what you intend to do with the report and its data.

- Use Report view when you want to filter the report data before printing a report or when you want to copy a selected portion of a report.
- Use Print Preview when you want to see what a report will look like when it is printed. Print Preview is the only view in which you can navigate the pages of a report, zoom in or out, or view a **multiple-column report**, which is a report that prints the same collection of field values in two or more sets across the page.
- Use Layout view when you want to modify a report while seeing actual report data.
- Use Design view when you want to fine-tune a report's design or when you want to add lines, rectangles, and other controls that are available only in Design view.

You'll open the rptVisitsAndInvoices report in Report view, and then you'll interact with its data in this view.

To view and filter the rptVisitsAndInvoices report in Report view:

1. Start Access, and then open the **CareCenter** database you worked with in the previous two modules.

   Trouble? If the security warning is displayed below the ribbon, click the Enable Content button.

2. Open the Navigation Pane if necessary, double-click **rptVisitsAndInvoices**, and then close the Navigation Pane. The rptVisitsAndInvoices report opens in Report view.

   In Report view, you can view the report prior to printing it, just as you can do in Print Preview. Report view also lets you apply filters to the report before printing it. You'll apply a text filter to the rptVisitsAndInvoices report.

3. Scroll down to Animal ID 12328, which has three report detail lines for Visit ID 1020, right-click **Injured wing** in the Reason column to open the shortcut menu, and then point to **Text Filters**. A submenu of filter options for the Text field opens. See Figure 7-1.

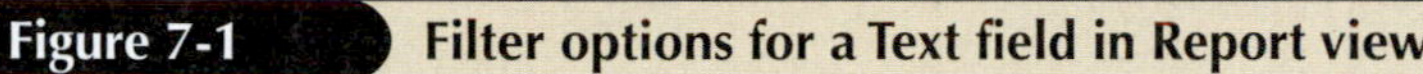

Figure 7-1 Filter options for a Text field in Report view

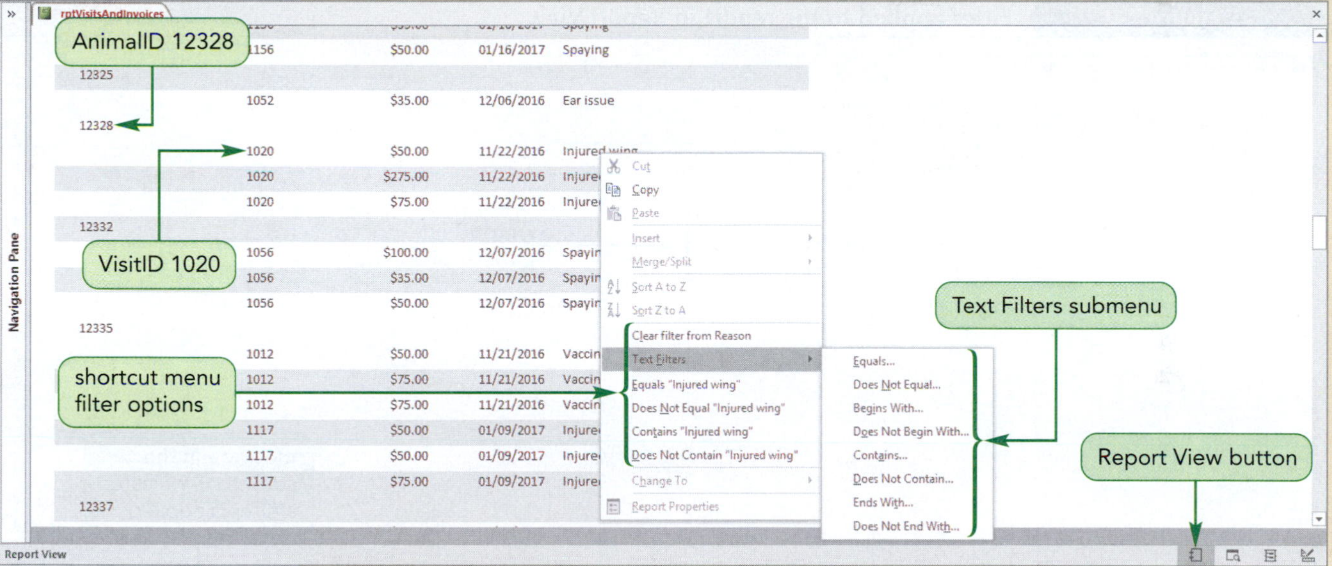

The filter options that appear on the shortcut menu depend on the selected field's data type and the selected value. Because you clicked the Reason field value without selecting a portion of the value, the shortcut menu displays filter options—various conditions using the value "Injured wing"—for the entire Reason field value. You'll close the menus and select a portion of the Reason column value to explore a different way of filtering the report.

4. Click a blank area of the screen to close the menus.

5. For Animal ID 12328: Visit ID 1020, double-click **wing** in the Reason column to select it, and then right-click **wing**. The filter options on the shortcut menu now apply to the selected text, "wing." Notice that the filter options on the shortcut menu include options such as "Ends With" and "Does Not End With" because the text you selected is at the end of the field value in the Reason column.

6. On the shortcut menu, click **Contains "wing"**. The report content changes to display only those visits that contain the word "wing" anywhere in the Reason column. Notice the results also show "Declawing" because the letter string "wing" appear within this word.

7. In the Reason column, double-click the word **Injured** for the Visit ID 1020 report detail line for Animal ID 12328, right-click **Injured** to open the shortcut menu, and then point to **Text Filters**. The filter options now include the "Begins With" and "Does Not Begin With" options because the text you selected is at the beginning of the field value in the Reason column.

   Kimberly wants to view only those visits that contain the phrase "Injured wing" in the Reason column.

8. Click a blank area of the screen to close the menus, and then click in a blank area again to deselect the text.

9. In the report detail line for Visit ID 1020, right-click **Injured wing** in the Reason column, and then click **Equals "Injured wing"** on the shortcut menu. Only the three invoices that contain the selected phrase are displayed in the report. See Figure 7-2.

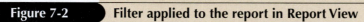

Figure 7-2 Filter applied to the report in Report View

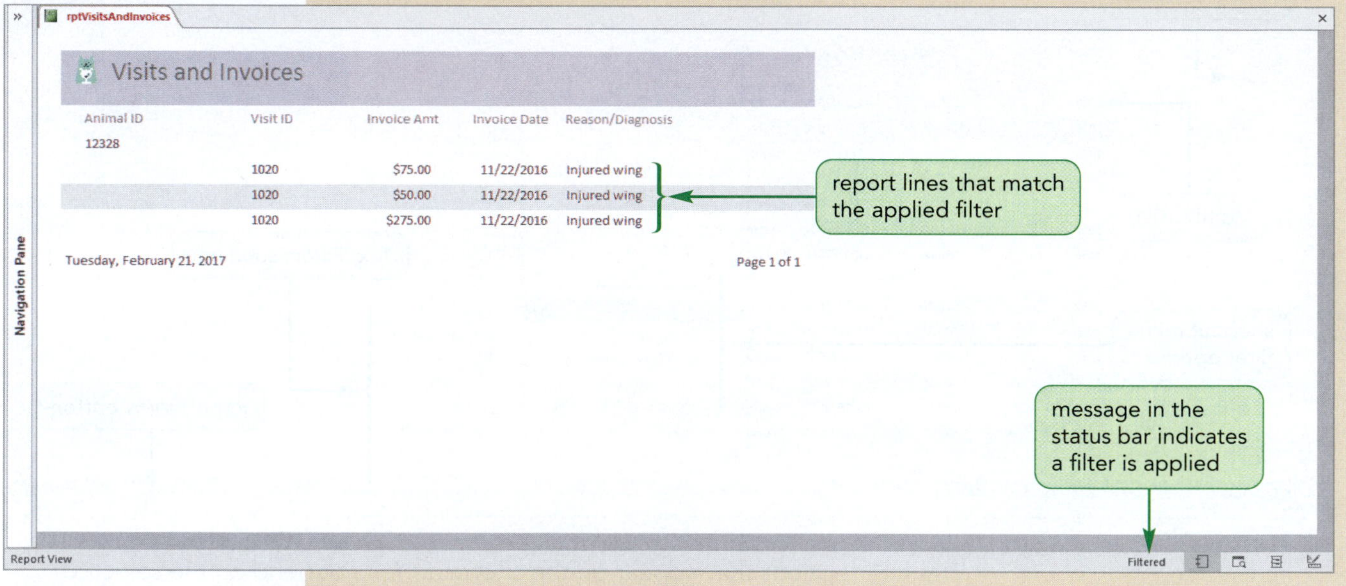

You can print the filtered report, or you can select the entire filtered report or a portion of it and copy it into another file so you can work with it in a different program.

Copying and Pasting a Report into Word

Sometimes it is helpful to copy a filtered report or a portion of a filtered report into another file, such as a Word document or an Excel spreadsheet. This allows you to distribute the report electronically in a format that others can easily access, or you can print the filtered report to distribute on paper. When you copy information contained in an Access object such as a report, it is placed on the Clipboard. The Clipboard is a temporary storage area on your computer on which text or objects are stored when you cut or copy them, and it's contents are available to all Windows programs. You can then paste the text or objects stored on the Clipboard into another file, such as a Word document or an Excel spreadsheet.

Kimberly would like you to create a Word document that contains the records from the Injured wing filter so she can provide this information to the veterinary technician who is monitoring the animal with these injuries. Next, you'll copy the entire filtered report to the Clipboard.

TIP

You can press the Ctrl + A keys to select all items in the report.

To copy the filtered report and paste it into a Word document:

1. Click to the left of the title graphic at the top of the report to select the report title control, drag down to the end of the last record in the report, and then release the mouse button to select the report title, field titles, and all of the records in the report. See Figure 7-3.

   Trouble? If you selected nothing, you clicked above the title graphic. Make sure the mouse pointer is to the left of the title graphic, but not above it, and then repeat Step 1.

   Trouble? If you selected only a portion of the report, press the Esc key to deselect your selection, and then repeat Step 1.

Figure 7-3 Selected filtered report in Report view

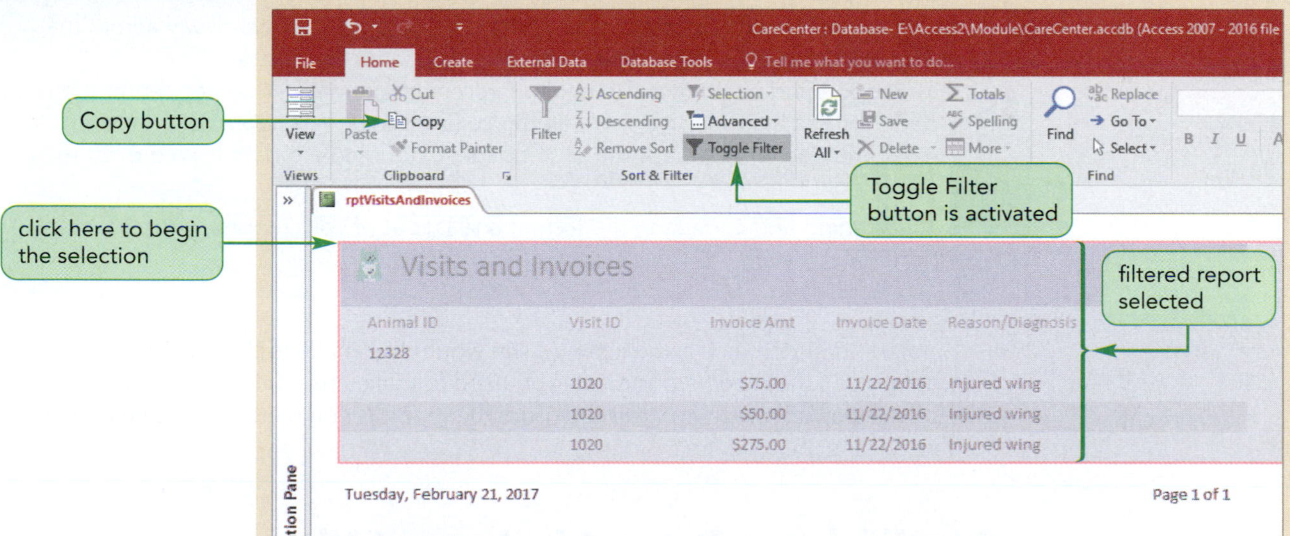

2. On the Home tab, in the Clipboard, click the **Copy** button.

   You'll copy this report data into a Word document.

3. Open Word, and then in Backstage view, click **Blank document**. A blank Word document opens.
4. On the Home tab, in the Clipboard group, click the **Paste** button to paste the report data into the document.
5. Save the Word document with the filename **Injuredwing** in the location where you are saving your files, and then close the Injuredwing document and exit Word. You return to the Access with the rptVisitsAndInvoices filtered report in Report view.
6. To the right of the records, click a blank area of the screen to deselect the report records, and then, in the Sort & Filter group, click the **Toggle Filter** button. The filters are removed from the report.

Viewing and working with a report in Report view often helps you to identify adjustments and modifications you can make to the report to enhance its readability. You can make modifications to a report in Layout view and Design view.

PROSKILLS

Written Communication: Enhancing Reports Created by the Report Tool and the Report Wizard

Creating a report using the Report tool or the Report Wizard can save time, but you should review the report to determine if you need to make any of the following types of common enhancements and corrections:

- Change the report title from the report object name (with an rpt prefix and no spaces) to one that has meaning to the users.
- Reduce the widths of the date and page number controls, and move the controls so that they are not printed on a separate page.
- Review the report in Print Preview, and, if the report displays excess pages, adjust the page margins and the placement of controls.
- Verify that all controls are large enough to fully display their values.
- Use page margins and field widths that display equal margins to the left and right of the data.
- Use a layout for the fields that distributes the data in a balanced way across the report, and use the same spacing between all columns of data.
- The report and page titles can be centered on the page, but do not center the report data. Instead, use spacing between the columns and reasonable column widths to make the best use of the width of the page, extending the data from the left margin to the right margin.

By fine-tuning and correcting the format and layout of your reports, you ensure the report's information is clearly conveyed to users.

Kimberly has identified some changes she would like made to the rptVistsAndInvoices report. Some of the report adjustments you need to make are subtle ones, so you need to carefully review all report controls to ensure the report is completely readable and usable for those using the report.

Modifying a Report in Layout View

You can make the report changes Kimberly wants in Layout view. Modifying a report in Layout view is similar to modifying a form in Layout view. When you open a report in Layout view, the Report Layout Tools Design, Arrange, Format, and Page Setup contextual tabs appear on the ribbon. You use the commands on these tabs to modify and format the elements of the report.

Kimberly wants you to decrease the width of columns and adjust the page margins in the report. She also wants you to rename some of the column headings, format the InvoiceAmt field values using the Standard format, resize the column headings, delete the picture from the Report Header section, remove the alternate row color from the detail and group header lines, and add a grand total of the InvoiceAmt field values. These changes will make the report more useful for Kimberly and her staff.

First, you will view the report in Layout view and observe how the information in the report is grouped and sorted.

To view the report in Layout view:

1. On the status bar, click the **Layout View** button, and then scroll to the top of the report (if necessary).
2. On the Report Layout Tools Design tab, in the Grouping & Totals group, click the **Group & Sort** button to open the Group, Sort, and Total pane at the bottom of the window. The Group & Sort button is a toggle button; you click this button to open and close this pane as needed. See Figure 7-4.

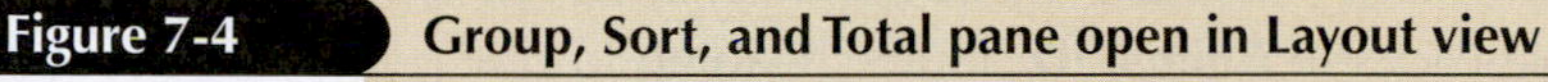

Figure 7-4 Group, Sort, and Total pane open in Layout view

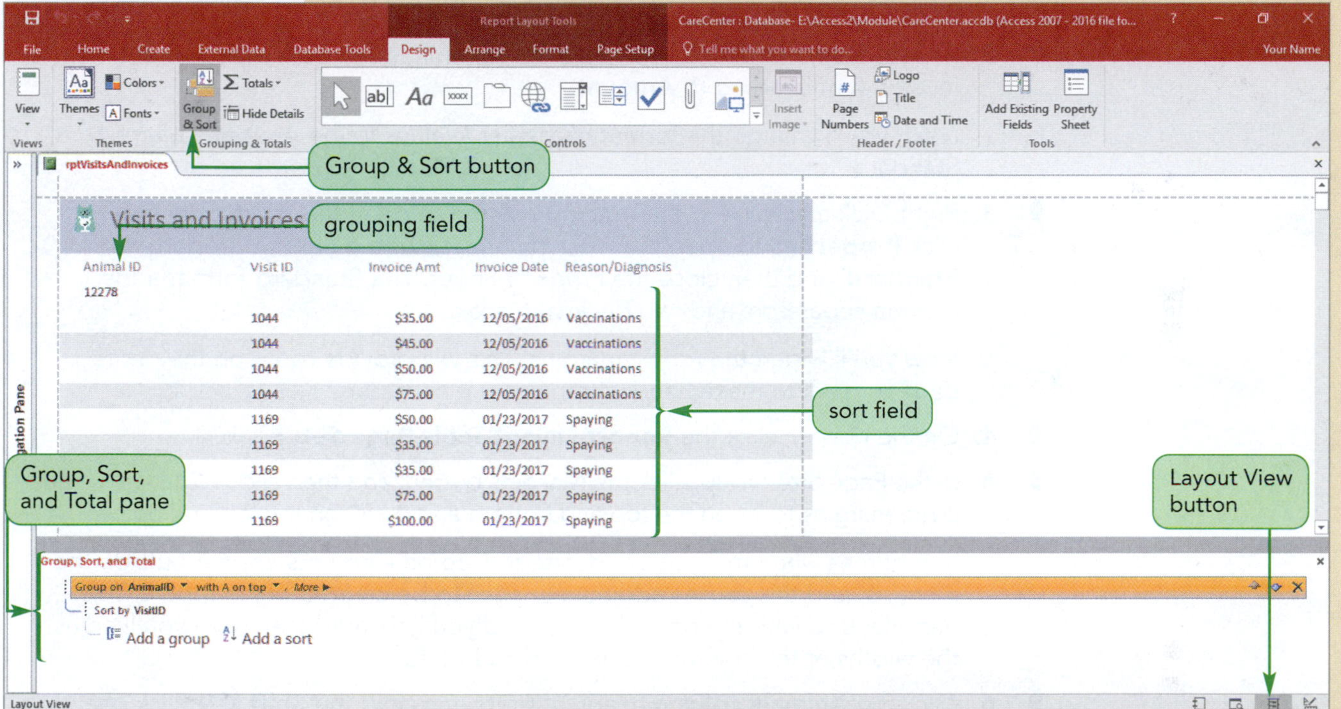

The rptVisitsAndInvoices report has a grouping field (the AnimalID field) and a sort field (the VisitID field). At the bottom of the window, the **Group, Sort, and Total pane** provides you with the options to modify the report's grouping fields and sort fields and the report calculations for the groups. A **grouping field** is a report sort field that includes a Group Header section before a group of records having the same sort field value and a Group Footer section after the group of records. These sections are defined with section bars in Design view. A Group Header section usually displays the group name and the sort field value for the group. A Group Footer section usually displays subtotals or counts for the records in that group. The rptVisitsAndInvoices report's grouping field is the AnimalID field, which is displayed in a Group Header section that precedes the set of visits for the Animal; the grouping field does not have a Group Footer section. The VisitID field is a secondary sort key, as shown in the Group, Sort, and Total pane.

Because you don't need to change the grouping or sort fields for the report, you'll close the pane and then make Kimberly's modifications to the report.

3. In the Grouping & Totals group, click the **Group & Sort** button to close the Group, Sort, and Total pane.

Now that you have an understanding of how the information in the report is grouped and sorted, you are ready to make the modifications to the report Kimberly has requested. First, you'll change the column headings for the first three columns to Animal#, Visit#, and Amount. Kimberly prefers to see all the detail data on one line, even when it means abbreviating column headings for columns whose headings are wider than the data. After reducing the column headings, you'll reduce the column widths, freeing up space on the detail lines to widen the Reason column.

To modify the columns in the report in Layout view:

1. Double-click the **Animal ID** column heading to change to editing mode, change it to **Animal#**, and then press the **Enter** key.
2. Repeat Step 1 to change the Visit ID column heading to **Visit#** and the Invoice Amt heading to **Amount**.

   Next, you'll change the format of the field values in the Amount column to Standard.
3. Right-click any value in the Amount column to open the shortcut menu, click **Properties** to open the Property Sheet, set the Format property to **Standard**, and then close the Property Sheet. The Standard format adds comma separators and two decimal places.

   Now you'll widen the report margins. This will provide room on the printed page for staff to make handwritten notes if necessary.
4. On the ribbon, click the **Report Layout Tools Page Setup** tab.
5. In the Page Size group, click the **Margins** button, and then click **Wide**. This sets page margins to 1" on the top and bottom and 0.75" on the left and right.

   Sometimes when margins are decreased, some elements appear outside the margins, and this causes additional pages to be created in the report. This has occurred with the page number, and you'll fix that later. Now you'll adjust the widths of the columns to fit the data better.
6. Click the **Animal#** column heading, press and hold the **Shift** key, click one of the AnimalID values in the column, and then release the **Shift** key. The Animal# column heading and all the values in this column are selected.
7. Position the pointer on the left border of the Animal# column heading selection box, and then when the pointer changes to ↔, drag the left border to the left so it aligns with the left edge of the gray report header box.
8. Drag the right border of the Animal# to the left until the border is just to the right of the # symbol in the column heading text. Now, you'll move the VisitID column to the left, closer to the Animal# column.
9. Click the **Visit#** column heading, press and hold the **Shift** key, click one the VisitID values in the column, and then release the **Shift** key. The Visit# column heading and all the VisitID values in this column are selected.
10. Using the pointer, drag the **Visit#** column to the left, until it is positioned such that the left border of the Visit# column heading selection box is aligned with the "t" in the word "Visits" in the report title. The column does not appear to move until you release the mouse button.

    Trouble? If the report scrolls to the bottom of the report after you release the mouse button in the drag operation, scroll back to the top of the report.

Now you'll resize and move the Amount heading and InvoiceAmt values to the left, closer to the VisitID column, and then you'll move the Date of Visit and Reason/Diagnosis columns to the left, closer to the Amount column.

11. Select the **Amount** column heading and the **InvoiceAmt** values in the column, and then drag the left border of the Amount column heading selection box to the right until it is positioned just to the left of the "A" in the column heading "Amount." The Amount column is resized to better fit the values in the column.
12. With the Amount column heading and the InvoiceAmt values still selected, drag the column heading to the left until the left border of its selection box aligns with the letter "I" in the word "Invoices" in the report's title.
13. Select the **Invoice Date** column heading and the **InvoiceDate** values, and then resize and reposition the selected column heading and column of values as shown in Figure 7-5.

Figure 7-5 **Resized columns in Layout view**

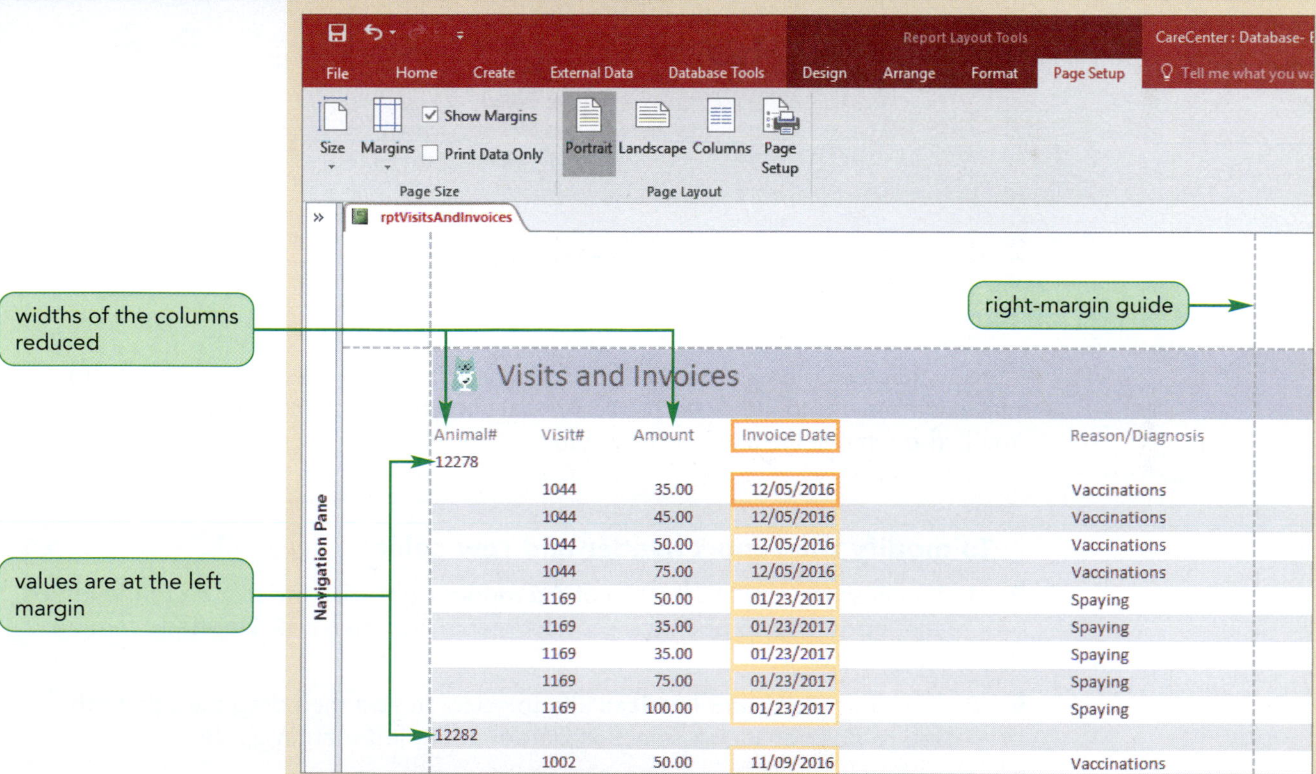

Now, you'll move the column for the Reason field to the left and resize it to better fit the data, aligning it with the page's right margin.

14. Select the **Reason/Diagnosis** column heading and field values, move them to the left, closer to the Date of Visit column, then resize the column heading and the column of values by dragging the right border of the selected items to the right margin of the report, as shown in Figure 7-6.

Figure 7-6 Adjusted column width

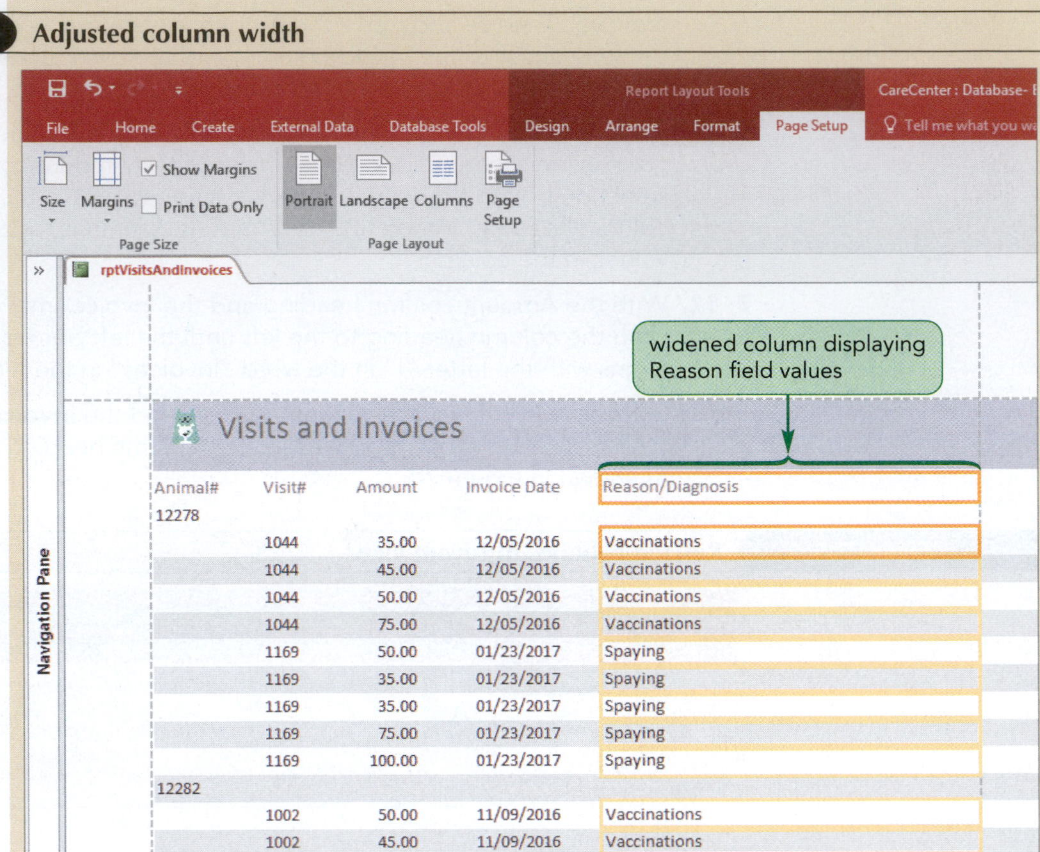

Now that the columns have been resized and repositioned, Kimberly asks you to make adjustments to the report header, which contains a picture and the report's title. You'll also remove the alternate row color.

To modify the report header and row color:

1. If necessary, scroll to the top of the report, right-click the picture to the left of the report title to open the shortcut menu, and then click **Delete** to remove the picture.
2. Click the **Visits and Invoices** title to select it, and then drag the title to the left to position its left selection border at the left-margin guide.
3. Drag the title's right selection border to the right to position it at the right-margin guide to increase the width of the title box to the full width of the page.
4. Click the **Report Layout Tools Format** tab, and then in the Font group, click the **Center** button to center the title in the report header.

   Kimberly finds the alternate row color setting in the group header and detail lines distracting, and asks you to remove this formatting.

5. To the left of the first AnimalID value in the first column, click to the left of the left-margin guide to select the group headers.
6. In the Background group, click the **Alternate Row Color** arrow to display the gallery of available colors, and then at the bottom of the gallery, click **No Color**. The alternate row color is removed from the AnimalID group header rows.

You've removed the alternate row color from the AnimalID values in the report, and next you'll remove the alternate row color from the detail lines. Because the Alternate Row Color button is now set to "No Color," you can just click the button to remove the color.

7. Next to the first VisitID in the first AnimalID record detail line, click to the left of the left-margin guide and then in the Background group, click the **Alternate Row Color** button to remove the alternate row color from the detail lines.

Kimberly's last change to the report is to add a grand total for the Amount field values. First, you must select the Amount column or one of the values in the column.

To add a grand total to the report in Layout view:

1. In the first detail line for VisitID 1044, click **45.00** in the Amount column. The values in this column are all selected.
2. Click the **Report Layout Tools Design** tab, and then in the Grouping & Totals group, click the **Totals** button to display the Totals menu. See Figure 7-7.

Figure 7-7 The Totals menu

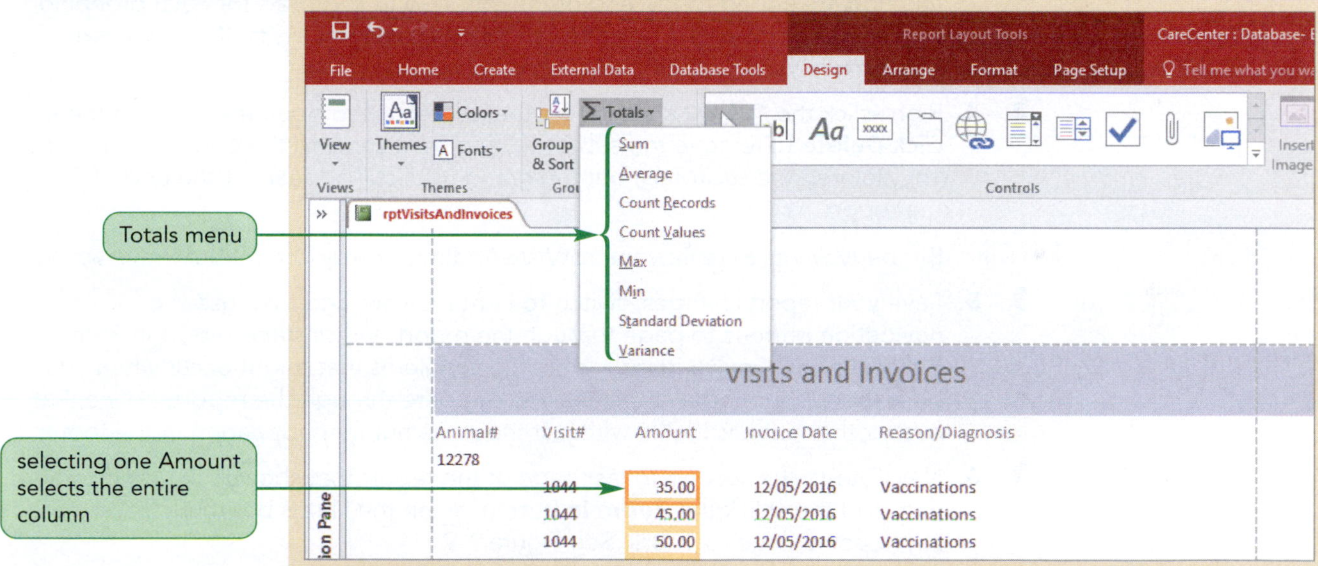

You can select one of the eight aggregate functions on the Totals menu to summarize values in the selected column. To calculate and display the grand total visit amount, you'll select the Sum aggregate function.

3. Click **Sum** in the Totals menu, scroll to the bottom of the report, and then if the last value in the Amount column displays as ######## instead of numbers, click **########** to select it, then drag the left selection border of the selected value to the left until the grand total of 12,015.00 displays.

   Notice subtotals for each group of visits are displayed for each AnimalID field value (125.00 for the last animal). See Figure 7-8.

   Trouble? If the field value box still contains ###### after you resize it, increase the width again until the grand total value of 12,015.00 is visible.

Figure 7-8 Report showing subtotals and a grand total of the Amount field values

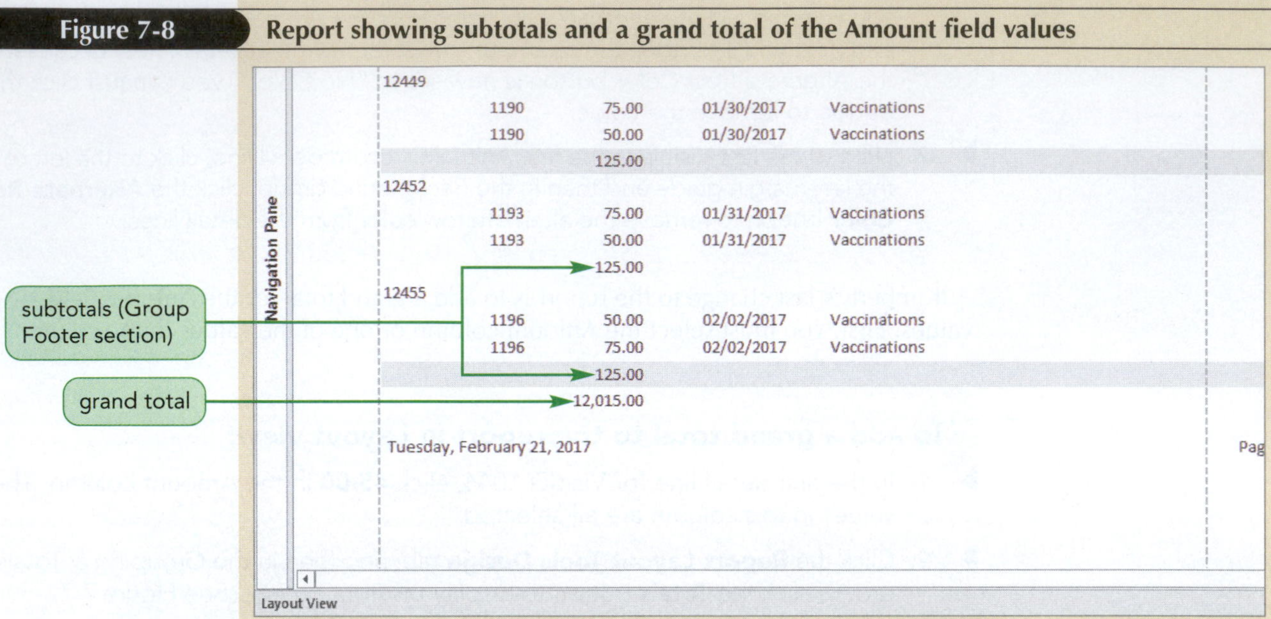

When you select an aggregate function in Layout view, the results of the function are added to the end of the report, and subtotals for each grouping field are also added. Because each Animal has so few visits, Kimberly asks you to remove the subtotals from the report.

4. Right-click the **125.00** subtotal for the last record to open the shortcut menu, click **Delete** to remove the subtotals, and then scroll to the end of the report. You deleted the subtotals, but the grand total still appears at the end of the report.

   Kimberly wants to review the rptVisitsAndInvoices report in Print Preview.

5. Save your report changes, switch to Print Preview, and then use the navigation buttons to page through the report. Viewing the report in Print Preview allows you to identify possible problems that might occur when you print the report. For example, as you navigate through the report, notice that every other page is blank, with just the page number appearing in the footer.

6. Navigate to the second to last page of the report that shows the grand total line, and then click the **Zoom In** button [+] on the status bar to increase the zoom percentage to 110%. See Figure 7-9.

Figure 7-9 The rptVisitsAndInvoices report in Print Preview

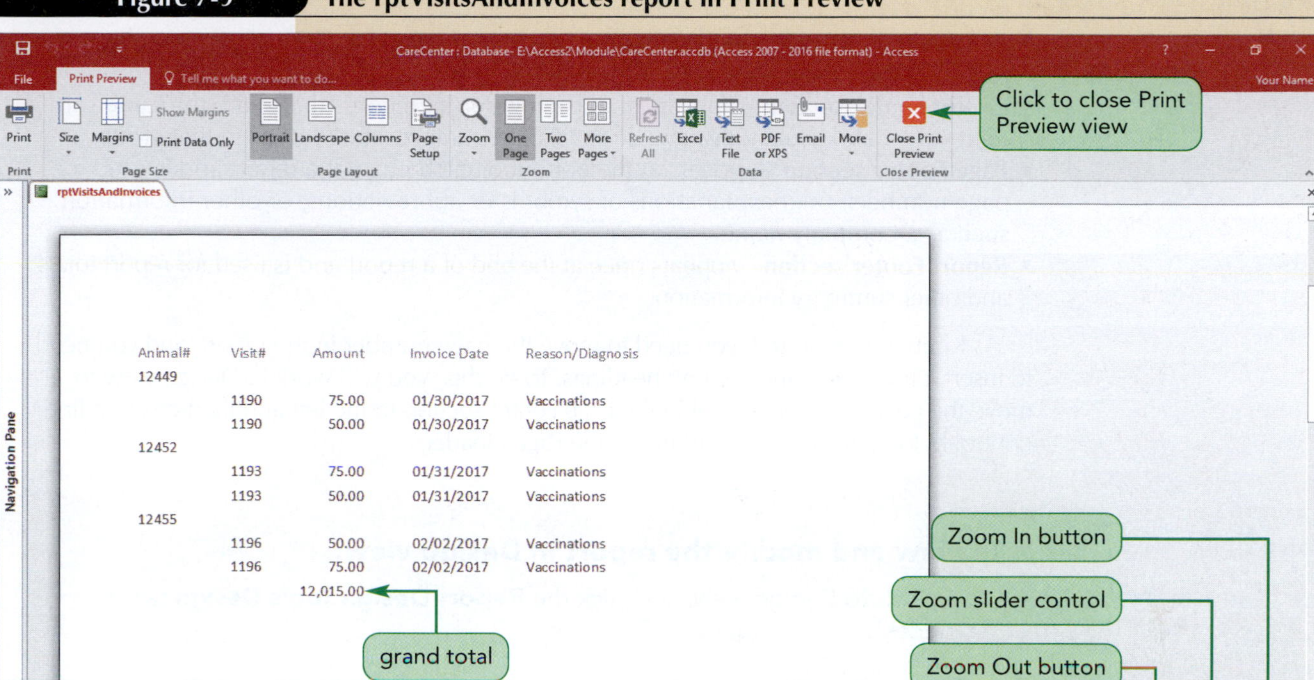

Trouble? Depending on the printer you are using, the last page of your report might differ. If so, don't worry. Different printers format reports in different ways, sometimes affecting the total number of pages and the number of records printed per page.

7. On the status bar, click the **Zoom Out** button [−] to decrease the zoom percentage to 100%, and close the Print Preview view and display the report in Layout view.

As you saw in Print Preview, the page numbers are outside the right margin and are causing extra pages in the report. Therefore, you need to reposition the page number that appears at the bottom of each page. Kimberly suggests you move the page number box to the left so that its right edge is aligned with the right edge of Reason field value box in the Detail section, thereby eliminating the extra pages in the report. She also wants you to add a line below the column heading labels. Although you can make Kimberly's modifications in Layout view, you'll make them in Design view so you can work more precisely.

Modifying a Report in Design View

Design view for reports is similar to Design view for forms, which you used in the previous module to customize forms. When you open a report in Design view, the Report Design Tools contextual tabs—Design, Arrange, Format, and Page Setup—appear on the ribbon, A report in Design view is divided into seven sections:

- **Report Header section**—appears once at the beginning of a report and is used for report titles, company logos, report introductions, dates, visual elements such as lines, and cover pages.
- **Page Header section**—appears at the top of each page of a report and is used for page numbers, column headings, report titles, and report dates.

- **Group Header section**—appears before each group of records that share the same sort field value, and usually displays the group name and the sort field value for the group.
- **Detail section**—contains the bound controls to display the field values for each record in the record source.
- **Group Footer section**—appears after each group of records that share the same sort field value, and usually displays subtotals or counts for the records in that group.
- **Page Footer section**—appears at the bottom of each page of a report and is used for page numbers, brief explanations of symbols or abbreviations, or other information such as a company name.
- **Report Footer section**—appears once at the end of a report and is used for report totals and other summary information.

As Kimberly requested, you need to move the page number in the report, and you need to insert a line below the column headings. To do this, you will work in Design view to move the page number control in the Page Footer section to the left and then create a line control below the column headings in the Page Header.

To view and modify the report in Design view:

1. Switch to Design view, and click the **Report Design Tools Design** tab, if necessary. See Figure 7-10.

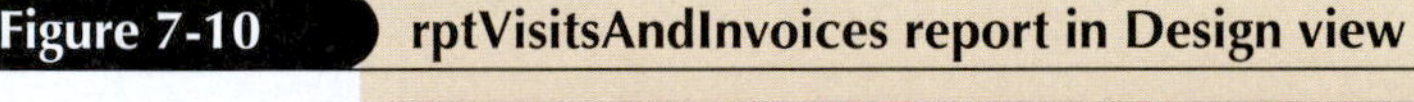

Figure 7-10 rptVisitsAndInvoices report in Design view

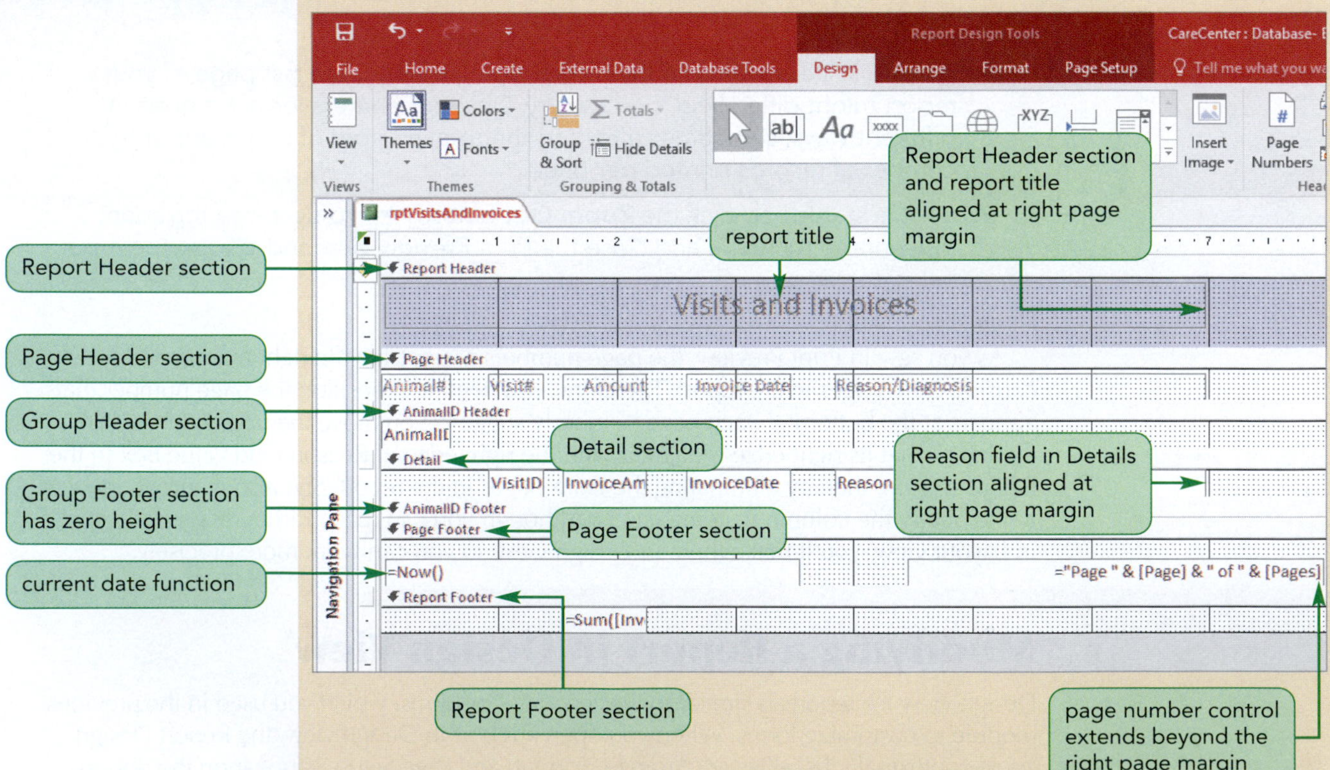

Notice that Design view for a report has most of the same components as Design view for a form. For example, Design view for forms and reports includes horizontal and vertical rulers, grids in each section, and similar buttons in the groups on the Report Design Tools Design tab.

Design view for the rptVisitsAndInvoices report displays seven sections: the Report Header section contains the report title; the Page Header section contains the column heading labels; the Group Header section (AnimalID Header) contains the AnimalID grouping field; the Detail section contains the bound controls to display the field values for each record in the record source (tblVisit); the Group Footer section (AnimalID Footer) isn't displayed in the report; the Page Footer section contains the current date and the page number; and the Report Footer section contains the Sum function, which calculates the grand total of the InvoiceAmt field values.

You will now move the page number control in the Page Footer section so that it is within the report's right page margin. To guide you in this, recall you earlier resized and repositioned the Reason/Diagnosis column in Layout view so it aligned to the right margin of the page. Therefore, you will right-align the page number control to the Reason field value box in the Detail section.

2. Click the **Page Number** control to select it (the control on the right side of the Page Footer section), and then press the ← key to move the control to the left until the right border of its selection box is roughly aligned with the right edge of the Reason field value control box in the Detail section.

   Trouble? If the page number control overlaps the date control in the Report Footer section, don't worry about it. The contents of both will still be displayed.

3. With the Page Number control still selected, press and hold the **Shift** key, click the **Reason** field value control box in the Detail section, and then release the **Shift** key. Both controls are now selected.

4. Right-click one of the selected controls, point to **Align** on the shortcut menu, and then click **Right**. Both controls are now right-aligned.

   Finally, you'll create the line in the Page Header section.

5. Drag the bottom border of the Page Header section down to increase the height approximately half an inch. You'll resize this again after the line is created.

6. On the Report Design Tools Design tab, in the Controls group, click the **More** button, and then click the **Line** tool.

7. In the Page Header section, position the plus symbol of the Line tool pointer approximately two grid dots below the column header boxes, press and hold the **Shift key**, drag to the right page margin, and then release the **Shift** key to create a horizontal line that spans the width of the page. Holding the Shift key while drawing or extending a line snaps the line to either horizontal or vertical—whichever is nearest to the angle at which the line is drawn.

8. If necessary, drag the lower edge of the Page Header section up so it is approximately two grid dots below the line. See Figure 7-11.

Figure 7-11 Modified report in Design view

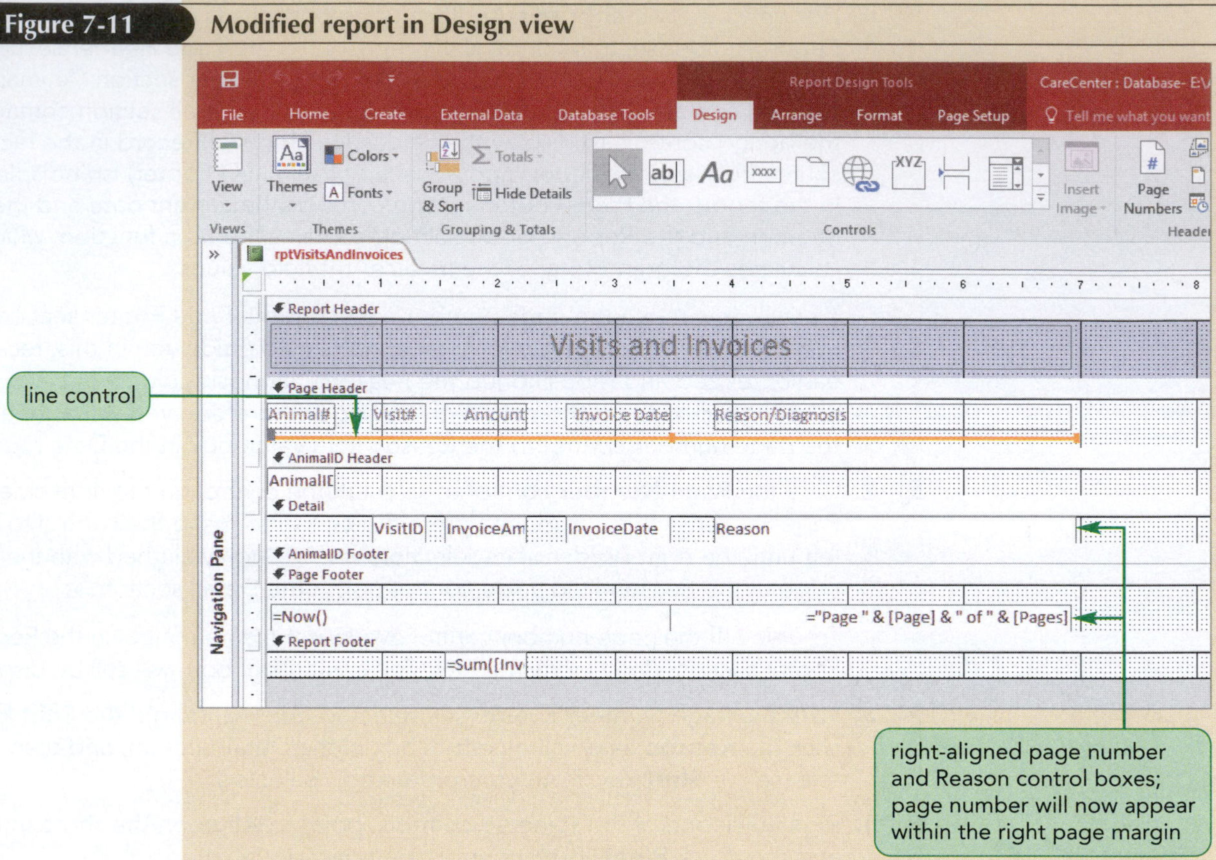

9. Save your report changes, switch to Print Preview, and then scroll and use the navigation buttons to page through the report, paying particular attention to the placement of the line in the Page Header section and the page number in the Page Footer section. The page number is right-aligned in the control box, so the text appears flush with the right margin. The data in the Reason field value text boxes are left-aligned, so this data does not appear flush with the right margin.

   Trouble? If you resize a field to position it outside the current margin, the report may widen to accommodate it, triggering a dialog box about the section width being greater than the page width. If this dialog box opens, click OK, manually move form elements as necessary so that no elements extend past 7 inches, and then adjust the report width to 7 inches.

10. Save and close the report.
11. If you are not continuing on to the next session, close the CareCenter database.

Kimberly is happy with the changes you've made to the rptVisitsAndInvoices report. In the next session, you create a new custom report for her based on queries instead of tables.

REVIEW

Session 7.1 Quick Check

1. What is a custom report?
2. Can a report be modified in Layout view?
3. Besides viewing a report, what other actions can you perform in Report view?
4. What is a grouping field?
5. List and describe the seven sections of an Access report.

Session 7.2 Visual Overview:

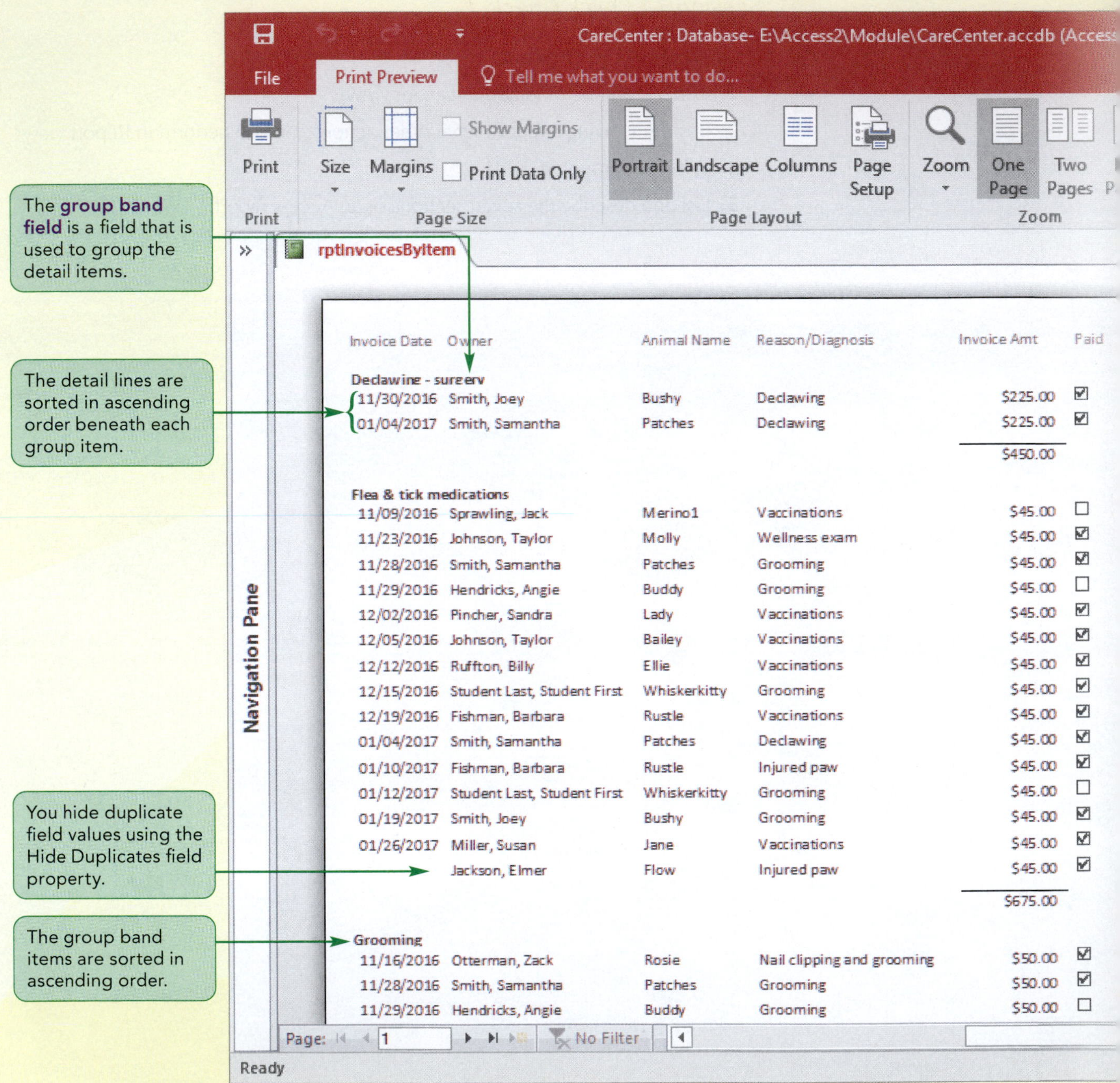

Custom Report in Print Preview

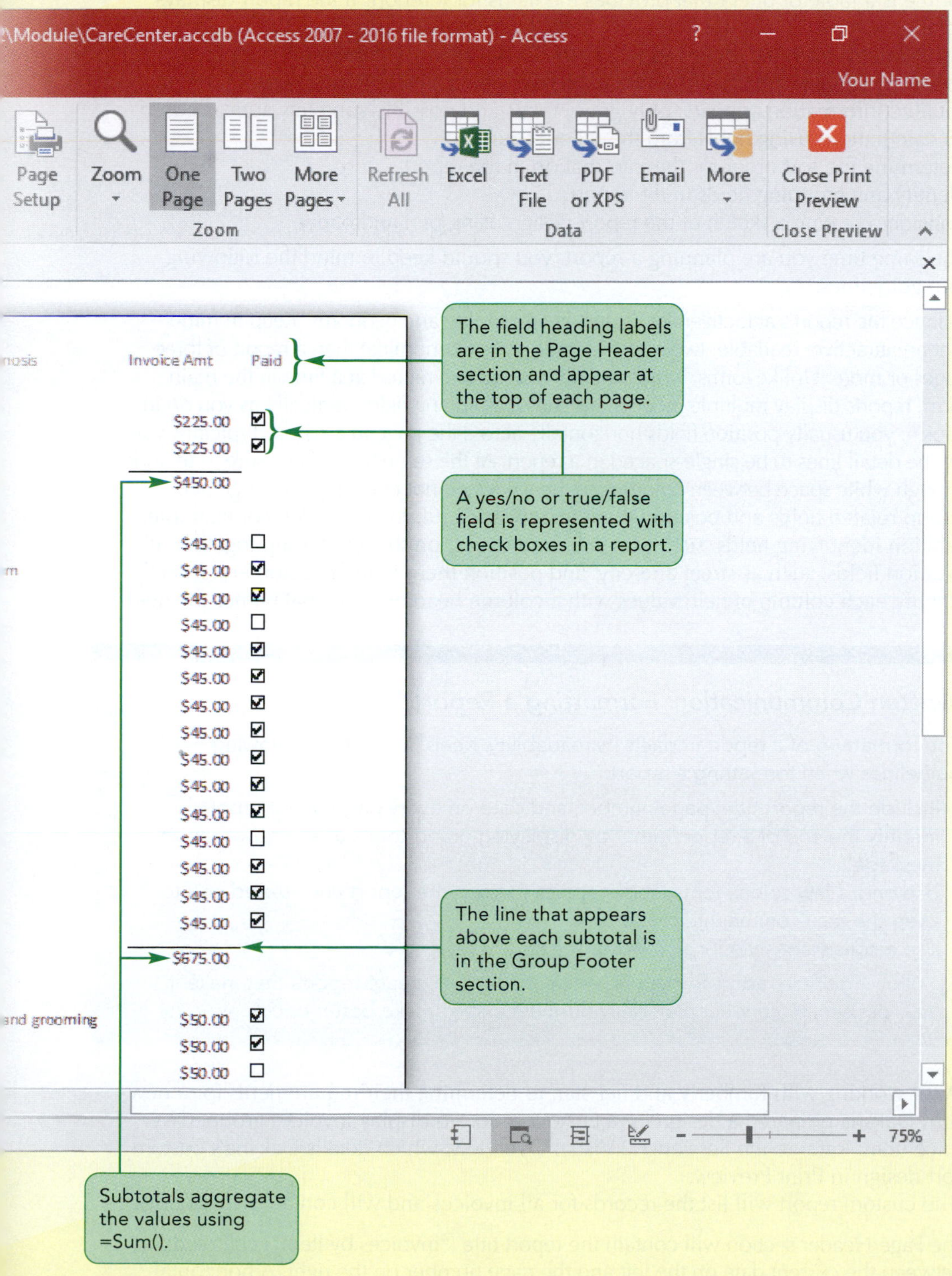

:\Module\CareCenter.accdb (Access 2007 - 2016 file format) - Access
Your Name
Page Setup
Zoom
One Page
Two Pages
More Pages
Refresh All
Excel
Text File
PDF or XPS
Email
More
Close Print Preview
Zoom
Data
Close Preview
Invoice Amt
Paid
$225.00
$225.00
$450.00
$45.00
$675.00
and grooming
$50.00
75%
The field heading labels are in the Page Header section and appear at the top of each page.
A yes/no or true/false field is represented with check boxes in a report.
The line that appears above each subtotal is in the Group Footer section.
Subtotals aggregate the values using =Sum().

Planning and Designing a Custom Report

Before you create a custom report, you should first plan the report's contents and its layout. When you plan a report, you should follow this general process:

- Determine the purpose of the report and its record source. Recall that the record source is a table or query that provides the fields for a report. If the report displays detailed information (a **detail report**), such as a list of all visits, then the report will display fields from the record source in the Detail section. If the report displays only summary information (a **summary report**), such as total visits by city, then no detailed information appears; only grand totals and possibly subtotals appear based on calculations using fields from the record source.
- Determine the sort order for the information in the report.
- Identify any grouping fields in the report.
- Consider creating a sketch of the report design using pen and paper.

At the same time you are planning a report, you should keep in mind the following layout guidelines:

- Balance the report's attractiveness against its readability and economy. Keep in mind that an attractive, readable, two-page report is more economical than a report of three pages or more. Unlike forms, which usually display one record at a time in the main form, reports display multiple records. Instead of arranging fields vertically as you do in a form, you usually position fields horizontally across the page in a report. Typically, you set the detail lines to be single-spaced in a report. At the same time, make sure to include enough white space between columns so the values do not overlap or run together.
- Group related fields and position them in a meaningful, logical order. For example, position identifying fields, such as names and codes, on the left. Group together all location fields, such as street and city, and position them in their customary order.
- Identify each column of field values with a column heading label that names the field.

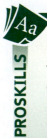

PROSKILLS

Written Communication: Formatting a Report

The formatting of a report impacts its readability. Keep in mind the following guidelines when formatting a report:

- Include the report title, page number, and date on every page of the report.
- Identify the end of a report either by displaying grand totals or an end-of-report message.
- Use only a few colors, fonts, and graphics to keep the report uncluttered and to keep the focus on the information.
- Use a consistent style for all reports in a database.

By following these report-formatting guidelines, you'll create reports that make it easier for users to conduct their daily business and to make better decisions.

After working with Kimberly and her staff to determine their requirements for a new report, Daksha prepared a design for a custom report to display invoices grouped by invoice item. Refer to the Session 7.2 Visual Overview, which details Daksha's custom report design in Print Preview.

The custom report will list the records for all invoices and will contain five sections:

- The Page Header section will contain the report title ("Invoices by Item") centered between the current date on the left and the page number on the right. A horizontal line will separate the column heading labels from the rest of the report page. From your work with the Report tool and the Report Wizard, you know that, by default, Access places the report title in the Report Header section and the date and page number in the Page Footer section. Kimberly prefers that the date, report title, and page number appear at the top of each page, so you need to place this information in the custom report's Page Header section.

- The InvoiceItemDesc field value from the tblInvoiceItem table will be displayed in a Group Header section.
- The Detail section will contain the InvoiceDate, InvoiceAmt, and InvoicePaid field values from the tblBilling table; the Reason field value from the tblVisit table; the AnimalName field value from the tblAnimal table; and the Owner calculated field value from the qryOwnersByName query. The detail records will be sorted in ascending order by the InvoiceDate field.
- A subtotal of the InvoiceAmt field values will be displayed below a line in the Group Footer section.
- The grand total of the InvoiceAmt field values will be displayed below a double line in the Report Footer section.

Before you start creating the custom report, you need to create a query that will serve as the record source for the report.

Creating a Query for a Custom Report

TIP

Create queries to serve as the record source for forms and reports. As requirements change, you can easily add fields, including calculated fields, to the queries.

As you know, the data for a report can come from a single table, from a single query based on one or more tables, or from multiple tables and/or queries. Kimberly's report will contain data from the tblInvoiceItem, tblBilling, tblVisit, and tblAnimal tables, and from the qryOwnersByName query. You'll use the Simple Query Wizard to create a query to retrieve all the data required for the custom report and to serve as the report's record source. A query filters data from one or more tables using criteria that can be quite complex. Creating a report based on a query allows you to display and distribute the results of the query in a readable, professional format, rather than only in a datasheet view.

To create the query to serve as the custom report's record source:

1. If you took a break after the previous session, make sure that the CareCenter database is open and the Navigation Pane is closed.
2. On the ribbon, click the **Create** tab.
3. In the Queries group, click the **Query Wizard** button to open the New Query dialog box, make sure **Simple Query Wizard** is selected, and then click the **OK** button. The first Simple Query Wizard dialog box opens.

   You need to select fields from the tblInvoiceItem, tblBilling, tblVisit, and tblAnimal tables and from the qryOwnersByName query, in that order.
4. In the Tables/Queries box, select **Table: tblInvoiceItem**, and then move the **InvoiceItemDesc** field from the Available Fields box to the Selected Fields box.
5. In the Tables/Queries box, select **Table: tblBilling**, and then move the **InvoiceItemID**, **InvoiceDate**, **InvoiceAmt**, and **InvoicePaid** fields, in that order, from the Available Fields box to the Selected Fields box.
6. In the Tables/Queries box, select **Table: tblVisit**, and then move the **Reason** field from the Available Fields box to the Selected Fields box.
7. In the Tables/Queries box, select **Table: tblAnimal**, and then move the **AnimalName** field from the Available Fields box to the Selected Fields box.
8. In the Tables/Queries box, select **Query: qryOwnersByName**, move the **Owner** calculated field from the Available Fields box to the Selected Fields box, and then click the **Next** button.

9. Make sure the **Detail (shows every field of every record)** option button is selected, and then click the **Next** button to open the final Simple Query Wizard dialog box.
10. Change the query name to **qryInvoicesByItem**, click the **Modify the query design** option button, and then click the **Finish** button. The query is displayed in Design view.

Next you need to set the sort fields for the query. The InvoiceItemDesc field will be a grouping field, which means it's the primary sort field, and the InvoiceDate field is the secondary sort field.

To set the sort fields for the query:

1. In the design grid, set the value in the InvoiceItemDesc Sort box to **Ascending** and then set the value in the InvoiceDate Sort box to **Ascending**.
2. Lengthen the query and table field lists as necessary to view all fields, drag the tables if necessary to position them so the join lines between them are visible, and then save your query changes. The completed query contains eight fields from four tables and one query, and the query includes two sort fields, the InvoiceItemDesc primary sort field and the InvoiceDate secondary sort field. See Figure 7-12.

Figure 7-12 Completed qryInvoicesByItem query in Design View

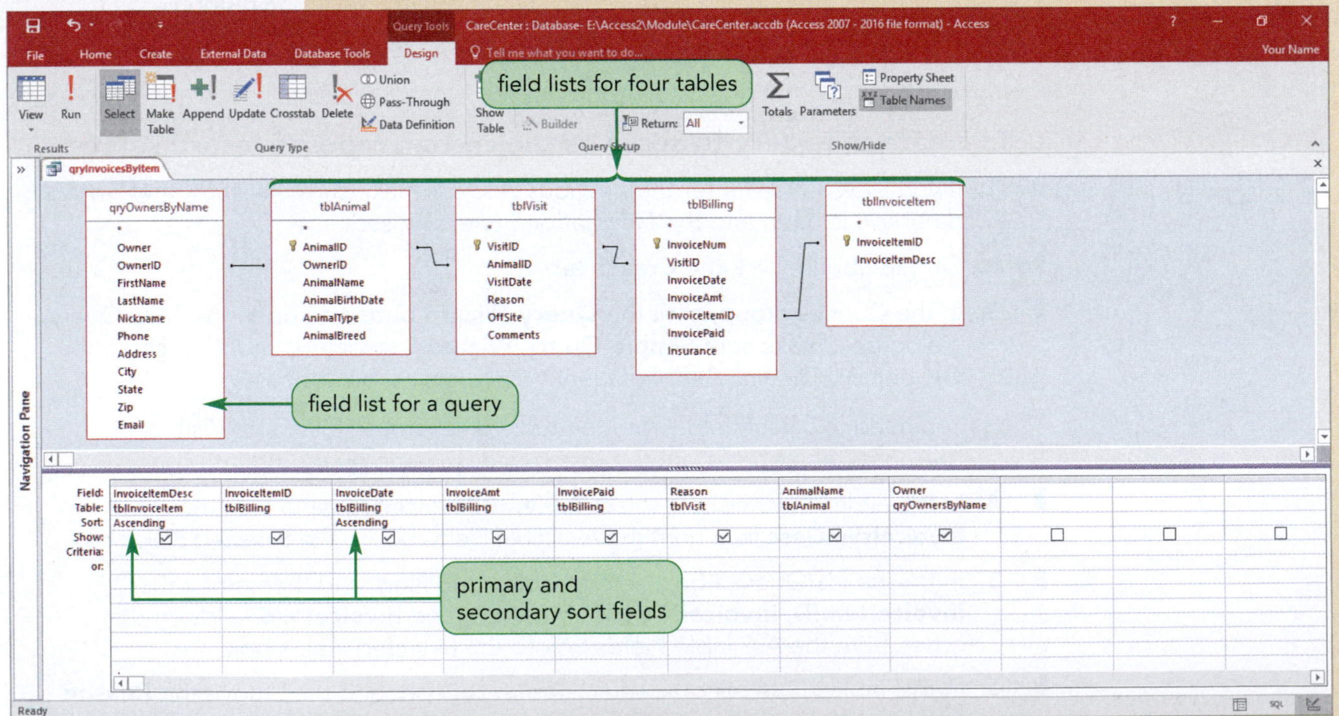

Before closing the query, you'll run it to view the query recordset.

3. If necessary, click the **Query Tools Design** tab, run the query, verify that it returns 202 records, and then save and close the query.

You'll use the qryInvoicesByItem query as the record source for the custom report.

Creating a Custom Report

Now that you've created the record source for the custom report, you could use the Report Wizard to create the report and then modify it to match the report design. However, because you need to customize several components of the report, you will create a custom report in Layout view and then switch between Layout and Design view to fine-tune the report.

INSIGHT

Making Report Design Modifications

You perform operations in Layout and Design views for reports in the same way that you perform operations in these views for forms. These operations become easier with practice. Remember to use the Undo button when necessary, back up your database frequently, save your report changes frequently, work from a copy of the report for complicated design changes, and compact and repair the database on a regular basis. You can also display the report in Print Preview at any time to view your progress on the report.

You'll create a blank report in Layout view, set the record source, and then add controls to the custom report.

To create a blank report and add bound controls in Layout view:

1. Click the **Create** tab, and then in the Reports group, click the **Blank Report** button. A new report opens in Layout view, with the Field List pane open, and the Report Layout Tools Design tab active on the ribbon. See Figure 7-13.

Figure 7-13 Blank report in Layout view

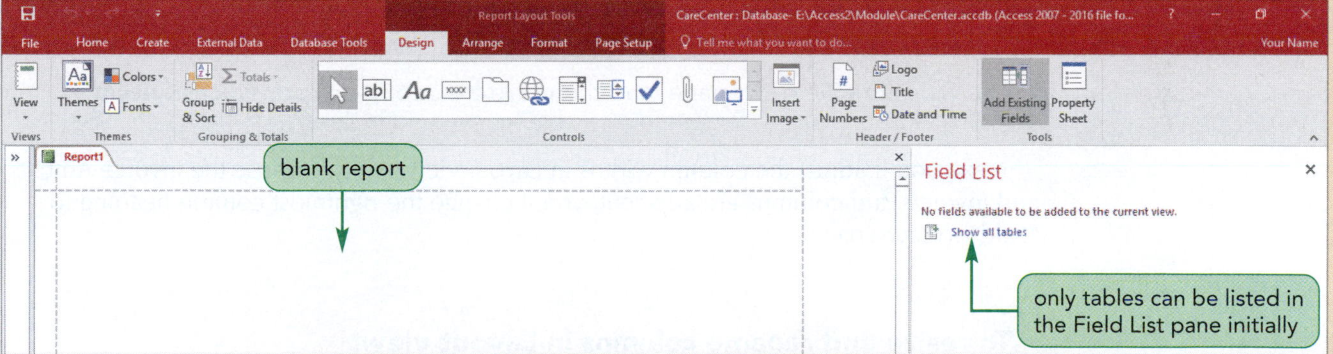

2. In the Tools group, click the **Property Sheet** button to open the Property Sheet for the report.
3. In the Property Sheet, click the **All** tab (if necessary), click the **Record Source** arrow, click **qryInvoicesByItem**, and then close the Property Sheet.
4. In the Tools group, click the **Add Existing Fields** button to open the Field List pane. The Field List pane displays the eight fields in the qryInvoicesByItem query, which is the record source for the report.

   Referring to Daksha's report design, you'll add six of the eight fields to the report in a tabular layout, which is the default control layout when you add fields to a report in Layout view.

5. In the Field List pane, double-click **InvoiceDate**, and then, in order, double-click **Owner**, **AnimalName**, **Reason**, **InvoiceAmt**, and **InvoicePaid** in the Field List pane. The six bound controls are displayed in a tabular layout in the report. See Figure 7-14.

Figure 7-14 Fields added to the report in Layout view

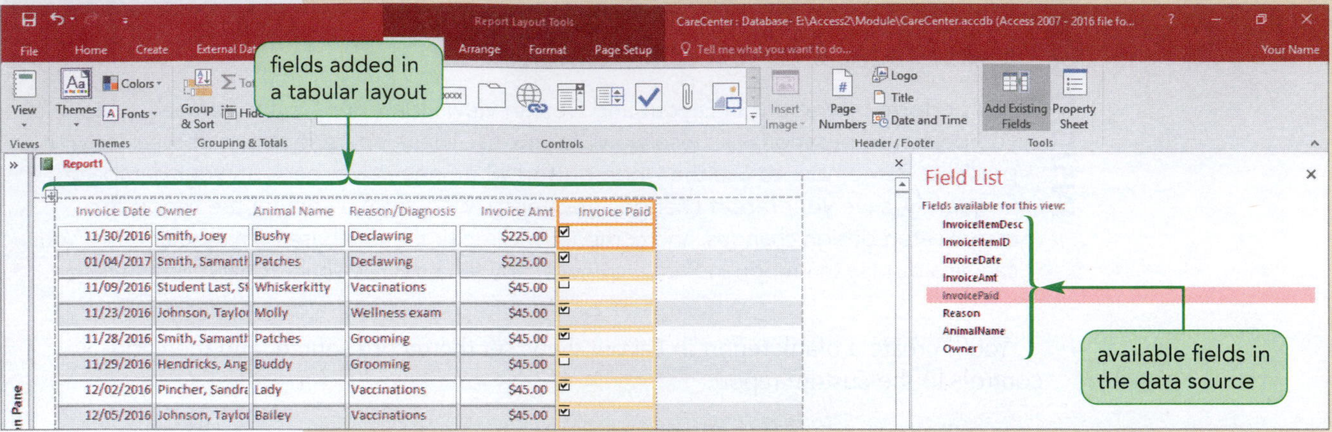

Trouble? If you add the wrong field to the report, click the field's column heading, press and hold the Shift key, click one of the field values in the column to select the column, release the Shift key, click the Home tab on the ribbon, and then in the Records group, click the Delete button to delete the field. If you add a field in the wrong order, click the column heading in the tabular layout, press and hold the Shift key, click one of the field values in the column, release the Shift key, and then drag the column to its correct position.

Later, you'll add the sixth field, the InvoiceItemDesc field, as a grouping field; for now you are done working with the Field List pane.

6. Close the Field List pane, and then save the report as **rptInvoicesByItem**.

Next, you'll adjust the column widths in Layout view. Also, because the Invoice Amt and Invoice Paid columns are adjacent, you'll change the rightmost column heading to "Paid" to save space.

To resize and rename columns in Layout view:

1. In the right-most column, double-click **Invoice Paid**, delete **Invoice** and the following space, and then press the **Enter** key.
2. Drag the right border of the Paid column heading selection box to the left to decrease the column's width so it just fits the column heading.
3. Click the **Owner** column heading to select the column, and then drag the right edge of the selection box to the right to increase its width, until it accommodates the contents of all data in the column. (You might need to scroll through the report to ensure all Owner field values are visible.)
4. Repeat Step 3 to resize the Animal Name and Reason columns, if necessary, as shown in Figure 7-15. (Note that Whiskerkitty is the longest animal name in the database.) You'll fine-tune the adjustments and the spacing between columns later in Design view.

Figure 7-15 Resized and renamed columns in Layout view

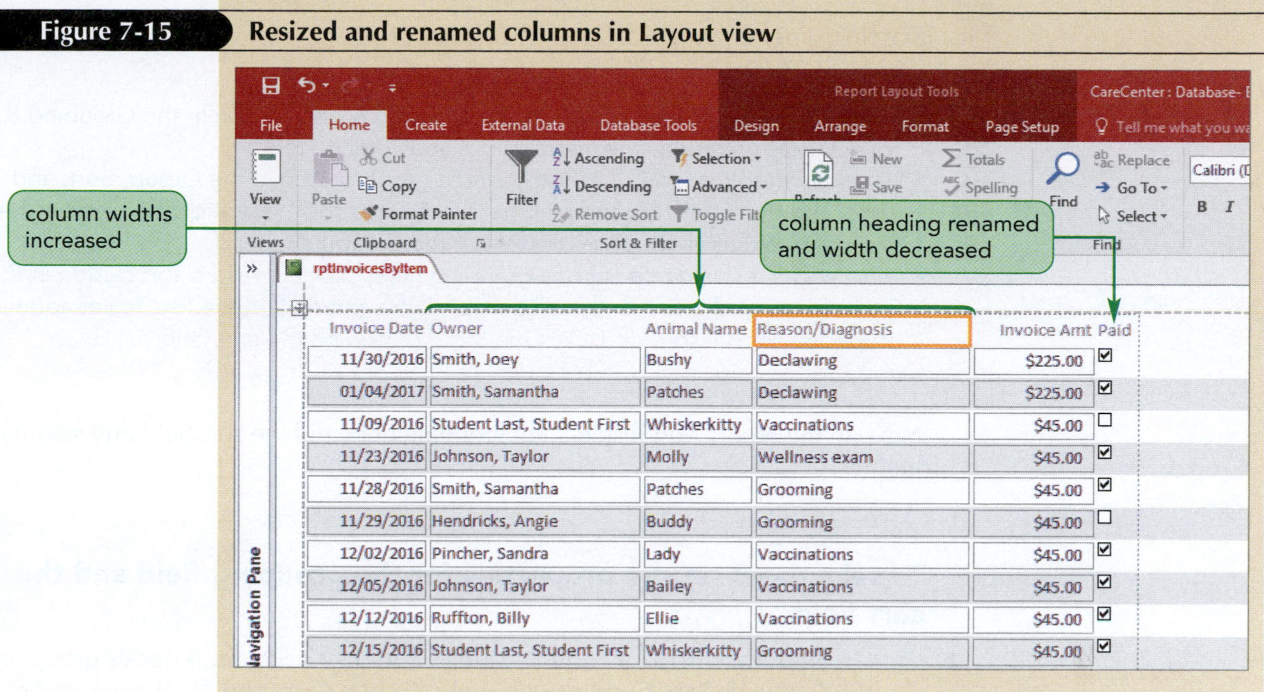

Next you need to add the sorting and grouping data to the report.

Sorting and Grouping Data in a Report

In Access, you can organize records in a report by sorting them using one or more sort fields. Each sort field can also be a grouping field. If you specify a sort field as a grouping field, you can include a Group Header section and a Group Footer section for the group. A Group Header section typically includes the name of the group, and a Group Footer section typically includes a count or subtotal for records in that group. Some reports have a Group Header section but not a Group Footer section, some reports have a Group Footer section but not a Group Header section, and some reports have both sections or have neither section.

You use the Group, Sort, and Total pane to select sort fields and grouping fields for a report. Each report can have up to 10 sort fields, and any of its sort fields can also be grouping fields.

In Daksha's report design, the InvoiceItemDesc field is a grouping field, and the InvoiceDate field is a sort field. The InvoiceItemDesc field value is displayed in a Group Header section, but the InvoiceItemDesc field label is not displayed. The sum of the InvoiceAmt field values is displayed in the Group Footer section for the InvoiceItemDesc grouping field.

REFERENCE

Sorting and Grouping Data in a Report

- Display the report in Layout view or Design view.
- If necessary, on the Design tab, click the Group & Sort button in the Grouping & Totals group to display the Group, Sort, and Total pane.
- To select a grouping field, click the Add a group button in the Group, Sort, and Total pane, and then click the grouping field in the list. To set additional properties for the grouping field, click the More button on the group field band.
- To select a sort field that is not a grouping field, click the Add a sort button in the Group, Sort, and Total pane, and then click the sort field in the list. To set additional properties for the sort field, click the More button on the sort field band.

Next, in the report, you'll select the grouping field and the sort field and set their properties.

To select and set the properties for the grouping field and the sort field:

1. On the Report Layout Tools Design tab, in the Grouping & Totals group, click the **Group & Sort** button to open the Group, Sort, and Total pane at the bottom of the Report window.
2. In the Group, Sort, and Total pane, click the **Add a group** button, and then click **InvoiceItemDesc** in the list. A Group Header section is added to the report with InvoiceItem as the grouping field, and group band options appear in the Group, Sort, and Total pane for this section. See Figure 7-16.

Figure 7-16 The InvoiceItemDesc as a grouping field in Layout view

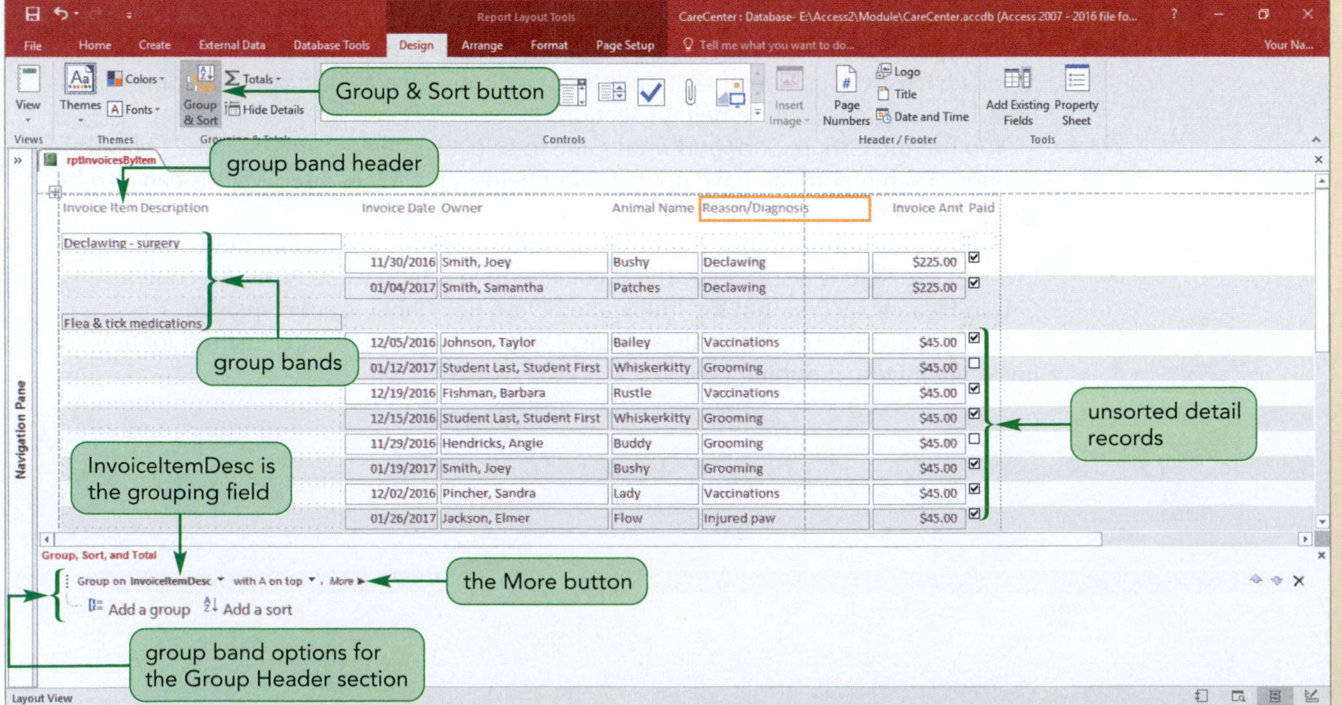

InvoiceItemDesc is now a bound control in the report in a Group Header section that displays a field value box. The group band options in the Group, Sort, and Total pane contain the name of the grouping field (InvoiceItem), the sort order ("with A on top" to indicate ascending), and the More button, which you click to display more options for the grouping field. You can click the "with A on top" arrow to change to descending sort order ("with Z on top").

Notice that the addition of the grouping field has moved the detail records to the right; you'll move them back to the left later in this module. Also, notice that the detail records are unsorted, but Daksha's design specifies an ascending sort on the InvoiceDate field. Next, you'll select this field as a secondary sort field; the InvoiceItem grouping field is the primary sort field.

3. In the Group, Sort, and Total pane, click the **Add a sort** button, and then click **InvoiceDate** in the list. The detail records appear in ascending order by InvoiceDate, and a sort band is added for the InvoiceDate field in the Group, Sort, and Total pane.

   Next, you'll display all the options for the InvoiceItemDesc group band field and set group band options as shown in Daksha's report design.

4. In the Group, Sort, and Total pane, click the **Group on InvoiceItemDesc (InvoiceItemDesc)**, and then click the **More** button to display all group band options in an orange bar at the top of the Group, Sort, and Total pane. See Figure 7-17. Next, you need to delete the Invoice Item label.

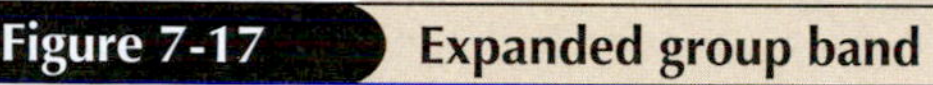

Figure 7-17 Expanded group band

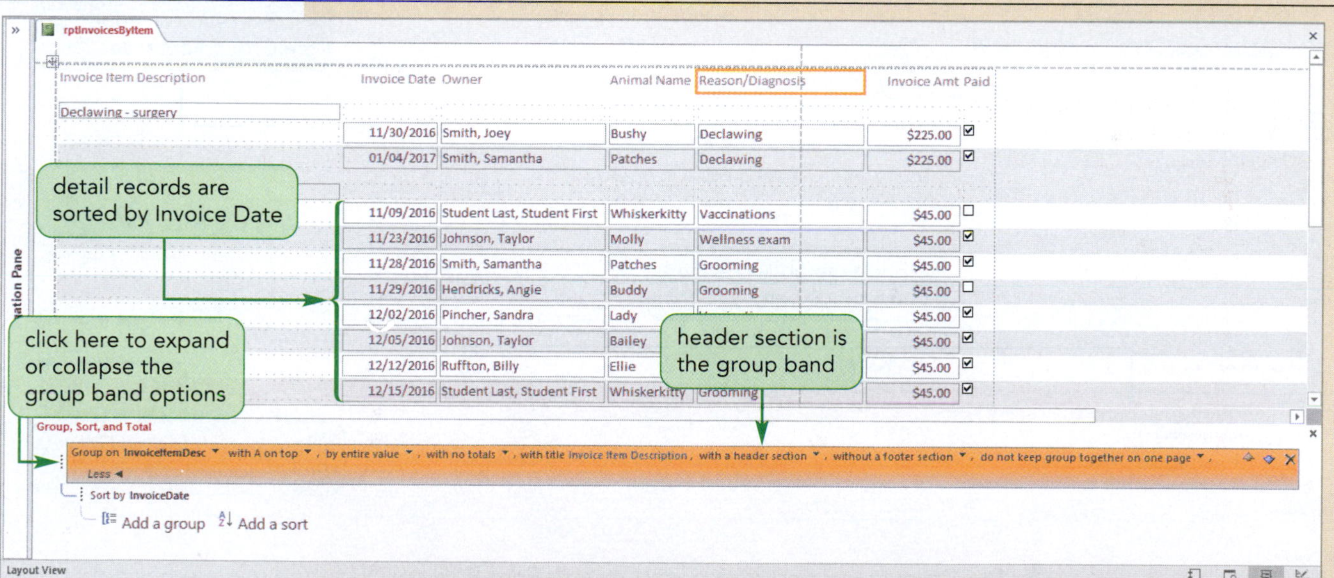

5. In the "with title Invoice Item Description" option, click the **Invoice Item Description** link to open the Zoom dialog box, press the **Delete** key to delete the expression, and then click the **OK** button. The Invoice Item label is deleted from the report, and the option in the group band options changes to "with title click to add."

   Next you'll set the Keep Together property. The **Keep Together property** prints a group header on a page only if there is enough room on the page to print the first detail record for the group; otherwise, the group header prints at the top of the next page.

6. In the group band options, click the **do not keep group together on one page** arrow, and then click **keep header and first record together on one page**.
7. In the group band options, click the **More** button to expand the options (if necessary), click the **without a footer section** arrow, and then click **with a footer section**. A Group Footer section is added to the report for the InvoiceItem grouping band field, but the report will not display this new section until you add controls to it.
8. In the group band options, click the **More** button to expand the options (if necessary), click the **with no totals** arrow to open the Totals menu, click the **Total On** arrow, click **InvoiceAmt**, make sure **Sum** is selected in the Type box, and then click the **Show Grand Total** check box.
9. In the group band options, click the **More** button to expand the options (if necessary), click the **with InvoiceAmt totaled** arrow, click the **Total On** arrow, click **InvoiceAmt**, and then click the **Show subtotal in group footer** check box. This adds subtotals in the Amount column, at the bottom of each group.
10. In the group band options, click the **More** button to expand the options (if necessary). The group band options show the InvoiceAmt subtotals, and a grand total added to the report. See Figure 7-18.

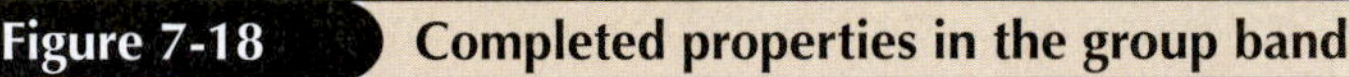

Figure 7-18 Completed properties in the group band

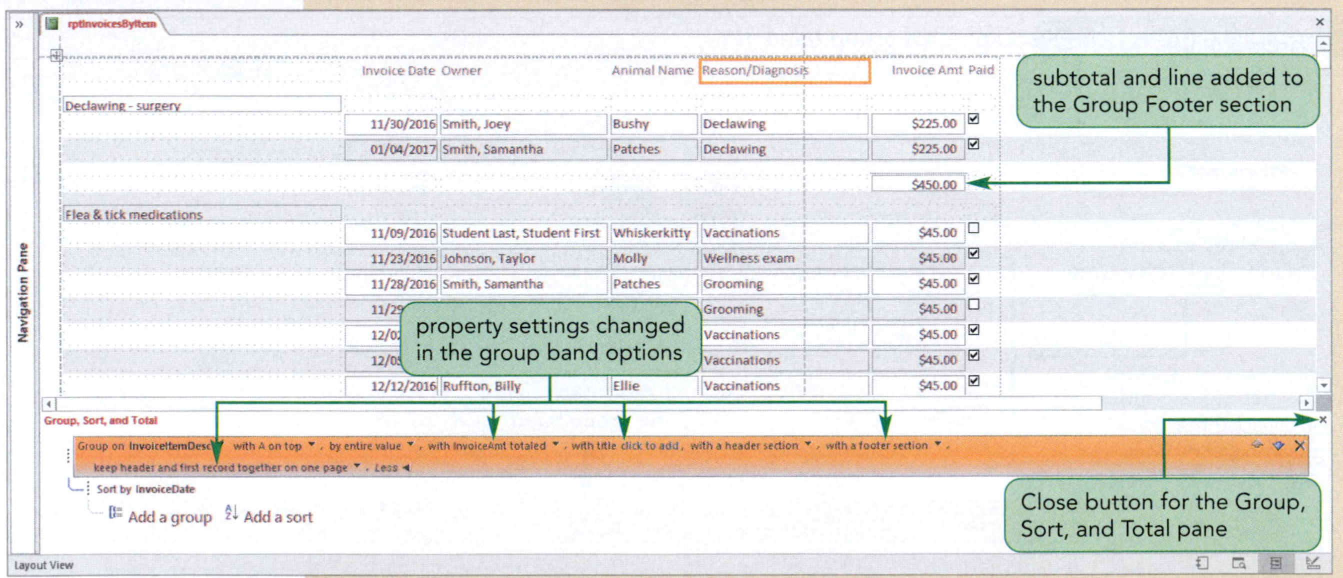

11. Save your report changes, switch to Print Preview, and then use the navigation buttons to review each page until you reach the end of the report—noticing in particular the details of the report format and the effects of the Keep Together property. Also, notice that because the grouping field forces the detail values to the right, the current report design prints the detail values across two pages.

Before you can move the detail values to the left onto one page, you need to remove all controls from the control layout.

To remove controls from a control layout in Layout view:

1. Switch to Layout view.
2. Click the layout selector ⊞, which is located at the top-left corner of the column heading line, to select the entire control layout. An orange selection border, which identifies the controls that you've selected, appears around the labels and field value boxes in the report, and a yellow outline appears around the other controls in the report.
3. Right-click one of the selected controls to open the shortcut menu, point to **Layout**, and then click **Remove Layout**. This removes the selected controls from the layout so they can be moved individually without affecting the other controls.

   Next you'll move all the controls to the left except for the InvoiceItemDesc field value box. You have to be careful when you move the remaining controls to the left. If you try to select all the column headings and the field value boxes, you're likely to miss the subtotal and grand total controls. The safest technique is to select all controls in the report, and then remove the InvoiceItemDesc field value box from the selection. This latter step, removing individual controls from a selection, must be done in Design view.
4. Switch to Design view, click the **Report Design Tools Format** tab, and then in the Selection group, click the **Select All** button. All controls in the report are now selected.
5. Press and hold the **Shift** key, click the **InvoiceItemDesc** control box in the InvoiceItemDesc Header section to remove this control from the selection, and then release the **Shift** key.
6. Press and hold the ← key to move the selected controls rapidly to the left edge of the report, and then release the ← key. See Figure 7-19.

Figure 7-19 All controls repositioned in the report

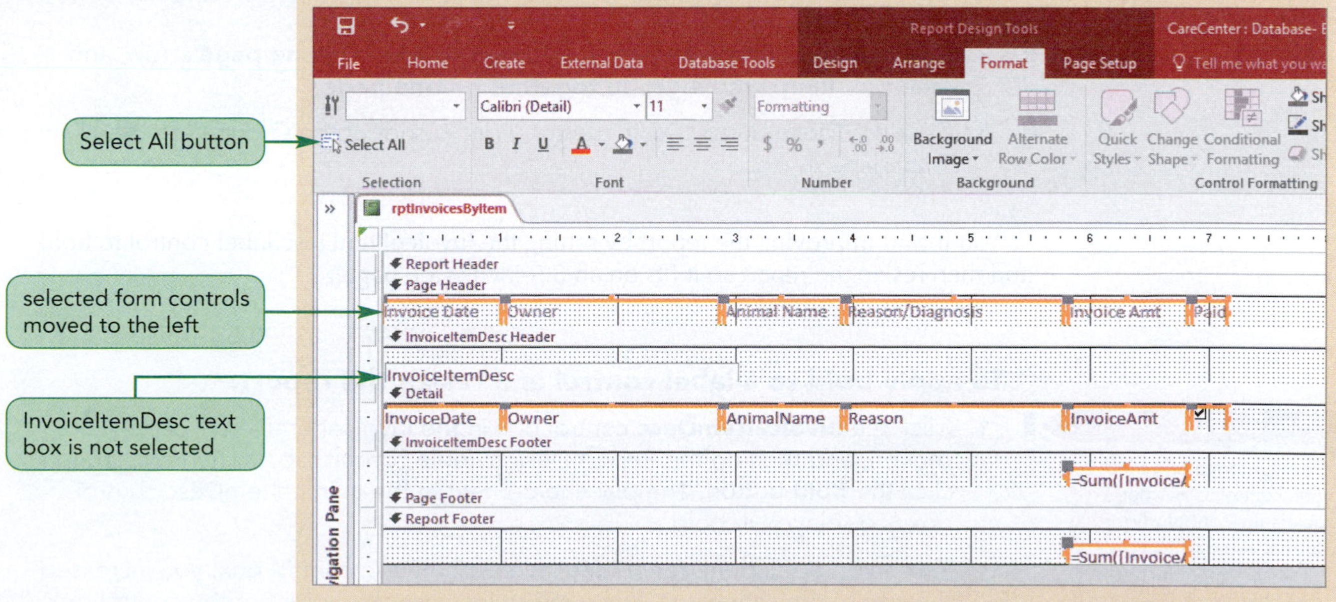

The grand total of the InvoiceAmt field values is displayed at the end of the report, and subtotals are displayed for each unique InvoiceItemDesc field value in the Group Footer section. It's possible for subtotals to appear in an orphaned footer section. An **orphaned footer section** appears by itself at the top of a page, and the detail lines for the section appear on the previous page. When you set the Keep Together property for the grouping field, you set it to keep the group and the first detail record together on one page to prevent an **orphaned header section**, which is a section that appears by itself at the bottom of a page. To prevent both types of orphaned sections, you'll set the Keep Together property to keep the whole group together on one page.

In addition, you need to fine-tune the sizes of the field value boxes in the Detail section, adjust the spacing between columns, and make other adjustments to the current content of the report design before adding a report title, the date, and page number to the Page Header section. You'll make most of these report design changes in Design view.

Working with Controls in Design View

As you learned when working with forms, Design view gives you greater control over the placement and sizing of controls than you have in Layout view and lets you add and manipulate many more controls; however, this power comes at the expense of not being able to see live data in the controls to guide you as you make changes.

The rptInvoicesByItem report has five sections that contain controls: the Page Header section contains the six column heading labels; the InvoiceItem Header section (a Group Header section) contains the InvoiceItemDesc field value box; the Detail section contains the six bound controls; the InvoiceItem Footer section (a Group Footer section) contains a line and the subtotal control; and the Report Footer section contains a line and the grand total control.

You'll format, move, and resize controls in the report in Design view. The Group, Sort, and Total pane is still open, so first you'll change the Keep Together property setting.

To change the Keep Together property:

1. In the Group, Sort, and Total pane, click the **More** button to display all group options.
2. Click the **keep header and first record together on one page** arrow, and then click **keep whole group together on one page**.
3. Click the **Close** button [X] in the top-right corner of the Group, Sort, and Total pane to close it.

You'll start improving the report by setting the InvoiceItemDesc label control to bold and then resize the report so it fits on an 8.5-inch-wide page.

To apply bold to a label control and resize the report:

TIP

To copy formatting from one control to another, select the control whose format you wish to copy, click the Format Painter tool on the Form Design Tools Format tab, and then click another control to apply the copied formatting.

1. Click the **InvoiceItemDesc** control box in the InvoiceItemDesc Header section, and then on the Report Design Tools Format tab, in the Font group, click the **Bold** button. The placeholder text in the InvoiceItemDesc control box is displayed in bold.

   When you bolded the font in the InvoiceItemDesc control box, you increased the size of the characters. You need to increase the height of the control box to fully display all characters.

2. Click the **InvoiceItemDesc** control box, and then increase the height of the control box from the top by one row of grid dots.

   The report's width is approximately 16 inches, which is much wider than the width of the contents of the report, so you'll reduce its width to fit a page that is 8.5 inches wide with narrow margins.

3. Click the **Report Design Tools Page Setup** tab, click the **Margins** button, and then click **Narrow**, if necessary.

4. Scroll to the right until you see the right edge of the report (where the dotted grid ends), position the pointer over the right edge of the report until it changes to ↔, drag to the left to the 8-inch mark on the horizontal ruler, and then drag the horizontal scroll box all the way to the left to display the entire report. See Figure 7-20.

Figure 7-20 **Width of the report reduced**

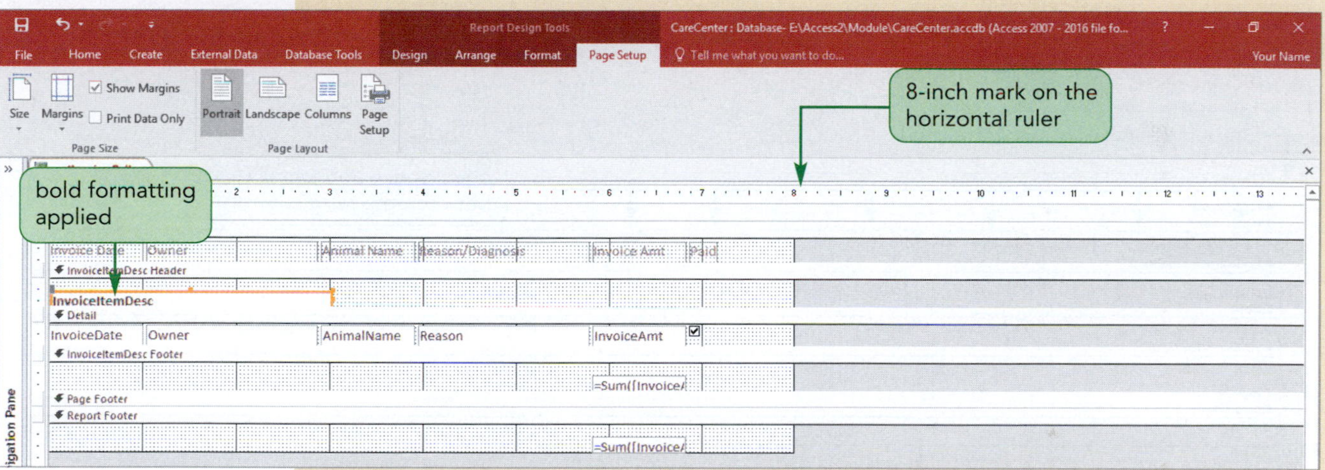

The field value control boxes in the Detail section are crowded together with little space between them. Your reports shouldn't have too much space between columns, but reports are easier to read when the columns are separated more than they are in the rptInvoicesByItem report. Sometimes the amount of spacing is dictated by the users of the report, but you also need to work with the minimum size of the form controls as well. To design this report to fit on a page with narrow margins, the report width will have to be 8.5 inches minus the left and right margins of 0.25 inches each, which results in a maximum report width of 8 inches (8.5"–0.25"–0.25"). This is the size you already used to reduce the report grid in Design view. Next, you'll add some space between the columns while ensuring they still fit in the 8-inch report width. First, you'll resize the Invoice Date and Owner columns in Layout view, and then you'll arrange the columns in Design view. You'll size the corresponding heading and field value boxes for each column to be the same width.

To move and resize controls in the report:

1. Switch to Layout view, click the **Invoice Date** column heading, press and hold the **Shift** key, and then click one of the **Invoice Date** field values to select all of the Invoice Date field value boxes.

2. Drag the right side of the controls to the left to reduce the size of the field value boxes to fit the data better.

TIP

You can resize labels and controls added with the Label tool using the To Fit command, but you can't resize field value boxes using the To Fit method.

3. Repeat Steps 1 and 2 for the Owner column heading and field values to reduce their widths to fit the data better, if necessary.

   Next you'll adjust the spacing between the controls to distribute them evenly across the page.

4. Switch to Design view, click the **Report Design Tools Format** tab, and then in the Selection group, click the **Select All** button to select all controls.
5. Press and hold the **Shift** key, and click the **InvoiceItemDesc** control to deselect it.
6. On the ribbon, click the **Report Design Tools Arrange** tab.
7. In the Sizing & Ordering group, click the **Size/Space** button, and then click **Equal Horizontal**. The form controls are shifted horizontally so the spacing between them is equal. See Figure 7-21.

Figure 7-21 **Equal horizontal spacing applied to controls in Design view**

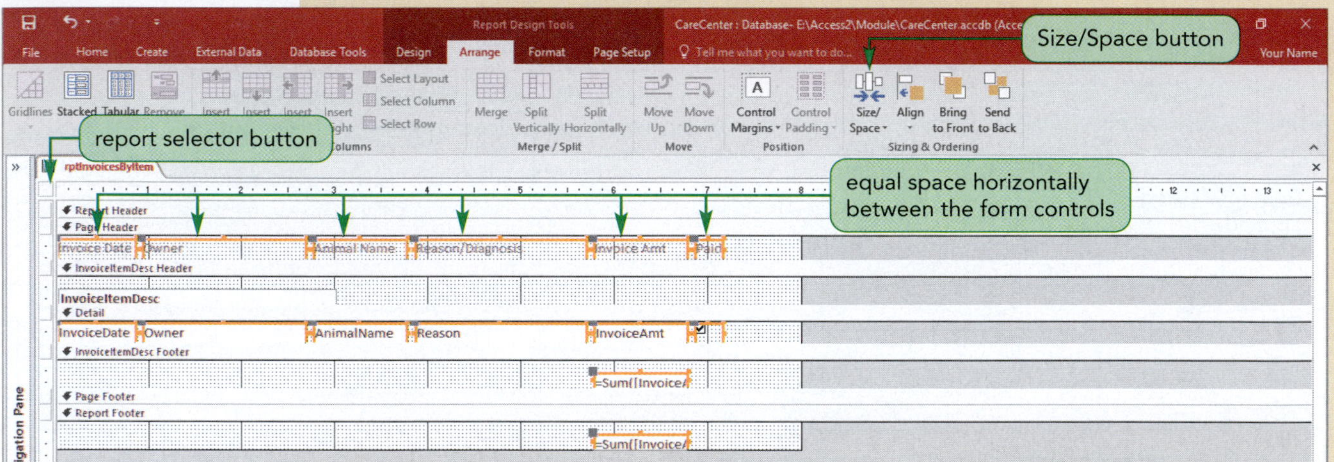

The Owner and Reason field value boxes may not be wide enough to display the entire field value in all cases. For the Owner and Reason field value boxes, you'll set their Can Grow property to Yes. The **Can Grow property**, when set to Yes, expands a field value box vertically to fit the field value when the report is printed, previewed, or viewed in Layout and Report views.

TIP

You can select two or more controls, and then set common properties for the selected controls, instead of setting them one control at a time.

8. Click the **Report Design Tools Design** tab, click the **Report Selector** button to deselect all controls, select the **Owner** and **Reason** field value control boxes in the Detail section, right-click one of the selected controls, and then on the shortcut menu click **Properties**.
9. On the Property Sheet, click the **Format** tab, scroll down the Property Sheet to locate the Can Grow property, and then if the Can Grow property is set to Yes, set it to **No**. The default setting for this feature may not work properly, so to ensure the setting is applied correctly, you must make sure it is first set to No.

   Trouble? If you don't see the Can Grow property on the Format tab, double-check to ensure you've selected the Owner and Reason controls in the Detail section, not in the Page Header section.

10. Change the Can Grow property value to **Yes**, close the Property Sheet, and then save your report changes.
11. Switch to Print Preview, and then review every page of the report, ending on the last page. See Figure 7-22.

Figure 7-22 The report changes in Print Preview

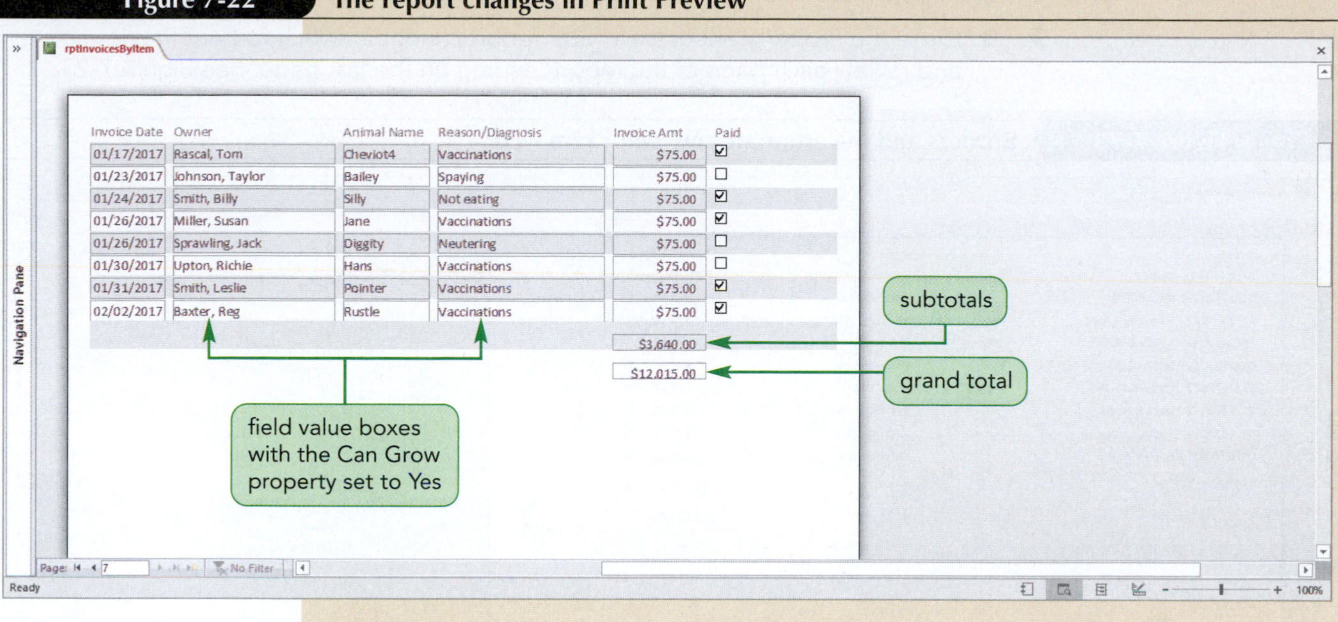

The groups stay together on one page, except for the groups that have too many detail lines to fit on one page. If necessary, the Can Grow property would expand the height of the Owner and Reason field value boxes.

Also, the lines that were displayed above the subtotals and grand total are no longer displayed, and the commas in the values are not fully visible. You'll add the totals lines back in the report and resize the field value boxes for the totals. First, Daksha thinks the borders around the field value boxes and the alternate row color are too distracting, so you'll remove them from the report.

To remove the borders and alternate row color:

1. Switch to Design view.
2. Click the **Report Design Tools Format tab**, and then in the Selection group, click the **Select All** button.
3. Right-click one of the selected controls, and then click **Properties** on the shortcut menu to open the Property Sheet.
4. Click the **Format** tab (if necessary) in the Property Sheet, click the right side of the Border Style box, and then click **Transparent**. The transparent setting removes the borders from the report by making them transparent.
5. Click the **InvoiceItemDesc Header** section bar, click the right side of the **Alternate Back Color** box in the Property Sheet, and then click **No Color** at the bottom of the gallery. This setting removes the alternate row color from the InvoiceItem Header section. You can also control the Alternate Back Color property using the Alternate Row Color button in the Background group on the Format tab, because the two options set the same property.
6. Click the **Detail** section bar, in the Background group, click the **Alternate Row Color button arrow**, and then click **No Color** at the bottom of the gallery. The Alternate Back Color property setting in the Property Sheet is now set to No Color.

7. Repeat Step 6 for the **InvoiceItemDesc Footer** section.
8. Close the Property Sheet, save your report changes, switch to Print Preview, and review each page of the report, ending on the last page. See Figure 7-23.

Figure 7-23 **Borders and the alternate row color removed**

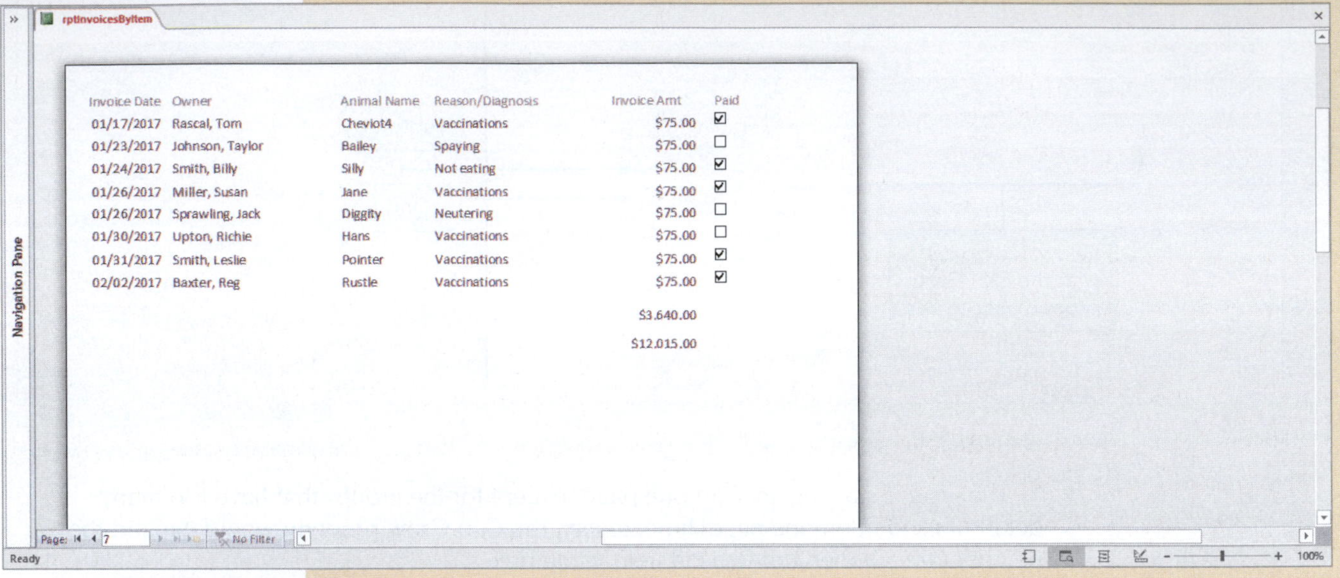

You still need to resize the subtotal and grand total field value boxes so that the comma separators fully display. In addition, you'll add lines to separate the values from the subtotals and grand total.

To resize the subtotals and grand totals field value boxes and add totals lines to the report:

1. Switch to Design view.
2. In the InvoiceItemDesc Footer section, click the calculated control box to select it, and then drag the upper-right sizing handle up to increase its height by one row of grid dots.
3. Repeat Step 2 to resize the calculated control box in the Report Footer section.
4. On the Report Design Tools Design tab, in the Controls group, click the **More** button to open the Controls gallery.
5. Click the **Line** tool, position the Line tool pointer's plus symbol in the InvoiceItemDesc Footer section in the upper-left corner of the calculated control box, press and hold the **Shift** key, drag from left to right so the line aligns with the top border of the calculated control box and ends at the upper-right corner of the calculated control box, release the mouse button, and then release the **Shift** key.
6. In the Report Footer section, click the calculated control box, press the ↓ key two times to move the control down slightly in the section, and then deselect all controls.

7. In the Controls group, click the **More** button, click the **Line** tool, position the pointer's plus symbol in the upper-left corner of the calculated control box, press and hold the **Shift** key, drag left to right so the line aligns with the top border of the calculated control box and ends at the upper-right corner of the calculated control box, release the mouse button, and then release the **Shift** key.

   The grand total line should have two lines separating it from the rest of the report. Next, you'll copy and paste the line you just created in the Report Footer section, and then align the copied line into position.

8. Right-click the selected line in the Report Footer section, and then click **Copy** on the shortcut menu.

9. Right-click the **Report Footer** section bar, and then click **Paste** on the shortcut menu. A copy of the line is pasted in the upper-left corner of the Report Footer section.

10. Press the ↓ key two times to move the copied line down in the section, press and hold the **Shift** key, click the first line in the Report Footer section to select both lines, and then release the **Shift** key.

11. Right-click the selected lines to open the shortcut menu, point to **Align**, and then click **Right**. A double line is now positioned above the grand total box.

12. Save your report changes, switch to Print Preview, and then navigate to the last page of the report. See Figure 7-24.

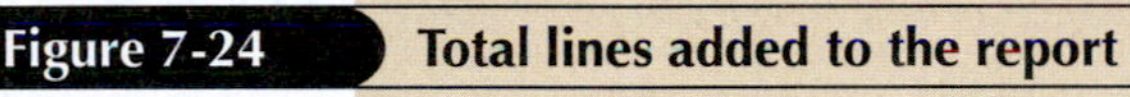

Figure 7-24 Total lines added to the report

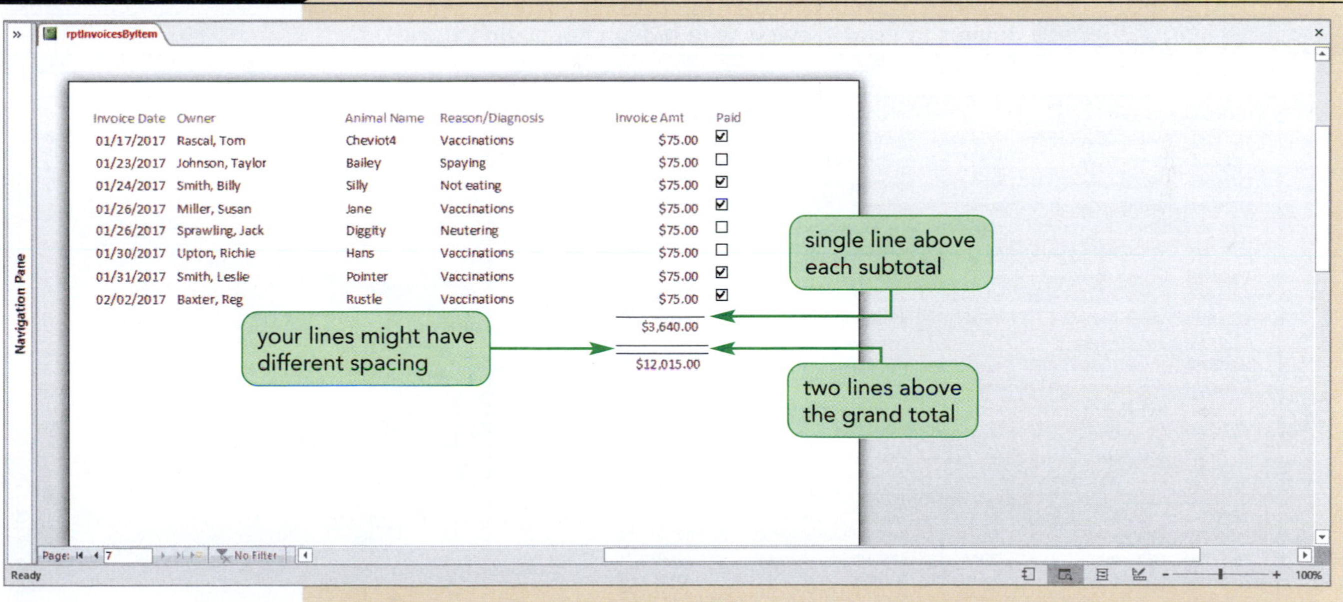

Your next design change to the report is to hide duplicate InvoiceDate field values in the Detail section. This change will make the report easier to read.

Hiding Duplicate Values in a Report

You use the **Hide Duplicates property** to hide a control in a report when the control's value is the same as that of the preceding record in the group. You should use the Hide Duplicates property only on fields that are sorted. Otherwise it may look as if data is missing.

For the rptInvoicesByItem report, the InvoiceDate field is a sort field. Two or more consecutive detail report lines can have the same InvoiceDate field value. In these cases, Daksha wants the InvoiceDate field value to appear for the first detail line but not for subsequent detail lines because he believes it makes the printed information easier to read.

To hide the duplicate InvoiceDate field values:

1. Switch to Design view, and then click a blank area of the screen to deselect all controls.
2. Open the Property Sheet for the InvoiceDate field value box in the Detail section.
3. Click the **Format** tab (if necessary), scroll down the Property Sheet, click the right side of the **Hide Duplicates** box, and then click **Yes**.
4. Close the Property Sheet, save your report changes, switch to Print Preview, navigate to page 1 (the actual page you view might vary, depending on your printer) to the Flea & tick medications group to see the two invoice records for 01/26/2017. The InvoiceDate field value does not display for the second of the two consecutive records with a 01/26/2017 date. See Figure 7-25.

TIP

For properties offering a list of choices, you can double-click the property name repeatedly to cycle through the option in the list.

Figure 7-25 Report in Print Preview with hidden duplicate values

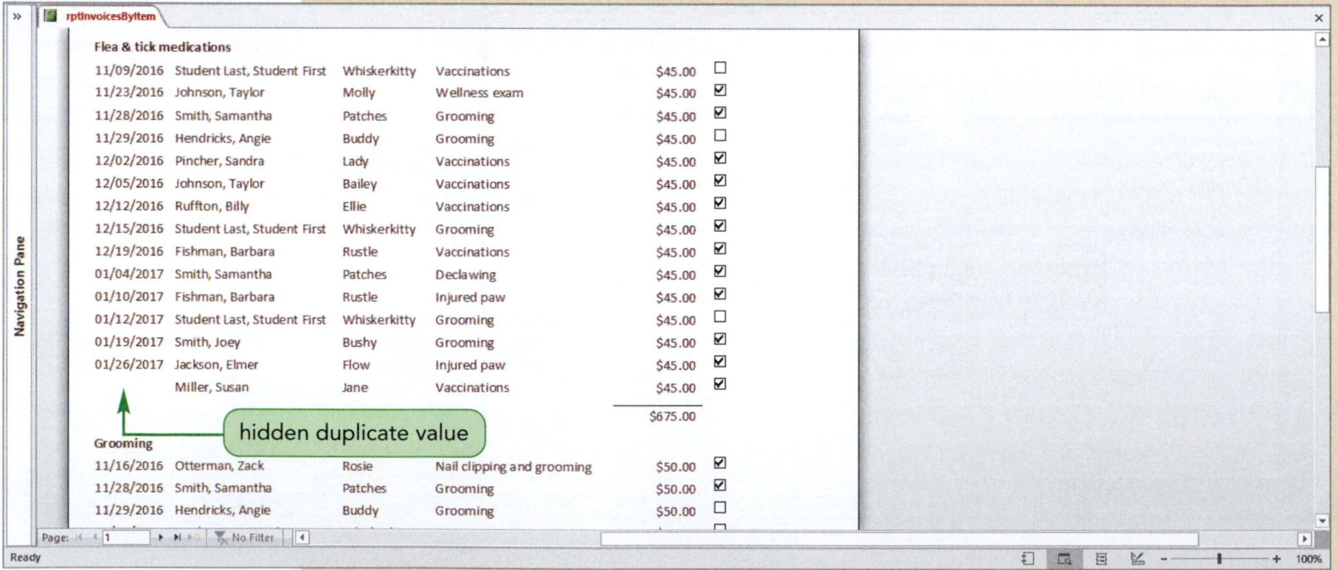

5. If you are not continuing on to the next session, close the CareCenter database.

You have completed the Detail section, the Group Header section, and the Group Footer section of the custom report. In the next session, you will complete the custom report according to Daksha's design by adding controls to the Page Header section.

REVIEW

Session 7.2 Quick Check

1. What is a detail report? A summary report?
2. The ______________ property prints a group header on a page only if there is enough room on the page to print the first detail record for the group; otherwise, the group header prints at the top of the next page.
3. A(n) ______________ section appears by itself at the top of a page, and the detail lines for the section appear on the previous page.
4. The ______________ property, when set to Yes, expands a field value box vertically to fit the field value when a report is printed, previewed, or viewed in Layout and Report views.
5. Why might you want to hide duplicate values in a report?

Session 7.3 Visual Overview:

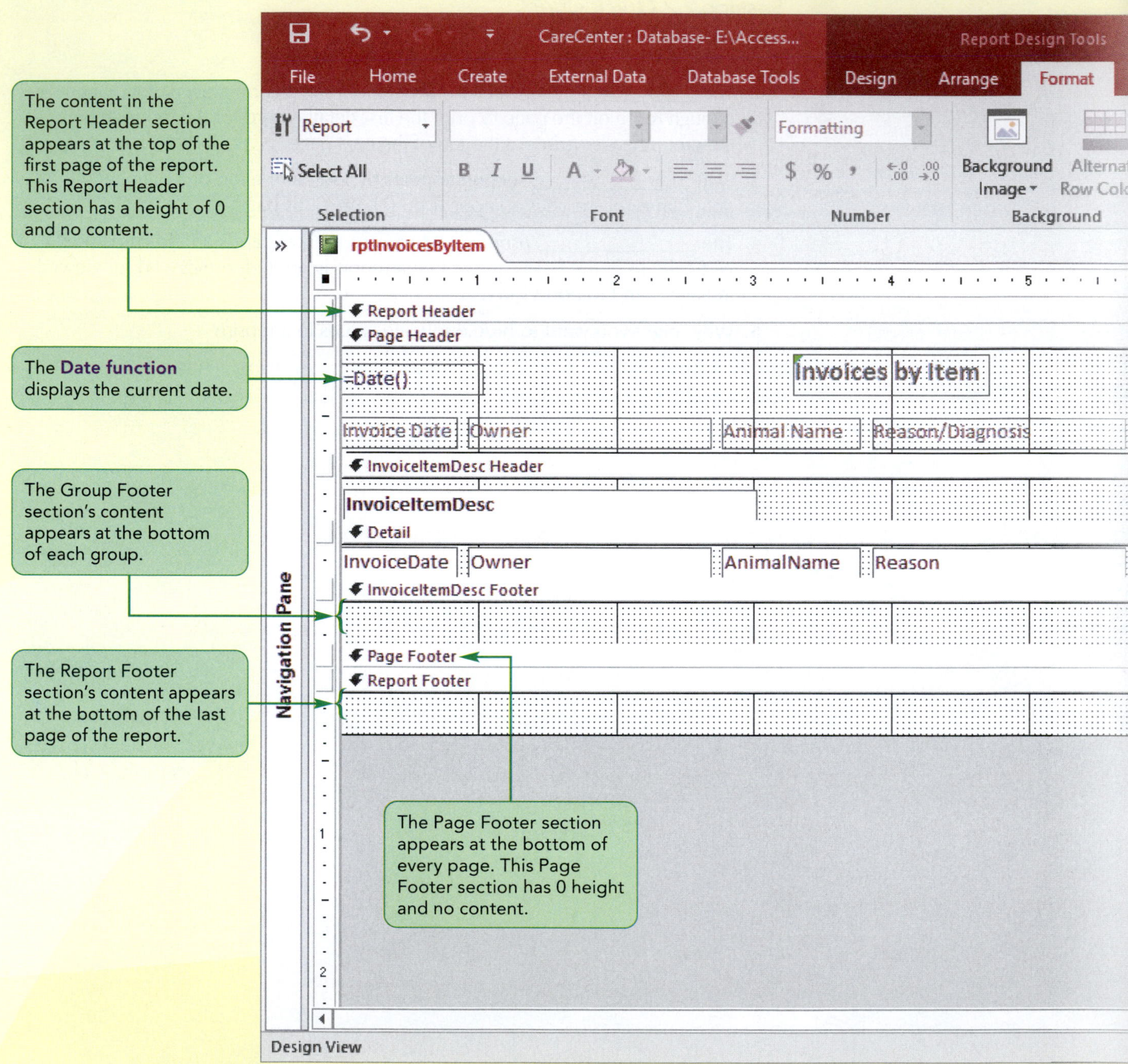

CareCenter : Database- E:\Access...
Report Design Tools
File
Home
Create
External Data
Database Tools
Design
Arrange
Format
Report
Select All
Formatting
Background Image
Alternat Row Colo
Selection
Font
Number
Background
rptInvoicesByItem
Navigation Pane
Report Header
Page Header
=Date()
Invoices by Item
Invoice Date
Owner
Animal Name
Reason/Diagnosis
InvoiceItemDesc Header
InvoiceItemDesc
Detail
InvoiceDate
Owner
AnimalName
Reason
InvoiceItemDesc Footer
Page Footer
Report Footer
Design View
The content in the Report Header section appears at the top of the first page of the report. This Report Header section has a height of 0 and no content.
The Date function displays the current date.
The Group Footer section's content appears at the bottom of each group.
The Report Footer section's content appears at the bottom of the last page of the report.
The Page Footer section appears at the bottom of every page. This Page Footer section has 0 height and no content.

Headers and Footers in Reports

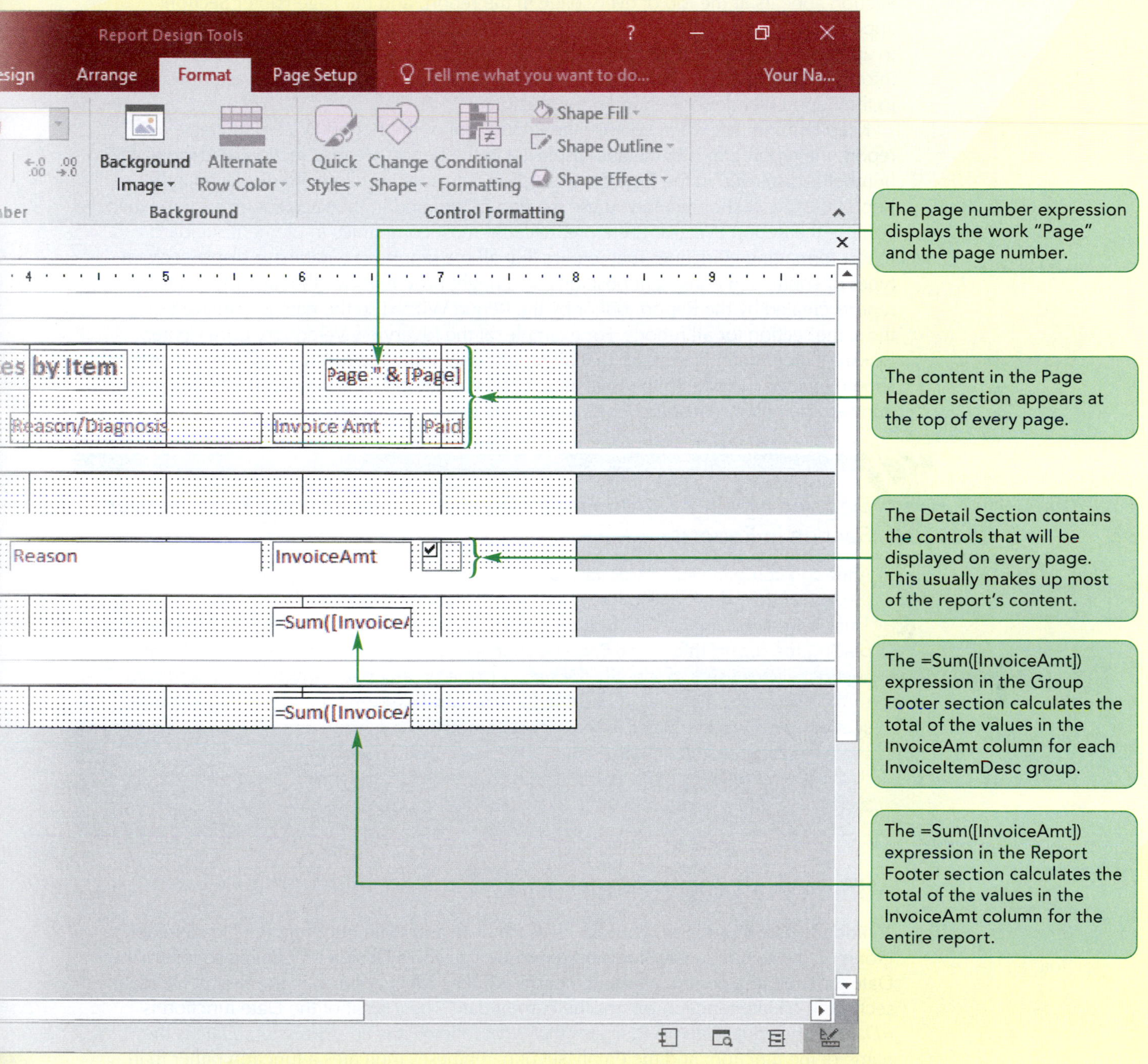
Report Design Tools
esign
Arrange
Format
Page Setup
Tell me what you want to do...
Your Na...
Background Image
Alternate Row Color
Quick Styles
Change Shape
Conditional Formatting
Shape Fill
Shape Outline
Shape Effects
nber
Background
Control Formatting
es by Item
Page " & [Page]
Reason/Diagnosis
Invoice Amt
Paid
Reason
InvoiceAmt
=Sum([InvoiceA
=Sum([InvoiceA
The page number expression displays the work "Page" and the page number.
The content in the Page Header section appears at the top of every page.
The Detail Section contains the controls that will be displayed on every page. This usually makes up most of the report's content.
The =Sum([InvoiceAmt]) expression in the Group Footer section calculates the total of the values in the InvoiceAmt column for each InvoiceItemDesc group.
The =Sum([InvoiceAmt]) expression in the Report Footer section calculates the total of the values in the InvoiceAmt column for the entire report.

Understanding Page Header and Page Footer Sections

Recall that in Access reports, the Report Header and Footer sections appear only once, at the top and bottom of the report, respectively. Comparatively, the Page Header Section appears at the top of every page in the report, and the Page Footer Section appears at the bottom of every page in the report. Therefore, if you want any information to appear consistently on every page in a multipage report, you want to place that information in the Page Header or the Page Footer sections of the report, as opposed to in the Report Header or Report Footer sections.

Keep in mind that when you use the Report tool or the Report Wizard to create a report, the report title is by default displayed in the Report Header section, and the page number is displayed in the Page Footer section. The date and time are displayed in the Report Header section when you use the Report tool and in the Page Footer section when you use the Report Wizard. Therefore, because most companies implement standard report-formatting guidelines that require that all the reports in a database display certain types of controls in consistent positions, you might have to move the date control for reports created by the Report tool or by the Report Wizard so the date is displayed in the same section for all reports. For example, at the Riverview Veterinary Care Center, Daksha's recommendations are that all reports, including the rptInvoicesByItem report, should include the date in the Page Header section, along with the report title, the page number, the column heading labels, and a line below the labels.

PROSKILLS

Decision Making: Determining Effective Content for the Page Header Section in Reports

Although company standards vary, a common standard for multipage reports places the report title, date, and page number on the same line in the Page Header section. This ensures this critical information appears on every page in the report. For example, placing the report title in the Page Header section, instead of in the Report Header section, allows users to identify the report name on any page without having to turn to the first page. Also, using one line to include this information in the Page Header section saves vertical space in the report compared to placing some of these controls in the Page Header section and others in the Page Footer section.

When you develop reports with a consistent format, the report users become more productive and more confident working with the information in the reports.

Adding the Date to a Report

To add the date to a report, you can click the Date and Time button in the Header/Footer group on the Report Layout Tools or Report Design Tools Design tab. Doing so inserts the Date function in a control (without a corresponding label control) in the Report Header section. The Date function returns the current date. The format of the Date function is *=Date()*. The equal sign (=) indicates that what follows it is an expression; *Date* is the name of the function; and the empty set of parentheses indicates a function rather than simple text.

REFERENCE

Adding the Date and Time to a Report

- Display the report in Layout or Design view.
- In Design view or in Layout view, on the Design tab, in the Header/Footer group, click the Date and Time button to open the Date and Time dialog box.
- To display the date, click the Include Date check box, and then click one of the three date option buttons.
- To display the time, click the Include Time check box, and then click one of the three time option buttons.
- Click the OK button.

In Daksha's design for the report, the date appears on the left side of the Page Header section. You'll add the date to the report and then cut the date from its default location in the Report Header section and paste it into the Page Header section. You can add the current date in Layout view or Design view. However, because you can't cut and paste controls between sections in Layout view, you'll add the date in Design view.

To add the date to the Page Header section:

1. If you took a break after the previous session, make sure that the CareCenter database is open, that the rptInvoicesByItem report is open in Design view, and that the Navigation Pane is closed.

   First, you'll move the column heading labels down in the Page Header section to make room for the controls you'll be adding above them.

2. In Design view, increase the height of the Page Header section by dragging the Page Header's bottom border down until the 1-inch mark on the vertical ruler appears.
3. Select all six label controls in the Page Header section, and then move the controls down until the tops of the label controls are at the 0.5-inch mark on the vertical ruler. You may find it easier to use the arrow keys, rather than the mouse, to position the label controls.

   Daksha's report design calls for a horizontal line below the labels. You'll add this line next.

4. On the Report Design Tools Design tab, in the Controls group, click the **More** button, click the **Line** tool, and then drag to create a horizontal line positioned one grid dot below the bottom border of the six label controls and spanning from the left edge of the Invoice Date label control and the right edge of the Paid label control.
5. Reduce the height of the Page Header section by dragging the bottom border of the section up until it touches the bottom of the line you just added.
6. In the Header/Footer group, click the **Date and Time** button to open the Date and Time dialog box, make sure the **Include Date** check box is checked and the **Include Time** check box is unchecked, and then click the third date format option button. See Figure 7-26.

Figure 7-26 Completed Date and Time dialog box

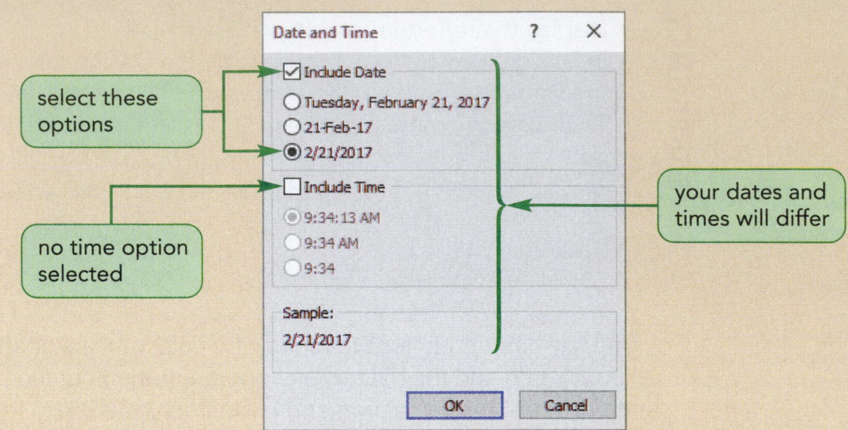

7. Click the **OK** button. The Date function control is added to the right side of the Report Header section.

8. Click the **Date function** control box, and then click the **layout selector** in the upper-left corner of the Report Header section. The Date function control box is part of a control layout with three additional empty control boxes. See Figure 7-27.

Figure 7-27 Date function added to the Report Header section

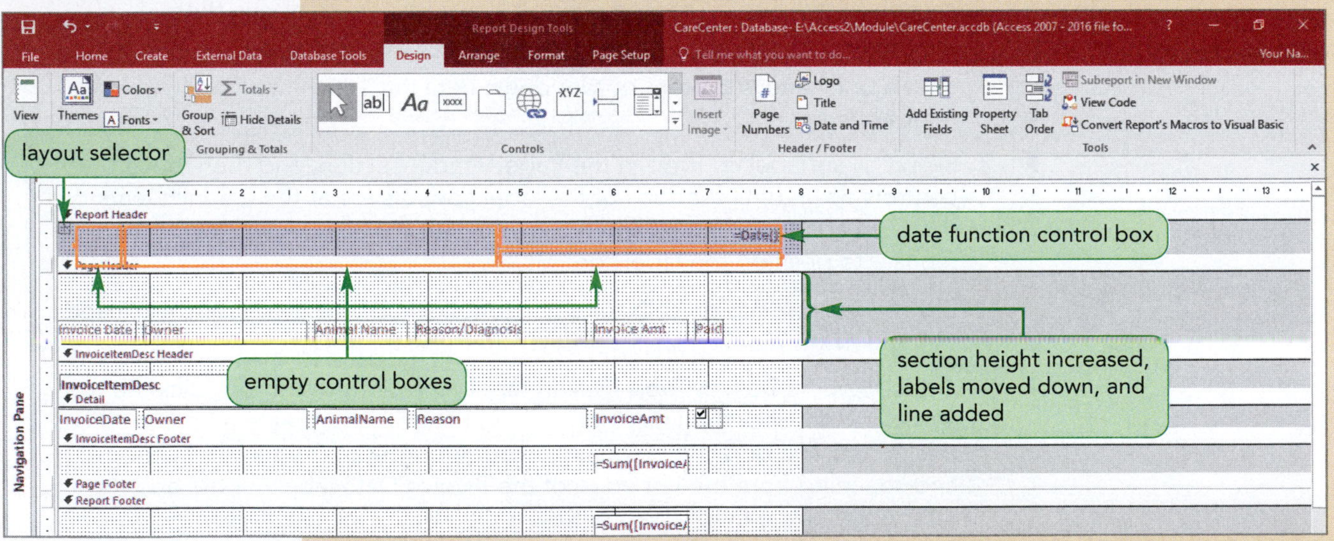

You need to remove these controls from the control layout before you work further with the Date function control box.

9. Right-click one of the selected control boxes, point to **Layout** on the shortcut menu, and then click **Remove Layout**. The three empty cells are deleted, and the Date function control box remains selected.

The default size for the Date function control box accommodates long dates and long times, so the control box is much wider than needed for the date that will appear in the custom report. You'll decrease its width and move it to the Page Header section.

10. Drag the left border of the Date function control box to the right until it is 1 inch wide.
11. Right-click the selected **Date function** control box to open the shortcut menu, click **Cut** to delete the control, right-click the **Page Header** section bar to select that section and open the shortcut menu, and then click **Paste**. The Date function control box is pasted in the upper-left corner of the Page Header section.
12. Save your report changes, and then switch to Print Preview to view the date in the Page Header section. See Figure 7-28.

Figure 7-28 **Date in Page Header Section in Print Preview**

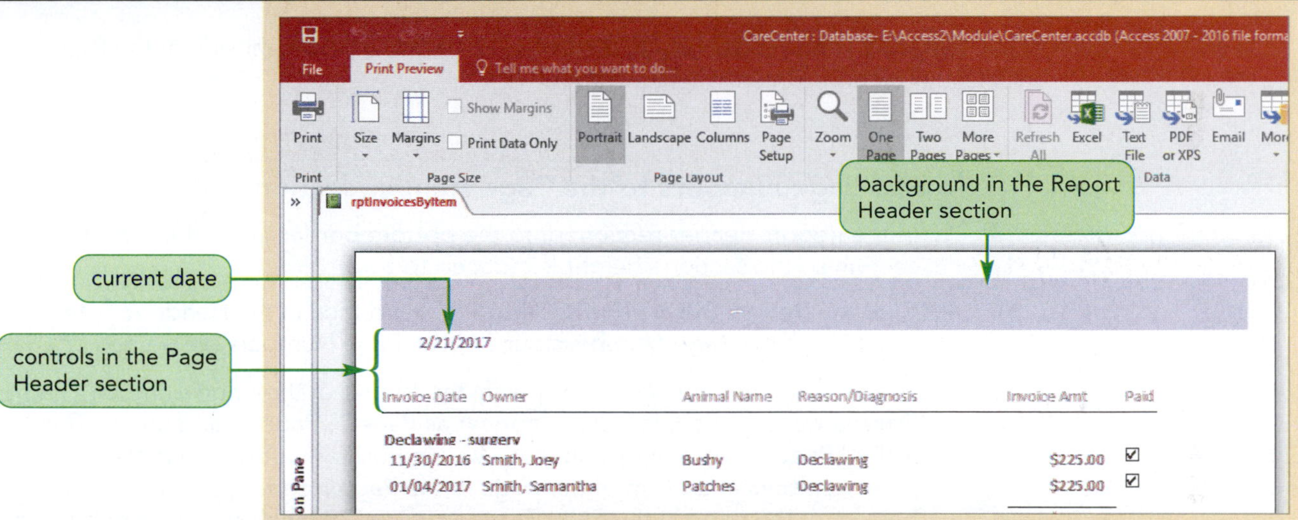

Trouble? Your year might appear with two digits instead of four digits as shown in Figure 7-28. Your date format might also differ, depending on your computer's date settings. These differences do not cause any problems.

Now that the date has been added to the Page Header section, you need to format and position it appropriately.

13. Switch to Design view, make sure the **Date function** control box is still selected, click the **Report Design Tools Format** tab, and then in the Font group, click the **Align Left** button.

If a report includes a control with the Date function, the current date will be displayed each time the report is run. If you instead want a specific date to appear each time the report is run, use a label control that contains the date, rather than the Date function.

You are now ready to add page numbers to the Page Header section. You'll also delete the empty Report Header section by decreasing its height to zero.

Adding Page Numbers to a Report

You can display page numbers in a report by including an expression in the Page Header or Page Footer section. In Report Layout Tools or Report Design Tools Design tab, you can click the Page Numbers button in the Header/Footer group to add a page number expression. The inserted page number expression automatically displays the correct page number on each page of a report.

REFERENCE

Adding Page Numbers to a Report

- Display the report in Layout or Design view.
- On the Design tab, click the Page Numbers button in the Header/Footer group to open the Page Numbers dialog box.
- Select the format, position, and alignment options you want.
- Select whether you want to display the page number on the first page.
- Click the OK button to place the page number expression in the report.

Daksha's design shows the page number displayed on the right side of the Page Header section, bottom-aligned with the date.

To add page numbers to the Page Header section:

1. In the Report Header section, drag the bottom border up to the top of the section so the section's height is reduced to zero.
2. Click the **Report Design Tools Design** tab, and then in the Header/Footer group, click the **Page Numbers** button. The Page Numbers dialog box opens.

   You use the Format options to specify the format of the page number. Daksha wants page numbers to appear as Page 1, Page 2, and so on. This is the "Page N" format option. You use the Position options to place the page numbers at the top of the page in the Page Header section or at the bottom of the page in the Page Footer section. Daksha's design shows page numbers at the top of the page.
3. In the Format section, make sure that the **Page N** option button is selected, and then in the Position section, make sure that the **Top of Page [Header]** option button is selected.

   The report design shows page numbers at the right side of the page. You can specify this placement in the Alignment box.
4. Click the **Alignment** arrow, and then click **Right.**
5. Make sure the **Show Number on First Page** check box is checked, so the page number prints on the first page and all other pages as well. See Figure 7-29.

Figure 7-29 **Completed Page Numbers dialog box**

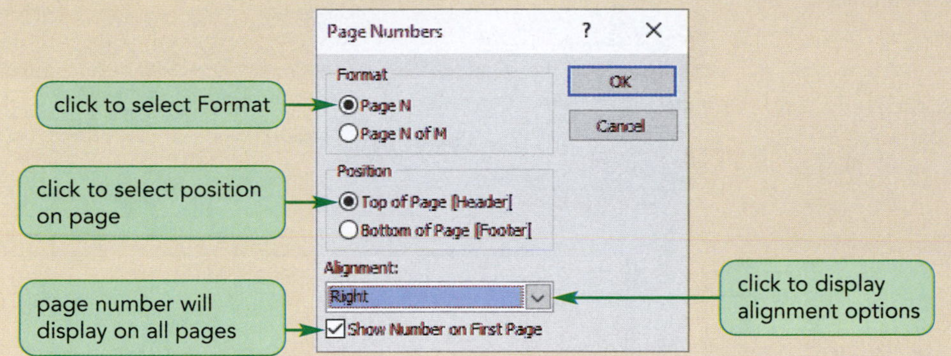

6. Click the **OK** button. A control box containing the expression *="Page " & [Page]* appears in the upper-right corner of the Page Header section. The expression *="Page " & [Page]* in the control box means that the printed report will show the word "Page" followed by a space and the page number. The page number control box is much wider than needed for the page number expression that will appear in the custom report. You'll decrease its width.
7. Click the **Page Number** control box, decrease its width from the left until it is 1 inch wide, and then move it to the left so its right edge aligns with the right edge of the Paid field value box. See Figure 7-30.

Figure 7-30 **Page number expression added to the Page Header section**

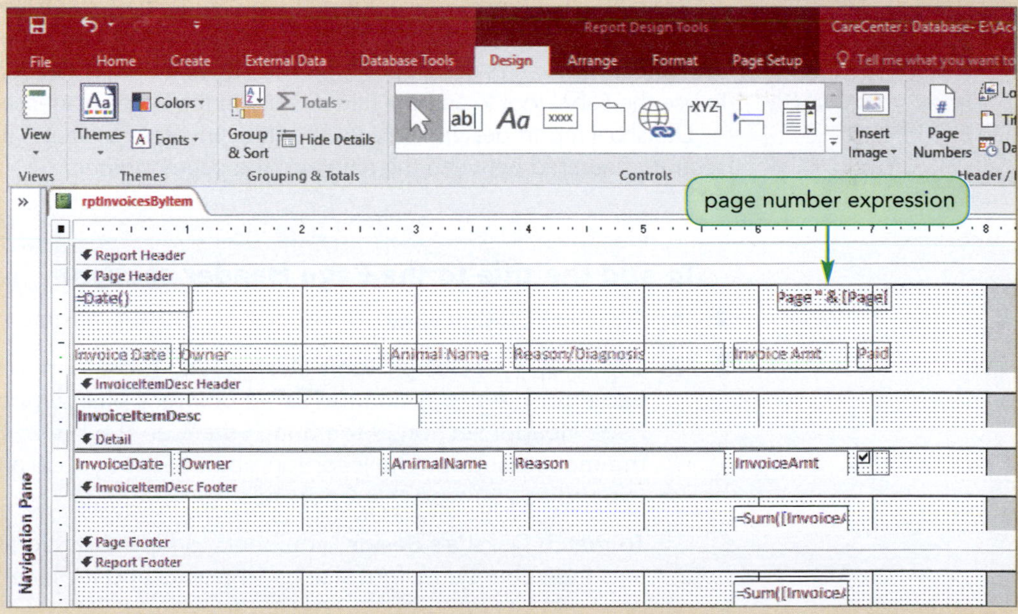

8. Save your report changes, and then switch to Print Preview. See Figure 7-31.

Figure 7-31 Date and page number in the Page Header section

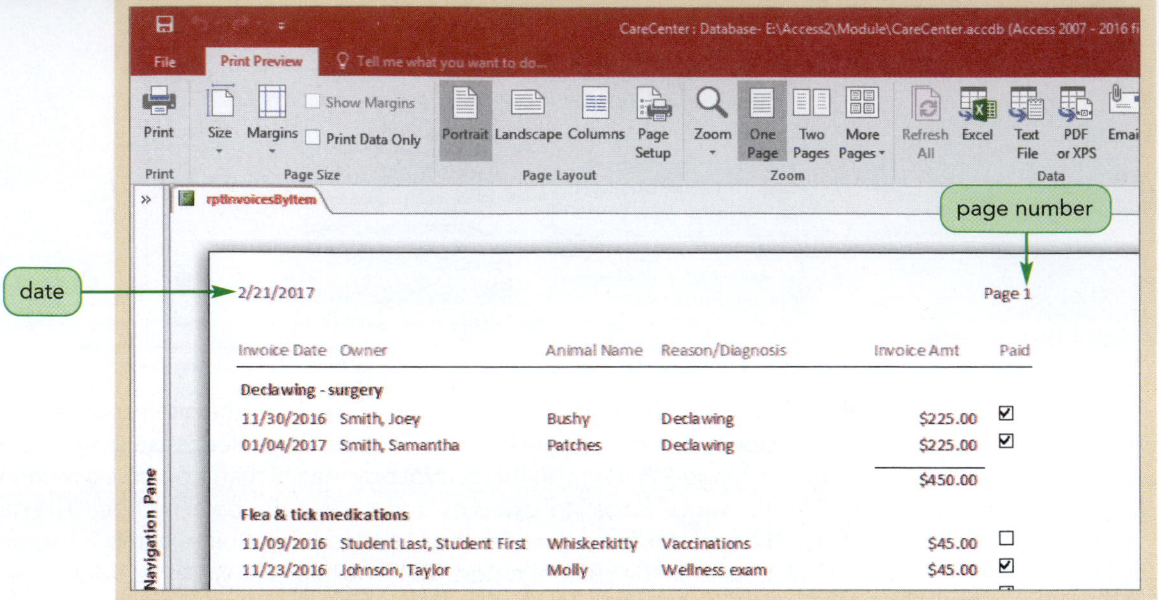

Now you are ready to add the title to the Page Header section.

Adding a Report Title to a Page Header Section

TIP

All reports should contain a title, either in the Report Header section to display only on the first page or in the Page Header section to display on all pages.

To add a title to a report, you use the Title button in the Header/Footer group on the Report Design Tools Design tab. However, doing so will add the title to the Report Header section, and Daksha's design positions the title in the Page Header section. It will be easier to use the Label tool to add the title directly in the Page Header section.

Daksha's report design includes the title "Invoices by Item" in the Page Header section, centered between the date and the page number.

To add the title to the Page Header section:

1. Switch to Design view.
2. On the Report Design Tools Design tab, in the Controls group, click the **Label** tool [Aa], position the Label pointer's plus symbol at the top of the Page Header section at the 3-inch mark on the horizontal ruler, and then click the mouse button. The insertion point flashes inside a narrow box, which will expand as you type the report title.

   To match Daksha's design, you need to type the title as "Invoices by Item" and then change its font size to 14 points and its style to bold.
3. Type **Invoices by Item** and then press the **Enter** key.
4. Click the **Report Design Tools Format** tab, in the Font group, click the **Font Size** arrow, click **14**, and then click the **Bold** button [B].
5. Resize the label control box to display the full title, increase the height of the label control box by two grid dots, and move the label control box to the right so it is centered at the 4-inch mark. See Figure 7-32.

Figure 7-32 Report title in the Page Header section

title font size

report title

center handles align with the 4-inch mark

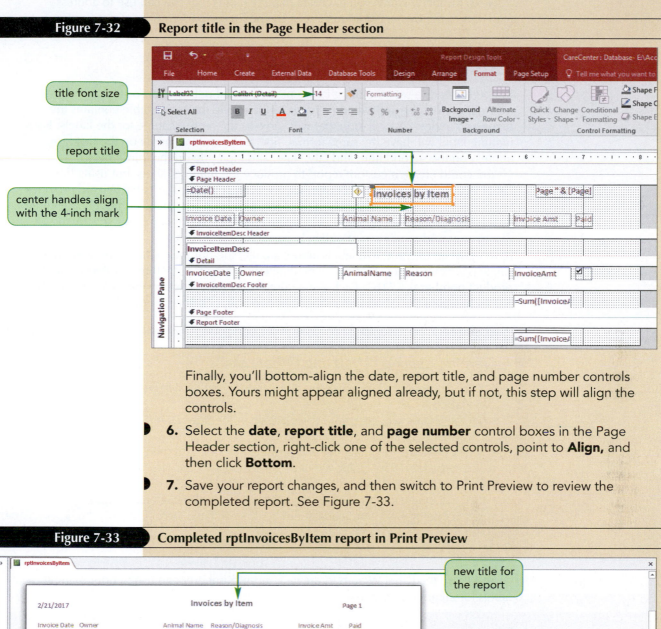

Finally, you'll bottom-align the date, report title, and page number controls boxes. Yours might appear aligned already, but if not, this step will align the controls.

6. Select the **date**, **report title**, and **page number** control boxes in the Page Header section, right-click one of the selected controls, point to **Align,** and then click **Bottom**.
7. Save your report changes, and then switch to Print Preview to review the completed report. See Figure 7-33.

Figure 7-33 Completed rptInvoicesByItem report in Print Preview

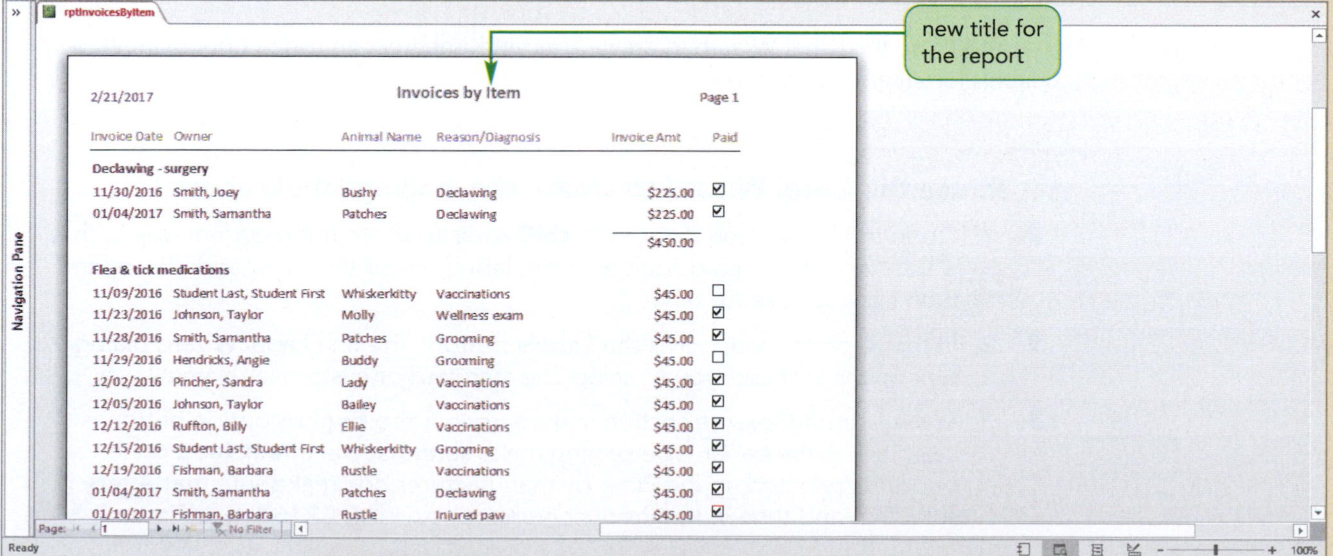

8. Close the report.

Next, Kimberly wants you to create mailing labels that she can use to address materials to the owners of animals seen by the Riverview Veterinary Care Center.

Creating Mailing Labels

Kimberly needs a set of mailing labels printed for all pet owners so she can mail a marketing brochure and other materials to them. The tblOwner table contains the name and address information that will serve as the record source for the labels. Each mailing label will have the same format: first name and last name on the first line; address on the second line; and city, state, and zip code on the third line.

You could create a custom report to produce the mailing labels, but using the Label Wizard is an easier and faster way to produce them. The **Label Wizard** provides templates for hundreds of standard label formats, each of which is uniquely identified by a label manufacturer's name and product number. These templates specify the dimensions and arrangement of labels on each page. Standard label formats can have between one and five labels across a page; the number of labels printed on a single page also varies. Kimberly's mailing labels are manufactured by Avery and their product number is C2163. Each sheet contains 12 labels; each label is 1.5 inches by 3.9 inches, and the labels are arranged in two columns and six rows on the page.

REFERENCE

Creating Mailing Labels and Other Labels

- In the Navigation Pane, click the table or query that will serve as the record source for the labels.
- On the Create tab, click the Labels button in the Reports group to start the Label Wizard and open its first dialog box.
- Select the label manufacturer and product number, and then click the Next button.
- Select the label font, color, and style, and then click the Next button.
- Construct the label content by selecting the fields from the record source and specifying their placement and spacing on the label, and then click the Next button.
- Select one or more optional sort fields, click the Next button, specify the report name, and then click the Finish button.

You'll use the Label Wizard to create a report Kimberly can use to print mailing labels for all animal owners.

To use the Label Wizard to create the mailing label report:

1. Open the Navigation Pane, click **tblOwner** to make it the current object that will serve as the record source for the labels, close the Navigation Pane, and then click the **Create** tab.
2. In the Reports group, click the **Labels** button. The first Label Wizard dialog box opens and asks you to select the standard or custom label you'll use.
3. In the Unit of Measure section make sure that the **English** option button is selected, in the Label Type section make sure that the **Sheet feed** option button is selected, in the Filter by manufacturer box make sure that **Avery** is selected, and then in the Product number box, click **C2163**. See Figure 7-34.

Figure 7-34 Label Wizard dialog box

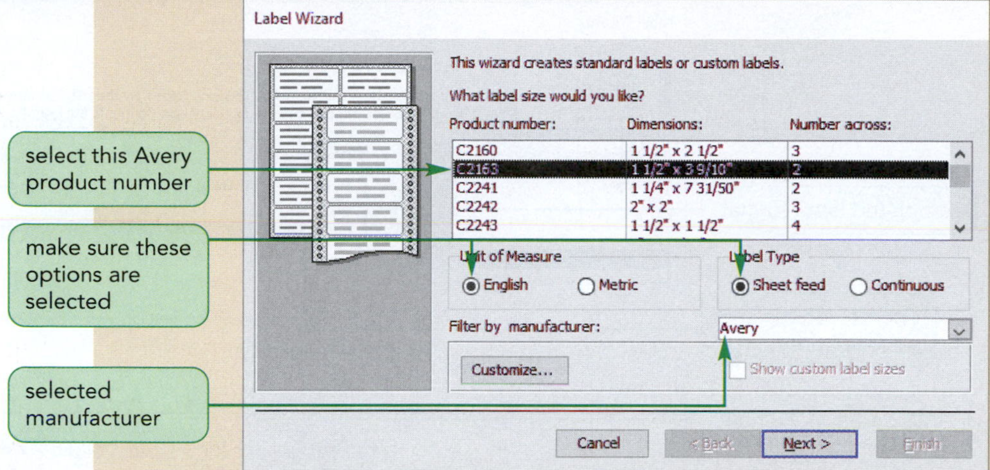

TIP

If your label manufacturer or its labels do not appear in the box, you can create your own custom format for them.

The top box shows the Avery product number, dimensions, and number of labels across the page for each of its standard label formats. You can display the dimensions in the list in either inches or millimeters by choosing the appropriate option in the Unit of Measure section. You specify in the Label Type section whether the labels are on individual sheets or are continuous forms.

4. Click the **Next** button to open the second Label Wizard dialog box, in which you choose font specifications for the labels.

   Kimberly wants the labels to use 10-point Arial with a medium font weight and without italics or underlines. The font weight determines how light or dark the characters will print; you can choose from nine values ranging from thin to heavy.

5. If necessary, select **Arial** in the Font name box, **10** in the Font size box, and **Medium** in the Font weight box, make sure the Italic and the Underline check boxes are not checked and that black is the text color, and then click the **Next** button. The third Label Wizard dialog box opens, in which you select the data to appear on the labels.

   Kimberly wants the mailing labels to print the FirstName and LastName fields on the first line, the Address field on the second line, and the City, State, and Zip fields on the third line. A single space will separate the FirstName and LastName fields, the City and State fields, and the State and Zip fields.

6. In the Available fields box, click **FirstName**, click the > button to move the field to the Prototype label box, press the **spacebar**, in the Available fields box click **LastName** (if necessary), and then click the > button. As you select fields from the Available fields box or type text for the label, the Prototype label box shows the format for the label. The braces around the field names in the Prototype label box indicate that the name represents a field rather than text that you entered.

   Trouble? If you select the wrong field or type the wrong text, click the incorrect item in the Prototype label box, press the Delete key to remove the item, and then select the correct field or type the correct text.

7. Press the **Enter** key to move to the next line in the Prototype label box, and then use Figure 7-35 to complete the entries in the Prototype label box. Make sure you type a comma and press the spacebar after selecting the City field, and you press the spacebar after selecting the State field.

Figure 7-35 Completed label prototype

Label Wizard

What would you like on your mailing label?

Construct your label on the right by choosing fields from the left. You may also type text that you would like to see on every label right onto the prototype.

Available fields: Address, City, State, Zip, Email

Prototype label:
{FirstName} {LastName}
{Address}
{City}, {State} {Zip}

completed label format

insert a comma and a space here

insert a space here

Cancel | < Back | Next > | Finish

8. Click the **Next** button to open the fourth Label Wizard dialog box, in which you choose the sort fields for the labels.

   Kimberly wants Zip to be the primary sort field and LastName to be the secondary sort field.

9. In the Available fields list, click the **Zip** field, click the > button to select Zip as the primary sort field, click the **LastName** field, click the > button to select LastName as the secondary sort field, and then click the **Next** button to open the last Label Wizard dialog box, in which you enter a name for the report.

10. Change the report name to **rptOwnerMailingLabels**, and then click the **Finish** button. The report is saved, and the first page of the report appears in Print Preview. Note that two columns of labels appear across the page. See Figure 7-36.

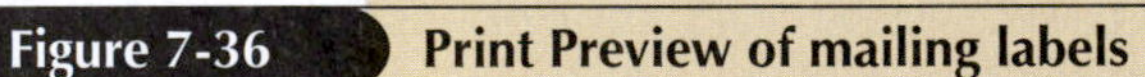

Figure 7-36 Print Preview of mailing labels

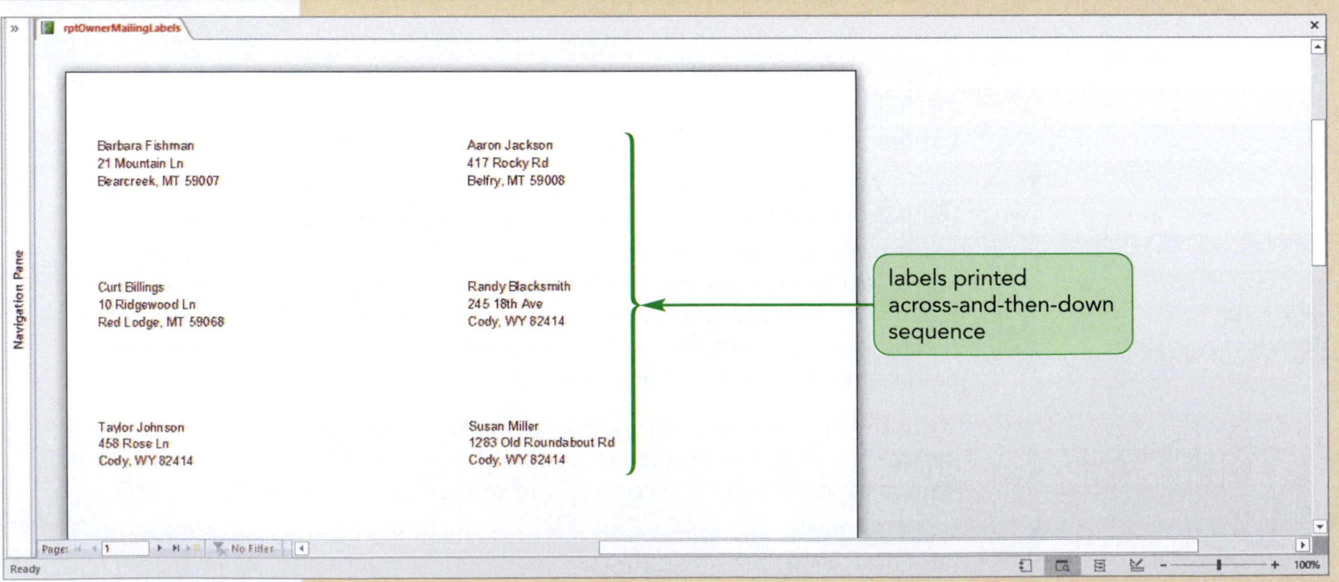

The rptOwnerMailingLabels report is a multiple-column report. The labels will be printed in ascending order by zip code and, within each zip code, in ascending order by last name. The first label will be printed in the upper-left corner on the first page, the second label will be printed to its right, the third label will be printed below the first label, and so on. This style of multiple-column report is the "across, then down" layout. Instead, Kimberly wants the labels to print with the "down, then across" layout because she prefers to pull the labels from the sheet in this manner. In this layout, the first label is printed, the second label is printed below the first, and so on. After the bottom label in the first column is printed, the next label is printed at the top of the second column. The "down, then across" layout is also called **newspaper-style columns** or **snaking columns**.

To change the layout of the mailing label report:

1. Switch to Design view. The Detail section, the only section in the report, is sized for a single label.

   First, you'll change the layout to snaking columns.

2. On the ribbon, click the **Report Design Tools Page Setup** tab.
3. In the Page Layout group, click the **Page Setup** button to open the Page Setup dialog box, and then click the **Columns** tab. The Page Setup dialog box displays the column options for the report. See Figure 7-37.

Figure 7-37 Columns tab in the Page Setup dialog box

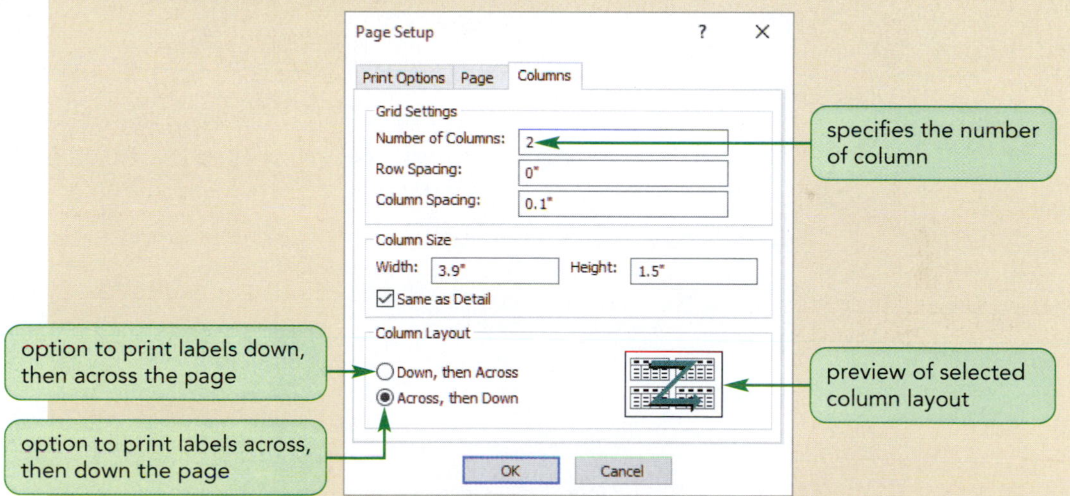

The options in the Page Setup dialog box let you change the properties of a multiple-column report. In the Grid Settings section, you specify the number of columns and the row and column spacing. In the Column Size section, you specify the width and height of each column set. In the Column Layout section, you specify the direction the information flows in the columns.

TIP

When you select a label using a manufacturer's name and product code, the options in the dialog box are set automatically.

4. Click the **Down, then Across** option button, and then click the **OK** button.

   You've finished the report changes, so you can now save and preview the report.

5. Save your report design changes, and then switch to Print Preview. The labels appear in the snaking columns layout.

   You've finished all work on Kimberly's reports.

6. Close the report, make a backup copy of the database, compact and repair the database, and then close it.

Kimberly is very pleased with the modified report and the two new reports, which will provide her with improved information and expedite her written communications with owners.

REVIEW

Session 7.3 Quick Check

1. What is the function and syntax to print the current date in a report?
2. How do you insert a page number in the Page Header section?
3. Must the page number reside only in the Page Header section?
4. Clicking the Title button in the Header/Footer group on the Report Design Tools Design tab adds a report title to the ______________ section.
5. What is a multiple-column report?

PRACTICE

Review Assignments

Data File needed for the Review Assignments: Supplier.accdb (cont. from Module 6)

Kimberly wants you to create a custom report for the Supplier database that prints all companies and the products they offer. She also wants you to customize an existing report. Complete the following steps:

1. Open the **Supplier** database you worked with in the previous two modules.
2. Modify the **rptSupplierDetails** report by completing the following steps:
   a. Change the report title to **Riverview Suppliers**.
   b. Remove the alternate row color from the detail lines in the report.
   c. Change the first column heading to Supplier ID. Change the fifth column heading to First Name and the sixth column heading to Last Name.
   d. In the Report Footer section, add a grand total count of the number of suppliers that appear in the report, make sure the calculated control box has a transparent border, and left-align the count with the left edge of the CompanyName field value box. Left-align the count value in the calculated control box.
   e. Add a label that contains the text **Suppliers:** to the left of the count of the total number of suppliers, aligned to the left margin, and aligned with the bottom of the count calculated control box.
   f. Set the margins to Normal, and adjust the width of the grid to 7.8 inches. Adjust the width of the controls in the Report Header to accommodate the corresponding data, ending up one grid point to the left of the width of the right margin.
   g. Move the page number control to the left until it is one grid dot to the left of the right margin. Right-align the page number value in the control box.
3. After you've completed and saved your modifications to the rptSupplierDetails report, filter the report in Report view, selecting all records that contain the word "supplies" in the Company field. Copy the headings and detail lines of the filtered report, and paste it into a new Word document. Save the document as **Supplies** in the location where you are storing your files. Close Word, save your changes to the Access report, and then close it.
4. Create a query that displays the Company and Category fields from the tblSupplier table and the ProductName, Price, and Units fields from the tblProduct table. Sort in ascending order by the first three fields in the query, and then save the query as **qrySupplierProducts**.
5. Create a custom report based on the qrySupplierProducts query. Figure 7-38 shows a sample of the completed report. Refer to the figure as you create the report. Distribute the fields horizontally to produce a visually balanced report.

Figure 7-38 Supplier database custom report

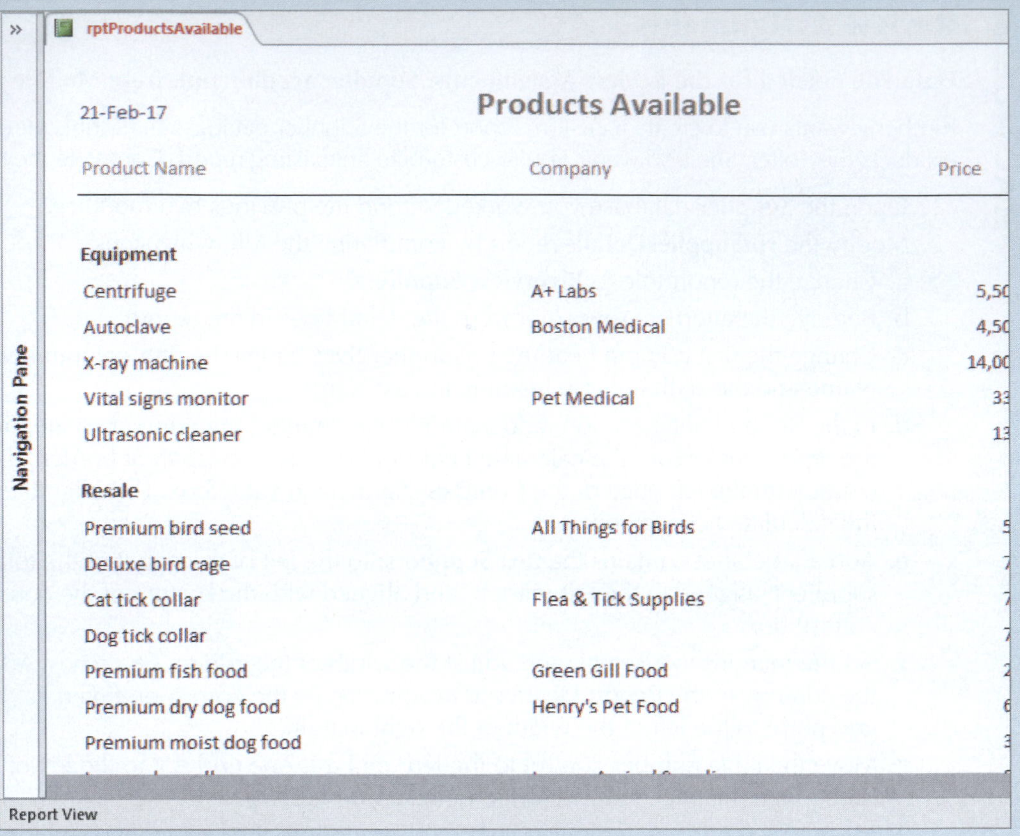

a. Save the report as **rptProductsAvailable**.
b. Use the Category field (from the tblSupplier table) as a grouping field, and use the Company field (from the tblSupplier table) as a sort field.
c. Hide duplicate values for the Company field.
d. Keep the whole group together on one page.
e. Remove the borders from the field value box.
f. Remove the alternate row color from the group header and detail line.
g. Add a Page title **Products Available** using 18-point font, centered horizontally.
h. Apply a text filter for companies that contain "Supplies" in the Company Name.

6. Create a mailing label report according to the following instructions:
   a. Use the tblSupplier table as the record source.
   b. Use Avery C2160 labels, and use the default font, size, weight, and color.
   c. For the prototype label, add the ContactFirst, a space, and ContactLast on the first line; the Company on the second line; the Address on the third line; and the City, a comma and a space, State, a space, and Zip on the fourth line.
   d. Sort by Zip and then by Company, and then name the report **rptCompanyMailingLabels**.
   e. Format the report with a three-column, across, then down page layout.
7. Make a backup copy of the database, compact and repair, and then close the Supplier database.

APPLY

Case Problem 1

Data File needed for this Case Problem: MoreBeauty.accdb (cont. from Module 6)

Beauty To Go Sue Miller wants you to create a custom report and mailing labels for the MoreBeauty database. The custom report will be based on the results of a query you will create. Complete the following steps:

1. Open the **MoreBeauty** database you worked with in the previous two modules.
2. Create a query that displays the OptionID, FeeWaived, OptionDescription, and OptionCost fields from the tblOption table, and the FirstName, and LastName fields from the tblMember table. Sort in ascending order by the OptionID, FeeWaived, and LastName fields, and then save the query as **qryOptionMembership**.
3. Create a custom report based on the qryOptionMembership query. Figure 7-39 shows a sample of the first page of the completed report. Refer to the figure as you create the report.

Figure 7-39 **MoreBeauty database custom report**

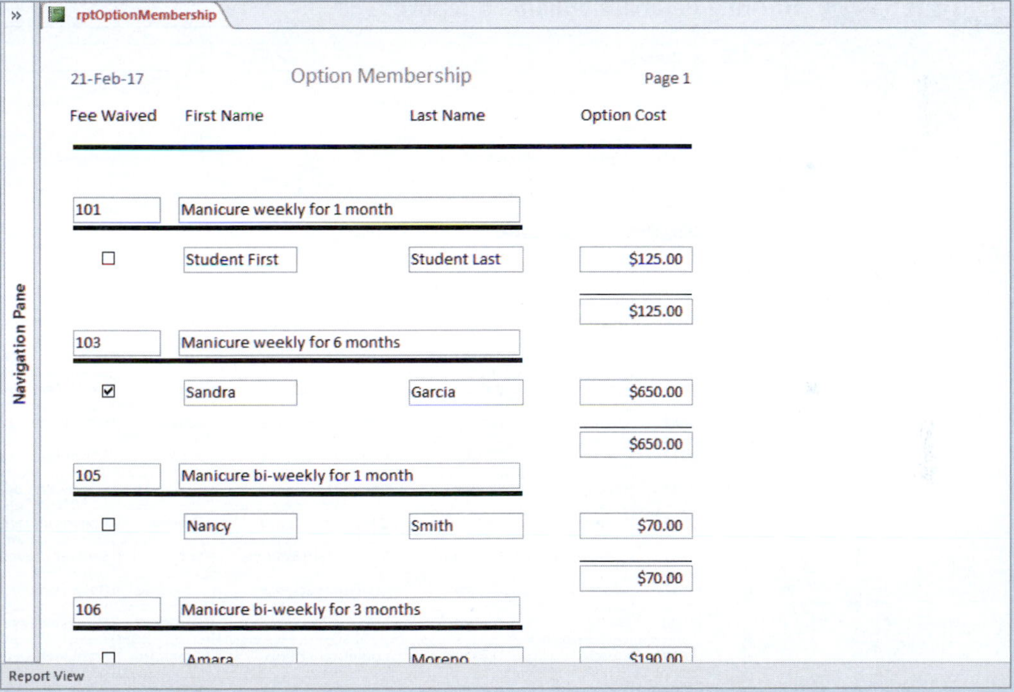

   a. Save the report as **rptOptionMembership**.
   b. Use the OptionID field as a grouping field.
   c. Select the FeeWaived field as a sort field, and the LastName field as a secondary sort field.
   d. Hide duplicate values for the FeeWaived field.
   e. Add the OptionDescription field to the Group Header section, and then delete its attached label.
   f. Keep the whole group together on one page.
   g. Use Narrow margins and spacing to distribute the columns evenly across the page.
   h. Remove the alternate row color for all sections.
   i. Use black font for all the controls, and set the lines' thickness to 3 pt.
4. Use the following instructions to create the mailing labels:
   a. Use the tblMember table as the record source for the mailing labels.
   b. Use Avery C2160 labels, and use the default font, size, weight, and color.

c. For the prototype label, place FirstName, a space, and LastName on the first line; Street on the second line; and City, a comma and space, State, a space, and Zip on the third line.
d. Sort by Zip and then by LastName, and then name the report **rptMemberLabels**.
e. Format the report with a three-column, across, then down page layout.

5. Make a backup copy of the database, compact and repair it, and then close the MoreBeauty database.

APPLY

Case Problem 2

Data File needed for this Case Problem: Tutoring.accdb (cont. from Module 6)

Programming Pros Brent Hovis wants you to modify an existing report and to create a custom report and mailing labels for the Tutoring database. Complete the following steps:

1. Open the **Tutoring** database you worked with in the previous two modules.
2. Modify the **rptTutorList** report. Figure 7-40 shows a sample of the first page of the completed report. Refer to the figure as you modify the report.

Figure 7-40 Tutoring database enhanced report

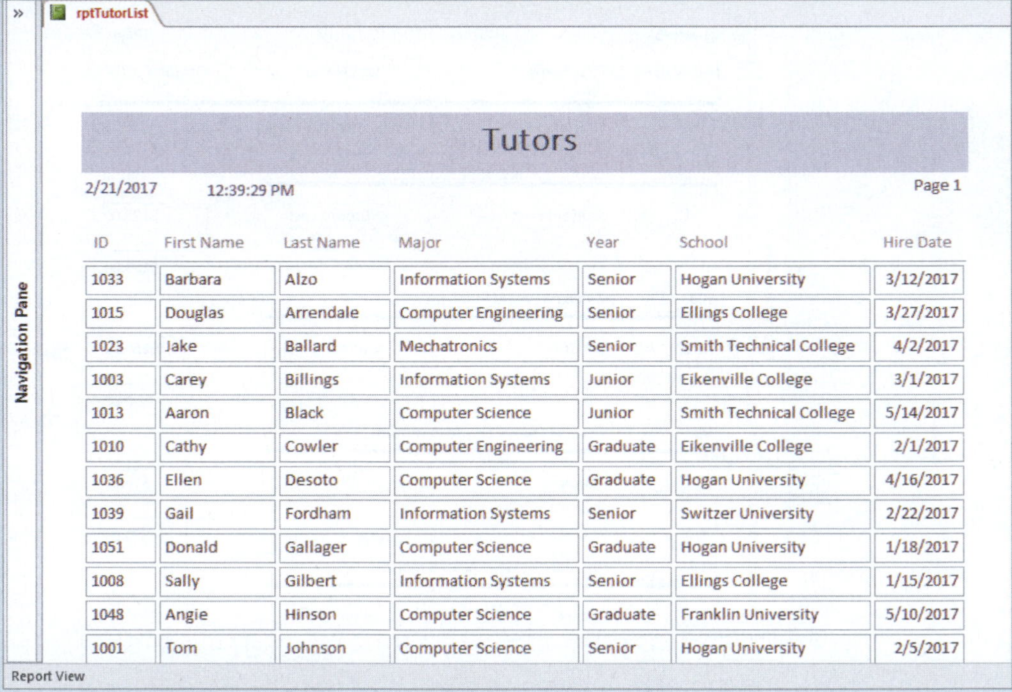

ID	First Name	Last Name	Major	Year	School	Hire Date
1033	Barbara	Alzo	Information Systems	Senior	Hogan University	3/12/2017
1015	Douglas	Arrendale	Computer Engineering	Senior	Ellings College	3/27/2017
1023	Jake	Ballard	Mechatronics	Senior	Smith Technical College	4/2/2017
1003	Carey	Billings	Information Systems	Junior	Eikenville College	3/1/2017
1013	Aaron	Black	Computer Science	Junior	Smith Technical College	5/14/2017
1010	Cathy	Cowler	Computer Engineering	Graduate	Eikenville College	2/1/2017
1036	Ellen	Desoto	Computer Science	Graduate	Hogan University	4/16/2017
1039	Gail	Fordham	Information Systems	Senior	Switzer University	2/22/2017
1051	Donald	Gallager	Computer Science	Graduate	Hogan University	1/18/2017
1008	Sally	Gilbert	Information Systems	Senior	Ellings College	1/15/2017
1048	Angie	Hinson	Computer Science	Graduate	Franklin University	5/10/2017
1001	Tom	Johnson	Computer Science	Senior	Hogan University	2/5/2017

a. Delete the picture at the top of the report.
b. Set Normal margins and a grid width of 7.8 inches.
c. Center the report title, and ensure the text is "Tutors", formatted in bold and 22-pt font.
d. Move the Hire Date column to the right margin, and center the Hire Date label value. Use horizontal spacing to evenly distribute the columns.
e. Remove the alternate row color from the detail lines in the report.
f. Change the page number format from "Page n of m" to "Page n," and right-align the text.
g. Move the date, time, and page number to the Page Header section.
h. Change the date format to short date, and left-align the date value.
i. Add a grand total control that calculates the total number of tutors, and add a label with the text "Total Tutors".
j. Sort the tutors by Last Name.

3. Create a query that displays, in order, the LastName and FirstName fields from the tblTutor table, the SessionType field from the tblContract table, the FirstName and LastName fields from the tblStudent table, and the NumSessions and Cost fields from the tblContract table. Sort in ascending order by the first three fields in the query, and then save the query as **qryTutorSessions**.
4. Create a custom report based on the qryTutorSessions query. Figure 7-41 shows a sample of the first page of the completed report. Refer to the figure as you create the report.

Figure 7-41 **Tutoring database custom report**

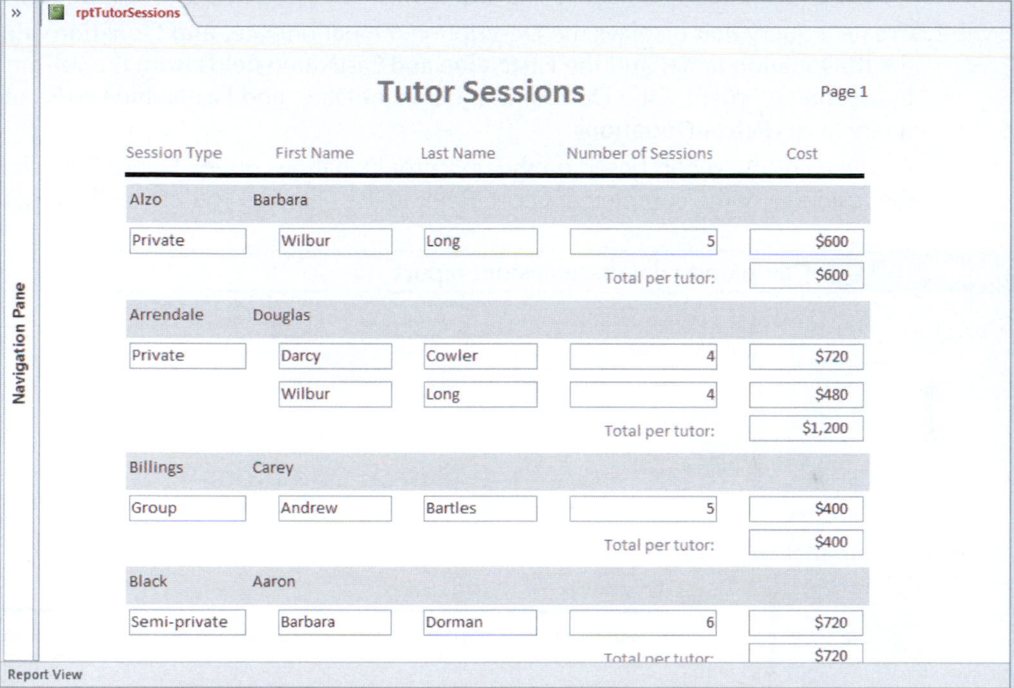

a. Save the report as **rptTutorSessions**.
b. The LastName field (from the tblTutor table) is a grouping field, and the FirstName field also appears in the Group Header section.
c. The SessionType field is a sort field, and the LastName field (from the tblStudent table) is a sort field.
d. Hide duplicate values for the SessionType field.
e. Use Wide margins, and set the grid width to 6.5 inches. Size fields as shown, and distribute horizontally using spacing to create a balanced look.
f. Set the background color for the grouped header and its controls to Gray-25% - Background 2 in the Theme colors.
g. In addition to the total for each tutor, give a grand total for all tutors with the label "Total for all tutors:"

5. Create a mailing label report according to the following instructions:
a. Use the tblStudent table as the record source.
b. Use Avery C2160 labels, use a 12-point font size, and use the other default font and color options.
c. For the prototype label, place FirstName, a space, and LastName on the first line; Address on the second line; and City, a comma and a space, State, a space, and Zip on the third line.
d. Sort by Zip and then by LastName, and then enter the report name **rptStudentMailingLabels**.
e. Change the page layout of the rptStudentMailingLabels report to three snaking columns.

6. Make a backup copy of the database, compact and repair it, and then close the Tutoring database.

CREATE

Case Problem 3

Data File needed for this Case Problem: Community.accdb (cont. from Module 6)

Diane's Community Center Diane Coleman asks you to create a custom report for the Community database so that she can better track donations made by donors and to create mailing labels. Complete the following steps:

1. Open the **Community** database you worked with in the previous two modules.
2. Create a query that displays the Description, DonationDate, and DonationValue fields from the tblDonation table, and the FirstName and LastName fields from the tblPatron table. Sort in ascending order by the Description, DonationDate, and LastName fields, and then save the query as **qryPatronDonations**.
3. Create a custom report based on the qryPatronDonations query. Figure 7-42 shows a sample of the first page of the completed report. Refer to the figure as you create the report.

Figure 7-42 Community database custom report

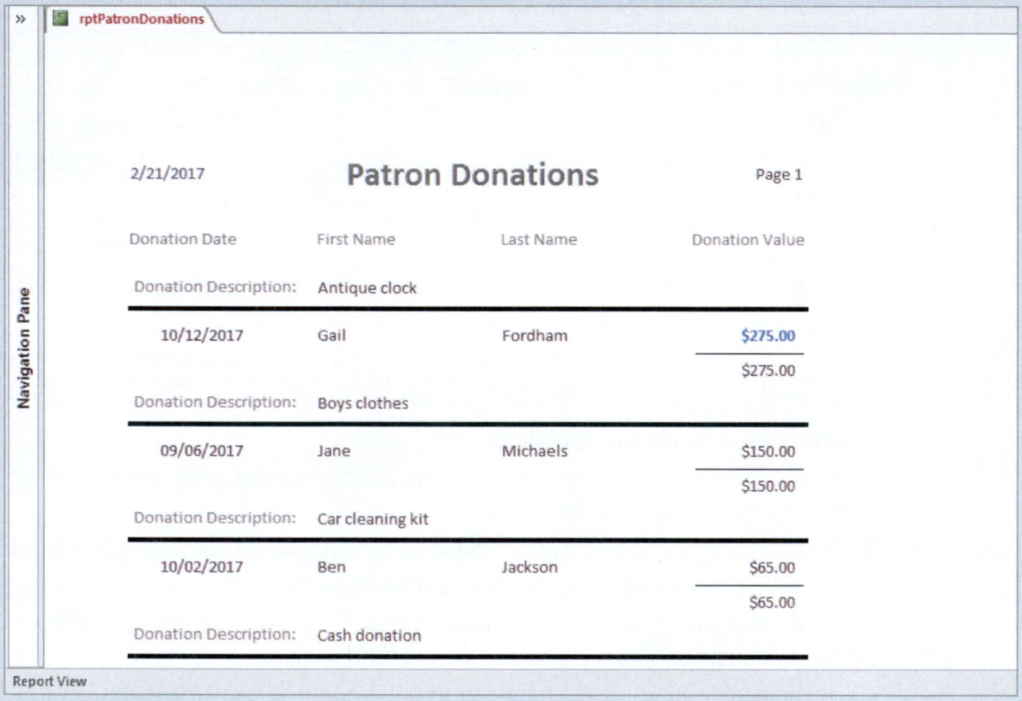

rptPatronDonations

Navigation Pane

2/21/2017 **Patron Donations** Page 1

Donation Date	First Name	Last Name	Donation Value
Donation Description:	Antique clock		
10/12/2017	Gail	Fordham	$275.00
			$275.00
Donation Description:	Boys clothes		
09/06/2017	Jane	Michaels	$150.00
			$150.00
Donation Description:	Car cleaning kit		
10/02/2017	Ben	Jackson	$65.00
			$65.00
Donation Description:	Cash donation		

Report View

a. Save the report as **rptPatronDonations**.
b. Use the Description field as a grouping field.
c. Select the DonationDate field as a sort field and the LastName field as a secondary sort field.
d. Hide duplicate values for the DonationDate field.
e. Use black font for all the controls.
f. Keep the whole group together on one page.
g. Use Wide margins, and set the grid width to 6 inches. Size fields as shown, and distribute horizontally, using spacing to create a balanced look.
h. Create a conditional formatting rule for the DonationValue field to display the value in blue, bold font when the amount is more than $200.
i. Make any additional changes to the layout and formatting of the report that are necessary for it to match Figure 7-42. Also include a grand total of all donations at the end of the report.

4. After you've created and saved the rptPatronDonations report, filter the report in Report view, selecting all records that contain "Jo" in the LastName field. Copy the entire filtered report, and paste it into a new Word document. Save the document as **PatronJo** in the location where you are storing your files. Close Word, and then save and close the Access report.
5. Diane's Community Center is having a fundraiser dinner, and Diane would like name tags for the patrons. Use the following instructions to create mailing labels that will be used as name tags:
   a. Use the tblPatron table as the record source for the mailing labels.
   b. Use Avery C2160 labels, and use a font size of 16, with Normal weight and black color.
   c. For the prototype label, place FirstName, a space, and LastName on the first line.
   d. Sort by LastName, and then type the report name **rptPatronNameTags**.
   e. Change the page layout of the rptPatronNameTags report to three snaking columns.
6. Make a backup copy of the database, compact and repair it, and then close it.

CREATE

Case Problem 4

Data File needed for this Case Problem: AppTrail.accdb (cont. from Module 6)

Hike Appalachia Molly and Bailey Johnson want you to create a custom report and mailing labels for the AppTrail database. Complete the following steps:

1. Open the **AppTrail** database you worked with in the previous two modules.
2. Create a query that displays the TourName field from the tblTour table; the HikerFirst, HikerLast, and State field from the tblHiker table; and the TourDate and People fields from the tblReservation table. Sort in ascending order by the TourName, State, and TourDate fields, and then save the query as **qryTourReservations**.
3. Create a custom report based on the qryTourReservations query. Figure 7-43 shows a sample of the first page of the completed report. Refer to the figure as you create the report.

Figure 7-43 AppTrail database custom report

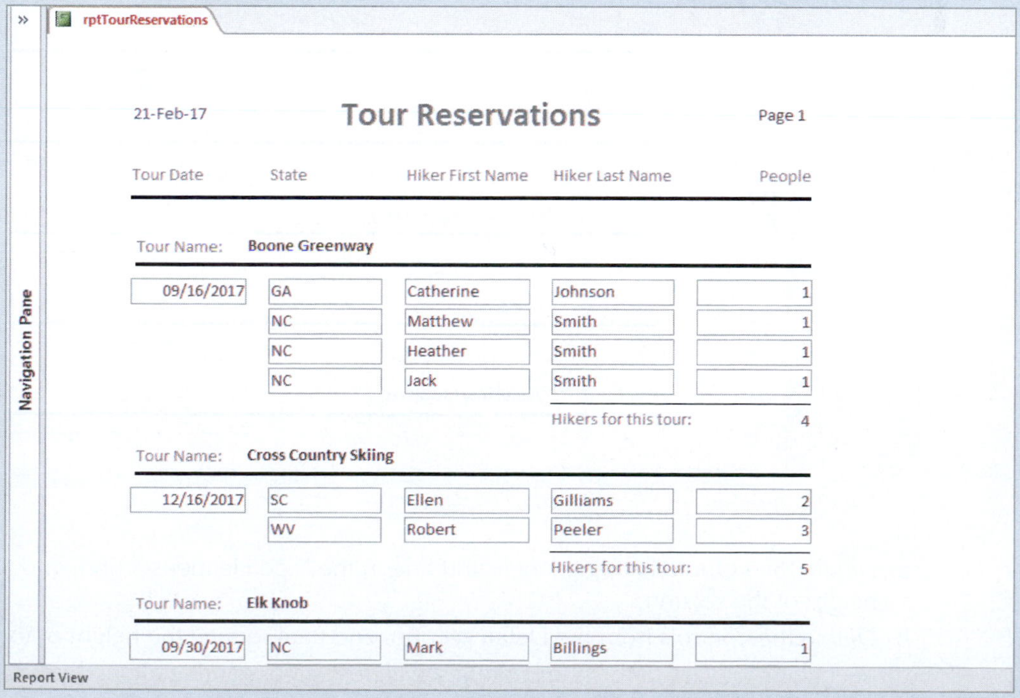

rptTourReservations

21-Feb-17 **Tour Reservations** Page 1

Tour Date	State	Hiker First Name	Hiker Last Name	People
Tour Name:	**Boone Greenway**			
09/16/2017	GA	Catherine	Johnson	1
	NC	Matthew	Smith	1
	NC	Heather	Smith	1
	NC	Jack	Smith	1
			Hikers for this tour:	4
Tour Name:	**Cross Country Skiing**			
12/16/2017	SC	Ellen	Gilliams	2
	WV	Robert	Peeler	3
			Hikers for this tour:	5
Tour Name:	**Elk Knob**			
09/30/2017	NC	Mark	Billings	1

Navigation Pane

Report View

a. Save the report as **rptTourReservations**.
b. Use the TourName field as a grouping field.
c. Select the TourDate field as a sort field and the State field as a secondary sort field.
d. Hide duplicate values for the TourDate field.
e. Use black font for all the controls, and display the Tour Name in bold.
f. Keep the whole group together on one page.
g. Add a grand total of all hikers for all dates at the end of the report.
h. Use Wide margins, and set the grid width to 6 inches. Size fields as shown, and distribute horizontally, using spacing to create a balanced look.
i. Remove the color for alternate rows, and then make any other layout and formatting changes necessary to match the report shown in Figure 7-43.

4. Use the following instructions to create the mailing labels:
   a. Use the tblHiker table as the record source for the mailing labels.
   b. Use Avery C2163 labels, with 12-point font size, Medium weight, and black color settings.
   c. For the prototype label, place HikerFirst, a space, and HikerLast on the first line; Address on the second line; City, a comma and a space, State, a space, and Zip on the third line.
   d. Sort by Zip, then by HikerLast, and then enter the report name **rptHikerLabels**.
   e. Change the page layout for the rptHikerLabels report to snaking columns.
5. Make a copy of the rptTourReservations report using the name **rptTourReservationsSummary**, and then customize it according to the following instructions. Figure 7-44 shows a sample of the first page of the completed report.

Figure 7-44 AppTrail database custom summary report

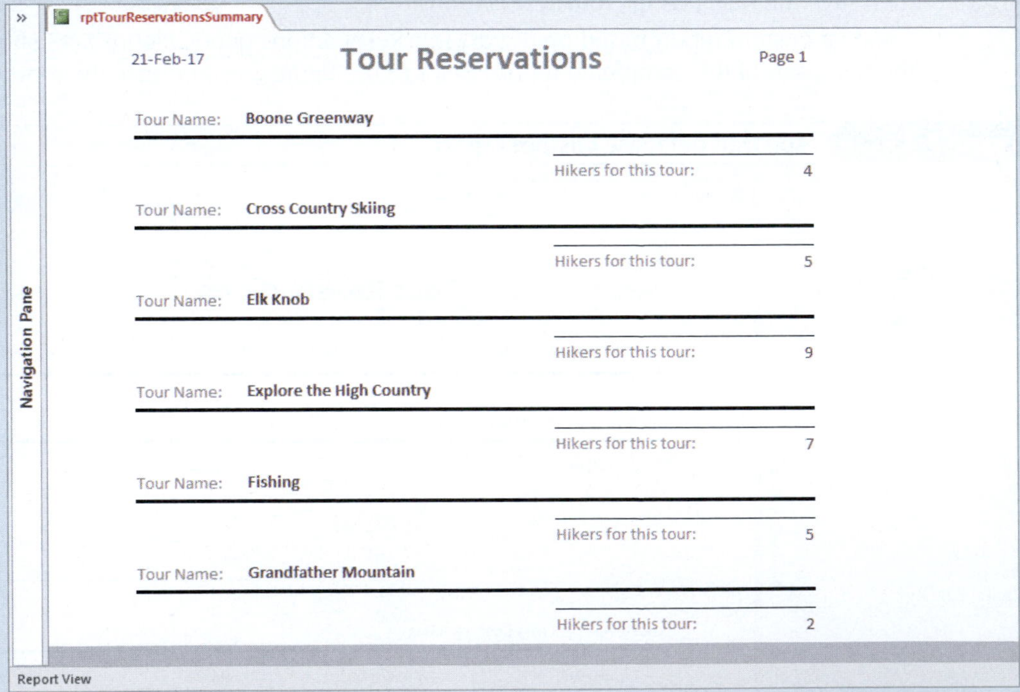

   a. Delete the column heading labels and line in the Page Header section, and then reduce the height of the section.
   b. Delete the controls from the Detail section, and then reduce the height of that section.
   c. Keep the subtotals for the number of reservations per tour and total number of hikers on all tours.
6. Make a backup copy of the database, compact and repair it, and then close the AppTrail database.

MODULE 8

Sharing, Integrating, and Analyzing Data

Importing, Exporting, Linking, and Analyzing Data in the CareCenter Database

OBJECTIVES

Session 8.1
- Export an Access query to an HTML document and view the document
- Import a CSV file as an Access table
- Use the Table Analyzer
- Import and export XML files
- Save and run import and export specifications

Session 8.2
- Create a tabbed subform using a tab control
- Create a chart in a tab control using the Chart Wizard
- Create and use an application part
- Export a PDF file
- Understand the difference between importing, embedding, and linking external objects
- Link data from an Excel workbook

Case | *Riverview Veterinary Care Center*

Kimberly Johnson is pleased with the design and contents of the CareCenter database. Kimberly feels that other employees would benefit from gaining access to the CareCenter database and from sharing data among the different applications employees use. Kimberly would also like to be able to analyze the data in the database.

In this module, you will import, export, and link data, and you will create application parts. You will also explore the charting features of Access.

STARTING DATA FILES

Module

CareCenter.accdb (*cont.*)
NewOwnerReferrals.accdb
PotentialOwners.csv
Referral.xml
Volunteer.xlsx

Review

Ads.xlsx
Partners.accdb
Payables.csv
Payments.xml
Supplier.accdb (*cont.*)

Case1

CreditCard.xml
MoreBeauty.accdb (*cont.*)
Schedule.xlsx

Case2

AddSubject.xml
NewStudentReferrals.accdb
Room.xlsx
Subject.csv
Tutoring.accdb (*cont.*)

Case3

Community.accdb (*cont.*)
Facility.csv
Volunteer.accdb

Case4

AppTrail.accdb (*cont.*)
PotentialTours1.xml
PotentialTours2.xml
Staff.xlsx

Session 8.1 Visual Overview:

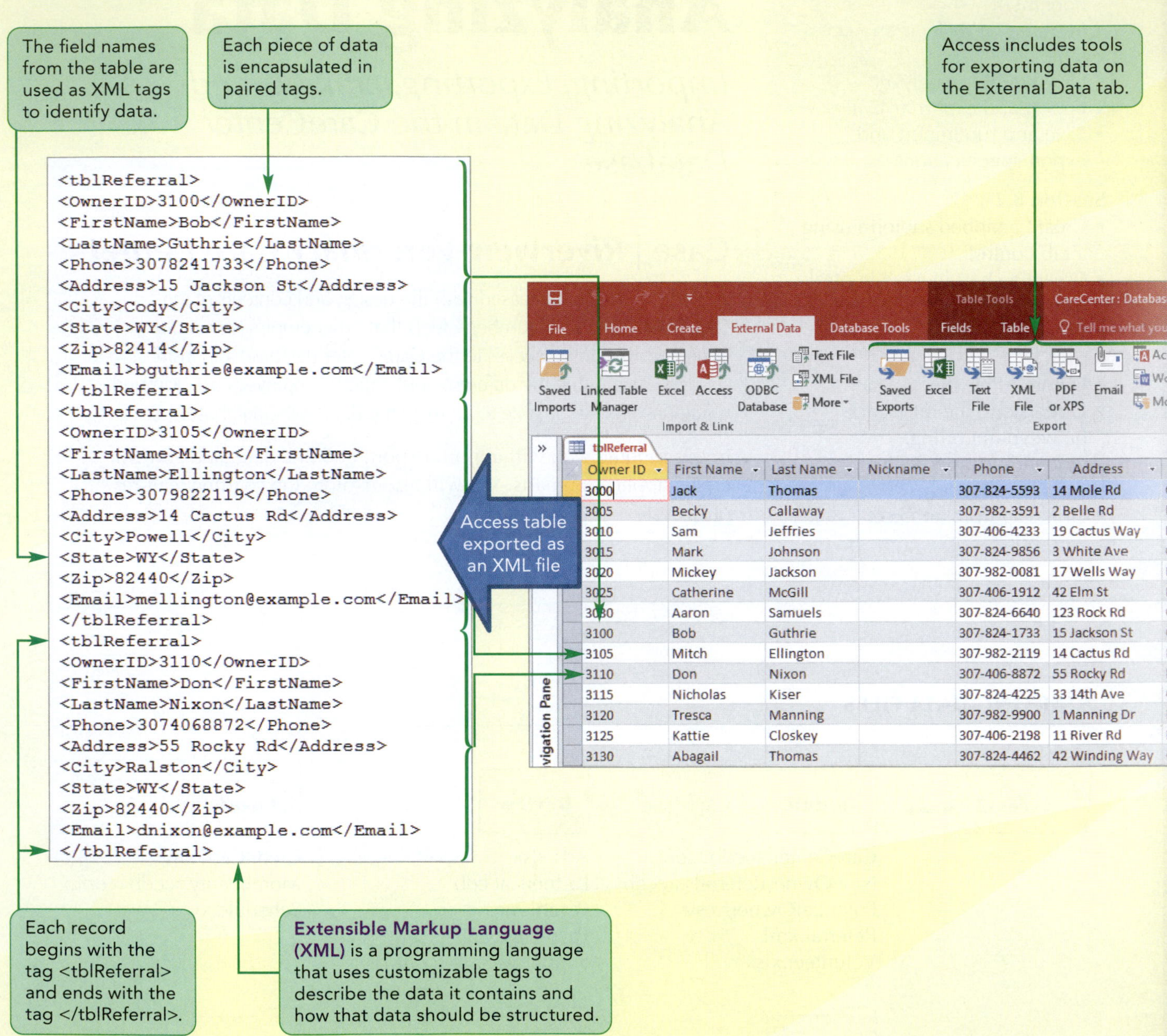

Exporting Data to XML and HTML

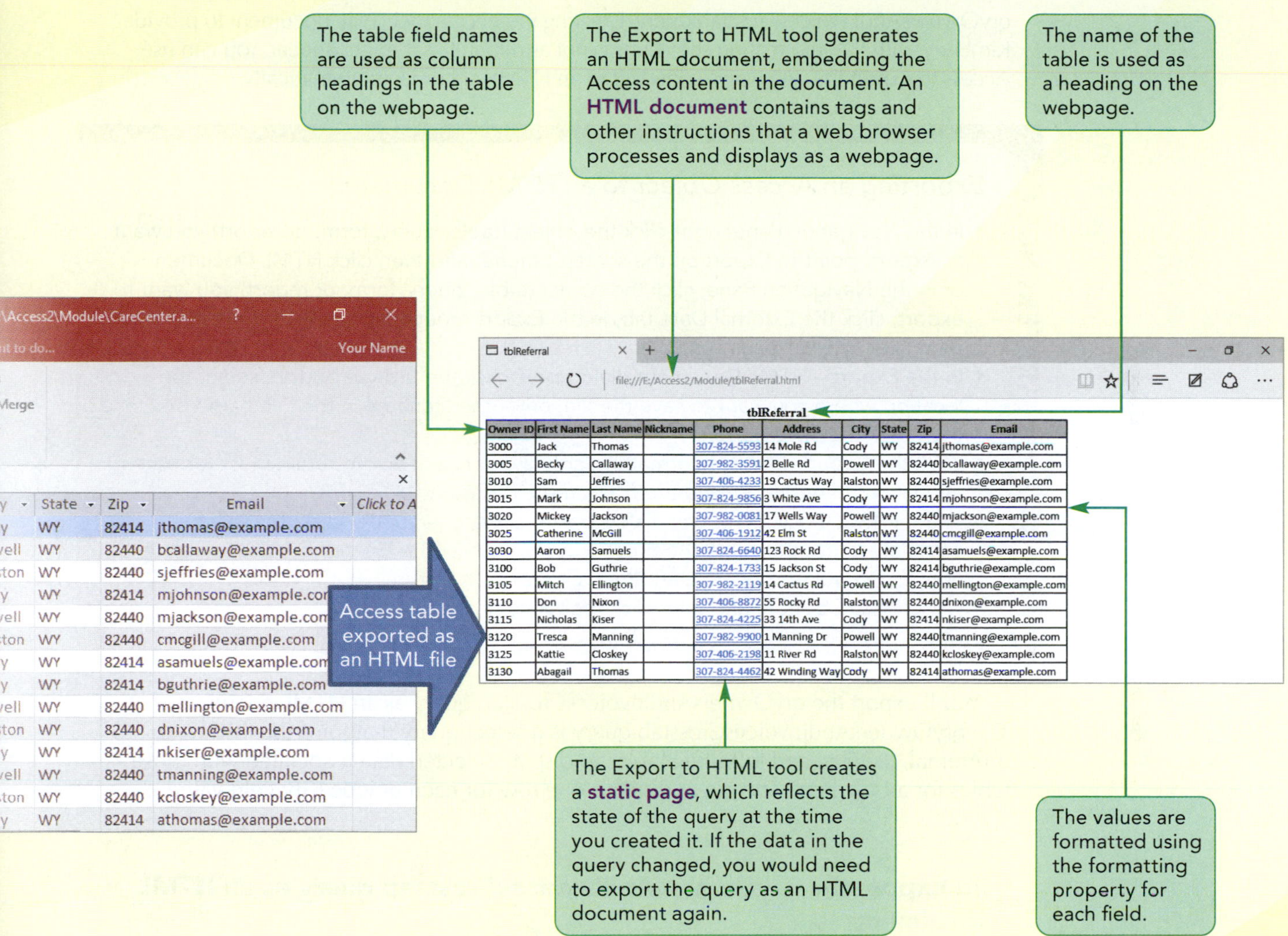
The table field names are used as column headings in the table on the webpage.
The Export to HTML tool generates an HTML document, embedding the Access content in the document. An HTML document contains tags and other instructions that a web browser processes and displays as a webpage.
The name of the table is used as a heading on the webpage.
tblReferral
file:///E:/Access2/Module/tblReferral.html
Access table exported as an HTML file
The Export to HTML tool creates a static page, which reflects the state of the query at the time you created it. If the data in the query changed, you would need to export the query as an HTML document again.
The values are formatted using the formatting property for each field.

tblReferral

Owner ID	First Name	Last Name	Nickname	Phone	Address	City	State	Zip	Email
3000	Jack	Thomas		307-824-5593	14 Mole Rd	Cody	WY	82414	jthomas@example.com
3005	Becky	Callaway		307-982-3591	2 Belle Rd	Powell	WY	82440	bcallaway@example.com
3010	Sam	Jeffries		307-406-4233	19 Cactus Way	Ralston	WY	82440	sjeffries@example.com
3015	Mark	Johnson		307-824-9856	3 White Ave	Cody	WY	82414	mjohnson@example.com
3020	Mickey	Jackson		307-982-0081	17 Wells Way	Powell	WY	82440	mjackson@example.com
3025	Catherine	McGill		307-406-1912	42 Elm St	Ralston	WY	82440	cmcgill@example.com
3030	Aaron	Samuels		307-824-6640	123 Rock Rd	Cody	WY	82414	asamuels@example.com
3100	Bob	Guthrie		307-824-1733	15 Jackson St	Cody	WY	82414	bguthrie@example.com
3105	Mitch	Ellington		307-982-2119	14 Cactus Rd	Powell	WY	82440	mellington@example.com
3110	Don	Nixon		307-406-8872	55 Rocky Rd	Ralston	WY	82440	dnixon@example.com
3115	Nicholas	Kiser		307-824-4225	33 14th Ave	Cody	WY	82414	nkiser@example.com
3120	Tresca	Manning		307-982-9900	1 Manning Dr	Powell	WY	82440	tmanning@example.com
3125	Kattie	Closkey		307-406-2198	11 River Rd	Ralston	WY	82440	kcloskey@example.com
3130	Abagail	Thomas		307-824-4462	42 Winding Way	Cody	WY	82414	athomas@example.com

Exporting an Access Query to an HTML Document

An HTML document contains tags and other instructions that a web browser, such as Microsoft Edge, Apple Safari, or Google Chrome, processes and displays as a webpage.

Kimberly wants to display the summary data in the qryOwnersAndInvoicesCrosstab query on the center's intranet so that all employees working in the office are able to view it. To store the data on the center's intranet, you'll create a webpage version of the qryOwnersAndInvoicesCrosstab query. Creating the necessary HTML document to provide Kimberly with the information she wants is not as difficult as it might appear. You can use Access to export the query and convert it to an HTML document automatically.

REFERENCE

Exporting an Access Object to an HTML Document

- In the Navigation Pane, right-click the object (table, query, form, or report) you want to export, point to Export on the shortcut menu, and then click HTML Document; or in the Navigation Pane, click the object (table, query, form, or report) you want to export, click the External Data tab, in the Export group, click the More button, and then click HTML Document.
- In the Export – HTML Document dialog box, click the Browse button, select the location where you want to save the file, enter the filename in the File name box, and then click the Save button.
- Click the Export data with formatting and layout check box to retain most formatting and layout information, and then click the OK button.
- In the HTML Output Options dialog box, if using a template, click the Select a HTML Template check box, click the Browse button, select the location for the template, click the template filename, and then click the OK button.
- Click the OK button, and then click the Close button.

You'll export the qryOwnersAndInvoicesCrosstab query as an HTML document. The qryOwnersAndInvoicesCrosstab query is a select query that joins the tblOwner, tblAnimal, tblVisit, and tblBilling tables to display selected data associated with those tables for all invoices. The query displays one row for each unique City field value.

To export the qryOwnersAndInvoicesCrosstab query as an HTML document:

1. Start Access, and then open the **CareCenter** database you worked with in the previous three modules.

   Trouble? If the security warning is displayed below the ribbon, click the Enable Content button.

2. Open the Navigation Pane (if necessary), right-click **qryOwnersAndInvoicesCrosstab** to display the shortcut menu, point to **Export**, and then click **HTML Document**. The Export - HTML Document dialog box opens.

3. Click the **Browse** button to open the File Save dialog box, navigate to the location where your Data Files are stored, select the text in the File name box, type **Crosstab**, make sure HTML Documents appears in the Save as type box, and then click the **Save** button. The File Save dialog box closes, and you return to the Export – HTML Document dialog box. See Figure 8-1.

Figure 8-1 Export – HTML Document dialog box

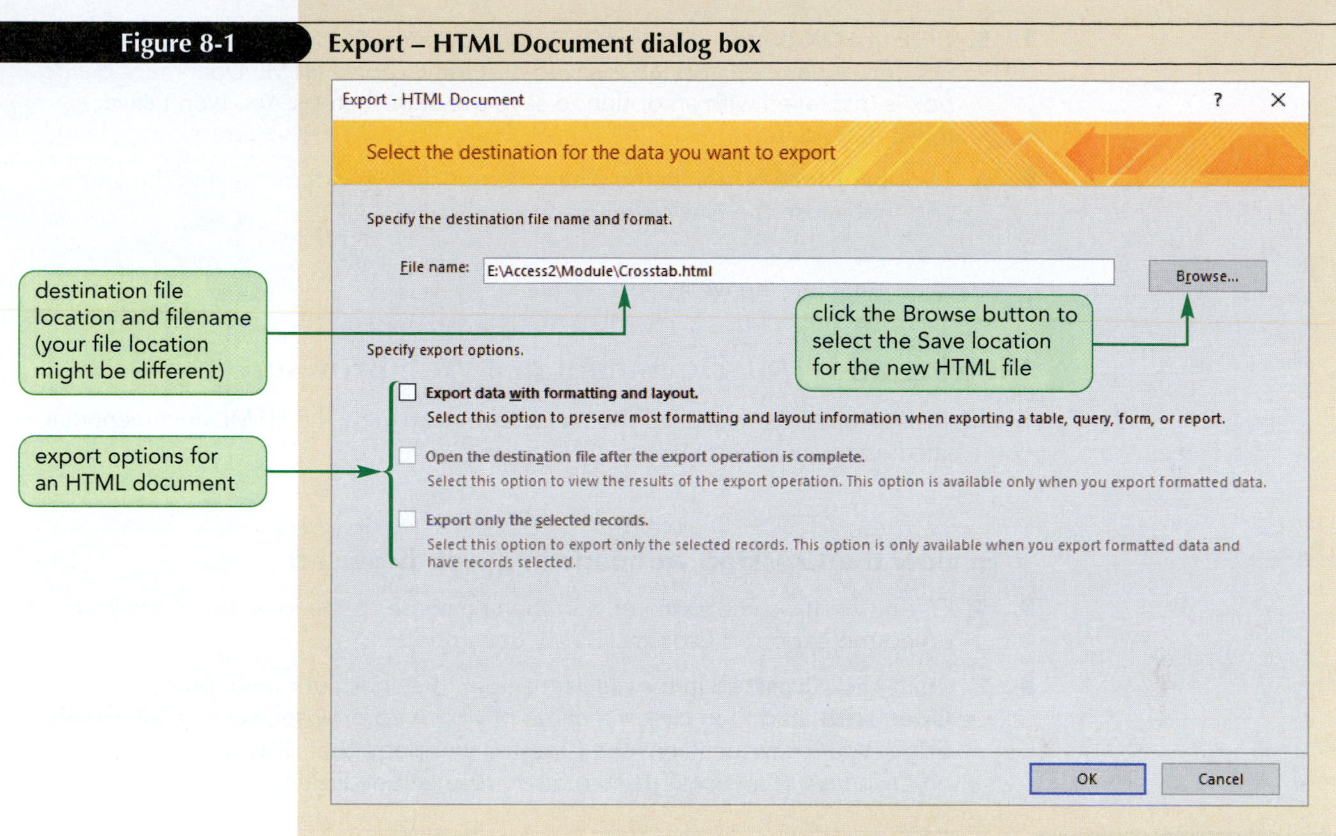
Export - HTML Document
Select the destination for the data you want to export
Specify the destination file name and format.
File name: E:\Access2\Module\Crosstab.html
Browse...
Specify export options.
Export data with formatting and layout.
Select this option to preserve most formatting and layout information when exporting a table, query, form, or report.
Open the destination file after the export operation is complete.
Select this option to view the results of the export operation. This option is available only when you export formatted data.
Export only the selected records.
Select this option to export only the selected records. This option is only available when you export formatted data and have records selected.
OK
Cancel
destination file location and filename (your file location might be different)
click the Browse button to select the Save location for the new HTML file
export options for an HTML document

The dialog box provides options for exporting the data with formatting and layout, opening the exported file after the export operation is complete, and exporting selected records from the source object (available only when you select records in an object instead of selecting an object in the Navigation Pane). You need to select the option for exporting the data with formatting and layout; otherwise the HTML document created will be poorly formatted and difficult to read.

4. Click the **Export data with formatting and layout** check box to select it, and then click the **OK** button. The Export - HTML Document dialog box closes, and the HTML Output Options dialog box opens. See Figure 8-2. In this dialog box you specify the coding to be used to save the HTML file, and you also have the option to save the exported data in a pre-existing HTML document template. The default option, Default encoding, is selected.

Figure 8-2 HTML Output Options dialog box

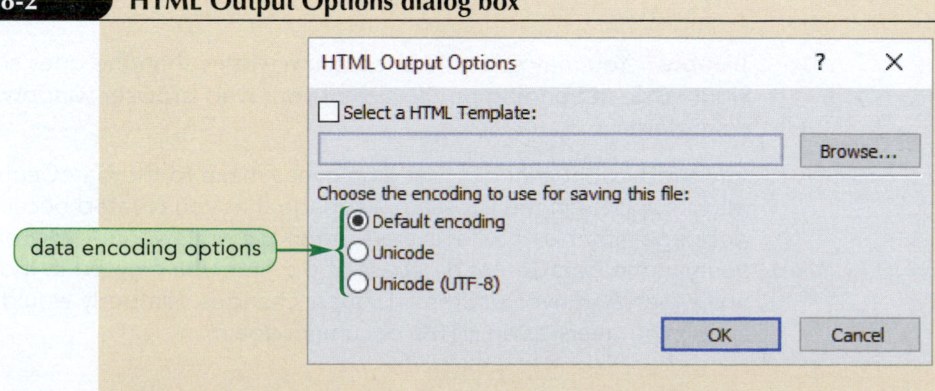
HTML Output Options
Select a HTML Template:
Browse...
Choose the encoding to use for saving this file:
Default encoding
Unicode
Unicode (UTF-8)
OK
Cancel
data encoding options

5. Click the **OK** button. The HTML Output Options dialog box closes, the HTML document named Crosstab is saved and the Export - HTML Document dialog box is displayed with an option to save the export steps. You won't save these export steps.
6. Click the **Close** button in the dialog box to close it without saving the steps, and then close the Navigation Pane.

Now you can view the webpage.

Viewing an HTML Document in a Web Browser

Kimberly asks to see the webpage you created. You can view the HTML document that you created using any web browser.

To view the Crosstab webpage in a web browser:

1. Open Windows File Explorer, and then navigate to the location where you saved the exported Crosstab HTML document.
2. Right-click **Crosstab** in the file list to open the shortcut menu, point to **Open with**, and then click the name of your web browser, such as **Microsoft Edge**. Your browser opens the Crosstab webpage that displays the qryOwnersAndInvoicesCrosstab query results. See Figure 8-3.

Figure 8-3 qryOwnersAndInvoicesCrosstab query displayed in Edge

path and filename for selected HTML file (your path might be different)

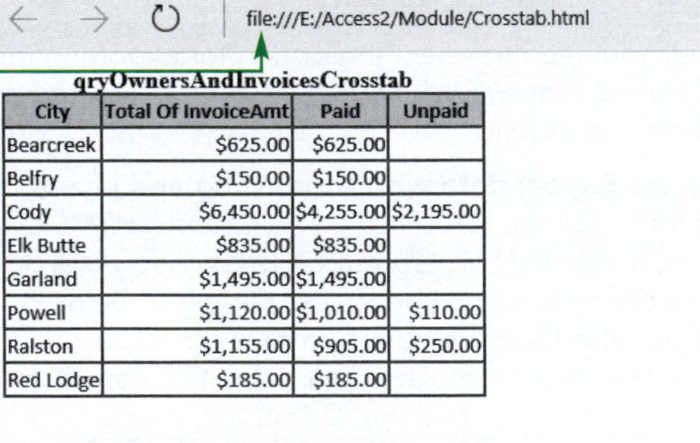

qryOwnersAndInvoicesCrosstab

City	Total Of InvoiceAmt	Paid	Unpaid
Bearcreek	$625.00	$625.00	
Belfry	$150.00	$150.00	
Cody	$6,450.00	$4,255.00	$2,195.00
Elk Butte	$835.00	$835.00	
Garland	$1,495.00	$1,495.00	
Powell	$1,120.00	$1,010.00	$110.00
Ralston	$1,155.00	$905.00	$250.00
Red Lodge	$185.00	$185.00	

Trouble? You may see different column widths than the ones shown in Figure 8-3, depending on the size of your web browser window. This is not a problem.

Any subsequent changes that employees make to the CareCenter database will not appear in the Crosstab webpage that you created because it is a static webpage—that is, it reflects the state of the qryOwnersAndInvoicesCrosstab query in the CareCenter database at the time you created it. If data in the qryOwnersAndInvoicesCrosstab query changes, Kimberly would need to export the query as an HTML document again.

3. Close your browser, and then click the **Close** button [X] on the Windows File Explorer window title bar to close it and to return to Access.

   Trouble? If the Access window is not active on your screen, click the Microsoft Access program button on the taskbar.

Now that you've completed your work creating the webpage, Kimberly has a file containing information for potential new owners that she needs to add to the CareCenter database. Instead of typing the information into new records, she asks you to import the data into the CareCenter database.

Importing a CSV File as an Access Table

Many people use Excel to manage a simple table, such as a table of contact information or product information. Kimberly has been maintaining an Excel workbook containing contact information for people who have called the Riverview Veterinary Care Center clinic to inquire about the services but have not yet booked appointments. Recall from your work in a previous module that she could use the Excel button on the External Data tab to access the Import Spreadsheet Wizard and import the Excel worksheet data. However, in this case, Kimberly has already exported the Excel data to a CSV file. A **CSV (comma-separated values) file** is a text file in which commas separate values, and each line is a record containing the same number of values in the same positions. This is a common format for representing data in a table and is used by spreadsheet applications such as Excel as well as database applications. A CSV file can easily be imported into the CareCenter database as a table. To do so, you use the Import Text Wizard, which you open by clicking the Text File button on the External Data Tab.

REFERENCE

Importing a CSV File into an Access Table

- On the External Data tab, in the Import & Link group, click the Text File button to open the Get External Data - Text File dialog box.
- Click the Browse button in the dialog box, navigate to the location where the file to import is stored, click the filename, and then click the Open button.
- Click the "Import the source data into a new table in the current database" option button, and then click the OK button.
- In the Import Text Wizard dialog box, click the Delimited option button, and then click the Next button.
- Make sure the Comma option button is selected. If appropriate, click the First Row Contains Field Names check box to select it, and then click the Next button.
- For each field, if necessary, select the column, type its field name and select its data type, and then click the Next button.
- Choose the appropriate option button to let Access create a primary key, to choose your own primary key, or to avoid setting a primary key, and then click the Next button.
- Type the table name in the Import to Table box, and then click the Finish button.

Kimberly's CSV file is named PotentialOwners, and you'll import the data as a new table in the CareCenter database.

To view and import the CSV file as an Access table:

1. Open Windows File Explorer, navigate to the **Access2 > Module** folder included with your Data Files, right-click **PotentialOwners (CSV)** in the file list to open the shortcut menu, click **Open with**, and then click **Notepad**.

   Trouble? If Notepad isn't an option when you click Open with, click Choose another app, click Notepad in the How do you want to open this file dialog box that opens, and then click the OK button.

2. Examine the contents of the PotentialOwners file. The file contains rows of data, with commas separating the individual pieces of data.

3. Close the Notepad window, and then close the File Explorer window. You return to the Access window.

   Trouble? If a dialog box appears prompting you to save the file, click Don't Save. You may have accidentally added or deleted a character, and you don't want to save this change to the file.

4. On the ribbon, click the **External Data** tab, and then in the Import & Link group, click the **Text File** button to open the Get External Data - Text File dialog box.

   Trouble? If the Export - Text File dialog box opens, you clicked the Text File button in the Export group. Click the Cancel button, and then repeat Step 4, being sure to select the Text File button in the Import & Link group.

5. Click the **Browse** button, navigate to the **Access2 > Module** folder included with your Data Files, click **PotentialOwners**, and then click the **Open** button.

6. In the Get External Data – Text File dialog box, click the **Import the source data into a new table in the current database** option button (if necessary). The selected path and filename appear in the File name box. See Figure 8-4.

Figure 8-4 Get External Data – Text File dialog box

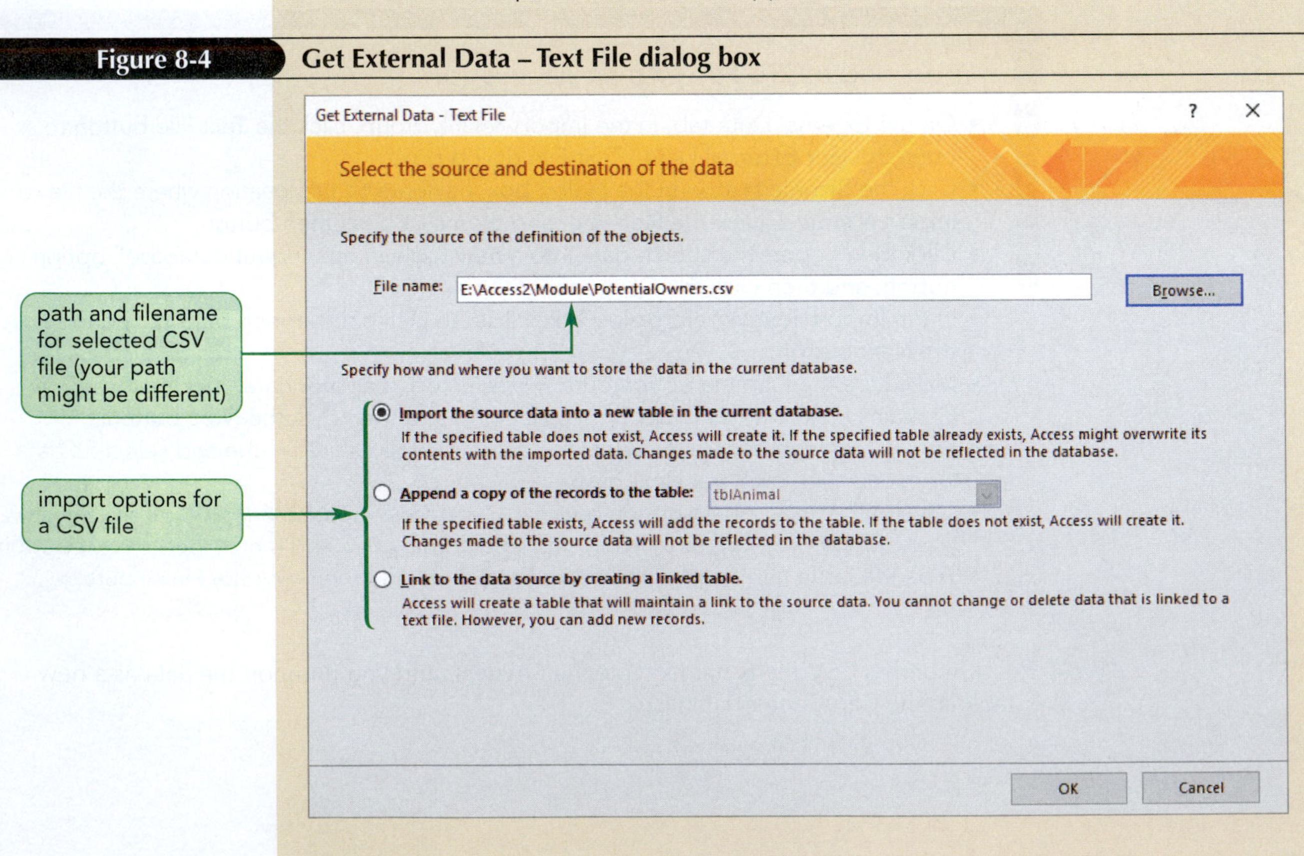

The dialog box provides options for importing the data into a new table in the database, appending a copy of the data to an existing table in the database, and linking to the source data. In the future, Kimberly wants to maintain the potential new owner data in the CareCenter database, instead of using her Excel workbook, so you'll import the data into a new table.

7. Click the **OK** button to open the first Import Text Wizard dialog box, in which you designate how to identify the separation between field values in each line in the source data. The choices are the use of commas, tabs, or another character to separate, or delimit, the values, or the use of fixed-width columns with spaces between each column. The wizard has correctly identified that values are delimited by commas.

8. Click the **Next** button to open the second Import Text Wizard dialog box, in which you verify the delimiter for values in each line. See Figure 8-5.

Figure 8-5 **Import Text Wizard dialog box specifying the delimiter for values in the CSV file**

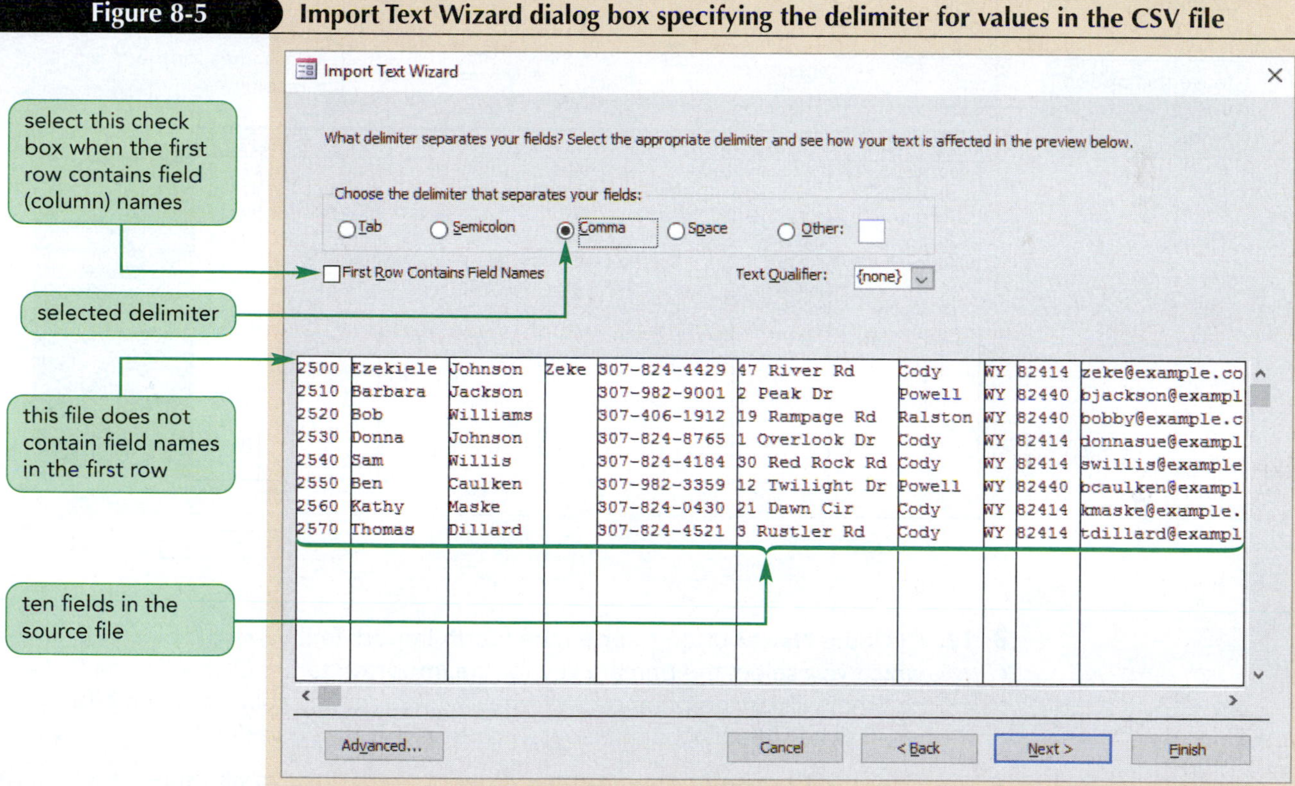

The CSV source file contains eight records with ten fields in each record. A comma serves as the delimiter for values in each line (record), so the Comma option button is selected. The first row in the source file contains the first record, not field names, so the "First Row Contains Field Names" check box is not checked. If the source file used either single or double quotation marks to enclose values, you would click the Text Qualifier arrow to choose the appropriate option.

9. Click the **Next** button to open the third Import Text Wizard dialog box, in which you enter the field name and set other properties for the imported fields. You will import all fields from the source file and use the default data type and indexed settings for each field, except for the first field's data type.

10. In the Field Name box, type **OwnerID**, click the **Data Type** arrow, click **Short Text**, and then click **Field2** in the table list. The heading for the first column changes to OwnerID (partially hidden) in the table list, and the second column is selected.

11. Repeat Step 10 for the remaining nine columns, making sure Short Text is the data type for all fields, typing **FirstName**, **LastName**, **Nickname**, **Phone**, **Address**, **City**, **State**, **Zip**, and **Email** in the Field Name box. See Figure 8-6.

Figure 8-6 **Field names and options as specified in the Import Text Wizard**

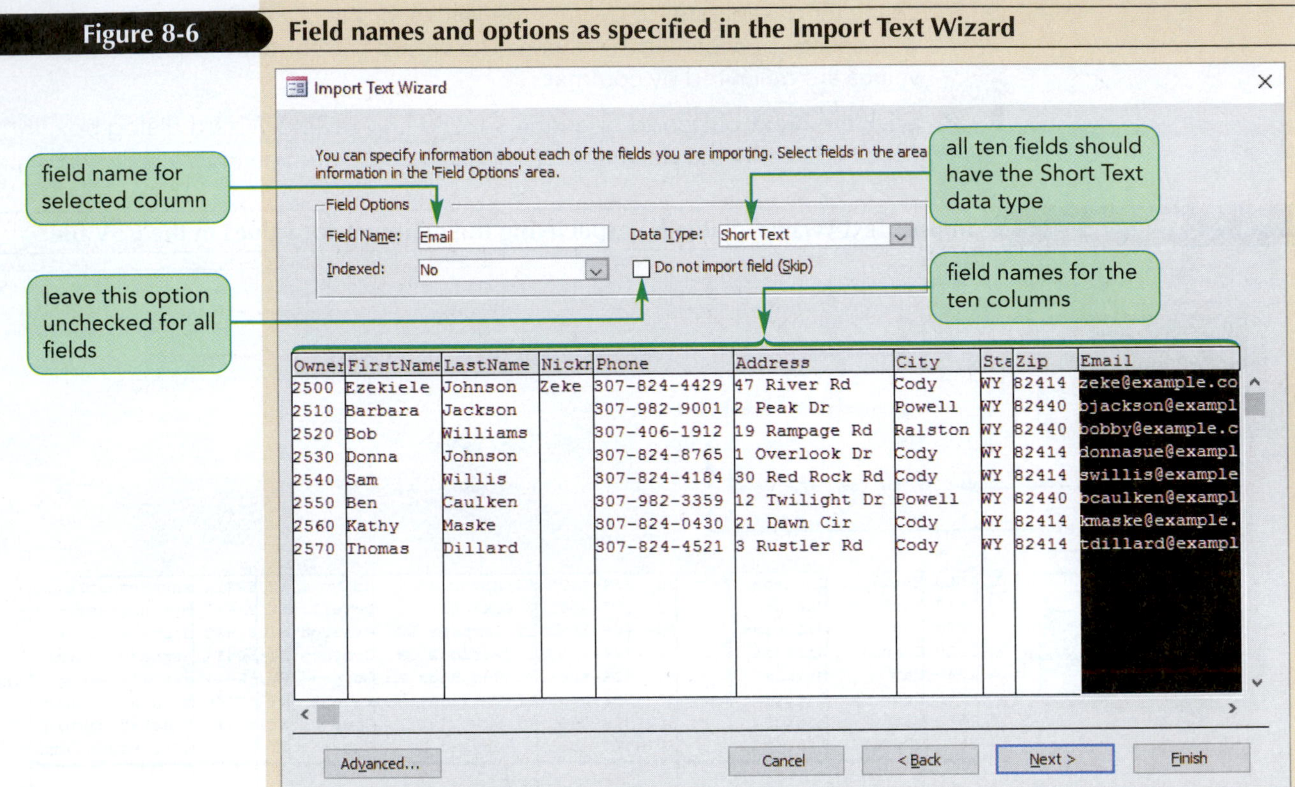

12. Click the **Next** button to open the fourth Import Text Wizard dialog box, in which you select the primary key for the imported table. OwnerID, the first column, will be the primary key. When you select this column as the table's primary key, the ID column created by the wizard will be deleted.

13. Click the **Choose my own primary key** option button, make sure **OwnerID** appears in the box for the option, click the **Next** button, type **tblPotentialOwners** as the table name in the Import to Table box, click the **I would like a wizard to analyze my table after importing the data** check box to select it, and then click the **Finish** button. An Import Text Wizard dialog box opens, asking if you want to analyze the table.

14. Click the **Yes** button to close the dialog box and start the Table Analyzer Wizard. You will continue working with this wizard in the next set of steps.

TIP

You can start the Table Analyzer Wizard directly by clicking the Database Tools tab and then clicking the Analyze Table button in the Analyze group.

After importing data and creating a new table, you can use the Import Text Wizard to analyze the imported table. The Table Analyzer Wizard identifies duplicate data in your table and displays a diagram and explanation in the dialog box describing the potential problem.

Analyzing a Table with the Table Analyzer

TIP

Read the Normalization section in the appendix titled "Relational Databases and Database Design" for more information about normalization and third normal form.

Normalizing is the process of identifying and eliminating anomalies, or inconsistencies, from a collection of tables in the database. The **Table Analyzer** analyzes a single table and, if necessary, splits it into two or more tables that are in third normal form. The Table Analyzer looks for redundant data in the table. When the Table Analyzer encounters redundant data, it removes redundant fields from the table and then places them in new tables. The database designer must always review the analyzer results carefully to determine if the suggestions are appropriate.

To use the Table Analyzer Wizard to analyze the imported table:

1. In the first Table Analyzer Wizard dialog box, click the first **Show me an example** button [>>], read the explanation, close the example box, click the second **Show me an example** button [>>], read the explanation, close the example box, and then click the **Next** button to open the second Table Analyzer Wizard dialog box. The diagram and explanation in this dialog box describe how the Table Analyzer solves the duplicate data problem.
2. Again, click the first **Show me an example** button [>>], read the explanation, close the example box, click the second **Show me an example** button [>>], read the explanation, close the example box, and then click the **Next** button to open the third Table Analyzer Wizard dialog box. In this dialog box, you choose whether to let the wizard decide the appropriate table placement for the fields, if the table is not already normalized. You'll let the wizard decide.
3. Make sure the **Yes, let the wizard decide** option button is selected, and then click the **Next** button. The wizard indicates that the City and State fields should be split into a separate table. Although this data is redundant, it is an industry practice to keep the city, state, and zip information with the address information in a table, so you'll cancel the wizard rather than split the table.
4. Click the **Cancel** button to close the Table Analyzer Wizard. You return to the final Get External Data - Text File dialog box, in which you specify if you want to save the import steps. You don't need to save these steps because you're importing the data only this one time.
5. Click the **Close** button to close the dialog box.

The tblPotentialOwners table is now listed in the Tables section in the Navigation Pane. You'll open the table to verify the import results.

To open the imported tblPotentialOwners table:

1. Open the Navigation Pane, if necessary.
2. Double-click **tblPotentialOwners** to open the table datasheet, and then close the Navigation Pane.
3. Resize all columns to their best fit, and then click **2500** in the first row in the OwnerID column to deselect all values. See Figure 8-7.

Figure 8-7 Imported tblPotentialOwners table datasheet

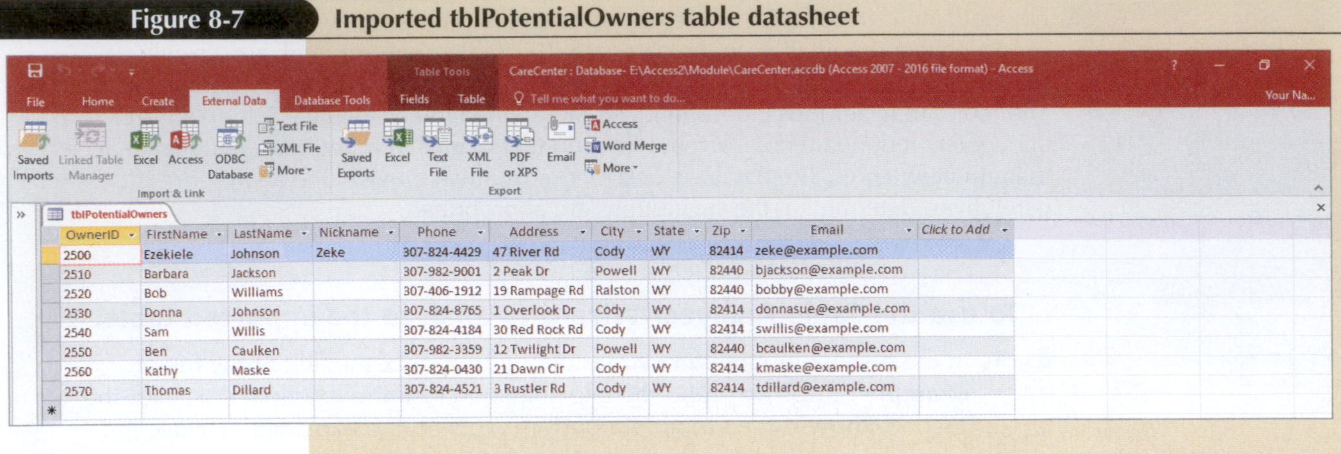

OwnerID	FirstName	LastName	Nickname	Phone	Address	City	State	Zip	Email	Click to Add
2500	Ezekiele	Johnson	Zeke	307-824-4429	47 River Rd	Cody	WY	82414	zeke@example.com	
2510	Barbara	Jackson		307-982-9001	2 Peak Dr	Powell	WY	82440	bjackson@example.com	
2520	Bob	Williams		307-406-1912	19 Rampage Rd	Ralston	WY	82440	bobby@example.com	
2530	Donna	Johnson		307-824-8765	1 Overlook Dr	Cody	WY	82414	donnasue@example.com	
2540	Sam	Willis		307-824-4184	30 Red Rock Rd	Cody	WY	82414	swillis@example.com	
2550	Ben	Caulken		307-982-3359	12 Twilight Dr	Powell	WY	82440	bcaulken@example.com	
2560	Kathy	Maske		307-824-0430	21 Dawn Cir	Cody	WY	82414	kmaske@example.com	
2570	Thomas	Dillard		307-824-4521	3 Rustler Rd	Cody	WY	82414	tdillard@example.com	

4. Save and close the table.

Next, Kimberly would like you to import data from another file containing new owner referrals from another veterinary care center. However, this data is not in an Access table; instead, it's stored in XML format.

Working with XML Files

Riverview Veterinary Care Center occasionally receives owner referrals from other clinics. Kimberly was provided an XML document that contains owner contact information from another veterinary care center, which she wants to add to the CareCenter database. XML (Extensible Markup Language) is a programming language that is similar in format to HTML but is more customizable and is suited to the exchange of data between different programs. Unlike HTML, which uses a fixed set of tags to describe the appearance of a webpage, developers can customize XML to describe the data it contains and how that data should be structured.

PROSKILLS

Teamwork: Exchanging Data Between Programs

If all companies used Access, you could easily exchange data between any two databases. However, not all companies use Access. One universal and widely used method for transferring data between different database systems is to export data to XML files and import data from XML files. XML files are used to exchange data between companies, and they are also used to exchange data between programs within a company. For example, you can store data either in an Excel workbook or in an Access table or query, depending on which program is best suited to the personnel working with the data and the business requirements of the company. Because the XML file format is a common format for both Excel and Access—as well as many other programs—whenever the data is needed in another program, you can export the data from one program as an XML file and then import the file into the other program. When collaborating with a team of users or sharing database information with other organizations, always consider the characteristics of the programs being used and the best format for exchanging data between programs.

Importing Data from an XML File

In Access, you can import data from an XML file directly into a database table. Kimberly's XML file is named Referral.xml, and you'll import it into a table called tblReferral in the CareCenter database.

REFERENCE

Importing an XML File as an Access Table

- On the External Data tab, in the Import & Link group, click the XML File button to open the Get External Data - XML File dialog box; or right-click the table name in the Navigation Pane, click Import, and then click XML File.
- Click the Browse button, navigate to the location of the XML file, click the XML filename, and then click the Open button.
- Click the OK button in the Get External Data - XML File dialog box, click the table name in the Import XML dialog box, click the appropriate option button in the Import Options section, and then click the OK button.
- Click the Close button; or if you need to save the import steps, click the Save import steps check box, enter a name for the saved steps in the Save as box, and then click the Save Import button.

Now you will import the Referral XML document as an Access table.

To import the contents of the XML document:

1. On the ribbon, click the **External Data** tab if necessary, and then in the Import & Link Group, click the **XML File** button. The Get External Data - XML File dialog box opens.
2. Click the **Browse** button to open the File Open dialog box, navigate to the **Access2 > Module** folder included with your Data Files, click **Referral**, and then click the **Open** button. The selected path and filename now appear in the File name box.
3. Click the **OK** button. The Import XML dialog box opens. See Figure 8-8.

Figure 8-8 Import XML dialog box

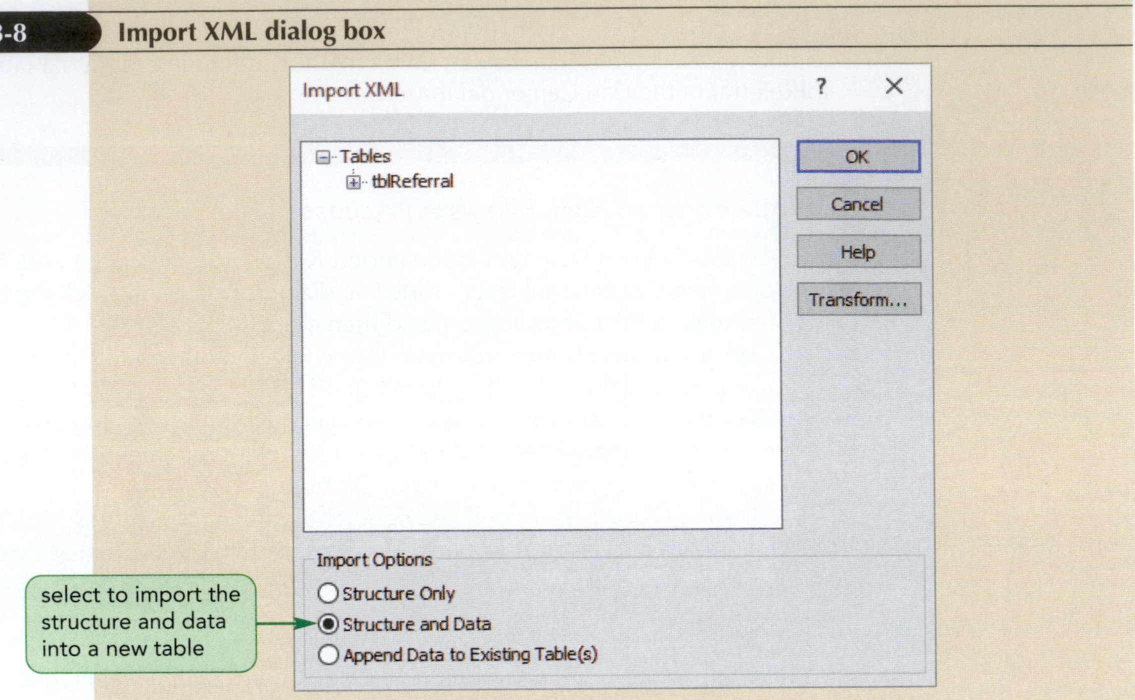

From the XML file, you can import only the table structure to a new table, import the table structure and data to a new table, or append the data in the XML file to an existing table. You'll choose to import the data and structure to a new table.

4. Make sure the **Structure and Data** option button is selected, click **tblReferral** in the box, and then click the **OK** button. The Import XML dialog box closes, and the last Get External Data - XML File Wizard dialog box displays. You'll continue to work with this dialog box in the next set of steps.

Saving and Running Import Specifications

If you need to repeat the same import procedure many times, you can save the steps for the procedure and expedite future imports by running the saved import steps without using a wizard. Because Kimberly will receive additional lists of owner referrals in the future, you'll save the import steps so she can reuse them whenever she receives a new list.

To save the XML file import steps:

1. In the Get External Data – XML File dialog box, click the **Save import steps** check box to select it. The dialog box displays additional options for the save operation. See Figure 8-9.

Figure 8-9 **Save Import Steps dialog box in the Get External Data - XML File Wizard**

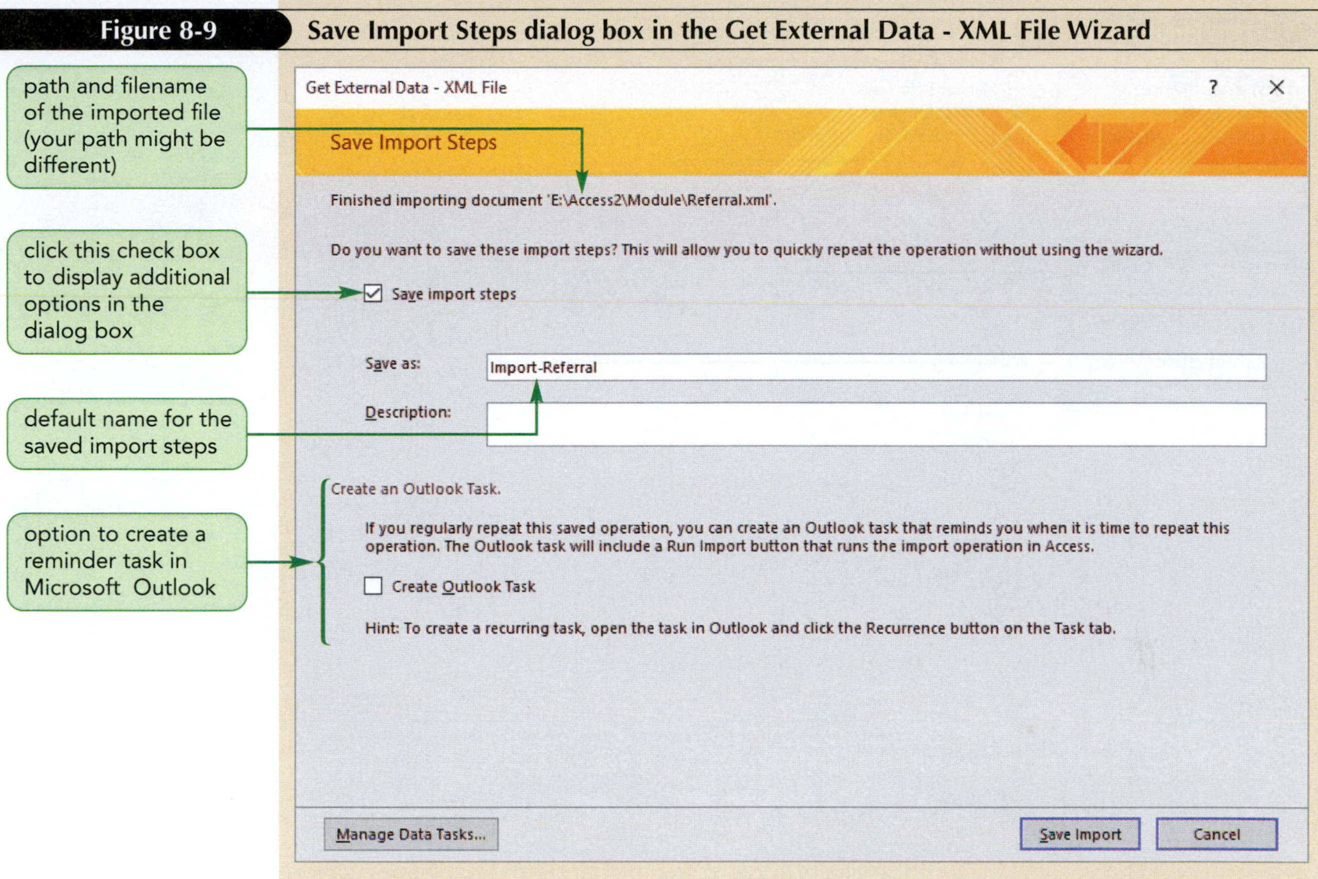
path and filename of the imported file (your path might be different)
click this check box to display additional options in the dialog box
default name for the saved import steps
option to create a reminder task in Microsoft Outlook
Get External Data - XML File
Save Import Steps
Finished importing document 'E:\Access2\Module\Referral.xml'.
Do you want to save these import steps? This will allow you to quickly repeat the operation without using the wizard.
Save import steps
Save as:
Import-Referral
Description:
Create an Outlook Task.
If you regularly repeat this saved operation, you can create an Outlook task that reminds you when it is time to repeat this operation. The Outlook task will include a Run Import button that runs the import operation in Access.
Create Outlook Task
Hint: To create a recurring task, open the task in Outlook and click the Recurrence button on the Task tab.
Manage Data Tasks...
Save Import
Cancel

You can accept the default name for the saved import steps or specify a different name, and you can enter an optional description. If the import will occur on a set schedule, you can also create a reminder task in Microsoft Outlook. You'll accept the default name for the saved steps, and you won't enter a description or schedule an Outlook task.

2. Click the **Save Import** button. The import steps are saved as Import-Referral, the Get External Data - XML File dialog box closes, and the data from the Referral.xml file has been imported into the CareCenter database with the name tblReferral. Before reviewing the imported table, you'll add a description to the saved import steps.

3. On the External Data tab, in the Import & Link group, click the **Saved Imports** button to open the Manage Data Tasks dialog box. See Figure 8-10.

   Trouble? If the Saved Exports tab is displayed in the Manage Data Tasks dialog box, then you selected the Saved Exports button instead of the Saved Imports button. Click the Saved Imports tab in the dialog box.

Figure 8-10 Saved Imports tab in the Manage Data Tasks dialog box

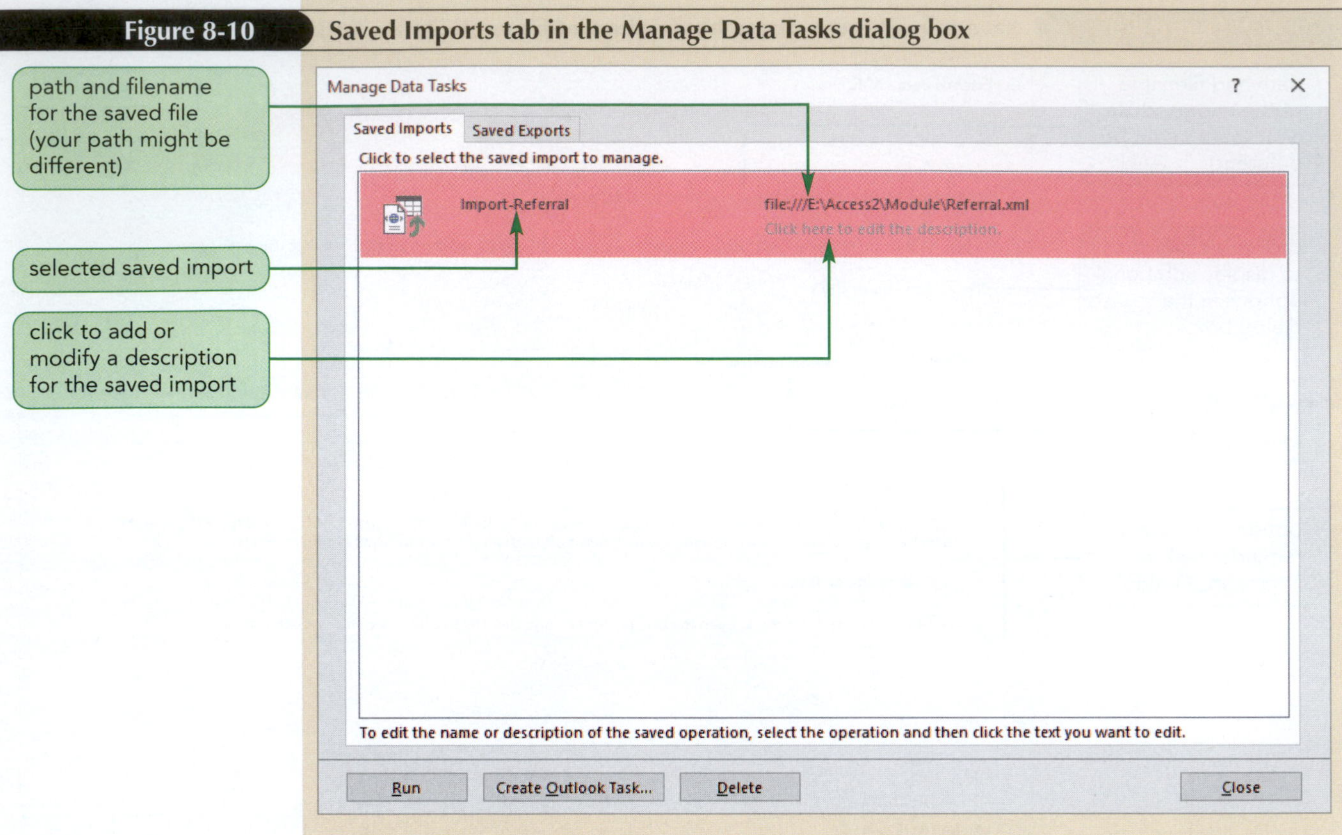

In this dialog box, you can change the name of a saved import, add or change its description, create an Outlook task for it, run it, or delete it. You can also manage any saved export by clicking the Saved Exports tab. You'll add a description for the saved import procedure.

4. Click the **Click here to edit the description** link to open a box that contains an insertion point, type **XML file containing owner referrals from other veterinary care centers**, click an unused portion of the highlighted selection band to close the box and accept the typed description, and then click the **Saved Exports** tab. You have not saved any export steps, so no saved exports are displayed.
5. Click the **Close** button to close the Manage Data Tasks dialog box.
6. Open the Navigation Pane, double-click the **tblReferral** table to open the table datasheet, close the Navigation Pane, resize all columns to their best fit if necessary, and then click **3000** in the first row in the Owner ID column to deselect all values. See Figure 8-11.

Figure 8-11 **Imported XML records in new tblReferral table**

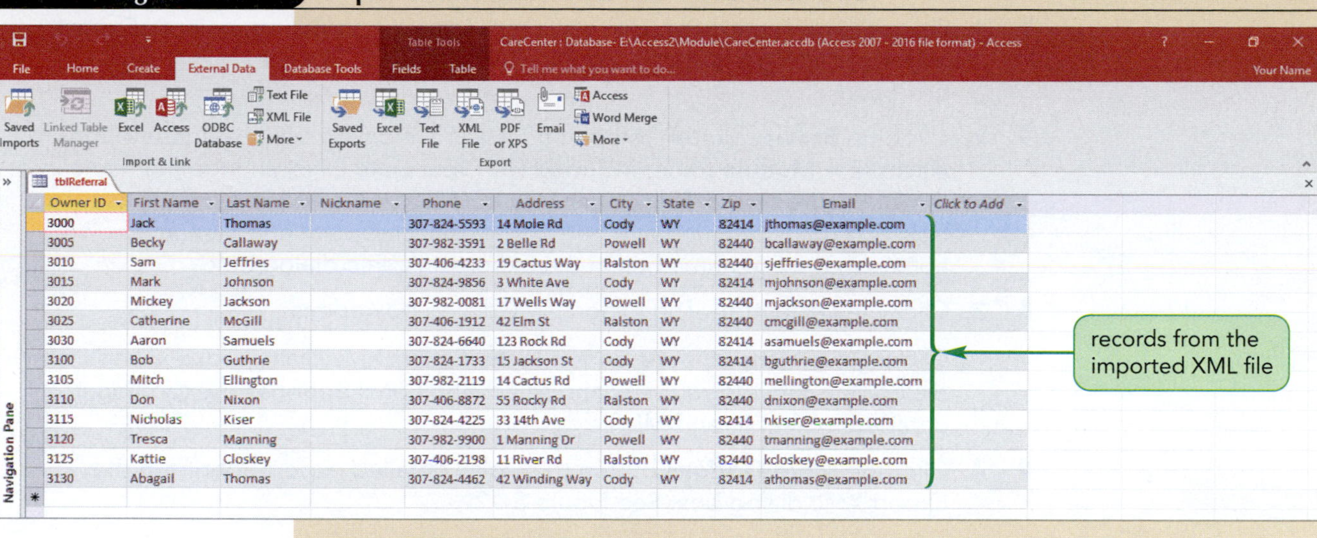

7. Save and close the table.

Next, Kimberly asks you to export the tblBilling table as an XML file.

Exporting an Access Table as an XML File

Riverview Veterinary Care Center uses an accounting system that accepts data in XML files. Kimberly wants to export the tblBilling table as an XML file so it can be tested with the accounting system.

REFERENCE

Exporting an Access Object as an XML File

- Right-click the object (table, query, form, or report) in the Navigation Pane, point to Export, and then click XML File; or click the object (table, query, form, or report) in the Navigation Pane, and then on the External Data tab, click the XML File button in the Export group.
- Click the Browse button in the Export - XML File dialog box, navigate to the location where you will save the XML file, and then click the Save button.
- Click the OK button in the dialog box, select the options in the Export XML dialog box, or click the More Options button and select the options in the expanded Export XML dialog box, and then click the OK button.
- Click the Close button; or if you need to save the export steps, click the Save export steps check box, enter a name for the saved steps in the Save as box, and then click the Save Export button.

You'll export the tblBilling table as an XML file now.

To export the tblBilling table as an XML file:

1. Open the Navigation Pane (if necessary), right-click **tblBilling**, point to **Export** on the shortcut menu, and then click **XML File**. The Export - XML File dialog box opens.
2. Click the **Browse** button to open the File Save dialog box, navigate to the **Access2 > Module** folder included with your Data Files, change the name in the File name box to **Billing**, make sure **XML** is specified in the Save as type box, and then click the **Save** button. The selected path and filename now appear in the File name box in the Export-XML File dialog box.
3. Click the **OK** button. The Export XML dialog box opens.

   Clicking the More Options button in the Export XML dialog box expands the dialog box and lets you view and select additional options for exporting a database object to an XML file.
4. Click the **More Options** button to display detailed export options in the Export XML dialog box. See Figure 8-12.

Figure 8-12 Data tab in the Export XML dialog box

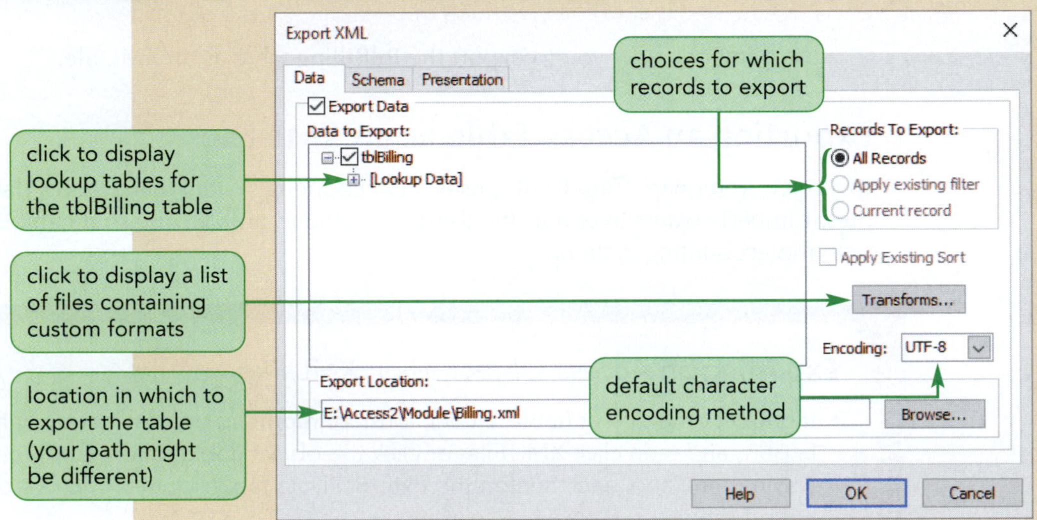

The Export Data check box, the Export Location box, and the Records To Export option group display the selections you made in the previous steps. You're exporting all records from the tblBilling table, including the data in the records and the structure of the table, to the Billing.xml file in the Access2 > Module folder. The encoding option determines how characters will be represented in the exported XML file. The encoding choices are UTF-8, which uses 8 bits to represent each character, and UTF-16, which uses 16 bits to represent each character. You can also click the Transforms button if you have a special file that contains instructions for changing the exported data.

The accounting software used by the center doesn't have a transform file and requires the default encoding, but Kimberly wants to review the tables that contain lookup data.

5. In the Data to Export box, click the **plus** box to the left of [Lookup Data], and then verify that the tblVisit check box and the tblInvoiceItem check box are not checked. Both the tblVisit table and tblInvoiceItem tables contain lookup data because they are in a one-to-many relationship with the tblBilling table. The accounting program requirements don't include any lookup data from the tblVisit table or tblInvoiceItem table, so you don't want the tblVisit check box or the tblInvoiceItem check box to be checked.

   The Data tab settings are correct, so next you'll verify the Schema tab settings.

6. Click the **Schema** tab. See Figure 8-13.

Figure 8-13 **Schema tab in the Export XML dialog box**

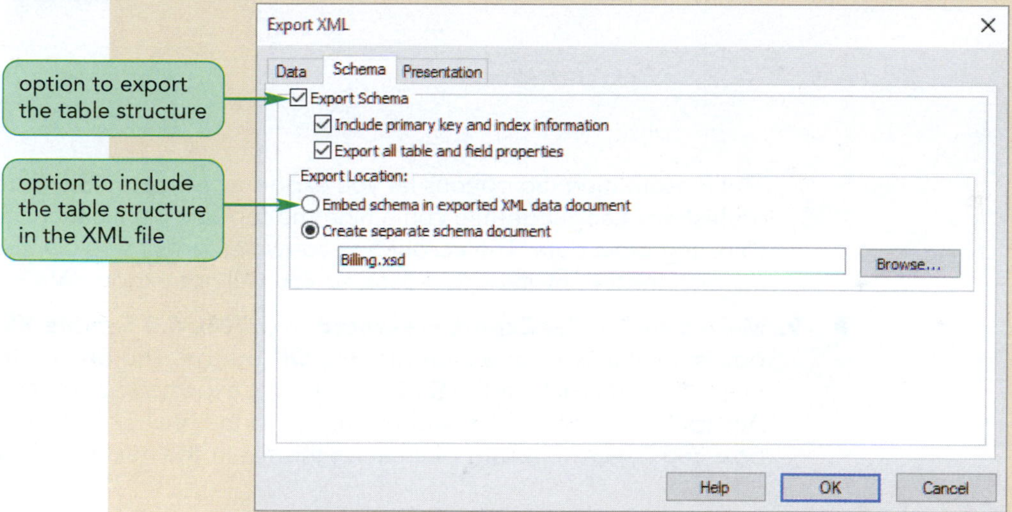

Along with the data from the tblBilling table, you'll be exporting its table structure, including information about the table's primary key, indexes, and table and field properties. An **XSD (XML Structure Definition) file** is a file that defines the structure of the XML file, much like the Design view of a table defines the fields and their data types. You can include this structure information in a separate XSD file, or you can embed the information in the XML file. The accounting software accepts a single XML file, so you'll embed the structure information in the XML file.

7. Click the **Embed schema in exported XML data document** option button. The Create separate schema document option button is now grayed out.
8. Click the **Presentation** tab. See Figure 8-14.

Figure 8-14 **Presentation tab in the Export XML dialog box**

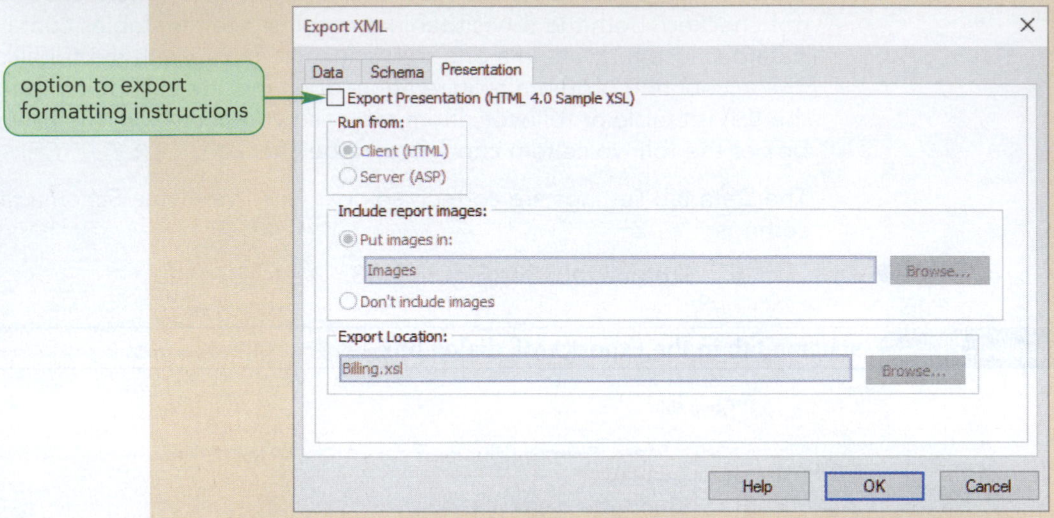

The Presentation tab options let you export a separate **XSL (Extensible Stylesheet Language) file** containing the format specifications for the tblBilling table data. The accounting software contains its own formatting instructions for any imported data, so you will not export an XSL file.

9. Make sure that the **Export Presentation (HTML 4.0 Sample XSL)** check box is not checked, and then click the **OK** button. The Export XML dialog box closes, the data in the tblBilling table is exported as an XML file to the Access2 > Module folder, and you return to the final Export - XML File dialog box. You'll see the results of creating this file in the next set of steps.

Kimberly plans to make further tests exporting the tblBilling table as an XML file, so you'll save the export steps.

Saving and Running Export Specifications

Saving the steps to export the tblBilling table as an XML file will save time and eliminate errors when Kimberly repeats the export procedure. You'll save the export steps and then run the saved steps.

To save and run the XML file export steps:

1. In the Export – XML File Wizard dialog box, click the **Save export steps** check box. The dialog box displays additional options for the save operation.

   The dialog box has the same options you saw earlier when you saved the XML import steps. You'll enter a description, and you won't create an Outlook task because Kimberly will be running the saved export steps only on an as-needed basis.

2. In the Description box, type **XML file accounting entries from the tblBilling table**. See Figure 8-15.

Figure 8-15 Saving the export steps

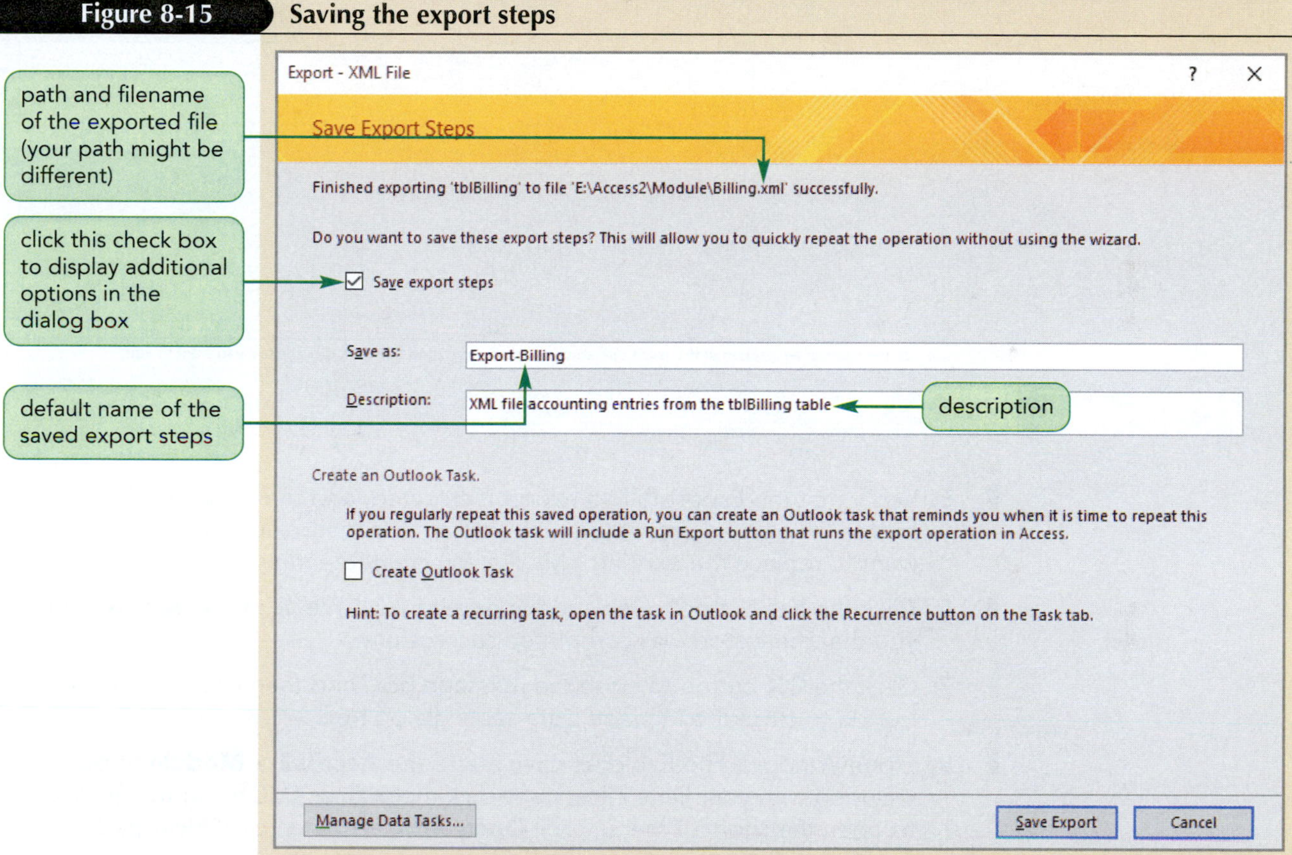
path and filename of the exported file (your path might be different)
click this check box to display additional options in the dialog box
default name of the saved export steps
description
Export - XML File
Save Export Steps
Finished exporting 'tblBilling' to file 'E:\Access2\Module\Billing.xml' successfully.
Do you want to save these export steps? This will allow you to quickly repeat the operation without using the wizard.
Save export steps
Save as:
Export-Billing
Description:
XML file accounting entries from the tblBilling table
Create an Outlook Task.
If you regularly repeat this saved operation, you can create an Outlook task that reminds you when it is time to repeat this operation. The Outlook task will include a Run Export button that runs the export operation in Access.
Create Outlook Task
Hint: To create a recurring task, open the task in Outlook and click the Recurrence button on the Task tab.
Manage Data Tasks...
Save Export
Cancel

3. Click the **Save Export** button. The export steps are saved as Export-Billing and the Export - XML File dialog box closes.

   Now you'll run the saved steps.

4. Click the **External Data** tab (if necessary), and then in the Export group, click the **Saved Exports** button. The Manage Data Tasks dialog box opens with the Saved Exports tab selected. See Figure 8-16.

   Trouble? If the Saved Imports tab is displayed in the Manage Data Tasks dialog box, then you selected the Saved Imports button instead of the Saved Exports button. Click the Save Exports tab in the dialog box.

Figure 8-16 Saved Exports tab in the Manage Data Tasks dialog box

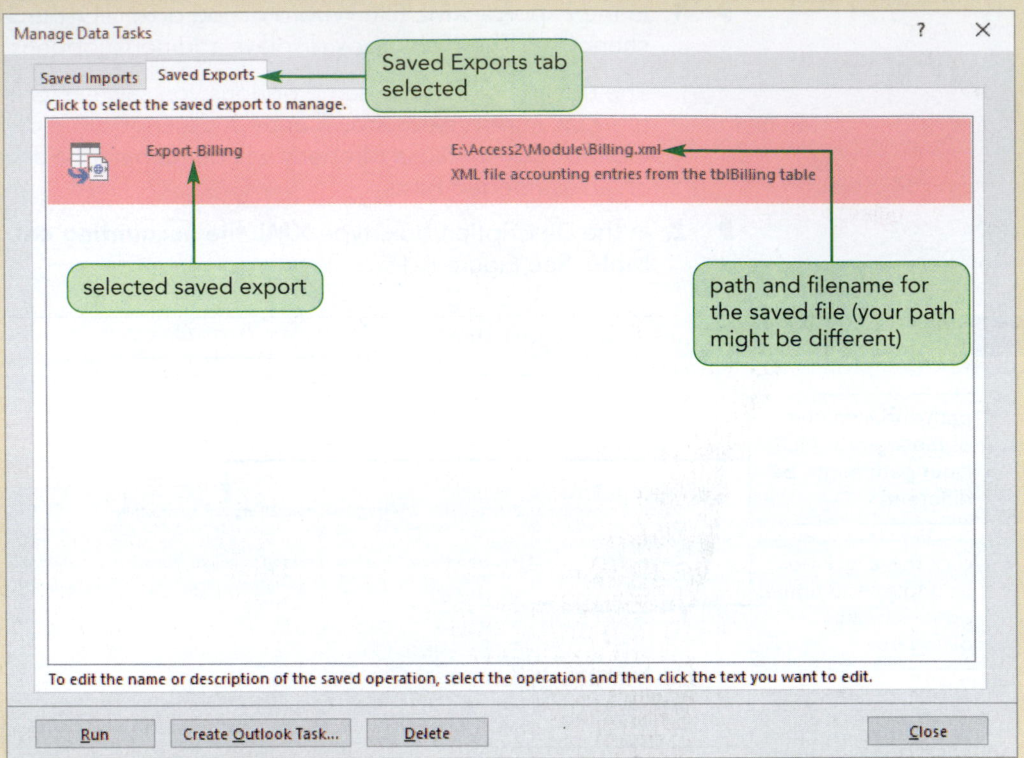

5. Verify that the Export-Billing export is selected, and then click the **Run** button. The saved procedure runs, and a message box opens, asking if you want to replace the existing XML file you created earlier.
6. Click the **Yes** button to replace the existing XML file. A message box informs you that the export was completed successfully.
7. Click the **OK** button to close the message box, and then click the **Close** button to close the Manage Data Tasks dialog box.
8. Open Windows File Explorer, navigate to the **Access2 > Module** folder included with your Data Files, right-click the **Billing** XML file in the file list to open the shortcut menu, click **Open with**, and then click **Notepad**. See Figure 8-17.

Figure 8-17 **Billing XML file in Notepad**

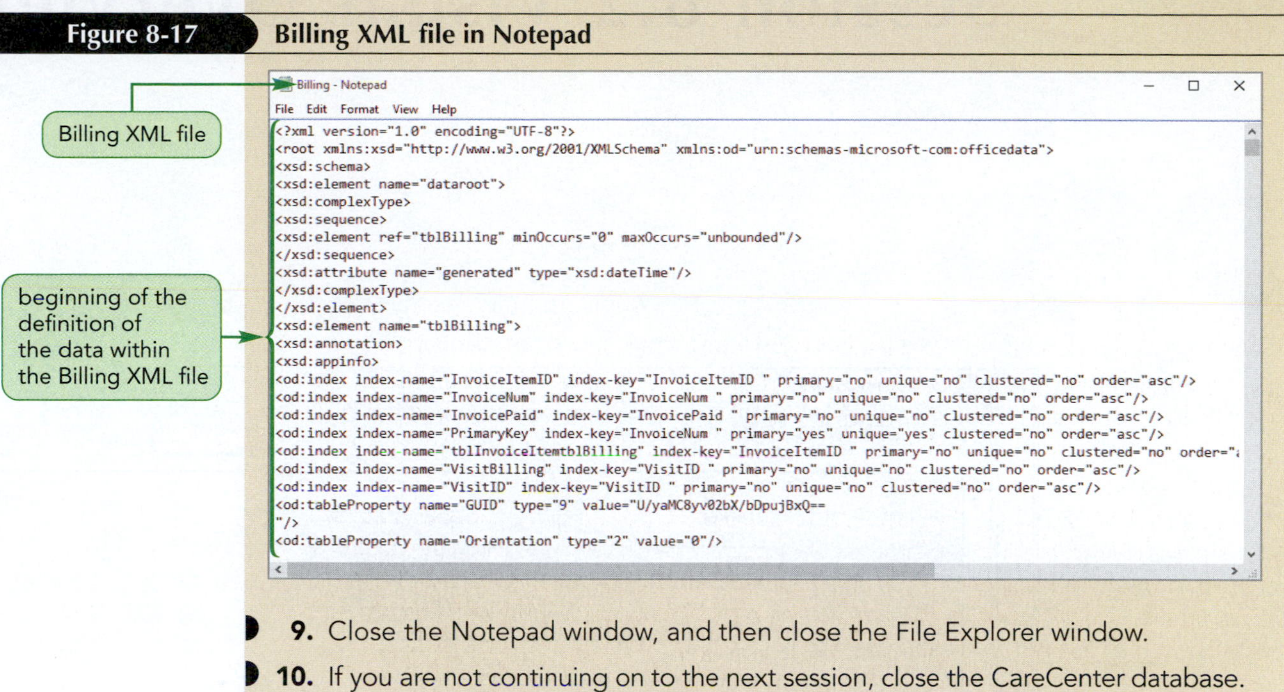

9. Close the Notepad window, and then close the File Explorer window.
10. If you are not continuing on to the next session, close the CareCenter database.

INSIGHT

Importing and Exporting Data

Access supports importing data from common file formats such as an Excel workbook, a text file, and an XML file. Additional Access options include importing an object from another Access database, importing data from other databases (such as Microsoft SQL Server, mySQL, and others), and importing an HTML document, an Outlook folder, or a SharePoint list.

In addition to exporting an Access object as an XML file or an HTML document, Access includes options for exporting data to another Access database, other databases (Microsoft SQL Server, mySQL), an Excel workbook, a text file, a Word document, a SharePoint list, or a PDF or XPS file. You can also export table or query data directly to Word's mail merge feature or export an object to an email message.

The steps you follow for other import and export options work similarly to the import and export steps you've already used.

You've imported and exported data, analyzed a table's design, and saved and run import and export specifications. In the next session, you will analyze data by working with a chart, creating and using an application part, linking external data, and adding a tab control to a form.

REVIEW

Session 8.1 Quick Check

1. What is HTML?
2. What is an HTML template?
3. What is a static webpage?
4. What is a CSV file?
5. What is the Table Analyzer?
6. _____________ is a programming language that describes data and its structure.

Session 8.2 Visual Overview:

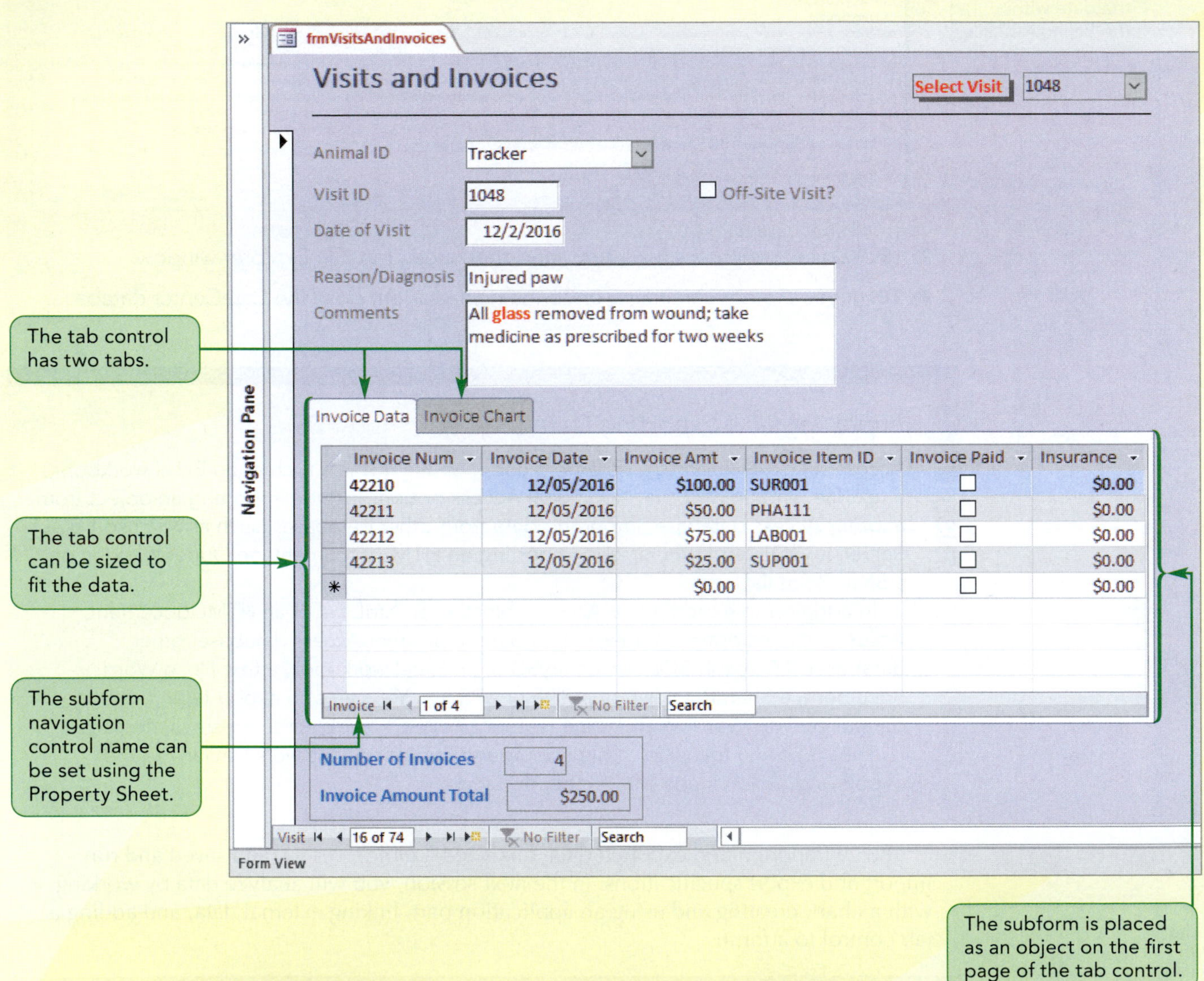

frmVisitsAndInvoices
Visits and Invoices
Select Visit
1048
Animal ID
Tracker
Visit ID
1048
Off-Site Visit?
Date of Visit
12/2/2016
Reason/Diagnosis
Injured paw
Comments
All glass removed from wound; take medicine as prescribed for two weeks
Navigation Pane
Invoice Data
Invoice Chart
Invoice Num
Invoice Date
Invoice Amt
Invoice Item ID
Invoice Paid
Insurance
42210 12/05/2016 $100.00 SUR001 $0.00
42211 12/05/2016 $50.00 PHA111 $0.00
42212 12/05/2016 $75.00 LAB001 $0.00
42213 12/05/2016 $25.00 SUP001 $0.00
$0.00 $0.00
Invoice 1 of 4 No Filter Search
Number of Invoices 4
Invoice Amount Total $250.00
Visit 16 of 74 No Filter Search
Form View
The tab control has two tabs.
The tab control can be sized to fit the data.
The subform navigation control name can be set using the Property Sheet.
The subform is placed as an object on the first page of the tab control.

Tab Control with a Chart

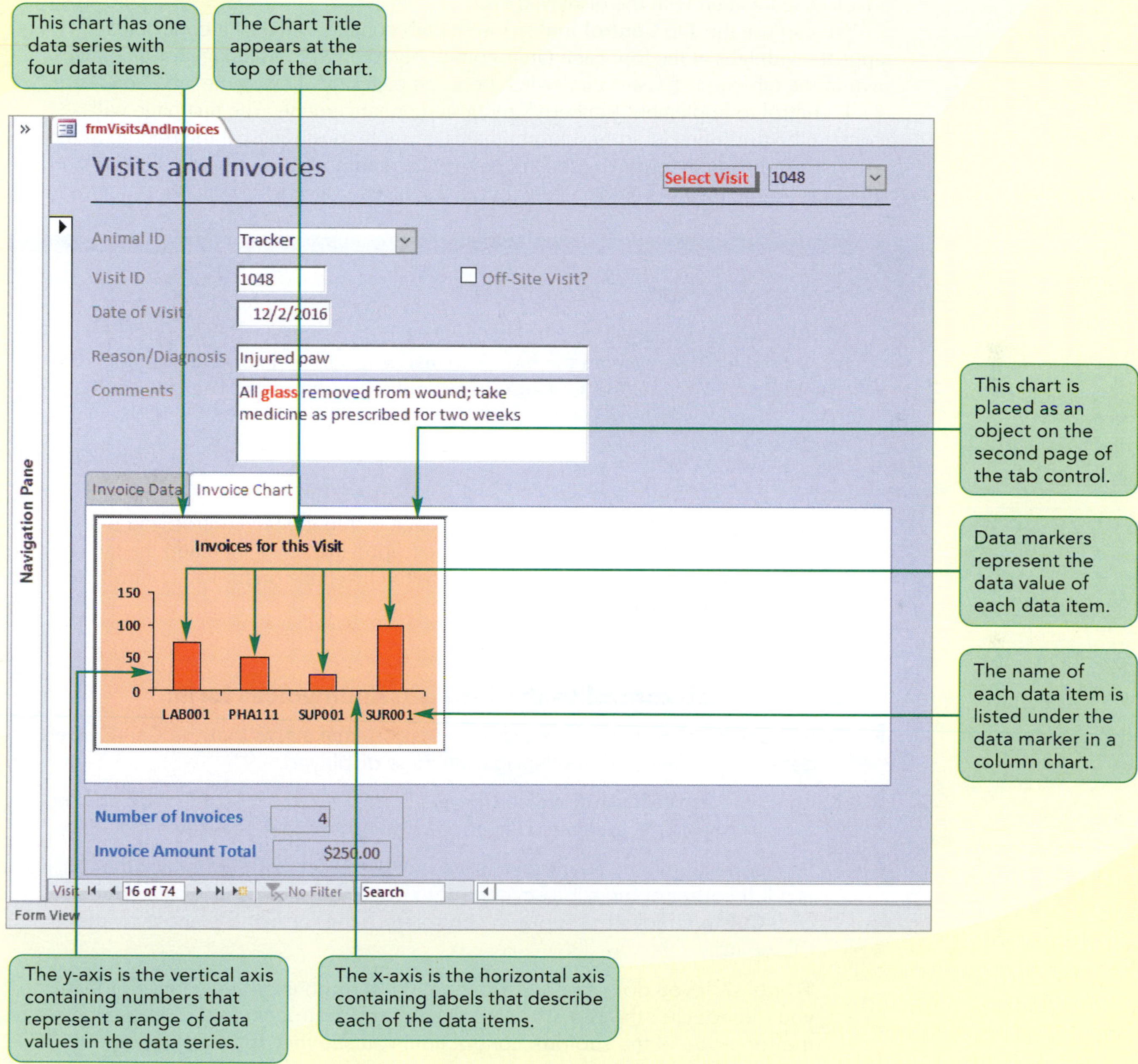

This chart has one data series with four data items.
The Chart Title appears at the top of the chart.
frmVisitsAndInvoices
Visits and Invoices
Select Visit
1048
Animal ID
Tracker
Visit ID
1048
Off-Site Visit?
Date of Visit
12/2/2016
Reason/Diagnosis
Injured paw
Comments
All glass removed from wound; take medicine as prescribed for two weeks
Navigation Pane
Invoice Data
Invoice Chart
Invoices for this Visit
150
100
50
0
LAB001
PHA111
SUP001
SUR001
Number of Invoices
4
Invoice Amount Total
$250.00
Visit
16 of 74
No Filter
Search
Form View
This chart is placed as an object on the second page of the tab control.
Data markers represent the data value of each data item.
The name of each data item is listed under the data marker in a column chart.
The y-axis is the vertical axis containing numbers that represent a range of data values in the data series.
The x-axis is the horizontal axis containing labels that describe each of the data items.

Using a Tab Control in a Form

Kimberly wants you to enhance the frmVisitsAndInvoices form in the CareCenter database to enable users to switch between different content. Recall the frmVistsAndInvoices form currently contains a main form displaying Visit data and the frmBillingSubform subform displaying the information for the billed invoices related to a displayed visit. Specifically, Kimberly wants users to be able to choose between viewing the frmBillingSubform subform or viewing a chart showing the invoices associated with the displayed visit.

You can use the **Tab Control tool** to insert a tab control, which is a control that appears with tabs at the top. Each tab is commonly referred to as a page, or tab page, within the tab control. Users can switch between pages by clicking the tabs. You'll use a tab control to implement Kimberly's requested enhancements. The first page will contain the frmBillingSubform subform that is currently positioned at the bottom of the frmVisitsAndInvoices form. The second page will contain a chart showing the invoice amounts for the invoices associated with the displayed visit.

INSIGHT

Working with Large Forms

When you want to work with a form that is too large to display in the Access window, one way to help you navigate the form is to manually add page breaks, where it makes sense to do so. You can use the **Page Break tool** to insert a page break control in the form, which lets users move between the form pages by pressing the Page Up and Page Down keys.

To expedite placing the subform in the first page within the tab control, you'll first cut the subform from the form, placing it on the Clipboard. You'll then add the tab control, and finally you'll paste the subform into the first page on the tab control. You need to perform these steps in Design view.

To add the tab control to the frmVisitsAndInvoices form:

1. If you took a break after the previous session, make sure that the CareCenter database is open with the Navigation Pane displayed.
2. Open the **frmVisitsAndInvoices** form in Form view to review the form and the frmBillingSubform, switch to Design view, and then close the Navigation Pane.
3. Scroll down until the subform is fully visible (if necessary), right-click the top-left corner of the subform control to open the shortcut menu, and then click **Cut** to remove the subform control from the form and place it on the Clipboard.

   Trouble? If you do not see Cut as one of the options on the shortcut menu, you did not click the top edge of the subform control correctly. Right-click the top edge of the subform control until you see this option on the shortcut menu, and then click Cut.
4. Increase the length of the Detail section to **7.0** inches.
5. Select the **Number of Invoices** label and control, the **Invoice Amount Total** label and control, and the rectangle control surrounding them, and then move the selected controls below the 6-inch horizontal line in the grid.
6. On the Form Design Tools Design tab, in the Controls group, click the **Tab Control** tool.

7. Position the + portion of the Tab Control tool pointer in the Detail section at the 2.75-inch mark on the vertical ruler and three grid dots from the left edge of the form, and then click the mouse button. A tab control with two tabs is inserted in the form.

8. Right-click in the middle of the tab control, and then when an orange outline appears inside the tab control, click **Paste** on the shortcut menu. The subform is pasted in the tab control on the left-most tab. See Figure 8-18.

Figure 8-18 Subform in the tab control

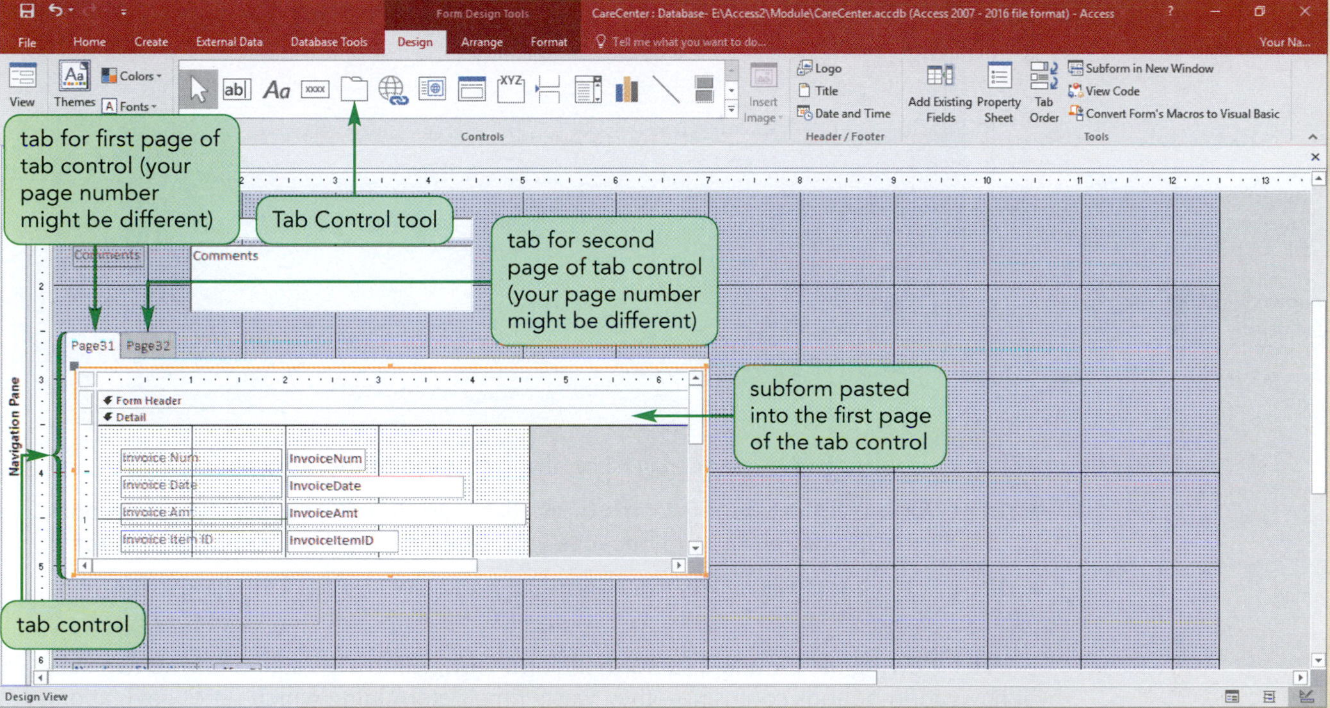

9. Switch to Form view, click the **Select Visit** arrow, click **1048** in the list, and then click **1048** in the Visit ID box to deselect all controls.

10. Scroll down to the bottom of the form. The left tab, which is labeled Page31 (yours might differ), is the active tab. See Figure 8-19.

Figure 8-19 Subform on the tab control in Form view

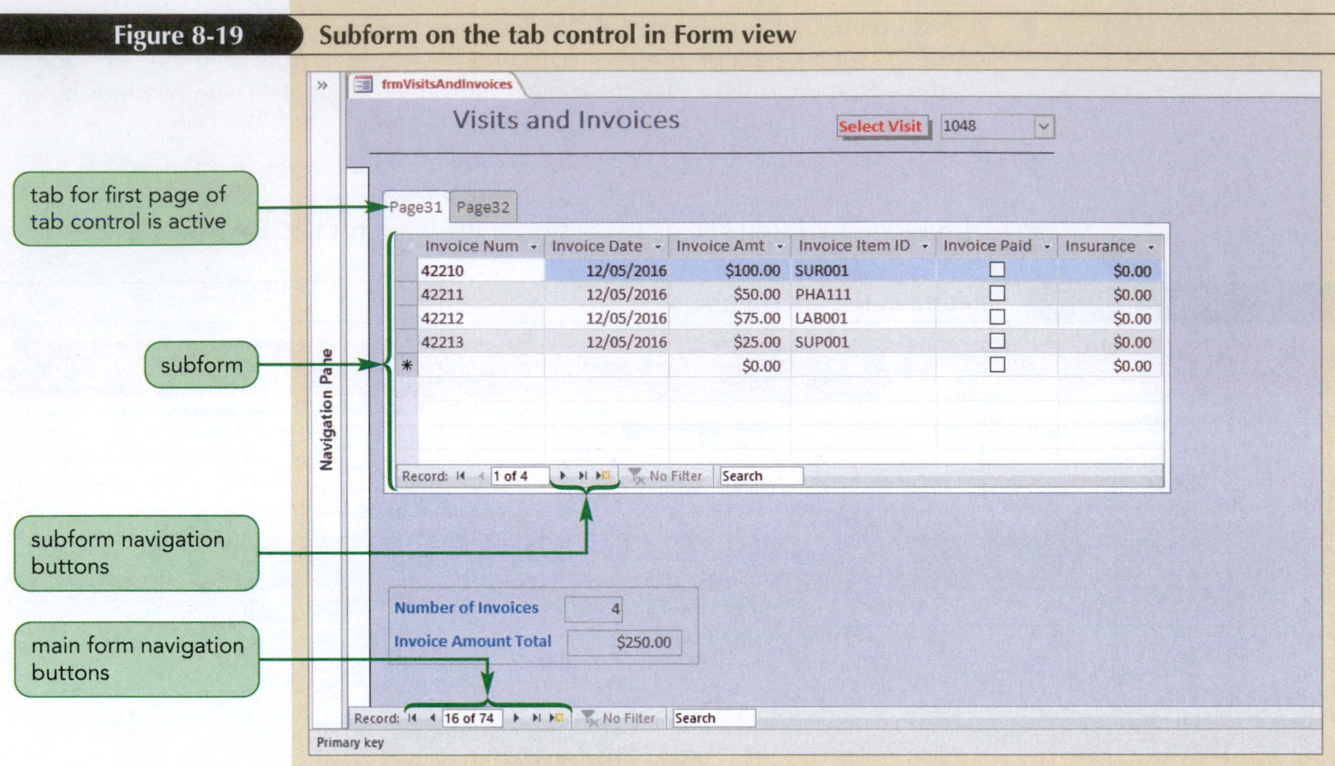

The subform is now displayed on the first page of the tab control.

11. Click the **right tab** of the tab control (labeled Page32) to display the second page. The page is empty because you haven't added any controls to it yet.

12. Click the **left tab** of the tab control again to display the frmBillingSubform.

After viewing the form and subform in Form view, Kimberly's staff finds the two sets of navigation buttons confusing—they waste time determining which set of navigation buttons applies to the subform and which to the main form. To clarify this, you'll set the Navigation Caption property for the main form and the subform. The **Navigation Caption property** lets you change the navigation label from the word "Record" to another value. Because the main form displays data about visits and the subform displays data about invoices, you'll change the Navigation Caption property for the main form to "Visit" and for the subform to "Invoice."

You'll also set the Caption property for the tabs in the tab control, so they indicate the label on the tabs indicate the contents of each page.

To change the captions for the navigation buttons and the tabs:

1. Switch to Design view, and then click the main form's form selector to select the form control in the main form, open the Property Sheet to display the properties for the selected form control, click the **All** tab (if necessary), click the **Navigation Caption** box, and then type **Visit**. See Figure 8-20.

Figure 8-20 Navigation Caption property set for the main form

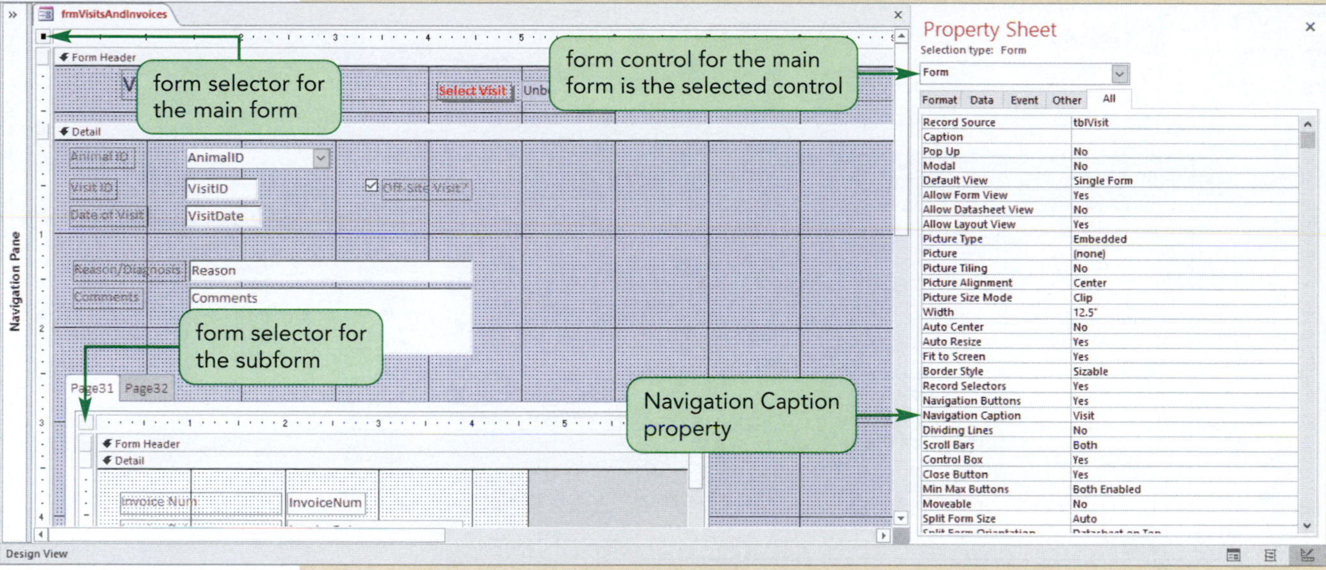

2. Click the **form selector** for the subform on the left-most tab to select the subform, click the **form selector** for the subform again to select the form control in the subform and to display the Property Sheet for the selected form control, click the **Navigation Caption** box, and then type **Invoice**. Navigation buttons don't appear in Design view, so you won't see the effects of the Navigation Caption property settings until you switch to Form view. Before you do that, you will set the Caption property for the two tabs in the tab control.
3. Click the **left tab** in the tab control, and then click the **left tab** in the tab control again to select it.
4. In the Property Sheet, in the Caption box, type **Invoice Data** and then press the **Tab** key. The Caption property value now appears on the left tab in the tab control. See Figure 8-21.

Figure 8-21 The Caption property set for the left tab of a tab control

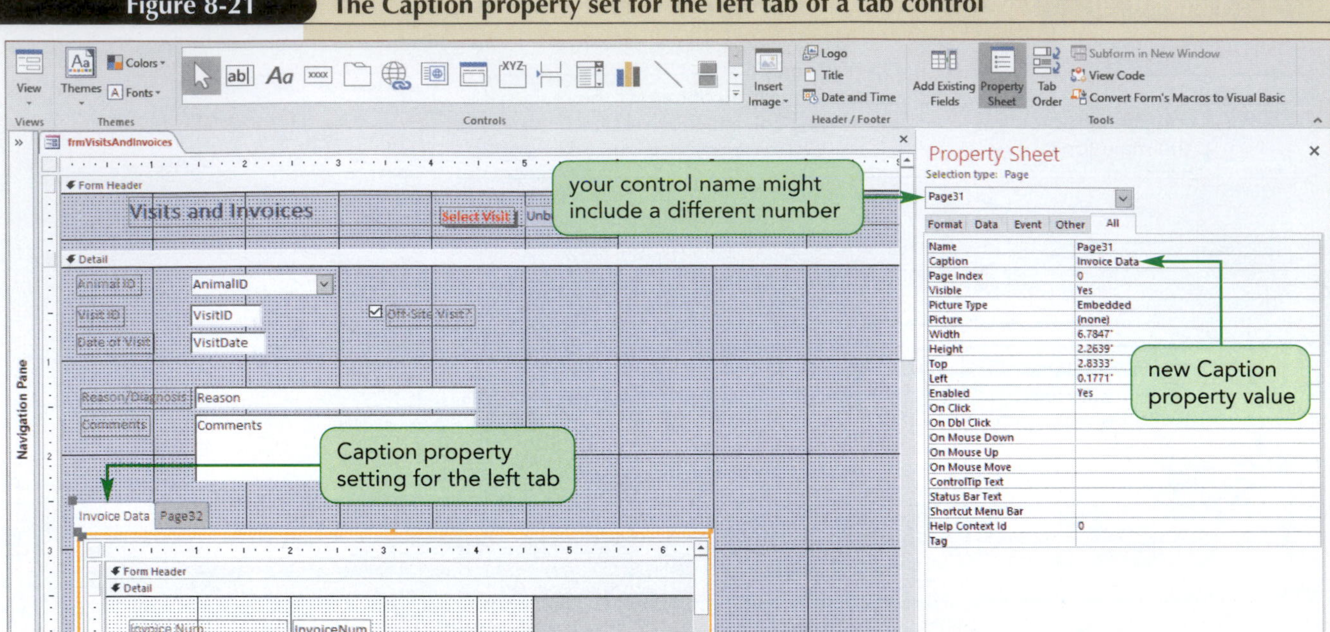

5. Click the **right tab** in the subform to select it, in the Property Sheet, in the Caption box, type **Invoice Chart**, press the **Tab** key, and then close the Property Sheet.
6. Save your form design changes, and then switch to Form view.
7. Click the **Select Visit** arrow, click **1048** in the list to display the information for this visit, click **1048** in the Visit ID box to deselect all controls, and then scroll to the bottom of the form. The tabs and the navigation buttons now display the new caption values. See Figure 8-22.

Figure 8-22 Modified report with tab control in Form view

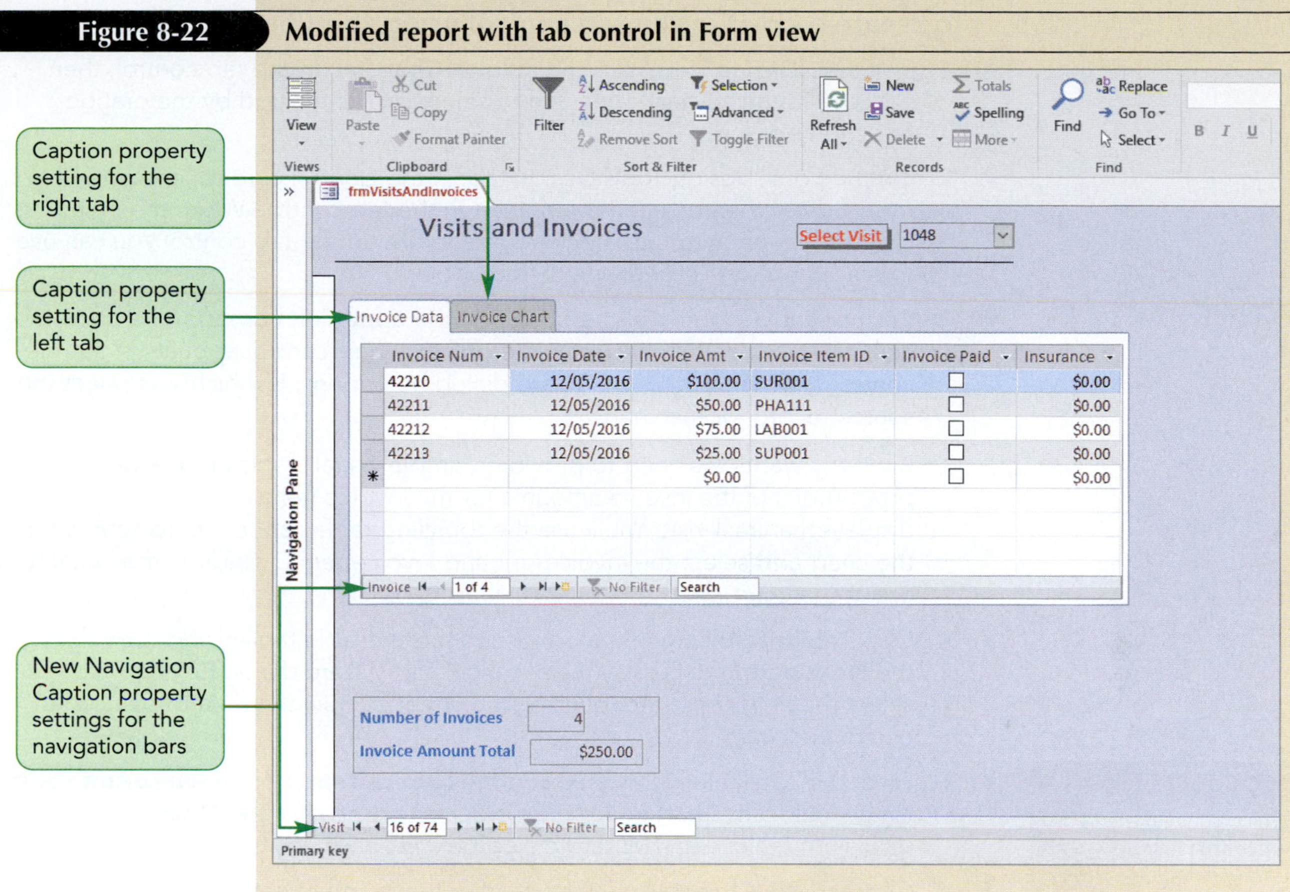

Next, Kimberly wants you to add a simple chart to the second page of the tab control. You will create the chart using the Chart Wizard.

Creating a Chart Using the Chart Wizard

The Chart Wizard in Access guides you in creating a chart in a form or report based upon data contained in the database. Once the chart is created, you can modify and format the chart using Microsoft Graph, a simple graphing tool included in Microsoft Office 365.

REFERENCE

Embedding a Chart in a Form or Report

- On the Report Design Tools or Form Design Tools Design tab, click the More button in the Controls group, and then click the Chart tool.
- Position the + portion of the pointer in the form or report, and then click the mouse button to start the Chart Wizard.
- Navigate through the Chart Wizard dialog boxes to select the record source, fields, chart type, specify a layout for the chart data, and select the fields that link the records in the database object to the chart's components, if necessary.
- In the Chart Wizard's last dialog box, enter a chart title, select whether to include a legend, and then click the Finish button.

The tblBilling table contains the information Kimberly wants displayed in chart form on the right tab in the tab control.

To create a chart in the tab control using the Chart Wizard:

1. Switch to Design view, click the **Invoice Chart** tab in the tab control, then click the **Invoice Chart** tab again to select it, as indicated by the orange selection border.
2. On the Form Design Tools Design tab, in the Controls group, click the **Chart** tool, and then position the pointer in the tab control. When the pointer is inside the tab control, the rectangular portion of the tab control you can use to place controls is filled with the color black.
3. Position the + portion of the pointer in the upper-left corner of the black tab control, and then click the mouse button. A chart control appears in the tab control, and the first Chart Wizard dialog box opens, in which you select the source record for the chart.

   Kimberly wants the chart to provide a simple visual display of the relative proportions of the invoice amounts for the invoice items for the currently displayed animal visit. You'll use the tblBilling table as the record source for the chart and select the InvoiceAmt and InvoiceItemID fields as the fields to use in the chart.
4. Click **Table: tblBilling** in the box listing the available tables, and then click the **Next** button to display the second Chart Wizard dialog box, in which you select the fields from the tblBilling table that contain the data to be used to create the chart.
5. From the Available Fields box, add the **InvoiceItemID** and **InvoiceAmt** fields to the Fields for Chart box, in that order, and then click the **Next** button to display the third Chart Wizard dialog box, in which you choose the chart type.
6. Click the **Pie Chart** button (first chart in the fourth row) to select the pie chart as the chart type to use for Kimberly's chart. The box on the right displays a brief description of the selected chart type. See Figure 8-23.

TIP

The order of the items is important. Be sure to add InvoiceItemID first, then InvoiceAmt.

Figure 8-23 Chart Wizard showing selected chart type

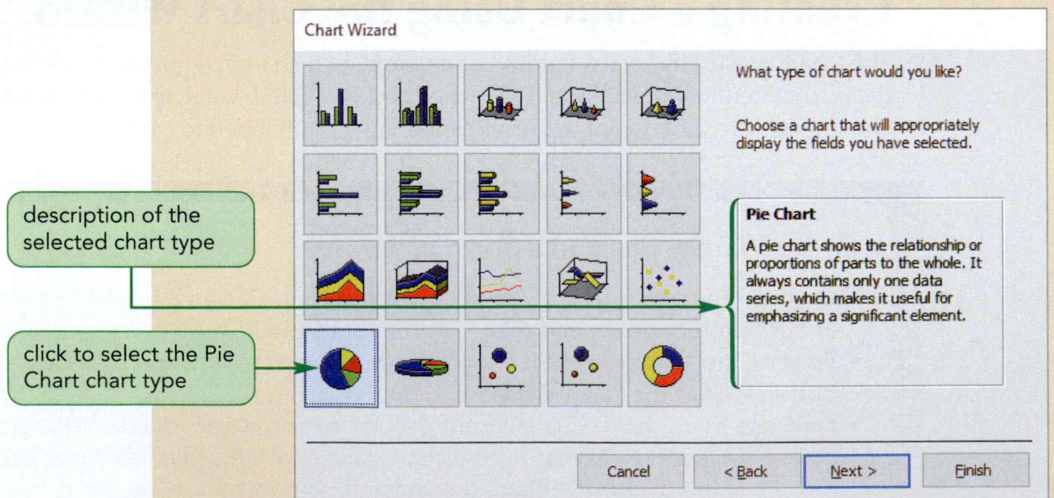

7. Click the **Next** button to display the next Chart Wizard dialog box, which displays a preview of the chart and options to modify the layout of the data in the chart. You'll use the default layout based on the two selected fields.

8. Click the **Next** button to display the next Chart Wizard dialog box, which lets you choose the fields that link records in the main form (which uses the tblVisit table as its record source) to records in the chart (which uses the tblBilling table as its record source). You don't need to make any changes in this dialog box because the wizard has already identified VisitID as the common field linking these two tables. You can use the VisitID field as the linking field even though you didn't select it as a field for the chart.
9. Click the **Next** button to display the final Chart Wizard dialog box, in which you enter the title that will appear at the top of the chart and choose whether to include a legend in the chart.
10. Type **Invoices for this Visit**, make sure the **Yes, display a legend** option button is selected, and then click the **Finish** button. The completed chart appears in the tab control.

    You'll view the form in Form view, where it's easier to assess the chart's appearance.

11. Save your form design changes, switch to Form view, display Visit ID **1048** in the main form, click the **Invoice Chart** tab to display the chart, and then scroll down to the bottom of the form (if necessary). See Figure 8-24.

Figure 8-24 Pie chart in the tab control

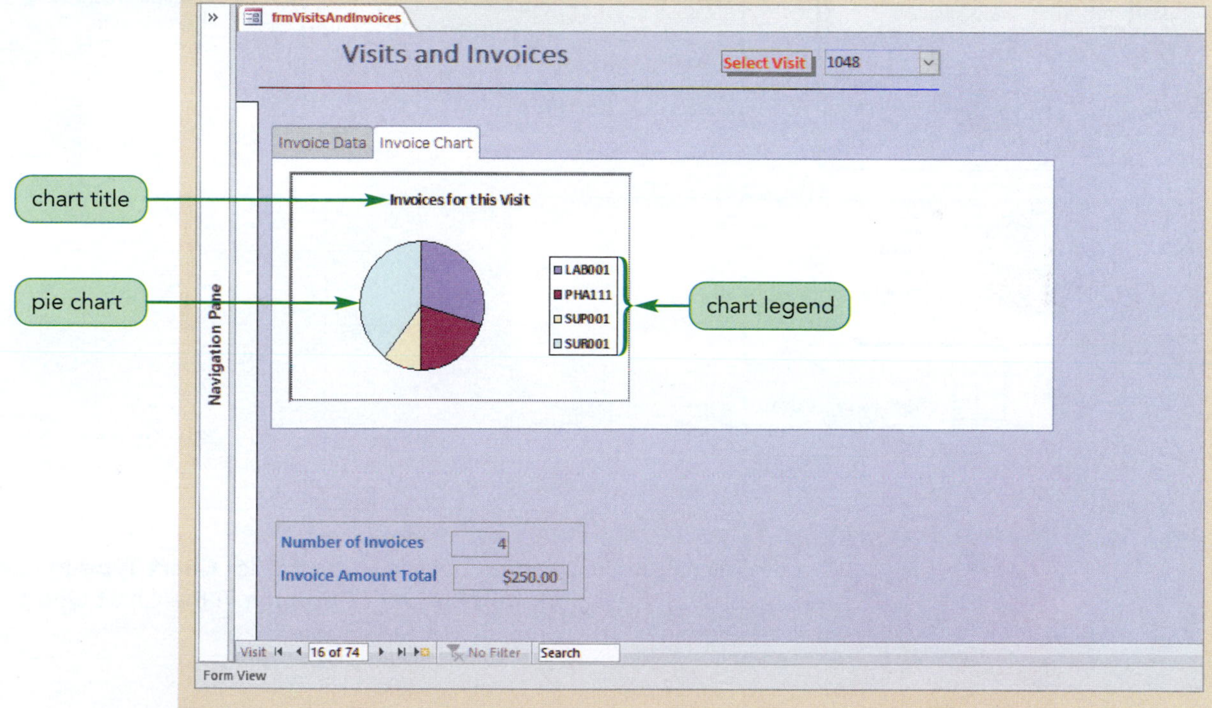

INSIGHT

Linking Record Sources

The record source for a primary main form must have a one-to-many relationship to the record source for a related subform or chart. The subform or chart object has its Link Master Fields property set to the primary key in the record source for the main form and its Link Child Fields property set to the foreign key in the record source for the subform or chart.

After viewing the chart, Kimberly decides it needs some modifications. She wants you to change the chart type from a pie chart to a bar chart, remove the legend, and modify the chart's background color. To make these formatting changes, you'll switch to Design view. To modify the chart, you need to access the Microsoft Graph tools. You can double-click the chart to display the Microsoft Graph menu bar and toolbar on the ribbon and open the datasheet for the chart, or you can right-click the chart and use the shortcut menu to open the chart in a separate Microsoft Graph window.

To edit the chart using Microsoft Graph tools:

1. Switch to Design view, right-click an edge of the chart object to open the shortcut menu, point to **Chart Object**, and then click **Open**. Microsoft Graph starts and displays the chart and datasheet in a separate window on top of the Access window. See Figure 8-25.

Figure 8-25 Chart in the Microsoft Graph window

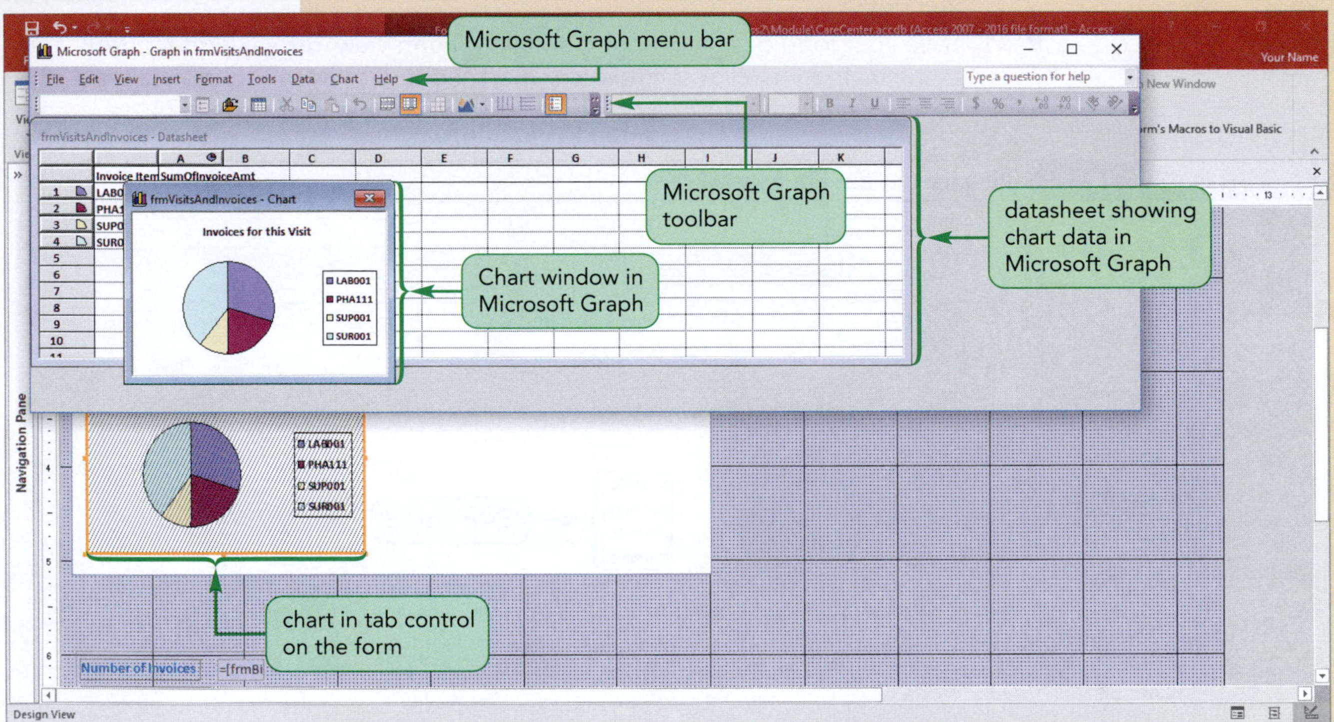

2. On the Microsoft Graph menu bar, click **Chart**, click **Chart Type** to open the Chart Type dialog box, and then click **Column** in the Chart type box to display the types of column charts. See Figure 8-26.

Figure 8-26 Microsoft Graph Chart Type dialog box

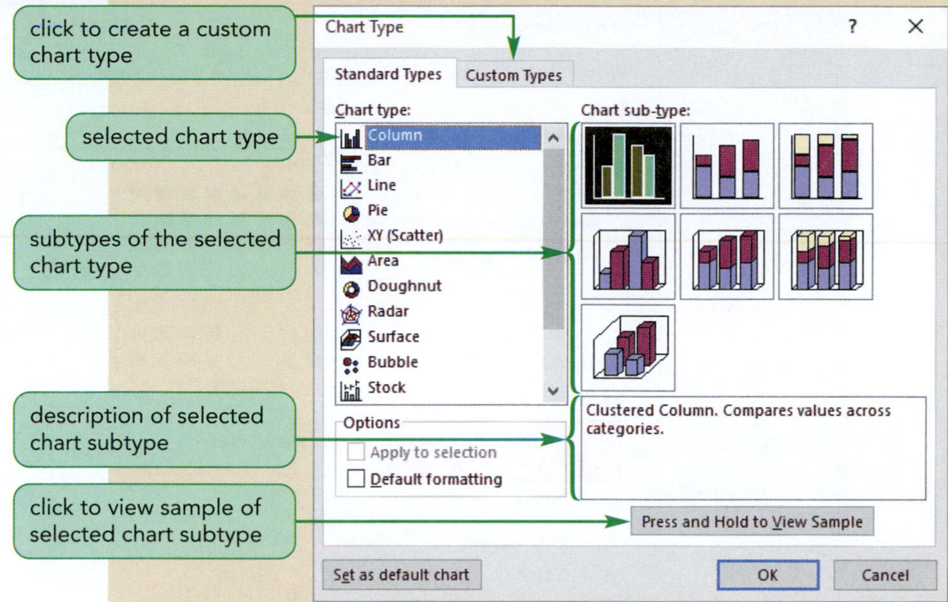

The column chart is the selected chart type, and the clustered column chart is the default chart subtype (row 1, column 1). A description of the selected chart subtype appears below the chart subtypes. You can create a custom chart by clicking the Custom Types tab. You can also use the Press and Hold to View Sample button to display a sample of the selected subtype.

3. Click the **Press and Hold to View Sample** button to view a sample of the chart, release the mouse button, and then click the **OK** button to close the dialog box and change the chart to a column chart in the Microsoft Graph window and in the tab control on the form.

4. On the Microsoft Graph menu bar, click **Chart**, click **Chart Options** to open the Chart Options dialog box, click the **Legend** tab to display the chart's legend options, click the **Show legend** check box to uncheck it, and then click the **OK** button. The legend is removed from the chart object in the Microsoft Graph window and in the tab control on the form.

To change the color or other properties of a chart's elements—the chart background (or chart area), axes, labels to the left of the y-axis, labels below the x-axis, or data markers (columnar bars for a column chart)—you need to double-click the chart element.

TIP

A data marker is a bar, dot, segment, or other symbol that represents a single data value.

5. In the Microsoft Graph Chart window, double-click one of the column data markers in the chart to open the Format Data Series dialog box, and then in the Area section, click the **orange** color (row 2, column 2) in the color palette. The sample color in the dialog box changes to orange to match the selected color. See Figure 8-27.

Figure 8-27 **Format Data Series dialog box in Microsoft Graph**

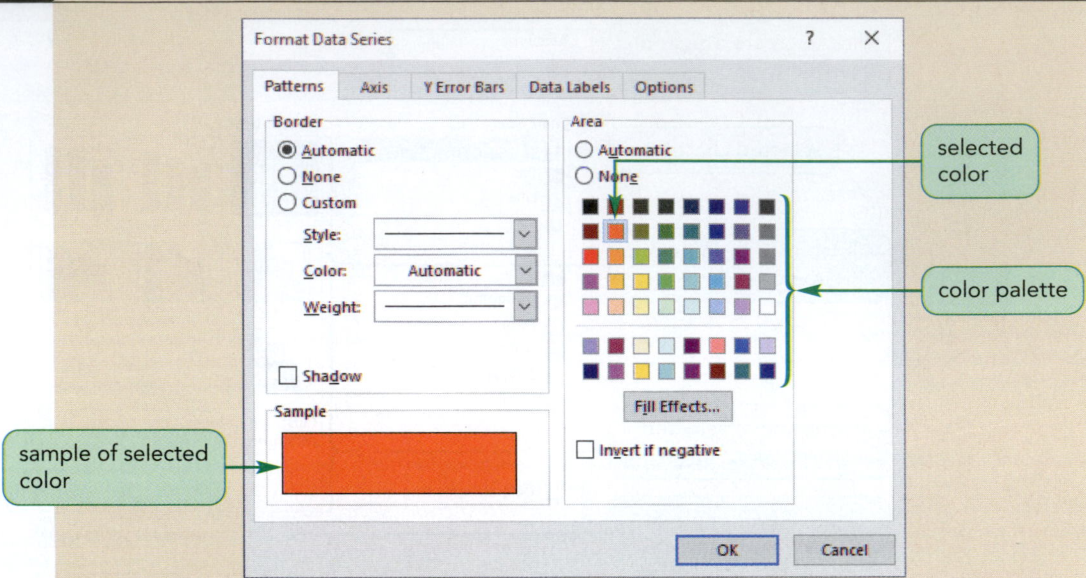

6. Click the **OK** button to close the dialog box. The color of the data markers in the chart in the Microsoft Graph window and in the form's tab control changes to orange.

   Trouble? If only one of the bars changed color, you selected one bar instead of the entire series. Click Edit, click Undo, and then repeat Steps 5 and 6.

7. In the Chart window, double-click the white chart background to the left of the title to open the Format Chart Area dialog box, in the Area section, click the **light orange** color (row 5, column 2) in the color palette, and then click the **OK** button. The chart's background color changes from white to light orange in the chart in the Microsoft Graph window and in the form's tab control.

8. Click **File** on the Microsoft Graph menu bar, and then click **Exit & Return to frmVisitsAndInvoices** to close the Microsoft Graph window and return to the form.

9. Save your form design changes, switch to Form view, display Visit ID **1048** in the main form, and then click the **Invoice Chart** tab to display the chart. Scroll down to the bottom of the form. See Figure 8-28.

Figure 8-28 Completed chart in Form view

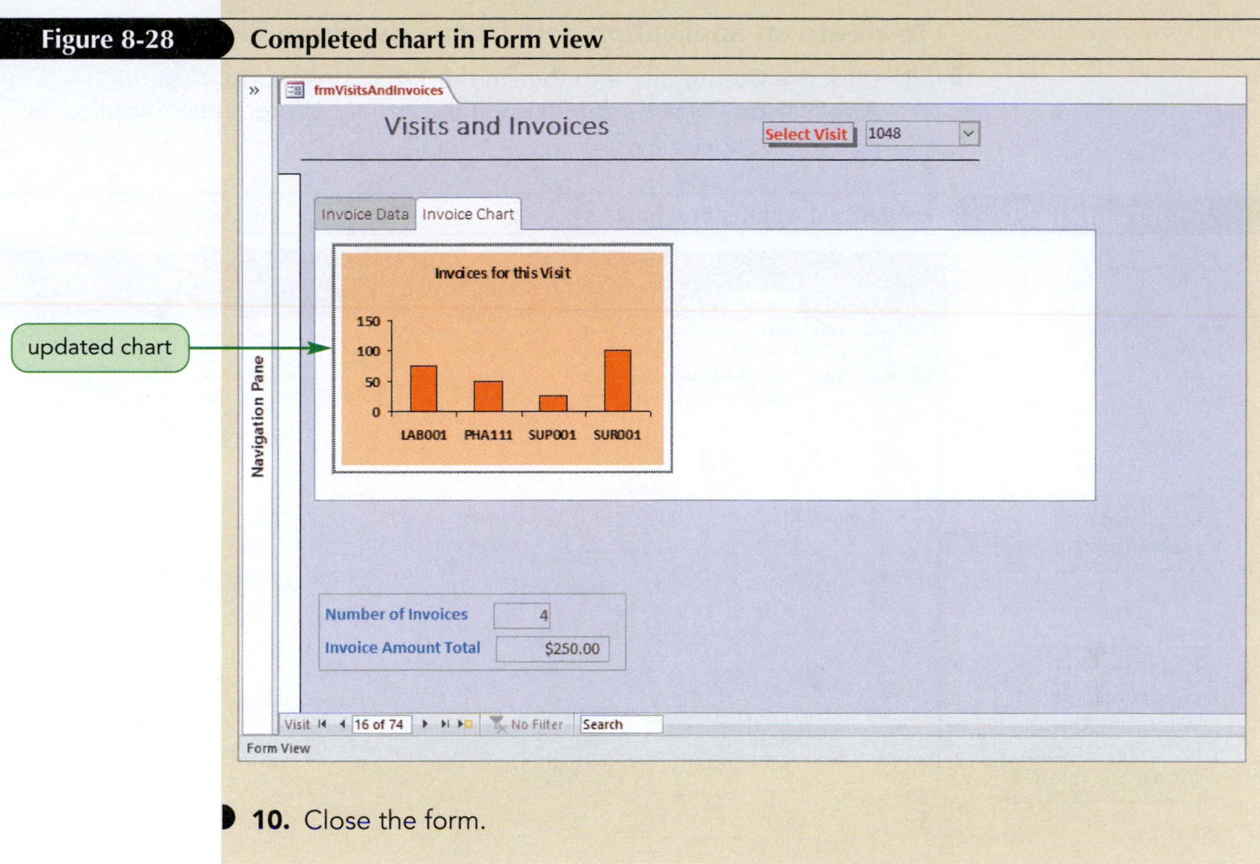

10. Close the form.

Sometimes it is useful to use a table structure from one database in other databases. One option would be to import the table structure only from the database file into each subsequent database, a method you used in an earlier module. Another option is to create an application part in one database, which can then easily be included in any Access database file on your computer.

Using Templates and Application Parts

A template is a predefined database that can include tables, relationships, queries, forms, reports, and other database objects and is used to create a new database file. On the New tab in Backstage view, a list of predefined templates are displayed. You can also create your own template from an existing database file. In addition to creating a database template, you can also create templates for objects using an **application part**, which is a specialized template for a specific database object that can be imported into an existing database. There are predefined application parts included with Access, and you can also create your own user-defined application part. Once you create a user-defined application part in one database, it is available to all Access databases created and stored on your computer.

You can use an application part to insert a predefined object from another database or template into an existing database. Like a template, an application part can contain tables, relationships, queries, forms, reports, and other database objects.

Kimberly would like to reuse a table structure from another database to create a new table in the CareCenter database. You'll use the NewOwnerReferrals.accdb database file to create an application part for the table structure, and then you'll import the new application part into the CareCenter database to use to create a table of referrals from online veterinary pharmacies.

To create an application part from a database file:

1. Click the **Create** tab, and then in the Templates group, click the **Application Parts** button to open the gallery of predefined application parts. See Figure 8-29.

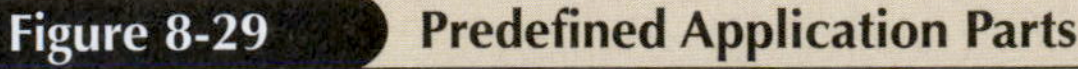

Figure 8-29 **Predefined Application Parts**

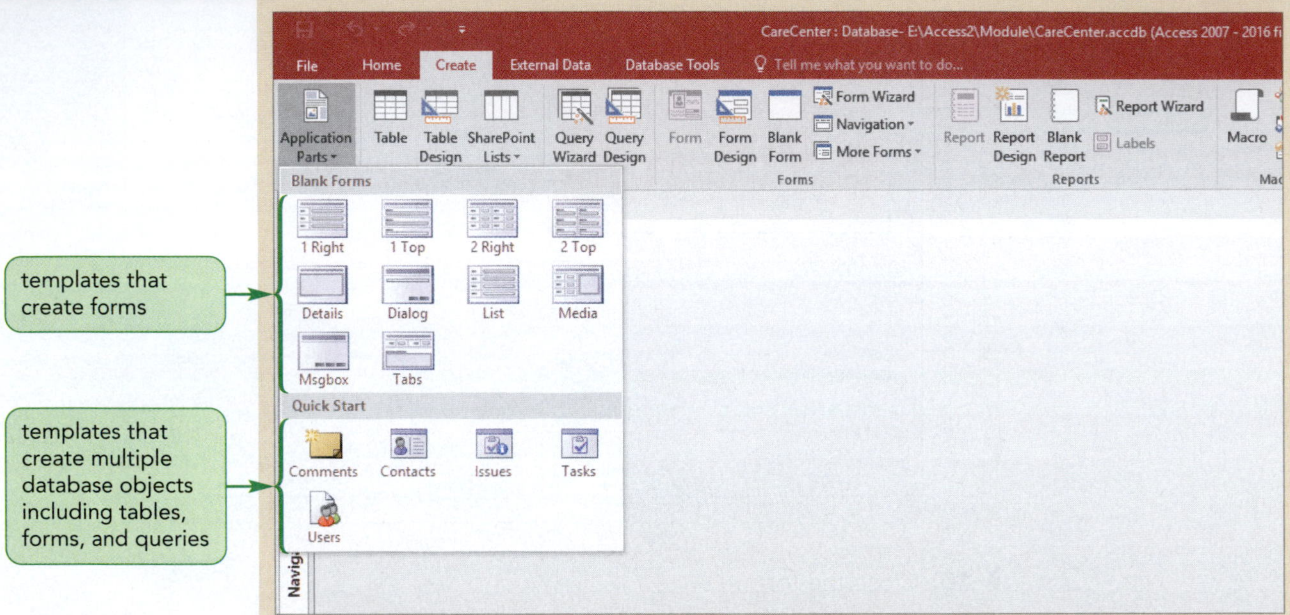

Note that there are Blank Forms and Quick Start Application Parts. If you or another user of your computer has created user-defined application parts, they also will appear in the gallery.

2. Close the CareCenter database file.
3. Open the **NewOwnerReferrals** database file from the **Access2 > Module** folder included with your Data Files, enabling the content if necessary.

   When you save this file as a template, all database objects that are in the file will be included in the template file. This file contains only the tblReferral table.

4. Click the **File** tab to open Backstage view, and then in the navigation bar, click **Save As**.
5. In Database File Types section of the Save Database As list, click **Template**. See Figure 8-30.

Figure 8-30 Save As options in Backstage View

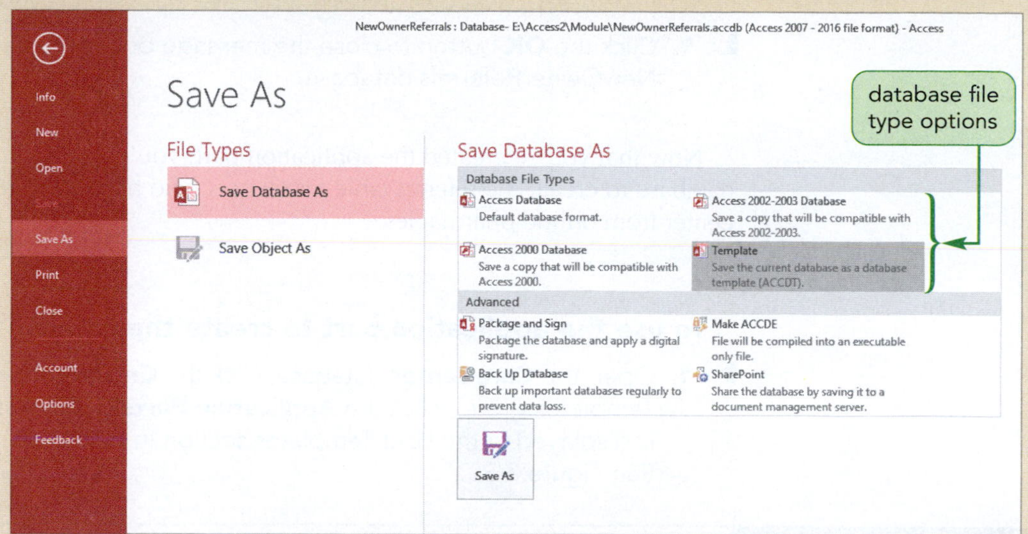

6. Click the **Save As** button. The Create New Template from This Database dialog box opens.
7. Click in the Name box, type **Referral**, click in the Description box, type **New owner referral**, and then click the **Application Part** check box to select it. See Figure 8-31.

Figure 8-31 Create New Template from This Database dialog box

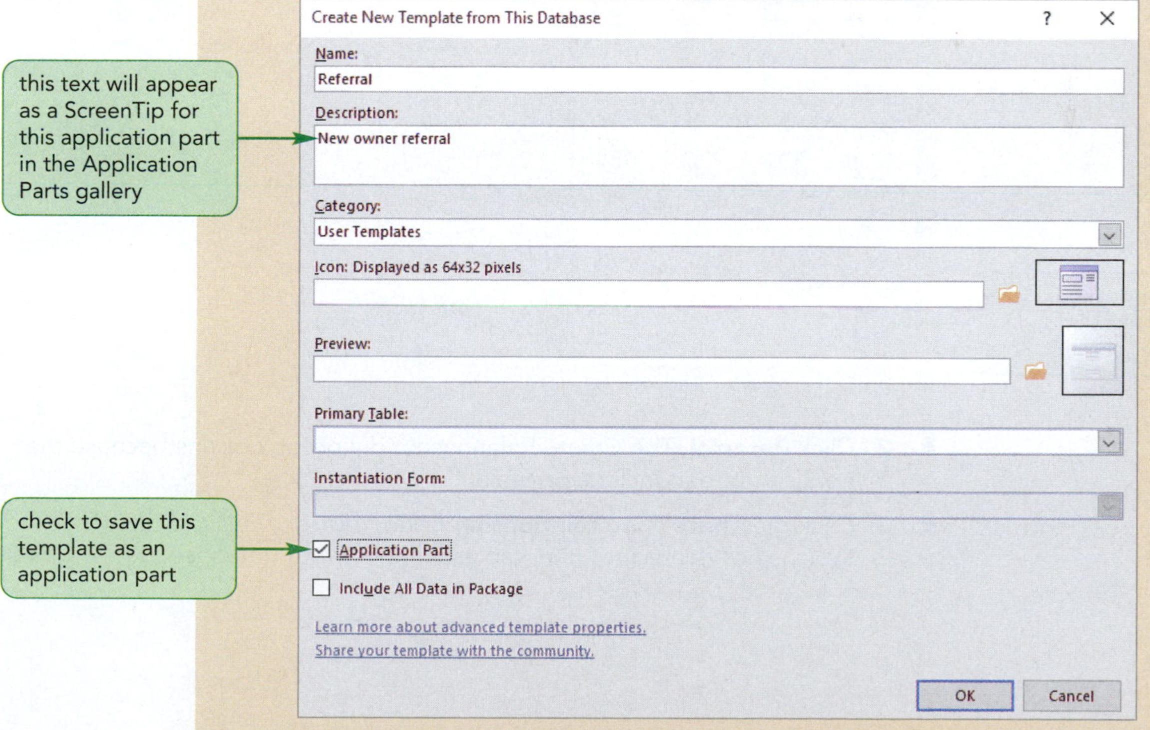

8. Click the **OK** button to close the dialog box. An alert box opens, indicating that the application part, as a template, has been saved.

9. Click the **OK** button to close the message box, and then close the NewOwnerReferrals database.

Now that you've created the application part, you'll use it in the CareCenter database to create the referral table for owners who have been referred to the care center from online pharmacies.

To use the application part to create the referral table:

1. Open the **CareCenter** database, click the **Create** tab, and then in the Templates group, click the **Application Parts** button. The Referral template is displayed in the User Templates section in the Application Parts gallery. See Figure 8-32.

Figure 8-32 Referral template in Application Parts Gallery

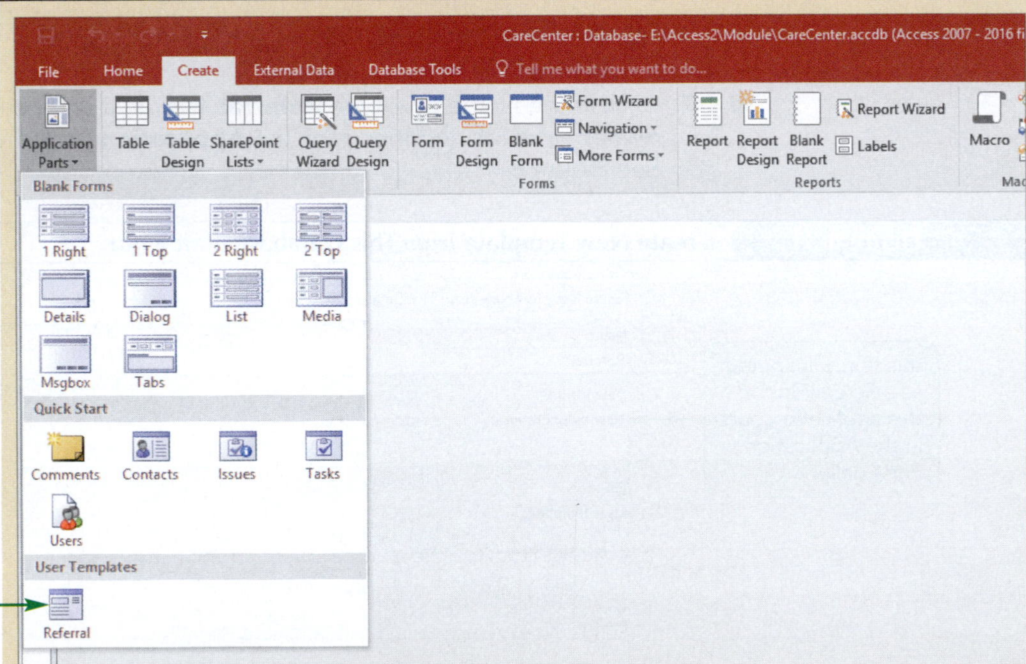

2. Click **Referral**. The Create Relationship dialog box opens because the application part includes a table.

3. Click the **There is no relationship** option button. This indicates that the new table is not related to other tables in the current database. See Figure 8-33.

Figure 8-33 Create Relationship dialog box

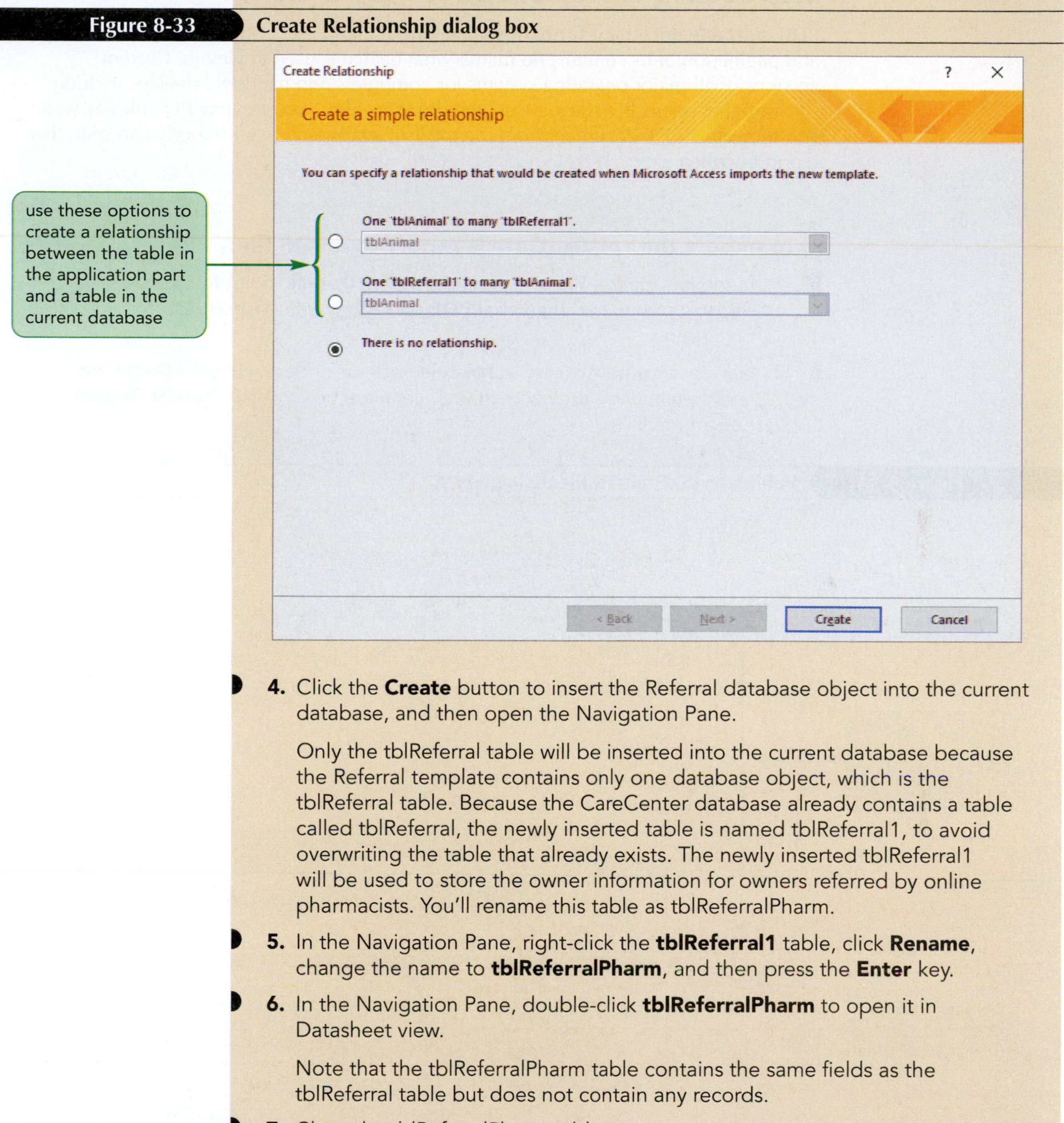

4. Click the **Create** button to insert the Referral database object into the current database, and then open the Navigation Pane.

   Only the tblReferral table will be inserted into the current database because the Referral template contains only one database object, which is the tblReferral table. Because the CareCenter database already contains a table called tblReferral, the newly inserted table is named tblReferral1, to avoid overwriting the table that already exists. The newly inserted tblReferral1 will be used to store the owner information for owners referred by online pharmacists. You'll rename this table as tblReferralPharm.

5. In the Navigation Pane, right-click the **tblReferral1** table, click **Rename**, change the name to **tblReferralPharm**, and then press the **Enter** key.

6. In the Navigation Pane, double-click **tblReferralPharm** to open it in Datasheet view.

   Note that the tblReferralPharm table contains the same fields as the tblReferral table but does not contain any records.

7. Close the tblReferralPharm table.

Kimberly would like to be able to send an electronic copy of the rptVisitDetails report that other people can view on their computers, rather than distributing printed reports. You can export tables, queries, reports, and other database objects as files that can be opened in other programs such as Excel and PDF readers. Kimberly would like to distribute rptVisitDetails as a PDF and asks you to export the report in this format.

Exporting a Report to a PDF File

PDF (portable document format) is a file format that preserves the original formatting and pagination of its contents no matter what device is used to view it. Current versions of all major operating systems for computers and handheld devices include software that opens PDF files. Most web browsers allow you to view PDF files as well. You'll create a PDF document from the rptVisitDetails report so Kimberly can send this report to colleagues.

To export the rptVisitDetails report to a PDF file:

1. In the Navigation Pane, right-click **rptVisitDetails**, point to **Export** on the shortcut menu, and then click **PDF or XPS**. The Publish as PDF or XPS dialog box opens.
2. Navigate to the **Access2 > Module** folder included with your Data Files, and then change the name in the File name box to **Visit Details Report**. See Figure 8-34.

Figure 8-34 Publish as PDF or XPS file dialog box

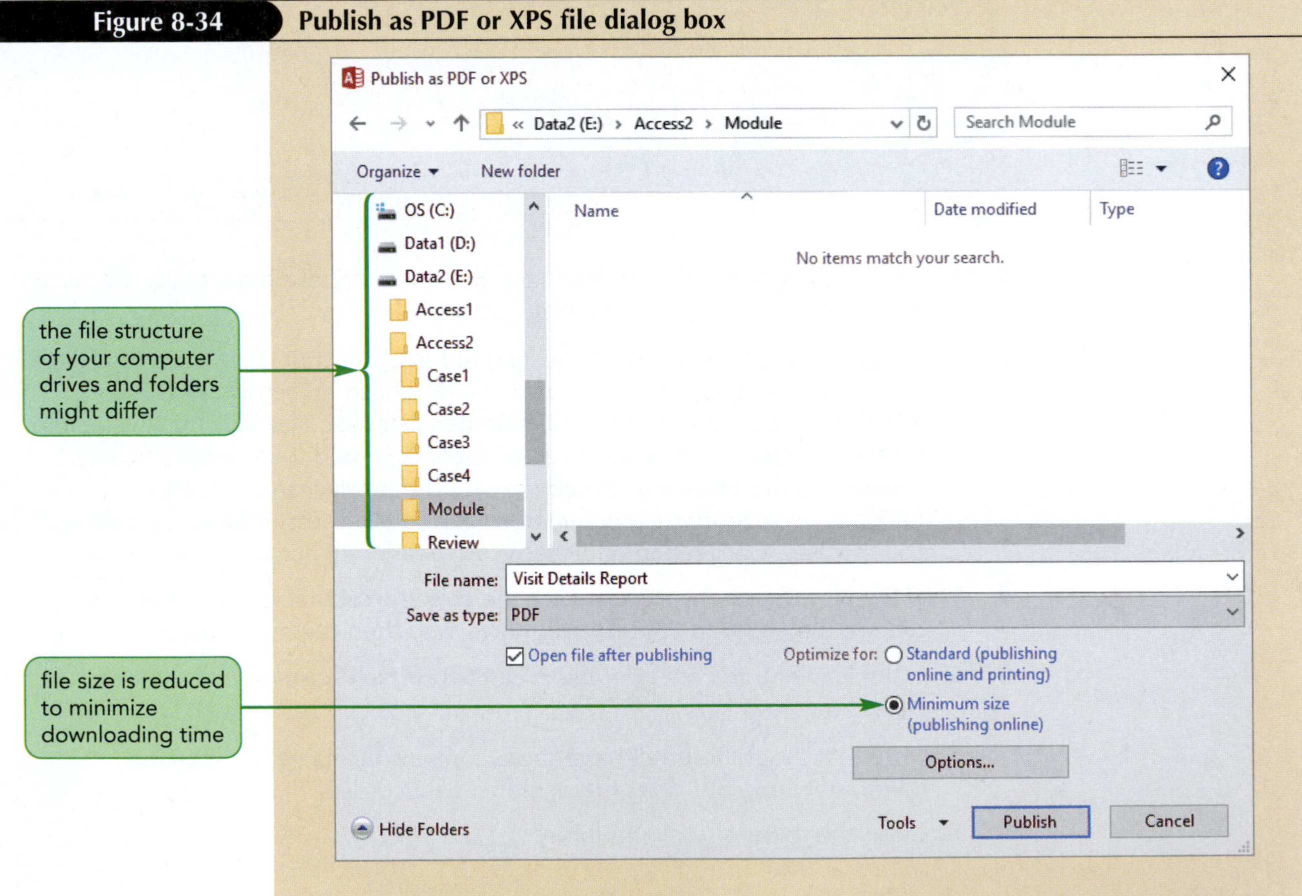

Kimberly would like people who are visually impaired to be able to use the PDF document with their screen readers. When a PDF file is saved using the minimum size option, there is no additional functionality for screen readers. You can include document structure tags that allow people using screen readers to navigate the document easily. Screen reader software voices the structure tags, such as a tag that provides a description of an image. Structure tags also reflow text so that screen readers understand the flow of information and can read it in a logical order. For instance, a page with a sidebar shouldn't be read as two columns; the main column needs to be read as a continuation of the previous page.

In order to add this functionality, you'll specify that document structure tags should be included.

3. Click the **Options** button. The Options dialog box opens.
4. Click the **Document structure tags for accessibility** check box to select it. See Figure 8-35.

Figure 8-35 Options dialog box for PDF file export

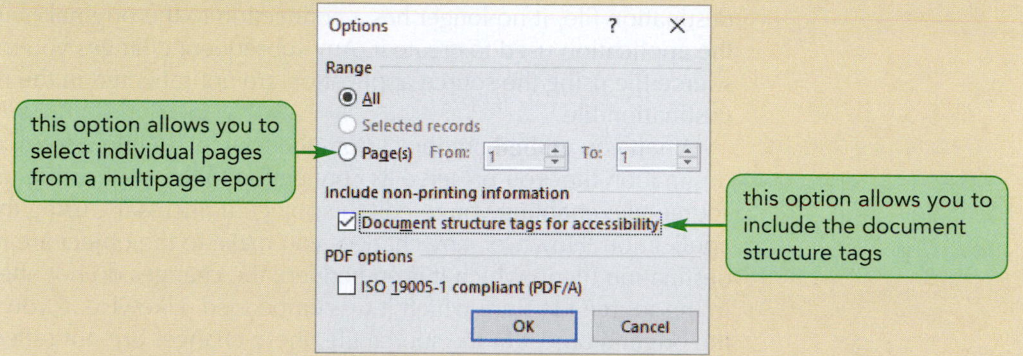

5. Click the **OK** button to close the Options dialog box, and then click the **Publish** button to close the Publish as PDF or XPS dialog box and to create the PDF file. The Export - PDF dialog box opens.

   Trouble? Depending on the operating system you're using, the PDF file may open. If it does, close the PDF file and return to Access.

6. In the Export - PDF dialog box, click the **Close** button to close the dialog box without saving the export steps.
7. Open Windows File Explorer, navigate to the **Access2 > Module** folder included with your Data Files, and then double-click the **Visit Details Report.pdf** to open the PDF file and examine the results.
8. Close the PDF file, and then close Windows File Explorer.

Kimberly is pleased to know that she can export database objects as PDF files. Now she would like your help with one additional external data issue. Her staff maintains an Excel workbook that contains contact information for people who volunteer at Riverview Veterinary Care Center. Kimberly wants to be able to use this data in the CareCenter database.

Integrating Access with Other Applications

As you know, when you create a form or report in Access, you include more than just the data from the record source table or query. You've added controls such as lines, rectangles, tab controls, and graphics in your forms and reports to improve their appearance and usability. You can also add charts, drawings, and other objects to your forms and reports, but Access doesn't have the capability to create them. Instead, you create these objects using other applications and then place them in a form or report using the appropriate integration method.

When you integrate information between two files created using different software applications, the file containing the original information, or object, is called the **source file**, and the file in which you place the information from the source file is called the **destination file**. In Access there are three ways for you to integrate objects created by other applications—importing, embedding, and linking.

As you know from your work thus far, when you import an object, you include the contents of a file in a new table or append it to an existing table, or you include the contents of the file in a form, report, or field. In this module you imported CSV and XML files as new tables in the CareCenter database, and the CSV and XML files you imported were created by other applications. After importing an object into a destination file, it no longer has a connection to the original object in the source file or the application used to create it. Any subsequent changes you make to the object in the source file using the source application are not reflected in the imported object in the destination file.

When you **embed** an object from the source file into a form, report, or field in the destination file, you preserve its connection to the application used to create it in the source file, enabling you to edit the object, if necessary, using the features of the source application. However, any changes you make to the object are reflected only in the destination file in which it is embedded; the changes do not affect the original object in the source file from which it was embedded. Likewise, if you make any changes to the original object in the source file, these changes are not reflected in the embedded object in the destination file.

When you **link** an object to a form, report, or field in a destination file, you maintain a connection between the object in the destination file to the original object in the source file. You can make changes to a linked object only in the source file. Any changes you make to the original object in the source file using the source application are then reflected in the linked object in the destination file. To view or use the linked object in a form, report, or field in the destination file, you must first open the source file in the source application.

PROSKILLS

Decision Making: Importing, Embedding, and Linking Data

How do you decide which integration method to use when you need to include in an Access database data that is stored in another file created in a different application?

- You should choose to import an object when you want to copy an object from a file created using a different application into a table, form, or report in the Access database, *and* you want to be able to manipulate and work with that object using Access tools, *and* you do not need these changes to the imported object to be reflected in the original object in the source file.
- Conversely, you should choose to embed or link the object when you want to be able to edit the copied object in the table, form, or report using the application with which the source object was created. You should embed the object when you *do not* want your changes to the embedded object in the destination file to affect the original object in the source file. You should choose to link the object when you want the object in the destination file to always match the original object in the source file.

The decision to import, embed, or link to an object containing data depends on how you will use the data in your database and what connection is required to the original data. You should carefully consider the effect of changes to the original data and to the copied data before choosing which method to use.

Linking Data from an Excel Worksheet

Kimberly's staff has extensive experience working with Excel, and one of her staff members prefers to maintain the data for people who volunteer in an Excel file named Volunteer. However, Kimberly needs to reference the volunteer data in the CareCenter database on occasion, and the data she's referencing must always be the current version of the data in the Volunteer Excel file. Importing the Excel workbook data as an Access table would provide Kimberly with data that's quickly out of date unless she repeats the import steps each time the data in the Excel workbook changes. Therefore, you'll link the data in the Excel file to a table in the CareCenter database. When the staff changes data in the Volunteer Excel workbook, the changes will be reflected automatically in the linked version in the database table. In addition, Kimberly won't be able to update the volunteer data from the CareCenter database, which ensures that only the staff members responsible for maintaining the Volunteer Excel workbook can update the data.

To link table data to an Excel file:

1. Click the **External Data** tab, and then in the Import & Link group, click the **Excel** button. The Get External Data - Excel Spreadsheet dialog box opens.

   Trouble? If the Export - Excel File dialog box opens, you clicked the Excel button in the Export group. Click the Cancel button and then repeat Step 1, being sure to select the Excel button from the Import & Link group.

2. Click the **Browse** button to open the File Open dialog box, navigate to the **Access2 > Module** folder included with your Data Files, click **Volunteer**, click the **Open** button, and then click the **Link to the data source by creating a linked table** option button. This option links to the data instead of importing or appending it. The selected path and filename are displayed in the File name box. See Figure 8-36.

Figure 8-36 Linking to data in an Excel workbook

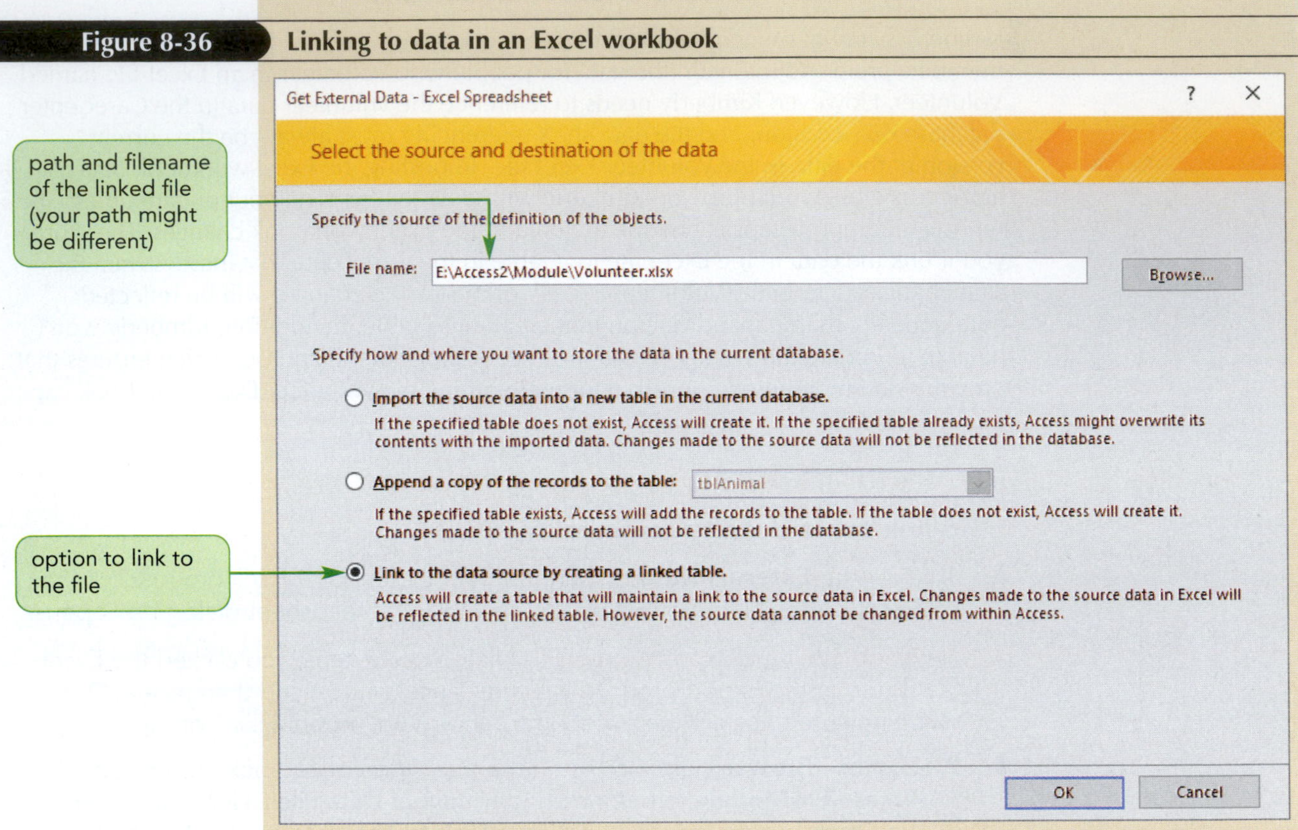

3. Click the **OK** button. The first Link Spreadsheet Wizard dialog box opens.

   The first row in the worksheet contains column heading names, and each row in the worksheet represents the data about a single volunteer.

4. Click the **First Row Contains Column Headings** check box to select it. See Figure 8-37.

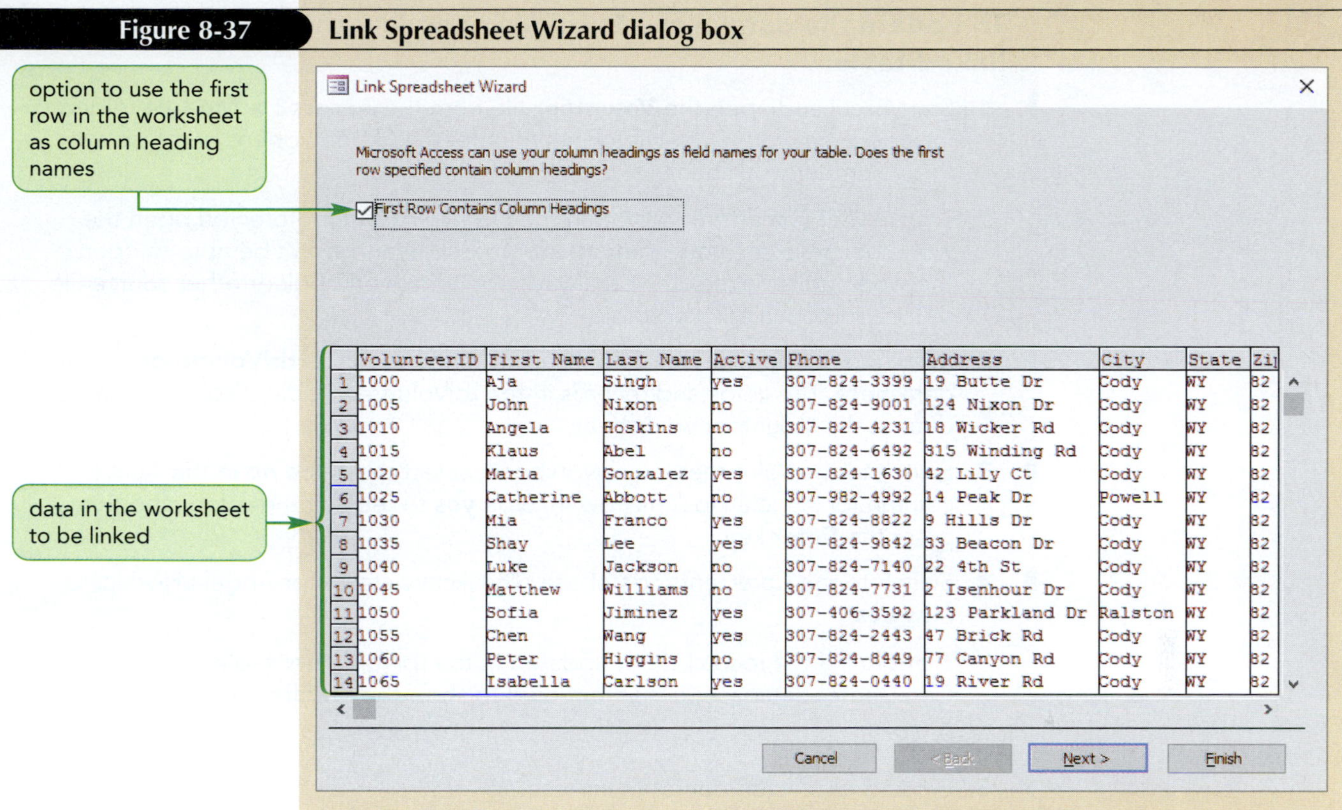

Figure 8-37 Link Spreadsheet Wizard dialog box

5. Click the **Next** button to open the final Link Spreadsheet Wizard dialog box, in which you choose a name for the linked table.
6. Change the default table name to **tblVolunteer** and then click the **Finish** button. A message box informs you that you've created a table that's linked to the workbook.
7. Click the **OK** button to close the message box. The tblVolunteer table is listed in the Navigation Pane, with an icon to its left indicating it is a linked table.

You can open and view the tblVolunteer table and use fields from the linked table in queries, forms, and reports, but you cannot update the data using the CareCenter database. You can only update the data only from the Excel workbook file. To open and view the tblVolunteer table in the CareCenter database, you must first open and leave open the Excel file to which the table is linked.

Kimberly tells you that the volunteer Hoskins had not been able to volunteer for a while, so her Active status was "no". She's now able to volunteer, and Kimberly would like to change her Active status to "yes". Next, you'll make a change to data in the Excel file and see the update in the linked table.

To update the data in the Excel file and view the data in the linked table:

1. Start Excel and open the **Volunteer** file from the **Access2 > Module** folder included with your Data Files. The Volunteer workbook opens and displays the Volunteer worksheet.

   Trouble? If you attempt to open the table in Access before you open the workbook in Excel, you'll get an error message and won't be able to open the workbook. Make sure you always open the workbook or other source file before you open a linked table.

2. Switch to the CareCenter database, and then open the **tblVolunteer** datasheet. The fields and records in the tblVolunteer table display the same data as the Volunteer worksheet.
3. Switch to the Volunteer Excel workbook, select the value **no** in the Active column for Angela Hoskins (row 4), type **yes** to replace the value, and then press the **Enter** key.
4. Switch to the CareCenter database. The Active status for Angela Hoskins is now **yes**.

   Trouble? If the record is not updated in the tblVolunteer table in the CareCenter database, click the record to show the update.

   You've completed your work for Kimberly and her staff.

5. Close the tblVolunteer table in Access.
6. Switch to the Volunteer workbook, save your changes to the workbook, and then exit Excel.
7. Make a backup copy of the CareCenter database, compact and repair the database, and then close it.

Knowing how to create tab controls and application parts, export data to PDF documents, and link to data maintained by other applications will make it easier for Kimberly and her staff to efficiently manage their data.

REVIEW

Session 8.2 Quick Check

1. The ______________ property lets you change the default navigation label from the word "Record" to another value.
2. What is the Microsoft Graph program?
3. What is a PDF file?
4. What is an application part?
5. What is the difference between an application part and a template?
6. How can you edit data in a table that has been linked to an Excel file?

PRACTICE

Review Assignments

Data Files needed for the Review Assignments: Ads.xlsx, Partners.accdb, Payables.csv, Payments.xml, and Supplier.accdb (cont. from previous module)

Kimberly wants you to integrate data in other files created with other applications with the data in the Supplier database, and she wants to be able to analyze the data in the database. Complete the following steps:

1. Open the **Supplier** database you worked with in the previous three modules.
2. Export the qrySupplierProducts query as an HTML document to the Access2 > Review folder provided with your Data Files, saving the file as **qrySupplierProducts**. Save the export steps with the name **Export-qrySupplierProducts**. Once saved, modify the description to be **HTML file containing the qrySupplierProducts query**.
3. Import the CSV file named **Payables**, which is located in the Access2 > Review folder, as a new table in the database. Use the names in the first row as field names, use Currency as the data type for the numeric fields, choose your own primary key, name the table **tblPayables**, run the Table Analyzer, record the Table Analyzer's recommendation, and then cancel out of the Table Analyzer Wizard without making the recommended changes. Do not save the import steps.
4. Import the data and structure from the XML file named **Payments**, which is located in the Access2 > Review folder included with your Data Files, as a new table named **tblPayments** in the database. Do not save the import steps, and then rename the table **tblPayment** (with no "s" on the end of the name).
5. Export the tblSupplier table as an XML file named **Supplier** to the Access2 > Review folder; do not create a separate XSD file. Save the export steps, and use the default name given.
6. The Riverview Veterinary Care Center also pays for advertisements, and information on this activity is contained in an Excel file named Ads. Create a table named **tblAds** in the **Supplier** database that links to the **Ads** Excel file, which is located in the Access2 > Review folder included with your Data Files. Change the cost of the flyer for Ad 5 to **$150**, and save the workbook.
7. Modify the **frmSuppliersWithProducts** form in the following ways:
    a. Add a tab control to the bottom of the Detail section, so the left edge is aligned with the left edge of the Notes label, and then place the existing subform on the first page of the tab control.
    b. Change the caption for the left tab to **Product Data** and for the right tab to **Product Chart.**
    c. Change the caption for the main form's navigation buttons to **Supplier.**
    d. Add a chart to the second page of the tab control. Use the tblProduct table as the record source, select the ProductName and Price, use the 3-D Column Chart type (row 1, column 2), do not include a legend, and use **Products Offered** as the chart title.
    e. Change the chart to a 3-D Clustered Bar chart, and change the purple colored data markers to pink.
8. Export the **tblPayment** table as a PDF file called **Payments**, using document structure tags for accessibility. Do not save the export steps.
9. Open the **Partners** database from the Access2 > Review folder, and then create and implement an application part as follows:
    a. Create an application part called **Vendor** with the description **New Vendor**, and do not include the data.
    b. Close the Partners database.
    c. Open the **Supplier** database and import the Vendor application part, which has no relationship to any of the other tables. Open the tblNewVendor table to verify the structure has been imported, but does not contain any records.
10. Make a backup copy of the database, compact and repair the database, and then close it.

APPLY

Case Problem 1

Data Files needed for this Case Problem: CreditCard.xml, MoreBeauty.accdb (cont. from previous module), and Schedule.xlsx.

Beauty To Go Sue Miller wants you to integrate data from files created with other applications with the data in the MoreBeauty database, and she wants to be able to analyze the data in the database. Complete the following steps:

1. Open the **MoreBeauty** database you worked with in the previous three modules.
2. Export the qryMemberNames query as an HTML document to the Access2 > Case1 folder using a filename of **MemberNames**. Save the export steps.
3. Export the rptOptionMembership report as a PDF document with a filename of **Option** to the Access2 > Case1 folder. Include the document structure tags for accessibility, and do not save the export steps.
4. Import the data and structure from the XML file named **CreditCard**, which is located in the Access2 > Case1 folder provided with your Data Files, as a new table. Save the import steps. Rename the table as **tblCreditCard**.
5. Export the tblOption table as an XML file named **Options** to the Access2 > Case1 folder; do not create a separate XSD file. Save the export steps.
6. Create a new table named **tblSchedule** by linking to the **Schedule** Excel file, which is located in the Access2 > Case1 folder provided with your Data Files. For ScheduleID 105, change the Day value to **Tuesday**.
7. Modify the **frmPlansWithMembers** form in the following ways:
   a. Add a tab control to the bottom of the Detail section, and place the existing subform on the first page tab of the tab control.
   b. Change the caption for the left tab to **Member Data** and for the right tab to **Member Chart**.
   c. Change the caption for the main form's navigation buttons to **Option** and for the subform's navigation buttons to **Member**.
   d. Add a chart to the second page of the tab control. Use the tblOption table as the record source, select the OptionID and OptionCost fields, use the Column Chart chart type, do not include a legend, and use **Option Cost** as the chart title.
   e. Change the color of the data marker to red (row 3, column 1 in the color palette.).
8. Make a backup copy of the database, compact and repair the database, and then close it.

CHALLENGE

Case Problem 2

Data Files needed for this Case Problem: AddSubject.xml, NewStudentReferrals.accdb, Room.xlsx, Subject.csv, and Tutoring.accdb (cont. from previous module)

Programming Pros Brent Hovis wants you to integrate data from other files created with different applications with the data in the Tutoring database, and he wants to be able to analyze the data in the database. Complete the following steps:

1. Open the **Tutoring** database you worked with in the previous three modules.
2. Export the rptTutorSessions report as a PDF document with a filename of **TutorSessions** to the Access2 > Case2 folder provided with your Data Files. Include the document structure tags for accessibility, and do not save the export steps.

3. Import the CSV file named **Subject**, which is located in the Access2 > Case2 folder, as a new table in the database. Use the names in the first row as field names, set the third column's data type to Currency and the other fields' data types to Short Text, choose your own primary key, name the table **tblSubject**, run the Table Analyzer, and record the Table Analyzer's recommendation, but do not accept the recommendation. Do not save the import steps.
4. Export the tblTutor table as an XML file named **Tutor** to the Access2 > Case2 folder; do not create a separate XSD file. Save the export steps.
5. Create a new table named **tblRoom** that is linked to the **Room** Excel file, which is located in the Access2 > Case2 folder provided with your Data Files. Add the following new record to the Room workbook: Room Num **6**, Rental Cost **$25**, and Type **Private**.

Explore 6. Import the XML file named **AddSubject** file, which is located in the Access2 > Case2 folder included with your Data Files, appending the records to the tblSubject table. Do not save any import steps. (*Hint:* Because you cannot import and append the data from the AddSubject XML file directly to the existing tblSubject table, first import the AddSubject XML file into a new table with an appropriate name (such as tblAddSubject), export this new table to an Excel file with an appropriate name (such as AddSubject), and then import and append the Excel data to the tblSubject table. Open the AddSubject table to verify the records with the SubjectID of 124 through 130 were appended. Close the tblAddSubject table. Remove the new table that was temporarily created (tblAddSubject). Finally, close the Tutoring database.)

Explore 7. Open the **NewStudentReferrals** database from the Access2 > Case2 folder provided with your Data Files, and then create and work with an application part as follows:

a. Create an application part called **NewStudentContact** with the description **New student referrals** and include the data.
b. Close the NewStudentReferrals database.
c. Open the **Tutoring** database and import the **NewStudentContact** application part, which has no relationship to any of the other tables. Open the tblContact table to verify the data has been imported.
d. Kimberly would like to import an empty tblContact table in the future. Delete the NewStudentContact application part by clicking the Application Parts button, right-clicking the NewStudentContact template, selecting Delete Template Part from Gallery, and then clicking Yes in the dialog box that opens.
e. Save and close the Tutoring database.
f. Open the **NewStudentReferrals** database, and then create an application part called **Contact** with the description **Contact information**, and do not include the data.
g. Close the NewStudentReferrals database.
h. Open the **Tutoring** database and then add the Contact application part. Note this will create a new table called tblContact1 because the tblContact table already existed. Open the tblContact1 table to verify that it does not contain records.

8. Make a backup copy of the database, compact and repair the database, and then close it.

CHALLENGE

Case Problem 3

Data Files needed for this Case Problem: Community.accdb (cont. from previous module), Facility.csv, and Volunteer.accdb.

Diane's Community Center Diane Coleman wants you to integrate data from other files created with different applications with data in the Community database, and she wants to be able to analyze the data in the database. Complete the following steps:

1. Open the **Community** database you worked with in the previous three modules.
2. Export the qryDonationsSeptemberOrLaterCrosstab query as an HTML document named **Crosstab** to the Access2 > Case3 folder. Save the export steps.
3. Export the rptPatronDonations report as a PDF document named **PatronDonations** to the Access2 > Case3 folder. Include the document structure tags for accessibility, and do not save the export steps.
4. **Explore** Import the CSV file named **Facility**, which is located in the Access2 > Case3 folder provided with your Data Files, as a new table in the database. Use the Short Text data type for all fields, choose your own primary key, name the table **tblTemporary**, and run the Table Analyzer. Accept the Table Analyzer's recommendations, which will be to create two tables. Rename the tables as **tblStorage** and **tblFacility**. (*Hint*: Use the Rename Table button to the right of "What name do you want for each table?") Make sure each table has the correct primary key. (*Hint*: Use the Set Unique Identifier button to set a primary key if necessary.) Let the Table Analzyer create a query. Do not save the import steps. Review the tblTemporary query, review the tblTemporary table (it might be named tblTemporary_OLD), and then review the tblStorage and tblFacility tables. Close all tables.
5. Export the tblDonation table as an XML file named **Donation** to the Access2 > Case3 folder; do not create a separate XSD file. Save the export steps. Once saved, modify the description as **Exported tblDonation table as an XML file**.
6. Modify the frmPatronDonations form in the following ways:
   a. Add a tab control to the bottom of the Detail section, and place the existing subform on the first page of the tab control.
   b. Change the caption for the left tab to **Donation Data** and for the right tab to **Donation Chart**.
   c. Change the caption for the main form's navigation buttons to **Donor** and for the subform's navigation buttons to **Donation**.
   d. Add a chart to the second page of the tab control. Use the tblDonation table as the record source, select the PatronID, DonationValue, and DonationDate fields, use the 3-D Column Chart type, include a legend, and use **Donations by Patron** as the chart title.
   e. Change the chart to a Clustered Bar chart.
7. Close the Community database.
8. Open the **Volunteer** database, which is located in the Access2 > Case3 folder provided with your Data Files. Create an application part called **Volunteer** with the description **Volunteer information**, and do not include the data. Close the Volunteer database.
9. Open the **Community** database. Create a table called **tblPotentialVolunteer** using the Volunteer application part.
10. Make a backup copy of the database, compact and repair the database, and then close it.

CHALLENGE

Case Problem 4

Data Files needed for this Case Problem: AppTrail.accdb (cont. from previous modules), PotentialTours1.xml, PotentialTours2.xml, and Staff.xlsx

Hike Appalachia Molly and Bailey Johnson want you to integrate data from other files created with different applications with the data in the AppTrail database, and they want to be able to analyze the data in the database. Complete the following steps:

1. Open the **AppTrail** database you worked with in the previous three modules.
2. Export the qryHikersWithoutReservations query as an HTML document named **HikersWithoutReservations** to the Access2 > Case4 folder. Do not save the export steps.
3. Import the data and structure from the XML file named **PotentialTours1**, which is located in the Access2 > Case4 folder provided with your Data Files, as a new table in the database. Do not save the import steps. Rename the new table **PotentialTours**. Open the PotentialTours table to verify the records were imported. Close the PotentialTours table.
4. **Explore** Import the data from the XML file named **PotentialTours2**, which is located in the Access2 > Case4 folder provided with your Data Files, appending the data to the PotentialTours table. *(Hint:* Because you cannot import and append the data from the PotentialTours2 XML file directly to the existing PotentialTours table, first import the PotentialTours2 XML file into a new table with an appropriate name, export this new table to an Excel file with an appropriate name (such as PotentialTours2), and then import and append the Excel data to the PotentialTours table.) Once the data is appended rename the PotentialTours table as **tblPotentialTours**. Open the tblPotentialTours table to verify the records were appended. Close the tblPotentialTours table. Remove the PotentialTours2 table from the database.
5. Export the qryTourReservations query as an XML file named **TourReservations** to the Access2 > Case4 folder; do not create a separate XSD file. Do not save the export steps.
6. Create a new table named **tblStaff** by linking to the **Staff** Excel file, which is located in the Access2 > Case4 folder provided with your Data Files. In the Staff Excel file, change the Job Title in the last record from Tour Assistant to **Tour Guide**. Open the tblStaff table to ensure the change was reflected. Close the tblStaff table.
7. Modify the frmHikersWithReservations form in the following ways:
   a. Add a tab control to the bottom of the Detail section, and place the existing subform on the first page of the tab control.
   b. Change the caption for the left tab to **Reservation Data** and for the right tab to **Reservation Chart**.
   c. Change the caption for the main form's navigation buttons to **Hiker** and for the subform's navigation buttons to **Reservation**.
   d. Add a chart to the second page of the tab control. Use the tblReservation table as the record source, select the TourDate, TourID, and People fields, use the Column Chart chart type, do not include a legend, and use **Reservations** as the chart title.
8. Export the rptTourReservations report as a PDF document named **TourReservations** to the Access2 > Case4 folder provided with your Data Files. Include the document structure tags for accessibility, and do not save the export steps.
9. Make a backup copy of the database, compact and repair the database, and then close it.

MODULE 3

POWERPOINT

Applying Advanced Formatting to Objects

Formatting Objects in a Presentation for a Study Abroad Company

OBJECTIVES

Session 3.1
- Create a SmartArt diagram
- Modify a SmartArt diagram
- Add an audio clip to a slide
- Create a chart
- Modify a chart
- Insert and format text boxes
- Apply a WordArt style to text

Session 3.2
- Correct photos using photo editing tools
- Remove the background from a photo
- Apply an artistic effect to a photo
- Create a custom shape
- Fill a shape with a texture and a custom gradient
- Add alt text to graphics
- Use the Selection pane

Case | *International Study Crossroads*

International Study Crossroads (ISC), located in Baltimore, Maryland, arranges semesters abroad for college students. They have partnerships with more than 20 colleges and universities in five countries and will be expanding into three more countries soon. Robert Cloud is a registration councilor for ISC. One of his duties is to attend college fairs and advertise the services ISC offers. He has created a presentation to advertise ISC at these fairs. He asks for your help in enhancing the presentation with some more advanced formatting of the presentation's content.

In this module, you will add interest to the presentation by creating a SmartArt graphic and a chart and by inserting an audio clip. You will also create a text box and use WordArt styles. You will improve the photos in the presentation using PowerPoint's photo editing tools. In addition, you will create a custom shape and apply advanced formatting to the shape. Finally, you will add text to describe some of the graphics to make the presentation more accessible for people who use screen readers.

STARTING DATA FILES

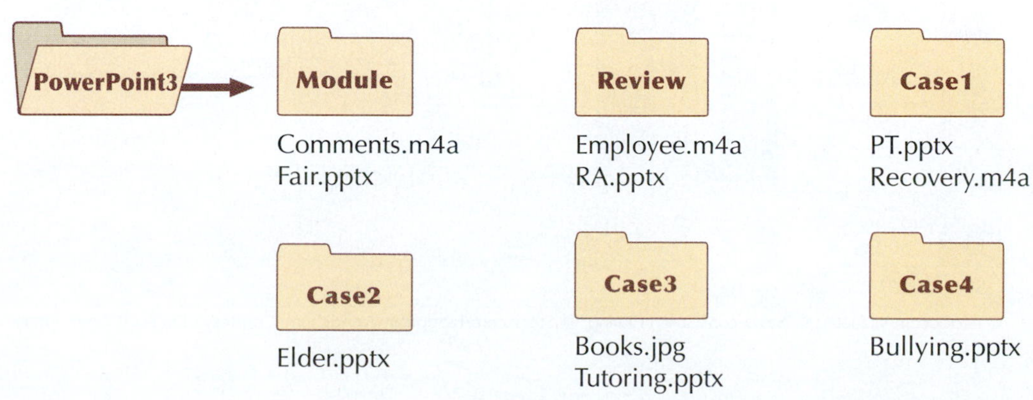

Session 3.1 Visual Overview:

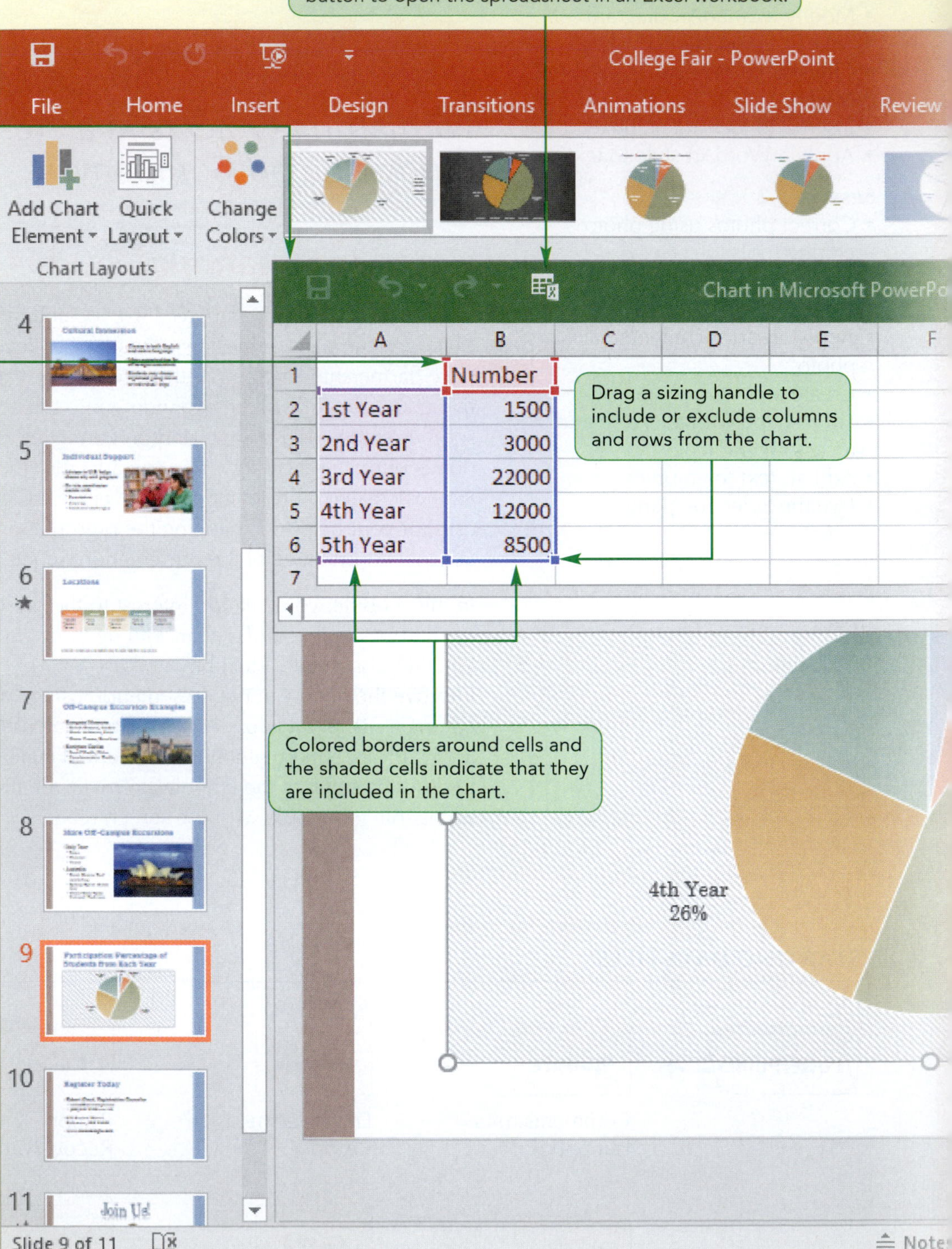
If you need additional tools and Excel is installed on your computer, click the Edit Data in Microsoft Excel button to open the spreadsheet in an Excel workbook.
When you insert a chart, a spreadsheet appears in which you enter the data to create the chart. A **spreadsheet** (called a worksheet in Microsoft Excel) is a grid of cells that contain numbers and text.
As in a table, the intersection of a row and a column is a **cell**, and you add data and labels in cells. Cells in a spreadsheet are referenced by their column letter and row number. This cell is cell B1.
Drag a sizing handle to include or exclude columns and rows from the chart.
Colored borders around cells and the shaded cells indicate that they are included in the chart.
College Fair - PowerPoint
File
Home
Insert
Design
Transitions
Animations
Slide Show
Review
Add Chart Element
Quick Layout
Change Colors
Chart Layouts
Chart in Microsoft PowerPo
A
B
C
D
E
F
Number
1st Year 1500
2nd Year 3000
3rd Year 22000
4th Year 12000
5th Year 8500
4th Year
26%
Join Us!
Slide 9 of 11
Notes

Creating a Chart on a Slide

When a chart is selected, the Chart Tools contextual tabs appear on the ribbon.

If you need to modify a chart's data, click the Edit Data button in the Data group on the Chart Tools Design tab.

Click these buttons to display menus of chart-related commands. These commands also appear on the Chart Tools contextual tabs.

A **data series** is the set of values represented in a chart by **data markers**. In a pie chart, there is only one data series represented. In a pie chart, each slice represents a **category** of data.

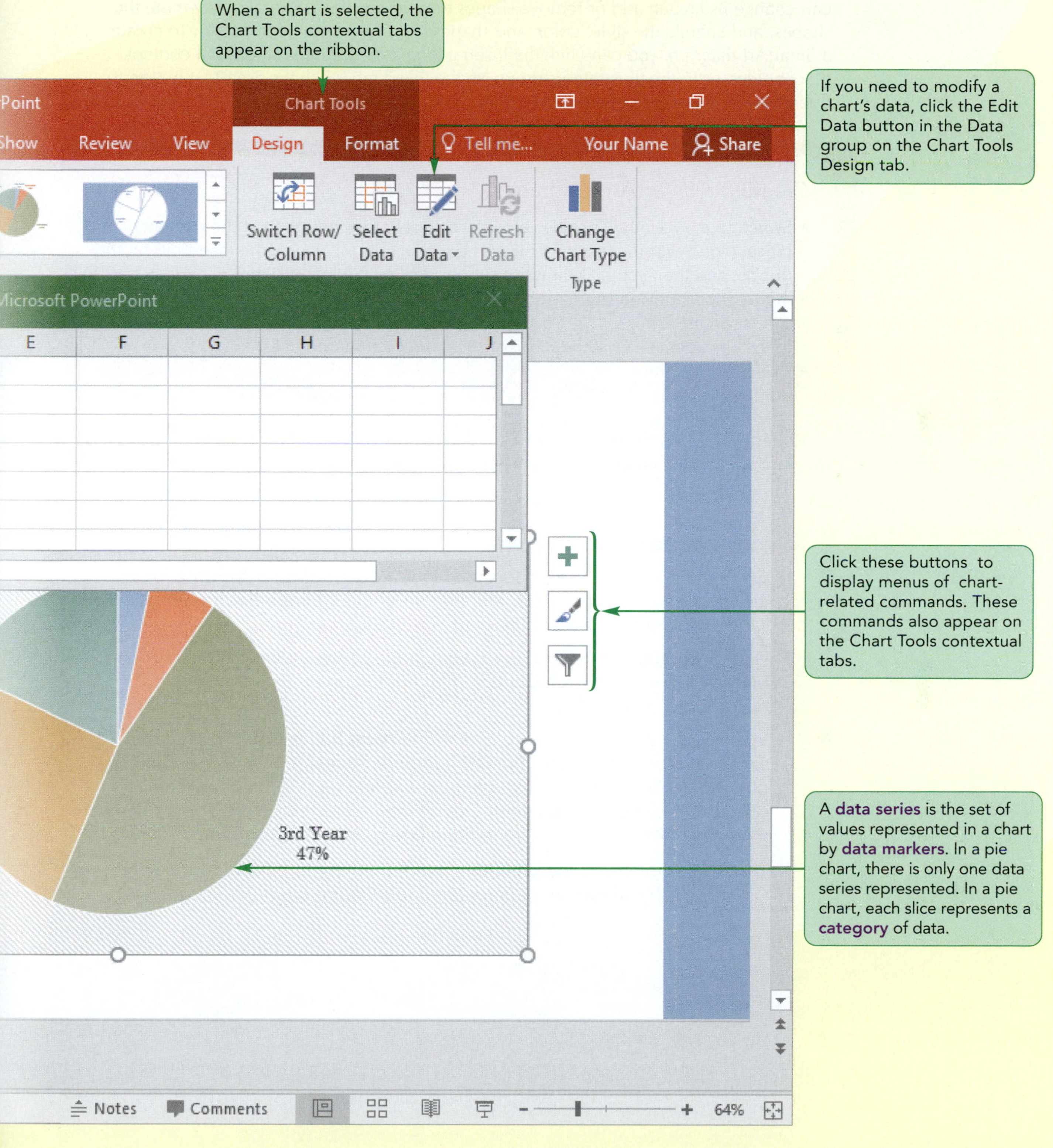

Creating SmartArt Diagrams

In addition to creating a SmartArt diagram from a bulleted list, you can create one from scratch and then add text or pictures to it. Once you create a SmartArt diagram, you can change its layout; add or remove shapes from it; reorder, promote, or demote the shapes; and change the style, color, and shapes used to create the SmartArt. To create a SmartArt diagram, you can click the Insert a SmartArt Graphic button in a content placeholder, or in the Illustrations group on the Insert tab, click the SmartArt button to open the Choose a SmartArt Graphic dialog box.

REFERENCE

Creating a SmartArt Diagram

- Switch to a layout that includes a content placeholder, and then in the content placeholder, click the Insert a SmartArt Graphic button; or click the Insert tab on the ribbon, and then in the Illustrations group, click the SmartArt button.
- In the Choose a SmartArt Graphic dialog box, select the desired SmartArt category in the list on the left.
- In the center pane, click the SmartArt diagram you want to use.
- Click the OK button.

Robert wants you to create a SmartArt diagram on Slide 6 of his presentation. The diagram will list the countries and cities in which ISC has programs.

To create a SmartArt diagram:

1. Open the presentation **Fair**, located in the **PowerPoint3 > Module** folder included with your Data Files, and then save it as **College Fair** to the location where you are saving your files.
2. Display **Slide 6** ("Locations"), and then in the content placeholder, click the **Insert a SmartArt Graphic** button. The Choose a SmartArt Graphic dialog box opens.
3. In the list on the left, click **List**, click the **Vertical Bullet List** layout (in the second row), and then click the **OK** button. A SmartArt diagram containing placeholder text is inserted on the slide with the text pane open next to the diagram, and the SmartArt Tools Design tab is selected on the ribbon. See Figure 3-1. The insertion point is in the first bullet in the text pane.

   Trouble? If the text pane is not displayed, click the Text Pane button in the Create Graphic group on the SmartArt Tools Design tab.

Figure 3-1 SmartArt inserted on Slide 6

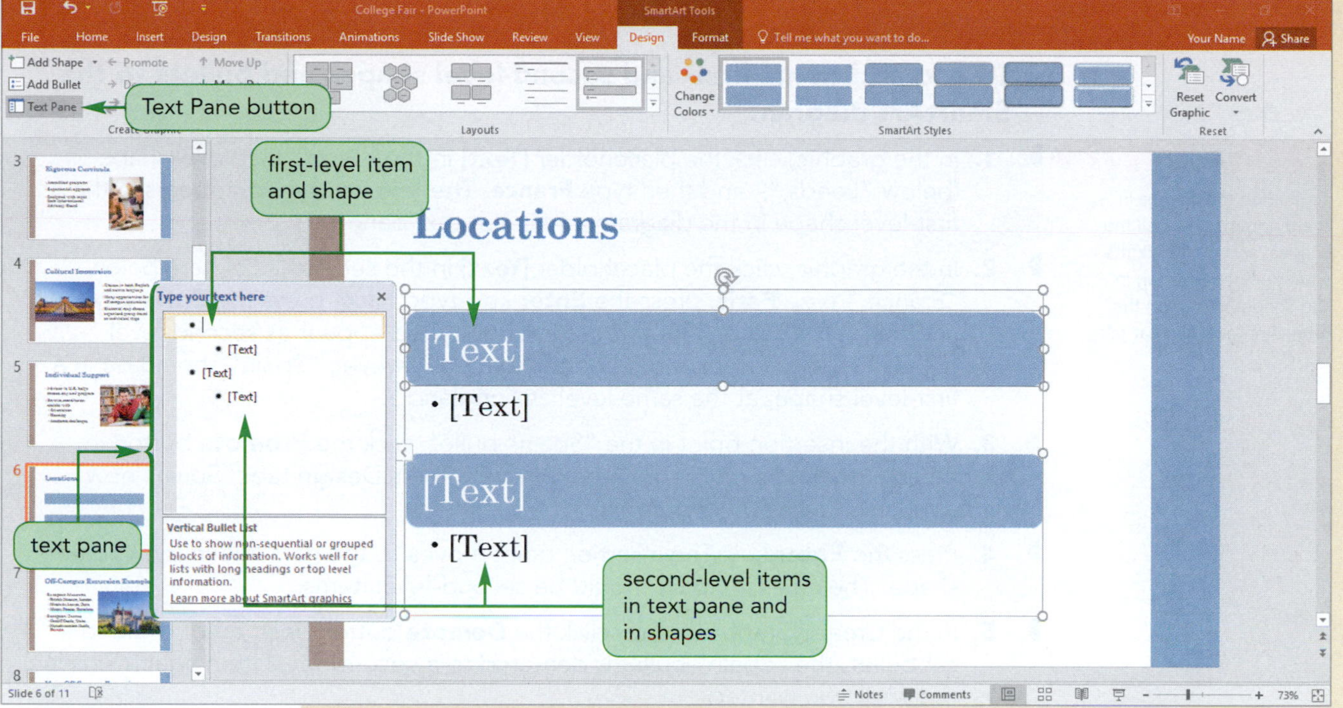

© iStock.com/sturti; © iStock.com/vichie81; © iStock.com/Susan Chiang; © iStock.com/Noppasin Wongchum

Now that you've added the diagram to the slide, you can add content to it. You will first add a first-level item and subitems to the diagram, and then reorder the shapes in the diagram.

To add text to the SmartArt diagram and move shapes:

1. With the insertion point in the first bulleted item in the text pane, type **England**. The text appears in the bulleted list in the text pane and in the top rectangle shape in the diagram.
2. In the text pane, in the first second-level bullet in the bulleted list, click **[Text]**. The placeholder text disappears and the insertion point appears.
3. Type **Oxford**. The text "Oxford" replaces the placeholder text in the second-level bullet.
4. Press the **Enter** key, type **London**, press the **Enter** key, and then type **Leeds**. The "London" bullet needs to be moved so it is the first second-level bullet.
5. In the text pane, click the **London** bullet, and then in the Create Graphic group, click the **Move Up** button. The London bullet moves up to become the first second-level bullet in the bulleted list.

With some SmartArt diagram layouts, you can click the Promote and Demote buttons in the Create Graphic group on the SmartArt Tools Design tab to move shapes up or down a level. But in other SmartArt diagrams, the insertion point must be in the text pane in order for this to work.

You need to add more first-level shapes to the SmartArt diagram. You do this using the Add Shape and Add Bullet buttons in the Create Graphic group on the SmartArt Tools Design tab.

TIP

To change the shapes in the diagram, select all the shapes, and then click the Change Shape button in the Shapes group on the SmartArt Tools Format tab.

To add additional first- and second-level shapes and bullets to the SmartArt diagram:

1. In the graphic, click the placeholder **[Text]** in the second first-level shape (below "Leeds,"), and then type **France**. The text you typed appears in the first-level shape in the diagram and in the text pane.
2. In the graphic, click the placeholder **[Text]** in the second-level item below "France," type **Paris**, press the **Enter** key, type **Nice**, press the **Enter** key, and then type **Spain**. The three items you typed appear as second-level bullets in the diagram and in the text pane. However, "Spain" should be in a first-level shape, at the same level as "England."
3. With the insertion point in the "Spain" bullet, click the **Promote** button in the Create Graphic group on the SmartArt Tools Design tab. "Spain" now appears in a first-level shape.
4. Press the **Enter** key. The insertion point moves to the next line in the "Spain" shape. The cities in Spain should be second-level items.
5. In the Create Graphic group, click the **Demote** button. Instead of creating a subbullet, the "Spain" bullet is demoted to a second-level item again. This is not what you wanted.
6. On the toolbar, click the **Undo** button twice. "Spain" again appears in the first-level shape in the diagram.
7. In the Create Graphic group, click the **Add Bullet** button. A second-level bullet is added below the "Spain" shape.
8. Type **Barcelona**, press the **Enter** key, type **Madrid**, press the **Enter** key, and then type **Seville**.
9. Click in the **Spain** shape, and then in the Create Graphic group, click the **Add Shape** button. A new first-level shape is added to the bottom of the diagram.
10. Type **Germany**, and then add **Berlin** and **Munich** as second-level bullets below Germany.
11. Add **Australia** in a new first-level shape with **Sydney** and **Newcastle** as second-level bullets below it, and then add **Japan** in a new first-level shape. Compare your screen to Figure 3-2.

Figure 3-2 SmartArt with text added

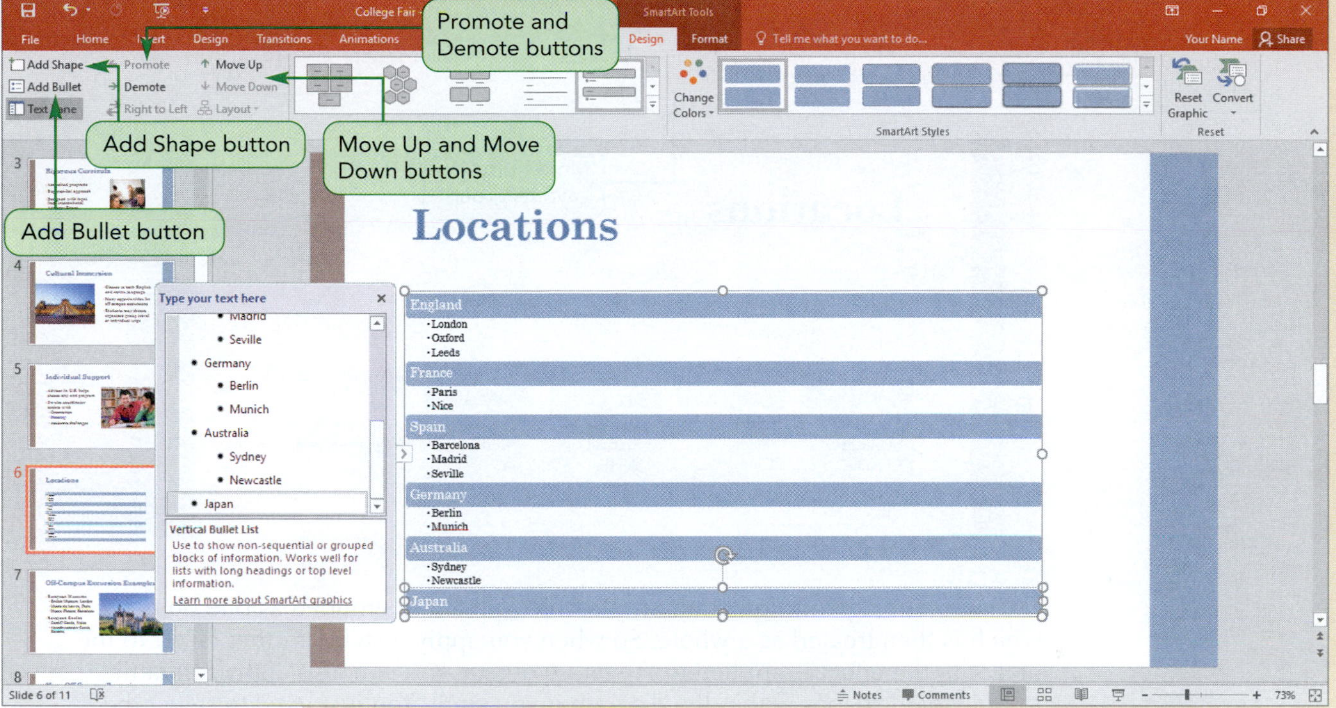

Modifying a SmartArt Diagram

There are many ways to modify a SmartArt diagram. For example, you can change the layout of the diagram so the information is presented differently. You will do this next.

TIP

To switch the order of the shapes, click the Right to Left button in the Create Graphic group on the SmartArt Tools Design tab.

To change the layout of the SmartArt diagram:

1. On the SmartArt Tools Design tab, in the Layouts group, click the **More** button. The gallery of layouts in the List category opens.
2. Click the **Horizontal Bullet List** layout (the fourth layout in the second row). The layout of the diagram changes to the new layout.
3. Click the **Japan** shape, and then press the **Delete** key. The text and the shape are deleted.

   Trouble? If nothing happened when you pressed the Delete key, make sure you clicked the top part of the Japan shape—the part that contains the text "Japan," and then press the Delete key again.

   Trouble? If one of the letters in the word "Japan" was deleted when you pressed the Delete key, click the border of the top part of the Japan shape, and then press the Delete key again.
4. In the text pane, click the **Close** button ✕. See Figure 3-3.

Figure 3-3 SmartArt after changing the layout

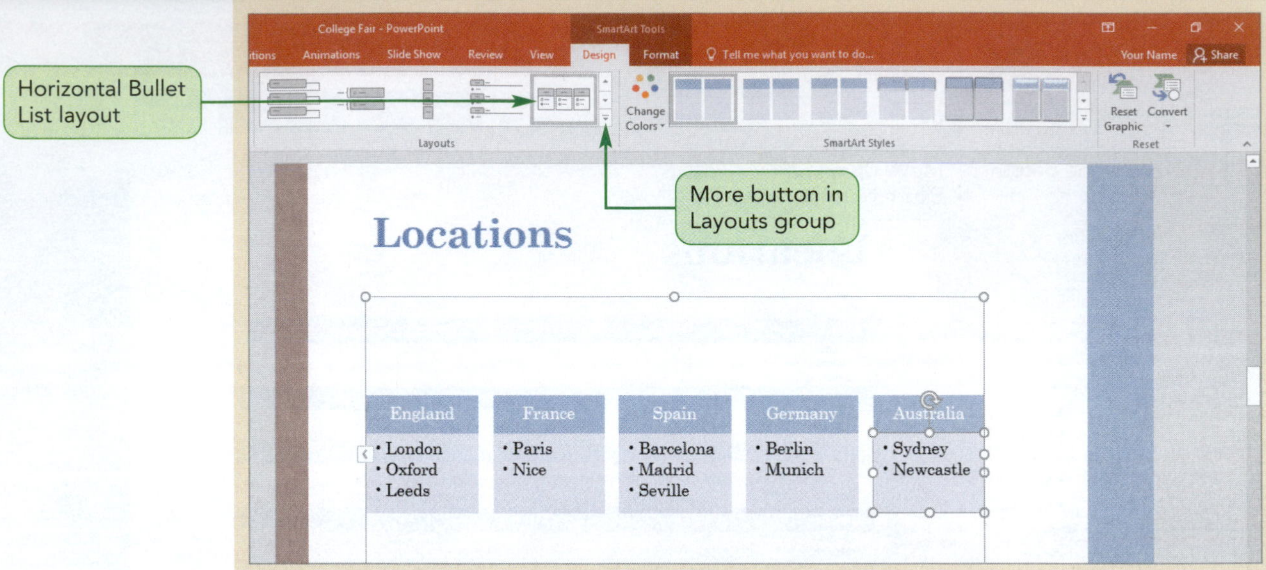

SmartArt diagrams contain multiple objects that are grouped as one object, which is then treated as a whole. So when you apply a style or other effect to the diagram, the effect is applied to the entire object. You can also apply formatting to individual shapes within the diagram if you want. You just need to select the specific shape first.

To apply a style to the SmartArt diagram and change its colors:

1. On the SmartArt Tools Design tab, in the SmartArt Styles group, click the **More** button to open the gallery of styles available for the graphic.
2. In the gallery, click the **Inset** style. The style of the graphic changes to the Inset style.
3. In the SmartArt Styles group, click the **Change Colors** button. A gallery of color styles opens.
4. Under Colorful, click the **Colorful – Accent Colors** style. See Figure 3-4.

Figure 3-4 SmartArt with color and style changed

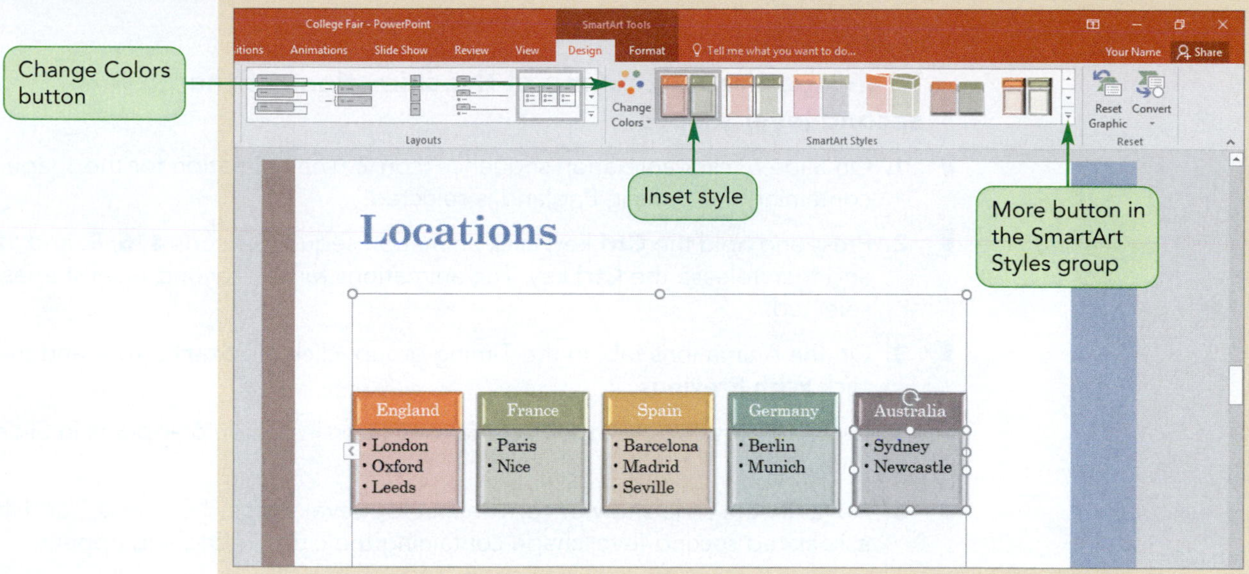

Animating a SmartArt Diagram

You animate a SmartArt diagram in the same way you animate any object. The default is for the entire object to animate as a single object. But similar to a bulleted list, after you apply an animation, you can use the Effect Options button and choose a different sequence effect. For example, you can choose to have each object animate one at a time.

Robert wants the shapes in the SmartArt diagram to appear on the slide one at a time during his presentation.

To animate the SmartArt diagram:

1. With Slide 6 displayed, on the ribbon, click the **Animations** tab.
2. In the Animation group, click the **Appear** animation. The animation previews, and the SmartArt diagram quickly appears on the slide. One animation sequence icon appears above and to the left of the diagram.
3. In the Animation group, click the **Effect Options** button. The selected effect is As One Object.
4. Click **One by One**. The animation previews, and each shape in the diagram appears one at a time. Ten animation sequence icons appear to the left of the diagram.
5. On the status bar, click the **Slide Show** button. Slide 6 appears in Slide Show view.
6. Advance the slide show twice. The first top-level shape, "England," appears, followed by the second-level shape containing the cities in England.
7. Advance the slide show eight more times. Each first-level shape appears, followed by its associated second-level shape.
8. Press the **Esc** key to end the slide show.

Robert wants the second-level shapes containing the cities to appear at the same time as the corresponding first-level shapes containing the countries. To make this happen, you need to change the start timing of each second-level shape to With Previous.

To change the start timing of the animations of the second-level shapes:

1. On Slide 6, click animation sequence icon **2**. The animation for the shape containing the cities in England is selected.
2. Press and hold the **Ctrl** key, click animation sequence icons **4**, **6**, **8**, and **10**, and then release the **Ctrl** key. The animations for the second-level shapes are selected.
3. On the Animations tab, in the Timing group, click the **Start** arrow, and then click **With Previous**.
4. On the status bar, click the **Slide Show** button. Slide 6 appears in Slide Show view.
5. Advance the slide show once. The first top-level shape, "England," and its associated second-level shape containing the cities in England appear.
6. Advance the slide show four more times. Each time the slide show is advanced, a first-level shape appears along with its associated second-level shape.
7. Press the **Esc** key to end the slide show.
8. Save the changes to the presentation.

INSIGHT

Converting a SmartArt Diagram to Text or Shapes

You can convert a SmartArt diagram to a bulleted list or to its individual shapes. To convert a diagram to a bulleted list, select the diagram, and then on the SmartArt Tools Design tab, in the Reset group, click the Convert button, and then click Convert to Text. To convert a group to its individual shapes, click Convert to Shapes on the Convert menu or use the Ungroup command on the Group menu on the Drawing Tools Format tab. In both cases, the shapes are converted from a SmartArt diagram into a set of grouped shapes. To completely ungroup them, you would need to use the Ungroup command a second time. Keep in mind that if you convert the diagram to shapes, you change it from a SmartArt object into ordinary drawn shapes, and you will no longer have access to the commands on the SmartArt Tools contextual tabs.

Adding Audio to Slides

Audio in a presentation can be used for a wide variety of purposes. For example, you might want to add a sound clip of music to a particular portion of the presentation to evoke emotion, or perhaps include a sound clip that is a recording of customers expressing their satisfaction with a product or service. To add a sound clip to a slide, you use the Audio button in the Media group on the Insert tab. When a sound clip is added to a slide, a sound icon and a play bar appear on the slide. Similar to videos, the options for changing how the sound plays during the slide show appear on the Audio Tools Playback tab. For the most part, they are the same options that appear on the Video Tools Playback tab. For example, you can trim an audio clip or set it to rewind after playing. You can also compress audio in the same way that you compress video.

REFERENCE

Inserting an Audio Clip into a Presentation

- Display the slide onto which you want to insert the sound.
- On the ribbon, click the Insert tab, click the Audio button in the Media group, and then click Audio on My PC.
- In the Insert Audio dialog box, navigate to the folder containing the sound clip, click the audio file, and then click the Insert button.
- If desired, click the Audio Tools Playback tab, and then in the Audio Options group:
  - Click the Start arrow, and then click Automatically.
  - Click the Hide During Show check box to select it to hide the icon during a slide show.
  - Click the Volume button, and then click a volume level or click Mute.

Robert wants you to add a sound clip to the presentation—a recording of a student praising the ISC. The recorded message is an MPEG-4 audio file, which is a common file format for short sound clips.

To add a sound clip to Slide 11:

1. Display **Slide 11** (the last slide), and then click the **Insert** tab on the ribbon.
2. In the Media group, click the **Audio** button, and then click **Audio on My PC**. The Insert Audio dialog box opens.
3. Navigate to the **PowerPoint3 > Module** folder, click the **Comments** file, and then click the **Insert** button. A sound icon appears in the middle of the slide with a play bar below it, and the Audio Tools Playback tab is selected on the ribbon. See Figure 3-5. As with videos, the default start setting is On Click.

TIP

To record an audio clip, click the Audio button, and then click Record Audio.

Figure 3-5 Sound icon on Slide 11

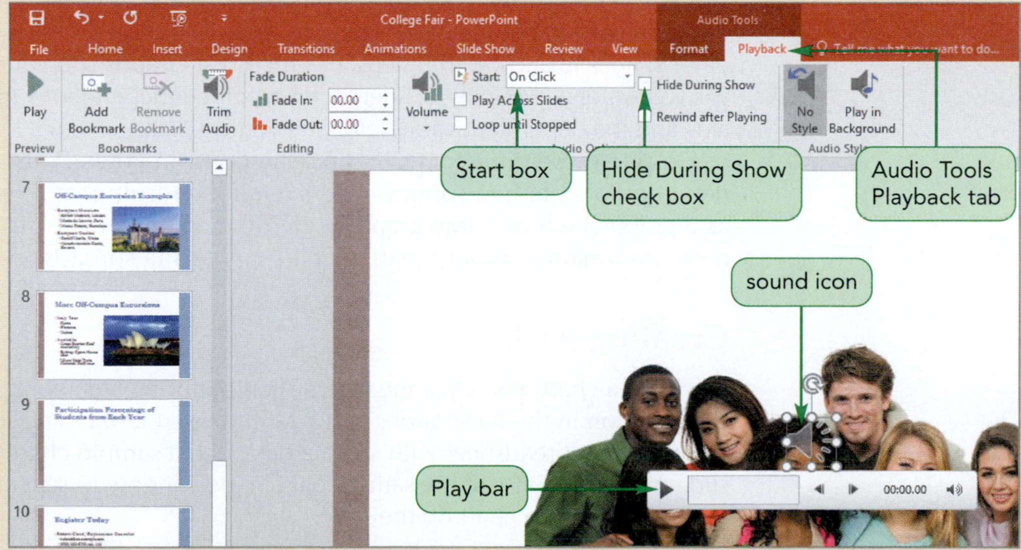

© iStock.com/Christopher Futcher; © iStock.com/Noppasin Wongchum; Courtesy of S. Scott Zimmerman

4. Drag the sound icon to the lower-right corner of the slide so it is positioned at the bottom of the blue bar.

5. On the play bar, click the **Play** button. The sound clip, which is a comment from a student complimenting the company on its programs, plays. Robert wants the clip to play automatically after the slide appears on the screen.
6. On the Playback tab, in the Audio Options group, click the **Start** arrow, and then click **Automatically**. Because the clip will play automatically, there is no need to have the sound icon visible on the screen during a slide show.
7. In the Audio Options group, click the **Hide During Show** check box to select it.
8. Save the changes to the presentation.

INSIGHT

Playing Music Across Slides

You can add an audio clip to a slide and have it play throughout the slide show. On the Audio Tools Playback tab, in the Audio Styles group, click the Play in Background button. When you select this option, the Start timing in the Audio Options group is changed to Automatically, and the Play Across Slides, Loop until Stopped, and Hide During Show check boxes become selected. Also, the Play in Background command changes the trigger animation automatically applied to media to an After Previous animation set to zero so that the sound will automatically start playing after the slide transitions. These setting changes ensure the audio clip will start playing when the slide appears on the screen during a slide show and will continue playing, starting over if necessary, until the end of the slide show. To change the settings so that the audio no longer plays throughout the slide show, click the No Style button in the Audio Styles group.

Adding a Chart to a Slide

The terms "chart" and "graph" often are used interchangeably; however, they do, in fact, have distinct meanings. **Charts** are visuals that use lines, arrows, and boxes or other shapes to show parts, steps, or processes. **Graphs** show the relationship between variables along two axes or reference lines: the independent variable on the horizontal axis and the dependent variable on the vertical axis.

Despite these differences in the definitions, in PowerPoint a chart is any visual depiction of data in a spreadsheet, even if the result is more properly referred to as a graph (such as a line graph). Refer to the Session 3.1 Visual Overview for more information about creating charts and using spreadsheets in PowerPoint.

Creating a Chart

To create a chart, you click the Insert Chart button in a content placeholder or use the Chart button in the Illustrations group on the Insert tab. Doing so will open a window containing a spreadsheet with sample data, and a sample chart will appear on the slide. You can then edit the sample data in the window to reflect your own data to be represented in the chart on the slide.

REFERENCE

Creating a Chart

- Switch to a layout that includes a content placeholder, and then click the Insert Chart button in the content placeholder to open the Insert Chart dialog box; or click the Insert tab, and then, in the Illustrations group, click the Chart button to open the Insert Chart dialog box.
- In the list on the left, click the desired chart type.
- In the row of styles, click the desired chart style, and then click the OK button.
- In the spreadsheet that opens, enter the data that you want to plot.
- If you need to chart fewer rows or columns than are shaded in the spreadsheet, drag the handle in the lower-right corner of the shaded area up to remove rows or to the left to remove columns.
- In the spreadsheet window, click the Close button.

Robert wants you to create a chart on Slide 9 to illustrate the percentage of students from each grade level that typically make up the total of participating students in a given year. A pie chart is a good choice when you want to show the relative size of one value compared to the other values and compared to the total set of values.

To create a chart on Slide 9:

1. Display **Slide 9** ("Participation Percentage of Students from Each Year"), and then, in the content placeholder, click the **Insert Chart** button. The Insert Chart dialog box opens. Column is selected in the list of chart types on the left, and the Clustered Column style is selected in the row of styles at the top and shown in the preview area. See Figure 3-6.

Figure 3-6 **Insert Chart dialog box**

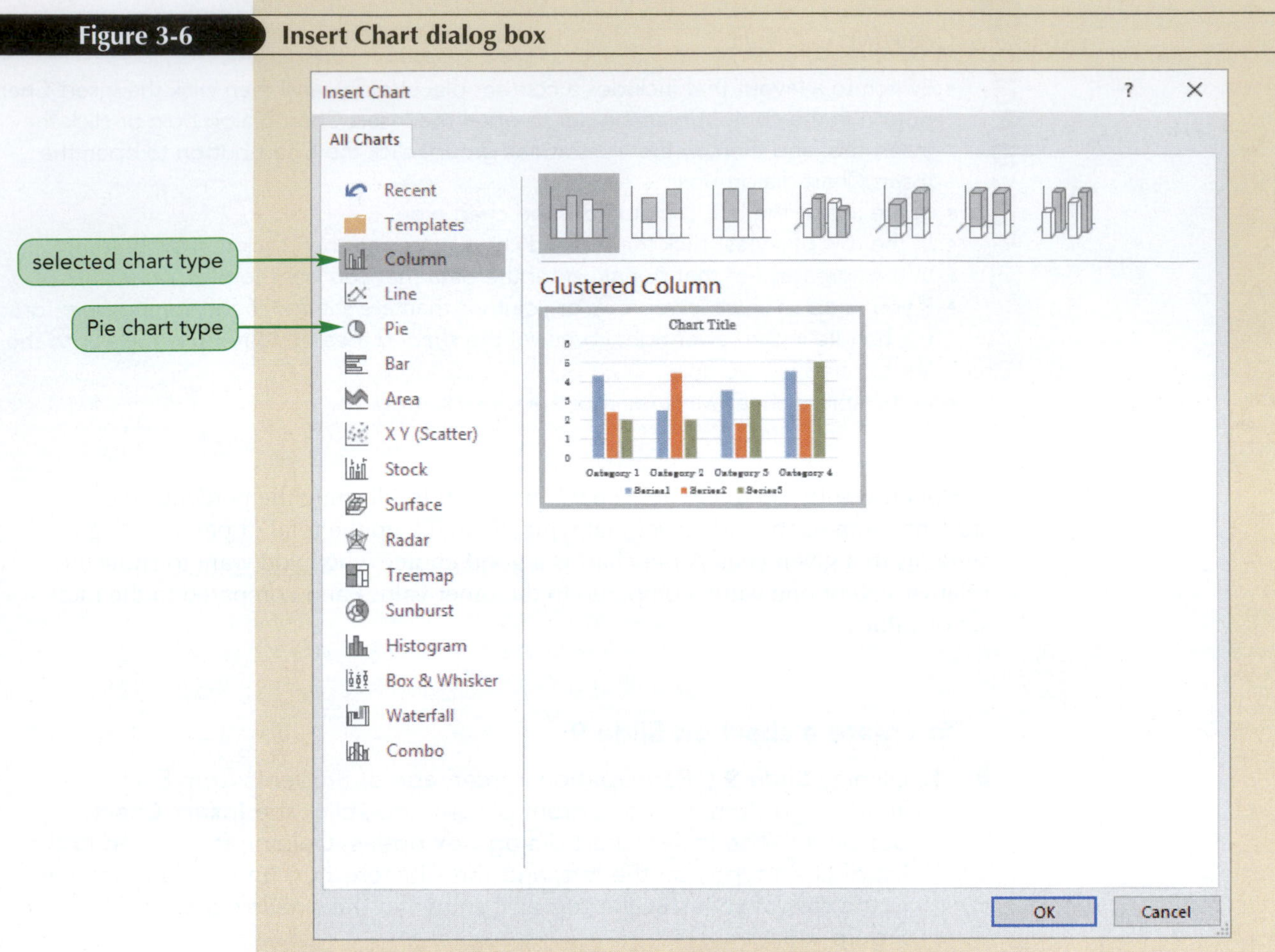

2. In the list of chart types, click **Pie**. The row of chart styles changes to pie chart styles. The Pie style is selected.
3. Click the **OK** button. A sample chart is inserted on Slide 9, and a small spreadsheet (sometimes called a datasheet) opens above the chart, with colored borders around the cells in the spreadsheet indicating which cells of data are included in the chart. See Figure 3-7.

Figure 3-7 Spreadsheet and chart with sample data

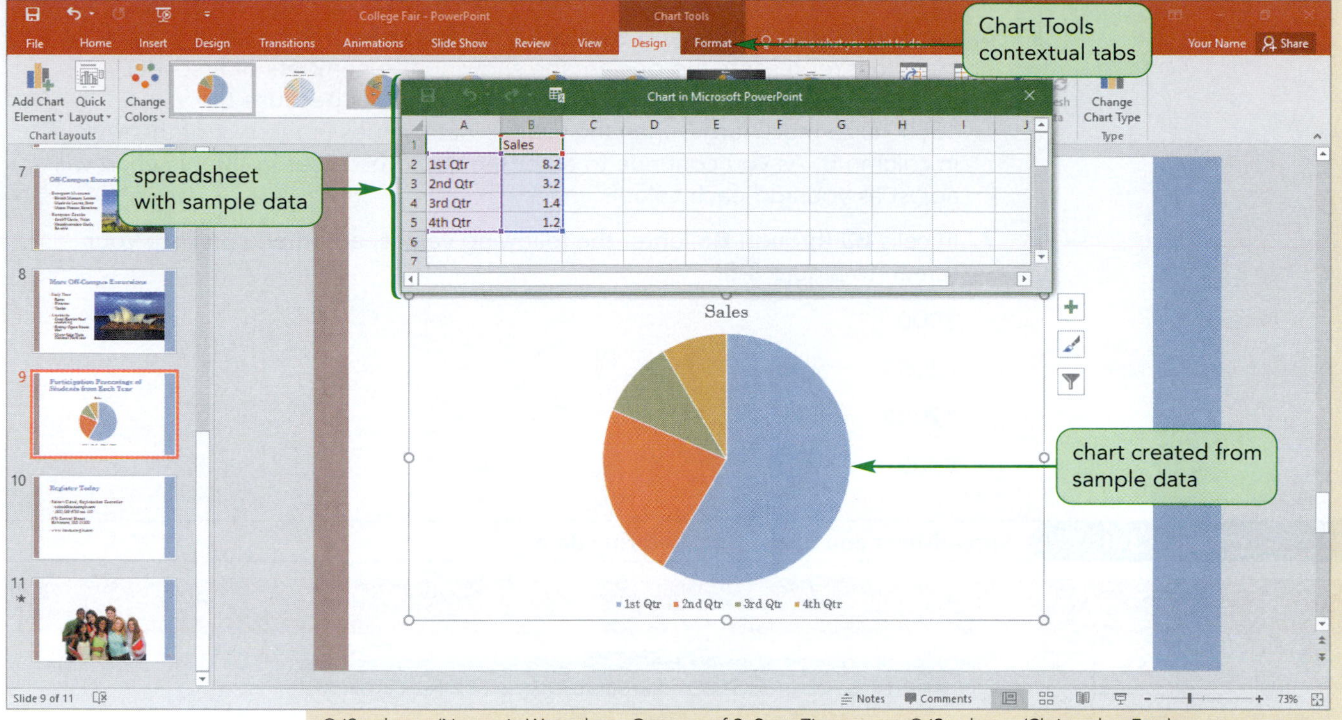

© iStock.com/Noppasin Wongchum; Courtesy of S. Scott Zimmerman; © iStock.com/Christopher Futcher

To create the chart for Robert's presentation, you need to edit the sample data in the spreadsheet. When you work with a spreadsheet, the cell in which you are entering data is the **active cell**. The active cell has a green border around it.

To enter the data for the chart:

1. In the spreadsheet, click cell **A2**. A green border surrounds cell A2, indicating it is selected.
2. Type **1st Year**, and then press the **Enter** key. Cell A3 becomes the active cell. In the chart, the category name in the legend for the blue pie slice changes to "1st Year."
3. Enter the following in cells **A3** through **A5**, pressing the **Enter** key after each entry:

   2nd Year

   3rd Year

   4th Year
4. In cell A6, type **5th Year**, and then press the **Enter** key. The active cell is cell A7, and the colored borders around the cells included in the chart expand to include cells A6 and B6. In the chart, a new category name is added to the legend. Because there is no data in cell B6, a corresponding slice was not added to the pie chart.

TIP

To add or remove a row or column from the chart, drag the corner sizing handles on the colored borders.

5. Click in cell **B1** to make it the active cell, type **Number**, and then press the **Enter** key. The active cell is now cell B2.
6. In cell **B2**, type **15000**, and then press the **Enter** key. The slice in the pie chart that represents the percentage showing the numbers of first-year students increases to essentially fill the chart. This is because the value 15000 is so much larger than the sample data values in the rest of the rows in column B. As you continue to enter the data, the slices in the pie chart will adjust as you add each value.
7. In cells **B3** through **B6**, enter the following values, and then compare your screen to Figure 3-8:

   3000

   22000

   12000

   8500

Figure 3-8 Spreadsheet and chart after entering data

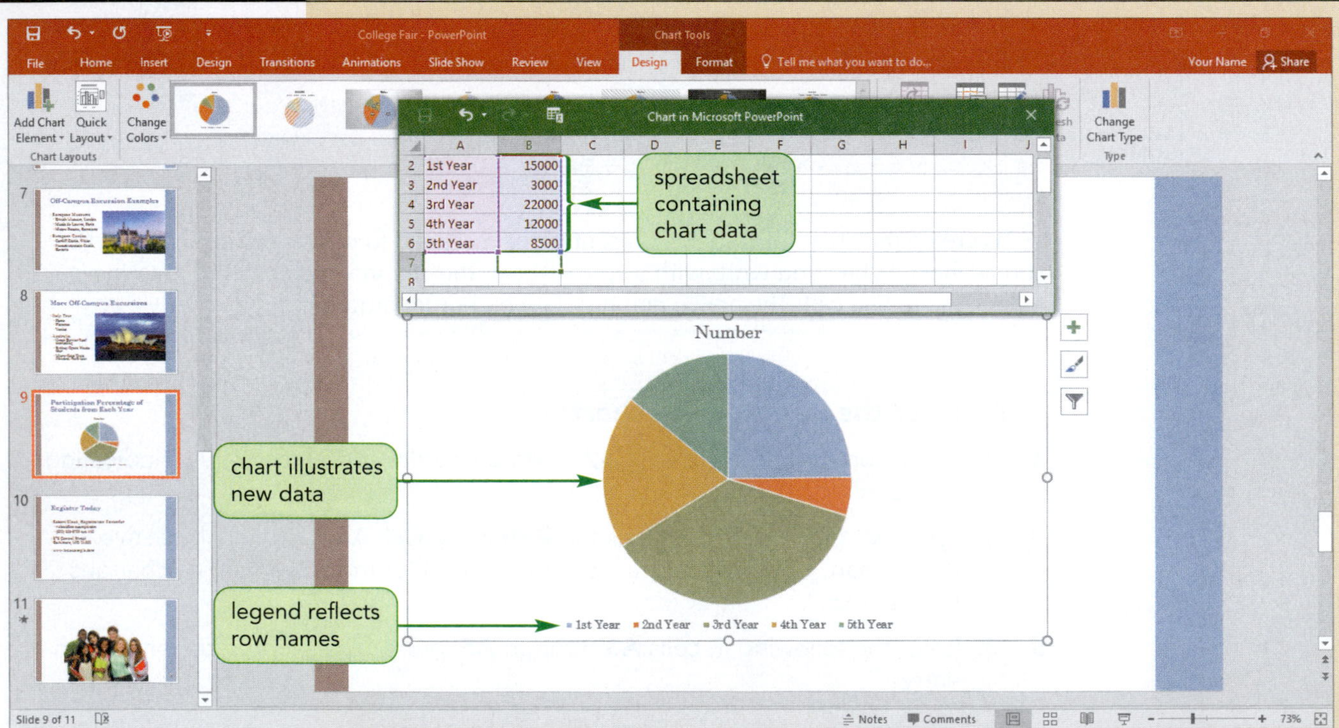

© iStock.com/Noppasin Wongchum; Courtesy of S. Scott Zimmerman; © iStock.com/Christopher Futcher

8. In the spreadsheet, click the **Close** button . The spreadsheet closes.
9. Save the changes to the presentation.

PROSKILLS

Decision Making: Selecting the Correct Chart Type

To use charts effectively, you need to consider what you want to illustrate with your data. To represent values, column charts use vertical columns, and bar charts use horizontal bars. These types of charts are useful for comparing the values of items over a period of time or a range of dates or costs. Line charts and area charts use a line to connect points that represent values. They are effective for showing changes over time, and they are particularly useful for illustrating trends. Line and area charts are a better choice than column or bar charts when you need to display large amounts of information and exact quantities that don't require emphasis. Pie charts are used to show percentages or proportions of the parts that make up a whole. Treemap and sunburst charts also show the proportion of parts to a whole, but these chart types also show hierarchies.

Modifying a Chart

Once the chart is on the slide, you can modify it by changing or formatting its various elements. For example, you can edit the data; apply a style; add, remove, or reposition chart elements; add labels to the chart; and modify the formatting of text in the chart.

You need to make several changes to the chart you created on Slide 9. First, Robert informs you that some of the data he provided was incorrect, so you need to edit the data. Remember that a pie chart shows the size of each value relative to the whole. Therefore, if you change the value corresponding to one pie slice, the rest of the slices will change size as well.

TIP

To switch to another type of chart, click the Change Chart Type button in the Type group on the Chart Tools Design tab.

To change the data used to create the chart:

1. On the Chart Tools Design tab, in the Data group, click the **Edit Data** button. The spreadsheet opens again above the chart. You need to change the number of first-year students who participate in the program. The 1st Year slice is the blue slice.
2. Click cell **B2**, type **1500**, and then press the **Enter** key. The blue slice in the pie chart decreases significantly in size, and the other slices in the pie chart adjust to reflect the new relative values.
3. On the spreadsheet, click the **Close** button. The spreadsheet closes.

Robert also wants you to make several formatting changes to the chart. There is no need for a title on the chart because the slide title describes the chart. Robert also wants you to remove the legend and, instead, label the pie slices with the category names and the percentage values. He also would like you to apply a different style to the chart.

To format and modify the chart:

1. On the Chart Tools Design tab, in the Chart Layouts group, click the **Quick Layout** button. A gallery of chart layouts specific to pie charts opens. Each layout includes different chart elements, such as the chart title and legend.
2. Point to several of the layouts to see which elements are added to the chart, and then click **Layout 1**. The category name and percentage of each slice is added as a label on the slices, and the legend is removed. With this layout, there is no need for the legend.

3. To the right of the chart, click the **Chart Styles** button. A gallery opens with the Style tab selected at the top.
4. Point to several of the styles to see the effect on the chart. In addition to changing the colors used, some of the styles include layouts and add or remove chart elements, similar to the Quick Layouts.
5. Click **Style 6**. This style adds the legend and a background of thin, slanted lines. See Figure 3-9.

Figure 3-9 Chart after changing the layout and applying a style

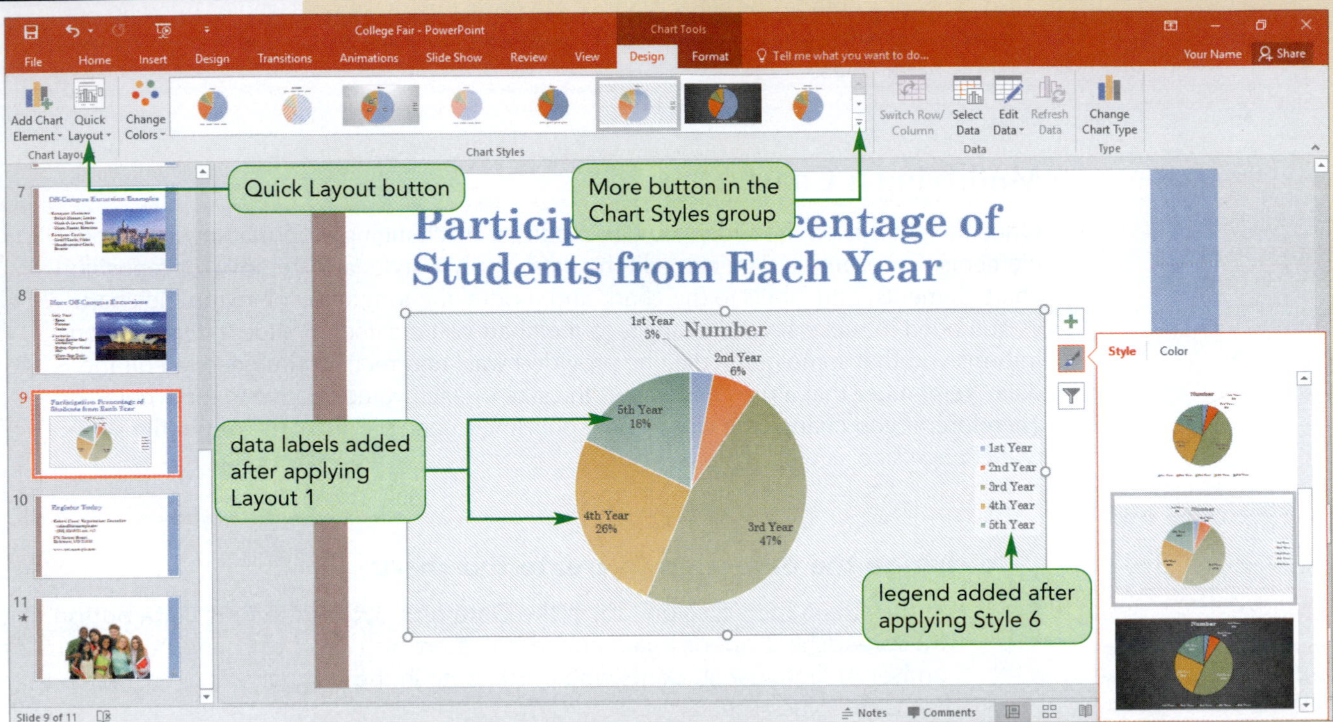

6. To the right of the chart, click the **Chart Elements** button. The CHART ELEMENTS menu opens to the right of the chart. The Chart Title, Data Labels, and Legend check boxes are all selected, which means these elements are shown on the chart.
7. On the CHART ELEMENTS menu, click the **Chart Title** check box, and then click the **Legend** check box to deselect them. The chart title and the legend are removed from the chart.
8. On the CHART ELEMENTS menu, point to **Data Labels**. An arrow appears.
9. Click the **arrow** to open the Data Labels submenu. See Figure 3-10.

TIP

Double-click a chart element to open a task pane containing additional commands for modifying that element.

Figure 3-10 Data Labels submenu on CHART ELEMENTS menu

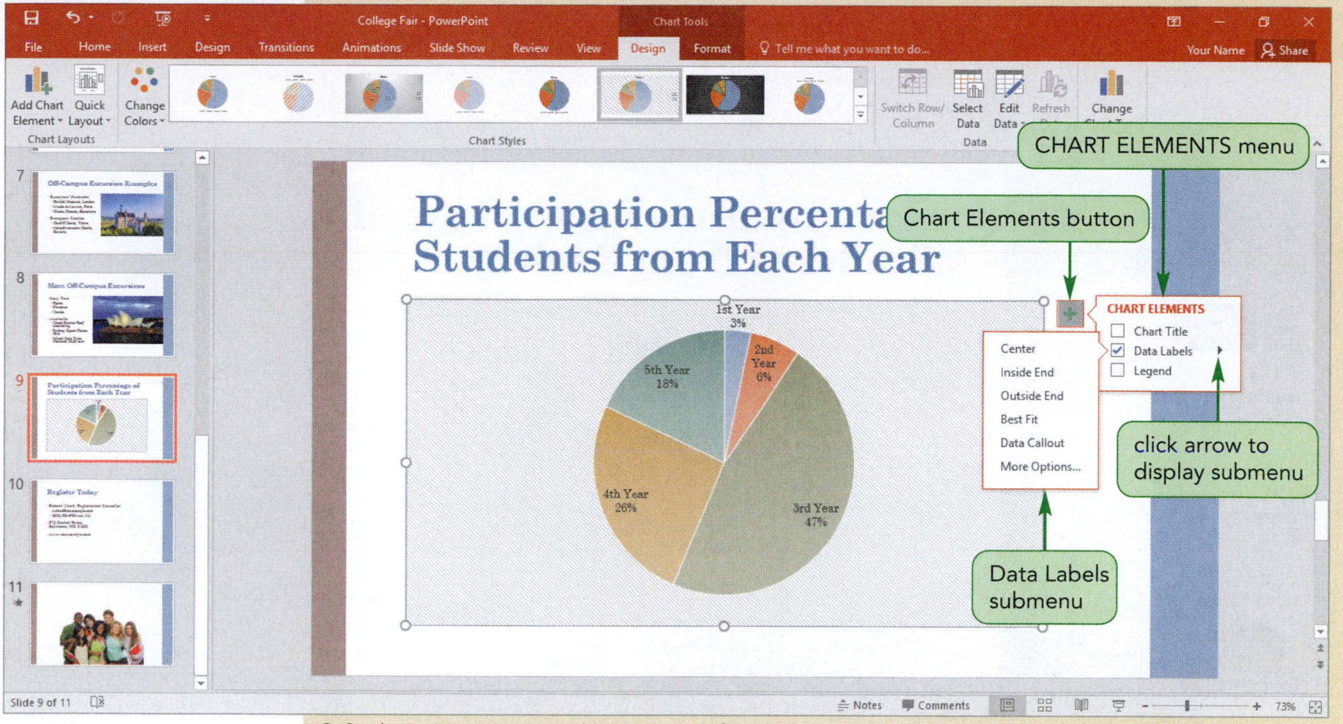

10. On the submenu, click **Outside End**. The data labels are positioned next to each pie slice.

The data labels are a little bit small, so Robert asks you to increase their font size. When you change the font size of data labels on a pie chart, it is sometimes necessary to move a label so it is better positioned. You'll do this next.

To change the point size of the data labels and adjust their position:

1. To the right of the chart, click the **Chart Elements** button [+] to close the menu, and then in the chart, click one of the data labels. All of the data labels are selected.
2. On the ribbon, click the **Home** tab, and then change the font size of the selected data labels to **14** points. The 1st Year data label is now too close to the 2nd Year data label.
3. Click the **1st Year** data label. Because all the data labels had been selected, now only the 1st Year data label is selected.
4. Position the pointer on the edge of the selected **1st Year** data label so that it changes to ✥, and then drag it to the left a little so that it is not touching the 2nd Year data label and so that the "3" is above the blue pie slice. See Figure 3-11.

Figure 3-11 Final chart on Slide 9

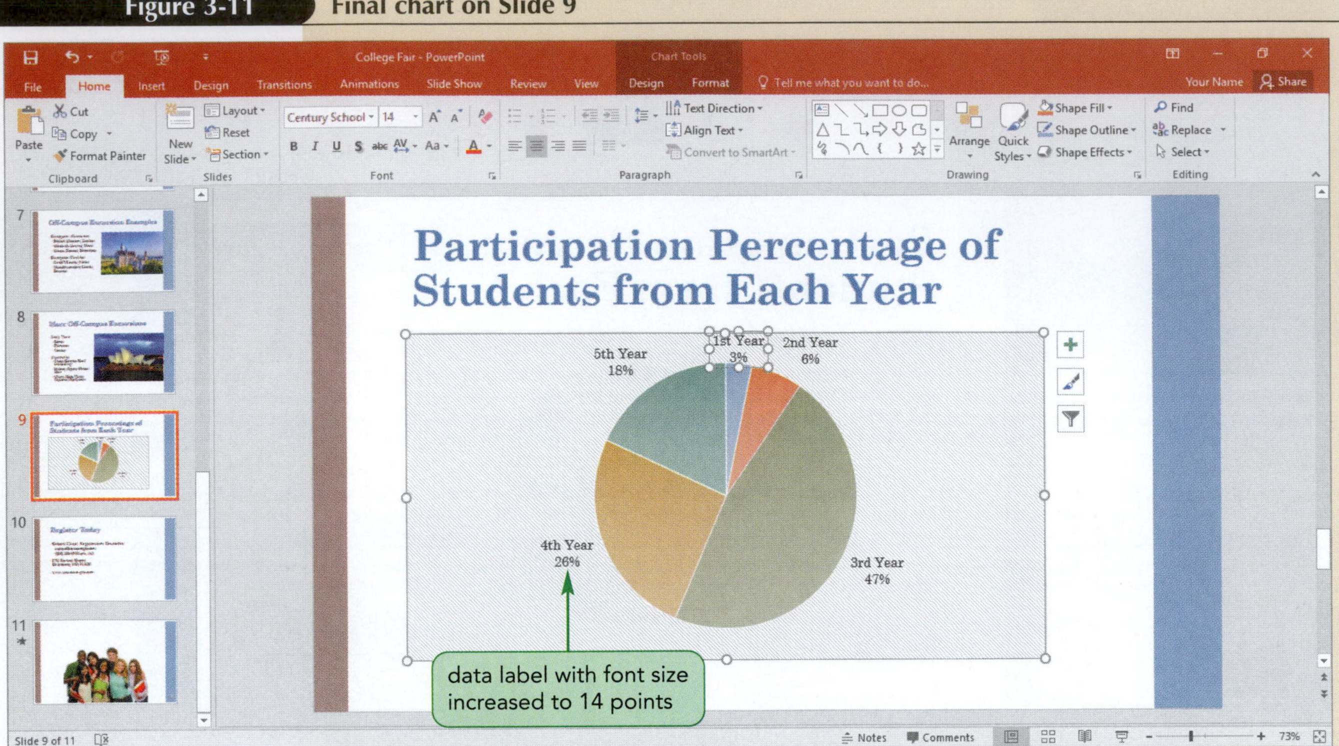

5. Save the changes to the presentation.

Inserting and Formatting Text Boxes

Sometimes you need to add text to a slide in a location other than in one of the text box placeholders included in the slide layout. You could draw any shape and add text to it, or you can add a text box shape. Unlike shapes that are filled with the Accent 1 color by default, text boxes by default do not have a fill. Another difference between the format of text boxes and shapes with text in them is that the text in a text box is left-aligned and text in shapes is center-aligned. Regardless of the differences, after you create a text box, you can format the text and the text box in a variety of ways, including adding a fill, adjusting the internal margins, and rotating and repositioning it.

Robert wants you to add text on Slide 6 that informs the audience of three new countries that will be available study abroad locations next spring. You will add a text box to accomplish this.

To add a text box to Slide 6:

1. Display **Slide 6** ("Locations"), and then click the **Insert** tab.
2. In the Text group, click the **Text Box** button, and then move the pointer to the slide. The pointer changes to ↓.
3. Position ↓ below the left edge of the first shape in the SmartArt, and then click and drag to draw a text box as wide as the England and France shapes and about one-half-inch high. See Figure 3-12.

Figure 3-12 Text box inserted on Slide 6

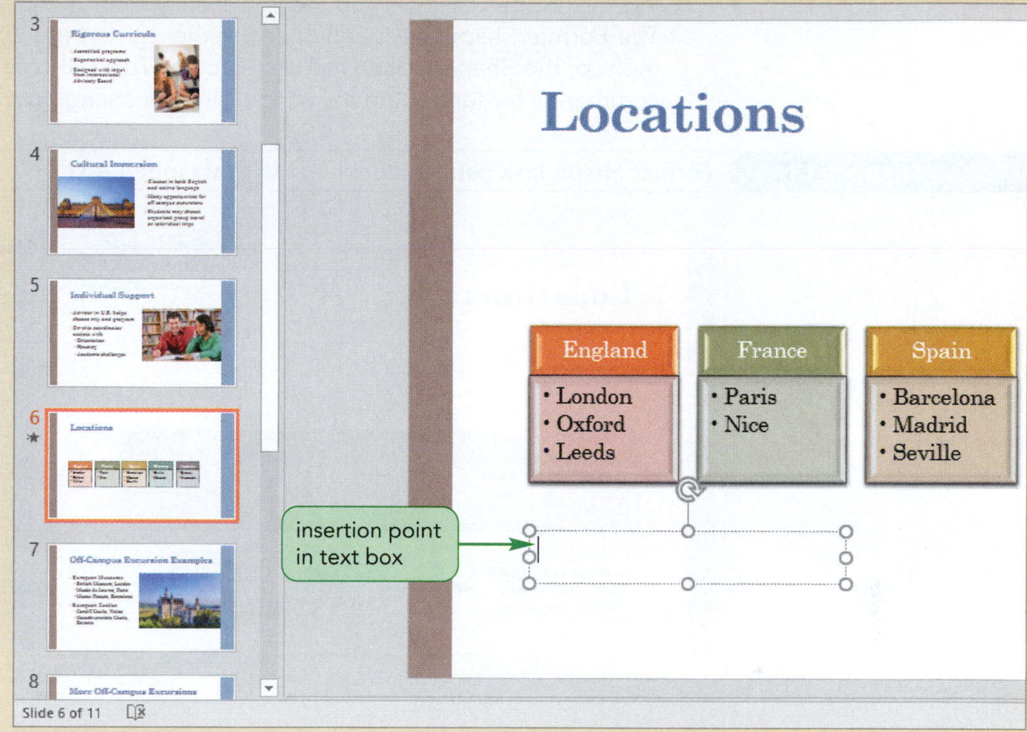

Trouble? If your text box is not the same size or is not positioned exactly as shown in Figure 3-12, don't worry. You'll adjust it later.

4. Type **Programs in South Africa, Japan, and Vietnam available next spring.** (including the period). As you type the text in the text box, the height of the text box changes, and the additional text wraps to the next line.

Trouble? If all the text fits on one line, drag the right-middle sizing handle to the left until some words appear on the next line so that you can complete the next sets of steps.

When you drag to create a text box, the default setting is for the text to wrap and for the height of the box to resize to accommodate the text you type. (If you simply click to place the text box, the text box will expand horizontally as wide as necessary to accommodate the text you type, even if it needs to flow off the slide.) This differs from text boxes created from title and content placeholders and shapes with text in them. Recall that text boxes created from placeholders have AutoFit behavior that reduces the font size of the text if you add more text than can fit. When you add text to a shape, if you add more text than can fit in that shape, the text extends outside of the shape.

Robert thinks the text below the SmartArt would look better if it were all on one line and italicized. You can widen the text box, or if you do not want the text to wrap to the next line regardless of how much text is in the text box, you can change the text wrapping option.

To modify and reposition the text box:

1. Right-click the text box, and then on the shortcut menu, click **Format Shape**. The Format Shape task pane opens to the right of the displayed slide. At the top, the Shape Options tab is selected. This tab contains categories of commands for formatting the shape, such as changing the fill. See Figure 3-13.

Figure 3-13 Format Shape task pane and text box with wrapped text

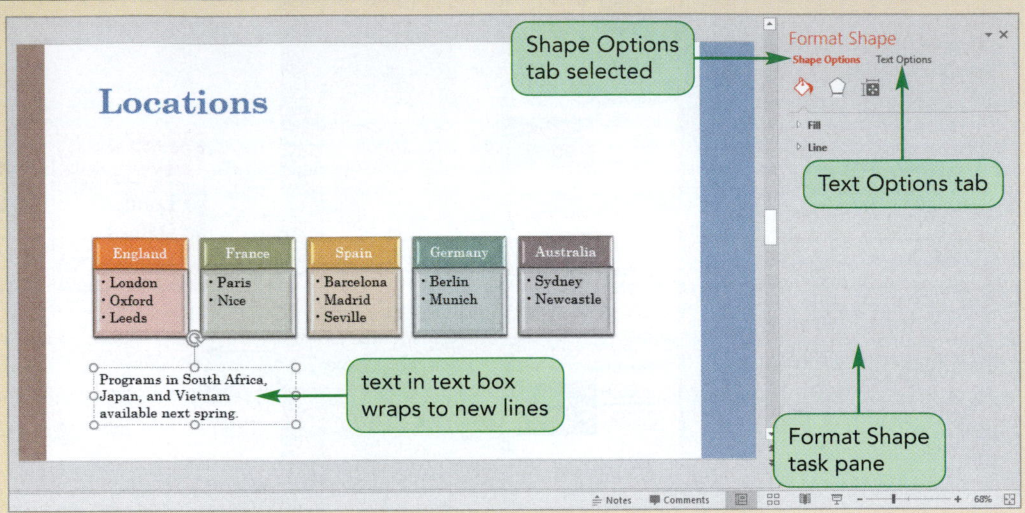

TIP

Clicking any of the Dialog Box Launchers on the Drawing Tools Format tab also opens the Format Shape task pane.

2. In the task pane, click **Text Options** to display the Text Options tab. This tab contains commands for formatting the text and how it is positioned.
3. Click the **Textbox** button. The task pane changes to show the Text Box section, containing options for formatting text in a text box. First you want to change the wrap option so the text does not wrap in the text box.
4. Click the **Wrap text in shape** check box to deselect it. The text in the text box appears all on one line. Next, you want to decrease the space between the first word in the text box and the left border of the box. In other words, you want to change the left margin in the text box.

   Trouble? If the Wrap text in shape check box is not selected, you clicked instead of dragging to create the text box in Step 3 in the previous set of steps. In this case, do not click the check box; leave it unselected.

5. Click the **Left margin down arrow**. The value in the box changes to 0", and the text shifts left in the text box.
6. Click the text box border to select all of the text in the text box, and then, in the Font group on the Home tab, click the **Italic** button *I*. The text in the text box is italicized.
7. Point to the border of the text box so that the pointer changes to the move pointer, press and hold the mouse button, and then drag the text box until its left edge is aligned with the left edge of the SmartArt and its top edge is aligned with the bottom edge of the SmartArt box, as shown in Figure 3-14.

Figure 3-14 Formatted and repositioned text box

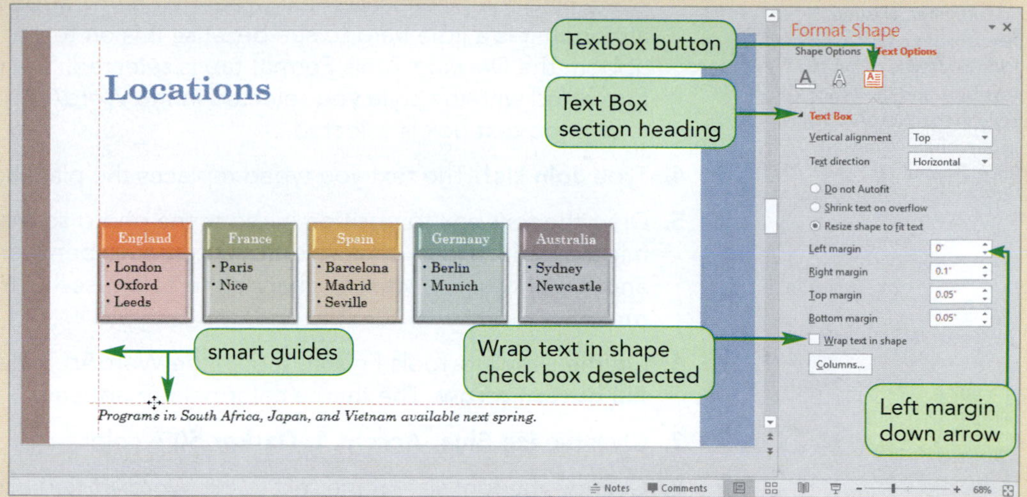

8. Release the mouse button.
9. In the Format Shape task pane, click the **Close** button, and then save the changes to the presentation.

Applying WordArt Styles to Text

WordArt is a term used to describe formatted, decorative text in a text box. WordArt text has a fill color, which is the same as the font color, and an outline color. To create WordArt, you can insert a new text box or format an existing one. You can apply one of the built-in WordArt styles or you can use the Text Fill, Text Outline, and Text Effects buttons in the WordArt Styles group on the Drawing Tools Format tab.

Robert would like you to add a text box that contains WordArt to Slide 11 that reinforces the invitation to register with ISC.

To create a text box containing WordArt on Slide 11:

1. Display **Slide 11** (the last slide), and then click the **Insert** tab.
2. In the Text group, click the **WordArt** button to open the WordArt gallery. See Figure 3-15.

Figure 3-15 WordArt gallery

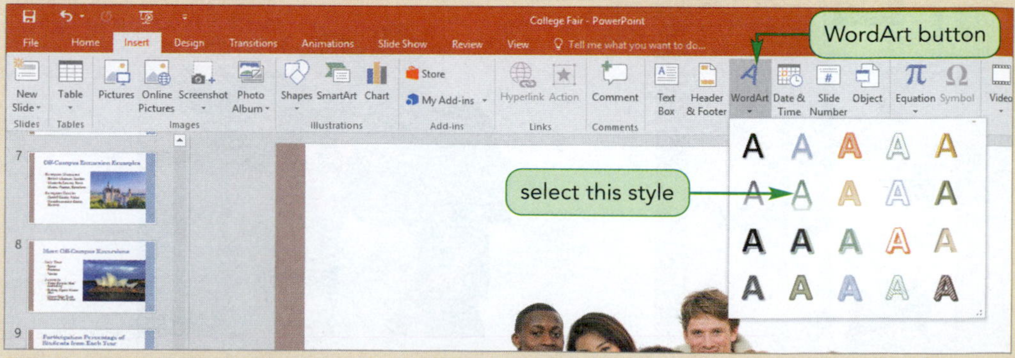

© iStock.com/Christopher Futcher; © iStock.com/Noppasin Wongchum; Courtesy of S. Scott Zimmerman

TIP

To format an existing text box on a slide with a WordArt style, select the text box, and then click a style in the WordArt Styles group on the Drawing Tools Format tab.

3. Click the **Gradient Fill – Green, Accent 1, Reflection** style. A text box containing the placeholder text "Your text here" appears on the slide, although it is a little hard to see because it is on top of the photo. On the ribbon, the Drawing Tools Format tab is selected. The placeholder text is formatted with the style you selected in the WordArt gallery. The placeholder text in the text box is selected.
4. Type **Join Us!**. The text you typed replaces the placeholder text.
5. Drag the text box to position it above the photo so that it is aligned with the middle of the slide and it is vertically centered between the top of the slide and the photo. You want to change the color used in the gradient fill from green to blue.
6. On the Drawing Tools Format tab, in the WordArt Styles group, click the **Text Fill button arrow**. The theme color palette appears.
7. Click the **Ice Blue, Accent 1, Darker 50%** color.
8. Change the font size of the text in the WordArt text box to **72** points.

The shape of text in a text box can be transformed into waves, circles, and other shapes. To do this, you use the options located on the Transform submenu, which is accessed from the Text Effects menu on the Drawing Tools Format tab.

Robert wants you to change the shape of the WordArt on Slide 11.

To change the shape of the WordArt by applying a transform effect:

1. With the WordArt on Slide 11 selected, click the **Drawing Tools Format** tab.
2. In the WordArt styles group, click the **Text Effects** button, and then point to **Transform**. The Transform submenu appears. See Figure 3-16.

Figure 3-16 Transform submenu on Text Effects menu

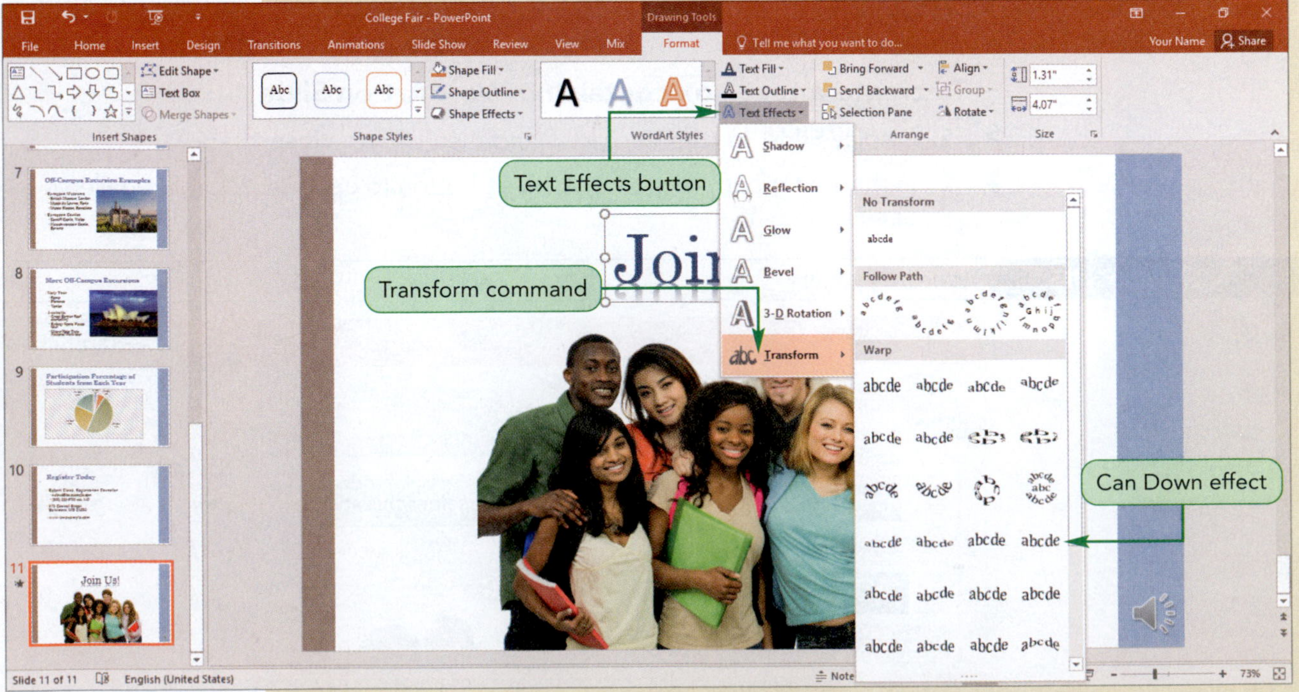

© iStock.com/Christopher Futcher; © iStock.com/Noppasin Wongchum; Courtesy of S. Scott Zimmerman

3. In the fourth row under Warp, click the **Can Down** effect. See Figure 3-17.

Figure 3-17 WordArt after applying Can Down transform effect

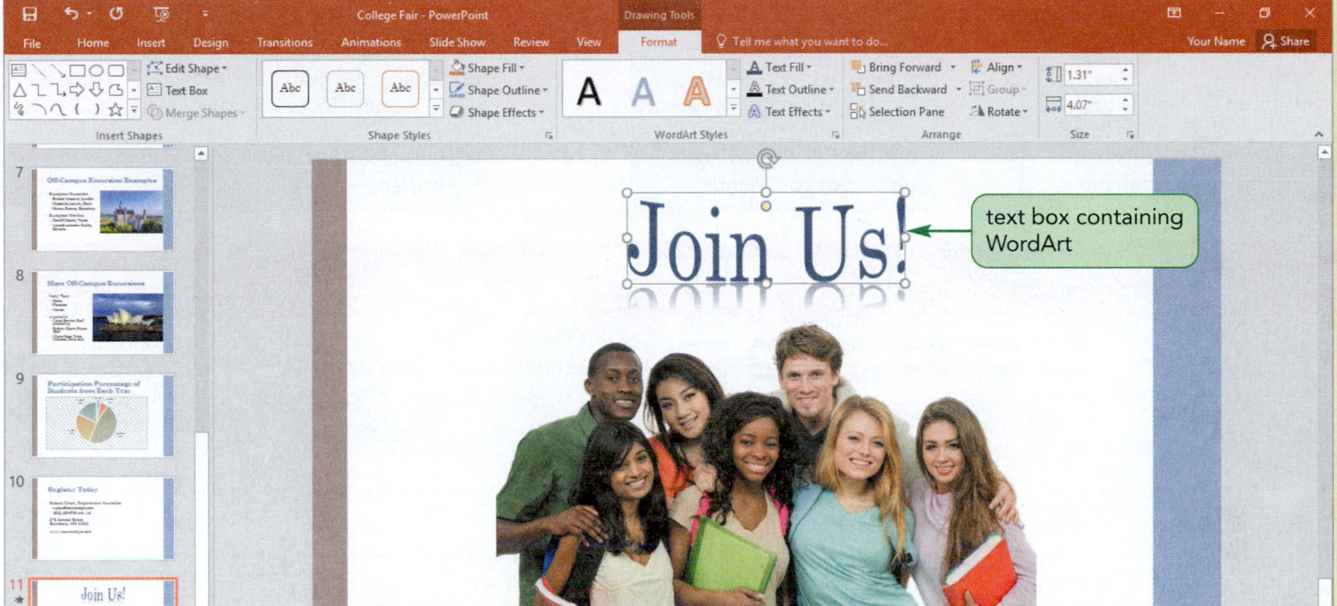

© iStock.com/Christopher Futcher; © iStock.com/Noppasin Wongchum; Courtesy of S. Scott Zimmerman

4. Save the changes to the presentation.

PROSKILLS

Decision Making: Selecting Appropriate Font Colors

When you select font colors, make sure your text is easy to read during your slide show. Font colors that work well are dark colors on a light background or light colors on a dark background. Avoid red text on a blue background or blue text on a green background (and vice versa) unless the shades of those colors are in strong contrast. These combinations might look fine on your computer monitor, but they are almost totally illegible to an audience viewing your presentation on a screen in a darkened room. Also avoid using red/green combinations, which color-blind people find illegible.

REVIEW

Session 3.1 Quick Check

1. How do you change the animation applied to a SmartArt diagram so that each shape animates one at a time?
2. What happens when you click the Play in Background button in the Audio Styles group on the Audio Tools Playback tab?
3. What is the difference between a chart and a graph?
4. What is a spreadsheet?
5. How do you identify a specific cell in a spreadsheet?
6. What is WordArt?

Session 3.2 Visual Overview:

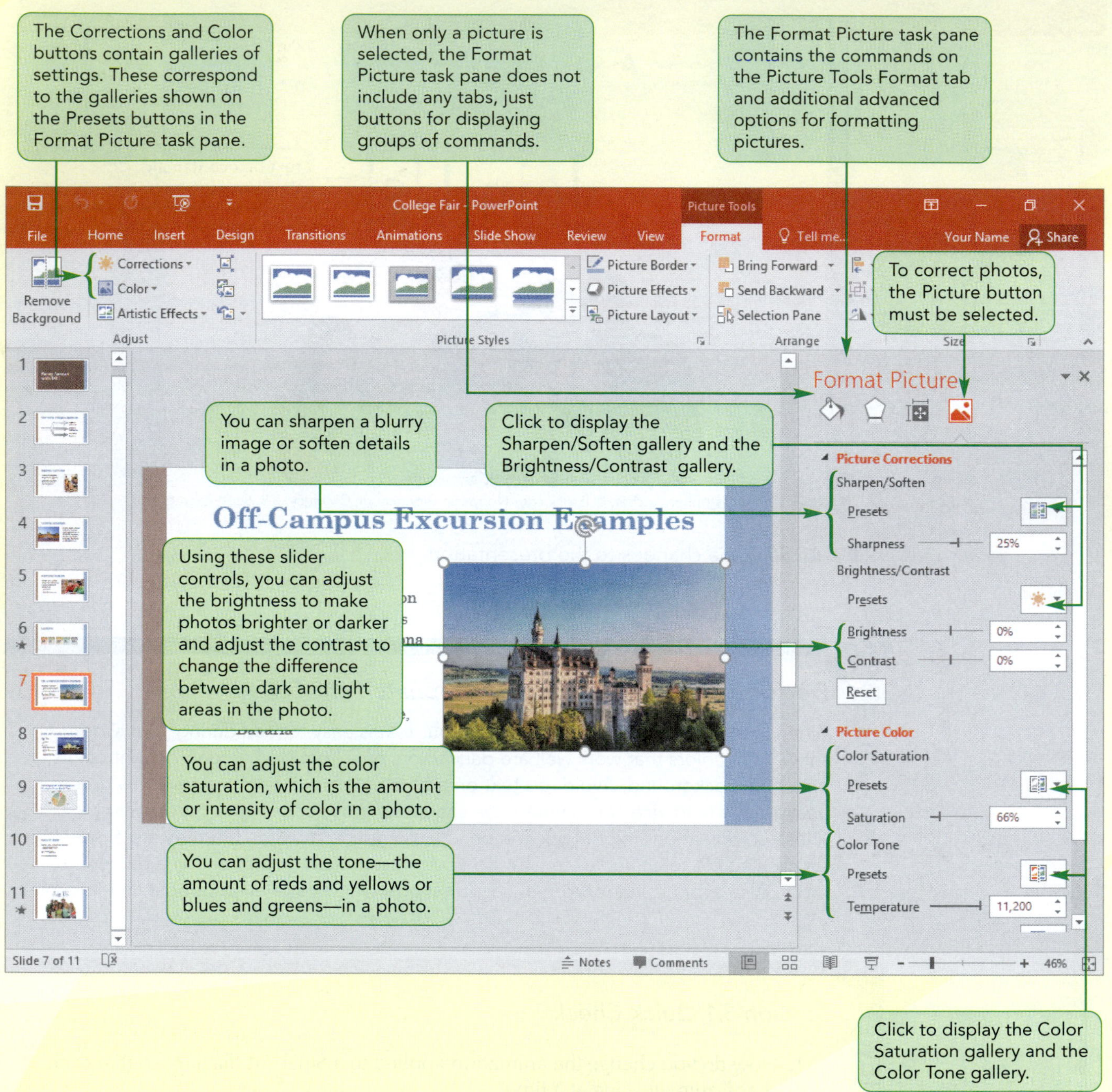
The Corrections and Color buttons contain galleries of settings. These correspond to the galleries shown on the Presets buttons in the Format Picture task pane.
When only a picture is selected, the Format Picture task pane does not include any tabs, just buttons for displaying groups of commands.
The Format Picture task pane contains the commands on the Picture Tools Format tab and additional advanced options for formatting pictures.
To correct photos, the Picture button must be selected.
You can sharpen a blurry image or soften details in a photo.
Click to display the Sharpen/Soften gallery and the Brightness/Contrast gallery.
Using these slider controls, you can adjust the brightness to make photos brighter or darker and adjust the contrast to change the difference between dark and light areas in the photo.
You can adjust the color saturation, which is the amount or intensity of color in a photo.
You can adjust the tone—the amount of reds and yellows or blues and greens—in a photo.
Click to display the Color Saturation gallery and the Color Tone gallery.
College Fair - PowerPoint
Picture Tools
File
Home
Insert
Design
Transitions
Animations
Slide Show
Review
View
Format
Tell me...
Your Name
Share
Remove Background
Corrections
Color
Artistic Effects
Adjust
Picture Styles
Picture Border
Picture Effects
Picture Layout
Bring Forward
Send Backward
Selection Pane
Arrange
Size
Off-Campus Excursion Examples
Format Picture
Picture Corrections
Sharpen/Soften
Presets
Sharpness
25%
Brightness/Contrast
Presets
Brightness
0%
Contrast
0%
Reset
Picture Color
Color Saturation
Presets
Saturation
66%
Color Tone
Presets
Temperature
11,200
Slide 7 of 11
Notes
Comments
46%

Formatting Shapes and Pictures

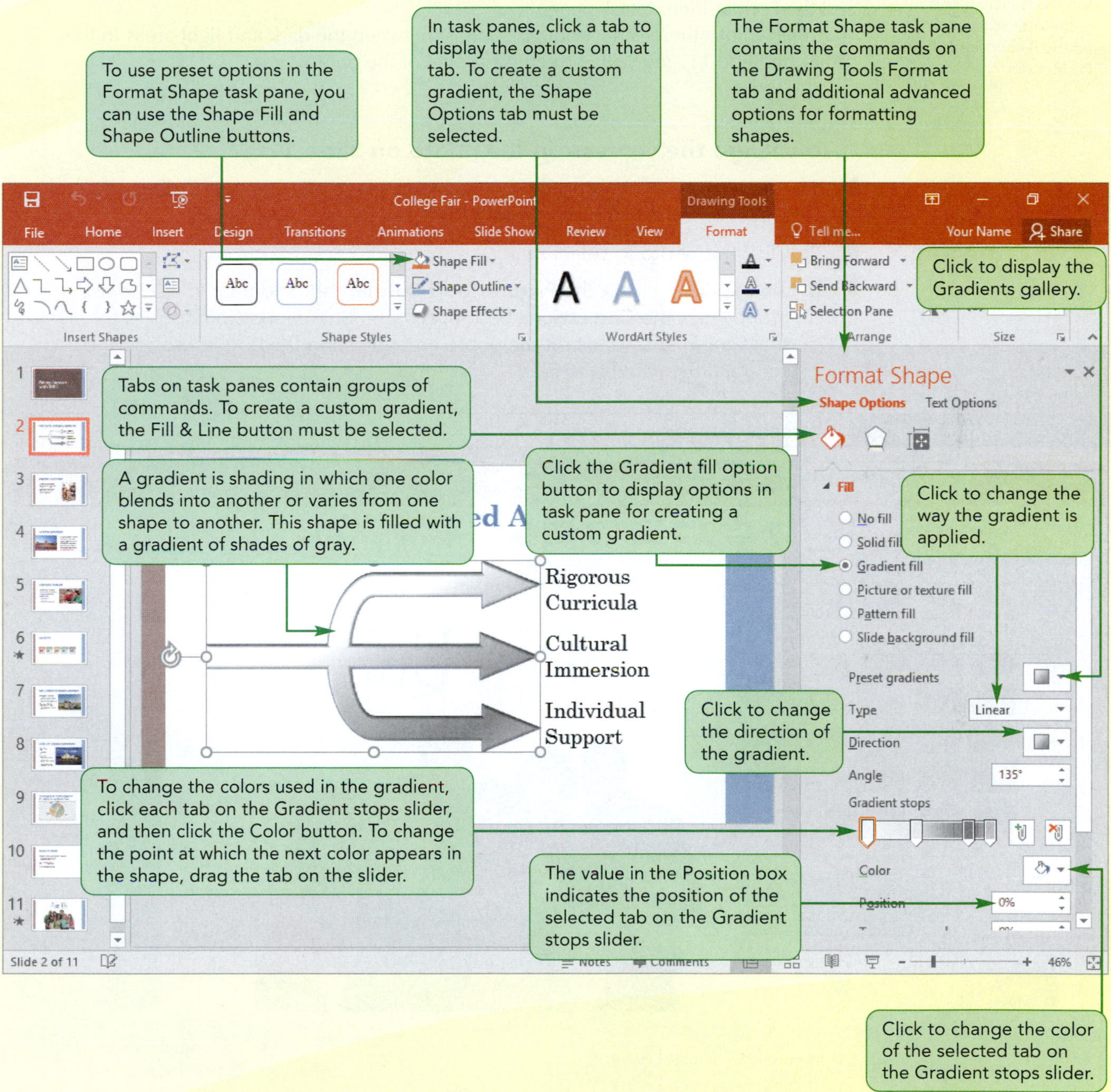
To use preset options in the Format Shape task pane, you can use the Shape Fill and Shape Outline buttons.
In task panes, click a tab to display the options on that tab. To create a custom gradient, the Shape Options tab must be selected.
The Format Shape task pane contains the commands on the Drawing Tools Format tab and additional advanced options for formatting shapes.
College Fair - PowerPoint
Drawing Tools
File
Home
Insert
Design
Transitions
Animations
Slide Show
Review
View
Format
Tell me...
Your Name
Share
Shape Fill
Shape Outline
Shape Effects
Bring Forward
Send Backward
Selection Pane
Insert Shapes
Shape Styles
WordArt Styles
Arrange
Size
Click to display the Gradients gallery.
Tabs on task panes contain groups of commands. To create a custom gradient, the Fill & Line button must be selected.
Format Shape
Shape Options
Text Options
A gradient is shading in which one color blends into another or varies from one shape to another. This shape is filled with a gradient of shades of gray.
Click the Gradient fill option button to display options in task pane for creating a custom gradient.
Click to change the way the gradient is applied.
Fill
No fill
Solid fill
Gradient fill
Picture or texture fill
Pattern fill
Slide background fill
Rigorous Curricula
Cultural Immersion
Individual Support
Preset gradients
Type
Linear
Direction
Angle
135°
Gradient stops
Click to change the direction of the gradient.
To change the colors used in the gradient, click each tab on the Gradient stops slider, and then click the Color button. To change the point at which the next color appears in the shape, drag the tab on the slider.
Color
Position
0%
The value in the Position box indicates the position of the selected tab on the Gradient stops slider.
Slide 2 of 11
46%
Click to change the color of the selected tab on the Gradient stops slider.

Editing Photos

TIP

If you make changes to photos and then change your mind, you can click the Reset Picture button in the Adjust group on the Picture Tools Format tab.

If photos you want to use in a presentation are too dark or require other fine-tuning, you can use PowerPoint's photo-correction tools to correct the photos. These photo-correction tools appear on the ribbon and in the Format Picture task pane. Refer to the Session 3.2 Visual Overview for more information about correcting photos and the Format Picture task pane.

Robert thinks there is not enough contrast between the dark and light areas in the photo on Slide 11. You will correct this aspect of the photo.

To change the contrast in the photo on Slide 11:

1. If you took a break after the previous session, make sure the **College Fair** presentation is open and **Slide 11** (the last slide) is displayed.
2. Click the photo to select it.
3. On the ribbon, click the **Picture Tools Format** tab, and then in the Adjust group, click the **Corrections** button. A menu opens, showing options for sharpening and softening the photo and adjusting the brightness and the contrast. See Figure 3-18.

Figure 3-18 Corrections menu

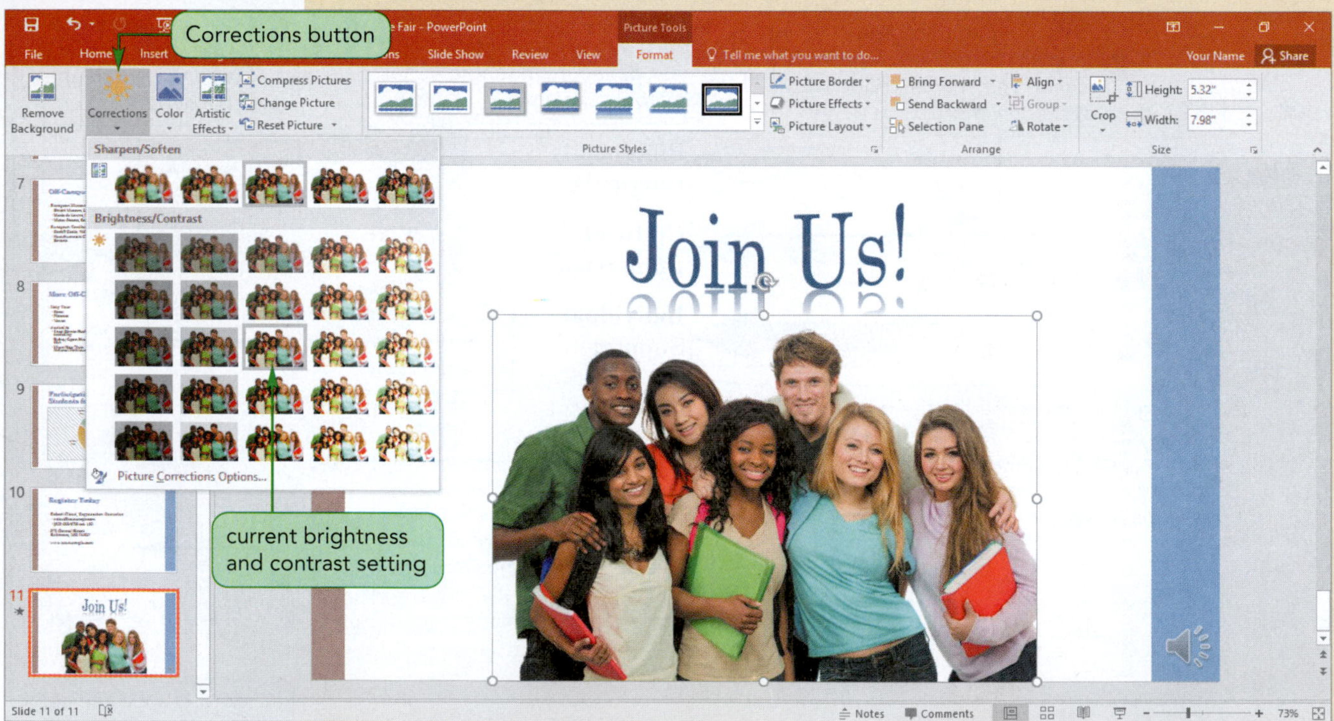

© iStock.com/Christopher Futcher

4. In the Brightness/Contrast section, click the **Brightness 0% (Normal) Contrast -20%** style (the third style in the second row). The contrast of the image changes. Because you chose a style with a Brightness percentage of 0%, the brightness of the photo is unchanged.

   You want to decrease the contrast just a little more. However, the gallery provides options that change the contrast in increments of 20 percent, which will be more of an adjustment than you are looking for. For selecting a more precise contrast setting, you need to open the Format Picture task pane.

TIP

You can also right-click the photo, and then click Format Picture on the shortcut menu to open the Format Picture task pane.

5. Click the **Corrections** button again, and then click **Picture Corrections Options**. The Format Picture task pane opens with the Picture button selected and the Picture Corrections section expanded.
6. Drag the **Contrast** slider to the left until the box next to the slider indicates -30%. The contrast increases slightly.

   Trouble? If you can't position the slider exactly, click the up or down arrow in the box containing the percentage as needed, or select the current percentage and then type -30.
7. Close the task pane.

Next, Robert wants you to adjust the photo on Slide 7. He wants you to make the colors in the photo more realistic, by reducing the saturation and the tone.

To change the saturation and tone of the photo on Slide 7:

1. Display **Slide 7** ("Off-Campus Excursion Examples"), click the photo to select it, and then click the **Picture Tools Format** tab on the ribbon, if necessary.
2. In the Adjust group, click the **Color** button. A menu opens with options for adjusting the saturation and tone of the photo's color. See Figure 3-19.

Figure 3-19 Color menu

© iStock.com/Noppasin Wongchum; Courtesy of S. Scott Zimmerman

TIP

To recolor a photo so it is all one color, click the Color button in the Adjust group on the Picture Tools Format tab, and then click a Recolor option.

3. Under Color Saturation, click the **Saturation: 66%** option. The colors in the photo are now less intense.
4. Click the **Color** button again.
5. Under Color Tone, click the **Temperature: 11200K** option. More reds and yellows are added to the photo, most noticeably in the skyline on the right side of the image.

Finally, Robert wants you to sharpen the photo on Slide 7 so that the objects in the photo are more in focus.

To sharpen the photo on Slide 7:

1. On Slide 7 ("Off-Campus Excursion Examples"), make sure the photo is still selected, and on the ribbon, the Picture Tools Format tab is the active tab.
2. In the Adjust group, click the **Corrections** button. The options for sharpening and softening photos appear at the top of the menu.
3. Under Sharpen/Soften, click the **Sharpen: 25%** option. The edges of the objects in the picture are sharper and clearer.
4. Save the changes to the presentation.

Removing the Background from Photos

Sometimes a photo is more striking if you remove its background. You can also layer a photo with the background removed on top of another photo to create an interesting effect. To remove the background of a photo, you can use the Remove Background tool. When you click the Remove Background button in the Adjust group on the Picture Tools Format tab, PowerPoint analyzes the photograph and marks parts of it to remove and parts of it to retain. If the analysis removes too little or too much of the photo, you can adjust it.

REFERENCE

Removing the Background of a Photograph

- Click the photo, and then click the Picture Tools Format tab on the ribbon.
- In the Adjust group, click the Remove Background button.
- Drag the sizing handles on the remove background border to make broad adjustments to the area marked for removal.
- In the Refine group on the Background Removal tab, click the Mark Areas to Keep or the Mark Areas to Remove button, and then click or drag through an area of the photo that you want marked to keep or remove.
- Click a blank area of the slide or click the Keep Changes button in the Close group to accept the changes.

Robert wants you to modify the photo of the Sydney Opera House on Slide 8 so that the background looks like a drawing, but the opera house stays sharp and in focus. To create this effect, you will need to work with two versions of the photo. You will use the Duplicate command to make a copy of the photo and then remove the background from the duplicate photo.

To duplicate the photo on Slide 8 and then remove the background from the copy:

1. Display **Slide 8** ("More Off-Campus Excursions" with the photo of the Sydney Opera House), click the photo to select it, and then, on the ribbon, click the **Home** tab, if necessary. The photo on Slide 8 is a photo of the Sydney Opera House in Sydney, Australia.
2. In the Clipboard group, click the **Copy button arrow**, and then click **Duplicate**. The photo is duplicated on the slide, and the duplicate is selected.
3. Point to the selected duplicate photo so that the pointer changes to ✥, and then drag it left to position it to the left of the original photo. The duplicate photo is on top of the bulleted list and extends beyond the slide border.

4. With the duplicate photo selected, click the **Picture Tools Format** tab on the ribbon.

5. In the Adjust group, click the **Remove Background** button. The areas of the photograph marked for removal are colored purple. A sizing box appears around the general area of the photograph that will be retained, and a new tab, the Background Removal tab, appears on the ribbon and is the active tab. See Figure 3-20. You can adjust the area of the photograph that is retained by dragging the sizing handles on the sizing box.

Figure 3-20 Photograph after clicking the Remove Background button

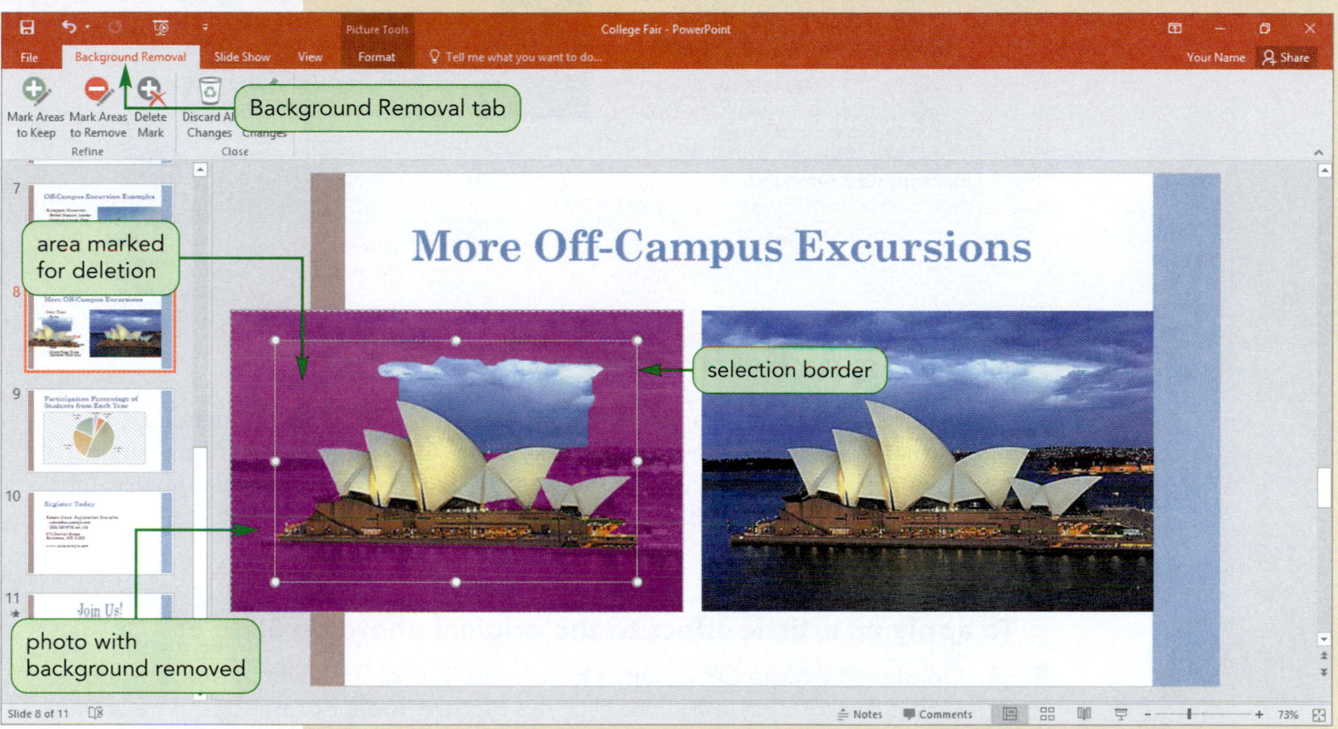

Courtesy of S. Scott Zimmerman; © iStock.com/Noppasin Wongchum; © iStock.com/Christopher Futcher

TIP

If the background of a photo is all one color, you can click the Color button in the Adjust group on the Picture Tools Format tab, click Set Transparent Color, and then click the color you want to make transparent.

6. Drag the top-middle sizing handle down to just above the tallest point of the opera house. Now only the opera house will be retained, and all of the sky and water will be removed.

   Trouble? If any of the background of the photo is colored normally, click the Mark Areas to Remove button in the Refine group on the Background Removal tab, and then drag through the area that should be removed.

7. On the Background Removal tab, in the Close group, click the **Keep Changes** button. The changes you made are applied to the photograph, and the Background Removal tab is removed from the ribbon. See Figure 3-21.

Figure 3-21 Duplicate photo with background removed

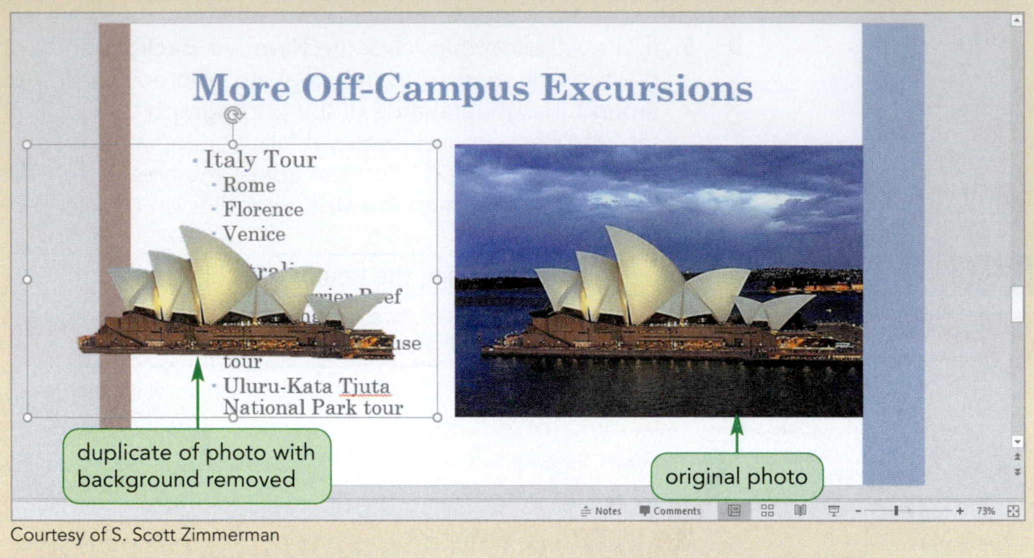

Courtesy of S. Scott Zimmerman

Applying Artistic Effects to Photos

You can apply artistic effects to photos to make them look like they are drawings, paintings, black-and-white line drawings, and so on. To make the opera house stand out in the photo, Robert wants you to apply an artistic effect to the original photo, and then place the photo with the background removed on top of it.

To apply an artistic effect to the original photo on Slide 8:

1. On Slide 8 ("More Off-Campus Excursions"), click the original photo with the visible background, and then click the **Picture Tools Format** tab, if necessary.
2. In the Adjust group, click the **Artistic Effects** button. See Figure 3-22.

Figure 3-22 Artistic Effects menu

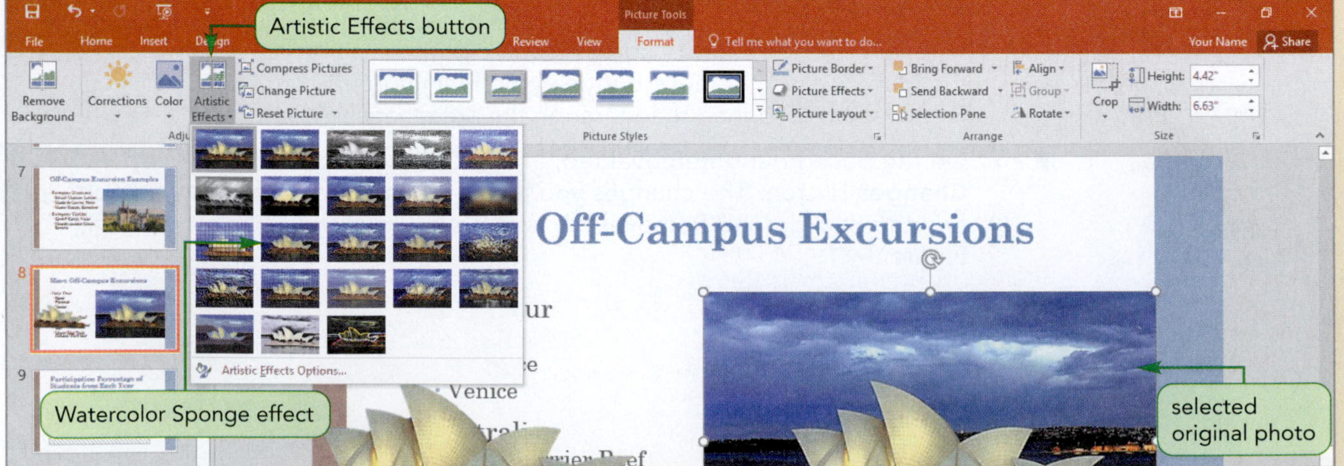

Courtesy of S. Scott Zimmerman; © iStock.com/Noppasin Wongchum

3. Click the **Watercolor Sponge** effect in the third row. The watercolor sponge effect is applied to the photo. Now you will place the photo with the background removed on top of the photo with the artistic effect.
4. Drag the photo with the background removed and position it directly on top of the opera house in the photo with the artistic effect applied. See Figure 3-23.

Figure 3-23 Final photo on Slide 8

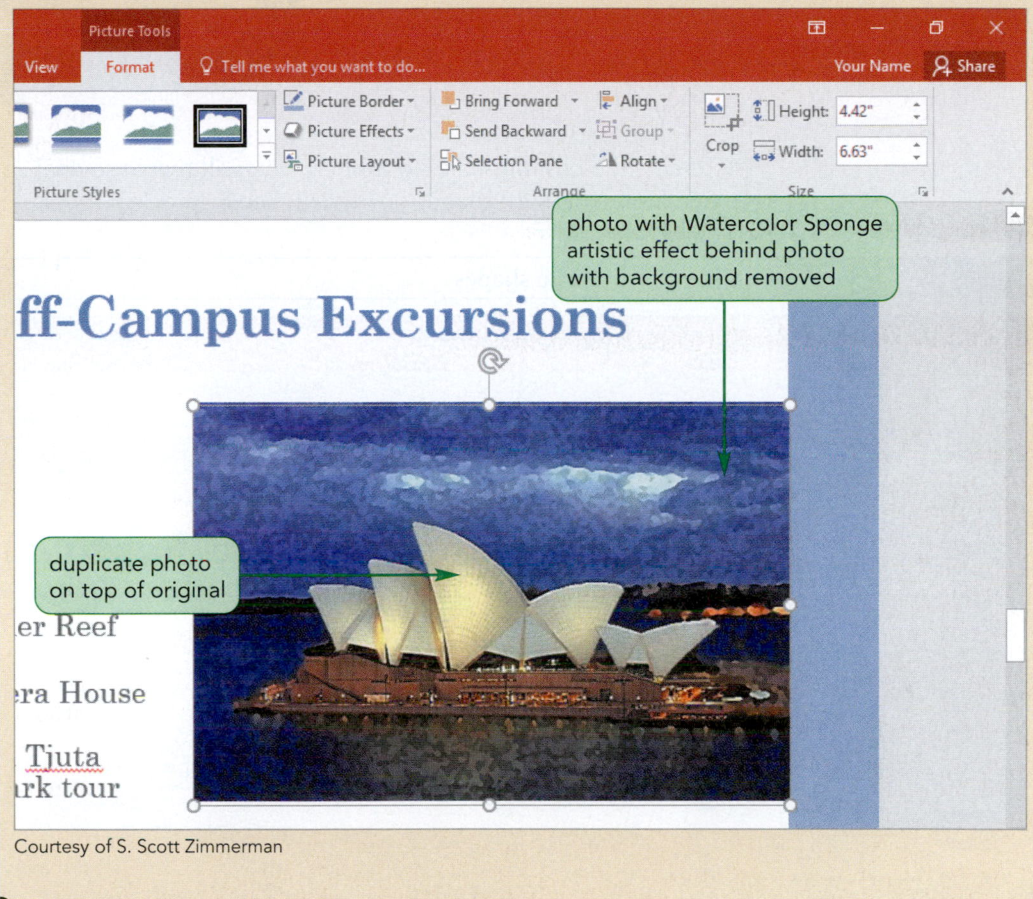

Courtesy of S. Scott Zimmerman

5. Save the changes to the presentation.

Creating a Custom Shape

You have learned how to insert and format shapes on slides. In PowerPoint you can also create a custom shape by merging two or more shapes. Then you can position and format the custom shape as you would any other shape.

ISC advertises that it offers three main advantages: rigorous curricula, cultural immersion, and individual support. To illustrate this three-pronged approach, Robert wants to use a graphic, but none of the built-in shapes or SmartArt diagrams matches the idea he has in mind. He asks you to create a custom shape similar to the one shown in Figure 3-24 to illustrate this concept.

Figure 3-24 Robert's sketch of the shape for Slide 2

To create the custom shape for Robert, you will merge several shapes. Robert already placed three of these shapes on Slide 2. See Figure 3-25.

Figure 3-25 Slide 2 with three shapes

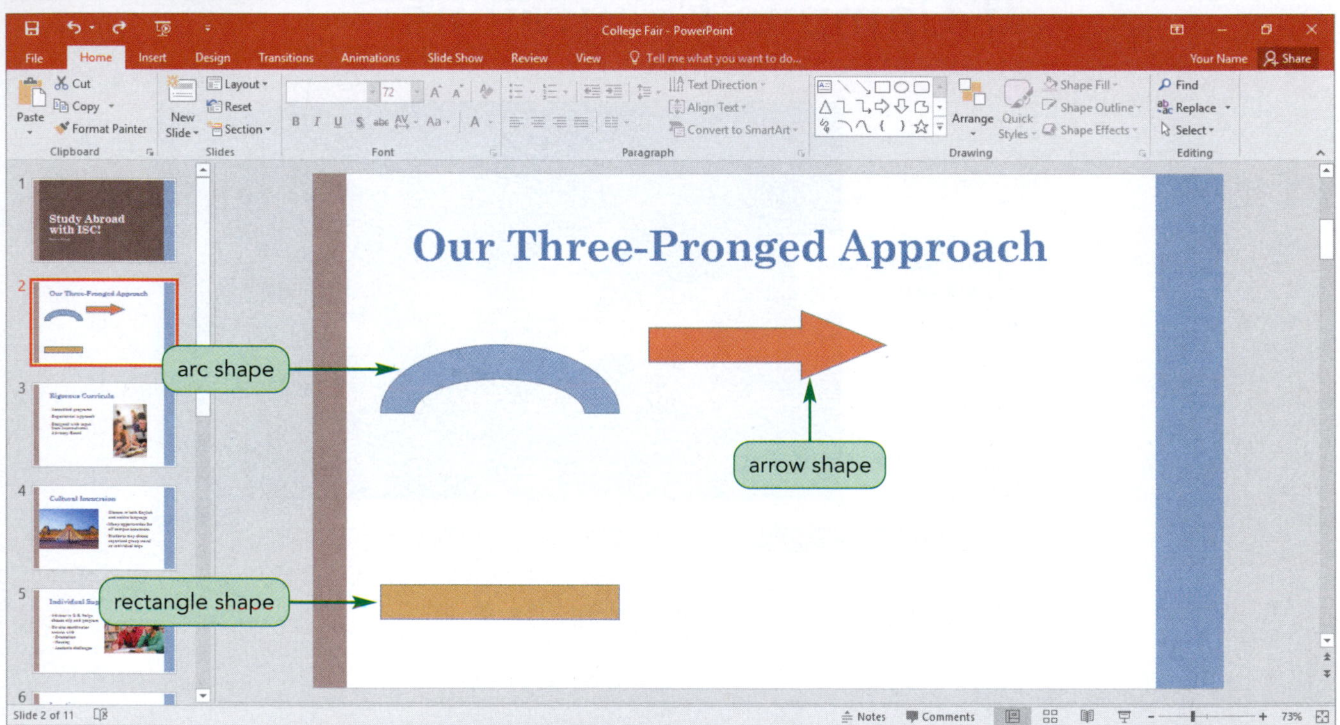

The first thing you need to do is duplicate the arrow shape twice to create the three prongs. Then you need to align the three arrow shapes.

TIP

You can also click the Align button in the Arrange group on the Format tab, and then click one of the alignment commands.

To align the three arrow shapes on Slide 2:

1. Display **Slide 2** ("Our Three-Pronged Approach"), and then duplicate the arrow shape twice.
2. Drag one of the duplicate arrows down until the smart guides indicate the bottom point of the arrow head is aligned with the top edge of the rectangle shape and so that its left and right ends are aligned with those of the original arrow.

3. Drag the other duplicate arrow so it is halfway between the top and bottom arrow, until the smart guides indicate that its left and right ends are aligned with those of the top and bottom arrows and so that there is the same amount of space between the top and middle arrow and between the middle and bottom arrow, as shown in Figure 3-26.

Figure 3-26 **Smart guides showing alignment of arrow shapes**

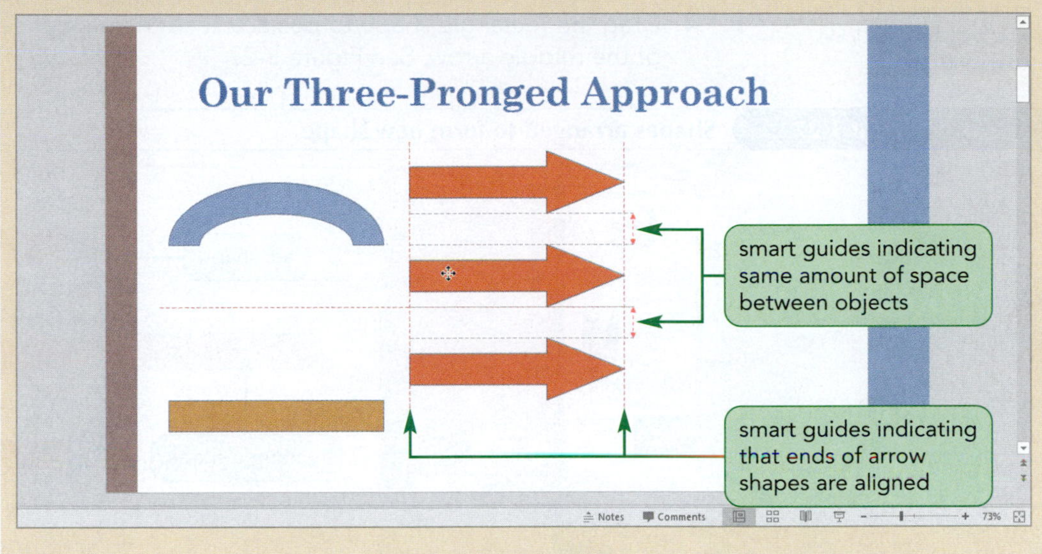

To create a custom shape, you need to use the commands on the Merge Shapes menu in the Insert Shapes group on the Drawing Tools Format tab. Each command has a different effect on selected shapes:

- **Union**—Combines selected shapes without removing any portions
- **Combine**—Combines selected shapes and removes the sections of the shapes that overlap
- **Fragment**—Separates overlapping portions of shapes into separate shapes
- **Intersect**—Combines selected shapes and removes everything except the sections that overlap
- **Subtract**—Removes the second shape selected, including any part of the first shape that is overlapped by the second shape

When you merge shapes, you place one shape on top of or touching another, and then you select the shapes. When you use the Union, Combine, Fragment, or Intersect command, the shape you select first determines the format of the merged shape. For example, if you select a red shape first and a blue shape second, and then you unite, combine, fragment, or intersect them, the merged shape will be red. When you use the Subtract command, the shape you select second is the shape that is removed.

You'll position the shapes and then merge them using the Union command.

Make sure the arc and arrow shape are touching or the shapes won't merge when you use the Union command.

To position the shapes and then merge them:

1. Click the **arc** shape to select it.
2. On the Home tab, in the Drawing group, click the **Arrange** button, point to **Rotate**, and then click **Rotate Left 90 degrees**.
3. Drag the arc shape and position it so that its ends touch the left end of the top arrow and bottom arrow shapes, making sure the shapes touch.
4. Drag the rectangle shape to position it so that its right end touches the end of the middle arrow. See Figure 3-27.

Figure 3-27 Shapes arranged to form new shape

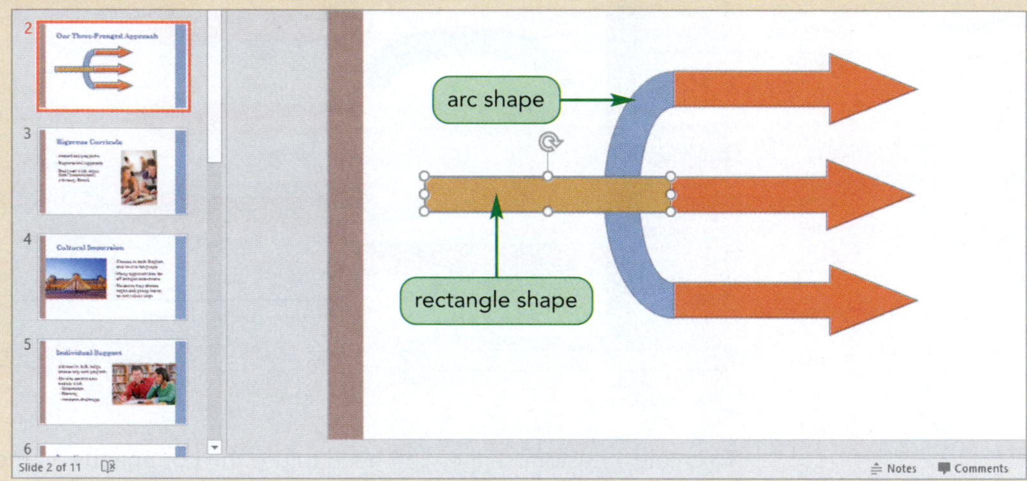

© iStock.com/sturti; © iStock.com/vichie81; © iStock.com/Susan Chiang

5. On the ribbon, click the **Drawing Tools Format** tab. In the Insert Shapes group, the Merge Shapes button is gray and unavailable. At least two shapes need to be selected to use the commands on the Merge Shapes menu.
6. Press and hold the **Shift** key, and then click the middle arrow. The rectangle and the middle arrow shape are now selected, and the Merge Shapes button is now available.
7. In the Insert Shapes group, click the **Merge Shapes** button, and then click **Union**. The two shapes are merged into a new shape formatted the same tan color as the rectangle shape because you selected the rectangle shape first.
8. Click the **arc** shape, press and hold the **Shift** key, click each of the arrow shapes including the merged shape, and then release the **Shift** key.
9. In the Insert Shapes group, click the **Merge Shapes** button, and then click **Union**. The four shapes are merged into a blue shape.

Applying Advanced Formatting to Shapes

You know that you can fill a shape with a solid color or with a picture. You can also fill a shape with a texture—a pattern that gives a tactile quality to the shape, such as crumpled paper or marble—or with a gradient. You'll change the fill of the custom shape to a texture.

To change the shape fill to a texture:

1. Make sure the custom shape is selected, and then click the **Drawing Tools Format** tab, if necessary.
2. In the Shape Styles group, click the **Shape Fill button arrow**, and then point to **Texture**. The Texture submenu opens. See Figure 3-28.

Figure 3-28 **Texture submenu on Shape Fill menu**

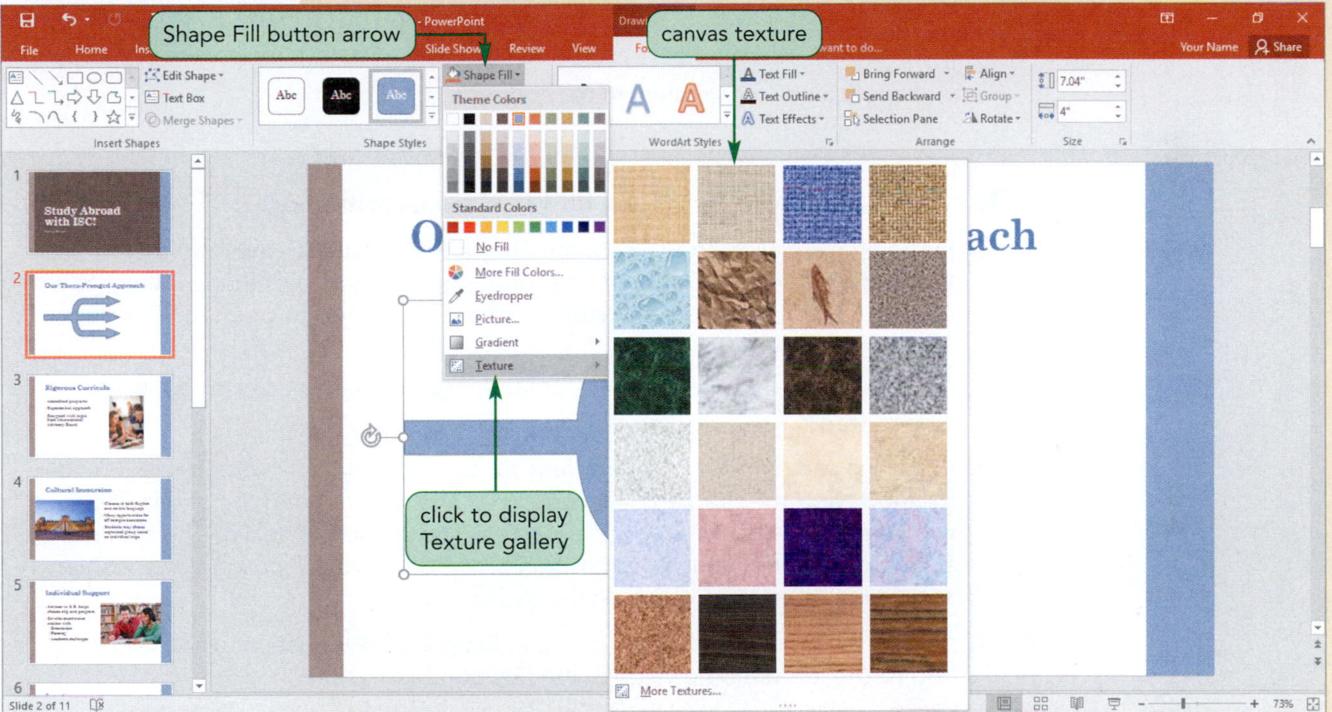

© iStock.com/sturti; © iStock.com/vichie81; © iStock.com/Susan Chiang

3. Click the **Canvas** texture, which is the second texture in the first row. The custom shape is filled with a texture resembling canvas. Robert doesn't like any of the textures as a fill for the shape. He asks you to remove the texture.
4. In the Shapes Styles group, click the **Shape Fill button arrow**, and then click **No Fill**. The texture is removed from the custom shape, and only the outline of the custom shape remains.

The texture did not achieve the effect Robert wanted for the shape. He now asks you to use a gradient to simulate the look of metal or silver. You can apply gradients on the Shape Fill menu that use shades of the Accent 1 color in the theme color palette. You can also create a custom gradient using the options in the Format Shape task pane. To create a custom gradient, you select the colors to use, specify the position in the shape where the color will change, and specify the direction of the gradient in the shape.

Refer to the Session 3.2 Visual Overview for more information about using the Format Shape task pane to create a custom gradient.

REFERENCE

Creating a Custom Gradient in a Shape

- Select the shape.
- Click the Drawing Tools Format tab.
- In the Shape Styles group, click the Shape Fill button arrow, point to Gradient, and then click More Gradients to open the Format Shape task pane.
- In the Format Shape task pane, on the Shape Options tab with the Fill & Line button selected, click the Gradient fill option button.
- On the Gradient stops slider, click a tab, drag it to the desired position on the slider, click the Color button, and then select a color.
- Repeat the above step for each tab.
- Click the Type arrow, and then click the type of gradient you want to use.
- Click the Direction button, and then click the direction of the gradient.

You will apply a custom gradient to the custom shape now.

To create a custom gradient fill for the custom shape:

1. In the Shape Styles group, click the **Shape Fill button arrow**, and then point to **Gradient**. The gradients on the submenu use shades of the Ice Blue, Accent 1 color. To create a custom gradient, you need to open the Format Shape task pane.
2. Click **More Gradients**. The Format Shape task pane opens with the Fill & Line button selected on the Shape Options tab.
3. In the Fill section, click the **Gradient fill** option button. The commands for modifying the gradient fill appear in the task pane, and the shape fills with shades of light blue. Under Gradient stops, the first tab on the slider is selected, and its value in the Position box is 0%. You will change the position and color of the second tab on the slider.
4. On the Gradient stops slider, drag the **Stop 2 of 4** tab (second tab from the left) to the left until the value in the Position box is **40%**.

   Trouble? If you can't position the slider exactly, click the Stop 2 of 4 tab, type 40 in the Position box, and then press the Enter key.

TIP

Click the Add gradient stop button to add another gradient stop to the slider; click the Remove gradient stop button to remove the selected gradient stop from the slider.

5. With the Stop 2 of 4 tab selected, click the **Color** button. The color palette opens.
6. Click the **White, Background 1, Darker 5%** color. Next you need to change the color of the third tab.
7. Click the **Stop 3 of 4** tab, click the **Color** button, and then click the **White, Background 1, Darker 50%** color.
8. Click the **Stop 4 of 4** tab, click the **Color** button, and then click the **Gray-50%, Accent 6, Lighter 60%** color.

   Next you will change the direction of the gradient. Above the Gradient stops slider, in the Type box, Linear is selected. This means that the shading will vary linearly—that is, top to bottom, side to side, or diagonally. You will change the direction to a diagonal.

9. Click the **Direction** button. A gallery of gradient options opens.
10. Click the **Linear Diagonal – Top Right to Bottom Left** direction. The shading in the shape changes so it varies diagonally. See Figure 3-29.

Figure 3-29 Custom shape with gradient fill

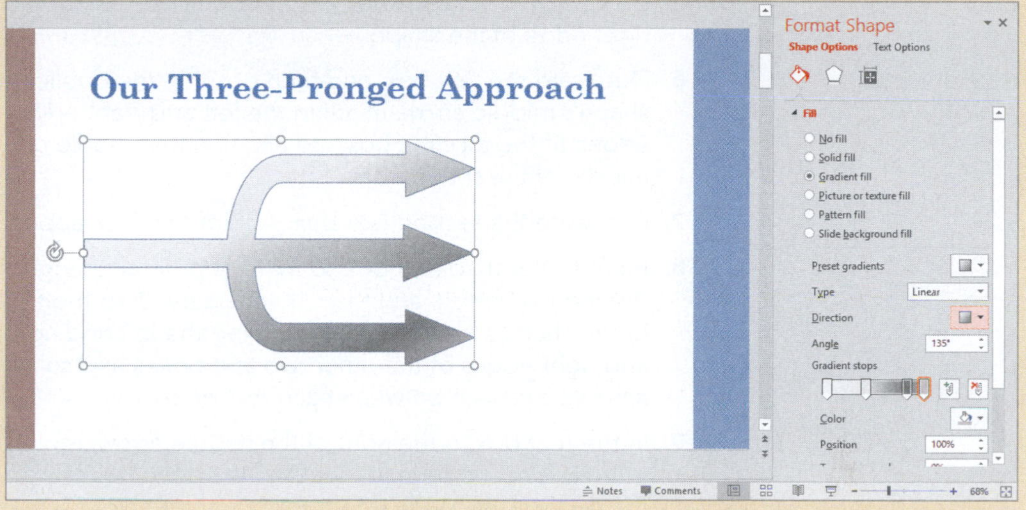

11. In the Format Shape task pane, click the **Close** button.

Although the gradient shading helped, the shape looks flat and doesn't really look metallic. To finish formatting the shape, you need to apply a bevel effect, which will give the edges a three-dimensional, rounded look.

To add a bevel effect to the custom shape:

1. On the ribbon, click the **Drawing Tools Format** tab, if necessary.
2. In the Shape Styles group, click the **Shape Effects** button. The menu that opens lets you choose from a variety of effects you can apply to shapes.
3. Point to **Bevel**, and then click the **Circle** bevel. The shape has a bevel effect.

TIP

To save a custom shape as a picture file so that you can use it in other files, right-click it, and then click Save as Picture on the shortcut menu.

Now you need to complete the slide by adding text boxes that list the three elements of the ISC approach. You will position the custom shape, and then place a text box next to each prong.

To add text boxes to Slide 2:

1. Drag the shape so its left edge aligns with the left edge of the title text box.
2. On the ribbon, click the **Insert** tab, and then in the Text group, click the **Text Box** button.
3. To the right of the shape's top arrow, drag to draw a text box approximately 2 inches wide, and then type **Rigorous Curricula**.

4. Change the font size of the text in the text box to **32** points. The text now appears on two lines in the text box.

   Trouble? If the text did not adjust to appear on two lines in the text box, drag the right-middle sizing handle to the left until it does.

5. Drag the text box to position it so that the top of the text box is aligned with the top of the shape and the left edge of the text box is aligned with the right edge of the shape.

6. Duplicate the text box, and then position the duplicate to the right of the shape's middle arrow, aligning the left and right edges with the left and right edges of the top text box and aligning the middle of the text box with the middle of the shape.

7. Duplicate the second text box. A third text box appears.

8. Point to the third text box so that the pointer changes to ✥, press and hold the mouse button, and then, if necessary, drag the third text box to the right of the shape's bottom arrow, aligning the left and right edges with the left and right edges of the other two text boxes and so that there is the same amount of space between each text box.

9. In the text box to the right of the middle arrow, replace the text with **Cultural Immersion**, and then in the text box to the right of the bottom arrow, replace the text with **Individual Support**. Compare your screen to Figure 3-30, and make any adjustments if necessary.

Figure 3-30 **Text boxes next to custom shape with beveled edge**

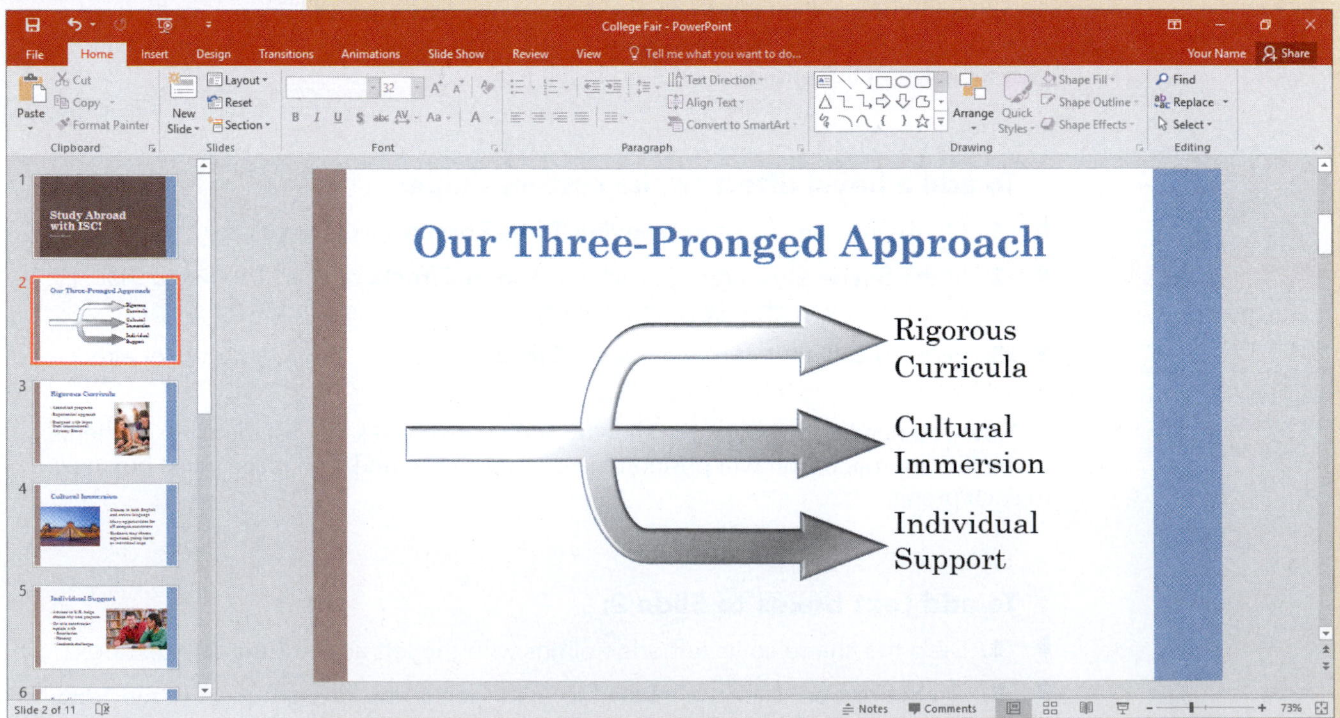

© iStock.com/sturti; © iStock.com/vichie81; © iStock.com/Susan Chiang

10. Save the changes to the presentation.

INSIGHT

Using the Format Shape and Format Picture Task Panes

Many options are available to you in the Format Shape and Format Picture task panes. Most of the commands are available on the Drawing Tools and Picture Tools Format tabs on the ribbon, but you can refine their effects in the task panes. For example, you can fill a shape with a color and then use a command in the Format Shape task pane to make the fill color partially transparent so you can see objects behind the shape. Because these task panes are so useful, you can access them in a variety of ways. Once a picture or shape is selected, you can do one of the following to open the corresponding task pane:

- Click any of the Dialog Box Launchers on the Drawing Tools or Picture Tools Format tab.
- Right-click a shape or picture, and then click Format Shape or Format Picture on the shortcut menu.
- Click a command at the bottom of a menu, such as the More Gradients command at the bottom of the Gradients submenu on the Fill Color menu or the Picture Corrections Options command at the bottom of the Corrections menu.

Making Presentations Accessible

People with physical impairments or disabilities can use computers because of technology that makes them accessible. For example, people who cannot use their arms or hands instead can use foot, head, or eye movements to control the pointer. One of the most common assistive technologies is the screen reader. The screen reader identifies objects on the screen and produces an audio of the text.

Graphics and tables cause problems for users of screen readers unless they have **alternative text**, often shortened to **alt text**, which is text added to an object that describes the object. For example, the alt text for a SmartArt graphic might describe the intent of the graphic. When a screen reader encounters an object that has alt text, it announces that an object is on the slide, and then it reads the alt text.

Adding Alt Text

You can add alt text for any object on a PowerPoint slide. Many screen readers can read the text in title text boxes and bulleted lists, so you usually do not need to add alt text for those objects. Most screen readers cannot read the text in SmartArt, in text boxes you draw, or in other shapes, so you will add alt text to the SmartArt diagram and the text box on Slide 6.

To add alt text for the SmartArt graphic:

1. Display **Slide 6** ("Locations").
2. Right-click the white area near any of the shapes in the SmartArt graphic to select the entire graphic.

Make sure you select the entire SmartArt object and not just one shape. If you right-click a shape, the alt text will be applied only for that individual shape.

3. On the shortcut menu, click **Format Object**. The Format Shape task pane opens with the Shape Options tab selected.
4. In the task pane, click the **Size & Properties** button, and then click **Text Box** to collapse that section, if necessary.

5. In the task pane, click **Alt Text** to expand the Alt Text section. A Title box and a Description box appear below the Alt Text section heading. See Figure 3-31.

Figure 3-31 Alt Text section in the Format Shape task pane

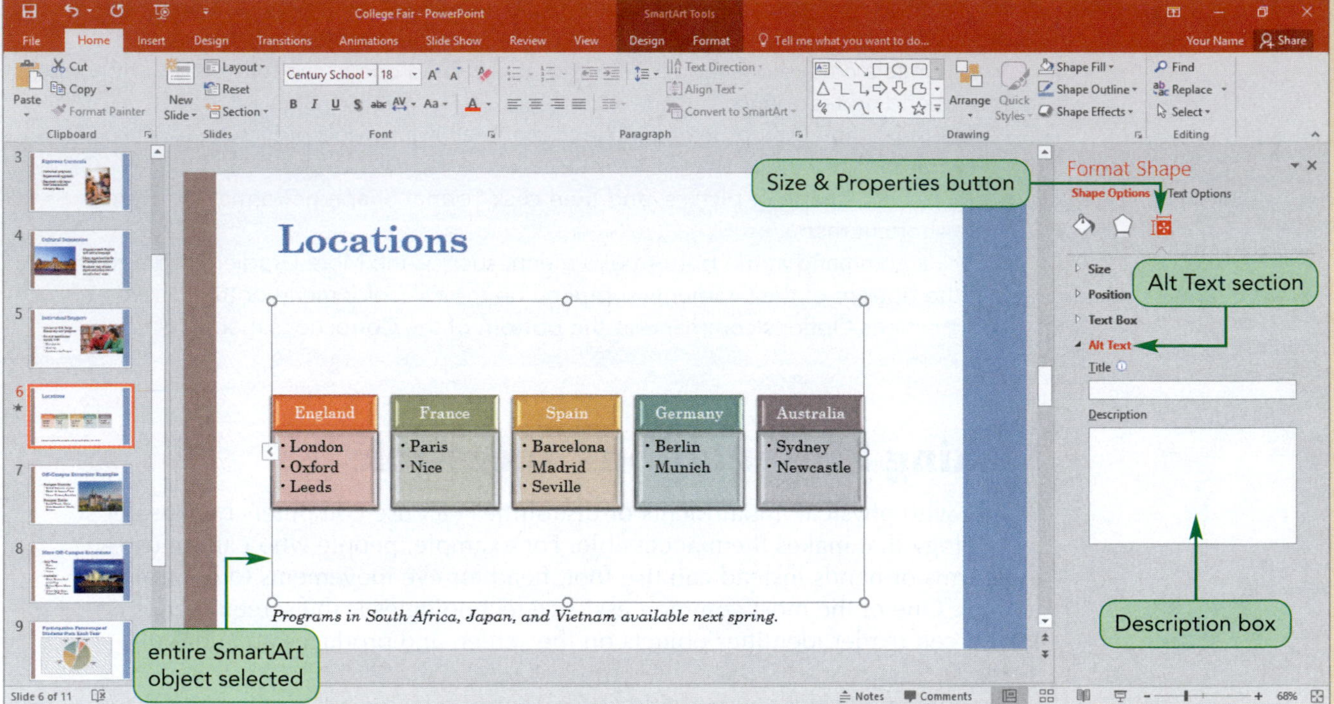

© iStock.com/sturti; © iStock.com/vichie81; © iStock.com/Susan Chiang; © iStock.com/Noppasin Wongchum; Courtesy of S. Scott Zimmerman

6. Click in the **Description** box, and then type **SmartArt graphic listing the ISC program countries and cities. The countries are England, France, Spain, Germany, and Australia.** (including the last period). This is the text a screen reader would read. (Note that in this case, if you were creating this slide for a real-life presentation, you should also add the city names to the Alt text.)
7. On Slide 6, click the text box at the bottom of the slide to select it. The Format Shape task pane changes to show an empty Description box. Now you will type alt text for the text box.
8. In the Format Shape task pane, click in the **Description** box, and then type **Note indicating that programs in South Africa, Japan, and Vietnam will be available next spring.** (including the period).

You also need to add alt text to the chart on Slide 9. To do this, you need to make sure that the chart area is selected and not just one element in the chart; otherwise the Alt Text commands will not be available in the task pane.

To select the chart area and add alt text to the chart on Slide 9:

1. Display **Slide 9** ("Participation Percentage of Students from Each Year"), and then click the chart.
2. On the ribbon, click the **Chart Tools Format** tab.
3. In the Current Selection group, click the **Chart Elements arrow** (the arrow on the top box in the group), and then click **Chart Area**, if necessary. Now the alt text will be added to the entire chart. In the task pane, the title is now Format Chart Area.
4. In the task pane, click the **Size & Properties** button. In the Alt Text section, the Description box is empty.
5. In the task pane, click in the **Description** box, and then type **Pie chart illustrating that 47% of students in the program are in their 3rd year, 26% are in their 4th year, 18% are in their 5th year, and a small percentage are in their 1st or 2nd year.** (including the period).
6. Close the Format Chart Area task pane.

Robert will add alt text for the rest of the graphics in the presentation later. Next, you need to make sure that the objects on slides will be identified in the correct order for screen readers.

Checking the Order Objects Will Be Read by a Screen Reader

When a person uses a screen reader to access a presentation, the screen reader selects and describes the elements on the slides in the order they were added. In PowerPoint, most screen readers first explain that a slide is displayed. After the user signals to the screen reader that he is ready for the next piece of information (for example, by pressing the Tab key), the reader identifies the first object on the slide. For most slides, this means that the first object is the title text box. The second object is usually the content placeholder on the slide. To check the order in which a screen reader will describe objects on a slide, you can use the Tab key or open the Selection pane. You'll check the order of objects on Slide 8.

To identify the order of objects on Slide 8:

1. Display **Slide 8** ("More Off-Campus Excursions"), and then click a blank area on the slide. The slide is active, but nothing on the slide is selected.
2. Press the **Tab** key. The title text box is selected.
3. Press the **Tab** key again. The bulleted list text box is selected next.
4. Press the **Tab** key. The photo is selected. However, remember that there are two photos here, one placed on top of the other. To see which one is selected, you can use the Selection pane.
5. On the Home tab, in the Editing group, click the **Select** button, and then click **Selection Pane**. The Selection pane opens. See Figure 3-32.

Figure 3-32 Selection pane listing objects on Slide 8

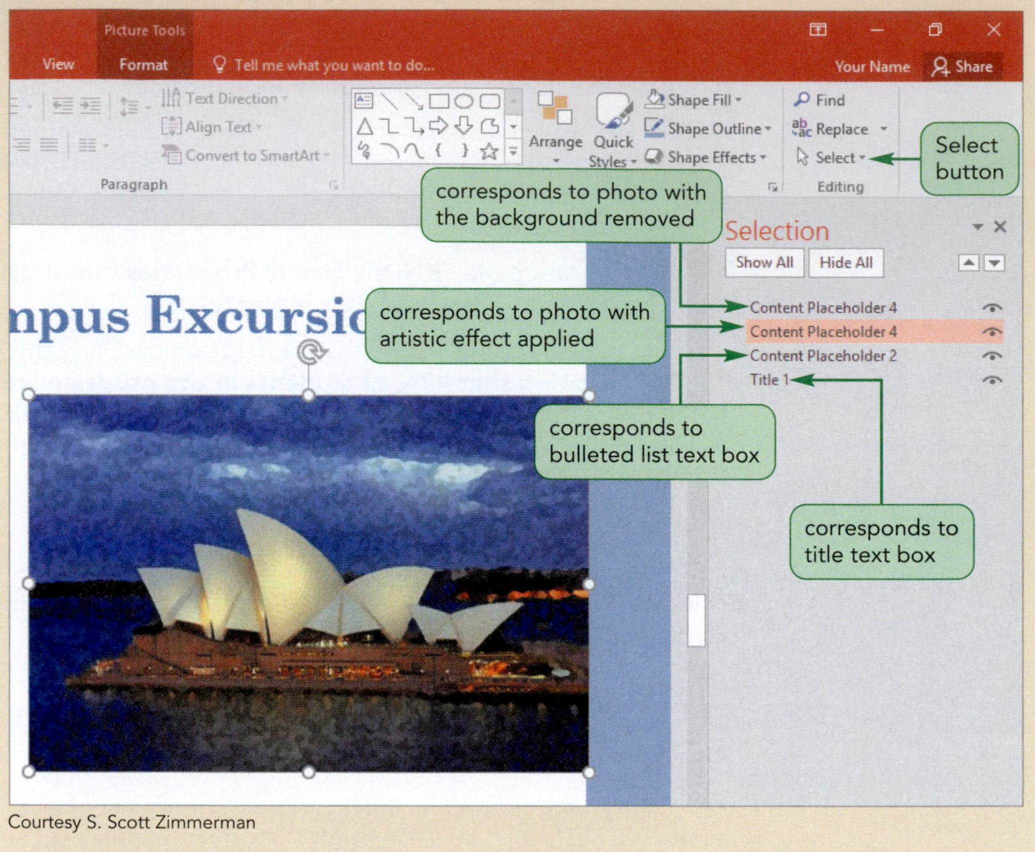

Courtesy S. Scott Zimmerman

In the Selection pane, the first object added to the slide appears at the bottom of the list, and the last object added appears at the top of the list. (The blue bar on the right side of the slide and the gray bar on the left side of the slide aren't listed in the Selection pane because they are part of the slide background.)

INSIGHT

Reordering Objects in the Selection Pane

If an object is listed in the wrong order in the Selection pane—for example, if the content placeholder was identified first and the title second—you could change this in the Selection pane. To do this, click the object you want to move, and then at the top of the pane, click the Bring Forward ▲ or Send Backward ▼ buttons to move the selected object up or down in the list.

Renaming Objects in the Selection Pane

In the Selection pane for Slide 8, there are two objects with the same name. This is because you duplicated the photo, so the name in the Selection pane was duplicated as well. To make it clearer which items on slides are listed in the Selection pane, you can rename each object in the list.

To rename objects in the Selection pane:

1. On the slide, click the photo to select it, if necessary, and then drag left so that the version of the photo with the background removed is to the left of the version of the photo with the artistic effect applied. In the Selection pane, the top Content Placeholder 4 is selected.
2. In the Selection pane, click the **selected Content Placeholder 4**. An orange border appears around the selected item. The insertion point appears in the selected text.
3. Press the **Delete** and **Backspace** keys as needed to delete "Content Placeholder 4," type **Photo with background removed**, and then press the **Enter** key. The name is changed in the Selection pane.
4. In the pane, click **Content Placeholder 4**, click it again, delete the text "Content Placeholder 4," type **Photo with artistic effect**, and then press the **Enter** key.
5. Drag the photo with the background removed back on top of the photo with the artistic effect applied.
6. Close the Selection pane.
7. Display **Slide 1** (the title slide), replace Robert's name in the subtitle with your name, and then save and close the presentation.

PROSKILLS

Decision Making: Selecting the Right Tool for the Job

Many programs with advanced capabilities for editing and correcting photos and other programs for drawing complex shapes are available. Although the tools provided in PowerPoint for accomplishing these tasks are useful, if you need to do more than make simple photo corrections or create a simple shape, consider using a program with more advanced features, or choose to hire someone with skills in graphic design to help you.

You have created and saved a custom shape and used advanced formatting techniques for shapes and photos in the presentation. Robert is pleased with the presentation. With the alt text you've added, he is also confident that users of screen readers will be able to understand the slide containing the SmartArt and the text box and the slide containing the chart.

REVIEW

Session 3.2 Quick Check

1. What are the five types of corrections you can make to photos in PowerPoint?
2. What happens when you use the Remove Background command?
3. What are artistic effects?
4. What happens when you merge shapes?
5. How do you create a custom gradient?
6. What is alt text?

PRACTICE

Review Assignments

Data Files needed for the Review Assignments: Employee.m4a, RA.pptx

Sara Allen is the human resources director at International Study Crossroads (ISC). Each year, she needs to hire resident advisors (RAs) for the program. The company requires one RA for every 50 students. Sara plans to attend career fairs at local colleges in Maryland, Washington, D.C., Virginia, Delaware, and southern Pennsylvania, and she asks you to help her create a presentation she can use to recruit new RAs. Complete the following:

1. Open the presentation **RA**, located in the PowerPoint3 > Review folder included with your Data Files, add your name as the Slide 1 subtitle, and then save it as **ISC RAs** to the location where you are storing your files.
2. On Slide 8 ("Interested in Applying?"), create a SmartArt diagram using the Circle Process layout, which is a Process type diagram. From left to right, replace the placeholder text in the shapes with **Fill out application**, **Submit information for CORI check**, and **Schedule drug test**.
3. Add a new first-level shape as the rightmost shape to the SmartArt diagram, and then replace the placeholder text in it with **Schedule interview**. Move the "Schedule interview" shape so it is the second shape in the diagram.
4. Change the style of the SmartArt diagram to the Powder style, and then change the color to Colorful – Accent Colors.
5. On Slide 9 (the last slide), add the audio clip **Employee**, located in the PowerPoint3 > Review folder. Set it to play automatically, and hide the icon during the slide show. Position the icon in the lower-right corner of the slide at the bottom of the orange bar.
6. On Slide 7 ("Number of Students by Country in 2016"), add a pie chart. In cells A2 through A6, type **England**, **France**, **Spain**, **Germany**, and **Australia**. In cell B1, type **2016**. In cells B2 through B6, type **14990**, **7233**, **9107**, **12997**, and **2673**.
7. Apply Layout 4 to the chart.
8. Click one of the data labels that was added, and then change the font color to Black, Text 1 and the font size to 16 points.
9. Change the position of the data labels to the Outside End option.
10. On Slide 5 ("Qualifications"), add a text box approximately 2 inches wide and one-half inch high. Type ***Criminal Offender Record Information**. Change the format of the text box so the text doesn't wrap and so that the left margin is zero.
11. Align the left edge of the text box with the left edge of the bulleted list text box, and align its top edge with the bottom edge of the picture and the bulleted list.
12. On Slide 9, insert a WordArt text box using the Fill - Orange, Accent 3, Sharp Bevel style. Replace the placeholder text with **Submit Your**, press the Enter key, type **Application**, press the Enter key, and then type **Today!**
13. Change the fill color of the WordArt text to Dark Red, Accent 1, and then change the font size of the text to 66 points. Add the Perspective Diagonal Upper Left shadow effect. (*Hint*: Use the Text Effects button in the WordArt Styles group on the Drawing Tools Format tab.)
14. Position the WordArt text box so it is entered horizontally and vertically on the slide. (*Hint*: Use the Align command in the Arrange group on the Drawing Tools Format tab.)
15. On Slide 5 ("Qualifications"), remove the background of the photo.
16. On Slide 6 ("Mandatory Training Dates"), change the color tone of the photo to Temperature: 7200K.
17. On Slide 3 ("What to Expect"), change the saturation of the photo to 66%.
18. On Slide 4 ("Locations"), sharpen the photo by 50%, and then change the contrast to 30%. Then apply the Pencil Sketch artistic effect to the photo.

19. On Slide 2, drag the gray doughnut shape on top of the large circle. Position the doughnut shape near the top right of the large circle so that smart guides appear indicating that the top and right of the two shapes are aligned. Subtract the doughnut shape from the larger circle by selecting the shape you want to keep—the large circle—first, and then selecting the shape you want to subtract—the gray doughnut shape—before using the Subtract command.
20. Drag the small yellow circle on top of the solid orange circle that was created in the merged shape. Position the yellow circle near the top right of the solid circle in the merged shape without overlapping the edges of the circles, and then subtract the yellow circle from the merged shape. The final shape should look like Figure 3-33.

Figure 3-33 **Merged shape**

21. On Slide 2, create a text box approximately 2 inches wide and 1 inch high. Type **ISC** in the text box. Deselect the Wrap text in shape option, if necessary. Change the font to Impact, and the font size to 48 points.
22. Drag the text box to the center of the white circle created when you subtracted the yellow circle in the merged shape. Select the merged shape first, and then select the text box. Use the Union command to combine the shapes.
23. Fill the merged shape with the From Bottom Left Corner gradient under Dark Variations on the Gradient submenu on the Shape Fill menu. Then customize the gradient by changing the position of the Stop 2 of 3 tab to 40% and changing the color of the Stop 3 of 3 tab to Dark Red, Accent 1, Lighter 80%.
24. Copy the merged shape. Display Slide 1 (the title slide), and then paste the copied shape to the slide. Resize the merged shape so that it is 1.4 inches square, and then position the shape to the left of "International Study Crossroads" so that its left edge is aligned with the left edge of the slide title text box and so that its top is aligned with the top of the "International Study Crossroads" text box. Delete Slide 2.
25. On Slide 6 ("Number of Students by Country in 2016"), add the following as alt text to the chart: **Pie chart showing the number of students in the program who went to each of the five countries.**
26. On Slide 7 ("Interested in Applying?"), add the following as alt text to the SmartArt shape: **SmartArt diagram listing four steps required to apply to be an RA.**
27. On Slide 7, edit the Content Placeholder 2 name in the Selection Pane to **SmartArt**.
28. Save and close the presentation.

APPLY

Case Problem 1

Data Files needed for this Case Problem: PT.pptx, Recovery.m4a

PT PLUS Ben and Helen Acosta, both physical therapists, opened their practice PT PLUS in Searcy, Arkansas, seven years ago. They have a state-of-the-art facility and equipment including a pool for aquatic therapy, and they have built a good reputation among local doctors and hospitals because patients referred to them have faster recovery times than average. They are preparing a bid for a local semi-pro football team to be the exclusive providers of physical therapy to the team members. As part of their bid, Helen prepared a PowerPoint presentation and asked you to finish it for her. Complete the following steps:

1. Open the presentation **PT**, located in the PowerPoint3 > Case1 folder included with your Data Files, add your name as the subtitle, and then save the presentation as **PT PLUS** to the location where you are storing your files.
2. On Slide 2 ("The PT PLUS Difference"), add a text box, and type ***American Board of Physical Therapy Specialties**. Turn off the Wrap text option, change the right margin to 0, and then right-align the text in the text box. Position the text box so that its right edge is aligned with the right edge of the title and bulleted list text boxes and its top edge is aligned with the bottom edge of the bulleted list text box.
3. On Slide 3 ("State of the Art Facility"), change the brightness of the photo on the left to -10% and the contrast to 30%.
4. On Slide 3, sharpen the photo on the right by 25%, change its saturation to 200%, and then change its tone to a temperature of 5900 K.
5. On Slide 4 ("Recovery Time Examples in Weeks"), add a clustered column chart in the content placeholder. Enter the date shown in Figure 3-34 in the spreadsheet to create the chart.

Figure 3-34 **Data for Slide 4**

	Industry Average	PT PLUS
Meniscus tear	8	5
Rotator cuff injuries	35	26
Achilles tendon rupture	24	18

6. Drag the small blue box in the lower-right corner of cell D5 up and to the left so that the blue border surrounds cells B2 through C4 and the data in column D and row 5 is removed from the chart.
7. Change the style of the chart to Style 2, and then change the colors of the chart to the Color 3 palette. (*Hint*: Use the Chart Styles button next to the chart.)
8. Move the legend so it appears below the chart, and then change the font size of the text in the legend to 16 points. Change the font size of the labels on the x-axis to 14 points, and then change the font size of the data labels to 16 points. (*Hint*: To modify all the data labels, select the data label above one color column and modify it, and then select the data label above a column of the other color and modify it.)
9. Remove the chart title.
10. On Slide 4, insert the audio clip **Recovery**, located in the PowerPoint3 > Case1 folder. Hide the icon during a slide show, and set it to play automatically. Position the sound icon centered below the chart.
11. Add the following alt text for the chart: **Chart showing that recovery times for certain injuries is faster at PT PLUS than the industry average.**
12. Save and close the presentation.

CHALLENGE

Case Problem 2

Data Files needed for this Case Problem: Elder.pptx

Keystone State Elder Services Shaina Brown is the director of Keystone State Elder Services, a company that provides in-home services for elderly and disabled people in Youngstown, Ohio, and surrounding cities so that they can continue to live at home rather than in a nursing home. Shaina travels to senior centers, churches, and other locations to explain the services her company provides. She started creating a PowerPoint presentation and asked you to help complete it by creating a logo based on her design, correcting photos, and adding SmartArt. Complete the following steps:

1. Open the file named **Elder**, located in the PowerPoint3 > Case2 folder included with your Data Files, add your name as the subtitle on Slide 1, and then save it as **Elder Services** to the location where you are storing your files.
2. On Slide 2, duplicate the red filled square shape three times. These are the four squares behind the center square in Figure 3-35. Arrange them as shown in Figure 3-35 so that there is about one-quarter inch of space between each square. Merge the four squares using the Union command.

Figure 3-35 **Logo for Keystone State Elder Services**

3. Apply the From Center Gradient style in the Light Variations set of gradient styles to the square. Customize this gradient by changing the Stop 1 of 3 tab to the Red, Accent 1 color, changing the Stop 2 of 3 tab to the Red, Accent 1, Darker 50% color, and changing the Stop 3 of 3 tab to Red, Accent 1, Lighter 40% color and changing its position to 80%. Then change the gradient Type to Linear and the direction to Linear Down.
4. Create a text box, type **KS**, press the Enter key, and then type **ES**. Turn off the Wrap text option if necessary, change the font to Copperplate Gothic Bold, change the font size to 40 points, and then use the Center button in the Paragraph group on the Home tab to center the text in the box. Change the size of the text box to 1.5″ square. Fill the text box shape with the White, Background 1 color. Apply the Preset 5 shape effect to this square (located on the Presets submenu on the Shape Effects menu).
5. Position the text box so it is centered over the custom shape, using the smart guides to assist you.

Explore 6. Group the custom shape and the text box. (*Hint*: Use the appropriate command on the Drawing Tools Format tab.)

Explore 7. Save the final grouped shape as a picture named **Logo** to the location where you are storing your files. (*Hint*: Right-click the shape.)

8. Delete Slide 2, and then insert the picture **Logo** on Slide 1 (the title slide). Resize it, maintaining the aspect ratio, so that it is approximately 2.6 inches by 2.6 inches (it may not be perfectly square). Position it to the left of the title so that it is bottom-aligned with the title text box and so that there is an equal amount of space between the logo and the slide title and the logo and the left side of the slide.
9. Add **Company logo** as alt text for the logo.
10. On Slide 2 ("Our Services"), change the saturation of the photo to 66%, and then change the tone to a temperature of 7200K.
11. On Slide 3 ("What We Do"), change the contrast of the photo to -20%, and sharpen it by 50%.
12. Add **Photo of a smiling woman at a keyboard** as alt text for the picture.
13. On Slide 4 ("How to Set Up Services"), insert a SmartArt diagram using the Sub-Step Process layout (in the Process category). Type the following as first-level items in the diagram:

    Schedule Services

    Set Up Assessment Appointment

    Answer Interview Questions

    Call Elder Line
14. Delete the second-level placeholders in the diagram. (*Hint*: Use the text pane.)

Explore 15. Reverse the order of the boxes in the diagram. (*Hint*: Use a command in the Create Graphic group on the SmartArt Tools Design tab.)

16. Change the style of the SmartArt diagram to the Cartoon style.
17. Add **SmartArt diagram listing the four steps to take to receive services.** as alt text for the SmartArt diagram.
18. On Slide 5 ("We Are Here for You"), insert the **Logo** file you created in the content placeholder on the left, and add **Company logo** as alt text for the logo on Slide 5.
19. Save and close the presentation.

CHALLENGE

Case Problem 3

Data Files needed for this Case Problem: Books.jpg, Tutoring.pptx

Total Learning Tutoring Total Learning Tutoring (TLT), in Durham, North Carolina, offers tutoring services for students of all ages who need extra help to keep up with their classwork or who want to learn additional material not offered in their classes. They also offer SAT and ACT test prep courses. Over the past three years, the popularity of their test prep courses has exploded. In addition, the number of students who enroll in ACT test prep courses instead of SAT test prep has increased significantly. Tom Shaughnessy, the owner of TLT, wants to expand and asks you to help him create a PowerPoint presentation that he can use when he talks to potential investors. Complete the following steps:

1. Open the presentation **Tutoring**, located in the PowerPoint3 > Case3 folder included with your Data Files, add your name as the subtitle, and then save the presentation as **Total Learning Tutoring** to the location where you are storing your files.
2. On Slide 1 (the title slide), apply the Photocopy artistic effect to the photo.
3. On Slide 2 ("Our Services"), insert the photo **Books**, located in the PowerPoint 3 > Case3 folder, in the content placeholder to the left of the bulleted list. Resize it, maintaining the aspect ratio, so it is 3.5" high. Position it so that its left edge is aligned with the left edge of the slide and so it is aligned with the middle of the bulleted list text box.

Explore 4. On Slide 2, make the background of the photo transparent. (*Hint*: Use the appropriate command on the Color menu on the Picture Tools Format tab.)

5. On Slide 2, increase the saturation of the photo to 200%, and then sharpen it by 25%.

6. On Slide 2, insert a text box below the bulleted list. Type ***for original SAT score between 300 and 1150 or an original ACT score between 13 and 29** in the text box. Change the font size of the text in the text box to 14 points, and italicize it. Turn off the Wrap text option, change the left and right margins of the text box to 0 inches, and then resize the text box so it just fits the text inside it. Position the text box so its left edge is aligned with the left edge of the bulleted list text box and its top edge is aligned with the bottom of the bulleted list text box.
7. On Slide 3 ("Tremendous Growth in Just Three Years"), change the contrast of the photo by -30%.
8. On Slide 4 ("SAT and ACT Prep Course Enrollment"), insert a clustered column chart using the data shown in Figure 3-36.

Figure 3-36 **Data for Slide 4**

	SAT Prep	ACT Prep
2014	201	87
2015	587	334
2016	922	885

9. In the spreadsheet, drag the small blue selection handle in the lower-right corner of cell D5 up one row and left one column to exclude the Series 3 column of data and the Category 4 row of data.
10. Change the style of the chart to Style 4.
11. Remove the chart title and the legend.

Explore 12. Add the data table, and remove the data labels. (*Hint*: Use the CHART ELEMENTS menu.)

13. Change the font color of the text in the data table to Black, Text 2, and the font size to 14 points.
14. Add **Column chart showing that SAT and ACT Prep course enrollment has increased over the past three years.** as alt text for the chart.
15. Change the colors used in the chart to the Color 4 palette. (*Hint*: Use the Chart Styles button next to the chart.)

Explore 16. Animate the chart with the entrance animation Appear. Modify the animation so that the chart grid animates first, then the three data markers for the SAT Prep data series one at a time, then the three data markers for the ACT Prep data series one at a time. Finally, modify the start timing of the chart grid animation so it animates with the previous action.

17. On Slide 5 ("Proposed Test Prep Course Expansion"), change the color tone of the photo to a temperature of 7200 K.
18. On Slide 7, format the text "Thank You!" as WordArt using the Gradient Fill – Brown, Accent 4, Outline – Accent 4 style. Center the WordArt in the text box, and then change the font size to 60 points.
19. Save and close the presentation.

RESEARCH

Case Problem 4

Data Files needed for this Case Problem: Bullying.pptx

Partners Counseling Patricia Burrell is one of the owners of Partners Counseling in Middletown, Connecticut. Partners Counseling is a group of therapists who specialize in providing therapy to children. Patricia has been hired by several school districts to talk to teachers and school support staff about ways they can identify and stop bullying. She asks you to help her create her presentation by researching statistics about bullying and ways to identify and prevent bullying. Complete the following steps:

1. Research bullying online. For example, look for statistics about the number of children who are bullied, suggested ways others can help, and ways to identify bullying. While you are researching the topic, look for information that can be presented in a chart or in a SmartArt graphic. Make sure you note the webpage addresses of the pages that contain the information you are going to use because you will need to include that on your slides.
2. Open the presentation **Bullying**, located in the PowerPoint3 > Case4 folder included with your data files. Add your name as the subtitle, and then save the presentation as **Stop Bullying** to the location where you are saving your files.
3. Based on your research, on Slide 3, create a chart that shows statistics about bullying, and then add a slide title that describes the data in the chart. On Slide 4 ("How to Help"), insert SmartArt containing suggestions for how to stop bullying. On Slide 5, add any additional information you think is helpful, such as describing a list of things that adults should not do, suggestions on how to stop bullying when it happens, or descriptions of times when the police should be called.
4. On Slide 2 ("What Is Bullying?"), change the tone of the photo to a temperature of 5900 K. On Slide 5, sharpen the photo by 50%.
5. On each slide that contains information from a webpage, include a text box at the bottom of the slide that contains **Data from** followed by the name of the website and the name of the webpage followed by the webpage address in parentheses.
6. Add appropriate transitions and animations.
7. Check the spelling in your presentation and proof it carefully.
8. Save and close the presentation.

MODULE 4

Advanced Animations and Distributing Presentations

Creating an Advanced Presentation for Agricultural Development

POWERPOINT

OBJECTIVES

Session 4.1
- Use guides to place objects
- Add more than one animation to an object
- Set animation triggers
- Use a picture as the slide background
- Create and edit hyperlinks
- Add action buttons
- Create a custom color palette

Session 4.2
- Create a self-running presentation
- Rehearse slide timings
- Record slide timings and narration
- Set options to allow viewers to override timings
- Inspect a presentation for private information
- Save a presentation in other formats

Case | *Division of Agricultural Development*

Brian Meyers works in the Division of Agricultural Development in the New Hampshire Department of Agriculture, Markets & Food. Over the past few years, small family-owned farms have contacted his office requesting suggestions and assistance in expanding and extending their cash flow into the fall and early winter seasons. In response, Brian will begin presenting on this topic at agricultural fairs and tradeshows across the state, and he wants your help in finishing the presentation he has created.

In this module, you will enhance Brian's presentation by adding multiple animations to objects and setting triggers for animations. You'll also add a picture as the slide background, create links, and create a self-running presentation including narration. Finally, you'll save the presentation in other formats for distribution.

STARTING DATA FILES

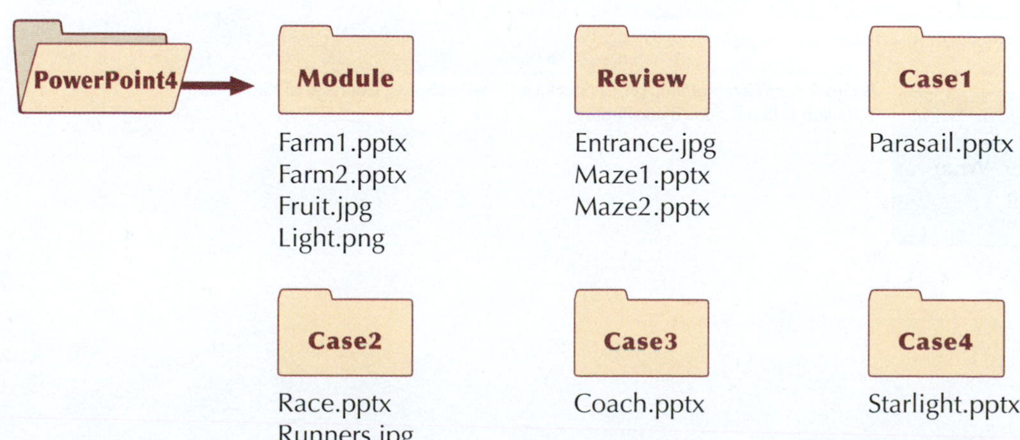

Session 4.1 Visual Overview:

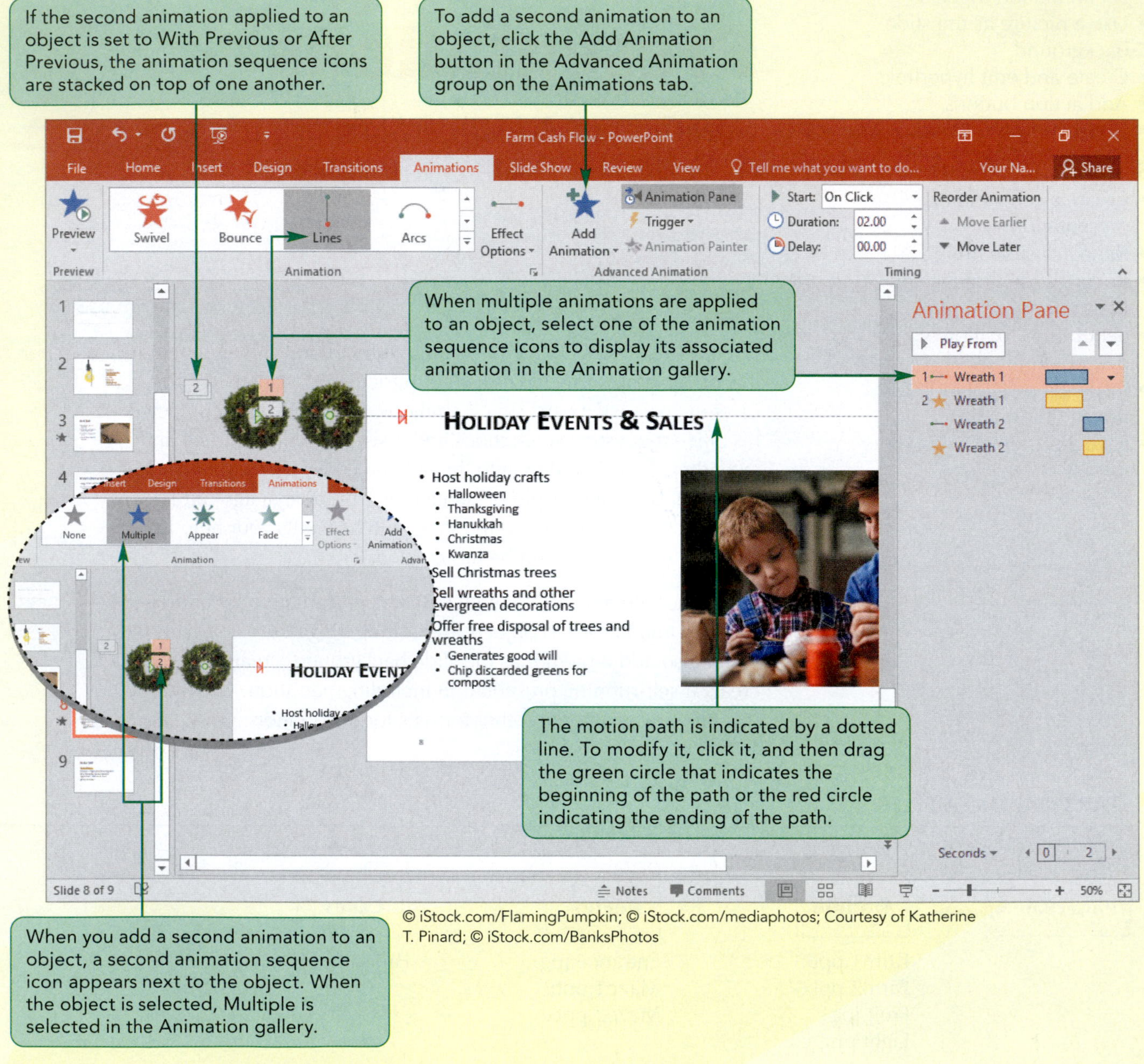

If the second animation applied to an object is set to With Previous or After Previous, the animation sequence icons are stacked on top of one another.
To add a second animation to an object, click the Add Animation button in the Advanced Animation group on the Animations tab.
When multiple animations are applied to an object, select one of the animation sequence icons to display its associated animation in the Animation gallery.
The motion path is indicated by a dotted line. To modify it, click it, and then drag the green circle that indicates the beginning of the path or the red circle indicating the ending of the path.
When you add a second animation to an object, a second animation sequence icon appears next to the object. When the object is selected, Multiple is selected in the Animation gallery.
Farm Cash Flow - PowerPoint
File
Home
Insert
Design
Transitions
Animations
Slide Show
Review
View
Tell me what you want to do...
Share
Preview
Swivel
Bounce
Lines
Arcs
Effect Options
Add Animation
Animation Pane
Trigger
Animation Painter
Start: On Click
Duration: 02.00
Delay: 00.00
Reorder Animation
Move Earlier
Move Later
Animation
Advanced Animation
Timing
Animation Pane
Play From
Wreath 1
Wreath 1
Wreath 2
Wreath 2
HOLIDAY EVENTS & SALES
Host holiday crafts
Halloween
Thanksgiving
Hanukkah
Christmas
Kwanza
Sell Christmas trees
Sell wreaths and other evergreen decorations
Offer free disposal of trees and wreaths
Generates good will
Chip discarded greens for compost
None
Multiple
Appear
Fade
Seconds
Slide 8 of 9
Notes
Comments
50%

© iStock.com/FlamingPumpkin; © iStock.com/mediaphotos; Courtesy of Katherine T. Pinard; © iStock.com/BanksPhotos

Understanding Advanced Animations

When an animation has a trigger, the number in the animation sequence icon is replaced with a lightning bolt. This is because the animation is no longer part of a sequence; it will occur only when the trigger is clicked.

The list of objects on the "On Click of" submenu corresponds to the objects on the slide. You can also see this list of objects in the Selection pane.

A **trigger** is an object, such as a text box or a graphic, on a slide that you click to start an animation.

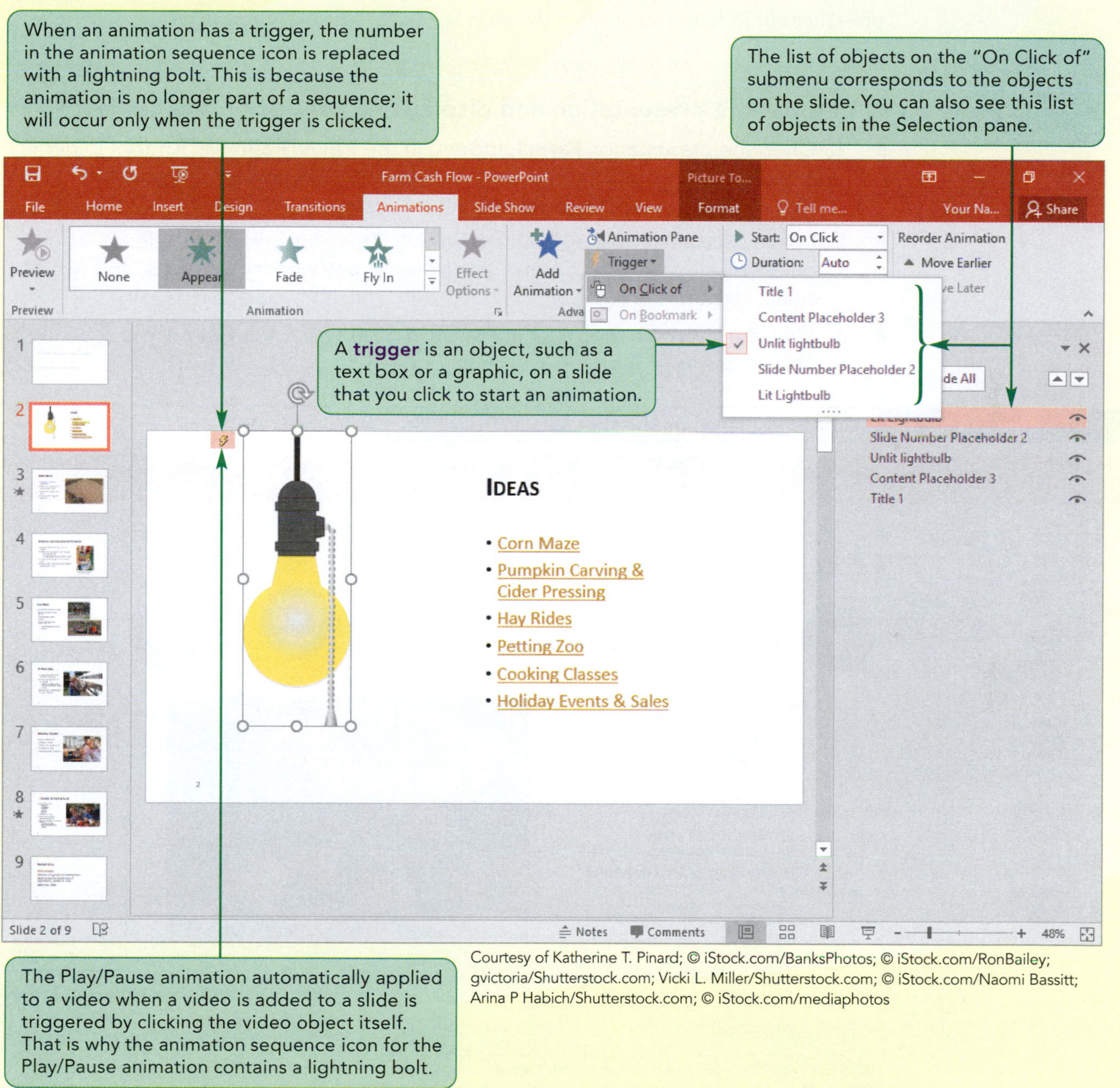

The Play/Pause animation automatically applied to a video when a video is added to a slide is triggered by clicking the video object itself. That is why the animation sequence icon for the Play/Pause animation contains a lightning bolt.

Courtesy of Katherine T. Pinard; © iStock.com/BanksPhotos; © iStock.com/RonBailey; gvictoria/Shutterstock.com; Vicki L. Miller/Shutterstock.com; © iStock.com/Naomi Bassitt; Arina P Habich/Shutterstock.com; © iStock.com/mediaphotos

Using Guides

You are already familiar with using smart guides, which are the dashed red lines that appear when you drag objects on a slide, to help you align objects. **Guides** are dashed vertical and horizontal lines that you can display and position on the slide in any location to help you place objects. When you drag a guide to reposition it, a ScreenTip appears, indicating the distance in inches from the center of the slide.

Brian wants you to apply motion path animations to some of the objects in his presentation. To help you position the objects, you will display the guides.

To open the presentation and display and reposition the guides:

1. Open the presentation **Farm1**, located in the **PowerPoint4 > Tutorial** folder included with your Data Files, and then save it as **Farm Cash Flow** to the location where you are saving your files.
2. Display **Slide 8** ("Holiday Events & Sales"). This slide contains a title, a bulleted list, an image of a man and a young boy working on crafts, and two small Christmas wreaths.
3. Click the **View** tab, and then in the Show group, click the **Guides** check box. The guides appear on the slide. See Figure 4-1.

Figure 4-1 Guides displayed on the slide

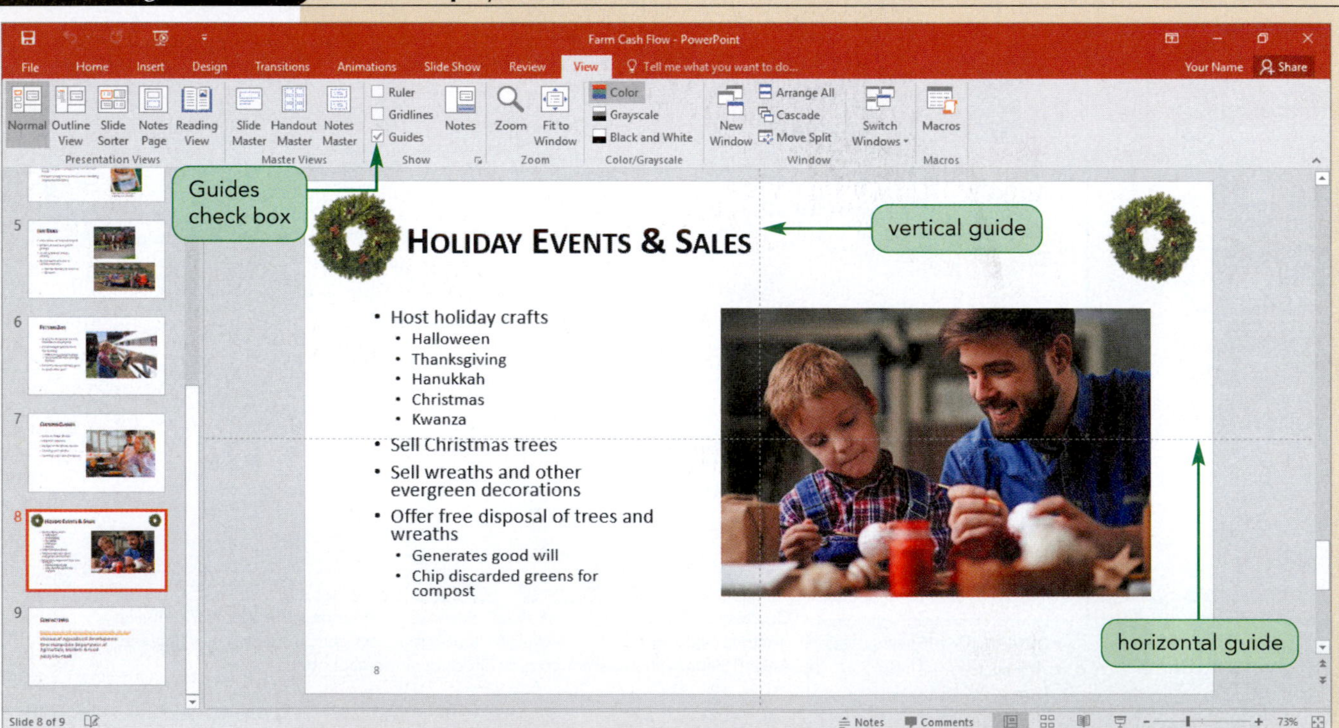

© iStock.com/FlamingPumpkin; © iStock.com/mediaphotos; © iStock.com/RonBailey; gvictoria/Shutterstock.com; Vicki L. Miller/Shutterstock.com; © iStock.com/Naomi Bassitt; Arina P Habich/Shutterstock.com

4. In a blank area of the slide, position the pointer on top of the horizontal guide so that the pointer changes to ÷, and then press and hold the mouse button. The pointer disappears and a ScreenTip appears in its place displaying 0.00. This indicates that the horizontal guide is in the middle of the slide.

   Trouble? If the pointer doesn't change, you are pointing to the bulleted list text box or the photo. Repeat Step 4, this time positioning the pointer on top of the guide in a blank area of the slide.

5. Drag the guide up until the ScreenTip displays 2.92, and then release the mouse button. The horizontal guide now intersects the middle of the wreaths at the top of the slide. Next, you will create a second vertical guide.
6. Position the pointer on top of the vertical guide so that the pointer changes to +||+, press and hold the **Ctrl** key, press and hold the mouse button, and then start dragging the guide to the right. A second vertical guide is created and moves right with the mouse pointer.
7. Continue dragging to the right until the ScreenTip displays **6.42**, release the mouse button, and then release the Ctrl key. The vertical guide you created is aligned with the right side of the wreath in the upper-right corner of the slide.
8. Drag the original vertical guide to the right until its ScreenTip displays 5.08 and it is aligned with the left side of the wreath. The guides are now positioned for your use in applying animations to the wreaths on the slide.

Adding More Than One Animation to an Object

You know how to apply an animation to an object and how to specify how the animation starts, its duration, and its speed. An object can have more than one animation applied to it. For example, you might apply an entrance animation to an object by having it fly into a slide, and then once the object is on the slide, you might want to animate it a second time to further emphasize a bullet point on the slide, or to show a relationship between the object and another object on the slide.

On Slide 8 in the presentation, Brian created list ideas for events that farm owners can conduct during the fall and winter holiday season. Brian wants you to add animations to the photos of wreaths on Slide 8 to add interest. He wants the wreaths to roll onto the slide.

To add a motion path animation to an object on Slide 8:

1. Click the wreath in the upper-right corner of the slide, and then on the ribbon, click the **Animations** tab.
2. In the Animation group, click the **More** button, scroll down to locate the Motion Paths section, and then click the **Lines** animation. The animation previews and the wreath moves down the slide. After the preview, the path appears below the wreath, and a faint image of the wreath appears at the end of the path. At the beginning of the path, the green circle indicates the path's starting point, and at the end of the path, the red circle indicates the path's ending point. See Figure 4-2.

Figure 4-2 Wreath with Lines motion path animation applied

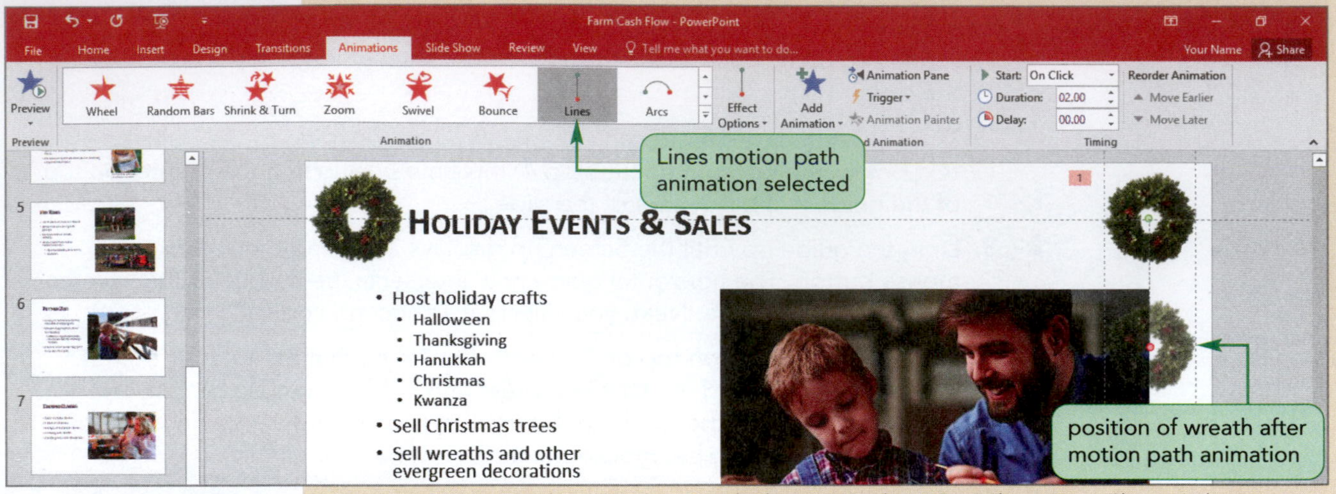

© iStock.com/FlamingPumpkin; © iStock.com/mediaphotos; © iStock.com/RonBailey; gvictoria/Shutterstock.com; Vicki L. Miller/Shutterstock.com; © iStock.com/Naomi Bassitt; Arina P Habich/Shutterstock.com

To have the wreath roll onto the slide, you need to position it in the area next to the slide. The area outside of the slide is part of the PowerPoint workspace, but anything positioned in this area will not be visible in any view except Normal view.

You will position the wreath to the left of the slide, and then change the direction of the Lines animation so that the wreath moves to the right instead of down. Then you will adjust the ending point of the motion path so that the wreath ends up in the upper-right corner of the slide when the animation is finished.

To move the wreath off the slide and modify the motion path animation:

1. Drag the wreath from the upper-right corner of the slide to the left until it is completely off of the slide, keeping its center aligned with the horizontal guide and the wreath in the upper-left corner. After you release the mouse button, the slide shifts to the right so there is some extra space to the left of the slide. See Figure 4-3.

Figure 4-3 Wreath positioned to the left of Slide 8

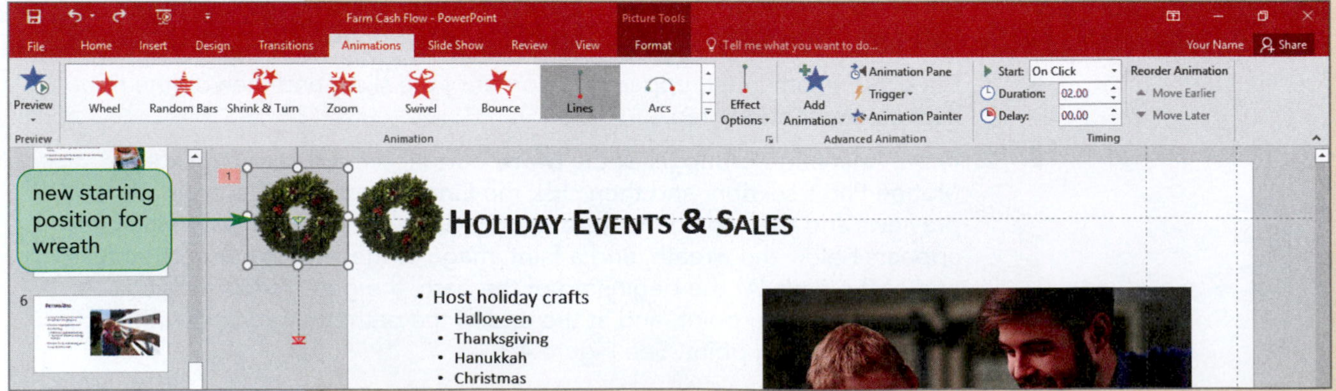

© iStock.com/FlamingPumpkin; © iStock.com/mediaphotos; © iStock.com/RonBailey; © iStock.com/Naomi Bassitt

2. In the Animation group, click the **Effect Options** button, and then click **Right**. The motion path changes to a horizontal line, the wreath moves right, and the circles at the beginning and end of the motion path change to arrows. You need to reposition the end point of the motion path so that the wreath ends up in the upper-right corner of the slide after the animation is finished. First you need to select the motion path.
3. Point to the motion path so that the pointer changes to ✥, and then click the motion path. The arrows on the ends of the motion path change to circles, and a faint copy of the image appears at the end of the motion path. Now you can drag the start and end points to new locations.

   Trouble? If you have trouble selecting the motion path, click the green or red arrow at the beginning or end of the path.
4. Position the pointer on top of the red circle so that it changes to ⤡, and then press and hold the **Shift** key. Pressing the Shift key while you adjust the motion path keeps the path a straight line.
5. Press and hold the mouse button. The pointer changes to +.
6. Drag the red circle to the right until the faint image of the wreath is in the upper-right corner of the slide between the two vertical guides, release the mouse button, and then release the Shift key. See Figure 4-4.

   Trouble? If the path moves so it is slanted, you released the Shift key before you released the mouse button. If you haven't released the mouse button yet, press and hold the Shift key, position the wreath, release the mouse button, and then release the Shift key. If you have released the mouse button, click the Undo button on the Quick Access Toolbar, and then repeat Steps 4 through 6.

Figure 4-4 Modified Lines motion path animation

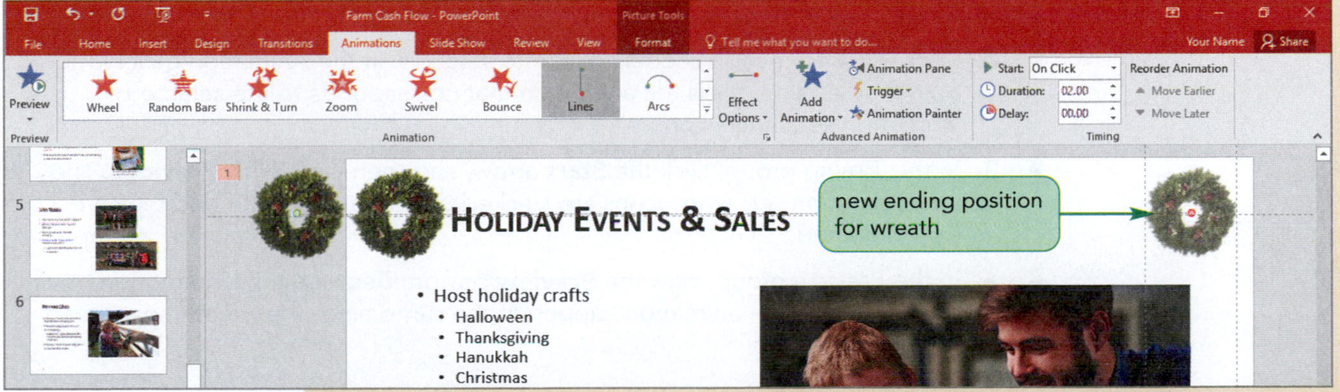

Brian wants the wreath to look like it is rolling onto the slide. To accomplish this effect you need to add a second animation to the wreath. To add a second animation to an object, you must use the Add Animation button in the Advanced Animation group on the Animations tab. If you try to add a second animation to an object by clicking an animation in the gallery in the Animation group, you will simply replace the animation already applied to the object.

To add a second animation to the wreath on Slide 8:

1. Click the wreath positioned to the left of the slide to select it, and then click the **Animations** tab, if necessary.
2. In the Advanced Animation group, click the **Add Animation** button.

   The same gallery of animations that appears in the Animation group appears.

3. In the Emphasis section of the gallery, click the **Spin** animation. The Spin animation previews, but you can't see it because the wreath is not on the slide. When the preview finishes, the slide shifts right again. Next to the wreath that is positioned to the left of the slide, a second animation sequence icon appears and is selected. In the Animation group, the Spin animation is selected, which means that animation sequence icon 2 corresponds to the Spin animation. You can preview both animations.
4. Click the **Preview** button. The wreath moves right onto the slide and stops in the upper-right corner, and then spins once in a clockwise direction.

Make sure you do not click another animation in the Animation group.

To make the wreath look like it is rolling onto the slide, you need to change the start timing of the Spin animation so it happens at the same time as the Lines animation—in other words, set its start timing to With Previous. Because two animations are applied to the object, you need to make sure that the correct animation sequence icon is selected and the correct animation is selected in the Animation group on the Animations tab before you make any changes.

To modify the start timing of the second animation applied to the wreath:

1. Click the wreath with the animations applied to it. In the Animation gallery, Multiple is selected. This indicates that more than one animation is applied to the selected object.
2. Click the **2** animation sequence icon to select it. In the Animation gallery, Spin is selected. This is the animation that corresponds to the selected animation sequence icon.
3. In the Timing group, click the **Start** arrow, and then click **With Previous**. The two animation sequence icons are stacked on top of the other and they are both selected.
4. In the Preview group, click the **Preview** button. Because the Line motion path and the Spin animation happen at the same time, the wreath appears to roll onto the slide.

Next, you need to apply the same animations to the wreath that is positioned in the upper-left corner of the slide. You can follow the same steps you took when you applied the animations to the first wreath, or you can copy the animations and then modify them. You will copy the animations.

To copy and modify the animations:

1. Click the wreath that has the animations applied to it so that Multiple is selected in the Animation group, and then in the Advanced Animation group, click the **Animation Painter** button.

2. Click the wreath that is in the upper-left corner of the slide. The animations are copied and previewed. Now you need to move the wreath in the upper-left corner of the slide off of the slide and then adjust its motion path.
3. In the status bar, click the **Zoom Out** button [−] twice to change the zoom percentage to 60%.
4. Drag the wreath in the upper-left corner of the slide off of the slide and position it to the left of the other wreath so that it is horizontally aligned with the other wreath and so that the vertical smart guide appears between the two wreaths. Now you need to change the end position of the motion path so that the leftmost wreath stops in the upper-left corner of the slide.
5. In the center of the leftmost wreath, point to the green arrow that indicates the beginning of the motion path applied to that wreath so that the pointer changes to ⁺⇖, and then click the green arrow. The motion path is selected and the arrows on either end change to circles.
6. Press and hold the **Shift** key, drag the red circle that indicates the end of the motion path to the left until the faint image of the wreath is in the upper-left corner of the slide between the slide title and the left edge of the slide, release the mouse button, and then release the Shift key.
7. Click a blank area of the slide to deselect the wreath, and then in the Preview group, click the **Preview** button. The first wreath rolls onto the slide and stops in the upper-right corner, then the second wreath rolls onto the slide and stops in the upper-left corner. You are finished using the guides so you can hide them.
8. Click the **View** tab, and then in the Show group, click the **Guides** check box. The guides no longer appear on the screen.

When previewing the slide, you might have noticed that when the first wreath rolled onto the slide, it seemed to slide part of the way instead of roll completely across the slide. And when the second wreath rolled onto the slide, it continued rolling after it was in position in the upper-right corner of the slide. You can adjust the Spin animation so the effect causes the wreaths to appear as if they are rolling into position and then stop. In this instance, the easiest way to do this is using the Animation Pane.

Using the Animation Pane

When multiple animations are applied to an object and the start timing of one of the animations is set to With Previous or After Previous, you can't select only one of the animation sequence icons because they are stacked on top of one another. To see a list of all the animations on a slide, you can open the Animation Pane. You'll examine the animations on Slide 8 in the Animation Pane.

To examine the animations on Slide 8 in the Animation Pane:

1. Click the **Animations** tab, and then in the Advanced Animation group, click the **Animation Pane** button. The Animation Pane opens. See Figure 4-5.

Figure 4-5 Animation Pane listing the animations on Slide 8

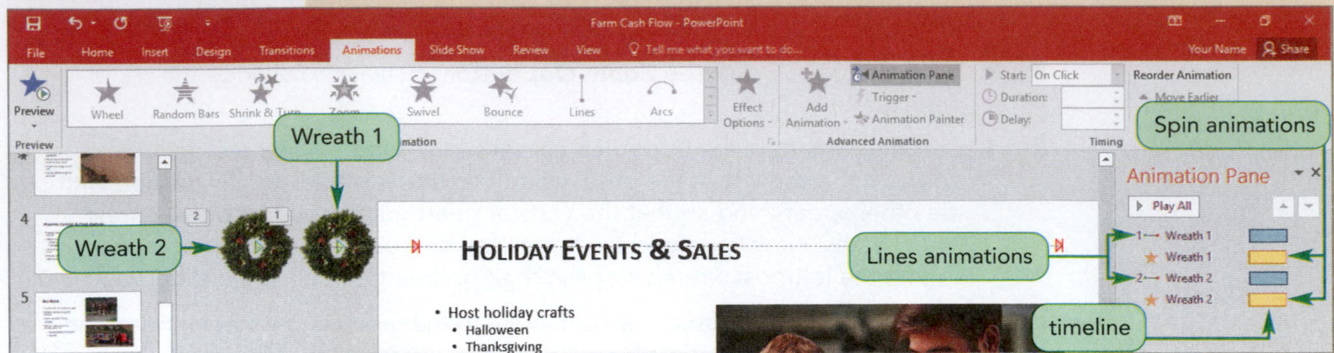

© iStock.com/FlamingPumpkin; © iStock.com/mediaphotos; © iStock.com/BanksPhotos; gvictoria/Shutterstock.com; Vicki L. Miller/Shutterstock.com

2. In the Animation Pane, point to the first animation in the list, Wreath 1. A ScreenTip appears, identifying the start timing (On Click), the animation (Right), and the full name of the object (Wreath 1). This is the Lines animation applied to the wreath that ends up in the upper-right corner of the slide. The horizontal line to the left of the object name indicates that this is a motion path animation, and the number 1 to the left of the object name is the same number that appears in the animation sequence icon for this animation.
3. In the Animation Pane, point to the second animation in the list, the second Wreath 1. This is the Spin animation applied to the wreath that ends up in the upper-right corner of the slide. There is no number to the left of this animation because this animation occurs automatically (With Previous), not when the slide show is advanced (On Click). The yellow star to the left of the object name indicates that this is an emphasis animation. (Entrance animations are indicated with a green star, and exit animations are indicated with a red star.)
4. To the right of the first animation in the list, Wreath 1, point to the blue rectangle so that the pointer changes to ↔. The rectangle indicates the length of the animation. The ScreenTip identifies the start time as 0s (zero seconds), which means it starts immediately after the slide show is advanced. The animation takes two seconds to complete so the ending time in the ScreenTip is 2s.
5. In the Animation Pane, click the **Close** button ☒.

TIP

The entrance animation Appear and the exit animation Disappear have no length so an arrow appears in the Animation Pane instead of a rectangle and the ScreenTip displays only a start time.

You will use the Animation Pane to select the Spin animation applied to each wreath so that you can modify them. To make the rolling effect appear more realistic, you will change the number of revolutions each wreath makes.

To select the Spin animations in the Animation Pane and modify them:

1. Click the **1** animation sequence icon. Because two animation sequence icons are stacked on top of one another, the Animation Pane opens automatically. In the Animation Pane, the two animations applied to the first wreath that animates are selected. In the Animation group on the Animations tab, Multiple is selected.
2. In the Animation Pane, click the **Wreath 1 Spin** animation (the second animation in the list). On the Animations tab, in the Animation group, the Spin animation is selected.

3. In the Animation group, click the **Effect Options** button. In the Amount section, Full Spin is selected. Because this wreath needs to travel all the way across the slide, two spins would look better.
4. On the Effect Options menu, click **Two Spins**. The menu closes. As the animation previews (which you can't see because the wreath is not on the slide), only the Wreath 1 Spin animation is shown in the Animation Pane, and a vertical line moves across the pane.
5. Press and hold the **Shift** key, click the **Wreath 1 Lines** animation in the Animation Pane, and then release the Shift key. The button at the top of the Animation Pane changes to the Play Selected button.
6. Click the **Play Selected** button. The two selected animations preview, with the wreath rolling onto the slide, spinning twice, and stopping in the upper-right corner.
7. In the Animation Pane, click the **Wreath 2 Spin** animation (the last animation in the list).
8. On the Animations tab, in the Animation group, click the **Effect Options** button, and then click **Half Spin**.
9. In the Animation Pane, click the **Wreath 1 Lines** animation, and then at the top of the pane, click the **Play From** button. The four animations preview.

The first wreath that animates continues to roll after it is in position. To fix this problem, you will slightly speed up the Spin animation applied to it by shortening its duration. The second wreath that animates seems to roll more slowly than the first wreath. To fix this, you will speed up both of the animations that are applied to the second wreath that animates (the wreath that ends up in the upper-left corner of the slide).

To modify the duration of animations:

1. In the Animation Pane, click the **Wreath 1 Spin** animation.
2. On the Animations tab, in the Timing group, click in the **Duration** box, type **1.75**, and then press the **Enter** key.
3. In the Animation Pane, click the **Wreath 2 Lines** animation.
4. On the Animations tab, in the Timing group, click in the Duration box, type **1**, and then press the **Enter** key.
5. Change the duration of the **Wreath 2 Spin** animation to **1.00** second. You will preview the modified animations in Slide Show view.
6. On the status bar, click the **Slide Show** button, and then press the **spacebar**. The first wreath rolls onto the slide and no longer has an extra spin at the end.
7. Press the **spacebar** again. The second wreath rolls on faster than before.
8. Press the **Esc** key to end the slide show and return to Normal view.

Brian wants the wreaths to roll onto the slide automatically after the slide transitions onto the screen during a slide show. In order for this to happen, the start timing of the Lines animations needs to be set to After Previous.

To change the start timing of the Lines animations:

1. In the Animation Pane, click the **Wreath 1 Lines** animation. An arrow appears to the right of the blue rectangle.
2. Click the **arrow** to the right of the blue rectangle. A menu appears. The first three commands are the same commands that appear when you click the Start arrow in the Timing group on the Animations tab. See Figure 4-6.

Figure 4-6 Menu for the selected Wreath 1 Lines animation

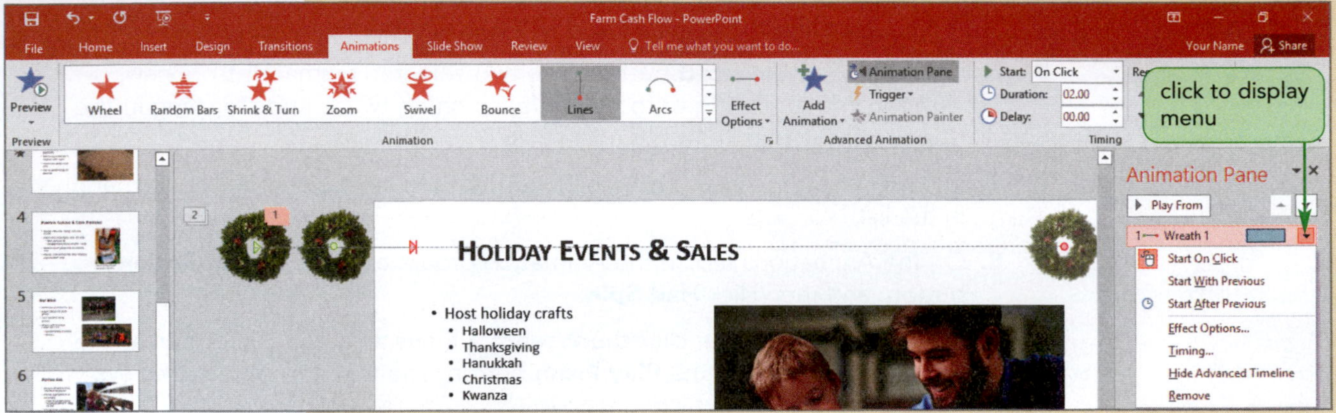

© iStock.com/FlamingPumpkin; © iStock.com/mediaphotos; © iStock.com/BanksPhotos; © iStock.com/RonBailey; gvictoria/Shutterstock.com; Vicki L. Miller/Shutterstock.com; © iStock.com/Naomi Bassitt

3. Click **Start After Previous**. Now the first wreath will roll onto the slide after the slide transitions. Notice that the number 1 that had been next to the animation changes to zero.
4. Click the **Wreath 2 Lines** animation, click the arrow that appears, and then click **Start After Previous**. The blue and yellow rectangles next to the Wreath 2 animations shift right to indicate that they won't start until after the previous animations finish. See Figure 4-7.

Figure 4-7 Modified timeline in the Animation Pane

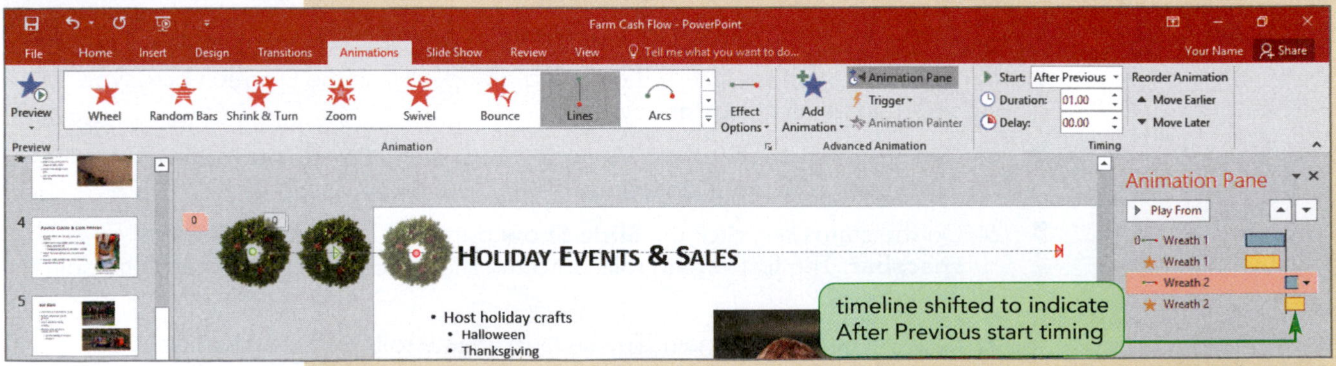

© iStock.com/FlamingPumpkin; © iStock.com/mediaphotos; © iStock.com/BanksPhotos; © iStock.com/RonBailey; gvictoria/Shutterstock.com; Vicki L. Miller/Shutterstock.com

5. Point to the blue rectangle to the right of the Wreath 2 Lines animation. The ScreenTip indicates that the animation will start two seconds after the slide show is advanced and will end three seconds after the slide show was advanced. Now preview the animations in Slide Show view.

6. On the status bar, click the **Slide Show** button. Slide 8 appears in Slide Show view, the first wreath rolls onto the slide, and then the second wreath rolls on.
7. Press the **Esc** key to end the slide show.
8. On the Animations tab, in the Advanced Animation group, click the **Animation Pane** button. The Animation Pane closes.
9. On the status bar, click the **Fit slide to current window** button. The slide increases in size.
10. Save the presentation.

Setting Animation Triggers

You would use a trigger for an animation that you want to be able to choose when it occurs while giving the presentation. Refer to the Session 4.1 Visual Overview for more information about triggers.

Brian created an overview slide listing his suggestions for increasing the cash flow for farms in the fall and early winter months. He included a graphic of an unlit lightbulb on the slide, and he wants to be able to click it during his presentation and have it change so it looks like he turned the light on. To do this, you need to insert a graphic of the lightbulb turned on and then apply an entrance animation to the lit bulb so that it appears when the unlit bulb is clicked; in other words, you need to make the unlit bulb a trigger for that entrance animation.

To set a trigger for an animation on Slide 2:

1. Display **Slide 2** ("Ideas"), and then, on the ribbon, click the **Home** tab. Slide 2 contains a title, a lightbulb graphic, and a bulleted list.
2. In the Editing group, click the **Select** button, and then click **Selection Pane**. The Selection pane opens.
3. On the slide, click the lightbulb. In the Selection pane, Content Placeholder 4 is selected.
4. In the Selection pane, click **Content Placeholder 4**, drag across **Content Placeholder 4** to select the text, type **Unlit Lightbulb**, and then press the **Enter** key.
5. Insert the picture **Light**, located in the PowerPoint 4 > Module folder. The same lightbulb graphic is added to the slide, but this one looks like the lightbulb is turned on. In the Selection pane, Picture 4 is added to the top of the list.
6. In the Selection pane, click **Picture 4**, drag across **Picture 4** to select the text, type **Lit Lightbulb**, and then press the **Enter** key.
7. On the slide, drag the lit version of the lightbulb graphic directly on top of the unlit version, using the smart guides to make sure the two graphics are perfectly aligned.
8. Click the **Animations** tab, and then in the Animation group, click the **Appear** entrance animation. The Appear animation is applied to the lit lightbulb. Now you need to make the unlit lightbulb the trigger for this animation.

TIP

To remove a trigger, select the animated object, click the Trigger button, and then click the checked object on the menu.

9. In the Advanced Animation group, click the **Trigger** button, and then point to **On Click of**. The same list of objects that appears in the Selection pane appears on the submenu.
10. Click **Unlit Lightbulb**. The animation sequence icon next to the light changes to a lightning bolt.
11. In the Selection pane, click the **Close** button.

Next you need to test the trigger. You'll view Slide 2 in Slide Show view and click the unlit lightbulb to make sure the lit bulb appears.

To test the animation trigger in Slide Show view:

1. On the status bar, click the **Slide Show** button. Slide 2 appears in Slide Show view displaying the slide title, the bulleted list, and the unlit version of the lightbulb graphic.
2. Click the lightbulb. The lightbulb appears to turn on, as the lit version of the lightbulb graphic appears on top of the unlit version.

   Trouble? If Slide 3 ("Corn Maze") appears instead of the lit bulb appearing on Slide 2, you clicked the slide area instead of clicking the lightbulb. Press the Backspace key to redisplay Slide 2, and then click the lightbulb graphic.
3. Press the **Esc** key to end the presentation, and then save the presentation.

Changing the Slide Background

The background of a slide can be as important as the foreground when you are creating a presentation with a strong visual impact. To change the background, you use the Format Background pane. When you change the background, you are essentially changing the fill of the background. The commands are the same as the commands you use when you change the fill of a shape. For example, you can change the color, add a gradient or a pattern, or fill it with a texture or a picture.

REFERENCE

Modify the Slide Background

- On the ribbon, click the Design tab, and then in the Customize group, click the Format Background button to open the Format Background pane with the Fill button selected and the Fill section expanded.
- Click one of the fill option buttons to select the type of fill you want to use.
- Use the option buttons, menus, and sliders that appear to customize the selected fill option.
- To apply the background to all the slides in the presentation, click the Apply to All button.

Brian wants you to add color to the slide background. You will do this now.

To fill the slide background with a gradient color:

1. Click the **Design** tab, and then in the Customize group, click the **Format Background** button. The Format Background pane opens. See Figure 4-8. This pane has only one button—the Fill button—and one section of commands—the Fill section. It contains the same commands as the Fill section in the Format Shape pane. The Solid fill option button is selected, indicating that the current background has a solid fill.

Figure 4-8 Format Background pane

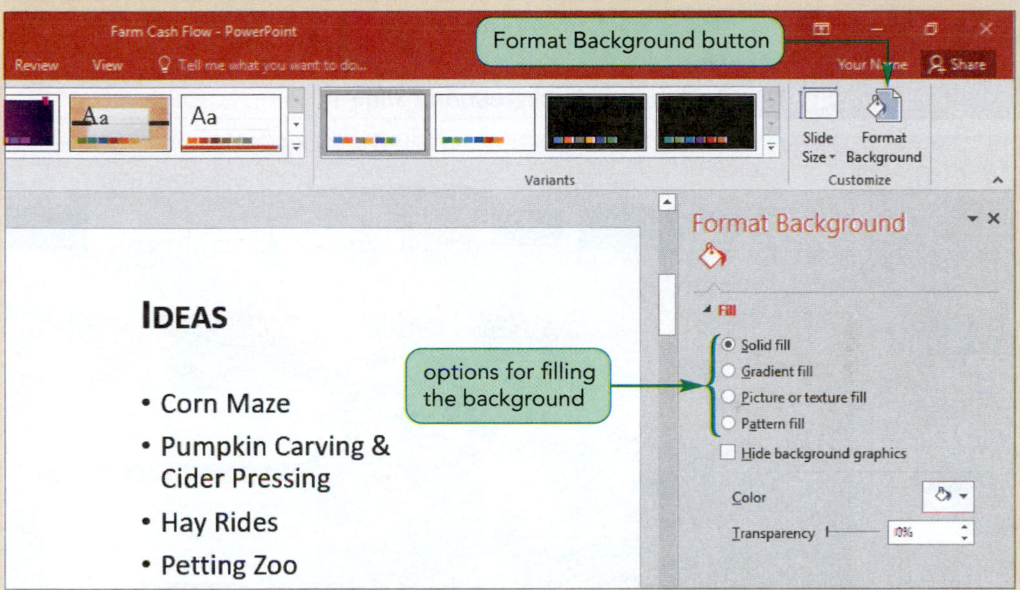

2. In the pane, click the **Color** button, and then click the **Olive Green, Accent 3** color. The slide background changes to the color you selected. This is too dark.
3. Click the **Gradient fill** option button. The slide is filled with a gradient of the color, and options for modifying the gradient fill appear in the Format Background pane.
4. Click the **Preset gradients** button, and then click the **Light Gradient – Accent 3** gradient. The gradient on the slide background changes so it is lighter at the top of the slide.
5. Click the **Type** arrow, and then click **Shade from title**. The gradient changes so that the darker shading is added along the top and sides of the slide.
6. At the bottom of the Format Background pane, click the **Apply to All** button. The gradient background is applied to all the slides in the presentation.

Brian wants the title slide to have a different background than the rest of the slides. You can display one image of a picture as the slide background, or you can tile it, which means to make the picture appear as repeating images across the slide. When you set an image to tile across the background, you can make the tiles smaller so that more tiles appear on the background.

You'll add a picture of fruit in bins at a fruit stand as the slide background of Slide 1, and then you will make it appear as tiles in the background for Slide 1.

To tile a picture in the background of Slide 1:

1. Display **Slide 1** (the title slide), and then in the Format Background pane, click the **Picture or texture fill** option button. The default texture is applied to the current slide background and the pane changes to include commands for inserting pictures.
2. In the Insert picture from section of the pane, click the **File** button. The Insert Picture dialog box opens.
3. Navigate to the **PowerPoint 4 > Module** folder, click **Fruit**, and then click the **Insert** button. The picture of fruit in a bin at a fruit stand fills the slide background of Slide 1. See Figure 4-9.

Figure 4-9 Picture in background of Slide 1

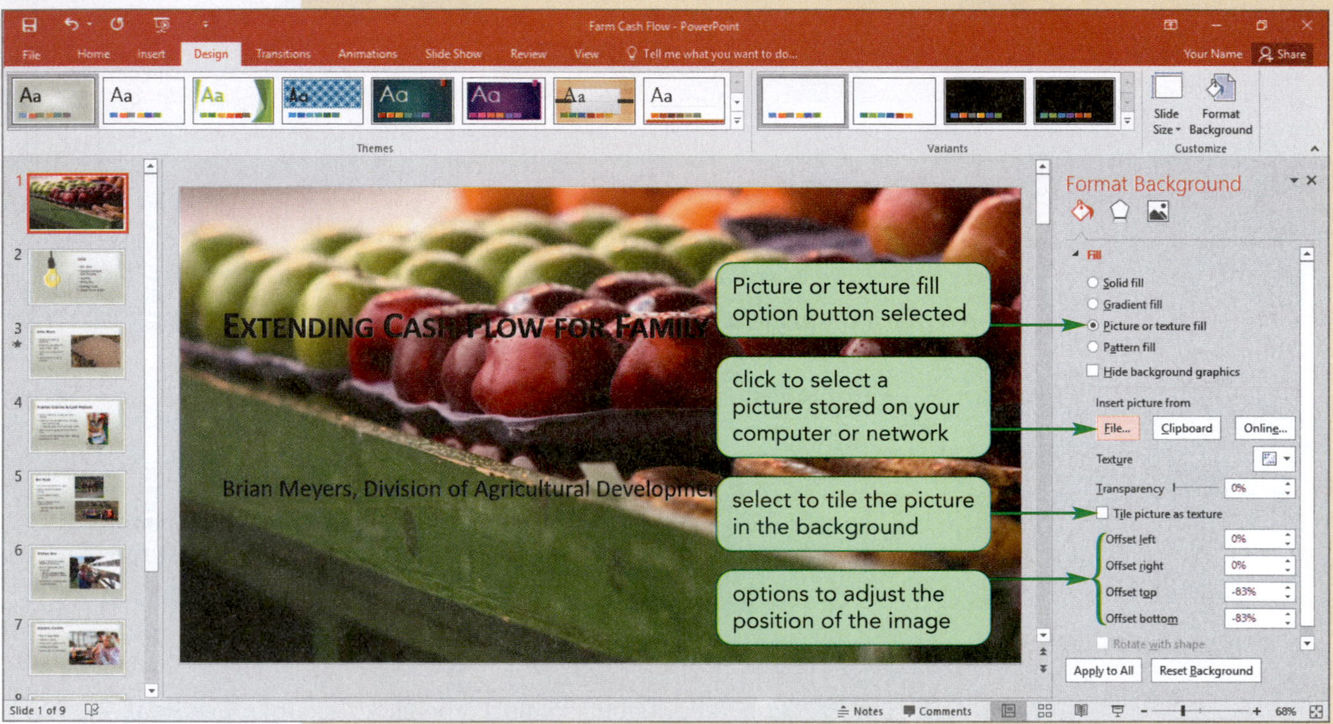

4. In the pane, click the **Tile picture as texture** check box to select it. The picture changes to a series of tiles on the slide. You want rows of tiles to appear.
5. Click in the **Scale X** box, delete the value in it, type **20**, and then press the **Enter** key. The tiles are resized narrower. To maintain the aspect ratio, you need to reduce the height of the tiles to the same percentage.
6. Click in the **Scale Y** box, delete the value in it, type **20**, and then press the **Enter** key. The tiles are resized vertically by the same amount that they were resized horizontally.
7. Scroll to the bottom of the Format Background pane, click the **Mirror type** arrow, and then click **Horizontal**. Each tile is duplicated and the duplicates are flipped horizontally to create mirror images. See Figure 4-10.

TIP

To adjust the position of the photo, use the offset options in the pane.

Figure 4-10 **Picture tiled in background of Slide 1 with a mirror effect**

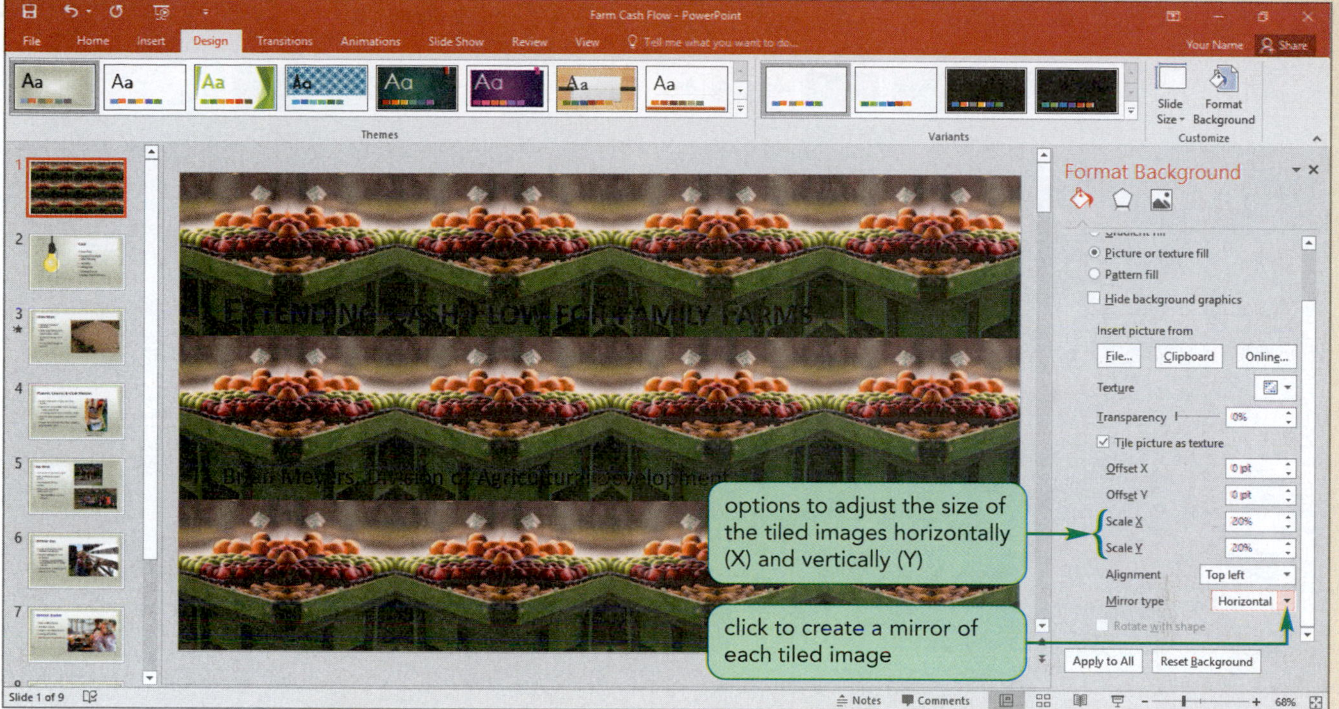

© iStock.com/cgering; Courtesy of Katherine T. Pinard; © iStock.com/BanksPhotos; © iStock.com/RonBailey; gvictoria/ Shutterstock.com; Vicki L. Miller/Shutterstock.com; © iStock.com/Naomi Bassitt; Arina P Habich/Shutterstock.com

The text on the slide is hard to see with the dark photo background.

8. Click the **title text**, press and hold the **Shift** key, and then click the **subtitle text**. The two text boxes on Slide 1 are selected. Note that the pane changed to the Format Shape pane.
9. Click the **Home** tab, in the Font group, click the **Font Color button arrow**, and then click the **White, Background 1, Darker 5%** color.

The text is still a little hard to see on the picture background. You could adjust the brightness and the contrast of the photo, or you could make the photo more transparent. You'll adjust the transparency of the photo now.

TIP

To view a presentation in black-and-white or grayscale, click the View tab, and then in the Color/Grayscale group, click the Grayscale button or the Black and White button.

To change the transparency of the background picture:

1. Click the **Design** tab, and then in the Customize group, click the **Format Background** button. The Format Background pane reappears.
2. In the pane, drag the **Transparency** slider to the right until the value in the Transparency box is 20%. Compare your screen to Figure 4-11.

   Trouble? If you can't position the slider so that 20% appears in the Transparency box, click the up or down arrows in the Transparency box as needed to change the value.

Figure 4-11 Tiled picture in slide background with transparency adjusted

© iStock.com/cgering; Courtesy of Katherine T. Pinard; © iStock.com/BanksPhotos; © iStock.com/RonBailey; gvictoria/Shutterstock.com; Vicki L. Miller/Shutterstock.com; © iStock.com/Naomi Bassitt; Arina P Habich/Shutterstock.com

3. In the Format Background pane, click the **Close** button ☒.
4. Save the presentation.

INSIGHT

Hiding Background Graphics

Some themes include graphics as part of the slide background. If you need to print slides with graphics in the background in black and white or grayscale, you might want to remove those graphics before printing the slides because the graphics could make the text difficult to read. To hide graphics in the background, select the Hide background graphics check box in the Format Background pane. Note that selecting this option will not hide anything you use as a fill for the background, such as the picture you added as the background in this module.

Creating and Editing Hyperlinks

If you've visited webpages on the Internet, you have clicked hyperlinks (or links) to "jump to"—or display—other webpages or files. In PowerPoint, a link on a slide accomplishes the same thing. You can convert any text or object on a slide to a link to another slide in the same presentation, a different file, or a webpage. A link can be customized to do several other actions as well.

To create a link, you use the Hyperlink button or the Action button in the Links group on the Insert tab. You can use either button to create most types of links; however the Action Settings dialog box allows you to also create a link to start a program and a few other advanced activities. In addition, when you use the Action button, you can create a link that responds when you simply point to it rather than click it.

Creating and Editing Text Links

As you know, when you type a webpage or an email address, it is automatically converted to a link. You can convert any text on a slide to a link. Text links are usually underlined and a different color than the rest of the text on a slide. After you click a text link during a slide show, the link changes to another color to indicate that it has been clicked, or followed.

Slide 9 contains Brian's email address formatted as a link. You can edit this link so that the text displayed on the slide is Brian's name instead of the email address.

To change the text displayed for a link:

1. Display **Slide 9** ("Contact Info"), and then click anywhere in the email address link on the slide.
2. Click the **Insert** tab, and then in the Links group, click the **Hyperlink** button. The Edit Hyperlink dialog box opens. In the Link to list on the left, the E-mail Address option is selected. The email address, preceded by the "mailto" instruction, appears in the E-mail address box. In addition, the email address that appears on the slide is in the Text to display box at the top of the dialog box. See Figure 4-12.

Figure 4-12 **Edit Hyperlink dialog box for a link to an email address**

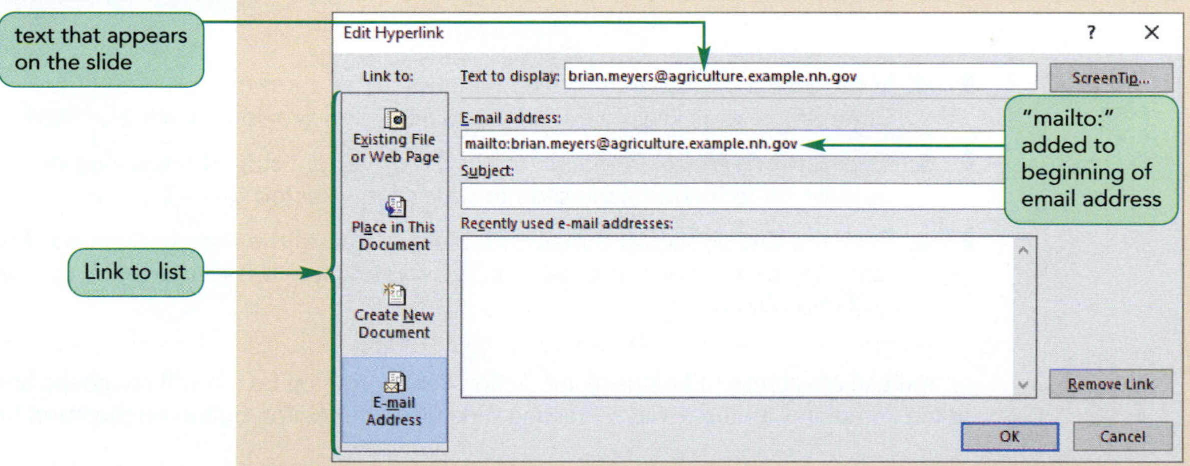

3. Click in the Text to display box, delete all the text, and then type **Brian Meyers**.
4. Click the **OK** button. The dialog box closes, and the email address on Slide 9 changes to the text you typed in the Edit Hyperlink dialog box, Brian Meyers.

Slide 2 in Brian's presentation is an overview slide. Each bulleted item on this slide names another slide in the presentation. Brian wants you to convert each bulleted item to a hyperlink that links to the related slide. One way to create hyperlinks is to use the Insert Hyperlink dialog box.

To create a hyperlink using the Insert Hyperlink dialog box:

1. Display **Slide 2** ("Ideas"), and then click the first bullet symbol. The text of the first bulleted item—"Corn Maze"—is selected.
2. Click the **Insert** tab, if necessary, and then in the Links group, click the **Hyperlink** button. The Insert Hyperlink dialog box opens. In the Link to list on the left, the E-mail Address option is selected. You need to identify the file or location to which you want to link. In this case, you're going to link to a slide in the current presentation.
3. In the Link to list on the left, click **Place in This Document**. The dialog box changes to show the Select a place in this document box, listing all the slides in the presentation. See Figure 4-13.

Figure 4-13 Insert Hyperlink dialog box displaying slides in this presentation

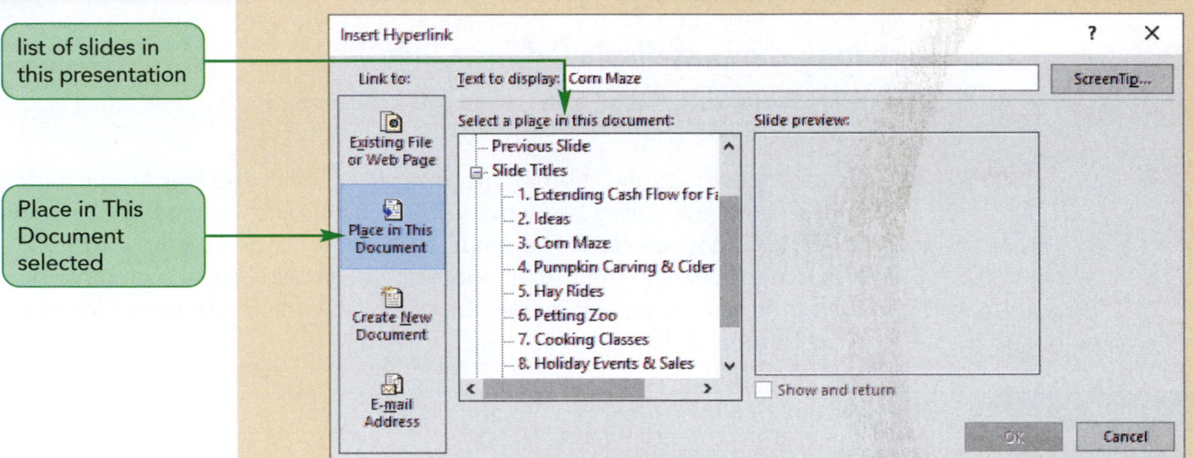

4. In the Select a place in this document list, scroll up to the top of the list. Commands for linking to the first, last, next, and previous slides are listed.
5. Click **3. Corn Maze**. The Slide preview on the right side of the dialog box displays Slide 3. This is the slide to which the selected text will be linked.
6. Click the **OK** button, and then click a blank area of the slide to deselect the text. The text of the first bullet is now a hyperlink and is formatted in yellow and underlined.

You can also create a link using the Action Settings dialog box. You'll create the link to the Pumpkin Carving & Cider Pressing slide using the Action button on the Insert tab.

To create a hyperlink using the Action Settings dialog box:

1. Click the second bullet in the list. The text of the second bulleted item, Pumpkin Carving & Cider Pressing, is selected.
2. On the Insert tab, in the Links group, click the **Action** button. The Action Settings dialog box opens with the Mouse Click tab selected. See Figure 4-14.

Figure 4-14 Action Settings dialog box

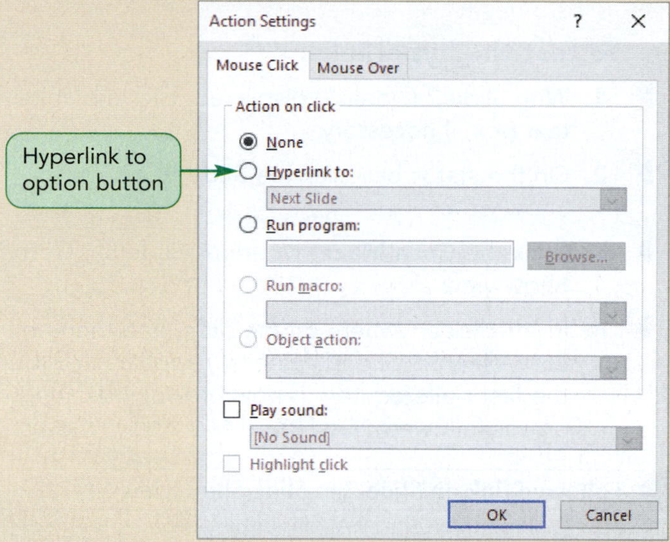

TIP

Click the Mouse Over tab to create a link that you only need to point to in order to display the linked slide or file.

3. In the Action on click section, click the **Hyperlink to** option button. The Hyperlink to box becomes available.
4. Click the **Hyperlink to** arrow. The commands on the list allow you to create hyperlinks to the same things you can link to using the Insert Hyperlink dialog box. You want to link to a specific slide in the current presentation.
5. Click **Slide**. The Hyperlink to Slide dialog box opens listing all the slides in the presentation. See Figure 4-15.

Figure 4-15 Hyperlink to Slide dialog box

© iStock.com/cgering

6. Click **4. Pumpkin Carving & Cider Pressing**, and then click the **OK** button. The Hyperlink to Slide dialog box closes and "Pumpkin Carving & Cider Pressing" appears in the Hyperlink to box.
7. Click the **OK** button. The dialog box closes and the second bulleted item is formatted as a link.
8. Change the next four bulleted items to links to Slides 5, 6, 7, and 8 respectively, using either the Hyperlink or the Action button.

Now you need to test the links you created. Links are not active in Normal view, so you will switch to Slide Show view.

To test the hyperlinks:

1. With Slide 2 ("Ideas") displayed, click a blank area of the slide to deselect the text box, if necessary.
2. On the status bar, click the **Slide Show** button. Slide 2 appears in Slide Show view.
3. Click the **Corn Maze** hyperlink. Slide 3 ("Corn Maze") appears in Slide Show view.
4. Right-click anywhere on the slide, and then on the shortcut menu, click **Last Viewed**. Slide 2 ("Ideas") appears in Slide Show view. The link text in the first bulleted item is now brown, indicating that the link had been clicked, or was followed. See Figure 4-16.

Figure 4-16 **Followed link on Slide 2 in Slide Show view**

IDEAS
• Corn Maze
• Pumpkin Carving & Cider Pressing
• Hay Rides
• Petting Zoo
• Cooking Classes
• Holiday Events & Sales
followed link
links that have not been followed

Courtesy of Katherine T. Pinard

5. Click each of the other links to verify that they link to the correct slides, using the Last Viewed command on the shortcut menu to return to Slide 2 each time.
6. Press the **Esc** key to end the slide show. Slide 2 appears in Normal view. The links are now all brown. They changed color because they have been clicked—followed—during a slide show. They will reset to the yellow color when you close and reopen the presentation.

   Trouble? If Slide 2 is not displayed, you did not return to Slide 2 in the Slide Show after clicking the last link. Display Slide 2.

   Trouble? If the links on Slide 2 are not brown, display any other slide, and then redisplay Slide 2.

Creating Object Links

You can also convert objects into links. Object hyperlinks are visually indistinguishable from objects that are not hyperlinks, except that when you move the mouse pointer over the object in Slide Show, Presenter, or Reading view, the pointer changes to 👆. Object links do not change in appearance after they have been clicked.

Although Brian can use commands on the shortcut menu in Slide Show view to return to Slide 2 after clicking a link to another slide, it would be easier for him to navigate during the slide show if you added a link to Slide 2 on each slide. You'll do this now by adding a shape that you format as a link on Slides 3 through 8.

To create a shape and format it as a link:

1. Display **Slide 3** ("Corn Maze").
2. On the Insert tab, in the Illustrations group, click the **Shapes** button, and then in the Rectangles group, click the **Rounded Rectangle** shape.
3. Click below the picture of the corn maze to insert the shape, resize it so it is one-half inch high and 1.2 inches wide, and then using the smart guides that appear, position it so that the shape's right edge is aligned with the right side of the photo and its center is aligned with the slide number.
4. With the shape selected, type **Ideas**, and then change the font size to **24** points and make the text bold.
5. On the ribbon, click the **Drawing Tools Format** tab.
6. In the Shape Styles group, click the **More** button, and then in the Presets section, click the **Transparent, Colored Outline – Olive Green, Accent 3** style. See Figure 4-17.

Figure 4-17 Ideas shape on Slide 3

© iStock.com/BanksPhotos

7. On the ribbon, click the **Insert** tab.
8. With the shape selected, in the Links group, click the **Hyperlink** button. The Insert Hyperlink dialog box opens. Because Slide 2 is the previous slide, you could select the Previous Slide location instead of clicking the slide number. However, you will be copying this link to other slides, so you will link specifically to Slide 2.
9. With Place in This Document selected in the Link to list, click **2. Ideas** in the Select a place in this document list, and then click the **OK** button. The shape does not look any different now that it is a link. You want the same link to appear on Slides 4 through 7. You can insert a shape on each slide and format it as a link, or you can copy the shape on Slide 3 and paste it on each slide.
10. With the **Ideas** shape selected, click the **Home** tab, and then in the Clipboard group, click the **Copy** button.

11. Display **Slide 4** ("Pumpkin Carving & Cider Pressing"), and then in the Clipboard group, click the **Paste** button. A copy of the Ideas link appears in the lower-right corner of the slide—the same position it was in on Slide 3.
12. Paste the Ideas link on Slide 5 ("Hay Rides"), Slide 6 ("Petting Zoo"), Slide 7 ("Cooking Classes"), and Slide 8 ("Holiday Events & Sales").

You need to test the Ideas links. Again, you must switch to Slide Show view to do this.

To test the Ideas shape links:

1. Display **Slide 2** ("Ideas"), and then on the status bar, click the **Slide Show** button .
2. Click the **Corn Maze** hyperlink. Slide 3 ("Corn Maze") appears in Slide Show view.
3. In the lower-right corner of the slide, click the **Ideas** shape. Slide 2 ("Ideas") appears on the screen.
4. On Slide 2 ("Ideas"), click each of the other links to display those slides, and then click the Ideas shape on each of those slides to return to Slide 2.
5. Press the **Esc** key to end the slide show and return to Slide 2 in Normal view.

Inserting Action Buttons

Finally, you want to add a link on Slide 2 that links to the last slide in the presentation, Slide 9 ("Contact Info"). Brian did not add a bulleted item in the overview on Slide 2 for Slide 9 because, as the final slide, it is meant to display only as the presentation is concluding. You will use an action button to do this. An action button is a shape that, when inserted, causes the Action Settings dialog box to be opened automatically, ready for you to specify the link. Some action buttons are preset to link to the first, last, next, or previous slides.

To insert an action button on Slide 2:

1. With Slide 2 ("Ideas") displayed, on the ribbon, click the **Insert** tab.
2. In the Illustrations group, click the **Shapes** button, scroll to the bottom of the gallery, and then in the Action Buttons section, click the **Action Button: End** shape.
3. Click below the bulleted list. The action button is inserted and the Action Settings dialog box opens. The Hyperlink to option button is selected, and Last Slide appears in the Hyperlink to box.
4. Click the **OK** button.
5. On the Drawing Tools Format tab, in the Shape Styles group, click the **More** button, scroll down, and then click the **Semitransparent – Olive Green, Accent 3, No Outline** style in the Presets section.
6. Resize the action button so it is one-half inch high and one inch wide, position it in the lower-right corner of the slide so it is in about the same position as the Ideas shape on the other slides, and then click a blank area of the slide to deselect the button. Compare your screen to Figure 4-18.

Figure 4-18 Action button on Slide 2

Courtesy of Katherine T. Pinard

Now you need to test the new link. Once again, you will switch to Slide Show view.

To test the shape link in Slide Show view:

1. On the status bar, click the **Slide Show** button. Slide 2 ("Ideas") appears in Slide Show view.
2. Click the action button. Slide 9 ("Contact Info") appears.
3. Press the **Esc** key to end the slide show. Slide 9 appears in Normal view.
4. Save the presentation.

INSIGHT

Linking to Another File

You can create a link to another file so that when you click the link during a slide show, the other file opens. The other file can be any file type; it doesn't need to be a PowerPoint file. To create a link to another file, open the Insert Hyperlink dialog box, click Existing File or Web Page in the Link to list, and then click the Browse for File button. To change the link destination of an action button to another file, open the Action Settings dialog box, click the Hyperlink to option button, click the Hyperlink to arrow, and then click Other PowerPoint Presentation or Other File. For either type of link, a dialog box opens in which you can navigate to the location of the file.

When you create a link to another file, the linked file is not included within the PowerPoint file; only the original path and filename to the files on the computer where you created the links are stored in the presentation. Therefore, if you need to show the presentation on another computer, you must copy the linked files as well as the PowerPoint presentation file to the other computer, and then you need to edit the path to the linked file so that PowerPoint can find the file in its new location. To update the path for a text or graphic link, right-click it, and then click Edit Hyperlink on the shortcut menu to open the Edit Hyperlink dialog box. To edit the path of a file linked to an action button, right-click the action button, and then click Hyperlink to open the Action Settings dialog box.

Customizing Theme Colors

As you know, each theme has its own color palette. In addition, you can switch to one of several built-in color palettes. However, sometimes, you might want to customize a palette. You can do so by changing one or all of the theme colors in a palette.

REFERENCE

Customizing Theme Colors

- On the ribbon, click the Design tab.
- In the Variants group, click the More button, point to Colors, and then click Customize Colors to open the Create New Theme Colors dialog box.
- Click the button next to the theme color you want to customize.
- Click a color in the Theme Colors section or in the Standard Colors section of the palette, or click More Colors, click a color in the Colors dialog box, and then click the OK button.
- Replace the name in the Name box with a meaningful name for the custom palette.
- Click the Save button.

In the Farm Cash Flow presentation, the color of the unfollowed text links is a little light on the colored slide background. To fix that, you will customize the link color in the color palette.

To create custom theme colors:

1. Make sure Slide 9 ("Contact Info") is displayed, and then on the ribbon, click the **Design** tab.
2. In the Variants group, click the **More** button, and then point to **Colors**. A menu of color palettes opens. See Figure 4-19. If you wanted to change the entire color palette, you could select one of these options. However, you want to change only the color of text links.

Figure 4-19 **Color palettes on Colors submenu**

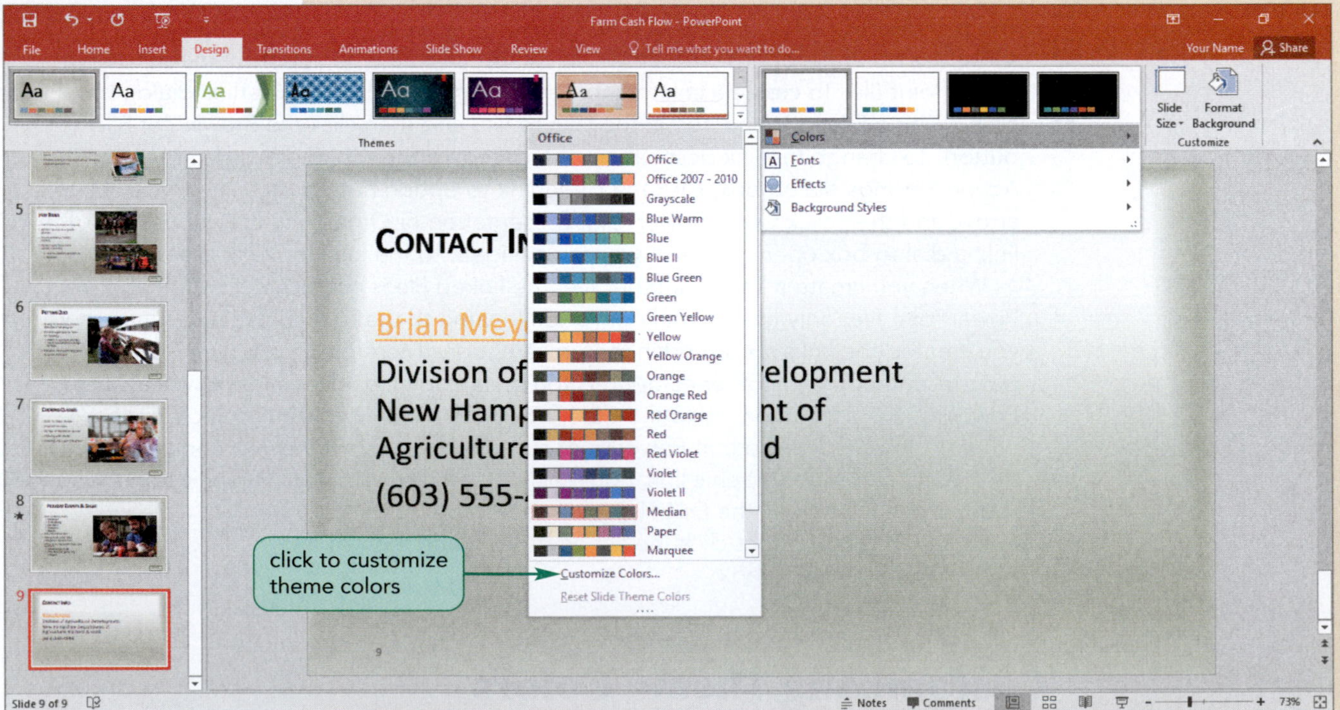

3. At the bottom of the menu, click **Customize Colors**. The Create New Theme Colors dialog box opens. See Figure 4-20. You want to change the color of hyperlinks to a darker shade.

Figure 4-20 **Create New Theme Colors dialog box**

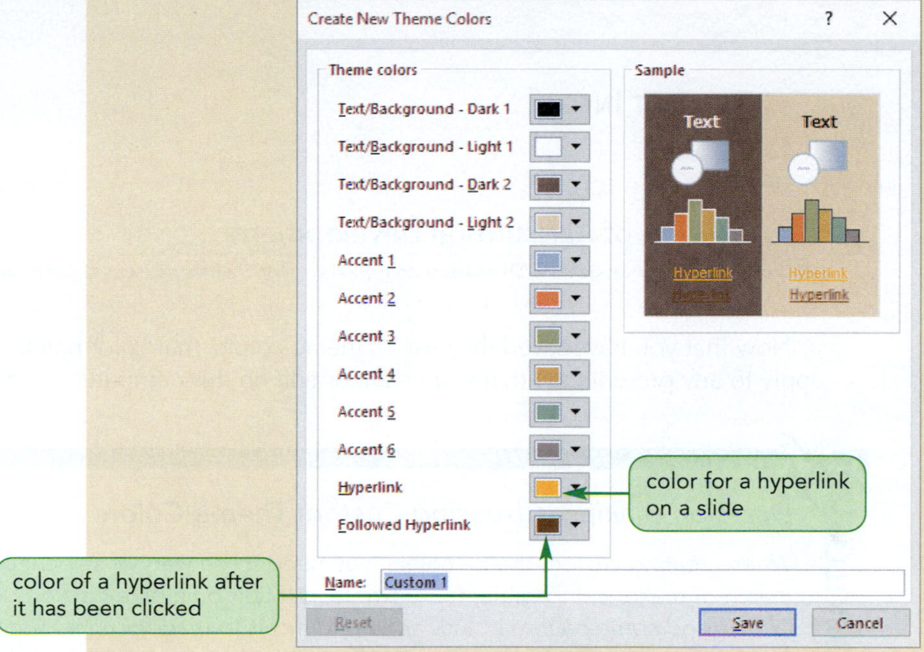

4. Click the **Hyperlink** button to display the complete Theme Colors and Standard Colors palettes.
5. In the Theme Colors section, point to the second to last color in the first row. The ScreenTip identifies this as Gold, Hyperlink. This is the current color for text hyperlinks.
6. Click the **Gold, Hyperlink, Darker 25%** color (second to last color in the column). The Hyperlink color is now the darker gold color you selected, and the top Hyperlink text in the Sample panel in the dialog box is now also darker.

TIP

Never place dark text on a dark background or light text on a light background.

7. Click in the **Name** box, delete the text "Custom 1," and then type **Custom Link Color**.
8. Click the **Save** button. The dialog box closes and the custom color is applied to the presentation. As you can see on Slide 9, the link is now the darker gold color you chose for unfollowed links. See Figure 4-21.

Figure 4-21 New link color on Slide 9

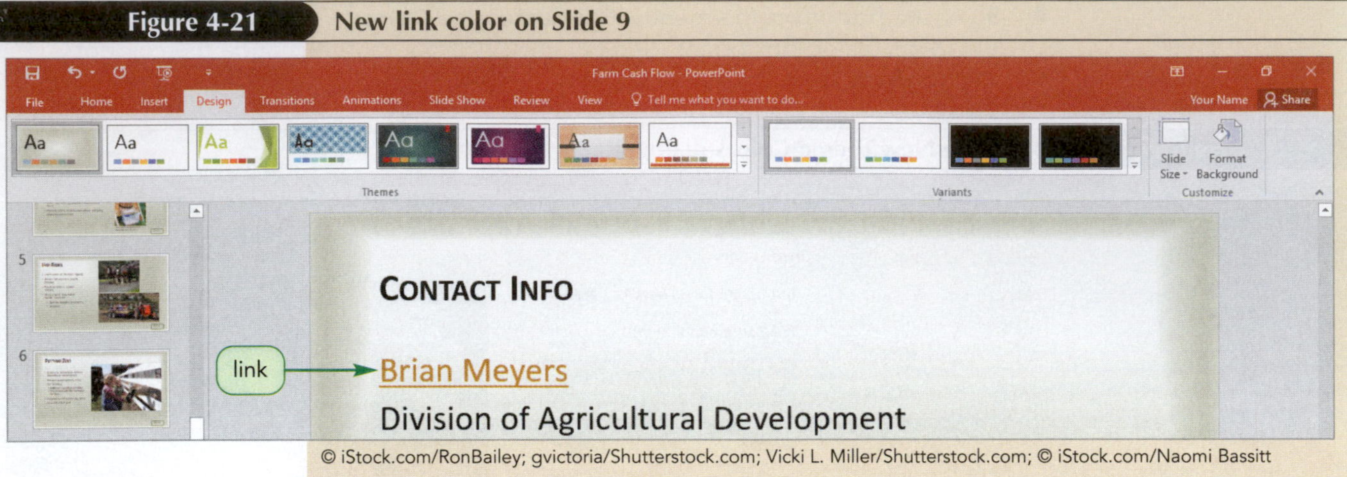

© iStock.com/RonBailey; gvictoria/Shutterstock.com; Vicki L. Miller/Shutterstock.com; © iStock.com/Naomi Bassitt

Now that you have saved the custom theme colors, that color palette is available to apply to any presentation that you create or edit on this computer.

PROSKILLS

Decision Making: Choosing Custom Theme Colors

When creating custom theme colors, you need to be wary of selecting colors that don't match or make text illegible; for example, red text on a blue background might seem like a good combination, but it's actually difficult to read for an audience at a distance from the screen. It's usually safer, therefore, to select one of the built-in theme color sets and stick with it or make only minor modifications. If you do create a new set of theme colors, select colors that go well together and that maximize the legibility of your slides.

Deleting Custom Theme Colors

When you save a custom theme color palette, the palette is saved to the computer. If you've applied the custom palette to a presentation, that color palette will stay applied to that presentation even if you delete the custom palette from the computer. You'll delete the custom theme color palette you created from the computer you are using.

To delete the custom color palette:

1. On the Design tab, in the Variants group, click the **More** button, and then point to **Colors**. The Custom Link Color palette you created appears at the top of the Colors submenu. If you had not given it a different name, it would be listed with the default name—Custom 1—which had appeared in the Create New Theme Colors dialog box.
2. Right-click the **Custom Link Color** palette, and then click **Delete**. A dialog box opens, asking if you want to delete these theme colors.
3. Click the **Yes** button to delete the custom theme colors. You can confirm that the color palette was deleted from your computer.
4. In the Variants group, click the **More** button, and then point to **Colors**. The Custom Link Color palette no longer appears on the Colors submenu.
5. Click a blank area of the slide to close the menu without making a selection.

6. Display **Slide 1** (the title slide), and then replace Brian Meyers' name in the slide subtitle with your name.
7. Save and close the presentation.

Brian is happy with the modifications you've made to the presentation so far. You applied two animations to pictures and modified motion path animations. You changed the slide background by filling all the slide backgrounds with a gradient and filling the title slide background with a tiled picture that you made somewhat transparent. You converted text and a shape to links and added an action button. Finally, you changed the color of linked text so that it can be more easily distinguished on the slides.

In the next session, you will create a self-running presentation by setting slide timings. You will then record a narration to accompany the self-running presentation. You also will save the presentation in other formats so it can be more easily distributed.

REVIEW

Session 4.1 Quick Check

1. What happens if you try to add a second animation by using the Animation gallery instead of the Add Animation button?
2. What is a trigger?
3. Name the five types of fill you can add to a slide background.
4. What items on a slide can be a link?
5. What is an action button?
6. What view(s) do you need to be in to test links?

Session 4.2 Visual Overview:

To set automatic timings manually, select the After check box. During a slide show, the slides will advance automatically after the time displayed in the After box.

When the On Mouse Click check box is selected, the slide show can be advanced by clicking the slide, even if there are saved slide timings. If the On Mouse Click check box is deselected, the slide show cannot be advanced by clicking a slide, although users can still use the keyboard or click links to display other slides.

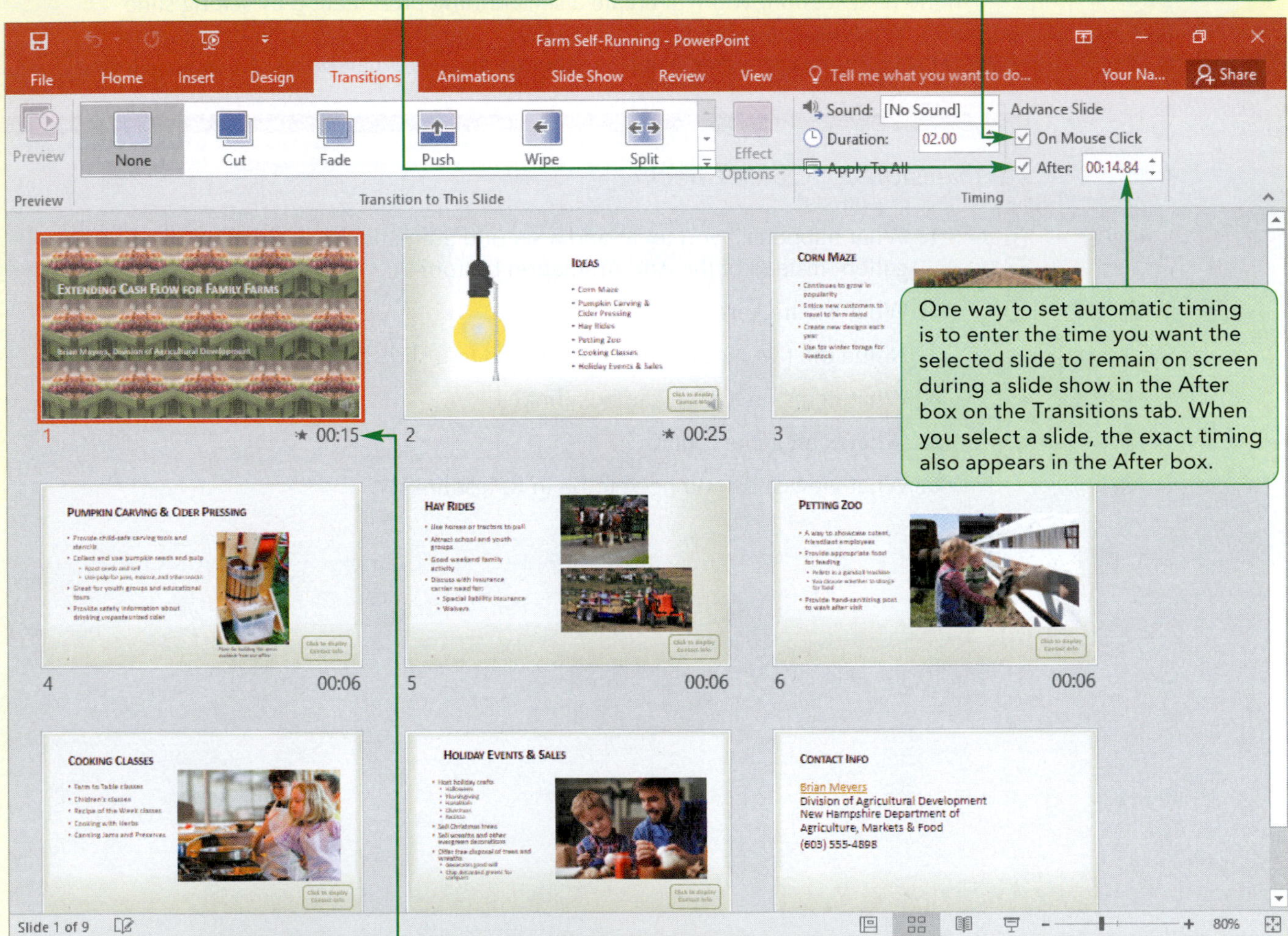

One way to set automatic timing is to enter the time you want the selected slide to remain on screen during a slide show in the After box on the Transitions tab. When you select a slide, the exact timing also appears in the After box.

Automatic timings indicate how many seconds a slide will stay on the screen before transitioning to the next slide during a slide show.

© iStock.com/cgering; Courtesy of Katherine T. Pinard; © iStock.com/BanksPhotos; © iStock.com/RonBailey; gvictoria/Shutterstock.com; Vicki L. Miller/Shutterstock.com; © iStock.com/Naomi Bassitt; Arina P Habich/Shutterstock.com; © iStock.com/mediaphotos

Automatic Slide Timings

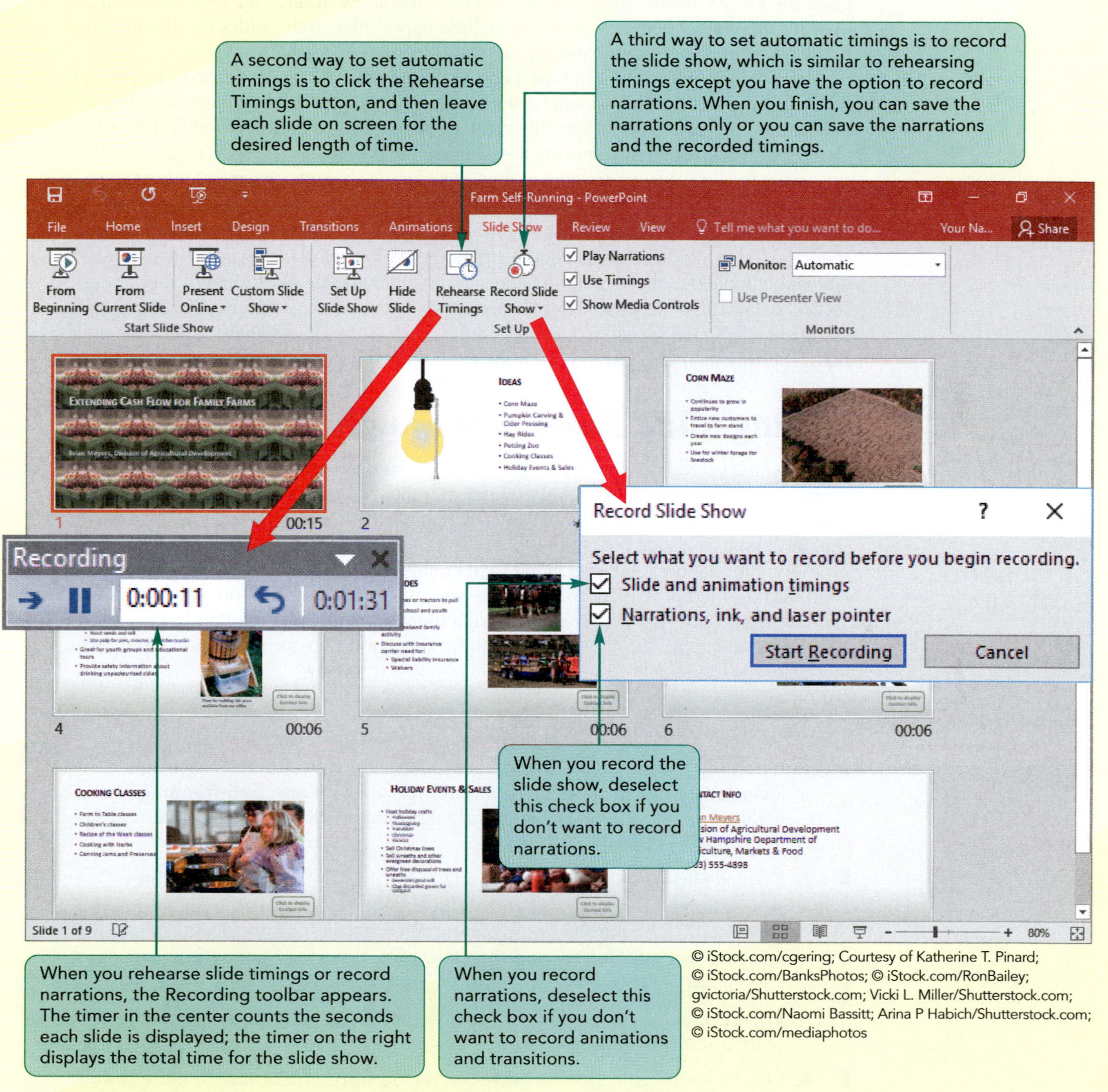
A second way to set automatic timings is to click the Rehearse Timings button, and then leave each slide on screen for the desired length of time.
A third way to set automatic timings is to record the slide show, which is similar to rehearsing timings except you have the option to record narrations. When you finish, you can save the narrations only or you can save the narrations and the recorded timings.
Farm Self-Running - PowerPoint
File
Home
Insert
Design
Transitions
Animations
Slide Show
Review
View
Tell me what you want to do...
Share
From Beginning
From Current Slide
Present Online
Custom Slide Show
Start Slide Show
Set Up Slide Show
Hide Slide
Rehearse Timings
Record Slide Show
Play Narrations
Use Timings
Show Media Controls
Set Up
Monitor: Automatic
Use Presenter View
Monitors
Recording
0:00:11
0:01:31
Record Slide Show
Select what you want to record before you begin recording.
Slide and animation timings
Narrations, ink, and laser pointer
Start Recording
Cancel
When you record the slide show, deselect this check box if you don't want to record narrations.
Slide 1 of 9
80%
When you rehearse slide timings or record narrations, the Recording toolbar appears. The timer in the center counts the seconds each slide is displayed; the timer on the right displays the total time for the slide show.
When you record narrations, deselect this check box if you don't want to record animations and transitions.

Understanding Self-Running Presentations

A self-running presentation advances without a presenter or viewer doing anything. Self-running presentations include settings that specify the amount of time that each slide is displayed as well as the time at which animations occur. Some self-running presentations include audio that takes the place of the presenter's oral explanations or gives the viewer instructions for watching the slide show. To give the user more control over his viewing experience, you can include hyperlinks on the slides or allow the user to advance the slide show manually using the mouse or keyboard.

Brian intends to use the Farm Cash Flow file for oral presentations, but he also wants to create a version of the file that will be self-running on a computer at agricultural fairs and tradeshows for people who are unable to attend his presentation. Brian modified the Farm Cash Flow presentation by removing the text hyperlinks on Slide 2 ("Ideas"). However, he does want to allow viewers to jump to the last slide, which contains contact information, if they want to skip some of the slides. So he replaced the action button on Slide 2 and the Ideas shape on Slides 3 ("Corn Maze") through 8 ("Holiday Events & Sales") with a new shape linked to Slide 9 ("Contact Info"). Brian also removed the trigger from the entrance animation applied to the lit bulb on Slide 2 and set it to appear automatically after a one-second delay. This is because in a self-running presentation, trigger animations do not occur automatically, so the lit bulb would never appear unless the viewer knew to click the unlit bulb. This modified presentation can now be set up as a self-running presentation.

Setting Slide Timings Manually

When setting up a slide show to be self-running, you need to specify how long each slide remains on the screen. The amount of time each slide stays on the screen might vary for different slides—a slide with only three bullet points might not need to remain on the screen as long as a slide containing six bullet points. See the Session 4.2 Visual Overview for more information about specifying slide timings.

In his modified presentation, Brian asks you to set the timings to four seconds per slide. Four seconds, of course, is not enough time for a viewer to read and understand the slide content, but the slide timings will be kept short here for instructional purposes.

To open the modified presentation and set slide timings:

1. Open the presentation **Farm2**, located in the **PowerPoint4 > Module** included with your Data Files, and then save it as **Farm Self-Running** to the location where you are saving your files. First you'll examine the animations that Brian applied.
2. Display **Slide 2** ("Ideas"), click the lit bulb graphic, and then click the **Animations** tab. The animation sequence icon does not contain a lightning bolt because Brian removed the trigger. In the timing group, After Previous appears in the Start box, and the Delay box is set for 1 second.
3. Display **Slide 7** ("Cooking Classes"), and then click the bulleted list. The Wipe entrance animation is applied to the list, and On Click appears in the Start box in the Timing group.
4. On the status bar, click the **Slide Sorter** button to switch to Slide Sorter view, scroll up, and then click the **Slide 1** thumbnail.
5. Press and hold the **Shift** key, scroll down, and then click the **Slide 9** ("Contact Info") thumbnail. All the slides are selected.
6. On the ribbon, click the **Transitions** tab. In the Timing group, the On Mouse Click check box is selected in the Advance Slide section. This means that the viewer can take an action to advance the slide show.

7. In the Timing group, click the **After** check box. The check box is selected, and 00:00 appears below each slide thumbnail. See Figure 4-22.

Figure 4-22 Transitions tab with After box selected

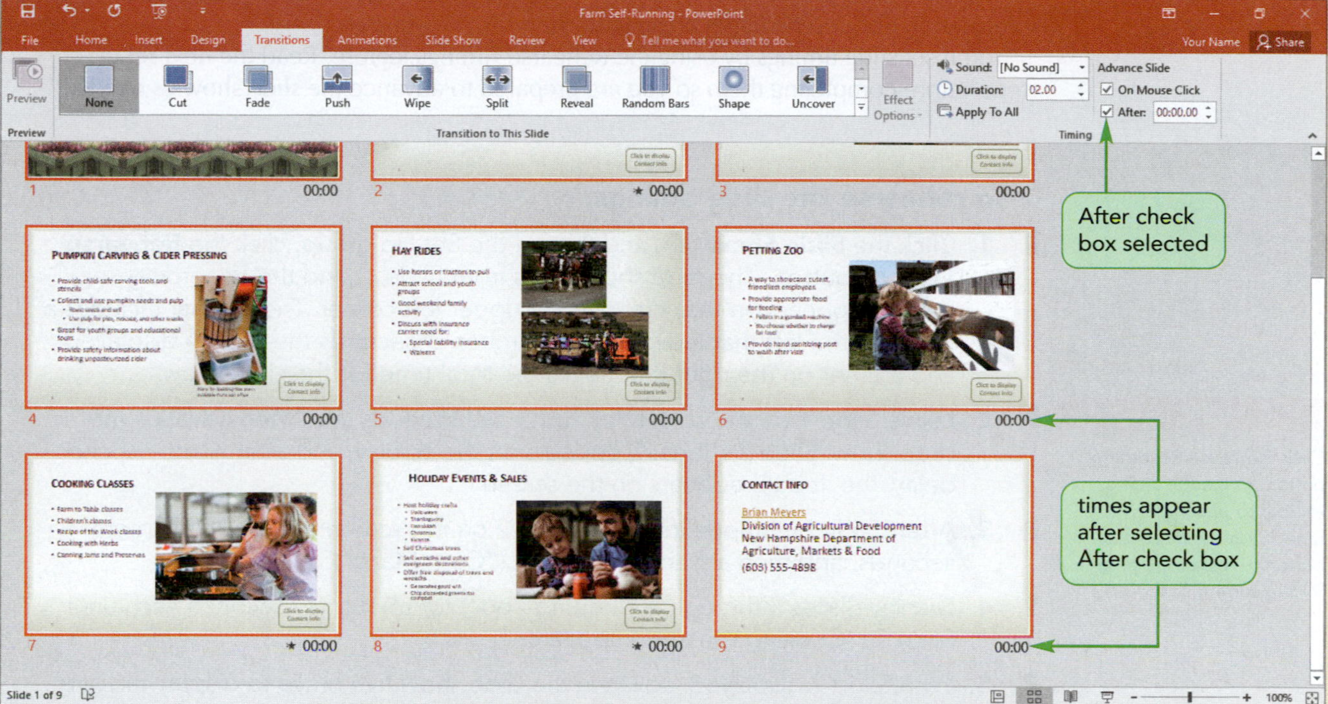

© iStock.com/cgering; © iStock.com/RonBailey; gvictoria/Shutterstock.com; Vicki L. Miller/Shutterstock.com; © iStock.com/Naomi Bassitt; Arina P Habich/Shutterstock.com; © iStock.com/mediaphotos

TIP

If you want to remove slide timings, select all the slides in Slide Sorter view, click the Transitions tab, and then click the After check box in the Timing group to deselect it.

8. In the Timing group, click the **After up arrow** four times to change the time to four seconds per slide. Under each slide thumbnail, the time changes to 00:04.
9. On the Quick Access Toolbar, click the **Start From Beginning** button. Watch as Slide 1 appears, then after four seconds, Slide 2 ("Ideas") appears. After one second, the lit bulb appears, and then three seconds later Slide 3 ("Corn Maze") appears.
10. Immediately click the mouse button. Slide 4 ("Pumpkin Carving & Cider Pressing") appears. You are able to advance the slide show by clicking the mouse button because you left the On Mouse Click check box on the Transitions tab selected.
11. Watch as the slide show advances through the rest of the slides. When Slide 7 ("Cooking Classes") appears, the animations occur automatically, even though they are set to start On Click. This is because the automatic timing overrides the On Click start setting.
12. When the black slide that indicates the end of the slide show appears, press the **spacebar**. The presentation appears in Slide Sorter view.

You could prevent viewers from advancing the slide show by clicking the mouse button by deselecting the On Mouse Click check box in the Timing group on the Transitions tab. Note, however, that the viewer will still be able to advance the slide show using the keyboard. If you do deselect the On Mouse Click check box, the viewer will still be able to click links and right-click the slide to display the shortcut menu.

Rehearsing Timings

Instead of guessing how much time each slide needs to remain displayed, you can ensure you have the right slide timing for each slide by rehearsing the slide show and then saving the slide timings. When you rehearse a slide show, the amount of time each slide is displayed during the slide show is recorded, as well as when you advance the slide show to play animations. See the Session 4.2 Visual Overview for more information about rehearsing presentations.

You'll set slide timings by using the Rehearse Timings feature. Read the next set of steps before completing them so you are prepared to advance the slide show as needed.

To rehearse the slide timings:

1. Click the **Slide Show** tab, and then in the Set Up group, click the **Rehearse Timings** button. The slide show starts from Slide 1, and the Recording toolbar appears on the screen in the upper-left corner. The toolbar includes a timer on the left that indicates the number of seconds the slide is displayed, and a timer on the right that tracks the total time for the slide show.
2. Leave Slide 1 on the screen for about five seconds, and then advance the slide show. Slide 2 ("Ideas") appears on the screen, and after a one-second delay, the lit bulb appears on the screen.
3. After the lit bulb appears, leave Slide 2 on the screen for about five more seconds, and then advance to Slide 3 ("Corn Maze").
4. Display Slides 3 through 6 ("Petting Zoo") for about five seconds each until Slide 7 ("Cooking Classes") appears.
5. With Slide 7 displayed, advance the slide show five times to display the five bulleted items, pausing briefly after each bulleted item appears, and then advance the slide show to display Slide 8 ("Holiday Events & Sales").
6. After the single wreath rolls onto the slide, wait five seconds, advance the slide show to display Slide 9, wait five seconds, and then advance the slide show once more. A dialog box opens asking if you want to save the timings.
7. Click the **Yes** button. The presentation appears in Slide Sorter view. The rehearsed time appears below each slide thumbnail. You can also see the timing assigned to the slides on the Transitions tab.
8. Click the **Transitions** tab, and then click the **Slide 1** thumbnail. In the Timing group, the recorded timing to the hundredth of a second for the selected slide appears in the After box. The rehearsed timing replaced the four-second slide timing you set previously.

TIP

Click the Pause Recording button on the Recording toolbar to pause the timer; click the Repeat button to restart the timer for the current slide.

After you rehearse a slide show, you should run it to evaluate the timings. If a slide stays on the screen for too much or too little time, stop the slide show, and then change that slide's time in the After box in the Timing group on the Transitions tab.

To play the slide show using the rehearsed slide timings:

1. On the Quick Access Toolbar, click the **Start From Beginning** button. The slide show starts and Slide 1 appears on the screen. The slide show advances to Slide 2 ("Ideas") automatically after the saved rehearsal timing for Slide 1 elapses. When Slide 7 ("Cooking Classes") appears, the animations occur automatically at the pace you rehearsed them.
2. When the final black slide appears, advance the slide show to end it.

Brian wants you to see what happens if the viewer tries to interact with the slide show and clicks one of the shapes that links to the last slide.

To interact with the self-running presentation:

1. Click the **Slide 2** thumbnail, and then on the status bar, click the **Slide Show** button. Slide 2 ("Ideas") appears in Slide Show view.
2. Move the mouse to display the pointer, and then in the lower-right corner, click the **Click to display Contact Info** shape. Slide 9 ("Contact Info") appears.
3. Press the **Backspace** key as many times as needed to display Slide 5 ("Hay Rides"). The slide show does not advance automatically to Slide 6.
4. Press the **spacebar**. Slide 6 ("Petting Zoo") appears, and the automatic timing is reactivated, so that after about five seconds, the next slide, Slide 7 ("Cooking Classes"), appears.
5. Right-click a blank area of the slide, and then on the shortcut menu, click **See All Slides**. The slides appear as thumbnails, similar to Slide Sorter view.
6. Click the **Slide 3** thumbnail. Slide 3 ("Corn Maze") appears in Slide Show view. After about five seconds, the slide show advances.
7. Press the **S** key. The slide show stops advancing automatically.
8. Press the **S** key again. The slide show resumes advancing automatically.
9. Press the **Esc** key to end the slide show.

TIP

You can also right-click a blank area of the screen, and then click Pause to stop the automatic slide advancement or click Resume to resume the automatic advancement.

Recording Narration and Timings

You can record narration to give viewers more information about your presentation's content. This is similar to what you did when you created a mix. When you use the Rehearse Timings command, only the amount of time a slide is displayed during the slide show and the time when animations occur are saved. If you want to record narration to play while a slide is displayed, you can use the Record Slide Show command. Using the Record Slide Show command is similar to the Rehearse Timings command, except you record narration while you rehearse the timing. When you record narration, the recorded audio for each slide is inserted on the slide as an audio object. Refer to the Session 4.2 Visual Overview for more information about recording narration.

If you add narration to a slide, you should not read the text on the slide—the viewers can read that for themselves. Your narration should provide additional information about the slides or instructions for the viewers as they watch the self-running presentation so that they know, for instance, that they can click action buttons to manually advance the presentation.

INSIGHT

Using the Record Sound Dialog Box

Another way to add narration is to click the Audio button in the Media group on the Insert tab, and then click Record Audio. To start recording, click the button with the red circle. When you are finished recording, click the button with the blue square.

REFERENCE

Recording Narration

- Click the Slide Show tab, click the Record Slide Show button arrow in the Set Up group, and then click Start Recording from Beginning or Start Recording from Current Slide.
- Speak into the microphone to record the narration for the current slide.
- Press the spacebar to go to the next slide (if desired), record the narration for that slide, and then continue, as desired, to other slides.
- End the slide show after recording the last narration; or continue displaying all the slides in the presentation for the appropriate amount of time, even if you do not add narration to each slide, and then end the slide show as you normally would.

Brian wants viewers to have some guidance in navigating through the presentation. You will record narration for Slides 1 and 2. You will also adjust the timing for these two slides to accommodate the accompanying narrations.

To record narration for Slides 1 and 2:

1. Make sure your computer is equipped with a microphone.

   Trouble? If your computer doesn't have a microphone, connect one, or check with your instructor or technical support person. If you can't connect a microphone, read the following steps but do not complete them.

2. On the ribbon, click the **Slide Show** tab.

TIP

To start recording on a slide other than Slide 1, click the Record Slide Show button arrow in the Set Up group, and then click Start Recording from Current Slide.

3. In the Set Up group, click the **Record Slide Show button arrow**, and then click **Start Recording from Beginning**. The Record Slide Show dialog box opens. You want to record both narration and timings, so you will not change the default settings.
4. Click the **Start Recording** button. The dialog box closes and the slide show starts from Slide 1. The Recording dialog box appears on the screen in the upper-left corner as it did when you rehearsed the slide timings.
5. Speak the following into the microphone: "**This presentation describes several ideas for increasing cash flow at your farm in the fall and early winter months. The presentation will advance automatically from one slide to the next.**"
6. Wait for a moment, press the **spacebar** to advance to Slide 2, wait for the light to "turn on," and then say into the microphone, "**To skip to the last slide, which contains contact information, click the button in the lower-right corner. To return to an earlier slide, click the right mouse button, click See All Slides, and then click the slide you want to view. To pause or resume the slide show, press S on the keyboard.**"
7. Wait five seconds, and then press the **Esc** key. The timer in the Recording toolbar stops, and then the newly recorded timings appear under the thumbnails for Slides 1 and 2 in Slide Sorter view.

   Trouble? If you advanced the slide show to Slide 4 instead of pressing the Esc key to end it, when Slide Sorter view appears again, double-click the Slide 3 thumbnail to display it in Normal view, click the Transitions tab, and then change the time in the After box to five seconds. Next, click the sound icon in the lower-right corner of Slide 3, and then press the Delete key to delete it. Return to Slide Sorter view.

TIP

To remove narration on a slide, delete the sound icon.

8. Double-click the **Slide 1** thumbnail to display it in Normal view, and then click the sound icon in the lower-right corner. This is the narration you recorded on Slide 1.
9. On the ribbon, click the **Audio Tools Playback** tab. In the Audio Options group, note that the start timing is set to Automatically, and the Hide During Show check box is selected.
10. On the Quick Access Toolbar, click the **Start From Beginning** button. The slide show starts, the recording that you made for Slide 1 plays, and then the slide show advances to Slide 2 a few seconds after the recorded time elapses. Five seconds after the recording on Slide 2 finishes playing, the slide show advances automatically to display Slide 3. The rest of the slides will continue to appear using the timings you set when you rehearsed the presentation.
11. Press the **Esc** key to end the slide show, and then save your changes.

Applying Kiosk Browsing

Brian wants you to set the presentation so that after the last slide appears, it will restart. He also doesn't want the viewer to be able to do anything other than click the links and press the Esc key to end the slide show. To do this, you'll set up the slide show to be browsed at a kiosk. If you apply kiosk browsing, every slide must have a link or timing assigned to it. Otherwise, after Slide 1 appears, and the viewer will be unable to advance the slide show.

To set up the presentation for browsing at a kiosk:

1. Click the **Slide Show** tab, and then in the Set Up group, click the **Set Up Slide Show** button. The Set Up Show dialog box opens. See Figure 4-23.

Figure 4-23 Set Up Show dialog box

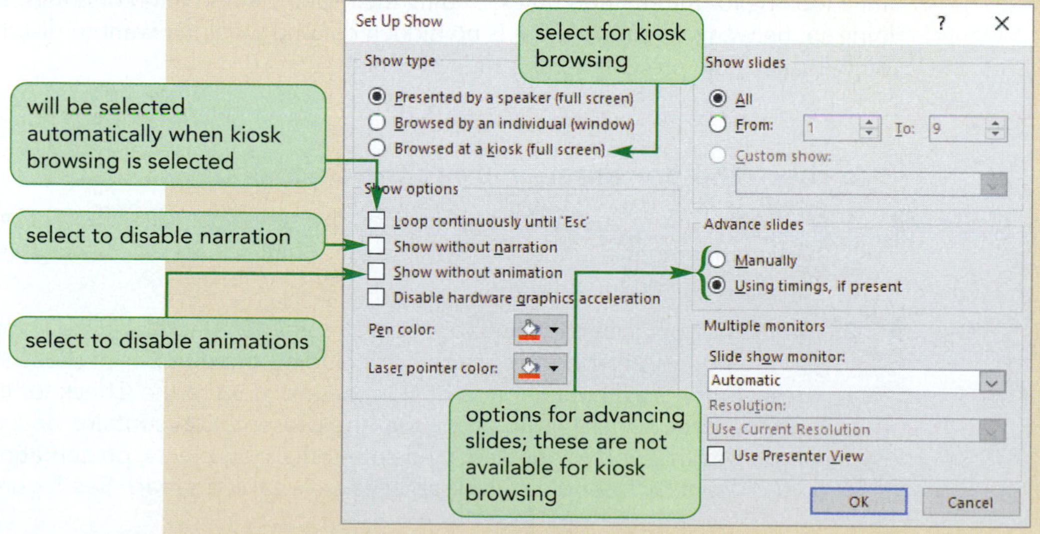

Note that the Advance slides section in the Set Up Show dialog box is similar to the options in the Timing group on the Transitions tab, but the options in this dialog box take precedence. For example, if the After check box is selected on the Transitions tab, but you select the Manually option button in this dialog box, the slide show will not advance automatically.

TIP

To change the resolution of the slide show, click the Slide show monitor arrow, click the monitor you are showing the slide show on, click the Resolution arrow, and then click the resolution you want to use.

2. In the Show type section, click the **Browsed at a kiosk (full screen)** option button. Under Show options, the Loop continuously until 'Esc' check box becomes selected. That option has also changed to light gray, indicating that you cannot deselect it. The options under Advance slides also cannot be changed now.
3. Click the **OK** button. The dialog box closes, and the presentation is set up for kiosk browsing.
4. Display **Slide 2** ("Ideas"), and then on the status bar, click the **Slide Show** button. Slide 2 appears in Slide Show view.
5. Click the **Click to display Contact Info** shape. Slide 9 ("Contact Info") appears.
6. Press the **spacebar**. The slide show does not advance, rather Slide 9 remains on the screen until the saved timing for Slide 9 elapses, and then the slide show automatically starts over with Slide 1.
7. After Slide 1 (the title slide) appears on the screen, press the **Esc** key to end the slide show.
8. Save the presentation.

Using the Document Inspector

The Document Inspector is a tool you can use to check a presentation for hidden data, such as the author's name and other personal information, objects that are in the presentation but are hidden or placed in the area next to a slide instead of on the slide, and speaker notes.

Brian wants to be able to send the presentation to small farmers who call into his office looking for information on expanding their selling season and offerings. Before doing so, he wants to ensure there is no hidden data he wouldn't want to distribute. You will check the presentation for hidden data.

To check the presentation using the Document Inspector:

1. With Slide 1 (the title slide) displayed, on the status bar, click the **Notes** button. Notice that there is a note on this slide that Brian added before he gave you the presentation to work with.
2. On the ribbon, click the **File** tab. The Info screen in Backstage view appears. On the right, file properties are listed, including the number of slides in the presentation and the author name. On the left, next to the Check for Issues button, a bulleted list informs you that the presentation contains document properties that you might want to delete, off-slide objects, presentation notes, and content that people with disabilities are unable to read. See Figure 4-24.

Figure 4-24 Info screen in Backstage view

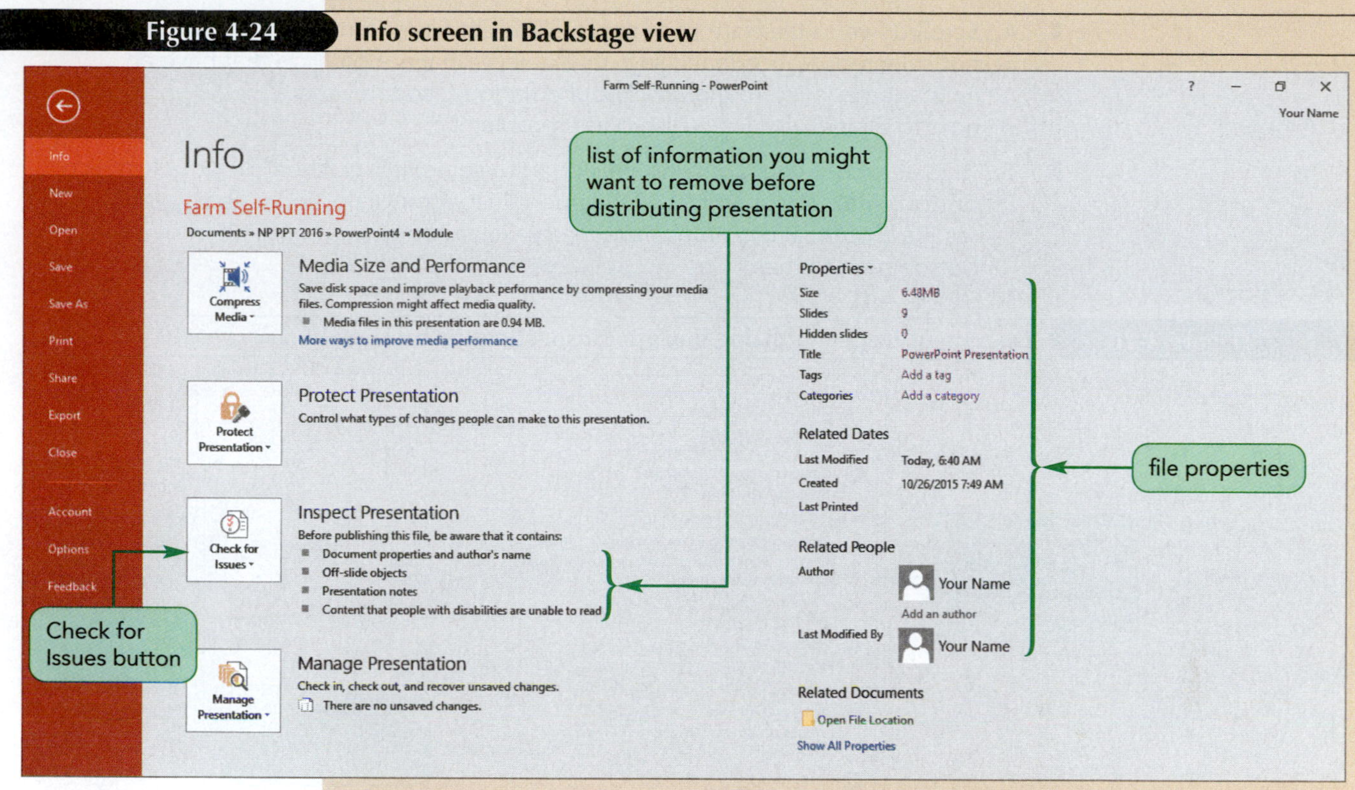

3. Click the **Check for Issues** button, and then click **Inspect Document**. The Document Inspector dialog box opens. All of the visible check boxes are selected. See Figure 4-25.

   Trouble? If a dialog box opens telling you that you need to save the presentation first, click the Yes button to save the presentation.

Figure 4-25 Document Inspector dialog box

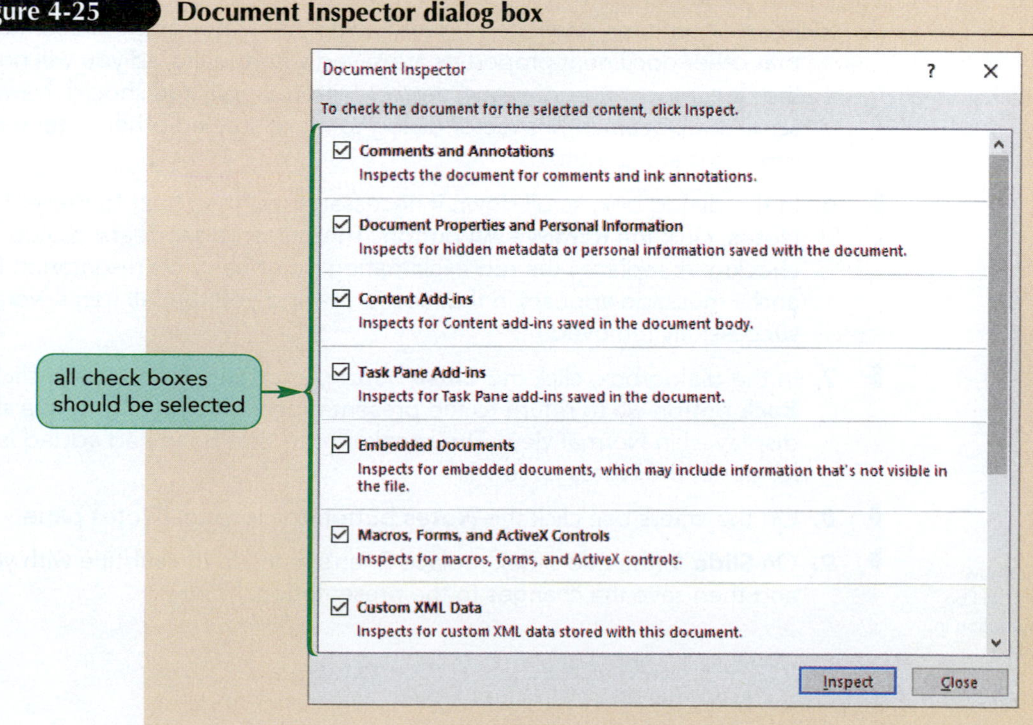

4. Scroll down to the bottom of the list. The Off-Slide Content check box is not selected. Notice that it says that objects that are off-slide that have an animation applied to them will not be flagged, so the wreath that is positioned next to Slide 8 will not be listed as a problem.

5. Click the **Off-Slide Content** check box to select it, and then click the **Inspect** button. After a moment, the Document Inspector dialog box displays the results. Potential problems have a red exclamation point and a Remove All button next to them. See Figure 4-26.

Figure 4-26 **Document Inspector dialog box after inspecting the presentation**

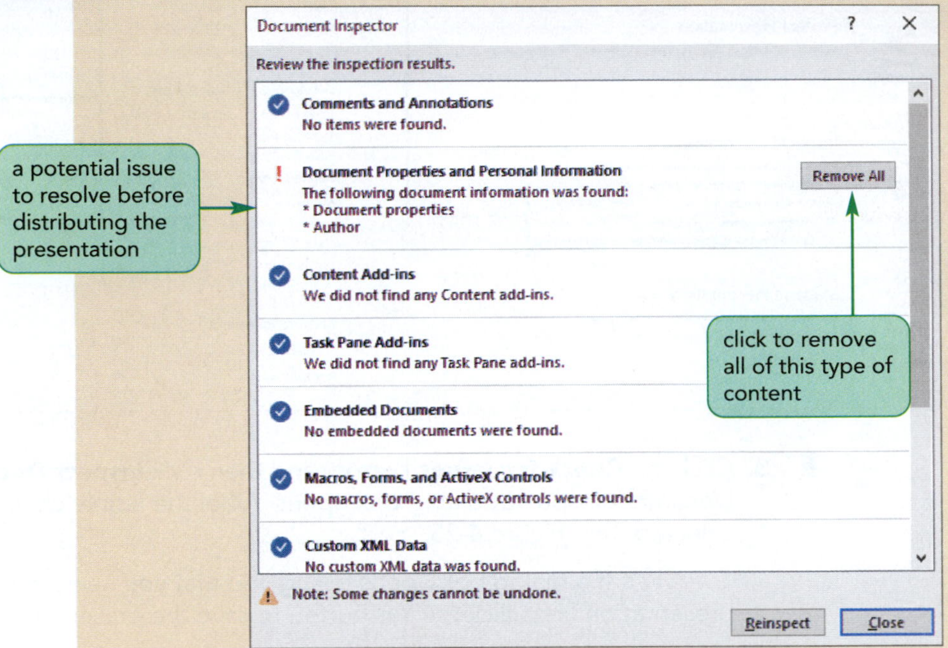

Brian doesn't mind that he is identified as the author of the presentation or that other document properties are saved with the file, so you will not remove the document properties and personal information. You should, however, scroll the Document Inspector dialog to make sure no other potential problems are identified.

6. In the dialog box, scroll down if necessary, and then next to Presentation Notes, click the **Remove All** button. The button disappears, a blue checkmark replaces the red exclamation point next to Presentation Notes, and a message appears in that section telling you that all items were successfully removed.

7. In the dialog box, click the **Close** button, and then, if necessary, click the **Back** button to return to the presentation with Slide 1 (the title slide) displayed in Normal view. The speaker note that Brian had added is no longer in the Notes pane.

8. On the status bar, click the **Notes** button to close the Notes pane.

9. On **Slide 1** (the title slide), replace Brian's name in the subtitle with your name, and then save the changes to the presentation.

Save the changes now because next you will be saving the presentation in a different format.

Packaging a Presentation for CD

Brian will present the slide show at various conventions and exhibitions around New Hampshire. He plans to bring his own laptop, but he knows it's a good idea to have backups. One way to back up a presentation is to use the Package a Presentation for CD feature. This puts all the fonts and linked files and anything else needed to burn and run the presentation on a CD or DVD or in a folder that you can put on a USB drive.

To package the presentation for CD:

1. Click the **File** tab, and then in the navigation bar, click **Export**. The Export screen appears in Backstage view.
2. Click **Package Presentation for CD**. The right side of the screen changes to display a description of this command.
3. Click the **Package for CD** button. The Package for CD dialog box opens. See Figure 4-27.

Figure 4-27 Package for CD dialog box

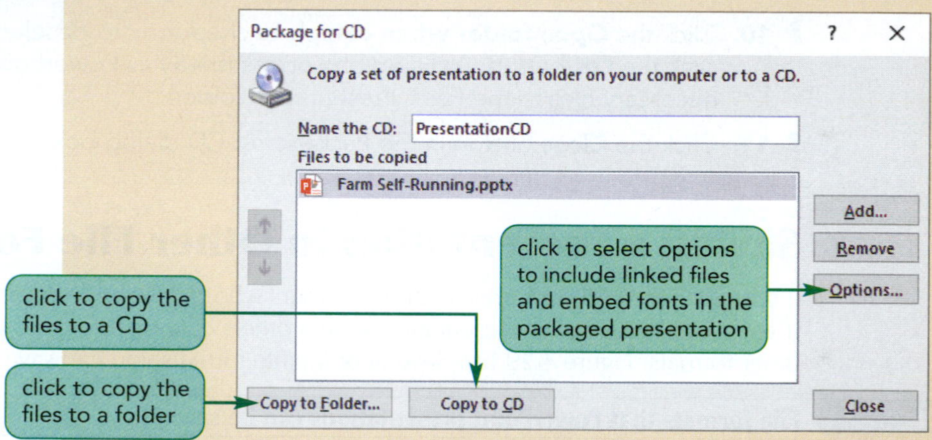

4. Click the **Options** button. The Options dialog box opens. See Figure 4-28.

Figure 4-28 Options dialog box when packaging a presentation for CD

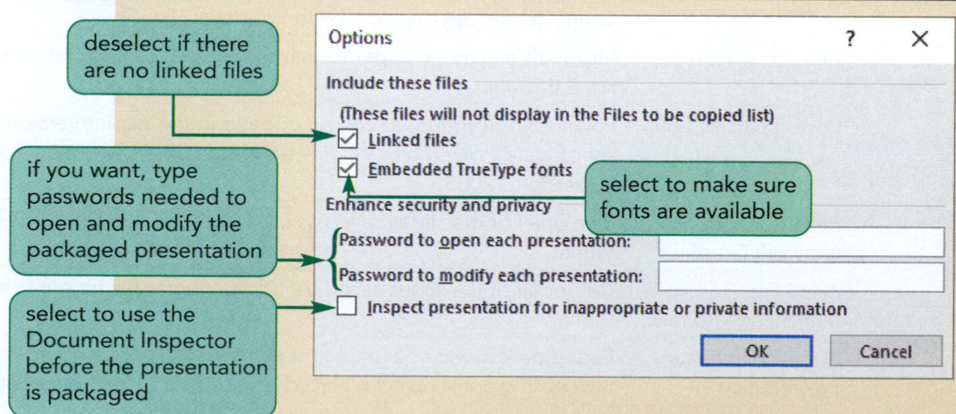

You will keep the Embedded TrueType fonts check box selected to ensure that you will have the fonts used in the presentation available if you run the packaged presentation on another computer. If your presentation contained

links to any other files, you would keep the Linked files check box selected to include those files in the package. However, the presentation file does not contain any linked files, so you will deselect that check box.

5. Click the **Linked files** check box to deselect it.
6. Click the **OK** button. The Package for CD dialog box is visible again.
7. Click the **Copy to Folder** button. The Copy to Folder dialog box opens. The default name for the folder you will create to hold the files of the packaged presentation—PresentationCD—appears in the Folder name box.

   Trouble? If you are copying your presentation to a CD, click the Cancel button to close this dialog box, insert a blank CD in the CD drive, click the Copy to CD button, click the No button when the dialog box opens asking if you want to copy the same files to another CD, and then skip to Step 10.
8. Click in the **Folder name** box, delete the text, and then type **Farm Presentation**.
9. Click the **Browse** button to open the Choose Location dialog box, navigate to the folder where you are storing your files, and then click the **Select** button. You return to the Copy to Folder dialog box.
10. Click the **Open folder when complete** check box to deselect it, and then click the **OK** button. A dialog box opens briefly as PowerPoint copies all the necessary files to the Farm Presentation folder.
11. Click the **Close** button in the Package for CD dialog box.

Saving a Presentation in Other File Formats

If you need to send your presentation to others who do not have PowerPoint 2016, or if you want to save your presentation so that others cannot change it, you can save it in other formats. Figure 4-29 lists several of the file formats you can save a presentation in.

Figure 4-29 File formats that PowerPoint presentations can be saved in

File Format	Description
PDF	Portable Document File format, a file format that can be opened on any make or model of computer, as long as a free PDF reader program is installed, such as the Reader app included with Windows 10.
XPS	Microsoft electronic paper format that displays the slides as a list that you can scroll through.
PowerPoint 97-2003	PowerPoint format that can be opened in the earlier versions of PowerPoint, specifically, PowerPoint 97, PowerPoint 2000, PowerPoint 2002, and PowerPoint 2003.
PNG Portable Network Graphics	One or all of the slides saved as individual graphic files in the PNG graphic format.
JPEG File Interchange Format	One or all of the slides saved as individual graphic files in the JPG graphic format.
PowerPoint Picture Presentation	Each slide is saved as a graphic object (as if you took a photo of each slide) and then each graphic object is placed on a slide in a new PowerPoint presentation.
PowerPoint Show	PowerPoint format that automatically opens in Slide Show view if you double-click the file in a File Explorer window.
OpenDocument Presentation	OpenDocument format, a free format that can be read by other presentation programs.
Outline/RTF	The text of the presentation is saved in a Word document.

INSIGHT

Checking a Presentation for Compatibility with Earlier Versions of PowerPoint

If you want to save a presentation in a format compatible with earlier versions of PowerPoint, you should first use the Compatibility Checker to identify features in the presentation that are incompatible with earlier versions of PowerPoint so that you can decide whether to modify the presentation. To do this, click the File tab, and then on the Info screen in Backstage view, click the Check for Issues button, and then click Check Compatibility.

Because the PDF format can be opened on any make or model of computer, it is a good format to choose if you don't know whether the people to whom you distribute the presentation have PowerPoint available. In addition, recipients cannot edit the presentation when it is saved as a PDF. When you save a presentation as a PDF, you can choose the number of slides to include on each page, similar to choosing the number of slides per handout when you print handouts.

Brian wants to be able to email the presentation to small farmers when they contact him for information about expanding their season or services. To ensure that the presentation can be opened and viewed by anyone, regardless of the type of computer they have and the programs they have access to, he asks you to save the presentation in the PDF format. You will save the presentation in the PDF format as a handout with all nine slides on a page.

TIP

You can save a presentation in different file types using the options on the Export screen in Backstage view.

To publish the presentation in PDF format:

1. Click the **File** tab to open Backstage view, and then click **Export** in the navigation bar. The Export screen appears with Create PDF/XPS Document selected.
2. Click the **Create PDF/XPS** button. Backstage view closes, and the Publish as PDF or XPS dialog box opens with PDF listed in the Save as type box. See Figure 4-30.

   Trouble? If XPS appears in the Save as type box instead of PDF, click the Save as type arrow, and then click PDF.

Figure 4-30 Publish as PDF or XPS dialog box

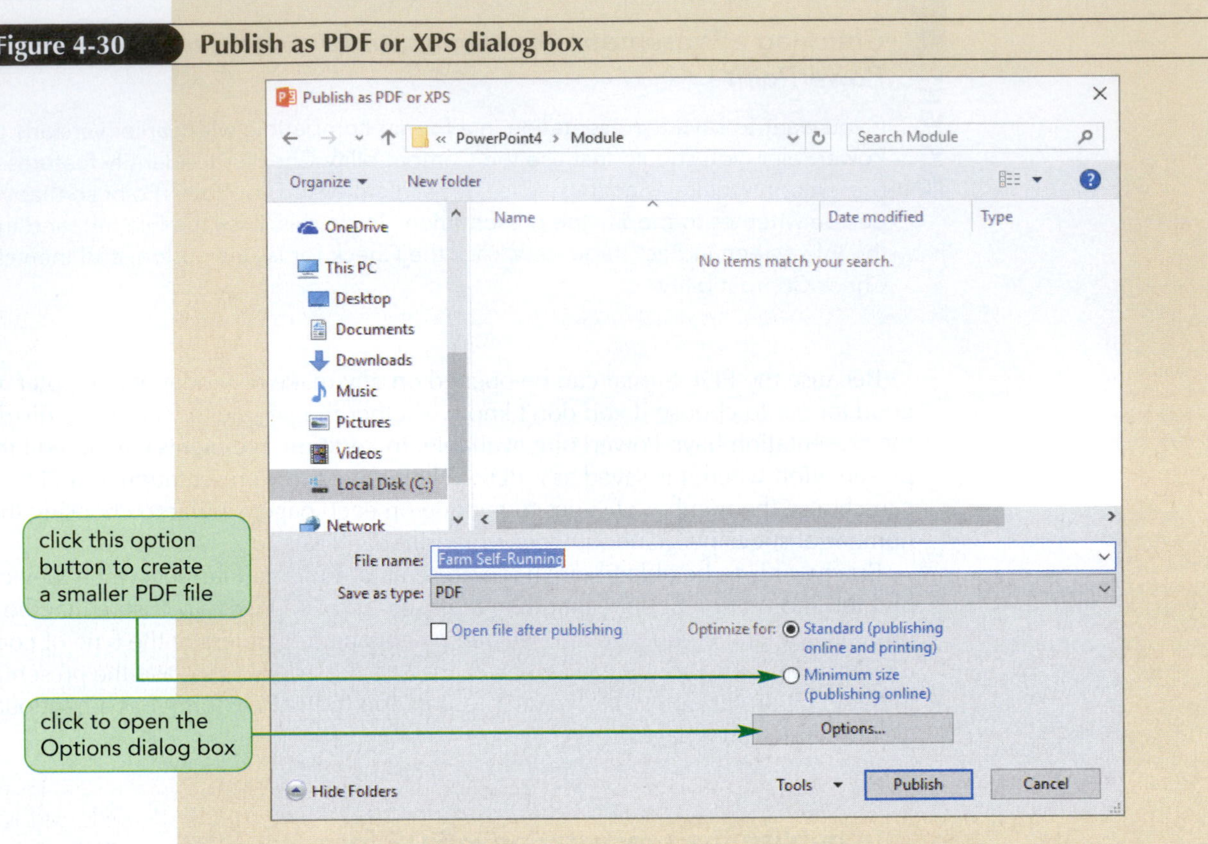

3. Navigate to the location where you are storing your files, if necessary, and then change the filename to **Farm PDF**. You want to create a smaller file size suitable for attaching to an email message.
4. Click the **Minimum size (publishing online)** option button. Now you need to set the option to save it as a handout.
5. Click the **Options** button. The Options dialog box opens. See Figure 4-31.

Figure 4-31 Options dialog box for saving a presentation as a PDF file

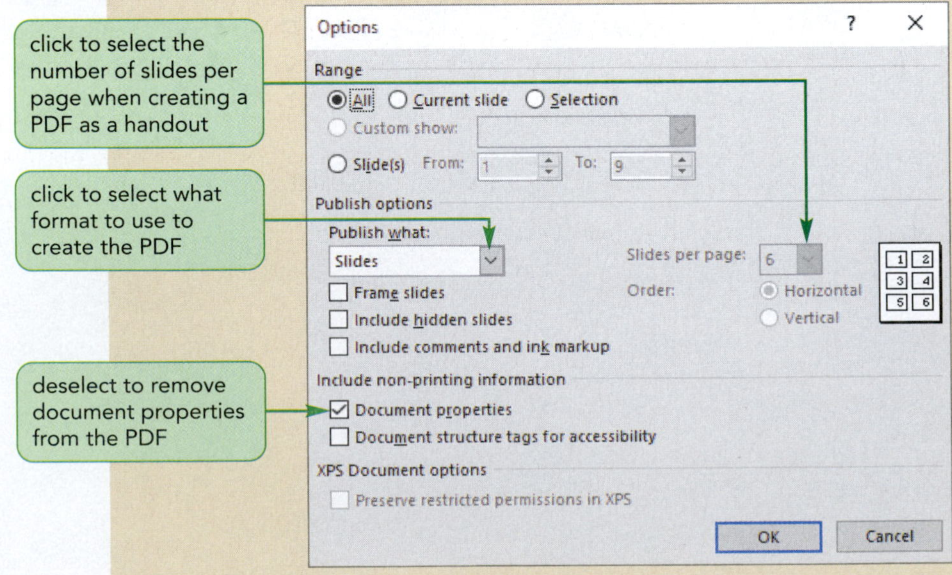

6. In the Publish options section, click the **Publish what** arrow, and then click **Handouts**.
7. In the Publish options section, click the **Slides per page** arrow, and then click **9**. Brian doesn't want the document properties to be included.
8. In the Include non-printing information section, click the **Document properties** check box to deselect it.
9. Click the **OK** button.
10. In the Publish as PDF or XPS dialog box, click the **Open file after publishing** check box to deselect it, if necessary.
11. Click the **Publish** button. A dialog box briefly appears as the presentation is saved in PDF format.

INSIGHT

Saving a Presentation as a Video

You can create a video of your presentation that can be viewed the same way you view any digital video, in an app such as the Movies & TV app included with Windows 10. On the Export screen in Backstage view, click Create a Video. Click the Presentation Quality box to select the video quality you want. Click the box below the box listing the quality to choose whether to use recorded timings and narrations. Then, in the Seconds spent on each slide box, set the number of seconds you want each slide to be displayed if you are not using timings and narrations or for any slides that do not have a saved time. Click the Create Video button to open the Save As dialog box. The MPEG-4 Video file type appears by default in the Save as type box, however, you can change that by clicking the Save as type arrow and then clicking Windows Media Video.

You have finished the Farm Self-Running presentation and ensured that Brian has the presentation in the formats he needs.

REVIEW

Session 4.2 Quick Check

1. How do you change the amount of time a slide stays on the screen during Slide Show view in a self-running presentation?
2. Do links work in a self-running presentation?
3. How do you prevent viewers from using normal methods of advancing the slide show in a self-running presentation?
4. What does the Document Inspector reveal?
5. Why would you package a presentation to a CD?
6. What does the Compatibility Checker reveal?

PRACTICE

Review Assignments

Data Files needed for the Review Assignments: Entrance.jpg, Maze1.pptx; Maze2.pptx

Some small farmers have asked Brian Meyers for suggestions on how to create a corn maze. Specifically, farmers have asked about how to design and build the maze, how to monitor customers in the maze, how to advertise the attraction, and how to set ticket prices. Brian created a presentation that he plans to use when he describes building a corn maze, and he wants your help to finish it. Complete the following steps:

1. Open the file **Maze1**, located in the PowerPoint4 > Review folder included with your Data Files, add your name as the subtitle, and then save the presentation as **Maze Suggestions** to the location where you are saving your files.
2. On Slide 2, display the guides, and then reposition the horizontal guide at 0.42 inches below the middle and the vertical guide at 2.17 inches to the right of center.
3. On Slide 2, position the maze to the left of the slide, keeping its top aligned with the bottom of the title text placeholder. Apply the Lines motion path animation with the Right effect. Adjust the ending of the lines motion path so that the center of the maze is on the intersection of the guides.
4. Add the Spin emphasis animation to the maze. Change its start timing to With Previous, and then change its duration to 1.75 seconds.
5. Change the start timing of the Lines animation to After Previous, and then view Slides 2 and 3 in Slide Show view to ensure that that the motion path applied to the maze on Slide 2 ends at the correct point on the slide so that that when Slide 3 transitions onto the screen it appears seamless.
6. Hide the guides.
7. On Slide 8 ("Pricing"), add the Zoom entrance animation to the text box containing the green dollar sign. Set the Zoom animation to occur when the viewer clicks the title text box.
8. Add a gradient fill to the background of all the slides in the presentation. Change the color of the Stop 1 of 4 tab to Gold, Accent 4, Darker 25%. (Note that after you apply this color, the name of the color changes to Dark Yellow, Accent 4, Darker 25%.) Change the color of the other three tabs to White, Background 1, Darker 5%. Change the Direction to Linear Right, and then change the position of the Stop 2 of 4 tab to 11%.
9. Add the photo **Entrance**, located in the PowerPoint4 > Review folder included with your Data Files, to the background of Slide 1 (the title slide). Tile the picture as texture, and then change the scale to 18% in both directions. Apply the vertical mirror effect.
10. Change the transparency of the photo background on Slide 1 to 50%.
11. On Slide 3 ("Plan"), format each of the bulleted items to links to the corresponding slides.
12. On Slide 4 ("Design and Build"), insert the Octagon shape, and then type **Plan** in the shape. Change the font size to 20 points. Resize the shape so it is 0.5 inches high and 0.9 inches wide. Apply the Intense Effect – Gold, Accent 4 shape style, and then position the shape in the lower-right corner of the slide so there is about one-eighth of an inch between the shape and the right side of the slide and between the shape and the bottom of the slide.
13. Format the Plan shape as a link to the previous slide.
14. Copy the Plan shape on Slide 4 ("Design and Build") to Slide 5 ("Operation"). Edit the link so that it links to Slide 3 ("Plan"), and then copy the Plan shape on Slide 5 to Slides 6 ("Overlooks"), 7 ("Marketing and Insurance"), and 8 ("Pricing").
15. On Slide 3 ("Plan"), insert the End action button to link to the last slide. Format the action button with the Colored Outline – Gold, Accent 4 shape style. Resize the action button so it is one-half inch square, and then position it so that its top is aligned with the bottom of the maze and there is about the same amount of space between its right side and the edge of the slide and between its bottom and the bottom of the slide.
16. Change the color palette so that links are Green, Accent 6, Darker 50%, and then delete the custom palette from your computer.

17. Save the presentation and close it.
18. Open the presentation **Maze2**, add your name as the subtitle, and then save it as **Maze Self-Running** to the location where you are saving your files.
19. Rehearse the timings, displaying the content of each slide for about five seconds, except Slide 2. Display Slide 2 only as long as it takes for the maze to slide onto the screen (one to two seconds) and then immediately display Slide 3. On Slide 3, after the path through the maze, the title, the bulleted list, and the TIPS shape appear, wait five seconds. On Slide 8, wait for the dollar sign to appear, and then wait five seconds.
20. Change the timing of Slide 9 to 10 seconds.
21. Display Slide 3 ("Plan"), and then start recording narration from the current slide. After the title, bulleted list, and TIPS shape appear on the screen, say, **"To skip to the last slide, which contains tips for running the corn maze attraction, click the button in the lower-right corner."** Wait five seconds, and then press the Esc key.
22. Set up the show to be browsed at a kiosk.
23. Run the Document Inspector and then remove anything found, except do not remove the document properties and personal information.
24. Save the changes to the presentation, and then package the presentation to a folder stored in the location where you are saving your files without including linked files. Name the folder **Maze Presentation**, and do not open the folder when complete.
25. Save the presentation file as a PDF named **Maze PDF** in the location where you are saving your files. Use the Minimum size option, remove the document properties, and create a handout with nine slides per page.
26. Close the file.

APPLY

Case Problem 1

Data Files needed for this Case Problem: Parasail.pptx

Carolina Coast Parasailing Ellie Nowicki founded Carolina Coast Parasailing on Hilton Head Island, South Carolina, in 2009. To promote her business, Ellie created a presentation that she gives at travel conventions and tradeshows. She also wants to run it on a kiosk at the hotels on the island. She asked you to help her finish the presentation. Complete the following steps:

1. Open the file **Parasail**, located in the PowerPoint 4 > Case1 folder included with your Data Files, add your name as the subtitle on the title slide, and then save it as **Carolina Coast Parasailing** in the location where you are saving your files.
2. Add a gradient to the background of all the slides. Set the first gradient tab to the Black, Background 1 color and position it at 10%. Change the color of the rest of the gradient tabs to Dark Teal, Background 2 color. Change the position of the second gradient tab to 65%.
3. On Slide 2 ("Come Fly with Us!"), insert the Round Diagonal Corner Rectangle shape and resize it so it is 1.3 inches high and 3.7 inches wide. Fill the shape with the Gold, Accent 5 color, and then apply the Cool Slant bevel effect. Type **Click here to reserve your adventure!** in the shape, change the font size to 20 points, and format the text as bold.
4. On Slide 2, display the guides, and then drag the horizontal guide down to 2.58 inches below center. (Note that in this presentation, this creates a second horizontal guide.) Position the shape so its center is aligned with the bulleted list on the right and so its bottom edge is aligned with the horizontal guide you dragged.
5. On Slide 2, format the shape you drew as a link to the webpage **www.carolinacoastparasailing.example.com/reservations.**

6. Copy the shape you created on Slide 2 to Slide 6 ("Reserve Today!"). On Slide 6, resize the shape so it is two inches high and four inches wide and increase the font size to 32 points. Drag the vertical guide to the right to position it 5.50 inches to the right of center, and then position the shape so its bottom edge is aligned with the horizontal guide in the center of the slide and its right edge is aligned with the vertical guide you just dragged.
7. Customize the color palette so that links are the Teal, Text 2, Lighter 60% color, and then delete the custom palette from your computer.
8. On Slide 3 ("Prices"), drag the silhouette image of the boat towing a parasailer to the left of the slide, keeping it aligned with the bottom of the slide. Animate the image with the Lines motion path and the Right effect, adjusting the end position of the path so it is on top of the vertical guide in the center of the slide. Set this animation to occur automatically after the previous action.
9. On Slide 3, add a second Lines motion path animation with the Right effect to the image. Position the end point of the second motion path to the right of the slide so that the faint image of the graphic is all the way off of the slide. Then adjust the starting point of the second Lines motion path so it is on top of the vertical guide in the center of the slide. Change the start timing of this animation to After Previous with a delay of one second.
10. On Slide 3, apply the Bold Reveal emphasis animation to the text box that contains the text "Price includes." Move this animation earlier so that the first Lines animation applied to the boat occurs first, then the emphasis animation applied to the text box, and finally the second Lines animation applied to the boat. Set the emphasis animation to occur automatically after the previous action with a delay of one-half second.
11. On Slide 4 ("Safety"), drag the life preserver off the slide to the left, keeping the top of the object aligned with the top of the slide. Apply the Lines motion path animation with the Right effect. Adjust the end point of the motion path so it is on top of the vertical guide positioned 5.50 inches to the right of center. Change the duration of the animation to 2.25 seconds, and change the start timing to After Previous.
12. On Slide 4, add the Spin emphasis animation to the life preserver. Set the Spin animation to occur at the same time as the Lines animation.
13. Rehearse the timings. Leave Slide 1 (the title slide) and Slide 2 ("Come Fly with Us!") displayed for five seconds. After Slide 3 ("Prices") appears, wait for the boat to move onto the slide, then for the text in the text box on the right to change to bold, then for the boat to leave the slide, and then wait for five seconds. After Slide 4 ("Safety") appears, wait for the life preserver to appear on the slide, wait five seconds and then advance the slide show. Leave the last two slides displayed for about five seconds each.
14. Record the presentation from the beginning. After Slide 1 appears, say, **"Carolina Coast Parasailing, where the fun never stops!"** Wait five seconds, and then press the Esc key to end the slide show.
15. Change the timing of Slide 2 ("Come Fly with Us!") to 10 seconds.
16. Set the slide show to be browsed at a kiosk.
17. Run the Document Inspector to remove notes, and then save the changes to the presentation.
18. Package the presentation in a folder named **Parasailing Presentation** in the location where you are saving your files. Do not include linked files.
19. Save the presentation as a PDF named **Carolina Coast Parasailing PDF** in the location where you are saving your files. Use the Minimum size option, remove the document properties, and create a handout with six slides per page.
20. Close the presentation.

TROUBLESHOOT

Case Problem 2

Data Files needed for this Case Problem: Race.pptx, Runners.jpg

Road Race Management Fiona Spaulding works for Road Race Management, a company in Wilmington, Delaware, that organizes road races for organizations and cities or provides guidance so that they can organize the races themselves. Harborside Homeless Shelter recently asked Road Race Management for assistance in organizing a new, annual road race whose proceeds will benefit the shelter. Fiona prepared a PowerPoint presentation and asked you to help her complete it. Complete the following steps:

1. Open the presentation **Race**, located in the PowerPoint4 > Case2 folder included with your Data Files, add your name as the subtitle, and then save the presentation with the filename **Race Planning**.
2. Add the picture **Runners**, located in the PowerPoint4 > Case2 folder, as the slide background. Change the transparency to 80%, and apply this to all the slides.
3. On Slide 1 (the title slide), change the background's transparency to 25%.
4. **Troubleshoot** On Slide 1, evaluate the problem changing the background caused and make any adjustments needed to correct this.
5. On Slide 6 ("Registration"), format the "Running in the USA" subbullet so it is a link to **www.runningintheusa.com**; format the "Road Race Runner" subbullet so it is a link to **www.roadracerunner.com**; and format the subbullet "Runner's World" so it is a link to **www.runnersworld.com**.
6. **Troubleshoot** On Slide 6, evaluate the problem formatting the text as links caused and correct it.
7. On Slide 7 ("Budget Items"), display the guides. Position the horizontal guide 3.58 inches below the center.
8. Reposition the text box that contains "Try to find a corporate sponsor" so its bottom edge is aligned with the horizontal guide and so its center is aligned with the vertical guide.
9. Animate the text box that contains "Try to find a corporate sponsor" with the Grow & Turn entrance animation, and then make the medal the trigger for this animation.
10. Add the Wave emphasis animation to the text box that contains "Try to find a corporate sponsor." Set its start timing to After Previous. Move this animation later so that it appears after the Trigger animation in the Animation Pane.
11. On Slide 7, animate the left gray and red ribbon with the Wipe entrance animation and the From Top effect, and set its start timing so that it animates automatically after the previous action. Then animate the right gray and red ribbon with the Wipe entrance animation and the From Bottom effect, and set its start timing so that it animates automatically after the previous action.
12. On Slide 8 ("Get the Word Out"), start recording from the current slide and say, **"Although every planning step is important, if you don't let people know about your new race, you won't have any participants."** Press the Esc key to end the slide show.
13. On Slide 9 ("Contact Information"), change the background to the Tan, Background 2 color.
14. Change the color palette so that links are Aqua, Accent 5, Darker 50%, and then delete the custom palette from your computer.
15. Save the changes to the presentation, and then close it.

CHALLENGE

Case Problem 3

Data Files needed for this Case Problem: Coach.pptx

Kid Coach Mara Riggs and John Sunjata own Kid Coach, a company that runs sports clinics for children in Thousand Oaks, California. They periodically visit schools and parent groups to explain the programs they offer. Mara created a presentation that they can use during these visits. She asked you to help her finish the presentation. Complete the following steps:

1. Open the presentation **Coach**, located in the PowerPoint4 > Case3 folder included with your Data Files, add your name as the subtitle, and then save the presentation with the filename **Kid Coach**.
2. On Slide 1 (the title slide), change the slide background to a gradient fill. Change the color of the Stop 1 of 4 gradient tab to the Turquoise, Accent 1, Darker 50% color. Change the color of the Stop 4 of 4 gradient tab to the White, Background 1, Darker 5% color. Change the color of the Stop 3 of 4 gradient tab to the Turquoise, Accent 1, Lighter 80% color, and then change its position to 97%. Change the color of the Stop 2 of 4 gradient tab to the Turquoise, Accent 1, Lighter 40% color, and then change its position to 92%. Change the type to Rectangular and the direction to From Center, if necessary. Do not apply the background to all the slides.
3. On Slide 1, change the color of the title and subtitle text to White, Background 1, Darker 5%.
4. On Slide 3 ("Sports Offered"), format each of the images as a link to the appropriate slide.
5. On Slide 4 ("Baseball Softball"), drag the white baseball off of the slide to the left and position it below the bottom-left corner of the slide. Apply the Lines animation to the baseball with the Up effect. Change the start timing to After Previous and the duration to 1.50. Do the same thing to the yellow softball, except position it off of the slide above the upper-left corner of the slide and leave the Lines effect as Down.
6. Create a copy of the vertical guide and drag the copy to 3.50 inches to the right of center. Create a copy of the horizontal guide and drag the copy to 1.75 inches above center. Then create another copy of the horizontal guide and drag it to 1.50 inches below center.
7. On Slide 4, adjust the ending points of both motion paths so they are each a diagonal line that ends on top of the intersections of the guides above and below center with the baseball ending above center and the softball ending below center.
8. On Slide 5 ("Lacrosse Soccer"), apply the entrance animation Fade to the lacrosse stick, set the start timing to After Previous, and set a delay of one-half second.
9. On Slide 5, drag the center horizontal guide down so it is 2.92 inches below center. (It will be aligned with the bottom of the blue and gray rectangles.)

Explore 10. Change the color of the bottom horizontal guide to red. (*Hint*: Right-click the guide.)

11. Drag the soccer ball off of the slide to the left keeping the ball between the two horizontal guides. (*Hint*: Press and hold the Alt key to have the ball not snap to the grid as you position it.)
12. Apply the Lines motion path animation to the soccer ball, and change its effect to Right. Drag the ending point of this animation to the right until the right edge of the soccer ball is touching the left side of the gray bar on the right side of the slide. (*Hint*: Again, press and hold the Alt key if needed to position the ending point where you want it.)
13. On Slide 5, apply a second Lines animation to the soccer ball, and change its effect to Left. Position its starting point on top of the ending point of the first motion path, and then position its end point on top of the vertical guide at 3.50 inches to the right of center.
14. On Slide 5, change the duration of the two Lines animations to one second. Set the start timing of both Lines animations to After Previous.

Explore 15. On Slide 5, add a 0.75-second bounce effect to the Lines animation. (*Hint*: Click the Dialog Box Launcher in the Animation group on the Animations tab to open the Effect Options dialog box for the Lines animation.)

16. On Slide 6 ("Basketball Volleyball"), drag the basketball straight up so it is above the slide, and then apply the Lines motion path animation. Drag the end point of the motion path down so that the bottom of the basketball is touching the bottom horizontal guide. Change its start timing to After Previous and its duration to 1.50 seconds.
17. On Slide 6, drag the vertical guide that is in the center of the slide to the left until it is 0.13 inches to the left of center. Apply a second Lines motion path to the basketball with the Right effect, and change its start timing to After Previous and its duration to 0.75 seconds. Adjust the start point so it is aligned with the end point of the first Lines animation that you applied to the basketball. Adjust the end point of the second Lines animation so that the right side of the basketball is touching the vertical guide you just moved.
18. On Slide 6, add the Spin emphasis animation as the third animation applied to the basketball. Change its start timing to With Previous and its duration to 0.75 seconds.
19. On Slide 6, drag the volleyball off of the slide to the left. Apply the Arcs motion path animation with the Up effect to the volleyball. Drag the end point of the arc path so that the bottom of the faint image of the volleyball is aligned with the bottom horizontal guide and the ending point is on top of the vertical guide positioned at 3.50 inches to the right of center. Finally, drag the top-middle sizing handle of the arc animation up until the top of the rectangle that defines the arc object is aligned with the smart guide that appears above "Basketball" above the bulleted list on the left. Change the start timing to After Previous.
20. On Slide 7 ("FAQs"), apply the Appear entrance animation to each answer, and then set the corresponding question for each question to be the trigger for that animation.

Explore 21. On Slide 8 ("Registration"), record the following: **"Go to www.kidcoach.example.com to register."** (*Hint*: Use the Audio button in the Media group on the Insert tab.) Set the audio clip to play automatically and hide it during the slide show.

22. Save the changes to the presentation, and then use the Document Inspector to remove document properties and the author's name.

Explore 23. Save Slide 1 (the title slide) as a PNG Portable Network Graphics file named **Kid Coach Slide 1** in the location where you are saving your files.

24. Save the presentation as a handout PDF with nine slides per page named **Kid Coach PDF** to the location where you are saving your files. Use the minimum size for publishing.
25. Save the changes, and then close the file.

CHALLENGE

Case Problem 4

Data Files needed for this Case Problem: Starlight.pptx

Starlight Fundraising Matt Elliott is an account manager at Starlight Fundraising, a company in Boulder, Colorado, that runs fundraisers for schools and nonprofit organizations. Starlight offers a wide variety of products that people can sell. All fundraising companies give a percentage of the profits to the schools and organizations, but the percentage that Starlight returns to the groups is among the highest. One of Matt's jobs is to convince schools to allow Starlight to run their fundraisers. He asked you to help him prepare his presentation. Complete the following steps:

1. Open the presentation **Starlight**, located in the PowerPoint4 > Case4 folder included with your Data Files, add your name as the subtitle, and then save the presentation with the filename **Starlight Fundraising**.
2. Display the guides, and then drag the horizontal guide up to 2.00 inches above the center and the vertical guide right to 4.29 inches to the right of the center.
3. On Slide 1 (the title slide), drag the picture of the star that is to the right of the slide title off of the slide to the right, and position it so that it is top-aligned with the subtitle text box.
4. Apply the Lines motion path animation to the star with the Up effect.

5. Change the ending of the motion path so it is on top of the intersection of the guides, and then hide the guides. Change the duration of the Lines animation to 0.50 seconds.
6. Add the Grow/Shrink emphasis animation to the picture of the star. Change its duration to one second, and set it to occur automatically after the previous action.

Explore 7. On Slide 1 only, add the 90% pattern to the slide background using the Foreground color Dark Blue, Text 2.

Explore 8. On Slide 2, format each shape in the SmartArt as a link to the corresponding slide.

9. On Slide 2, add the End action button that links to the last slide. Resize it so it is 0.6 inches high and one inch wide. Apply the Semitransparent – Blue, Accent 1, No Outline shape style to the action button. Position the action button in the lower-left corner of the slide about one-eighth inch from the left and bottom edges of the slide.
10. On Slide 3 ("Large Variety of Items"), open the Selection pane to see that each picture is listed and that the bulleted list is actually five separate text boxes. Apply the Appear entrance animation to each of the five images. For each Appear animation, set a trigger so that when you click the corresponding text box, the image appears.
11. On Slide 3, insert a rounded rectangle, and then type **Overview** in the rectangle. Resize the rectangle so it is 0.6 inches high and 1.5 inches wide. Apply the Intense Effect – Blue, Accent 1 shape style, and then make the text bold. Position the Overview shape in the lower-left corner so there is about one-eighth of an inch between it and the left and bottom sides of the slide.
12. Format the Overview shape as a link to Slide 2 ("Overview"), and then copy this shape to Slide 4 ("High Percentage of Sales Returned to School") and Slide 5 ("Dedicated Support").
13. Use the Document Inspector to remove off-slide content. Save the changes to the presentation.
14. Use the Package Presentation for CD command to package the presentation to a folder named **Fundraising Presentation** in the location where you are storing your files, making sure to embed fonts and without including linked files.

Explore 15. Save the presentation as an outline in the RTF format with the filename **Starlight Fundraising Outline**. (*Hint*: Use the Save as type box in the Save As dialog box.)

Explore 16. Save the presentation in a format compatible with PowerPoint 97-2003 in the location where you are saving your files. Name the file **Starlight Fundraising Earlier Version**.

17. Close the presentation.

INDEX

E

G

H

I

K

L

P

Q

R